ABOVE THE TRENCHES

A Complete Record of the
Fighter Aces and Units of the
British Empire Air Forces
1915-1920

ABOVE THE TRENCHES

A Complete Record of the Fighter Aces and Units of the British Empire Air Forces 1915-1920

Christopher Shores Norman Franks
& Russell Guest

GRUB STREET · LONDON

Published by
Grub Street
The Basement
10 Chivalry Road
London SW11 1HT

Copyright © 1990 Grub Street, London
Text copyright © 1990 Christopher Shores, Norman Franks, Russell Guest

Reprinted 1996

Map by kind permission of Wing Commander Jefford

British Library Cataloguing in Publication Data
Shores, Christopher 1937-
Above the trenches: a complete record of the fighter aces
and the units of the British Empire air forces 1915-1920.
1. World War 1. Air operations by fighter aeroplanes.
Pilots
I. Title II. Franks, Norman III. Guest, Russell
940.441

ISBN 0-948817-19-4

All rights reserved. No part of this publication may be reproduced, stored in a retrieval system, or transmitted in any form or by any means, electronic, mechanical, photocopying, recording, or otherwise, without the prior permission of the copyright owner.

Typeset by Pearl Graphics, Hemel Hempstead

Printed and bound by The Bath Press, Bath

ACKNOWLEDGEMENTS

The authors wish to acknowledge the help of many World War I air historians who over the years have been only too happy to help with the mammoth task of adding information to *Above the Trenches*. Each one is in our debt.

Frank 'Bill' Bailey (USA), Winfried Bock (Germany), Chaz Bowyer (England), George Brown (USA), Harry Creagan (Canada), Stu Leslie (England), the late Steve St Martin (USA), Gerald Muir (Australia), O.A. Slater (USA), Chas Schaedel (Australia), Paul Sortehaug (New Zealand), Stewart Taylor (Canada), and of course the Keeper and staff of the Public Records, Kew, England.

There are also the many former WWI aces whom the authors have met or corresponded with over the years, most of whom, alas, have since flown their last patrol.

Contents

Introduction

Much has been written regarding the fighting 'aces' of the First World War — some of it well-researched and of considerable historical merit, but a good deal representing cheap and sensational journalism of the worst kind, in which mistakes, mis-representations and oft-repeated half-truths have been served up repeatedly. Certain charismatic or favoured pilots have received massive coverage, whilst the majority, many of whom had no less interesting and noteworthy careers, have been given scant mention, if at all.

This book began as an attempt to provide a companion volume to *Aces High: The Fighter Aces of the British and Commonwealth Air Forces in World War II* (by Christopher Shores and Clive Williams, published by Neville Spearman Ltd. 1966). From the very start, research quickly indicated that difficulties of interpretation and terminology existed which would make this a more problematic and less exact exercise. These difficulties may be summarized under five headings:-

i) Claim terminology;
ii) Submission of claims;
iii) Shared victories;
iv) Two-seater crews;
v) Balloons;

Claim terminology

With the birth of aerial fighting various methods were employed to compute pilots' scores arising from time to time during the war years, and from nation to nation. The conditions prevalent on the Western Front made it easier for the Germans to confirm the claims of their pilots than was the case for the Allies, since most combats took place over, or behind the German lines. There were two main reasons for this phenomenon; firstly the determination of the British air commanders to sustain offensive action, even when aerial supremacy was in enemy hands, and secondly the prevailing westerly wind, which tended to blow combatant aircraft further to the east, or to slow down the return flights of Allied aircraft towards their bases in the West.

In the early days (1915-16) pilots of the Royal Flying Corps and Royal Naval Air Service were credited with a 'victory' if they shot down an enemy aircraft, drove it down 'out of control', forced it to land within Allied *or* enemy lines, or drove it down in an obviously damaged condition. Clearly many of these 'victories' were of a moral, rather than actual nature; frequently both crew and aircraft survived to fight another day. However, having regard to the very primitive armament, and the total lack of previous experience or training for such combat, to be able to prevent an opposing aircraft and its crew from carrying out their function and to drive them away, damage them, or so harrass the crew as to force them to land, was clearly a most noteworthy achievement. Several of the victories of the early British 'aces' such as Hawker, Ball and others, were of this type, as will become clear in the body of the book.

By early 1917 air fighting had become a more established practice, and specialised aircraft were being produced in great numbers. Although training in the arts required was still rudimentary in the extreme, and was given mainly at unit level, the chances of success had grown considerably and victories credited were limited to aircraft destroyed or driven down 'out of control', where there seemed to be little likelihood of the victim recovering; credit was also given for aircraft forced to land in Allied lines where these were subsequently captured. This was to become the basis on which scores were to be calculated throughout the rest of the war, with but little modification.

During the war the Headquarters of the RFC on the Western Front issued detailed Communiques, reporting daily actions. These were for internal use within the Services, and provided a synopsis of all activities of the Corps (after 1 April 1918, of the RAF), both in air fighting and other notable activities. These Communiques included the majority of daily claims, both destroyed and 'out of control', until late May 1918. Thereafter details of the latter category were deleted due to their sheer volume. In the past this has given the impression to some researchers that 'out of control' claims were no longer included in pilots' total scores subsequent to this date, but this is not in fact the case. They continued to be credited to pilots for the purposes of medal citations etc., until the end of the war. Indeed Brigade and Wing Headquarters also maintained listings of units' victories and individual pilots' claims, contrary to popular belief.

Submission of claims

In the RFC, RNAS, and later in the RAF, squadrons wrote out 'Combat Reports' for each pilot following an engagement, and these were sent to the Wing Headquarters, to which the squadrons were attached. The Wing Commander allowed or disallowed each claim made in these reports, but then passed them on up to Brigade Headquarters. It is clear that by 1918 Wing Commanders took considerable care to eliminate duplications of claims, and to cut them down on the number of 'out of control' submissions.

Brigades followed this procedure, and it was possible to have a claim disallowed by a Wing, only to be allowed by Brigade, or for a claim disallowed by both to appear in the Communique. The main weakness of the system lay in the lack of any centralized review process, which meant that two or more patrols from different units involved in the same fight, would each tend to claim all the German aircraft seen spinning down. Additionally, the RFC/RAF operated their records from 4 pm (1600 hours) on Day 'Y' to 4 pm on Day 'X'. Consequently, activity in the late afternoon of Day 'Y' is often reported in Communiques as having occurred on the next day. This has led to a number of claims previously being listed twice, once from the Combat Reports on Day 'Y' and once more from Day 'X's Communique. This factor also plays havoc with daily and weekly totals.

The activities of some squadrons, particularly those of 5 Group on the Belgian coast, were not included in the Communiques at all. Consequently the daily or weekly totals mentioned in the Communiques do not refer to the total British activity, units such as 204, 210 and 213 Squadrons failing to feature for the duration of their service with the Group!

In this book a source of confirmation for each claim has been included wherever possible, but this becomes very difficult for 'out of control' claims after 19 May 1918, when these ceased to be listed. However, an attempt has been made to indicate some higher level organisation's acceptance of all claims. Some units have proved more difficult than others to reconstruct full listings of all claims, due to the destruction of their records. In particular, 48 Squadron lost a lot of its papers when the unit headquarters were bombed in 1918, while 22 and 60 Squadrons both lost portions of their records during fires in the squadron offices. Naturally, the passage of time has reduced the number of combat reports and squadron records that have survived. Some Wings (11, for example) kept most of the copies of combat reports submitted by all the units operating under their command — although some months are missing — but other Wings, Brigades and Squadrons retained none at all.

It needs to be remembered that by 1917 the scale of air fighting was vast. It was quite common for the British air forces alone to submit 30 or more claims a day. In 1918 there were numerous days when the RAF claimed over 50 victories, and of course, losses were on an equally large scale. The air war had developed in three years into a large, well-organised and sophisticated science.

There is no doubt that had claims been assessed as in the Second War, 'out of control' claims would have been classed as 'probably destroyed', and would not have been included in scores. For this reason they cannot be considered truly comparable. It has to be said that none of the other combatant nations added 'unconfirmed' (i.e. out of control, in British parlance) claims to credited scores, so that the totals of the leading British aces of 1914-18 are not properly comparable with those of, say, Guynemer, Fonck, Nungesser or Madon of France, von Richthofen, Udet or Voss of Germany, Baracca or Scaroni of Italy, or with Brumowski, Fiala or Linke-Crawford of the Austro-Hungarian Empire, since in almost every case the accepted and published British Empire totals overstate the case. Only the British, and later the United States Air Service, accepted claims for victories made by pilots without independent verification from the ground. In the French, Italian and Belgian air forces (i.e. the other Allied air forces) no ground witnesses or wreckage meant no confirmations, and thus only 'probable' victories. It is worth noting that both the United States Air Service and the Austro-Hungarians allowed 'forced to land' claims until the end of the war. Equally, it is clearly difficult to compare fairly the pilots of the different periods between 1915 and 1918 on the same basis. By 1918 new pilots were starting to receive combat training before posting to the front, during which the benefit of the experiences of the pilots of 1917 were passed on to them. In the

RNAS in particular, 11 (Naval) and 12 (Naval) Squadrons were effectively operational training units, preparing new graduates for the conditions they would meet over the front. Aircraft too had rapidly become infinitely stronger and more reliable, equipped with double the fire-power and with effective gun synchronisation gear. The level of experience of existing squadrons had obviously become much higher, and tactics had become established, rather than needing to be devised in the midst of battle.

Shared victories

A further vexing question which arose was over the subject of shared victories. It was noted at the start that all scores quoted for pilots in this war were in whole numbers, and never included mention of shares, unlike the listings for the RAF and USAAF in World War Two. Frequently in past publications, it has been stated that shared victories in the war under review were credited to one pilot only — generally the newest and most inexperienced, to give him a little confidence.

Research shows this not to have been the case in the majority of such situations; in the vast majority of cases shared victories involving two or more pilots were credited to each pilot as a whole individual victory, but obviously as one addition only to the squadron's overall score. This explains why in some unit histories the sum of the scores credited to leading individual pilots substantially exceeded the total listed for the unit. In some squadrons victories shared by several pilots were awarded as 'Flight' victories or 'Patrol' victories without mentioning pilots' names, whilst in others — particularly RNAS units — the victory was split between all pilots involved. There was clearly no policy in this respect in force.

Again, if such fractional shares were aggregated in the manner employed by, say, the US 8th Air Force in 1943-5, personal totals would frequently have been further reduced. Once more the problem of international comparability is fraught with difficulty. All nations except the Germans (but including the Austro-Hungarians) treated shared victories as being credited to each participating pilot's personal score as a full victory during this war. This continued to be the basis which was again employed by the French in 1939-45, and to some extent by the RAF and by the US forces during the first year or so of their involvement in that later war. In Italy however, 7 Brigade only very rarely allocated shared victories.

Certainly during this research it became clear that most squadrons, Wings and Brigades were very score-conscious — far more so than the public has been given to believe in the past. There were frequent cases where a commanding officer appeared to relish the idea of having a high-scoring pilot in his unit, and every effort seems to have been made to increase his score as much as possible. Sometimes this was for morale and encouragement purposes for young pilots to maintain a proper 'offensive spirit' — often in the face of severe difficulties. A particular consideration was also the allocation of medals, which was to a large extent based on victory totals. A prime example occurred in the case of Donald MacLaren of 46 Squadron, a unit very concerned to do this. MacLaren's quoted score of 54 included many shared victories, some with three, or in one case even with four, other pilots.

Two-seater crews

To complicate matters further, claim totals of the pilots of two-seater fighting machines do not give a true comparison with the scores of those flying single-seaters. As the First War two-seater had no real opposite number in World War Two, there is no established basis in this case — indeed most two-seater fighters were operated by the British during 1914-18. In the case of the Sopwith 1½ Strutter and Bristol F2A and B Fighters, the overall claims made both by the pilot with the front gun and the gunner in the rear cockpit, tended to be credited to the pilot, whilst the observer/gunner was credited only with the number he actually claimed with his gun. No 'team' scores were developed at the time.

In the case of Vickers FB 5s and FE 2s, nearly all claims resulted from fire by the gunner, but these victories too, were also credited to the pilot. Also Bristol Fighter crews frequently 'shared' a victory, where for instance, the pilot fired a burst, flew past, and the gunner then finished off the victim. Some units like 20 and 22 Squadrons kept separate lists for pilots and gunners during 1918, but others — 11, 48, 62 and 88 Squadrons — did not.

On the same basis, a number of bomber and Corps reconnaissance crews were also credited with five or more victories, generally where a particularly accurate observer/gunner was carried, or where the pilot was unusually aggressive. It has been necessary to reach a compromise solution here: pilots of two-seater Scouts have been included, with the total claims made by themselves and their observer/gunners. Pilots of other two-seater types have not generally been included unless they also flew scout aircraft and gained some victories whilst flying these. Scout pilots who also gained victories whilst gunners in other aircraft types are also included. Separate listings have been prepared of 'ace' gunners in fighter aircraft, and of pilots and observers in bomber and reconnaissance units, and these are separately included. Biographical notes are included only of the two top-scoring bomber pilots (D.A. Stewart and E. Dickson), and of the most successful Corps reconnaissance crew (C.R. Pithey/H. Rhodes).

Balloons

All the warring nations during World War One included the destruction of observation kite-balloons in pilots' scores, the British being no exception. Research has proven this statement beyond doubt, and many pilots had more than half a dozen of these highly-defended targets in their personal tallies. By 1918 generally only those balloons that burnt were regarded as destroyed. Sometimes in 1916-17, balloons that 'crumpled up and fell' (all the gas escaped, but did not burn) have been regarded as destroyed, as were balloons last seen 'smoking'. Both Bishop and Fullard, for example, claimed balloons in this category; Bishop's were generally left out of his score, while Fullard's were included by the squadron, but not by higher authority.

Another difficulty arose; balloons claimed in 1917 and early 1918 were recorded on a separate form from that used for claims against aircraft. These forms were seldom retained in collections of combat reports, and there is a strong likelihood that the number of balloon claims for which details are available is well below the number actually achieved. 40 Squadron for instance, undertook some balloon 'strafes' in May 1917 which are listed in the RFC Communiques, but for which not all claim forms have been found, whilst those that do exist do not mention precise times, nor the serial numbers of the successful aircraft.

General observations

The above comments have been made to explain the constraints under which the authors have worked, and to assist in understanding how they arrived at the format of this book. It will be noted that unlike other 'ace' books, there is no definitive listing of the pilots by claimed score. This is because the authors do not feel that in many cases these are directly comparable, or give any useful guide to merit. Indeed score has been used as no more than a yardstick to give coverage of the more interesting and successful scout pilots in an established and readily understandable framework. They have been included in a strictly alphabetical order, their achievements set out for the reader to study and to draw his or her own conclusions from. The scores listed are believed to be as accurate as possible, but must still be considered approximate in some cases.

In the early days of air fighting the most successful pilots were the great individualists — aggressive fighters like Ball or Bishop, who preferred to fly and hunt alone. As the war in the air progressed, and the numbers on either side increased, opportunities for this type of fighting diminished, and the patrol leader came into his own — typified by such pilots as Mannock and McCudden. The latter could also be an individualist on occasion, but generally was better able to operate at the head of a practised team. Much of McCudden's score for instance, was achieved against reconnaissance two-seaters which penetrated over the British lines at high level, and which he intercepted alone. For those pilots who continued to prefer flying alone, and who had the necessary determination, these opponents offered themselves throughout the whole war. This is not to say that attacking two-seaters was in any way a 'soft option'; some of the best were killed or wounded attacking such opponents, falling victim to gunners who were either good marksmen, or lucky.

A touchy question concerns the introduction of the term 'ace' and its general recognition. There is no doubt that this description for a pilot with five victories in the air was first coined by the French. However, it has often been stated that it was virtually unknown to the RFC. One story which has circulated concerned a French pilot who had landed at the base of a British scout squadron, and proudly introduced himself as an 'ace'. Asked what this meant, he explained the term to his allies, many of whom turned out to have higher scores than him, but who professed never to have heard this description before.

How much credence can be given to this tale is uncertain when regard is given to a statement in William 'Billy' Bishop's book *Winged Warfare*, which was published in 1918, and written immediately following the author's period of service with 60 Squadron in 1917. Here Bishop wrote that in June 1917 he was presented by his groundcrew with a special blue spinner to fit over the propeller boss of his Nieuport 17, in recognition of his having become an 'ace' by shooting down five enemy aircraft. If this term was so well-known as to precipitate a presentation of this kind from ground personnel in mid-1917, it seems unlikely that it was not equally well-known to the pilots of 1918. In his letters home to his family, published in a recent biography of Arthur Rhys-Davids, while this modest and self-effacing pilot of 1917 does not specifically mention the term 'ace', he is clearly at pains to keep record of his personal score.

It has already been indicated above the extent to which the British air forces maintained 'game books' of unit and personal successes throughout the war, but it is also certain that the British air authorities, with their known distaste for the individual glorification of military personnel, and their national enthusiasm for the team rather than for the individual, refused to capitalise upon the exploits of their leading scout pilots. This was in direct contrast to other nations which lionized them and publicized them for propaganda and public morale purposes.

This is not to say that there was no publicity at all. Each day the 'score' for the previous day's actions was published in the daily papers in Britain. Such totals were tallied up into monthly, quarterly and yearly scores. However, despite pressure from the media, mention of who the pilots achieving these successes were, was rarely made. For the discerning public, the best source of further information was to peruse the pages of the *London Gazette* to ascertain the victory credits mentioned in the decoration citations — which in certain cases were repeated in the daily press — or to read the obituary notices of leading pilots which were frequently published following their deaths in action.

There was, however, no system for the awarding of medals, even for comparable periods. Certainly it can be said that Bristol Fighter pilots received far fewer decorations than did the pilots of single-seaters with similar scores. As the war drew to a close, less medals were handed out, and an increasing proportion of those that were awarded were for other activities — particularly ground attack duties.

CHAPTER ONE

Background to the Air War, 1914-18, and a Brief Account of the War in Russia, 1918-20

When war broke out in Europe on 4 August 1914, the aeroplane was initially viewed by the military as a vehicle for reconnaissance, and it was for that purpose that each of the combatants employed their machines during the opening months of the conflict. Inevitably, aircraft of the opposing forces soon began to meet each other in the air whilst performing their important but mundane tasks, and at first were content to leave each other in peace. Such a state of affairs did not suit the more aggressive young airmen of the various air services, and soon they were carrying aloft carbines, revolvers, grenades and any other weapons which they could shoot at or drop on their opponents, in an effort to prevent them from completing their allocated tasks.

The development of the military aeroplane was closely following that of the light machine gun, and indeed gun-carrying and firing tests had already been undertaken by several nations before the war — initially as a method of attacking ground targets. Consequently it was not long before a pilot of the Royal Flying Corps had mounted a Lewis gun on his machine to be manned by the observer, in an effort to intercept German reconnaissance aircraft that were appearing over his airfield. However, so low-powered were the early machines then in use that the additional weight of the gun adversely affected their performance, and he was ordered to remove it.

The way ahead was already clear however, and as more powerful, reliable aircraft arrived at the front, it became accepted practise to fit a movable machine gun for use by the observer in two-seaters. Initially the reason for the carriage of such a weapon was defensive rather than offensive, in order to allow the crew to complete their reconnaissance or artillery co-operation duties unscathed.

From the very beginning of the war a few fast, light, single-seater aircraft had been available, and had been supplied to units for high-speed scouting behind the enemy's lines. As they carried no observer, these aircraft also carried no machine gun, but soon individual pilots, who saw the potential offered by the higher performance and greater manoeuvrability generally offered, began arranging 'lash-up' mountings for one or two carbines in order to add a certain offensive capability. Almost without exception these scouts were at the time tractor aeroplanes, i.e. with the propeller at the front, pulling the aircraft along. The presence of the propeller in this location posed a major problem to the pilots in obtaining a clear field of fire in the direction he could most effectively employ a gun with any degree of accuracy — forwards!

On the other hand many of the Allied two-seaters were 'pusher' types, with the propeller at the rear, like a ship. In such aircraft the observer was located in front of the pilot, with an unlimited view of the ground, and consequently a similarly unlimited field of fire in a forward direction. The first British aeroplane to be designed with specific offensive duties in mind was the Vickers FB 5, which was a two-seater biplane of this pusher configuration. Soon known colloquially as the 'Gun Bus', examples first arrived in France during February 1915 to equip 5 Squadron, RFC, the first victory to be gained by the crews of one of these aircraft occurring in May.

At this time the French Air Service had been receiving a number of Morane monoplanes which gave similar promise of offensive potential, the first escadrilles for such duties being raised during March with the Type 'L' version of the new aircraft. This had a machine gun mounted on the fuselage immediately in front of the pilot, aimed to fire over the arc of the tractor propeller. This was a far from ideal solution however, proving very difficult to aim and fire in flight with any degree of accuracy. However, a month later, a well-known pre-war French aviator, Roland Garros, who was serving in Escadrille MS 23, devised a forward-firing mounting for his Morane Parasol, fixing a Hotchkiss machine gun directly in front of the cockpit to fire in the line of flight. To prevent the gun shooting off the propeller of his own aircraft, wedges of armoured steel were fitted to the back of each blade to deflect any bullets which did not pass between them. This installation was crude, dangerous, but quite effective. It frequently damaged the blades and threw the engine out of balance, but it often worked. Flying what was undoubtedly the first true single-seater fighting scout, Garros shot down three German aeroplanes during the first half of April and damaged others, causing much concern to the German Air Service.

On 19 April 1915, Garros suffered engine trouble and landed behind the German lines. Despite an attempt to destroy his machine, Garros was captured and the Germans, well aware that they had inadvertently come into possession of the tormentor of their reconnaissance crews, passed the wreckage to Anthony Fokker in order that copies might be fabricated at once. The Fokker engineers realised immediately the limitations of the Garros modification. They were also aware that systems for the mechanical interruption of machine gun fire through a revolving propeller had already been invented and patented. Without more ado, they set to and produced their own version of such a system, whereby the revolutions of a cam actuated by the engine stopped the gun firing whenever a propeller blade was directly in line with the muzzle. This, the first true interrupter gear to be produced and tested, was fitted to a Fokker M5K (A III) monoplane for demonstration to the German clients. Impressed, they ordered immediate production of the aircraft, which went into service as the EI.

Aerial combats now began to escalate as more fighting aircraft appeared on both sides of the lines, and during May the number of attacks on Allied reconnaissance aircraft over the Ypres area reached a sufficient level to cause concern. Consequently, 11 Squadron, RFC, which had been formed on 14 February 1915 as the first unit fully equipped with FB 5s, was despatched hurriedly to France. The French were moving with greater speed towards the production of a dedicated specialist fighting scout however, and during the summer were able to introduce the first examples of two new tractor biplanes, the two-seater Nieuport 10 and the single-seater Nieuport 11 'Bebe' — the latter the progenitor of a long and distinguished line of fighters.

Meanwhile the first attempt at a single-seater fighting scout for the RFC had been produced by local field modifications undertaken in 6 Squadron by Captain L.G. Hawker, a flight commander and already a veteran airman, aided by Air Mechanic E.J. Elton. Hawker, a trained engineer, designed an attachment for a Lewis gun to be fitted on the side of a Bristol Scout, one of which was available to his flight. This mounting allowed the gun to fire forward and outward at such an angle that it just missed the propeller arc. Although possessing similar disadvantages to the first French attempts, Hawker was quick to try out the aircraft in action, and on 25 July 1915 twice engaged German aircraft, shooting down one in flames and driving down two others. For this performance and previous "good work", he received the Victoria Cross, the first 'fighter pilot' to be so honoured. His Squadron had now received a few examples of a new two-seater pusher biplane, similar in general arrangement to the FB 5, but of higher performance. This, the FE 2B, was soon to become a major item of RFC equipment, but was not yet generally available. In one of these, with a gunner in the front cockpit, Hawker was to gain several more victories during the summer, to become the first RFC 'ace'. He was closely followed by Captain C.G. Bell of 10 Squadron, who was also engaging German aircraft in a modified Bristol Scout during this period. It is also interesting to note that Hawker's able assistant, Elton, subsequently trained as a pilot and became a successful air fighter in his own right.

The Royal Naval Air Service was also developing armed scouts, having experimented with machine gun-armed Sopwith Tabloids, and having acquired a small number of Sopwith-designed and manufactured 'Gun Buses'. It was in the Dardanelles however, that armed Naval aircraft were first in action, French-built Nieuport 11s being put into service here in July, followed the next month by Lewis gun-armed Bristol Scouts.

On the Western Front the first production Fokker EIs had been issued to the German Feldfliegerabteilungen during July, one or two initially serving with each unit to protect the two-seaters. Leutnant Kurt Wintgens was to claim the first victory in an EI on 1 July. Development of the EI, which was in fact a rather poor aircraft, had continued at Fokker's factory, the EII and EIII following in August and September respectively. Air fighting remained scattered and infrequent at this time, but the desirability of grouping fighting scouts into larger, more specialized units to allow control of the air to be obtained and exercised over a complete area had become obvious to the Germans also. To provide protection to other aircraft in such areas, and to meet the larger formations of Allied aircraft which were now appearing, three Kampfeinsitzer Kommandos (KEK) were formed, and at once proved successful. Losses by the RFC rose alarmingly during 1915, and the period known as the 'Fokker Scourge' had arrived. Once operating in numbers, the Fokkers quickly proved too fast and manoeuvrable for 11 Squadron's 'Gun Buses', which had been gaining a fair number of successes during the late summer and early autumn. By November these aircraft were clearly outclassed, and the British began casting around for a replacement. 18 Squadron reached France during this month, but this unit too was equipped with the FB 5, and it was to be April 1916 before more appropriate aircraft were to arrive (FE 2Bs) to re-equip the unit.

1916

The year did not begin well for the Allied air services, as the initiative held so firmly by them during 1915 passed inexorably into the hands of the Germans. Desperate efforts were made to reverse the situation during January, a new fighting unit (20 Squadron) being rushed out to France on 23rd, fully equipped with the new FEs. During the same month the French were able to form their first unit to be fully equipped with the Nieuport 11 — Escadrille N3. Meanwhile as an initial precaution a special RFC order was issued, decreeing that at least three escorting aircraft must accompany each reconnaissance two-seater over the front for the time being.

In England at this time production was underway of a new British single-seater fighting scout known as the DH2; its designer was Geoffrey De Havilland who had already been responsible for the successful FE 2 series. Indeed, the first single-seater scout unit for the RFC — 24 Squadron — had commenced formation with these aircraft in December 1915 under the command of none other than Captain Hawker, VC, DSO. Hampered by the lack of a viable interrupter gear, De Havilland's aircraft was again a pusher biplane, the pilot sitting in a nascelle in front of the engine with a single Lewis gun firing forward, provided with a limited amount of traverse and elevation. In practice pilots found it preferable to clamp the gun in a fixed position on the line of flight, allowing the whole aircraft to be aimed at an adversary, as was later to be the norm with tractor scouts. Typically, this modification was initially forbidden by officialdom!

24 Squadron arrived in France in early February 1916, followed during March by the similarly equipped 29 Squadron. Other new units were also being hastened to the Western Front with more FE 2Bs, 25 Squadron arriving in February, 23 Squadron in March and 22 Squadron in April. Together with the French Nieuports, these new machines swiftly proved to have the measure of the Fokker monoplanes, which enjoyed a relatively low performance, despite their effective armament. Once all the new units had become established in action, they soon wrested back superiority in the air from the Germans. A second single-seater type entered service over the front with the RFC during March with the arrival of the Martinsyde G 100s of 27 Squadron. Known as the 'Elephant', the Martinsyde was a tractor biplane which featured a top-wing Lewis gun mounting, similar to that used by the Nieuport types, and firing above the airscrew. A rather large and cumbersome machine, it was to serve with several units, though only 27 Squadron would ever be fully equipped with the type. Designed as a reconnaissance, rather than a fighting scout, it proved effective against initial opposition, and saw a fair amount of action during its early days at the front, some dozen or so victories being claimed by its pilots. It quickly became outclassed however, and as soon as more effective types became available, was relegated to long-range bombing duties.

While all the new units were starting to reach France, the Germans undertook their first substantial concentration of fighting scouts in the Verdun area, where the French were just opening a large-scale offensive on the ground. Here two new groupings, Kampfeinsitzer Kommando Sud and Nord were to gain a remarkable success, Leutnant Oswald Boelcke swiftly rising to prominence as their leading fighter pilot.

While the RFC continued to prepare new squadrons for the front with aircraft capable of dealing with the Fokkers, British engineers pressed on with work to allow the introduction of a useable and reliable interrupter gear to allow the installation of guns on the more promising tractor configuration. While Fokker had developed a mechanical gearing, activated by the engine via linked rods, the British sought to develop a hydraulic system which had been first invented by a Rumanian engineer, Constantinescu. During March a Vickers machine gun was fitted above the engine of a Bristol Scout, linked to an early example of one of these designs, and was despatched to France for trials; much initial trouble was experienced with the installation at this stage however.

During April a new two-seater tractor biplane arrived in France to join 5 Wing of the Royal Naval Air Service at Coudekerque, where by the end of the month a complete flight had been re-equipped. This was the oddly named Sopwith 1½ Strutter, which, although initially armed only with a flexibly mounted Lewis gun for the observer, proved to have so excellent a performance that it was chosen to be the first type fitted with production examples of the interrupter gear, allowing a nose-mounted Vickers to be added to its armament. In this guise it could double as either fighter or bomber, although the RNAS was soon producing a single-seat version for long-range bombing duties. Initially the aircraft entered service to provide escorts to 5 Wing's Breguet V and Caudron G IV bombers, but so outstanding did it prove that a number were agreed to be transferred to the RFC, and before April was out 70 Squadron was being formed to receive the new aircraft. The first Flight was ready to move to France on 24 May, followed during the next two months by the rest of the unit.

Late May also saw the arrival of 60 Squadron from England, but without aircraft. This new unit was swiftly equipped with French Morane-Saulnier types — initially one Flight each of Type N 'Bullet' monoplanes, Type BB biplanes and Type L and LA Parasols; the latter were quickly replaced with more Type Ns.

In France the Nieuport factory had also been hard at work, developing the successful Type 11. Before the spring was out the RFC was to benefit from their efforts also, receiving a number of new Type 13 and 16 single-seaters which were issued to augment the equipment of 11 and 29 Squadrons. During May the most famous of the Nieuport Scouts, the classic Type 17, entered service on the Western Front with the French Escadrille N.57, while a few of these excellent aircraft soon found their way into British hands, serving with 1 Squadron alongside that unit's various two-seaters. In addition a very limited number of Bristol Scouts were fitted with Lewis guns mounted above the top wing in a manner similar to that employed on the Nieuports, these being supplied to augment the equipment of 11 and 25 Squadrons. A third DH 2 unit — 32 Squadron — also reached France during May.

On 29 April 1916 Lord Doune, a pilot in 25 Squadron, with Lt R.V. Walker as the gunner/observer in his FE, engaged a Fokker of Flg Abteilung 18 in combat, shooting down this aircraft which turned out to be flown by the son of Prinz Ernst von Sachsen-Meingen. The 'Fokker Scourge' was fast coming to an end, and by the start of June 1916 the RFC's fighting squadrons on the Western Front had become a force to be reckoned with.

UNIT	AIRCRAFT	BASE
1 Squadron	Nieuport 17, Morane Biplane and Parasol, Martinsyde S 1	Bailleul
11 Squadron	FB 5, Nieuport 13, Bristol Scout D	Savy
20 Squadron	FE 2B	Clairmarais
22 Squadron	FE 2B	Bertangles
23 Squadron	FE 2B	Le Hameau
24 Squadron	DH 2	Bertangles
25 Squadron	FE 2B, Bristol Scout	Lozinghem
27 Squadron	Martinsyde G 100	Fienvillers
29 Squadron	DH 2, Nieuport 16	Abeele
32 Squadron	DH 2	Treizennes
60 Squadron	Morane Type N, Morane Type BB	Vert Galant
70 Squadron	Sopwith 1½ Strutter	Fienvillers

The RFC was soon to be joined by other British fighting scouts, for during the early summer the RNAS formed a fighter unit known as A Squadron at Furnes for the defence of the supply ports on the Channel coast. This unit was soon seeing a fair amount of action, while at the same time testing prototypes of various new scouts ordered by the Admiralty.

With the approach of finer weather a great offensive on the Somme was planned by the British Army. By this time the RFC had regained a marked ascendency in the air, which was underlined on 18 June when in a fight between Fokker monoplanes and FE 2Bs of 25 Squadron, the first of the great German aces, Leutnant Max Immelmann, was shot down and killed by Corporal J.H. Waller, gunner in 2nd Lt G.R. McCubbin's aircraft. Later that same month the Nieuport Scout squadrons undertook an all-out offensive against German observation balloons, which were tethered close behind the enemy lines and were used for artillery spotting. These heavily defended targets were attacked with le Prieur rockets, mounted on the interplane struts of the aircraft, and fired electrically. Within two days eight of the kite balloons had been destroyed.

By the end of June a further development of the FE 2 series, the FE 2D, which was fitted with a 250 hp engine, had begun arriving at the front, being supplied initially to 20 Squadron. The first examples of a new single-seat pusher, very similar in general appearance to the DH 2, known as the FE 8, also arrived and were issued to 29 Squadron, replacing the latter's few Nieuport 16s alongside the predominant DHs.

On 1 July the Somme offensive began, and on this first day the RFC had available 81 single-seat scouts, only six of which were Nieuport 17s — the best available. During the day Major L.W.B. Rees, commanding officer of 32 Squadron, made a single-handed attack on ten German two-seaters in his DH 2, for which he received the Victoria Cross. There was considerable aerial fighting over the following weeks, the Sopwith 1½ Strutters of 70 Squadron gaining a number of successes, mainly whilst engaged in escorting 27 Squadron's Martinsydes on bombing raids. The Nieuports were also very active, a young Lieutenant named Albert Ball starting to build up a large total of claims whilst flying these aircraft with 11 Squadron. DH 2s remained much in evidence, and on 21 July, 24 Squadron claimed a total of nine German machines out of 25 engaged during two encounters. 60 Squadron's Moranes proved vulnerable however, and so heavy were losses that in mid-August the unit had to be pulled out of the line to be re-built. Nieuport Scouts and their pilots from 11 Squadron were transferred to this unit, which was brought up to strength with these aircraft, while 11 Squadron fully re-equipped with FE 2Bs.

Despite the RFC's mastery at this time, the demand for more fighting scouts was increasing. During July, 19 Squadron arrived at St Omer equipped with another 'new' type, the BE 12, while 21 Squadron, which was at Fienvillers, replaced its RE 7 two-seaters with these aircraft. This ill-fated tractor biplane was a single-seat 'development' of the reconnaissance BE 2C, carrying a Vickers gun on the side of the fuselage and an interrupter gear to allow forward fire. Possessing the inherent stability of its predecessor, the aircraft was not a success as a fighter on the Western Front, although 21 Squadron did manage to bring down a few enemy machines initially. 17 Squadron in the Middle East also received a few of these aircraft to supplement its BE 2s, also receiving a few Bristol Scout Ds and Nieuport Scouts to form a fighter flight. Other BE 12s were employed on Home Defence duties.

In August, 40 Squadron, the first unit fully equipped with FE 8s, arrived in France following delays associated with teething troubles with the aircraft. 30 July also saw the arrival far to the south, in the French zone, of 3 Naval Wing, equipped with 1½ Strutters — both bombers and fighters — for strategic bombing duties over Germany.

Needless to say, the Germans had been quick to respond to the Allies' new aerial challenge with their customary vigour and inventiveness, and had swiftly produced three new scouts to replace the Fokker Eindeckers. These were all tractor biplanes, one of which — the Fokker DIII — was fitted with a rotary engine, the other two — the Halberstadt DII and the Albatros DI — being powered by water-cooled units. The first two each carried one synchronised machine gun (some Fokker DIIs had two), but the Albatros, which was undoubtedly the most promising of the trio, carried two — a notable improvement in firepower. New German fighter units known as Jagdstaffeln (Jasta) were also being formed, the excellent Leutnant Oswald Boelcke commanding Jasta 2. Boelcke claimed his 20th victory (a DH 2) in one of the new Fokker DIIIs on 2 September, while on 17th of that month he led his unit into action as a formation for the first time, during the Battle of Flers-Courcelette. Eight BEs from 12 Squadron and six FE 2Bs of 11 Squadron were attacked, two of the former and four of the latter being shot down. One of the successful pilots during this ominous action was later to become probably the world's most famous fighter pilot — Manfred von Richthofen, soon to be known as the 'Red Baron'. By the end of September Boelcke's personal score had risen to 29, and it was becoming clear that the RFC was in trouble again — particularly the BE 12 squadrons.

Development was continuing apace in England however, and during the autumn of 1916, 2 Naval Squadron, which formed part of the Dover Defence Flight, received a new scout from the Sopwith factory, soon to be known unofficially as the Pup. This delightful little aircraft was also supplied to 1 Naval Wing at Dunkerque, where it joined that unit's Nieuports, and immediately demonstrated its capabilities, its pilots accounting for eight opposing aircraft between 24 September and 30 October. Although armed only with one Vickers gun, this rotary-engined biplane, which began a line of successful scouts from the Sopwith stable, was quickly found to be the equal of the new Halberstadt and Albatros scouts, and superior to the Fokker DIII, which soon disappeared from the front. It was not long before the RFC pilots were clamouring for the new Sopwith Scout!

Meanwhile however, two more fighting units had reinforced the RFC in France, 41 Squadron with already obsolescent FE 8s, and 45 Squadron with 1½ Strutters. Although the latter were now somewhat outclassed by the Albatros DI, and its successor the DII, which was also starting to reach the Jastas, 45 was to become the most successful of the 1½ Strutter squadrons, claiming 88 victories in 11 months — no less than 13 of these being claimed by Lt G.H. Cock and his gunners before he was shot down and made a prisoner in July 1917. The French now introduced a new scout which was to prove very successful. This was the Spad S VII, which soon began replacing the Nieuport 17s in the French Escadrilles de Chasse. Although a Spad was evaluated by 60 Squadron during October, the RFC was at the time expecting to re-equip its units with other types from England in the near future, and the Nieuports therefore remained in service with British units for a longer period.

Although outclassed by the newer German types, the 1½ Strutters and FE 2Ds were capable of holding their own, due mainly to the presence of the second crew member with his flexible gun. It was the DH 2, FE 8 and BE 12, and the older Corps reconnaissance types (mainly BE 2s) which suffered most to the newly regained German superiority, which only the Nieuport 17s and Pups were able to challenge on anything approaching equal terms.

Despite their renewed ascendency, the Germans suffered some heavy losses, not least of these being Oswald Boelcke, their leading ace. Boelcke had gained his 40th success on 26 October, but two days later, when about to engage 24 Squadron, he collided with a fellow pilot and was killed in the ensuing crash. The RFC dropped a laurel wreath over the German lines in tribute to the memory of a gallant foe, as they had done when Immelmann was killed.

At this time the RFC's own top-scorer was Albert Ball who had made some 31 claims, but who was about to be sent home to England for a rest. He gained much newspaper publicity as a result of which he was the first British fighter pilot to become a public idol — at the age of 20. The Germans and French had quickly realised the morale and propaganda value to be gained by publicizing the exploits of their outstanding pilots, and the extent to which public interest and support for the air services could be enhanced by this. Consequently men like Boelcke, von Richthofen and Georges Guynemer, the French ace, became national heroes and household names. The British authorities — with their traditional distaste for publicity of this sort for individuals — generally refused to release similar information, and unless the announcement of the award of a Victoria Cross or other high award made publicity unavoidable, the RFC — and to an even greater extent, the RNAS — remained nameless services to the public at large.

During September, General Trenchard had been obliged to order the BE 12 squadrons to cease operating as fighters and fly instead as bombers, to prevent their total extinction. So manifest had German superiority become by November that the RFC in some desperation sought aid from the Navy. The RNAS was in the process of increasing its own fighting scout component, and during the last two months of the year formed a number of new units from a variety of nuclei. At Furnes 'A' Squadron became 1 Naval Squadron with Nieuport 17s and Bristol Scout Cs, while at Dunkerque's St Pol airfield the similarly equipped 'C' Squadron became 3 Naval. At Coudekerque 5 Wing's 'A' Squadron, flying 1½ Strutters, became 4 Naval, while at Dover 6 Naval was formed, moving to Petite Synthe in December with Nieuports. Specifically to aid the RFC, 8 Naval was formed at St Pol from personnel drawn from 1, 4 and 5 Wings, and was equipped initially with one flight of Nieuports, one of Pups and one of 1½ Strutters. During October this latter unit was despatched to Vert Galand on the Western Front, where on 16 November the 1½ Strutters were replaced by more Pups, further examples of which also replaced the Nieuports by the end of the year. By this time 20 victories had been claimed by the pilots of this unit.

On 18 November the Army launched the last of the desperately costly attacks on the Somme, and five days later the RFC suffered a grievous loss when Major Hawker, VC, DSO, still commanding 24 Squadron, was shot down and killed in a classic dogfight by Manfred von Richthofen as the latter's 11th victory. This action seemed to set the scene for what was to come in the new year which was fast approaching.

1917

The winter of 1916/17 brought to an end major operations on the ground, both this factor and the weather resulting in a consequent reduction in aerial activity. Both sides of the lines, the combatants seized upon the opportunity further to improve the size and quality of their air forces prior to renewed activity in the spring. During December 1916 the first RFC unit to receive Sopwith Pups — 54 Squadron — arrived in France, followed in January 1917 by the third and last of the Corps' 1½ Strutter squadrons, No. 43. Following its exertions during the late autumn, 8 Naval Squadron returned to St Pol, its place on the Western Front being taken by 3 Naval, which had now also re-equipped with Pups, as had 4 Naval Squadron.

8 Naval was now to receive the new Sopwith Triplane, a development of the Pup with an additional wing and a more powerful engine. Constructed initially for the Navy, the Triplane had been ordered for both the RNAS and the RFC. The British authorities had also now decided to acquire the French Spad S VII, which had been ordered for both air services, both from the manufacturers in France, and via construction under licence in the United Kingdom. In a move to rationalize equipment and get the maximum number of squadrons to the front in the minimum time, an inter-service agreement was now negotiated whereby the RNAS took over all Triplane production and the RFC accepted all the Spads. In consequence both 1 and 8 Naval Squadrons were re-equipped with the new Sopwith during February, and on 15th the former unit joined 3 Naval on the Western Front under RFC control.

On 8 March, 48 Squadron arrived in France from England, equipped with another new type, the Bristol F2A two-seater, soon to be known generally as the Bristol Fighter; this aircraft had been designed for a similar role to the earlier 1½ Strutter. Four days later 66 Squadron followed, equipped with more Pups, while 29 Squadron exchanged the ageing DH 2s for Nieuport 17s. On 9th of this month however, the equally outclassed FE 8s had suffered a major setback when a patrol of nine of these aircraft from 40 Squadron were attacked by von Richthofen's Jasta 11; five were brought down and the rest all damaged. At the end of the month this unit too was hastily re-equipped with Nieuports. The only pilot to achieve any degree of success with the ill-fated FE 8 had been Lt E.L. Benbow, MC, who had claimed eight victories whilst flying this type.

It was not only the older types which suffered badly however, for on 5 April, six of 48 Squadron's new Bristol Fighters, led by Captain W. Leefe Robinson, VC, were intercepted by Richthofen's Albatri, and four Bristols, including that flown by the leader, were shot down. Consequently the German master-fighter reported adversely on the new opponent, rather than on the tactics that had been employed, which had been the true cause of this reverse. Leefe Robinson, until recently a Home Defence pilot, who had gained his Victoria Cross for shooting down a Zeppelin, was inexperienced in the ways of the Western Front. Against the advice of his fellow flight commanders, he had sought to operate the aircraft as traditional two-seaters, flying straight and level, relying on the gunners for defence, rather than employing the excellent performance of the aircraft to dogfight like single-seaters, but with the added benefit of the rear seat gunner. Worse, he had ordered that all oil be removed from the guns to prevent their freezing up in the bitter cold of high altitude in early spring, and when attacked, all the gunners' Lewis guns had failed to operate! However, 48's other flights were soon employing their new mounts with considerable success.

By now the German Air Service had 37 Jastas available, most equipped with Albatros DIIs, or the newer and faster DIIIs. Although inferior in overall numbers to the Allies, they had the edge in performance over most of the aircraft facing them, and were about to inflict the heaviest casualties yet. 'Bloody April' of 1917 would cost the RFC no less than 316 aircrew, as the Battle of Arras opened the spring campaigning season.

Better British equipment was on the way, and on 8 April 56 Squadron arrived in France, having been formed to bring the new SE 5 scout into service. This aircraft, powered like the Albatros by a water-cooled engine, was the first Allied fighter designed to carry two guns to actually see active service. It was armed with a Vickers in front of the pilot, synchronised to fire through the propeller, and a Lewis gun on the top wing. This latter weapon could be pulled down on its Foster mounting to be reloaded, or to fire upwards — an arrangement that had been put to good effect on occasions by pilots of the Nieuport Scout, especially by one of 56 Squadron's new flight commanders, Capt Albert Ball, who at the time was still the RFC's top-scorer. At the same time 19 Squadron exchanged its BE 12s for the first British Spad S VIIs, and resumed fighting duties, while 46 Squadron replaced its Nieuport 12 two-seaters with Sopwith Pups. At Coudekerke on the coast, 4 Naval Squadron also replaced its 1½ Strutters with Pups at the time, while 6 Naval moved to La Bellevue to operate under RFC control, also operating two-gun fighters — Nieuport Scouts which had been fitted, like the SE 5, with both a Vickers and a Lewis gun.

The Arras battle opened on 9 April, and two days later Flight Sub Lieutenant J.S.T. Fall demonstrated impressively the capabilities of the Pup, claiming two Albatros and one Halberstadt scouts shot down single-handed in one dogfight. However despite this, and other isolated successes by British pilots, the German Air Service (as already noted) was taking a fearful toll of the RFC, Rittmeister von Richthofen's Jasta 11 inflicting particularly great execution. Their leader achieved considerable prominence during the month, claiming five victories on 28 April to take his total to over 50. One of the Jasta's victims was Major H.D. Harvey-Kelly, commander of 19 Squadron, who had been the first RFC pilot to land in France after war was declared in 1914. The Triplane squadrons were making their mark however, and two pilots, Roderick Dallas of 1 Naval and Robert Little of 8 Naval, were beginning long runs of success. By the end of the month von Richthofen was reporting that the Sopwith Triplane was the best Allied scout at the front, and was superior to the Albatros DIII, and even the improved DV, which was just about to be introduced.

On 1 May von Richthofen returned to Germany on leave, and almost as if this were a signal, German aerial activity slackened. Early in this month the RFC again undertook an all-out assault on the German kite balloons, whilst the Nieuport units carried out many ground strafing sorties. Some of the Nieuport pilots were by now achieving sizeable personal victory totals, notable amongst these being Jenkins, Campbell, Hazell and Fullard, all members of 1 Squadron, all of whom would attain scores of 20 or more. Another Nieuport pilot in 60 Squadron, Capt W.A. Bishop, was also appearing frequently in the RFC's Communiques. 56 Squadron's SE 5s were also starting to make their mark in the hands of pilots such as Rhys-Davids, Hoidge and G.C. Maxwell, while the squadron's famous flight commander, Ball, was rapidly adding more victories to maintain his position at the top. However on 7 May, after a month at the front, he crashed to his death after an engagement in cloud; the award of a Victoria Cross was announced shortly after his loss.

In mid May, 10 Naval, another newly-formed Triplane squadron, was attached to the RFC. One of the flight commanders was a Canadian, Raymond Collishaw, who had already gained several victories and who was during the next two months, to become probably the supreme exponent of the Sopwith Triplane, his all-Canadian 'Black Flight' claiming a record number of victories for the period. Considerable re-equipment of RFC units also took place during May, 11 Squadron receiving the latest Bristol F2B Fighters to replace its FE 2Bs, while 24 and 32 Squadrons exchanged their long-outdated DH 2s for De Havilland's latest scout, the DH 5. This aircraft featured back-stagger wings, giving it a most distinctive appearance. It had gained an unenviable, if rather undeserved reputation for being a difficult aircraft to fly. Certainly its altitude performance was not good compared with the Pup, SE 5 or Spad, and it was armed only with one machine gun. 23 Squadron had replaced its FE 2Bs with Spad S VIIs, taking these into action during the month, while 4 Naval Squadron at Dunkirk took delivery of the first of another of the war's classic fighters, the Sopwith Camel. Although tricky and unforgiving to fly, once mastered, the Camel was quite incredibly manoevrable and soon became famous for fighting its way out of trouble, rather than flying away from it. Fitted with a variety of rotary engines and armed with two Vickers guns — the most effective armament to date on an Allied aircraft — this little machine was to become the most numerous scout in the RFC and RNAS, and was to be credited with shooting down more of its opponents than any other type during the war.

One of the more successful Allied offensives commenced on 7 June when a series of vast mines which had been planted beneath the German front line positions in secret tunnels dug by the engineers, were set off in the largest man-made explosion ever seen or heard up to that time, opening the Battle of Messines. June was also marked by a feat which was to bring the RFC another Victoria

Cross when 'Billy' Bishop of 60 Squadron returned to report a lone dawn attack on a German airfield, during which he claimed to have shot down three hostile scouts which took off to try and intercept him.

By now the SE 5 had been refined into the improved SE 5A, the first of these reaching 56 Squadron at this time. However on 13th German Gotha bombers made a large-scale daylight attack on London, which resulted in a public outcry over the lack of adequate defence for the capital. In consequence 56 Squadron was posted from France to the London area, while the Pups of 66 Squadron were sent to Calais, placed to intercept any further bombers en route. No repeat raid was made during the next few weeks, and both units soon returned to the front.

A British monoplane scout, the Bristol M1, had been developed, and was approaching service readiness during early 1917. When the DH 5s of 24 and 32 Squadrons had proved disappointing, and 56 Squadron had been suffering various technical problems with its SE 5s, it had been hoped that the new aircraft might prove to be a viable alternative. However an inbred distrust of the monoplane configuration by the British authorities led to delays, and finally in June all available aircraft of this type were despatched instead to the Middle East.

Several leading pilots continued to score well during June, although rather strangely one of the most successful was Capt F.H. Thayre of 20 Squadron, who with his gunner/observer, Capt F.B. Cubbon, were to become the highest scoring of all FE 2 crews, accounting for 20 enemy machines with this type.

The first successes with the Camel were achieved on 5 June, when Flight Commander A.M. Shook of 4 Naval Squadron claimed an Albatros DV shot down and a two-seater out of control. During the month 3 and 6 Naval Squadron re-equipped with this new scout, while 8 and 9 Naval also began to replace their existing machines with them. The RFC's 70 Squadron also converted to Camels from 1½ Strutters, and by the end of July, 45 Squadron also began to receive batches of these machines. 41 Squadron at last got rid of its surviving single-seat pushers when DH 5s were received to replace their FE 8s, and 60 Squadron began converting from Nieuports to SE 5s.

The Germans too were upgrading their equipment, the first Albatros DVs and DVAs reaching the front during May, several Jastas having these new aircraft on strength by the summer. On 6 July, having returned to Jasta 11 after a long leave of absence from the front, Manfred von Richthofen was shot down in combat with an FE 2D, and was wounded in the head, once again being off operations for some weeks as a result.

For the first time during this month, Allied scouts operated as fighter-bombers, carrying light Cooper bombs to drop on targets of opportunity. It was also at this time that Capt Arthur Coningham of 32 Squadron became the most notable exponent of the DH 5, claiming nine victories during a period of just two weeks in mid July. During July and August the three great Naval aces claimed their last successes with the Triplane; Little's score had now reached 37, 24 of them gained whilst flying a Triplane (and he was also the first Camel 'ace'), while Dallas' total had reached 20. Collishaw, Fall and Little were now closely following the RFC's 'Billy' Bishop towards passing Ball's total.

Meanwhile in the Mediterranean area 17 Squadron had moved from Egypt to Macedonia, where quite a lot of combat was taking place in the air. The unit's most deadly opponent was the chivalrous German ace, von Eschwege, but it was here that even the despised BE 12 found an exponent in Capt G.W. Murlis-Green, who claimed half a dozen victories whilst flying this type.

On the Western Front the British now continued their offensive in Flanders by launching the Battle of Ypres on 31 July. This was designed to advance along the Belgian coast up to Ostende, capturing Bruges and Zeebrugge in order to offset the German submarine campaign which was being conducted largely from these seaport bases. During this battle much use was made of scouts in the ground attack role, co-ordinated with the infantry advance, and here the DH 5s were to prove their particular suitability for this task, although the purpose of the new offensive was not to be achieved.

By now the variety of fighting machines in use on the Western Front by the British forces had reached an all-time high.

RFC

UNIT	AIRCRAFT	BASE
1 Squadron	Nieuport 17,	Bailleul
11 Squadron	Bristol F2B	La Bellevue
19 Squadron	Spad S VII	Estree Blanche
20 Squadron	FE 2D	Boisdinghem
22 Squadron	FE 2B	Le Hameau
23 Squadron	Spad S VII	La Lovie
24 Squadron	DH 5	Baizieux
27 Squadron	Martinsyde G 100	Clairmarais
29 Squadron	Nieuport 17	Poperinghe
32 Squadron	DH 5	Droglandt
40 Squadron	Nieuport 17	Bruay
41 Squadron	DH 5	Lealvillers
43 Squadron	Sopwith 1½ Strutter	Auchel
45 Squadron	Sopwith Camel	St Marie-Cappel
46 Squadron	Sopwith Pup	Bruay and Sutton's Farm (temporarily detached to Home Defence)
48 Squadron	Bristol F2B	Bray Dunes
54 Squadron	Sopwith Pup	Leffrinckhoucke
56 Squadron	SE 5/5A	Estree Blanche
60 Squadron	Nieuport 17/SE 5	Le Hameau
66 Squadron	Sopwith Pup	Estree Blanche
70 Squadron	Sopwith Camel	Estree Blanche

RNAS

UNIT	AIRCRAFT	BASE
1(N) Squadron	Sopwith Triplane	Bailleul
3(N) Squadron	Sopwith Camel	Furnes
4(N) Squadron	Sopwith Camel	Bray Dunes
6(N) Squadron	Sopwith Camel	Bray Dunes
8(N) Squadron	Sopwith Triplane/Camel	Mont St Eloi
9(N) Squadron	Sopwith Triplane/Camel	Leffrinckhoucke
10(N) Squadron	Sopwith Triplane	Droglandt
Seaplane Defence Flight	Sopwith Pup	St Pol

18 and 25 Squadrons had exchanged their FE 2Bs for DH 4s during June, becoming bomber units, and 27 Squadron was about to join them in this new role. At home in England, the number of Home Defence squadrons had now risen to 12 — Nos 33, 36, 37, 38, 39, 44, 50, 51, 75, 76, 77 and 78, while 112 Squadron was also being formed, and 61 Squadron was about to be so. On 22 August however, the last daylight raid on England was made, and the main purpose of these units became superfluous. A few days later the first severe night raid by German aeroplanes was made and several of these Home Defence squadrons began training for nocturnal operations.

On the Western Front, the Germans now began grouping chosen Jagdstaffeln into Jagdgeschwadern for larger-scale air superiority operations. During major operations individual Jastas would also be gathered into more temporary groupings known as Jagdgruppen. The first of the new permanent Jagdgeschwadern was JG I, based at Courtrai under the command of Manfred von Richthofen, and incorporating as well as his old Jasta 11, Jastas 4, 6 and 10. During August two pre-production examples of a new Triplane scout, produced by Anthony Fokker as a result of the admiration expressed by the Germans for the performance of the Sopwith machine of this configuration, were supplied to JG I for experimental use. One was allocated to the Baron himself, but was passed by him to Oberleutnant Kurt Wolff, and the other for his successful Jasta commander, Leutnant Werner Voss. Von Richthofen was not at first very impressed with the new aircraft, but Voss quickly put its exceptional manoeuvrability to telling use. Meanwhile on 1 September Richthofen claimed his 60th victim while flying the new Triplane.

Voss was to shoot down 10 Allied machines between 30 August and 23 September to raise his own score to 48, but on the latter day while attempting to shoot down an SE 5 of 60 Squadron, he became involved in a long, and now classic dogfight with six SE 5As of 56 Squadron led by James McCudden. After putting up a wonderful fight, aided briefly by a lone Albatros scout, Voss at last fell victim to Lt Rhys-Davids, dying as Germany's second highest-scoring scout pilot of the war up to this time. 56 Squadron was now considered the RFC's premier unit, the 200th victory being claimed by its pilots on 30 September. This total had already been achieved by 20 Squadron during early August; astonishingly, all this latter unit's claims had been gained in FE 2Ds!

On the British side there was again no leading ace at the front. During August Bishop's claims had equalled, or passed, Ball's score, but after his 47th he had been posted to Home Establishment, returning to Canada to be married. Collishaw and Little, who had both been close to his heels, had also left the front, and the position was wide open.

During September 68 Squadron arrived in France equipped with DH 5s; this unit was composed entirely of Australian Flying Corps personnel. In the same month 43 Squadron, whose obsolescent 1½ Strutters had been suffering severe casualties, exchanged these machines for Camels, marking the end of the former aircraft's first-line service with the British forces. Two further new units to arrive during this month were 28 Squadron, equipped with Camels, and 84 Squadron with SE 5As. In October a fifth DH 5 squadron, 64, arrived, but even as this unit became operational, 41 Squadron was getting rid of these aircraft in favour of the much superior SE 5A. 40 Squadron also converted to the latter aircraft at this time.

In the middle of August the first production examples of Fokker's Triplane, known now as the DrI, were delivered to JG I, but a few days later two experienced pilots were killed in crashes in these aircraft, and all the new machines were grounded pending an investigation. By this time another new German scout had appeared at the front; the Pfalz DIII was not unlike the Albatros in appearance, though rather more graceful. It was not however, to be as affective as the DV.

On 2 November, 1 Naval Squadron's attachment to the RFC ended and the last Sopwith Triplanes left the front — before ever meeting any of the new Fokker Triplanes in combat. The unit retained its machines for a few more weeks while based on the Channel coast, before re-equipping with the ubiquitous Camels. The last Triplane victory was gained on 1 November by Flight Lieutenant H.V. Rowley.

The RFC continued to bring as many squadrons as possible up to date and to the front. Early in November 46 Squadron exchanged its Pups for Camels, while 3 and 65 Squadrons, the former previously an army co-operation unit, began to go into action with the same type of aircraft. The Battle of Cambrai opened on 20 November, the British for the first time employing tanks in a massed attack, without the usual preliminary artillery bombardment. Supported by the Camels of 3 and 46 Squadrons, and by the DH 5s of 64 and 68 (AFC) Squadrons which carried out ground attack sorties, the British forces took the Germans completely by surprise on this quiet sector of the front, and broke through into open country beyond. At the start of the Battle the RFC had 134 scouts available in the immediate area, faced by only the 12 of a single German Jasta. Unfortunately for the Allies, the offensive lacked reserves and could not be exploited. As a result it was soon held up and driven back. Three days after the initial attack, JG I arrived from Flanders, and very heavy fighting developed in the air.

During November, Capt P.F. Fullard of 1 Squadron accidentally broke a leg and was invalided home, having become the top-scorer at the front by this time. However fate had put an end to his run of successes before he could overtake Bishop's or Ball's earlier totals. Another pilot to leave France at this time was Capt A.E. McKeever, a Canadian with 11 Squadron, who with his observers had claimed 31 victories on Bristol Fighters, the highest score to be attained on this type throughout the war. At the end of the month the Fokker DrI was at last cleared for combat, and the RFC was then faced with increasing numbers of this dangerous new opponent.

Meanwhile in Italy, where all had been quiet for some time, the Austro-Hungarians launched a sudden strong offensive at Caporetto, and the Italian forces were soon in headlong flight. In order to bolster up their allies, Britain and France both sent expeditionary forces which helped to stabilize the line in Northern Italy. Accompanying the British contingent went three Camel squadrons, the first of which left France in November. This initial unit was 28 Squadron, only recently arrived on operations; it was followed by 66 Squadron, newly converted from Pups, and the very experienced

45 Squadron. These units were to serve on the Italian front throughout the coming year of 1918, faced initially by a joint German and Austro-Hungarian air force, but after March solely by the latter. Their main opponents were to be Offag-built Albatros DIIIs, Aviatiks, Berg DIs and Phoenix Scouts, as well as several types of two-seaters, most notably of Brandenburg construction.

As yet another winter arrived, the DH 5s began to be phased out of service. 24 Squadron (December), 32, 64 and 68 (AFC) Squadrons (January 1918) all converting to SE 5As. 54 Squadron exchanged the last Pups at the front for Camels, and sufficient modern fighters were now available to allow a few SE 5As to be sent to the Middle East for use by 17 and 47 Squadrons in Macedonia and 111 Squadron in Egypt. These units also received some examples of the production model of the Bristol monoplane, the M IC. Although not used in France due to the continued high level of prejudice, this aeroplane was highly thought of by all pilots who flew it, and was considered by many of them to be superior to any other British fighter operational during 1918.

1918

Late in 1917, 19 Squadron had supplemented, then replaced its decidedly dated Spad S VIIs with the improved two-gun S XIII, and during December 23 Squadron had been similarly re-equipped. In January 1918 however, 19 Squadron exchanged its French fighters for the first examples of a completely new scout, the Sopwith Dolphin. This aeroplane featured back-staggered wings similar to those of the DH 5, and for this reason there was some initial prejudice against it from amongst pilots who had not flown it. A break-away from previous Sopwith practice in that it was powered by a water-cooled, rather than a rotary engine, it was to prove an excellent fighter, with an outstanding high-altitude performance. Throughout its early life it was dogged by engine trouble, but later models proved far more reliable.

The Dophin was particularly unusual in that it incorporated an attempt virtually to double the firepower of existing scouts. Main armament remained a pair of fixed Vickers guns above the engine, but facility existed for two moveable Lewis guns to be provided on a mounting above the cockpit for upward fire. In practice this was found to be unwieldy, and rarely was more than one carried, most pilots preferring to rely only on the twin Vickers. Later in the war provision was made for two further Lewis guns to be fixed on the lower wing planes, firing outside the propeller arc; these could not, of course, be re-armed in flight, and added considerably to the weight of the aircraft. Again, little favour was found for this modification with pilots at the front.

The start of the new year saw the arrival of two more new Camel units, 71 and 80 Squadrons, together with 79, which was equipped with more of the new Dolphins. Like 67 and 68 Squadrons (the former in Egypt), 71 was an all-Australian unit, and early in 1918 these three squadrons were to be re-numbered 1, 2 and 4 Squadrons, Australian Flying Corps.

Mention should also be made of the channel coast area, where aerial activity had been steadily increasing during 1917. Initially seaplanes of the German Marine units had faced their opposite numbers from the Royal Naval Air Service's St Pol Defence Flight. Each side had supplemented these aircraft with growing numbers of fighting scouts, the RNAS Flight receiving Sopwith Pups in mid 1917 to provide cover and defence for the units of the British Grand Fleet. These were replaced by Camels during September, and by the turn of the year the flight had grown into a full squadron, 13 Naval, which was under the command of Squadron Commander Raymond Collishaw, who was now back in action.

Over the Western Front meanwhile Captain James McCudden of 56 Squadron claimed three victories on 16 February 1918 to become the first Empire pilot to pass 50. However the spring of 1918 brought approaching crisis for the Allies. Bled white at Verdun, demoralized by mutinies and consequent summary executions, the French armies were in no condition for anything other than defensive operations. The British forces, seriously weakened by the costly offensives of the previous year, had just taken over an extra 28 miles of front line from the French. The despatch of forces to Italy had further aggravated manpower shortages, and although American troops were expected following their nation's entry into the war during 1917, none had yet arrived. The Germans, greatly strengthened in the West following the conclusion of their armistice with Russia, knew that they must strike now if they were to have any chance of winning the war before the enormous potential manpower and industrial might of the USA could become manifest.

Preparations had therefore been made for a large-scale offensive on the British 3rd and 5th Army fronts to the north and south of Arras. In the air many Corps units (Feldfliegerabteilungen) had been converted to the Schlacht role, providing close ground attack support to the land forces, whilst the number of Jastas had been increased to 80 — although many were understrength and equipped with obsolescent aircraft. However other sectors of the front were denuded to allow 326 fighting scouts to be gathered to support the attack. Although Anglo-French aerial strength was now much greater along the front as a whole, in the area under threat the British could only initially muster 261 scouts. Just prior to the German assault RFC scout squadrons had been reorganised to a strength of 24 aircraft, while sufficient administrative back-up at last allowed unit commanders to fly regularly in action if they so desired, their duties in the past having been mainly of a desk-bound nature.

Despite some two years of almost constant action, Manfred von Richthofen was still at the front with his JG I, an inspiration to all German scout pilots. On 12 March his unit shot down four out of nine Bristol Fighters of 62 Squadron, although next day the latter unit gained its revenge when one of its crews helped to shoot down the Baron's brother, Lothar, who was badly wounded.

Thus on 21 March 1918 the long-awaited German push began, supported by large numbers of ground strafing aircraft. All available British squadrons were thrown into the defence, most units flying ground attack sorties. As reinforcements were rushed to the area, aerial engagements increased sharply as large formations of opposing scouts battled in the skies above, each seeking to prevent the other playing havoc with the low-flying support units.

As the fighting grew, 29 Squadron which was the last unit at the front still flying Nieuport Scouts, claimed the final successes with these aircraft on 23rd, before withdrawing briefly to re-equip with SE 5As. Next day Captain John Trollope, MC, of 43 Squadron claimed six victories between dawn and dusk in his Camel.

25 March was the day of greatest crisis, as despite a famous "backs to the wall" order, the British were forced to withdraw. Squadrons were occasionally shelled out of their airfields by approaching German forces, although some evacuations had begun as early as 22nd. As confusion increased some records were lost or destroyed, making March 1918 one of the worst documented months of the air war as a result. During this period many new British aces built up their scores rapidly. A few subsequently became well-known names, but most remained in almost total obscurity. From March until the end of the war many pilots were to claim more than 20 victories, but most did not receive even the little publicity that had followed the exploits of the pilots of 1917. Such men as Proctor, MacLaren, McElroy, Carter, and many others were in the thick of the fighting at this time.

On 1 April 1918 there occurred a momentous change — although this was scarcely even noticed in the heat of the battle! The Royal Flying Corps and the Royal Naval Air Service merged to form a new and totally independent third force — the Royal Air Force. The Naval squadrons were all renumbered in the 200 range, so that 1 Naval became 201, 3 Naval became 203 and so on; the RNAS's special officers' ranks were changed for the old Army ones that had been employed by the RFC. Only after the end of the war would the RAF's unique new rank structure become adopted (see below for comparative ranks).

Comparative Rank Structure

ROYAL FLYING CORPS	ROYAL NAVAL AIR SERVICE	ROYAL AIR FORCE
2nd Lieutenant	Flight Sub Lieutenant	Pilot Officer
Lieutenant	Flight Lieutenant	Flying Officer
Captain	Flight Commander	Flight Lieutenant
Major	Squadron Commander	Squadron Leader
Lieutenant Colonel	Wing Commander	Wing Commander
Brigadier General		Group Captain
Major General		Air Commodore
Lieutenant General		Air Vice-Marshal
General		Air Marshal
Field Marshal		Air Chief Marshal

The change occurred at a time when the air service could be said to be having a really decisive effect on the outcome of the battles on the ground for the first time. Despite their initial numerical inferiority, the British squadrons had so continually and effectively attacked German troops, supply columns, and bases as to have a disruptive effect upon the advance. This was in no small part responsible for preventing a complete breakthrough to the Channel coast.

On 9 April the Germans attacked again, this time in the Lys area, in a hitherto quiet sector manned by inexperienced Portuguese troops; a rapid breakthrough was achieved. Once more the RAF was thrown in, and on 12th another 43 Squadron pilot, Captain Henry Woollett, repeated Trollope's success of a few days earlier, also claiming six enemy aeroplanes in a single day. On 21st Rittmeister Manfred von Richthofen, top-scoring fighter pilot of the war and victor in over 80 combats, was shot down and killed whilst in action with Camels of 209 Squadron. Capt A.R. Brown, DSC, was officially credited with the 'Red Baron's' demise, but Australian machine gunners also claimed to have brought him down. Controversy has continued over these respective claims ever since, but that submitted by the gunners would, on the face of it, appear to possess the greater merit.

Meanwhile during April 74 Squadron with SE 5As, 87 Squadron with Dolphins and 88 Squadron with Bristol Fighters all arrived in France, followed in May by 85 Squadron with SE 5As. At the same time 23 Squadron exchanged its Spad S XIIIs for Dolphins, thereby effectively standardising RAF scout equipment in France on four types — Camels, SE 5As, Dolphins and Bristol F2Bs. First examples of two new German scouts now began appearing with the Jastas to challenge them, both possessing excellent performances. The Siemens-Schuckert DIII was to be met only in small numbers, but the Fokker DVII (often identified as the Fokker Biplane) was to become the RAF's main opponent for the rest of the war; first with a Mercedes engine and later in its more dangerous guise with a BMW engine.

85 Squadron was commanded by Major 'Billy' Bishop, VC, who speedily sought to regain his ascendency as leading RAF ace. By mid-June, usually flying alone, as was his preferred practise, he had claimed 25 victories in under a month to bring his total to 72. At the request of the Canadian government he was then removed from the front and returned to England to help form the new Canadian Air Force. During this period the Germans had opened their last great offensive on 27 May, and by 30th had reached the Marne, but here they were held.

On the Italian front a new unit had been formed in early March 1918 when Z Flight, which had been operating Bristol Fighters under the administration of 34 Squadron, an RE 8 'Corps' unit, was expanded into 139 Squadron. A number of pilots had been doing well on this front, notably Captain W. Barker, who became commanding officer of the new unit after serving with 28 and 66 Squadrons, and Captain M.B. Frew of 45 Squadron. Lieutenant A. Jerrard of 66 Squadron was engaged in a fight with a reported 19 Austro-Hungarian aircraft whilst accompanied by only two other pilots on 30 March. According to the reports of the other two, he shot down three of these before being shot down and taken prisoner himself; in consequence, the award of a Victoria Cross was announced. During June the Austro-Hungarians also launched a final major offensive on this front, but this too was held. By the end of that month it had become clear that the Central Powers had 'shot their bolts'.

In the Middle East also, the RAF was growing in size. 72 Squadron had arrived at Basra in Mesopotamia (Iraq) with a variety of aircraft, while 150 Squadron was formed in Macedonia from fighter flights in 17 and 47 Squadrons, becoming the first fighting unit in the area, equipped with a mixed bag of SE 5As, Bristol M1Cs, Nieuports, and later, Camels. In Palestine too, 67 Squadron with its all-Australian personnel was becoming 1 AFC Squadron, and had received Bristol Fighters to replace an earlier miscellany of BE 12s, Martinsyde G 100s and other types. The Bristols had been received from 111 Squadron, which had previously operated these alongside Nieuports, but now used these and SE 5As. These two units were to see considerable action, gaining control of the skies in this area.

Since considerably earlier in the war, units of American volunteer pilots had been formed by the French, operating on that sector of the front. Many other American citizens had joined the RFC or RNAS direct, and had seen service with these forces, with which most of them remained until the close of hostilities. During the spring of 1918 however, a number of pilots of the United States Air Service had been sent to Britain to receive operational training and combat experience with British squadrons, many of them serving with RAF units throughout the summer. The US authorities also purchased 143 Clerget-engined Sopwith Camels for the equipment of a nominal four squadrons, two of which were to operate initially in the British sector under RAF control. The first of these to go into action (on 13 July) was the 148th Aero Squadron, followed within a week by the 17th Aero Squadron. They were to remain a part of the 65th Wing until the last few weeks of the war, when they were transferred to the American sector to become a part of the 4th Pursuit Group. Since all their actual operational flying was under RAF control and several of their leading pilots had served first with RAF units, these squadrons are considered to be within the scope of this book, as are all Americans with the RFC, RNAS or RAF.

June had seen the introduction to France of a specialised night-fighter squadron, similar to those fighting Gothas over London. German night raids on Allied supply dumps and airfields had become dangerously effective and this unit, 151 Squadron, equipped with Camels, was sent to oppose these attacks. In July one of the last two RAF scout units to enter operational service before the war ended, arrived at the front; this was 92 Squadron, equipped with SE 5As, and under the command of Major Arthur Coningham, DSO, MC, of DH 5 fame. In 85 Squadron Bishop's place had been taken by Major 'Mick' Mannock, DSO, MC, previously a flight commander with 74 Squadron, who was rapidly building up an impressive score also. However on 26 July he was shot down and killed after successfully attacking a two-seater. After the war, when his exploits became better-known to the authorities, the award of a Victoria Cross was made posthumously. Mannock was virtually unknown outside the air force, though highly-regarded within the service as a leader and tactician. The citation for this award credited him with 50 victories, but subsequently his biographer, 'Taffy' Jones — himself a notable ace in 74 Squadron — claimed that Mannock had gained 73 victories, putting him ahead of Bishop as RAF top-scorer. This total was never officially denied by the Air Ministry and came to be accepted. Many years of detailed research has indicated that it is unlikely that Mannock ever did in fact claim this number of victories, although every effort has been made here to arrive at a definitive listing for him.

On 8 August the Allied forces opened their final great offensive, and from the start all went well, tanks and aircraft playing an important part. On 21st the Battle of Bapaume was fought, followed on 26th by the Battle of the Scarpe. Two days later the final Somme battle commenced. By this time the Sopwith Camel had reached a stage where it was in many respects outclassed by the BMW-Fokker DVII which now equipped many of the most successful German Jastas. Although the British aircraft's wonderful sensitivity and manoeuvrability still allowed an experienced pilot to use to advantage the machine's good points, and to more than hold his own in close combat, losses had begun to rise alarmingly. On 26 August the 17th Aero Squadron lost six of 11 Camels in a fight with JG III; although five of the attackers were claimed in return, none were actually lost. On 5 September 4 AFC Squadron, which had suffered very few losses since July, lost four out of five Camels to eight Fokkers (of JG III), only claiming one 'out of control' in return. However replacement was already in hand, a new rotary-engined Sopwith scout, the Snipe, arriving at the front in September. In the meantime RAF scout squadrons had started operating at least in pairs, a Camel unit flying lower down, covered by an SE 5A unit, and sometimes by both SE 5As and Dolphins. When all three types were used, the Dolphins, which enjoyed an extremely high service ceiling, covering both lower units from upwards of 18,000 feet. Indeed the Dolphin squadrons had really got into their stride during August and September, pilots like R.B. Bannerman and F.W. Gillett of 79 Squadron, A.W. Vigars and A.A.N.D. Pentland of 87 Squadron building up creditable scores with this type of aeroplane.

Further new German types were also appearing, and in August the first examples of the Siemens DIV, an improved version of the DIII, reached selected units, while six pre-production Fokker EV high-wing monoplanes arrived with Jasta 6. One of these was involved in a crash within days of arrival, and as with the Fokker Triplane, the aircraft were at once grounded. However the excellent DVIIs were now being supplemented by the similar Pfalz DXII. Problems with the E V were ironed out, and late in September production versions, now known as the DVIII, began to arrive at the front.

It should be emphasized that, whilst the German Army on the ground was losing its struggle, the Air Service was by no means defeated in the air war, although cuts in training standards had resulted in heavy losses of inexperienced pilots, and fuel for the aircraft was in critically short supply. Following the death of von Richthofen, several new 'champions' had emerged, amongst whom Ernst Udet's star was rising the most rapidly. The losses which the outnumbered German scout pilots were to inflict on the growing mass of Allied aircraft during the final months of the war, far outstripped those of any other period, the inexperienced Americans suffering particularly heavily.

Nonetheless, by mid-September the Allies had recovered all the ground lost during the preceding spring, and on 27th of that month an assault was launched on the Hindenburg Line. These fortifications — the Germans' last real hope — fell remarkably quickly; by 8 October they were all in Allied hands. On 14 October a successful attack was made in the Lys area, and on 17th a Camel of 210 Squadron landed in Ostende, from which port the Germans had just withdrawn.

Action in the air continued to the very last. On 27 October the great ace of the Italian front, Major W. Barker, who had come to France with a personal Sopwith Snipe and was on attachment to 201 Squadron for a 'refresher course' on current activities, flew a lone patrol prior to returning to England. He became involved in a classic and oft-recorded combat with a large number of German fighters after shooting down a two-seater, and in the dogfight reportedly shot down three Fokkers before being brought down himself. In the action he had been seriously wounded three times, his performance bringing the award of a Victoria Cross. Only one further scout pilot was to be so honoured, Captain Anthony Beauchamp Proctor of 84 Squadron, the top RAF 'balloon-buster', receiving the award for his sustained record of success.

By late 1918 aerial operations had developed to a degree of complexity and expertise that approached that of World War II. Indeed the RAF's skills in ground attack, co-operation with tanks, and fighter sweeps were mainly to be lost in the inter-war years due to the need to cling obsessively to the concept of the independent bombing force in order to ensure and protect the fledgling from re-absorbtion by the Army and Navy. Not until 1943/4 were the lessons of 1918 fully to be relearned and put into practise again.

During the closing weeks of the war, Snipes were arriving in France in growing numbers. 4 AFC Squadron joined 43 Squadron in taking these into action late in October, while 208 Squadron began to convert to these fighters also, although too late to use them. 45 Squadron arrived back from Italy to join the Independent Air Force, where the unit was to escort this body's strategic bombers over German territory. Whilst awaiting long-range Snipes, the squadron resumed operations briefly with its faithful Camels.

An idea of the intensity of the air fighting at this time can be gained from the events of 30 October when the RAF alone lost 41 scouts in actions, whilst submitting claims for 67 German aircraft. Even the new Snipes could suffer reverses in such conditions, and on 4 November, 4 AFC Squadron lost three in one combat (two falling to one of the really great German aces of the year, Karl Bolle) in addition to two lost earlier in the day.

Late in October the Allies in Italy gained a great victory at Vittorio Veneto and the Austro-Hungarians collapsed — and with them the whole Hapsburg Empire. The Turkish Army had also been defeated in the Middle East, and only in Germany did fighting continue against a backdrop of revolution and starvation at home. As the Allied advance continued unabated, the whole structure of German society began to collapse, and on 11 November the Armistice was signed, fighting on the Western Front finally coming to an end. The RAF Order of Battle for its fighting scouts at this time had grown to:-

UNIT	AIRCRAFT	BASE	UNIT	AIRCRAFT	BASE
1 Squadron	SE 5A	Bouvincourt	70 Squadron	Camel	Droglandt N.
3 Squadron	Camel	Lechelle	73 Squadron	Camel	Malencourt
11 Squadron	F2B	Mory	74 Squadron	SE 5A	Marcke
19 Squadron	Dolphin	Abscon	79 Squadron	Dolphin	Reckem
20 Squadron	F2B	Iris Farm	80 Squadron	Camel	Bertry W.
22 Squadron	F2B	Aniche	84 Squadron	SE 5A	Bertry
23 Squadron	Dolphin	Bertry E.	85 Squadron	SE 5A	Escaucourt

24 Squadron	SE 5A	Busigny	87 Squadron	Dolphin	Soncamp
29 Squadron	SE 5A	Marcke	88 Squadron	F2B	Bersee
32 Squadron	SE 5A	Pronville	92 Squadron	SE 5A	Bertry E.
39 Squadron	F2B	Bavichove	94 Squadron	SE 5A	Senlis
40 Squadron	SE 5A	Aniche	151 Squadron	Camel (NF)	Bancourt
41 Squadron	SE 5A	Holluin E.	152 Squadron	Camel (NF)	Carvin
43 Squadron	Snipe	Bouvincourt	201 Squadron	Camel	La Targette
46 Squadron	Camel	Busigny	203 Squadron	Camel	Bruille
48 Squadron	F2B	Reckem	204 Squadron	Camel	Heule
54 Squadron	Camel	Merchin	208 Squadron	Snipe	Maretz
56 Squadron	SE 5A	La Targette	209 Squadron	Camel	Bruille
60 Squadron	SE 5A	Quiery	210 Squadron	Camel	Boussieres
62 Squadron	F2B	Villers-les-Cagnicourt	213 Squadron	Camel	Bergues
64 Squadron	SE 5A	Aniche	2AFC Squadron	SE 5A	Auchel
65 Squadron	Camel	Bisseghem	4AFC Squadron	Snipe	Auchel

Independent Air Force

45 Squadron	Camel	Bettancourt

Attached (USAS)

17th Aero Squadron	Camel	ex-Petite Synthe	148th Aero Squadron	Camel	ex-Cappelle

Italy

28 Squadron	Camel	Treviso	66 Squadron	Camel	San Pietro
139 Squadron	F2B	Grossa			

Middle East / Mediterranean

72 Squadron	Spad S VII/ SE 5A/M1C G 100	Baghdad, Mesopotamia	150 Squadron	M1C/SE 5A/ Camel	Kirce, Salonika
111 Squadron	SE 5A	Kantara, Palestine	222 Squadron (part)	Camel (one flight)	Thasos; Greece
145 Squadron	SE 5A	Ramleh, Palestine	1AFC Squadron	F2B	Haifa, Palestine

Home Defence

33 Squadron	Avro 504(NF)	Kirton-in-Lindsay	76 Squadron	F2B	Ripon
36 Squadron	F2B	Usworth	77 Squadron	Avro 504 (NF)	Penston
37 Squadron	Camel	Stow Maries	78 Squadron	Camel	Sutton's Farm
44 Squadron	Camel	Hainault Farm	90 Squadron	Avro 504 (NF)	Buckminster
50 Squadron	Camel	Bekesbourne	112 Squadron	Camel	Throwley
51 Squadron	Camel	Marham	141 Squadron	F2B	Biggin Hill
61 Squadron	SE 5A/Camel	Rochford	143 Squadron	Camel	Detling

1918-1920

The close of hostilities between the Allies and the Central Powers was not to see the immediate conclusion of fighting in Europe, or an end to aerial warfare. Bolshevik forces in Russia were being opposed on several fronts by the forces remaining loyal to the short-lived Kerensky government, or to the old Tsarist regime. These latter disparate elements were receiving growing support from the Western nations, hostile to the new incumbents, and eager to see the old 'status quo' reinstated. Although they were at best equivocal regarding the desirability of full involvement, most felt aggrieved by the Bolsheviks' precipitate withdrawl from the war in 1917, which had led to the reverses suffered on the Western Front during the spring of 1918.

The result was that early in 1919 the Soviets found themselves faced by the following hostile forces:-

i) General Kolchak's White Army in Siberia, supported by American, Japanese and Canadian forces.
ii) White Russian and British troops in North Russia, around Archangel.
iii) The efficient, tough army of newly-independent Poland, anxious to protect their own territory and wrest the Ukraine from the Bolsheviks; the Poles enjoyed the support of France.
iv) A White Army in the Baltic states, marching on Petrograd.
v) A White Russian army moving in the Ukraine.
vi) The Cossacks in open rebellion in South Russia.
vii) General Denikin's Army, mainly comprised of officers of the old Imperial Army, moving out of the Caucasus. Denikin would receive British support, and become Commander-in-Chief of the combined forces in the Kuban and the Don Cossacks.

Many personnel who had served during the Great War volunteered to fly in Russia, and for this reason a brief account of operations has been included. Whilst the British government was finally to bow to public opinion and join other countries in presenting at least the face of non-intervention, initially this was far from being the case. Money was provided to pay, feed and equip Denikin's forces, and as these possessed no air support, personnel of 17 and 47 Squadrons were despatched to South Russia with a number of DH 5 and 9A bombers and Sopwith Camel fighters, forming a new 47 Squadron for operations here. The unit was set up in the Aegean area, sailing aboard a seaplane carrier to Baku via Constantinople (Istanbul). Here it entrained for Petrousek, one of the senior pilots initially being Major J.O. Andrews, DSO, MC. Even as the unit began operating in support of Denikin's forces, Major Raymond Collishaw, DSO, DSC, DFC, was recruiting for the unit in England amongst officers on the point of demobilisation, and in May 1919 his group of volunteers arrived to replace the servicemen who had been drafted to the area.

At this time other RAF volunteers were being shipped to Archangel to support the armies in North Russia, flying DH 4s and 9As, some RE 8s and Short 184 seaplanes. Amongst those serving on this front were a number of ex-scout pilots including notably Major G. Bowman, Captains Ira Jones, Alan Jerrard VC, Keith Park, Oliver Bryson, Thomas Williams and R.L. Chidlaw-Roberts. This group were subsequently to receive two Sopwith Camels and some Nieuport two-seaters to provide escort to the bombers and Corps aircraft, but no aerial fighting ensued on this front. In July 1919 a pair of Snipes were delivered, but were employed mainly in the ground attack role.

In the south 47 Squadron was divided into three flights under Collishaw's overall command, two of these equipped with the De Havilland bombers, the third with the Camels. This latter flight was led by Captain S.M. Kinkead, DSO, DSC, DFC, and other pilots of note serving under him included Aten, Daly, Burns-Thompson and Fulford. The Bolshevik air units facing them were equipped mainly with aircraft of French manufacture, plus a few captured German and Austro-Hungarian types. While aerial clashes were to prove relatively rare events, the occasional attempts by these elements to prevent the British machines undertaking their designated duties did give some pilots opportunities to become involved in dogfights and to claim victories.

Most successful in this role was Sam Kinkead, who added ten more aircraft to his wartime tally, while Marion Aten claimed at least five, and Daly added sufficient victories over 'Red' aircraft to increase his overall total to seven. Although mainly flying with the bombers, Collishaw himself added one victory over an Albatros. Another ex-scout pilot flying bombers on this front was Leonard Slatter, DSC, DFC, who was to be awarded an OBE for his work in Russia between July 1919-March 1920.

The civil war on the steppes of Russia was essentially a cavalry battle, with no specific front lines. Hundreds of thousands of horsemen were employed by each side, and on the featureless, flat and open land the Bolshevik units were to suffer great losses to air attack. Supplies for these forces were moved down the River Volga, the vessels employed also providing ready targets for the airmen. On one occasion a flotilla of small destroyers and other ships was moved from the Baltic to the Volga via canals, in an effort to force the capture of the city of Czaritzsin (later known as Stalingrad). Moored in a semicircle around the city in preparation to carry out a bombardment, they came under attack by aircraft of 47 Squadron which claimed to have sunk 17 vessels with anti-submarine bombs!

By late 1919 Denikin's forces were within 120 miles of Moscow, while Kolchak's army had occupied all Siberia, and the Baltic forces were threatening Petrograd. At this point cohesion and success began to desert the 'White' forces. In Siberia US and Japanese detachments were at loggerheads, while Kolchak's forces were overwhelmed by treachery. In an unfortunately worded speech, Denikin alienated the Cossacks, on whose support he relied greatly. All these sudden reversals caused a general collapse of the anti-Bolshevik forces on a thousand mile front, and as the Cossacks withdrew to their homelands on the Don, the Bolshevik cavalry under General Budenny had little more to do than follow up the retreat and drive the remnants of Denikin's disintegrated army into the Black Sea. Following this disastrous reverse, the remaining forces in the Baltic area soon withdrew and dispersed. By the spring of 1920 all counter-revolutionary elements in Russia had withdrawn or been overwhelmed.

CHAPTER TWO

The Squadrons

At the end of each unit history a list is given of the pilots who gained five or more victories flying with that unit. Where a higher figure is given in brackets after the number of victories quoted, this relates to that individual's total claims for the war. Ranks given are the highest achieved whilst serving with the squadron in question; those pilots who became aces, but achieved less than five victories with any particular unit are not listed in this section of the book.

1 Squadron

Formed in May 1912 as an Airship Company, the squadron became an RFC unit in May 1914 after a short period under Naval Control. Reformed as an aeroplane unit with a variety of machines, with which a move to France was made in March 1915. 20 victories had been claimed by the end of 1916, nine by pilots of single-seater aircraft. In February 1917 it officially became a scout squadron, equipped initially with Nieuport 17s, supplemented later with Types 23 and 27. Re-equipment with SE 5s and SE 5As took place in early 1918. Some 340-350 victories were claimed, 31 pilots being credited with five or more successes. Five of these claimed 20 or over.

Capt P.F. Fullard	40	Capt G.B. Moore	10	Lt E.E. Owen	6
Capt P.J. Clayson	29	Lt B.H. Moody	9	Capt H.A. Rigby	6
Capt W.C. Campbell	23	Capt W.W. Rogers	9	Lt D.E. Cameron	5
Capt L.F. Jenkin	22	Capt C.S.I. Lavers	8	2/Lt L. Cummings	5
Capt T.F. Hazell	20(43)	Capt W.V.T. Rooper	8	Lt K.J.P. Laing	5
Lt H.A. Kullberg	19	Lt J.C. Bateman	7	Lt F.P. Magoun	5
Capt H.G. Reeves	13	2/Lt E.S.T. Cole	7(8)	Capt K.C. Mills	5
Sgt G.P. Olley	11	Capt W.D. Patrick	7	Lt F. Sharpe	5
Capt R.A. Birkbeck	10	Capt C.J. Quintin-Brand	7(12)	Lt W.A. Smart	5
Capt C.C. Clark	10	Maj E.O. Grenfell	6(8)		
1/Lt D. Knight	10	Lt E.T.S. Kelly	6		

3 Squadron

Formed in May 1912, this unit was one of the first to move to France in August 1914, with an assortment of aircraft types. The unit possessed a number of early fighting scouts, but little combat occurred during the first three years at the front, only five claims being made. In October 1917 Sopwith Camels were received and the unit became a fighting squadron, taking part in many ground attack sorties throughout 1918. In this latter period some 120 aerial victories were claimed, Capt D.J. Bell and eight other pilots each achieving at least five victories.

Capt D.J. Bell	17(20)	Lt A.W. Franklyn	6	Lt D.J. Hughes	5
Lt G.R. Riley	13	Capt H.L. Wallace	6(14)	2/Lt W.H. Maxted	5
Capt W. Hubbard	10	1/Lt L.A. Hamilton	5(10)	Capt N.R. Smuts	5

11 Squadron

Formed at Netheravon in February 1915, the unit received Vickers FB 5 'Gunbus' fighting scouts during July, taking these to France on 25th of that month as the first RFC all-fighter unit at the front. By 1916 numbers of DH 2s and Nieuport Scouts had been added to the squadron's equipment, and two of the unit's pilots had gained early fame. These were Lt G.S.M. Insall, who was awarded the Victoria Cross for an action in November 1915, and Lt Albert Ball, who flew with the unit from May to August 1916. In the latter month 'C' Flight was transferred to 60 Squadron with all available Nieuports, and at the same time the squadron was re-equipped with FE 2Bs. These were replaced with Bristol F2B Fighters in June 1917, remaining the unit's equipment for the rest of the war. By November 1918 nearly 300 victories had been claimed, at least 17 pilots being credited with five or more of these. The most successful pilot was Capt Andrew McKeever, who claimed 31 during the summer and autumn of 1917.

Capt A.E. McKeever	31	Lt J.B. Quested	8	Lt C.R. Smythe	6
Capt J.S. Chick	16	Lt H.W. Sellars	8	Capt H.A. Hay	5
Capt E.S. Coler	16	Sgt D.W. Beard	7(8)	2/Lt C.G.O. McAndrew	5
Lt A. Ball	11(44)	Capt S.W. Price	7	Capt J.P. Seabrook	5
Capt F. Libby	9(14)	Capt L.W.B. Rees	6(8)	Sgt T.F. Stephenson	5
Lt R.F.S. Mauduit	9	2/Lt H. Scandrett	6(7)	2/Lt M.S. West	5

17 Squadron

Formed at Gosport in February 1915, this squadron was ordered to the Middle East, where it flew BE 2Cs, BE 12s and AW FK 8s. In July 1916 it began moving flight by flight from Egypt to Salonika in Northern Greece, to operate over the Macedonian Front in a multi-role capacity. The unit's most outstanding pilot at this time was Capt G.W. Murlis-Green, who achieved a number of victories. By 1918 the flight which undertook fighter operations had been fully re-equipped with SE 5As, but in April this was amalgamated with a similar flight from 47 Squadron to form 150 Squadron. 26 victories had been claimed up to this point.

Lt G.E. Gibbs	10	Capt G.W. Murlis-Green	7(8)

18 Squadron

Formed in May 1915 at Northolt, the squadron served initially as a training unit before being posted to France in November 1915, equipped mainly with Vickers FB 5s, but also with a few DH 2s. In April 1916 re-equipment with FE 2Bs followed, the unit then undertaking artillery observation and contact patrols on the Somme, as well as fighting and reconnaissance sorties. Bombing was also undertaken, and in June 1917 the squadron became a bomber unit, receiving DH 4s. Two pilots claimed five or more victories while the unit was operating in the fighting role.

Lt V.H. Huston	6

19 Squadron

Formed at Castle Bromwich in September 1915, the unit moved to France in July 1916, equipped with BE 12s. Due to the failure of these aircraft in the fighting role, bomber operations were flown during November, but early in 1917 Spad S VIIs were received, allowing an effective fighting role to be resumed. These aircraft were supplemented and then replaced by Spad S XIIIs later in the year, notable exponents of this aircraft with the unit including Capt J. Leacroft, Capt F. Sowrey, and Lt A.A.N.D. Pentland. In January 1918 the unit became the first to receive Sopwith Dolphins. 269 victories were claimed, 22 pilots gaining five or more.

Maj A.D. Carter	29	Capt C.V. Gardner	10	Capt J.D. de Pencier	7
Capt J. Leacroft	22	Capt R.A. Del Haye	9	Lt L.H. Ray	7
Lt A.B. Fairclough	14(19)	Capt J.D. Hardman	9	Lt J.G.S. Candy	6
Capt O.C. Bryson	12	Capt F.M. McQuiston	9(10)	Lt C.R.J. Thompson	6
Capt G.B. Irving	12	2/Lt A.A.N.D. Pentland	9(23)	Lt J.A. Aldridge	5
Capt F. Sowrey	12(13)	2/Lt E. Olivier	8	Lt A.W. Blake	5
Capt P. Huskinson	11	Lt N.V. Hustings	7	Capt J. Manley	5

20 Squadron

Formed at Netheravon in September 1915, the unit moved to France on 23 January 1916 with the first FE 2Bs to see action. In one of these Sgt T. Mottershead won a Victoria Cross on 7 January 1917. During early 1917 FE 2Ds with 250 hp engines were received, these proving to be a substantial improvement. As a result the unit's crews were to have claimed 220 victories by September 1917 when re-equipment with Bristol Fighters occurred. Operations in the fighter-reconnaissance role continued until the end of the war, by which time the squadron had made 630 claims, 75 of these during May 1918 alone. This was by a wide margin the highest total for any British scout unit, and no fewer than 42 pilots had claimed five or more victories. Leading amongst these was Capt F.A Thayre, who claimed 20 whilst flying FE 2s, and Capt D. Latimer, the overall top-scorer with 28 on Bristols.

Capt D. Latimer	28	Lt C.R. Richards	11	Capt A.G.V. Taylor	7
Capt W. McK. Thomson	26	Lt R.G. Bennett	9	Lt N.S. Boulton	6
Capt H.G.E Luchford	24	Capt D.C. Cunnell	9	Lt J.H. Colbert	6
Capt T.P. Middleton	20(27)	Sgt F. Johnson	9(16)	Lt R.E. Conder	6
Capt W. Beaver	19	Capt W. Durrand	8	Lt Col H.E. Hartney	6(7)
Capt H.P. Lale	19(23)	Capt V.E. Groom	8	Lt M. McCall	6
Capt F.J.H. Thayre	19(20)	Capt F.G. Harlock	8	Lt D.E. Smith	6(9)
Capt A.T. Iaccaci	17	Capt G.H. Hooper	8(11)	Lt G.P.S. Reid	6
Capt P.T. Iaccaci	17	Capt R.K. Kirkman	8	Lt F.F. Babbage	5
Capt R.M. Makepeace	16(17)	Capt H.L. Satchell	8	Lt E.H. Lindup	5
Capt D.G. Cooke	13	Capt T.C. Traill	8	Capt D. McGoun	5(9)
Capt O.H.D Vickers	13	Lt L.H.T. Capel	7	Maj G.R.M. Reid	5
Lt D.J. Weston	13	Capt T. Colvill-Jones	7(11)	Capt F.D. Stevens	5
Capt R.M. Trevethan	12	Capt H.W. Joslyn	7	Sgt J.J. Cowell	1(+15 as observer)
Lt G.E. Randall	11	Capt A.N. Solly	7(9)		

21 Squadron

Formed at Netheravon in July 1915 with RE 7s, the unit moved to France in January 1916 to undertake the bombing and long-range reconnaissance role. In July 1916 came re-equipment with BE 12s, with which fighting as well as bombing duties were attempted. In this role the squadron achieved little success, top-scorer being Lt J.B. Brophy with four victories. In February 1917 the BEs were replaced by RE 8s and the unit became a Corps squadron — a function in which it was to achieve some note in terms of aerial victories.

22 Squadron

Formed at Gosport in September 1915, the unit went to France in April 1916 with FE 2Bs. Re-equipment with Bristol F2B Fighters followed in July 1917, which aircraft for some months the unit operated in a pure fighting role unlike most other similarly-equipped squadrons, which also undertook the reconnaissance function. In consequence much action was seen, allowing nearly 390 aircraft and balloons to be claimed, 27 pilots and seven gunners claiming five or more such victories. Most outstanding pilots were Captains S.F.H. Thompson, A.C. Atkey, W.F.J. Harvey and J.E. Gurdon, whilst the most successful observer/gunner was Lt C.G. Gass, who flew mainly with Atkey and emerged as the RFC's top-scoring gunner of the war.

Capt S.F.H. Thompson	30	Lt C.W.M. Thompson	12	Lt T.W. Martin	6
Capt A.C. Atkey	29(38)	Capt H.F. Davison	11	Maj R. Stuart-Wortley	6
Capt J.E. Gurdon	28	Lt S.A. Oades	11	Capt W.L. Wells	6(10)
Capt W.F.J. Harvey	26	Lt H.H. Beddow	10	Capt J.V. Aspinall	5(6)
Sgt E.J. Elton	16	Capt G.W. Bulmer	10	Capt C.S. Duffus	5
Capt F.G.C. Weare	15	Capt S.W. Wallage	10	Lt C.E. Hurst	5
Capt C.M. Clement	14	Lt L.W. King	9	Capt W.J. Mostyn	5
Lt F.G. Gibbons	14	Lt F.C. Stanton	7	Lt T.H. Newsome	5
2/Lt E.C. Bromley	12	Lt J.C. Bush	6	Lt I.O. Stead	5

23 Squadron

Formed at Gosport in September 1915 with a mixed bag of aircraft, this unit went to France in March 1916 equipped with FE 2Bs and Martinsyde G 100 'Elephants'. In February 1917 it was selected for re-equipment with French Spad S VIIs, with which it was engaged above the Third Battle of Ypres during June of that year. In December the improved S XIII version of the Spad was received, but in April 1918 came re-equipment with Sopwith Dolphins. The unit claimed over 230 victories and produced 19 aces.

Capt W.J.C.K. Cochran-Patrick	18(21)	2/Lt B. Doran	7	Capt A.B. Fairclough	5(19)
Capt D.U. McGregor	12	Capt H.F.S. Drewitt	7	2/Lt R.W. Farquhar	5(6)
Capt J.W. Pearson	12	Capt J. Fitz-Morris	7(15)	Lt H.A.F. Goodison	5
Lt C.T. Warman	12	Lt H.A. White	7	2/Lt D. Langlands	5
Lt F.J. Gibbs	11	Capt A.E. McKay	6(10)	Lt J.F.N. MacRae	5
Lt S.C. O'Grady	9	Capt L.D. Baker	5		
2/Lt G.I.D. Marks	8	Lt H.N. Compton	5		

24 Squadron

Formed at Hounslow in September 1915 as the first single-seat scout squadron of the RFC, the unit moved to France on 7 February 1916 under the leadership of Major L.G. Hawker VC, DSO. In May 1917, having claimed 85 hostile machines shot down and 30 more driven down, the squadron converted to DH 5s, but with these the pace of success diminished. Only a further 20 or so successes were recorded before the end of the year, when SE 5As were received. By the close of hostilities the score had risen to 175 destroyed and 122 out of control, 33 pilots being credited with five or more. Indeed during the early months of 1918 virtually every pilot who claimed was to be included in this category. The unit's top-scorer was Capt T.F. Hazell who claimed 23 of his 43 victories with the squadron.

Capt T.F. Hazell	23(43)	2/Lt J.J. Dawe	8	2/Lt H.B. Redler	7(10)
Capt I.D.R. MacDonald	20	Lt R.G. Hammersley	8	1/Lt H.L. Bair	6
Capt H.D. Barton	19	Capt E.C. Pashley	8	2/Lt S. Cockerell	6(7)
Capt A.K. Cowper	19	Capt J.O. Andrews	7(12)	2/Lt S.E. Cowan	6(7)
Lt W.C. Lambert	18	Capt B.P.G. Beanlands	7(8)	2/Lt J.A.E.R. Daley	6
Capt G.E.H. McElroy	16(46)	Capt A.J. Brown	7(8)	Capt K. Crawford	5
Lt H.B. Richardson	15	2/Lt C.M.G. Farrell	7	Lt H.C. Evans	5
Lt R.T. Mark	14	2/Lt G.B. Foster	7	2/Lt T.M. Harries	5(11)
Lt P.A. Langan-Byrne	10	Lt A.G. Knight	7(8)	Capt G.O. Johnson	5(11)
Capt A. Wilkinson	10(19)	Capt C.N. Lowe	7(9)	Capt W.H. Longton	5(11)
Capt S.H. Long	9(10)	2/Lt P.A. McDougall	7	Capt H.W. Woollett	5(35)

25 Squadron

Formed at Montrose in September 1915, the unit moved to France in February 1916 with FE 2Bs. On 18 June 1916 2/Lt G.R. McCubbin and his gunner, Cpl J.H. Waller, were instrumental in shooting down the first great German ace, Max Immelmann. The unit's service in the fighting role was brief however, terminating when it became a bomber unit in June 1917, equipped with DH 4s.

2/Lt J.L. Leith	8(9)	Capt C.H.C. Woollven	6	Capt N.W.W. Webb	5(14)
Capt R.G. Malcolm	8	Capt J.H.R. Davey	5(6)		
Capt L.L. Richardson	7	Sgt J.H.R. Green	5		

27 Squadron

Formed at Hounslow in November 1915, the unit moved to France on 2 March 1916, equipped with Martinsyde G 100 'Elephants'. 27 Squadron was the only unit to be fully equipped with these large, heavy scouts, which were soon relegated to day bombing and reconnaissance duties. Nonetheless several pilots managed to gain some successes and invaluable experience whilst flying these aircraft, and amongst these Lts J. Gilmour, D.J. Bell, C.J.W. Darwin, R.W. Chappell and S. Dalrymple were all destined to become notable with other units in due course. In November 1917 the squadron re-equipped with DH 4 bombers.

28 Squadron

Formed in November 1915 at Gosport, the unit undertook training and Home Defence duties, receiving FE 2Bs in July 1917, and then Sopwith Camels two months later. In October 1917 a move was made to France in time for the Third Battle of Ypres, but at the end of the month the unit was ordered to the Italian front, where it served from mid-November until the end of the war, a year later. 111 aircraft were claimed destroyed, and 25 more out of control; Lt C.M. McEwan with 27 victories headed the list of 11 aces.

Lt C.M. McEwan	27	Capt S. Stanger	10(13)	Capt T.F. Williams	6(14)
Capt W.G. Barker	22(50)	Lt A.G. Cooper	7	Capt J.E. Hallonquist	5
Lt H.B. Hudson	13	Capt P. Wilson	7	Lt A.G. Jarvis	5
Capt J. Mitchell	11	Capt J. Mackereth	6(7)		

29 Squadron

Formed at Gosport in November 1915, the unit proceeded to France in March 1916 without flying equipment. Here in the following month it was provided with DH 2s, the first victory being claimed on 29 May 1916. In March 1917 re-equipment with Nieuport 17s took place, these later being supplemented by Types 24 and 27. The squadron was to fly Nieuports longer than any other RFC scout unit, not receiving SE 5As until April 1918. Considerable success was nonetheless achieved with these aircraft, and by the end of the war the squadron 'bag' stood at 385; 26 pilots claimed five or more, headed by Capt T.S. Harrison with 22.

Capt T.S. Harrison	22	Capt E.W. Molesworth	12(18)	Capt A.G. Jones-Williams	8(11)
Capt C.H.R Lagesse	20	Lt H.C. Rath	12	Lt C.M. Wilson	8
Capt C.G. Ross	20	Lt E.O. Amm	10	Lt E.S. Meek	6
Lt A.E. Reed	19	Lt E.G. Davies	10	Lt A.W.B. Miller	6
Lt C.J. Venter	16	Capt R.H. Rusby	10	2/Lt S.M. Brown	5
Capt J.D. Payne	14	Capt A.S. Shepherd	10	Lt P. De Fontenay	5
Capt E.C. Hoy	13	Capt G.W. Wareing	9	2/Lt J.T.B. McCudden	5(57)
Lt W.B. Wood	13	Capt J.G. Coombe	8	Lt F.J. Williams	5
Capt F.J. Davies	12	2/Lt D.F. Hilton	8		

32 Squadron

Formed at Netheravon in January 1915, the unit was equipped with DH 2s which it took to France on 28 May. Here on 1 July the commanding officer, Major L.W.B. Rees, was awarded a Victoria Cross. Early in 1917 a few Nieuport Scouts were received, but in May full re-equipment took place with DH 5s. Capt A. Coningham, one of the flight commanders, was to become the most successful pilot flying this type of scout, claiming nine victories in one month during the summer. In January 1918 SE 5As replaced the De Havillands, and by November over 175 victories had been claimed, 16 pilots gaining five or more of these, including several Americans. The unit's most successful pilot was Capt W.A. Tyrell who claimed 18, twice being credited with three in one day.

Capt W.A. Tyrell	18	Capt W.B. Green	7	Lt B. Rogers	6
Capt A. Coningham	10(14)	Lt F.L. Hale	7	Lt S.R.P. Walter	6
Capt A.A. Callender	8	Capt H.W.G. Jones	7	Lt H.J. Edwards	5
Capt W.R.G. Pearson	8	Lt StC.C. Tayler	7(10)	Capt G.E.B. Lawson	5
Capt A. Claydon	7	Capt W.G.S. Curphey	6		
2/Lt J.O. Donaldson	7	Lt M.J.J.G. Mare-Montembault	6		

40 Squadron

Formed at Gosport in February 1916 with the first FE 8 'pusher' scouts, the unit despatched 'A' Flight to France in August of that year, followed by 'B' and 'C' Flights later in the month. Over 20 victories were claimed with FE 8s, eight of these by Lieutenant E.L. Benbow, but during March 1917 Nieuport Scouts began arriving as replacements, and these remained in service until October, when the unit re-equipped with SE 5As. Lieutenant E.C. Mannock served with the squadron with distinction during the Nieuport-equipped period, whilst in 1918 'notables' included Captain G.E.H. McElroy, who claimed 31 victories during two periods of service with the unit, Lt I.L. Roy, an Indian pilot who shot down ten aircraft in 13 days, and an American, Lt L. Bennett, who claimed nine balloons and three aircraft in just 25 sorties. At the end of the war 350 victories had been claimed over aircraft and balloons.

Capt G.E.H. McElroy	30(46)	Capt G.H. Lewis	10(12)	Capt G.J. Strange	7
Capt E.C. Mannock	16(61)	Lt I.L. Roy	10	Lt J.L. Barlow	6
Capt A.E. Godfrey	13(14)	Capt J.H. Tudhope	10	Capt W.A. Bond	5
Maj A.W. Keen	13(14)	Maj R.S. Dallas	9(32)	Capt G.B. Crole	5
Lt L. Bennett	12	Capt E.L. Benbow	8	Capt G.C. Dixon	5(9)
Lt R.G. Landis	12	Capt I.F. Hind	8	Capt R.N. Hall	5
Capt I.P.R. Napier	12	Capt H.E.O. Ellis	7	Lt D.F. Murman	5
Capt W.L. Harrison	11(12)	Lt W. MacLanachan	7	Lt J.W. Wallwork	5

41 Squadron

Formed at Gosport in July 1916 with FE 8s, the unit took these to France in October where it gained a few successes. In July 1917 re-equipment took place with DH 5s, but these were then exchanged for SE 5As only a month later, although Lts Winnicott and Thomas had time to gain some successes with them first. By the close of hostilities 124 aircraft and ten balloons had been claimed destroyed, plus 112 more out of control. The unit's two most outstanding pilots were both Canadians — Captains W.G. Claxton and F.R. McCall.

Capt W.G. Claxton	37	Maj G.H. Bowman	9(33)	Lt S.A. Puffer	7
Capt F.R. McCall	32(35)	Capt R.W. Chappell	9(11)	Lt H.E. Watson	6
Capt W.E. Shields	24	Lt A.S. Hemming	8	Capt L.J. MacLean	5
Capt E.J. Stephens	13	Lt F.H. Taylor	8(10)	Capt M. Thomas	5
Capt F.O. Soden	11(27)	Lt E.F.H. Davis	7	Lt W.J. Gillespie	5
Lt R. Winnicott	10	Lt M.P. MacLeod	7		

43 Squadron

Formed at Stirling in April 1916, the unit served first at Northolt on Home Defence duties. In January 1917 it was equipped with Sopwith 1½ Strutters, moving to France under the command of Major W. Sholto-Douglas. Re-equipment with Camels followed in September 1917, which were exchanged a year later for the first Sopwith Snipes to reach the front. During March and April 1918 Captains Trollope and Woollett each claimed six aircraft shot down in one day, Woollett becoming the unit's top-scorer. Nine other pilots claimed five or more victories from the squadron's total of 122.

Capt H.W. Woollett	30(35)	Capt H.H. Balfour	9	Lt G. A. Lingham	6
Capt C.F. King	22	Lt H.C. Daniel	9	Lt J.H.G. Womersley	5
Capt C.L. Trollope	18	Lt G.C. Bailey	8		
Capt C.C. Banks	11(12)	Lt R.J. Owen	7		

44 Squadron

Formed at Hainault Farm in July 1917 with Sopwith 1½ Strutters as a Home Defence unit, the squadron received Camels within a month of formation. Experimentation with night flying proved the Camel suitable for this work, and brought the first night victory over a Gotha bomber. The unit continued on these duties for the rest of the war, but achieved no further victories. Several notable pilots were to serve with the unit between tours of duty at the front.

45 Squadron

Formed at Gosport in March 1916, the squadron moved to France in October of that year, equipped with Sopwith 1½ Strutters. A few Nieuport two-seaters were added to these for a brief spell during April 1917, but in July re-equipment with Camels commenced, and in November the unit moved to Italy. In September 1918 the squadron returned to France to operate as part of the Independent Air Force, escorting bombers into German territory for raids on industrial targets. Whilst awaiting re-equipment with long-range Snipes, some ten final victories were claimed, five of them by Capt J.W. Pinder, to raise the squadron's total for the war to 316. Capt M.B. Frew was top-scorer with 25, while Capt G.H. Cock claimed an outstanding 12 whilst flying 1½ Strutters. 30 pilots claimed five or more victories.

Capt M.B. Frew	23	Lt R.J. Dawes	8(9)	Lt E.D. Clarke	6
Capt C.E. Howell	19	Capt N.C. Jones	8(9)	Lt A.J. Haines	6
Capt G.H. Cock	13	Lt C.H. Masters	8	Lt T.M. Harries	6(11)
Capt J. Cottle	13	Lt H.M. Moody	8	Lt O.L. McMaking	6
Capt R.J. Brownell	12	2/Lt T.F. Williams	8(14)	Lt A. Rice-Oxley	6
Capt J.C.B. Firth	11	Capt W.A. Wright	8	Lt F.S. Bowles	5
Lt K.B. Montgomery	11(12)	Lt J.H. Dewhirst	7	Lt J.E. Child	5
Capt M.R. James	10(11)	Lt E.A.L.F Smith	7	Lt E. McN. Hand	5
Capt N. Macmillan	9	Lt J.D. Belgrave	6(18)	Capt A.T. Harris	5
Lt P. Carpenter	8(24)	Lt C.G. Catto	6	Capt J.W. Pinder	5(17)

46 Squadron

Formed at Wyton in April 1916, the unit moved to France in October as a Corps unit, equipped with Nieuport two-seaters. Re-equipment with Sopwith Pups followed during the spring of 1917, and in July the unit returned to England for six weeks on Home Defence duties following the first daylight raids by Gothas on London. Returning to France, the now-obsolescent Pups were exchanged for Camels in November, following a period of heavy losses; the new aircraft were first employed during the Battle of Cambrai. During the German offensive of March 1918 the squadron undertook much low attack work in support of the Army, while also managing to claim 21 victories in one 24 hour period ending 23 March. In all, 184 victories were claimed, Capt D.R. MacLaren emerging as the top-scorer with 54 victories in eight months.

Capt D.R MacLaren	54	Capt C.A. Brewster Joske	7(8)	Lt C.H. Sawyer	6
Capt G.E. Thomson	21	Capt A.G. Lee	7	Lt P.M. Tudhope	6
Capt C.J. Marchant	9	Lt R.K. McConnell	7	Lt H.G.W. Debenham	5(6)
Lt H.N.C Robinson	8(10)	Capt C.O.W. Odell	7	Lt V.M. Yeates	5
Lt J.H. Smith	8	Capt M.D.G. Scott	7(12)		
Lt A.G. Vlasto	8	2/Lt M.M. Freehill	6(7)		

47 Squadron

Formed at Beverley in March 1916 for Home Defence duties with BE 12s, the unit was sent overseas to Salonika in September of that year, taking with it a variety of BE 2Cs, Avro 504s and AW FK 3s. In 1917 BE 12s were once again received, together with some DH 2s for air fighting, one flight becoming fighter-equipped. In April 1918, when more than ten victories had been claimed, the flight was detached with a similar flight from 17 Squadron, to form 150 Squadron. Following the Armistice the squadron was sent to South Russia early in 1919 to support the anti-Bolshevik forces, and here — known as 'A' Squadron, RAF Mission — it once again featured a fighter flight, this time equipped with Sopwith Camels. Some months of fighter operations were undertaken over South Russia under the command of Major Raymond Collishaw, and a number of victories were claimed, Capt S.M. Kinkead adding further to his war-time score as the flight's most successful pilot, while an American officer, Lt M. Aten, also claimed five victories.

Capt S.M. Kinkead	?10(35/40)	Lt M.H. Aten	5

48 Squadron

Formed at Netheravon in April 1916, the unit received the first of the new Bristol F2A Fighters in early 1917. These were taken to France on 8 March 1917, but were initially incorrectly employed by one flight, and in consequence during their first action on 5 April lost four out of six to Jasta 11, including that flown by Capt W. Leefe-Robinson, VC. Properly employed as a fighting scout however, the Bristol soon showed that it was a match for opposing single-seaters, particularly when in the hands of pilots such as A.M. Wilkinson and F.P. Holliday. The improved F2B version soon arrived, and by the end of the war the unit had claimed 317 victories, 32 pilots becoming aces. Most successful amongst these was K.R. Park, who rose rapidly from Lieutenant to Major commanding the unit, claiming 20 victories along the way.

Maj K.R. Park	20	Capt F.C. Ransley	9	2/Lt W.O.B. Winkler	6
Capt F.P. Holliday	17	Capt A.M. Wilkinson	9(19)	Capt F.J. Cunninghame	5
2/Lt R.L. Curtis	15	Lt R.D. Coath	7(8)	2/Lt H.W. Elliott	5
Capt J.H.T. Letts	13	2/Lt H.A. Hartley	7	Lt R.B. Hay	5
Capt B.E. Baker	12	2/Lt T.P. Middleton	7(28)	Sgt N. Hunt	5
Capt H.A. Oaks	11	2/Lt W.T. Price	7	Lt R.H. Little	5
Capt L.A. Payne	11	Capt C.R. Steele	7	2/Lt H.J. Pratt	5
Capt R. Dodds	10	Capt J.E. Drummond	6	Lt A.G. Riley	5
2/Lt J.A.W. Binnie	9	Capt N.C. Millman	6	Lt N. Roberts	5
Capt J.T. Milne	9	2/Lt T.G. Rae	6	2/Lt E.G.H.C. Williams	5
Capt C.G.D. Napier	9	Capt O.J.F. Scholte	6(8)		

54 Squadron

Formed at Castle Bromwich in May 1916, the squadron was the first RFC unit to be equipped with Sopwith Pups, which it took to France in December of that year. More than 55 victories had been claimed when these were replaced by Camels a year later, the unit then undertaking much ground strafing work throughout much of 1918, as well as adding at least 80 more victories. Ground attack duties could be expensive however, and some 40 Camels were lost between February and April 1918. The unit top-scorer was Capt E.J. Salter with nine victories, while 10 more pilots claimed at least five each.

Capt E.J. Salter	9	Capt F.M. Kitto	6(9)	Maj R.S. Maxwell	5(9)
Capt H.H. Maddocks	7	Lt O.M. Sutton	6(7)	Capt O. Stewart	5
Capt G.H. Hackwill	6(9)	Capt M.E. Gonne	5	Capt W.V. Strugnell	5(6)
Capt F.N. Hudson	6	Lt G.A. Hyde	5		

56 Squadron

Formed at Gosport in June 1916, the squadron was the first to receive the new SE 5 fighter, which it took to France in April 1917. It was the nearest to an 'elite' unit ever to be formed in the RFC, and included in its initial establishment Capt Albert Ball, VC. Like 46 Squadron, the unit was withdrawn to England for six weeks during June and July 1917 due to the threat posed to London by the appearance of the Gotha bombers. SE 5As subsequently supplemented and then replaced the original SE 5s, and by the end of the war 427 victories had been claimed, including six balloons. 26 pilots claimed five or more victories, Capt McCudden gaining 51 of his total of 57 whilst with the unit, but losses were heavy, 40 pilots being killed, 20 wounded and 31 taken prisoner.

Capt J.T.B. McCudden	51(57)	Lt M.E. Mealing	14	Capt L.W. Jarvis	7
Lt R.T.C. Hoidge	27(28)	Capt A. Ball	13(44)	Lt H.J. Walkerdine	7
Capt G.C. Maxwell	26	Capt W.R. Irwin	11	Capt W.S. Fielding-Johnson	6
Lt A.P.F. Rhys-Davids	25	Lt T. Durrant	10(11)	Capt P.B. Prothero	6(8)
Capt G.H. Bowman	22(33)	2/Lt R.H. Sloley	9	Capt W.O. Boger	5
Capt R.A. Mayberry	21	Capt E.W. Broadberry	8	Capt D. Grinnel-Milne	5(6)
Lt L.M. Barlow	20	Lt K.W. Junor	8	Lt C.H. Jeffs	5
Capt H.J. Burden	16	Lt C.A. Lewis	8	Lt H.A.S. Molyneux	5
Capt C.M. Crowe	14(15)	2/Lt K.K. Muspratt	8		

60 Squadron

Formed at Gosport in April 1916, the unit went to France the following month equipped with three types of Moranes — Bullets, Biplanes and Parasols. Following very heavy losses during the opening weeks of the Somme battles, it was withdrawn from the front and was rebuilt around the Nieuport Scouts and pilots of 'C' Flight, 11 Squadron. Nieuports formed the main equipment until replaced by SE 5s in July 1917, these later giving way to SE 5As. 320 victories were to be claimed, 47 of them by Captain W.A. Bishop, the unit's most successful pilot. Over 20 others became aces, but more than 70 pilots were reported killed or missing while serving with the squadron.

Capt W.A. Bishop	47(72)	Capt R.L. Chidlaw-Roberts	9(10)	Capt W.E. Molesworth	6(18)
Lt A. Ball	20(44)	Capt J.E. Doyle	9	2/Lt S.L.G. Pope	6
Capt F.O. Soden	16(27)	Capt K.L. Caldwell	8(25)	Capt J.B. Crompton	5
Capt H.A. Hamersley	13	Lt G.M. Duncan	8	Lt W.M. Fry	5(10)
Capt J.D. Belgrave	12(18)	Capt H.G. Hegarty	8	Capt J.W. Rayner	5
Capt A.W. Saunders	12	Capt W.J. Rutherford	8	Maj A.J.L. Scott	5
Capt A. Beck	11	Capt A.D. Bell-Irving	7	Lt R.K. Whitney	5
Capt W.J.A. Duncan	11	Lt J.S. Griffith	7	Lt G.C. Young	5
2/Lt W.C. Jenkins	10	Lt S.B. Horn	6(13)		

62 Squadron

Formed at Filton in August 1916, the squadron was at first used as a training unit until mobilized for front line service late in 1917. It departed for France in February 1918, equipped with Bristol F2B Fighters, claiming 76 aircraft destroyed and 85 out of control by the end of the war. Capt W.E. Staton was top-scorer with 26.

Capt W.E. Staton	26	Lt C.H. Arnison	9	Lt W.K. Swayze	6
Capt G.E. Gibbons	17	Capt L. Campbell	7	2/Lt P.S. Manley	5
Capt T.L. Purdom	13	Capt E.T. Morrow	7		
Capt G.F. Hughes	11	Lt D.A. Savage	6		

64 Squadron

Formed at Sedgeford in June 1917, the unit was equipped with DH 5s, which it took to France in October of that year, undertaking ground attack sorties during the Battle of Cambrai. In January 1918 SE 5As were received, allowing the unit to claim over 130 aerial victories, Capt J.A. Slater heading the list of 11 aces with a personal score of 22.

Capt J.A. Slater	22(24)	Capt C.W. Cudemore	10(15)	Lt B.A. Walkerdine	6
Capt E.R. Tempest	17	Capt W.H. Farrow	9(10)	Capt E.D. Atkinson	5(10)
Capt P.S. Burge	11	Capt D. Lloyd-Evans	8	Capt R.S. McClintock	5
Lt T. Rose	11	Lt C.A. Bissonette	6		

65 Squadron

Formed at Wyton in August 1916, the squadron received Camels a year later and moved to France with these during October 1917. During the next 12 months some 200 victories were claimed, including 17 by eight pilots during a single action on 4 November 1918. Capt J. Gilmour claimed 35 of his victories whilst with the squadron.

Capt J. Gilmour	36(39)	Capt A.A. Leitch	7	Capt G.M. Cox	5
Capt J.L.M. White	22	Capt E.G. Brookes	6	Lt E.C. Eaton	5
Capt M.A. Newnham	18	Maj J.A. Cunningham	6(10)	Lt G.O.D. Tod	5
Lt T.M. Williams	9	Lt H.L. Symons	6		
2/Lt W.H. Bland	7	Lt G. Bremridge	5		

66 Squadron

Formed at Filton in June 1916, the squadron went to France in March 1917 equipped with Sopwith Pups. It was moved to Calais in June, and then back to England for several weeks of Home Defence duties, following the first daylight raid on London by Gotha bombers. It was replaced by 46 Squadron early in July, returning to France. In October 1917 re-equipment with Camels took place, and next month the unit moved to the Italian front, where considerable success was claimed. Whilst there Captain A. Jerrard was awarded a Victoria Cross for an action during which he was shot down and became a prisoner, on 30 March 1918. At least 250 victories were claimed over France and Italy, allowing 19 pilots to be credited with five or more victories each.

Capt W.G. Barker	16(50)	Capt H.B. Bell	10	Lt H.K. Boysen	5
Capt P. Carpenter	16(24)	Lt C. McEvoy	9	Lt W.C. Hilborn	5(6)
Lt H.K. Goode	15	2/Lt H.R. Eycott-Martin	8	Capt T.V. Hunter	5
Lt F.S. Symondson	13	Lt W.M. MacDonald	8	Lt J.S. Lennox	5
Lt G.A. Birks	12	Lt A. Gerrard	7	Lt W.A. Pritt	5
Capt C.M. Maud	11	Lt A. Paget	6		
Lt G.F.M. Apps	10	Capt J.O. Andrews	5(12)		

67 Squadron/1 AFC Squadron

Originally formed in Australia in 1915 as a general reconnaissance and bombing unit, the squadron was despatched to the Middle East to serve in Egypt early in 1916. Here it operated a diverse collection of aircraft, including Martinsyde G 100s, BE 2Cs and a number of Bristol Scouts. Subsequently a quantity of BE 12s were supplied to increase the unit's ability to defend itself, although these failed to achieve any conspicuous success. RE 8s and up-engined Martinsydes were received during late 1917, but in 1918 when 111 Squadron was re-equipped with SE 5As, this latter unit's Bristol Fighters were then passed to 1AFC, which achieved some notable successes with them. On a number of occasions the unit's pilots were conspicuously successful in forcing down German aircraft in combat and then destroying them on the ground. Indeed, by August 1918 full aerial superiority in the area had been gained. Over 50 victories were claimed by the unit, and some eight of its pilots became aces.

Capt R.M. Smith	12	Lt G.C. Peters	7	Lt E.S. Headlam	5
Lt E.P. Kenney	7	Lt A.V. Tonkin	6	Lt C.S. Paul	5
Lt P.J. McGiness	7	Capt A.R. Brown	5		

68 Squadron/2 AFC Squadron

Formed at Heliopolis, Egypt, with Australian personnel in October 1916, the unit was shipped to France, arriving in September 1917 and being equipped with DH 5s. These were replaced by SE 5As in January 1918, at which time the unit was renumbered 2 Squadron, Australian Flying Corps. About 170 victories were claimed, 16 pilots gaining five or more of these.

Capt F.R. Smith	16	Lt G.H. Blaxland	8	Lt J.J. Wellwood	6
Capt R.C. Phillips	15	Capt R.W. Howard	8	Capt A.G. Clark	5
Capt R.L. Manuel	12	Lt F. Alberry	7	Lt G.J. Cox	5

Capt H.G. Forrest	11	Lt E.E. Davies	7	Capt E.L. Simonson	5
Capt A.T. Cole	9	Lt C.O. Stone	7		
Capt E.D. Cummings	9	Lt R.W. McKenzie	6		

70 Squadron

Formed at Farnborough in April 1916, the squadron was the first in the RFC to equip with Sopwith 1½ Strutters. The aircraft received had actually been transferred from the RNAS. The unit moved to France in flights during May-August 1916, under the command of Major A.W. Tedder. During July 1917 it became the first RFC unit to receive Sopwith Camels, operating these fighters until the end of the war. 287 victories were claimed, Capt F.G. Quigley being credited with 33 of these and 18 other pilots with five or more each.

Capt F.G. Quigley	33	Lt G.R. Howsam	12(13)	Lt D.H.S. Gilbertson	5
Capt J. Todd	18	Capt C.F. Collett	11	Lt E.C. Gribben	5
Capt F.H. Hobson	15	Lt A. Koch	10	Capt F.H. Laurence	5
Capt F.C. Gorringe	14	Lt K.B. Watson	9	Capt J.T. Morgan	5
Capt O.A. Heron	14	Capt N.W. Webb	9(14)	Lt E.H. Peverell	5
Capt S.T. Liversedge	13	Lt K.G. Seth-Smith	7		
Capt W.M. Carlaw	12	2/Lt E.B. Booth	5		

71 Squadron/4 AFC Squadron

Formed at Castle Bromwich in March 1917 with Australian volunteers, the unit received Camels as its equipment in December 1917, departing at once for France with these. It was renumbered 4 Squadron, Australian Flying Corps, in January 1918, and was to prove one of the most aggressive and successful Camel units at the front during the year. In October 1918 it was one of the first units to re-equip with Sopwith Snipes, 35 victories in a month with these new mounts bringing the squadron's total to some 220. Capt A.H. Cobby, the AFC top-scorer, was the unit's leading pilot with 29 victories, ten other pilots also being aces.

Capt A.H. Cobby	29	Capt T.C.R. Baker	12	Lt A.J. Palliser	7
Capt R. King	26	Lt L.E. Taplin	12	Lt N.C. Trescowthick	7
Capt E.J.K. McCloughry	21	2/Lt T.H. Barkell	7	Capt G.F. Malley	6
Capt H.G. Watson	14	Capt G. Jones	7		

72 Squadron

Formed at Upavon in July 1917, the unit was sent to the Middle East, arriving at Basra (now in Iraq) for operations over Mesopotamia, as three detached flights, 'A' with DH 4s, SE 5As and Spad SVIIs; 'B' with Martinsyde G 100s, and 'C' with Bristol M1C monoplanes. These flights aided various elements of the British Army as it drove the Turks out of the area, being mainly involved in ground attack work as few hostile aircraft were to be met over the area.

73 Squadron

Formed at Upavon in July 1917, the unit moved to France in January 1918 equipped with Camels. Patrols and ground attack work — some of it while attached to the Tank Corps for direct support duties — brought the squadron 120 aerial victories, ten pilots claiming five or more, of whom the most successful was Capt O.M. Baldwin.

Capt O.M. Baldwin	16	Lt E.J. Lussier	11	Capt T.S. Sharpe	6
Capt G.L. Graham	13	2/Lt R.W. Chandler	7	Capt G.E.H. Pidcock	5(6)
Lt W.S. Stephenson	12	Lt N. Cooper	6		
Capt W.H. Hubbard	11(12)	Capt M. LeBlanc Smith	6		

74 Squadron

Formed at Northolt in July 1917, the squadron was led to France at the end of March 1918 by Major K.L. Caldwell, equipped with SE 5As. Here it was to claim 140 aircraft destroyed and 85 out of control for the relatively modest loss of 15 pilots killed or taken prisoner. Of the 17 pilots who claimed five or more victories, Capt E.C. Mannock gained 36 of his total with the unit, while Capt J.I.T. Jones was credited with 37 in just three months.

Capt J.I.T. Jones	37	Lt F.S. Gordon	9	Lt H.G. Clements	6
Capt E.C. Mannock	36(61)	2/Lt F.J. Hunt	9	Lt G.W.G. Gauld	5
Capt B. Roxburgh-Smith	22	Capt C.B. Glynn	8	Lt P.F.C. Howe	5
Maj K.L. Caldwell	16(25)	Lt G.R. Hicks	8	Lt F.L. Luff	5
Capt A.C. Kiddie	14	Capt W.E. Young	8(11)	1/Lt H.G. Shoemaker	5
Capt S. Carlin	10	Lt H.E. Dolan	7		

79 Squadron

Formed at Gosport in August 1917, the squadron went to France in February 1918 equipped with Sopwith Dolphins. Victories over 77 aeroplanes and nine balloons were claimed, five pilots becoming aces, of whom the most successful was an American, Capt F.W. Gillet.

Capt F.W. Gillet	20	Capt F.I. Lord	12	Lt E. Taylor	5
Capt R.B. Bannerman	17	Lt J.H. McNeaney	5		

80 Squadron

Formed in August 1917 at Montrose, the unit moved to France in January 1918 after equipping with Camels. Here it undertook much ground support work, particularly in co-operation with the Tank Corps as an anti-tank gun suppression unit. In this role the unit suffered relatively heavy casualties without much opportunity for aerial combat, but one flight commander, Capt H.A. Whistler, gained considerable success, claiming 23 victories from the unit's total of approximately 60.

Capt H.A. Whistler	23

84 Squadron

Formed at Beaulieu in January 1917, the unit subsequently received SE 5s and SE 5As. It was led to France by Major W. Sholto-Douglas on 23 September 1917, where it became a premier fighting unit and the RAF's top balloon-busting squadron. 323 victories were claimed, 54 of them by Capt A.W.B. Proctor, who was awarded a Victoria Cross. 25 pilots were credited with five or more victories.

Capt A.W. Beauchamp Proctor	54	Capt R. Manzer	11	Lt C.L. Stubbs	7
Capt W.A. Southey	20	Capt J.S. Ralston	11(12)	Lt G.A. Vaughn	7(13)
Capt C.F. Falkenburg	17	Capt F.E. Brown	10	Lt G.O. Johnson	6(11)
Capt R.A. Grosvenor	16	2/Lt W.H. Brown	9	2/Lt J.A. McCudden	6(8)
Capt S.W. Highwood	16	Lt J.F. Larsen	9	Lt C.R. Thompson	6
Capt H.W.L. Saunders	15	Capt K.M.StC. Leask	8	Capt J.M. Child	5(8)
Capt J.V. Sorsoleil	14	Lt P.K. Hobson	7	Lt C.F.C. Wilson	5
Lt E.A. Clear	12	Lt H.O. MacDonald	7		
Lt N.W.R. Mawle	12	Lt W.J.B. Nel	7		

85 Squadron

Formed at Upavon in August 1917, the unit initially received Sopwith Dolphins, but these were exchanged early in 1918 for SE 5As. On 22 May 1918 the unit went to France, commanded by Major W.A. Bishop, VC, DSO, MC, who was to claim his final 25 victories in a short period with the squadron, before being sent home to Canada. He was replaced by Major E.C. Mannock, until the latter's death in action a few weeks later, and then by another notable ace, Major C.M. Crowe. 99 victories were claimed, eight pilots gaining five or more each.

Maj W.A. Bishop	25(72)	Capt A.C. Randall	8(10)	Capt S.B. Horn	7(13)
Capt M.C. McGregor	10(11)	Lt J.W. Warner	8	Lt W.H. Longton	6(11)
Maj E.C. Mannock	8(61)	Lt A. Cunningham-Reid	7		

87 Squadron

Formed from a nucleus at the Central Flying School, Upavon, in September 1917, the squadron was despatched to France in April 1918 equipped with Sopwith Dolphins. Operating against high-flying German reconnaissance two-seaters during the initial months after arrival, on one occasion the unit despatched eight of these in one ten day period. By the end of the war more than 90 victories had been claimed for the loss of only six pilots killed in action and three lost as prisoners. Eight pilots became aces, of whom Capt A.W. Vigers was the most successful.

Capt A.W. Vigers	14	Capt H.J. Larkin	11	Lt R.M. Macdonald	5
Capt A.A.N.D. Pentland	13(23)	Capt H.A.R. Biziou	8	Lt C.E. Worthington	5
Lt L.N. Hollinghurst	11	Maj C.J.W. Darwin	5		

88 Squadron

Formed at Gosport in July 1917, the unit was equipped with Bristol F2B Fighters, with which it proceeded to France in April 1918 to undertake the fighter-reconnaissance role. Here the squadron helped to develop air-to-air wireless telegraphy, and also took part in many bombing raids. In combat it claimed 147 victories, of which 20 were credited to Lieutenant K.B. Conn, the leading of the unit's 11 aces. Losses amongst the two-man crews were very light, amounting only to two killed, five wounded and ten missing.

Lt K.B. Conn	20	Lt A. Williamson	9	Lt W.A. Wheeler	6
Capt E.G Johnston	19(20)	Lt G.F. Anderson	8	Lt R.J. Cullen	5
Capt A. Hepburn	16	Lt J.P. Findlay	6	Lt G.R. Poole	5
Capt C. Findlay	14	Capt W.G. Westwood	6		

92 Squadron

Formed in September 1917 at London Colney, the unit went to France in July 1918 with SE 5As, under the command of Major A. Coningham. Here during its brief service, 38 aircraft were claimed shot down and 18 out of control. The outstanding pilot was an American, Captain O.J. Rose, who claimed 16 victories; five others were credited with five or more.

Capt O.J. Rose	16	Capt W.E. Reed	7(9)	Capt J.M. Robb	6(7)
Lt T.S. Horry	8	Lt E.F. Crabb	6	Lt H.B. Good	5

111 Squadron

Formed in Palestine in August 1917 from a flight of 14 Squadron, the unit initially received a variety of fighting types, mainly Bristol Fighters. During January 1918 Nieuports and SE 5As became more numerous, subsequently allowing the Bristols to be passed to 1 AFC Squadron. By the end of the war some 59 victories had been claimed on this distant front, eight of them by Captain R.M. Drummond, who twice claimed three in a single engagement. Three other pilots also became aces, while the commanding officer, Major F.W. Stent MC, himself claimed four. The squadron fought over Palestine, Syria, Egypt and Iraq.

Capt R.M. Drummond	8	Capt A.H. Peck	8	Lt C.R. Davidson	5(6)
2/Lt A.L. Fleming	8				

139 Squadron

Formed at Villaverla, Italy, in July 1918 from 'Z' Flight of 34 Squadron with Bristol F2B fighters, the unit undertook fighter-reconnaissance sorties over the Italian front for the rest of the war. Commanding officer was Major W.G. Barker, who generally flew in his personal Sopwith Camel which he had brought with him from his previous unit. He was to claim eight of the unit's 27 victories whilst flying this.

Maj W.G. Barker	8(50)	Lt W.C. Simons	8

150 Squadron

Formed in Salonika in April 1918 by the amalgamation of the fighter flights from 17 and 47 Squadrons, the unit initially equipped with Sopwith Camels, SE 5As and Bristol M1C monoplanes. 80 further victories were to be added to the 36 or so already claimed by the flights; 10 pilots became aces either with victories in 17 or 47 Squadron and then with 150 Squadron, or with the latter unit only.

Capt G.G. Bell	12(16)	Lt F.D. Travers	9	Capt G.C. Gardiner	6
Lt C.B. Green	11	Capt F.G. Saunders	8	Lt L. Hamilton	6
Lt D.A. Davies	10	Lt A.E.deM. Jarvis	7		
Capt A.G. Goulding	9	Lt J.C. Preston	7		

151 Squadron

Formed at Hainault Farm in June 1918 from flights of night fighter Camels drawn from 44, 78 and 112 Squadrons, the unit was intended for night defensive and intruder duties in France. A move to that country was made late in the month, where command was taken by Major C.J. Quintin-Brand, and one flight was attached to 101 Squadron for intruder sorties behind German lines. 21 bombers were to be claimed shot down during the hours of darkness, Lieutenant A.V. Blenkiron adding to earlier victories to become an ace, while the most successful pilot was Major Quintin-Brand himself, who claimed four victories to add to his previous successes as a scout pilot.

1 Naval/201 Squadron

Formed at Furnes, Dunkirk, in December 1916 from the earlier RNAS 'A' Squadron, which had been a part of No. 1 Wing, the unit initially equipped with Sopwith Pups and a few Nieuports, but had become fully equipped with Sopwith Triplanes by January 1917. Immediately thereafter it moved to the Western Front, coming under RFC control until November of that year. It then returned to the coast and converted to Camels, remaining there until February 1918, when it once again returned to RFC control. On 1 April it became 201 Squadron, RAF. Very heavy casualties were suffered during ground attack operations in August 1918, but by the end of the war over 250 victories had been claimed and 18 pilots had become aces, the most successful of whom was Captain S.M. Kinkead with 29. Other pilots of note had included Minifie and Rosevear, while the unit had been commanded by two outstanding fighters, Roderick Dallas and Charles Booker.

Capt S.M. Kinkead	29(35/40)	Capt M.H. Findlay	12(14)	Maj C.D. Booker	6(29)
Capt S.W. Rosevear	25	Capt C.B. Ridley	11	Flt Lt T.G. Culling	6
Capt R.P. Minifie	21	Flt Cdr H.V. Rowley	9	Flt Cdr C.A. Eyre	6
Sqn Cdr R.S. Dallas	16(32)	Lt A.G.A. Spence	9	Flt Cdr F.H.M. Maynard	6
Capt G.B. Gates	16	Flt Cdr T.F.N. Gerrard	8(10)	Capt R. McLaughlin	6
Capt R.C.B. Brading	13	Capt J.H. Forman	7(9)	Lt H.L. Wallace	6(14)

3 Naval/203 Squadron

Formed in late 1916 at Dunkirk from 'C' Squadron, No 1 Wing, by mid January 1917 the unit had been strongly reinforced with pilots from No 3 Wing which had previously been a strategic bombing formation, operating on the southern French front. Equipped with Sopwith Pups released by 8 Naval Squadron, which had converted to Triplanes, it operated under RFC control from mid February until the end of May, proving to be one of the most successful units during this period. The unit returned to Naval control at Dunkirk in June and re-equipped with Sopwith Camels. A period of little decisive air action followed, until October when the squadron moved to England for a brief rest. It returned to Dunkirk in January 1918, and in March once more moved south to come under RFC control. On 1 April it became 203 Squadron, RAF, at which time it was commanded by Major R. Collishaw who claimed his last 19 victories of the war while leading the squadron. The most successful pilot was Captain L.H. Rochford, who claimed 29 victories, while 22 further pilots claimed five or more to contribute to the unit total of around 250.

Capt L.H. Rochford	29	Capt H.F. Beamish	11	Flt Sub Lt W.H. Chisham	7
Capt A.T. Whealy	23(27)	Sqn Cdr A. Breadner	10	Flt Sub Lt E. Pierce	7(9)
Maj R. Collishaw	19(60)	Lt A.B. Ellwood	10	Flt Lt H.S. Kerby	6(9)
Lt J.A. Glen	15	Flt Sub Lt J.J. Malone	10	Flt Sub Lt G.B. Anderson	5
Capt E.T. Hayne	15	Capt J.D. Breakey	9	Capt L.D. Bawlf	5
Lt W. Sidebottom	14	Lt F.J.S. Britnell	9	Flt Sub Lt A.W. Carter	5(17)
Flt Cdr F.C. Armstrong	13	Flt Lt F.D. Casey	9	Flt Lt H.G. Travers	5
Flt Lt J.S.T. Fall	13(36)	Capt R.A. Little	9(47)		

4 Naval/204 Squadron

Formed at Cudekirke in December 1916 from 'A' Squadron, No 5 Wing, the unit was initially equipped with Sopwith 1½ Strutters and was mainly involved in bombing operations. However in March 1917 conversion to Sopwith Pups followed, and a move was made to Bray Dunes in April, where the unit was to remain for the rest of the year. In June 1917 the squadron became the first unit to receive Sopwith Camels, the first victories for this type being recorded on 5 June. In April 1918 it became 204 Squadron, RAF, and by 5 May it had claimed a total of 49 aircraft shot down and 43 out of control. A further 140 victories had been added by the end of the war, Captain C.R.R. Hickey heading the list of 19 squadron aces with 22 victories. The squadron remained at the northern end of the front throughout 1918, engaging in many large-scale engagements with the German MarineFeld-Jastas during the latter part of the year.

Capt C.R.R. Hickey	21	Lt W.B. Craig	9	Capt T.W. Nash	6
Capt A.J. Enstone	13	Lt R.McI. Gordon	9	Lt R.M. Bennett	5
Capt R.McN. Keirstead	13	Flt Lt L.W.F. Smith	8	Flt Sub Lt S.E. Ellis	5
Capt J.E.L. Hunter	12	Capt C.P. Allen	7	2/Lt J.D. Lightbody	5
Capt A.M. Shook	12	2/Lt H.G. Clappison	6	Lt O.J. Orr	5
Capt A.J.B. Tonks	12	Capt G.H.D Gossip	6		
Flt Cdr A.J. Chadwick	11	Flt Lt G.W. Hemming	6		

6 Naval Squadron

Formed in December 1916 at Petite Synthe, the unit was attached to the RFC in March 1917, at which time it was equipped with Nieuport Scouts. It took part in the severe air fighting of the early months of that year, during which time its most successful pilot was Flight Commander E.W. Norton. In June 1917 re-equipment with Sopwith Camels began, but its life as a fighting squadron ended in August, by which time 35 victories had been claimed. It reformed in January 1918 as a bomber unit with DH 4s, subsequently becoming 206 Squadron, RAF, in April of that year.

Flt Cdr E.W. Norton	8(9)	Flt Cdr B.P.H.De Roeper	5

8 Naval/208 Squadron

Formed at St Pol in October 1916 with Sopwith Pups, Nieuport Scouts and 1½ Strutters, the unit was placed under RFC control after initial service at Dunkirk. After a few weeks at the front it had become fully equipped with Pups, subsequently converting to Camels during July-August 1917, one flight at a time. In March 1918 the unit moved to England for a rest, before again coming under RFC control on its return to France later that month. On 1 April 1918 it became 208 Squadron, RAF, and at the end of October that year re-equipped with Sopwith Snipes. Several famous pilots served with 8 Naval, notably R.A. Little, R.J.O. Compston and C.D. Booker; Little gained 38 of his 47 victories while with the unit, while W.L. Jordan claimed 39. In total 298 victories were claimed and 26 pilots became aces.

Capt W.L. Jordan	39	Flt Sub Lt H. Day	10(11)	Lt R.C.D'A. Gifford	6
Flt Cdr R.A. Little	37(47)	Lt R.L. Johns	9	Flt Sub Lt P.A. Johnstone	6
Flt Cdr R.J.O. Compston	25	Lt J.S. McDonald	9	Flt Cdr G.G. Simpson	6(8)
Flt Cdr C.D. Booker	23(29)	Flt Cdr R.B. Munday	9	Flt Cdr A.R. Arnold	5
Lt E.G. Johnstone	17	Flt Lt R.R. Thornley	9	Flt Cdr S.J. Goble	5(10)

Capt W.E.G. Mann	13	Capt R. McDonald	8	Lt M.C. Howell	5
Flt Cdr G.W. Price	12	Lt P.M. Dennett	7	Lt W.H. Sneath	5
Flt Sub Lt R.R. Soar	12	Capt G.K. Cooper	6		
Capt J.B. White	12	Lt H.H.S. Fowler	6		

9 Naval/209 Squadron

Formed at St Pol in the Dunkirk area in February 1917, the squadron began life with a mixture of Sopwith Pups and Triplanes, and Nieuport Scouts. By June it was fully equipped with Triplanes and later that month was attached to the RFC, remaining so until September. By then it had been re-equipped with Camels, which it operated over the Channel area until early in 1918, when it flew to England for a short rest. Recalled to France in March 1918, it was again attached to the RFC, now flying Bentley-engined Camels. On 21 April, having become 209 Squadron, RAF, at the start of that month, the unit was involved in the famous engagement with Jagdgeschwader I in which Freiherr Manfred von Richthofen met his death. Between its formation and 25 April 1918, the unit claimed 68 destroyed and 39 out of control, adding 58 more victories by November 1918, plus three forced down and captured, for a final total of 168. The squadron was most particular in crediting shares in victories to its various pilots, the most successful of whom was Flt Cdr J.S.T. Fall, who claimed 23 of his total of 36 with the unit. At least 17 other pilots claimed five or more.

Flt Cdr J.S.T Fall	23(36)	Flt Cdr F.E. Banbury	11	Lt M.S. Taylor	8
Capt S.T. Edwards	16	Flt Sub Lt A.V. Wood	11	Lt C.G. Edwards	7
Capt O.M. Redgate	16	Capt O.C. LeBoutillier	10	Lt F.J.W. Mellersh	5
Capt R.M. Foster	15(16)	Capt A.R. Brown	9(10)	Flt Sub Lt H.G. Mott	5
Flt Lt H.F. Stackard	15	Lt J.H. Siddall	9	Lt K.M. Walker	5
Capt W.R. May	13	Capt J.K. Summers	8		

10 Naval/210 Squadron

Formed at St Pol in February 1917 from pilots of No 3 Wing RNAS, with Sopwith 1½ Strutters and Nieuport single- and two-seaters, the unit moved to Furnes where it was re-equipped with Sopwith Triplanes. These were employed over the Western Front under RFC control from May 1917, being replaced by Camels during the following August. Flight Commander R. Collishaw proved to be the most successful of the unit's pilots at this time. In April 1918 the unit became 210 Squadron, RAF, undertaking much ground attack work during the months that followed. By November 1918, 345 victories had been claimed and 29 pilots had become aces, but with 105 casualties the squadron had been the hardest-hit British scout unit of the war.

Flt Cdr R. Collishaw	34(60)	Lt W.S. Jenkins	12	Flt Lt H.J.T. Saint	7
Capt W.M. Alexander	23	Capt H.A. Patey	11	Flt Cdr J.E. Sharman	7(8)
Flt Sub Lt E.V. Reid	19	Lt C.W. Payton	11	Lt P. Boulton	6
Capt E. Swale	17	Lt I.C. Sanderson	11	Lt F.V. Hall	6(7)
Capt L.P. Coombes	15	Capt H.T. Mellings	10(15)	Capt W.G.R. Hinchliffe	6
Lt K.R. Unger	14	Flt Sub Lt D.F. Fitzgibbon	8	Flt Sub Lt G.E. Nash	6
Flt Cdr W.A. Curtiss	13	Capt H.B. Maund	8	Lt C.F. Pineau	6
Lt S.C. Joseph	13	Lt A. Buchanan	7	Flt Lt G.E. Trapp	6
Capt J.G. Manuel	13	Lt A.L. Jones	7	Lt G.A. Welsh	5
Capt A.W. Carter	12(17)	Flt Lt J.A. Page	7		

11 Naval Squadron

Formed at Dunkirk in March 1917 as a fighter unit, the squadron served mainly as an operational training unit. Its three flights were to be equipped with Sopwith Pups, Triplanes and Camels, with which a certain amount of combat was seen on occasions, 2 or 3 victories being claimed by the unit's personnel. It was disbanded at the end of August 1917 due to shortage of pilots, but was to be reformed as a bomber unit in January 1918, subsequently becoming 211 Squadron, RAF.

13 Naval/213 Squadron

Formed at Dover in June 1917 on a one flight basis, the unit moved to Dunkirk shortly afterwards where it was known initially as the St Pol Seaplane Defence Flight. In this role it was equipped with Sopwith 1½ Strutters and Pups. During September it was expanded to full squadron strength to give cover to the North Sea Fleet, and was re-equipped with Camels, becoming 13(N) Squadron in January 1918. On 1 April it became 213 Squadron, RAF, but continued its oversea role, also undertaking a good deal of ground attack work during the last months of the war. Credited with about 110 victories, the squadron produced 14 aces by the war's end, most successful of whom was Captain G.C. MacKay, who claimed 18.

Capt G.C. MacKay	18	Lt C.J. Sims	9	Flt Cdr M.J.G. Day	5
Capt J.E. Greene	15	Capt M.L. Cooper	6	Maj R. Graham	5
Capt C.P. Brown	14	Lt G.S. Hodson	6(10)	Lt W.E. Gray	5
Capt J.de'C. Paynter	9(10)	Lt D.S. Ingalls	6	Lt H.C. Smith	5
Capt J.W. Pinder	9(17)	Capt L.H. Slatter	6(7)	Lt A.H. Turner	5

17th Aero Squadron, US Air Service

Formed in the USA in 1917, this unit was sent to France where it entered action in July 1918, flying Sopwith Camels as part of the British 65th Wing. Later, under III Brigade, the squadron took part in the August offensives, while during September many low strafing missions were flown. In October the unit was posted to the American front to join the 4th Pursuit Group, but the war ended before it got back into action. 53 aircraft were claimed shot down and 11 others out of control, but losses included 13 killed and six taken prisoner, six Camels being lost during a single action with JG III on 26 August. The unit's leading pilot was Lieutenant Howard Burdick with eight victories, while four others claimed five or more.

Lt H. Burdick	8	1/Lt G.A. Vaughn	6(13)	2/Lt R.M. Todd	5
2/Lt H.C. Knotts	7	1/Lt L.A. Hamilton	5(10)		

148th Aero Squadron, US Air Service

Formed at Kelly Field, Texas, in late 1917, the unit was posted to France where it went into action under British control on 20 July 1918. However patrols had actually begun a few days earlier, the first victory being claimed on 13 July. The unit moved to the American front on 29 October, but was too late to see any further action here. Claims totalled 47 destroyed and 19 out of control, Captain Elliot White Springs claiming 12 victories, while four others claimed at least five.

1/Lt E.W. Springs	12(16)	1/Lt H.R. Clay	8	1/Lt C.L. Bissell	6
1/Lt F.E. Kindley	11(12)	1/Lt J.O. Creech	7		

Scout Pilots Claiming Five or More Victories Prior to the Formation of Scout Squadrons

Name	Squadron	Score	Name	Squadron	Score
Maj L.G. Hawker	6	7	FSL H.T. Mellings	2W(N)	5(15)
Maj C.G. Bell	10	5+	FSL R.H. Mulock	1W(N)	5
Capt H.W. Medlicot	2	5+			

Scout Aces Gaining Less Than Five Victories With Any One Squadron

Name	Squadron	Score	Name	Squadron	Score
Maj C. Draper	3W, 6(N), 8(N), 208	9	Capt W. Cairnes	19, 74	5
Capt A.T. Drinkwater	57, 40	9	Maj J.C. Callaghan	18, 87	5
Capt J.W. Aldred	3, 70, 3	8	1st Lt L.K. Callahan USAS	85, 148th	5
Capt G.L. Lloyd	60, 40	8	Capt S. Dalrymple	27, 139	5
Capt H. Meintjes	60, 56	8	Capt E.B. Drake	Manston, 209	5
Maj C.M.B. Chapman	24, 29	7	Maj E.L. Foot	11, 60	5
Capt E.D. Crundall	8(N), 210	7	Lt W.B. Giles	43, 74	5
Lt R.H. Daly	10(N), 47	7	Flt Lt E.R. Grange	1W, 8(N)	5
Capt I.H.D. Henderson	19, 56	7	Capt J.P. Hales	9(N), 203	5
Flt Cdr N.M. Macgregor	6(N), 10(N)	7	Lt R.A. Hewat	19, 87	5
Capt A.H. Orlebar	19, 73, 43	7	Capt E.Y. Hughes	46, 3	5
Capt D.M. Tidmarsh	24, 48	7	Capt J.D. Latta	5, 1, 60, 66	5
Maj A.M. Vaucour	70, 45	7	Capt T.C. Luke	66, 209	5
Capt H.G. White	20, 29	7	Capt L.M. Mansbridge	1, 23	5
Lt C.G. Brock	1(N), 209, 3	6	2/Lt W.S. Mansell	22, 1	5
Capt D.M.B Galbraith	1W, A, 8(N)	6	Lt R.F. McRae	4 AFC, 46	5
Capt H.J Hamilton	1, 29	6	Capt R.H.G. Neville	21, 23	5
Lt R.A. Hewat	19, 87	6	Capt T.A. Oliver	1, 29	5
Capt N. Keeble	1W, 202	6	Capt E.R. Pennell	27, 84	5
Capt A.T. Loyd	22, 25, 32	6	Maj C.E.M. Pickthorne	32, 84	5
Lt W.G. Meggitt	25, 22	6	1st Lt O.A. Ralston USAS	85, 148th	5
Maj R. Raymond-Barker	48, 11, 3	6	Maj W.D.S. Sanday	2, 70, 19	5
Capt R. Sykes	9(N), 203, 201	6	Capt R.H.M.S. Saundby	24, 41, Orfordness	5
Lt J.S. Turnbull	56, 41	6	Capt S.P. Smith	6, 46	5
Capt D'U.V. Armstrong	60, 151	5	1st Lt W.D. Tipton USAS	3, 17th	5
Capt F. Billinge	20, 32, 56	5	Capt L.E. Whitehead	60, 65	5
Lt A.V. Blenkiron	25, 56, 151	5	Flt Cdr R.R. Winter	6(N), 9(N)	5
Capt A.J. Bott	70, 111	5	Capt E.L. Zink	18, 32	5

Interpretation of the Claim Lists

A few words are necessary regarding interpretation of the claim lists appended to each pilot's biographical notes. A glossary of the abbreviations employed is also set out below.

Reading from left to right, the first column indicates the numerical sequence of the claims, running from one onwards. The addition of a small 's' indicates a shared victory. In such cases the identities of the other pilots involved and, where possible, the serial numbers of the aircraft which they were flying, are indicated at the end of the list. Unless stated otherwise, all the pilots sharing may be assumed to be from the same unit. In the case of two-seater crews, identity of those sharing the claim is given in the order pilot/observer.

The second column is headed by the year, beneath which are set out the specific dates within that year on which each claim occurred.

The third column indicates the types claimed, whether aeroplane or balloon (see glossary for meanings of abbreviations used). The fourth column is headed by an identification of the type of aircraft flown when the claims were made, beneath which is the individual serial number of the aircraft in which each specific claim was made. These serials where possible have been checked with surviving operational record books and the RNAS equivalent. However some units made multiple claims on one combat report and listed for example, the names of five pilots followed by five serial numbers. It can only be assumed that the first pilot was allocated the first machine identified, and so on. Further, some combat reports are extremely indistinct, while a fair percentage contain typing errors.

The fifth column indicates the squadron in which the pilot was serving when making the claim. In the sixth column is the location of the claim (it is strongly recommended that a reliable map of the area be referred to if any checking or dispute regarding identities of claiming pilots on any particular date is intended). The place names separated by a hyphen indicate a location between the identified locations. A series of numbers, such as 57C L27 are map references employed for locational purposes by certain squadrons. The time of the engagement is given in the seventh column. All times have been converted to a 24 hour clock for the avoidance of confusion. The RAF adopted such a system in 1918. Where two times are separated by a hyphen, this indicates either the time of departure and the time of return of the patrol undertaken, or in some instances the duration of a particularly long engagement. A small 'c' before the time noted indicates 'circa' (approximately). Where in columns four, six or seven a series of dashes appear, this indicates that information relevant to this claim has not been discovered. This particularly applies to units which had their records destroyed (e.g. 23 Squadron). Column eight is the classification of the claim made (see glossary for explanation of terms). The final column indicates the source or sources of the information set out. The main sources have been the Royal Flying Corps and Royal Naval Air Service Communiques, combined after April 1918 into the Royal Air Force Communiques; the 5 Group Communique and the RFC and RAF War Diaries. Also where possible Brigade and Wing Records have been used. This is particularly necessary for 'out of control' claims in 1918. It was also evident during research that there are various omissions of particular units at various times from the higher command records.

At the end of each entry a total is given, broken down by type of claim made. Finally where the identity of the aircraft claimed can be ascertained with a reasonable degree of certainty, this is provided with the name of the pilot or crew and the unit. This must not be considered definitive, since German records are incomplete.

Glossary

1. Aircraft Claimed

C	Unidentified two-seater
D	Unidentified Scout
Alb.	Albatros
Halb.	Halberstadt
Hann.	Hannover
SS	Siemens Schuckert

(All other aircraft types are identified by their full designation.)

2. Identities of Aircraft Types Flown

Nieup	Nieuport Scout
Strutter	Sopwith 1½ Strutter
Triplane	Sopwith Triplane
Bristol	Bristol F2A or F2B Fighter unless otherwise indicated

(All other aircraft types are identified by their full names or designation.)

3. Abbreviations for Classifications of Claims

DES	Destroyed
DES(F)	Destroyed in flames
CAPT	Landed in Allied lines (this may or may not indicate intact)
OOC	Out of control
FTL	Forced to land (NB in Palestine this category was only allowed if the aircraft had also been strafed on the ground)
DD	Driven down
FTL/DES	Forced to land and crashed

4. Abbreviations for Sources and Comment Thereon

A. Official Documents

AIR 1/number		File in which a particular Report was found. This is used where no other evidence is available.
BG WD	Brigade War Diary:	Usually prefaced by the number of the Brigade in Roman numerals; this indicates confirmation within the Brigade War Diary.
Citation		Mention in the citation to a medal award or recommendation.
CR	Combat Report	
DL	Dunkirk List:	A list maintained which indicated all claims accepted by the RNAS in France; although it contains errors, it provides a useful confirmation of RNAS claims.
DOS	Daily Operational Summary:	An RNAS document.
DRO	Daily Return of Operations:	RNAS document relating to squadrons operating under Naval control; when units operated under RFC control, these became ORBs.
5 GR and/or 5 GR Comm	5 Group Communique:	This Group operated on the Channel coast, and after 1 April 1918 remained under Naval control; hence none of its activities are mentioned in the RAF Communiques; the Group produced its own Communiques, e.g. 204 Squadron's claims do not appear in the main Communiques until late October 1918 when the unit finally came under RAF control.

OH	Official History:	Particularly with regard to Australian and Canadian pilots.
Pbr	Probationary Observer:	Particular rank for an observer before gaining 'observer's' insignia and becoming a Second Lieutenant.
ORB	Operational Record Book	
RAF and date	RAF Communique of date specified:	The date given was often that after the action in respect of claims made in the late afternoon. No reliance can be placed upon the date in the Communiques being the correct date.
RAF WD	RAF War Diary	
RC	Record of Combats:	Certain squadrons maintained such records (e.g. very few combat reports have been found for 66 squadron, but the Record of Combats for each pilot lists most of the details).
RFC and date	RFC Communique of date specified:	Comments as for RAF Communique.
RFC WD	RFC War Diary	
RNAS and date	RNAS Communique of date specified:	Comments as for RAF Communique. (NB The authors have been unable to discover RNAS Communiques for the period May-early July, 1917).
SD	Squadron Diary:	In particular those hand-written diaries kept by 24 and 32 Squadrons detailing all operations.
SQ REC or SR	Squadron Records:	Used for some units where lists of claims were maintained, but no combat reports exist.
Sq Vic List	Squadron Victory List:	A few units maintained full lists of claims, e.g. 41 and 204 Squadrons.
Summ.	Summary:	E.g. in respect of one combat for 20 Squadron on 4 February 1918, a Summary of the claims has been found, but no supporting combat records are in existence.
US 133	Study 133 of the USAF Academy:	A listing of all US Air Service claims made during World War I, prepared by the Academy at Maxwell Air Force Base, Alabama.
203 WD	203 Squadron War Diary:	A highly detailed, but unofficial history.
WS	Wing Summary:	Usually prefaced by the Wing number (e.g. 11 WS); 11 Wing particularly retained copies of all their combat reports from late 1916 until the end of the war, apart from about two months in early 1918). These are generally grouped as an Appendix to a War Diary. Indicates a claim (usually 'out of control') for which confirmation is lacking, generally because no other documents have been found for the period in question.

B. Unofficial Sources

AC	*Air Command*, R. Dodds and R. Collishaw.
ADOGB or ADGB	*Air Defence of Great Britain*, C. Cole and F. Cheesman, in relation to claims over Great Britain.
AR	Alex Revell — indicating his two books on various 56 Squadron pilots.
CB	Chaz Bowyer — indicates either his biography of Albert Ball, or *For Valour*.
C&C	*Cross & Cockade* — indicates references to an article in either the Journal of *Cross & Cockade US* or *Cross & Cockade Great Britain/International* — particularly with regard to 62 Squadron.
CEM	*Courage of the Early Morning*, Bishop.
Jackson	Only reference available for the claims of certain pilots in South Russia in 1919.
Mac	The books of Norman Macmillan — *Offensive Patrol* and *Into the Blue*.
RLR	Raymond Rimmel — indicating his book *The Zeppelin Fighters*.

SS	Secondary Source — i.e. an unspecified book.
TBYW	*Those Brave Young Wings*, R. Dodds.
TFE	*The Flying Elephants*, Chaz Bowyer.
TS	*Tiger Squadron*, J.I.T. Jones.

5. Abbreviations for German and Austro-Hungarian Ranks and Unit Designations

A. German

i. Units

BG	Bogohl	(Bomber Group)
FA	FliergerAbteilung	(Reconnaissance Unit)
FA(A)	FliegerAbteilung(A)	(Artillery Spotting Unit)
KEK	KampfeinsitzerKommando	(Single-seat Fighter Detachment)
KSt	Kampfstaffel	(Bomber Unit)
Sch	Schlasta	(Ground Attack Unit)
SchSt	Schutzstaffel	(Escort Unit)

ii. Ranks

Fl	Flieger	(Private)
Uffz	Unteroffizier	(Corporal)
Fw	Feldwebel	(Sergeant)
Serg	Sergeant(Artillerie)	(Artillery Sergeant)
FwLt	FeldwebelLeutnant	(Master Sergeant)
Vzfw	Vizefeldwebel	(Sergeant Major)
Offstlvtr	OffizierStellvertreter	(Warrant Officer)
Fh	Fähnrich	(Ensign)
Lt	Leutnant	(2nd Lieutenant)
Oblt	Oberleutnant	(1st Lieutenant)
Hpt	Hauptmann	(Captain)
Rttm	Rittmeister	(Cavalry Captain)
Flgm	Flugmaat	(Flying Mate — Naval)
FlgObm	FlugObermaat	(Flying 1st Mate — Naval)
LtzS	Leutnant zur See	(Lieutenant — Naval)

B. Austro-Hungarian

i. Units

Flik	Fliegerkompanie	(J) indicates Fighter (D) indicates Reconnaissance etc.

ii. Ranks

FP	Feldpilot	(Private)
Zgfhr	Zugsführer	(Junior NCO)
KorpP	KorporalPilot	(Corporal)
Fw	Feldwebel	(Sergeant)
StFw	Stabsfeldwebel	(Staff Sergeant)

NB OffizierStellvertreter and above, the ranks are as for the German forces (see above).

CHAPTER THREE

The Aces – Biographical and Claim Notes

ALBERRY Frank Lieutenant 2 AFC

An Australian, born on 29 September 1892 in Hobart, Tasmania, Alberry worked his way to England as a young man and joined the British Army, from which he subsequently deserted to return home. On the outbreak of war he joined the Australian infantry, serving with distinction in the Dardanelles and then in France as a Lewis gun section commander. He was wounded in action in July 1916, having his right leg amputated as a result. He was subsequently awarded the DCM. On recovery he petitioned King George V personally to be allowed to transfer to the RFC, and following flying training was posted to 2AFC Squadron in France to fly SE 5As. Here he gained seven victories during the last two months of the war. He returned to Australia and became involved in the timber business, rejoining the RAAF for recruiting duties during World War II. He died in 1969 at the age of 77.

	1918		SE 5A					
1	16 Sep	Fokker DVII	D6995	2AFC	N W Lille	0730	DES(F)	CR/ORB/RAF 25
2	17 Sep	Fokker DrI	D6995	2AFC	Lille	1020	OOC	CR/ORB/OH
3	17 Sep	Fokker DrI	D6995	2AFC	Lille	1020	OOC	CR/ORB/OH
4	18 Oct	Fokker DVII	D6995	2AFC	N Tournai	1230	OOC	CR/ORB/OH
5	28 Oct	Fokker DVII	D6995	2AFC	Bandour	1120	OOC	CR/ORB/OH
6	28 Oct	Fokker DVII	D6995	2AFC	Bandour	1120	DES	CR/ORB/RAF 31
7	4 Nov	Fokker DVII	D6995	2AFC	Houtaing	1310	OOC	CR/ORB/OH

TOTAL: 2 destroyed, 5 out of control = 7.

ALDRED John William Captain 5, 70, 3

Born on 26 August 1884, Aldred served with the Royal Lancashire Regiment before transferring to the RFC, with which force he became an observer in 5 Squadron from 30 August 1916 until 3 April 1917. During this period he claimed two enemy aircraft shot down and was awarded an MC. Following pilot training, he returned to France on 21 October 1917 and served with 70 Squadron, claiming three victories before being promoted to Captain and made a flight commander in 3 Squadron on 3 April 1918. During May 1918 he claimed a further three victories and received a Bar to his MC.

	1917		BE 2C					
1*	16 Feb	Alb. DII	2533	5	Hebuterne	0930	DES(F)	CR/RFC 16.2
2**	16 Feb	Alb. DII	2533	5	Hebuterne	0930	OOC	CR/RFC 16.2
			Camel					
3s***	9 Nov	Alb. DV	B2396	70	Staden	1610	OOC	CR/RFC 9.11
	1918							
4	5 Feb	C	B5179	70	Houthoulst-Staden	1335	OOC	CR/RFC 5.2
5	12 Mar	Alb. DV	B7471	70	Menin-Wervicq	1245	DES	CR/RFC 12.3
6	15 May	LVG. C	C1675	3	Map 57C G26	0934	DES(F)	CR/RFC 16.5
7	15 May	LVG. C	C1655	3	Map 57D L5	1030	OOC	CR/RFC 16.5
8s†	19 May	C	C1655	3	Map 57D R13	0650	CAPT	CR/RFC 19.5

TOTAL: 2 and 1 shared destroyed, 4 and 1 shared out of control = 8.

*Pilot: Sgt H.G. Smith: The aircraft destroyed was flown by Lt Hans Gutermuth of Jasta 5, who was killed. **Shared with Lt C. Runnels-Moss 70 Sqn, in B2423. ***70 Sqn claimed 4 DES and 3 OOC, Flgr G. Boit of Jasta 51 was killed, probably by Capt F.G. Quigley. †Shared with Lt F.J. Brotheridge 3 Sqn, in D6433.

ALDRIDGE John Arthur Lieutenant 19

Lieutenant Aldridge joined the RFC in June 1917 and served with 19 Squadron during the spring and summer of 1918, flying Dolphins. He claimed four aircraft out of control, shared in the destruction of a fifth, and forced one enemy scout down to land in a damaged condition.

	1918		Dolphin					
1	21 Apr	Pfalz DIII	C3833	19	Steenwerck	1915	OOC	CR/RAF 21.4
2	27 May	Alb. DV	C3833	19	E Arras	1055	OOC	CR/ORB/SR
3s*	1 Jul	LVG. C	C3833	19	W Steenwerck	1430	DES	CR/RAF 1.7
4	2 Jul	Fokker DrI	C3833	19	Estaires	0530	OOC	CR/ORB/SR
5	27 Sep	Fokker DVII	C3833	19	N W Cambrai	0735	OOC	CR/ORB/SR

TOTAL: 1 shared destroyed, 4 out of control = 5.

*Shared with Capt G.B. Irving C3996, Lt J.D.I. Hardman C3818.

ALEXANDER William Melville Captain 10(N), 210

A Canadian from Toronto, born 8 November 1897, he joined the RNAS in 1916 and first served in 3 Wing in France in early 1917, flying Sopwith 1½ Strutters. When the wing was disbanded in April he was posted to the newly-forming 10(N) Squadron equipped with Sopwith Triplanes, and served in Raymond Collishaw's famous 'Black Flight'. During the summer of 1917 he was constantly in action, claiming 11 victories. In mid-August the unit converted to Camels, and in these he continued to fly with the squadron, becoming a flight commander. By spring 1918 the unit had become 210 Squadron, RAF, and his score had risen to 23. He returned to Home Establishment in May, after 465 hours of war flying. He died in Canada on 4 October 1988.

	1917		Triplane					
1s*	2 Jun	C	N5487	10N	St Julien	0700-0900	OOC	CR/ORB
2	4 Jun	Alb. DIII	N5487	10N	N E Ypres	0850	OOC	CR/ORB/WS/DL
3	6 Jun	Alb. DIII	N5487	10N	Polygon Wood	1150	OOC	CR/RFC 6.6
4	6 Jul	Alb. DIII	N5487	10N	Deulemont	1100	OOC	CR/RFC 6.7
5	6 Jul	Alb. DIII	N5487	10N	Deulemont	1100	OOC	CR/RFC 6.7
6	11 Jul	Alb. DV	N5487	10N	Polygon Wood	2045	OOC	CR/RFC 11.7
7	20 Jul	Alb. DV	N5487	10N	Menin-Messines	0805	DES(F)	CR/RFC 20.7
8	28 Jul	Alb. DV	N5487	10N	Dadizeele	1950	OOC	CR/RFC 28.7
			Camel					
9	16 Aug	Alb. DV	N6368	10N	Wervicq	0850	OOC	CR/RFC 16.8
			Triplane					
10	20 Aug	Alb. DV	N6302	10N	Roubaix	1530	OOC	CR/RFC 20.8
11	21 Aug	Alb. DV	N6302	10N	E Menin	1830	OOC	CR/RFC 21.8
			Camel					
12	23 Sep	Alb. DV	B3910	10N	Houthoulst	1125	OOC	CR/RFC 23.9
	1918							
13	23 Jan	Alb. DV	B6289	10N	Staden	1450	OOC	CR/RNAS 23.1
14	6 Mar	Alb. DV	B7215	10N	S E Dixmude	0830	OOC	CR/RNAS 6.3
15	10 Mar	C	B7215	10N	Roulers	1545	DES	CR/RNAS 16.3
16	10 Mar	Alb. DV	B7215	10N	S E Dixmude	1600	OOC	CR/RNAS 10.3
17	24 Mar	Alb. DV	B7215	10N	Menin-Roulers	0920	OOC	CR/RNAS 24.3
18	24 Mar	Alb. DV	B7215	10N	Menin-Roulers	0920	OOC	CR/RNAS 24.3
19	3 Apr	C	B7215	210	Roulers	1130	DES	CR/DOS/?
20	11 Apr	C	B7215	210	E Estaires	1515	OOC	CR/RAF 11.4
21	11 May	Alb. DV	D3348	210	Armentieres	1925	DES(F)	CR/RAF 11.5
22	18 May	Pfalz DIII	D3348	210	Bac St Maur	2005	DES	CR/RAF 18.5
23	27 May	Pfalz DIII	D3348	210	Bailleul	0820	OOC	CR/?

TOTAL: 5 destroyed, 17 and 1 shared out of control = 23.
*Shared with F/Lt R. Collishaw N5490, FSL E.V. Reid N5483, FSL G.E. Nash N5492.

ALLEN Charles Philip Captain 204

Born on 3 April 1899, this native of Liverpool joined 204 Squadron on 5 April 1918, serving throughout the summer and autumn, becoming a flight commander in November, just before the end of the war. All his victories were claimed against Fokker DVIIs. He was awarded the Crown of Belgium decoration.

	1918		Camel					
1	29 Jun	Fokker DVII	D3332	204	S Ghistelles	1445	OOC	CR/ORB/5 GR
2	15 Aug	Fokker DVII	D8222	204	Menin	1905	OOC	CR/ORB/5 GR
3	24 Sep	Fokker DVII	D8222	204	Pervyse	1850	OOC	CR/ORB/5 GR
4	27 Oct	Fokker DVII	D9600	204	S Ghent	0910	DES	CR/RAF 27.10
5	27 Oct	Fokker DVII	D9600	204	S Ghent	0910	OOC	CR/?
6	30 Oct	Fokker DVII	B7860	204	Nazereth	1315	DES(F)	CR/RAF 30.10
7	4 Nov	Fokker DVII	F6037	204	Melle	0845	OOC	CR/?

TOTAL: 2 destroyed, 5 out of control = 7.

AMM Edgar Oxenham Lieutenant 29

Born 19 August 1898 in Johannesburg, South Africa, he joined 29 Squadron in July 1918. Here he claimed three enemy aircraft during August and one more plus a balloon in September, receiving a DFC for these actions, which was gazetted on 3 December. His tenth and final victory was claimed on 9 November, but during the same combat he was shot down. Taken prisoner, he was released two days later due to the Armistice. A Bar to his DFC was gazetted in June 1919; he also received a Croix de Guerre from the French.

	1918		SE 5A					
1	12 Aug	Fokker DVII	D6964	29	S E Bailleul	1940	DES(F)	CR/RAF 12.8
2	17 Aug	Hann. C	E5974	29	E Estaires	0830	DES	CR/RAF 17.8

3	18 Aug	Halb. C	E5974	29	S E Bailleul	1752	DES	CR/RAF 18.8
4	16 Sep	Fokker DVII	E5974	29	Bois Warneton	0835	DES	CR/RAF 16.9
5	29 Sep	Balloon	C1135	29	E Armentieres	1000	DES	CR/RAF 29.9
6	5 Oct	Fokker DrI	C1133	29	N W Courtrai	0855	DES	CR/RAF 5.10
7	8 Oct	Fokker DVII	F853	29	S E Roulers	1339	OOC	CR/11 WS
8	8 Oct	Fokker DVII	F853	29	N Roulers	1425	DES	CR/RAF 8.10
9	9 Nov	Fokker DVII	C1141	29	S E Audenarde	0945	OOC	CR/11 WS
10	9 Nov	Fokker DVII	C1141	29	Laerne-Lemberge	1035	DES(F)	CR/11 WS

TOTAL: 8 destroyed, 2 out of control = 10.

ANDERSON George Benson Flight Lieutenant 3W, 3(N)

A Canadian from Ottawa, born on 26 December 1890, Anderson joined the RNAS and served in 3 Wing, and then in 3(N) Squadron from spring 1917 until early 1918. He was an excellent example of a slow, steady scorer, who took nearly a year on operations to gain five victories.

	1917		Pup					
1	23 Apr	Alb. DII	N5194	3N	Croiselles	0630	OOC	CR/RFC 23.4
			Camel					
2	22 Aug	Alb. DIII	B3858	3N	St Pierre Capelle	1550	OOC	CR/RNAS 22.8
3s*	10 Sep	DFW. C	B3895	3N	Furnes	1800	CAPT	CR/RNAS 23.9
4	11 Sep	Alb. DV	B3940	3N	Thorout	1100	OOC	CR/DOS/?
	1918							
5	23 Jan	DFW. CV	B3940	3N	Houthoulst Forest	1500	OOC	CR/RNAS 23.1

TOTAL: 1 shared captured, 4 out of control = 5.
*Shared with F/Cdr R.F. Redpath B3785, FSL E.T. Hayne B3866, FSL G. Harrower B3782, FSL H.F. Beamish N6377.

ANDERSON Gerald Frank Lieutenant 88

A South African from Newcastle, Natal, who was born on 24 February 1898, Gerald Anderson served with 88 Squadron in 1918, flying Bristol Fighters. He claimed three victories with his front gun, while his various observers claimed an additional five from the rear seat whilst flying with him. During the fight on 30 October 1918 he and Lt C.M.W. Elliott each claimed a Fokker shot down, but they were both wounded during this action, subsequent to which Anderson was awarded a DFC.

	1918		Bristol					
1*	17 Jul	Halb. C	----	88	Map 20X 26	----	DES(F)	Sq Rec
2	31 Jul	Pfalz DIII	D8062	88	Fromelles	0915	OOC	CR/Sq Rec
3**	15 Sep	Fokker DVII	—	88	E Seclin	----	OOC	Sq Rec
4**	27 Sep	Fokker DVII	E2451	88	Lambersart	0755	OOC	CR/Sq Rec
5**	4 Oct	Fokker DVII	E2451	88	Quesnoy	1145	OOC	CR/Sq Rec
6	23 Oct	Fokker DVII	----	----	----	----	OOC	CR/Sq Rec
7	30 Oct	Fokker DVII	----	----	----	----	OOC	CR/Sq Rec
8***	30 Oct	Fokker DVII	----	----	----	----	DES(F)	CR/Sq Rec

TOTAL: 2 destroyed, 6 out of control = 8.
*Observer: Lt H.R Goss. **Observer: Lt T.S. Chiltern. ***Observer: Lt C.W.M. Elliott.
SOURCE: Sq Rec refers to claims listed in the 'Squadron Game Book'.

ANDREWS John Oliver Major 24, 66, 209

John Andrews transferred to the RFC from the Royal Scottish Regiment early in the war, and in June 1915 joined 5 Squadron as an observer on Avro 504s. After notable work with this unit, he was selected for pilot training and early in 1916 was posted to 24 Squadron which was forming with DH 2s. In France with this unit he quickly showed himself to be a first-class air fighter, becoming a flight commander. For his work he received an MC and Bar, and whilst with the squadron claimed some seven victories and six other aircraft driven down. After a brief rest from operations he helped form 66 Squadron on Sopwith Pups as a flight commander, entering action with this unit in April 1917. By the end of July he had claimed a further five victories, plus five more driven down or forced to land. His final total of destroyed and out of control aircraft was thus 12, his quoted score of 24 including 12 driven down or forced to land. At this stage he was awarded a DSO, and he later commanded 209 Squadron. In 1919 he led 221 Squadron in the Mediterranean and in South Russia. He remained in the RAF, becoming a Group Captain in 1937, and retired with the rank of Air Vice Marshal. He was still known to be alive in 1985.

	1916		DH 2					
1	21 Jul	Fokker E	5948	24	Allaines	0800	DES	CR/RFC 21.7
2	9 Aug	C	5925	24	S Mory	0630	OOC	CR/IV Bg W.D.
3	2 Sep	D	5998	24	N Les Boeufs	1925	DES	CR/RFC 2.9
4s*	6 Sep	C	5998	24	E Flers	1830	DES	CR/RFC 6.9

5	2 Nov	Halb. DII	5998	24	N W Bapaume	c1500	DES	CR/RFC 2.11
6s**	17 Nov	D	5998	24	Bapaume	1530	DES(F)	CR/IV Bg W.D.
7s***	22 Nov	Alb. DI	5998	24	Les Boeufs	1310	CAPT	CR/RFC 22.11
	1917		Pup					
8	30 Apr	Alb. C	A6177	66	Brebieres-Fresnes	0845	DES	CR/AIR 1 1970
9	2 May	Alb. DII	A6177	66	Orchies	1415	DES	CR/RFC 2.5
10	13 May	Alb. DIII	B1703	66	----	0625-0815	OOC	ORB/RFC 13.5
11	7 Jun	C	B1703	66	Gheluvelt	0800	DES	CR/RFC 7.6
12	11 Jul	Alb. C	B1703	66	Henin Lietard	1035	DES	CR/RFC 11.7

TOTAL: 1 shared captured, 7 and 1 shared destroyed, 3 out of control = 12.

*Shared with Lt R.H.M.S. Saundby, in 5928. **Shared with Lt R.H.M.S. Saundby, in 5925. ***Shared with Lt K. Crawford, in 5925. This was Oblt S. Kirmaier, an ace and Commander of Jasta B.

Andrews also had 7 driven down claims in 1916, plus 3 driven down and 2 forced to land in 1917. These, if added to his score, would bring it to the generally quoted 24.

APPS Gordon Frank Mason Lieutenant 66

Born in Kent in 1899, Apps was commissioned in the RFC in August 1917. He saw service as a Camel pilot in Italy, flying in 66 Squadron. He claimed nine victories, and the award of the DFC was gazetted in September 1918.

	1918		Camel					
1	11 Mar	Berg D	B5190	66	N Valstagna	1140	OOC	ORB/SR/14 W
2	28 Mar	Alb. DIII	B5190	66	Spresiano	1520	DES	ORB/SR/14 W
3	4 May	Alb. DIII	B2497	66	Vidor	0945	DES(F)	ORB/SR/14 W
4*	4 May	Alb. DIII	B2497	66	Moriago-Vidor	0945	DES	ORB/SR/14 W
5	24 May	Alb. DIII	B5190	66	Mt Coppola	1045	DES	ORB/SR/14 W
6	21 Jun	Alb. DV	B9410	66	Sola di La-Oderzo	0905	DES	ORB/SR/14 W
7	21 Jun	Alb. DV	D9410	66	Motta	1820	OOC	ORB/SR/14 W
8	28 Jun	Alb. DIII	D8101	66	Cismon	1030	DES	ORB/SR/14 W
9	13 Jul	Berg D	B7358	66	Cismon-S Godega	0705	DES	ORB/SR/14 W
10s**	16 Jul	C	B7358	66	S Giustana	1015	DES	ORB/SR/14 W

TOTAL: 7 and 1 shared destroyed, 2 out of control = 10.

*One of these was StFw A. Dombrowski of Flik 68j, who crash landed Albatros DIII, 153:195. **Shared with Lt A.E. Baker in D9418.

ARMSTRONG D'Urban Victor Captain 60, 78, 39, 151

Named after his home town of Durban, South Africa, Armstrong joined the RFC in 1915 and was posted to 60 Squadron in 1916, where he claimed his first victory. Sent to England, he joined 44 (Home Defence) Squadron with which unit he served throughout 1917, then becoming a flight commander in 78 Squadron. He subsequently transferred to 151 Squadron which became the first RAF night fighter unit in France, receiving a DFC for the four victories he gained there. Whilst in England he had become a noted exponent of aerobatics in the Sopwith Camel — especially at low level — but this led to his downfall, for on 13 November 1918 whilst stunting in C6713 near Bouvincourt, he crashed and was killed.

	1916		Nieuport					
1*	9 Nov	Alb. DI	A211	60	Havrincourt	1000	DES	CR/RFC 9.11
	1918		Camel					
2	29 Jun	LVG. C	C6713	151	Estree area	2035	OOC	ORB/RAF 29.6
3	8 Aug	C	C6713	151	Estree	0030	DES(F)	CR/RAF 7.8
4s**	24 Aug	Gotha G	C6713	151	Arras	2220	CAPT	CR/RAF 25.8
5***	17 Sep	Fried. G	C6713	151	Fletre	2240	CAPT	CR/RAF 18.9

TOTAL: 1 and 1 shared captured, 2 destroyed, 1 out of control = 5.

*Note: 60, 11 and BE 2's were involved in a fight in which at least three destroyed claims were given. It is believed all three were given to 60, as 11 Sqn records indicate they got none and the BE's got one out of control. **Shared with Lt F.C. Broome D6102; Lt Bratke KIA, Vzfw Heinrich and Vzfw Lehmann POWS from 15/BG III. ***This was Uffz Noeller, Lt Freck, Uffz Kagelmacher, Lt M. Scherf all KIA of 8/BG VI.

ARMSTRONG Frederick Carr Flight Commander 3(N)

A tall, fair-haired Canadian, born in Toronto on 19 June 1895, he was known as 'Army'. He joined the RNAS in 1915, serving first with 3 Wing before being posted to 3(N) Squadron at Dunkirk, at the beginning of 1917. In July he took command of C Flight, and by 24 March 1918 had claimed 15 victories and been awarded the DSC and French Croix de Guerre. On 25 March he took off on a Special Patrol, but was seen to go down in flames south of Ervillers in Camel B7218.

	1917		Pup					
1	6 Apr	Halb. DII	N6178	3N	Bourlon Wood	1020	OOC	CR/ORB/D.L.
2s*	12 Apr	Alb. DII	N6178	3N	Pronville	1030	OOC	CR/RFC 12.4
3s**	2 May	Alb. C	N6178	3N	Bourlon Wood	0700	DES(F)	CR/ORB/D.L.
4s***	6 May	Alb. DIII	N6178	3N	Bourlon Wood	1905	OOC	CR/RFC 6.5
5s†	7 Jul	Seaplane	N6465	3N	6m N Ostend	1110	DES	CR/RNAS 7.7
			Camel					
6	16 Sep	Alb. DV	B3808	3N	Thorout	1140	DES	CR/RNAS 16.9
7	16 Sep	Alb. DV	B3808	3N	Thorout	1145	OOC	CR/RNAS 16.9
	1918							
8	29 Jan	Alb. DV	B7193	3N	Roulers	1315	OOC	CR/RNAS 29.1
9	11 Mar	Alb. DV	B7218	3N	Drocourt	1120	DES	CR/RFC 11.3
10	21 Mar	Pfalz DIII	B7220	3N	Esquerchin	1150	OOC	CR/RFC 21.3
11	22 Mar	Alb. DV	B7218	3N	Marquion	1300	DES	CR/RFC 22.3
12	23 Mar	Pfalz DIII	B7185	3N	Vaulx-Beugnatre	1700	DES(F)	CR/RFC 23.3
13s††	24 Mar	Alb.DV	B7218	3N	Vaux	1530	OOC	CR/RFC 24.3

TOTAL: 4 and 2 shared destroyed, 4 and 3 shared out of control = 13
*Shared with FSL E. Pierce in N6171. **Shared with FSL A.T. Whealy in N6194, FSL E. Pierce in N6171. ***Shared with FSL H.S. Kerby in N6465. †Shared with F/Cdr J.S.T. Fall in N6364, FSL J.A. Glen in N6183, FSL L.H. Rochford in N6162. ††Shared with F/L S. Smith B7214, FSL R.C. Berlyn B7274, F/Lt E.T. Hayne B7231, F/Lt L.D. Bawlf B7192, F/Cdr A.T. Whealy B7220, F/Lt E. Pierce B7227, FSL J.S. Britnell B7229.

ARNISON, Charles Henry Lieutenant 62

Lieutenant Arnison was commissioned in the RFC in September 1917, and flew in 62 Squadron during the spring of 1918, being awarded an MC and DFC. During April his gunner was Lt S. Parry, with whom he claimed five victories before the latter was shot dead during a combat on 3 May. He then flew with Lieutenants H.E. Merritt and C.P. Wells. On 16 May 1918, Arnison and Wells were shot down in Bristol Fighter C4859 near Corbie by Leutnant Hans Kirchstein of Jasta 6 as the German's 15th victory. Arnison crash-landed in Allied lines and pulled his observer clear of the wreckage whilst under heavy shell-fire. Wells was dead however, and Arnison also suffered wounds that prevented his return to action.

	1918		Bristol					
1*	12 Apr	Alb. DV	C4859	62	E Estaires	1420	OOC	C&C/RAF 12.4
2*	21 Apr	Pfalz DIII	C4859	62	Estaires-Lille	1000	OOC	C&C/RAF 21.4
3*	21 Apr	Pfalz DIII	C4859	62	Estaires-Lille	1000	OOC	C&C/RAF 21.4
4*	3 May	Alb. DV	C4859	62	E Armentieres	1115	OOC	C&C/RAF 3.5
5*	3 May	Alb. DV	C4859	62	E Armentieres	1116	OOC	C&C/RAF 3.4
6*	3 May	Alb. DV	C4859	62	E Armentieres	1117	DES(F)	C&C/RAF 3.5
7**	9 May	Pfalz DIII	C4859	62	S Herlies	----	DES	C&C/RAF 9.5
8**	9 May	Pfalz DIII	C4859	62	N E La Bassee	----	OOC	C&C/RAF 9.5
9***	15 May	C	C4859	62	Albert-Ayette	1745	DES	C&C/RAF 15.5

Total: 3 destroyed, 6 out of control = 9
*Observer: Lt S. Parry. **Observer: Lt H.E. Merritt. ***Observer: Lt C.D. Wells.

ARNOLD Anthony Rex Major 8(N), 79

Born on 26 August 1896 in Fareham, Hampshire, Arnold joined the RNAS on 30 June 1916 and was involved on Home Defence duties initially. On his second operational sortie during the night of 2/3 September, he crashed on landing after chasing a Zeppelin. Early in 1917 he was posted to 8(N) Squadron in France to fly Pups and Triplanes. He had claimed five victories by mid June when he was awarded a DSC. Following a period back in England as an instructor, he was promoted Major in the new RAF and took command of 79 Squadron on Dolphins. He was subsequently awarded a DFC for ground-attack work; he was also awarded a Belgian Croix de Guerre. He remained in the RAF after the war, and by January 1936 had become a Group Captain.

	1917		Triplane					
1	8 Apr	Alb. DIII	N5477	8N	Beaumont	1530	OOC	CR/RFC 8.4
2s*	21 Apr	Alb. DIII	N5458	8N	Thelus-Vitry	1845	CAPT	CR/RFC 21.4
3	21 Apr	Alb. DIII	N5458	8N	Thelus	1850	DES(F)	CR/RFC 21.4
4	3 May	Alb. DIII	N6290	8N	Henin-Lietard	1810	OCC	CR/RFC 3.5
5	13 Jun	Alb. DV	N6290	8N	Douai	2000	OOC	CR/RFC 13.6

TOTAL: 1 shared captured, 1 destroyed, 3 out of control = 5.
*Shared with Lt R.G. Malcolm & 2/Lt J.B. Weir, 25 Sqn in 4839.

ASPINALL John Vincent Captain 22, 11

After service in the Worcestershire Regiment, he joined 22 Squadron as an FE 2B pilot in late 1916. He subsequently served as a flight commander in 11 Squadron on Bristol Fighters in spring 1918. Aspinall was killed in action on 15 May 1918 when his Bristol and another flown by Lieutenant H.W. Sellars were shot down by German scouts, Offstvtr Josef Mai of Jasta 5 claiming one as his 11th victory over Contalmaison at 1815, while Leutnant Hans Kirchstein of Jasta 6 claimed another, five minutes later over Orvillers. The missing Bristol crews were jointly credited with having shot down one of their opponents before their demise.

	1916		FE 2B					
1*	21 Oct	Fokker E	7012	22	Biefvillers	1405	DES	CR/RFC 21.10
	1917							
2**	28 Jan	Alb. DI	7681	22	Villers au Flos	1045	DES	CR/RFC 28.1
3s***	6 Apr	Alb. DIII	----	22	St Quentin	0800	DES	CR/RFC 6.4
4s†	8 Apr	Alb. DIII	----	22	Regny	0700	DES	CR/RFC 8.4
5††	13 Apr	Alb. DIII	4983	22	Itancourt	1830	DES	CR/RFC 13.4
	1918		Bristol					
6s†††	15 May	Fokker DR I	C4882	11	Mametz	1720	OOC	CR/RAF 15.5

TOTAL: 3 and 2 shared destroyed, 1 out of control = 6.
*Observer: 2/Lt W.M. Taylor. **Observer: 2/Lt J.M.R. Miller. ***Observer: 2/Lt M.K. Parlee; shared with Capt C.M. Clement/2/Lt L.G. Davies, Capt Gladstone/Lt Friend, Lt J.F. Day/2/Lt J.K. Campbell. †Observer: 2/Lt M.K. Parlee; shared with Capt C.M. Clement/2/Lt L.G. Davies, Capt L.W. Beale/Lt G.G. Bell, Lt J.F. Day/Lt W.M. Taylor, Lt C.A.M. Furlonger/Lt C.W. Lane, Lt H.G. Spearpoint/2/Lt J.K. Campbell. ††Observer: 2/Lt M.K. Parlee. †††Observer: Lt de la Cour; shared with Lt H.W. Sellars/Lt C.C. Robson C845.

ATEN Marion Hughes Captain 203, 47

An American, and son of a famous Texas Ranger Captain, 'Bunny' Aten went to Canada to join the RAF, and late in the war joined 203 Squadron to fly Camels. Before he had a chance to gain any victories, he crashed his aircraft and broke his arm badly; the war ended while he was still in hospital. Recruited by his old Commanding Officer, Raymond Collishaw, he agreed to join 47 Squadron which was to go to South Russia, where he arrived in early summer 1919, serving with the Camel Flight of this unit. He was to become one of the flight's most successful pilots, gaining the squadron's first victory over a Nieuport Scout of the Red air force. His second victory occurred when a Fokker Triplane he was chasing in a dive, broke up and crashed before he had fired a shot. His final two victories occurred in one day in May, when escorting an RE 8. He first shot down a Nieuport in flames, and then had a long fight with an all-black Fokker DVII which had just shot down his flight commander, Major S.M. Kinkead, and he managed to send this down. He had encountered this aircraft several times before, and later learned that it was reputed to have been flown by the Bolshevik's top-scoring pilot, who had shot down about 12 aircraft, mainly bombers of the White air force. Aten's fighter was twice hit and forced to land on the steppes during operations in Russia, but each time he returned safely. He was awarded a DFC subsequently. A series of retreats then virtually put an end to any effective operational flying, and the flight was on the last train to enter the port of Rostov before the bridge leading into the town was blown up. He returned to England forthwith, and served with the RAF for several more years before returning to the United States. He published the story of his exploits *Last Train over Rostov Bridge*, in 1961, but died shortly thereafter.

	1919		Camel					
1	? Apr	Nieuport	----	47	Volga River-Tsaritsyn	----	DES	Jackson
2	? Apr	Spad ?	----	47	Tsaritsyn area	----	DES	Jackson
3	1-7 May	Nieuport	----	47	Tsaritsyn area	----	DES	Jackson
4	? Aug	Nieuport	----	47	Tsaritsyn area	----	DES	Jackson
5*	? Aug	Fokker DVII	----	47	Tsaritsyn area	----	DES(F)	Jackson

TOTAL: 5 Destroyed = 5
*The pilot of the Fokker was supposedly a 12 victory ace.

ATKEY, Alfred Clayburn Captain 18, 22

Born on 16 August 1894, in Minebow, Saskatchewan, Atkey was working on the *Toronto Evening Telegram* as a journalist at the outbreak of war. Although little-known, this Canadian was to become the most successful two-seater pilot of the war, he and his observers claiming 38 machines shot down, 29 of them while flying Bristol Fighters. He was trained in early 1917 in 27 and 28 Reserve Squadrons, before becoming a bomber pilot in 18 Squadron, flying DH 4s from 8 September 1917. It was said that he handled a 'Four' like a Sopwith Pup, he and his gunners claiming nine enemy scouts whilst engaged on bombing raids. In late April 1918 he was posted to 22 Squadron as 'A' Flight commander, presumably to allow his obvious talents a more appropriate outlet. Here he chose Lt C.G. Gass as his observer, this team then accounting for 29 enemy aircraft in less than one month! On the evening of 7 May Atkey and Gass, in company with John Gurdon and his observer John Thornton, became involved with some 20 German scouts, the ensuing battle becoming famous in the annals of the RAF as 'Two against Twenty'. Atkey and Gass claimed five of the German aircraft, while Gurdon claimed three more. Two days later Atkey and Gass were again to claim five in one day. On a later sortie the end of one of the top planes of their Bristol was shot away and Gass had to climb out onto the lower wing to balance the aircraft so that Atkey could fly it home. Atkey was posted to Home Establishment in June; he was awarded the MC and Bar. Lieutenant C.G. Gass had transferred to the RFC after serving as a private, a sergeant, and later as an officer in the 2/24th London Regiment until the end of 1917. He was awarded the MC, having participated in 38 claimed victories with various pilots, some 17 of these being credited to his rear gun — 13 of them whilst flying with Atkey; he was the most successful gunner in the RAF. Gass left the RAF in 1919, but rejoined in World War II, becoming a Squadron Leader; Atkey died on 10 February 1971.

	1918		DH 4					
1*	4 Feb	SS DIII	A7798	18	Messines	1115	OOC	CR/RFC 4.2
2*	4 Feb	SS DIII	A7798	18	Messines	1115	OOC	CR/RFC 4.2
3**	15 Mar	Pfalz DIII	----	18	Avelin	1245	OOC	CR/IV BG WD
4***	16 Mar	Alb. DV	----	18	Fromelles	1520	OCC	CR/IV BG WD
5†	25 Mar	C	A7833	18	Bapaume-Flers	1610	DES(F)	CR/RFC 26.3
6†	25 Mar	Alb. DV	A7833	18	Bapaume	1615	OOC	CR/RFC 26.3
7s††	12 Apr	Pfalz DIII	----	18	Estaires	1025	DES(F)	CR/RAF 12.4
8s†††	12 Apr	Pfalz DIII	----	18	Estaires	1025	OOC	CR/IV BG WD
9‡	21 Apr	Pfalz DIII	A8064	18	Aubers	1400	OOC	CR/RAF 21.4
			Bristol F2B					
10‡‡	7 May	D	B1164	22	10m N E Arras	1845	DES(F)	CR/RAF 7.5
11‡‡	7 May	D	B1164	22	10m N E Arras	1845	DES(F)	CR/RAF 7.5
12‡‡	7 May	D	B1164	22	10m N.E Arras	1845	DES	CR/RAF 7.5
13‡‡	7 May	D	B1164	22	N.E Arras	1850	DES	CR/RAF 7.5
14‡‡	7 May	D	B1164	22	N.E Arras	1850	DES	CR/RAF 7.5
15‡‡	9 May	D	B1253	22	Lille	0940	DES(F)	CR/RAF 9.5
16‡‡	9 May	D	B1253	22	Lille	0940	OOC	CR/RAF 9.5
17‡‡	9 May	D	B1253	22	Lille	0940	OOC	CR/RAF 9.5
18‡‡	9 May	Pfalz DIII	B1253	22	N Douai	1840	DES	CR/RAF 9.5
19‡‡	9 May	Pflaz DIII	B1253	22	N Douai	1840	DES(F)	CR/RAF 9.5
20‡‡	15 May	Pfalz DIII	B1253	22	N W Lille	1020	OOC	CR/RAF 15.5
21‡‡	15 May	Pfalz DIII	B1253	22	N W Lille	1020	OOC	CR/RAF 15.5
22‡‡	19 May	Alb. C	C4747	22	S Douai	1050	DES	CR/RAF 19.5
23‡‡	19 May	LVG. C	C4747	22	W Lille	1845	OOC	CR/RAF 19.5
24‡‡	19 May	LVG. C	C4747	22	W Lille	1845	OOC	CR/RAF 19.5
25‡‡	20 May	Halb. C	C4747	22	Lille-Armentieres	1045	OOC	CR/10 WS
26‡‡	20 May	Halb. C	C4747	22	Lille-Armentieres	1045	OOC	CR/10 WS
27‡‡	20 May	Halb. C	C4747	22	Lille-Armentieres	1045	OOC	CR/10 WS
28‡‡	22 May	Alb. DV	B1253	22	2m S E Arras	1030	DES	CR/10 WS
29‡‡	22 May	DFW. C	B1253	22	Armentieres	1915	OOC	CR/10 WS
30‡‡	27 May	Pfalz DIII	B1253	22	N E Lens	2000	DES	CR/RAF 27.5
31‡‡	27 May	Pfalz DIII	B1253	22	Meurchin	2000	OOC	CR/10 WS
32‡‡	27 May	Pfalz DIII	B1253	22	N E Lens	2000	OOC	CR/10 WS
33‡‡	30 May	Pfalz DIII	B1253	22	Armentieres	1940	DES	CR/RAF 30.5
34‡‡	30 May	Pfalz DIII	B1253	22	S Armentieres	1940	OOC	CR/10 WS
35‡‡	31 May	Pfalz DIII	B1253	22	Armentieres	1030	OOC	CR/10 WS
36‡‡	31 May	Pfalz DIII	B1253	22	Armentieres	1030	OOC	CR/10 WS
37‡‡	2 Jun	C	B1253	22	N E Lens	1015	OOC	CR/10 WS
38‡‡	2 Jun	C	B1253	22	N E Lens	1015	OOC	CR/10 WS

TOTAL: 13 and 1 shared destroyed, 23 and 1 shared out of control = 38.
*Observer: Lt C.R.H. Ffolliott. **Observer: 2/Lt L.A. Mayne. ***Observer: Sgt M.B. Kilroy. †Observer: Lt J.M. Brisbane. ††Observer: Sgt H. Hammond. †††Observer: Sgt H. Hammond: shared with; Lt F.J. Morgan/Sgt M.B. Kilroy, 2/Lt H.R. Gould/Capt M.S.E. Archibald, Capt A.G. Waller/2/Lt J. Waugh. ‡Observer: Lt P. Anderson. This was probably Lt Paul Strahle of Jasta 57 who forced landed after being shot up by a two seater. No other claims fit the time and location of Strahle's combat. ‡‡Observer: Lt C.G. Gass.

ATKINSON Edward Dawson Captain 1, 56, 64

Born on 10 November 1891 in Scotland, Atkinson transferred from the Indian Army Reserve of Officers to the RFC, and after pilot training went to 1 Squadron in May 1916, becoming a flight commander in 1917. On 1 May 1917, in combat with four Albatros Scouts, he encountered one painted all red and flown by an 'exceptionally good pilot'; this was Karl Schaefer of Jasta 28. Atkinson was attacked by this aircraft, and his scout was considerably damaged, but after a long fight he managed to escape and return over Allied lines, where he force-landed at Elverdinghe; his Nieuport was a write-off, Schaefer being credited with this as his 24th victory. Atkinson claimed three victories before returning to Home Establishment as an instructor. In April 1918 he managed to return to active service for a refresher course under combat conditions; flying first with 56, then with 64, and on occasion with 22 Squadron, he thereby gained experience in SE 5As, and Bristol Fighters. After less than a month at the front he had claimed a further seven enemy machines, before returning to England to continue his instructional duties. The award of a DFC was gazetted on 3 August 1918. He received the AFC in 1919 and became a Squadron Leader in 1924.

	1917		Nieuport					
1	25 Mar	Balloon	----	1	Warneton-Wervicq	c1700	DES	CR/RFC 25.3
2	22 Apr	Alb. DII	A6624	1	Lille	0705	OOC	CR/RFC 22.4
3	29 Apr	Alb. C	A6678	1	Armentieres	1740	OOC	CR/RFC 30.4
	1918		SE 5A					
4s*	3 May	Rump. C	B8494	56	Montauban	0955	DES	CR/RFC 3.5
5s*	3 May	Rump. C	B8494	56	S E Bapaume	1015	OOC	CR/?
6	26 May	Alb. DV	D6861	64	Erquinghem-Lys	1930	OOC	CR/?
7	28 May	Alb. DV	D6861	64	Bapaume-Bancourt	0750	DES	CR/RAF 28.5
8	28 May	Halb. C	D6861	64	Bapaume-Bancourt	0855	DES	CR/RAF 28.5
9	31 May	Pfalz DIII	D6861	64	E. Merris	0620	OOC	CR/?
10	31 May	Palfz DIII	----	64	La Bassee	1940	DES	CR/RAF 31.5

TOTAL: 1 balloon, 4 destroyed, 5 out of control = 10.
*Observer: shared with Lt T. Durrant B183, Lt W.R. Irwin C5435.

BABBAGE F. Lieutenant 20

Lieutenant Babbage flew with 20 Squadron during the spring and summer of 1917. Initially flying FE 2Ds with Air Mechanic B. Aldred as gunner, he claimed two victories during May. Later in the summer he began flying Bristol Fighters, claiming a further three victories in the early autumn to bring his score to five.

	1917		FE 2D					
1*	6 May	Alb. C	A1935	20	Hollebeke	1745	CAPT	CR/RFC 6.5
2**	7 May	Alb. DIII	A1935	20	S E Courtrai	1100	DES	CR/RFC 7.5
			Bristol					
3***	11 Sep	Alb. DV	A7193	20	E Menin	1400	DES(F)	CR/RFC 11.9
4***	27 Sep	Alb. DV	A7255	20	Moorslede	1300	DES	CR/RFC 27.9
5†	27 Oct	Alb. DV	B1104	20	Moorslede	1510	OOC	CR/RFC 27.10

TOTAL: 1 captured, 3 destroyed, 1 out of control = 5.
*Observer: 2AM B. Aldred; probably Uffz F. Stegmann/Vzfw J. Wenzl, of Schlasta 27, who were killed. **Observer: 2AM B. Aldred. ***Observer: 2/Lt R.C. Purvis. †Observer: Gnr J. McMechan.

BAILEY Geoffrey Grierson Lieutenant 43

'Lumpy' Bailey attended the Westminster School before joining the RFC; after training he was posted to 43 Squadron. He served with this unit throughout 1918, being awarded a DFC, which was gazetted on 3 August.

	1918		Camel					
1	16 Feb	Alb. DIII	B7297	43	Henin Lietard	1125	DES(F)	CR/RFC 16.2
2	12 Apr	Alb. DV	C8262	43	Cagnicourt	1030	DES	CR/RAF 12.4
3	12 Apr	Alb. DV	C8262	43	La Gorgue	1030+	OOC	CR/RAF 12.4
4	3 May	Alb. DV	C8262	43	Vieux Berquin	1140	OOC	CR/RAF 3.5
5	9 May	Alb. DV	C8262	43	S Nieppe Forest	1510	OOC	CR/RAF 9.5
6	30 May	Alb. DV	C8262	43	N Combles	1450	DES	CR/RAF 30.5
7*	30 May	Alb. DV	C8262	43	Combles	1500	DES	CR/RAF 30.5
8	9 Aug	Fokker DVII	E1485	43	Pertain	0640	OOC	CR/ORB/?

TOTAL: 4 destroyed, 4 out of control = 8.
*43 claimed 7 in this fight; Jasta 34 lost 2, with possibly 1 more lost from Jasta 32.

BAIR Hilbert Leigh 1st Lieutenant 24

Born in New York on 15 November 1894, Bair joined the USAS on 18 July 1917. Attached to the RAF for experience, he was posted to 24 Squadron on 5 July 1918, and was awarded a DFC on 19 September, by which time he had claimed five victories. In October he joined the 25th Aero Squadron, USAS, and was subsequently awarded an American DSC. In World War II he served as a Lieutenant Colonel in the Army Air Force. He died in White Plains, New York, in autumn 1985.

	1918		SE 5A					
1s*	10 Aug	Fokker DVII	C1945	24	N E Rosieres	0750	OOC	CR/SR
2	19 Aug	Fokker DVII	B8505	24	Fresnoy	1130	DES	CR/SR
3s**	19 Aug	Fokker DVII	B8505	24	Fresnoy	1130	OOC	CR/SR
4s***	30 Aug	Alb. C	B8505	24	Bus	0630	DES	CR/RAF 30.8
5	8 Sep	Fokker DVII	B8505	24	N St Quentin	0820	DES	CR/RAF 8.9
6s†	15 Sep	Hannover C	B8505	24	Hainescourt Wood	1855	DES	CR/RAF 15.9

TOTAL: 2 and 2 shared destroyed, 2 shared out of control = 6.

*Shared with Capt W. Selwyn C8840, 2/Lt T.M. Harries C8844 and Lt W.C. Lambert B8395. **Shared with Capt W. Selwyn, C8840. ***Shared with Lt H.D. Barton C8840, 2/Lt T.M. Harries E6006. †Shared with Capt H.D. Barton C8840.

BAKER Brian Edmund Major 48, 141

Born on 31 August 1896, he served in the Rifle Brigade at the outbreak of war, and transferred to the RFC in August 1915. He went to France with a total of 12 hours' flying time in his logbook, to join 13 Squadron, flying BEs. In 1917 he was posted to 48 Squadron which had the new Bristol Fighters, to take command of a flight. On 22 July he intercepted a formation of Gotha bombers, shooting one down into the sea as it was returning from a raid on England. He was awarded a DSO and MC before returning to Home Establishment to command 141 (Home Defence) Squadron at Biggin Hill in 1918. After the war he went to the CFS, then to Egypt to command 4 FTS. In 1935 he was a Wing Commander and took a post as SAFC aboard the aircraft carrier HMS 'Courageous'. He retired as Air Marshal Sir Brian Baker, KBE, CB, DSO, MC, AFC, and died on 8 October 1979.

	1917		Bristol					
1s*	15 Jun	Alb. DIII	A7149	48	N Vitry	2020	DES(F)	CR/RFC 16.6
2s**	21 Jul	Alb. DV	A7107	48	Slype	1800	OOC	CR/RFC 22.7
3***	22 Jul	Gotha	A7146	48	N W Ostend	1040	DES	CR/RFC 22.7
4s†	27 Jul	Alb. DIII	A7170	48	N E Nieuport	1710	DES(F)	CR/RFC 27.7
5††	28 Jul	Alb. DIII	A7170	48	Ghistelles-Zevecote	0815	DES(F)	CR/RFC 28.7
6†††	19 Aug	Alb. DV	A7170	48	Ostend	0650	OOC	CR/RFC 19.8
7‡	21 Oct	Alb. DIII	A7170	48	Ostend	1300	OOC	CR/RFC 21.10
8‡	31 Oct	Pfalz DIII	A7170	48	N E Dixmude	1615	OOC	CR/IV BG WD
9‡‡	11 Nov	Alb. DIII	A7170	48	N E Dixmude	1710	OOC	CR/RFC 11.11
10‡‡‡	11 Nov	Alb. DIII	A7170	48	N E Dixmude	1710	OOC	CR/RFC 11.11
11§	29 Nov	Alb. DIII	A7170	48	Houthoulst Wood	1445	OOC	CR/RFC 29.11
12‡‡	29 Nov	Alb. DIII	A7170	48	Armesvelde-Zarren	1530	CAPT	CR/IV BG ?

TOTAL: 1 captured, 1 and 3 shared destroyed, 6 and 1 shared out of control = 12.

*Observer: Lt H. Munro; shared with Lt J.A.W. Binnie/AM V. Reed in A7223. **Observer: 2/Lt G.R. Spencer; shared with Lt R. Dodds/Lt T.C.S. Tuffield in A7153 and Lt R.D. Coath/2/Lt L.H. Tanner in A7164. ***Observer: 2/Lt G.R. Spencer; shared with Lt R.D. Coath/2/Lt A.D. Merchant A7164. The squadron reported the wreck was still visible sticking up out of the water four hours later. †Observer: Lt G.R. Spencer; shared with F/S/L J.H. Forman of 6N in Camel N6358. ††Observer: Lt G.R. Spencer; shared with Lt J.A.W. Binnie/Cpl V. Reed A7123. †††Observer: Lt H. Munro. ‡Observer: Lt E.F. Dixon. ‡‡Observer: 2 AM B. Jackman. ‡‡‡Observer: 2AM B. Jackman; Vzfw H. Werner KIA?. §Observer: 2 AM B. Jackman; possibly Lt W. Blume of J26, who was WIA.

BAKER Lovell Dickens Captain 23

After service with the Dublin Fusiliers, Baker flew Spads with 23 Squadron from the summer of 1917 until March 1918, by which time he had become a flight commander. His last victory was over an LVG two-seater which he and Lt Goodison forced down inside Allied lines at Champien aerodrome.

	1917		Spad					
1	9 Sep	Alb. DIII	B3510	23	Passchendaele	1140	OOC	CR/11 WS
2*	29 Oct	Alb. DV	A6642	23	Passchendaele	1555	DES(F)	CR/RFC 29.10
3	12 Dec	Alb. DV	B3640	23	Staden-Oostnieuwkerke	1500	OOC	CR/11 WS
	1918							
4	12 Mar	DFW. C	B6842	23	N E Brissay	1050	OCC	CR/RFC 12.3
5s**	23 Mar	LVG. C	B6842	23	W Champien aerodrome	1125	CAPT	CR/RFC 23.3

TOTAL: 1 shared captured, 1 destroyed, 3 out of control = 5.

*Probably Lt Fritz Berkemeyer, of Jasta 27 who was killed. **Shared with 2/Lt H.A.F. Goodison in B6845.

BAKER Thomas Charles Richmond Captain 4 AFC

Born on 2 May 1897 in Smithfield, South Australia, Baker was educated in Adelaide, leaving school to become a bank clerk in 1914. He enlisted on 29 July 1915 in the 16th Battery, 6th Field Artillery Brigade. He was awarded an MM on 15 December 1916 for an action near Guedecourt repairing broken telephone lines under fire. Shortly afterwards he received a Bar to this award. Transferring to the AFC in September 1917, he was sent to France in June 1918 with a total of 57 hours 40 minutes flying. Serving with 4 AFC Squadron on Camels, he was to claim six victories by early October, when the unit re-equipped with Snipes, becoming a flight commander at this time. On 4 November he was involved in a fight with a large formation of Fokker DVIIs from JG III and was one of three Snipe pilots shot down and killed, while flying E8065. Two of these three Snipes were claimed by Rittmeister Karl Bolle, commander of Jasta 'Boelcke'. The award of a DFC was gazetted on 8 February 1919.

	1918		Camel					
1	31 Jul	Fokker DVII	E1482	4AFC	S W Estaires	1135	OOC	CR/ORB/OH
2	7 Aug	Alb. DV	E1482	4AFC	S Laventie	1405	DES	CR/RAF 7.8
3	24 Aug	Balloon	E1482	4AFC	N E Estaires	1530	DES	CR/RAF 24.8
4	30 Aug	DFW. C	E1482	4AFC	E Laventie	0615	DES	CR/RAF 30.8
5	1 Oct	Alb. C	E1482	4AFC	Habourdin	0810	DES	CR/RAF 1.10
6	2 Oct	Fokker DVII	E1482	4AFC	E Fromelles	0750	DES	CR/RAF 2.10
			Snipe					
7	26 Oct	Fokker DVII	E8069	4AFC	E Tournai	1545	OOC	CR/ORB/OH
8	28 Oct	Fokker DVII	E8092	4AFC	S E Tournai	1200	DES	CR/RAF 28.10
9	28 Oct	Fokker DVII	E8092	4AFC	Ath	1455	OOC	CR/ORB/OH
10	28 Oct	Fokker DVII	E8092	4AFC	Ath	1500	DES	CR/RAF 28.10
11	29 Oct	Fokker DVII	E8092	4AFC	Marcourt-Tournai	1610	DES	CR/RAF 29.10
12	30 Oct	Fokker DVII	E8065	4AFC	Leuze	1455	OOC	CR/ORB/OH

TOTAL: 1 balloon, 7 destroyed, 4 out of control = 12.

BALDWIN Owen Morgan Captain 73

Joining 73 Squadron early in 1918, Baldwin gained his first victories during the big German offensive of March and April, also carrying out many ground attack sorties. By late July he had accounted for eight enemy aircraft including three of the highly manoeuvrable Fokker Triplanes, and was awarded a DFC, which was gazetted on 21 September. On 15 September he claimed four Fokker DVIIs and a two-seater during two sorties. He was promoted flight commander during this period, and by the end of September had brought his score to 16. A Bar to his DFC was gazetted on 3 December 1918.

	1918		Camel					
1	7 Apr	Fokker DrI	D1832	73	S Cerisy	1200	DES	CR/RAF 7.4
2	12 Apr	Alb. DV	D1832	73	Lestrem	1240	DES(F)	CR/RAF 12.4
3*	11 Jun	C	D1832	73	E Mery	1415	DES	CR/RAF 11.6
4	9 Jul	Fokker DrI	D1898	73	Monchaux, N Douai	1205	DES	CR/RAF 9.7
5	16 Jul	Fokker DVII	D1898	73	S Roncheres	2000	DES	CR/RAF 16.7
6	22 Jul	Fokker DrI	D1898	73	S Paars	1810	DES	CR/RAF 22.7
7	22 Jul	Fokker DVII	D1898	73	Bazoches	1815	DES	CR/RAF 22.7
8	29 Jul	Fokker DVII	D1898	73	N E Soissons	1950	OOC	CR/?
9	19 Aug	Fokker DVII	D1898	73	Combles	0810	DES	CR/RAF 19.8
10	15 Sep	Fokker DVII	D1898	73	Cambrai	1105	DES	CR/RAF 15.9
11	15 Sep	Fokker DVII	D1898	73	Cambrai	1110	OOC	CR/?
12	15 Sep	C	D1898	73	La Folie	1120	DES	CR/RAF 15.9
13	15 Sep	Fokker DVII	D1898	73	S Gouy sous Bellone	1815	DES	CR/RAF 15.9
14	15 Sep	Fokker DVII	D1898	73	S Gouy sous Bellone	1815	OOC	CR/?
15	17 Sep	Rumpler C	D1898	73	E Cambrai	1230	DES	CR/RAF 17.9
16	27 Sep	LVG C	E7178	73	N Graincourt	1410	DES(F)	CR/RAF 27.9

TOTAL: 13 destroyed, 3 out of control = 16.
*Possibly Uffz B. Conze/Flgr K. Busch; KIA near here.

BALFOUR Harold Harrington Major 43

Born in Camberley, Surrey on 1 November 1897, he joined the King's Royal Rifle Company in 1914. He learned to fly at his own expense and requested a transfer to the RFC, but was posted to France and served with his regiment for three months before his transfer came through. Completing his training, he flew with 60 Squadron in 1916 before returning to England to become a test pilot at Martlesham. In 1917 he went back to France as a flight commander with 43 Squadron, flying 1½ Strutters, but was injured in a crash in April.

Towards the end of the year he again returned to England to the School of Special Flying at Gosport. In November 1917 he was posted to 40 Squadron, but managed to return to 43 Squadron for another tour with the unit, now flying Camels. He was awarded an MC in May 1917, a Bar to this in April 1918, and the Croix de Guerre. With the rank of Major he commanded a training school in Norfolk during 1918-19, then took a post at the RAF College, Cranwell. He retired from the RAF in 1926, going into politics and becoming a prominent and respected MP. In 1938 he was Under-Secretary of State for Air, having previously been Minister of Aviation. He was made Lord Balfour of Inche, and remained an active member of the House of Lords for many years. He was also President of the Society of World War I Aero Historians, Great Britain (Cross & Cockade) until 1985. He died in late 1988.

	1917		Strutter					
1*	6 Mar	Halb D	A1097	43	Givenchy-Lens	1100	OOC	CR/RFC 6.3
2**	3 Apr	Alb. DIII	A970	43	Izel	1435	DES(F)	CR/RFC 3.4
	1918		Camel					
3	16 Feb	Alb. DV	B5620	43	Courrieres	1115	OOC	CR/RFC 16.2
4	16 Feb	Alb. DV	B5620	43	S Courrieres	1115	DES	CR/RFC 16.2
5s***	17 Feb	C	B5620	43	E Pont a Vendin	0920	OOC	CR/RFC 17.2
6	18 Feb	Alb. DV	B5620	43	E Henin Lietard	1010	DES(F)	CR/RFC 18.2
7†	18 Feb	Alb. DV	B5620	43	E Henin Lietard	1010	OOC	ORB/RFC 18.2
8	11 Mar	DFW. C	B5620	43	Fromelles	1240	OOC	CR/RFC 11.3
9	12 Mar	Rumpler C	B5620	43	Laventie	1045	DES(F)	CR/RFC 12.3

TOTAL: 3 destroyed, 5 and 1 shared out of control = 9.
*Observer: 2/Lt A. Roberts; 43 claimed 3, Lt Lubbert of Jasta 11 was WIA. **Observer: 2/Lt A. Roberts. ***Shared with Lt C.F. King B5608, and 2/Lt Grandy B6272. †Shared with 2/Lt Grandy B6272, 2/Lt C.F. King B5608, 2/Lt C.R. Maasdorp B5409, 2/Lt N. Orcutt B5628.

BALL Albert Captain 13, 11, 8, 60, 56

Albert Ball was born in Nottingham on 14 August 1896. When war was declared he joined the 2/7th Battalion, Sherwood Foresters, later transferring to the RFC, and being posted to 13 Squadron in February 1916. He then went to 11 Squadron on 7 May 1916, exactly one year to the day before he would be killed in action. He quickly proved himself to be one of the pioneer single-seat fighter pilots, but was posted to 8 Squadron for a short period, where only two seaters were available. However he soon managed to get back to 11 Squadron and its Nieuport Scouts. When, following the Battle of the Somme, part of 11 Squadron joined 60 Squadron, Ball went to the new unit. Now a full-time fighter pilot, he soon became Britain's leading air fighter in terms of successful combats. Already awarded an MC, in September he received the DSO and Bar; by the time he returned to England in October he had achieved some 31 victories, including some driven down or forced to land, although it is very difficult at this early stage of the air war to differentiate between 'driven down' and 'out of control' claims.

After a period as an instructor he became a flight commander with the newly-formed 56 Squadron and returned to France with this unit on 7 April 1917. In one month he claimed 12 destroyed and one out of control, his last-known victory being over an Albatros DIII of Jasta 20 on 6 May. This brought his score to at least 44 destroyed and out of control, and forced to land, although precise details vary. On the evening of the next day, Ball was posted missing in action, his fate being unknown for many years. It can now be accepted that, having shot down Lt Lothar von Richthofen of Jasta 11 (who was forced to land, although unhurt) Albert Ball was seen to come spinning down out of cloud upside down and crashed into the ground; he died of his injuries soon afterwards. He was given a full military funeral by the Germans. It does not appear that he had been shot down, and it is surmised that he either suffered vertigo, or was struck on the head by a pan of ammunition whilst seeking to reload his Lewis gun — a not unknown occurrence. He was awarded a second Bar to his DSO, and then posthumously a Victoria Cross, announced on 8 June 1917. His mother and father received this coveted decoration from King George V on 22 July of that year. His morale and inspirational value to the RFC was unsurpassed.

	1916		Bristol					
1*	16 May	Alb. C	5312	11	Givenchy-Beaumont	0845	OOC/DD	CR/RFC 16.5
			Nieup					
2**	29 May	LVG. C	5173	11	Beaumont	0800	OOC	CR/RFC 29.5
3	29 May	LVG. C	5173	11	Oppy	0830	FTL	CR/RFC 29.5
4	1 Jun	Fokker E	5173	11	1m W Douai a/d	1010	FTL	CR/RFC 1.6
5	25 Jun	Balloon	5173	11	----	1600	DES	CR/RFC 25.6
6	2 Jul	Roland CII	A134	11	Mercatel-Arras Rd	1730	DES	CR/RFC 2.7?
7	2 Jul	Aviatik C	A134	11	Lens area	1800	DES	CR/RFC 2.7?

8	16 Aug	Roland CII	A201	11	S E St Leger	0910	FTL	CR/RFC 16.8
9	22 Aug	Roland CII	A201	11	W Bapaume	C1900	DES	CR/RFC 22.8
10	22 Aug	Roland CII	A201	11	Vaux	c1930	DES(F)	CR/RFC 22.8
11***	22 Aug	Roland CII	A201	11	Vaux-Maurepas	c1945	DES	CR/RFC 22.8
12	25 Aug	Roland CII	A201	60	S Arras	1100	OOC	SR/CB
13•	28 Aug	Roland CII	A201	60	S E Bapaume	0700	FTL	CR/RFC 28.8
14	28 Aug	Roland CII	A201	60	E Ayette	c1900	DES	CR/RFC 28.8
15	28 Aug	C	A201	60	N Grevillers	1900	FTL	CR/RFC 28.8
16	31 Aug	Roland CII	A201	60	S E Bapaume	1830	DES	CR/RFC 31.8
17†	31 Aug	Roland CII	A201	60	S E Bapaume	1830	FTL	CR/RFC 31.8
18	15 Sep	Fokker DII	A200	60	E Beugny	0955	DES	CR/RFC 15.9
19††	15 Sep	Roland CII	A212	60	N E Bertincourt	1900	DES	CR/CB
20	21 Sep	Roland D	A213	60	N Bapaume	c1600	FTL	CR/RFC 21.9
21	21 Sep	Roland D	A213	60	St Leger	c1605	DES	CR/RFC 21.9
22	21 Sep	Roland CII	A213	60	Bucquoy	c1800	DES	CR/RFC 21.9
23†††	22 Sep	Fokker D	A213	60	E Bapaume	c1700	DES	CR/RFC 22.9
24‡	23 Sep	Roland CII	A213	60	Mory	1800	DES(F)	CR/RFC 23.9
25‡‡	25 Sep	Alb. C	A213	60	Bapaume-Cambrai	1830	DES(F)	CR/RFC 26.9
26	28 Sep	Alb. C	A213	60	Haplincourt	1745	DES	CR/RFC 28.9
27	28 Sep	Alb. C	A213	60	Bapaume	c1915	FTL	CR/RFC 28.9
28‡‡‡	28 Sep	Alb. C	A213	60	N E Bapaume	c1930	FTL	CR/RFC 28.9
29s§	30 Sep	Alb. C	A201	60	Velu	1055	DES(F)	CR/RFC 30.9
30	30 Sep	Roland C	A213	60	Graincourt	1830	OOC	CR/RFC 30.9
31§§	30 Sep	Roland C	A213	60	Cambrai	1845	OOC	CR/RFC 30.9
	1917		Nieuport					
32••	23 Apr	Alb. C	B1522	56	Abancourt-Tilloy Rd	0645	DES	CR/RFC 23.4
			SE 5					
33	23 Apr	Alb. DIII	A4850	56	Cambrai-Selvigny	1145	DES(F)	CR/RFC 23.4
34	26 Apr	Alb. DIII	A4850	56	N E Cambrai	1920-2000	DES	CR/RFC 26.4
35•••	26 Apr	S.S. DI	A4850	56	E Cambrai	1920-2000	DES(F)	CR/RFC 26.4
36	28 Apr	Alb. C	A4850	56	Fontaine	1650-1745	DES	CR/RFC 28.4
37	1 May	Alb. C	A8898	56	Marquoin	1700	DES	CR/RFC 1.5
38	1 May	Alb. C	A8898	56	S W Cambrai	1950	OOC	CR/RFC 1.5
39	2 May	Alb. DIII	A4855	56	Halte-Vitry	0740	DES	CR/RFC 2.5
40§§§	2 May	Alb. C	A4855	56	Sailly	0810	DES	CR/RFC 2.5
41	4 May	Alb. DIII	A8898	56	Graincourt	1850-2000	DES	CR/AR/CB
42	5 May	Alb. DIII	A8898	56	Lens-Carvin	1830-1900	DES	CR/RFC 5.5
43	5 May	Alb. DIII	A8898	56	Lens-Carvin	1830-1900	DES	CR/RFC 5.5
			Nieuport					
44¶	6 May	Alb. DIII	B1522	56	Sancourt	1930	DES	CR/RFC 6.5

TOTAL: 1 balloon, 27 and 1 shared destroyed, 6 out of control, and 9 forced to land = 44
NB: On 1 October 1916, Ball claimed three enemy aircraft as forced to land. Unlike those of 28th September, they are not mentioned as such in the communiques. Ball's score could therefore be much higher, but the total of 44 derived here is taken from the total in his V.C. citation.
*There is some doubt as to whether this aircraft was out of control or driven down. The aircraft was last seen at 2000 ft. on its back, after a vertical dive. The aircraft, from KG 3/17 was force landed by its wounded pilot. **This aircraft was last seen in a vertical dive. Whether this is out of control, or driven down, is an open question. ***The last aircraft was flown by Offz W. Cymera of Kampfstaffel 1 who was wounded, the observer Lt Hans Becker died of wounds. Cymera later became an ace. This was the first 'hat-trick' in the RFC. †Ball notes his score as being 17. ††This was Uffz Carstens/Oblt du Cornu, of Kasta 13 who were both wounded, du Cornu died two days later. †††Lt Winand Grafe, KIA, of Jasta 2. ‡Possibly Lt E. Kliche, Oblt H. Miner, both KIA in the vicinity. ‡‡The crew were Flgr Tewes/Lt M. Hoffman of FA (A) 237. Tewes was wounded and Hoffman was killed. ‡‡‡Ball notes his score as being 28. §Shared with 2/Lt C.L. Roberts/Lt Collins in FE 2 7014 of 11 Sqn. §§Although claimed as two seaters, one of these was almost certainly Lt Ernst Diener of Jasta 2 who was killed. The communique notes that two Rolands were driven out of control without specifying a pilot. Ball made the only claims in the area at this time. The RFC communique for 1 October notes Ball 'drove down two patrolling machines out of control near Gommecourt'. This would appear to be a late confirmation of the 30th September claims. This list gives Ball's total as 1 balloon, 16 destroyed, 5 out of control and 9 forced to land, that are all mentioned in the communiques. §§§Possibly Lt K. Prill/Lt A Reichle of FA 26, lost over Bullecourt. • Ltn Joachim von Arnim and Ltn Böhne, Ft Abt 207, pilot killed, ob landed a/c Nr Transloy. ••Believed to be Ltn Hugo Siebel. •••Possibly Vzfw Emil Eisenhuth, Jasta 3, killed (in AbDIII). ¶Vzfw Jager of Jasta 20, who was wounded.

BANBURY Fred Everest Flight Commander 9(N)

Born in Regina, Saskatchewan, Canada, on 27 October 1893, Banbury became a law student at Toronto University. He learned to fly at the Curtiss Company's School in the USA, and gained his certificate with the best grades in the school. He came to England in July 1916 with the initial intake of some 200 Canadians for the RNAS, and after training was posted to France to join 9 Naval Squadron upon its formation in March 1917. He became a flight commander in July and was awarded a DSC. On 1 April 1918, the day the RAF was formed, he crashed five minutes after take off (it was surmised as a result of a heart attack) and was killed.

	1917		Pup					
1s*	31 May	C	N6188	9N	Ostend	1615	OOC	CR/DRO/DL
2	1 Jun	Halb. C	N6188	9N	Westende-Ghistelles	0915	OOC	DRO/DL
			Camel					
3s**	25 Jul	C	B3820	9N	off Westende	1730	OOC	CR/DRO/DL
4s***	5 Sep	Alb. C	B3832	9N	Middelkerke-Nieuport	0800	OOC	CR/DRO/?
5s†	13 Sep	Alb. DV	B3832	9N	E Leke	c1430	OOC	CR/DRO/?
6s††	28 Sep	Alb. DV	B6230	9N	Dixmude	1610	DES	CR/DRO/?
7s†††	2 Oct	C	B6230	9N	Ostend-Slype	1450	OOC	CR/RNAS 2.10
8s‡	27 Oct	Alb. DV	B6230	9N	Slype	1040	OOC	CR/DRO/?
9	28 Oct	Alb. DV	B6230	9N	Schoore	1230	DES	CR/RNAS 28.10
10s‡‡	23 Nov	Alb. DV	B6230	9N	S Dixmude	1220	OOC	CR/RNAS 23.11
	1918							
11s‡‡‡	26 Mar	C	B7247	9N	1m S of Becelaere	0725	CAPT	CR/DRO/?

TOTAL: 1 shared captured, 1 and 1 shared destroyed, 1 and 7 shared out of control = 11.
*Shared with FSL A. Shearer in N6193, FSL H.F. Stackard in 9916. **Shared with FSL J.W. Pinder B3870, FSL Snell B3813, FSL O.M. Redgate B3832, FSL H.G. Mott. ***Shared with F/Cdr S.T. Edwards B3829, FSL A.R. Brown B3818, FSL O.M. Redgate B3810, FSL A.V. Wood B3897. †Shared with F/Cdr S.T. Edwards B6217, FSL Oakley B3880, FSL J.P. Hales B3898, FSL Ingleson B3817. ††Shared with FSL O.M. Redgate, FSL J.P. Hales, FSL M.S. Taylor, FSL C.G. Edwards. †††Shared with FSL O.M. Redgate. ‡Shared with F/Cdr S.T Edwards B6217, FSL F.J.W. Mellersh B6204, FSL J.P. Hales B6342, FSL J. de C. Paynter B3830, FSL Narbeth B3883, FSL A.V. Wood B3884, FSL M.S. Taylor B3892, F/Cdr H.F. Stackard B6327. ‡‡Shared with FSL J.P. Hales N6342. ‡‡‡Shared with FSL Squire D3328, FSL O.M. Redgate B7250, FSL M.S. Taylor B7200.

BANKS Charles Chaplin Captain 44, 43

A schoolmaster before the war, 'Sandy' Banks joined the RFC, and after training, joined 44 (Home Defence) Squadron flying Camels. With this unit he shared in the destruction of a Gotha bomber. Awarded an MC, he was posted to 43 Squadron on the Western Front on 8 February 1918, becoming a flight commander. He remained with the unit throughout the rest of the war, and during early September converted to Sopwith Snipes. He claimed his three final victories with these new fighters, receiving a DFC which was gazetted on 8 February 1919. He had achieved an unusual victory on 31 May 1918, when he shot down a Friedrickshafen two-seater at night over the Western Front, the first occasion that such a success had been achieved. His son was a fighter pilot in World War II; shot down, he fought alongside Italian partisans until captured and executed.

	1918		Camel					
1s*	28 Jan	Gotha	B3827	44	Frund's Farm	2210	CAPT	Co/Ch
2	6 Apr	Alb. DV	D1815	43	Guillaucourt	1735	DES	CR/RAF 6.4
3	12 Apr	Alb. DV	D1815	43	Bois du Biez	1115	DES	CR/RAF 12.4
4	3 May	Alb. DV	D1815	43	E Villers-Brettoneaux	1130	DES	ORB/RAF WD
5	8 May	Fokker DrI	D1815	43	S E Bailleul	1315	OOC	CR/RAF 8.5
6	31 May	Fried. G	D1894	43	----	2350	CAPT	CR/RAF 1.6
7	10 Jun	Alb. DV	D1809	43	W Monchy	1915	DES	CR/RAF 11.6
8	13 Jun	Pfalz DIII	D1894	43	Ribecourt	0840	DES	CR/RAF 13.6
9**	29 Aug	Fokker DVII	F9514	43	Somain	0830	DES	CR/RAF 29.8
			Snipe					
10s***	27 Sep	Fokker DVII	E8028	43	Cambrai	0925	OOC	CR/ORB/?
11	1 Oct	Fokker DVII	E8028	43	Quiercy	1030	OOC	CR/ORB/?
12	30 Oct	Fokker DVII	E8028	43	Aulnoye	1335	OOC	CR/ORB/?

TOTAL: 1 and 1 shared captured, 6 destroyed, 4 out of control = 12.
*Shared with Capt G.H. Hackwill in B2402. This was Gotha GV 938/16. The crew, Lt F. von Thomsen, Uffz K. Ziegler, Uffz W. Reiden, were all killed. **This was Vzfw Knobel, of Jasta 57, who was severely wounded. ***Shared with Capt C.F. King E8031.

BANNERMAN Ronald Burns Captain 79

Born in 1890, Ronald Bannerman, from Dunedin, New Zealand, joined the RFC on 29 March 1917, and was posted to 79 Squadron in summer 1918 to fly Sopwith Dolphins. During August he was to claim five aircraft and a balloon, for which he was awarded a DFC, gazetted on 2 November. In September he was to add seven more victories, including two in one day, and was promoted Captain. He was awarded a Bar to his DFC early in October, but then went on leave. He returned later in that month, claiming four more victories before the war ended to bring his score to 17, only one of which was claimed as out of control. During World War II he rose to the rank of Air Commodore and was made a CBE. He died on 2 August 1978.

	1918		Dolphin					
1	4 Aug	Fokker DVII	C3879	79	Neuve Eglise	0840	DES	CR/RAF 4.8
2	20 Aug	C	C3879	79	Estaires	1845	DES(F)	CR/RAF 20.8
3	22 Aug	DFW. C	D8075	79	W Bailleul	0945	DES	CR/RAF 22.8
4	24 Aug	Balloon	C3879	79	W Armentieres	1305	DES	CR/RAF 24.8
5	29 Aug	Hannover C	C3879	79	E Estaires	1740	DES	CR/RAF 29.8
6	31 Aug	C	C3879	79	N E Estaires	1915	DES	CR/?
7	7 Sep	C	C3879	79	N E Ploegsteert	1100	DES	CR/RAF 7.9
8	16 Sep	C	C3879	79	N Hollebeke	1145	DES	CR/RAF 16.9
9	16 Sep	C	C3879	79	Hooge	1200	DES	CR/RAF 16.9
10	19 Sep	Fokker DVII	C3879	79	E Houthoulst Wood	0735	DES	CR/RAF 19.9
11	21 Sep	C	C3879	79	S W Hollebeke	1015	DES	CR/RAF 21.9
12	28 Sep	Fokker DVII	C3879	79	S W Comines	1235	DES	CR/RAF 28.9
13	29 Sep	Hannover C	C3879	79	Estaires	1740	DES	CR/RAF 29.9
14	27 Oct	Halb. C	C3879	79	E Avelghem	0815	OOC	CR/?
15	1 Nov	Fokker DVII	C3879	79	Audenarde	1500	DES	CR/RAF 1.11
16	2 Nov	Halb. C	E4716	79	Salsique	1000	DES	CR/RAF 2.11
17	4 Nov	C	E4716	79	Baeggem	1245	DES	CR/RAF 4.11

TOTAL: 16 destroyed, 1 out of control = 17.

BARKELL, Thomas Henry Lieutenant 4 AFC

Born in Randwick, Sydney, Australia, in 1892, Barkell was a motor mechanic at the outbreak of war, and joined the AFC. Posted to France, he served with 4 AFC Squadron, initially flying Sopwith Camels in which he claimed four aircraft shot down, the last two on 22 September, when his own engine was hit and he just managed to regain British lines before crashing. The squadron converted to Sopwith Snipes, and on 26 October he claimed the first two victories for the unit with these aircraft, but on 29th he was hit again, and this time was wounded in the leg whilst over Tournai. He landed E8032 at Peronne, far from his own base. He was awarded a DFC for seven victories.

	1918		Camel					
1	7 Sep	LVG. C	F1415	4AFC	Henin Lietard	0700	DES	CR/RAF 7.9
2	16 Sep	Fokker DVII	E7191	4AFC	Frelinghien	0820	DES	CR/RAF 16.9
3	22 Sep	Fokker DVII	E7191	4AFC	E Armentieres	0820	OOC	CR/ORB/OH
4	22 Sep	Fokker DVII	E7191	4AFC	Armentieres	0820	OOC	CR/ORB/OH
			Snipe					
5	9 Oct	Balloon	E8052	4AFC	W Douai	0955	DES	CR/ORB/OH
6	26 Oct	Fokker DVII	E8032	4AFC	E Tournai	1545	DES(F)	CR/RAF 26.10
7	26 Oct	Fokker DVII	E8032	4AFC	E Tournai	1545	OOC	CR/ORB/OH

TOTAL: 4 destroyed, 3 out of control = 7.

BARKER William George Major 9, 4, 15, 28, 66, 139, 201

Born in Dauphin, Manitoba, on 3 November 1894, Barker joined the 1st Canadian Mounted Rifles in December 1914. He arrived in France in September 1915 as a machine gunner, when the unit converted to the infantry role. One winter in the trenches was enough for Barker, who was over six feet tall, and in March 1916 he transferred to the RFC as an observer on probation with 9 Squadron. He was commissioned the following month, and posted to 4 Squadron, which also flew BE 2s, but then on 7 July joined 15 Squadron. On 21 July he claimed to have driven down a Roland two-seater, but this claim was not to be included in his subsequent score. He drove down another aircraft on 15 August, but was then posted for pilot training on 16 November 1916. An MC for his services as an observer was awarded on 10 January 1917. After training he returned to 15 Squadron on 24 February, and on 25 March drove down a scout; he was awarded a Bar to his MC on 18 July. Since late April he had been flying RE 8s, but he was wounded by 'Archie' (anti-aircraft fire) whilst over the lines in one of these on 7 August, and was then posted to England as an instructor.

Here he employed every endeavour to shorten his stay, continually breaking low flying regulations. These efforts were successful, for he was then given the choice of joining 56 Squadron or a new unit, 28

Squadron, which was forming on Camels at Yatesbury; in either case he was to be a flight commander. He chose Camels, because of their manoeuvrability, and was consequently appointed to command 'A' Flight of the latter unit a few days after his arrival.

He moved back to France with his new unit on 8 October 1917, where he at once showed prowess as a fighter pilot. That very evening he led an unofficial patrol, shooting down an Albatros DV which he did not claim. His first confirmed claim was made on 20 October, two more following before the month was out. On 7 November the unit was posted to Italy in support of the Italians against the Austro-Hungarians and Germans, and here he was to claim the first three RFC victories on this front. By the end of December his score had reached seven, confirmed by the citation to his DSO, which indicated his total as five aircraft and two balloons. On Christmas Day he and Steve Hudson slipped off on an unauthorised flight to shoot up an enemy airfield where they dropped a placard wishing their opponents 'Merry Christmas'! The German 14 Army 'Wochenbericht' (Weekly Reports of the German air force in Italy) noted that two Camels shot up the airfield of Fliegerabteilung (A) 204, damaging several hangars and four aircraft. Next day the Germans attempted a revenge raid on Allied airfields, but lost six aircraft; the captured crews of some of these were found to be drunk! In January Barker claimed one aircraft and two balloons shared, followed by four more aircraft and five shared balloons in February. Three more in March brought his total to 22. When the commanding officer's post became vacant, he was passed over — probably due to the number of unauthorised sorties he had indulged in. Dissatisfied, he applied for a posting, and on 10 April exchanged with a flight commander in 66 Squadron, also in Italy. Here he achieved more successes, claiming 16 victories by mid-July. He was then posted to command 139 Squadron which had been formed from a Bristol Fighter flight in 34 Squadron, but was permitted to take his Camel, B6313, with him. With this unit he undertook an unusual sortie during the night of 9 August when he flew a Savoia-Polilia SP 4 bomber to land a spy behind the Austrian lines; for this he received the Italian Medaglio d'Argento (Silver Medal) for Military Valour on 12 September 1918.

Barker's Camel, B6313, is a story in itself. He first flew the aircraft on 30 September 1917, and for the last time on 29 September 1918, by which time he had accounted for 379 hours 25 minutes of the aircraft's total flight time of 404 hours 10 minutes. He claimed all his eight victories with 139 Squadron whilst flying this aircraft, bringing his score to 46 — all in B6313. The citation to the Bar to his DSO stated that up to 20 July, Barker had been credited with 33 aircraft and nine balloons. Four claims followed by 18 September, bringing his score in Italy to 43, the highest for any pilot on that front, including Baracca, the Italian top-scorer and Bruwmowski of Austro-Hungary. B6313 had become the single most successful fighter aircraft in the history of the RAF; it was dismantled on 2 October 1918, and Barker attempted to retain its clock as a souvenir. He was asked to return it next day — such is the gratitude of officialdom !

He then returned to the United Kingdom to become commander of a school of air fighting at Hounslow, but managed to persuade the authorities that to carry out his job properly after so long in Italy, it was necessary for him to have a 'refresher' course to get up to date on the latest conditions and techniques on the Western Front. Taking one of the new Sopwith Snipes, E8102, he joined 201 Squadron (which was still flying Camels) with a ten day roving commission, but failed to see any combat. On 27 October he took off to return to England, but could not resist one last look at the front first. Now at last, he found a two-seater which he shot down, the crew baling out. After two years of combat flying and a year as a fighter pilot, Barker now made his first serious mistake; he was taken by surprise by 15 Fokker DVIIs, one of which opened fire and wounded him in the thigh. He fainted, but recovered to find himself in the midst of all 15 Fokkers, and in a terrific battle, during which he was wounded in the other thigh and one elbow, managed to shoot down three of the scouts in flames and drive down the others before his badly-damaged aircraft crash-landed in Allied lines. This action took place in full view of Allied troops, initial press reports crediting him with between six and ten aircraft destroyed or out of control! He was in fact credited with four destroyed (including the two-seater) to bring his score to 50 — 46 of these being destroyed, the highest such ratio of the war for an RFC, RNAS or RAF pilot. Awarded the Victoria Cross for his last fight, he was sufficiently recovered from his wounds to receive this from King George V on 30 November 1918, to add to his DSO and Bar, MC and two Bars, Croix de Guerre and Medaglio d'Argento. Barker had been an outstanding fighter pilot and commander, as illustrated by the following tribute, paid to him by a fellow pilot from the Italian Front: "He was one of the finest Camel pilots I have ever seen. Apart from the usual 'stunts', he seemed to have an uncanny sense of just how much his machine was capable of doing in an emergency. He was a dead shot and God help the enemy aircraft which tangled with him on anything like equal terms. He was dedicated to his service and worked himself and his pilots assiduously to maintain fitness and efficiency over the line. New pilots to his flight were lucky. He looked after them as a hen does her chicks and many of the survivors must owe their lives to his skill and care. He could have cut quite a few more 'notches' for himself had it not been for his consideration for the other pilots of his patrols. In person he was unassuming and likeable."

Leaving the RAF in April 1919, he went into partnership with Billy Bishop, the other Canadian fighter VC, in civil aviation, but this venture soon failed. Barker then served in the new Canadian Air Force from

1920-24, before starting a tobacco business. In January 1930 he became Vice President of the Fairchild Aviation Corporation of Canada, but on 12 March of that year was killed in a flying accident at Rockliffe, Ottawa.

	1917		Camel					
1*	20 Oct	Alb. DIII	B6313	28	Roulers	1215	DES	CR/RFC 20.10
2**	26 Oct	Alb. DV	B6313	28	W Roulers	1215	DES(F)	CR/RFC 26.10
3***	26 Oct	Alb. DV	B6313	28	Roulers-Thielt	1220	DES	CR/RFC 26.10
4†	29 Nov	Alb. DV	B6313	28	Pieve di Soligo	1215	DES	CR/7 BG
5††	3 Dec	Alb. DIII	B6313	28	N E Conegliano	1245	DES(F)	CR/7 BG
6†††	3 Dec	Balloon	B6313	28	N E Conegliano	1250	DES	CR/7 BG
7	29 Dec	Balloon	B6313	28	N E Pieve di Soligo	0845	DES	CR/7 BG
	1918							
8‡	1 Jan	Alb. DV	B6313	28	N W Vittorio	1100	DES(F)	CR/7 BG
9s‡‡	24 Jan	Balloon	B6313	28	2km E Conegliano	1620	DES	CR/7 BG
10s‡‡	24 Jan	Balloon	B6313	28	E Conegliano	1620	DES	CR/7 BG
11‡‡‡	2 Feb	Phonix DI	B6313	28	1km S W Conegliano	1050	DES(F)	CR/7 BG
12	2 Feb	C	B6313	28	Gera	1050	DES	CR/7 BG
13§	5 Feb	Alb. DIII	B6313	28	3km N W Oderzo	1200	DES	CR/7 BG
14	5 Feb	C	B6313	28	Cornure	1215	DES	CR/Cit/?
15s‡‡	12 Feb	Balloon	B6313	28	Fossamerlo	1445	DES	CR/7 BG
16s‡‡	12 Feb	Balloon	B6313	28	Fossamerlo	1445	DES	CR/7 BG
17s‡‡	12 Feb	Balloon	B6313	28	Fossamerlo	1445	DES	CR/7 BG
18s‡‡	12 Feb	Balloon	B6313	28	Fossamerlo	1445	DES	CR/7 BG
19s‡‡	12 Feb	Balloon	B6313	28	Fossamerlo	1445	DES	CR/7 BG
20	18 Mar	Alb. DIII	B6313	28	Villanova	1245	DES	CR/7 BG
21	19 Mar	Alb. DIII	B6313	28	Bassiano	1245	OOC	CR/7 BG
22	19 Mar	Alb. DIII	B6313	28	N Cismon	1250	DES	CR/7 BG
23	17 Apr	Alb. DIII	B6313	66	E Vittorio	1100	DES	ORB/SR/7 BG
24	8 May	C	B6313	66	Annone-Cessalto	1920	DES	ORB/SR/14 W
25§§	11 May	Alb. DV	B6313	66	Torre di Mosto	1045	DES	ORB/SR/14 W
26	20 May	Alb. DV	B6313	66	Levico	0800	OOC	ORB/SR/14 W
27	20 May	Alb. DV	B6313	66	Levico	0803	DES	ORB/SR/14 W
28	21 May	Lloyd C	B6313	66	N Treviso	0750	CAPT	ORB/SR/14 W
29	23 May	C	B6313	66	S Motta	1215	DES(F)	ORB/SR/14 W
30	24 May	Alb. DV	B6313	66	Grigno-Val Sugana	1045	DES	ORB/SR/14 W
31§§§	24 May	Alb. DV	B6313	66	Val Sugana	1050	DES	ORB/SR/14 W
32	3 Jun	Berg C	B6313	66	Fiume-Feltre	0830	DES	ORB/SR/14 W
33	9 Jun	Berg D	B6313	66	Levico	1020	DES	ORB/SR/14 W
34	9 Jun	Berg D	B6313	66	Levico	1025	DES	ORB/SR/14 W
35#	21 Jun	Alb. DV	B6313	66	Motta	0900	DES	ORB/SR/14 W
36	25 Jun	Berg D	B6313	66	Susegana	0910	OOC	ORB/SR/14 W
37	13 Jul	Berg D	B6313	66	Conegliano-Godega	0705	DES	ORB/SR/14 W
38	13 Jul	Alb. DV	B6313	66	1m S Godega a/d	0708	DES	ORB/SR/14 W
39	18 Jul	C	B6313	139	S Gallio	0805	DES	CR/OP/14 W
40s##	18 Jul	C	B6313	139	2m N Asiago	0810	DES	CR/OP/Cit
41	20 Jul	Alb. DV	B6313	139	Motta	—	DES	C&CB/14 W
42###	20 Jul	Alb. DV	B6313	139	Motta	—	DES	C&CB/14 W
43s¶	23 Jul	Alb. DV	B6313	139	Godega a/d	—	DES	C&CB/14 W
44	18 Sep	D	B6313	139	4m S Feltre	1000	OOC	C&CB/14 W
45	18 Sep	D	B6313	139	S Feltre	1000	OOC	C&CB/14 W
46¶¶	18 Sep	D	B6313	139	3m N Queroe	1005	DES	C&CB14 W
			Snipe					
47	27 Oct	Rumpler C	E8102	201	Mormal Woods	0825	DES(F)	CR/RAF 27.10
48	27 Oct	Fokker DVII	E8102	201	Mormal Woods	0830	DES(F)	CR/RAF 27.10
49	27 Oct	Fokker DVII	E8102	201	Mormal Woods	0830	DES(F)	CR/RAF 27.10
50	27 Oct	Fokker DVII	E8102	201	Mormal Woods	0830	DES(F)	CR/RAF 27.10

TOTAL: 1 captured, 2 and 7 shared balloons, 33 and 2 shared destroyed, 5 out of control = 50.

*Possibly Lt W. Lange of Jasta B, who was killed. **Lt O. Schober of Jasta 18 was killed in action. ***Offstv J. Klein of Jasta 18, who was damaged and may have force-landed. †This was Lt Haertl of Jasta 1, who was wounded. This victory is often given as Rttm N. von Hideghethy of Flik 24, but he crashed in the Astico valley, 80km due west of Barker's fight, whereas Jasta 1 operated in the area of the engagement. ††This was Lt F. von Kerssenbrock of Jasta 39, who was killed. †††Possible Lt M. Riegert of BK 10, who was killed. ‡ This was Offstv K. Lang of Jasta 1, who was killed. ‡‡Shared with Lt H.B. Hudson B6356. ‡‡‡This was FwP A. Koritzky of Flik 28d, killed in 228.43. §This was Zgsf J. Schantl in 153.76 from Flik 19d, who was killed. §§66 made three claims; Zgsfhr S Gyurgyev in 153:145 of Flik 61j, was killed. §§§This was a fight between 66 Sqn and Flik 55j during which Offstv Josef Kiss was killed, probably by Lt G. Birks, and Fw Kasza was damaged. #66 made three claims; Oblt F. Dechant in 153:188 of Flik 51j was killed. ##Shared with Lt G.T.C. May D9414 of 66. 14 W apparently gave sole credit to May, but 139 and Barker's citation note Barker shared it. ###One of these was probably Zgsf F. Sommer in 253:17 of Flik 61j. ¶Shared with Lt H.C. Walters/Lt C.T. Davies in Bristol C916. Possibly? Cserich of Flik 74j, killed in 138:166. ¶¶The pilot baled out successfully; this was Zgsf Ludwig Thaler of Flik 14d.

BARLOW John Lancashire Lieutenant 40

Barlow flew Nieuport Scouts with 40 Squadron in 1917. On 9 June he went out alone to attack the enemy's balloon lines, but sighted a formation of 12 hostile aircraft, consisting of both two-seaters and scouts. He dived to attack, claiming one two-seater and one Albatros Scout shot down. On 23 September 1917 he was killed in a flying accident in B1670.

	1917		Nieuport					
1	9 Jun	Alb. DIII	A6789	40	Don	0720	DES	CR/RFC 9.6
2	9 Jun	Aviatik C	A6789	40	1m E of Wingles	0730	OOC	CR/RFC 9.6
3	2 Jul	C	A6771	40	E Lens	2030	OOC	CR/RFC 3.7
4	21 Jul	Alb. DV	B1670	40	Douai	1930	OOC	CR/AIR 1/1222
5	9 Aug	Balloon	B1670	40	Lens area	0930	DES	ORB/C&C V4 N4
6	9 Aug	Alb. DV	B1670	40	Vitry en Artois	2015	OOC	CR/RFC 10.8

TOTAL: 1 balloon, 1 destroyed, 4 out of control = 6.

BARLOW Leonard Monteagle Lieutenant 56

Born 5 June 1898, in Islington, London, he trained as an electrical engineer. As soon as he reached the age of 18 in 1916, he joined the RFC, and after training was posted to 56 Squadron which was just forming with the first SE 5s. Upon arrival in France he quickly proved himself to be one of the outstanding pilots of the unit, and by 24 September he had accounted for 14 enemy aircraft. Next day over Houthulst Forest single-handed he attacked four scouts, two Pfalz and two Albatros, and in three minutes claimed three of these shot down; the two Albatros were flown by Oberleutnant Weigand and Unteroffizier Werkmeister of Jasta 10. He claimed two more aircraft before the end of the month, and in October was posted home for a rest. One reason for his success (and the source of his nickname — 'The Gadget King') had been his ingenuity, by which he had arranged both his guns, the Vickers and the Lewis, to fire from the same trigger. During his five months in combat he received an MC and two Bars. He was killed on 5 February 1918, before he could return to the front, when a Sopwith Dolphin which he was testing at Martlesham Heath, broke up at 150 feet and caught fire; he was buried three days later in Bardon Hill Cemetary.

	1917		SE 5					
1s*	24 Apr	Alb. C	A4858	56	Bellone	1140	OOC	CR/RFC 24.4
2	27 May	C	A4858	56	Plouvain	0615-0700	DES	CR/RFC 27.5
3	27 May	C	A4858	56	Plouvain	0615-0700	DES	CR/RFC 27.5
4	13 Jul	Alb. DV	A8910	56	Moorslede	2000	OOC	CR/RFC 13.7
5s**	17 Jul	Alb. DV	A8910	56	Roulers-Menin Rd	2015	DES	CR/RFC 17.7
6	26 Jul	Alb. DV	B507	56	Roulers-Menin Rd	1930-2030	DES	CR/RFC 26.7
7	5 Aug	Alb. DV	B507	56	N E Dadizeele	1930-2030	DES	CR/RFC 5.8
8	14 Aug	C	B507	56	Moorslede	0930-1030	DES	CR/RFC 14.8
9	17 Aug	Alb. DV	B507	56	Moorslede	1920-1945	DES	CR/RFC 17.8
10	17 Aug	Alb. DV	B507	56	Wervicq	1920-1945	OOC	CR/RFC 17.8
11	20 Aug	Alb. DV	B507	56	E Roulers	1850-1930	DES	CR/RFC 20.8
12	20 Aug	Alb. DV	B507	56	E Polygon Wood	1850-1930	OOC	CR/RFC 20.8
13	16 Sep	Alb. DV	B511	56	Wervicq	1830	DES	CR/RFC 16.9
14***	24 Sep	C	B511	56	S Houthoulst Forest	1715-1830	DES	CR/RFC 24.9
15	25 Sep	Alb. DV	B511	56	Houthoulst Forest	1740	DES(F)	CR/RFC 25.9
16	25 Sep	Pfalz DIII	B511	56	Houthoulst Forest	1740	DES(F)	CR/RFC 25.9
17†	25 Sep	Pfalz DIII	B511	56	Houthoulst Forest	1740	DES	CR/RFC 25.9
18	27 Sep	Alb. DV	B511	56	Menin-Roulers Rd	1730-1845	OOC	CR/RFC 27.9
19	28 Sep	Alb. DV	B511	56	S Houthoulst Forest	0815-0840	OOC	CR/RFC 28.9
20s††	1 Oct	Alb. DV?	B511	56	Westroosebeke	1700-1815	OOC	CR/RFC 1.10

TOTAL: 12 and 1 shared destroyed, 6 and 1 shared out of control = 20.
*Shared with Capt C.M. Crowe in A4860, and Lt M.A. Kay in A4866. **Shared with Capt I.H.D. Henderson A8909, 2/Lt A.P.F. Rhys-Davids A4863, 2/Lt K.K. Muspratt A8913, Lt V.P. Cronyn A4856. ***Lt von Esmarch/Lt H. Fleischer KIA F A A 266, at Houthoulst by Barlow and/or Rhys-David. †Oblt H. Weigand and Uffz Werkmeister of Jasta 10 were both killed, and possibly another member of Jasta 10 wounded. ††Shared with Capt J.T.B. McCudden B4853, Lt A.P.F. Rhys-Davids B525, Lt M.H. Coote B1, Lt D.J. Reason A8961.

BARTON Horace Dale Captain 24

A South African born on 22 November 1891, he served for eight months in German South-West Africa and then 16 months in German East Africa, before joining the RFC. After training, he went to 84 Squadron in November 1917, then to 24 Squadron on 3 January 1918. Following a slow start, he rapidly became one of the stars of the squadron, was promoted to Captain, and awarded the DFC and Bar. On 17 June he was involved in the action which resulted in the German ace, Leutnant Kurt Wusthoff (27 victories) being captured, while on 28 July, while leading a patrol, Barton forced down a German two-seater inside British lines.

	1918		SE 5A					
1s*	18 Feb	DFW. C	B120	24	La Fere	0830	OOC	CR/ORB/5 BG
2	8 Mar	Fokker DrI	C1751	24	S E La Fere	1500	DES(F)	CR/RFC 8.3
3	12 Mar	Alb. DV	C1751	24	Bellenglise	1045	OOC	CR/5 BG
4**	16 May	Fokker DrI	C6417	24	S Proyart	1915	DES	CR/RAF 16.5
5	6 Jun	Alb. DV	C6481	24	Moreuil	1130	OOC	CR/ORB/SR
6s***	17 Jun	Fokker DVII	C6481	24	Cachy	1200	CAPT	CR/RAF 17.6
7	27 Jun	Fokker DVII	C6481	24	Chipilly	1925	OOC	CR/ORB/SR
8s†	1 Jul	LVG. C	C6481	24	Meaulte	0830	OOC	CR/ORB/SR
9	16 Jul	Balloon	C6481	24	62D R22 central	1345	DES	CR/ORB/SR
10s††	26 Jul	DFW. C	C6481	24	N W Royaucourt	0730	CAPT	CR/RAF 26.7
11s†††	4 Aug	DFW. C	C6481	24	N Suzanne	0900	DES	CR/RAF 4.8
12	28 Aug	Pfalz DIII	C8840	24	62C N Barleux area	1915	DES	CR/RAF 28.8
13s‡	30 Aug	Alb. C	C8840	24	Bus, near Sailly	0630	DES	CR/RAF 30.8
14	8 Sep	Fokker DVII	C8840	24	Le Catelet	0815	OOC	CR/ORB/5 BG
15	15 Sep	Alb. C	C8840	24	Cambrai	1830	OOC	CR/ORB/5 BG
16s‡‡	15 Sep	Hannover C	C8840	24	Hannescourt	1855	DES	CR/RAF 15.9
17	20 Sep	LVG. C	C8840	24	Wassigny	0630	DES	CR/RAF 20.9
18	22 Sep	Fokker DVII	C8840	24	E Bourlon Wood	1040	DES	CR/RAF 22.9
19s‡‡‡	2 Oct	Balloon	C8840	24	Clary	1635	DES	CR/5 BG

TOTAL: 1 and 1 shared balloons, 2 shared captured, 5 and 3 shared destroyed, 5 and 2 shared out of control = 19.
*Shared with Lt R.T. Mark B67, Lt A.K. Cowper B664. **Probably Lt Hans Joachim Wolff, of Jasta 11, who was killed. ***Shared with Capt I.D.R. MacDonald D3444, Capt G.O. Johnson C1084, of 24 and Lt C.E. Walton of 23 in C4185. Lt Kurt Wusthoff, a 27 victory ace, on his first flight with Jasta 15, who was taken prisoner. †Shared with Capt C.N. Lowe E1293. ††Shared with 2/Lt C.M.G. Farrell E1293, 2/Lt J.J. Palmer C1861, Lt J.A. Miller C6466, Lt F.S. Passmore C1938. Uffz Neuendorff/Lt Bolgiehn of FAA 232, captured intact. †††Shared with 2/Lt C.M.G. Farrell D6937. 24 claimed 3 two seaters, Lt O. Kiehn/Lt P. Martini of FAA 207 were killed. ‡Shared with Lt H.L. Bair B8505, Lt T.M. Harries E6006. ‡‡Shared with Lt H.L. Bair B8505. ‡‡‡Shared with Lt W.C.G. Geraghty in B8505.

BATEMAN John Courade Lieutenant 1

Born in Woodford, Essex, in 1899, he was commissioned on 21 June 1917, gained his wings on 29 September, and joined 1 Squadron in France on 31 October. Here he flew Nieuports until spring 1918, and then SE 5As.

	1918		SE 5A					
1s*	9 Mar	Balloon	A8930	1	Lomme	1435	DES	CR/RFC WD
2	10 Mar	Balloon	B641	1	Roulers-Staden	0740	DES	CR/RFC WD
3	25 Apr	Pfalz DIII	B8254	1	Houthem	1855	OOC	CR/ORB WD
4s**	2 May	LVG. C	B8254	1	Houthoulst	1325	OOC	CR/ORB/?
5s***	9 Jun	Fokker DVII	B8254	1	Dickebusch	0630	CAPT	CR/RAF 9.6
6s†	23 Jun	Pfalz DIII	B8254	1	.5m N W Lestrem	0600	DES	CR/ORB/?
7s††	1 Jul	Halb. C	B8254	1	Messines	0805	DES(F)	CR/RAF 1.7

TOTAL: 1 and 1 shared balloon, 1 shared captured, 2 shared destroyed, 1 and 1 shared out of control = 7.
*Shared with Capt H.J. Hamilton B32, 2/Lt A McN Denovan B511, 2/Lt J.O. Chantler B4851, 2/Lt E.E. Owen A8932, 2/Lt F.J. Chown B597. **Shared with Lt K.C. Mills C5374. ***Shared with Capt P.J. Clayson C1114, Lt H.A. Kullberg C8842, Lt D. Knight C1106, Lt E.S. Crossley D6881, Lt K.J.P. Laing C1898, Lt E.E. Owen B8512, 2/Lt H.B. Parkinson C6458, Lt H.B. Bradley C1102, Lt C.B. Henderson C1849, Gefr Preiss of Jasta 14 was captured. †Shared with Capt P.J. Clayson C1114, Lt H.A. Kullberg C1835, Lt D. Knight C1894, Lt C.B. Henderson C1849. ††Shared with Lt H.A. Kullberg C1835, Lt W.A. Smart C1092.

BAWLF Louis Drummond Captain 3(N), 203

A Canadian from Winnipeg, born on 19 November 1896, Bawlf joined 3 Naval Squadron in spring 1917 serving with this unit for over a year. He subsequently became a flight commander in what became 203 Squadron, RAF, during the summer of 1918. His brother, 'Barney' Bawlf, also served in the unit, but was killed in a flying accident on 21 April 1918. This affected Louis deeply, and he was posted to Home Establishment in August.

	1917		Camel					
1s*	27 Jul	Seaplane	B3805	3N	20m off Ostend	1415	DES	CR/RNAS 27.7

	1918							
2	18 Feb	Alb. DV	D6417	3N	Dixmude-Thorout	1140	OOC	CR/RNAS 18.2
3	22 Mar	Alb. DV	B7192	3N	Marquion	1230	OOC	CR/RFC 22.3
4s**	24 Mar	Alb. DV	B7192	3N	Vaux	1530	OOC	CR/RFC 24.3
5	22 Jul	DFW. C	D3415	203	Bauvin	0645	DES	CR/RAF 22.7

TOTAL: 1 and 1 shared destroyed, 2 and 1 shared out of control = 5.
*Shared with F/Cdr J.S.T. Fall N6364, FSL J.A. Glen B3782, FSL H.F. Beamish N6377, FSL A.B. Ellwood B3781. **Shared with F/Cdr F.C. Armstrong B7218, FSL S. Smith B7274, FSL R.C. Berlyn, F/Lt E. Pierce B7227, FSL F.J. Britnell B7229.

BEAMISH Harold Francis Captain 3(N), 203

Born in Havelock North, New Zealand on 7 July 1896, he was known as 'Kiwi'. He joined the RNAS in June 1916, going to Crystal Palace in July and then on to Cranwell. He arrived at Dunkirk on 9 January 1917 and was posted to 3 Naval Squadron with which he served until 17 August 1918. Early in 1917 he got lost after a dogfight and had to land to locate his position. He saw German soldiers running towards him, but to his relief saw British 'Tommies' with them, realizing that the Germans were prisoners. He was awarded a DSC, and became a flight commander during 1918. He returned to New Zealand for a rest and was still on leave when the war ended. Discharged from the RAF, he became a sheep and cattle farmer. He died on 26 October 1986.

	1917		Pup					
1	23 Apr	Alb. DIII	N6202	3N	Croiselles area	0630	OOC	CR/RFC 23.4
			Camel					
2s*	27 Jul	Seaplane	N6377	3N	20m off Ostend	1415	DES	CR/RNAS 27.7
3	5 Sep	Alb. DV	N6377	3N	S E Middelkerke	1840	OOC	CR/RNAS 5.9
4s**	10 Sep	DFW. C	N6377	3N	Furnes	1800	CAPT	CR/RNAS 10.9
5	23 Sep	Alb. DV	N6377	3N	Middelkerke	1100	OOC	CR/RNAS 23.9
	1918							
6	3 May	Fokker DrI	B3855	203	Neuve-Eglise area	1135	OOC	CR/RAF 3.5
7	9 May	Fokker DrI	B3385	203	1m E Herlies	1140	DES	CR/RAF 9.5
8s***	15 May	LVG. C	B3855	203	Salome, E La Basee	1145	DES	CR/RAF 15.5
9	16 May	Pfalz DIII	B3855	203	N La Basee	1120	DES	CR/RAF 16.5
10s†	17 May	Alb. DV	B3855	203	S Merville	1120	DES	CR/RAF 17.5
11s††	18 May	Rumpler C	B3855	203	Merville	1120	DES(F)	CR/RAF 18.5

TOTAL: 1 shared captured, 1 and 4 shared destroyed, and 5 out of control = 11.
*Shared with F/Cdr J.S.T. Fall N6364, FSL J.A. Glen B3782, FSL L.D. Bawlf B3805, FSL A.B. Ellwood B3781. **Shared with F/Cdr R.F. Redpath B3785, FSL E.T. Hayne B3866, FSL G. Harrower B3782, FSL G.B. Anderson B3895. ***Shared with Lt W.W. Goodnow B7198, Lt A.N. Webster B3788, Lt J.D. Breakey D3384, Lt H.W. Skinner B7231, Lt E.T. Hayne D3376. †Shared with Lt W.W. Goodnow B6212, Lt R. Sykes B6378, Lt J.D. Breakey D3384, Lt H.W. Skinner B7231. ††Shared with Lt J.D. Breakey D3384.

BEANLANDS Bernard Paul Gascoigne Captain 70, 24

Beanlands transferred to the RAF from the Hampshire Regiment and flew as a pilot in 70 Squadron during 1916 on Sopwith 1½ Strutters. Converting to single-seat scouts, he was posted to 24 Squadron as a flight commander. He was awarded an MC on 10 January 1918, but was wounded in a fight on 22 March 1918. He died on 8 May 1919 as a result of an accident.

	1916		Strutter					
1s*	6 Sep	Roland C	A1902	70	Elincourt	1845	DES(F)	CR/RFC 6.9
	1917		DH 5					
2	25 Aug	C	A9165	24	Bellenglise	0600	DES(F)	CR/RFC 25.8
3s**	25 Aug	C	A9165	24	Bellenglise	0600	OOC	CR/RFC 25.8
4***	13 Nov	Alb. DIII	A9304	24	Schoorbakke	1230	CAPT	CR/RFC 13.11
5	13 Nov	Alb. DIII	A9304	24	Schoorbakke	1230	OOC	CR/RFC 13.11
6s†	18 Nov	Alb. DIII	A9304	24	Nieuport-Dixmude	1105	OOC	CR/RFC 18.11
7	30 Nov	Alb. DV	A9304	24	E Bourlon Wood	1255	OOC	CR/SR/?
	1918		SE 5A					
8s††	18 Mar	C	C1081	24	Villers Le Sec	1140	OOC	CR/RFC 18.3

TOTAL: 1 captured, 1 and 1 shared destroyed, 2 and 3 shared out of control = 8.
*Observer: Lt C.A. Good; shared with Capt W.J.S. Sanday/Lt Busk A3431, Lt Selby/Lt Thomas A394. This aircraft was manned by Vzfw F. Fahlbusch/Lt H. Rosencrantz of Kampfstfl 1, a 5 victory ace crew who were killed at Malincourt, about 1km further north west of Elincourt. **Shared with 2/Lt W.B. Ives A9389. ***This was probably Maat F. Heinze of MFJ 2 who was killed. †Shared with 2/Lt D. Sutherland. 48 and 24 made 3 claims; Lt F. Kuke of Jasta 33 was killed at Wynghene, in this area. ††Shared with Lt H.B. Redler B7824.

BEARD Donald Wainwright Lieutenant 4, 11

Born in Cheshire on 20 May 1895, he joined the RFC on 20 August 1913 as 2nd Class Air Mechanic 839 Beard. When war broke out he went to France as ground crew in 4 Squadron, but frequently volunteered to fly. On 20 July 1916 he flew as an observer in a BE 2C with Capt Copeland, and shot down a Pfalz Eindekker scout after his pilot had been badly wounded. He then landed the aircraft from the front cockpit with the spare control stick which all BEs carried. For this valiant effort he received an MM and was allowed to return to England to train as a pilot. First as a Sergeant from 26 November 1917, then as a 2nd Lieutenant, he served almost until the end of the war in 11 Squadron. He left the RAF in 1919, and was believed to have still been alive at the time of writing.

	1916		BE 2C					
1*	20 Jul	Pfalz E	----	4	----	----	DES	C&C (GB) 7/3
	1918		Bristol					
2**	9 Mar	Pfalz DIII	C4846	11	Douai	1130	OOC	CR/RFC 9.3
3**	15 Mar	Alb. DV	C4846	11	Rumilly	1115	DES	CR/RFC 15.3
4**	15 Mar	Alb. DV	C4846	11	Rumilly	1115	OOC	CR/RFC 15.3
5**	15 Mar	Alb. DV	C4846	11	Rumilly	1115	OOC	CR/RFC 15.3
6†	22 Mar	Alb. DV	C4846	11	Queant	1835	DES(F)	CR/RFC 23.3
7††	9 May	Pfalz DIII	C807	11	Albert-Combles	1220	OOC	CR/RAF 9.5
8††	9 May	Pfalz DIII	C807	11	1m W of Combles	1225	DES	CR/RAF 9.5

TOTAL: 4 destroyed, 4 out of control = 8.

*Pilot: Capt Copeland. **Observer: Sgt H.W. Scarnell. †Observer: 2/Lt H.M. Stewart. ††Observer: Sgt V.H. Davis

BEAUCHAMP PROCTOR Anthony Frederick Weatherby Captain 84

Anthony Proctor was born on 4 September 1894 in South Africa, and was attending the University of Cape Town when war broke out. Obtaining a second year degree, he left to join the Duke of Edinburgh's Own Rifles and served in the campaign in German South-West Africa. Following this, he transferred to the South African Field Telegraph and Postal Corps as a signaller, but in August 1915 was demobilized and returned to college. He completed his studies and in March 1917 was recruited into the RFC by an old boy of his school, Major A.M. Miller. Travelling to England, he was commissioned and undertook pilot training, joining newly-formed 84 Squadron in late July. On 21 September this unit was sent to France, where he gained his first victory on 3 January 1918. He was awarded an MC after claiming three scouts shot down on 17 March to raise his score to nine. Only five feet two inches in height, he found landing and taking off in the SE 5A difficult despite having a specially built-up seat and adjusted controls to suit his stature. He crashed B539 on landing on 11 March as a result of this. He was awarded a Bar to his MC in the field on 28 May, and early in June was able successfully to turn his attention to balloons, which fascinated him. By 11 June he had destroyed 12 aircraft and four balloons, and driven down 12 more aircraft out of control; this total included three and two shared on 19 May.

On 15 June he was posted to Home Establishment for a rest, receiving the award of one of the first DFCs on 2 July; he rejoined the unit on 6 August. During the next two months he was constantly in action, and by 8 October had raised his total to 54, all gained in under 11 months; this total includes 16 kite balloons, the highest number destroyed by any Empire pilot. On 8 October he shot down a two-seater, but was then hit by ground fire and wounded in the arm. He continued to attack a balloon without success, but on return was hospitalized, where he remained for the rest of the war. On 2 November the award of a DSO was gazetted, followed on 30 November by the Victoria Cross 'for deeds of bravery between 8 August and 6 October 1918'. He left hospital in March 1919 and carried out a tour of the United States to aid the Liberty Loan drive. On return in July he attended the RAF College, Cranwell, being granted a permanent commission as a Flight Lieutenant in November. On 27th of that month he was invested at Buckingham Palace with his VC, DSO and DFC. In February 1920 he returned to South Africa on an extended leave, coming back the following December to join 24 Squadron. Here he flew Sopwith Snipes, forming a formation aerobatic team. On 21 June 1921 he took off for a routine practice flight with the other members of the team, but during a slow loop his aircraft went into a vicious spin, and unable to regain control, he was killed in the ensuing crash. His body was returned to South Africa for burial.

	1918		SE 5A					
1	3 Jan	C	B539	84	N E St Quentin	1500	OOC	CR/RFC 3.1
2s*	15 Feb	C	B539	84	S Le Catelet	1545	OOC	CR/AIR 1/1794
3	17 Feb	Alb. DV	B539	84	S E St Quentin	1045	OOC	CR/RFC 17.2
4	19 Feb	Alb. DV	B539	84	S E La Fere	1020	DES	CR/RFC 19.2
5	28 Feb	Pfalz DIII	B539	84	S E La Fere	1630	OOC	CR/RFC 28.2
6**	15 Mar	DFW. C	D259	84	S Villaret	0820	CAPT	CR/RFC 15.3
7	17 Mar	Alb. DV	D259	84	Busigny	1140	OOC	CR/RFC 17.3
8	17 Mar	Alb. DV	D259	84	W Busigny	1142	OOC	CR/RFC 17.3

9***	17 Mar	Pfalz DIII	D259	84	4m W Busigny	1145	DES	CR/RFC 17.3
10	23 Apr	Fokker DrI	C1772	84	Framerville	1640	DES	CR/RAF 23.4
11	9 May	Alb. DV	C1772	84	W Villers-Brettoneaux a/d	1510	OOC	CR/Air 1/1794
12	10 May	Rumpler C	C1772	84	S E Bray	1410	DES	CR/RAF 10.5
13	17 May	Alb. DV	C1772	84	Hangest	1330	DES	CR/RAF 17.5
14	19 May	C	C1772	84	Vauvillers	0945	OOC	CR/?
15	19 May	Alb. DV	C1772	84	Wiencourt	1000	DES	CR/RAF 19.5
16†	19 May	Alb. DV	C1772	84	Cachy	1835	CAPT	CR/RAF 19.5
17s††	19 May	Alb. DV	C1772	84	S E Villers-Brettoneaux	c1835	DES	CR/RAF 19.5
18s††	19 May	Alb. DV	C1772	84	S E Villers-Brettoneaux	c1835	DES	CR/RAF 19.5
19	27 May	Alb. DV	C1772	84	S Mezieres	1950	OOC	CR/?
20	29 May	Alb. DV	D333	84	S E Fricourt	1850	OOC	CR/?
21	31 May	Alb. DV	D333	84	near Hangest	1245	OOC	CR/?
22	1 Jun	Balloon	D333	84	S E Fricourt	1235	DES	CR/RAF 1.6
23s†††	5 Jun	Rumpler C	D333	84	2000yds W Moreuil	1235	DES	CR/RAF 5.6
24	6 Jun	Balloon	D333	84	N W Proyart	1010	DES	CR/RAF 6.6
25	6 Jun	Balloon	D333	84	N Bray	1025	DES	CR/RAF 6.6
26	11 Jun	Alb. DV	D333	84	5m E Montdidier	1350	OOC	CR/?
27	11 Jun	Pfalz DIII	D333	84	N Cayeux	1430	DES	CR/RAF 11.6
28	13 Jun	Balloon	D333	84	E Contoire	0800	DES	CR/?
29	8 Aug	Balloon	D6856	84	Rosieres	1440	DES	CR/RAF 8.8
30	11 Aug	Fokker DVII	D6856	84	Villers Carbonnel	1810	OOC	CR/?
31	14 Aug	Fokker DVII	D6856	84	Villers Carbonnel	1055	DES(F)	CR/RAF 14.8
32	14 Aug	Fokker DVII	D6856	84	Estrees	1130	OOC	CR/?
33‡	16 Aug	DFW. C	D6856	84	Estrees	1015	DES(F)	CR/RAF 16.8
34	21 Aug	Alb. C	D6856	84	Fay	1530	DES	CR/RAF 21.8
35	22 Aug	Balloon	D6856	84	Assevillers	0940	DES	CR/RAF 22.8
36	22 Aug	Balloon	D6856	84	Hem	0945	DES	CR/RAF 22.8
37	24 Aug	Fokker DVII	D6856	84	Brie	1815	OOC	CR/?
38	24 Aug	Fokker DVII	D6856	84	E Brie	1830	DES(F)	CR/RAF 24.8
39	25 Aug	Fokker DVII	D6856	84	S Tempeux	1020	DES	CR/RAF 25.8
40s‡‡	25 Aug	Rumpler C	D6856	84	S Vrely	1120	CAPT	CR/RAF 25.8
41s‡‡‡	27 Aug	Balloon	D6856	84	Flaucourt	0840	DES	CR/RAF 27.8
42	27 Aug	Balloon	D6856	84	Mt St Quentin	0945	DES	CR/RAF 27.8
43s§	29 Aug	Fokker DVII	D6856	84	1m E Somme, S Brie	1925	DES	CR/RAF 29.8
44	7 Sep	Balloon	D6856	84	Cambrai-St Quentin	1135	DES	CR/RAF 7.9
45s§§	15 Sep	Balloon	C1911	84	Bellicourt	0850	DES	CR/RAF 15.9
46	24 Sep	Balloon	E6028	84	Gouy	0915	DES	CR/?
47	27 Sep	Balloon	C1911	84	2m W Crevecoeur	0850	DES	CR/RAF 27.9
48	1 Oct	Fokker DVII	C1911	84	S E Fontaine	1605	DES	CR/?
49	1 Oct	Fokker DVII	C1911	84	S E Ramicourt	1640	DES(F)	CR/? 20 Sqn
50	2 Oct	Balloon	C1911	84	Selvigny	0830	DES	CR/?
51	3 Oct	Fokker DVII	C1911	84	Mont d'Origny	1025	OOC	CR/?
52	3 Oct	Balloon	C1911	84	Mont d'Origny	1145	DES	CR/RAF 3.10
53s§§§	5 Oct	Balloon	C1911	84	W Bohain	1155	DES	CR/RAF 5.10
54	8 Oct	Rumpler C	C1911	84	N E Mametz	1130	DES	CR/RAF 8.10

TOTAL: 2 and 1 shared captured, 13 and 3 shared balloons, 15 and 4 shared destroyed, 15 and 1 shared out of control = 54.
* Shared with 2/Lt J.A. McCudden C5310. ** This was Gefr Amman/Lt Wagner, both KIA, of FAA 207. ***In this region at this time 84 claimed 3 destroyed and 4 out of control. One known loss was Vzfw Adolf Schreder of Jasta 17, who was killed at Busigny. †This was Lt H. Witt, of Jasta 37, or 46, who was killed. ††Shared with Lt H.O. Macdonald C8719, Lt B. Oliver C9519, Lt E.E. Biccard C6442. †††Shared with Lt W.A. Southey C5399. ‡The observer jumped out, apparently without a parachute. ‡‡Shared with Lt I.P. Corse D6897, Lt N.H. Goudie D6917. ‡‡‡Shared with Lt I.P. Corse, Lt J.E. Boudwin. §Shared with Lt C.F. Falkenburg D6920. §§Shared with Capt D. Carruthers. §§§Shared with 2/Lt A.E. Hill F5477.

BEAVER Wilfred Captain 20

Although living in Montreal, Canada, Beaver was an American citizen. He joined 20 Squadron in late 1917, and was promoted flight commander during the heavy fighting of spring 1918, at which time he was awarded an MC. He brought his score to 19 by mid-June. He flew with various gunners, his main companions being Corporal Mather, Lieutenant H.E. Easton and Sergeant E.A. Deighton.

	1917		Bristol					
1*	13 Nov	Alb. DV	B883	20	S E Houthoulst Wood	1500	DES	CR/RFC 13.11
2**	2 Dec	Alb. DV/C?	B883	20	S E Passchendaele	1030	DES	CR/RFC 2.12
3**	5 Dec	Alb. C	B883	20	Dadizeele	0925	OOC	CR/RFC 5.12

	1918							
4†	3 Jan	Alb. C	B883	20	N E Moorslede	1545	DES	CR/RFC 3.1
5†	6 Jan	Alb. C	B883	20	Houthoulst Forest	1210	OOC	CR/RFC 6.1
6†	3 Feb	Alb. DV	B1156	20	Roulers-Menin Rd	1245	DES(F)	CR/RFC 3.2
7†	4 Feb	Alb. DV	----	20	Roulers	1415	OOC	Summ/AIR 1/689
8†	5 Feb	Alb. DV	B1156	20	Roulers	1120	OOC	CR/RFC 5.2
9†	5 Feb	Alb. DV	B1156	20	Roulers	1120	OOC	CR/RFC 5.2
10†	16 Feb	C	C4826	20	Menin	1140	OOC	CR/RFC 16.2
11†	23 Mar	Alb. DV	B1114	20	Menin-S Roncq	1220	DES	CR/RFC 23.3
12††	25 Apr	Alb. DV	C817	20	N Ploegsteert Wood	1935	DES(F)	CR/RAF 25.4
13†††	3 May	Alb. DV	C817	20	Gheluvelt	1105	DES	CR/RAF 3.5
14‡	9 May	Alb. DV	C817	20	E Warneton-Comines	1330	DES	CR/RAF 9.5
15‡	27 May	Alb. DV	C889	20	N E Armentieres	1125	DES(F)	CR/RAF 27.5
16‡‡	27 May	Fokker DrI	C889	20	N E Armentieres	1125	OOC	CR/RAF 27.5
17‡‡	27 May	Fokker DrI	C889	20	N E Armentieres	1125	DES	CR/RAF 27.5
18‡	29 May	Fokker DrI	C889	20	Bac St Maur	1825	DES	CR/RAF 29.5
19‡	13 Jun	Alb. DV	C889	20	N W Armentieres	0800	OOC	CR/AIR 1/186

TOTAL: 12 destroyed, 7 out of control = 19.

*Observer: 2/Lt C.J. Agelasto. **Observer: AM M. Mather. †Observer: 2/Lt H.E. Easton. ††Observer: Cpl. M. Mather; possibly Lt A. King, of Jasta 40, who was wounded †††Observer: Capt N.W. Taylor. ‡Observer: Sgt E.A. Deighton. ‡‡Observer: Sgt E.A. Deighton, who claimed the two Triplanes.

BECK Alexander Captain 60

An Anglo-Argentinian who was at school in England at the start of the war, Beck joined the RFC, and after pilot training was posted to 60 Squadron in July 1917. When his parents discovered he was in France, they informed the authorities that he was under age and as a result he was posted home in August, although he had already flown 13 sorties over the lines. In March 1918, having reached the required age, he returned to 60 Squadron, becoming a flight commander and receiving a DFC. His 11th victory, claimed on 1 November 1918, was the squadron's last of the war.

	1918		SE 5A					
1	8 Aug	Fokker DVII	D6945	60	Folier-Rosieres	1255	DES	CR/C&C V11 N4
2	14 Aug	Hannover C	D6945	60	Riencourt	0615	DES	CR/C&C V11 N4
3	14 Aug	Alb. DV	D6945	60	Guemappe	0945	DES	CR/RAF 14.8
4s*	31 Aug	LVG. C	D6945	60	Inchy	1020	DES	CR/RAF 31.8
5	28 Sep	LVG. C	F5455	60	Cambrai	0825	DES	CR/RAF 28.9
6	3 Oct	Fokker DVII	F5455	60	Esnes	0815	OOC	CR/C&C V11 N4
7	9 Oct	LVG. C	F5455	60	Bohain	1140	CAPT	CR/RAF 9.10
8	22 Oct	Halb. C	F5455	60	Ovillers	1615	CAPT	CR/C&C V11 N4
9s**	26 Oct	LVG. C	F5455	60	Le Quesnoy	1325	DES	CR/RAF 26.10
10	29 Oct	Fokker DVII	D6953	60	Mormal	1450	OOC	CR/C&C V11 N4
11s***	1 Nov	Fokker DVII	D6134	60	Mormal Woods	1600	DES	CR/RAF 1.11

TOTAL: 2 captured, 4 and 3 shared destroyed, 2 out of control = 11.

*Shared with Lt A.R. Oliver in D6887. **Shared with Lt H.C.M. Orpen in E6029. The observer baled out. ***Shared with Lt F.W. McCarthy E6007, and 2/Lt W.B. Newth D380.

BEDDOW Herbert Howell Lieutenant 22

Joining the RFC in October 1917, Lieutenant Beddow flew with 22 Squadron throughout 1918, claiming 10 victories.

	1918		Bristol					
1*	26 May	Alb. DV	B1209	22	S E Armentieres	1945	DES	CR/RAF 26.5
2**	8 Aug	Pfalz DIII	D7998	22	N E Vitry	1030	OOC	CR/ORB/?
3***	13 Aug	Pfalz DIII	E2499	22	Auberchicourt	1100	OOC	CR/ORB?
4***	13 Aug	Pfalz DIII	E2499	22	Auberchicourt	1100	OOC	CR/ORB/?
5***	16 Aug	Pfalz DIII	D7998	22	Lille	1035	DES	CR/RAF 16.8
6***	16 Aug	Fokker DVII	D7998	22	Lille	1035	DES	CR/RAF 16.8
7s†	22 Aug	Halb. C	----	22	N E Bailleul	1910	DES	CR/RAF 22.8
8***	27 Aug	Fokker DVII	D7998	22	Vitry	0630	OOC	CR/ORB/?
9***	2 Sep	Fokker DVII	D7998	22	Arras-Cambrai	0915	DES	CR/RAF 2.9
10††	5 Sep	Fokker DVII	D7998	22	Douai	1700	OOC	CR/ORB/?

TOTAL: 4 and 1 shared destroyed, 5 out of control = 10.

*Observer: Sgt J. Goodman. **Observer: 2/Lt W.A. Cowie. ***Observer: 2/Lt T.J. Birmingham. †Observer: 2/Lt T.J. Birmingham; shared with Capt W.F.J. Harvey/Capt. D.E. Waight, and Lt I.O. Stead/2/Lt W.A. Cowie. ‡‡Observer: 2/Lt W.V. Tyrrell.

BELGRAVE James Dacres Captain 45, 61, 60

Born in Chinor in 1897, Belgrave enlisted in the Oxford and Bucks Light Infantry in December 1914, going to France in April 1915; he served at the front until he was wounded in November. He remained in France until he joined the RFC in July 1916. After receiving his pilot training, he was posted to 45 Squadron, flying Sopwith 1½ Strutters; in these he and his observers claimed six victories and he was awarded an MC. He then served in 61 Squadron on Home Defence duties, flying Pups and SE 5As, twice engaging Gothas without success. In April 1918 he was posted to 60 Squadron as a flight commander, and in under two months he claimed a further 11 victories. Then on 13 June he took off on patrol at 0415 with two other pilots. Engaging a two-seater, he was seen to shoot this down in conjunction with Lt G.M. Duncan, but his own aircraft and that of Lt R.G. Lewis were both shot down, either by return fire from the German aircraft, or from the ground. Belgrave crashed and was killed.

	1917		Strutter					
1*	7 Feb	Alb. D	7775	45	Menin	1200	OOC	CR/RFC 7.2
2**	18 Mar	C	A2384	45	N E Ploegsteert Wood	1630	DES(F)	CR/RFC 18.3
3***	5 May	Alb. DIII	A2382	45	Becelaere	1145	OOC	CR/RFC 5.5
4***	7 May	Alb. DIII	A2382	45	Lille	1845	DES(F)	CR/RFC 7.5
5***	24 May	Alb. DIII	A8223	45	Zonnebeke	1945	OOC	CR/RFC 25.5
6†	27 May	Alb. DIII	----	45	Roulers	0630	OOC	CR/RFC 27.5
	1918		SE 5A					
7	15 May	Alb. DV	C1056	60	Arras-Cambrai Rd.	1945	DES	CR/RAF 15.5
8	15 May	Alb. DV	C1056	60	Croisilles	1950	OOC	CR/RAF 15.5
9	16 May	Alb. DV	B151	60	Bapaume	1615	OOC	CR/RAF 16.5
10	18 May	DFW. C	B151	60	Carnoy	1115	OOC	CR/?
11	18 May	Alb. DV	B151	60	Carnoy	1130	DES	CR/RAF 18.5
12	21 May	LVG. C	D5988	60	Courcelette	0930	OOC	CR/?
13s††	23 May	Alb. DV	D5988	60	Fricourt	0550	DES	CR/RAF 23.5
14†††	28 May	LVG. C	D5988	60	Albert	0510	DES(F)	CR/RAF 28.5
15	5 Jun	Fokker DrI	D5988	60	Proyart	1930	DES(F)	CR/RAF 5.6
16s††	9 Jun	Hannover C	D5988	60	Arras	1045	DES(F)	CR/RAF 9.6
17s††	9 Jun	Hannover C	D5988	60	Arras	1050	OOC	CR/?
18s‡	13 Jun	C	D5988	60	4m E Albert	0445	DES	CR/RAF 13.6

TOTAL: 7 and 2 shared destroyed, 7 and 2 shared out of control = 18.
*Observer: Sub Lt Thompson. **Observer: Lt E.G. Truscott. ***Observer: 2/Lt C.G. Stewart. †Observer: 2/Lt G.A.H. Davies. ††Shared with Lt A.W. Saunders in B137. †††Lt A. Schroedter/Lt R.E. Wittler, FAA 224; both killed at Albert. ‡Shared with Lt H.A. Gordon in E1261.

BELL Charles Gordon Major 10, 41

Gordon Bell learnt to fly at Brooklands in 1910 (Pilot's Certificate No.100, awarded 4 July 1911) and became a well-known aviator before the war started; in fact by 1914 he had flown no less than 63 different aeroplane types! Joining the RFC in late 1914, he went to France and flew BEs and Bristol Scouts with 10 Squadron during 1915. For this period he was one of the most aggressive pilots in France, constantly engaging enemy aircraft in his Bristol and having numerous combats. His exact total of victories is not known, but at least five have been recorded, including two forced to land. Returning to England due to ill health in December 1915, he took command of the embryo 41 Squadron in 1916 at Gosport; here one of the pilots he later helped to train was future VC, James McCudden. Bell was well-known for his stammer, his monocle and his ready wit, and the air force lost a great man when he was killed during a test flight at Villacoubley on 29 July 1918.

	1915		Bristol	Scout				
1	19 Sep	LVG. C	----	10	S Don	0700	FTL	RFC WD
2	13 Oct	Alb. C	----	10	W Lens	1500	OOC	RFC 13.10
3	13 Oct	LVG. C	----	10	E Lille	1510	FTL	RFC 13.10
4	16 Nov	Alb. C	----	10	Lille	----	OOC	RFC WD
5	30 Nov	LVG. C	----	10	Henin Lietard	----	DES	RFC 30.11

TOTAL: 1 destroyed, 2 out of control, 2 forced to land = 5.

BELL Douglas John Captain 27, 78, 3

A South African, born on 16 September 1893, Bell joined the RFC on 1 June 1916, and was posted to 27 Squadron in October 1916 to fly Martinsyde G 100s. During offensive day bombing missions he had several combats with enemy machines, during which he claimed three victories. He was promoted flight commander in March 1917. Posted to England, he served in 78 (Home Defence) Squadron during 1917, where on the night of 25/26 September, flying Sopwith 1½ Strutter A1040 with 2/Lt G.G. Williams, he shot up a Gotha at 2015 south of Brentwood, firing at it for some 15 minutes. Apparently this bomber ditched in the North Sea and was lost, but this first victory for the home defence squadrons was never confirmed. In 1918 he returned to France to become a flight commander with 3 Squadron on 13 February with which unit he brought his score to 20 in less than two months, being awarded a Bar to his MC. Then on 27 May, he and Lieutenant L.A. Hamilton went up after a German two-seater, but Bell was hit and crashed to his death in C6370, possibly shot down by the reconnaissance crew, Gefreiter Rosenau/Leutnant de Reserve Heinzelmann.

	1917		Martinsyde					
1	1 May	Alb. DIII	----	27	Epinoy area	----	OOC	RFC 1.5/TFE
2s*	4 Jun	Alb. DIII	A6262	27	W St Denis Westrem	1415	DES	CR/RFC 4.6
3	4 Jun	Alb. DIII	A6262	27	Hausbeke	1415	OOC	CR/RFC 4.6
	1918		Camel					
4	11 Mar	Alb. DV	C1615	3	Queant-Pronville	1730	OOC	CR/RFC 11.3
5	13 Mar	Alb. DV	C1615	3	Villers	1545	DES(F)	CR/RFC 13.3
6	16 Mar	Alb. DV	C1615	3	Cambrai	0915	DES	CR/RFC 16.3
7	16 Mar	C	C1615	3	Cambrai	0930	DES	CR/RFC 16.3
8s**	17 Mar	Alb. DV	C1615	3	Cagnicourt	1330	DES(F)	CR/RFC 17.3
9	22 Mar	Alb. DV	C1615	3	Havrincourt Wood	1430	DES(F)	CR/RFC 22.3
10	23 Mar	Balloon	C1615	3	Queant	1540	DES	Sqn WD
11	23 Mar	Alb. DV	C1615	3	Queant	1545	OOC	CR/RFC 23.3
12	23 Mar	Alb. DV	C1615	3	Queant	1545	OOC	CR/RFC 23.3
13s***	27 Mar	LVG. C	C1615	3	—	c0700	DES	Sqn WD
14	1 Apr	Fokker DrI	C6730	3	Combles	1815	DES	CR/RAF 1.4
15s†	8 Apr	Balloon	C6730	3	N Mory	0655	DES	CR/RAF 8.4
16s††	11 Apr	Alb. C	----	3	Ervillers	1600	DES(F)	CR/RAF 11.4
17	12 Apr	Alb. DV	C6730	3	Albert	1900	DES	CR/RAF 12.4
18	12 Apr	Alb. DV	C6730	3	Pozieres	1915	OOC	CR/RAF 12.4
19	20 Apr	Fokker DrI	C6730	3	N E Villers Brettoneaux	1750	DES	CR/RAF 20.4
20s†††	27 May	C	C6730	3	57D R32	1240	OOC	CR/?

TOTAL: 1 and 1 shared balloons, 7 and 4 shared destroyed, 6 and 1 shared out of control = 20.
*Shared with Lt D.V.D. Marshall in A1573. **Shared with 2/Lt A.A.M. Arnot in B5448. Uffz H. Kehr KIA of Jasta 3. ***Shared with Lt G.R. Riley and Lt W.C. Dennett. †Shared with Capt C.B. Ridley in B7428 of 201. ††Shared with Lt L.A. Hamilton, Lt A.W. Franklyn and Lt Mayer. †††Shared with Lt L.A. Hamilton and Lt W. Hubbard.

BELL Gerald Gordon Captain 22, 17, 47, 150

A Canadian, he first served with the Canadian Infantry in the 38th Battalion in France, before transferring to the RFC. During 1917 he flew as an observer with 22 Squadron on FE 2Bs, participating in three victories whilst with this unit. He then trained as a pilot, and was posted to 47 Squadron in Salonika to fly scouts as a flight commander; here he claimed one victory during April 1918. The scouts in 17 and 47 Squadrons were then detached to form 150 Squadron, and during the rest of the spring and summer he claimed a further nine victories, half of these being shared; he commanded 'A' Flight whilst with the squadron. His tour ended late in 1918 and he then returned to Canada, where he was still living in Ontario when last heard of.

	1917		FE 2B					
1s*	8 Apr	Alb. DII	A5454	22	Regny	0700	DES	CR/RFC 9.4?
2**	3 May	Alb. DIII	A855	22	----	1730	OOC	CR/RFC 3.5
3**	29 Jul	C	----	22	Tortequesne	0650	OOC	CR/?
	1918		SE 5A					
4s***	13 Apr	Alb. DIII	B692	47	1500yds S of Brajkovic	0730	DES	CR/BG
5s†	13 May	Alb. DIII	B695	150	Livanovo	0800	DES	CR/BG
6s††	15 May	Alb. DV	B28	150	Hudova	0530	OOC	CR/BG
7	1 Jun	SS DIII	B692	150	Casandale	1505	DES(F)	CR/BG
8s†††	15 Jun	Alb. DV	B692	150	Marinopolje	0915	OOC	CR/BG
9s†	18 Jun	Alb. DV	B692	150	N Paljorca	0750	DES	CR/BG
10s‡	23 Jun	Alb. DV	B6925	150	Hill 5401-Rupel Pass	0745	DES	CR/BG
11	9 Jul	Rumpler C	B6945	150	Angista	0800	OOC	CR/BG
12s‡‡	19 Jul	Alb. DV	B692	150	W Livanova airfield	0800	DES	CR/BG
13s‡‡‡	5 Aug	SS DIII	D3495	150	3000yds N W Hudova	0815	DES	CR/BG
14	15 Aug	LVG. C	D3495	150	Seres Uesnik	1200	OOC	CR/BG
15	21 Aug	LVG. C	D3495	150	Girejik-Derbend	0910	OOC	CR/BG
16	18 Sep	Fokker D	D3495	150	Karali	0630	DES(F)	CR/BG

TOTAL: 2 and 7 shared destroyed, 4 and 3 shared out of control = 16.
*Pilot: Lt L.W. Beale; shared with Capt C.W. Clement/2/Lt L.G. Davies A5461, Lt J.F.A. Day/2/Lt W.M. Taylor 7681, 2/Lt J.V.A. Aspinal/2/Lt M.K. Parlee A796, 2/Lt Furlonger/2/Lt C.W. Lane 4883, and Lt H.G. Spearpoint/2/Lt J.K. Campbell 4891. **Pilot: 2/Lt E.A.H. Ward. ***Shared with Lt C.B. Green in B30. †Shared with Capt A.G. Goulding. ††Shared with Lt F.D. Travers in B688. †††Shared with Capt G.M. Brawley in B613 and Lt L. Hamilton in B28. ‡Shared with Lt L. Hamilton in B28. ‡‡Shared with Capt G.M Brawley in B694, Lt A.E. Jarvis in B30 Lt W. Ridley in C9501. ‡‡‡Shared with Lt J.A. Beeny in B695.

BELL Hilliard Brooke Captain 66

A Canadian from Toronto, born in January 1897, he served with the Canadian Field Artillery until he joined the RFC in July 1917. He was posted to Italy after training, where he flew with 66 Squadron from 16 October. He was subsequently promoted Captain and awarded an MC and the Italian Bronze Medal for Military Valour. Bell died on 16 September 1960.

	1917		Camel					
1	16 Dec	Alb. DV	B5223	66	N E Casa de Felice	1400	OOC	ORB/SR/14 W
	1918							
2*	4 Feb	Alb. DIII	B4628	66	.5m S W St Giacomo Di Veglia	1250	DES(F)	ORB/SR/7 BG
3**	6 Feb	Aviatik C	B5172	66	S E Giacomo Di Veglia	0820	DES	ORB/SR/7 BG
4	16 Mar	Berg D	B5180	66	La Parada	1200	OOC	ORB/SR/14 W
5	19 Mar	Alb. DIII	B5180	66	St Giacomo Di Veglia	1025	DES	ORB/SR/14 W
6***	23 Apr	Alb. DIII	B5180	66	Mt Moscaigh	0850	DES(F)	ORB/SR/14 W
7	3 May	Alb. DIII	B5180	66	Ormelle	1150	DES	ORB/SR/14 W
8	10 May	Alb. DIII	B5180	66	Mt Meatta	0930	DES(F)	ORB/SR/14 W
9	1 Jul	Pfalz DIII	D9388	66	Coma-Vezzano	0900	DES	ORB/SR/14 W
10	4 Jul	Pfalz DIII	D9388	66	W Asiago	0750	DES	ORB/SR/14 W

TOTAL: 8 destroyed, 2 out of control = 10.

*Vzfw Rudolf Wiessner of Jasta 39, was shot down in flames and killed at this location and time. **Lt Kurt Muehrwald, an observer of FA2 was killed. ***Fw Alois Lehmann, from Flik 55j, was shot down and killed in Albatros DIII 153:160.

BELL-IRVING Alan Duncan Captain 7, 60

Born in Vancouver, Canada, on 28 August 1894, he first served with the Gordon Highlanders, but later transferred to the RFC and flew as an observer with 7 Squadron. He was shot down on 20 September 1915, escaping unhurt, but suffered wounds on a later occasion on 14 December. He undertook pilot training on recovery, joining 60 Squadron in May 1916, where he made seven claims including one balloon. He was again shot down on 21 October, surviving unharmed, but on 9 November was shot down in Nieuport A272 (probably by Leutnant Hohne of Jasta 2) and was wounded again on this occasion; he received an MC and Bar, and Croix de Guerre whilst with the unit. After leaving hospital he returned to Home Establishment, where he served with — and later commanded — the School of Special Flying at Gosport; he left the RAF in 1919. During World War II he served with the RCAF, becoming an Air Commodore, OBE; he died on 24 April 1965. There is considerable confusion over the name Bell-Irving, as there were four pilots of this name in the RFC and RNAS, and two other Bell-Irvings in the Army; all were related.

	1916		Morane					
1	28 Aug	Roland C	A166	60	Bapaume	1840	DES	CR/C&C V11 N4
			Nieup					
2	14 Sep	Balloon	A203	60	Avesnes les Bapaume	1845	DES	CR/RFC 15.9
3	23 Sep	Roland CII	A203	60	Croisilles	1230	DES	CR?/RFC 23.9
4	30 Sep	Roland C	A203	60	Villers au Flos	1040	DES(F)	CR?/RFC 30.9
5	30 Sep	Roland C	A203	60	Villers au Flos	1045	DES(F)	C&C V11 N4
6	15 Oct	C	A203	60	Ervillers	1200	DES	C&C V11 N4
7	15 Oct	C	A203	60	Ervillers	1200	OOC	C&C V11 N4

TOTAL: 6 destroyed, 1 out of contol = 7.

BENBOW Edwin Louis Captain 40, 85

Known as 'Lobo', he joined the Royal Field Artillery and went to France in February 1915, serving with his battery for 12 months. Transferring to the RFC, he flew for eight months as an observer before being selected for pilot training. In 1916 he was posted to 40 Squadron and became the only pilot to fly the FE 8 in combat with a reasonable degree of success. At the end of his tour with 40 he became an instructor, and then joined Major Bishop's newly-formed 85 Squadron as a flight commander. Returning to France in May 1918, 'Lobo' was killed in action on 30th of that month without having added to his score, when he was shot down in SE 5A C1861 by Oberflugmeister Schonfelder of Jasta 7 as the latter's eighth victory.

	1916		FE 8					
1	20 Oct	Alb. DI	7627	40	E Lens	1205	DES	CR/RFC 20.10
2	22 Oct	C	7627	40	Vimy	1050	DES(F)	CR/RFC 22.10
3	16 Nov	Alb. C	7627	40	Provin-Annoeullin	1135	DES	CR/RFC 16.11
4	4 Dec	Alb. DI	7627	40	N E Arras	1250	DES?	CR/RFC 4.12
5	20 Dec	Alb. C	7627	40	Lens	1205	DES	CR/RFC 20.12
	1917							
6s*	14 Feb	Alb. DII	A4871	40	N E Arras	1515	DES	CR/AIR 1/141
7	15 Feb	Alb. DII	A4871	40	W Douai	1120	OOC	CR/RFC 15.2
8	6 Mar	Alb. DII	A4871	40	Givenchy	1050	DES(F)	CR/RFC 6.3

TOTAL: 6 and 1 shared destroyed, 1 out of control = 8.

*Shared with Lt C.O. Usbourne in 6426; late confirmation by AA.

BENNETT Jnr. Louis Lieutenant 40

Born on 22 September 1894, in Weston, West Virginia, Louis Bennett was an American who was studying at Yale University from 1913-17, and who enlisted in the RFC in Toronto, Canada, on 9 October 1917. After initial training, he arrived in England on 25 February 1918, and on completion of training in May he was posted to 90 (Home Defence) Squadron. Anxious to get into action, he was posted to France in July, joining George McElroy's 'C' Flight in 40 Squadron on 21st of that month. He shot down a Fokker DVII out of control on 15 August for his first victory, and two days later destroyed his first balloon. Developing a taste for attacking these, he sent down four in flames in one day on 19th, adding two more on 22nd, by which time his score stood at 10. Two days later he again attacked balloons, being seen to destroy another two. He made for a third, but was hit by AA fire from Machine Gun Detachments 920 and 921, and his aircraft burst into flames. He jumped out at a height of about 100 feet, breaking both legs. Carried to hospital by the crews of the guns which had shot him down, he died while his injuries were being dressed. His phenomenal 12 victories, including nine balloons within ten days, happened too swiftly for him to be awarded a decoration before his death; in fact he only flew on 25 sorties in his brief career on the Western Front.

	1918		SE 5A					
1	15 Aug	Fokker DVII	E3947	40	Brebieres	1200	OOC	CR/AIR 1 1222
2s*	17 Aug	LVG. C	E3947	40	E Henin Lietard	0740	DES	CR/RAF 17.8
3	17 Aug	Balloon	E3947	40	S E Merville	0800	DES	CR/Air1 1222
4	19 Aug	Balloon	E3947	40	E Merville	1000	DES	CR/RAF 19.8
5	19 Aug	Balloon	E3947	40	E Merville	1010	DES	CR/RAF 19.8
6	19 Aug	Balloon	E3947	40	E Merville	1340	DES	CR/RAF 19.8
7	19 Aug	Balloon	E3947	40	E Merville	1341	DES	CR/RAF 19.8
8	22 Aug	Balloon	C9258	40	W Don	0620	DES	CR/RAF 22.8
9	22 Aug	Balloon	C9258	40	E La Bassee	0630	DES	CR/RAF 22.8
10	23 Aug	LVG. C	C9258	40	S Quierry la Motte	0715	DES	CR/RAF 23.8
11	24 Aug	Balloon	E3947	40	Provin	1225	DES	CR/Air1 1222
12	24 Aug	Balloon	E3947	40	Hantay	1230	DES	CR/Air1 1222

TOTAL: 9 balloons, 1 and 1 shared destroyed, 1 out of control = 12.
*Shared with Lt F.H. Knobel in E3183.

BENNETT Rex George Lieutenant 20

Bennett joined the RFC as an equipment officer in September 1915, but later volunteered for aircrew duties, training as a pilot. He joined 20 Squadron during the early months of 1918, claiming nine victories, five with his front gun and four by his observers in the rear cockpit; he flew with a different observer on each of the latter occasions. He was reported missing on 28 May 1918 in Bristol Fighter C4763 with Lt G.T.C. Salter. They left at 0917 and were possibly in the aircraft identified as a 'De Havilland 4' which was shot down in flames at La Gorgue by Leutnant K. Baier of Jasta 18; alternatively they may have been one of two 'DH 4s' claimed by Flak. No claims at all were submitted by the Germans for Bristols on this date.

	1918		Bristol					
1*	30 Jan	Alb. DIII	C6404	20	W Ghistelles	1420	OOC	CR/RFC 30.1
2**	4 Feb	Alb. DV	----	20	Menin-Roulers Rd.	c1415	DES(F)	Summ/RFC 4.2
3**	4 Feb	Alb. DV	----	20	Menin-Roulers Rd.	c1415	OOC	Summ/RFC 4.2
4***	17 Feb	Pfalz DIII	C4604	20	Moorslede	1120	OOC	CR/RFC 17.2
5†	21 Feb	Alb. DV	C4604	20	S W Comines	1210	DES	CR/RFC 21.2
6††	27 Mar	Alb. DV	C4641	20	W Cappy	1100	DES	CR/SR
7†††	28 Mar	Pfalz DIII	C4641	20	La Boiselle	0900	OOC	CR/RFC 28.3
8‡	15 May	Alb. DV	----	20	Wervicq	1115	OOC	SR/?
9‡	15 May	Alb. DV	----	20	Wervicq	1115	OOC	SR/?

TOTAL: 3 destroyed, 6 out of control = 9.
*Observer: 2AM Matthews. **Observer: 1AM Mather. ***Observer: Cpl F. Archer. †Observer: Cpl E. Veale. ††Observer: Lt T.C. Noel. †††Observer: Lt J.D. Boyd. ‡Observer: 2/Lt P.G. Jones.

BENNETT Risdon Mackenzie Lieutenant 204

Born on 12 February 1900 in Beckenham, Kent, he served in 204 Squadron during the summer of 1918. He was shot down by AA fire over Thorout in Camel D8187 on 28 September 1918, and was reported missing. At 18½ years of age, Bennett may have been the youngest ace to be killed during the First War.

	1918		Camel					
1	31 Jul	Fokker DVII	D3354	204	Roulers	1930	DES	CR/5 GP Comm
2	15 Aug	Pfalz DIII	D3354	204	Menin	1900	DES	CR/5 GP Comm
3	15 Aug	Fokker DVII	D3354	204	Menin	1905	OOC	CR/5 GP Comm
4s*	16 Sep	Fokker DVII	D8187	204	Blankenburghe-Zeebrugge	1855	DES(F)	CR/5 GP Comm

5	16 Sep	LVG. C	D8187	204	Blankenberghe	1900	DES	CR/5 Gp Comm

TOTAL: 3 and 1 shared destroyed, 1 out of control = 5.
*Shared with Capt C.R.R. Hickey F3942, 2/Lt N. Smith D8188, Lt F.G. Bayley, 2/Lt J.R. Chisman.

BILLINGE Frank Captain 20, 32, 56

Born 19 December 1894 in London, Frank Billinge was an original member of 20 Squadron in 1916 as an observer, gaining one victory with this unit. On 31 August 1916 he was posted to Home Establishment for flying training, upon completion of which he returned to France, joining 32 Squadron on 24 November on DH 2s. Promoted flight commander on 12 March 1917, he served until 1 June, claiming two further victories. On 6 February 1918 he returned to the front as a flight commander with 56 Squadron on SE 5As, adding two final victories to his total.

	1916		FE 2B					
1*	13 Feb	A.G.O. C	6336	20	W Mouscron	1615	DES	CR/RFC 13.3
	1917		DH 2					
2s**	23 Jan	C	----	32	Ervillers	1515	DES(F)	ORB/SD/?
3s***	27 Jan	C	----	32	Courcelles-Achiet	0945	DES(F)	ORB/RFC 27.1
	1918		SE 5A					
4s†	19 Feb	C	B4880	56	S W Rumaucourt	1240	OOC	CR/RFC 19.2
5	22 Mar	Alb. DV	B4880	56	S E Queant	1525	OOC	CR/RFC 22.3

TOTAL: 1 and 2 shared destroyed, 1 and 1 shared out of control = 5.
*Pilot: Lt J.T. Kirton. **Shared with Capt L.P. Aizlewood, Lt G.J. King, Lt T.A. Gooch, Lt St C.C. Taylor, Lt A.C. Randall, 2/Lt A. Coningham. ***Shared with Capt J.M. Robb, Lt T.A. Gooch, Lt H.D. Davis, Lt C.E.M. Pickthorne, Lt Eccles, Lt M.L. Taylor. †Shared with Capt L.W. Jarvis B53.

BINNIE James Alexander Weatherhead Lieutenant 48

After serving with the Highland Light Infantry, Binnie joined the RFC, receiving his wings in 1917. He served with 48 Squadron during the summer of that year, flying with Corporal V. Reed as his gunner.

	1917		Bristol					
1*	15 Jun	Alb. DIII	A7123	48	S W Douai	1940	OOC	CR/RFC 16.6
2s**	15 Jun	Alb. DIII	A7123	48	N Vitry	2020	DES(F)	CR/RFC 16.6
3***	13 Jul	Alb. DV	A7151	48	Slype	0940	DES(F)	CR/RFC 13.7
4s†	28 Jul	Alb. DV	A7123	48	Ghistelles-Zevecote	0815	DES(F)	CR/RFC 28.7
5***	19 Aug	Alb. DV	A7220	48	Ostend	0650	OOC	CR/?
6††	22 Aug	Alb. DV	A7220	48	Ghistelles	0900	DES(F)	CR/RFC 22.8
7***	26 Aug	Alb. DV	A7220	48	W Middelkerke	0830	DES	CR/RFC 26.8
8†††	26 Aug	Alb. DV	A7220	48	W Middelkerke	0830	OOC	CR/RFC 26.8
9§	11 Sep	DFW. C	A7220	48	Dixmude	1015	OOC	CR/RFC 11.9

TOTAL: 3 and 2 shared destroyed, 4 out of control = 9.
*Observer: AM. V. Reed. **Observer: AM V. Reed; shared with Capt B.E. Baker/Lt H. Munro in A7149. ***Observer: Cpl V. Reed. †Observer: Cpl V. Reed; shared with Capt B.E. Baker/Lt G.R. Spencer in A7170. Possibly Lt Crusemann of Jasta 17. ††Observer: Cpl V. Reed; possibly Lt Koenemann of Jasta B, killed in action at Lombartzyde. 48 made 6 claims in the fight. †††Observer: Cpl V. Reed; Uffz Carl Conradt of Jasta 17 killed. §Observer: Lt T.C.S. Tuffield.

BIRKBECK Robert Alexander Captain 1

Born in October 1898 in Bournemouth, Robert Birkbeck joined 1 Squadron on 10 June 1917, claiming 10 victories with this unit. He was later promoted to Captain, leaving the unit on 17 February 1918; he was later awarded a DFC, which was gazetted on 3 June 1918. This was somewhat unusual, since all his claims were made six months before this medal was inaugurated. He may therefore have seen service elsewhere subsequently, in a non fighting scout role.

	1917		Nieuport					
1	22 Jul	Alb. DV	B1582	1	Menin	1900	OOC	CR/RFC 23.7
2	10 Aug	Alb. DV	B1582	1	Quesnoy	1430	OOC	CR/RFC 10.8
3	16 Aug	Alb. DV	B1582	1	Passchendaele	0930	OOC	CR/RFC 16.8
4s*	1 Oct	DFW. C	B6753	1	Houthoulst	1110	OOC	CR/RFC 1.10
5**	9 Oct	Alb. DV	B6753	1	S Polygon-Wood	1515	DES(F)	CR/RFC 9.10
6**	9 Oct	Alb. DV	B6753	1	S Polygon-Wood	1515	OOC	CR/RFC 9.10
7	12 Oct	C	B6753	1	Comines	1145	DES	CR/RFC 12.10
8	21 Oct	DFW. C	B6753	1	Nieppe	1145	OOC	CR/RFC 21.10
9	31 Oct	DFW. C	B6753	1	S Houthem	1030	DES	CR/RFC 31.10
10	9 Nov	DFW. C	B6826	1	S E Houthoulst Wood	1600	OOC	CR/RFC 9.11

TOTAL: 3 destroyed, 6 and 1 shared out of control = 10.
*Shared with Capt W.V.T. Rooper B6767, Lt F.G Baker B3630 and Lt L. Cummings in B6790. **1 Sqn made 6 claims; Lt R. Wagner of Jasta 26 was killed.

BIRKS Gerald Alfred Lieutenant 66

From Montreal, Canada, he joined the RFC in 1917 and on 10 March 1918 joined 66 Squadron in Italy at the age of 23. He was awarded an MC and Bar, both gazetted on 16 September, and was credited with 12 enemy machines destroyed. On 24 May 1918, in company with Capt W.G.Barker and Lt Apps, he was involved in a prolonged fight with an enemy formation which resulted in the claiming of four Austro-Hungarian machines shot down; one of these (almost certainly that shot down by Birks) was that flown by the Hungarian ace, Josef Kiss (19 victories), commander of Flik 55j. It is notable that in almost every fight in which he was involved, Austrian aircraft were lost. Birks is known to have shot down a second Austro-Hungarian ace, Lt Patzelt (five victories) as well as Lt Kiss. He was one of the most accurate claimers and proficient fighter pilots in the RAF. Gerald Birks attended the World War I Aces' Reunion in 1981.

	1918		Camel					
1*	18 Mar	Rumpler C	B6424	66	Pravisdomini	0825	DES	ORB/SR/14 W
2**	24 Mar	C	B2497	66	S E Conegliano	1145	DES(F)	ORB/SE/14 W
3***	2 May	Alb. DV	B6424	66	Levico	1145	DES	ORB/SR/14 W
4†	4 May	Alb. DV	B6424	66	Vidor	0945	CAPT	ORB/SR/14 W
5†	4 May	Alb. DV	B6424	66	Vidor	0950	CAPT	ORB/SR/14 W
6††	11 May	Alb. DV	B7358	66	Torre di Mosto	1645	DES(F)	ORB/SR/14 W
7†††	19 May	Berg D	D1913	66	Borgo	0735	DES	ORB/SR/14 W
8†††	19 May	Berg D	D1913	66	Borgo	0740	DES	ORB/SR/14 W
9‡	20 May	Berg D	D1913	66	Valdobiadene	1200	DES	ORB/SR/14 W
10‡‡	24 May	Berg D	B6424	66	Lamon	1045	DES	ORB/SR/14 W
11‡‡‡	9 Jun	Alb. DV	D8101	66	Levico	1020	DES(F)	ORB/SR/14 W
12§	21 Jun	Alb. DV	D8101	66	Motta	0910	DES	ORB/SR/14 W

TOTAL: 3 captured, 9 destroyed = 12.

*Aircraft 161:69 Schneeberger KIA Flik 43d. **The crew Suski/Poelzi of Flik 50d were killed in 69:81. ***153:176 Lt K. Kosiuski of Flik 68j was wounded and crash landed. †Both these aircraft were totally destroyed. Lt F. Frisch in 153:210 and Lt K. Patzelt in 153:182, both of Flik 68j were killed. Patzelt was a 5 victory ace. ††66 made 3 claims, Zgsfhr Slavko Gyurgyev of Flik 61j was killed. †††Possibly Oblt K. Benedek in 328:18, and Flgr Czemy 328:28 of Flik 14k, who were both killed. ‡2 claims 1 loss, Korp S. Szijarto of Flik 42j, crash landed 153:163. ‡‡See also the entry for Capt W.G. Barker. It is probable that Birks was primarily responsible for shooting down Oblt Josef Kiss of Flik 55j in 422:10. Kiss, the fifth most successful Austro-Hungarian ace with 19 victories, was killed. ‡‡‡2 claims 1 loss; Fw L. Telessy of Flik 9j in 153:151 died of wounds. §3 claims 1 loss; Oblt F. Dechant of Flik 51j, in 153:188 was killed.

BISHOP William Avery Lieutenant Colonel 21, 60, 85

Born on 8 February 1894 at Owen Sound, Ontario, Canada, he attended the Royal Military College in 1911 and then joined the Canadian Mounted Rifles. Sent to England at the outbreak of war as a young Lieutenant, he soon tired of the inaction of the cavalry and applied to join the RFC in July 1915. As an observer he served with 21 Squadron in France during the autumn, but was injured in a crash and admitted to hospital. Following this experience, he requested pilot training, and after qualification was posted to 60 Squadron flying Nieuport 17s, in March 1917. He claimed his first victory on his first patrol over the lines and by the end of a fortnight had claimed a total of five. An aggressive and 'lone wolf' type of pilot, he flew his share of patrols and when off duty went out on his own. He was promoted to Captain in April and received the MC in May, followed shortly afterwards by a DSO. On 2 June he was out alone to attack an enemy airfield and returned with his machine badly shot about, claiming to have shot down three enemy scouts which had attempted to take off and intercept him. For this action he received the Victoria Cross. By late July he had claimed 36 victories flying the Nieuport, when the squadron re-equipped with SE 5s, Bishop being very impressed by the performance of the new aircraft. Following the award of the VC, he was promoted to Major, and a Bar to his DSO was announced before he was posted to England, having now claimed a total of 45 aircraft and two balloons destroyed or driven down. He was claimed by his Wing Headquarters to be the highest-scoring RFC pilot of the day (no mention being made at the time of RNAS pilots!).

In September 1917 he returned to Canada on a recruiting drive, married his sweetheart, and then came back to England as Chief Instructor at a gunnery school, taking time out to write his autobiography *Winged Warfare*. He was then given command of 85 Squadron which was forming, and led this unit to France on 22 May 1918. Again flying many lone patrols, he claimed a further 25 victories between 27 May and 19 June, no less than five of them being claimed on this latter date during his final flight over the front. For this he received the DFC. His score by his own count was 72, a figure confirmed by Wing HQ. It should be mentioned however that most of his victories were credited without any confirmation by other pilots or ground observers. Indeed his claims on 2 June 1917, which resulted in his receiving the VC, were not corroborated by any other witness, an almost unprecedented case for this decoration; nevertheless, he was a most colourful fighter during his period at the front. The whole question as to the veracity of many of Bishop's claims has been the subject of much controversy for many years, culminating in a full scale Senate Inquiry in Canada following a TV documentary questioning their legitimacy. The authors feel that it is not appropriate in the context of this book to enter into such controversy, or to make judgements, but merely to record what was claimed and accepted at the time.

In August 1918 Bishop was posted to Canadian HQ to help form the Canadian Air Force. After the war he returned to Canada, going into partnership with 'Billy' Barker, VC, to form a commercial aviation concern. During World War II he served as an Air Marshal in charge of training. He died on 11 September 1956. His biography *Courage of the Early Morning*, written by his son, was published in 1967.

	1917		Nieuport					
1	25 Mar	Alb. DII	A306	60	N St Leger	1700	DES	CR/CEN/?
2	31 Mar	Alb. DII	A6769	60	S Gavrelle	0730	DES	CR/RFC 31.3
3	7 Apr	Alb. DIII	A6769	60	Arras	1700	OOC	CR/RFC 7.4
4	7 Apr	Balloon	A6769	60	Vis en Artois	1701	DES	CR/RFC 7.4
5s*	8 Apr	Alb. C	A6769	60	Douai-Flesquieres	0930	DES	CR/RFC 8.4
6	8 Apr	Alb. DIII	A6769	60	N E Arras	0930	OOC	CR/RFC 8.4
7	8 Apr	Alb. DIII	A6769	60	Vitry en Artois	1010	OOC	CR/RFC 8.4
8	20 Apr	C	B1566	60	Biache St Vaast	1458	DES(F)	CR/RFC 20.4
9	22 Apr	Alb. DIII	B1566	60	E Vimy	1120	OOC	CR/RFC 22.4
10	23 Apr	Alb. C	B1566	60	Vitry en Artois	1530	DES	CR/RFC 23.4
11	23 Apr	Alb. DIII	B1566	60	E Vitry	1559	DES	CR/RFC 23.4
12	27 Apr	Balloon	B1566	60	Vitry en Artois	0855	DES	CR/C&C/CEM
13	29 Apr	Halb. DII	B1566	60	E Epinoy	1155	DES(F)	CR/RFC 29.4
14	30 Apr	C	B1566	60	S E Lens	1115	DES	CR/RFC 30.4
15	2 May	Alb. CIII	B1566	60	E Epinoy	1010	DES	CR/RFC 2.5
16	2 May	Alb. CIII	B1566	60	E Epinoy	1012	OOC	CR/RFC 2.5
17s**	4 May	AEG C IV	B1566	60	Brebieres-Vitry	1336	DES	CR/RFC 4.5
18	7 May	Alb. DIII	B1566	60	N Vitry	0950	OOC	CR/RFC 7.5
19	7 May	Alb. DIII	B1566	60	Brebieres	1500	OOC	CR/RFC 7.5
20	26 May	Alb. DIII	B1566	60	Izel les Esquerchin	1016	OOC	CR/C&C/CEM
21	27 May	C	B1566	60	Dourgies-Monchy	0940	DES	CR/RFC 27.5
22	31 May	Alb. DIII	B1566	60	Epinoy	0711	DES	CR/RFC 31.5
23	2 Jun	Alb. DIII	B1566	60	Estourmel area	0430	DES	CR/RFC 2.6
24	2 Jun	Alb. DIII	B1566	60	Estourmel area	c0435	DES	CR/RFC 2.6
25	2 Jun	Alb. DIII	B1566	60	Estourmel area	c0440	DES	CR/RFC 2.6
26	8 Jun	Alb. DIII	B1566	60	N Lille	1210	DES	CR/RFC 8.6
27	24 Jun	Alb. DIII	B1566	60	Beaumont	1123	DES(F)	CR/RFC 24.6
28	25 Jun	Alb. DIII	B1566	60	Dury	1205	OOC	CR/RFC 25.6
29	26 Jun	Alb. DIII	B1566	60	Annay-N Etaing	1055	DES(F)	CR/RFC 26.6
30	26 Jun	Alb. DIII	B1566	60	Annay-N Etaing	1056	OOC	CR/RFC 26.6
31	28 Jun	Alb. DIII	B1566	60	Drocourt-La Bassee	1130	DES	CR/RFC 28.6
32	10 Jul	Alb. DIII	B1566	60	Vitry-Quiery	2010	OOC	CR/RFC 11.7
33	12 Jul	Alb. DIII	B1566	60	Vitry-Douai	1340	DES	CR/RFC 12.7
34	17 Jul	Alb. DIII	B1566	60	Havrincourt	1945	DES(F)	CR/RFC 17.7
35	17 Jul	Alb. DIII	B1566	60	Marquion- Queant	1955	DES	CR/RFC 17.7
36	20 Jul	Alb. DIII	B1566	60	6m S E Havrincourt	1205	OOC	CR/RFC 20.7
			SE 5A					
37	28 Jul	Alb. DIII	A8936	60	Phalempin	1810	DES(F)	CR/RFC 28.7
38	29 Jul	Alb. DIII	A8936	60	Beaumont	0710	OOC	CR/RFC 29.7
39	5 Aug	Alb. DIII	A8936	60	Hendecourt- Monchy	2000	DES(F)	CR/RFC 5.8
40	5 Aug	Alb. DIII	A8936	60	Hendecourt-Monchy	2000	OOC	CR/RFC 5.8
41	6 Aug	Alb. DIII	A8936	60	Brebieres	1545	DES	CR/RFC 6.8
42	9 Aug	Alb. DIII	A8936	60	Escourt St Quentin	0900	DES	CR/RFC 9.8
43	13 Aug	Alb. DIII	A8936	60	5m S Douai	1902	DES(F)	CR/C&C/CEM
44	13 Aug	Alb. DIII	A8936	60	5m S Douai	1902	DES(F)	CR/C&C/CEM
45	15 Aug	Alb. DV	A8936	60	Henin Lietard	2020	OOC	CR/RFC 15.8
46	16 Aug	C	A8936	60	Harnes	1903	DES	CR/RFC 16.8
47	16 Aug	Alb. DV	A8936	60	Carvin	1905	DES	CR/RFC 16.8
	1918							
48	27 May	C	C6490	85	E Passchendaele	1632	DES	CR/RAF 27.5
49	28 May	Alb. DV	C6490	85	S W Cortemarck	1555	DES	CR/RAF 28.5
50	28 May	Alb. DV	C6490	85	S W Cortemarck	1555	DES	CR/RAF 28.5
51	30 May	C	C6490	85	Roulers	1542	DES	CR/RAF 30.5
52	30 May	Alb. DV	C6490	85	Roulers	1545	DES	CR/RAF 30.5
53	30 May	Alb. DV	C6490	85	.5m N Armentieres	1953	DES	CR/RAF 30.5
54	31 May	Pfalz DIII	C6490	85	Quesnoy	1505	DES	CR/RAF 31.5

55	31 May	Pfalz DIII	C6490	85	2m N Estaires	2015	DES	CR/RAF 31.5
56	1 Jun	Pfalz DIII	C6490	85	La Gorgue	2010	DES	CR/RAF 1.6
57	2 Jun	Pfalz DIII	C6490	85	S Armentieres	2015	DES	CR/CEM
58	4 Jun	Alb. DV	C6490	85	3m off Nieuport	1128	DES(F)	CR/RAF 4.6
59	4 Jun	Alb. DV	C6490	85	Leffinghe	1137	OOC	CR/CEM
60	15 Jun	Pfalz DIII	C1904	85	E Estaires	1855	DES	CR/RAF 15.6
61	16 Jun	C	C1904	85	E Armentieres	2020	DES	CR/RAF 16.6
62	16 Jun	Alb. DV	C1904	85	Armentieres	2025	DES	CR/RAF 16.6
63	17 Jun	C	C1904	85	Staden-Hooglede	1025	DES(F)	CR/RAF 17.6
64	17 Jun	C	C1904	85	Sailly sur la Lys	1050	DES	CR/RAF 17.6
65	17 Jun	Alb. DV	C1904	85	Laventie	1055	DES	CR/RAF 17.6
66***	18 Jun	Alb. DV	C1904	85	N E Ypres	1045	DES	CR/RAF 18.6
67***	18 Jun	Alb. DV	C1904	85	N E Ypres	1045	DES	CR/RAF 18.6
68	19 Jun	Pfalz DIII	C1904	85	1.5m E Ploegsteert	0958	DES	CR/RAF 19.6
69	19 Jun	Pfalz DIII	C1904	85	E Ploegsteert	0958	DES	CR/RAF 19.6
70	19 Jun	Pfalz DIII	C1904	85	E Ploegsteert	0958	DES	CR/RAF 19.6
71	19 Jun	Pfalz DIII	C1904	85	E Ploegsteert	1000	DES	CR/RAF 19.6
72	19 Jun	C	C1904	85	Ploegsteert-Neuve-Eglise	1010	DES	CR/RAF 19.6

TOTAL: 2 Balloons, 52 and 2 shared destroyed, 16 out of control = 72.
*Shared with Major A.J.L. Scott in A6647. **Shared with Lt W.M. Fry in B1597. ***Possibly Lt R. Heins and Uffz Kohler of Jasta 56, both WIA.

BISSELL Clayton Lawrence Captain 148US

Born on July 29 1896 in Kone, Pennsylvania, Captain Bissell was a member of the USAS, and flew Camels with the 148th Aero Squadron under RAF command during the summer and autumn of 1918. He received a DFC and a US DSC, and remained in the USAAC after the war, rising to the rank of Major General. During World War II he served mainly in China. Bissell died on 24 September 1972.

	1918		Camel					
1	21 Aug	Fokker DVII	F1400	148	Velu	1940	OOC	CR/?
2	4 Sep	Fokker DVII	F5943	148	S W Marquion	0710	DES	CR/RAF 4.9
3	4 Sep	Fokker DVII	F5943	148	W Marquion	0715	DES	CR/RAF 4.9
4	3 Oct	Fokker DVII	F6201	148	Wambaix	1107	DES(F)	CR/US 133
5	28 Oct	Fokker DVII	F7329	148	N E Jenlain	1205	DES	CR/RAF 28.10
6	28 Oct	Fokker DVII	F7329	148	N E Jenlain	1208	DES	CR/RAF 28.10

TOTAL: 4 destroyed, 2 out of control = 6.

BISSONETTE Charles Arthur Lieutenant 64, 24

An American from Los Angeles, Bissonette joined the RFC in March 1917 and flew SE 5As with 64 Squadron from November 1917 to June 1918; he claimed four victories during the March-May period, and then on 31 May caused two Albatros DVs to collide, both being reported to have crashed. These were credited to him, raising his total to six. In September 1918 he joined 24 Squadron for a second tour, but gained no further victories.

	1918		SE 5A					
1s	17 Mar	Pfalz DIII	----	64	Biache	1135	OOC	CR/RFC 17.3
2	23 Mar	C	C9493	64	Havrincourt Wood	1110	DES	CR/RFC 23.3
3	9 May	Halb. C	C9517	64	Monchy	1042	OOC	CR/RAF 9.5
4	9 May	Pfalz DIII	C9517	64	Boiry	1043	OOC	CR/RAF 9.5
5**	31 May	Alb. DV	----	64	La Bassee	1940	DES	CR/RAF 31.5
6**	31 May	Alb. DV	----	64	La Bassee	1940	DES	CR/RAF 31.5

TOTAL: 3 destroyed, 3 out of control = 6.
*Shared with Lt J.F.T. Barrett, Lt Stringer, Capt E.R. Tempest, Lt Hendrie. **These two aircraft collided.

BIZIOU Henry Arthur Richard Captain 87

Born on 18 September 1896, 'Weegee' Biziou, as he was called, joined RFC as an observer in 1916. After pilot training and completing a course at the School of Special Flying, Gosport, he joined 87 Squadron and went to France in April 1918. On 6 May he claimed the Squadron's first victory, destroying a Rumpler two-seater. By the end of the war he was a Captain and had received the DFC, having claimed eight victories. In 1919 he went to the Royal Aircraft Establishment at Farnborough, where he was killed in a flying accident on 14 July, when he collided with a Bristol Fighter.

	1918		Dolphin					
1	6 May	Rumpler C	C4165	87	Gheluvelt	1740	DES(F)	CR/RAF 6.5
2	8 Jul	DFW. C	C8072	87	Aveluy Wood	0925	DES	CR/RAF 8.7

3	21 Aug	Alb. DV	C8072	87	Bapaume	1815	DES	CR/RAF 21.8
4	16 Sep	Fokker DVII	E4493	87	N Cambrai	1735	DES	CR/?
5	16 Sep	Fokker DVII	E4493	87	N Cambrai	1735	OOC	CR/?
6	20 Sep	Fokker DVII	E4493	87	Noyelles	1530	DES	CR/?
7	22 Sep	Fokker DVII	E4493	87	Bourlon Wood	0840	DES	CR/RAF 22.9
8	22 Sep	Fokker DVII	E4493	87	Bourlon Wood	0840	DES	CR/RAF 22.9

TOTAL: 7 destroyed, 1 out of control = 8.

BLAKE Arthur Winston Lieutenant 19

Lieutenant Blake transferred to the RFC in August 1917 and flew Sopwith Dolphins with 19 Squadron in the early summer of 1918, claiming five victories. After the war he returned to his native South Africa where he joined the SAAF, but was killed in a flying accident on 14 December 1922.

	1918		Dolphin					
1s*	2 May	Alb. DV	C3843	19	S Armentieres	1745	DES(F)	CR/RAF 2.5
2	19 May	Pfalz DIII	C3796	19	E La Bassee	1015	OOC	CR/RAF 19.5
3	31 May	Pfalz DIII	C3840	19	W Armentieres	0800	OOC	CR/ORB/?
4s**	5 Jun	Fokker DrI	C3796	19	N E Arras	1210	OOC	CR/ORB/?
5	31 Jul	Pfalz DIII	C3796	19	S Douai	1950	DES	CR/RAF 31.7

TOTAL: 1 and 1 shared destroyed, 2 and 1 shared out of control = 5.

*Shared with Lt A.B. Fairclough C3796. **Shared with Capt J.D. de Pencier C3902.

BLAND William Harry Lieutenant 65

Bland joined the RFC in January 1918 and after training was posted to 65 Squadron in the autumn. During this period the squadron was engaged in some intensive air fighting in which he played a full part, gaining seven victories before the war ended. He received the Croix de Guerre from the French.

	1918		Camel					
1	5 Sep	Fokker DVII	F6154	65	E Ostend	1345	OOC	CR/ORB/?
2	4 Oct	Fokker DVII	E1415	65	Lendelede	1750	DES	CR/RAF 4.10
3	4 Oct	Fokker DVII	E1415	65	Lendelede	1750	OOC	CR/ORB/?
4	30 Oct	Fokker DVII	E7160	65	W Audenarde	1320	OOC	CR/ORB/?
5	30 Oct	Fokker DVII	E7160	65	Audenarde	1320	OOC	CR/ORB/?
6	4 Nov	Fokker DVII	E7160	65	S E Ghent	0855	OOC	CR/ORB/?
7	4 Nov	Fokker DVII	E7160	65	S E Ghent	0855	DES(F)	CR/RAF 4.11

TOTAL: 2 destroyed, 5 out of control = 7.

BLAXLAND Gregory Hamilton Captain 2AFC

Blaxland was born in Broken Hill, New South Wales, Australia, on 10 March 1896, and was studying electrical engineering at Fremantle when war broke out. Initially serving with the 10th Australian Light Horse, he joined the AFC in June 1917 and was posted to 2AFC Squadron in France on 21 February 1918. After two early victories in the spring of 1918, he mistakenly shot down Adjutant Renault of SPA 86 in his Spad on 4 May, killing the pilot. The squadron attempted to cover this up, but were unsuccessful. In consequence the commanding officer was posted, and on 12 May so was Blaxland. He served in 8 Training Squadron, AFC, where he was injured in a flying accident on 1 July. Upon recovery in late September 1918, he returned to 2AFC Squadron, claiming six Fokker DVIIs shot down during the last month of the war. He became a flight commander on 9 November, but perhaps because of his unfortunate mistake, he did not receive a decoration. The great grandson of a famous explorer, he married in 1927, obtained a B.Ed. at Sydney University and died on 25 August 1969.

	1918		SE 5A					
1s*	4 Apr	C	B571	2AFC	Amiens-Corbie Rd	1730	DES(F)	CR/RAF 2.4
2s**	6 Apr	C	----	2AFC	Lamotte	1500	DES	CR/RAF 6.4
3	10 May	DFW. C	B571	2AFC	Morcourt	1810	OOC	CR/RAF 10.5
3	4 Oct	Fokker DVII	D6903	2AFC	Lille	1000	OOC	CR/ORB/OH
4	14 Oct	Fokker DVII	C1125	2AFC	Grand Ennestieres	1015	DES(F)	CR/RAF 14.10
5	14 Oct	Fokker DVII	C1125	2AFC	Grand Ennestieres	1015	OOC	CR/RAF 14.10
6	18 Oct	Fokker DVII	F5457	2AFC	S Tournai	1230	DES	CR/RAF 18.10
7***	28 Oct	Fokker DVII	F5457	2AFC	Blaton-Peruwelz	1120	DES(F)	CR/RAF 28.10
8	4 Nov	Fokker DVII	F5457	2AFC	Houtaing	1245	OOC	CR/ORB/OH

TOTAL: 3 and 1 shared destroyed, 4 out of control = 8.

*Shared with 2/Lt A.G. Clark in D3429. **Shared with 2/Lt A.G. Clark, Lt L.J. Primose, Lt A.L. Paxton. ***The pilot baled out O.K. 2AFC claimed 2 baled out; one who did was Uffz M. Schell of Jasta 58.

BLENKIRON, Alfred Victor Lieutenant 22, 23, 25, 56, 151

Born on 4 June 1895, Alfred Blenkiron transferred to the RFC from the Somerset Light Infantry in 1916. He flew many sorties as an observer, serving with 22 Squadron from 17 March-8 August 1916; with 23 Squadron from 5-14 October 1916, and with 25 Squadron from 3 December 1916-1 June 1917. He was awarded the MC, which was gazetted in March 1917, for an action in which he shot down an attacking enemy scout although he was wounded. He had previously claimed one victory. Recovering from his wound, he undertook pilot training and was then posted to 56 Squadron on 3 December 1917, flying SE 5s, with which he claimed two more enemy machines. Later in 1918 he returned to Home Establishment and joined the newly-formed 151 Night Fighter Squadron, equipped with Camels. After this unit moved to France he claimed his fifth victory on the night of 14/15 August, when he destroyed a Friedrichshafen G III of Bogohl 3.

	1917		FE 2B					
1*	23 Jan	Halb. DII	4925	25	E Lens	1130	DES	CR/RFC 23.1
2**	29 Jan	Alb. DII	A784	25	Harnes	1050	DES(F)	CR/RFC 29.1
			SE 5A					
3	15 Dec	Alb. DV	B56	56	Bourlon Wood	0900	OOC	CR/RFC 15.12
	1918							
4	25 Jan	C	B66	56	S W Cambrai	1410	OOC	CR/RFC 25.1
			Camel					
5***	14/15 Aug	Fried GIII	D9577	151	Bapaume	1045	CAPT	CR/RAF 15.8

TOTAL: 1 captured, 2 destroyed, 2 out of control = 5.
*Pilot: Lt B. Mews. **Pilot: 2/Lt W. Shirtcliffe. ***This was a crew of Bogohl 3.

BOGER William Otway Captain 11, 56

A Canadian, born on 19 June 1896, he transferred to the RFC from the Canadian cavalry (Strathcona's Horse), with which he had served from August 1914 to September 1916. He flew as an observer on FE 2Bs with 11 Squadron during 1916, but was wounded in action on 23 December of that year. After training as a pilot he joined 56 Squadron on 24 May 1918 and quickly claimed five victories, being awarded the DFC. He failed to return from a patrol on 10 August, and was probably shot down and killed by Leutnant Veltjens, the 35 victory ace of Jasta 15.

	1918		SE 5A					
1	13 Jun	Fokker DrI	C9567	56	Le Sars	1115	OOC	CR/?
2	30 Jun	LVG. C	C9567	56	E. Legast Wood	1045	DES	CR/RAF 30.6
3	24 Jul	Pfalz DIII	D6096	56	Mericourt	2020	OOC	CR/?
4	24 Jul	Pfalz DIII	D6096	56	Cappy	2050	DES(F)	CR/RAF 25.7
5	8 Aug	Fokker DVII	D6096	56	N E Chaulnes	1905	OOC	CR/?

TOTAL: 2 destroyed, 3 out of control = 5.

BOND William Arthur Captain 40

After serving in the King's Own Yorkshire Light Infantry, Bond transferred to the RFC, and joined 40 Squadron early in 1917, flying Nieuport Scouts. During the early summer he claimed five enemy aircraft in a month. He was promoted to flight commander in July, but was killed in action on 22nd of that month in Nieuport B1688 at Sallaumines, probably by Uffz Beyer and Lt Ebert of Flg.Abt.235, although the squadron claimed that he had been shot down by AA fire. He had been awarded a DSO, MC and Bar.

	1917		Nieuport					
1	10 May	C	B1545	40	2m S W Douai	1640	OOC	CR/RFC 10.5
2s*	28 May	Alb. DIII	B1545	40	N E Douai	1950	OOC	CR/RFC 28.5
3	28 May	Alb. DIII	B1545	40	N E Douai	2020	OOC	CR/RFC 28.5
4	5 Jun	Alb. DIII	B1545	40	Fampoux	2050	DES	CR/RFC 6.6
5	9 Jun	Alb. DIII	B1545	40	N Douai	2020	OOC	CR/RFC 9.6

TOTAL: 1 destroyed, 4 out of control = 5.
*Shared with Lt A.E. Godfrey in B1684.

BOOKER, Charles Dawson Major 5W, 8(N), 1(N), 201

Booker was born at Speldhurst, Kent, on 21 April 1897, but resided in Australia until 1911, attending Melbourne Grammar School. Returning to England with his parents, he then became a pupil at Bedford Grammar School, joining the RNAS direct from there on 8 September 1915. He served in 5 Naval Wing from May 1916 and then from 26 October 1916 joined 8 Naval Squadron as a Flight Lieutenant to fly Pups, and later, Triplanes. He became a brilliant exponent of the Triplane, gaining most of his 29 victories on this type flying N5482 which was named 'Maud'. He became a Flight Commander on 18 May 1917 and was awarded the DSC and French Croix de Guerre. One of his most memorable combats occurred on 11 August 1917; taking off on the evening patrol, he led three other machines into a dogfight that was in progress over 'No Mans'

Land'. After shooting down one black Albatros in collaboration with W.L. Jordan, he was then attacked by two others. Reggie Soar shot one of these off his tail, but the other, flown by Leutnant Victor Schobinger of Jasta 12, damaged Booker's machine and he came down just inside the British lines, where German artillery began to shell him. Later it was discovered that the pilot he had shot down was Hauptmann Adolf Ritter von Tutschek (27 victories), commander of Jasta 12, who was badly wounded in the shoulder.

Booker was posted home in October for a rest, but on 18 March 1918 was promoted to take command of 1 Naval Squadron (which was just about to become 201 Squadron, RAF) in France. On 27 May he had the sad task of identifying the body of his old friend Bob Little, who had been shot down near his aerodrome. He claimed his final victory, on 13 August but was himself shot down when going to the aid of a new pilot from his squadron who was in trouble with some enemy scouts. Booker fell to Leutnant Ulrich Neckel, an ace of Jasta 12, crashing west of Rosieres, and died of the wounds he had suffered. Jasta 12 was the same unit that had been responsible for shooting down Booker a year earlier, and a contemporary description of the engagement recorded: "He left the aerodrome at about 10.30 am... and took a new pilot up with him to show him the new line. Just at this time there happened to be about 60 Fokker biplanes on the lines, and he was immediately attacked by ten of them. His first thoughts went to his new pilot, and he successfully drove five Fokkers from his tail, enabling him to cross the line. He then dealt with the remaining five, shot three down and was himself driven down by the remaining two. He died a gallant death, the bravest of all. By his death the squadron has sustained a great loss, and I cannot tell you how much we all miss him. He took over our squadron in March, not an easy task at the time, and since then his work has been incomparable."

	1918		Pup					
1*	23 Jan	Alb. DIII	N5197	8N	N E Bapaume	1135	OOC	CR/RFC 23.1
			Triplane					
2	7 Apr	Alb. DII	N5455	8N	Lens	1745-1930	OOC	CR/RNAS DL
3	14 Apr	LVG. C	N5481	8N	Henin Lietard	0910	OOC	CR/RFC 14.4
4	26 Apr	Alb. DIII	N5482	8N	Drocourt	1720	DES(F)	CR/RFC 27.4
5	30 Apr	Alb. DIII	N5482	8N	Douai	0700	OOC	CR/RFC 30.4
6	4 May	C	N5492	8N	Henin Lietard	1335	OOC	CR/RFC 4.5
7	6 May	Alb. DIII	N5450	8N	Lens-Henin Lietard	1815	OOC	CR/RFC 6.5
8	10 May	C	N5482	8N	E Douai	0730	OOC	CR/ORB/DRO
9	12 May	Alb. DIII	N5482	8N	Henin-Lietard-Vitry	0800	OOC	CR/ORB/DRO
10s**	23 May	Alb. DIII	N5482	8N	W Douai	1545	DES	CR/RFC 23.5
11s***	24 May	Alb. DIII	N5482	8N	Douai	0750	DES	CR/RFC 24.5
12s***	24 May	Alb. DIII	N5482	8N	Douai	0751	OOC	CR/RFC 24.5
13	24 May	Alb. DIII	N5482	8N	Willerval	0835	DES(F)	CR/RFC 24.5
14	28 May	Alb. DIII	N5482	8N	W Douai	2020	OOC	CR/DRO 28.5
15	11 Jun	Alb. DV	N5482	8N	Lens	2020	OOC	CR/ORB/
16s†	12 Jun	C	----	8N	Arras	0855	CAPT	CR/RFC 12.6
17	14 Jun	Alb. DV	N5482	8N	Arras-Cambrai	2015	OOC	CR/RFC 15.6
18††	17 Jul	Alb. DV	N5482	8N	Quiery la Motte	0930	OOC	CR/RFC 17.7
19	20 Jul	Rumpler C	N5447	8N	Thelus	0830	OOC	CR/RFC 20.7
20s††	22 Jul	Alb. DV	N5482	8N	Quiery la Motte	0735	OOC	CR/RFC 22.7
21s†††	11 Aug	Alb. DV	N5482	8N	Acheville	1930	DES	CR/RFC 11.8
22s‡	18 Aug	Alb. DV	N5460	8N	Henin Lietard	1830	OOC	CR/RFC 19.8
			Camel					
23s‡‡	27 Sep	Alb. DV	B6227	8N	Souchez	1855	CAPT	CR/RFC 27.9
	1918							
24s‡‡‡	15 May	Alb. DV	D1852	201	Bapaume	0645	DES	CR/RAF 15.5
25s§	23 May	Alb. DV	D1852	201	Arras-Cambrai	0845	OOC	CR/?
26	31 Jul	Fokker DVII	D9642	201	S W Armentieres	2050	DES	CR/RAF 31.7
27§§	13 Aug	Fokker DVII	D9642	201	W Rosieres	1100	DES	SR/SS
28§§	13 Aug	Fokker DVII	D9642	201	W Rosieres	1100	DES	SR/SS
29§§	13 Aug	Fokker DVII	D9642	201	W Rosieres	1100	DES	SR/SS

TOTAL: 2 shared captured, 6 and 4 shared destroyed, 12 and 5 shared out of control = 29.
*Probably one of two Jasta B pilots killed by 'wing failure'. **Shared with F/Lt R.A. Little in N5493. ***Shared with FSL R. MacDonald in N5472. †Shared with FSL C.H.B. Jenner-Parsons, FSL R.R.Soar. Lt Pieveling/Lt Nieberle POW of FAA 288. ††Shared with FSL R.R. Soar in N6292. †††Shared with FSL W.L. Jordon in Camel N6372: This was Oblt Adolf Ritter von Tutschek, the commanding officer of Jasta 12, who was wounded. ‡Shared with F/L R.B. Munday N5421, FSL E.D. Crundall N5465. ‡‡Shared with FSL J.H. Thompson of 8N and Lt J.H. Tudhope B3617 of 40 Sqn. The pilot Oblt Hans Waldhausen of Jasta 37 became a prisoner. Waldhausen was an ace. ‡‡‡Shared with Capt S.M. Kinkead, Lt H.L. Wallace, Lt R.S.S. Orr, Lt R. Hemmens, Lt J.H. Forman, Lt M.H. Findlay, Lt R. McLaughlin, B.C.B. Brading. §Shared with Capt S.M. Kinkead in B7190. §§These were confirmed as destroyed in a letter from the squadron to Bookers' old school describing his death, and in other secondary sources.

BOOTH Edward Borgfeldt Lieutenant 70

A Canadian, Booth flew with 70 Squadron in the latter half of 1917. After his second claim on 12 October, he was shot down unhurt by Leutnant Hans Klein, the commander of Jasta 10 in the Richthofen Circus as Klein's 18th victory. Booth was to make three more claims before he was injured on 11 November 1917 when his Camel, B2387, crashed on landing after hitting some infantrymen on the airfield. He saw no further active service.

	1917		Camel					
1	20 Sep	Alb. DV	B6206	70	Houthoulst Forest	1130	OOC	CR/RFC 20.9
2	12 Oct	Alb. DV	B6206	70	S E Houthoulst	1730	OOC	CR/RFC 12.10
3s*	20 Oct	C	B6366	70	Rumbeke	1115	DES	CR/RFC 20.10
4s**	27 Oct	Alb. DV	----	70	Roulers	1400	OOC	CR/RFC 27.10
5	9 Nov	C	B2447	70	E Ypres	0700	OOC	CR/RFC 9.11

TOTAL: 1 shared destroyed, 3 and 1 shared out of control = 5.
*Shared with 2/Lt F.G. Quigley B2356 and 2/Lt C.W. Primeau B2349. **Shared with Major Nethersole, Capt Lawrence, Lt Goode, Lt Hobson and Lt Primeau.

BOTT Alan John Captain 70, 111

After service with the Royal Garrison Artillery, he joined the RFC, and went to France in 1916 as an observer with 70 Squadron, flying in 1½ Strutters; his pilot on most occasions was 'Bunny' Vaucour. During one hectic fight their machine was set on fire, but Bott managed to dowse the flames by crawling along inside the rear fuselage to beat them out with his gauntlets. He was awarded the MC for this action, and for accounting for four enemy machines. In 1917 he learned to fly, was promoted to Captain, and was posted to the Middle East to join 111 Squadron as a flight commander in the Sinai desert. Here he claimed two enemy aeroplanes shot down before he himself was brought down on 22 April 1918 and taken prisoner. He wrote several books on his experiences under the pen name of *Contact*. He was later a journalist, drama critic and publisher, helping found Pan Books in 1947; he died in 1952.

	1916		Strutter					
1*	2 Sep	Fokker E	A892	70	Bourlon Wood	1905	DES	CR/RFC 2.9
2*	2 Sep	Fokker E	A892	70	Ytres-Sailly	1925	OOC	CR/RFC 2.9
3*	15 Sep	Fokker E	A892	70	Hendicourt	1840	DES	CR/RFC 15.9
	1918		Nieuport					
4	14 Apr	C	B3595	111	10m N E Arsum	1755	FTL/DES	CR/40 WWD
5	15 Apr	C	B3595	111	S E Tul Keram	1700	DES	CR/40 WWD

TOTAL: 4 destroyed, 1 out of control = 5.
*Pilot: 2/Lt A.M. Vaucour.

BOULTON Nicholson Stuart Lieutenant 20

Lieutenant Boulton joined the RFC as a cadet on 26 July 1917 and served with 20 Squadron during the late summer of 1918. He was credited with six Fokker DVIIs, three destroyed and three out of control, all during mid September. On each occasion that claims were made he was accompanied by a different gunner, and five of his victories were credited to the rear gun position. He failed to return on 29 September when shot down by Leutnant Josef Mai of Jasta 5, while flying E2561 with 2/Lt C.H. Chase as gunner.

	1918		Bristol					
1*	15 Sep	Fokker DVII	E2493	20	N E St Quentin	1110	OOC	CR/?
2**	16 Sep	Fokker DVII	E2467	20	W Lesdin	0825	OOC	CR/?
3***	20 Sep	Fokker DVII	E2493	20	N E St Quentin	1015	DES	CR/RAF 20.9
4†	23 Sep	Fokker DVII	E2213	20	N E St Quentin	1815	DES	CR/RAF 23.9
5†	23 Sep	Fokker DVII	E2213	20	N E St Quentin	1815	DES	CR/RAF 23.9
6†	23 Sep	Fokker DVII	E2213	20	N E St Quentin	1820	OOC	CR/?

TOTAL: 3 destroyed, 3 out of control = 6.
*Observer: Lt G.W. Pearce. **Observer: Sgt J. Dodds. ***Observer: Sgt E.G. Mitchell. †Observer: 2/Lt H.L. Edwards.

BOULTON Percy Lieutenant 210

Percy Boulton was born in Stoke-on-Trent on 8 October 1898. He joined 210 Squadron on 7 July 1918, claiming his first victory in August. By October he had claimed six Fokker DVIIs, receiving a DFC.

	1918		Camel					
1	11 Aug	Fokker DVII	D9615	210	Zonnebeke	0930	OOC	CR/5 GP
2	11 Aug	Fokker DVII	D9615	210	Vladsloo-Eesen	1835	DES(F)	CR/5 GP
3	24 Sep	Fokker DVII	E4383	210	S St Pierre Capelle	1440	DES	CR/5 GP
4	28 Sep	Fokker DVII	E4383	210	E Staden	1725	DES	CR/5 GP

5	29 Sep	Fokker DVII	E4383	210	Wijnendaele Wood	0800	OOC	CR/5 GP
6	14 Oct	Fokker DVII	E4383	210	S E Roulers	1415	DES	CR/5 GP

TOTAL: 4 destroyed, 2 out of control = 6.

BOWLES, Francis Stephen Lieutenant 45

Born on 31 October 1899 in Thornton Heath, Surrey, and an old boy of Whitgift School, Bowles served with 45 Squadron in Italy during 1918 at the age of 18. When the unit returned to France late in the war to join the Independent Air Force, Lt Bowles failed to return from a patrol on 3 November, but obviously survived as he was on the Air Force List in 1919. He served in World War II as an accounts officer, becoming a Flight Lieutenant.

	1918		Camel					
1s*	13 May	C	B2426	45	Frison	0630	DES	CR/14 W
2	15 Jun	C	B5181	45	Ponte di Piave	1330	OOC/CAPT?	CR/ORB
3	20 Jul	Alb. DV	B5181	45	S E Feltre	0720	DES	ORB/14 W
4	20 Jul	Alb. DIII	B5181	45	Feltre-Cesana	0720	DES	ORB/14 W
5	5 Aug	D	D9392	45	Grappa	1030	OOC	ORB/?

TOTAL: 2 and 1 shared destroyed, 1 out of contol, 1 out of control or captured = 5.
*Shared with Lt E.H. Masters B2379.

BOWMAN Geoffrey Hilton Major 29, 56, 41

Born on 2 May 1891, and commissioned in the Royal Warwickshire Regiment early in the war, Lieutenant Bowman transferred to the RFC on 20 March 1916. He joined 29 Squadron on 7 July, on completion of training, to fly DH 2s. His first victory was over a Roland with which he collided head-on; the second was a run-away German kite balloon, which he shot down whilst it was drifting over the Allied lines, but he crashed while trying to land alongside the wreckage; he was rested on 16 December 1916. On 11 May 1917 he was posted to 56 Squadron as 'C' Flight commander, flying SE 5s, and by the end of June had claimed a further five victories, followed by eight more in July. He continued to claim throughout the summer and autumn, receiving an MC on 17 September and a Bar on 27 October. By November his score had risen to 22. He had a narrow escape on 5 December when his wing spars broke whilst diving to attack a balloon. On 9 February 1918 he was posted, albeit with reluctance on his part, to command 41 Squadron. 'Beery' as he was known because of his florid complexion, claimed nine more victories with this unit, including a share in a Fokker DVII forced down inside Allied lines on 10 October 1918 (Leutnant Schaefer of Jasta 16). At this stage he received an order which stated "Major Bowman is forbidden to leave the ground on any pretext whatsoever, without the personal permission of the GOC,II Brigade", since he was now considered such an experienced and valuable pilot that the authorities wished to keep him alive! His score at the end of the war was at least 32, and he received the DSO and DFC, together with the Belgian Croix de Guerre. In 1919 he served in Russia and continued to serve with the RAF, rising to the rank of Wing Commander in 1929. He joined Headquarters, 23 Group, in 1934, but retired that year, joining the Royal Aircraft Establishment in 1935. Recalled to duty in 1939, he served until December 1941; he died on 25 March 1970.

	1916		DH 2					
1	3 Sep	Roland	5984	29	E Linselles	c1030	DES	CR/RFC 3.9
2	27 Sep	Balloon	7857	29	Mt Kemmel	1800	DES	CR/RFC 27.9
	1917		SE 5A					
3	6 Jun	Alb. DV	A8900	56	N Roulers	0900	OOC	CR/RFC 6.6
4	6 Jun	Alb. DV	A8900	56	N Roulers	0900	OOC	CR/RFC 6.6
5	14 Jun	C	A8900	56	N Quesnoy	1840	OOC	CR/RFC 14.6
6	14 Jun	Alb. DIII	A8900	56	S W Roulers	1930	OOC	CR/RFC 14.6
7	17 Jun	DFW. C	A8900	56	Lille	0845-0900	OOC	CR/RFC 17.6
8	7 Jul	Alb. DIII	A8900	56	Louvrin	0830-0915	OOC	CR/RFC 7.7
9	12 Jul	Alb. DV	A8900	56	E Polygon Wood	1930-2030	DES	CR/RFC 12.7
10*	16 Jul	Alb. DIII	A8900	56	Polygon Wood	1815-1915	DES	CR/RFC 16.7
11	20 Jul	Alb. DIII	A8900	56	Zonnebeke	1915-2030	OOC	CR/RFC 20.7
12	27 Jul	Alb. DV	A8900	56	2m W Roulers	1930-2045	DES	CR/RFC 27.7
13	27 Jul	Alb. DV	A8900	56	Houthoulst Wood	1930-2045	DES	CR/RFC 27.7
14	17 Aug	Alb. DV	B2	56	S Moorslede	0615-0715	DES	CR/RFC 17.8
15	22 Aug	Alb. DV	B2	56	N Houthoulst Wood	1845-1920	OOC	CR/RFC 22.8
16**	14 Sep	Alb. DV	B2	56	N E Menin	0900	DES	CR/RFC 14.9
17***	28 Sep	Alb. DV	B2	56	E Westroosebeke	1720	DES	CR/RFC 28.9
18	2 Oct	Alb. DV	B2	56	Moorslede	1030-1145	OOC	CR/RFC 2.10
19	27 Oct	Alb. DV	B2	56	S W Iseghem	1015-1230	OOC	CR/RFC 27.10
20	29 Oct	Alb. DV	B2	56	Moorslede	1455-1625	DES	CR/RFC 29.10
21†	23 Nov	Alb. DV	B2	56	E Cambrai	1520	DES	CR/DES 23.11

22	30 Nov	Alb. DV	C5303	56	W Cantaing	1430	DES	CR/RFC 30.11
	1918							
23	25 Jan	C	C9533	56	N W Rumilly	1410	DES	CR/RFC 25.1
24	30 Jan	Alb. DV	C9533	56	S Cambrai	1415	DES	CR/RFC 30.1
25	16 Feb	LVG. C	C9533	41	Bantouzelle	0800	OOC	CR/RFC 16.2
26	26 Feb	C	C9533	41	Berjaumont Wood	1350	DES	CR/RFC 26.2
27	17 Jul	Rumpler C	D6179	41	S W Bapaume	0845	OOC	CR/?
28	9 Aug	Fokker DVII	D6179	41	Cappy	1730	OOC	CR/?
29	16 Sep	Fokker DVII	E4092	41	Houthloulst	1410	OOC	CR/?
30	25 Sep	Rumpler C	E4092	41	N E Ypres	1830	DES(F)	CR/?
31††	10 Oct	Fokker DVII	E4092	41	N Moorslede	1645	CAPT	CR/RAF 10.10
32	15 Oct	Fokker DVII	E4092	41	S Lichtervelde	0740	DES	CR/RAF 15.10

TOTAL: 1 shared captured, 1 balloon, 15 destroyed, 15 out of control = 32.

*probably the ace Vzfw Fritz Krebs of Jasta 6, who was killed. **56 made 4 claims, one loss was probably Lt G.W. Groos of Jasta 11 who was wounded. ***Lt Karl Menckhoff of Jasta 3, who crash landed. †Probably Lt K.A. von Schonebeck of Jasta 11 who force landed. ††Shared with Capt F.O. Soden in F5545 Lt J. Schafer KIA of Jasta 16.

BOYSEN Howard Koch Lieutenant 66

An American from Dallas, Texas, and Chicago, Boysen, who was born in 1892, joined the RFC on 16 June 1917 at the age of 26. He served with 66 Squadron from 22 August 1917, flying Sopwith Pups and then Camels in Italy. He was injured when he crashed B2472 whilst trying to land in fog on 29th January 1918, and left the squadron. He received the Italian Silver Medal for Military Valour.

	1917		Camel					
1*	8 Dec	Alb. DV	B2363	66	Valstagna	1310-1530	OOC	ORB/SR/?
	1918							
2	3 May	Alb. DIII	B7389	66	Ormelle	1145	DES(F)	ORB/SR/7 Bg
3	10 May	Alb. DIII	B5171	66	Mt Meatta	0930	DES	ORB/SR/7 Bg
4s**	26 May	LVG. C	B5180	66	Salina	0615	DES	ORB/SR/7 Bg
5***	30 May	Alb. DIII	B5180	66	Moreno	1555	DES	ORB/SR/7 Bg

TOTAL: 3 and 1 shared destroyed, 1 out of control = 5.

*Believed to be Lt Bertelsmeier of Jasta 39 who was captured. **Shared with Lt C. McEvoy B7353. ***This was probably Offstellv Karl Gebhard of Flik 41j in 153:219.

BRADING Reginald Carey Brenton Captain 1(N), 201

Born on 4 May 1899 in Croydon, Surrey, he joined the RNAS on 12 June 1917. After operational training with 12(N) Squadron at the end of 1917, he was posted to 1(N) Squadron (201 Squadron from April 1918), being promoted flight commander in mid July. He was awarded the DFC and Bar for his score of 13. His last victim was Flieger Braun of Jasta 23, who baled out but was killed either due to his parachute not opening properly, or to a bad landing. In 1919 Brading served in the Baltic, flying against the Bolsheviks as a Flying Officer, and was Mentioned in Despatches. During 1921 he flew a Snipe in the RAF aerobatic team.

	1918		Camel					
1s*	2 May	C	B6421	201	N Albert	1010	OOC	CR/RAF 2.5
2s**	15 May	Alb. DV	----	201	Bapaume-Mory	0645	DES	CR/RAF 15.5
3	15 May	Alb. DV	B5749	201	E Albert	1745	OOC	CR/RAF 15.5
4	9 Jun	DFW. C	D9582	201	S E Arras	1200	OOC	CR/?
5	28 Jun	Alb. DV	B7968	201	Bois de Tailles	0945	OOC	CR/?
6	29 Jul	Fokker DVII	B5749	201	Bailleul area	1120	DES(F)	CR/RAF 29.7
7	29 Jul	Fokker DVII	B5749	201	Armentieres	1120	OOC	CR/?
8	8 Aug	Fokker DVII	C64	201	Bray	1520	OOC	CR/?
9	2 Sep	Fokker DVII	B6398	201	Heudicourt	0630	OOC	CR/?
10	2 Sep	Fokker DVII	B6398	201	Lagnicourt	0715	DES	CR/RAF 2.9
11	6 Sep	Fokker DVII	B6398	201	Cambrai	1845	OOC	CR/?
12	15 Sep	Pfalz DXII	B6398	201	1m W Cambrai	0845	DES	CR/RAF 15.9
13***	16 Sep	Fokker DVII	C196	201	S E Cambrai	1735	DES	CR/RAF 16.9

TOTAL: 5 destroyed, 6 and 2 shared out of control = 13.

*Shared with Capt S. Kinkead B6429, Lt H.L. Wallace B6359, Lt R.E. Bright B7267, 2/Lt H. Riddell B7225, Lt A.G.A. Spence B7278. **Shared with Major C.D. Booker, Capt S.M. Kinkead, Lt H.L. Wallace, Lt R.S.S. Orr, Lt R. Hemmens, Lt J.H. Forman, Lt M.H. Findlay, Lt R. McLaughlin. ***The pilot of this aircraft baled out. This was probably Flgr S. Braun of Jasta 23 who baled out, but died when his parachute failed.

BREADNER Lloyd Samuel Major 3W, 3(N)

Born on 17 July 1894 in Carleton Place, Ontario, Canada, 'Bread' Breadner enlisted in the RNAS and came to Europe, beginning operational flying in 3 Naval Wing in 1916. By the end of the year he was promoted to Flight Lieutenant, and early in 1917 he joined 3 Naval Squadron, flying Sopwith Pups; in May he became a flight commander. By this time the unit was flying with the RFC on the Western Front, where he claimed to have destroyed four aircraft, sent three more down out of control, and forced a number of others to land; one of those destroyed was a Gotha GIII of Kagohl III/15, the first Gotha brought down by a British fighter on the Western Front. His DSC was gazetted on 22 May 1917, but from the end of this month until September he did not claim any further victories. Then, the squadron having been re-equipped with Camels, and he having been promoted to Squadron Commander, he claimed three more to bring his score to ten. He returned to the United Kingdom on 23 January 1918, and later in the year, with the new RAF rank of Major, he took command of 204 Training Squadron. After the war he joined the RCAF, and in 1940 became Chief of the Air Staff with the rank of Air Chief Marshal. He died in Boston, USA, in 1953.

	1917		Pup					
1	6 Apr	Halb. DII	N5199	3N	Bourlon Wood	1020	DES	CR/RFC 6.4
2	11 Apr	Alb. C	N6181	3N	Cambrai	0845	DES(F)	CR/RFC 11.4
3	11 Apr	Alb. DIII	N6181	3N	Cambrai	0855	DES	CR/RFC 11.4
4*	23 Apr	Gotha GII	N6181	3N	Vron	1030	CAPT	CR/RFC 23.4
5	23 Apr	Alb. DIII	N6181	3N	Bourlon Wood	1730	OOC	CR/RFC 23.4
6	29 Apr	Alb. DIII	N6181	3N	S E Cambrai	1115	OOC	CR/RFC 29.4
7	23 May	Alb. DIII	N6197	3N	Awoignt-Bourlon	1345	OOC	CR/RFC 23.5
			Camel					
8	3 Sep	Alb. DV	B3782	3N	Belhutte	0725	DES	CR/RNAS 3.9
9	3 Sep	Alb. DV	B3782	3N	Belhutte	0730	OOC	CR/RNAS 3.9
10	11 Sep	Alb. DV	B3782	3N	Thorout	1150	OOC	CR/RNAS 11.9

TOTAL: 1 captured, 4 destroyed, 5 out of control = 10.
*Lt K. Schweren, Lt O. Wirsch, Offstv A. Hecher POWS, of KG III/15.

BREAKEY John Denis Captain 3(N), 203

Born on 19 May 1899, in Sheffield, Yorkshire, he joined the RNAS in 1917, becoming a Flight Sub Lieutenant in October. He was posted to France where he went to 3 Naval Squadron. Initially in 'A' Flight, he soon proved a competent scout pilot, being awarded a DFC and becoming a Captain and flight commander in August 1918. In 1919 he served as a Flying Officer in Russia, receiving a Bar to his DFC. He remained in the RAF, becoming commanding officer of 201 Squadron at Calshot in April 1935. He subsequently rose to the rank of Air Vice-Marshal as AOC Malaya, 1945-50, and then as AOC 21 Group, Training Command. He died in 1966, having become a CB and CBE for his services.

	1918		Camel					
1*	15 May	LVG. C	D3384	203	Salome, E La Bassee	1145	DES	CR/RAF 15.5
2	16 May	Pfalz DIII	D3384	203	N La Bassee	1120	OOC	CR/RAF 16.5
3s**	17 May	Alb. DV	D3384	203	Merville	1120	DES	CR/RAF 17.5
4s***	18 May	Rumpler C	D3384	203	Merville	1120	DES(F)	CR/RAF 18.5
5	25 Aug	DFW. C	D9651	203	N Hem	1300	DES	CR/RAF 25.8
6	20 Sep	Fokker DVII	----	203	Haynecourt	1530	OOC	?/Rochford
7	26 Sep	Fokker DVII	D9651	203	S W Lieu St Amand	1300	DES(F)	CR/RAF 26.9
8	29 Sep	LVG. C	D9651	203	Sensee Canal, Hem	0730	DES	CR/RAF 29.9
9	2 Oct	Fokker DVII	D9592	203	Morenchies	0850	DES	CR/RAF 2.10

TOTAL: 4 and 3 shared destroyed, 2 out of control = 9.
*Shared with Capt H. Beamish B3855, 1/Lt W Goodnow B7198, Lt A.N. Webster B3788, Lt H.W. Skinner B7123, Lt E.T. Hayne D3376. **Shared with Capt H.F. Beamish B3855, 1/Lt W.W. Goodnow B6212, Lt R. Sykes B6378, Lt H.W. Skinner B7331. ***Shared with Capt H.F. Beamish D3855.

BREMRIDGE Godfrey Lieutenant 65

Joining the RFC in July 1917 he flew Sopwith Camels with 65 Squadron from late 1917 until March 1918, during which time he claimed five victories.

	1917		Camel					
1s*	18 Dec	Alb. DV	B6335	65	Roulers	1415	OOC	CR/RFC 18.12
2s**	28 Dec	C	B5597	65	N W Houthoulst Wood	1115	OOC	CR/RFC WD
	1918							
3***	25 Jan	C	B5597	65	Warneton	1245	DES(F)	CR/RFC 25.1
4	3 Feb	Alb. DV	B5597	65	S W Roulers	1035	OOC	CR/?
5†	9 Mar	Fokker DrI	B5597	65	Westroosebeeke	1640	DES(F)	CR/RFC 9.3

TOTAL: 2 destroyed, 1 and 2 shared out of control = 5.
*Shared with Lt G. Knocker. **Shared with Lt C.B. Matthews B2487. ***The Germans lost Gefr W. Schreiber and Offz O. Haas at Warneton. †The Fokker had a light blue tail. Lt Naujork of Jasta 36, whose unit markings were light blue tails, was killed.

BREWSTER-JOSKE Clive Alexander Captain 1, 46

An Australian, born in Fiji in October 1896, he was educated in Melbourne, Victoria. He left for England in September 1914 to join the British Army and served in the 37th Division, reaching the front in July 1915 as a 2nd Lieutenant. He joined the RFC on 15 November 1915 as an observer, and became a pilot in August 1916. He flew Sopwith Pups in 46 Squadron during 1917, becoming a patrol leader of some merit; in September he was awarded the unit's first decoration — an MC. He returned to Home Establishment in November. After the war he returned to Fiji, becoming a prominent figure in the local community. In 1939 he commanded the Fiji Military Forces as a Lieutenant Colonel, but in 1940 joined the RAAF, becoming a Group Captain in Training and Administration. He died in 1947.

	1916		Parasol					
1s*	29 Feb	?	5119	1	Passchendaele	----	DES(F)	CR/RFC 29.2
	1917		Pup					
2	2 Jun	Alb. DIII	B1709	46	Houthoulst	1800	OOC	CR/RFC 3.6
3	7 Jun	Alb. DIII	B1709	46	Wervicq-Comines	1030	DES	CR/RFC 7.6
4	17 Jun	Alb. DV	B1709	46	Lens	1930	OOC	CR/SR/?
5	3 Sep	Alb. DV	B1716	46	Menin	1030	DES	CR/RFC 3.9
6	4 Sep	Alb. DV	A7335	46	E Menin	0800	OOC	CR/11 WS
7	16 Sep	Alb. DIII	A7335	46	Ecoust St Quentin	1315	OOC	CR/RFC 16.9
8s**	22 Sep	Alb. DIII	A7335	46	N Brebieres	1015	DES	CR/RFC 22.9

TOTAL: 2 and 2 shared destroyed, 4 out of control = 8.
*Pilot: Capt R.A. Saunders; shared with Capt Powell in FE 8, 5 Sqn. **Shared with Lt R.L.M. Ferrie A7324.

BRITNELL Frederick John Shaw Captain 3(N), 203

Born on 16 April 1899, in High Wycombe, Buckinghamshire, Britnell joined the RNAS on 3 June 1917, flying with 3 Naval Squadron. Known as 'Duke' from his early training days, he was a popular figure with his fellow officers. He received both the DSC and DFC.

	1918		Camel					
1	10 Mar	Alb. DV	B7251	3N	2m S E Lens	1315	OOC	CR/ORB/WS
2s*	24 Mar	Alb. DV	B7228	3N	Vaux	1530	OOC	CR/ORB/WS
3s**	15 May	DFW. CV	B7251	203	1m E Pont du Hem	1050	DES	CR/RAF 15.5
4	16 May	Pfalz DIII	B7251	203	N La Bassee	1120	OOC	CR/RAF 16.5
5s***	27 Aug	DFW. CV	D9611	203	S Combles	1210	DES	CR/RAF 27.8
6	16 Sep	Fokker DVII	D9611	203	Haynecourt	1840	DES(F)	CR/RAF 16.9
7	20 Sep	Fokker DVII	D9611	203	Haynecourt	1530	OOC	CR/?
8	26 Sep	Fokker DVII	B9611	203	Haynecourt	1315	DES(F)	CR/?
9	2 Oct	Balloon	----	203	Cambrai area	----	DES	Rochford/?

TOTAL: 1 balloon, 2 and 2 shared destroyed, 3 and 1 shared out of control = 9.
*Shared with F/Cdr F.C. Armstrong B7218, FSL S. Smith B7274, FSL R.C. Berlyn B7274, F/Lt E.T. Hayne B7231, FSL L.D. Bawlf B7192. F/Cdr A.T. Whealy B7220, F/Lt E. Pierce B7227. **Shared with Capt A.T. Whealy B7220. ***Shared with Capt A.T. Whealy in D9641.

BROADBERRY Edric William Captain 56

Born 14 December 1894, he served at Gallipoli with the Essex Regiment. He joined the RFC and learnt to fly at Aboukir, Egypt; returning to England, he was then posted to 56 Squadron on 20 April 1917. On 12 May he assisted Gerald Maxwell in shooting down a German scout and eight days later claimed his second victory. From then until he was wounded, he scored quicker than any other pilot in the squadron with the sole exception of Hoidge. On 11 July he claimed his ninth victory and was awarded the MC. He was shot down in A8918 on 12 July and was wounded in the leg, possibly by pilots of Jasta 4 or Marinefeldjasta 1. He remained in the RAF after the war and in 1936 was a Squadron Leader at the Air Observers' School at North Coates; by 1941 he was a Group Captain. He retired in 1947 and died in the early hours of Boxing Day, 1967.

	1917		SE 5A					
1s*	12 May	Alb. DIII	A8903	56	E Lens	0845	DES	CR/RFC 12.5
2**	20 May	Alb. DIII	A8903	56	Guesnain	1410	OOC	CR/RFC 20.5
3s***	23 May	Alb. DIII	A8903	56	Aubigny	1900-1915	OOC	CR/RFC 23.5
4	26 May	C	A8903	56	Gouy-sons-Bellone	1930	OOC	CR/RFC 26.5
5	27 May	Alb. DIII	A8903	56	E Bugnicourt	1900-2000	OOC	CR/Wing WD
6	7 Jun	C	A8918	56	Poelcapelle	0850-0940	DES	CR/RFC 7.6
7	7 Jun	C	A8918	56	Ledeghem	0850-0940	OOC	CR/RFC 7.6
8	11 Jul	C	A8918	56	Houthoulst Wood	1930	OOC	CR/RFC 11.7

TOTAL: 1 and 1 shared destroyed, 5 and 1 shared out of control = 8.
*Shared with Lt G.C. Maxwell A8902. **Possibly Lt K Francke of Jasta B, who was killed. ***Shared with Capt P.B. Prothero A8909.

BROCK Cecil Guelph Lieutenant 1(N), 9(N), 3, 209

Although born in Southsea, Hampshire, on 24 May 1897, Brock was resident in Winnipeg, Canada, when war broke out. Commissioned in the RNAS on 28 October 1916, he served with 1 Naval Squadron from 4 June to 13 August 1917, and then with 209 Squadron from 1 April. He was involved in the famous engagement on 21st of that month when von Richthofen was killed. He was posted to 3 Squadron on 13 June, where he completed his war service.

	1917		Triplane					
1	3 Jul	Alb. DIII	N5373	1N	Tenbrielen	1835	OOC	CR/RFC 4.7
2s*	17 Jul	Alb. DV	N5485	1N	4m E Messines	2005	OOC	CR/ORB/?
3	9 Aug	Alb. DV	N5373	1N	Moorslede	0740	OOC	CR/RFC 9.8
	1918		Camel					
4s**	22 Apr	C	----	209	Albert	0610	CAPT	CR/RAF 22.4
5s***	13 Jul	C	D7835	3	57C S11	0710	OOC	CR/?
6s†	16 Jul	?	D7835	3	57C A15	1210	DES	CR/RAF 16.7

TOTAL: 1 shared captured, 1 shared destroyed, 2 and 2 shared out of control = 6.

*Shared with FSL E Anthony N6296, F/Lt C.B. Ridley N6304, FSL G.B. Scott N5455, FSL H.L. Everitt N6308, FSL H.V. Rowley N5373, FSL A.G.A. Spence N6300, F/Cdr F.H.M. Maynard N5479. **Shared with Capt O.C. LeBoutillier, Lt M.S. Taylor, Lt M.A. Harker, Lt R.M. Foster; Flgr Raschke/Lt K. Schneider KIA, of F.A.A. 219. ***Shared with Lt A. Hamilton D6635. †Shared with 2/Lt J.G. Fleet D9435.

BROMLEY Ernest C Lieutenant 22

Joining 22 Squadron in the spring of 1918 to fly Bristol Fighters, he teamed up with Lieutenant J.H. Umney, and on 6 May claimed his first victory, with the front gun. On 5 June, flying with Lieutenant C.G. Gass, Bromley claimed a two-seater, Gass accounting for an attacking scout. Both Bromley and Umney received MCs, the latter adding three more victories to his personal score while flying with other pilots.

	1918		Bristol					
1*	6 May	Alb. DV	C4747	22	Roeux	1845	OOC	CR/RAF 6.5
2*	8 May	C	C4747	22	S E Arras	1005	DES	CR/RAF 8.5
3*	9 May	Pfalz DIII	C4747	22	N Douai	1840	OOC	CR/RAF 9.5
4*	16 May	Pfalz DIII	C4747	22	Douai	1005	DES	CR/RAF 16.5
5*	16 May	Pfalz DIII	C4747	22	Douai	1015	DES	CR/RAF 16.5
6*	22 May	D	A7243	22	S E Arras	1030	OOC	CR/?
7*	30 May	Pfalz DIII	C961	22	Armentieres	1940	OOC	CR/?
8*	31 May	Pfalz DIII	C961	22	Laventie	1915	DES	CR/RAF 31.5
9*	2 Jun	C?	C961	22	E Lens	1015	OOC	CR/?
10*	2 Jun	C?	C961	22	E Lens	1015	OOC	CR/?
11**	5 Jun	Halb. C	C961	22	S Laventie	1030	DES	CR/RAF 5.6
12**	5 Jun	Alb. DV	C961	22	S Laventie	1036	OOC	CR/RAF 5.6

TOTAL: 5 destroyed, 7 out of control = 12.

*Observer: Lt J.H. Umney. **Observer: Lt C.G. Gass.

BROOKES Eric Guy Captain 65

Brookes flew Sopwith Camels with 65 Squadron in 1918. By the beginning of August he was acting Captain, and on 8th of that month led a patrol which forced two Fokker DVIIs down inside Allied lines, one of which crashed; however, he failed to return from a sortie later that day, last being seen north of Harbonnieres in Camel D8119. The award of a DFC was gazetted on 3 August.

	1918		Camel					
1*	25 May	Alb. DV	C8291	65	Albert	1945	DES	CR/ORB/?
2	18 Jun	Fokker DrI	C8291	65	Morcourt	0930	DES(F)	CR/RAF 18.6
3	18 Jun	Alb. DV	C8291	65	Morcourt	0930	OOC	CR/ORB/?
4	2 Jul	Pfalz DIII	C8291	65	Bayonvillers	2027	OOC	CR/ORB/?
5s**	8 Aug	Fokker DVII	D8119	65	Proyart	1225	CAPT	CR/RAF 8.8
6s**	8 Aug	Fokker DVII	D8119	65	Proyart	1225	CAPT	CR/RAF 8.8

TOTAL: 2 shared captured, 2 destroyed, 2 out of control = 6.

*Probably Lt A. Angermund of Jasta 76, who was wounded. **Shared with Lt J.L.M. White, Lt G.O.D. Tod, Lt F. Edsted, Lt C. Tolley, Lt D. Oxley.

BROWN Alfred John Captain 24, 23

Brown served with 24 Squadron from mid 1917, becoming a flight commander in December. Awarded an MC, he was rested on 15 March 1918. In July 1918 he joined 23 Squadron, but on 31 August he and two members of his flight were shot down by Oberleutnant E. von Wedel, Leutnant J. Schulte-Frohlinde and Leutnant F. von Kockritz during an evening patrol. Brown force-landed D5232 safely, as did one of his wingmen, but the third member of the patrol went down in flames.

	1917		DH 5					
1	21 Sep	Alb. DV	B362	24	Anneux-Rumilly	1705	DES	CR/RFC 21.9
2	10 Dec	Alb. DV	B4918	24	Honnecourt	1200	OOC	CR/Air1/169/SRB
	1918		SE 5A					
3s*	6 Mar	Alb. DV	C9494	24	St Quentin	1015	OOC	CR/RFC 6.3
4s**	11 Mar	C	C9494	24	E Bellenglise	1315	OOC	CR/RFC 11.3
5	11 Mar	Pfalz DIII	C9494	24	Ribemont	1815	OOC	CR/RFC 12.3
6	12 Mar	C?	C9494	24	S W St Quentin	1840	DES	CR/RFC 12.3
7	13 Mar	Alb. DV	C9494	24	Bellicourt	1245	OOC	CR/RFC 13.3
			Dolphin					
8s***	23 Aug	DFW. C	D3732	23	Maricourt-Suzanne	1850	OOC	CR/?

TOTAL: 2 destroyed, 3 and 3 shared out of control = 8.

*Shared with Lt A.K. Cowper in B664. **Shared with 2/Lt P.J. Nolan C5301, Lt R.T. Mark C6397, 2/Lt H.B. Richardson C1070, Lt E.W. Lindeburg B125; probably Vfw Diehl/Lt Ordelheide of FAA 271. ***Shared with Lt C. Bridge D3717, Lt S. Symondson D5233.

BROWN Arthur Roy Captain 9(N), 11(N), 4(N), 209

A Canadian from Carleton Place, Ontario, where he was born on 23 December 1893, Roy Brown was selected for pilot training in the RNAS in 1915, qualifying as a pilot on 24 November. He was posted to the United Kingdom in December, but was injured in an aircraft crash on 2 May 1916, and spent three months in hospital with a damaged back. On recovery he returned to advanced training, but further illness delayed his joining an operational unit until April 1917 when he was posted to 9(N) Squadron on the Western Front, to fly Triplanes. He did not remain with the unit long, being posted in rapid succession to 11(N), 4(N) and back to 11(N) Squadron, and it was here while flying Sopwith Pups, that he gained his first victory in July. In the early autumn he rejoined 9(N) Squadron and on 6 October received a DSC for having shot down four enemy aircraft out of control. Two further victories in the Ostend area followed during October, and the following month he went on leave.

He returned to the squadron and on 15 February 1918 became Flight Commander. On 21 April, having claimed 9 victories, he saw a Camel of his flight flown by Lieutenant 'Wop' May, being chased by a Fokker Triplane flown by the famous Rittmeister Freiherr Manfred von Richthofen, at that time credited with 80 victories. He dived on the Baron's aircraft, and after a chase, the Triplane crashed. Richthofen had been killed by one bullet, and his death was claimed by Australian machine gunners on the ground as well as by Brown; to this day no final agreement as to the victor has been reached, although it does seem generally accepted now that the gunners were responsible. Nine days later Brown was admitted to hospital with influenza and a nervous condition, and received a Bar to his DSC while there, the citation officially crediting him with the victory over von Richthofen. In June he was discharged and joined 2 School of Aerial Fighting as an instructor. On 15 July he was involved in a very bad accident when he fainted in the air, and suffered a fractured skull, neck and back. He nonetheless recovered, spending five months in hospital, but it was five years before he could be considered fully fit again. He retired from the RAF in April 1919 and became an accountant in Canada. He worked at various jobs and finally organised a small airline, but this failed just before World War II. In 1939 he tried to join the RCAF, but was turned down, and he then became Advisory Editor to *Canadian Aviation* magazine. In 1943 he ran unsuccessfully for political office, but on 9 March the following year he died of a heart attack.

	1917		Pup					
1	17 Jul	Alb. DIII	A6174	11N	S E Nieuport	1845	OOC	CR/RNAS 17.7
			Camel					
2s*	5 Sep	C	B3818	9N	Middelkerke-Neiuport	0800	OOC	CR/DRO/?
3	15 Sep	DFW. C	B3893	9N	Westende-Zevecote	1300	OOC	CR/RFC 15.9
4	20 Sep	Alb. DV	B3893	9N	Leke	1510	OOC	CR/RFC 20.9
5	13 Oct	DFW. C	B3893	9N	Ostend	0900	DES(F)	CR/RNAS 13.10
6	28 Oct	Alb. DV	B6617	9N	Pervyse	1220	OOC	CR/RNAS 28.10
	1918							
7	22 Mar	C	B7270	9N	N E Houthoulst Wood	1530	DES	CR/RFC 22.3
8s**	11 Apr	Alb. DV	B7270	209	Albert	c1700	OOC	CR/RAF 11.4
9s***	12 Apr	Fokker DrI	B7270	209	Warfusee-Abancourt	0830	DES(F)	CR/RAF 12.4
10†	21 Apr	Fokker DrI	B7270	209	Vaux sur Somme	1100	CAPT	CR/RAF 21.4

TOTAL: 1 captured, 2 and 1 shared destroyed, 4 and 2 shared out of control = 10.
Note: Brown's score is often given as 13; this would include counting 3 driven down with 11N in 1917. Brown also made a claim on 20 April 1918, which was disallowed.
*Shared with F/Cdr S.T. Edwards B3829, FSL O.M. Redgate B3810, FSL A. Wood B3897, F/Lt F.E. Banbury B3832. **Shared with Lt C.G. Edwards D3331. ***Shared with Lt F.J.W. Mellersh D3326. †Supposedly Rttm M. von Richthofen, the commander of Jagdgeschwader 1.

BROWN Allan Runciman Captain 1AFC

Born on 24 April 1895, and a draper in Launceston, Tasmania, before the war, Brown served with the Australian Artillery before transferring to the AFC. Posted to 1AFC Squadron in Egypt, he flew Bristol Fighters with Lieutenant G. Finlayson as his observer/gunner. On almost every occasion that they met enemy aircraft in decisive combat, this crew forced them to land on the flat desert, and then destroyed them with bombs and machine gun fire. On one occasion they forced down one aircraft within Allied lines and on 16 July 1918 attacked four Albatros scouts and forced them all to land hurriedly, but without destroying them. Their final victim was shot down and captured on 22 August, to bring their score to at least six, but before this they had been recommended for decorations. On 8 February 1919 the awards of DFCs for pilot and gunner were gazetted.

	1918		Bristol					
1*	3 May	C	B1149	1AFC	S W Suweilah	0700	FTL/DES	CR/BG Summ
2**	8 Jun	C	A7200	1AFC	S E Amman a/d	0700	FTL/DES	CR/BG Summ
3***	27 Jun	AEG. C	B1149	1AFC	Kutrani	0645	FTL/DES	CR/BG Summ
4s†	28 Jul	Rumpler C	B1284	1AFC	Wadi Fara	1200	FTL/DES	CR/BG Summ
5††	22 Aug	Rumpler C	B1284	1AFC	Ramleh	1315	CAPT	CR/BG Summ

TOTAL: 1 captured, 2 and 2 shared forced to land and destroyed = 5.
*Observer: Lt G. Finlay; shared with Lt G.V. Oxenham/Lt H.A. Letch B1225. **Observer: Lt H.A. Letch. ***Observer: Lt G. Finlay. †Observer: Lt G. Finlay. Shared with Lt C.S. Paul/Lt W.J.A. Weir C4627; both crews machined gunned the Rumpler crew on the ground. ††Observer: Lt G. Finlay. The crew were Lt Sakonski/Lt Moser of FA 301.

BROWN Colin Peter Captain 13(N), 213

Born on 20 December 1898, Colin Brown was educated at Dulwich College, London. He joined the RNAS in June 1917, going to the Seaplane Base at Dunkirk, which later became 13 Naval Squadron. He became a very aggressive and able pilot, attacking enemy aircraft as well as many targets on the sea and on land, including night strafing attacks on Zeebrugge harbour. In 1918 he became a flight commander, being awarded the DFC and Bar while with 213 Squadron for claiming 14 victories during 374 hours of war flying. He remained in the RAF, flying in Iraq in 1929-30 and becoming commanding officer of 26 Squadron in 1934. He was a Wing Commander at Air Ministry in 1938, and from 1940-42 was SASO, No 60 Group. In 1950 he was at the Air Ministry again, and retired as an Air Vice-Marshal,CBE. He died on 19 October 1965.

	1917		Camel					
1s*	13 Nov	Alb. DV	B6300	13N	E Nieuport	1145	DES	DOS/AIR 1/59
	1918							
2	27 Apr	Alb. DV	B7274	213	Uytkerke	1515	OOC	CR/DRO/?
3	8 May	Alb. DV	B7226	213	Wenduyne	1950	OOC	CR/5 GP Comm
4	14 Jul	Fokker DVII	D8177	213	Ostend	0925	DES(F)	CR/5 GP Comm
5**	31 Jul	Rumpler C	D3341	213	8m N E Nieuport	1040	DES	CR/5 GP Comm
6s***	11 Aug	Alb. C	D9490	213	7m N E Dixmude	0955	OOC	CR/5 GP Comm
7s†	21 Aug	C	D9649	213	S Zevecote	1650	DES	CR/5 GP Comm
8	25 Aug	Fokker DVII	F5913	213	10m N Ostend	1840	OOC	CR/5 GP Comm
9	24 Sep	Fokker DVII	D8177	213	S W Thorout	1445	DES	CR/5 GP Comm
10	24 Sep	Fokker DVII	D8177	213	1m S W Thorout	1450	DES	CR/5 GP Comm
11	29 Sep	Fokker DVII	D8177	213	1m E Roulers	1200	OOC	CR/5 GP Comm
12	4 Oct	Fokker DVII	D8177	213	Rumbeke	0930	DES(F)	CR/5 GP Comm
13	4 Oct	Fokker DVII	D8177	213	Rumbeke	0930	DES	CR/5 GP Comm
14	4 Oct	Fokker DVII	D8177	213	Rumbeke	0930	DES	CR/5 GP Comm

TOTAL: 7 and 2 shared destroyed, 4 and 1 shared out of control = 14.
*Shared with FSL Lawson B6410, FSL Moyle B6212. The details of this combat are unclear. The DOS refers to a combat report that is missing. That Brown scored on this day is noted in the list of claims kept by the squadron. **This was shot into the sea, and the crew rescued by a RN destroyer. It is believed this is the crew in the photo of Brown with 2 POW. ***Shared with Lt D.S. Ingalls C73. †Shared with Lt H.C. Smith D3341, Lt D.S. Ingalls N6376.

BROWN Frederic Elliott Captain 2, 84

A Canadian from Quebec, born in 1895, Brown served initially with the Royal Dublin Fusiliers before joining the RFC to fly as an observer in 2 Squadron from August 1916 to April 1917. After becoming a pilot he was posted to 84 Squadron on 1 November 1917, later becoming a most able flight commander in February 1918; he received the MC and Bar and claimed ten victories, but was injured in a landing crash on 31 March, leaving the squadron as a result. Returning to Canada in 1919 he became a successful businessman in Montreal until his death in Toronto on 15 September 1971.

	1917		SE 5A					
1s*	8 Nov	Alb. DV	----	84	E Poelcapelle	1415	OOC	CR/RFC 8.11
	1918							
2	16 Feb	Alb. DV	C5364	84	St Quentin	1020	OOC	CR/RFC 16.2
3	16 Feb	Alb. DV	C5364	84	St Quentin	1045	OOC	CR/RFC 16.2
4	16 Feb	C	C5364	84	N La Fere	1100	DES	CR/RFC 16.2
5s**	11 Mar	Alb. DV	C5364	84	Lavergies	1040	DES	CR/RFC 11.3
6	13 Mar	Alb. DV	B8337	84	Homblieres	1210	DES	CR/RFC 13.3
7	17 Mar	Alb. DV	B8337	84	Bussigny	1140	OOC	CR/RFC 17.3
8	17 Mar	Alb. DV	B8337	84	W Bussigny	1145	OOC	CR/RFC 17.3
9	18 Mar	Alb. DV	B8337	84	S E Sequehart	1140	OOC	CR/RFC 18.3
10	22 Mar	Pfalz DIII	B8337	84	Fayet	1145	DES	CR/RFC 22.3

TOTAL: 3 and 1 shared destroyed, 5 and 1 shared out of control = 10.
*Shared with Capt J.M. Child B562. **Shared with Lt G.O. Johnson B699.

BROWN Sydney MacGillvary Lieutenant 29

Born in Brooklyn, New York, on 10 August 1895, Sydney Brown joined the RFC in July 1917. After training he was posted to 29 Squadron on 4 July 1918, and on 12 August claimed a Fokker DVII for his first victory. He remained with the unit for the rest of the war, claiming three more aircraft and a balloon. He was awarded a DFC, gazetted on 9 February 1919.

	1918		SE 5A					
1	12 Aug	Fokker DVII	C1132	29	S E Bailleul	1940	DES	CR/RAF 12.8
2	19 Aug	DFW. C	E5999	29	Bailleul-Nieppe Rd	1120	DES	CR/RAF 19.8
3	28 Sep	Fokker DVII	E5999	29	Menin	1625	DES	CR/RAF 29.8
4	27 Oct	Balloon	E5999	29	E Tournai	0920	DES	CR/RAF 27.10
5	28 Oct	Fokker DVII	E5999	29	S W Avelghem	1600	DES	CR/RAF 28.10

TOTAL: 1 balloon, 4 destroyed = 5.

BROWN William Henry Lieutenant 84

Born in British Columbia, Canada, on 12 March 1894, Lieutenant Brown saw two years' service with 1st Canadian Signals Corps. Transferring to the RFC, he joined 84 Squadron on 6 August 1917 and went with the unit to France. Having survived the high initial casualties suffered by the inexperienced squadron, Brown developed slowly as a fighting pilot, gaining one victory in November and another in December. He then claimed five in three combats in March 1918. By early April his score had risen to nine, but on 8th he returned to Home Establishment. At this time only Proctor, Larsen and Stubb, apart from the commanding officer, remained of the squadron's original pilots — and like Brown, all had become aces. Brown was awarded an MC, gazetted on 22 June 1918.

	1917		SE 5A					
1	26 Nov	Alb. DV	B559	84	Fonsomme-Mt.d'Origny	0800	OOC	CR/RFC 26.11
2s*	23 Dec	C	B559	84	N St Quentin	1300	OOC	CR/RFC 23.12
	1918							
3	10 Mar	C	C5384	84	Bellicourt	1420	OOC	CR/RFC 10.3
4**	17 Mar	Fokker DrI	C9263	84	Crevecoeur	1730	OOC	CR/RFC 17.3
5	18 Mar	Alb. DV	C9263	84	St Souplet	1130	OOC	CR/RFC 18.3
6	18 Mar	Alb. DV	C9263	84	St Souplet	1130	OOC	CR/RFC 18.3
7	25 Mar	C	C9267	84	Flers	0920	DES	CR/RFC 25.3
8s***	25 Mar	C	C9267	84	Flers	0930	DES(F)	CR/RFC 25.3
9	3 Apr	Alb. DV	C9263	84	W Villers Brettoneaux	1200	OOC	CR/RAF 3.4

TOTAL: 1 and 1 shared destroyed, 6 and 1 shared out of control = 9.
*Shared with Capt E.R. Pennell B4886. **Possibly Lt W. Steinhauser, who was forced to land at Briaste, north of Crevecoeur. ***Shared with Capt R.A. Grosvenor C1077.

BROWNELL Raymond James Captain 45

Born in Tasmania on 17 May 1894, Brownell was educated at Scotch College, Melbourne, Victoria. He served with the Australian Artillery in Gallipoli and France, being awarded an MM before he transferred to the RFC late in 1916, when some 200 members of the Australian forces were recruited. In 1917 he was posted to 45 Squadron in France and went with this unit to Italy in November. Flying initially under Captain Norman Macmillan in 'A' Flight, he was later promoted to Captain and awarded an MC, claiming 12 victories. On his first patrol on 10 September 1917 he had the good fortune to find himself behind a German two-seater, opened fire and saw the enemy go down in flames. After the war he joined the RAAF, becoming a Wing Commander in 1936. In that year he came to England on an exchange scheme with the RAF, and was second in command of No. 3 FTS at Grantham. He retired with the rank of Air Commodore and the CBE. Brownell wrote an autobiography which was published in 1978, entitled *From Khaki to Blue*, he died prior to its publication, however, on 12 April 1974.

	1917		Camel					
1	10 Sep	DFW. C	B2323	45	Houthoulst Wood	1720	DES(F)	CR/RFC 10.9
2s*	20 Sep	C	----	45	Paschendaele	1825	DES(F)	CR/RFC 20.9
3	1 Oct	Alb. DV	B2323	45	Quesnoy	1220	OOC	CR/RFC 1.10
4	20 Oct	Alb. DV	----	45	Kastelhoek	1240	OOC	CR/RFC 20.10
5s**	27 Oct	Alb. DV	----	45	N E Comines	1015	DES	ORB/RFC 27.10
6	31 Dec	Alb. DIII	B2430	45	Piave de Soligo	0945	DES	CR/7 BG
7s***	31 Dec	Alb. DV	B2430	45	Paderno	1030	CAPT	CR/7 BG
	1918							
8	10 Jan	Alb. DIII	B2430	45	Portobuffolo	1615	DES	CR/7 BG
9	11 Jan	Alb. DIII	B2430	45	St Stino	1535	DES	CR/7 BG
10†	30 Jan	DFW. C	B6283	45	Saletto	1045	DES(F)	CR/7 BG
11	17 Apr	Alb. DIII	B3872	45	Oderzo	0915	OOC	CR/7 BG
12	18 Apr	Balloon	B3872	45	Piave River	----	DES	FKTB/OP

TOTAL: 1 balloon, 1 shared captured, 5 and 2 shared destroyed, 2 and 1 shared out of control = 12.
*Shared with Lt H.M. Moody, 2/Lt E.A.L.F. Smith. **Shared with Lt J.E. Child, 2/Lt M.B. Frew. ***Shared with Lt H.M. Moody B6238; Lt A. Thurm KIA of Jasta 31. †Korp Berger/Oblt Lifka KIA Flik 58b.

BRYSON Oliver Campbell Captain 19

Born on 18 August 1896, Oliver Bryson joined the Queen's Own Dorset Yeomanry Cavalry in 1914, but he was soon wounded in action. Transferring to the RFC in 1915 while serving in Egypt, he was posted to 19 Squadron in July 1917. He was awarded the MC and promoted to Captain while serving with this unit, with which he remained until early 1918. He stayed in the RAF after the war, serving in Russia in 1919 and in India 1928-31; he became a Squadron Leader in 1933 when he was in charge of engines at the CFS. Promotion to Wing Commander followed in 1935, and to Group Captain in November 1938. He retired from the service in August 1943 with the MC,DFC and Bar, and the Albert Medal.

	1917		Spad					
1	25 Aug	C	B3569	19	N W Houthoulst Wood	1835	OOC	ORB/RFC 25.8
2	25 Sep	Alb. DIII	B3646	19	S E Houthem	1815	DES	ORB/RFC 25.9
3	24 Oct	Alb. DIII	A6780	19	N N E Menin	0850	OOC	CR/RFC 24.10
4	31 Oct	Alb. DV	A6780	19	S Westroosebeke	0950	OOC	CR/RFC 31.10
5	12 Nov	Alb. DV	A6780	19	E Gheluwe	1020	OOC	CR/RFC 12.11
6s*	29 Nov	Alb. DV	A6780	19	E Becelaere	1245	OOC	CR/ORB 11 WS
7s**	6 Dec	C	A6780	19	E Roulers	1542	OOC	CR/ORB/11 WS
8s***	8 Dec	Rumpler C	A6780	19	Tenbrielen-Wervicq	1335	OOC	CR/RFC 8.12
9s†	18 Dec	C	A6802	19	Comines	1035	OOC	CR/RFC 18.12
10s††	19 Dec	C	A6780	19	W Passchendaele	1130	DES	CR/RFC 19.12
11s†††	22 Dec	Alb. DIII	A6780	19	S Quesnoy	1420	DES(F)	CR/RFC 22.12
	1918		Dolphin					
12	8 Mar	Alb. DV	C3837	19	Gheluvelt	1110	DES	ORB/RFC 8.3

TOTAL: 2 and 2 shared destroyed, 5 and 3 shared out of control = 12.
*Shared with Lt N.W. Hustings B1660, Capt G.W. Taylor B6805. **Shared with Lt A.B. Fairclough B6836, Lt R.G. Holt B6802, Lt E. Olivier A6714. ***Shared with Lt A.B. Fairclough B3528, Capt G.W. Taylor B6805. †Shared with Lt A.B. Fairclough B3528. ††Shared with Lt A.B. Fairclough B3528. †††Shared with Lt E.J. Blyth B3563, Lt E. Olivier A6714, Lt A.B. Fairclough B6802, Capt G.W. Taylor B6805, Major A.D. Carter A8836, Lt H.E. Galer A8834.

BUCHANAN Archie Lieutenant 210

Born on Long Island, New York, on 5 October 1892, Archie Buchanan left the US to join the RAF, and was posted to 210 Squadron on 11 June 1918. Serving in Belgium, and flying along the Flanders coast, he claimed six enemy aeroplanes and a balloon, for which he was awarded the DFC. On 17 October he landed his Camel at Ostend and was informed by the local populace that he was the first of the Allies to enter the town since the Germans had left that morning. On 30 October he was shot down by a Fokker DVII while flying Camel F3242 east of Valenciennes during the morning, spending the last 12 days of the war as a prisoner.

	1918		Camel					
1	30 Jun	Balloon	D9669	210	N E Estaires	1110	DES	CR/RAF 30.6
2s*	20 Jul	Fokker DVII	D6909	210	S E Ostend	0945	OOC	CR/CR/5 GP Comm
3	31 Jul	Fokker DVII	D6909	210	N W Wervicq	1830	DES	CR/5 GP Comm
4	11 Aug	Pfalz DIII	D3422	210	2m S Westende	1050	OOC	CR/5 GP Comm
5	16 Sep	Fokker DVII	D3422	210	6m N Zeebrugge	1115	DES	CR/5 GP Comm
6	29 Sep	Fokker DVII	D3422	210	Wijnendaele Wood	0800	DES	CR/5 GP Comm
7	29 Sep	Fokker DVII	D3422	210	Wijnendaele Wood	0805	OOC	CR/5 GP Comm

TOTAL: 4 destroyed, 2 and 1 shared out of control = 7.
*Shared with Capt H.T. Mellings D5914.

BULMER George William Captain 22

Born in the United States of British parents in Dixon, Illinois, on 1 September 1898, Bulmer settled in Canada; he served with 22 Squadron during the spring and summer of 1918, flying Bristol Fighters. Over a four month period he claimed 11 victories, two of the first three falling to the rear gun, and at least seven of the rest to the front gun. He was awarded an MC and DFC, and became a flight commander during July 1918.

	1918		Bristol					
1*	6 Mar	Pfalz DIII	C4810	22	E La Bassee	1115	OOC	CR/RFC 6.3
2**	16 Mar	Pfalz DIII	C4810	22	Henin Lietard	1030	OOC	CR/RFC 16.3
3**	16 Mar	Pfalz DIII	C4810	22	Henin Lietard	1030	OOC	CR/RFC 16.3
4**	23 Mar	Alb. DV	A7251	22	Bussy	1100	DES	CR/RFC 23.3
5***	6 May	Pfalz DIII	C4888	22	Fresnoy	1025	OOC	CR/RAF 6.5
6**	8 May	Pfalz DIII	C4888	22	Brebieres	1015	DES	CR/RAF 8.5
7**	16 May	Balloon	C4888	22	1m N E Neuf Berquin	1045	DES	CR/ORB/?
8**	17 May	C	C4888	22	S E Douai	1200	DES	CR/RAF 17.5
9†	9 Jul	C	C4888	22	N Bois de Phalempin	1100	DES(F)	CR/RAF 9.7
10†	? Jul	----	----	22	----	----	DES	RAF 8/14.7

TOTAL: 1 balloon, 5 destroyed and 4 out of control = 10.
*Observer: 2/Lt S.J. Hunter. **Observer: 2/Lt P.S. Williams. ***Observer: Lt H.E. Elsworth. †Observer: 2/Lt J. McDonald.

BURDEN Henry John Captain 56

Born in Canada on 28 April 1893, 'Hank' Burden joined the Canadian Forestry Company, with which he served in France from August 1916 until April 1917. Transferring to the RFC, he was posted to 56 Squadron in February 1918. During his time with this unit he claimed 16 air victories and also three aircraft destroyed on the ground during an attack on Epinoy airfield on 1 August. On 10 August he claimed five Fokker Biplanes shot down in two actions. The awards of both the DSO and DFC were gazetted on 2 November. Returning home, he remained associated with flying, and in 1938 was a member of the Air Advisory Committee. He was also the brother-in-law of W.A. Bishop. He died on 28 March 1960.

	1918		SE 5A					
1	21 Mar	Alb. DV	D283	56	Inchy	1315-1345	OOC	CR/RFC 21.3
2s*	23 Mar	C	D283	56	Moreuil	0740	DES	CR/RFC 23.3
3	2 May	Pfalz DIII	C1096	56	S E Martinpuich	1125	DES	CR/RAF 2.5
4	10 May	Alb. DV	C1096	56	S Bray	1930	DES	CR/RAF 10.5
5	18 Jun	Alb. DV	C1096	56	Suzanne	0850	DES	CR/RAF 18.6
6	10 Aug	Fokker DVII	C1096	56	N Chalus	1000	DES	CR/RAF 10.8
7	10 Aug	Fokker DVII	C1096	56	E Chalus	1000	DES	CR/RAF 10.8
8	10 Aug	Fokker DVII	C1096	56	Puzeaux	1030	DES	CR/RAF 10.8
9	10 Aug	Fokker DVII	C1096	56	E Roye	2010	DES	CR/RAF 10.8
10	10 Aug	Fokker DVII	C1096	56	E Roye	2010	DES	CR/RAF 10.8
11	12 Aug	Fokker DVII	C1096	56	Ham	1645	OOC	CR/RAF 12.8
12	12 Aug	Fokker DVII	C1096	56	Ham	1645	DES	CR/RAF 12.8
13	12 Aug	Fokker DVII	C1096	56	Ham	1645	DES	CR/RAF 12.8
14	13 Aug	DFW. C	C1096	56	Pozieres	1015	DES	CR/RAF 13.8
15	15 Aug	LVG. C	C1096	56	Croisilles	1900	DES	CR/RAF 15.8

16	22 Aug	Fokker DVII	D6126	56	Peronne	1315	DES	CR/RAF 22.8

TOTAL: 13 and 1 shared destroyed, 2 out of control = 16.
*Shared with Lt M.E. Mealing C5389, 2/Lt H.J. Walkerdine B8266, Capt L.W. Jarvis C5430, Lt E.D.G. Galley B59, 2/Lt W.S. Maxwell B119.

BURDICK Howard 1st Lieutenant 17 US

Howard Burdick, from Brooklyn, New York, was a member of the USAS who served in the 17th Aero Squadron. Here he claimed eight victories and was awarded an American DSC. During World War II his son Clinton D. Burdick, was an ace with the 356th Fighter Group of the US 8th Air Force.

	1918		Camel					
1	18 Sep	LVG. C	F2141	17US	Rumilly	1100	DES(F)	CR/RAF 18.9
2	24 Sep	Fokker DVII	F2141	17US	N W Havrincourt	1040	DES	CR/RAF 24.9
3	28 Sep	LVG. C	F2141	17US	51a/1/78d	1745	DES(F)	CR/RAF 28.9
4	28 Sep	Fokker DVII	F2141	17US	51b/X/12d	1810	DES	CR/US 133
5s*	2 Oct	DFW. C	F2141	17US	E Awoignt	0910	DES	CR/RAF 2.10
6s**	14 Oct	Halb. C	H830	17US	E Bazeul	0710	DES	CR/RAF 14.10
7s***	14 Oct	Fokker DVII	H830	17US	N E Hausey	1400	DES	CR/?
8	25 Oct	Fokker DVII	H830	17US	Mormal Woods	1055	DES(F)	CR/RAF 25.10

TOTAL: 5 and 3 shared destroyed = 8.
*Shared with 1/Lt G.A. Vaughn H828. **Shared with 1/Lt G.A. Vaughn H828, 2/Lt L. Myers F2007. ***Shared with 1/Lt G.A. Vaughn H828; the Fokker was forced to crash-land and then the pilot was shot dead on the ground.

BURGE Philip Scott Captain 64

Burge served in the Army in the early years of the war, being awarded an MM before joining the RFC. Commissioned a 2nd Lieutenant, he qualified as a pilot on 24 May 1917 and joined 64 Squadron on 14 October. He subsequently rose to become a flight commander and was awarded an MC during 1918. On 24 July 1918 he was hit during a dogfight whilst flying SE 5A D6900, and was seen to go down in flames west of Seclin just after 1800 hours. The Germans later confirmed his death, which was probably caused by Unteroffizier Marat Schumm of Jasta 52.

	1918		SE 5A					
1	23 Mar	Fokker DrI	B125	64	Bourlon Wood	1530	DES	CR/RFC 23.3
2s*	30 Mar	C	B76	64	Croisilles	1150	DES	CR/RFC 30.3
3	1 Apr	Alb. DV	B125	64	Mericourt	0715	OOC	CR/RAF 1.4
4s**	3 May	Rumpler C	B58	64	Mercatel	1055	DES	CR/RAF 3.5
5	16 May	Alb. DV	----	64	S W Brebieres	0940	DES	CR/RAF 16.5
6	16 May	Alb. DV	----	64	Brebieres	0941	OOC	CR/RAF 16.5
7	20 May	Halb. C	C641	64	S W Armentieres	0740	DES	CR/RAF 20.5
8	21 May	Halb. C	----	64	S W Laventie	1050	DES	CR/?
9	19 Jul	Fokker DrI	D6900	64	S Lille	0835	DES	CR/RAF 19.7
10s***	20 Jul	Rumpler C	----	64	Drocourt	0945	DES	CR/RAF 20.7
11	22 Jul	Alb. DV	----	64	Harnes	2010	DES	CR/RAF 22.7

TOTAL: 6 and 3 shared destroyed, 2 out of control = 11.
*Shared with Capt J.A. Slater D289. **Shared with Lt W.C. Daniels B2, Lt B.A. Walkerdine C6447. ***Shared with Capt E.R. Tempest, Lt W.R. Henderson.

BUSH James Cromwell Lieutenant 22

A clergyman's son from Dorset, who had previously served with the Dorset Regt, Bush flew FE 2Bs with 22 Squadron during 1917. Once the unit equipped with Bristol Fighters he began to achieve success, flying either with Air Mech A. Whitehouse (later famous as the aviation journalist 'Arch' Whitehouse, who was to write some colourful but rather unreliable accounts of his service with the squadron) or with Lt W.W. Chapman. Bush claimed six victories and received an MC, but he and Lt Chapman were shot down and killed on 7 October 1917 in Bristol A7280, by Lt Haebler of Jasta 36 near Kruishoek.

	1917		Bristol					
1s*	12 Aug	Alb. DV	A7174	22	Lens-Douai	1930	DES(F)	CR/RFC 13.8
2s**	12 Aug	Alb. DV	A7174	22	Lens	1945	OOC	CR/RFC 13.8
3***	17 Aug	Alb. DV	A7174	22	Staden	1915	OOC	CR/?
4***	5 Sep	Alb. DV	A7185	22	E Houthoulst Wood	1900	DES(F)	CR/RFC 5.9
5***	1 Oct	Alb. DV	B1114	22	Westroosebeke	1750	OOC	CR/RFC 1.10
6†	2 Oct	C	B1123	22	N Courtrai	1041	DES	CR/RFC 2.10

TOTAL: 2 and 1 shared destroyed, 2 and 1 shared out of control = 6.
*Observer: 1 AM A.G. Whitehouse; shared with Capt C.M. Clement/Lt R.B. Carter in A7172 and Lt M.W. Turner/Lt Edson. **Observer: 1 AM A.G. Whitehouse; shared with Capt C.M. Clement/Lt R.B. Carter in A7172. ***Observer: Lt W.W. Chapman. †Observer: 1 AM A.G. Whitehouse.

CAIRNES W.J. Captain 19, 74

An Irishman, Cairnes served with 19 Squadron during the spring and summer of 1917 after previous service on Home Defence duties. During this period he was promoted to flight commander due to his skill, and to heavy casualties suffered by the unit. He claimed at least three victories flying Spads with the squadron before he was posted back to Home Establishment as an instructor. In early 1918 he returned to France as a flight commander in the newly-formed 74 Squadron, now flying SE 5As. By the end of May his score was reputed to be six, but appears only to be five, due to an 'out of control' claim being disallowed. However, on 1 June he was shot down by Leutnant Paul Billik of Jasta 52, one wing being seen to come off his aircraft (C6443) before it crashed north-east of Estaires.

	1917		Spad					
1	19 May	Alb. C	B1565	19	E Croisilles	0645	DES	CR/RFC WD
2	19 May	Alb. DIII	B1565	19	N Vitry	0740	DES	CR/RFC 19.5
3	7 Jun	Alb. DV	B1565	19	Warneton	1320	OOC	CR/??
	1918		SE 5A					
4	21 Apr	Alb. DV	----	74	Armentieres	2000	OOC	TS/?
5	30 May	Alb. DV	C6443	74	Steenwerck	1515	OOC	CR/11 WS

TOTAL: 2 destroyed, 3 out of control = 5.

CALDWELL Keith Logan Major 8, 60, 74

Born in Wellington, New Zealand, on 16 October 1895, Keith Caldwell joined the New Zealand Territorial Infantry at the outbreak of war. In August 1915 he joined a private flying club and was taught to fly in a flyingboat, and then a Caudron converted as a seaplane. He left for England in December and joined the RFC in April 1916. Completing his flying training, he was posted to France on 19 July, joining 8 Squadron ten days later; here he flew many missions and gained one victory in combat. In November he went to 60 Squadron, staying with this unit until 12 October 1917 with only one break of ten weeks' sick leave during March and April; he became a flight commander in May. In September he received an MC and was posted to the Special School of Flying at Gosport the following month. He then served at the RFC's Aerial Gunner School at Ayr, before a period at CFS. He was then given command of 74 Squadron and led it to France in April 1918, remaining in command until the end of the war. He received the DFC and Bar, together with the Belgian Croix de Guerre, and brought his victory total to 25, surviving a mid-air collision.

Known as an excellent pilot but a very poor shot, it was considered that had his marksmanship been better, he would probably have become one of the greatest aces of the war. After the close of hostilities, 'Grid', as he was known, returned to New Zealand and took up farming. In 1925 he married Dorothy Gordon, sister of F.S. Gordon who had flown in 74 Squadron. Caldwell kept in touch with flying, by serving in the reserve and joining private flying clubs. During World War II he held various training and administrative posts in the RNZAF. In 1945 he was AOC,RNZAF Headquarters in London, receiving the CBE and attaining the rank of Air Commodore. When that war ended he returned to his family in New Zealand and resumed farming until his death on 28 November 1980. In his later years Caldwell was of much assistance to historians interested in the men of his two famous units, 60 and 74 Squadrons.

	1916		BE 2D					
1*	18 Sep	Roland CII	5735	8	Grevillers-Bucquoy	1930	DES	CR/RFC 18.9
			Nieup					
2s**	11 Dec	Alb. C	----	60	Dainville	1030	CAPT	CR/RFC 11.12
	1917							
3	14 Jun	Alb. DIII	B1654	60	Drocourt	0955	OOC	CR/RFC 14.6
4s***	4 Jun	Alb. DIII	B1654	60	Vitry	2020	DES	CR/C&C V11 N4
5	24 Jun	Alb. DIII	B1654	60	Douai	2010	DES	CR/RFC 25.6
6s†	24 Jun	Alb. DIII	B1654	60	Douai	2010	OOC	CR/C&C C11 N4
7	3 Jul	Alb. DIII	B1654	60	Graincourt	1750	OOC	CR/RFC 4.7
8s††	15 Jul	Alb. DIII	B1654	60	Vitry	1950	DES	CR/RFC 15.7
			SE 5A					
9	15 Sep	Alb. C	B534	60	St Julien	1600	DES	CR/RFC 15.9
	1918							
10	12 Apr	Alb. DV	C5396	74	S E Deulemont	1935	DES	CR/RFC 12.4
11	21 May	Pfalz DIII	C5396	74	2m W Ypres	1900	DES	CR/RAF 21.5
12	28 May	Pfalz DIII	C5396	74	I 36	1935	OOC	CR/11 WS
13	31 May	Pfalz DIII	C5396	74	1m W Ploegsteert Wood	1950	OOC	CR/11 WS
14	1 Jun	Pfalz DIII	C5396	74	2m E Dickebusch	1945	OOC	CR/11 WS
15	15 Jul	Fokker DVII	D6864	74	2m S Roulers	0850	DES	CR/RAF 15.7
16	29 Jul	Pfalz DIII	D6864	74	1m E Dickebusch	1945	OOC	CR/11 WS
17	30 Jul	Fokker DVII	D6864	74	W Armentieres	1130	OOC	CR/11 WS
18	23 Aug	Fokker DVII	----	74	S E Houthoulst Wood	1925	DES	CR/RAF 23.8

19	4 Sep	Fokker DVII	D6864	74	S Lille	1930	DES	CR/RAF 4.9
20	17 Sep	Fokker DVII	----	74	N Courtrai	1825	DES	CR/RAF 17.9
21†††	17 Sep	Fokker DVII	----	74	N W Coutrai	1840	OOC	CR/11 WS
22	21 Sep	Fokker DVII	----	74	Lille	1845	OOC	CR/11 WS
23	24 Sep	SS DIV	----	74	3m E Armentieres	1030	OOC	CR/11 WS
24	14 Oct	Fokker DVII	C1139	74	Ledgehem	1100	DES	CR/RAF 14.10
25	30 Oct	Fokker DVII	----	74	Quaremont	0825	DES	CR/11 WS

TOTAL: 1 shared captured, 11 and 2 shared destroyed, 10 and 1 shared out of control = 25.
*Observer: Capt P.E. Welchman. **Shared with Capt E. Grenfell, Lt H. Meintjes, Lt A.P.V. Daly, Lt A.D. Whitehead, Lt L.S. Weedon. No. 174/16 captured pilot died of wounds, Lt Baldamus POW. ***Shared with Lt W.M. Fry B1619, Lt Collier B1605; Lt H. Becker WIA, Jasta 12. †Shared with Lt D.C.G. Murray B1605, Lt A.R. Adam B1569. ††Shared with Lt W.E. Jenkins B1629, Lt W.B. Sherwood B1605. †††Probably Vzfw H. Popp of Jasta 77 KIA.

CALLAGHAN Joseph Creuss Major 18, 87

An Irishman born in 1893, Callaghan spent the pre-war years in Texas, returning home in 1914 to join the Royal Munster Fusiliers. He transferred to the RFC on 1 September 1915, and in April 1916 joined 18 Squadron, claiming one victory on 24th of that month while flying an FE 2B. In January 1917 he became an instructor at No 2 School of Aerial Gunnery at Turnberry, before being posted as commanding officer of 87 Squadron on Sopwith Dolphins in January 1918, leading this unit to France. Here he claimed four more victories before, on 2 July, he was seen to attack a formation of Fokker DVIIs single-handed. He was shot down and killed by Leutnant Franz Buchner the commander of Jasta 13, who ended the war with 40 victories.

	1916		FE 2B					
1*	26 Apr	Fokker E	5232	18	----	----	DES	RFC WD/RFC 26.4
	1918		Dolphin					
2	29 May	Rumpler C	D3671	87	Villers-Brettoneaux	1940	OOC	CR/?
3	1 Jun	LVG. C	D3671	87	W Bertangles	1415	DES	CR/RAF 1.6
4	28 Jun	Alb. DV	D3671	87	Bapaume-Queant	0815	DES	CR/RAF 28.6
5	28 Jun	Alb. DV	D3671	87	Bapaume	0915	OOC	CR/?

TOTAL: 3 destroyed, 2 out of control = 5.
*Observer: Lt J. Mitchell, who was killed in action in this fight.

CALLAHAN Lawrence Kingsley 1st Lieutenant 85, 148 US

Born on 11 January 1894, Larry Callahan, an American from Chicago, Illinois, joined the US Air Service and was posted to the United Kingdom to undertake advanced training attached to the RFC, and then to obtain operational experience at the front with a British squadron. In April 1918 he was posted to France with 85 Squadron, RAF, and with this unit claimed three victories during the early summer. He was then posted to the 148th Aero Squadron, USAS, converting from SE 5As to Camels. With this latter unit he claimed two further victories to bring his score to five; he was awarded a British DFC. Callahan was featured in E.W. Springs' book *Warbirds* after the war, which was based on the letters of J.McG. Grider, who had been killed in action, and with whom Springs and Callahan had served in 85 Squadron. Callahan served with the USAAF during World War II, and died on 17 September 1977.

	1918		SE 5A					
1	16 Jun	C	D6871	85	Estaires	0720	DES	CR/RAF 16.6
2	13 Jul	Fokker DVII	C1935	85	Armentieres	2030	DES	CR/RAF 14.7
3	24 Jul	Fokker DVII	C1947	85	Neuve Eglise	1040	OOC	CR/?
			Camel					
4	3 Oct	Fokker DVII	V8253	148US	Esnes	1110	DES	CR/RAF 3.10
5	28 Oct	Fokker DVII	C8253	148US	N W Jenlain	1205	DES	CR/US 133

TOTAL: 4 destroyed, 1 out of control = 5.

CALLENDER Alvin Andrew Captain 32

An American, Callender was born in New Orleans on 4 July 1893. He enlisted in the RFC in Canada in June 1917, and following training in England, was posted to 32 Squadron on 15 May 1918, one of many Americans to serve with that unit. Callender was shot down on 10 June, but survived unhurt. By early September he was promoted to flight commander, and by 30 October had claimed eight victories. However on this date he was shot down again while flying SE 5A E6010 — probably the victim of Oblt Greiesheim of Jasta 'Boelcke'; he subsequently died of his wounds, having fallen within British lines. A very fine collection of his letters and photographs was privately published in 1978, entitled *War in an Open Cockpit*. It is a lasting memorial to one of the least-known American aces.

	1918		SE 5A					
1	28 May	Pfalz DIII	C1884	32	Armentieres	1830	OOC	CR/ORB/SR?
2	6 Jun	Fokker DVII	C1884	32	Montdidier	1900	OOC	CR/ORB/SR?

3	8 Jul	Fokker DVII	C1903	32	Bauvin, N E Lens	0810	OOC	CR/ORB/SR?
4	25 Jul	Fokker DVII	C1903	32	Fismes	1930	DES(F)	CR/RAF 25.7
5	10 Aug	Fokker DVII	C9565	32	Peronne	1140	OOC	CR/ORB/SR?
6	16 Sep	Fokker DVII	E6010	32	Sancourt	1810	OOC	CR/ORB/SR?
7	24 Sep	Fokker DVII	E6010	32	N Bourlon Wood	1705	OOC	CR/ORB/SR?
8	24 Sep	Fokker DVII	E6010	32	N Bourlon Wood	1710	OOC	CR/ORB/SR?

TOTAL: 1 destroyed, 7 out of control = 8.

CAMERON Douglas Evan 2nd Lieutenant 1

From Hythe, Sussex, Douglas Cameron was born on 18 January 1893. He was commissioned on 11 March 1918, joining 1 Squadron at the front on 19 June. He remained with the unit throughout the rest of the war, and was demobilized on 6 January 1919.

	1918		SE 5A					
1s*	15 Sep	Pfalz DXII	F6429	1	Recourt	1705	CAPT	CR/RAF 15.9
2	29 Sep	Fokker DVII	H7257	1	Bohain	0945	OOC	CR/ORB/?
3s**	1 Oct	Fokker DVII	H7257	1	N E St Quentin	1710	OOC	CR/ORB/?
4s***	28 Oct	Fokker DVII	H7257	1	Trelon	1530	DES	CR/RAF 28.10
5s***	28 Oct	Fokker DVII	H7257	1	Trelon	1530	OOC	CR/ORB/?

TOTAL: 1 shared captured, 1 destroyed, 1 and 2 shared out of control = 5.
*Shared with Lt B.H. Moody B8501, Capt G.W.D. Allen F5912, Capt C.S.T. Lavers E5969 and Capt W.E. Staton/Lt L.R. Mitchell of 62. Lt P. Vogel of Jasta 23 died of wounds. **Shared with Capt C.S.T. Lavers C9292, Lt B.H. Moody B8501, Lt F.M. Squires E6009, 2/Lt F.A.S. Nesbitt B7881, 2/Lt C.R. Boyd C9065, Lt W.A. Smart D6973, 2/Lt L.H. Phinney D6951, Capt W. Pallister F5473, Lt W. Newby E1353, Lt C.W. Arning E4023, 2/Lt W. Joffe B8427, 2/Lt Dickenson C1812. ***Shared with Lt B.H. Moody B8501.

CAMPBELL Lynn Captain 62

A Canadian from Hamilton, Ontario, this officer flew Bristol Fighters with 62 Squadron in 1918, where he was credited with six victories, four being shared with his observers. By the latter half of the year he had been promoted to Captain, but was killed in action on 9 October 1918 in E2256 with Sub Lieutenant W. Hodgkinson, his regular observer. They were probably flying the 43rd victim of Leutnant Paul Baumer of Jasta 'Boelcke'.

	1918		Bristol					
1*	12 Apr	Alb. DV	----	62	E Estaires	1420	OOC	CR/RAF 12.4
2*	8 Jul	Fokker DrI	B1339	62	N W Carvin	0715	DES	CR/RAF 8.7
3*	3 Aug	?	----	62	----	----	OOC	SR/C&C/V17 N4
4*	8 Aug	?	----	62	----	----	OOC	SR/C&C/V17 N4
5*	12 Aug	?	----	62	----	----	DES	SR/RAF 12.8
6**	16 Sep	Fokker DVII	----	62	----	----	OOC	CR/C&C? V17 N4
7*	9 Oct	Fokker DVII	E2256	62	Preseau	----	DES	SR/RAF 9.10

TOTAL: 3 destroyed, 4 out of control = 7.
*Observer: 2/Lt W. Hodgkinson. **Observer: 2/Lt I. Egan.

CAMPBELL William Charles Captain 1

A relatively old pilot, born it is believed, in 1889 of a Scottish father and French mother, he joined the RFC in 1916 and he became one of the most successful of the RFC's Nieuport Scout pilots. Campbell served with 1 Squadron from 1 May 1917, gaining all his 23 victories in a period of three months. He was awarded an MC and Bar, and was promoted to flight commander. He was subsequently also awarded a DSO, receiving this in September, during which month he was posted home as an instructor. Five of his victories were balloons, making him the first 'Balloon Buster ace' in the RFC.

	1917		Nieuport					
1	14 May	C	B1635	1	Polygon Wood	1115	DES	CR/RFC 14.5
2	19 May	Balloon	A6670	1	Ploegsteert	0730	DES	CR/RFC 19.5
3	21 May	Alb. DIII	A6670	1	S Armentieres	2000	DES	CR/RFC 21.5
4	3 Jun	C	B1700	1	Gapaard	1525	DES	CR/RFC 2.6
5	4 Jun	LVG. C	B1700	1	Handzaeme	0745	DES(F)	CR/RFC 4.6
6	9 Jun	Alb. DIII	B1700	1	Oosthoek	0825	OOC	CR/RFC 9.6
7	9 Jun	Alb. DIII	B1700	1	Oosthoek	0830	OOC	CR/RFC 9.6
8	9 Jun	Alb. DIII	B1700	1	Houthem	1400	DES	CR/RFC 9.6
9	15 Jun	Halb. D	B1700	1	Becelaere	0845	OOC	CR/RFC 15.6
10	16 Jun	Alb. C	B1700	1	Houthem	0900	DES	CR/RFC 16.6
11	16 Jun	Alb. C	B1700	1	E Houthem	0910	DES	CR/RFC 16.6
12	16 Jun	C	B1700	1	Quesnoy	0940	DES	CR/RFC 16.6
13s*	21 Jun	Alb. DV	B1700	1	S Polygon Wood	1050	OOC	CR/RFC 21.6
14s**	23 Jun	C	B1700	1	Wulverghem-Houthem	1520	OOC	CR/RFC 23.6
15	16 Jul	Alb. DV	B3466	1	Poelcapelle	1920	DES	CR/RFC 16.7

Captain W.M. 'Mel' Alexander, DSC, a Canadian who flew with)(Naval) and 210 Squadron, 1917-18. *(R.C. Bowyer)*

Major B.E. Baker, DSO, MC, AFC, a very successful Bristol ghter pilot who served with 48 Squadron in 1917. He is seen here e following year in England whilst serving with 141 (Home efence) Squadron. He later became Air Marshal Sir Brian Baker. *R.C. Bowyer)*

A.C. Atkey, MC & Bar (Canadian) and his gunner, C.G. Gass, C, were an extremely successful Bristol Fighter team with 22 uadron in 1918. Atkey emerged as the top-scoring two-seater pilot the war. *(C.G. Gass)*

Captain E.D. 'Spider' Atkinson, DFC, AFC, (left) gained victories th both 1 and 64 Squadrons. He is seen here with Gerald J.C. axwell, MC, DFC, (56 Squadron) while both were at Turnberry in 18. *(MoD)*

3

4

1. Three Sopwith Dolphin pilots of 79 Squadron, 1918; (l to r) Captain R. Bannerman, DFC, (NZ), Lieutenant C.L. Lindburg (1 victory) and Captain F.W. Gillet, DFC, (American). *(S. St Martin)*

2. Captain Albert Ball, VC, DSO & 2 Bars, MC, Britain's first great ace in 1916. Often flying alone, he was probably the RFC's most aggressive pilot until his death in combat in May 1917. *(R.C. Bowyer)*

3. Captain H.F. 'Kiwi' Beamish, DSC, a New Zealander with the RNAS, flew wit 3(Naval)/203 Squadron in 1917-18 befor returning home to his farm. *(P. Sortehaug,*

4. Major W.G. Barker, VC, DSO, & Ba MC & 2 Bars, a Canadian who flew as a observer before becoming a pilot. He claimed most of his victories in Italy in 1917-18, but was awarded his Victoria Cross for a solo action over France late ir the war whilst attached to 201 Squadron *(Public Archive of Canada)*

1. Another recipient of the Victoria Cross was Captain Anthony Beauchamp Proctor (third from left), who was also awarded the DSO, MC, & Bar and DFC while with 84 Squadron during 1917-18. 'Proccy' came from South Africa and was that colony's highest-scoring pilot. Also in this picture are Lieutenant Simpson, Captain S.W. Highwood, DFC & Bar, and far right, Lieutenant J.E. Boudwin, USAS (2 victories). *(H.W.L. Saunders via Bruce & Leslie)*

2. Sergeant D.W. Beard, MM, piloted FE 2Bs with 11 Squadron during 1917-18, after service – and a victory – with a Corps squadron. *(R. Vann)*

3. Captain J.D. Belgrave, MC & Bar, flew with 45 and 60 Squadrons before his death in action, aged 21. He had previously been wounded while serving with the army in France.

4. Sergeants V.H. Davis (left) and H.W. Scarnell were both successful gunner/observers who flew with Sergeant Beard in 11 Squadron. *(R. Vann)*

1. Captain D.J. Bell, MC & Bar, a South African, served in 27 Squadron and then with 3 Squadron, flying Camels, until his death in action. *(Geo Williams)*

2. Louis Bennett Jr., an American who served with 40 Squadron in 1918. In just 25 sorties he shot down nine balloons and three aircraft before he was brought down by ground fire. *(via Geo Williams)*

3. Montreal-born G.A. Birks flew with 66 Squadron in Italy, where he was awarded the MC & Bar. *(S. St Martin)*

4. Major W.A. Bishop, VC, DSO & Bar, MC, DFC, ÇdeG; this well-known pilot flew with 60 Squadron in 1917, being awarded the Victoria Cross. He then commanded 85 Squadron during early 1918. *(P. Rosie)*

1. Major C.D. Booker, DSC, served with 8(Naval) Squadron, then commanded 201 Squadron, gaining over 20 victories before his own death in action.

2. Lieutenant C. Boothroyd, a successful gunner/observer with 20 Squadron during 1918. *(S. St Martin)*

3. Lloyd Breadner received his DSC while with 3(Naval) Squadron in 1917; he later commanded 204 Squadron in 1918. This Canadian subsequently became an Air Chief Marshal in the RCAF. *(R.C. Bowyer)*

4. Arthur Roy Brown, DSC & Bar, a Canadian from Ontario, flew with 9(Naval)/209 Squadron during 1917-18 and is still considered by some to have shot down Manfred von Richthofen in April 1918. *(Public Archive of Canada)*

1

3

2

1. Captain C.P. Brown, DFC & Bar, 13(Naval)/213 Squadron, 1917-18. Another successful pilot who later became an Air Vice-Marshal in the RAF.

2. The American, Sydney M. Brown, DFC, of 29 Squadron, 1918, is seen here in front of a Dolphin. *(R.C. Bowyer)*

3. Captain R.C. Brownell, MC, MM, from Tasmania, was awarded his MM whilst serving with the Australian artillery at Gallipoli and in France. He then became a scout pilot with 45 Squadron. *(S. St Martin)*

4. C.L. 'Grid' Caldwell, MC, DFC & Bar, served with 60 Squadron then commanded the famous 74 Squadron in 1918. A New Zealander, he served in the RNZAF in World War II. *(P. Sortehaug)*

1. Captain Sydney 'Timber Toes' Carlin, MC, DFC, DCM, lost a leg in the army, but overcame this handicap to become a successful scout pilot with 74 Squadron in 1918. He flew again in World War II.

2. Peter Carpenter, DSO, MC & Bar, flew Camels in Italy with both 45 and 66 Squadrons, 1917-18.

3. Major A.D. Carter, DSO & Bar, from Canada, claimed over 30 victories while flying Spads and Dolphins with 19 Squadron; he was shot down and captured in May 1918.

4. Flight Sub Lieutenant A.J. Chadwick, DSC, from Canada, flew with 4(Naval) Squadron at Dunkirk in 1917. *(R.C. Bowyer)*

1. Captain J.M. Child, MC, flew Spads with 19 Squadron, then SE 5As with 84 Squadron, before becoming an instructor in England, where he was killed.

2. Top-scorer with 4 AFC Squadron in 1918 was A.H. Cobby, DSO, DFC & 2 Bars. He later served with the RAAF as an Air Commodore. *(RAAF)*

3. A group of pilots at Turnberry in 1918 with Captain Roy Chappell, MC, first on the left; he flew with 27 and 41 Squadrons. Next are two former 84 Squadron pilots, Captains H.W.L. Saunders, MC, DFC, MM, and J.V. Sorsoleil, MC. Beyond them is Lieutenant A.B. Yuille, who shot down two Gotha night bombers with 151 Squadron. Far right is Captain P.J. Clayson, MC, DFC, formerly with 1 Squadron. *(H.W.L. Saunders via Bruce & Leslie)*

4. Flight Lieutenant W.H. Chisam served with 3(Naval) Squadron. He is seen here with a Sopwith Pup named 'Aileen' at Walmer, Kent. *(R.C. Bowyer)*

4

3

1. Captain Clive Collett, MC & Bar, from New Zealand, flew with 70 Squadron, claiming the RFC's first Camel victory. *(P. Sortehaug)*

2. One of the great Naval fighting pilots on the Western Front was the Canadian, Major Ray Collishaw, DSO & Bar, DSC, DFC, who claimed 60 victories with many more inconclusive engagements. He later went on to add two more victories in Russia in 1919. *(R. Collishaw)*

3. Captain L.P. Coombes, DFC, from London, was only 18 when the war ended, but he had seen action with 210 Squadron and had claimed 14 aircraft shot down. *(L.P. Coombes)*

4. Jesse Orin Creech, USAS, from Washington, DC, claimed eight victories with the 148th Aero Squadron, USAS, which operated under British command. *(S. St Martin)*

1. Major C.M. 'Billy' Crowe, MC, DFC, flew with 16, 56, 60 and 85 Squadrons between 1916-18, commanding both the latter units. *(P. Rosie)*

2. Captain W.G.S. Curphy, MC & Bar, (left) flew with 32 Squadron in 1916-17, but was killed in May 1917. Next to him are Lieutenant Henty, Lieutenant F.H. Coleman (4 victories), Lieutenant M.J. Mare-Montembault and Captain R.E. Wilson. Both of the latter were shot down by Oswald Boelcke, although the former survived to fly again, and was subsequently shot down by von Tutschek and captured. *(R.C. Bowyer)*

3. Captain E.D. Crundell, DFC, AFC, flew with 8(Naval) Squadron and later 210 Squadron; he served as a Wing Commander in World War II. *(R.C. Bowyer)*

4. Major R.S. Dallas, DSO, DSC & Bar, from Australia, flew with 1(Naval) Squadron during 1915-17, then commanded 40 Squadron in 1918. He claimed more than 32 victories before he was killed in action.

1. Dolphin pilots of 19 Squadron; (l to r): Lieutenant T.A. Aldridge (5 victories), Captain R.A. Del'Haye, DFC, (10 victories), Lieutenant C. Montgomery-Moore, DFC, (4 victories), Captain J.W. Crane (4 victories) and Lieutenant W.F. Gordon. *(via R.C. Bowyer)*

2. Captain Ellwood, DSC, 3(Naval) Squadron, 1917-18. He was later Air Marshal Sir Aubrey Ellwood. *(R.C. Bowyer)*

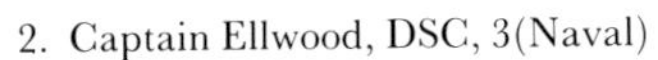

3. Captain A.B. Fairclough, MC, of 19 and 23 Squadrons, 1917-18. *(S. St Martin)*

4. Carl F. Falkenberg, DFC & Bar, a Canadian who flew SE 5As with 84 Squadron. *(Franks collection)*

1

1. Captain J.S.T. Fall, DSC & 2 Bars, AFC, served with 3 and 9(Naval) Squadrons during 1917. With 36 victories by December 1917 he was one of the earliest high-scorers of the RNAS. *(Franks collection)*

2. Captain W.M. Fry, MC, gained victories with 60, 23 and 79 Squadrons. He served as a Wing Commander in World War II. *(W.M. Fry)*

3. Lieutenant A.L. Fleming, MC, flew in Palestine with 111 Squadron. *(IWM)*

4. Captain M.B. Frew, DSO, MC & Bar, AFC, 45 Squadron, 1917-18. He remained in the RAF after the war, gaining a Bar to his DSO for service in Kurdistan in 1932; he later became Air Vice-Marshal Sir Matthew Frew. *(Franks collection)*

3

2

4

Captain D.M.B. Galbraith, DSC & Bar, (Naval) Squadron. *(R.C. Bowyer)*

Captain P.F. Fullard, DSO, MC & Bar, FC, flew with 1 Squadron in 1917, ecoming the highest-scoring pilot on the ieuport Scout in the RFC. He later became Air Commodore. *(via R.C. Bowyer)*

3. Captain G.E. Gibbons, MC, DFC, (right) with his observer, Lieutenant S.A.W. Knights, 62 Squadron, 1918. *(G. Muir)*

4. Captain John Gilmour, DSO, MC & 2 Bars, served with 27 and 65 Squadrons, and then commanded 28 Squadron in Italy. He was one of the lesser-known high-scoring scout pilots of the war. *(Franks collection)*

1. Captain C.B. Glynn, DFC, 74 Squadron. *(Franks collection)*

2. Major S.J. Goble, DSO, DSC, from Australia (right), flew with 8(Naval) and then commanded 5(Naval)/205 Squadron. Later he became an Air Commodore in the RAAF. Far left is Captain Euan Dickson, DSC & Bar, a flight commander in 205 Squadron in 1918 who emerged as one of the top-scoring bomber pilots of the war, whose biography is included here. *(P. Sortehaug)*

3. Three Camel pilots of 66 Squadron in Italy; Captain Harry Goode, DSO, DFC, AFC, Captain Peter Carpenter, DSO, MC & Bar (front), who also flew with 45 Squadron, and Captain C.M. Maude, DFC, CdesG. *(S. St Martin)*

4. Fred Gordon, a New Zealander with 74 Squadron in 1918, who later became the brother-in-law of 'Grid' Caldwell, his commanding officer. *(P. Sortehaug)*

1. Captain G.E. Gibbs, MC & 2 Bars (left) (17 and 150 Squadrons) and Captain A.G. Goulding, MC, DFC, (a Canadian who served in 17,47 and 150 Squadrons) are seen in Salonika with the crew of an enemy aircraft which they had jointly shot down on 20 March 1918. Gibbs later rose to the rank of Air Marshal and was knighted. *(G.E. Gibbs)*

2. Victor Groom, DFC, (2nd from right) flew with 20 Squadron in 1918. He is seen here with some of the squadron's observer/gunners, (l to r) C.G. Boothroyd, Ernest Hardcastle, DFC, (Groom's own gunner), D.E. Smith and J. Hills. *(E. Hardcastle)*

3. Captain H.J. Hamilton, MC, flew with 1 and 29 Squadrons before his death in a flying accident in June 1918. *(Franks collection)*

4. Major Ronnie Graham, DSO, DSC, DFC, joined the RNAS in 1915 and served with the St. Pol Seaplane Defence Flight, subsequently 13(Naval)/213 Squadron, 1917-18. He retired from the RAF as an Air Vice-Marshal. *(Franks collection)*

1. Captain J.D.I. Hardman, DFC, 19 Squadron, 1918. He was later Air Chief Marshal Sir Donald Hardman. *(J.D.I. Hardman)*

2. Captain A.T. Harris, AFC, flew with 45 Squadron in 1917. In World War II he commanded Bomber Command as Air Chief Marshal Sir Arthur Harris. *(A.T. Harris)*

3. Captain W.F.J. Harvey, DFC & Bar, 22 Squadron, 1918. *(W.F.J. Harvey)*

4. Major Lanoe Hawker, VC, DSO, gained early victories with 6 Squadron, then commanded 24 Squadron. He was shot down and killed by von Richthofen on 23 November 1916. *(R.C. Bowyer)*

16	16 Jul	Alb. DV	B3466	1	Zonnebeke	1940	DES	CR/RFC 16.7
17	16 Jul	Alb. DV	B3466	1	Zonnebeke	1942	OOC	CR/RFC 16.7
18	21 Jul	Alb. DV	B3474	1	N Polygon Wood	0750	DES	CR/RFC 21.7
19	21 Jul	Balloon	B3474	1	Wervicq	0800	DES	CR/RFC 21.7
20	22 Jul	Balloon	B3474	1	W Lille	0730	DES	CR/RFC 22.7
21	24 Jul	Alb. DV	B3474	1	E Polygon Wood	0800	OOC	CR/RFC 24.7
22	28 Jul	Balloon	B3474	1	Westroosebeke-Gheluwe	1350	DES	CR/RFC 28.7
23	28 Jul	Balloon	B3474	1	S E Houthoulst	1410	DES	CR/RFC 28.7

TOTAL: 5 balloons, 11 destroyed, 5 and 2 shared out of control = 23.
*Shared with Lt T.M. McFerran B3495. **Shared with Sgt G.P. Olley B1681

CANDY John Geoffrey Sadler Lieutenant 19

An ex-member of the Royal Sussex Regiment, Candy transferred to the RFC and joined 19 Squadron on 5 July 1917. He was awarded an MC early in 1918.

	1917		Spad					
1s*	26 Aug	DFW. C	B3352	19	Moorseele	0540	DES	CR/RFC 16.8
2s**	30 Sep	C	B3615	19	Gheluwe	0900	OOC	ORB/RFC 30.9
3s***	9 Oct	Alb. C	B3615	19	Moorslede	1040	OOC	CR/RFC WD
4s†	11 Nov	Alb. DIII	A6773	19	Gheluwe-Menin	1620	OOC	CR/RFC 11.11
5s††	13 Nov	Alb. DV	B6760	19	N Comines	1445	DES	CR/RFC 13.11
6	29 Dec	Alb. DV	B1660	19	N Houthoulst Forest	1010	OOC	CR/RFC 29.12

TOTAL: 2 shared destroyed, 1 and 4 shared out of control = 6.
*Shared with Lt H.C. Ainger B3616, 2/Lt A.A.N.D. Pentland B3620, Lt A.E. Boeree B3520, Lt R.L. Graham B3618. **Shared with Capt F. Sowrey A6777, Lt Delamere B3489, Lt R.M. Strang B1697, Lt R.A. Hewat A6662. ***Shared with Lt R.A. Hewat A6662, Capt F. Sowrey A6777. †Shared with Lt A.H. Rice B1581. ††Shared with Major A.D. Carter B3498.

CAPEL Leslie Howard Tandy Lieutenant 60, 20

On completion of training, Capel was posted to 60 Squadron in France, on 29 January 1918. After undertaking 11 sorties, he crashed on landing on 17 February, and was at once posted to 20 Squadron to fly Bristol Fighters. Here his first victories were gained with Corporal M.B. Mather in the rear seat, but most of his combat flying was accomplished in company with Sergeant E. Deighton. Of his seven victories, four were credited to the front gun and three to the rear.

	1918		Bristol					
1*	9 Mar	Alb. DV	B1191	20	S Menin	0800	OOC	CR/RFC 9.3
2*	9 Mar	Alb. DV	B1191	20	S Menin	0800	OOC	CR/RFC 9.3
3**	11 Apr	C	C4616	20	S Armentieres	1515	DES	CR/RAF 11.4
4***	31 May	Alb. DV	C4604	20	N Laventie	0730	DES	CR/RAF 31.5
5**	17 Jun	Pfalz DIII	C4604	20	N Comimes	0740	OOC	CR/?
6**	17 Jun	Pfalz DIII	C4604	20	N E Gheluvelt	0755	DES	CR/RAF 17.6
7**	23 Jun	Pfalz DIII	C4604	20	Laventie	0730	DES	CR/RAF 23.6

TOTAL: 4 destroyed, 3 out of control = 7.
*Observer: Cpl M.B. Mather. **Observer: Cpl E. Deighton. ***Observer: Pbr F.J. Ralph.

CARLAW Walter Macfarlane Captain 70

Joining 70 Squadron in 1918, Carlaw made his first claim on 11 March when he shared with three others in destroying a balloon. Next day he drove down a scout out of control, but he did not claim again until late July, by which time he had become a flight commander. He was awarded a DFC, ending the war with 12 victories.

	1918		Camel					
1s*	11 Mar	Balloon	----	70	Menin	1230	DES	CR/RFC 11.3
2	12 Mar	Alb. DV	B7473	70	N W Gheluwe	1300	OOC	CR/RFC 12.3
3	29 Jul	Fokker DVII	D9442	70	E Armentieres	1915	DES	CR/RAF 29.7
4	31 Jul	Fokker DVII	D9442	70	Wervicq	1745	DES	CR/RAF 31.7
5	31 Jul	Fokker DVII	D9442	70	N Menin	1745	OOC	CR/11C WS
6	19 Aug	Fokker DVII	D9442	70	Warneton-Comines	1950	DES	CR/RAF 19.8
7	28 Sep	Fokker DVII	B7162	70	N E Gheluwe	1150	DES	CR/RAF 28.9
8	3 Oct	Fokker DVII	B7176	70	E Roulers	1710	DES	CR/RAF 3.10
9	3 Oct	Fokker DVII	B7176	70	Roulers	1710	DES	CR/RAF 3.10
10	7 Oct	Fokker DVII	B7162	70	Lichtervelde	0845	DES	CR/RAF 7.10
11**	7 Oct	Fokker DVII	B7162	70	Lichtervelde	0845	OOC	CR/11 WS
12	14 Oct	Fokker DVII	N7883	70	S E Roulers	1425	OOC	CR/11 WS

TOTAL: 1 shared balloon, 7 and 1 shared destroyed, 3 out of control = 12.
*Shared with Capt Quigley, 2/Lt A. Koch, Lt Seth-Smith. **Carlaw and Lt O.A.P. Heron claimed 4 Fokkers in this fight. The only known loss was Vzfw Paul Groll of Jasta 40.

CARLIN Sydney Captain 74

Sydney Carlin, a Yorkshireman born in 1889, worked as a farmer near Hull before the war. Joining the Royal Engineers, he was awarded a DCM on 5 August 1915, and was later commissioned. In 1916 while under fire he laid out a fire trench, brought up his section, dug the trench and held it with his men against counter attacks. He was seriously wounded during this encounter, losing a leg, and was awarded an MC, gazetted on 20 October 1916. On recovering, he transferred to the RFC, where he was known as 'Timbertoes' due to his wooden leg, and became an instructor at CFS, before joining 74 Squadron on 26 May 1918 to fly SE 5As. On 31 May, having returned to France with this unit, he suffered an engine failure while in combat and crashed, but was unhurt, claiming his first victim a couple of weeks later. He then concentrated on hunting balloons, and by early August had destroyed four of these and two aircraft, for which he was awarded a DFC. He remained in combat throughout the summer, bringing his score to ten. He narrowly escaped death again in early September when he collided in the air with his commanding officer, Keith Caldwell, though both managed to land their damaged aircraft safely. Carlin was shot down in D6958 on 21 September by Uffz Westphal of Jasta 29 as the latter's second victory, and was taken prisoner. Between 1919 and 1939, Carlin farmed in Kenya. On the outbreak of World War II he returned to the United Kingdom and enlisted. He was only allowed to become an air gunner this time, flying mainly in a 264 Squadron Defiant night fighter. However he managed to get several trips as rear gunner in a bomber flown by Sqn Ldr Percy Pickard of *No Moon Tonight* fame, who he had known in Kenya; they flew together in a Wellington of 311 (Czech) Squadron. Carlin, now with 151 Squadron, was killed during a surprise air attack on his airfield on 9 May 1941, at which time he was 48 years old.

	1918		SE 5A					
1	13 Jun	DFW. C	C6459	74	S E Zillebeke Lake	1015	DES	CR/RAF 13.6
2	18 Jun	Pfalz DIII	C6459	74	S W Zillebeke Lake	0810	OOC	CR/11 WS
3	19 Jul	Balloon	D6922	74	Nieppe Village	0915	DES	CR/RAF 19.7
4	20 Jul	Balloon	D6922	74	2m S W Armentieres	0830	DES	CR/RAF 20.7
5	28 Jul	Balloon	D6922	74	S Armentieres	0540	DES	CR/RAF 28.7
6	30 Jul	Fokker DVII	D6922	74	E Dickebusch Lake	1805	DES	CR/RAF 30.7
7	2 Aug	Balloon	D6922	74	Erquinghem	0600	DES	CR/RAF 2.8
8	10 Aug	Fokker DVII	----	74	E Messines	1905	DES	CR/RAF 10.8
9	4 Sep	Balloon	D6091	74	N E Armentieres	0745	DES	CR/RAF 4.9
10	15 Sep	Fokker DVII	----	74	N E Lille	1850	DES(F)	CR/RAF 15.9

TOTAL: 5 balloons, 4 destroyed, 1 out of control = 10.

CARPENTER Peter Captain 45, 66

This very successful Camel pilot claimed 23 victories. After completing his training he was posted to 45 Squadron in the summer of 1917, making his first claim on 20 September. Moving to the Italian front at the end of the year with his unit, he was posted as a flight commander to 66 Squadron at the end of January 1918, becoming that unit's most successful pilot. He was awarded a DSO, MC and Bar, together with the Italian Bronze Medal for Military Valour. On 30 March he was involved in a fight which resulted in Alan Jerrard being awarded the Victoria Cross — on Carpenter's and Eycott-Martin's report. Carpenter claimed one of the six Albatros scouts that were reported shot down in this action. Only three were in fact damaged, the account of this fight simply not matching the Austro-Hungarian records.

	1917		Camel					
1	20 Sep	Alb. DV	B2314	45	E Ypres	1200	OOC	CR/RFC 20.9
2	21 Oct	Alb. DV	—	45	Lille	0945	DES(F)	CR/RFC 21.10
3s*	31 Oct	Alb. C	----	45	E Quesnoy	1030	DES	CR/RFC 31.10
4	8 Nov	Alb. C	----	45	S Passchendaele	1025	DES	CR/RFC 8.11
5	15 Nov	Rumpler C	B5782	45	N E Houthoulst Wood	0910	DES	CR/RFC 15.11
	1918							
6	10 Jan	Alb. DIII	B3929	45	Ceggia-Staffolo	1025	DES	ORB/7 Bg
7	15 Jan	Alb. DIII	B3929	45	Vazzolo	1030	DES	ORB/7 BG
8	26 Jan	Alb. DIII	B3929	45	Novesta	1335	DES	ORB/7 Bg
9	27 Feb	Alb. DIII	B6424	66	St Dona di Piave	1205	DES	ORB/SR/7 Bg
10	11 Mar	Berg DI	B2500	66	N Valstagna	1140	DES(F)	ORB/SR/7 Bg
11	21 Mar	Berg DI	B7383	66	Ghirano	1240	DES	ORB/SR/7 Bg
12	21 Mar	Berg DI	B7383	66	Cimadolmo	1240	OOC	ORB/SR/7 Bg
13	30 Mar	Alb. DIII	B7387	66	3m S Mansue	1140	DES	ORB/SR/7 Bg
14	11 Apr	C	B7387	66	Arcade	1130	OOC	ORB/SR/14 W
15	17 Apr	Alb. DV	B7387	66	Borgo	0940	DES	ORB/SR/14 W
16	31 May	Alb. DV	B7387	66	W Feltre	0650	DES	ORB/SR/14 W

17	9 Jun	Alb. DV	B7387	66	S Sebastiano	0710	DES(F)	ORB/SR/14 W
18	10 Jun	LVG. C	B7387	66	N E Feltre	1420	DES	ORB/SR/14 W
19	15 Jun	LVG. C	B7387	66	S Feltre	0550	OOC	ORB/SR/14 W
20	15 Jun	Alb. DV	B7387	66	Feltre	0820	DES	ORB/SR/14 W
21	14 Jul	Alb. DIII	B7387	66	W Feltre	0820	DES	ORB/SR/14 W
22	31 Aug	Alb. DV	E1489	66	W Staffolo	1020	DES	ORB/SR/14 W
23s**	8 Oct	Alb. C	C3290	66	S W Vadeo	1120	DES	ORB/SR/14 W
24	25 Oct	Alb. DV	E1489	66	Feltre	0955	OOC	ORB/SR/14 W

TOTAL: 15 and 2 shared destroyed, 7 out of control = 24.
*Shared with Lt J.C.B. Firth B6354. **Shared with Lt H.K. Goode E7211.

CARTER Albert Desbrisay Major 19

A Canadian from Pointe de Bute, New Brunswick, Carter was a professional soldier who was commissioned in March 1911. He served in the Infantry, becoming a Major during February 1916, but he was wounded in action. On recovery he transferred to the RFC, qualifying as a pilot in summer 1917. For four months he was engaged on coastal patrol duties and then, in autumn was posted to France where he flew Spad S VIIs and S XIIIs with 19 Squadron. His victories at once began to mount rapidly, and he became a flight commander on 4 November. The award of a DSO was made on 2 January 1918. The squadron then converted to the new Sopwith Dolphin, and with these he proved just as successful, claiming 14 further victories by 16 May. He was awarded a Bar to his DSO, but on 19 May was shot down behind German lines in Dolphin C4017 by Leutnant Paul Billik of Jasta 52, and became a prisoner of war. Billik shot down at least four Commonwealth aces, 'Nick' Carter being his 16th victim. After the conclusion of hostilities, Carter returned to the United Kingdom, but was killed early in 1919 when a Fokker DVII which he was test flying broke up in the air.

	1918		Spad					
1	31 Oct	C	B3498	19	Becelaere-Gheluvelt	1020	OOC	CR/RFC 31.10
2	31 Oct	Alb. DV	B3498	19	Becelaere-Gheluvelt	1340	DES	CR/RFC 31.10
3	8 Nov	C	B3498	19	S Gheluvelt	0925	DES	CR/RFC 8.11
4	9 Nov	C	B3498	19	Moorslede	1100	OOC	CR/11 WS/WD
5s*	13 Nov	Alb. DV	B3498	19	N Comines	1445	DES	CR/RFC 13.11
6s**	15 Nov	C	A8834	19	Zandvoorde	1015	DES	CR/RFC 15.11
7s***	18 Nov	Alb. C	A8834	19	S Passchendaele	1045	OOC	CR/RFC 18.11
8	23 Nov	Alb. DV	A8834	19	Westroosebeke-Moorslede	1025	OOC	CR/RFC 23.11
9	15 Dec	C	A8834	19	Comines	0950	DES(F)	CR/RFC 15.12
10	18 Dec	Pfalz DIII	A8834	19	Gheluwe	1500	OOC	CR/RFC 18.12
11	18 Dec	Alb. DV	A8834	19	Gheluwe-Moorslede	1530	OOC	CR/RFC 18.12
12	19 Dec	Alb. DV	A8834	19	Hollebeke	1545	OOC	CR/RFC 20.12
13s†	22 Dec	Alb. DV	A8834	19	S Quesnoy	1420	DES(F)	ORB/WD 22.12
14	28 Dec	Alb. DV	A8834	19	N W Houthoulst Wood	1005	OOC	ORB/RFC 28.12
15	29 Dec	Alb. DV	A8834	19	Houthoulst Wood	1015	OOC	ORB/RFC 29.12
	1918		Dolphin					
16	15 Mar	Pfalz DIII	C4017	19	S Halluin	1115	OOC	CR/RFC 15.3
17	15 Mar	Pfalz DIII	C4017	19	S Halluin	1130	DES	CR/RFC 15.3
18	17 Mar	Alb. DV	C4017	19	Oostnieuwkerke	1235	DES	CR/RFC 17.3
19s††	24 Mar	C	C4017	19	W Roulers	1040	OOC	ORB/RFC 24.3
20	10 Apr	C	C4017	19	Neuve Chapelle	1015	DES	ORB/RAF 10.4
21	21 Apr	Pfalz DIII	C4017	19	Steenwerck	1915	OOC	CR/RAF 21.4
22	23 Apr	Pfalz DIII	C4017	19	N La Bassee	1820	DES	ORB/RAF 23.4
23s†††	23 Apr	Pfalz DIII	C4017	19	N La Bassee	1820	DES	ORB/RAF 23.4
24	23 Apr	Pfalz DIII	C4017	19	N La Bassee	1820	DES	ORB/SR/?
25	2 May	Fokker DrI	C4017	19	S Armentieres	1745	OOC	ORB/RAF 2.5
26s†††	8 May	Alb. DV	C4017	19	S E Bailleul	1020	DES	CR/RFC 8.5
27	15 May	Fokker DrI	C4132	19	Quesnoy	1825	DES	CR/RAF 15.5
28	15 May	Fokker DVII	C4132	19	Wervicq	1825	OOC	CR/RAF 15.5
29s‡	16 May	C	C4132	19	Bucquoy	1110	DES(F)	CR/RAF 16.5

TOTAL: 9 and 6 shared destroyed, 12 and 2 shared out of control = 29.
*Shared with Lt J.G.S. Candy B6760. **Shared with 2/Lt E. Olivier A6784. ***Shared with 2/Lt E. Olivier A6784, Lt A. Reid-Walker B6817. †Shared with Capt O.C. Bryson A6780, 2/Lt E.J. Blyth B3563, 2/Lt E. Oliver A6784, Lt A.B. Fairclough A6802, Capt G.W. Taylor A6805, 2/Lt H.E. Galer A8836. ††Shared with Lt G.B. Irving C3838. †††Shared with Lt G.B. Irving C3799. ‡Shared with Lt J.D. Hardman C3818.

CARTER Alfred William Major 3W, 3(N), 10(N), 210

Born in Calgary, Alberta, on 29 April 1894, this Canadian joined the RNAS in May 1916 and in November was a pilot with No 3 Wing. In March 1917 he was posted to 3 Naval Squadron, claiming five victories whilst flying Sopwith Pups with this unit before being posted again, this time to 10 Naval Squadron as a flight commander in July 1917. Here he brought his score to eight and was awarded a DSC, but was posted to Home Establishment after only a month with the unit. In February 1918 he returned to 210 Squadron, RAF, as it would become in April, and raised his total to 16 by 11 June, when he was injured in a crash. Back in England he became an instructor, but returned once again to France to command the unit at the end of October. On 10 November he led the squadron in a strafing attack on an enemy landing ground which resulted in two LVGs being destroyed. 'Nick' Carter remained in the RAF after the war, rising to the rank of Air Marshal; he received an OBE and MBE and retired in 1953, but died in Canada on 17 December 1986.

	1917		Pup					
1	6 Apr	Halb. DIII	N6160	3N	Bourlon Wood	1020	OOC	CR/RFC 6.4
2	23 Apr	Alb. DIII	N6179	3N	Epinoy	1730	DES	CR/RFC 23.4
3	23 Apr	Alb. DIII	N6179	3N	Epinoy	1800	OOC	CR/RFC 23.4
4	29 Apr	Alb. DIII	N6179	3N	S E Cambrai	1115	OOC	CR/DRO/DL
5	27 May	Alb. DIII	N6474	3N	E Bullecourt	0740	OOC	CR/RFC 27.5
			Triplane					
6	17 Jul	Alb. DV	N6302	10N	Roulers	2000	OOC	CR/RFC 17.7
7	23 Jul	Alb. DV	N6302	10N	Houthoulst Forest	2025	OOC	CR/RFC WD
8	24 Jul	Alb. DV	N6302	10N	Langemarck	1230	OOC	CR/RFC 24.7
9	27 Jul	Alb. DV	N6302	10N	W Tourcoing	1930	OOC	CR/RFC 27.7
	1918		Camel					
10	19 Feb	Alb. DV	B7202	10N	S Zillebeke Lake	1150	DES(F)	CR/ORB/
11	10 Apr	LVG. C	B6228	210	Neuf Berquin	1245	CAPT	CR/RAF 10.4
12	12 Apr	Balloon	----	210	----	----	DES	Bg Summ/?
13	8 May	Alb. DV	D3364	210	Armentieres	1055	OOC	CR/?
14s*	9 May	Rumpler C	D3364	210	Bailleul	1145	OOC	CR/RAF 9.5
15s**	9 May	Alb. C	D3364	210	1m N Aubers	1615	DES	CR/RAF 9.5
16	31 May	Fokker DrI	D3399	210	2m S Estaires	1130	DES	CR/RAF 26.5
17	5 Jun	Fokker DrI	D3399	210	2m E Bailleul	1010	DES	CR/RFC 5.6

TOTAL: 1 balloon, 5 and 1 shared destroyed, 9 and 1 shared out of control = 17.
*Shared with Capt E.S. Arnold B7227, Lt S.C. Joseph B6228. **Shared with Capt E.S. Arnold B6242, Lt F.V. Hall C62.

CASEY Francis Dominic Flight Commander 2W, 3(N)

Born on 3 August 1890, this Irishman joined the RNAS in 1916 and served with No 2 Wing as an observer. He was posted to 3 Naval Squadron after training as a pilot, serving with this unit during the first half of 1917, becoming a flight commander and receiving the DSC for nine victories. He was very keen on stunting, and on 11 August, immediately after a return from leave, took off for a test flight. He began to spin, but failed to recover in time and crashed, receiving fatal injuries.

	1917		Pup					
1	17 Mar	Halb. DII	N6163	3N	N E Bapaume	1040	OOC	CR/RFC 17.3
2	8 Apr	Alb. DIII	N6182	3N	N E Pronville	1500	OOC	CR/RFC 8.4
3	21 Apr	Alb. DIII	N6182	3N	Hendecourt	1730	DES	CR/RFC 21.4
4	21 Apr	Alb. DIII	N6182	3N	Hendecourt	1730	OOC	CR/RFC 21.4
5	23 Apr	Alb. DIII	N6182	3N	Cagnicourt	1730	OOC	CR/RFC 24.4
6s*	24 Apr	DFW. C	N6182	3N	Morchies-Louverval	1650	CAPT	CR/RFC 24.4
7	26 Apr	Alb. DIII	N6182	3N	Cambrai	1915	OOC	CR/RFC 27.4
8	29 Apr	Alb. DIII	N6182	3N	Bantouzelle-Cambrai	1100	DES(F)	CR/RFC 29.4
9	2 May	Alb. DIII	N6182	3N	Moevres	1120	OOC	CR/ORB/DL

TOTAL: 1 shared captured, 2 destroyed, 6 out of control = 9.
*Shared with FSL J.J. Malone N6208, F/Lt Travers N6169. This was Uffz M. Haase POW/Lt K. Kelm POW FA 26.

CATTO Charles Gray Lieutenant 45

An American, Catto was born in Dallas, Texas, on 7 November 1896, but was a medical student at Edinburgh University in Scotland in 1914. He tried to enlist, but his parents refused permission and he was only allowed to complete his education provided that he did not then join the Army; he therefore joined the RFC in June 1917! After training he went to Italy to join 45 Squadron in March 1918. Flying Camels, he claimed five enemy machines, one of which — a Brandenburg two-seater — fell inside Allied lines. This machine came from Flik 8D, and was flown by Flugsfuhrer Alois Gnamusch and Leutnant Rudolf Huss. After the war Catto returned to Edinburgh University to complete his studies, and then to the US where he became a doctor in his native Texas; he died on 24 June 1972.

	1918		Camel					
1s*	19 May	Aviatik C	B6412	45	Mel	0625	DES(F)	CR/14 W
2s**	22 May	C	B6372	45	Levada	0920	DES	CR/14 W
3***	7 Jun	Brand C	B3872	45	Cismon	0935	CAPT	CR/14
4	15 Jun	Aviatik C	D9392	45	Mt Campo-Poselaro	0745	OOC	CR/14 W
5	20 Jun	Alb. DIII	D9392	45	Nerversa	1040	OOC	ORB/14 W
6	5 Aug	D	D8243	45	Mt Grappa	1030	DES	ORB/14 W

TOTAL: 1 captured, 1 and 2 shared destroyed, 2 out of control = 6.
*Shared with Capt N.C. Jones B6372. **Shared with Capt G. Bush B3867. ***Flgr A. Gramusch/Lt R. Huss of Flik 80.

CHADWICK Arnold Jaques Flight Commander 5W, 4(N)

A Canadian, born on 23 August 1895, Chadwick flew Sopwith 1½ Strutters with No 5 Naval Wing on bombing raids early in 1916, until shot down while bombing Zeppelin sheds on 2 October. He evaded capture and got into Holland; following repatriation, he joined 4(N) Squadron in April 1917, becoming a flight commander in July. Having claimed 11 victories, including one on 25 June, claimed when single-handed he attacked a formation of nine, he was obliged to ditch Camel N6369 off La Panne at 1610 hours on 28 July. He was not rescued, and drowned; the award of a DSC was gazetted the following month.

	1917		Pup					
1	26 Apr	Alb. DII	N9899	4N	Steenbrugh	1530	OOC	CR/RNAS 26.4
2	25 May	Alb.C	N6176	4N	10m off Bray Dunes	0535	DES	CR/DRO/DL
3s*	25 May	Gotha	N6176	4N	15m N Westende	1830	DES	CR/DRO/DL
4s**	26 May	C	N6176	4N	S W Furnes	0845	DES	CR/DRO/DL
5	3 Jun	Alb. DV	N6176	4N	Cortemarck	1640	DES	CR/DRO/DL
			Camel					
6	25 Jun	Alb. C	N6345	4N	Roulers	1030	DES(F)	CR/DRO/DL
7	3 Jul	C	N6370	4N	Ghistelles	1800	OOC	CR/RNAS 3.7
8s***	6 Jul	Alb. C	N6370	4N	S W Ghistelles	1440	DES	CR/RNAS 6.7
9	10 Jul	Alb. DV	N6369	4N	Ghistelles	1950	OOC	CR/RNAS 10.7
10s†	10 Jul	Alb. DV	N6369	4N	Ghistelles	1955	OOC	CR/RNAS 10.7
11††	25 Jul	Seaplane	N6369	4N	30m N N E Ostend	1930	DES	CR/RNAS 25.7

TOTAL: 3 and 4 shared destroyed, 3 and 1 shared out of control = 11.
*Shared with F/Lt G.H.T. Rouse N6198, FSL L.F.W. Smith N6168, FSL E.W. Busby N5196. **Shared with FSL A.J. Enstone B6187. ***Shared with FSL S.E. Ellis N6337. †Shared with FSL R. Kierstead N6362. ††Shared with FSL A.J. Enstone B3841, FSL R. Kierstead N6370.

CHANDLER Robert North Lieutenant 73

A Londoner, 'Chubby' Chandler joined 73 Squadron on 18 December 1917 and flew Camels until September 1918. He claimed seven victories with the unit as well as taking part in many ground attack sorties, and was awarded a DFC, gazetted on 9 February 1919. He subsequently emigrated to Canada where he joined the RCAF in 1940; he retired in 1946 as a Wing Commander.

	1918		Camel					
1	24 Mar	Alb. DV	B9261	73	Vraignes	1045	OOC	CR/RFC 24.3
2	11 Apr	Alb. DV	D1800	73	5m S E Villers Brettoneaux	1910	OOC	CR/RAF 11.4
3	11 Jun	Fokker DVII	D1922	73	E Bus	1600	DES	CR/RAF 11.6
4s*	21 Jul	Fokker DrI	C8296	73	N E Oulchy le Chateau	2000	DES	CR/RAF 21.7
5	22 Jul	Fokker DVII	B7867	73	Bazoches	1810	DES	CR/?
6	29 Jul	Fokker DVII	D1922	73	N E Soissons	1945	DES	CR/RAF 29.7
7s**	8 Aug	C	D1922	73	Nesle	1720	DES	CR/RAF 8.8

TOTAL: 3 and 2 shared destroyed, 2 out of control = 7.
*Shared with Major R.H. Freeman, Capt M. Smith, Lt G.L. Graham, Lt W.S. Stephenson, 2/Lt K.S. Laurie, Lt W. Sidebottom, Lt J. Balfour, Lt W.G. Peters. **Shared with Lt G.L. Graham, Lt E.J. Lussier B2525.

CHAPMAN Charles Meredith Bouverie Major 24, 29

Born on 9 January 1887, he was commissioned in the East Kent Regiment in January 1913. He transferred to the RFC on 1 July 1915 and the following year was a pilot with 24 Squadron, flying DH 2s in France. With these he claimed at least three enemy aircraft and was awarded an MC. In 1917 he was promoted to Captain and became a flight commander, in 29 Squadron, flying Nieuport Scouts; he took command of this unit in July. Adding a further four victories to his score, he was made a Chevalier of the Order of Leopold by the Belgian Government. One of his victories was over an Albatros DIII flown by Leutnant Georg Simon of Jasta 11, who landed inside Allied lines to become a prisoner. On 1 October 1917, 29 Squadron's airfield at Poperinghe was bombed, Chapman being hit by fragments and dying of the wounds received. His brother, Lieutenant W.W. Chapman, an observer in 22 Squadron, was shot down and killed on the day following Charles' funeral.

	1916		DH 2					
1	22 Jun	LVG. C	6016	24	Courcelles	1915	DES	CR/4 BG WD
2	14 Jul	Fokker E	5992	24	Beaulencourt	1940	DES	CR/4 BG WD
3	20 Jul	Fokker E	5924	24	High Wood	2045	DES(F)	CR/RFC 20.7
	1917		Nieuport					
4	11 May	Alb. DIII	B1517	29	Biache	1040	OOC	CR/RFC 11.5
5*	4 Jun	Alb. DIII	B1517	29	Fontaine-les Croisilles	1820	CAPT	CR/RFC 4.6
6	27 Jun	Alb. DIII	B3452	29	Croisilles-Pronville	1850	OOC	CR/RFC 27.6
7	17 Sep	Alb. DIII	B3485	29	3m E Staden	0820	OOC	CR/RFC 17.9

TOTAL: 1 captured, 3 destroyed, 3 out of control = 7.
*Lt Georg Simon of Jasta 11 POW.

CHAPPELL Roy Williamson Captain 27, 41

Born on 31 December 1896, he joined a South African cavalry regiment in December 1915, and served in the German South West Africa campaign. Chappell came to England in 1916, attending the Inns of Court OTC and being commissioned in the RFC. After training on Farmans and Martinsydes he was posted to France and to 27 Squadron in September, flying G.100 Elephants in action. He flew many bombing sorties and claimed at least two victories before returning to England in May 1917 to become an instructor at the CFS. In October he joined 41 Squadron as a flight commander, and while with this unit was awarded an MC, bringing his score to 11. In July 1918 he again returned to Home Establishment, serving at Turnberry. During 1919 he flew with 24 Squadron before going to 84 Squadron in Iraq in 1922. He became a test pilot at Henlow in 1924, and from 1925 to 1928 was Language Officer at the British Embassy in Tokyo. Later, in 1930, he was an instructor in air fighting with the Japanese Navy. Promoted Squadron Leader, he served in Palestine before returning to Tokyo in 1934 as Air Attache with the rank of Wing Commander. Promoted to Group Captain in 1938, he finally retired from the RAF in 1946 with the rank of Air Commodore, settling in Sussex.

	1916		Martinsyde					
1	27 Sep	D	----	27	----	----	OOC	RFC 27.9
	1917							
2s*	17 Mar	C	A1573	27	N Havrincourt Wood	1320	OOC	CR/RFC 17.3
	1918		SE 5A					
3	2 Feb	Alb. DV	B663	41	Erchin	1430	DES	CR/RFC 2.2
4	2 Feb	Alb. DV	B663	41	Erchin	1430	OOC	CR/RFC 2.2
5	6 Mar	Pfalz DIII	B624	41	Niergnies	1000	OOC	CR/RFC 6.3
6	16 Mar	LVG. C	B624	41	Brebieres	1145	DES(F)	CR/RFC 16.3
7	23 Mar	Alb. DV	B624	41	Bourlon Wood	1130	OOC	CR/RFC 23.3
8	24 Mar	Fokker DrI	B624	41	Sailly	1455	OOC	CR/RFC 24.3
9	24 Mar	Fokker DrI	B624	41	Havrincourt	1500	OOC	CR/RFC 24.3
10	25 Mar	Alb. DV	B624	41	Sailly	1040	DES	CR/RFC 25.3
11	16 May	C	C5436	41	S E Arras	0750	OOC	CR/RFC 16.5

TOTAL: 3 destroyed, 7 and 1 shared out of control = 11.
*Shared with Lt W.S. Canter 7499.

CHICK John Stanley Captain 11

Flying with 11 Squadron from November 1917, Johnny Chick claimed his first victory on the first day of 1918. On 12 March he and his observer, Lieutenant P. Douglas, claimed five enemy scouts out of control during a single engagement. On 15 May he and Lieutenant E.C. Gilroy claimed four victories in two patrols. By that date he had brought his score to 16, been awarded an MC, and had become a flight commander. After the war he remained in the RAF, serving with 20 Squadron during the early 1920s; he later flew in the RAF Aerobatic Teams of 1923, 1929 and 1930. By 1934 he was a Squadron Leader commanding the Cambridge University Air Squadron at Duxford, and in 1939 became Wing Commander with the Air Force Cross. In 1942 he took command of Luqa airfield, Malta, during the siege of that island. He died on 21 January 1960.

	1918		Bristol					
1*	1 Jan	Alb. DV	C4846	11	Crevecoeur	1330	OOC	CR/RFC 1.1
2**	28 Jan	DFW. C	----	11	N Bourlon Wood	1315	OOC	CR/RFC 28.1
3***	12 Mar	C	C4847	11	S Cambrai	1115	OOC	CR/RFC 12.3
4***	12 Mar	Fokker DrI	C4847	11	Caudry	1145	OOC	CR/RFC 12.3
5***	12 Mar	Fokker DrI	C4847	11	Caudry	1150	OOC	CR/RFC 12.3
6***	12 Mar	Fokker DrI	C4847	11	Caudry	1155	OOC	CR/RFC 12.3
7***	12 Mar	Fokker DrI	C4847	11	Caudry	1155	OOC	CR/RFC 12.3
8***	13 Mar	Alb. DV	C4847	11	S Cambrai	1345	OOC	CR/RFC 13.3
9***	15 Mar	Alb. DV	A7153	11	Rumilly	1115	DES(F)	CR/RFC 15.3
10***	15 Mar	Alb. DV	A7153	11	Rumilly	1115	OOC	CR/RFC 15.3
11†	9 May	Pfalz DIII	C4845	11	S Albert	1220	OOC	CR/RAF 9.5
12†	9 May	Pfalz DIII	C4845	11	S Albert	1220	OOC	CR/RAF 9.5
13†	15 May	C	C797	11	Brebieres	0600	DES(F)	CR/RAF 15.5
14†	15 May	Fokker DrI	C797	11	S E Albert	1720	DES	CR/RFC 15.5
15†	15 May	Pfalz DIII	C797	11	S E Albert	1721	DES	CR/RAF 15.5
16†	15 May	Fokker DrI	C797	11	S E Albert	1722	OOC	CR/RAF 15.5

TOTAL: 4 destroyed, 12 out of control = 16.

*Observer: Lt H.R. Kinkead. **Observer: Capt R.M. Makepeace; Makepeace was a pilot in 20 Sqn. ***Observer: Lt P. Douglas. †Observer: Lt E.C. Gilroy.

CHIDLAW-ROBERTS Robert Leslie Captain 2, 18, 60, 40

Born in May 1896, he joined the RFC from Sandhurst in May 1915 and became an observer with 2 Squadron, flying with this unit for six months on the Western Front. He then trained as a pilot and joined 18 Squadron, completing eight months of operations, mainly at night, before being posted to 60 Squadron to fly SE 5As in August 1917. On 16 September 1917 he shot down Leutnant Alfred Bauer of Jasta 17, and on 23 September was involved in the last heroic fight of Werner Voss; in fact Voss put several bullets into Chidlaw's rudder before 56 Squadron came to the rescue. He was later promoted to Captain, awarded an MC, and on 9 January 1918 he shared in shooting down Leutnant Max Muller, the 36 victory ace and commander of Jasta 'Boelcke'. Posted home for a rest in January, he served with 28 Training Squadron before returning to France to take command of 'A' Flight, 40 Squadron in summer 1918. He shared in the destruction of a German kite balloon, bringing his score to ten. He was one of the very few pilots to fly operationally in every year of the war from 1915 to 1918. In 1919 he served in Russia. He died on 1 June 1989.

	1917		SE 5A					
1	14 Sep	Alb. DV	B4864	60	E Menin	1645	OOC	CR/C&C VII N4
2*	16 Sep	Alb. DIII	A8932	60	S Houthem	1830	DES(F)	CR/RFC 16.9
3s**	21 Sep	Alb. DV	A8932	60	Langemarck	1815	DES	CR/RFC 21.9
4s**	21 Sep	C	A8932	60	Langemarck	1816	DES	CR/RFC 21.9
5s***	22 Sep	Alb. DV	A8932	60	S E Zonnebeke	1045	OOC	CR/RFC 22.9
6s†	18 Nov	DFW. C	B536	60	N E Westrosebeke	1105	DES	CR/RFC 18.11
7	23 Nov	Alb. DV	B536	60	W Dadizeele	1010	DES	CR/RFC 23.11
	1918							
8s††	3 Jan	C	C5311	60	Comines-Menin	1240	DES(F)	CR/RFC 3.1
9s†††	9 Jan	Alb. DV	B626	60	Moorslede	1145	DES(F)	CR/RFC 9.1
10s‡	29 Sep	Balloon	E4086	40	N E Cambrai	1340	DES	CR/?

TOTAL: 1 shared balloon, 2 and 5 shared destroyed, 1 and 1 shared out of control = 10.

*3 claims, 1 loss; Lt A. Bauer KIA of Jasta 17. **Shared with Lt I.O. Whiting B4864. ***Shared with Capt H.A. Hammersley B539. †Shared with Capt H.A. Hammersley B4867. ††Shared with 2/Lt C.F. Cunningham B626. †††Shared with Capt F.O. Soden C5332, and Capt G. Zimmer/2/Lt H. Somerville of 21 Sqn in an RE 8. Lt Max Muller, the 36 victory commander of Jasta Boelcke, jumped out and was killed. ‡Shared with 2/Lt G.S. Smith E3946, Lt Field E4037.

CHILD James E Lieutenant 45

Jimmy Child joined 45 Squadron in France in the late summer of 1917 and went to Italy with the unit in November. Flying Camels, he claimed five victories. On 10 March 1918 while on patrol, the formation in which he was flying was attacked in error by several Italian scouts, and in the brief engagement which followed he may have shot one down.

	1917		Camel					
1	11 Sep	Alb. DIII	----	45	E Ypres	1200	OOC	CR/RFC 11.9
2s	27 Oct	Alb. DV	----	45	N E Comines	1015	DES	CR/ORB/FRC 11.9
3	8 Nov	Junkers J1	----	45	Westroosebeke	1025	DES	CR/RFC 8.11
	1918							
4	22 Feb	Alb. DIII	B2443	45	Salgareda	1300	DES(F)	CR/7 BG
5	7 Jul	LVG. C	C1975	45	Val d'Assa	c0900	DES	CR/14W

TOTAL: 3 and 1 shared destroyed, 1 out of control = 5.

*Shared with Lt M.B. Frew, 2/Lt R.J. Brownell.

CHILD James Martin Captain 4, 19, 84

Born in Leytonstone, North London, on 20 October 1893, Child was resident in Canada at the outbreak of war. Returning home, he joined the army, but in 1916 transferred to the RFC from the Manchester Regiment. After pilot training he went to France with 4 Squadron, later joining 19 Squadron in July 1916. Initially he flew BE 12s with this unit, and later Spads. During May 1917 he was promoted to Captain and received a Mention in Despatches. After a rest from operations, he joined 84 Squadron as a flight commander, and by the end of the year had raised his score to eight, receiving an MC. With the commanding officer and other flight commanders, he had undertaken the difficult and costly task of 'blooding' a new and untried unit, laying the framework for the success which 84 Squadron would achieve in 1918. From the Belgian authorities Child received the Order of Leopold and the Croix de Guerre. In February 1918 he returned to England as an instructor. He was posted to Canada, but was killed there on 23 August 1918 whilst trying to rescue a fellow airman from an aeroplane accident.

	1917		Spad					
1	23 Apr	Alb. C	B1537	19	N W Douai	1520	DES	CR/RFC 23.4
2	25 May	Alb. DIII	B1537	19	W Douai	0645	OOC	CR/RFC 25.5
3	7 Jun	DFW. C	B3502	19	S W Menin	0915	DES	CR/RFC 7.6
			SE 5A					
4	21 Oct	Alb. DIII	B562	84	Gheluvelt	0825	OOC	CR/RFC 21.10
5s*	8 Nov	Alb. DV	B562	84	E Poelcapelle	1415	OOC	CR/RFC 8.11
6	22 Nov	Alb. DV	B562	84	N E Bourlon Wood	1145	DES	CR/RFC 22.11
7**	22 Nov	DFW. C	B562	84	Flesquires	1150	CAPT	CR/RFC 22.11
8	30 Nov	Alb. DV	B562	84	Malincourt	1230	DES	CR/RFC 30.11

TOTAL: 1 captured, 4 destroyed, 3 out of control = 8.
*Shared with Lt F.E. Brown. **Flgr Elser/Lt Steiner of FAA 269.

CHISAM William Hargrove Flight Lieutenant 3(N)

Born in 15 November 1894 in Carlisle, he joined the RNAS as a Flight Sub Lieutenant with effect from 3 January 1916. After flying in England on Home Defence sorties from Walmer, he was posted to Dunkirk and then to 3 Naval Squadon, serving with 'B' Flight from August 1917 until March 1918. He claimed seven victories before he was wounded in the hand during a fight on 26 March.

	1917		Camel					
1	3 Sep	Alb. DV	B3909	3N	Stelhilde	0730	OOC	CR/RNAS 3.9
2	11 Sep	Alb. DV	N6364	3N	Thorout	1100	OOC	CR/RNAS 11.9
	1918							
3s*	9 Mar	DFW. C	----	3N	Henin-Lietard	1120	DES(F)	CR/ORB/?
4	10 Mar	Alb. DV	B7223	3N	E Lens	1315	OOC	CR/RFC 10.3
5	16 Mar	Alb. C	B7222	3N	Hermies	1035	DES	CR/RFC 16.3
6s**	21 Mar	Alb. C	B7223	3N	4m E Bapaume	1645	DES(F)	CR/RFC 21.3
7	24 Mar	Alb. DV	B7223	3N	Beaumetz	1715	OOC	CR/RFC 24.3

TOTAL: 1 and 2 shared destroyed, 4 out of control = 7.
*Shared with FSL J.A. Glen B7185. **Shared with F/Cdr L.H. Rochford B7203, FSL O.P. Adam B3798, FSL K.D. Macleod B7222, FSL J.A. Glen B7185, FSL A.B. Ellwood B7229, FSL C.S. Devereux B7228. FSL L.A. Sands B7216, FSL R.C. Berly B7224, FSL E.T. Hayne B7231.

CLAPPISON Henry Gordon Captain 204

Harry Clappison, a Canadian from Hamilton, Ontario, was born on 1 October 1898. Joining the RAF, he was posted to 204 Squadron in August 1918 and from mid September to the end of the war claimed victories over six Fokker DVIIs, two of them claimed as destroyed and four out of control. He became a flight commander on 4 November. Later he served with the RCAF, and in 1946 received the OBE by which time he had reached the rank of Air Commodore.

	1918		Camel					
1	20 Sep	Fokker DVII	F3243	204	5m N E Dixmude	1025	DES(F)	CR/5 BG Comm
2	26 Sep	Fokker DVII	F3243	204	Blankenberghe	1045	OOC	CR/5 BG Comm
3	23 Oct	Fokker DVII	F3243	204	Termonde	1005	OOC	CR/Sq Vic List
4	27 Oct	Fokker DVII	B7860	204	Ghent	0910	DES	CR/RAF 27.10
5	30 Oct	Fokker DVII	D9600	204	Nazereth	1315	OOC	CR/Sq Vic List
6	1 Nov	Fokker DVII	D9596	204	Soffeghem	1315	OOC	CR/Sq Vic List

TOTAL: 2 destroyed, 4 out of control = 6.

CLARK A.G. Captain 2AFC

Born in August 1896 in Sydney, Clark joined the Australian Light Horse on the outbreak of war, later transferring to the AFC. Serving with 2AFC Squadron early in 1918, he claimed five victories by the spring, being promoted to flight commander early in April.

	1918		SE 5A					
1	21 Feb	Alb. DV	B4895	2AFC	Brebieres	1045	DES	CR/RFC 21.2
2	24 Mar	Alb. DV	B4895	2AFC	Vaulx-Bourlon Wood	1230	OOC	CR/RFC 24.3
3s*	2 Apr	C	D3429	2AFC	Amiens-Corbie	1730	DES	CR/RAF 2.4
4s**	6 Apr	C	D3429	2AFC	Lamotte	1500	DES	CR/RAF 6.4
5	12 Apr	Alb. DV	B4895	2AFC	Lorgies	1100	OOC	CR/RAF 12.4

TOTAL: 1 and 2 shared destroyed, 2 out of control = 5.
*Shared with Lt G.H. Blaxland B571. **Shared with Lt G.H. Blaxland, Lt L.J. Primrose, 2/Lt A.L. Paxton.

CLARK Cecil Christian Captain 1

From Norwich, Clark was born in 1898 and transferred to the RFC in 1916 after service with the Royal Field Artillery. He joined 1 Squadron on 1 February 1917 to fly Nieuport Scouts. After claiming three initial victories, his name disappeared from the squadron for about a year. In April 1918 he reappeared as a flight commander, now on SE 5As. During the spring of this year he claimed a further seven victories, including a balloon and a share in a Pfalz DIII on 21 April. On 8 May he was shot down north-east of Kemmell in B4890 by Leutnant Harry von Bülow of Jasta 36; he was wounded and taken prisoner.

	1917		Nieuport					
1	15 Mar	Alb. DII	----	1	Zandvoorde	1545	OOC	CR/RFC 15.3
2s*	17 Mar	Alb. DII	A6672	1	Courtrai-Menin	1045	OOC	CR/RFC 17.3
3	28 Mar	Halb. D	A6672	1	Lesquin	1045	OOC	CR/RFC 28.3
	1918		SE 5A					
4s**	21 Apr	Pfalz DIII	C1107	1	Lompret	1210	DES	CR/RAF 21.4
5	21 Apr	Balloon	B4810	1	Laventie	1710	DES	ORB/?
6	23 Apr	Fokker DrI	B4810	1	S Courtrai	1920	DES(F)	CR/RAF 23.4
7	25 Apr	Pfalz DIII	B4810	1	Houtham	1850	OOC	CR/RAF 25.4
8s***	29 Apr	Pfalz DIII	C1106	1	Kemmel-Wytschaete	0650	DES	RC/RAF 29.4
9	29 Apr	Alb. DV	C1106	1	Wytschaete	1145	OOC	CR/RAF 29.4
10	7 May	C	B4810	1	S Dickebusch	1645	DES	CR/ORB/AA

TOTAL: 1 balloon, 2 and 2 shared destroyed, 4 and 1 shared out of control = 10.
*Shared with Lt J.A. Slater A6624. **Shared with Lt K.C. Mills C5374. ***Shared with Lt P.J. Clayson C1095.

CLARKE Edward Denman Captain 45

Born on 21 May 1898, he was educated at Eton. During the war he flew with 45 Squadron, which he joined in 1917. After initially flying Sopwith 1½ Strutters, he converted to Camels, but he was shot down by ground fire on 26 October 1917 during the Battle of Passchendaele, and was wounded; he was awarded an MC. After the war he remained associated with aviation, and from 1937 to 1960 was Managing Director of Saunders-Roe, being made a CBE. He died on 5 September 1966.

	1917		Strutter					
*1	23 Aug	Alb. DV	A1048	45	Bellewarde Lake	0915	OOC	CR/?
			Camel					
2	3 Sep	Alb. DIII	B2327	45	Zandvoorde	1310	DES(F)	CR/RFC 3.9
3	14 Sep	Alb. DV	B2327	45	E Merckem	1424	OOC	CR/RFC 14.9
4	20 Sep	Alb. DV	B2327	45	Passchendaele	1120	DES	CR/RFC 20.9
5s	26 Sep	C	B2327	45	E Zillebeke	1650	DES	CR/RFC 26.9
6	20 Oct	Alb. DV	----	45	Kastelhoek	1240	OOC	CR/RFC 20.10

TOTAL: 3 destroyed, 3 out of control = 6.
*Observer: Lt G.A. Brooke.

CLAXTON William Gordon Captain 41

Born in Gladstone, Manitoba, on 1 June 1899, Claxton joined the RFC in Canada in 1917 and after training at Camp Borden, arrived in the United Kingdom late in the year. He showed early promise as an aerial marksman while at CFS, and in March 1918 was posted to France to join 41 Squadron. He soon gained the nickname of 'Dozy' for his impeturbability under fire, as he often returned with badly damaged machines. He had to force-land on 13 June, and was shot-up again on 16th and 27th of that month. He claimed his first victory in late May, and soon received a DFC, gazetted on 3 August, for three destroyed, three out of control and a balloon. His score rose very rapidly and by the end of June he had claimed 20 victories, including two on 27th, three on 28th, two on 29th and six on 30th — 13 in four days! After being on leave during July, he continued at the same pace throughout early August, being recommended for a DSO after his 31st victory, the award being gazetted on 2 November. He was promoted to flight commander, but on 17 August, after victories over 35 aircraft and two balloons, he and F.R. McCall, a fellow Canadian with a similar high score in the same squadron, were involved in a fight with a large number of German scouts; Claxton was wounded in the head, crashing in enemy lines. Skilful cranial surgery by a German doctor saved his life. He had been shot down by Leutnant Hans Gildmeister of Jasta 20. After the war Claxton returned to Canada where be became a financial journalist, writing for several papers including the *Toronto Evening Telegram* until his death on 28 September 1967.

	1918		SE 5A					
1	27 May	Fokker DrI	B38	41	E Estaires	1915	OOC	CR/SR
2	28 May	Pfalz DIII	B38	41	Oppy-Gavrelle	1145	OOC	CR/SR
3	28 May	Pfalz DIII	D3927	41	Estaires	1415	OOC	CR/SR
4	12 Jun	C	D6120	41	Caix	1345	OOC	CR/SR
5	13 Jun	DFW. C	D6120	41	Bois de Champien	0950	DES	CR/RAF 13.6
6	16 Jun	Fokker DVII	D6125	41	Grevillers	2010	DES	CR/SR
7	17 Jun	Balloon	C8879	41	Chuignes	0915	DES	CR/RAF 17.6
8	17 Jun	Pfalz DIII	C8879	41	E Combles	0945	DES	CR/RAF 17.6
9	27 Jun	Halb. C	D6120	41	Goyencourt	2015	DES	CR/RAF 27.6
10	27 Jun	Pfalz DIII	D6120	41	Bray	2040	OOC	CR/SR
11	28 Jun	Pfalz DIII	D6186	41	Bray-Peronne	2010	OOC	CR/SR
12	28 Jun	Pfalz DIII	D6186	41	Bray-Peronne	2010	OOC	CR/SR
13	28 Jun	Fokker DVII	D6186	41	W Peronne	2015	OOC	CR/SR
14	29 Jun	Pfalz DIII	D6186	41	S Maricourt	1915	DES	CR/RAF 29.6
15	29 Jun	Fokker DVII	D6186	41	Chaulnes	1940	OOC	CR/SR
16	30 Jun	Pfalz DIII	D6120	41	Bray	0815	DES(F)	CR/RAF 30.6
17	30 Jun	Alb. DV	D6120	41	E Maricourt	0820	DES	CR/RAF 30.6
18	30 Jun	Alb. DV	D6120	41	W Cappy	0845	DES	CR/RAF 30.6
19	30 Jun	Pfalz DIII	D6120	41	Caix	0845	OOC	CR/SR
20	30 Jun	Pfalz DIII	D6120	41	E Mametz Wood	1750	DES	CR/RAF 30.6
21	30 Jun	DFW. C	D6120	41	W Proyart	1830	DES(F)	CR/RAF 30.6
22	2 Jul	Alb. DV	D6125	41	Lamotte	2020	OOC	CR/SR
23	4 Jul	Fokker DrI	D6065	41	Proyart	1330	OOC	CR/SR
24	4 Jul	Pfalz DIII	D6065	41	E Harbonnieres	1400	DES	CR/RAF 4.7
25	5 Jul	Pfalz DXII	D6000	41	S Cappy	2015	DES	CR/RAF 5.7
26s*	30 Jul	Alb. C	F5910	41	Guillancourt	1240	DES	CR/RAF 30.7
27s**	31 Jul	Alb. C	E1309	41	Pozieres	1210	DES	CR/RAF 31.7
28	1 Aug	Alb. C	C1895	41	E Vignaucourt	0800	DES	CR/RAF 1.8
29	1 Aug	Hannover C	C1895	41	E Moreuil	0820	OOC	CR/SR
30	1 Aug	DFW. C	F5910	41	E Albert	2040	OOC	CR/SR
31	8 Aug	Fokker DVII	F5910	41	E Chuignes	1530	DES	CR/RAF 8.8
32	9 Aug	Balloon	F5910	41	N E Bray	0745	DES	CR/RAF 9.8
33	9 Aug	Fokker DVII	F5910	41	E Estrees	1625	DES(F)	CR/RAF 9.8
34	10 Aug	Fokker DVII	F5910	41	S Mametz	2015	DES	CR/RAF 10.8
35	11 Aug	Fokker DVII	D3921	41	Estrees	2030	DES	CR/SR
36	12 Aug	Fokker DVII	D5984	41	N Bayonvillers	0930	OOC	CR/SR
37	13 Aug	Halb. C	F5910	41	Cappy-Frise	0800	OOC	CR/SR

TOTAL: 2 balloons, 18 and 2 shared destroyed, 15 out of control = 37.
*Shared with Capt F.R. McCall E1289. **Shared with Capt F.R. McCall E1289.

CLAY Jnr. Henry Robinson 1st Lieutenant 43, 148 US

Henry Clay, a pilot of the USAS from Fort Worth, Texas, received his advanced training from the RFC as a member of the first detachment of US cadets to be sent to Oxford for this purpose. He was then posted for operational experience to the newly-formed RAF, flying Camels with 43 Squadron during the spring of 1918. In the summer he was posted to the similarly-equipped 148th Aero Squadron, USAS, which was serving under British control, as 'C' Flight commander. Here he brought his score to eight by October, but he was then assigned to command the 41st Aero Squadron, which was not to see action before the war ended. He received a DFC from the British and a US DSC, but died of influenza at Coblenz on 17 February 1919.

	1918		Camel					
1	18 Aug	Fokker DVII	D8180	148US	3m N Noyon	1555	DES	CR/RAF 18.8
2	21 Aug	Fokker DVII	D8180	148US	Velu-Beaumetz	1940	OOC	CR/?
3	25 Aug	Fokker DVII	D8180	148US	N Bapaume-Cambrai Rd.	1856	DES	CR/RAF 25.8
4s*	27 Aug	DFW. C	D8180	148US	Remy	1305	DES	CR/RAF 27.8

5	4 Sep	Fokker DVII	E1506	148US	Sains les Marquion	0710	DES	CR/RAF 4.9
6	4 Sep	Fokker DVII	E1506	148US	Marquion	0714	DES	CR/RAF 4.9
7	24 Sep	Fokker DVII	E1586	148US	Bourlon-Espinoy	0735	DES(F)	CR/US 133
8s**	27 Sep	Halb. C	E1580	148US	Fontaine-Notre-Dame	0955	DES	CR/RAF 27.9

TOTAL: 5 and 2 shared destroyed, 1 out of control = 8.
*Shared with 1/Lt T.L. Moore. **Shared with 1/Lt E.W. Springs E1550.

CLAYDON Arthur Captain 32

After coming to Europe in the Canadian Field Artillery, Claydon transferred to the RFC in 1917, and following training was posted to 32 Squadron. This unit was flying DH 5s at the time, and during November he claimed his first two victories. In January 1918 the squadron re-equipped with SE 5As, and he was promoted to flight commander during May. He was constantly in action during the spring and early summer, claiming six further victories. Claydon was reported missing on 8 July in C1089 over Carvin at 0840 hours; he was another victim of Leutnant Paul Billik of Jasta 52. The award of a DFC was gazetted after his death.

	1917		DH 5					
1s*	20 Nov	C	A9300	32	Passchendaele	0800	DES(F)	CR/ORB/11 WS
	1918		SE 5A					
2	8 May	Pfalz DIII	C1089	32	Dury-Vitry	0935	OOC	CR/RAF 8.5
3	8 May	Pfalz DIII	C1089	32	Vitry	1015	DES(F)	CR/RAF 8.5
4	28 May	Pfalz DIII	C1089	32	N W Armentieres	1845	OOC	CR/ORB/SR
5	12 Jun	Fokker DVII	C1089	32	Cuvilly	1630	DES	CR/RAF 12.6
6	13 Jun	Alb. DV	C1089	32	Couchy	0600	DES	CR/RAF 13.6
7	25 Jun	C	C1089	32	Fleurbaix-Laventie	1815	DES(F)	CR/RAF 25.6

TOTAL: 4 destroyed, 2 and 1 shared out of control = 7.
*Shared with Lt A.L. Cuffe B4924, 2/Lt W.A. Tyrrell B4916.

CLAYSON Percy Jack Captain 1

Born in Croydon in May 1896, he joined the RNAS on the outbreak of war and served in France for two and a half years from December 1914; he then transferred to the RFC. Joining 1 Squadron on the last day of October 1917, Clayson did not gain his first victory until three and a half months later, but his score then rose quickly. He was awarded an MC on 9 April 1918, and during May became a flight commander. On 9 June he saw three Fokker Triplanes attacking three SE 5As of 29 Squadron, and diving to assist them, shared with his patrol in forcing one Triplane to land in Allied lines, where Gefreiter Preiss of Jasta 14 was captured. The award of a DFC was announced three days later, and by the end of July his final score had reached 29; he was posted to Home Establishment on 3 August. He later flew in 6 and 70 Squadrons during the 1920s.

	1918		SE 5A					
1*	16 Feb	Alb. DV	B4881	1	Bailleul	1130	CAPT	CR/RFC 16.2
2	28 Feb	Alb. DV	B8930	1	Gheluvelt	1715	OOC	CR/RAF 1.3
3s**	11 Mar	C	A8908	1	Ypres	1810	OOC	CR/RFC 11.3
4s***	13 Mar	Pfalz DIII	A8908	1	Wieltje	1220	DES	ORB/RFC 13.3
5	27 Mar	Alb. DV	A8908	1	Achiet le Grand	0935	DES	CR/RFC 27.3
6	21 Apr	Pfalz DIII	C1095	1	N W Pacaut Wood	0915	OOC	CR/ORB/?
7s†	29 Apr	Pfalz DIII	C1095	1	Kemmel-Wytschaete	0650	DES	CR/RAF 29.4
8	2 May	Pfalz DIII	C1095	1	S E Bailleul	1350	OOC	CR/RAF 2.5
9	14 May	Alb. DV	C1102	1	Dickebusch	1735	DES	CR/RAF 14.5
10s††	27 May	C	C1114	1	1m S Bailleul	1425	DES(F)	ORB/RAF 27.5
11s††	27 May	C	C1114	1	Kemmel	1450	DES	ORB/RAF 27.5
12	27 May	Alb. DV	C1114	1	Steenwerck	1940	DES	CR/RAF 27.5
13s†††	28 May	DFW. C	C1849	1	Meteren-Bailleul	0635	OOC	CR/ORB/?
14s‡	28 May	DFW. C	C1849	1	Meteren-Vieux-Berquin	0635	DES	CR/RAF 28.5
15	29 May	Alb. DV	C1114	1	Merville-Neuf Berquin	1630	DES	CR/RAF 29.5
16s‡‡	29 May	Halb. C	C1114	1	1m E Vieux Berquin	1645	DES	CR/RAF 29.5
17s‡‡‡	1 Jun	Pfalz DIII	C1114	1	Armentieres	1940	OOC	CR/ORB/?
18	2 Jun	Alb. DV	C1114	1	N Pacaut Wood	0940	DES	CR/RAF 2.6
19§	6 Jun	Alb. DV	C1114	1	Ploegsteert Wood	0740	DES(F)	CR/RAF 6.6
20s§	6 Jun	Pfalz DIII	C1114	1	Ploegsteert	0745	DES(F)	CR/RAF 6.6
21s§§	9 Jun	Fokker DrI	C1114	1	Dickebusch	0630	CAPT	CR/RAF 9.6
22	13 Jun	Pfalz DIII	C1114	1	Passchendaele area	2035	DES(F)	CR/RAF 13.6
23s§§§	15 Jun	Balloon	C1114	1	S Estaires	1315	DES	CR/RAF 15.6
24s#	23 Jun	C	C1114	1	.5m N W Lestrem	0600	DES	CR/ORB/?
25s##	27 Jun	LVG. C	C1114	1	E Meteren	0427	DES(F)	CR/RAF 27.6
26###	30 Jun	Fokker DVII	C1114	1	Wulverghem	1900	DES(F)	CR/RAF 30.6
27s¶	2 Jul	Hannover C	C1114	1	Ploegsteert Wood	1110	DES(F)	CR/RAF 2.7

28	4 Jul	Fokker DVII	C1114	1	Salome	2045	OOC	CR/ORB/?
29	14 Jul	Fokker DVII	C1114	1	Neuf Berquin-Estaires	1735	OOC	CR/ORB/?

TOTAL: 1 shared balloon, 1 and 1 shared captured, 9 and 9 shared destroyed, 5 and 3 shared out of control = 29.
*Lt Bastgen, of Jasta 30 POW. **Shared with Capt H.J. Hamilton B32. ***Shared with Capt H.J. Hamilton B32, 2/Lt L.W. Mawbey B632, Capt G.B. Moore B511, Lt H.A. Rigby C9624, 2/Lt A.E. Sweeting A8932, Capt W.D. Patrick B641, 2/Lt W.M.R. Gray A8904, 2/Lt A. Hollis B520. †Shared with Capt C.C. Clark C1106. Possibly Gefr Peisker of Jasta 7 who was forced to land in this area at this time. ††Shared with Lt D. Knight C6479, Lt B.H. Moody C1092, Lt H.A. Kullberg D337, Lt E.T.S. Kelly B130. †††Shared with Lt E.M. Forsyth B733, Lt B.H. Moody C1092, Lt E.E. Owen B8512, Lt A.F. Scroggs C6416, Capt K.S. Henderson C1112, Lt K.J.P. Laing B8504, Lt H.B. Bradley C1102, Lt H.A Kullberg B8254, Lt D. Knight C6479. ‡Shared with Lt E.M. Forsyth B733, Lt B.H. Moody C1092, Lt E.E. Owen B8512, Lt A.F. Scroggs C6416, Capt K.S. Henderson C1112, Lt K.J.P. Laing B8504, Lt H.B. Bradley C1102, Lt H.A. Kullberg B8254, Lt D. Knight C6479. ‡‡Shared with Lt A.F. Scroggs C6416. ‡‡‡Shared with Capt C.S.T. Lavers C1110, Lt W.A. Smart C1092, Lt L.W. Mawbey B130, Lt E.M. Newman C1101, Lt E.T.S. Kelly B733, Lt H.A. Kullberg B8512, Lt C.B. Henderson C1849, Lt D. Knight C1106, 2/Lt H.S. Hennessey D377. §One of these was Vzfw Otto Heller of Jasta 40 who was killed. §§Shared with Lt H.B. Bradley C1102, 2/Lt H.B. Parkinson C6458, Lt E.E. Owen B8512, Lt H.A. Kullberg C8842, Lt D. Knight C1106, Lt E.S. Crossley D6881, Lt J.C. Bateman B8254, Lt K.J.P. Laing C1898, Lt C.B. Henderson C1849. This was Gefr Preiss, of Jasta 14, who was captured. §§§Shared with Lt H.A. Kullberg C1853, Lt G.W. Bellin B6881. #Shared with Lt D. Knight C1894, Lt J.C. Bateman B8254, Lt H.A. Kullberg C1835, Lt C.B. Henderson C1849. ##Shared with Lt H.A. Kullberg C1835, Lt D. Knight C1894. Probably Lt G. Kuter/Lt J. Frankstein of FAA 213, who were killed. ###Probably Lt Carl of Jasta 51 who was killed. ¶Shared with Lt D. Knight C1106.

CLEAR Edward Arnold Lieutenant 84

A Londoner, born on 28 May 1896, Clear joined the RFC as a ground mechanic and served in Egypt for 20 months. Accepted for pilot training, he took his early instructions at Heliopolis and Aboukir, then returned to England and the CFS. Commissioned in September 1917, he was sent to 84 Squadron in October where he flew SE 5As. He served with the unit until June 1918, was awarded an MC, and claimed 12 German aircraft shot down, all of which were confirmed as destroyed. He remained in the RAF for some years as a Flying Officer until he was forced to retire through ill health in 1935.

	1918		SE 5A					
1	29 Jan	C	B627	84	S E Bellicourt	1325	DES(F)	CR/RFC 29.1
2	10 Mar	C	C5326	84	W Estrees	1420	DES	CR/RFC 10.3
3	15 Mar	Alb. DV	C1075	84	Mesnil St Laurent	0945	DES	CR/RFC 15.3
4*	17 Mar	Fokker DrI	C1075	84	Crevecoeur	1730	DES	CR/RFC 17.3
5*	17 Mar	Alb. DV	C1075	84	Crevecoeur	1730	DES	CR/RFC 17.3
6**	18 Mar	Fokker DrI	C1075	84	W Busigny	1135	DES	CR/RFC 18.3
7	30 Mar	Alb. DV	C1075	84	S Somme at Cerisy	0930	DES	CR/RFC 30.3
8	12 Apr	Hannover C	C1075	84	Longueval	1150	DES	CR/RAF 12.4
9	12 Apr	Pfalz DIII	C1075	84	W Plessier	1810	DES	CR/RAF 12.4
10***	25 Apr	Pfalz DIII	C1075	84	E Wiencourt	1700	DES	CR/RAF 25.4
11	25 Apr	C	C1075	84	S Hangard Wood	1710	DES	CR/RAF 25.4
12	28 May	Alb. DV	C1871	84	N E Moreuil	1330	DES	CR/RAF 28.5

TOTAL: 12 destroyed = 12.
*The above aircraft collided. Possibly aircraft of Jasta 17 and 12. **Probably Flgr Ihde of Jasta 10 who was killed. ***84 made 8 claims for fighters. Jasta 34 lost two aircraft, Lt W. Meyer KIA, Oblt Dieterle was wounded.

CLEMENT Carleton Main Captain 22

Clement, a Canadian, was born on 15 May 1896 and attended Toronto University. He served as a private in the 47th Battalion, Canadian Expeditionary Force, before transferring to the RFC, where he was commissioned in March 1916. He joined 22 Squadron during the summer of 1916, flying obsolescent FE 2Bs, and received an MC for two destroyed and five out of control. By mid August 1917, after over a year of continuous action, he had brought his score to 14, the last five while flying Bristol Fighters. However on 19 August he and his observer, Lieutenant R.B. Carter, left on an evening patrol in A7172 and were shot down near Langemarck by Leutnant Böhner's gun crew of Flakzug 99, being killed. At the time he was by far the most successful pilot on the squadron, General Trenchard sending a telegram to the unit regretting his loss. He had also received a Croix de Guerre and been Mentioned in Despatches.

	1916		FE 2B					
1*	4 Dec	Alb. DI	7703	22	Baraste	1010	OOC	CR/RFC 4.12
	1917							
2s**	4 Feb	Alb. DII	A5461	22	Rocquigny	1400	DES	CR/RFC 4.2
3s***	6 Apr	Alb. DIII	----	22	St Quentin	0800	DES	CR/RFC 6.4
4s†	8 Apr	Alb. DIII	----	22	Regny	0700	DES	CR/RFC 8.4
5††	9 May	Alb. DIII	A5461	22	Honnecourt	1545	OOC	CR/RFC 9.5
6††	9 May	Alb. DIII	A5461	22	S W Lesdains	1545	DES	CR/RFC 9.5

7‡	5 Jun	Alb. DV	A5461	22	N W Lesdains	0715	DES	CR/RFC 5.6
8‡	5 Jun	Alb. DV	A5461	22	N W Lesdains	0730	OOC	CR/RFC 5.6
			Bristol					
9‡‡	29 Jul	C	A7174	22	Tortequesne	0650	DES(F)	CR/RFC 29.7
10‡‡‡	10 Aug	Alb. DV	A7172	22	Aubigny au Bac	1845	OOC	CR/RFC 10.8
11§	12 Aug	Alb. DV	A7172	22	Biache St Vaast	1915	OOC	CR/RFC 13.8
12§	12 Aug	Alb. DV	A7172	22	Biache St Vaast	1915	DES(F)	CR/RFC 13.8
13s§§	12 Aug	Alb. DV	A7172	22	Douai-Lens	1930	OOC	CR/RFC 13.8
14s§§§	12 Aug	Alb. DV	A7172	22	Lens	1945	OOC	CR/RFC 13.8

TOTAL: 4 and 3 shared destroyed, 5 and 2 shared out of control = 14.

*Observer: 2/Lt J.K. Cambell. **Observer: 2/Lt M.K. Parlee. Shared with 2/Lt E.C. Pashley, 24 Sqn. ***Observer: 2/Lt L.G. Davies: shared with Capt Gladstone/Lt Friend, Lt J. Aspinall/2/Lt M.K. Parlee, Lt J.F. Day/2/Lt J.K. Campbell. †Observer: 2/Lt L.G. Davies: shared with Capt L.W. Beale/Lt G.G. Bell, Lt J.F. Day/Lt Taylor, Lt J. Aspinall/2/Lt M.K. Parlee, Lt Furlonger/Lt W.C. Lane, Lt H.G. Spearpoint/2/Lt J.K. Campbell. ††Observer: 2/Lt M.K. Parlee. ‡Observer: 2/Lt L.G. Davies; one of these was Lt K. Schneider, a 15 victory ace, and acting C.O. of Jasta 5. ‡‡Observer: 2/Lt L.G. Davies. ‡‡‡Observer: Pte D.W. Clement. §Observer: Lt R.B. Carter. §§Observer: Lt R.B. Carter; shared with Lt M.W. Turner/Lt Edson, Lt J.C. Bush/AM A. Whitehouse. §§§Observer: Lt R.B. Carter; shared with Lt J.C. Bush/AM A. Whitehouse.

CLEMENTS Harris G. Lieutenant 74

'Clem' Clements was born at Chilum, Kent, in January 1893, but emigrated to Canada as a young man. On the outbreak of war he joined the Alberta Regiment where he was commissioned, but the unit was not posted to France. Late in 1917 he volunteered for a transfer to the RFC, and after training joined 74 Squadron in February 1918, moving with the unit to France in April. Here he was to claim six victories during May and June. On 21 May his engine failed while he was attacking a two-seater over Armentieres and although he crashed into the trenches, he was unhurt. His last confirmed victory was over a Rumpler CV of Flg Abt 48 which crashed inside Allied lines, but not before the crew, Leutnant Josef Keller and Fw Lt Kurt Schott had fallen from their machine to their deaths. Clements left 74 in September and became an instructor at London Colney. He did not return to Canada after the war, but left the RAF in 1919 and never flew again. His two sons were both killed in action with Bomber Command during World War II, but Clements remained in retirement in Leicester until his death on 6 May 1983.

	1918		SE 5A					
1s*	12 Apr	Alb. DV	----	74	Bois de Phalempin	1440	DES	CR/RAF 12.4
2s**	3 May	LVG. C	----	74	S Merville	1855	DES	CR/RAF 3.5
3	29 May	Alb. DV	C9584	74	Lille-Roubaix	2055	DES	CR/RAF 29.5
4s***	6 Jun	Pfalz DIII	----	74	2m W Roulers	1935	DES	CR/RAF 6.6
5s†	9 Jun	Alb. C	----	74	S Mt Kemmel	0805	DES	CR/RAF 9.6
6††	30 Jun	Rumpler C	C1779	74	N E Cassel	1305	CAPT	CR/RAF 30.6

TOTAL: 1 captured, 1 and 4 shared destroyed = 6.

*Shared with Capt E.C. Mannock, Lt H.E. Dolan, Lt B. Roxburgh-Smith, Lt P.F.C. Howe. **Shared with Capt E.C. Mannock, Lt H.E. Dolan, Lt A.C. Kiddie; This was Uffz Schoning/Lt Beuttler of FA 32, who were killed. ***Shared with 7 others. †Shared with Capt E.C. Mannock, Lt A.C. Kiddie, Capt W.E. Young. ††This was Flgr K. Schott/Lt J. Keller of FA 48; Keller was killed.

COATH Robert D. Lieutenant 48, 11

Coath flew Bristol Fighters on the Western Front with 48 and 11 Squadrons in 1917 before being wounded on 23 November. He claimed eight victories, although when he died in 1967 a score of 14 was recorded in his obituary. From 1935 to 1962 he was airport manager at Portsmouth aerodrome, a post he had taken up upon retirement from the RAF with the rank of Wing Commander.

	1917		Bristol					
1*	13 Jul	Alb. DIII	A7106	48	Slype	0915	OOC	CR/RFC 13.7
2s**	21 Jul	Alb. DIII	A7164	48	Slype	1800	OOC	CR/RFC 21.7
3***	12 Aug	Alb. DIII	A7164	48	Slype	1045	DES(F)	CR/RFC 12.8
4***	12 Aug	Alb. DIII	A7164	48	Slype	1045	OOC	CR/RFC 12.8
5†	21 Aug	Alb. DV	A7213	48	E Westende	1940	DES(F)	CR/4 BG Sum
6†	22 Aug	Alb. DV	A7213	48	3m S W Ostende	0900	DES	CR/RFC 22.8
7†	22 Aug	Alb. DV	A7213	48	Slype-Westende	0915	OOC	CR/RFC 22.8
8††	27 Oct	Alb. DV	A7128	11	Ribicourt	1115	OOC	CR/RFC 27.8

TOTAL: 3 destroyed, 4 and 1 shared out of control = 8.

*Observer: 2/Lt A.W. Merchant. **Observer: Lt L.H. Tanner; shared with Capt B.E. Baker/Lt G.R. Spencer A7107, Lt R. Dodds/Lt T.C.S. Tuffield A7153. ***Observer: 2 AM Walker. †Observer: Lt A.D. Light. ††Observer: 2/Lt K.F. Jones.

COBBY Arthur Henry Captain 4 AFC

Arthur Cobby was born in Melbourne, Australia, on 26 August 1894. A bank clerk before the war, he joined the AFC on 22 December 1916 and went to France early in 1918 with 71 Squadron. This unit was shortly afterwards re-designed 4 AFC Squadron. Although his book, *High Adventure*, mentions an early victory on 3 February 1918, this was actually credited as driven down, the only confirmed victory going to Captain O'Hara-Wood; Cobby's first victories were gained on 21 March. An extremely aggressive, but very cunning pilot, he was in action throughout the German offensive in the spring of 1918, strafing troops and airfields, attacking balloons, and claiming numbers of aircraft. The award of a DFC was announced on 3 August, and this was followed by two Bars on 21 September, the citations stating that he had claimed 21 enemy aircraft and balloons. He had been promoted to flight commander on 14 May, and was posted to England as an instructor on 4 September; the award of a DSO followed. The highest-scoring pilot of the AFC, he was credited with 29 victories.

He served in the RAAF on his return to Australia, becoming a Wing Commander in 1933 before resigning in 1936 to become Controller of Operations with the Civil Aviation Board, although he remained in the Citizen Air Force Reserve. He also wrote his autobiography, *High Adventure*, which was published at the time of the outbreak of World War II. Cobby returned to active service on 25 July 1940 as Director of Recruiting; by August 1942 as an Air Commodore, he had become operational commander of the RAAF in Western Australia. He was awarded a George Medal for actions on 7 September 1943 when a Catalina flyingboat in which he was a passenger, crashed on landing. Although injured, he played a major part in rescuing other survivors. Subsequently, after commanding the RAF Staff College, he commanded an operational Group in the South-West Pacific area from July 1944, which became the 1st Tactical Air Force on 21 October 1944. He left the Air Force as an Air Commodore, CBE, DSO, DFC, GM, in 1946 to return to Civil Aviation, and died of natural causes on 11 November 1955.

	1918		Camel					
1	21 Mar	Alb. DV	B2535	4AFC	S Brebieres	0905	OOC	CR/RFC 21.3
2	21 Mar	Alb. DV	B2535	4AFC	S Brebieres	0905	DES	CR/RFC 21.3
3	30 Mar	Pfalz DIII	B2535	4AFC	S E Arras	1215	DES	CR/RFC 30.3
4	10 Apr	Alb. DV	B2535	4AFC	S E Estaires	0940	DES	CR/RAF 10.4
5	20 May	Pfalz DIII	D1893	4AFC	Neuve-Eglise	0745	DES	CR/ORB/OH
6	21 May	Balloon	D1893	4AFC	Merville	1100	DES	CR/RAF 21.5
7	30 May	Alb. DV	D1929	4AFC	Estaires	1650	DES(F)	CR/RAF 30.5
8	30 May	Balloon	D1929	4AFC	Estaires	1657	DES	CR/RAF 30.5
9	1 Jun	Balloon	D1929	4AFC	N Estaires	0920	DES	CR/RAF 1.6
10	1 Jun	Alb. DV	D1929	4AFC	Estaires	0935	DES	CR/RAF 1.6
11	17 Jun	Pfalz DIII	D1929	4AFC	E Laventie	1950	DES	CR/RAF 17.6
12	17 Jun	Pfalz DIII	D1929	4AFC	E Laventie	1950	DES	CR/ORB/OH
13*	19 Jun	Pfalz DIII	D1929	4AFC	Nieppe Forest	1845	DES	CR/RAF 19.6
14	25 Jun	Pfalz DIII	D1929	4AFC	Estaires-Laventie	1935	DES	CR/RAF 25.6
15	26 Jun	Pfalz DIII	D1929	4AFC	S E Armentieres	1805	DES	CR/RAF 26.6
16	28 Jun	LVG. C	D1929	4AFC	E Outtersteene	1455	DES	CR/RAF 28.6
17	28 Jun	Pfalz DIII	D1929	4AFC	S E Estaires	1505	DES(F)	CR/RAF 28.6
18	28 Jun	Halb. C	D1929	4AFC	Wytschaete	1840	DES	CR/RAF 28.6
19	2 Jul	Balloon	D1969	4AFC	Bac St Maur	1535	DES	CR/RAF 3.7
20	2 Jul	Fokker DrI	D1969	4AFC	N E La Bassee	1600	DES	CR/RAF 3.7
21	9 Jul	A.G.O. C	E1416	4AFC	N E Gravelin	1940	DES	CR/RAF 9.7
22	14 Jul	Balloon	E1416	4AFC	Estaires-La Bassee	0718	DES	CR/RAF 14.7
23	15 Jul	Pfalz DIII	E1416	4AFC	Armentieres	1725	DES(F)	CR/RAF 15.7
24	15 Jul	Pfalz DIII	E1416	4AFC	Armentieres	1725	DES	CR/RAF 15.7
25	6 Aug	LVG. C	E1416	4AFC	S E Bac St Maur	2050	DES	CR/RAF 6.8
26**	7 Aug	C	E1416	4AFC	Lestrem	1235	DES	CR/RAF 7.8
27	7 Aug	Pfalz DIII	E1416	4AFC	S E Armentieres	1245	DES	CR/RAF 7.8
28s***	16 Aug	Fokker DVII	----	4AFC	Wavrin	1315	DES	CR/RAF 16.8
29	4 Sep	Fokker DVII	E1416	4AFC	Wattignies area	0715	OOC	CR/ORB/OH

TOTAL: 1 captured, 5 balloon, 20 and 1 shared destroyed, 2 out of control = 29.
*This was Uffz Max Mertens of Jasta 7. The tail-skid of this aircraft is in the Australian War Memorial, Canberra. **Possibly Uffz Tegtmeier/Uffz M. Kanz of Schlasta 13. ***Shared with Lt D.C. Carter, Lt R. King, Lt J.R. Edols, 2/Lt M.H. Eddie, Lt N.C. Trescowthick.

COCHRAN-PATRICK William John Charles Kennedy Major 1AD, 70, 23, 60

Born in Ireland on 25 May 1896, son of Sir Noel Cochran-Patrick, he received his university education at Cambridge. He served initially with the Rifle Brigade before joining the RFC, and gained his wings at Farnborough in April 1915. Later he became a test pilot at No 1 Aeroplane Depot, St Omer, and was still so employed because of his exceptional flying abilities, when on 20 April 1916 he fought an action which gained for him an MC. Taking off to intercept an intruding two-seater, he attacked it three times in his Nieuport Scout and forced it to crash; he then landed alongside his victim. He was then posted to 70 Squadron to fly 1½ Strutters, and here he gained two more victories, although on both occasions his observers were killed during the action. Promoted to Captain, he went to 23 Squadron where he flew Spads in 1917, serving with great distinction during the late spring and early summer, being awarded a Bar to his MC, and later a DSO; he had by then raised his score to 21, one of the first RFC pilots to pass 20. In July he was promoted to Major and took command of 60 Squadron, a post which he held until the end of the year when he returned to England to take up a position in the Training Division of the Air Board; in 1918 he was back at No 1 Aeroplane Depot. After the war he did much work flying on aerial surveys, but he was killed in a crash at Johannesburg, South Africa, on 27 September 1933.

	1916		Nieuport					
1*	26 Apr	LVG. C	5172	1AD	Hazebrouck	—	CAPT	RFC 26.4/ C&C V14 N3
			Strutter					
2**	14 Sep	EA	----	70	Bapaume	----	OOC	RFC 14.9? C&C (US) V20 N4
3***	15 Sep	Scout	A1912	70	Equancourt-Epehy	0715	DES	CR/RFC 15.9
	1917		Spad VII					
4	22 Apr	Alb. DIII	B1524	23	Fontaine Notre Dame	1830	OOC	CR/RFC 23.4
5	22 Apr	Alb. DIII	B1524	23	Flesquires	1900	OOC	CR/5 Bg
6	26 Apr	C	B1524	23	Baralle	1905	OOC	CR/RFC 27.4
7	30 Apr	Alb. DIII	B1527	23	Inchy en Artois	1640	DES(F)	CR/RFC 30.4
8	2 May	Alb. DIII	B1527	23	Brebieres	1715	OOC	CR/RFC 3.5
9†	11 May	Alb. DIII	B1580	23	W Bourlon Wood	1905	DES(F)	CR/RFC 12.5
10s††	13 May	Alb. DIII	B1580	23	Etaing	1905	OOC	CR/5 Bg
11s†††	13 May	Alb. DIII	B1580	23	Roucourt	1910	DES(F)	CR/RFC 13.5
12	20 May	Alb. DIII	----	23	----	----	DES	RFC 20.5
13	8 Jun	Alb. DIII	B1580	23	Roulers	0600	OOC	CR/RFC 8.6
14	13 Jun	Alb. DIII	B1580	23	Menin-Ypres	1730	OOC	CR/5 BG
15‡	16 Jun	Alb. C	----	23	----	PM	OOC	RFC 16.6
16s‡‡	24 Jun	Alb. DV	B1580	23	St Jean	1630	DES(F)	CR/RFC 25.6
17	6 Jul	Alb. DIII	B1580	23	Passchendaele	1415	DES	CR/RFC 6.7
18s‡‡‡	6 Jul	C	B1580	23	Zandvoorde	1430	DES	CR/RFC 6.7
19	7 Jul	Alb. DV	B1580	23	Roulers	1850	OOC	CR/RFC 8.7
20§	7 Jul	C	B1580	23	Houthoulst Wood	1940	DES(F)	CR/RFC 8.7
21	16 Jul	Alb. DV	----	23	Roulers	----	DES	RFC 16.7

TOTAL: 1 captured, 6 and 4 shared destroyed, 9 and 1 shared out of control = 21.

*The crew were killed pilot ?/observer Lt Georg V. Puttkammer. **Observer: 2/Lt E.W. Burke, who was killed in the fight. ***Observer: Capt F.G. Glenday, who was fatally wounded in the fight. †This was Offz Stlvtr Edmund Nathanael, an 11 victory ace from Jasta 5 who was shot down in flames by a Spad over Bourlon Wood. ††Shared with 2/Lt R.W. Farquhar B1530. †††Shared with 2/Lt G.C. Stead B1527. ‡The 5 BG summ (AIR 1/2219) notes that on the "PM of 16 June" Patrick shot down an aircraft out of control. The combat report is missing. It is possible this was late on the 15 June, reported a day late. ‡‡Shared with 2/Lt S.C.O'Grady B3464, 2/Lt G.I.D. Marks B1698. ‡‡‡Shared with 2/Lt G.I.D. Marks, 2/Lt D.U. Macgregor. §Shared with 2/Lt D.U. MacGregor B3488.

COCK Geoffrey Hornblower Captain 45

Born on 7 January 1896, he joined the 28th London Regiment, the Artists' Rifles OTC, in December 1915. He was seconded to the RFC in June 1916 and trained with 25 Reserve Squadron. After receiving his wings in September (RAF Certificate No 2157) he was posted to 45 Squadron, going to France with the unit on 14 October 1916, flying Sopwith 1½ Strutters; in May 1917 he became 'B' Flight commander and was awarded the MC. He was shot down in combat by Hauptmann Willi Reinhard of Jasta 11 on 22 July, and taken prisoner. At that time he was the last of the original pilots who had flown to France in the previous October. During his period in action he flew 97 sorties and with his observers claimed 19 enemy machines (which appear to have included a number of 'driven down' claims), of which Cock considered 15 as 'certainties' — nine by the front gun and six by the rear. He was by far the most successful pilot on 1½ Strutters in terms of victories. After an abortive attempt to escape, he was eventually repatriated in December 1918 and remained in the RAF, commanding 9 Squadron at Boscombe Down in 1935. He retired with the rank of Group Captain in 1943.

	1917		Strutter					
1*	6 Apr	Alb. DIII	A1075	45	Lille	1030	DES	CR/RFC 6.4
2*	6 Apr	Alb. DIII	A1075	45	Lille	1030	OOC	CR/RFC 6.4
3*	7 May	S.S. DI	A8260	45	Don-Lille	1830	OOC	CR/RFC 7.5

4*	9 May	Alb. DIII	A8260	45	N W Seclin	1650	DES	CR/RFC 9.5
5s**	9 May	Alb. DIII	A8260	45	N W Seclin	1700	DES	CR/RFC 9.5
6***	20 May	Alb. DIII	A8226	45	Lille	1630	OOC	CR/RFC 20.5
7†	27 May	Alb. DIII	A1016	45	Menin	0630	OOC	CR/RFC 27.5
8††	28 May	Alb. DIII	A8299	45	Menin	1300	DES(F)	CR/RFC 28.5
9*	16 Jun	Alb. DV	----	45	Warneton	1800	OOC	CR/RFC 16.6
10†††	6 Jul	Alb. DIII	----	45	N W Comines	1500	OOC	CR/RFC 6.7
11†††	7 Jul	Alb. DIII	----	45	Wervicq	1700	OOC	CR/RFC 7.7
12‡	13 Jul	Alb. DIII	----	45	E Polygon Wood	1515	OOC	CR/RFC 13.7
13‡‡	22 Jul	Alb. DIII	B2576	45	Warneton	1035	DES(F)	Sq Rec/Mac

TOTAL: 3 and 1 shared destroyed, 9 out of control = 13.
*Observer: 2/Lt J.T.G. Murison. **Observer: 2/Lt J.T.G. Murison. Shared with 2/Lt W.A. Wright/2/Lt E.T. Caulfield-Kelly A8225. ***Observer: 2/Lt A.S. Carey. †Observer: 2/Lt E.T. Caulfield-Kelly. ††2/Lt W.G. Corner. †††Observer: Lt C.T.R. Ward. ‡Observer: Lt V.R.S. White. ‡‡Observer: 2/Lt W.C. Moore.

COCKERELL Stanley Captain 24, 50, 112, 78, 151

One of the RFC's earliest scout pilots, Cockerell from Osterley Park, Middlesex, went to France with 24 Squadron on DH 2s in early 1916 as a Sergeant. On 10 October he was wounded in action. On recovery from his injuries, he was commissioned and returned to the squadron, claiming further victories during early 1917. When the unit converted to DH 5s in the late spring, he gained the first victory in one of the new aircraft for this unit. Returning to England, he was promoted to Captain and flew with a Home Defence unit for some time, before being posted to 151 Squadron flying Camels on night-fighter sorties over France. He flew many night patrols and bombing raids, harassing enemy night-bomber aerodromes. On the night of 2 August 1918, after dropping four bombs on Guizencourt airfield, he saw and attacked a Gotha as it was preparing to land, causing it to crash about two miles from the base — his seventh victory.

	1916		DH 2					
1s*	14 Sep	Fokker DII	7873	24	Manancourt	2045	DES(F)	CR/RFC 14.9
2	30 Sep	Alb. DI?	A2556	24	Grevillers	0945	OOC	CR/BG Sum
	1917							
3s**	4 Feb	C	A2541	24	Templeux	1315	OOC	CR/RFC 4.2
4	6 Feb	C	A2581	24	Velu	1415	OOC	CR/RFC 6.2
5	2 Apr	Alb. DIII	A2581	24	Gouzeaucourt	0850	DES	CR/RFC 2.4
			DH 5					
6	25 May	Alb. DIII	A9363	24	Ligny	1145	DES	CR/RFC 25.5
	1918		Camel					
7	2 Aug	Gotha	----	151	Guizencourt	night	DES	RAF 2.8

TOTAL: 4 destroyed, 2 and 1 shared out of control = 7.
*Shared with Lt A.G. Knight 5931. **Shared with Lt Begbie A2544, Lt Evans A2563.

COLBERT John Henry Lieutenant 20

Colbert flew with a number of different observers in 20 Squadron in the summer of 1918, claiming six victories, three with his front gun.

	1918		Bristol					
1*	18 May	Pfalz. DIII	B1168	20	N Neuf Berquin	1140	DES	CR/RFC 18.5
2**	31 May	Pfalz DIII	B1168	20	E Estaires	0745	DES	CR/RAF 31.5
3***	31 May	Pfalz DIII	B1168	20	Armentieres	1850	DES(F)	CR/RAF 31.5
4*	24 Jul	Fokker DVII	D7951	20	3m N Comines	2000	DES	CR/RAF 24.7
5*	29 Jul	Fokker DVII	D7951	20	N W Wervicq	2010	DES	CR/RAF 29.7
6†	21 Aug	Fokker DVII	E1258	20	N Menin	1920	DES	CR/RAF 21.8

TOTAL: 6 destroyed = 6.
*Observer: Lt R.W. Turner. **Observer: 2/Lt P.W. Wilson. ***Observer: Lt A. Mills. †Observer: Lt H.L. Edwards.

COLE Adrian Trevor Captain 1 AFC, 2 AFC

An Australian from Melbourne, where he was born on 19 June 1895, 'King' Cole joined the AFC and was posted to Egypt in 1917 to fly with 67 Squadron (later 1AFC Squadron). On 21 April 1917, flying a Martinsyde Elephant, he was shot down over Tel el Sheria by ground fire and forced to land, but a fellow pilot landed and picked him up. On 26 June he and another pilot landed to pick up the pilot of a BE 2 whose engine had seized. The other pilot took off two-up, escorted by Cole, but his engine then seized also, and he had to land again. Cole then tried to take both pilots in his Martinsyde, but his engine also stopped and he crash-landed. After a long walk through 'No Mans' Land', they were finally picked up by a Light Horse detachment. Converting to Bristol Fighters, he was awarded an MC on 16 August 1917 for attacking six aircraft which were about to strafe Allied cavalry. He was then posted to France, joining 2AFC Squadron on SE 5As as a flight commander in the early summer of 1918. During the next five months he claimed ten victories, receiving a DFC after the fourth of these. He joined the RAAF upon its formation and became Director of Training, and then Commandant of Point Cook in 1926. He was Deputy Chairman of the McRobertson-Miller Air Race in 1934. Cole had a distinguished career in World War II, including being the Fighter Controller during the Dieppe Raid of 19 August 1942. He ended his service as an Air Vice-Marshal.

	1918		SE 5A					
1s*	2 Jun	Pfalz DIII	D3962	2AFC	Clery	1905	DES	CR/ORB/OH
2	2 Jun	Fokker DrI	D3962	2AFC	Estrees	1930	DES	CR/RAF 2.6
3**	17 Jul	Fokker DrI	C1934	2AFC	Armentieres	1730	DES(F)	CR/RAF 17.7
4	7 Aug	Fokker DVII	C1934	2AFC	Herrin	0630	OOC	CR/ORB/OH
5	19 Aug	Fokker DVII	D6948	2AFC	E Habourdin	0950	OOC	CR/ORB/OH
6	19 Aug	Fokker DVII	D6948	2AFC	Epinoy	1000	OOC	CR/ORB/OH
7s***	25 Aug	DFW. C	D6948	2AFC	Epinoy	1130	DES	CR/RAF 25.8
8	25 Sep	Pfalz DIII	D6964	2AFC	Habourdin-Perenchies	1835	DES	CR/ORB/OH
9†	28 Oct	Fokker DVII	D6964	2AFC	Peruwelz	1120	DES(F)	CR/RAF 28.10

TOTAL: 6 destroyed, 3 out of control = 9 (Cole had one "driven down" claim with 1 AFC, thus his score is usually quoted as 10.
*Shared with Lt W.Q. Adams, Lt F.R. Smith, Lt H.E. Hamilton. **This was Lt Otto Franke of Jasta 30, who was killed. ***Shared with Lt J.J. Wellwood D6968. †Cole and Lt G.H. Blaxland both claimed Fokkers whose pilots baled out.

COLE Edwin Stuart Travis Lieutenant 60, 1

Born in Bristol in 1895, Cole was living in Canada on the outbreak of war. He was commissioned in 1916, qualifying as a pilot in July and joining 60 Squadron on 5 August to fly Nieuport Scouts. He claimed one victory during September, but was then posted to 1 Squadron when this unit began flying the same aircraft type. Here he claimed seven further victories during the spring of 1917, and received an MC, which was gazetted on 18 June. Early in World War II he participated in a disastrous attempt to ferry Blenheim bombers across France to the Middle East, from which his crew were the sole survivors*.
*NB. The full story of this operation can be found in *Malta: The Hurricane Years, 1940-41*, Christopher Shores and Brian Cull with Nicola Malizia, Grub Street, 1987.

	1916		Nieuport					
1	15 Sep	Roland CII	A174	60	Bapaume	0945	OOC	CR/RFC 15.9
	1917							
2	4 Mar	LVG. C	A6619	1	N Ypres	1415	DES	CR/RFC 4.3
3	28 Mar	Alb. DIII	A6603	1	Lesquin	1045	OOC	CR/RFC 28.3
4	8 Apr	Balloon	A6603	1	Quesnoy	0820	DES	CR/RFC 8.4
5	22 Apr	Balloon	A6790	1	Wervicq	0720	DES	CR/RFC 22.4
6	29 Apr	Alb. DIII	B1508	1	Ypres-Menin Rd	1530	OOC	CR/RFC 29.4
7	30 Apr	Halb. DII	A6690	1	N Ypres	1145	OOC	CR/RFC 30.4
8*	1 May	Alb. DIII	B1508	1	Roulers-Elverdinghe	1200	CAPT	CR/RFC 1.5

TOTAL: 2 balloons, 1 shared captured, 1 destroyed, 4 out of control = 8.
*Lt Kuttscher of Jasta 28 was killed in allied lines. Shared with Lt F. Sharpe B1550.

COLER Eugene Seeley Lieutenant 11

An American from Newark, New Jersey, born on 13 January 1896, who joined the Canadian forces, Coler flew with 11 Squadron in 1918 where he had a very intense and hectic combat career. He first claimed in May — a triple victory in one patrol — but then no more until August when he and his gunner Lieutenant C.W. Gladman, accounted for five Fokker DVIIs, although during this fight Gladman was wounded. Coler received the DFC for this action, and went on to bring his score to 16 before being wounded on 16 September by a member of Jasta 'Boelcke', as a result of which he crash-landed. After the war he returned to university, became a doctor, and set up practice in New York. In 1942 he joined the USAAF as a Major in the 319th Bomb Group, serving in North Africa and later with the 8th Air Force in England. After the second war he was again recalled in 1951, going to England as Divisional Air Surgeon at Headquarters, 7th Air Division, until he died on 30 August 1953 in Gerrard's Cross, Buckinghamshire with the rank of Colonel. He had received the Legion of Merit, Air Medal and Bronze Star Medal. Coler's service with the RAF is unique — he never claimed less than two victories in a fight!

	1918		Bristol					
1*	9 May	Pfalz DIII	C792	11	Albert-Combles	1220	OOC	CR/RAF 9.5
2*	9 May	Pfalz DIII	C792	11	Albert-Combles	1220	OOC	CR/RAF 9.5
3*	9 May	Pfalz DIII	C792	11	Albert-Combles	1220	OOC	CR/RAF 9.5
4*	13 Aug	Fokker DVII	D7912	11	Peronne	0840	DES(F)	CR/RAF 13.8
5*	13 Aug	Fokker DVII	D7912	11	Peronne	0840	OOC	CR/RAF 13.8
6*	13 Aug	Fokker DVII	D7912	11	Peronne	0841	OOC	CR/?
7*	13 Aug	Fokker DVII	D7912	11	Peronne	0842	DES(F)	CR/RAF 13.8

8*	13 Aug	Fokker DVII	D7912	11	Peronne	0842	DES(F)	CR/RAF 13.8
9**	30 Aug	Fokker DVII	E2215	11	N W Havrincourt	1840	DES	CR/?
10**	30 Aug	Pfalz DXII	E2215	11	N W Havrincourt	1840	DES	CR/?
11***	6 Sep	Fokker DVII	E2215	11	W Cambrai	1030	DES	CR/RAF 6.9
12***	6 Sep	Fokker DVII	E2215	11	W Cambrai	1030	OOC	CR/?
13†	15 Sep	Fokker DVII	E2215	11	2m W Esnes	1200	DES	CR/RAF 15.9
14†	15 Sep	Fokker DVII	E2215	11	2m W Esnes	1200	DES	CR/RAF 15.9
15†	16 Sep	Pfalz DXII	E2215	11	E Cambrai	0830	DES	CR/RAF 16.9
16†	16 Sep	Fokker DVII	E2215	11	E Cambrai	0830	DES	CR/RAF 15.9

TOTAL: 10 destroyed, 6 out of control = 16.
*Observer: Lt C.W. Gladman. **Observer: 2/Lt B.E.J.D. Tuke. ***Observer: Lt D.P. Conyngham. †Observer: Lt E.J. Corbett.

COLLETT Clive Franklyn Captain 70

Born on 28 August 1886, Clive Collett, a New Zealander from Blenheim, joined the RFC in 1914, gaining his Royal Aero Club certificate on 29 January 1915, and being commissioned the following March. He was injured in a crash while flying an aircraft from France to England, where during 1916 he became a test pilot. In January 1917 he made an experimental parachute jump from a BE 2C, then joining 70 Squadron in the summer as a flight commander when the unit was newly converted to Camels. By September he had claimed 12 victories and had been awarded an MC and Bar. On 9 September he had claimed 3 shot down, but was himself wounded, probably by Leutnant Ludwig Hanstein of Jasta 35. Collett later again flew as a test pilot, but on 23 December 1917 was killed when flying a captured Albatros Scout over the Firth of Forth. It is interesting to note that one of Collett's victims during his final combat was Leutnant Karl Hammes of Jasta 35, whose severe wounding ended a four-victory combat career. His voice was obviously not affected at any rate, for he later became a star of Viennese opera in the 1930s, before being killed in action over Poland in 1939.

	1917		Camel					
1	27 Jul	Alb. DV	B3756	70	Ypres	2045	DES	CR/RFC 27.7
2	5 Aug	Alb. DV	B3768	70	Roulers-Bixschoote	1945	OOC	CR/RFC 5.8
3	10 Aug	Alb. DV	B3768	70	N E Polygon Wood	2005	DES	CR/RFC 10.8
4	13 Aug	C	B3889	70	N W Dixmude	1945	DES	CR/9 W WD
5	13 Aug	Alb. DV	B3889	70	N Thorout	2005	DES	CR/RFC 13.8
6	18 Aug	Alb. DV	B3889	70	E Gheluvelt	1940	DES	CR/RFC 18.8
7	22 Aug	Alb. DV	B3889	70	Gheluwe	0850	OOC	CR/RFC 22.8
8	5 Sep	Alb. DV	B6234	70	Roulers	1845	DES	CR/RFC 5.9
9s*	9 Sep	C	B2341	70	Gheluvelt	1705	OOC	CR/RFC 9.9
10	9 Sep	C	B2341	70	N E Houthoulst Wood	1725	DES	CR/RFC 9.9
11**	9 Sep	Alb. DV	B2341	70	N E Houthoulst Wood	1750	DES	CR/RFC 9.9

TOTAL: 8 destroyed, 2 and 1 shared out of control = 11.
*Shared with Lt N.C. Saward B3928. **This was Lt K. Hammes of Jasta 35.

COLLISHAW Raymond Lieutenant Colonel 3W, 10(N), 13(N), 203, 47

Born on 22 November 1893, in Nanaimo, British Columbia, Canada, Ray Collishaw became a seaman on leaving school. In January 1916 he joined the RNAS, and after training was posted to No 3 Wing to fly Sopwith 1½ Strutters on long-range bombing sorties and other duties. He was shot down on 27 December, but survived unhurt, and in February 1917 was posted to 3(N) Squadron to fly Sopwith Pups, gaining two victories on this type. In April he joined the newly-formed 10(N) Squadron, equipped with Sopwith Triplanes, and during late April and early May accounted for four more enemy aircraft in the Dunkirk area, following which, in late May the squadron was posted to join 11 Wing, RFC, on the Western Front. The Triplanes had already made a name for themselves as one of the most deadly fighters at the front at this time, and Collishaw soon became one of the outstanding exponents of the type. While in 3(N) Squadron, his flight had painted the cowlings of their Pups black to distinguish them from the other flights, and now as flight commander he introduced this idea to his new unit, the famous 'Black Flight' thus being born; cowlings and wheel covers of the Triplanes were painted in this manner, and each aircraft was given a name beginning with the prefix 'Black'; Collishaw's usual mount was N5492 'Black Maria'. All members of the flight were Canadians, and included Flight Sub Lieutenants W.M. Alexander, G.E. Nash, E.V. Reid and J.E. Sharman, all of whom became aces. Between 30 May and the end of July Collishaw personally claimed 30 victories, to bring his score to 38 including one destroyed and five apparently out of control on 6 July — the first pilot to claim six victories in one day!

During this period an event occurred which has been much misrepresented since. On 24 June one member of the 'Black Flight', Nash, was shot down by the German ace Leutnant Karl Allmenröder, the acting Commander of Jasta 11, and was taken prisoner. Three days later Collishaw may have shot down Allmenröder; many accounts of their "long, swirling, twisting dogfight" were written, but Collishaw's own account, if more mundane, is much stranger. On 27 June he saw an Albatros Scout at extreme range, pulled up the nose of his aircraft and fired. He saw the Albatros appear to stagger, then go down in a glide, but he did not bother to put in a claim. Nash, in captivity, heard church bells ringing that night in a nearby village, and was informed that they were for the death of Allmenröder, who had been killed by a burst of fire from a Triplane, fired at extreme range! Collishaw did not learn of this until after the war, and though it does seem likely that he had indeed shot down the German ace, he never claimed, nor was credited with this victory, which is not included in his score. On 15 July Collishaw was again shot down, but again was unhurt, and five days later was awarded a DSC. On 28 July he was ordered back to Canada on leave, and on 11 August was awarded a DSO.

He returned to France in November, taking command of 13(N) Squadron on the Channel, now flying Sopwith Camels; at this time he claimed at least two more victories. In January 1918 he was again posted to 3(N) Squadron, this unit also now flying Camels, but was initially ordered not to fly combat. In April the squadron became 203 Squadron, RAF, and in June he again entered action, claiming 19 further victories by the end of September, all in Camel D3417. He received a DFC in August and a Bar to his DSO in September, but on 1 October returned to the United Kingdom, where he was promoted to Lieutenant Colonel, assisting in the setting up of the Canadian Air Force. During his air fighting he had also taken part in at least 100 indecisive fights and had driven down over 15 aircraft during these.

He remained in the RAF after the war and in early 1919 led 47 Squadron to South Russia to assist the White forces. Flying a Camel with the Fighter Flight after the unit became 'A' Squadron, whenever he could get away from administrative duties, he shot down an Albatros Scout of the Red Air Force, and also shared in a second victory to bring his score for the 1916-1919 period to 60, although some of these — like a lot of RNAS out of control claims for 1917, were classified as 'apparently out of control'. During 1940-41 he commanded No 201 Group in the Western Desert of Egypt and Libya, and then No 12 Group of Fighter Command in the Midlands of England. He retired to Vancouver in 1943 with the rank of Air Vice-Marshal, having received a CB and OBE. For many years until his death in 1976 he was much engaged in air historical research, and co-wrote his autobiography, *Air Command.*

	1916		Strutter					
1	25 Oct	Scout	9407	3W	Luneville	----	DES	AC/TBYW
2	25 Oct	Scout	9407	3W	Luneville	----	OOC	AC/TBYW
	1917			Pup				
3	15 Feb	Halb. DII	N6160	3N	Bapaume	1200	OOC	CR/RFC 15.2
4	4 Mar	Halb. DII	N6160	3N	Bapaume	1105	OOC	CR/DOR/DL
			Triplane					
5	28 Apr	Alb. DII	N5490	10N	Ostend	c2000	DES	CR/AC/?
6	30 Apr	Alb. DII	N5490	10N	E Courtemarck	1730	DES	CR/RNAS 1.5
7	9 May	Alb. DIII	N5490	10N	E Dixmude	1955	OOC	CR/DOR/DL
8	12 May	Seaplane	N5490	10N	Ostend	0750	DES	CR/RNAS 12.5
9	1 Jun	Alb. DIII	N5490	10N	S Wervicq	0920	DES(F)	CR/RFC 1.6
10s*	2 Jun	C	N5490	10N	St Julien	0900	OOC	CR/ORB/AC
11	3 Jun	Alb. DIII	N5490	10N	Roubaix	1915	DES(F)	CR/RFC 4.6
12	4 Jun	Alb. DIII	N5490	10N	Lille	2000	DES(F)	CR/AC/?
13s**	5 Jun	Alb. C	N5490	10N	Wervicq	0850	DES(F)	CR/RFC 5.6
14s***	5 Jun	Alb. C	N5490	10N	N W Poelcapelle	0900	OOC	CR/RFC 5.6
15	6 Jun	Alb. DIII	N5490	10N	Polygon Wood	1050	DES(F)	CR/RFC 6.6
16	6 Jun	Alb. DIII	N5490	10N	Polygon Wood	1105	DES(F)	CR/RFC 6.6
17	6 Jun	Alb. DIII	N5490	10N	Polygon Wood	1110	OOC	CR/RFC 6.6
18	7 Jun	Alb. DIII	N5490	10N	Menin-St Julien	0845	OOC	CR/RFC 7.6
19	15 Jun	C	N5492	10N	St Julien-Houthem	1055	OOC	CR/RFC 15.6
20	15 Jun	C	N5492	10N	Menin	1715	OOC	CR/RFC 15.6
21	15 Jun	Alb. DV	N5492	10N	Moorslede	1740	OOC	CR/RFC 15.6
22	15 Jun	Alb. DV	N5492	10N	Moorslede	1740	DES	CR/RFC 15.6
23	17 Jun	Alb. DV	N5492	10N	Roulers	1910	OOC	CR/RFC 18.6
24	24 Jun	Alb. DV	N5492	10N	Moorslede	0810	DES	CR/RFC 24.6
25	2 Jul	C	N5492	10N	Poelcapelle Stn.	1100	DES	CR/RFC 2.7
26†	6 Jul	Alb. DV	N5492	10N	Deulemont	1100	DES	CR/RFC 6.7
27†	6 Jul	Alb. DV	N5492	10N	Menin	1110	OOC	CR/RFC 6.7
28†	6 Jul	Alb. DV	N5492	10N	Menin	1110	OOC	CR/RFC 6.7
29†	6 Jul	Alb. DV	N5492	10N	Menin	1110	OOC	CR/RFC 6.7
30†	6 Jul	Alb. DV	N5492	10N	Menin	1110	OOC	CR/RFC 6.7
31†	6 Jul	Alb. DV	N5492	10N	Menin	1110	OOC	CR/RFC 6.7
32	11 Jul	Alb. DV	N5492	10N	Moorslede	2040	OOC	CR/RFC 11.7
33	12 Jul	Alb. DV	N5492	10N	Polygon Wood	0745	OOC	CR/RFC 12.7
34	20 Jul	Alb. DV	N5492	10N	Menin-Messines	0805	DES	CR/RFC 20.7
35	21 Jul	Alb. DV	N5492	10N	Passchendaele	2000	OOC	CR/RFC 22.7
36	21 Jul	Alb. DV	N5492	10N	Passchendaele	2000	OOC	CR/RFC 22.7

37	27 Jul	Alb. DV	N533	10N	N Menin	1945	DES	CR/RFC 27.7
38††	27 Jul	Alb. DV	N533	10N	Polygon Wood	1950	OOC	CR/RFC 27.7
			Camel					
39†††	10 Dec	Alb. C	B6390	13N	Dunkerque	1145	DD	CR/AC/?
40	19 Dec	Alb. DV	B6390	13N	Ostend	1520	OOC	CR/RNAS 19.12
	1918							
41	11 Jun	Pfalz DIII	D3417	203	E Outtersteene	1835	DES	CR/RAF 11.6
42	11 Jun	Pfalz DIII	D3417	203	W Armentieres	1835	OOC	CR/WD/AC
43	15 Jun	Fokker DVII	D3417	203	Ervillers	2040	DES	CR/RAF 15.6
44	26 Jun	Fokker DVII	D3417	203	Bussy, N Noyon	2000	DES	CR/RAF 26.6
45	30 Jun	Pfalz DIII	D3417	203	Houthoulst Wood	1905	OOC	CR/WD/AC
46‡	4 Jul	DFW. C	D3417	203	N E Dixmude	2130	OOC	CR/WD/AC
47‡	4 Jul	DFW. C	D3417	203	N E Dixmude	2130	OOC	CR/WD/AC
48	20 Jul	DFW. C	D3417	203	S E Merville	1100	DES	CR/RAF 20.7
49	20 Jul	DFW. C	D3417	203	Miraumont	1140	OOC	CR/WD/AC
50‡‡	22 Jul	C	D3417	203	Dorignies	0355	DES	CR/RAF 22.7
51‡‡	22 Jul	Alb. DV	D3417	203	Scarpe River	0535	DES	CR/RAF 22.7
52	9 Aug	DFW. C	D3417	203	2000yds N E Locon	1520	DES	CR/RAF 9.8
53	10 Aug	Fokker DVII	D3417	203	W Bray	1925	DES	CR/RAF 10.8
54	10 Aug	Fokker DVII	D3417	203	W Bray	1930	OOC	CR/1 BG/AC
55	15 Aug	Fokker DVII	D3417	203	S Damery	2000	DES	CR/RAF 15.8
56	5 Sep	Fokker DVII	D3417	203	Inchy-en-Artois	----	CAPT	CR/RAF 5.9
57	24 Sep	Fokker DVII	D3417	203	Epinoy	0705	DES	CR/1 BG
58	26 Sep	Fokker DVII	D3417	203	Lieu St Amand	1305	DES	CR/RAF 26.9
59	26 Sep	Fokker DVII	D3417	203	E Lieu St Amand	1308	DES	CR/RAF 26.9
	1919							
60	9 Oct	Nieuport	B6396	47	20m N Czaritsyn	----	DES	AC/.

TOTAL: 1 captured, 27 and 1 shared destroyed, 28 and 2 shared out of control, 1 driven down = 60.
*Shared with FSL E V Reid N5483, FSL W. M. Alexander N5487, FSL G.E. Nash N5492. **Shared with FSL K.G. Boyd B5478, FSL Fitzgibbon N5466, FSL G.E. Nash N6302, FSL E.V. Reid. ***Shared with FSL D.F. Fitzgibbon N5466. †The RNAS credited Collishaw with 6 out of control, but the RFC Communique noted 1 out of control, and 5 apparently out of control. Collishaws' score, like all others, includes apparently out of control claims. It will not add up unless credited with all six. ††The entire daily records of flights for Naval 10, still exist. All the above claims, except for 28th April and 4th June, are mentioned in the ORB. All other claims made for Collishaw in his co-written autobiography and other secondary sources are incorrect. †††Although only claimed as a driven down, Collishaw counted this in a list of his victories prepared when he joined 3N. Unless this was confirmed late, it should not have been counted in his score. ‡These two aircraft collided, and spun into cloud locked together. ‡‡3N records contain telegrams from various generals congratulating Collishaw for his 50th and 51st victories.
NB: AC is *Air Command*, Collishaw's autobiography, and TBYM is *Those Brave Young Men* by R. Dodds. There have been many lists published for Collishaw's claims, and the details of these and his autobiography all differ. This list accepts only those claims made with some primary evidence, with the exceptions noted above. There are occasions when published sources, including his autobiography, have Collishaw making claims on days when he was not flying according to 10N, 13N and 203 Squadron records. That this was not neccessary, can be seen from the above list. It is interesting to note that the scores of the four top scoring pilots of the war have all given similar difficulties with post war compilation. This list gives the best available summary of how Collishaw's WW 1 total was derived. He may have made another claim in Russia.

COLVILL-JONES Thomas Captain 20, 48

Colvill-Jones, an Anglo-Argentinian from Buenos Aires, joined 20 Squadron in the latter part of 1917, claiming his first victory on 18 October. He added three more during January 1918, and on 4 February, flying with the successful gunner, Captain Hedley, claimed an Albatros Scout and a balloon. C-J was promoted to Captain and posted as a flight commander to 48 Squadron, where he claimed four more victories to bring his score to 11. He was reported missing on 25 April, last being seen going after enemy aircraft above Wiencourt in the late afternoon. It was later learned that he had died of wounds on 24 May 1918 in Limburg prisoner-of-war camp.

	1917		Bristol					
1*	18 Oct	Alb. DV	B1139	20	Gheluvelt	1610	DES	CR/RFC 18.10
2**	27 Nov	Alb. DIII	B1122	20	Westroosebeke	1525	OOC	CR/RFC 27.11
	1918							
3***	3 Jan	C	B1122	20	N Moorslede	1425	DES(F)	CR/RFC 13.1
4*	19 Jan	Alb. DV	----	20	E Moorslede	----	OOC	CR/RFC 19.1
5*	28 Jan	Alb. DV	B1122	20	N W Westroosebeke	1350	OOC	CR/RFC 28.1
6†	4 Feb	Balloon	----	20	28K 5C	1055	DES	CR/RFC 4.2
7†	4 Feb	Alb. DV	----	20	Roulers-Menin Rd.	c1415	DES	CR/RFC 4.2
8††	22 Mar	Alb. DV	C4864	48	1m S E Monchy-Legache	1620	DES	CR/RFC 22.3

9†††	24 Mar	LVG.C	C4864	48	E Ham	1340	DES	CR/RFC 24.3
10‡	4 Apr	Alb. DV	C4831	48	S E Villers Brettoneaux	1330	DES	CR/RAF 4.4
11‡‡	23 Apr	Pfalz DIII	B1126	48	W Bray	1550	OOC	CR/RAF 23.4

TOTAL: 1 balloon, 6 destroyed, 4 out of control = 11.

*Observer: Lt L.H. Phelps. **Observer: Capt L.R. Speakman. ***Observer: 2/Lt H.G. Crowe. †Observer: Capt J.H. Hedley. ††Observer: 2/Lt J.A. Galbraith. †††Observer: 2/Lt D. Wishart-Orr. ‡Observer: 2/Lt W. Hart. ‡‡Observer: 2/Lt J.M.J. Moore.

COMPSTON Robert John Orton Major 8(N), 40

Born the son of a vicar on 9 January 1898, Compston joined the RNAS in August 1915. In 1916, after a period on Home Defence, he was posted to 8 Naval Squadron, and except for brief periods on leave, flew with this unit until the end of February 1918. He was once wounded in action in September 1917, but soon recovered. He was promoted to flight commander and received the DSO, DSC and two Bars whilst with the squadron. After leaving 8 Naval for a rest, he became Commanding Officer of 40 Squadron, RAF, in August 1918. He died on 28 January 1962, having served with the RAF again during World War II.

	1916		Nieuport					
1	26 Dec	Alb. C	8750	8N	2m N Cambrai	1000	OOC	CR/RFC 26.12
	1917		Triplane					
2	5 Apr	Halb. DII	N5471	8N	S E La Bassee	1245	OOC	CR/RFC 5.4
3	30 Apr	Aviatik C	N5471	8N	E Douai	0645	OOC	CR/RFC 30.4
4	30 Apr	Aviatik C	N5471	8N	W Douai	0700	OOC	CR/RFC 30.4
5	2 May	C	N5471	8N	N E Douai	0950	OOC	CR/RFC 2.5
6s*	10 May	Alb. C	N5471	8N	E Douai	0730	OOC	CR/RFC 10.5
7	3 Jun	C	N5471	8N	Vitry-Douai	0745-0905	OOC	ORB/RFC 3.6
8**	4 Jun	C	N5471	8N	E Lens	0945	DES(F)	CR/RFC 4.6
9***	12 Jun	Alb. DIII	N6299	8N	Lens	0950	OOC	CR/RFC 12.6
10s†	16 Jun	C	N6299	8N	Loos-E Lens	0830	CAPT	CR/RFC 16.6
			Camel					
11	8 Nov	Alb. DIII	B6340	8N	Oppy	0820	DES(F)	CR/RFC 8.11
12	22 Nov	LVG. C	B6340	8N	Vitry en Artois	1055	OOC	CR/RFC 22.11
13s††	5 Dec	Rumpler C	B6340	8N	----	----	OOC	CR/RFC 6.12
14s†††	6 Dec	DFW. C	B6340	8N	Drocourt-Douai	1125	OOC	CR/RFC 6.12
15	28 Dec	DFW. C	B6319	8N	Harnes-Pont a Vendin	1240	DES(F)	CR/RFC 28.12
	1918							
16s‡	1 Jan	Hannover C	B6340	8N	Fampoux	1128	CAPT	CR/RFC 1.1
17s‡‡	1 Jan	Alb. DV	B6340	8N	Neuvireuil	1530	OOC	CR/RFC 1.1
18s‡‡‡	3 Jan	DFW. C	B6340	8N	Arras	1005	DES	CR/RFC 3.1
19	3 Jan	DFW. C	B6340	8N	Epmay Wood	1120	OOC	CR/RFC 3.1
20s§	6 Jan	Alb. DV	B6340	8N	Quiery la Motte	1150	OOC	CR/RFC 6.1
21s§§	2 Feb	C	B6340	8N	Ostricourt-Douai	1130	DES	CR/RFC 2.2
22s§§	2 Feb	Alb. DV	B6340	8N	Carvin	1215	OOC	CR/RFC 2.2
23	3 Feb	DFW. C	B6340	8N	S E Douai	1125	OOC	CR/RFC 3.2
24s#	3 Feb	DFW. C	B6340	8N	Sallaumines	1225	DES	CR/RFC 3.2
25	18 Feb	Alb. DV	B7203	8N	Douai	1115	OOC	CR/RFC 18.2

TOTAL: 2 shared captured, 2 and 4 shared destroyed, 11 and 6 shared out of control = 25.

*Shared with FSL E.A. Bennetts N5442. **Shared with F/L R.R. Thornley N5465, FSL E.A. Bennetts N5492. ***Possibly Uffz Otto Rosenfeld of Jasta 12, who was wounded. †Shared with F/Lt R.R. Thornely N5465; the crew were Vzfw H. Totsch, KIA, and Lt K. Riegel, POW, of F.A.A. 211. ††Shared with FSL P.M. Dennett, FSL E.G. Johnstone. †††Shared with FSL W.L. Jordon, FSL P.M. Dennett. ‡Shared with FSL G.K. Cooper B6321, Capt E.C. Mannock of 40 in B665. This was Vzfw F. Korbacher/Lt W. Klein who were killed from FAA 288. ‡‡Shared with FSL A.J. Dixon B6319. ‡‡‡Shared with FSL W.L. Jordon B6319, FSL P.M. Dennett B6447. Probably Lt J. Lampart/Lt A. Zipperer of FA 46, who were killed. §Shared with FSL W.L. Jordon B6447. §§Shared with FSL R.L. Johns, FSL H. Day, FSL W.F. Crundall. #Shared with FSL W.F. Crundall B6356, FSL E.G. Johnstone B6377.

COMPTON Harry Neville Lieutenant 23

Lieutenant Compton, a Canadian from Westholme, British Columbia, served with 23 Squadron during the summer and autumn of 1918, during which time he claimed five victories. His DFC was gazetted on 3 June 1919.

	1918		Dolphin					
1	1 Jul	Alb. DV	D3715	23	N E Hangest	2045	DES	CR/V BG
2	7 Jul	Pfalz DIII	C3810	23	N Proyart	1900	DES	CR/RAF 7.7
3	6 Sep	Fokker DVII	D3754	23	St Quentin	0915	DES(F)	CR/RAF 6.9
4	28 Oct	Fokker DVII	C4130	23	Bois de Nouvion	1130	OOC	CR/V BG
5s*	1 Nov	DFW. C	C4130	23	Petit Bart	1200	DES	CR/RAF 1.11

TOTAL: 3 and 1 shared destroyed, 1 out of control = 5.

*Shared with Capt J.W. Pearson F5961, Lt E.J. Taylor E4139.

CONDER Reginald Edward Lieutenant 20

Conder flew FE 2Ds in 20 Squadron early in 1917, and with Air Mechanic J.J. Cowell as gunner, claimed six victories during the month of May.

	1917		FE 2D					
1*	29 Apr	Alb. DIII	A6539	20	Courtrai	1700	OOC	CR/RFC 29.4
2**	5 May	Alb. DIII	A6400	20	Poelcapelle	1710	OOC	CR/RFC 6.5
3**	20 May	Alb. DIII	A6412	20	Menin	0920	OOC	CR/RFC 20.5
4**	25 May	Alb. DIII	A6415	20	Wervicq	0850	OOC	CR/RFC 25.5
5**	26 May	Alb. DIII	A6415	20	Comines	1030	OOC	CR/RFC 26.5
6**	26 May	Alb. DIII	A6415	20	S E Ypres	2010	DES(F)	CR/RFC 27.5

TOTAL: 1 destroyed, 5 out of control = 6.
*Observer: 2/Lt H.G. Neville. **Observer: AM J.J. Cowell.

CONINGHAM Arthur Major 32, 90

Born in Brisbane, Australia, on 19 January 1895, he spent his early life in Wellington, New Zealand. He served with the New Zealand Expeditionary Force in Somaliland and Egypt at the beginning of the war. Invalided out of the service with typhoid in 1916, his military career seemed to be at an end. However, he came to England that same year and joined the RFC. In 1917 he served with 32 Squadron from early in the year, flying DH 2s and DH 5s, becoming a flight commander. During July he claimed at least nine enemy machines (which was no mean achievement when flying the DH 5), receiving the DSO and MC. The following year he took command of 92 Squadron and led it to France during June. He flew at the head of his unit whenever possible, adding five more victories to his score and being awarded a DFC. He was twice wounded in action, once with 32 Squadron and once with 92. He remained in the RAF after the war, and his nickname of 'Maori' gradually became 'Mary', by which he was known for the rest of his life. During World War II he held various commands, becoming AOC of the Western Desert Air Force in North Africa from late 1941 to early 1943. He then became AOC of 2nd Tactical Air Force until 1945, attaining the rank of Air Marshal; for his services he was knighted Sir Arthur. On 30 January 1948 he was lost on a civil flight to Bermuda when a passenger in an Avro Tudor of British South American Airways. At the time of going to print, his biography by Vincent Orange had just been published.

	1917		DH 2					
1s*	23 Jan	C	----	32	Ervillers	1515	DES(F)	CR/ORB/?
			DH 5					
2	11 Jul	Alb. DV	A9179	32	W Gheluvelt	1530	OOC	CR/RFC 11.7
3	12 Jul	Alb. DV	A9179	32	Gheluvelt	1225	DES	ORB/RFC 12.7
4s**	20 Jul	C	A9179	32	Zandvoorde	0950	OOC	CR/RFC 20.7
5	20 Jul	Alb. DV	A9179	32	Zandvoorde	1015	OOC	CR/RFC 20.7
6	20 Jul	Alb. DV	A9179	32	Wervicq	1115	DES	CR/RFC 20.7
7***	27 Jul	Alb. C	A9179	32	N Polygon Wood	0900	DES	CR/RFC 27.7
8	27 Jul	Alb. DV	A9179	32	E Houthoulst Wood	2025	OOC	CR/RFC 27.7
9	30 Jul	Alb. DV	A9179	32	Langemarck	1900	OOC	ORB/RC/
10	30 Jul	Alb. DV	A9179	32	Langemarck	1905	OOC	ORB/RC/
	1918		SE 5A					
11s†	29 Jul	C	D6883	92	N Estaires	1130	DES	CR/RAF 29.7
12	11 Aug	Fokker DVII	D6883	92	Nesle	1130	OOC	CR/ORB/?
13	11 Aug	Fokker DVII	D6883	92	Nesle	1130	DES	CR/RAF 11.8
14	5 Sep	Fokker DVII	D6993	92	1m W Cambrai	1100	DES	CR/RAF 5.9

TOTAL: 4 and 3 shared destroyed, 6 and 1 shared out of control = 14.
*Shared with Capt L.P. Aizlewood. Lt G.J. King, Lt F. Billinge, Lt T.A. Gooch, Lt St C.C. Taylor, Lt A.C. Randell. **Shared with Lt G.A. Wells A9386. ***Shared with Lt H.J. Edwards A9372, Lt G.A. Wells A9374, Lt E. Pownall A9396. †Shared with Lt E. Shapard D6915.

CONN Kenneth Burns Lieutenant 88

Born on 11 July 1896 in Ashton, Ontario, in Canada, Kenneth Conn was a dancer before the war. He served with the 3rd Reserve Battalion and the 234th Battalion, Canadian Expeditionary Force, 1915-16. He joined the RFC in March 1917, and went to 88 Squadron, flying Bristol Fighters in 1918 until the Armistice, by which time he was the unit's top-scorer. With his various rear seat observers, he accounted for 21 enemy aircraft, yet strangely his DFC was awarded for ground attack missions. During one air fight on 16 September, he attacked one Fokker and it spun down, colliding with another — both crashed. After the war he joined the RCAF, but was injured in a crash in 1921 that ended his flying career. During World War II he again served with the RCAF, reaching the rank of Group Captain, becoming Director of Staff Duties at Air Force HQ. When this war ended, he returned to his position as General Manager of University Tours Ltd., Toronto.

	1918		Bristol					
1*	5 Jun	Alb. DV	C787	88	Messines	2015	DES	CR/RAF 5.6
2*	5 Jun	Alb. DV	C787	88	Messines	2015	DES	CR/RAF 5.6
3**	28 Jun	Halb. C	C787	88	Houthoulst Forest	2000	DES(F)	CR/RAF 28.6
4***	29 Jun	Fokker DVII	C787	88	Ghistelles	2010	DES	CR/RAF 29.6
5s†	29 Jun	Fokker DVII	C787	88	Ghistelles	2010	DES	CR/RAF 29.6
6*	1 Jul	Fokker DVII	C787	88	W Westroosebeke	1945	DES(F)	CR/RAF 1.7
7*	1 Jul	Fokker DVII	C787	88	W Westroosebeke	1945	OOC	CR/SR
8***	19 Aug	Fokker DVII	E2216	88	Oignies	1025	OOC	CR/SR
9s††	19 Aug	Fokker DVII	E2216	88	Oignies	1025	OOC	CR/SR
10†††	4 Sep	Fokker DrI	E2216	88	Provin	0930	OOC	CR/SR
11*	5 Sep	Fokker DVII	E2216	88	N E Armentieres	1845	OOC	CR/SR
12*	16 Sep	Fokker DVII	E2216	88	N E Habourdin a/d	1750	DES	CR/RAF 16.9
13*	16 Sep	Fokker DVII	E2216	88	N E Habourdin a/d	1750	DES	CR/RAF 16.9
14*	20 Sep	Fokker DVII	E2216	88	Quesnoy	0750	OOC	CR/SR
15s‡	20 Sep	Fokker DVII	E2216	88	S E Quesnoy	0755	DES	CR/RAF 20.9
16‡‡	3 Oct	Fokker DVII	E2216	88	Meurchin	1730	DES	CR/RAF 3.10
17‡‡‡	23 Oct	Fokker DVII	E2216	88	Beclers	1710	DES	CR/RAF 23.10
18§	30 Oct	Fokker DVII	E2612	88	Peruwelz	0855	DES	CR/RAF 30.10
19§	30 Oct	Fokker DVII	E2612	88	Peruwelz	0855	DES	CR/RAF 30.10
20§	4 Nov	Fokker DVII	E2216	88	Foucaumont	1308	DES	CR/RAF 4.11

TOTAL: 12 and 2 shared destroyed, 5 and 1 shared out of control = 20.
*Observer: 2/Lt B. Digby-Worsley. **Observer: 2/Lt B.H. Smyth; possibly Lt M. Handschuher/Lt A. Knadgen of FAA 288b who were killed. ***Observer: 2/Lt B.H. Smyth. †Observer: 2/Lt B.H. Smyth; shared with Capt K.R. Simpson/Sgt C. Hill, Lt R.J. Cullen/Lt E.H. Ward, Lt A.W. Wheeler/Lt T.S. Chiltern. ††Observer: Lt B.H. Smyth, shared with Capt E.C. Johnson/2/Lt J. Rudkin C4867. †††Observer: Sgt C.M. Maxwell. ‡Observer: 2/Lt B. Digby-Worlsey; shared with Capt E.C. Johnston/Lt W.I.N. Grant, Lt G.R. Poole/Sgt C. Hill. ‡‡Observer: Lt A.B. Radford. ‡‡‡Observer: 2/Lt D.A. Vavasour. §Observer: 2/Lt K.C.W. Craig.

COOKE Douglas Graham Captain 20

Cooke joined 20 Squadron in the winter of 1917-18, and gained his first victory on 22 January. Three more victories followed in February and another in March. He was awarded an MC and promoted flight commander, adding a further seven victories to his score during the spring. Of the total of 13 claims, nine fell to his front gun.

	1918		Bristol					
1*	22 Jan	Alb. DV	A7256	20	S W Roulers	1110	OOC	CR/RFC 22.1
2*	22 Jan	Alb. DV	A7256	20	S Moorslede	1115	DES(F)	CR/RFC 22.1
3**	4 Feb	Alb. DV	----	20	Roulers	c1415	OOC	SR/RFC 4.2
4**	5 Feb	Alb. DV	C4605	20	N Staden	1120	OOC	CR/RFC 5.2
5**	5 Feb	Alb. DV	C4605	20	N Staden	1120	OOC	CR/RFC 5.2
6***	9 Mar	Alb. DV	C4605	20	S Comines	0800	OOC	CR/RFC 9.3
7*	21 Apr	Alb. DV	C4749	20	N Wervicq	1100	OOC	CR/RAF 21.4
8*	3 May	Fokker DrI	C4749	20	S E Hollebeke	1720	DES(F)	CR/RAF 3.5
9*	3 May	Alb. DV	C4749	20	S E Ypres	1730	OOC	CR/11 W/SR
10*	8 May	Fokker DrI	C4749	20	Comines-Wervicq	1650	DES	CR/RAF 8.5
11†	17 May	Alb. DV	----	20	E Armentieres	0815	OOC	CR/11 W/SR
12††	19 May	Pfalz DIII	C4749	20	Estaires	1025	DES(F)	CR/RAF 19.5
13††	19 May	Pfalz DIII	C4749	20	Laventie	1030	DES	CR/RAF 19.5

TOTAL: 6 destroyed, 7 out of control = 13.
*Observer: Lt H.G. Crowe. **Observer: 2/Lt C.J. Agelasto. ***Observer: 2/Lt J.J. Scaramanga. †Observer: 2/Lt E. Hardcastle. ††Observer: Lt S.H.P. Masding.

COOMBE James Geoffrey Captain 21, 29

Born 1 April 1894, Coombe was commissioned in the Lincoln Regiment in 1915. In August of that year he transferred to the RFC and served as an observer in 21 Squadron. He then undertook pilot training, and was posted to 29 Squadron in October 1917, claiming his first victory on 8 November; two more followed before the end of the year, and then another three in January 1918. His final claim was made on 18 March, and during this month he was promoted to flight commander. He left the squadron when it withdrew to re-equip with SE 5As.

	1917		Nieuport					
1	8 Nov	C	B6821	29	Houthoulst	c1600	OOC	CR/RFC 8.11
2	26 Nov	Alb. DV	B6821	29	Gulleghem	1430	OOC	CR/RFC 26.11
3	16 Dec	Alb. DV	----	29	Roulers area	1020	OOC	SR/RFC 16.12
	1918							
4	24 Jan	C	B6832	29	N E Roulers	1230	OOC	CR/RFC 24.1
5	28 Jan	Alb. DV	B6836	29	S Roulers	1220	OOC	CR/RFC 28.1
6	30 Jan	Alb. DV	B6836	29	W Roulers	1225	OOC	CR/RFC 30.1
7	18 Feb	Alb. DIII	B6820	29	N W Courtemarck	1120	DES	CR/ORB/?
8	18 Mar	Pflaz DIII	B6786	29	S E Rumbeke	1145	OOC	CR/RFC 18.3

TOTAL: 1 destroyed, 7 out of control = 8.

COOMBES Lawrence Percival Captain 10(N), 210

Born in India on 9 April 1899, Coombes was educated at the City of London School. He joined the RNAS in July 1917 and after training at Crystal Palace, Chingford and Cranwell, went to France to join 12 Naval Squadron in January 1918. After two weeks with this holding unit he went to 10 Naval, which became 210 Squadron, RAF, in April. He became a flight commander and received the DFC; by the time he returned to England on 9 August he had claimed 15 victories. For the remainder of the war he was with 204 Training Depot Squadron at Eastchurch; he left the service in March 1919. That summer, in company with Charles Kingsford-Smith and Derek Shepperson, he toured Oxford, Abingdon and several Lancashire towns, flying and 'barnstorming' in three BE 2Es. He then went to London University and completed his engineering degree. He later worked at the Royal Aircraft Establishment, Farnborough, the MAEE at Felixstowe, and in 1927 he accompanied the Schneider Trophy Team to Venice as technical officer. He returned to the RAE in 1930, and in 1938 was chosen to establish an aeronautical research laboratory for the Australian Government in Melbourne. In 1960 he was seconded to the United Nations to advise on the establishment of similar laboratories in India, and also became Chairman of CAARC, and Chief Supervisor at the Aero Research Laboratory in Australia. He died in Melbourne on 2 June 1988.

	1918		Camel					
1	24 Mar	Alb. DV	B6358	10N	Menin-Roulers	0920	DES(F)	CR/RNAS 24.3
2	9 Apr	Alb. DV	B6358	210	N La Bassee	1545	DES(F)	CR/RAF 9.4
3	8 May	Alb. DV	B7252	210	Armentieres	1055	OOC	CR/ORB/?
4	11 May	Alb. DV	B7252	210	Armentieres	1925	OOC	CR/ORB/?
5s*	27 May	Pfalz DIII	B7153	210	Bailleul	0820	OOC	CR/ORB/?
6s**	1 Jun	C	B7153	210	3m S Bailleul	1745	DES	CR/RAF 1.6
7	10 Jun	Fokker DVII	D3387	210	S E Kemmel	0815	OOC	CR/ORB/?
8	23 Jun	Fokker DVII	D3387	210	3m S W Armentieres	2000	DES	CR/RAF 23.6
9s***	26 Jun	Fokker DVII	D3387	210	1m W Armentieres	1920	DES	CR/RAF 26.6
10s†	26 Jun	Fokker DVII	D3387	210	Ypres-Dickebusch	1945	OOC	CR/ORB/?
11s†	26 Jun	Pfalz DIII	D3387	210	Ypres-Dickebusch	1945	OOC	CR/ORB/?
12s†	26 Jun	Pfalz DIII	D3387	210	Ypres-Dickebusch	1945	OOC	CR/ORB/?
13	6 Jul	Pfalz DIII	D3387	210	Lestrem	1155	DES(F)	CR/RAF 6.7
14s††	31 Jul	Fokker DVII	D9673	210	Nieuport-Dixmude	1115	OOC	CR/5 GR Comm
15s††	31 Jul	Fokker DVII	D9673	210	Wervicq	1825	OOC	CR/5 GR Comm

TOTAL: 4 and 2 shared destroyed, 3 and 6 shared out of control = 15.

*Shared with Lt C.W. Payton C66. **Shared with Lt C.W. Payton B7146. ***Shared with Lt K.R. Unger D9608, Lt I.C. Sanderson B7155; this was Obflgm K. Schonfelder of Jasta 7, a 13 victory ace who was killed. †Shared with Lt K.R. Unger D9608, Lt I.C. Sanderson B7155. ††Shared with Lt I.C. Sanderson E1405.

COOPER Arthur Gabbettis Lieutenant 28

Born in Essex, Cooper joined the RFC and was posted to 28 Squadron in 1917, serving with the unit both in France and Italy. He returned to England on 4 July 1918.

	1917		Camel					
1	27 Oct	Alb. DV	B6364	28	Roulers	1343	OOC	CR/RFC 27.10
2s*	29 Dec	Alb. DV	B6362	28	Lentaia	1500	DES(F)	CR/RFC 7 BG
	1918							

3	19 May	Alb. DV	D1911	28	Arsie	0715	DES(F)	CR/ORB 14 W
4	19 May	Alb. DV	D1911	28	Arsie	0716	DES	CR/ORB/14 W
5	19 May	Alb. DV	D1911	28	Arsie	0717	OOC	CR/ORB/?
6**	18 Jun	Alb. DV	D1911	28	Cessalto	1840	DES	CR/ORB/14 W
7	20 Jun	Alb. DV	D8103	28	Montello	1100	DES	CR/ORB/14 W

TOTAL: 4 and 1 shared destroyed, 2 out of control = 7.
*Shared with Lt C.M. McEwan B2461. **This was Fwp Hugo Konig of Flik 51j, who was killed in 153:214.

COOPER Gerald Kempster Captain 8(N), 208

Cooper was born in Catford, South London, on 13 November 1897 and joined the RNAS on 9 September 1916. After a period on Home Defence duties he was posted to 8 Naval Squadron in December 1917. Before he left in late May 1918 for a rest, he had claimed five enemy machines shot down out of control. He returned to the unit (now 208 Squadron, RAF) in August with the rank of Captain, claiming one more victory on 1 September.

	1918		Camel					
1s*	1 Jan	Hannover C	B6321	8N	Fampoux	1138	CAPT	CR/RFC 1.1
2s**	6 Apr	Fokker DrI	B7189	208	Lens	1130	OOC	CR/RAF 6.4
3	8 May	Alb. DV	D1873	208	Provin	1115	OOC	CR/RAF 8.5
4	18 May	Pfalz DIII	D1919	208	S Merville	1150	OOC	CR/RAF 18.5
5s***	22 May	C	----	208	2m N E Lens	0800	OOC	CR/ORB/?
6	1 Sep	Fokker DVII	E1587	208	Ecourt St Quentin	1850	OOC	CR/ORB/?

TOTAL: 1 shared captured, 3 and 2 shared out of control = 6.
*Shared with F/Cdr R.J.O. Compston B6340 and Capt E.C. Mannock of 40 Sqn in B665; Vzfw F. Korbacher/Lt W. Klein of FAA 288 both killed. **Shared with Capt T.F.N. Gerrard B7196, Lt W.H. Sneath B7187. ***Shared with Capt W.L. Jordon, Lt R.L. Johns, Lt J.S. McDonald, Lt E.G. Johnstone, Lt P.M. Dennett, Lt H.H.S. Fowler.

COOPER Maurice Lea Captain 213

Born on 18 December 1898, in Dublin, Maurice Cooper received his education in York. He joined the RNAS on 29 April 1917 as a Flight Sub Lieutenant, and served with 13(N)/213 Squadron, claiming six victories with this unit between December 1917 and 30 July 1918, becoming a flight commander. He was awarded a DFC on 15 June, but was killed on 2 October 1918 when his Camel (F3951) was hit by machine gun fire from the ground whilst he was bombing a train north-east of Gitsberg; his fighter spun straight into the ground.

	1917		Camel					
1s*	5 Dec	C	B6407	13N	4m N W Wenduyne	1505	DES	CR/RNAS 5.12
	1918							
2s**	29 Jan	Seaplane	B6410	13N	100 yards off Blankenberghe Pier	1400	DES	DOR/RNAS 29.1
3s***	12 Mar	C	B6410	13N	Ostend-Wenduyne	0905	DES(F)	CR/RNAS 12.3
4†	1 Apr	Seaplane C	B6416	213	Zeebrugge	c1430	DES(F)	DOR/5 GR 1.4
5s††	7 Jul	Alb. DV	B3326	213	Middelkerke	1140	OOC	CR/5 GR 7.7
6	30 Jul	Alb. DV	D3326	213	Bruges	1150	OOC	CR/5 GR 30.7

TOTAL: 1 and 3 shared destroyed, 1 and 1 shared out of control = 6.
*Shared with FSL J.W. Pinder B6357, FSL G.C. MacKay N6335, FSL J. de C Paynter B6391. **Shared with FCdr L.H. Slatter B7186, FSL J. de C Paynter B3782, FSL J.E. Greene B3989, FSL G.C. McKay B6407. ***Shared with FSL J.E. Greene, FSL G.C. MacKay B6400, FSL Bell B7226. †This was FlObmt M. Behrendt/Lt D.R. Hauptvogel of Seeflug 1, who were killed. ††Shared with Lt G.D. Smith B8368, Lt Jenner B6448, Lt Allott D9647, Lt Rankin B7270, Lt C.J. Sims D9627.

COOPER Norman Lieutenant 73

An American, whose real name was E.S. Tooker, he served with the 3rd Canadian Divisional Supply Column as a private from June 1916 until August 1917, when he decided to join the RFC. Following training, he went to 73 Squadron, flying Camels until the end of the war, receiving a DFC. He took part in many low level ground attacks and the recommendation for his award credited him with eight victories; his actual score would appear to be six.

	1918		Camel					
1s*	25 Jul	LVG. C	D6484	73	Cohan	1945	DES	CR/RAF 25.7
2s**	30 Jul	LVG. C	F6063	73	N Vezilly	1400	DES	CR/RAF 30.7
3	19 Aug	Fokker DVII	F6063	73	S E Combles	0810	DES	CR/RAF 19.8
4	25 Aug	Fokker DVII	F6063	73	N E Bapaume	1830	DES(F)	CR/RAF 25.8
5	15 Sep	Fokker DVII	C3312	73	Cambrai	1100	OOC	CR/?
6	15 Sep	Fokker DVII	C3312	73	N E Bourlon Wood	1815	DES	CR/RAF 15.9

TOTAL: 3 and 2 shared destroyed, 1 out of control = 6.
*Shared with Lt W.S. Stephenson C8296. **Shared with Lt E.J. Lussier, Lt A. McConnel-Wood.

COTTLE Jack Captain 45

Jack Cottle was born in Plymouth, Devon, on 19 June 1892, but his early life was spent in Zululand, where he was known by a Zulu name which meant 'the man with the funny elbows'! In 1914 he joined the South African Mounted Rifles and served with them until he transferred to the RFC in 1917, being commissioned on 27 July. Posted to 45 Squadron in Italy, he flew with this unit until the end of the war, being awarded a DFC and claiming his 13th and final victory when the squadron returned to France in the final months of 1918 to join the Independent Air Force. After the war he decided to stay in the RAF, becoming a flight commander in 79 Squadron in 1919, and subsequently serving in India with 48 Squadron. He later married a Major in the Women's Indian Army. He served in Iraq in 1924, and was seconded to the Egyptian Air Force in 1932. He became a Group Captain in 1940 and retired from the RAF in 1942, being re-employed until 1944. He then retired to India where he died on 15 August 1967. He received an MBE, and had also been awarded the Italian Silver Medal for Military Valour in 1918.

	1918		Camel					
1s*	10 Mar	DFW. C	B6354	45	S E Salgarada	1130	DES	CR/ORB/7 BG
2**	18 May	Alb. DIII	B5181	45	Poncegno, W Borgo	0715	DES(F)	CR/ORB/14 W
★	5 Jul	LVG. C	B7380	45	Astica-Pederiva	1815	DES(F)	ORB/?
3	12 Jul	LVG. C	D8113	45	Mt Cismon	0945	DES	ORB/14 W
4***	31 Jul	Phonix D1	D8237	45	Fontane	0915	DES(F)	ORB/14 W
5	5 Aug	D	D8237	45	Mt Grappa	1030	DES	ORB/14 W
6	20 Aug	C	D8237	45	Torre an Levenza	1045	DES	CR/ORB/14 W
7	20 Aug	C	D8237	45	S Asiago	1910	CAPT	CR/ORB/14 W
8	31 Aug	Alb. DIII	D8237	45	Peralto	0935	DES	CR/ORB/14 W
9†	31 Aug	Alb. DIII	D8237	45	Arsiero	0940	CAPT	CR/ORB/14 W
10††	31 Aug	Alb. DIII	D8237	45	Posino	0945	CAPT	CR/ORB/14 W
11	31 Aug	C	D8327	45	Valsugana, Pesina	1035	OOC	CR/ORB/14 W
12	3 Nov	Fokker DVII	D8211	45	Herbeville	1155	OOC	CR/ORB/
13	5 Nov	Rumpler C	D8327	45	E Diaze	1200	DES	CR/ORB/IAF

TOTAL: 3 captured, 7 and 1 shared destroyed, 2 out of control = 13.
*Shared with 2/Lt R.J. Dawes B6412. **Probably Flp J. Skvor of Flik 27, who was killed in 153:233. ***This was Fw J. Acs of Flik 60j, who landed severely damaged. †This was Oblt Josef Purer of Flik 3j who was killed in 153:234. ††This was Stfw Otto Forster of Flik 3j, who was wounded and taken prisoner in 253:03. ★Although set on fire, the aircraft went down under control, and was only credited as a 'driven down'.

COWAN Sidney Edward Captain 24, 29

Born near Dublin in 1897, Cowan was an original member of 24 Squadron in September 1915. One of the very first aces of the RFC, he was a true pioneer of single-seat fighter piloting and tactics. His second victory, a two-seater, he strafed on the ground, killing the crew. Cowan nearly regretted this as his engine then failed, forcing him to land near his victims behind enemy lines. However he got the engine going again, and managed to take off and return to his own airfield. He was awarded the MC and two Bars, claiming seven victories. On 17 November 1916 he collided with another British aircraft and was killed; at this time he was 'C' Flight commander in 29 Squadron. His elder brother, Captain P.C. Cowan, was also a scout pilot and was killed in action almost a year later on 8 November 1917.

	1916		DH 2					
1	4 May	C	5966	24	Hem-Clery	0900	DES	CR/RFC 4.5
2	1 Jul	C	5964	24	Pys	0745	OOC	CR/RFC 1.7
3	29 Jul	Roland CII	6000	24	Morval-Vaux Wood	1400	DES	CR/RFC 29.7
4	3 Aug	LVG. C	5904	24	Sailly	1530	OOC	CR/RFC 3.8
5	9 Aug	C	5998	24	Le Sars	0730	DES	CR/IV BG
6	16 Sep	Fokker DII?	5964	24	Sailly-Saillisel	1015	DES(F)	CR/RFC 16.9
7	17 Nov	Halb. DII	A2555	29	----	----	OOC	RFC 17.11

TOTAL: 4 destroyed, 3 out of control = 7.

COWELL J.J. Sergeant 20

Cowell served as a 2nd Class Air Mechanic in 20 Squadron, flying as a gunner in FE 2Ds from April to August 1917 with pilots including Lieutenants R.E. Conder, R.M. Trevathan, C.R. Richards and O.H.D. Vickers. He was one of the two top-scoring observer/gunners with the unit during the year, being awarded DCM, MM and Bar. Posted to Home Establishment to train as a pilot, he returned to 20 Squadron in summer 1918 as a Sergeant to fly Bristol Fighters. On 29 July he and his observer claimed a Fokker DVII shot down to bring his total claims to 16, but next day while flying E2471 near Ypres with Corporal C. Hill as observer, he was shot down by Leutnant Fritz Röth of Jasta 16 for that pilot's 17th victory.

	1917		FE 2D					
1*	5 May	Alb. DIII	A6400	20	Poelcapelle	1710	OOC	CR/RFC 6.5
2**	13 May	C	A6412	20	Reckem a/d	1040	DES	CR/RFC 13.5
3*	20 May	Alb. DIII	A6412	20	Menin	0920	OOC	CR/RFC 20.5
4*	25 May	Alb. DIII	A6415	20	Wervicq	0850	OOC	CR/RFC 25.5
5*	26 May	Alb. DIII	A6415	20	Comines	1030	OOC	CR/RFC 26.5
6*	26 May	Alb. DIII	A6415	20	S E Ypres	2010	DES(F)	CR/RFC 27.5
7***	2 Jun	Alb. DIII	A6480	20	Gheluvelt	0945	DES	CR/RFC 2.6
8†	29 Jun	Alb. DV	A6376	20	Becelaere	1610	OOC	CR/RFC 29.6
9†	12 Jul	Alb. DV	A6376	20	E Ploegsteert Wood	1700	DES	CR/RFC 12.7
10†	12 Jul	Alb. DV	A6376	20	E Ploegsteert Wood	1715	OOC	CR/RFC 12.7
11††	17 Jul	Alb. DV	A6468	20	Polygon Wood	1945	DES(F)	CR/RFC 17.7
12††	17 Jul	Alb. DV	A6468	20	28Q 28	1950	DES	CR/RFC 17.7
13†	20 Jul	Alb. DV	A6376	20	Wervicq	0955	OOC	CR/ORB/11 W
14†	22 Jul	Alb. DV	A6376	20	Menin-Wervicq	1650	OOC	CR/RFC 22.7
15	28 Jul	Alb. DV	A6376	20	E Messines	1845	OOC	CR/RFC 28.7
	1918		Bristol					
16†††	29 Jul	Fokker DVII	E2471	20	N W Wervicq	2010	OOC	CR/ORB/11 W

TOTAL: 6 destroyed, 10 out of control = 16.
*Pilot: 2/Lt R.E. Conder. **Pilot: 2/Lt M.P. Scott. ***Pilot: 2/Lt R.M. Trevethan. †Pilot: 2/Lt O.H.D. Vickers. ††Pilot: Lt C.R. Richards. †††Observer: Cpl. C. Hill.

COWPER Andrew King Captain 24

Born on 16 November 1898 in Sydney, Australia, Cowper joined 24 Squadron on 26 August 1917, where he first flew the DH 5 fighter, claiming his first two victories on this type. He then converted to SE 5As and took part in a number of successful combats during February 1918 whereby he increased his score to nine. The award of an MC was gazetted on 22 April, but in the meantime during March 1918 he had been extremely active, becoming a flight commander on 24th and claiming a further 11 victories for which he received two Bars to his decoration. He left for Home Establishment on 11 April 1918, and later in 1919 served with 79 Squadron based in Germany with the occupation forces. Cowper died in his native Australia during the 1970s.

	1917		DH 5					
1s*	28 Oct	Alb. DIII	A9232	24	Ramscapelle	1230	DES	CR/RFC 29.10
2	9 Nov	Alb. DIII	A9232	24	Beerst	0845	OOC	CR/SR
	1918		SE 5A					
3s**	18 Feb	DFW. C	B664	24	La Fere	0830	OCC	CR/RFC WD
4	18 Feb	Pfalz DIII	B664	24	2-3m E St Quentin	1430	OOC	CR/RFC 18.2
5s***	19 Feb	Rumpler C	B664	24	Servais	0840	DES(F)	CR/RFC 19.2
6s***	19 Feb	DFW. C	B664	24	Bernot	0850	DES	CR/RFC 19.2
7	26 Feb	Fokker DrI	B664	24	E Laon	0840	DES	CR/RFC 26.2
8†	26 Feb	Pfalz DIII	B664	24	La Fere	0900	CAPT	CR/RFC 26.2
9s††	6 Mar	Alb. DV	B664	24	St Quentin	1015	OOC	CR/RFC 6.3
10†††	8 Mar	Rumpler C	B664	24	Bellenglise	0800	DES	CR/RFC 8.3
11	13 Mar	Alb. DV	C5428	24	Mezieres	1235	OOC	CR/RFC 13.3
12s‡	15 Mar	Rumpler C	C5428	24	N Premonte	1020	DES	CR/RFC 15.3
13	17 Mar	Pfalz DIII	B8407	24	S W Ramicourt	1820	DES	CR/RFC 17.3
14	18 Mar	Pfalz DIII	B8407	24	Itancourt	1145	OOC	CR/RFC 18.3
15	21 Mar	Alb. DV	B8407	24	Bellicourt	1415	OOC	CR/RFC 21.3
16	21 Mar	Alb. DV	B8407	24	S Havrincourt	1700	DES(F)	CR/RFC 21.3
17s‡‡	23 Mar	C	B8407	24	E Matigny	1145	DES	CR/ORB/
18s‡‡‡	23 Mar	Rumpler C	B8407	24	Nesle	1815	DES	CR/RFC 24.3
19	29 Mar	Alb. C	B8411	24	Warfusee	1500	DES	CR/RFC 29.3

TOTAL: 1 captured, 6 and 6 shared destroyed, 5 and 1 shared out of control = 19.
*Shared with 2/Lt W.B. Ives A9471. **Shared with 2/Lt H.D. Barton B120, Lt R.T. Mark B67. ***Shared with Lt P.A. MacDougall B120, Lt R.T. Mark B67, Lt H.G. Hemmarsley B891. †This was Uffz Hageler of Jasta 15, who was taken prisoner. ††Shared with Capt. A.J. Brown C9494. †††Probably Gefr W. Behm/Gefr W. Sellenbohme of Sch 5. ‡Shared with Lt R.T. Mark C9494, Lt H.B. Richardson B8257. ‡‡Shared with Capt W.L. Wells/Cpl W. Beales C4707 of 48 Sqn. ‡‡‡Shared with Lt P.J. Nolan B8411, Lt C.M.G. Farrell B63.

COX George J. Lieutenant 2AFC

Born in Melbourne, Victoria, on 17 July 1894, this Australian flew with 2AFC Squadron on the Western Front in 1918. On 27 August he was flying in a formation led by Captain Robey Manuel an hour before midday when they encountered 28 Fokker and Pfalz scouts at 17,000 feet. Cox claimed three of these to bring his score to five. Before he could gain any further successes, he was forced to land behind German lines. The squadron recorded that the engine of his SE 5A, F5965, had failed, but his own statement following his repatriation from captivity at the end of the war, differed. He had seen an enemy aircraft over Lille at 1,500 feet and had been about to attack, when he collided with 'something' which knocked the engine out of its bearers, causing him to spin down more or less out of control, and crash; he had obviously been hit by an artillery shell.

	1918		SE 5A					
1	30 May	Pfalz DIII	D3451	2AFC	Bapaume	1515	DES(F)	CR/RAF 30.5
2	2 Jun	Pfalz DIII	D3451	2AFC	Chuignes	1930	OOC	CR/ORB/OH
3	27 Aug	Fokker DVII	F5965	2AFC	Sains les Marquion	1050	DES(F)	CR/RAF 27.8
4	27 Aug	Fokker DVII	F5965	2AFC	Sains les Marquion	1051	OOC	CR/ORB/OH
5	27 Aug	Pfalz DIII	F5965	2AFC	Lecluse	1055	OOC	CR/ORB/OH

TOTAL: 2 destroyed, 3 out of control = 5.

COX George Montague Captain 65

Born on 31 October 1892 in Calcutta, India, he joined the Royal Berkshire Regiment in 1914, serving until 1916 when he transferred to the RFC. After training, he went to 65 Squadron in 1917. In 1918 he was promoted to Captain and awarded the MC having claimed five victories. Leaving 65, he took command of No 2 Test Flight in France until the end of the war. He became a Squadron Leader in 1919, and in 1935 he was an instructor with over 3,000 hours' flying experience.

	1917		Camel					
1	15 Nov	Alb. DIII	B2411	65	Dadizeele	0740	OOC	CR/11 W
	1918							
2	14 Jan	C	B2411	65	Westroosebeke	1155	DES	CR/RFC 14.1
3	9 Mar	Fokker DrI	B2411	65	Becelaere-Dadizeele	1010	DES	CR/RFC 9.3
4	13 Mar	C	B2411	65	Houthem	1605	OOC	CR/RFC 13.3
5	17 May	Pfalz DIII	C8272	65	Demuin	1045	DES	CR/RAF 17.5

TOTAL: 3 destroyed, 2 out of control = 5.

CRABB Earl Frederick Lieutenant 92

Earl Crabb was a Canadian who flew SE 5As with 92 Squadron in 1918. He was awarded a DFC, gazetted on 2 November of that year.

	1918		SE 5A					
1	22 Jul	Fokker DVII	C8896	92	S Bailleul	1930	DES	CR/RAF 22.7
2	7 Aug	Fokker DVII	C8896	92	S E Steenwerck	0815	DES(F)	CR/RAF 7.8
3	14 Oct	Fokker DVII	E5792	92	S E Le Cateau	1630	DES	CR/RAF 14.10
4s*	27 Oct	DFW. C	E5792	92	Mormal Wood	0630	DES(F)	CR/RAF 27.10
5	27 Oct	Fokker DVII	E5792	92	Maroilles	1030	OOC	CR/ORB/80 W
6	29 Oct	Fokker DVII	E5792	92	E Le Quesnoy	1030	OOC	CR/ORB/80 W

TOTAL: 3 and 1 shared destroyed, 2 out of control = 6.
*Shared with Capt W.S. Philcox, Lt T.S. Horry.

CRAIG William Benson Lieutenant 204

From Smith's Falls, Ontario, Craig was born on 2 August 1895. He transferred to the RNAS from the Canadian Field Artillery, and in May 1918 joined 204 Squadron, RAF. He opened his scoring with a double on 15 August, followed by a triple on 16 September and a double on 20th. This sort of pace could not be maintained, and after one more claim Craig was killed in action on 26 September in Camel D3374 off Blankenberghe. He was awarded a DFC on 5 October 1918.

	1918		Camel					
1	15 Aug	Fokker DVII	D9268	204	E Ypres	0825	DES(F)	CR/5 GP Comm
2	15 Aug	Fokker DVII	D9268	204	E Ypres	0825	DES	CR/5 GP Comm
3	16 Sep	Fokker DVII	D3374	204	Blankenberghe	1905	DES	CR/5 GP Comm
4	16 Sep	Fokker DVII	D3374	204	Blankenberghe	1907	OOC	CR/5 GP Comm
5	16 Sep	Fokker DVII	D3374	204	Blankenberghe	1910	OOC	CR/5 GP Comm
6	20 Sep	Fokker DVII	D3374	204	N E Dixmude	1025	OOC	CR/5 GP Comm
7	20 Sep	Fokker DVII	D3374	204	S W Ostend	1030	OOC	CR/5 GP Comm
8	24 Sep	Fokker DrI	D3374	204	Dixmude	1845	DES(F)	CR/5 GP Comm

TOTAL: 4 destroyed, 4 out of control = 8.

CRAWFORD Kelvin Captain 24, 60

Kelvin Crawford was an Englishman who flew DH 2s and DH 5s with 24 Squadron from 17 October 1916, becoming a flight commander on 21 March 1917. He claimed five victories before returning to Home Establishment on 3 July. In March 1918 he was posted to 60 Squadron, but was killed in action on 11 April in SE 5A C5445 near Bucquouoy during an evening sortie — probably a victim of Vizefeldwebel Otto Könnecke of Jasta 5.

	1916		DH 2					
1	26 Oct	Halb. DII	A2459	24	Bapaume	0800	OOC	CR/RFC 26.10
2s*	22 Nov	Alb. DII	5925	24	Les Boeufs	1310	CAPT	CR/RFC 22.11
3s**	20 Dec	Alb. DI	6008	24	Velu	1200	DES(F)	CR/IV BG
	1917							
4s***	2 Apr	Alb. DII	5925	24	Gouzeaucourt	0850	DES(F)	CR/RFC 2.4
			DH 5					
5	10 May	Alb. DIII	A2581	24	Villers Guislain	1450	DES	CR/RFC 10.5

TOTAL: 1 shared captured, 1 and 2 shared destroyed, 1 out of control = 5.
*Shared with Capt J.O. Andrews 5998. This was Oblt S. Kirmaier the commander of Jasta B. **Shared with Capt S.H. Long A305. ***Shared with Capt C.R. Cox/2/Lt L.C. Welford 4855, of 22 Sqn. This was probably Lt H. Konig of Jasta B who was killed.

CREECH Jesse Orin 1st Lieutenant 148 US

Born on 22 August 1896 in Harlan, Kentucky, Creech served with the 148th Aero Squadron, USAS, under RAF command in autumn 1918, claiming eight victories. He was awarded a US DSC, but was shot down on 2 September, together with five other Camel pilots of the unit; he survived this experience at the hands of Jasta 'Boelcke' and returned to duty. Jesse Creech died on 16 February 1948, aged 52.

	1918		Camel					
1	15 Aug	Fokker DVII	D8166	148US	E Chaulnes	1623	OOC	CR/US 133
2	25 Aug	Hannover C	D8166	148US	N E Vaulx-Vraucourt	1805	DES	CR/RAF 25.8
3	6 Sep	Fokker DVII	D6574	148US	100y N E Bourlon	0705	DES	CR/RAF 6.9
4	15 Sep	Fokker DVII	F7176	148US	Epinoy	1840	DES	CR/RAF 15.9
5s*	17 Sep	Fokker DVII	F7176	148US	Epinoy	1700	DES	CR/RAF 17.9
6	26 Sep	Fokker DVII	F7176	148US	E Boulon Wood	1325	DES	CR/RAF 26.9
7	28 Oct	Fokker DVII	F7176	148US	N W Jenlain	1205	DES	CR/RAF 28.10

TOTAL: 5 and 1 shared destroyed, 1 out of control = 7.
*Shared with 1/Lt F.E. Kindley E1539.
NB: Creech is often listed as having 2 victories on 15 Sep. There is no record of any second claim being made or confirmed.

CROLE Gerard Bruce Captain 40, 43

A Scot, Gerard Crole had been a pupil at Edinburgh Academy and had become a Bachelor of Arts at Oxford University before joining the 2nd Dragoon Guards in 1914. Transferring to the RFC, he served with 40 Squadron in 1917, subsequently becoming a flight commander in 43 Squadron in September of that year, and being awarded an MC. He was shot down during a mission to Douai on the morning of 22 November 1917 in Camel B6267, and became a prisoner for the duration of the war. Post war, he attended Edinburgh University, graduating as a solicitor.

	1917		Nieup					
1	25 Jun	Alb. DV	B1552	40	N E Douai	2000	OOC	CR/RFC 25.6
2s*	25 Jun	Alb. DV	B1552	40	5m E La Bassee	2040	DES	CR/RFC 25.6
3**	2 Jul	Alb. DV	B1552	40	N W Douai	1050	DES(F)	CR/RFC 2.7
4	15 Aug	Alb. DV	A6793	40	E La Bassee	1845	OOC	CR/BG Summ
5	23 Aug	DFW. C	A6793	40	N E Lens	0600	DES(F)	CR/RFC 23.8

TOTAL: 2 and 1 shared destroyed, 2 out of control = 5.
*Shared with Lt L.G. Blaxland B1682. **Probably Lt Fortstmann of Jasta 30, who was killed.

CROMPTON John Bonnicher Captain 60

A Candian from Toronto, he arrived in France in August 1917, joining 60 Squadron where he was to fly the SE 5A. Crompton's first three victories were claimed in September, and one more was credited to him before the end of the year. He claimed a further three during the first quarter of 1918, becoming a flight commander on 5 January, but on 16 March a medical board declared him to be unfit for further active service over the front and he returned to Home Establishment. He is not to be confused with H.D. Crompton, who also served with 60 Squadron during the same period.

	1917		SE 5A					
1s*	5 Sep	Alb. DV	A8918	60	Sailly en Ostrevent	1900	OOC	CR/RFC 6.9
2	20 Sep	C	B543	60	Roulers-Menin	1200	OOC	CR/RFC 20.9
3s**	25 Sep	Alb. DV	B512	60	Goenberg	1200	DES	CR/RFC 25.9
4	12 Oct	Alb. DV	B519	60	De Ruite	0915	DES	CR/RFC 12.10
	1918							
5s***	1 Jan	DFW. C	A8901	60	W Roulers	1050	OOC	CR/RFC 1.1

TOTAL: 1 and 1 shared destroyed, 1 and 2 shared out of control = 5.
*Shared with Lt S.B. Horn A8936. **Shared with Lt G.L. Young B533. ***Shared with Capt F.O. Soden C5332.

CROWE Cyril Marconi Major 4, 8, 16, 56, 60, 85

Born on 6 January 1894, 'Billy' Crowe joined the RFC, serving initially as an observer in 4 Squadron from 3 January to 25 May 1915. Training as a pilot, he then joined 8 Squadron on 4 December 1915, remaining with this unit only until 4 February 1916, then serving with 16 Squadron from March 1916-March 1917. In April 1917 he went to 56 Squadron as a flight commander, exchanging his BE for an SE 5. During the summer of 1917 he was awarded an MC and claimed eight victories. In a hectic air battle on 7 May when Albert Ball was lost, he actually had his goggles shot off his face, but without injury. Crowe did much to develop the 'dive and climb' tactics that utilized the best aspects of the SE 5's performance. He was an instructor at CFS from August 1917-3 March 1918, and was promoted to acting Major, returning to 56 for a brief refresher course before being taken ill on 9 April; during this short stay he claimed five more enemy machines. On 9 July he took command of 60 Squadron after the death of Jimmy McCudden, but his stay was a short one, for on 30 July, when returning from a 13 Wing party at Dieppe, the car he was driving struck a tree and two of his passengers, Major Foggin and Captain Scholte, were killed. Crowe was court-martialled and reduced to Captain for one month. He was then posted to 85 Squadron which he commanded until the end of the war, being awarded a DFC. During World War II he served again in the RAF, becoming a Wing Commander. He died in 1974.

	1917		SE 5					
1s*	24 Apr	C	A4860	56	Bellone	1110	DES	CR/RFC 24.4
2s**	29 Apr	Alb. DII	A4860	56	Waziers	1500	OOC	CR/RFC 29.4
3s**	29 Apr	Alb. DII	A4860	56	Bugnicourt	1500	OOC	CR/RFC 29.4
4	30 Apr	Alb. DII	A4860	56	Douai	0845	DES	CR/RFC 30.4
5	23 May	C	A8902	56	Tilloy	1915-2015	OOC	CR/RFC 23.5
6s***	24 May	Alb. DIII	A8910	56	S Douai	1900-2000	OOC	CR/RFC 24.5
7	25 May	Alb. DIII	A8910	56	Courcelles	0630-0730	OOC	CR/RFC 25.5
8	27 May	Alb. DIII	A8910	56	Erchin	0615-0715	DES	CR/RFC 27.5
9	16 Jun	C	A8910	56	Passchendaele	0845-0930	DES	CR/RFC 16.6
	1918		SE 5A					
10	18 Mar	C	B4891	56	W Maquigny	1110	OOC	CR/RFC 18.3
11	18 Mar	C	B4891	56	N E Rumaucourt	1145	DES	CR/RFC 18.3
12	28 Jun	Pfalz DIII	C1848	56	Dompierre	2020	OOC	CR/?
13	1 Jul	Fokker DVII	C1848	56	N E Albert	0540	DES	CR/RAF 1.7
14s†	1 Jul	Fokker DrI	C1848	56	N E Albert	0540	DES	CR/RAF 1.7
15	16 Sep	Fokker DVII	B8354	85	Sauchy-Couchy	1845	DES	CR/RAF 16.9

TOTAL: 6 and 2 shared destroyed, 4 and 3 shared out of control = 15.
*Shared with 2/Lt L.M. Barlow A4858, 2/Lt M.A. Kay A4866. **Shared with Lt J.O. Leach A4856, Lt M.A. Kay A4866. ***Shared with 2/Lt R.T.C. Hoidge A8910, 2/Lt A.P.F. Rhys Davids A4868, 2/Lt K.K. Muspratt A4861, 2/Lt J.S. Turnbull A8913. †Shared with Capt G.C. Maxwell D6126.

CRUNDALL Edward Duncan Captain 8(N), 210

Born on 9 December 1896, he joined the RNAS in 1914. In 1916 he was posted to 8 Naval Squadron and while with this unit claimed three victories by 10 May 1917. On this date he was shot down and forced to land in N5464 near Bethune by OffStellv Alois Heldman of Jasta 10, suffering wounds. In 1918 he was posted as a flight commander to 210 Squadron, RAF, claiming at least four more hostile aeroplanes, and receiving the DFC. After the war he did much civil flying and air charter work until 1937; in 1939 he rejoined the RAF, commanding 116 Calibration Squadron until 1945, receiving the AFC. After World War II he opened charter routes to South Africa and French Equatorial Africa, during which time he brought his total flying hours to over 8,500. His autobiography, *Fighter Pilot on the Western Front*, was published in 1975.

	1917		Triplane					
1	14 Apr	Alb. C	N5464	8N	Henin-Lietard	0905	OOC	CR/RFC 14.4
2	14 Apr	Alb. C	N5464	8N	Henin-Lietard	0905	OOC	CR/RFC 14.4
3s*	18 Aug	Alb. DV	N5465	8N	Henin-Lietard	1830	OOC	CR/RFC 19.8
	1918		Camel					
4	30 Jul	Pfalz DIII	B7860	210	5m E Dixmude	1000	OOC	CR/5 GP Comm
5	1 Aug	Fokker DVII	B7860	210	N Lille	1925	OOC	CR/5 GP Comm
6	9 Aug	Fokker DVII	B7860	210	Zonnebeke	0725	DES	CR/5 GP Comm
7	9 Aug	Fokker DVII	B7860	210	2m S E Staden	0730	DES	CR/5 GP Comm

TOTAL: 2 destroyed, 4 and 1 shared out of control = 7.
*Shared with F/Cdr C.D. Booker N5460, F/Lt R.B. Munday N5421.

CUDEMORE Charles William Captain 40, 29, 64

Born on 19 November 1897 in Essex, Charles Cudemore served with the King's Scottish Light Infantry before transferring to the RFC in December 1916. He first saw action flying Nieuport Scouts with 40 Squadron from 23 April 1917, and on 7 May took part in a balloon strafe with his flight, making two of the seven claims which were submitted. After three weeks at No 1 Aeroplane Depot, he joined 29 Squadron on 20 July, making three more claims and engaging in some 25 indecisive combats. He was posted to Home Establishment on 8 October 1917, after 274 hours of war flying. Promoted to Captain, he next joined 64 Squadron as a flight commander in August 1918, and by the end of the war had added a further ten victories to his score during 80 sorties. He was awarded the DFC, and after the war emigrated to Canada, where he joined the RCAF.

	1917		Nieup					
1s*	7 May	Balloon	A6744	40	S Quiery la Motte	0935	DES	ORB/RFC 7.5
2	7 May	Balloon	A6744	40	S Quiery la Motte	0935	DES	ORB/RFC 7.5
3**	28 Jul	Alb. DV	B1609	29	Gheluvelt	1100	DES	CR/RFC 27.7
4	11 Aug	C	B1645	29	N Roulers	1845	OOC	CR/RFC 11.8
5	3 Sep	Alb. DIII	A271	29	Poelcapelle	0715	OOC	CR/RFC 3.9
	1918		SE 5A					
6s***	11 Aug	Fokker DVII	D6952	64	Roye	0815	OOC	CR/ORB/?
7	12 Aug	Fokker DVII	D6952	64	Chaulnes	0715	DES	CR/RAF 12.8
8	16 Aug	Rumpler C	D6952	64	Le Catelet	1010	OOC	CR/?
9	25 Aug	Fokker DVII	D6952	64	Haucourt	0900	OOC	CR/?
10	24 Sep	Fokker DVII	D6952	64	S Cambrai	1030	OOC	CR/?
11s†	25 Sep	Hannover C	D6952	64	Bourlon	1740	OOC	CR/?
12	29 Sep	Fokker DVII	D6952	64	N W Cambrai	1115	DES	CR/RAF 29.9
13	29 Sep	Fokker DVII	D6952	64	N W Cambrai	1115	OOC	CR/?
14	4 Nov	Pfalz DXII	F5500	64	Bavay	0750	OOC	CR/?
15	9 Nov	Fokker DVII	F5500	64	Givry	1515	OOC	CR/?

TOTAL: 1 and 1 shared balloons, 3 destroyed, 10 out of control = 15.
*Shared with Lt R.N. Hall B1542. **29 Sqn made another claim by Sgt Hervey-Bathurst at this time and place, the known loss was Lt A. Niederhoff, an ace of Jasta 11, who was killed. ***Shared with Capt E.R. Tempest B74, Lt T. Rose C1860, Lt G.L. Wood E1391, Capt T. St.P. Bunbury E5977. †Shared with Lt J. Bullough H7259, Lt A.H.B. Youell E1277, Lt A.G. Donald F5452, Lt G.W. Graham C9249, Lt R.B. Francis C9242.

CULLEN Robert James Lieutenant 88

Cullen first saw service as a Bombardier in the Lowland Brigade Field Artillery, but on 17 December 1915 he was commissioned in the Black Watch. He transferred to the RFC in January 1917, and flew Bristol Fighters in 88 Squadron during 1918; with his regular observer, Lieutenant E.A. Ward, he claimed five enemy aircraft. He became a section leader, but during a fight with MFJ 2 near Beveren on 29 June he was hit and wounded in the leg after he had claimed two and one shared victories in D8022. Prior to this on 18 May, he had been forced to land in Allied lines due to damage sustained while gaining his second victory in C780, probably by Offstellv Behneke of Jasta 51.

	1918		Bristol					
1*	15 May	Alb. DV	C780	88	Ghistelles	0635	DES	CR/RAF 15.5
2*	18 May	Alb. DIII	C780	88	Zandvoorde	0800	OOC	CR/SR
3*	29 Jun	Fokker DVII	D8062	88	W Ghistelles	2010	OOC	CR/SR
4*	29 Jun	Fokker DVII	D8062	88	W Ghistelles	2010	DES	CR/RAF 29.6
5s**	29 Jun	Fokker DVII	D8062	88	Ghistelles	2010	DES	CR/RAF 29.6

TOTAL: 2 and 1 shared destroyed, 2 out of control = 5.
*Observer: Lt E.H. Ward. **Observer: Lt E.H. Ward; shared with Capt K.R. Simpson/Sgt C. Hill, Lt K.B. Conn/2/Lt B.H. Smyth C787, Lt W.A. Wheeler/2/Lt T.S. Chiltern C774.

CULLING Thomas Grey Flight Sub-Lieutenant 1(N)

Joining the RNAS in 1916, Flight Sub-Lieutenant Culling, a New Zealander from Auckland, born on 31 May 1896, flew Sopwith Triplanes in 1 Naval Squadron during the spring of 1917, claiming six victories during April and May. He was awarded a DSC during May, but was shot down and killed in Triplane N5491 on 8 June near Warneton by Flugmeister Bossler of Marinefeldjasta 1.

	1917		Triplane					
1	6 Apr	C	N5444	1N	4m N E St Quentin	1150	OOC	CR/RFC 6.4
2	22 Apr	Alb. DIII	N5444	1N	Arleux	1720	OOC	CR/RFC 22.4
3	23 Apr	C	N5444	1N	W Douai	0800	OOC	CR/RFC 23.4
4	5 May	Alb. DIII	N5444	1N	4m E Lens	1900	OOC	CR/RFC 6.5
5*	19 May	Alb. DIII	N5444	1N	Estrees	1030	OOC	CR/RFC 19.5
6	20 May	C	N5444	1N	Henin-Lietard	0540	DES	CR/RFC 20.5

TOTAL: 1 destroyed, 5 out of control = 6.
*1N made 2 claims at 1030, one was Lt Schock of Jasta 12, who was killed.

CUMMINGS Eric Douglas Captain 2AFC

Born on 13 April 1896 in Franklin, Tasmania, Cummings served with the Australian Army Service Corps before transferring to the AFC. Posted to 2AFC Squadron in early 1918, he gained his first victory on 3 May when he claimed a grey and white Triplane. He was then attacked by four more Triplanes and was shot down — probably by Lieutenant Karl Bolle of Jasta 'Boelcke' — crashing in 'No Man's Land'. Thrown clear of the wreck, he was rescued by Australian infantrymen and was soon back on operations, claiming three victories during June and July. Awarded a DFC, he was promoted to flight commander by September; he had brought his score to nine when the Armistice brought an end to the fighting.

	1918		SE 5A					
1	3 May	Fokker DrI	B168	2AFC	Meteren	1130	DES	CR/RAF 3.5
2	1 Jun	Pfalz DIII	B195	2AFC	E Pozieres	0900	DES	CR/RAF 1.6
3	31 Jul	LVG. C	C6473	2AFC	E Laventie	1115	DES(F)	CR/ORB/OH
4	31 Jul	LVG. C	C6473	2AFC	Merville	1115	OOC	CR/ORB/OH
5s*	15 Sep	Alb. C	C6473	2AFC	W Macquart	1720	DES	CR/RAF 15.9
6	14 Oct	Fokker DVII	C6473	2AFC	W Cysoing	1010	DES	CR/RAF 14.10
7	14 Oct	Fokker DVII	C6473	2AFC	E Grusan	1015	OOC	CR/RAF 14.10
8	14 Oct	Fokker DVII	C6473	2AFC	Hertain	1020	OOC	CR/RAF 14.10
9s**	1 Nov	LVG. C	C6473	2AFC	Antoing	1415	OOC	CR/ORB/OH

TOTAL: 4 and 1 shared destroyed, 3 and 1 shared out of control = 9.
*Shared with Lt E.E. Davies D6860. **Shared with Lt E.E. Davies E5765.

CUMMINGS Lumsden Captain 1

Born in Toronto, Canada, in 1896, Cummings was commissioned into the RFC in October 1915, but did not receive his wings until 13 June 1917. He joined 1 Squadron in August of that year and was promoted Captain on 24 January 1918. He went into hospital on 9 February, and did not return to the front.

	1917		Nieuport					
1	20 Sep	DFW. C	B3631	1	Gheluvelt	1210	DES	CR/RFC 20.9
2	1 Oct	C	B6790	1	Keiberg	1100	DES	CR/RFC 1.10
3s*	1 Oct	DFW. C	B6790	1	Houthoulst	1110	OOC	CR/RFC 1.10
4	15 Nov	Alb. DV	B6815	1	Gheluwe	1156	OOC	CR/RFC 15.11
5	24 Nov	Alb. DV	B6815	1	Moorslede	0845	OOC	CR/ORB/?

TOTAL: 2 destroyed, 2 and 1 shared out of control = 5.
*Shared with Capt W.V.T. Rooper B6767, 2/Lt R.A. Birckbeck B6753, Lt F.G. Baker B3630.

CUNNELL Douglas Charles Captain 20

Cunnell was commissioned on 2 November 1915 in the Hampshire Regiment, transferring to the RFC during 1915. He flew FE 2Ds as a flight commander in 20 Squadron, first claiming on 2 May 1917; three more victories followed. Then on 6 July whilst in combat with a formation of red Albatros Scouts from Jasta 11, he and his gunner, Lieutenant Woodbridge, claimed four of their opponents out of control. A fifth was hit and seen to spin away, but was not claimed. The pilot of this latter aircraft was in fact Manfred von Richthofen, the leading German ace, who was wounded in the head and consequently carried out a forced landing. A few days later, on

12th Cunnell's gunner, Lieutenant Bill, claimed an Albatros, but Cunnell was then himself hit and killed. Bill took over the controls and flew the aircraft back to base.

	1917		FE 2D					
1*	2 May	Alb. DIII	A6431	20	Comines	1115	DES(F)	CR/RFC 2.5
2**	26 May	Alb. DIII	A6431	20	Comines-Quesnoy	1035	DES	CR/RFC 26.5
3***	31 May	Alb. DIII	A6430	20	Comines	1920	DES	CR/RFC 1.6
4†	5 Jun	Alb. DV	A6414	20	Coucou	0810	DES(F)	CR/RFC 5.6
5††	6 Jul	Alb. DV	A6512	20	Wervicq	1030	OOC	CR/RFC 6.7
6††	6 Jul	Alb. DV	A6512	20	Wervicq	1030	OOC	CR/RFC 6.7
7††	6 Jul	Alb. DV	A6512	20	Wervicq	1030	OOC	CR/RFC 6.7
8††	6 Jul	Alb. DV	A6512	20	Wervicq	1030	OOC	CR/RFC 6.7
9†††	11 Jul	Alb. DV	A6512	20	Wervicq-Menin	1400	DES(F)	CR/RFC 11.7

TOTAL: 5 destroyed, 4 out of control = 9.
*Observer: 2 AM A.H. Sayers. **Observer: Lt W.T. Gilson. ***Observer: Lt W.C. Cambray. †Observer: Sgt A.H. Sayers. ††Observer: 2/Lt A.E. Woodbridge. One of these was probably Rttm M. von Richthofen, the commander of JG I, who was wounded. †††Observer: Lt A.G. Bill.

CUNNINGHAM Jack Armand Lieutenant Colonel 18, 6, 65, 65w

Jack Cunningham flew as a pilot with 18 Squadron in 1915-16, in Vickers, De Havilland and Bristol Scouts. He had many engagements and forced an enemy aircraft to land; he was then posted to 6 Squadron to fly BE 2Cs. He later became an instructor with 47 Reserve Squadron, and was subsequently promoted to Major. In late 1917 he took command of 65 Squadron, flying Camels. Leading this unit to France, he claimed six victories before being promoted to command 65 Wing in 1918 with the rank of Lieutenant Colonel. During August he shot down his tenth enemy aeroplane. For his gallantry and leadership he received the DSO, DFC, and Croix de Guerre, also being made a Chevalier of the Order of Leopold.

	1915		Vickers FB					
1*	28 Nov	LVG. C	2343	18	La Bassee	----	DD	RFC WD
			Bristol Scout					
2	29 Dec	Aviatik C	----	18	Provin	----	DD	RFC WD
	1916		DH 2					
3	5 Feb	Alb. C	5916	18	Carvin	----	FTL	RFC 5.2
	1917		Camel					
4	18 Dec	Alb. DV	B2418	65	Roulers	1415	DES	CR/RFC 18.12
5	18 Dec	Alb. DV	B2418	65	Hooglede	1420	OOC	CR/RFC 18.12
	1918							
6	5 Feb	Alb. DV	B5632	65	Beythem	1335	DES	CR/RFC 5.2
7	12 Mar	Alb. DV	B5632	65	Westroosebeke	1135	DES	CR/RFC 12.3
8	17 Mar	Alb. DV	N5632	65	Zuidhoek	1125	DES	CR/RFC 17.3
9	3 Apr	Alb. DV	D1791	65	E Demuin	1200	DES	CR/RAF 3.4
10	13 Aug	C	----	65W	Belgian Coast	c0530	DES	RAF 12-18.8

TOTAL: 6 destroyed 1 out of control, 2 driven down and 1 FTL = 10.
*Observer: 1 AM. Smith.

CUNNINGHAME Frederick Joseph Captain 48

Joining 48 Squadron during 1918, Cunninghame claimed his first victory on 2 July. Promoted to flight commander, he claimed another in September, followed by three more during October, two of his five claims falling to the rear gun on 3 October, manned on this occasion by Lieutenant R.A. Brunton, MC.

	1918		Bristol					
1*	2 Jul	Pfalz DIII	C950	48	S E Foucaucourt	1950	OOC	CR/?
2**	28 Sep	Fokker DVII	E2532	48	S E Roulers	1445	DES	CR/RAF 28.9
3**	3 Oct	Fokker DVII	E2507	48	Inglemunster	1750	DES	CR/RAF 3.10
4**	3 Oct	Fokker DVII	E2507	48	Ingemunster	1810	DES(F)	CR/RAF 3.10
5***	14 Oct	Fokker DVII	E2507	48	W Thielt	0855	OOC	CR/11 W

TOTAL: 3 destroyed, 2 out of control = 5.
*Observer: 2/Lt H. Knowles. **Observer: Lt R.A. Brunton. ***Observer: Lt T.C. Jones.

CUNNINGHAM-REID Alec Stratford Lieutenant 85

After service with the Royal Engineers, he joined the RFC in 1917 and the following year was posted to 'Billy' Bishop's newly-formed 85 Squadron, going to France with this unit in May. He received a DFC, which was gazetted in August, and by the end of the war had claimed eight victories. He remained in the RAF for a while in a staff position, but then left and took part in politics, becoming a Member of Parliament for Warrington from 1922-29, and St Marylebone from 1932-45; he also wrote several books before his death at Valbonne, France, on 26 March 1977, aged 78.

	1918		SE 5A					
1	16 Jun	Balloon	D6859	85	Kruiseik	1230	DES	CR/11 W
2	17 Jun	C	D6859	85	E Bailleul	0630-0645	DES	CR/RAF 17.6
3s*	18 Jun	C	D6859	85	Voormezeele	0450	DES	CR/RAF 18.6
4	25 Jun	Alb. DV	D6859	85	Nieppe	1845	OOC	CR/11 W
5	25 Jun	C	D6859	85	Voormezeele area	1915	DES	CR/11 W
6	29 Jun	Pfalz DIII	C1922	85	Kemmel	2017	DES	CR/RAF 29.6
7	3 Jul	Pfalz DIII	C1922	85	Bruges-Thielt	1215	DES	CR/RAF 3.7

TOTAL: 1 balloon, 4 and 1 shared destroyed, 1 out of control = 7.
*Shared with Capt A.C. Randall B7870.

CURPHEY William George Sellar Captain 32

One of the original pilots of 32 Squadron, he went to France flying DH 2s in the summer of 1916. He was in the thick of the fighting over the Somme and had many combats. In the new year he was promoted to Captain, and claimed his fifth victory on 4 February 1917, but in so doing received a slight head wound when he was forced to land A2536 by Leutnant Erwin Böhme of Jasta 'Boelcke'. On 14 May the patrol was attacked by six Albatros Scouts. In the fight which followed one of his pilots shot down one of these off Curphey's tail, but he was hit by another flown by Hauptmann Franz Walz of Jasta 'Boelcke'. His machine, A2622, caught fire and he went down in flames as the German's seventh victory, falling to the east of Lagnicourt. He received the MC and Bar.

	1916		DH 2					
1	22 Aug	LVG. C	7851	32	N Bapaume	1745	OOC	CR/RFC 22.8
2	28 Sep	LVG. C	A2536	32	Miraumont	1605	DES	ORB/RFC 28.9
3s*	30 Sep	C	A2535	32	Grevillers	1435	DES	ORB/RFC 30.9
	1917							
4	4 Feb	Alb. DII	A2536	32	Achiet	1535	OOC	ORB/RFC 4.2
5s**	4 Feb	Alb. DII	A2536	32	Ablainville	1600	DES	ORB/RFC 4.2
6s***	7 Feb	Alb. DII	----	32	Gommecourt	1430	OOC	ORB/SD/AA

TOTAL: 2 and 1 shared destroyed, 3 out of control = 6.
*Shared with Capt L.P. Aizlewood A2536. **Shared with Capt J.M. Robb, Lt H.D. Davis; possibly Lt von Scheele of Jasta Boelcke who was killed. ***Shared with Lt H.D. Davis.

CURTIS Ralph Luxmore Lieutenant 48

Lieutenant Curtis served with 48 Squadron during the summer of 1917, claiming 15 victories, making him one of the most successful Bristol Fighter pilots of that year. His usual gunner, who participated in many of the victories, was 2nd Lieutenant D.P.F. Uniacke. Curtis and Uniacke were shot down near Roulers in A7224 on 21 September 1917, falling as the 14th victory of Oberleutnant Hermann Goering, commander of Jasta 27; they became prisoners for the duration of the war.

	1917		Bristol					
1*	16 Jun	Alb. DIII	A7107	48	Fresnes les Montauban	0730	DES	CR/RFC 16.6
2**	3 Jul	C	A7149	48	Queant	0910	OOC	CR/RFC 3.7
3**	5 Jul	Alb. DV	A7153	48	Bapaume	2020	OOC	CR/III BG
4**	7 Jul	Alb. DV	A7107	48	Vitry	0550	DES	CR/III BG
5**	28 Jul	Alb. DIII	A7121	48	Ghistelles	0815	OOC	CR/RFC 28.7
6**	16 Aug	Alb. DV	A7151	48	St Pierre Capelle	1955	DES(F)	CR/RFC 16.8
7**	16 Aug	Alb. DV	A7151	48	St Pierre Capelle	2000	OOC	CR/RFC 16.8
8**	20 Aug	Alb. DV	A7224	48	Ghistelles	2005	OOC	CR/RFC 20.8
9**	22 Aug	Alb. DV	A7224	48	Ostend	0907	DES	CR/RFC 22.8
10**	22 Aug	Alb. DV	A7224	48	Ostend	0908	OOC	CR/RFC 22.8
11s***	2 Sep	Alb. DV	A7224	48	5m E Dixmude	0930	OOC	CR/RFC 2.9
12**	5 Sep	DFW. C	A7170	48	Middelkerke	0840	OOC	CR/RFC 5.9
13†	5 Sep	Alb. DV	A7155	48	off Westende	1200	DES(F)	CR/RFC 5.9
14**	14 Sep	Alb. DV	A7224	48	Ghistelles	1640	DES	CR/RFC 14.9
15s††	17 Sep	C	A7224	48	Leke	0915	OOC	CR/RFC 17.9

TOTAL: 6 destroyed, 7 and 2 shared out of control = 15.
*Observer: 2/Lt L.W. Allen. **Observer: 2/Lt D.P.F. Uniacke. ***Observer: 2/Lt D.P.F. Uniacke, shared with Lt K.R. Park/2/Lt A.D. Light A7170. †Observer: 2/Lt H. Munro: This was Lt Pernet, of Jasta Boelcke who was killed. ††Observer: 2/Lt D.P.F. Uniacke; shared with Sgt J. Oldham/2 AM W. Walker.

CURTIS Wilfred Austin Flight Commander 6(N), 10(N)

A Canadian from Havelock, Ontario, Curtis was born on 21 August 1893; he joined the RNAS on 11 August 1916, first serving with 6(N) Squadron. On 28 August 1917 he joined 10(N) Squadron, and during the next two and a half months claimed ten victories — two destroyed and eight out of control. During this period he was promoted to Flight Lieutenant on 29 October, and later on 2 January 1918, to Flight Commander. His final score was 13, and he was awarded a DSC and Bar. In World War II he served in the RCAF, and rose to the rank of Air Marshal, becoming Chief of Air Staff in Canada in 1947. He retired from the service in 1953, and died on 7 August 1977.

	1917		Camel					
1	6 Sep	Alb. DV	N6342	10N	S E Dixmude	0800	OOC	CR/RFC 6.9
2	27 Sep	Alb. DV	B6244	10N	N E Westroosebeke	1605	OOC	CR/RFC 27.9
3	1 Oct	Alb. DV	B6444	10N	N E Passchendaele	1415	OOC	CR/RFC 1.10
4	15 Oct	C	B6202	10N	S E Zarren	1345	OOC	CR/RFC 15.10
5s*	21 Oct	C	B6202	10N	Dixmude	1330	DES(F)	CR/RFC 21.10
6s**	21 Oct	Alb. DV	B6202	10N	N E Dixmude	1331	DES	CR/DL
7s***	27 Oct	Alb. DV	B6202	10N	N E Dixmude	1320	OOC	CR/RFC 27.10
8	4 Nov	Alb. DV	B6202	10N	N Dixmude	1505	OOC	CR/RFC 4.11
9	4 Nov	Alb. DV	B6202	10N	N Dixmude	1505	OOC	CR/RFC 4.11
10	15 Nov	Alb. DV	B6202	10N	Keyem	1245	OOC	CR/RFC 15.11
11s†	5 Dec	Alb. DV	B5663	10N	Keyem-Leke	1535	DES	CR/RNAS 5.12
	1918							
12	14 Jan	Alb. DV	B6450	10N	E Houthoulst Wood	1135	OOC	CR/RNAS 14.1
13	23 Jan	C	B6450	10N	Staden	1450	DES	CR/RNAS 23.1

TOTAL: 1 and 3 shared destroyed, 8 and 1 shared out of control = 13.

*Shared with FSL H.L. Nelson B6289, FSL H.J. Emery B6203. **Shared with FSL H.L. Emery B6203. ***Shared with FSL K.V. Stratton B6225. †Shared with FSL F.V. Hall B6320.

DALEY John Edwin Albert Robertson Lieutenant 13, 24

Transferring from the British West Indies Regiment to the RFC, he flew as an observer with 13 Squadron in early 1917. On 27 February he and his pilot were attacked by six hostile scouts and Daley managed to hit one of these, which dived steeply into its own lines. However the pilot was also hit, and Daley had to leave his observer's cockpit and climb into the pilot's seat. Half sitting on the latter's lap, with one leg out on the wing, he succeeded in bringing the machine safely back to base. On 14 March 1918 he went to 24 Squadron after taking pilot training, and with this unit claimed six victories flying SE 5As, being awarded a DFC. Daley was fatally injured in a flying accident on 3 July 1918 in B8261, dying five days later.

	1918		SE 5A					
1	26 Mar	D	B79	24	Croix	1415	DES(F)	CR/RFC 26.3
2	9 May	Alb. DV	B8261	24	Hangard Wood	1915	DES	CR/RAF 9.5
3	2 Jun	SS DIII	B8261	24	Contoire	1115	DES	CR/RAF 2.6
4	27 Jun	Alb. DV	B8261	24	Chipilly	1925	OOC	CR/ORB/?
5	29 Jun	Alb. DV	C1085	24	N Le Quesnel	1850	DES(F)	CR/ORB/?
6	1 Jul	Balloon	B8261	24	Warfusee	0845	DES	CR/RAF 1.7

TOTAL: 1 balloon, 4 destroyed, 1 out of control = 6.

DALLAS Roderic Stanley Major 1W, 1(N), 40

Born on 30 July 1891 at Mount Stanley, Queensland, Australia, Dallas enlisted in the Australian Army in 1913 and was commissioned. When he applied for a transfer to the RFC soon after the outbreak of war, he was rejected. However he was then accepted by the RNAS and commenced training in June 1915. On 3 December he joined 1 Naval Wing at Dunkirk where he flew reconnaissance sorties in both single and two-seaters. He claimed his first victory on 22 April 1916, and by February 1917 he had claimed seven enemy machines shot down, driven down, forced to land, or driven off; two of these claims had been made whilst flying the prototype Sopwith Triplane, N500, the rest being gained in Nieuport Scouts. By this time he had received the DSC and become a flight commander. In the new year 1 Wing became 1 Naval Squadron and began to equip fully with Triplanes; in April 1917 the unit was attached to the RFC, going down to the Somme Front. Here April was to prove a very successful month for Dallas, who claimed eight more victories. Continuing to serve on this front until the early summer, he was awarded a Bar to his DSC; he had been given command of 1(N) Squadron on 14 June, and he continued to lead the unit until mid-March 1918. Following the formation of the RAF on 1 April 1918, he was posted to command 40 Squadron with which unit he shot down nine more enemy machines.

In spite of a wound received when ground strafing on 14 April, 'Breguet', as he was called, continued to fly in combat. On 1 June he flew an early bombing sortie over Estaires, then later, at 1010 am took off alone and headed for the front. Patrolling along the lines, just west of the foremost trenches, he was surprised and attacked by three Fokker Triplanes of Jasta 14 which crossed the lines to intercept the lone SE 5A. Dallas was hit by fire from Leutnant Hans Werner, the unit's commander, and crashed near Lievin, where he was buried; it was the German's sixth victory. With a score of 32, Dallas was second only to Robert Little as leading Australian scout pilot of the war.

	1916		Nieuport					
1	22 Apr	C	3987	1W	Middelkerke	c0530	OOC	DRO/RNAS 23.4
2	20 May	Seaplane	3993	1W	4m off Blankenberghe	0700	DES	DRO/RNAS 20.5
3	21 May	C	3991	1W	5m N Dunkerque	c1400	OOC	DRO/RNAS 21.5
			Triplane					
4	1 Jul	C	N500	A	6m off La Panne	----	OOC	DRO/RNAS 1.7
			Nieuport					
5	9 Jul	Fokker EIII	3994	A	Mariakerke	1510	OOC	DRO/RNAS 9.7
			Triplane					
6	30 Sep	D	N500	A	S W St Pierre Capelle	----	OOC	DRO/RNAS 30.9
	1917							
7	1 Feb	LVG. C	N5436	A	880y N Dixmude	----	DES	DRO/RNAS 1.2
8	5 Apr	Alb. DII	N5436	1N	2m E S E St Quentin	1200	OOC	CR/RFC 5.4
9	8 Apr	C	N5436	1N	2m E Cambrai	1445	OOC	CR/RFC 8.4
10	22 Apr	Alb. DIII	N5436	1N	Arleux	1722	DES	CR/RFC 22.4
11	22 Apr	Alb. DIII	N5436	1N	Arleux	1725	DES(F)	CR/RFC 22.4
12	23 Apr	Alb. C	N5436	1N	W Douai	0800	OOC	CR/RFC 23.4
13	24 Apr	Alb. DIII	N5436	1N	S E Lens	0815	OOC	CR/RFC 24.4
14	30 Apr	Rumpler C	N5436	1N	Haynecourt	0835	DES	CR/RFC 30.4
15	30 Apr	Alb. DIII	N5436	1N	Haynecourt	0925	OOC	CR/RFC 30.4
16	5 May	Alb. DIII	N5436	1N	4m E Lens	1900	OOC	CR/RFC 6.5
17	19 May	Alb. DIII	N6296	1N	Henin-Lietard	1945	OOC	CR/RFC 19.5
18	22 Jul	Alb. C	N5466	1N	Lille	0930	DES	CR/RFC 22.7
19	12 Aug	Alb. DV	N6308	1N	E Wervicq	0800	DES	CR/RFC 12.8
20	16 Aug	Alb. DV	N534	1N	Gheluwe	0845	DES	CR/RFC 16.8
			Camel					
21	15 Nov	DFW. C	B6427	1N	Ruggevelde	0915	DES	CR/RFC 15.11
22	6 Dec	DFW. C	B6431	1N	Ostend	0730	OOC	CR/RNAS 6.12
	1918							
23	12 Mar	Rumpler C	B6427	1N	Dixmude	1115	CAPT	CR/RNAS 12.3
			SE 5A					
24	11 Apr	DFW. C	C4879	40	La Bassee	1840	DES	CR/RAF 11.4
25	12 Apr	Alb. DV	B178	40	S Estaires	1925	DES	CR/SR/?
26	2 May	Alb. DV	D3511	40	Brebieres	1450	DES	CR/RAF 2.5
27	8 May	Pfalz DIII	D3511	40	Brebieres	1745	DES	CR/RAF 8.5
28	15 May	Alb. C	D3511	40	E La Bassee	0715	OOC	CR/RAF 15.5
29	18 May	Rumpler C	D3511	40	Lille	1200	DES(F)	CR/RAF 18.5
30s*	20 May	Pfalz DIII	----	40	Merville	2000	OOC	CR/?
31	22 May	Pfalz DIII	D3511	40	W Lille	1115	OOC	CR/?
32	27 May	Pfalz DIII	D3520	40	Hantay, E Billy	2015	DES	CR/RAF 27.5

TOTAL: 1 captured, 15 destroyed, 15 and 1 shared out of control = 32.
*Shared with 2/Lt I.F. Hind, Lt H.H. Wood, Lt C.O. Rusden, Capt G.H. Lewis, 1/Lt D.S. Poler.

DALRYMPLE Sydney Captain 27, 24, 139

Joining the RFC in 1915, Dalrymple trained as a pilot and was posted to 27 Squadron on Martinsyde 'Elephants'. He became a flight commander in June, and flew many bombing raids during which he had several air combats, claiming at least one enemy machine. From 22 May to 12 July 1917 he served as a flight commander with 24 Squadron, then in 1918 was posted to Italy as a Captain with 139 Squadron, flying Bristol Fighters. Whilst mainly engaged on reconnaissance sorties, he was also involved in several fights during which he and his observers claimed four victories. For his long service he was awarded the DFC.

	1916		Martinsyde					
1	1 Jul	Roland C	----	27	Cambrai area	0930-1130	DES	TFE/RFC 1.7
	1918		Bristol					
2*	8 Aug	Berg DI	D8084	139	Levico	----	DES	C&C V4 N3 C&C(US) V24 N 4
3*	8 Aug	Berg DI	D8084	139	Caldonazzo	----	DES(F)	C&C V4 N3 C&C (US) V4 N4
4**	13 Sep	Alb. DIII	D8081	139	Trento	----	DES(F)	C&C V4 N3 C&C (US) V24 N4

5**	13 Sep	Alb. DIII	D8081	139	Trento	----	DES(F)	C&C V4 N3 C&C (US) V24 N4

TOTAL: 5 destroyed = 5.
*Observer: 2/Lt H. Baldwin. These two were probably Zgsfhr K. Linner, 122:02 and FwP J. Pinkalsky, 122:12, of Flik 9j, who were both killed. **Observer: 2/Lt G.Beagle.

DALY Rowan Heywood Lieutenant MDF, 10(N), 47

'Bill' Daly, born on 30 March 1898, became a pilot in the RNAS. In 1917 he was based in England on Home Defence duties. During one raid by enemy bombers on 7 July of that year he took off and claimed one of these shot down, chasing a second back to the European coast. He was then posted to France, where he joined 10 Naval Squadron, claimed his third victory on 26 September, but being wounded himself during the combat. At the end of the war he volunteered to go with Ray Collishaw to serve with the fighter flight of 47 Squadron in South Russia. Operating with Kinkead, Aten, and others, he personally shot down two Russian aircraft and shared in the destruction of at least two others. With the RNAS he received the DSC, and against the Bolsheviks, the DFC. He died in an aerial collision near Northampton in 1923.

	1917		Triplane					
1	7 Jul	Gotha GIII	N5382	M	15m off Ostend	c1130	DES(F)	C&C ADOGB
			Camel					
2	24 Sep	C	N6359	10N	Houthoulst	1610	OOC	CR/RFC 24.9
3	26 Sep	Alb. DIII	N6359	10N	N E Houthoulst	1100	DES	CR/RFC 26.9
	1919							
4	- Apr	Spad	----	47	Tsaritsyn area	----	DES	Jackson/?
5	7-14 May	Spad	----	47	Volga River	----	DES	Jackson/?
6s	7-14 May	----	----	47	----	----	DES	?
7s	- May	----	----	47	----	----	DES	?

TOTAL: 4 and 2 shared destroyed, 1 out of control = 7.

DANIEL Hector C. Captain 43

'Daisy' Daniel was a South African who served with 43 Squadron, 1917-18. He was awarded an MC in July 1918, claiming nine victories before being posted to England where he later received an AFC. In 1919 he was a Captain in Major H.H. Balfour's training school in Norfolk, but in 1921 he returned home to join the new SAAF. Here he gained high rank, becoming a Lieutenant Colonel by 1939 as Director of Air and Technical Services, and later being promoted Brigadier. Shortly after World War II he took his own life in a Pretoria hospital.

	1918		Camel					
1	17 Feb	C	B5595	43	E Pont a Vendin	1240	OOC	CR/RFC 17.2
2	9 Mar	DFW. C	B5595	43	N E Pont a Vendin	c1015	DES	CR/RFC 9.3
3	24 Mar	Alb. DV	C8240	43	Bullecourt	1130	DES	CR/RFC 24.3
4	6 Apr	Fokker DrI	C8240	43	Abancourt	1430	DES(F)	CR/RAF 6.4
5	6 Apr	Fokker DrI	C8240	43	Abancourt	1435	OOC	CR/RAF 6.4
6	12 Apr	Alb. DV	D6428	43	La Gorgue	1030	DES	CR/RAF 12.4
7	12 Apr	Alb. DV	D6428	43	La Gorgue	1030	DES	CR/RAF 12.4
8	12 Apr	Alb. DV	D6428	43	N E La Gorgue	1700	DES	CR/RAF 12.4
9	30 May	Alb. DV	C8240	43	Flers	1445	DES	CR/RAF 30.5

TOTAL: 7 destroyed, 2 out of control = 9.

DARWIN Charles John Wharton Major 27, 87

Born in Durham on 12 December 1894, he was known as 'Johnny'. A graduate of the Royal Military College, Sandhurst, he served in France with the Coldstream Guards, 1914-16. Transferring to the RFC, he first flew with 27 Squadron on Martinsyde Scouts before returning to England to become a flight commander at the CFS, Upavon, in 1917. Under his leadership 87 Squadron was subsequently formed, and when the unit went to France in April 1918 he decided to retain the rank of Captain so as to go with it. When the CO, Major Callaghan, was killed Darwin was promoted to take his place. He claimed five enemy aircraft shot down and received the DSO in 1919. After the war he took various posts at both the CFS and Cranwell, retiring from the RAF in 1928. He then became London manager for the Bristol Aeroplane Company until World War II. With the rank of Squadron Leader, he died suddenly on 26 December 1941. His son was a fighter pilot in 87 Squadron in World War II; he was later killed in action in North Africa with 274 Squadron.

	1918		Dolphin					
1	31 May	LVG. C	C4158	87	Gentelles	1100	DES	CR/RAF 31.5
2	6 Jun	Rumpler C	C4158	87	Moreuil	0550	DES	CR/RAF 6.6
3	28 Jul	Rumpler C	C4158	87	Amiens	0835	OOC	CR/?
4	21 Aug	Fokker DVII	C4158	87	Biefvillers	1745	DES	CR/RAF 21.8
5	26 Sep	LVG. C	C4158	87	Bois Lateau	c1120	DES	CR/?

TOTAL: 4 destroyed, 1 out of control = 5.

DAVEY Horace Balfour Captain 25, 11

After service with the North Staffordshire Regiment, Davey transferred to the RFC and trained as a pilot, gaining his RFC ticket on 6 March 1916. From May 1916 he served with 25 Squadron until posted as a flight commander to 11 Squadron the following October. He was rested early in 1917, becoming an instructor at 59 TDS, but returned to 11 Squadron in May 1918 as commanding officer, holding this post until July.

	1916		FE 2B					
1*	16 May	Fokker E	5209	25	S Lille	0925	DES	CR/RFC 16.5
2s**	17 Jun	Fokker E	6938	25	Don	1130	OOC	CR/RFC WD
3***	2 Jul	Fokker E	5238	25	Lille	1930	DES	CR/RFC WD
4s†	20 Jul	Fokker E	5238	25	E Lens	1830	DES	CR/RFC WD
5s†	20 Jul	Fokker E	5238	25	E Lens	1830	DES	CR/RFC WD
6††	22 Nov	LVG. C	7694	11	E Arras	1400	CAPT	CR/RFC 22.11

TOTAL: 1 captured, 2 and 1 shared destroyed, 2 out of control = 6.

*Observer: Cpl L. van Schaick. **Observer: 2/Lt J.B. Hinchcliffe shared with 2/Lt J.R.B. Savage/2 AM Robinson 5201, Lt L.L. Richardson/Lt M.V. Lewes. ***Observer: Cpl W. Paull. †Observer: Capt H.C. Morley shared with Lt L.L. Richardson/2 AM L.S. Court 6932. ††Observer: Lt A.L. Harrow-Bunn; Flgr Friedrich Simon and Lt Ewald Fisher were killed.

DAVIDSON Charles Robert Lieutenant 14, 111

After service with the Highland Light Infantry, Davidson transferred to the RFC and joined 14 Squadron in Palestine early in 1917. When 111 Squadron was formed in September as the fighter unit for the Middle East, he was transferred. His first two victories with the unit were gained whilst flying Vickers FB 19 Scouts, the remainder on Bristol Fighters. He left the unit on 9 January 1918, receiving an MC five days later; he was aged 20 at this time.

	1917		Vickers Bullet					
1s*	23 Sep	C	----	14	Beit Hanun	1600	OOC	CR/5W WD
2	4 Oct	Alb. DIII	5233	111	Huj-Beit Hanun	1140	OOC	CR/5W WD
			Bristol					
3**	17 Dec	C	A7192	111	5m N Bireh	1115	FTL/DES	CR/40W WD
4**	22 Dec	C	A7192	111	4m N E Nebulus	1430	FTL/DES	CR/40W WD
5†	28 Dec	C	A7192	111	Nebulus Valley	1600	FTL/DES	CR/40W WD
6**	29 Dec	Alb. DIII	A7202	111	8m S W Samaria	0830	OOC	CR/40W WD

TOTAL: 3 forced to land, strafed and destroyed, 3 out of control = 6.

*Shared with Lt H.E. Sheppard 5233. **Observer: 2/Lt A. Simmons. †Observer: 2 AM F.J. Knowles.

DAVIES Douglas Arthur Lieutenant 150

After service with the 1/4th Territorial Force Battalion, Wiltshire Regiment, he transferred to the RFC and was later posted to Salonika to fly in 150 Squadron. This unit had a mixed complement of scouts, including a few Sopwith Camels, one of which he always flew. He first claimed on 12 June 1918, when he shot down two Albatros DVs. By the end of August his score had reached ten and he was awarded a DFC.

	1918		Camel					
1	12 Jun	Alb. DV	C1599	150	12m N Guevgueli	0600	DES(F)	CR/BG
2*	12 Jun	Alb. DV	C1599	150	N Guevgueli	0800	DES	CR/BG
3**	17 Jul	Alb. DV	C1599	150	Hudova	0735	DES	CR/BG
4**	17 Jul	Alb. DV	C1599	150	Hudova	0735	DES	CR/BG
5	17 Jul	Alb. DV	C1599	150	Balinge	c0900	OOC	CR/BG
6s***	23 Jul	Alb. DV	C1599	150	N E Boluntili	0730	DES	CR/BG
7	8 Aug	D	C1599	150	Piravo	c0800	OOC	CR/BG
8	8 Aug	D	C1599	150	Boluntili	0810	OOC	CR/BG
9s†	18 Aug	Alb. DV	C1599	150	N Lake Doiran	0745	OOC	CR/BG
10s†	18 Aug	Alb. DV	C1599	150	N Lake Doiran	0745	OOC	CR/BG

TOTAL: 4 and 1 shared destroyed, 3 and 2 shared out of control = 10.

*150 claimed 4 Albatros, one was Oblt K. Grashoff, the commander of Jasta 38, who was killed. **The above two aircraft collided. ***Shared with Lt J.C. Preston C6643. †Shared with Lt H.N. Jennings, Lt J.C. Preston, Lt H.A.E. Matthews.

DAVIES Ernest Edgar Captain 2AFC

An Australian, born on 16 March 1890, at Kerang, Victoria, and a barrister and solicitor in Swan Hill, Victoria, before the war, Davies joined the Light Horse initially, later transferring to the AFC. Posted to 2AFC Squadron in France in the summer of 1918, he claimed his first victory on 27 August. On 18 October, while on a bombing mission, his SE 5A was hit in the oil tank by ground fire, but he managed to crash unhurt in Allied lines. His most successful day was on 4 November, by which time he had become a flight commander; he claimed three Fokker DVIIs on this date to bring his score to seven. He was later awarded a DFC.

	1918		SE 5A					
1	27 Aug	Fokker DVII	D6860	2AFC	S Douai-Lecluse	1055	DES	CR/RAF 27.8
2s*	15 Sep	Alb. C	D6860	2AFC	W Macquart	1720	DES	CR/RAF 15.9
3	1 Oct	C	D6860	2AFC	Ligny	0925	OOC	CR/ORB/OH
4s*	1 Nov	LVG. C	E5765	2AFC	Antoing	1415	OOC	CR/ORB/OH
5	4 Nov	LVG. C	E5765	2AFC	Elleselles-Renaix	0810	DES	CR/RAF 4.11
6	4 Nov	Fokker DVII	E5765	2AFC	Houtaing	1300	OOC	CR/ORB/OH
7	4 Nov	Fokker DVII	E5765	2AFC	Houtaing	1300	OOC	CR/ORB/OH

TOTAL: 2 and 1 shared destroyed, 3 and 1 shared out of control = 7.
*Shared with Capt E.E. Cummings C6473.

DAVIES Edgar George Lieutenant 29

Born on 4 November 1898, Lieutenant Davies, from Tufnell Park, North London, joined the RFC on 4 November 1917. He was posted to 29 Squadron on 1 September 1918 with 100 hours flying experience. Here he was to claim victories over nine aircraft and a balloon during the last two months of the war. He was awarded a DFC after his fifth victory, and subsequently with a Bar to this decoration. He remained with 29 Squadron in Germany after the war, but was killed in a crash on 6 February 1919. He was also awarded the Belgian Croix de Guerre.

	1918		SE 5A					
1	16 Sep	Fokker DVII	D6916	29	E Lille	0920	DES	CR/RAF 16.9
2	29 Sep	Balloon	F853	29	S E Comines	0955	DES	CR/RAF 29.9
3	2 Oct	Fokker DVII	C9071	29	W Roulers	1520	DES	CR/RAF 2.10
4	7 Oct	Fokker DVII	E6030	29	E Courtrai	0855	DES	CR/RAF 7.10
5	27 Oct	Fokker DVII	H7162	29	S E Renaix	0950	DES	CR/ORB/11 WS
6	28 Oct	Fokker DVII	H7162	29	E Avelghem	1600	DES	CR/RAF 28.10
7	3 Nov	DFW. C	H7162	29	Celles	1430	DES(F)	CR/RAF 3.11
8	9 Nov	Rumpler C	H700	29	Laethan-St Marie	1000	DES(F)	CR/RAF 9.11
9	9 Nov	Fokker DVII	H700	29	N E Audenaarde	1005	DES	CR/RAF 9.11
10	10 Nov	Fokker DVII	F5660	29	Moorleghen	1345	DES	CR/RAF 10.11

TOTAL: 1 balloon, 9 destroyed = 10.

DAVIES Francis James Captain 29

Born on 20 October 1889, Davies, who was from Warwickshire, joined the RFC in May 1917 and qualified as a pilot in August of that year. He joined 29 Squadron in January 1918, at which time it was the last RFC unit on the Western Front still operating Nieuport Scouts. It was in one of these that he claimed his first victory on 18 March. The unit then converted to SE 5As, and early in the summer he became a flight commander. He received a DFC on 10 September, having raised his score to 11 by 12 August. On this latter date he was wounded in action whilst flying D6944, and as a consequence crashed on landing. He saw no further action before the war ended.

	1918		Nieuport					
1	18 Mar	Pfalz DIII	B6815	29	S E Rumbeke	1145	OOC	CR/RFC 18.3
			SE 5A					
2	19 May	Alb. DV	D5957	29	S Bailleul	1100	DES	CR/RAF 19.5
3s*	26 May	DFW. C	----	29	S Bailleul	1835	DES	CR/RAF 26.5
4	27 May	Alb. DV	D5967	29	Becelaere	0525	OOC	ORB/?
5	29 May	Alb. DV	D3931	29	Armentieres	1950	OOC	ORB/?
6	30 May	Alb. DV	D6159	29	Armentieres	1520	DES	CR/RAF 30.5
7	18 Jun	C	D5963	29	Merville	0815	DES(F)	CR/RAF 18.6
8	27 Jun	Halb. C	D6874	29	W Armentieres	1415	OOC	CR/ORB/?
9	4 Jul	Rumpler C	----	29	W Armentieres	1835	DES	CR/RAF 4.7
10	14 Jul	Halb. C	D5963	29	N E Estaires	0530	DES(F)	CR/RAF 14.7
11	9 Aug	Hannover C	D6944	29	W Laventie	1735	DES	CR/RAF 9.8
12	11 Aug	Balloon	D6944	29	Courtrai	1345	DES	CR/RAF 11.8

TOTAL: 1 balloon, 6 and 1 shared destroyed, 4 out of control = 12.
*Shared with Lt C.G. Ross, Capt R.H. Rusby D5963.

DAVIS Ernest Francis Hartley Lieutenant 41

From Saskatchewan, Canada, he flew with 41 Squadron from 31 October 1917 until 21 July 1918. He took part in many combats and was credited with seven victories.

	1917		SE 5A					
1s*	6 Dec	Alb. DV	B666	41	Sailly	1450	OOC	CR/RFC 6.12
	1918							
2	23 Mar	Alb. DV	C6396	41	Bourlon Wood	1130	OOC	CR/RFC 23.3
3	12 Apr	Alb. DV	C6396	41	Bac St Maur	1515	DES	CR/RAF 12.4
4	30 Jun	Alb. DV	D6023	41	E Albert	2015	OOC	CR/SR/?
5	2 Jul	Pfalz DIII	D6023	41	E Caveux	2020	DES	CR/RAF 2.7
6s**	4 Jul	Fokker DVII	D6023	41	Proyart	1330	OOC	CR/SR/?
7s**	4 Jul	Fokker DVII	D6023	41	Proyart	1330	OOC	CR/SR/?

TOTAL: 2 destroyed, 3 and 2 shared out of control = 7.
*Shared with Capt M. Thomas B633, 2/Lt Anderson B596. **Shared with Capt F.R. McCall D6154.

DAVISON Hiram Frank Lieutenant 22

Lieutenant Davison, a Canadian, joined 22 Squadron early in 1918, and flew the Bristol Fighter. All his air combats were compressed into the month of March, when his unit was heavily engaged during the German spring offensive. In 24 days he claimed nine victories with his front gun while his gunner, Lieutenant J.L. Morgan, sent down two more from the rear cockpit, for a total of 11. Davison was awarded an MC, gazetted on 22 June 1918. During one combat on 8 March he sent down two scouts out of control, the pilot of one being seen to fall out of his cockpit onto the centre section. Davison was wounded on 13 April, and did not see further action.

	1918		Bristol					
1*	6 Mar	Alb. DV	B1152	22	Douai	1400	OOC	CR/RFC 6.3
2*	8 Mar	Alb. DV	B1152	22	Lille-Douai	1245	OOC	CR/RFC 8.3
3*	8 Mar	Alb. DV	B1152	22	Lille-Douai	1245	OOC	CR/RFC 8.3
4*	8 Mar	Pfalz DIII	B1152	22	Douai	1310	DES	CR/RFC 8.3
5*	13 Mar	Pfalz DIII	B1155	22	Annoeullin	1615	DES(F)	CR/RFC 13.3
6*	25 Mar	Alb. DV	A7243	22	N Havrincourt Wood	0800	OOC	CR/RFC 25.3
7*	26 Mar	Pfalz DIII	A7243	22	E Albert	1245	DES(F)	CR/RFC 26.3
8*	27 Mar	Fokker DrI	B1164	22	Albert	1130	OOC	CR/RFC 27.3
9*	27 Mar	Fokker DrI	B1164	22	S E Albert	1135	DES	CR/RFC 27.3
10*	29 Mar	C	A7243	22	S E Hangard	1530	DES	CR/RFC 29.3
11*	29 Mar	Rumpler C	A7243	22	E Bervillers	1610	OOC	CR/RFC 29.3

TOTAL: 5 destroyed, 6 out of control = 11.
*Observer: 2/Lt J.L. Morgan.

DAWE James Jeffery Lieutenant 24

James Dawe of Rickmansworth, Hertfordshire, joined the RFC in 1917 and on 20 November became a scout pilot with 24 Squadron. Surviving his first combats, he soon began to build a modest score, but was killed in combat over Rosieres in SE 5A B611 on 7 June when he fell victim to Leutnant Fritz Rumey of Jasta 5; he was aged 19 at the time of his death.

	1918		SE 5A					
1s*	26 Feb	Fokker DrI	B85	24	E Samoussy	0900	DES	CR/RFC 26.2
2	6 Mar	Fokker DrI	B85	24	La Fere	1340	OOC	CR/RFC 6.3
3s**	16 Mar	Rumpler C	C1789	24	Lesdins	1700	OOC	CR/RFC 16.3
4	10 Apr	Alb. DV	B611	24	N E Moreuil	1145	OOC	CR/RAF 10.4
5	12 Apr	Pfalz DIII	B611	24	Hangard-Moreuil	1615	DES	CR/RAF 12.4
6	19 May	Pfalz DIII	B611	24	Chaulnes/Albert	0835	OOC	ORB/?
7	31 May	Pfalz DIII	C1081	24	Becquigny	1730	DES	CR/RAF 31.5
8s***	3 Jun	LVG. C	B611	24	S E Marcelcave	1120	DES	CR/RAF 3.6

TOTAL: 2 and 2 shared destroyed, 3 and 1 shared out of control = 8.
*Shared with Lt I.D.R. MacDonald C1057, Lt J.A. Poultet C9494, 2/Lt H.V.L. Tubbs C9542, Lt R.T. Mark B67, 2/Lt H.B. Richardson B124. **Shared with Lt H.V.L. Tubbs D272. ***Shared with Capt I.D.R. MacDonald D3444.
N.B. Dawe claimed an Out of Control on 12 March, which was disallowed.

DAWES Richard Jeffries Captain 45, 28

A Canadian from Montreal, who joined the RFC, Dawes flew Camels in France and Italy. He first served with 45 Squadron, claiming five victories before being posted to 28 Squadron where he claimed one more. This was an Aviatik two-seater which he forced down over the Piave Valley after firing 650 rounds at it. Promoted to Captain, he returned to 45 Squadron, was awarded a DFC, and brought his score to nine before he returned to Home Establishment at the end of June.

	1917		Camel					
1	20 Oct	Alb. DIII	----	45	Kastelhoek	2040	OOC	CR/RFC 20.10
2	31 Dec	Alb. DIII	B6412	45	Piave de Soligo	0945	OOC	CR/ORB/?
	1918							
3	14 Jan	Alb. DIII	B6412	45	Borgo	1500	DES	CR/7 BG
4	27 Jan	DFW. C	B6412	45	Conegliano	1340	OOC	CR/14 W
5s*	10 Mar	DFW. C	B6412	45	S E Salgarada	1130	DES	CR/7 BG
6	3 May	Aviatik C	B7359	28	Mt Santo	0915	DES	CR/ORB/?
7	3 Jun	Alb. DV	B6412	45	Campo	0905	OOC	CR/ORB/?
8	7 Jun	Alb. DIII	B6412	45	Piovena	0930	DES	CR/14 W
9	15 Jun	Aviatik C	B6412	45	Mt Campo-Poselaro	0745	DES	CR/14 W

TOTAL: 4 and 1 shared destroyed, 4 out of control = 9.
*Shared 2/Lt J. Cottle B6354.

DAY Harold Flight Lieutenant 10(N), 8(N)

Born on 17 April 1897 in Abergaveney, Wales, Day joined the RNAS on 28 January 1917. As a Flight Sub Lieutenant he flew Sopwith Camels with 10(N) Squadron from 25 July until he was taken ill on 12 September. On recovery he was transferred to 8(N) Squadron on 3 October. Between December 1917 and February 1918 he was to claim 11 victories, but on 5 February as he dived at high speed on an Albatros DV near Harnes, N6379 was seen to break up and he crashed to his death; he was claimed shot down by Leutnant G. Shuster of Jasta 29. Day received a DSC before his death.

	1917		Triplane					
1	12 Aug	Alb. DV	N5437	10N	Wervicq	1130	OOC	CR/RFC 12.8
			Camel					
2s*	6 Dec	DFW. C	----	8N	Loison, S E Lens	1045	OOC	CR/RFC 6.12
3s*	27 Dec	DFW. C	----	8N	Lens-Henin Lietard	1435	OOC	CR/RFC 27.12
4s**	28 Dec	DFW. C	B6379	8N	Vitry	1100	OOC	CR/RFC 28.12
	1918							
5	4 Jan	C	B3821	8N	5m N Bourlon Wood	1120	OOC	CR/RFC 4.1
6	6 Jan	C	B6371	8N	Fresnoy	1300	DES	CR/RFC 6.1
7	22 Jan	Alb. DV	B6371	8N	Vitry	1120	OOC	CR/RFC 22.1
8	29 Jan	Alb. DV	B6371	8N	S Scarpe River	1140	OOC	CR/RFC 29.1
9s***	2 Feb	C	----	8N	Douai-Ostricourt	1130	DES	CR/RFC 2.2
10s***	2 Feb	Alb. DV	----	8N	Carvin	1215	OOC	CR/RFC 2.2
11s†	5 Feb	Alb. DV	B3832	8N	S Pont a Vendin	1245	DES	CR/RFC 5.2

TOTAL: 1 and 2 shared destroyed, 4 and 4 shared out of control = 11.
*Shared with F/Cdr D.W. Price. **Shared with F/Cdr D.W. Price B6229. ***Shared with F/Cdr R.J.O. Compston, F/Cdr R. Macdonald, FSL R.L. Johns. †Shared with F/Lt R. Macdonald B6387, FSL W.H. Sneath B6356, FSL H.H.S. Fowler B3832.

DAY Miles Jeffrey Game Flight Commander 13(N)

Born on 1 December 1896, Miles Day become an experienced test pilot at the Royal Navy's Isle of Grain establishment before seeing any operational service. On 19 December 1917 he joined 13(N) Squadron, gaining five victories in six weeks for which he was awarded a DSC. On 27 February 1918 he was shot down in flames in Camel N6363 by a seaplane crewed by Flugmeister Dreyer/Leutnant Frantz of Seeflug II, falling into the sea 25 miles west of Dunkirk.

	1918		Camel					
1	3 Jan	C	N6349	13N	Dunkirk	1400	OOC	CR/RNAS 3.1
2	25 Jan	Fokker DrI	N6363	13N	Staden	1525	OOC	CR/RNAS 25.1
3s*	30 Jan	C	N6363	13N	2m N Ostend	1420	DES	CR/RNAS 30.1
4	2 Feb	Rumpler C	N6363	13N	Oostkerke	1245	CAPT	CR/RNAS 2.2
5s**	19 Feb	Seaplane	N6363	13N	E Ostend	1355	DES(F)	CR/RNAS 19.2

TOTAL: 1 captured, 2 shared destroyed, 2 out of control = 5.
*Shared with FSL J. deC Paynter B3782. **Shared with FSL J.C. Stovin N6349, FSL E.V. Bell B3773, FSL J. deC Paynter B3782, FSL G.D. Smith N6345.

DEBENHAM Horace Gilbert Wanklyn Captain 46, 208

Born in Essex on 9 September 1897, Debenham first flew as an observer with 46 Squadron when the unit was equipped with Nieuport two-seaters. Selected to become a pilot, he returned to the unit on 22 November 1917 following training, and in the early months of 1918 gained five victories while serving in 'B' Flight. He was then posted to 208 Squadron on 10 May as a flight commander, claiming one further victory with this unit.

	1918		Camel					
1s*	16 Feb	C	B9195	46	51B V2	0830	OOC	CR/RFC 16.2
2	22 Mar	Alb. DV	C1659	46	Doignies	1330	OOC	CR/RFC 22.3
3	22 Mar	C	C1659	46	Doignies	1415	OOC	CR/ORB/?
4	23 Mar	Alb. DV	C1637	46	Lagnicourt	0950	DES	CR/RFC 23.3
5s**	2 Apr	Alb. C	----	46	Courcelles	1245	DES	CR/RAF 2.4
6	18 May	Pfalz DIII	D1781	208	Merville	1200	OOC	CR/RAF 18.5

TOTAL: 1 and 1 shared destroyed, 3 and 1 shared out of control = 6.
*Shared with Capt G.E. Thomson B9137. **Shared with Capt S.P. Smith, Lt A.G. Vlasto, 2/Lt D.R. MacLaren, 2/Lt R.K. McConnell.

De FONTENAY Philip August Lieutenant 29

Born on 13 November 1897 in Mauritius, he served for five months in the French Foreign Legion before joining the RFC in January 1917. He was posted to 29 Squadron in July of that year, after a very brief stay with 40 Squadron, and flew Nieuport Scouts until early in 1918, claiming five victories. He was posted to Home Establishment on 30 January 1918.

	1917		Nieuport					
1	20 Sep	C	B1618	29	St Julien	1030	DES	CR/RFC 20.9
2	12 Nov	Alb. C	B3578	29	Houthoulst Forest	1440	OOC	CR/RFC 12.11
3s*	15 Dec	Alb. DV	B3625	29	Westroosebeke	1400	OOC	CR/RFC 15.12
	1918							
4	24 Jan	Alb. DV	----	29	N E Roulers	1230	DES	ORB/RFC 24.1
5	28 Jan	C	B6826	29	Staden	1200	OOC	CR/RFC 28.1

TOTAL: 2 destroyed, 3 out of control = 5.
*Shared with Lt E.S. Meek B6812.

DEL'HAYE Roger Amedee Captain 13, 19

Born in France on 9 January 1891, he was educated at the University of Paris. Emigrating to Canada, he became a British subject in 1914 and joined the RFC in October 1915. He flew over his native country with 13 Squadron on RE 8s from April 1916 to May 1917, during which time he drove down a German two-seater. Converting to single-seater scouts, he went to 19 Squadron in May 1918 and flew Dolphins. He became a very capable fighter and soon took command of a flight, being awarded the DFC and the Belgian Croix de Guerre. He ended the war with nine victories, eight of which were Pfalz Scouts. Between the wars he was a Dominion income tax assessor from 1921-1929, and from that year until 1939 he managed an airport at Regina, Canada. He served in the RCAF Reserve, commanding 120 Bomber Squadron in 1936. In 1940 he became a Wing Commander, and then a Group Captain in 1941. As an Air Commodore in 1944 he was killed taking off solo in a Harvard on 18 November, spinning from 1000 feet. He was buried in Montreal.

	1918		Dolphin					
1	17 Jun	Fokker DrI	C3792	19	Lens	0920	OOC	CR/ORB/?
2	30 Jun	Pfalz DIII	C3792	19	Armentieres	2000	OOC	CR/ORB/?
3	4 Jul	Pfalz DIII	C3792	19	Esterelles	1700	DES(F)	CR/RAF 4.7
4	16 Jul	Pfalz DIII	C3792	19	Armentieres	1230	DES	CR/RAF 16.7
5	16 Jul	Pfalz DIII	C3792	19	Armentieres	1230	OOC	CR/RAF/?
6	16 Sep	Pfalz DIII	D5236	19	N Lille	0940	DES	CR/RAF 16.9
7s*	27 Sep	Pfalz DIII	D5236	19	Haynecourt	0725	DES	CR/RAF 27.9
8	27 Sep	Pfalz DIII	D5236	19	Aubigny	1250	OOC	CR/ORB/?
9	1 Oct	Pfalz DIII	D5236	19	E Cambrai	0850	OOC	CR/ORB/?

TOTAL: 3 and 1 shared destroyed, 5 out of control = 9.
*Shared with Lt C. Montgomery-Moore B7855.

DENNETT Pruett Mullens Lieutenant 8(N), 208

From Southsea, Hampshire, where he was born on 21 January 1899, Dennett joined the RNAS on 25 March 1917 and was commissioned a Flight Sub Lieutenant on 27 August of that year, joining 8 Naval Squadron some months later. By June 1918 he had claimed eight victories, five of which were shared. On 2 June he was shot down and killed in Camel D1854 near Estaires by Oberflugmeister Schönfelder of Jasta 7.

	1917		Camel					
1s*	6 Dec	C	----	8N	Henin-Lietard	0900	OOC	CR/RFC 6.12
	1918							
2s**	3 Jan	Hannover C	B6447	8N	Arras	1005	DES	CR/RFC 3.1
3s***	4 Jan	DFW. C	B6319	8N	Oppy-Monchy	1130	DES	CR/RFC 4.1
4s†	19 Jan	Alb. DV	B6447	8N	Wingles	1125	OOC	CR/RFC 19.1
5	19 Jan	Alb. DV	B6447	8N	Henin-Lietard	1515	OOC	CR/RFC 19.1
6	17 Apr	Alb. DV	D1873	208	1m S Merville	0715	DES	CR/RAF 17.4
7s††	22 May	C	----	208	2m N E Lens	0800	OOC	CR/?

TOTAL: 1 and 2 shared destroyed, 1 and 3 shared out of control = 7.
*Shared with F/Cdr R.J.O. Compston, FSL E.G. Johnstone. **Shared with F/Cdr R.J.O. Compston B6340, FSL W.L. Jordon B6319. ***Shared with FSL W.L. Jordon B6447, FSL E.G. Johnstone B6376, FSL A.J. Dixon B6278. †Shared with FSL W.L. Jordon B6369, FSL E.G. Johnstone B6377. ††Shared with Capt W.L. Jordon, Lt R.L. Johns, Lt J.S. MacDonald, Lt E.G. Johnstone, Capt G.K. Cooper, Lt H.H.S Fowler.

De PENCIER John Dartnell Captain 19

Born in Canada, son of the Bishop of New Westminster, he joined 19 Squadron in October 1917, flying Spads, and later, Dolphins. He claimed seven victories, but on one occasion landed with a hole in his stomach which the doctor and his comrades thought was a mark made by a spent bullet. After lunch he discovered blood on his bed, when a second examination revealed that a bullet had gone right through him without causing serious damage. He was given seven days leave in England to recover. In June 1918 he was promoted to Captain, and in 1919 was with 1 RCAF Squadron in England, but was killed on 17 May 1920.

	1917		Spad					
1s*	30 Oct	DFW. C	A6971	19	W Dadizeele	0620	OOC	CR/11 WS
2	29 Dec	Alb. DV	B1581	19	Houthoulst Forest	1020	OOC	CR/RFC 29.12
	1918		Dolphin					
3	26 Feb	Fokker DrI	C3841	19	Comines	1005	OOC	ORB/RFC WD
4	21 Apr	Alb. DV	C4019	19	Estaires	1400	OOC	CR/RAF 21.4
5	20 May	Pfalz DIII	C4019	19	N E Estaires	1755	DES	CR/RAF 20.5
6s**	5 Jun	Fokker DrI	C3902	19	N E Arras	1210	OOC	CR/ORB/SR/?
7s***	6 Jun	DFW. C	C3829	19	Vieux Berquin	0715	OOC	CR/ORB/?
8	13 Jul	Fokker DVII	C3829	19	Bois de Biez	2005	OOC	CR/ORB/?

TOTAL: 1 destroyed, 4 and 3 shared out of control = 8.
*Shared with Lt C.R.J. Thompson B6817. **Shared with Lt A.W. Blake C3796. ***Shared with Capt G.B. Irving C3799, Lt F. McQuistan C3902, Lt C.V. Gardner C4159.

De ROEPER Bruno Philip Henry Major 6(N)

An RNAS pilot, he flew anti-Zeppelin patrols in BE 2Cs during 1916 before joining 6 Naval Squadron in France, where he flew Nieuport Scouts and Sopwith Camels in 1917. On 25 May he dived down in his Nieuport to attack a German two-seater, but the enemy observer got in an accurate burst of fire, hitting De Roeper's machine and wounding him in the jaw. He was out of action until July, but during that time 6 Naval had converted to Camels and he was promoted to Flight Lieutenant. He returned to action to claim at least four more victories on the new aircraft. He was then posted as an instructor, a role he continued to fill for the rest of the war, being promoted Squadron Commander in January 1918.

	1917		Nieuport					
1	20 May	Alb. C	N3209	6N	N W Bohain	1140	OOC	CR/RFC 20.5
			Camel					
2	22 Jul	C	N6341	6N	3m N E Dixmude	2040	OOC	CR/4 BG
3	15 Aug	Alb. DIII	B3882	6N	Ghistelles	1740	OOC	CR/4 BG
4s*	17 Aug	Aviatik C	B3882	6N	1m E Westende	1815	OOC	CR/4 BG
5s**	20 Aug	C	B3882	6N	Moere	1050	OOC	CR/4 BG

TOTAL: 3 and 2 shared out of control = 5.
*Shared with FSL N.M. MacGregor B3833, FSL R.E. Carroll N6381. **Shared with FSL N.M. MacGregor B3833.

DEWHIRST James Henry Lieutenant 45

From Yorkshire, he joined the RNAS, serving for two and a half years, all but eight months of this time being spent in the field. In 1918 he joined 45 Squadron, RAF, in Italy, where he was credited with the destruction of six enemy aircraft. On 19 June three of 45's pilots fought with several enemy aircraft, claiming six destroyed and one out of control; three were claimed by Dewhirst. It is now known that the actual result of this engagement was the loss to the Austro-Hungarians of two Albatros DIIIs totally destroyed and one badly damaged. Dewhirst claimed two further aircraft out of control during his service, but these were not confirmed. He received the French Croix de Guerre in September 1918. Whilst flying in France after the unit had returned to join the Independent Air Force, he made his last claim a few days before the war ended. The award of a DFC was gazetted in 1919.

	1918		Camel					
1	24 Mar	Berg DI	B6282	45	8m N W Asiago	1030	OOC	CR/ORB/7 BG
2	4 May	Berg DI	B6282	45	2.5m W Feltre	1030	DES	CR/ORB/14 W
3	1 Jun	Alb. DV	B7360	45	S Feltre	0945	DES	CR/ORB/14 W
4	19 Jun	Alb. DIII	D1910	45	Mt Verena	0935	DES	ORB/14 W
5	19 Jun	Alb. DIII	D1910	45	Mt Verena	0935	DES(F)	ORB/14 W
6*	19 Jun	Alb. DIII	D1910	45	Asiago	0935	DES	ORB/14 W
7	5 Nov	Fokker DVII	E7204	45	N Parroy	1550	DES	CR/8 BG WD

TOTAL: 6 destroyed, 1 out of control = 7.

*In this fight Capt C.E. Howell D9394 claimed 2 destroyed and Lt C.H. Masters 1 destroyed and 1 out of control. Flik 9j lost FwP Michael Messner in 153:47 and Zgsfhr Franz Cerda in 153:71, both killed, and Lt Alfred Hessenberger damaged in 153:187.

DICKSON Euan Captain 10(N), 5(N), 205

A New Zealander, born in Thames on 31 March 1892, Dickson joined the RNAS on 30 July 1916, and was posted to 10(N) Squadron on 31 March. On 29 April however, he was posted to 5(N) Squadron where he was to become one of the two most successful bomber pilots of the war in terms of aerial combat. Flying DH 5s, he claimed 14 victories — two of them shared — between December 1917 and May 1918, by which time the unit had become 205 Squadron. He was awarded a DSC and Bar and a DFC.

	1917		DH 4					
1*	8 Dec	Alb. DV	N5962	5N	Aertrycke a/d	1140	OOC	CR/DRO/5 GP
	1918							
2**	17 Feb	Alb. DV	N6000	5N	off Ostend, to sea	1210	OOC	DRO/?
3**	18 Feb	Alb. DV	N6000	5N	St Pierre Capelle	c1300	OOC	DRO/?
4***	16 Mar	Alb. DV	A7739	5N	Bohain-Le Catelet	c1100	DES	CR/RFC 16.3
5***	18 Mar	Alb. DV	A7620	5N	Beaurevoir	1054	OOC	CR/RFC 18.3
6†	27 Mar	Alb. DV	A7620	5N	Rainecourt	1530	DES	CR/RFC 27.3
7†	28 Mar	Pfalz DIII	A7620	5N	Foucaucourt	0950	OOC	CR/RFC 28.3
8††	6 Apr	Pfalz DIII	A7739	205	Abancourt	1550	OOC	CR/RAF 6.4
9†††	22 Apr	Fokker DrI	A7739	205	Chaulnes	1615	OOC	CR/ORB/?
10†††	23 Apr	Fokker DrI	A7739	205	Chaulnes	1940	OOC	CR/ORB/?
11†††	3 May	Pfalz DIII	D9237	205	Chaulnes-Rosieres	1542	OOC	CR/ORB/?
12s‡	3 May	Pfalz DIII	D9237	205	Chaulnes-Rosieres	1545	DES(F)	CR/ORB/?
13s‡	3 May	Pfalz DIII	D9237	205	Chaulnes-Rosieres	1545	OOC	CR/ORB/?
14†††	18 May	Alb. DV	D9238	205	4-6m W Chaulnes	1130	DES(F)	CR/RAF 18.5

TOTAL: 3 and 1 shared destroyed, 9 and 1 shared out of control = 14.

*Observer: AGL Shaw. **Observer: A.G.L. Naylor. ***Observer: Sub/Lt Scott. †Observer: Sub/Lt Stewart. ††Observer: 2/Lt Scott. †††Observer: AG C.V. Robinson. ‡Observer: AG C.V. Robinson. both of these were shared with 8 other crews.

DIXON George Clapham Captain 43, 85, 40

A Canadian from Vancouver, he served initially with the Highland Light Infantry before joining the RFC in April 1917. From May to September 1917 he flew as an observer with 43 Squadron on Sopwith 1½ Strutters, participating in two victories; he returned to Home Establishment on 20th of the latter month. After pilot training he returned to France to 85 Squadron with the rank of Captain in July 1918, and by August had claimed two victories; he was then posted to 40 Squadron as a flight commander. With 40 he claimed four more victories and destroyed a kite balloon, before he was wounded on 16 September.

	1917		Strutter					
1s*	16 Jun	Alb. DIII	A8785	43	N Lens	0630	DES(F)	CR/RFC 16.6
2**	13 Aug	Alb. DV	A8785	43	Pont a Vendin	1930	OOC	CR/RFC 13.8

	1918		SE 5A					
3	13 Jul	Pfalz DIII	D6923	85	Armentieres	2030	DES	CR/RAF 13.7
4	14 Jul	Pfalz DIII	D6923	85	Estaires	0855	OOC	CR/?
5	21 Aug	Fokker DVII	C9258	40	S W Cambrai	1750	OOC	CR/?
6	22 Aug	Balloon	E3979	40	Hantay	0605	DES	CR/RAF 22.8
7	29 Aug	Fokker DVII	E3979	40	Saudemont	1150	OOC	CR/?
8	1 Sep	DFW. C	E3979	40	S E Henin-Lietard	0815	OOC	CR/?
9	2 Sep	Fokker DVII	E3979	40	W Ecourt St Quentin	1435	OOC	CR/?

TOTAL: 1 balloon, 1 and 1 shared destroyed, 5 and 1 shared out of control = 9.
*Pilot: 2/Lt C.H. Harriman; shared with Capt K.L. Gopsill/2/Lt J. Bonner-Smith A8335, Sgt A.V. Webb/Lt W. Gaunt A7798, 2/Lt L.S.V. Gedge/Pte Blatherwick A8229, Lt C.G. Moore/Lt W.B. Giles A1903, 2/Lt J.H.G. Womerersley/A.M. O'Shea. **Pilot: 2/Lt C.H. Harriman.

DODDS Robert E. Captain 48

A Canadian from Hamilton, Ontario, he flew in 48 Squadron during the summer and autumn of 1917, then becoming a flight commander at the beginning of 1918. He flew with several different gunners, and was awarded the MC. The citation, gazetted in May 1918, gave him credit for 11 victories. Post war Dodds reached high office in the Canadian transport bureaucracy.

	1917		Bristol					
1s*	21 Jul	Alb. DIII	A7153	48	Slype	1800	OOC	CR/RFC 21.7
2**	22 Aug	Alb. DIII	A7222	48	Ghistelles	0905	OOC	CR/RFC 22.8
3***	3 Sep	Alb. DIII	A7222	48	N Dixmude	0815	DES(F)	CR/RFC 3.9
4***	3 Sep	Alb. DIII	A7222	48	N Dixmude	0815	OOC	CR/RFC 3.9
5†	21 Oct	Alb. DV	B1134	48	Clemskerke	1245	OOC	CR/SR/?
	1918							
6††	9 Jan	Rumpler C	B1182	48	Caudry	1140	OOC	CR/RFC 9.1
7††	9 Jan	Alb. DV	B1182	48	Wallencourt	1150	OOC	CR/RFC 9.1
8†††	8 Mar	Pfalz DIII	----	48	La Fere	AM	DES(F)	Cit
9†††	8 Mar	Pfalz DIII	----	48	La Fere	AM	DES(F)	Cit
10†††	8 Mar	C	C4606	48	Bellecourt-Quesnoy	1600	OOC	CR/5 BG

TOTAL: 3 destroyed, 6 and 1 shared out of control = 10.
*Observer: Lt T.C.S. Tuffield; shared with Capt B.E. Baker/Lt G.R. Spencer A7146, Lt R.D. Coath/2/Lt K. Tanner A7164. **Observer: Lt T.C.S. Tuffield. ***Observer: Lt T.C.S. Tuffield; The first of these was Hptm O Hartmann an ace, and commander of Jasta 28. †Observer: Lt H.A. Cooper. ††Observer: 2/Lt W. Hart. †††Observer: Lt D Wishart-Orr.

DOLAN Henry Eric Lieutenant 74

Lieutenant Dolan served as an artillery officer, and in this role was awarded an MC. He transferred to the RFC, and after training was posted to 74 Squadron, serving in 'Mick' Mannock's flight. He claimed four aircraft shot down during the squadron's first month at the front in April 1918, and added three more in early May, bringing his total to seven in just one month. On 12th he was seen to spiral down and crash near Wulverghem during a fight with Albatros and Pfalz Scouts, almost certainly the victim of Leutnant Raven von Barnekow of Jasta 20; his death was confirmed by the Germans on 18 June.

	1918		SE 5A					
1	12 Apr	Alb. DV	B173	74	E Merville	0825	DES	CR/RAF 12.4
2	21 Apr	Fokker DrI	----	74	Steenwerck	0915	OOC	2 BG WD
3	29 Apr	Alb. DV	B173	74	S Dickebusch Lake	1140	DES	CR/RAF 29.4
4s*	30 Apr	Halb. C	B173	74	Dickebusch Lake	1440	CAPT	CR/RAF 30.4
5s**	3 May	LVG. C	B173	74	S Merville	1855	DES	CR/RAF 3.5
6***	7 May	Fokker DrI	C1112	74	E Zillebeke Lake	1525	DES	CR/RAF 7.5
7s†	11 May	Pfalz DIII	----	74	N E Armentieres	1740	DES	CR/RAF 11.5

TOTAL: 1 shared captured, 3 and 2 shared destroyed, 1 out of control = 7.
*Shared with Capt E.C. Mannock D278; Flgr Zimmerman/Vzfw Speer KIA, Sch. 10. **Shared with Capt E.C. Mannock, Lt H.G. Clements, Lt A.C. Kiddie; This was Uffz Schoning/Lt Beuttler KIA of FA 32. ***74 made 2 claims; one was probably Offstvtr W. von der Weppen, of Jasta 27, who was killed. †Shared with Capt E.C. Mannock; this was Lt O. Aeckerle KIA of Jasta 47.

DONALDSON John Owen Captain 32

An American born on 14 May 1897 in Fort Yates, North Dakota, and a member of the USAS, Donaldson flew with 32 Squadron where he became a flight commander. In a period of just over one month during the summer of 1918 he claimed at least seven Fokker DVIIs, receiving a DFC and Bar and a US DSC. On 1 September he was shot down by Leutnant Theodor Quandt of Jasta 36, and became a prisoner. He may have made a claim during this fight, but if so, it was never confirmed. Donaldson was killed in a crash on 7 September 1930.

	1918		SE 5A					
1	22 Jul	Fokker DVII	E1361	32	Mont Notre Dame	1810	DES(F)	CR/RAF 22.7
2	25 Jul	Fokker DVII	E5939	32	Fismes	1900	OOC	CR/?
3	8 Aug	Fokker DVII	B8374	32	Licourt	1815	DES	CR/RAF 8.8
4	9 Aug	Fokker DVII	E5939	32	Licourt	1100	DES(F)	CR/RAF 9.8
5	10 Aug	Fokker DVII	E5939	32	Peronne	1130	OOC	CR/?
6*	25 Aug	Fokker DVII	E5939	32	Hancourt	0650	DES	CR/RAF 25.8
7	29 Aug	Fokker DVII	E5939	32	Cambrai	0750	OOC	CR/?

TOTAL: 4 destroyed, 3 out of control = 7.
*The pilot of this aircraft baled out successfully.

DORAN T.A. Lieutenant 23

Doran served with 23 Squadron from April 1917 when Spads were received; he had claimed seven victories by mid August of that year.

	1917		Spad					
1	2 May	Alb. DIII	----	23	Brebieres	1715	OOC	CR/RFC 2.5
2	13 May	Alb. DIII	A262	23	Vis en Artois	0735	OOC	CR/V BG WD
3	13 May	Alb. DIII	A262	23	Vis en Artois	0735	OOC	CR/V BG WD
4	14 Jun	Alb. DIII	B1530	23	Roulers	2015	OOC	CR/RFC 14.6
5s*	28 Jul	C	B1530	23	E Polygon Wood	0850	DES	CR/RFC 28.7
6	10 Aug	Alb. DV	B3550	23	S Houthoulst Forest	0545	OOC	CR/RFC 10.8
7s**	14 Aug	C	----	23	E St Julien	1915	DES	CR/V BG WD

TOTAL: 2 shared destroyed, 5 out of control = 7.
*Shared with 2/Lt W.R. Brookes B1581. **Shared with 2/Lt S.C.O'Grady, 2/Lt G.I.D. Marks, 2/Lt C.F. Briggs.

DOYLE John Edgcombe Captain 56, 60

Born on 18 April 1893 in Cleveden, Somerset, Doyle served for 12 months with an infantry regiment in France. Joining the RFC in September 1916, he served with 88 Squadron in England until he eventually went to 56 Squadron on 25 March 1918, and then on 17 July was posted as a flight commander to 60 Squadron. Here he claimed nine victories and received the DFC. In a fight with several Fokker DVIIs near Cambrai on 5 September, he was shot down in E1397 by Leutnant E. Koepsch of Jasta 4, and was wounded in the leg. He was taken prisoner and his injured limb had to be amputated. In the 1930s he wrote several articles for flying magazines, some telling of his experiences.

	1918		SE 5A					
1	22 Jul	Pfalz DIII	E1288	60	Aveluy Wood	0540	OOC	CR/?
2s*	8 Aug	Hannover C	E1397	60	Foucaucourt	1640	DES	CR/RAF 8.8
3	8 Aug	Hannover C	E1397	60	Estrees	1655	DES	CR/RAF 8.8
4s**	9 Aug	Hannover C	E1288	60	Croisilles	0835	DES	CR/RAF 9.8
5	14 Aug	Alb. DV	E1397	60	Guemappe	0955	DES	CR/RAF 14.8
6	23 Aug	DFW. C	E1397	60	Croisilles	0955	DES	CR/RAF 23.8
7	3 Sep	Fokker DVII	D6953	60	Inchy	1010	DES	CR/?
8s***	5 Sep	Fokker DVII	E1397	60	Avesnes	1810	DES	CR/RAF 5.9
9	5 Sep	Fokker DVII	E1397	60	Avesnes	1810	OOC	CR/?

TOTAL: 4 and 3 shared destroyed, 2 out of control = 9.
*Shared with Lt R.K. Whitney C8886; both crew baled out safely! **Shared with Lt R.K. Whitney C8886. ***Shared with Lt O.P. Johnson E5991.

DRAKE Edward Barfoot Captain MDF, 9(N), 209

Edward Drake served initially with the Manston Defence Flight of the RNAS, on Home Defence duties. With this unit he was credited with shooting down a Gotha bomber on 22 August 1917 during a German air raid on Southern England. Shortly after this, he was posted as a reinforcement to 9(N) Squadron in France, and after this unit became 209 Squadron, RAF, he was to add four further victories to his total. On 29 September 1918 he was reported missing, presumed shot down by ground fire in E4376.

	1917		Camel					
1*	22 Aug	Gotha G. IV	B3844	Mn	Off Dover	1120	DES	ADGB
	1918							
2	2 May	Alb. DV	D3345	209	Cayeux	1845	OOC	CR/?
3	3 Jun	Fokker DrI	D3345	209	3m N W Montdidier	2000	OOC	CR/?
4**	27 Jun	Pfalz DIII	D3345	209	Warfusee	2050	DES(F)	CR/RAF 27.6
5	8 Aug	Fokker DVII	C1672	209	N W Rosieres	1915	DES	CR/RAF 8.8

TOTAL: 3 destroyed, 2 out of control = 5.
*This aircraft was destroyed. Details not known. **This was Lt Steinbrecher of Jasta 46 who made the first successful operational parachute escape.

DRAPER Christopher Major 3W, 6(N), 8(N), 208

Born in Liverpool on 15 April 1892, Draper was a pre-war pilot (Royal Aero Club Certificate No 646, dated 13 October 1913). He joined the RNAS in January 1914, serving at several stations in England during 1914-15. In 1916 he participated in various armaments experiments before becoming an original member of 3 Wing as a Flight Commander, leading the escort section of Sopwith 1½ Strutter fighters. In three fights in November 1916 he claimed four enemy aircraft shot down. Following the disbandment of the Wing, Draper was posted to 6(N) Squadron on Camels, and here he made one further claim before becoming commanding officer of 8(N) Squadron in September 1917. With this unit he shared in the destruction of a balloon at night and claimed one aircraft out of control. His final claim was made on 8 May 1918. For his services he was awarded a DSC, and subsequently wrote his autobiography, *The Mad Major* in the 1950s. He died on 16 January 1979.

	1916		Strutter					
1*	10 Nov	Fokker D	9407	3W	Landorf	1210	OOC	WR/3W
2*	10 Nov	C	9407	3W	Landorf	1210	OOC	WR/3W
3**	23 Nov	EA	9722	3W	----	1400-1515	DES	WR/3W
4s***	24 Nov	EA	9407	3W	N E Deline	1300	DES	WR/3W
	1917		Camel					
5	6 Jun	Alb. DV	N3101	6N	N W Cambrai	1200	DES	CR/ORB/DL
6	6 Jun	Alb. DV	N3101	6N	N W Cambrai	1200	OOC	CR/ORB/DL
7	11 Sep	Alb. DV	B3922	8N	E Douai	1355	OOC	CR/ORB/DL
8s†	3 Oct	Balloon	----	8N	Douai Area	c2300	DES	ORB/SR/DL
	1918							
9	8 May	DFW. C	D1928	208	Scarpe River	1945	OOC	CR/RAF 8.5

TOTAL: 1 shared balloon, 2 and 1 shared destroyed, 5 out of control = 9.
*Observer: Sub/Lt L.V. Pearkes. **Observer: Sub/Lt Barker. ***Shared with F/Lt C.B. Dalison/Sub/Lt F.E. Fraser. †Shared with F/Cdr R.B. Munday.

DREWITT Herbert Frank Stacey Captain 23, 79

A New Zealander from Christchurch, born in 1895, Drewitt joined 23 Squadron in 1917 and flew Spads. Early in January 1918 he became a flight commander and was subsequently awarded an MC. He later flew Sopwith Dolphins in 79 Squadron, but does not appear to have gained any further victories on this type. He later received an AFC. He died of illness in England on 4 January 1927.

	1917		Spad					
1	17 Oct	C	B6761	23	Dixmude-Houthoulst	1105	DES(F)	CR/RFC 17.10
2	27 Oct	Alb. DV	B6761	23	N W Roulers	1220	OOC	CR/RFC 27.10
	1918							
3	24 Jan	Alb. DV	A6654	23	Comines	1220	OOC	CR/RFC 24.1
4	11 Mar	C	B6848	23	Beaurevoir	1135	OOC	CR/RFC 11.3
5	12 Mar	Alb. DV	B6738	23	E Bellenglise	1045	DES	CR/RFC 12.3
6s*	15 Mar	DFW. C	B6738	23	Brissey	1015	DES	CR/RFC 15.3
7**	16 Mar	C	B6738	23	Pontruet	0720	DES(F)	CR/RFC 16.3

TOTAL: 3 and 1 shared destroyed, 3 out of control = 7.
*Shared with Lt G.G. Macphee B6861. **This was Vzfw E Greiff/Vzfw X Zollinger, of Schusta 6b, who were shot down in flames at Bellenglise, about 400 metres north of Pontruet.

DRINKWATER Arthur Thomas Captain 57, 40

Born in 1894 in Queenscliff, Victoria, this Australian joined the RFC in November 1916, and flew DH 4 bombers with 57 Squadron during the summer of 1917, he and his observers claiming six victories by mid November. Following a period off operations, he was posted to 40 Squadron in August 1918, becoming a flight commander in October. He had increased his score to nine by the end of the war.

	1917		DH 4					
1*	18 Aug	Alb. DV	A2138	57	Courtrai	1920	OOC	CR/RFC 19.8
2*	20 Aug	Alb. DV	A2132	57	Houthoulst Forest	1130	OOC	CR/RFC 20.8
3*	21 Sep	Alb. DV	A7581	57	Dadizeele	1050	DES	CR/RFC 21.9
4*	21 Sep	Alb. DV	A7581	57	Dadizeele	1050	DES	CR/RFC 21.9
5*	12 Nov	Alb. DV	A7424	57	S E Houthoulst Wood	1145	OOC	CR/RFC 12.11
6*	12 Nov	Alb. DV	A7424	57	S E Houthoulst Wood	1145	OOC	CR/RFC 12.11
	1918		SE 5A					
7	17 Sep	Fokker DVII	E5982	40	S E Cambrai	0955	OOC	CR/?
8	1 Oct	Halb. C	F5527	40	N Cambrai	1245	DES(F)	CR/RAF 1.10
9	9 Oct	Fokker DVII	E4036	40	N E Cambrai	0740	OOC	CR/?

TOTAL: 3 destroyed, 6 out of control = 9.
*Observer: Lt F.T.S. Menendez.

DRUMMOND Jack Elmer Captain 48

Lieutenant Drummond, a Canadian, joined 48 Squadron early in 1918, and began claiming during March. On 6 April he shot down a Triplane but was wounded in the ankle. He was soon back in action and early in June was promoted to flight commander. His fifth and sixth victories were shared between the front and rear guns of his Bristol Fighter.

	1918		Bristol					
1*	8 Mar	Alb. DIII	B1265	48	N E Laon	1100	OOC	CR/RFC 8.3
2**	6 Apr	Fokker DrI	B1299	48	S Lamotte	1540	DES(F)	CR/RAF 6.4
3***	21 May	Fokker DrI	C805	48	S Combles	1850	DES	CR/RAF 21.5
4s†	10 Jun	Alb. DV	----	48	Roye	1745	DES(F)	CR/RAF 10.6
5††	29 Jun	Pfalz DIII	C926	48	Hangest	2010	DES	CR/RAF 29.6
6††	2 Jul	Pfalz DIII	C926	48	880y S Soyecourt	0840	DES	CR/RAF 2.7

TOTAL: 4 and 1 shared destroyed, 1 out of control = 6.
*Observer: 2/Lt N Sillars. **Observer: 2/Lt H.F. Lamb. ***Observer: 2/Lt L.C. Walmsley. †Shared with Capt C.R. Steele, Capt F.C. Ransley, 2/Lt H.A. Oaks, 2/Lt N.Y. Lewis, Lt E.D. Shaw; The CR did not mention the observers! ††Observer: Lt J.A. Galbraith.

DRUMMOND Roy Maxwell Major 67, 111

Known as 'Peter', he was born in Australia on 2 June 1894, in Perth. He served with the Australian Imperial Force, 1914-16, as a private in the Medical Corps. Joining the RFC, he served with 67 Squadron, AFC, early in 1917, receiving an MC; he was flying on 20 March, taking part in the engagement that resulted in Lieutenant McNamara being awarded the VC. Drummond then became a Captain with 111 Squadron in Palestine, 1917-18. For his work with this unit, with which he claimed eight victories flying Bristol Fighters and Nieuports, he received the DSO and Bar. By the end of the war he was a Major, and during the 1920s was attached to the RAAF. In 1930 he attended the Imperial Defence College, and shortly afterwards became a Wing Commander; he received the OBE, then took command of RAF Northolt in 1936. Various commands in the Middle East, 1937-43, followed, where he became Deputy to Arthur Tedder; he then served on the Air Council, 1943-45. He was knighted KCB, but was killed in an aircraft accident on 27 March 1945 while flying to Canada. He had attained the rank of Air Marshal.

	1917		Bristol					
1*	12 Dec	Alb. DV	A7202	111	Tul Keram	1030	OOC	CR/BG WD
2**	12 Dec	Alb. DV	A7202	111	4m N W Tul Keram	1035	DES	CR/BG WD
3**	12 Dec	Alb. DV	A7202	111	Wadi Auja	1045	DES	CR/BG WD
4*	14 Dec	Alb. DV	A7202	111	1m N Beisan	0945	DES	CR/BG WD
	1918		Nieuport					
5s***	19 Mar	C	B3597	111	Kefra-Saba	1545	DES	CR/BG WD
7	27 Mar	Alb. DV	B3597	111	N E Purdisia	0830	DES	CR/BG WD
8	27 Mar	Alb. DV	B3597	111	Teiyibeh	0845	OOC	CR/BG WD

TOTAL: 6 and 1 shared destroyed, 1 out of control = 8.
*Observer: 2 AM F.J. Knowles. **Observer: 2 AM F.J. Knowles; one was possible Lt Heinrich Deilmann, KIA at Tul Keram. ***Shared with 2/Lt H.E. Walker B3595.

DUFFUS Chester Stairs Major 22, 25

A Canadian from Halifax, Nova Scotia, Duffus flew with 22 Squadron throughout 1916, claiming his first two victories during August of that year; he was awarded an MC on 14 November. Following his fourth victory on 4 December 1916, he was forced to land near Bapaume in FE 2B 4883. He claimed one further victory later in that month. Subsequently he commanded 25 Squadron.

	1916		FE 2B					
1s*	17 Aug	C	6931	22	W Pozieres	1020	CAPT	CR/RFC 17.8
2**	23 Aug	Fokker E	6931	22	Bapaume	1310	OOC	CR/IV BG
3***	16 Oct	D	4855	22	Guedecourt	1440	OOC	CR/RFC 16.10
4†	4 Dec	Alb. DI	4883	22	Barastre	1015	OOC	CR/RFC 4.12
5s††	11 Dec	C	7697	22	Bapaume	1000	DES(F)	CR/RFC 11.12

TOTAL: 1 shared captured, 1 shared destroyed, 3 out of control = 5.

*Observer: Cpl A. Winterbottom; shared with Capt J.G. Swart/2/Lt L.C.L. Cook. Possibly OfzStv K. Branicke/Lt P. Wagner. **Observer: Cpl A. Winterbottom. ***Observer: Cpl F. Johnson. †Observer: 2/Lt G.O. McEntee. ††2/Lt G.O. McEntee; shared with Capt S.H. Long A305, 2/Lt E.C. Pashley 7930 of 24 Sqn.

DUNCAN Gordon Metcalfe Captain 60

Born in Edinburgh on 25 March 1899, Gordon Duncan joined the RFC on 20 June 1917, being posted to 60 Squadron on 27 March 1918, where he carried out his first patrol on 10 April; during this he was shot-up and forced to land. Following this, he served successfully until 19 June, when he was injured in a force-landing caused by mechanical failure. After a month in hospital, he rejoined the unit and in three days in early August he accounted for four Fokker DVIIs during the intense aerial fighting associated with the battle of Amiens; on the last day of that month he claimed a DFW two-seater. In two days in early September three more Fokker DVIIs became his victims, and he was awarded a DFC, which was gazetted on 3 December 1918. On 15 September he was posted to 56 Squadron as a flight commander, but he was not to add further to this score with this unit.

	1918		SE 5A					
1	8 Aug	Fokker DVII	D6178	60	Peronne	1400	DES	CR/RAF 8.8
2	9 Aug	Fokker DVII	D6178	60	Nesles	1520	DES	CR/RAF 9.8
3	9 Aug	Fokker DVII	D6178	60	Chaulnes	1530	OOC	CR/?
4	10 Aug	Fokker DVII	D6178	60	Foucaucourt	0645	DES	CR/RAF 10.8
5	31 Aug	DFW. C	D6960	60	Bapaume	1020	DES	CR/?
6	4 Sep	Fokker DVII	D6960	60	Cambrai	0635	DES	CR/RAF 4.9
7	5 Sep	Fokker DVII	D6960	60	Avesnes	1820	DES	CR/RAF 5.9
8	5 Sep	Fokker DVII	D6960	60	Avesnes	1825	OOC	CR/?

TOTAL: 6 destroyed, 2 out of control = 8.

DUNCAN William James Arthur Captain 60

A Canadian from Toronto, he joined the RFC at the end of 1916 and was posted to 60 Squadron in September 1917 after receiving his wings. On 1 April 1918 he forced down Vizefeldwebel Weimar of Jasta 56 inside Allied lines, the German pilot later succumbing to his wounds. Duncan remained with the squadron until June 1918, becoming a flight commander in May and receiving an MC and Bar; he returned to Home Establishment on 30 June. Post war he became a leading professional ice hockey player.

	1917		SE 5A					
1	6 Nov	DFW. C	B512	60	N E Polygon Wood	0840	DES	CR/RFC 6.11
2s*	19 Nov	DFW. C	B608	60	S W Becelaere	1520	OOC	CR/RFC 19.11?
3s*	19 Nov	Alb. C	B608	60	S E Passchendaele	1545	DES	CR/RFC 19.11?
	1918							
4s**	4 Feb	Alb. DV	C1056	60	Ypres	1120	DES(F)	CR/RFC 4.2
5	9 Mar	Alb. DV	C9536	60	Gheluwe	1145	OOC	CR/RFC 9.3
6s***	30 Mar	LVG. C	C9536	60	Becourt	1150	DES	CR/RFC 30.3
7†	1 Apr	Alb. DV	C9536	60	Gentelles	1015	CAPT	CR/RAF 1.4
8s††	6 May	Alb. DV	B567	60	Guillaucourt	1915	DES	CR/RAF 6.5
9	17 May	Alb. DV	C9536	60	Bapaume	1110	DES	CR/RAF 17.5
10	3 Jun	LVG. C	D5992	60	Contalmaison	2015	DES	CR/RAF 3.6
11	5 Jun	Balloon	D5992	60	Irles	0925	DES	CR/RAF 5.6

TOTAL: 1 captured, 4 and 4 shared destroyed, 1 and 1 shared out of control = 11.

*Shared with 2/Lt W.E. Jenkins B623. **Shared with 2/Lt J.O. Priestley B103. ***Shared with 2/Lt J.S. Griffith C1069. †Vzfw Weimar of Jasta 56, who was killed. ††Shared with 2/Lt J.S. Griffith D3503.

DURRAND William Lieutenant 20

Lieutenant Durrand served with 20 Squadron, and during the summer of 1917 flew FE 2Ds, claiming four victories on these aircraft, with a different gunner on each occasion. In September this Canadian converted to Bristol Fighters after claiming the unit's last FE 2D victory on 21st. He then teamed-up with Lieutenant A.E. Woodbridge, and during the autumn accounted for three more enemy aircraft to bring his score to eight and received the MC.

	1917		FE 2D					
1*	8 Jun	Alb. DIII	A1965	20	Comines	0745	DES(F)	CR/RFC 8.6
2**	17 Jul	Alb. DV	A6548	20	Polygon Wood	0845	OOC	CR/RFC 17.7
3s***	17 Aug	Alb. DV	A6456	20	E Polygon Wood	2000	DES	CR/RFC 17.8
4†	21 Sep	Alb. DV	B1892	20	Becelaere	1100	OOC	CR/RFC 21.9
			Bristol					
5††	27 Sep	Alb. DV	A7245	20	Moorslede	1300	DES(F)	CR/RFC 27.9
6†††	17 Oct	DFW. C	A7141	20	Wervicq-Menin	0925	DES	CR/RFC 17.10
7†††	27 Oct	Alb. DV	A7298	20	S W Roulers	1310	DES	CR/RFC 27.10
8†††	8 Nov	Alb. DV	A7253	20	N E Houthoulst Wood	1330	DES	CR/RFC 8.11

TOTAL: 5 and 1 shared destroyed, 2 out of control = 8.

*Observer: Sgt E.H. Sayers. **Observer: 2/Lt S.F. Thompson. ***Observer: 2/Lt J.P. Flynn; shared with Lt R.M. Makepeace/Gnr J. McMechan B1597. †Observer: Lt A.N. Jenks. This was the last claim in daylight by an FE 2D. ††Observer: Sgt W.J. Benger. †††Observer: 2/Lt A.E. Woodbridge.

DURRANT Trevor Captain 55, 56

Born in Woking, Surrey, on 21 January 1893, this pilot joined the RFC on 5 August 1916 and served from November of that year to June 1917 as an observer in 55 Squadron. After undertaking pilot training, he was posted to 56 Squadron on 7 December 1917, and flew with this unit until May 1918. During this period he flew 42 offensive patrols and four special missions; in combat he was credited with ten victories. On 16 May 1918 he took off on patrol in B183 at 1850 and was last seen north-east of Albert, fighting several Fokker Triplanes; he did not return, having been shot down by Leutnant Hans Kirschtein of Jasta 6.

	1917		DH 4					
1*	4 May	Alb. DIII	A7415	55	Denain	1215	OOC	CR/RFC WD
	1918		SE 5A					
2	25 Jan	C	B35	56	S Cambrai	1415	OOC	CR/RFC 25.1
3	21 Mar	Alb. DV	B35	56	Inchy	1315-1345	OOC	CR/RFC 21.3
4	6 Apr	C	B183	56	N Lamotte	1845	DES(F)	CR/RAF 6.4
5**	11 Apr	Alb. DV	B183	56	W Pozieres	1830	DES(F)	CR/RAF 11.4
6	2 May	Pfalz DIII	B183	56	S E Martinpuich	1125	OOC	CR/RAF 2.5
7	3 May	Rumpler C	B183	56	S Pozieres	0940	DES	CR/RAF 3.5
8s***	3 May	Rumpler C	B183	56	Montauban	0945	DES	CR/RAF 3.5
9s***	3 May	Rumpler C	B183	56	Montauban	0945	OOC	CR/RAF 3.5
10s†	9 May	Rumpler C	B183	56	Achiet le Grand	1050	OOC	CR/RAF 9.5
11	13 May	LVG. C	B183	56	S W Beaucourt	0605	DES	CR/RAF 13.5

TOTAL: 4 and 1 shared destroyed, 4 and 2 shared out of control = 11.

*Pilot: Lt P.J. Barnett. **This was Pnr A. Kohler, of Jasta 35, who was forced to crash land. ***Shared with Capt E.D. Atkinson B8494, Lt W.R. Irwin C5435. †Shared with Capt E.D.G. Galley B8376.

EATON Edward Carter Lieutenant 65

Eaton, a Canadian, went to France in late 1917 with 65 Squadron, flying Sopwith Camels. On 23 November he shared with two other pilots the squadron's first claim, when they sent down an Albatros Scout out of control. He went on to claim a total of six victories, but was reported missing in action on 26 June 1918 in D6630 north-east of Albert; he fell to one of the leading pilots of Jasta 5, Vizefeldwebel Fritz Rumey, as his 25th victory.

	1917		Camel					
1s*	23 Nov	Alb. DIII	B2413	65	2m E Passchendaele	1525	OOC	CR/ORB/?
	1918							
2	4 Jan	Alb. DV	B2394	65	Passchendaele	1045	OOC	CR/RFC 4.1
3s**	16 Feb	Alb. DV	B5621	65	Moorslede-Dadizeele	0735	DES	CR/ORB/?
4s***	20 May	Fokker DrI	D6630	65	S E Albert	2030	DES	CR/RAF 20.5
5	28 May	Pfalz DIII	D6630	65	Bois de Tailleux	0955	OOC	CR/ORB/?

TOTAL: 1 and 1 shared destroyed, 2 and 1 shared out of control = 5.

*Shared with Capt L.S. Weedon B2394, Lt B. Balfour B5221. **Shared with Lt H.D. Harrington B2416. ***Shared with Capt J. Gilmour D8118.

EDWARDS Cedric George Lieutenant 9(N), 209

Born on 5 June 1899 in St. Albans, Hertfordshire, Edwards was a pupil at Mill Hill School, North London. He joined the RNAS in June 1917, completing his training in France with 12(N) Squadron at the end of the year. Early in 1918 he joined 9(N) Squadron — later 209 Squadron — and with this unit claimed seven victories, receiving a DFC. He was killed by a direct hit from anti-aircraft fire on 27 August 1918, whilst flying Camel B6371 near Jigsaw Wood.

	1918		Camel					
1*	11 Apr	Alb. DIII	D3331	209	Albert	1700	OOC	CR/RAF 11.4
2	20 Apr	Fokker DrI	D3331	209	Clery	1100	OOC	CR/ORB/?
3	24 Apr	Pfalz DIII	D3351	209	Warfusee-Abancourt	1850	DES	CR/RAF 24.4
4	9 Jun	LVG. C	B6371	209	Mericourt	0830	DES	CR/RAF 9.6
5s**	9 Jun	LVG. C	B6371	209	Proyart	1130	OOC	CR/RAF 9.6
6s***	8 Aug	Halb. C	D9588	209	Harbonnieres	1905	DES(F)	CR/RAF 8.8
7	11 Aug	Fokker DVII	B6371	209	Assevillers	0840	DES	CR/RAF 11.8

TOTAL: 3 and 1 shared destroyed, 2 and 1 shared out of control = 7.

*Shared with Capt A.R. Brown B7270. **Shared with Lt J.H. Siddall B6369. ***Shared with Capt R.M. Foster C61, Capt T.C. Luke C142, Lt K.M. Walker C199, Lt M.A. Harker D9625.

EDWARDS Herbert James Captain 32, 92

Born on 20 November 1896 in Victoria, Australia, he joined the army in England on 4 August 1915, having failed a medical for the Australian Army. Transferring to the RFC in September 1916, he joined 32 Squadron in May 1917. He was promoted Captain on 1 January 1918, but ended his first tour soon afterwards. Posted as one of the original flight commanders in the new 92 Squadron, he left the unit due to ill health and saw no further service. Returning to Australia after the war, he lived in Mayborough, Victoria, until his death on 10 September 1967.

	1917		DH 5					
1s*	25 Jul	Alb. DIII	A9374	32	N Polygon Wood	c0830	OOC	ORB/SR/?
2s**	27 Jul	C	A9372	32	N Polygon Wood	0545	DES	ORB/RFC 27.7
3s***	10 Aug	Alb. C	A9431	32	E Zillebeke Lake	2025	CAPT	ORB/RFC 10.8
4	17 Aug	Alb. C	A9439	32	Zonnebeke	1025	DES	CR/RFC 17.8
5s†	3 Sep	Alb. C	A9439	32	Poelcapelle	0350	DES(F)	CR/ORB/SR?

TOTAL: 1 shared captured, 1 and 2 shared destroyed, 1 shared out of control = 5.

*Shared with Lt S.R.P. Walter A9407, 2/Lt J. Simpson A9404, 2/Lt W.R. Fish A9396. **Shared with Capt A. Coningham A9179, Lt G.A. Wells A9374, Lt E. Pownall A9396. ***Shared with Lt G.A. Wells A9472. †Shared with Capt D. Joy B345, Lt W.E. Sandys A9374, 2/Lt W.O. Cornish A9179.

EDWARDS Stearne Tighe Captain 3W, 11(N), 6(N), 9(N), 209

Born in Canada on 13 February 1893, he grew up in Carleton Place, Ontario, where he was firm friends with Roy Brown and D.M. Galbraith — both also future aces. He sailed for England in November 1915 after having gained his pilot's certificate — No 350 of the Aero Club of America, dated 13 October 1915 — at his own expense. Joining the RNAS, he became an original member of 3 Wing in 1916, flying on operations until February 1917. On 9 March he joined 11(N) Squadron as a fighter pilot, then joining 6(N) Squadron on 19 April. When this unit was disbanded in July 1917 he transferred to 9(N) Squadron, where he received a DSC for an action on 23 September when he claimed two Albatros Scouts shot down. He went on to receive a Bar to this decoration, becoming a flight commander on 30 January 1918. On 16 May 1918 he helped to force down a Fokker Triplane piloted by Leutnant Hubner of Jasta 4, who was taken prisoner. Now totally exhausted, Edwards suffered a nervous collapse on 23 May, and was hospitalised. Upon recovery he became an instructor, but he was critically injured in a flying accident on 12 November 1918 and died on 22nd.

	1917		Camel					
1s*	5 Sep	Alb. C	B3829	9N	Middelkerke	0800	OOC	CR/ORB/?
2s**	21 Sep	DFW. C	B6217	9N	Zarren	1700	OOC	CR/RFC 22.9
3	23 Sep	Alb. DV	B6217	9N	off Ostend	0730	DES	CR/RFC 23.9
4	23 Sep	Alb. DV	B6217	9N	880y N Dixmude	0820	DES	CR/RFC 23.9
5s***	28 Sep	Alb. DV	B6217	9N	Dixmude	1610	DES	CR/RFC 28.9
6s†	2 Oct	Alb. C	B6217	9N	E Slype	1450	OOC	CR/RNAS 2.10
7s††	27 Oct	Alb. DV	B6217	9N	N E Nieuport	1435	OOC	CR/RNAS 27.10
	1918							
8s†††	3 Feb	Alb. C	B6351	9N	Staden	0840	DES	CR/RNAS 3.2
9‡	2 Apr	Alb. DIII	B7199	209	S Halluin	1115	DES	CR/RAF 2.4
10s‡‡	2 Apr	Alb. DIII	B7199	209	S Halluin	1115	OOC	CR/RAF 2.4
11s	12 Apr	C	B7199	209	W Amiens	1715	CAPT	CR/RAF 12.4

12	2 May	Alb. DV	B7199	209	Brie	1815	OOC	CR/RAF 2.5
13	2 May	Alb. DV	B7199	209	Cayeux	1845	DES	CR/RAF 2.5
14	15 May	Pfalz DIII	B6398	209	E Rosieres	1045	OOC	CR/RAF 15.5
15s§	16 May	Fokker DrI	B6398	209	W Corbie	1615	CAPT	CR/RAF 16.9
16	19 May	C	B7199	209	S Albert	1100	OOC	CR/?

TOTAL: 2 shared captured, 4 and 2 shared destroyed, 3 and 5 shared out of control = 16.
*Shared with FSL A.R. Brown B3818, FSL O.M. Redgate B3810, FSL A.W. Woods B3897, FSL F. Banbury B3832. **Shared with FSL O.M. Redgate B3818. ***Shared with FSL F. Banbury B6330, FSL O.M. Redgate B3818. FSL J.P. Hales B3832, FSL M.S. Taylor B5652. †Shared with F/Cdr J.S.T. Fall B3898. ††Shared with FSL F.J.W. Mellersh B6204, FSL J.P. Hales N6342, FSL J.E. Paynter B3830, FSL F. Banbury B6230, FSL C.A. Narbeth B3883, FSL A.W. Woods B3884, FSL M.S. Taylor B3892, FSL H.F. Stackard B6327. †††Shared with FSL O.M. Redgate D3566. ‡This was Uffz Wenn of Jasta 57 who was killed. ‡‡Shared with Lt J.H. Siddall. §Shared with Lt M.S. Taylor, Lt W.R. May; this was Lt Hubner of Jasta 4, who was captured.

ELLIOTT Hugh William Lieutenant 48

Flying with 48 Squadron during summer 1917, Elliott claimed five victories, all whilst flying with Lieutenant J.W. Ferguson as his gunner. No further successes came his way until 25 January 1918, when the rear gun, now manned by Lieutenant R.S. Herring, sent down an Albatros DIII flown by Leutnant Heinrich Kroll, Staffelführer of Jasta 24, who was obliged to force-land his damaged aircraft.

	1917		Bristol					
1*	3 Jul	Alb. DV	A7123	48	Queant	0930	DES(F)	CR/RFC 3.7
2*	7 Jul	Alb. DV	A7146	48	Vitry	0550	OOC	CR/RFC 7.7
3*	21 Jul	Alb. DV	A7131	48	Slype	1800	OOC	CR/RFC 22.7
4*	2 Sep	Alb. DV	B1108	48	Beerst	0915	DES	CR/RFC 2.9
	1918							
5**	25 Jan	Alb. DIII	B1187	48	N E St Quentin	1425	OOC	CR/RFC 25.1

TOTAL: 2 destroyed, 3 out of control = 5.
*Observer: 2/Lt J.W. Ferguson. **Observer: Lt R.S. Herring; probably Lt H. Kroll, the commander of Jasta 24, who was forced to land.

ELLIS Herbert Edward Oscar Lieutenant 40

Ellis was commissioned in the Royal Engineers on 16 March 1915, and had been awarded an MC prior to transferring to the RFC in 1916. He joined 40 Squadron early in 1917, and during April claimed two victories plus one shared. On 4 May over Douai aerodrome he attacked a number of Albatros Scouts; he reported shooting one down which crashed, and forcing another to crash-land, whereupon it stood on its nose. Attacked by another Albatros, he became involved in a dogfight during which he ran out of ammunition. Drawing his Colt automatic pistol, he fired seven shots at his opponent, whereupon the enemy scout side-slipped, broke up and crashed.

	1917		Nieuport					
1	13 Apr	Alb. C	B1519	40	Courrieres	1130	DES	CR/RFC 13.4
2s*	23 Apr	Halb. C	A6789	40	Lens	1140	OOC	CR/RFC 23.4
3	26 Apr	Alb. DIII	B1519	40	E Salome	1920	DES	CR/RFC 27.4
4	28 Apr	Aviatik C	B1519	40	Salome	1000	DES	CR/RFC 28.4
5	4 May	Alb. DIII	B1545	40	S Douai	1950	DES	CR/RFC 5.5
6	4 May	Alb. DIII	B1545	40	S Douai	1950	DES(col)	CR/RFC 5.5
7	4 May	Alb. DIII	B1545	40	S Douai	1950	DES	CR/RFC 5.5

TOTAL: 6 destroyed, 1 shared out of control = 7.
*Lt K. Mackenzie B1548.

ELLIS Sydney Emerson Flight Sub Lieutenant 4(N)

Born on 15 January 1896 in Kingston, Ontario, this Canadian joined the RNAS in August 1916. Posted to 4(N) Squadron as a Flight Sub Lieutenant, he claimed three aircraft destroyed and three out of control. He was one of the first two Camel pilots to claim when he shot down a Gotha bomber out of control on 4 July 1917. On 12 July he took off in N6337, got into a spin and crashed, being killed instantly.

	1917		Pup					
1	25 May	Alb. DIII	N6475	4N	2m S E Ghistelles	1500	DES	CR/DOS/DL/SR
2	4 Jun	Alb. DIII	N6475	4N	3-4m E Dixmude	0830	DES	CR/DOS/DL/SR
			Camel					
3	4 Jul	Gotha G	----	4N	30m N W Ostend	0830	OOC	CR/DOS/DL/SR
4s*	6 Jul	Alb. C	N6337	4N	S W Ghistelles	1440	DES	CR/DOS/DL/SR
5s**	7 Jul	Seaplane	N6337	4N	Ostend	1110	OOC	CR/DOS/DL/SR

TOTAL: 2 and 1 shared destroyed, 1 and 1 shared out of control = 5.
*Shared with F/Lt A.J. Chadwick N6370. **Shared with FSL J.S.T. Fall N6364 of 3N.

ELLWOOD Aubrey Beauclerk Lieutenant 3(N)

Born on 3 July 1897, the son of the Rev C.E. Ellwood, he was educated at Marlborough and joined the RNAS in June 1916. In April 1917 he was posted to 'B' Flight of 3 Naval Squadron, and flew with this unit until May 1918, by which time it had become 203 Squadron, RAF. He received the DSC and claimed ten victories. Remaining in the service he attained the rank of Air Marshal. At one time he was Director General of Personnel, and from 1947-50 was AOC in C, Bomber Command, and then of Transport Command, 1950-52. Created a KCB in 1949, he was living in retirement at the time of writing.

	1917		Camel					
1s*	27 Jul	Seaplane	B3781	3N	20m off Ostend	1415	DES	CR/RNAS 27.7
	1918							
2s**	30 Jan	Alb. DV	B6408	3N	Gheluvelt	1045	OOC	CR/RNAS 30.1
3s**	30 Jan	Alb. DV	B6408	3N	Gheluvelt	1045	OOC	CR/RNAS 30.1
4s***	8 Mar	C	B7229	3N	Tortequesne	1200	DES(F)	CR/RFC 8.3
5	10 Mar	Alb. DV	B7229	3N	Lens	1315	OOC	CR/RFC 10.3
6s†	16 Mar	Hannover C	B7229	3N	Gavrelle	1120	DES(F)	CR/RFC 16.3
7	22 Mar	Alb. DV	B7229	3N	Marquion	1230	OOC	CR/RFC 22.3
8	23 Mar	Alb. DV	B7229	3N	Marquion	1235	OOC	CR/WS/?
9s††	23 Mar	Alb. DV	B7229	3N	Noreuil	1725	DES	CR/RFC 23.3
10s†††	9 Apr	Alb. C	B7229	203	Givency	1610	DES(F)	CR/RAF 9.4

TOTAL: 5 shared destroyed, 3 and 2 shared out of control = 10.
*Shared with FSL J.S.T. Fall B6364, FSL J.A. Glen B3782, FSL H.F. Beamish N6377, FSL L.D. Bawlf B3805. **Shared with F/Lt L.H. Rochford B6401, FSL J.A. Glen B6242. ***Shared with FSL K.D. Macleod B7232, FSL C.S. Deveraux B7230. †Shared with F/Lt L.H. Rochford B7203, FSL J.A. Glen B7185. ††Shared with FSL K.D. Macleod B7222. †††Shared with Capt R.A. Little B7231, Lt J.A. Glen B7185.

ELTON Ernest John Sergeant 22

Elton joined the RFC as an air mechanic early in the war and in 1915 was with 6 Squadron in France. He helped to design and manufacture Lanoe Hawker's machine gun mounting on his Bristol Scout, and was undoubtedly influenced by Hawker's successes and strong personality. Eventually Elton was accepted for pilot training, and in 1918 was posted to 22 Squadron as a Sergeant, flying Bristol Fighters. On 26 February, when he and his gunner, Sergeant C. Hagan, claimed their first two victories, they were then themselves shot down but survived. Elton became the most successful NCO pilot in the RFC, for he and his observer/gunners accounted for 16 enemy machines in 32 days, ten with his front gun and six with the rear. Elton received the DCM and MM, and from the Italian Government, the Italian Bronze Medal.

	1918		Bristol					
1*	26 Feb	Alb. DV	----	22	E Lens	1130	DES	CR/RFC 26.2
2*	26 Feb	Alb. DV	----	22	E Lens	1130	DES	CR/RFC 26.2
3**	6 Mar	Alb. DV	B1162	22	Douai	1400	DES	CR/RFC 6.3
4**	6 Mar	Alb. DV	B1162	22	S E Douai	1410	OOC	CR/RFC 6.3
5***	8 Mar	Alb. DV	B1162	22	S E Lille	1245	DES	CR/RFC 8.3
6**	11 Mar	Alb. DV	B1152	22	Vendville-Faches	1425	DES	CR/RFC 11.3
7**	11 Mar	Alb. DV	B1152	22	Lille	1430	OOC	CR/RFC 11.3
8**	13 Mar	Alb. DV	B1162	22	S S W Lille	1620	DES	CR/RFC 13.3
9**	13 Mar	Pfalz DIII	B1162	22	S S W Lille	1630	DES	CR/RFC 13.3
10†	16 Mar	Alb. DV	B1162	22	Carvin	1030	DES	CR/RFC 16.3
11†	16 Mar	Alb. DV	B1162	22	Carvin	1045	DES(F)	CR/RFC 16.3
12†	18 Mar	Alb. DV	B1162	22	Carvin	1030	DES	CR/RFC 18.3
13†	26 Mar	Pfalz DIII	B1162	22	E Albert	1245	DES	CR/RFC 26.3
14†	29 Mar	C	B1162	22	Rosieres	1530	DES	CR/RFC 29.3
15†	29 Mar	C	B1162	22	Lihons	1535	DES	CR/RFC 29.3
16†	29 Mar	C	B1162	22	Vauvillers	1540	DES	CR/RFC 29.3

TOTAL: 14 destroyed, 2 out of control = 16.
*Observer: Sgt John Charles Hagen. **Observer: 2/Lt G.S.L. Hayward. ***Observer: Sgt S. Belding. †Observer: Lt R. Critchley.

ENSTONE Albert James Captain 4(N), 204

Born on 25 August 1895 in Birmingham, Enstone joined 4(N) Squadron on its formation in April 1917. Based close to the Channel coast, he was first in action in the spring of that year, flying Sopwith Pups. His unit was the only one to see much action against the Siemens-Schukert DI, the German copy of the Nieuport 17, and at least one of his early claims was against these types. 4(N) was the first squadron to take the Camel into action in June 1917, and on this new mount he flew both against Gotha bombers on their way to raid England, and against German seaplanes. By early 1918 he had been awarded a DSC (1 August 1917) and been promoted to the position of flight commander; he continued to serve with the squadron after 1 April 1918 when it became 204 Squadron, RAF, his rank then changing to Captain. He received a DFC during the summer, and when he left the squadron was credited with 13 victories, 10 destroyed and three out of control. He had also driven down 11 more aircraft, three of them Gothas. He left the unit for Home Establishment on 13 August 1918.

	1917		Pup					
1	9 May	C	N6187	4N	Ghistelles	0730	DES	CR/RNAS 9.5
2	12 May	SS DI	N6187	4N	5m off Zeebrugge	0720	DES	CR/RNAS 12.5
3s*	26 May	C	N6187	4N	S W Furnes	0845	DES	CR/DOS/DL
4	5 Jun	EA	N6187	4N	2m N E Nieuport	1915	DES	CR/DOS/DL
			Camel					
5	7 Jul	Seaplane C	N6347	4N	19m off Ostend	1115	DES	CR/RNAS 7.7
6	14 Jul	C	N6370	4N	1m S E Ghistelles	0420	DES	CR/RNAS 14.7
7s**	25 Jul	Seaplane	N6370	4N	30m N N E Ostend	1930	OOC	CR/RNAS 25.7
8	30 Sep	Alb. DV	B3841	4N	Rattevalle	1200	OOC	CR/RNAS 30.9
9	9 Nov	DFW. C	B3841	4N	S E Pervyse	1435	OOC	CR/RNAS 9.11
	1918							
10	24 Mar	Alb. DV	B3841	4N	S Thorout	1140	DES(F)	CR/RNAS 24.3
11	30 Jun	Fokker DVII	D6624	204	5m N Blankenberghe	1445	DES(F)	CR/5 GP Comm
12	30 Jun	Fokker DVII	D6624	204	N Blankenberghe	1445	DES	CR/5 GP Comm
13	1 Jul	Hansa. W 12	D6624	204	Middelkerke	1710	DES	CR/5 GP Comm

TOTAL: 9 and 1 shared destroyed, 2 and 1 shared out of control = 13.
*Shared with FSL A.J. Chadwick N6176. **Shared with F/Cdr A.J. Chadwick N6369, FSL R, Mc Kierstead N6370.

EVANS Henry Cope 2nd Lieutenant 24

Evans was born in Camberley, Surrey, in 1879, and saw service with the army during the Boer War. In 1914 he was living in Canada and joined the Alberta Dragoons, serving in France from February to September 1915, during which period he was badly gassed. He transferred to the RFC as an observer on 23 September, and in 1916 undertook pilot training. He joined 24 Squadron on 4 July, where he was awarded a DSO for shooting down four aircraft in two weeks. He was killed in action on 3 September 1916 after achieving his fifth victory.

	1916		DH 2					
1	20 Jul	Roland CII	7842	24	Fleurs	2020	OOC	CR/RFC 20.7
2*	21 Jul	C?	5924	24	Combles	2025	DES	CR/RFC 21.7
3	6 Aug	LVG. C	7876	24	E Bois de Vaux	0915	DES	CR/RFC 6.8
4	8 Aug	Roland CII	7878	24	E Bapaume	1200	DES	CR/RFC 8.8
5	9 Aug	C	7878	24	Achiet le Grand	0815	DES	CR/SR/?

TOTAL: 4 destroyed, 1 out of control = 5.
*This was Lt W. Schramm, of A.K.N. who was killed.

EYCOTT-MARTIN Harold Ross Lieutenant 66

From Haywards Heath, Sussex, where he was born in 1896, Eycott-Martin was commissioned in the Royal Engineers on 26 October 1915, before joining the RFC. He qualified as a pilot on 29 February 1917 and was posted initially to 41 Squadron in May, but was injured when he crashed an FE 8 whilst taking off one week after joining the unit. On 7 February 1918 he joined 66 Squadron in Italy, flying Camels, and received an MC on 5 April of that year. On 30 March he had taken part in the action which resulted in Alan Jerrard being awarded the VC, and claimed two of the enemy scouts reported destroyed during that engagement. In all, he was credited with eight victories over German and Austrian machines.

	1918		Camel					
1	21 Feb	Aviatik C	B5623	66	N E Motta	0710	DES	ORB/SR/7 BG
2	21 Mar	Berg DI	B7283	66	Portobuffalo a/d	1255	DES	ORB/SR/14W
3	30 Mar	Alb. DIII	B7283	66	Mansue	1140	DES	CR/ORB/SR/14W
4	30 Mar	Alb. DIII	B7283	66	Mansue	1151	DES	CR/ORB/SR/14W
5	10 May	Alb. DV	B7283	66	S W Caldonazzo	1050	DES	ORB/SR/14W
6	26 May	Berg DI	B7283	66	S W Feltre	0925	DES	ORB/SR/14W
7	15 Jun	Brand. C	D9390	66	Feltre a/d	0820	DES(F)	ORB/SR/14W
8	22 Jun	Brand. C	B7283	66	Bassano	1555	DES(F)	ORB/14W

TOTAL: 8 destroyed = 8.

EYRE Cyril Askew Flight Commander 1(N)

Although born in Britain, on 25 April 1896, and a graduate of Magdalen College, Oxford, he joined the RNAS in Toronto, Canada, in 1915, being commissioned as a Flight Sub Lieutenant in October of that year. By June 1916 he was on operations with 'A' Squadron on Sopwith Pups; later this became 1(N) Squadron, re-equipped with Triplanes, and by July 1917 he had claimed six victories. On 7 July 1917 he was shot down and killed in N6291, one of three Triplanes which fell to Leutnants Kurt Wolff and Alfred Niederhoff of Jasta 11 and Leutnant Krüger of Jasta 4; it is believed that Eyre was Niederhoff's victim.

	1917		Triplane					
1	4 May	Alb. DIII	N5435	1N	Wancourt	0830-1030	OOC	ORB/RFC 4.5
2	19 May	Alb. DIII	N5435	1N	Henin-Lietard	1945	OOC	CR/RFC 19.5
3s*	15 Jun	C	N5444	1N	St Jean, N E Ypres	1200	CAPT	CR/RFC 15.6
4	21 Jun	Alb. DV	N5444	1N	St Julien	1745	OOC	CR/RFC 21.6
5	3 Jul	Alb. DIII	N6291	1N	Tenbrielen	0945	OOC	ORB/RFC 3.7
6	3 Jul	Alb. DIII	N6291	1N	E Gheluvelt	1835	DES(F)	ORB/?

TOTAL: 1 captured, 1 destroyed, 4 out of control = 6.
*Lt Reichstein/Lt Raddatz KIA? of FA 7.

FAIRCLOUGH Arthur Bradfield Captain 19, 23

Born in Canada, he joined the Canadian Machine Gun Corps and served in France before transferring to the RFC in May 1917. Posted to 19 Squadron in November, he flew both Spads and Dolphins before being promoted to Captain and joining 23 Squadron as a flight commander in May 1918. He claimed 14 victories with 19 Squadron and a further five with 23 Squadron, bringing his total to 19. He was awarded the MC in March 1918. He died on 9 December 1968.

	1917		Spad					
1s*	6 Dec	C	A6836	19	E Roulers	1542	OOC	CR/RFC WD
2s**	8 Dec	Rumpler C	B3528	19	Tenbrielen-Wervicq	1335	OOC	CR/RFC 8.12
3s***	18 Dec	C	B3528	19	Comines	1035	OOC	ORB/RFC WD
4	18 Dec	Alb. DV	A6795	19	Gheluvelt	1250	DES	CR/RFC 18.12
5	19 Dec	C	A6805	19	E Hooglede	0805	OOC	CR/RFC 19.12
6s†	19 Dec	C	B3528	19	W Passchendaele	1130	DES	CR/RFC 19.12
7s††	22 Dec	Alb. DIII	A6802	19	S Quesnoy	1420	DES(F)	CR/RFC 22.12
8	29 Dec	Alb. DV	A6802	19	Houthoulst Forest	1010	OOC	CR/RFC 29.12
9	29 Dec	Alb. DV	A6802	19	Houthoulst Forest	1015	DES(F)	CR/RFC 29 .12
	1918		Dolphin					
10s†††	17 Mar	Alb. DV	C3940	19	N E Menin	1215	DES(F)	CR/RFC 17.3
11s‡	23 Mar	C	C3940	19	E Lille	1540	DES(F)	CR/RFC 23.3
12	22 Apr	Alb. DV	C3796	19	Bois Du Biez	1030	OOC	CR/RAF 22.4
13	23 Apr	Pfalz DIII	C3796	19	N La Bassee	1820	OOC	CR/RAF 23.4
14s‡‡	2 May	Alb. DV	C3796	19	S Armentieres	1745	DES(F)	CR/RAF 2.5
15s‡‡‡	29 Jun	Fokker DVII	C8070	23	Hangard	1030	DES(F)	CR/RAF 29.6
16	29 Jun	Fokker DVII	C8070	23	Hangard	1830	OOC	CR/?
17	1 Jul	Alb. DV	D3669	23	Hangest	2040	DES	CR/RAF 1.7
18	4 Jul	Pfalz DIII	C8074	23	Hamel	1020	DES	CR/RAF 4.7
19s§	5 Jul	Rumpler C	D3669	23	S E Mezieres	1030	DES(F)	CR/RAF 5.7

TOTAL: 5 and 6 shared destroyed, 5 and 3 shared out of control = 19.
*Shared with Capt O.C. Bryson A6780, 2/Lt E. Olivier A6714, Lt R.G. Holt A6802. **Shared with Capt O.C. Bryson B6780, Capt G.W. Taylor A6805. ***Shared with Capt O.C. Bryson A6802. †Shared with Capt O.C. Bryson A6780. ††Shared with Capt O.C. Bryson A6780, Lt E.J. Blyth B3563, 2/Lt E. Olivier A6714, Capt G.W. Taylor A6805, Major A.W. Carter A8836, Lt H.E. Galer A8834. †††Shared with 2/Lt E. Olivier C3902. 19 claimed 4 or 5 with one known loss being Lt Jahnsen of Jasta 17. ‡Shared with Capt J. Leacroft C3829. ‡‡Shared with Lt A.W. Blake C3843. ‡‡‡Shared with Lt A.P. Pehrson, Lt C.C.A. Sherwood, Lt H.A. White, Lt Bentley, Lt Adam, Lt Macpherson. §Shared with Lt A.B. Sinclair D5233.

FALKENBERG Carl Frederick Captain 84

A Canadian, born in Newfoundland on 4 February 1897, Falkenberg joined the Quebec Regiment before transferring to the RFC. After training, he joined 84 Squadron, RAF, flying SE 5As, and gained his first victory on 29 April 1918, sharing with pilots of 70 Squadron in forcing a DFW to land in Allied territory. From June to October he was much in action, claiming regularly. He was awarded a DFC, gazetted on 2 November, for four destroyed and four out of control. A Bar followed, gazetted on 3 December, for having destroyed four more plus a balloon, and two out of control since his DFC, for a total of 15; his final score was 17. Falkenberg's brother was shot down and taken prisoner in 1918 whilst serving with 46 Squadron.

	1918		SE 5A					
1s*	29 Apr	DFW. C	----	84	S E St Gratien	1900	CAPT	CR/RAF 29.4
2	11 Jun	Alb. DV	D6882	84	Montdidier	1345	OOC	CR/?
3s**	17 Jun	Fokker DrI	D6890	84	Chaulnes	0940	OOC	CR/?
4	25 Jun	Pfalz DIII	D6890	84	Chipilly	1330	OOC	CR/?
5	24 Jul	Alb. DV	D6928	84	Peronne	1845	OOC	CR/?

6	28 Jul	Halb. C	D6920	84	1m S Foucaucaourt	0930	DES	CR/RAF 28.7
7	1 Aug	Fokker DVII	D6920	84	Suzanne a/d	1000	OOC	CR/?
8	11 Aug	Fokker DVII	D6980	84	Estrees	0945	DES	CR/RAF 11.8
9	16 Aug	Fokker DVII	D6980	84	Estrees	0945	DES	CR/RAF 16.8
10s***	23 Aug	Rumpler C	D6920	84	Maricourt	1120	DES	CR/RAF 23.8
11s†	29 Aug	Fokker DVII	D6920	84	1m E Somme, S Brie	1925	DES	CR/RAF 29.8
12	16 Sep	Fokker DVII	E6024	84	Montigny	1400	OOC	CR/?
13	20 Sep	Fokker DVII	E6024	84	Mont d'Origny	1015	OOC	CR/?
14	20 Sep	Fokker DVII	E6024	84	Mont d'Origny	1030	DES	CR/RAF 20.9
15	24 Sep	Balloon	E6024	84	Cambrai	1350	DES	CR/RAF 24.9
16	29 Sep	Fokker DVII	E6024	84	Beaurevoir	1030	DES	CR/RAF 29.9
17	4 Oct	Fokker DVII	E6024	84	Cambrai	0845	OOC	CR/?

TOTAL: 1 balloon, 1 shared captured, 4 and 2 shared destroyed, 7 and 1 shared out of control = 17.
*Shared with Lt H.W.L. Saunders B8403, Lt J. Todd C1670 and Lt V.C. Chapman C7471 of 70 Sqn. This was Uffz Krug/Lt Adler of FAA 218. **Shared with Capt J.V. Sorsoleil C1834, Lt A. Matthews B682. ***Shared with 1/Lt G.A. Vaughn E4012. †Shared with Capt A.W.B. Proctor D6856.

FALL Joseph Stewart Temple Flight Commander 3(N), 9(N)

Joe Fall, from Millbank, British Columbia, was born in Canada on 17 November 1895 and joined the RNAS in 1915. After pilot training he was sent to 3 Naval Squadron during the latter part of 1916, flying Sopwith Pups. In July 1917 he became a Flight Lieutenant; in May he received a DSC for an action on 11 April when he claimed three enemy scouts shot down. On 30 August he was promoted to Flight Commander and posted to 9 Naval Squadron, having at this time claimed 13 victories, eight of which had been officially confirmed as destroyed. With 9 Naval he became a most competent flight commander, always encouraging his young pilots to join him in attacking enemy machines. By the end of the year when he returned to England he had brought his score to 36; it will be noted that 11 of these were shared by him with his flight members. For his work he received two Bars to his DSC. He remained in the RAF after the war and was a Squadron Leader in the mid 1930s. In 1935 he was testing automatic flying controls at the Home Aircraft Depot at Henlow and became a Wing Commander in 1936. Promotion to Group Captain followed in 1940, and then retirement in 1945, following which he returned to Canada.

	1917		Pup					
1	6 Apr	Halb. DII	N6158	3N	Bourlon Wood	1020	DES	CR/RFC 6.4
2	11 Apr	Alb. DII	N6158	3N	Cambrai	0900	OOC	CR/RFC 11.4
3	11 Apr	Alb. DII	N6158	3N	Cambrai	0905	DES	CR/RFC 114
4	11 Apr	Alb. DII	N6158	3N	Cambrai	0905	DES	CR/RFC 11.4
5	23 Apr	Alb. DIII	N6205	3N	Bourlon Wood	1730	OOC	CR/RFC 24.4
6	29 Apr	Alb. DIII	N6205	3N	Bois de Gaard	1100	DES	CR/RFC 29.4
7	1 May	Alb. DIII	N6205	3N	Epinoy	1045	OOC	CR/ORB/DL
8	23 May	Alb. DIII	N6479	3N	W Bourlon	1345	OOC	CR/RFC 23.5
			Camel					
9s*	7 Jul	Seaplane	N6364	3N	6m N Ostend	1110	DES	CR/RNAS 7.7
10s**	7 Jul	Seaplane	N6364	3N	1m N W Ostend	1115	DES	CR/RNAS 7.7
11	7 Jul	Alb. DV	N6364	3N	Ostend	1220	DES(F)	CR/RNAS 7.7
12s***	27 Jul	Seaplane	N6364	3N	20m off Ostend	1415	DES	CR/RNAS 27.7
13	17 Aug	Alb. DV	N6364	3N	S Ostend	1820	OOC	CR/RNAS 17.8
14s†	3 Sep	Alb. DV	B3898	9N	S E Pervyse	1830	DES	CR/RFC 3.9
15s††	4 Sep	DFW. C	B3898	9N	Nieuport-Middelkerke	2140	DES	CR/RFC 4.9
16s†††	6 Sep	Alb. C	B3898	9N	Middelkerke	1335	OOC	CR/ORB/?
17s‡	9 Sep	Alb. DV	B3898	9N	Middelkerke	1905	OOC	CR/RFC 10.9
18s‡‡	11 Sep	Alb. DV	B3898	9N	Leke	1730	DES(F)	CR/RFC 11.9
19s‡‡‡	11 Sep	Alb. DV	B3898	9N	Leke	1730	DES	CR/RFC 11.9
20s§	14 Sep	Alb. DV	B3898	9N	1m N W Leke	1715	DES	CR/RFC 14.9
21s§§	16 Sep	DFW. C	B3883	9N	E Mariakerke	1645	DES(F)	CR/RFC 16.9
22s§§§	24 Sep	Alb. DIII	B3892	9N	Leke	1545	OOC	CR/ORB/?
23	24 Sep	Alb. DIII	B3892	9N	Middelkerke	1625	OOC	CR/RFC 24.9
24	30 Sep	Alb. C	B3898	9N	Middelkerke	1055	DES	CR/RNAS 30.9
25s#	2 Oct	Alb. C	B3898	9N	E Slype	1450	OOC	CR/RNAS 2.10
26	16 Oct	Alb. C	B6228	9N	Zarren	0950	DES	CR/RNAS 16.10
27	17 Oct	Fokker DV	B3897	9N	E Middelkerke	1100	OOC	CR/RNAS 17.10
28s##	21 Oct	C	B3898	9N	E Slype	1300	DES(F)	CR/DOS/?
29###	31 Oct	Alb. DV	B3898	9N	Dixmude	1140	OOC	CR/RNAS 31.10

30	4 Nov	Alb. DV	B3883	9N	Dixmude	0945	OOC	CR/RNAS 4.11
31	13 Nov	Alb. C	B3883	9N	Slype	1345	DES	CR/RNAS 13.11
32s¶	13 Nov	Alb. C	B3883	9N	Pervyse	1435	DES	CR/RNAS 13.11
33	6 Dec	DFW. C	B6370	9N	Moorslede	1030	DES	CR/RNAS 6.12
34	6 Dec	Alb. DV	B6370	9N	2m S Staden	1145	DES	CR/RNAS 6.12
35¶¶	8 Dec	Alb. DV	B6370	9N	N E Houthoulst Wood	1445	DES	CR/RNAS 8.12
36	22 Dec	Alb. C	B6231	9N	S E Quesnoy	1530	DES	CR/RNAS 22.12

TOTAL: 11 and 12 shared destroyed, 10 and 3 shared out of control = 36.
*Shared with FSL J.A. Glen N6183, FSL L.H. Rochford N6162, FSL F.C. Armstrong N6465, FSL R.F.P. Abbott. **Shared with FSL J.A. Glen N6183. ***Shared with FSL J.A. Glen B3782, FSL L.D. Bawlf B3805, FSL H.F. Beamish N6377, FSL A.B. Ellwood B3781. †Shared with FSL J.E. Scott B3907, FSL A.W. Wood B3884, FSL H.F. Stackard B6204. This was probably FlM Brenner of MFJ 1, who was wounded. ††Shared with FSL J.E. Scott B3907, FSL H.F. Stackard B6204. †††Shared with FSL A.W. Wood B3884, FSL H.F. Stackard B6204, FSL J.E. Scott B3907, FSL H.L. Wallace B3892. ‡Shared with FSL H.F. Stackard B6204. ‡‡Shared with FSL H.F. Stackard B3863, FSL A.W. Wood B3884. This was probably LtzS Gotz of MFJ 1. ‡‡‡Shared with FSL H.F. Stackard B3863, FSL A.W. Wood B3884. §Shared with FSL C.A. Narbeth B3905, FSL A.C. Campbell-Orde B3829. §§Shared with FSL H.L. Wallace B3892, FSL A.W. Wood B3904. §§§Shared with FSL H.F. Stackard B3885, FSL A.W. Wood. #Shared with F/Cdr S.T. Edwards B6217. ##Shared with FSL A.W. Wood N6348. ###Possibly Uffz K. Reinhold of Jasta 24, who was wounded and forced to land. ¶Shared with FSL A.W. Wood B3884. ¶¶Probably Lt Daube of Jasta B, who was killed.

FARQUHAR Robert Wallace 2nd Lieutenant 18, 23

Robert Farquhar served with 18 Squadron in 1916, later transferring to 23 Squadron where he became one of the first exponents of the Spad, claiming three and two shared victories by 2 July 1917. No other details of this officer are known.

	1917		FE 2B					
1*	4 Feb	Alb. DII	A5460	18	N le Sars	1600	OOC	CR/RFC 4.2
			Spad					
2	4 May	Alb. DIII	----	23	Cambrai	c1040	OOC	RFC 4.5
3s**	13 May	Alb. DIII	B1530	23	Etaing	1905	OOC	CR/?
4	26 May	Aviatik C	B1530	23	Lens	1130	OOC	CR/RFC 26.5
5s***	23 Jun	Alb. DV	----	23	N E Ypres	----	DES(F)	CR/RFC 23.6
6	7 Jul	Alb. DV	B1530	23	Zillebeke	1040	OOC	CR/RFC 7.7

TOTAL: 1 shared destroyed, 4 and 1 shared out of control = 6.
*Observer: 2/Lt C.N. Blennerhasset. **Shared with Capt C.K.C. Patrick B1580. ***Shared with 2/Lt D.P. Collis, 2/Lt D.A.A. Sheperson.

FARRELL Conway McAlister Grey Captain 24, 56

Born on 22 May 1898 in Regina, Saskachewan, this Canadian was commissioned on 12 October 1917 and joined 24 Squadron on 11 March 1918. On 22 August he was awarded a DFC, gazetted in November, for seven victories. He was transferred to 56 Squadron on 29 August as a flight commander, but was injured in an accident on 6 October 1918.

	1918		SE 5A					
1s*	23 Mar	Rumpler C	B63	24	Nesle	1815	DES	CR/RFC 4.3
2s**	4 Apr	Rumpler C	C1099	24	St Nicholas	1730	CAPT	CR/RAF 4.4
3	16 May	Alb. DV	C1099	24	Foucaucourt	1915	OOC	CR/RAF 16.5
4s***	26 Jul	DFW. C	E1293	24	Royaucourt	0730	CAPT	CR/RAF 28.7
5s†	4 Aug	DFW. C	D6937	24	N Suzanne	0900	DES	CR/RAF 4.8
6	4 Aug	DFW. C	D6937	24	Fricourt	1005	OOC	CR/ORB/SR/?
7	10 Aug	Fokker DVII	E4022	24	N E Le Quesnoy	1400	DES	CR/RAF 10.8

TOTAL: 2 shared captured, 1 and 2 shared destroyed, 2 out of control = 7.
*Shared with Lt A.K. Cowper B8407, Lt P.J. Nolan B8411. **Shared with Lt R.T. Mark B8411, this was the crew Uffz Brocklebank/2 Lt Behnecke of FA 33, who were captured. ***Shared with Lt H.D. Barton C6481, Lt J. Palmer C1861, Lt W.J. Miller C6466, Lt F.S. Passmore C1938. This was aircraft 342/18, Uffz Neuendorf/Lt Bolgeihn of FAA 232. †Shared with Lt H.D. Barton C6481. Possibly Lt Otto Kiehn/Lt Peter Martini of FAA 207, who were killed near here. 24 Sqn made the only 3 claims for two seaters on 4 August.

FARROW William Hastings Captain 47, 64

William Farrow served as a Sergeant in the Royal Engineers before transferring to the RFC on 14 June 1916. Later that year he joined 47 Squadron in Macedonia, flying Armstrong Whitworth two-seaters. On a sortie in December 1916 he attacked an enemy machine, getting in three long bursts; the German aircraft reared up and hit Farrow's undercarriage, then went spinning down into cloud with its top wing crumpled. On 5 April 1917 he was attacked by an Albatros Scout and wounded, but it would seem that the German was also hit and went down to crash near Bogdanci. Returning to England, he had a spell off operations as an instructor, and was then posted to 64 Squadron on 27 April 1918, becoming a flight commander in July. He gained nine victories with the squadron before he was injured and had to go into hospital on 26 September. For his work he was awarded the DFC.

	1916		AW FK2						
1s*	22 Dec	C	5528	47	Hudova	1030	OOC	CR/BG Summ	
	1918		SE 5A						
2	17 May	Fokker DrI	C6448	64	Lagnicourt	1925	DES(F)	CR/RAF 17.5	
3	27 May	Alb. DV	C6402	64	Cagnicourt	1100	OOC	CR/?	
4	31 May	Pfalz DIII	----	64	La Bassee	1940	DES	CR/RAF 31.5	
5	31 May	Pfalz DIII	----	64	La Bassee	1942	OOC	CR/?	
6	21 Aug	Fokker DVII	E5941	64	N E Douai	1630	DES	CR/RAF 21.8	
7	22 Aug	Fokker DVII	E5941	64	Queant	1000	DES(F)	CR/RAF 22.8	
8	25 Aug	Fokker DVII	E5941	64	Haucourt	0900	OOC	CR/ORB/?	
9	2 Sep	Fokker DVII	E5941	64	Aubencheul	1200	OOC	CR/ORB/?	
10	5 Sep	Fokker DVII	C1874	64	N E Cambrai	1015	DES	CR/RAF 5.9	

TOTAL: 5 destroyed, 4 and 1 shared out of control = 10.
*Observer: Lt F.C. Brooks; shared with 2/Lt H.J. Gibson/2/Lt A.P. Adams 6199.

FIELDING-JOHNSON William Spurrett Captain 3, 56

Born on 8 February 1892, he served in the Leicestershire Yeomanry, and was awarded an MC in France. In 1915 he transferred to the RFC, joining 3 Squadron on 16 October as an observer on Morane Parasols. On 19 January 1916 his pilot crashed badly and Fielding-Johnson was injured. Recovering, he undertook pilot training and in October 1917 joined 56 Squadron where he received a Bar to his MC and became an acting flight commander. By the time he left the unit in 1918 he had claimed six victories. During World War II he saw service as an air gunner and in that conflict was awarded a DFC. He died in 1953.

	1918		SE 5A					
1	17 Feb	Alb. DV	B37	56	Fresnoy	1445	OOC	CR/RFC 17.2
2	19 Feb	Alb. DV	B37	56	N Lehaucourt	1150	DES	CR/RFC 19.2
3	15 Mar	Alb. DV	B37	56	N Bourlon Wood	1050	DES(F)	CR/RFC 15.3
4s*	15 Mar	C	B37	56	S E Inchy	1150	DES	CR/RFC 15.3
5	18 Mar	Pfalz DIII	B37	56	N Buissy	0650-0750	DES	CR/RFC 18.3
6	18 Mar	Pfalz DIII	B37	56	E Marquion	0650-0750	DES	CR/RFC 18.3

TOTAL: 4 and 1 shared destroyed, 1 out of control = 6.
*Shared with Lt M.E. Mealing B595; probably Uffz W, Stein/Lt W. Somme of FAA 293b, who were killed.

FINDLAY Charles Captain 88

Born in Scotland on 22 June 1891, he was a student working for an arts degree in Glasgow in 1914. Although a married man, he enlisted in March 1915 in the 52nd Division, Mounted Field Ambulance, but then accepted a commission in the 6th Battalion(TA), Highland Light Infantry. He joined his regiment at Kantara, Egypt, and fought in the Sinai campaign until December 1916. He then transferred to the RFC, returning to England for pilot training with 52 Training Squadron. When in May 1917 he qualified, he was posted to the unit as an instructor. In July he went as a member of staff to the Gunnery School in Ayrshire until early 1918, when he requested a posting to a fighter unit and succeeded in being sent to 88 Squadron, which was forming at Kenley. The squadron went to France in April, flying Bristol Fighters. With his observers he claimed 14 victories, nine with the front gun and five with the rear; his machine was not once hit by an enemy bullet. He took part in several attacks on aerodromes and helped to test wireless telegraphy between aircraft. Knowing the Germans could pick up their messages, 88 Squadron often amused themselves by addressing rude remarks to the enemy with their new apparatus. Findlay was awarded the DFC, and remained in the RAF after the war, receiving the AFC in 1934. He commanded 9 Squadron, and was later CO of RAF Wyton. He retired as a Group Captain in 1941, but was re-employed until 1946.

	1918		Bristol					
1*	30 Jul	Pfalz DIII	C4601	88	Richebourg	1035	OOC	CR/SR/?
2*	6 Aug	Fokker DVII	C4601	88	Ploegsteert	1045	DES(F)	CR/SR/?
3*	11 Aug	Fokker DVII	C4601	88	Clery	1135	OOC	CR/SR/?
4*	11 Aug	Fokker DVII	C4601	88	Clery	1135	OOC	CR/SR/?
5*	11 Aug	Fokker DVII	C4601	88	Mericourt	1700	DES(F)	CR/RAF 11.8
6*	11 Aug	Fokker DVII	C4601	88	Mericourt	1700	DES(F)	CR/RAF 11.8
7*	12 Aug	Fokker DVII	C4601	88	E Biaches	1005	DES	CR/RAF 12.8
8**	4 Sep	Fokker DVII	C4601	88	S Don	0930	DES	CR/RAF 4.9
9**	5 Sep	Fokker DVII	C4601	88	E Perenchies	1850	DES	CR/RAF 5.9
10***	2 Oct	Fokker DVII	E2412	88	La Bassee	0815	DES	CR/RAF 2.10
11***	2 Oct	Fokker DVII	E2412	88	La Bassee	0820	DES(F)	CR/RAF 2.10
12***	7 Oct	Fokker DVII	E2412	88	Annapes	0635	DES	CR/RAF 7.10
13***	30 Oct	Fokker DVII	F2533	88	Havinnes	0855	DES(F)	CR/RAF 30.10
14***	30 Oct	Fokker DVII	F2533	88	Havinnes	0855	DES(F)	CR/RAF 30.10

TOTAL: 11 destroyed, 3 out of control = 14.
*Observer: 2/Lt B. Digby-Worsley. **Observer: 2/Lt C.T. Gauntlett. ***Observer: Lt I.W.F. Agaberg.

FINDLAY John Pierce Lieutenant 88

From South Africa, he joined the RFC in August 1917 and served with 88 Squadron in 1918. Flying Bristol Fighters, he claimed five victories and one of his observers got a sixth. Findlay was wounded in the stomach by a bullet during August, but was back in action in September. After the war he returned to South Africa.

	1918		Bristol					
1*	31 May	Alb. DV	C785	88	Ostend	1950	OOC	CR/SR/?
2*	2 Jun	Alb. DV	C785	88	Ostend	1945	OOC	CR/SR/?
3**	29 Jul	Fokker DVII	E2474	88	Bois Grenier	1830	DES(F)	CR/RAF 29.7
4***	6 Sep	Fokker DVII	E2474	88	N Douai	1845	OOC	CR/?
5s†	4 Oct	Fokker DVII	E2474	88	1n S E Lille	1745	DES	CR/RAF 4.10
6	4 Oct	Halb. C	E2474	88	1m S E Lille	1745	DES	CR/SR/RAF 4.10

TOTAL: 2 and 1 shared destroyed, 3 out of control = 6.
*Observer: 2/Lt G.W. Lambert. **Observer: 2/Lt R.E. Hasell. ***Observer: 2/Lt W. Tinsley. †Observer: 2/Lt R.E. Hasell; shared with Lt I.G. Fleming/Lt H.G. Eldon.

FINDLAY Maxwell Hutcheon Captain 6(N), 1(N), 201

Born in Aberdeen, Scotland, on 17 February 1898, he spent his early life in Canada, returning to join the Black Watch on the outbreak of war. He later transferred to the RNAS and in 1917 joined 6 Naval Squadron where he gained two victories. Posted to 1(N) Squadron, he remained with this unit until the end of May 1918, by which time it had become 201 Squadron, RAF. He was awarded the DSC, gazetted in April 1918, and later the DFC. He remained in the RAF after the war, serving in Afghanistan and Waziristan until 1921 when he retired and became a farmer. He kept in close touch with flying and in the 1930s he became sales manager and instructor at Brooklands School of Flying. In October 1936 he took part in the Johannesburg Air Race, flying a twin-engined Airspeed Envoy. Taking off from an airfield in Northern Rhodesia, he crashed and was killed.

	1917		Camel					
1	22 Jul	Alb. DV	N6339	6N	W. Steene	1750	OOC	CR/ORB/?
2	20 Aug	Alb. DV	N6339	6N	Middelkerke	0720	OOC	CR/RFC 20.8
3	15 Nov	Alb. DV	B6419	1N	N Dixmude	1355	OOC	CR/RNAS 15.11
4	4 Dec	Alb. DV	B6419	1N	Houthoulst	1115	OOC	CR/RNAS 4.12
	1918							
5	8 Mar	Alb. DV	B6419	1N	Roulers	1400	OOC	CR/RNAS 8.3
6	10 Mar	Alb. DV	B6419	1N	2m N W Menin	1530	DES	CR/RNAS 10.3
7	16 Mar	Alb. DV	B6419	1N	E Roulers	1115	DES	CR/RNAS 15.3
8s*	16 Mar	Alb. DV	B6419	1N	E Roulers	1625	OOC	CR/RNAS 15.3
9	21 Mar	Alb. DV	B6419	1N	3m S W Nieuport	0720	DES(F)	CR/RNAS 21.3
10	9 May	Alb. DV	B6431	201	Bapaume	1315	DES	CR/RAF 9.5
11s**	15 May	Alb. DV	----	210	Bapaume-Mory	0645	DES	CR/RAF 15.5
12	17 May	Alb. DV	B3884	201	6m S E Arras	1900	DES	CR/RAF 17.5
13	30 May	C	D9589	201	N E Albert	1015	OOC	CR/?
14	30 May	Alb. DV	B7226	210	Achiet le Grand	1955	OOC	CR/?

TOTAL: 5 and 1 shared destroyed, 8 out of control = 14.
*Shared with FSL H.L. Wallace B6359. **Shared with Maj C.D. Booker, Capt S.M. Kinkead, Lt R. Hemmens, Lt J.H. Forman, Lt R. McLaughlin, Lt H.L. Wallace, Lt R.C.B. Brading, Lt R.S.S. Orr.

FIRTH John Charles Bradley Captain 45

Born on 8 August 1894, John Firth served with 45 Squadron in France and Italy, 1917-18, where he received the MC and the Italian Bronze Medal for Military Valour. In his squadron he was known to be quite fearless in action, and he became a very competent flight commander. On one occasion in November 1917 during the Battle of Passchendaele, he constantly flew through the British barrage to attack enemy troops and positions. In air combat he accounted for 11 enemy machines. After the war he went into business with the Firth Steel Company, becoming very successful before dying in tragic circumstances on 23 August 1931.

	1917		Strutter					
1*	12 Jul	Alb. DIII	A1036	45	E Messines	1315	OOC	CR/SR/11 WS
2*	22 Jul	Alb. DIII	A1036	45	Menin	1030	OOC	CR/RFC 22.7
			Camel					
3	25 Sep	Alb. C	B2374	45	Passchendaele	1450	OOC	CR/RFC 25.9
4	26 Sep	Alb. DIII	B2350	45	Passchendaele	1130	DES	CR/RFC 26.9
5	27 Oct	Alb. DIII	B6354	45	N E Comines	1025	DES(F)	CR/RFC 27.10
6s**	31 Oct	C	B6354	45	E Quesnoy	1030	DES	CR/RFC 31.10
7	5 Nov	Alb. DV	B6354	45	Poelcapelle	1150	OOC	CR/RFC 5.11
8	8 Nov	Alb. DV	B6423	45	Houthoulst Forest	1610	OOC	CR/RFC 8.11
9	15 Nov	Alb. DV	B6423	45	E Comines	0945	OOC	CR/RFC 15.11
	1918							
10s***	2 Jan	C	B6423	45	E Conegliano	1045	DES(F)	CR/7 BG Summ
11	27 Mar	Alb. DV	B6423	45	Ceggia	1205	OOC	CR/7 BG

TOTAL: 2 and 2 shared destroyed, 7 out of control = 11.
*Observer: 2/Lt J.H. Hartley. **Shared with Lt P. Carpenter. ***Shared with Lt H.T. Thompson B4609. This was Korp. Josef Ranke/Lt Georg Repa of Flik 50.

FITZGIBBON Desmond Fitzgerald Flight Lieutenant 10(N)

Born on 1 November 1890 in Hampstead, London, Fitzgibbon joined the RNAS on 28 May 1916. After service with 3 Wing, he joined 10(N) Squadron on 5 May 1917, flying Sopwith Triplanes. During June he destroyed a two-seater and claimed four more victories out of control, adding a fifth late in August. The squadron then converted to Camels, and with this new aircraft he drove down three Albatros Scouts out of control during September. He was posted to Home Establishment on 15 October and was awarded a DSC, gazetted on 2 November 1917.

	1917		Triplane					
1s*	5 Jun	Alb. C	N5466	10N	Wervicq	0850	DES(F)	CR/RFC 5.6
2s**	5 Jun	Alb. C	N5466	10N	N W Poelcapelle	0900	OOC	CR/RFC 5.6
3	15 Jun	Halb. DII	N5458	10N	St Julien	1055	OOC	CR/RFC 15.6
4	15 Jun	Alb. DV	N5458	10N	Moorslede	1740	OOC	CR/RFC 15.6
5	25 Aug	Alb. DV	N5389	10N	N Polygon Wood	1930	OOC	CR/RFC 25.8
			Camel					
6	14 Sep	Alb. DV	B6202	10N	Tenbrielen	1630	OOC	CR/RFC 14.9
7	26 Sep	Alb. DV	B6202	10N	Westroosebeke	1100	OOC	CR/RFC 26.9
8	27 Sep	Alb. DV	B6202	10N	N E Westroosebeke	1610	OOC	CR/RFC 27.9

TOTAL: 1 shared destroyed, 6 and 1 shared out of control = 8.
*Shared with F/Lt R. Collishaw N5490, FSL K.G. Boyd N5478, FSL G.E. Nash N5492, FSL E.V. Reid N6302. **Shared with F/Lt R. Collishaw N5490.

FITZ-MORRIS James Captain 11, 25, 23

Records have shown James Fitz-Morris as J.F. Morris, Fitzmorris and Fitzmaurice! After serving with the Highland Light Infantry, this Scot from Polemont, Stirling, flew as an observer in 11 Squadron on Vickers Gun Buses in 1915, later becoming a pilot. He then joined 25 Squadron on 1 July 1917, flying FE 2s and then DH 4s, usually with a Canadian observer, Lieutenant D.L. Burgess; they claimed seven victories and both received MCs. Fitz-Morris then went as a flight commander to 23 Squadron, flying Spads in early 1918, accounting for at least seven more enemy machines; he was awarded a Bar to his MC. On 24 March 1918 he was shot down and slightly wounded, but was back in action within a few days.

	1917		DH 4					
1*	7 Jul	Alb. DV	A7505	25	Dorignies	0940	OOC	CR/RFC 11.7
2*	11 Jul	Alb. DV	A7505	25	5m W Douai	1300	OOC	CR/?
3*	22 Jul	Alb. DV	A7505	25	Lille	1430	DES(F)	CR/RFC 22.7

4*	5 Aug	Alb. DV	A7505	25	Perenchies	1720	DES(F)	CR/RFC 5.8
5*	14 Aug	Alb. DV	A7505	25	N E Dourges	1300	DES	CR/RFC 14.8
6*	14 Aug	Alb. DV	A7505	25	N E Dourges	1300	DES	CR/RFC 14.8
7*	15 Aug	Alb. DV	A7505	25	La Bassee	1015	DES(F)	CR/RFC 15.8
	1918		Spad					
8	1 Mar	Alb. DV	B6856	23	St Quentin	1030	OOC	CR/RFC 1.3
9	7 Mar	Rumpler C	B6846	23	Urvillers	0810	DES(F)	CR/RFC 7.3
10s**	9 Mar	Rumpler C	B6846	23	S Masnieres	0915	DES	CR/?
11	12 Mar	C	B6856	23	St Quentin	1030	OOC	CR/RFC 12.3
12	21 Mar	Alb. DV	B6856	23	Aubencheul au Bois	1420	DES	CR/RFC 21.3
13	24 Mar	C	B6856	23	Canizy	1400	DES(F)	CR/RFC 24.3
14***	24 Mar	Pfalz DIII	B6856	23	Viefville	1415	CAPT	CR/RFC 24.3

TOTAL: 1 captured, 8 and 1 shared destroyed, 4 out of control = 14.
*Observer: Lt D.L. Burgess. **Shared with Lt J.F.N. MacRae B6847, Lt G.W.R. Pidsley B3479. ***Possibly Oblt Cordes of Jasta 16.

FLEMING Austin Lloyd Captain 111

Fleming qualified as a pilot in February 1917, and served with 6th Training Wing at Maidstone from March to May. He was then posted to Palestine and joined 111 Squadron later in the year. In 1918 he was awarded the MC for an action when he attacked a German two-seater escorted by two scouts, forcing the two-seater to land. This combat, on 29 January 1918, had an interesting sequel 41 years later when this Canadian pilot presented to 111 Squadron a Spandau machine gun taken from the downed aircraft. Of his eight victories, his first two were claimed whilst flying a Bristol F 2B, the others in an SE 5A.

	1918		Bristol					
1*	17 Jan	C	A7192	111	Kalkilieh	0920	DES	CR/BG Summ
2s**	18 Jan	C	A7198	111	Jaffa-Arsuf	1130	DES	CR/BG Summ
			SE 5A					
3	23 Jan	Alb. DIII	B358	111	Tul Keram	1145	DES	CR/BG Summ
4	24 Jan	C	B538	111	N W Tul Keram	1130	DES	CR/BG Summ
5***	29 Jan	C	B538	111	S W Junction Station	1530	CAPT	CR/BG Summ
6	10 Mar	Alb. DIII	B540	111	E Bireh	0930	DES	CR/BG Summ
7	12 Apr	Alb. DV	B6242	111	Tul Keram	0715	OOC	CR/BG Summ
8	12 Apr	Alb. DV	B6242	111	Tul Keram	0720	OOC	CR/BG Summ

TOTAL: 1 captured, 5 destroyed, 2 out of control = 8.
*Observer: Cpl F.J. Knowles. **Observer: Cpl F.J. Knowles; shared with Lt D.B. Aitken/Lt L.A.J. Barbe A7196. ***Fleming killed the pilot and the observer landed it and became a POW.

FOOT Ernest Leslie Major 11, 60, 56

One of the most famous of the early pilots of the RFC, 'Feet' Foot served in 11 Squadron during 1916, gaining three victories in FE 2s. During this period he was the closest friend of Albert Ball. On 16 September 1916 he was posted to 60 Squadron as a flight commander, where he claimed one victory in a Spad which was on test with the unit, then one more in a Nieuport. He was shot down in flames in Nieuport Scout A162 over Serre on 26 October by Leutnant Hans Imelmann of Jasta 2, but managed to crash-land unhurt. Soon after this experience, on 3 November, he was posted home for a rest. On 10 March 1917 he joined 56 Squadron as it was forming on the first SE 5s, as one of the original flight commanders, but he was injured in a car accident the evening before the unit left for France, and was not to fly operationally again. On 23 June 1923 he was piloting a Bristol Monoplane M1D, G-EAUP, when one wing tore away; the aircraft crashed near Chertsey and Foot was killed.

	1916		FE 2B					
1*	9 Sep	?	7016	11	Irles	1630	DES	CR/3 BG WD
2*	9 Sep	LVG. C	7016	11	Irles	1630	DES	CR/3 BG WD
3*	15 Sep	D	7016	11	Ligny	0930	DES	CR/RFC 15.9
			Spad					
4	28 Sep	Alb. C	A253	60	Avesnes les Bapaume	1810	DES	CR/RFC 28.9
			Nieuport					
5	21 Oct	Roland CII	A212	60	Riencourt	1600	OOC	C&CB V11 N4

TOTAL: 4 destroyed, 1 out of control = 5.
*Observer: 2/Lt G.K. Welsford.

FORMAN James Henry Captain 6(N), 1(N), 201, 70

A Canadian from Kirkfield, Ontario, born on 1 February 1896, he joined the RNAS, and after training went to 6(N) Squadron, flying Camels during the summer of 1917. He claimed one victory before being posted to 1(N) Squadron which was still on Sopwith Triplanes, and flying this type he gained his second victory before the unit also converted to Camels. He remained with the squadron throughout the spring of 1918; when it became 201 Squadron, RAF, he was promoted to Captain and later received a DFC. He accounted for eight victories by the middle of May when he was again posted, this time to 70 Squadron for 'Special Service'. He was shot down and became a prisoner on 8 September, on which date 70 Squadron lost eight of 12 Camels to JG III. In the early 1920s Forman saw service with the RCAF, and also served during World War II as a Flight Lieutenant.

	1917		Camel					
1	27 Jul	Alb. DV	N6358	6N	N E Nieuport	1710	DES(F)	CR/RFC 27.7
			Triplane					
2s*	18 Oct	DFW. C	N5479	1N	E Poelcapelle	1030	OOC	CR/RFC 18.10
			Camel					
3s**	12 Nov	Pfalz DIII	B5651	1N	Dixmude	1545	DES(F)	CR/RNAS 12.11
4	29 Nov	Alb. DV	B6409	1N	Middelkerke	1415	OOC	CR/RNAS 29.11
	1918							
5	12 Apr	Fokker DrI	B7280	201	S E Albert	1500	OOC	CR/RAF 12.4
6	9 May	Alb. DV	B7280	201	Bapaume	1315	OOC	CR/RAF 9.5
7s***	15 May	Alb. DV	----	201	Bapaume	0645	DES	CR/RAF 15.5
8	16 May	Fokker DrI	D3392	201	S Albert	1920	DES(F)	CR/RAF 15.5
9	10 Aug	LVG. C	E1472	70	La Creche-Bailleul	2045	OOC	CR/?

TOTAL: 2 and 2 shared destroyed, 5 out of control = 9.
*Shared with FSL S.M. Kinkead N5465. **Shared with FSL S.M. Kinkead N5465; probably Obflgm K. Meyer of MFJ 1, who was killed. ***Shared with Maj C.D. Booker, Capt S.M. Kinkead, Lt M.H. Findlay, Lt R. Hemmens, Lt R. McLaughlin, Lt H.L. Wallace, Lt R.C.B. Brading, Lt R.S.S. Orr.

FORREST Henry Garnet Captain 43, 32, 2AFC

Born on 5 December 1895 in Melbourne, Victoria, Henry Forrest worked as a clerk until the outbreak of World War I, when he joined the Australian Infantry. Later transferring to the AFC, he was one of the first pilots to be sent to France, being attached initially to 43 Squadron and then to 32 Squadron in order to gain operational experience. In November he joined 68 Squadron (later 2AFC Squadron) and on 1 December damaged a large three-seater, twin-engined aircraft. His first victory was not achieved until March 1918, by which time his squadron had re-equipped with SE 5As. Operating as a flight commander, he claimed 11 victories during the spring and early summer, and was awarded a DFC. He was posted to Home Establishment on 19 July. Currently in the Australian War Memorial at Canberra there is an SE 5A painted to represent C9539 in which Forrest gained all his victories.

	1918		SE 5A					
1	22 Mar	C	C9539	2AFC	N E St Quentin	1510	OOC	CR/RFC 22.3
2	22 Mar	Alb. DV	C9539	2AFC	Bullecourt	1530	DES	CR/RFC 22.3
3	22 Mar	Alb. DV	C9539	2AFC	Bullecourt	1530	DES	CR/RFC 22.3
4	23 Mar	C	C9539	2AFC	N E Bapaume	1515	DES(F)	CR/RFC 23.3
5	30 Mar	C	C9539	2AFC	Quesnel	0800	OOC	CR/RFC 30.3
6s*	2 Apr	C	C9539	2AFC	S E Demuin	0700	DES	CR/RAF 2.4
7	12 Apr	C	C9539	2AFC	Vielle Chapelle	1700	DES	CR/RAF 12.4
8	9 May	DFW. C	C9539	2AFC	Ervillers	1900	OOC	CR/ORB/OH
9	2 Jun	Pfalz DIII	C9539	2AFC	Estrees	0805	OOC	CR/ORB/OH
10	2 Jun	Pfalz DIII	C9539	2AFC	Albert	0900	OOC	CR/ORB/OH
11	2 Jun	Fokker DrI	C9539	2AFC	Chuignes	1930	DES	CR/RAF 2.6

TOTAL: 5 and 1 shared destroyed, 5 out of control = 11.
*Shared with Lt R.L. Manuel B184.

FOSTER George Buchanan Lieutenant 24

This Canadian flew SE 5As with 24 Squadron from 8 March to 27 August 1918, claiming seven victories and receiving a DFC.

	1918		SE 5A					
1	12 Apr	Pfalz DIII	C1081	24	N Moreuil a/d	1100	DES	CR/RAF 12.4
2	20 Apr	Pfalz DIII	C1081	24	Morcourt	1000	DES	CR/RAF 20.4
3	7 Jun	Fokker DrI	C1081	24	Rosieres	1145	DES	CR/RAF 7.6

4	25 Jun	Fokker DrI	C1081	24	Contalmaison	1130	OOC	CR/ORB/SR/?
5s*	22 Jul	Balloon	D6918	24	Proyart	0730	DES	CR/RAF 22.7
6s**	31 Jul	Hannover C	D6918	24	Caix	1100	DES	CR/RAF 31.7
7	10 Aug	Hannover C	D6918	24	S Rosieres	1410	DES	CR/RAF 10.8

TOTAL: 1 shared balloon, 4 and 1 shared destroyed, 1 out of control = 7.
*Shared with Capt T.F. Hazell E1388. **Shared with Capt T.F. Hazell E1388, 2/Lt E.P. Crossen E1392.

FOSTER Robert Mordaunt Captain 54, 209

Born on 3 September 1898, Foster served with the Royal Fusiliers before he joined the RFC in June 1916. He was posted to 54 Squadron flying Pups in 1917, and claimed at least one victory. After a spell on Home Defence with 44 Squadron, he joined 209 Squadron as a flight commander in April 1918. By the end of the war he had been awarded the DFC and claimed a further 15 victories. After the war he served in India from 1919-1923. He became a Wing Commander in July 1937, and from 1939-41 was with Bomber Command. He later held various staff positions and retired from the RAF as Air Chief Marshal Sir Robert Foster, KCB, CBE, DFC.

	1917		Pup					
1	6 Jun	Alb. DIII	A6167	54	S W Cambrai	1200	DES	CR/RFC 6.6
	1918		Camel					
2s*	21 Apr	Alb. C	B3838	209	Le Quesnel	1025	DES(F)	CR/RAF 21.4
3s**	22 Apr	DFW. CV	----	209	Albert	0610	CAPT	CR/RAF 22.4
4s***	27 Apr	Alb. DV	B6276	209	E Villers Brettoneaux	1445	DES	CR/RAF 27.4
5	4 May	Pfalz DIII	B3858	209	1m S. Hamel	1555	OOC	CR/ORB/?
6s†	16 May	LVG. C	B3858	209	Villers Brettoneaux	0940	DES(F)	CR/RAF 16.5
7	30 May	Alb. DV	B3858	209	N W Meaulte	1130	OOC	CR/ORB/?
8s††	17 Jun	LVG. C	B3858	209	Ailly-sur-Noye	0830	CAPT	CR/RAF 17.6
9	29 Jun	Fokker DVII	B3858	209	Harbonnieres	2010	DES(F)	CR/RAF 29.6
10s†††	1 Aug	Fokker DVII	C61	209	Bailleul	0945	DES	CR/RAF 1.8
11s‡	8 Aug	Halb. C	C61	209	Harbonnieres	1905	DES(F)	CR/RAF 8.8
12‡‡	12 Aug	Fokker DrI	C61	209	S W Proyart	0905	CAPT	CR/RAF 12.8
13	30 Aug	Fokker DVII	C61	209	Recourt-Dury	1040	OOC	CR/?
14	15 Sep	Fokker DVII	C61	209	Ecoust St Quentin	1700	DES	CR/RAF 15.9
15	15 Sep	Fokker DVII	C61	209	Ecoust St Quentin	11720	DES	CR/RAF 15.9
16s‡‡‡	4 Nov	Pfalz DXII	C61	209	Athies	0730	OOC	CR/?

TOTAL: 1 and 2 shared captured, 4 and 5 shared destroyed, 3 and 1 shared out of control = 16.
*Shared with Capt O.C. Le Boutillier D3338, Lt M.S. Taylor. **Shared with Capt O.C. Le Boutillier, Lt M.S. Taylor, Lt M.A. Harker, Lt C.G. Brock. This was Flgr O. Raschke/Lt K. Schneider of FAA 219 in DFW. CV 7752/17, who were killed. ***Shared with Lt O.M. Redgate B7270. †Shared with Capt O.C. Le Boutillier D3338. ††Shared with Lt R.D. Gracie D3328. †††Shared with Lt W.R. May F5925. ‡Shared with Lt C.G. Edwards D9588, Capt T.C. Luke C142, Lt K.M. Walker C199, Lt M.A. Harker D9625. ‡‡This was Ofstvtr Blumenthal of Jasta 53, who was captured. ‡‡‡Shared with Lt E.W. Mills F3946, Lt E.K. Langton H6998.

FOWLER Herbert Howard Snowdon Lieutenant 8(N)

Born in Toronto on 18 December 1894, Herb Fowler was brought up in Bowmansville, Ontario. He began training as a pilot at a civil school, but it closed before he gained his wings. Inducted into the RNAS on 7 December, he was sent to England to complete his training, and was then posted to 12(N) Squadron in France on 23 July 1917. On 18 August he joined 8(N) Squadron to begin operations, serving in Charlie Booker's 'C' Flight on Triplanes. The following month the unit re-equipped with Camels, which he first flew on 11th. In February 1918 Fowler suffered ear trouble, and did not fly until late March. When he completed his last patrol on 1 June 1918 he had flown 166 hours, 15 minutes over the lines. Upon arrival in England he was medically examined and found to have become almost totally deaf, and in consequence he was discharged from the RAF, arriving home in Canada in July. After the war his hearing became partially restored, and he worked in a manufacturing concern until his death from a heart attack on 26 January 1962.

	1918		Camel					
1s*	5 Feb	Alb. DV	B3832	8N	S Pont-a-Vendin	1245	DES	CR/RFC 5.2
2s**	16 Feb	Alb. DV	B3832	8N	Pronville	1115	DES(F)	CR/ORB/?
3	8 May	Alb. DV	C8266	208	Provin	1115	OOC	CR/RAF 8.5
4s***	9 May	Alb. DV	C8266	208	Phalempin	1345	OOC	CR/RAF 9.5
5	18 May	Alb. DV	C8266	208	S Merville	1150	OOC	CR/RAF 18.5
6s†	22 May	C	----	208	N E Lens	0800	OOC	CR/?

TOTAL: 2 shared destroyed, 2 and 2 shared out of control = 6.
*Shared with F/Cdr R. McDonald B6387, FSL H. Day N6379, FSL W.H. Sneath N6356. **Shared with F/Cdr G.W. Price B6379, FSL W.H. Sneath N6356. ***Shared with Lt G.A. Wightman. †Shared with Capt W.L. Jordan, Lt R.L. Johns, Lt J.S. Macdonald, Lt E.G. Johnstone, Capt G.K. Cooper, Lt P.M. Dennett.

FRANKLYN Adrian Winfrid Lieutenant 3

Born on 1 April 1899 in Hounslow, Middlesex, Lieutenant Franklyn joined 3 Squadron in January 1918 and flew with the unit throughout the spring and summer. Three times he shared in destroying two-seaters, and on three occasions he claimed enemy scouts, a different type in each case. He was awarded an MC, gazetted on 22 June 1918.

	1918		Camel					
1	22 Mar	Alb. DV	C1611	3	S E Havrincourt	1430	DES	CR/RFC 22.3
2s*	11 Apr	C	----	3	Ervillers	1600	DES(F)	CR/RAF 11.4
3s**	9 Jun	Alb. C	D6431	3	57 D R 3	1100	DES	CR/RAF 12.6
4s***	20 Jul	Hannover C	D6628	3	Ayette	1020	OOC	CR/?
5	4 Sep	Fokker DrI	F2125	3	51 B W 21	1010	DES	CR/RAF 4.9
6	5 Sep	Fokker DVII	----	3	51 B M 14	1145	DES(F)	CR/RAF 5.9

TOTAL: 3 and 2 shared destroyed, 1 shared out of control = 6.
*Shared with Capt D.J. Bell, Lt C.E. Mayer, Lt L.A. Hamilton. **Shared with Lt W. Hubbard B2491. ***Shared with Capt H.L. Wallace C1698.

FREEHILL Maurice Michael Captain 46, 80

Born on 21 January 1899, Freehill joined the RFC in April 1917 and after training was posted to 46 Squadron on 26 January 1918. By September his score had risen to six and at the end of the month he was promoted to Captain and posted to 80 Squadron, where he gained one further victory. In the 1930s he was a Flight Lieutenant.

	1918		Camel					
1	23 Mar	C	B9149	46	Bullecourt	1300	DES	CR/RFC 23.3
2s*	3 Apr	C	B5636	46	57 D L32	1245	DES	CR/RAF 3.4
3s*	20 Apr	Alb. C	B5636	46	Harnes	1000	DES	CR/RAF 20.4
4	30 May	Fokker DrI	B5636	46	Estaires	1930	OOC	CR/RAF 30.5
5s**	7 Aug	Fokker DVII	B9291	46	S W Armentieres	0810	DES	CR/RAF 7.8
6	15 Aug	Fokker DVII	B9291	46	S E Peronne	1810	OOC	CR/RAF 15.8
7	4 Oct	Fokker DVII	H773	80	Beaurevoir	0900	OOC	CR/ORB/?

TOTAL: 1 and 3 shared destroyed, 3 out of control = 7.
*Shared with Capt C.J. Marchant B9211. **Shared with Lt A.L. Aldridge D9407.

FREW Matthew Brown Captain 45

'Bunty' Frew was born in Rutherglen, near Glasgow, Scotland, on 7 April 1895. He joined the Highland Light Infantry in 1914, and served in France from January 1915 to March 1916, before transferring to the RFC in August 1916. After training he joined 45 Squadron on 28 April 1917, flying Sopwith 1½ Strutters and then Camels. He fought in France and Italy, gaining the DSO, MC and Bar, together with the Italian Silver Medal and Belgian Croix de Guerre; he also became a Commander of the Greek Royal Order of George I, with Swords. On 15 January 1918 his Camel was hit by anti-aircraft fire. He got the machine down safely but had displaced his neck, which forced him to return to England a month later. Here he became an instructor at the CFS until the end of hostilities. He served in North Kurdistan in 1931-32, adding a Bar to his DSO, and later commanded 111 and 10 Squadrons. He became a Wing Commander in 1934 and a Group Captain in 1938. After holding various posts during World War II, he retired in 1948 having reached the rank of Air Vice-Marshal and been knighted Sir Matthew Frew, KBE,CB,DSO,MC,AFC. He retired to Pretoria, South Africa, where he died in May 1974.

	1917		Strutter					
1*	5 Jun	Alb. DIII	----	45	Menin	1015	OOC	CR/RFC 5.6
2*	5 Jun	Alb. DIII	----	45	Warneton	1020	DES(F)	CR/RFC 5.6
3**	16 Jul	Alb. DIII	----	45	Polygon Wood	0910	DES(F)	CR/RFC 16.7
4**	28 Jul	Alb. DIII	----	45	S Comines	1700	DES	CR/RFC 28.7
5**	10 Aug	Alb. DIII	----	45	3m E Comines	1830	OOC	CR/RFC 10.8
			Camel					
6	3 Sep	Alb. DIII	----	45	Zandvoorde	1315	OOC	CR/RFC 3.9
7	4 Sep	Alb. C	----	45	N E Comines	1445	OOC	CR/RFC 4.9
8	4 Sep	Alb. C	----	45	N E Comines	1450	OOC	CR/RFC 4.9
9	11 Sep	Alb. DIII	----	45	Kortewilde	0920	OOC	CR/RFC 11.9
10	21 Sep	Alb. DIII	----	45	N Comines	1815	DES(F)	CR/RFC 22.9
11	10 Oct	Alb. DV	----	45	Dadizeele	1430	OOC	CR/RFC 10.10
12	10 Oct	Alb. DV	----	45	Dadizeele	1430	DES	CR/RFC 10.10
13	21 Oct	Alb. DV	----	45	Lille	0945	OOC	CR/RFC 21.10
14s***	26 Oct	Junkers CL	----	45	Houthoulst Forest	1025	DES	CR/RFC 26.10
15s†	27 Oct	Alb. DV	----	45	N E Comines	1015	DES	CR/RFC 27.10

16	27 Oct	Alb. DV	----	45	E Moorslede	1025	DES	CR/RFC 27.10
	1918							
17	11 Jan	Alb. DIII	B6372	45	Motta	1530	DES	CR/7 BG Summ
18	15 Jan	C	B6372	45	Vazzolo	1030	DES(F)	CR/7 BG Summ
19	15 Jan	Alb. DV	B6372	45	Vazzolo	1030	DES(F)	CR/7 BG Summ
20	15 Jan	Alb. DV	B6372	45	Vazzolo	1030	DES	CR/7 BG Summ
21	27 Jan	Alb. DIII	B6372	45	Conegliano	1342	DES(F)	CR/7 BG Summ
22	4 Feb	Alb. DV	B6372	45	Barbisano Collato	1115	DES	CR/7 BG Summ
23	4 Feb	Alb. DV	B6372	45	Susegana	1120	OOC	CR/14 W Summ

TOTAL: 12 and 2 shared destroyed, 9 out of control = 23.

*Observer: 2/Lt M.J. Dalton. **Observer: 2/Lt G.A. Brooke. ***Shared with Lt K.B. Montgomery. †Shared with 2/Lt J.E. Child, 2/Lt R.J. Brownell.

FRY William Mays Captain 12, 11, 60, 23, 79

Born on 14 November 1896, he served in France as a Territorial infantry private in 1914. Returned to England in December as under age, he was commissioned in the Somerset Light Infantry, but transferred to the RFC in December 1915. After training he went to 12 Squadron, flying BE 2Cs. He then served with 11 Squadron and when, after the Battle of the Somme, 'C' Flight was absorbed into 60 Squadron, Fry and Albert Ball were two of the pilots involved. He flew with 60 Squadron during the summer of 1917 as 'Billy' Bishop's deputy leader, before returning to England with an MC. He was not happy to be away from the front and persuaded his superiors to put him back on operations. After a brief spell with 87 Squadron which was forming, he was given command of 'C' Flight in 23 Squadron, flying Spads. With 23 he claimed at least five victories, including an Albatros Scout shared with 70 Squadron on 6 January 1918; the pilot of this was Walter von Bülow of Jasta 'Boelcke', victor of 28 combats. From 23 Squadron he went to 79 Squadron which had just formed on Dolphins; before he left this unit he had claimed his 11th victory. He remained in the RAF after the war, becoming a Wing Commander before retiring. During World War II he returned to the service from 1939-45. His autobiography, *Air of Battle*, was published in 1974.

	1917		Nieuport					
1	2 May	Alb. DIII	B1503	60	Drocourt	1545	OOC	CR/SR/?
2s*	4 May	AEG. CV	B1597	60	Brebieres-Vitry	1330	DES	CR/RFC 4.5
3	13 May	Alb. DIII	B1602	60	Dury	1430	DES	CR/RFC 13.5
4**	19 May	Alb. DIII	B1602	60	Gouy-en-Artois	1010	CAPT	CR/RFC 19.5
5s***	16 Jun	Alb. DIII	B1619	60	Vitry	2020	OOC	CR/SR/RFC/?
			Spad					
6	20 Nov	Type ?	A8864	23	Passchendaele	1530	OOC	CR/RFC 20.11
7	12 Dec	Alb. DV	A8864	23	Staden	1500	OOC	CR/RFC 12.12
	1918							
8	4 Jan	Alb. DV	B6845	23	E Becelaere	1110	DES	CR/RFC 4.1
9†	6 Jan	Alb. DV	B3640	23	S Passchendaele	1400	CAPT	CR/RFC 6.1
			Dolphin					
10††	23 Jan	Alb. DV	B6847	23	Houthoulst Forest	----	DES(F)	SS
			Dolphin					
11	11 May	Fokker DrI	C4131	79	Bray	----	DES	RAF 11.5

TOTAL: 2 captured, 4 and 1 shared destroyed, 4 out of control = 11.

*Shared with Capt W.A. Bishop B1566. **This was Lt Georg Noth, of Jasta B, who was taken prisoner. ***Shared with Capt K.L. Caldwell B1654, Lt J. Collier B1605. Probably Lt H. Becker, later a 24 victory ace, of Jasta 12, who was wounded. †This was Lt W. von Bulow, a 28 victory ace and commander of Jasta B; Capt F.G. Quigley was also involved in this fight. ††Lt Gustav Mandelt, Jasta 36, who was killed.

FULLARD Philip Fletcher Captain 1

Born at Hatfield on 27 June 1897, Fullard attended school in Norwich where he excelled in sports; in 1914 he played centre half for the Norwich City reserves at soccer. He joined the Inns of Court Officer Training College in 1915, serving with the Royal Fusiliers the following year. Learning to fly at his own expense, he then transferred to the RFC, but after training with 24 Reserve Squadron and at the Central Flying School, he was made an instructor in December 1916 because of his exceptional flying ability. Subsequently he was posted to France late in April 1917, joining 1 Squadron early in May, which at that time was flying Nieuport Scouts; he made his first patrol in one of these on 4 May. Like several outstanding pilots, he maintained his own guns and ammunition, which resulted in his never suffering a jam whilst in action. All his victories were gained while flying Nieuports, and on 26 September he was awarded both the MC and Bar; these were followed on 27 October by a DSO, his score at the time of the recommendation being 14 destroyed and 18 out of control. He had one very narrow escape on 4 June when, after sending down an Albatros Scout out of control, he was attacked by an all-red Albatros. Fortunately for him, this latter was itself attacked and shot down by an SE 5, and Fullard went on to claim another scout shot down. On 15 November Fullard, who had become a flight commander in late July, claimed two Albatros Scouts to bring his score to 40, but two days later broke his leg while playing football, and returned to the United Kingdom to convalesce. Probably due to the intense strain he had been under for several months, Fullard's leg was slow to heal and he was not fully fit until September 1918. He remained in the RAF after the war, being posted to the USA on special duties in 1919, and on his return joined the Army of Occupation in the Rhineland. Promoted to Squadron Leader in 1929, he took command of 2 Squadron in 1933, and by 1941 had reached the rank of Air Commodore, becoming AOC, 246 Group. He received a CBE and AFC, and retired from the RAF at the end of the war. Fullard, unlike most high-scoring pilots, attributed his victories to his piloting skill, rather than his gunnery. He died on 24 April 1984.

	1917		Nieuport					
1	26 May	Alb. DIII	B1559	1	Lompret	1040	OOC	CR/RFC 26.5
2	28 May	Alb. DIII	B1559	1	Warneton	1210	OOC	CR/ORB/SR/?
3	4 Jun	Alb. DV	B1553	1	Roulers	0800	OOC	CR/RFC 4.6
4s*	4 Jun	Alb. DV	B1533	1	Roulers	0815	DES	CR/RFC 4.6
5	8 Jun	Alb. DV	B1553	1	Becelaere	0630	DES(F)	CR/RFC 5.6
6	14 Jun	Alb. DV	B3486	1	Moorslede	2040	OOC	CR/RFC 15.6
7	15 Jun	Alb. DV	B3486	1	Comines-Houthem	c0845	OOC	CR/RFC 15.6
8	7 Jul	Alb. DV	B1666	1	Roulers	2040	OOC	CR/RFC 8.7
9	11 Jul	Alb. DV	B1666	1	N Comines	2015	OOC	CR/RFC 11.7
10	11 Jul	Alb. DV	B1666	1	Verlinghem	2030	OOC	CR/RFC 11.7
11	13 Jul	Alb. DV	B1666	1	Zandvoorde-Wervicq	2015	OOC	CR/RFC 13.7
12	17 Jul	Alb. DV	B3459	1	Polygon	0950	OOC	CR/RFC 17.7
13	22 Jul	Alb. DV	B3459	1	N E Lille	1100	OOC	CR/RFC 22.7
14	22 Jul	Alb. DV	B3459	1	Marcq	1110	DES	CR/RFC 22.7
15	28 Jul	C	B3459	1	Korentje	0950	DES	CR/RFC 28.7
16s**	9 Aug	C	B3459	1	Houthoulst Forest	1050	CAPT	CR/RFC 9.8
17	9 Aug	Alb. DV	B3459	1	Becelaere	2015	OOC	CR/RFC 10.8
18***	10 Aug	DFW. C	B3459	1	HaboURDin	1815	DES	CR/RFC 10.8
19	12 Aug	DFW. C	B3459	1	E Tenbrielen	0750	OOC	CR/RFC 12.8
20	15 Aug	Alb. DV	B3459	1	Poelcapelle	1800	DES	CR/RFC 15.8
21	15 Aug	Alb. DV	B3459	1	Poelcapelle	1810	OOC	CR/RFC 15.8
22	16 Aug	Alb. DV	B3459	1	Poelcapelle area	0800	DES	CR/RFC 16.8
23	16 Aug	Alb. DV	B3459	1	Pont Rouge	0805	OOC	CR/RFC 16.8
24	16 Aug	Alb. DV	B3459	1	Lille-Perenchies	2010	OOC	CR/RFC 16.8
25	19 Aug	Alb. DV	B3459	1	Roncq-Menin	1700	DES	CR/RFC 19.8
26	21 Aug	Alb. DV	B3459	1	Houthoulst	1900	OOC	CR/RFC 21.8
27	22 Aug	DFW. C	B3459	1	Poelcapelle	1835	DES	CR/RFC 22.8
28	5 Oct	C	B6789	1	Bousbecque	1645	DES	CR/RFC 5.10
29	7 Oct	DFW. C	B6789	1	Wervicq	0635	OOC	CR/RFC 7.10
30	8 Oct	C	B6789	1	Wervicq	1420	OOC	CR/RFC 8.10
31	14 Oct	DFW. C	B6789	1	Gheluvelt	1700	OOC	CR/RFC 14.10
32	17 Oct	C	B6789	1	Quesnoy	0945	OOC	CR/RFC 17.10
33	17 Oct	C	B6789	1	S E Ledgehem	1030	DES	CR/RFC 17.10
34	17 Oct	Alb. DV	B6789	1	Moorslede	1425	OOC	CR/RFC 17.10
35s†	24 Oct	C	B6789	1	Moorslede	0625	OOC	CR/RFC 24.10
36	27 Oct	DFW. C	B6789	1	N W Roulers	0940	DES	CR/RFC 27.10
37	27 Oct	DFW. C	B6789	1	Becelaere	1010	DES	CR/RFC 27.10
38	30 Oct	Pfalz DIII	B6789	1	N Westroosebeke	0900	DES	CR/RFC 30.10
39	15 Nov	Alb. DV	B6789	1	Zandvoorde	1155	DES	CR/RFC 15.11
40	15 Nov	Alb. DV	B6789	1	Zandvoorde	1156	DES	CR/RFC 15.11

TOTAL: 1 shared captured, 15 destroyed, 22 and 2 shared out of control = 40.

*Shared with F/Cdr T.F.N. Gerrard N5479 of 1N; this was possibly Ofzstvtr Matthias Denecke of Jasta 18 who was fatally wounded. **Shared with 2/Lt W.V.T. Rooper B1675; this was Uffz Walter Stulcken/Lt Johann Schmidt of FAA 238. ***Probably Uffz A. King/Lt G. von Langen of KG 1. †Shared with 2/Lt W.D. Patrick B6768.

NB: Neither of the two balloons generally credited to Fullard were confirmed by either Wing, Brigade, the RFC War Diary, or the Communiques.

GALBRAITH Daniel Murray Bayne Captain 1W, A, 8(N)

Born in Carleton Place, Ontario, Canada, on 27 April 1895, Murray Galbraith was a student at the outbreak of war, and with his friends Roy Brown and Stearne Edwards, trained to fly in the US at his own expense, receiving Aero Club of America certificate No 356 on 3 November 1915. He then joined the RNAS, serving initially at Dover from 29 May 1916, and then with 1 Naval Wing from 12 June. He joined 8(N) Squadron upon its formation on 17 October 1916, and by this time already had three victories. Flying Nieuports and Pups with

8(N), he claimed three more, receiving the DSC and Bar and a French Croix de Guerre. On 23 November 1916 he single-handedly attacked six enemy two-seaters, shooting down one, driving off another and forcing three more to land. On 1 December 1916 he was rested, and after a spell as an instructor, flew on anti-submarine operations in Italy in 1918. He joined the Canadian Air Force after the war, but was killed in a car accident on 29 March 1921.

	1916		Nieuport					
1	15 Jul	Seaplane	3963	1W	10m off Ostend	1600	DES(F)	DRO/RNAS 15.7
2	28 Sep	Seaplane	3992	1W	18m off Calais	c1100	DES	DRO/RNAS 28.9
			Pup					
3	22 Oct	Seaplane	----	A	2.5m off Blankenberghe	1530	DES	DRO/RNAS 22.10
4	10 Nov	Roland D	N5193	8N	Bapaume	1450	OOC	CR/RFC 10.11
5	16 Nov	LVG. C	N5193	8N	Pys-Miraumont	1530	OOC	CR/RFC 16.11
6	23 Nov	LVG. C ?	N5196	8N	E Cambrai	1440	DES	CR/RFC 23.11

TOTAL: 4 destroyed, 2 out of control = 6.

GARDINER George Cecil Captain 14, 17, 47, 150

After service as an observer with 14 Squadron in Palestine, Captain Gardiner flew in Salonika in 1917 with 47 Squadron. His first victory was gained over an Albatros two-seater, claimed by himself and another pilot whilst flying BE 12s. His next combat occurred while he was flying a DH 2; attacked by an Albatros DIII, he fired three shots at his opponent whereupon his Lewis gun jammed. He broke off combat and returned to base, not making any claim. However infantrymen had seen the fight and reported watching the Albatros fall to earth and crash as a result of his brief fire; this victory was therefore credited to him. He was posted as a flight commander to 17 Squadron and then in April 1918 the scouts of 17 and 47 Squadrons were amalgamated into the new 150 Squadron. With this unit he flew Camels, claiming five further victories during the summer months; he was awarded a DFC during June. In 1919 he returned to 17 Squadron. He had become a Squadron Leader with 4 FTS by 1934, having in the meantime been awarded a DSO, while from the French came the Legion d'Honneur and Croix de Guerre avec Palme.

	1917		BE 12					
1s*	1 Oct	Alb. C	----	47	Beles	1030-1130	OOC	CR/BG Summ/?
			DH 2					
2**	? Nov	Alb. DIII	----	47	----	----	DES	SR/
	1918		Camel					
3	6 Jun	Alb. DIII	C1598	150	Mravin	1130	OOC	CR/BG Summ
4s***	12 Jun	Alb. DV	C1586	150	S S E Pardovica	0805	DES	CR/BG Summ
5s†	25 Jun	C	C1586	150	1m E Cestovo	1820	DES	CR/BG Summ
6	3 Sep	Alb. DV	D6544	150	W Cerniste Hospital	0820	DES	CR/BG Summ

TOTAL: 2 and 2 shared destroyed, 1 and 1 shared out of control = 6.

*Shared with 2/Lt A.F. Buckley 6554. **Apparently confirmed late by infantry. ***Shared with Lt C.B. Green in SE 5A B695. †Shared with Capt G.M. Brawley in SE 5A B694.

GARDNER Cecil Vernon Captain 19

Posted to 19 Squadron on 22 January 1918 after completing pilot training, Cecil Gardner flew Sopwith Dolphins with this unit during the summer of that year. He became 'B' Flight Commander, claimed ten victories, and was awarded a DFC. On 11 August he attacked and shot down a Pfalz Scout, from which he observed the pilot to jump out and descend safely by means of a parachute. He was wounded in action on 27 September, crashing near Bapaume in E4501; he died three days later.

	1918		Dolphin					
1s*	6 Jun	DFW. CV	C4129	19	Vieux Berquin	1715	OOC	ORB/?
2	9 Jun	DFW. CV	C4057	19	Neuf Berquin	0945	DES	CR/ORB/SR
3	1 Jul	Pfalz DIII	D5236	19	Fleurbaix	1755	OOC	CR/ORB/SR
4	4 Jul	Pfalz DIII	C3788	19	Esterelles	1700	OOC	CR/ORB/SR
5	15 Jul	Fokker DVII	C3792	19	Bois du Biez	2005	DES(F)	CR/RAF 13.7
6	31 Jul	Pfalz DIII	D5236	19	S Douai	1950	DES	CR/RAF 31.7
7**	11 Aug	Pfalz DIII	D5236	19	Estrees	1700	DES(F)	CR/RAF 11.8
8	11 Aug	Fokker DVII	D5236	19	Brie	1755	DES	CR/RAF 11.8
9s***	16 Sep	Fokker DVII	C3818	19	Lille	0940	OOC	CR/ORB/SR
10	27 Sep	Fokker DVII	E4501	19	Haynecourt	0730	DES	CR/RAF 27.9

TOTAL: 6 destroyed, 2 and 2 shared out of control = 10.

*Shared with Capt G.B. Irving C3799, Lt F. McQuistan C3902 and Capt J.D. De Pencier C3829. **This was Uffz Max Bauer of Jasta 23, who baled out safely. ***Shared with Lt J.D. Hardman C3769.

GATES George Brian Captain 1(N), 201

Born on 21 July 1899 in Hove, Sussex, George Gates joined the RNAS on 22 June 1917 and after training was posted to 1(N) Squadron at the start of 1918. During the spring, after the unit had become 201 Squadron, RAF, he began claiming, and by the end of August had five aircraft and two balloons to his credit. He claimed heavily during September, was promoted to Flight Commander and awarded a DFC, but was wounded in action. He was subsequently awarded a Bar to his DFC.

	1918		Camel					
1	15 Mar	Pfalz DIII	B7233	1N	E Dixmude	1145	DES	CR/DOS/?
2	16 May	Fokker DrI	B6401	201	S Albert	1920	OOC	CR/RAF 16.5
3	16 Jun	Rumpler C	D3419	201	S E Villers-Brettoneaux	1945	DES(F)	CR/RAF 16.6
4s*	16 Jul	Balloon	D3419	201	Achiet le Grand	1735	DES	CR/RAF 28.7
5	19 Jul	Balloon	B7190	201	Fricourt	1220	DES	CR/RAF 28.7
6	10 Aug	Halb. C	F5941	201	S E Rosieres	1615	DES(F)	CR/RAF 10.8
7	10 Aug	Halb. C	F5941	201	S E Rosieres	1620	DES(F)	CR/RAF 10.8
8	3 Sep	Hannover C	F5941	201	Moeuvres area	1310	DES(F)	CR/RAF 3.9
9	3 Sep	Alb. C	D9672	201	E Metz en Couture	1925	DES(F)	CR/RAF 3.9
10**	7 Sep	Alb. C	F5941	201	Noyelles	1020	DES	CR/RAF 7.9
11***	8 Sep	Alb. C	F5941	201	Cantaing	0650	DES(F)	CR/RAF 8.9
12	14 Sep	LVG. C	F5941	201	Villers-Plouich	1325	DES(F)	CR/RAF 14.9
13s†	16 Sep	LVG. C	F5941	201	Haynecourt	0905	DES	CR/RAF 16.9
14	23 Sep	LVG. C	F5941	201	N Bourlon Wood	1725	DES	CR/RAF 23.9
15	27 Sep	Balloon	F5941	201	57 C L 12c	1130	DES	CR/RAF 27.9
16††	29 Sep	Balloon	----	201	Bantouzelle	c1800	DES	SS

TOTAL: 3 and 1 shared balloons, 10 and 1 shared destroyed, 1 out of control = 16.
*Shared with Lt R.S.S. Orr D9648. **The observer parachuted successfully. ***One of the crew parachuted successfully. †Shared with Lt J.M. Mackay D9672; both baled out successfully. ††The log book of Capt Ron Sykes of 201, cited in C&C (G.B.) V2 N2 gives precise details of this action.

GAULD George William Gladstone Lieutenant 74

Lieutenant Gauld, a Canadian from Mimico, Ontario, served in 74 Squadron during the latter part of 1918, during which time he claimed five victories, including two Fokker DVIIs on 1 November. He was awarded a DFC.

	1918		SE 5A					
1s*	30 Jul	Rumpler C	----	74	Cassel-Ypres	1210	DES(F)	CR/RAF 1.8
2**	2 Aug	LVG. C	C6468	74	Dickebusch	0930	CAPT	CR/RAF 2.8
3	26 Oct	Fokker DVII	----	74	Cordes	1455	OOC	CR/11 WS
4***	1 Nov	Fokker DVII	----	74	W Audenarde	1550	CAPT	CR/RAF 1.11
5	1 Nov	Fokker DVII	----	74	W Audenarde	1550	OOC	CR/?

TOTAL: 1 and 1 shared captured, 1 shared destroyed, 2 out of control = 5.
*Shared with Capt J.I.T. Jones D6895, 1/Lt H.G. Shoemaker E1389. **Shared with Lt F.S. Gordon D3438; this was Vzfw Anton Daron/Lt Ludwig Molitor of FAA 268, both of whom were killed. ***The pilot baled out of his flaming aircraft and was captured.

GERRARD Thomas Francis Netterville Major A, 1(N) 208, 209

Born on 30 August 1897, the son of Brigadier General E.L.Gerrard DSO, 'Teddy' Gerrard joined the RNAS in 1915, becoming operational at the Dunkirk Seaplane Base in December of that year. On 10 June 1916 he joined 'A' Squadron, flying scouts, but in September was posted to Cranwell as an instructor. By December he had been promoted to Flight Commander, and shortly afterwards joined 1(N) Squadron on its formation with Sopwith Triplanes. He received the DSC and Croix de Guerre, claiming eight more victories. On 4 June he engaged a formation of 15-20 German scouts, sending one down 'out of control' and sharing in the destruction of another with Fullard of 1 Squadron, RFC. Leaving France, he went to 256 Squadron in England; he returned to the front in early summer 1918, where after a short stint with 208 Squadron, he took command of 209 Squadron during June, a post he held until the end of the war. He remained in the RAF, becoming an instructor at the CFS in the 1920s. In July 1921 he took part in the second Hendon Air Pageant, flying in a formation of five CFS Snipes led by Squadron Leader Chris Draper. Some time later, during a game of polo, he fell from his horse and hit his head. He appeared unhurt initially, but shortly afterwards collapsed and died in the Officers' Mess.

	1916		Nieuport					
1	8 Jul	Fokker E	3889	A	2m off Ostend	1405	OOC	DOS/RNAS 8.7
	1917		Triplane					
2	14 Apr	E/A	N5440	1N	Epinoy	0820	OOC	ORB/DL/?
3	24 Apr	Alb. DIII	N5440	1N	Noyelles	1115	DES	CR/RFC 24.4
4	24 Apr	Alb. DIII	N5440	1N	S Wancourt	1120	OOC	CR/ORB/?

5	29 Apr	Alb. DIII	N5440	1N	Epinoy	1110	OOC	CR/RFC 29.4
6	19 May	Alb. DIII	N5440	1N	Henin-Lietard	1945	OOC	CR/RFC 19.5
7	4 Jun	Alb. DIII	N5440	1N	Moorslede-Menin	0750	OOC	CR/RFC 4.6
8s*	4 Jun	Alb. DIII	N5440	1N	Moorslede-Menin	0800	DES	CR/RFC 4.6
9	7 Jun	Alb. DIII	N6291	1N	Ypres	0600	DES	CR/RFC 7.6
	1918		Camel					
10s**	6 Apr	Fokker DrI	B7196	208	Lens	1130	OOC	CR/RAF 6.4

TOTAL: 2 and 1 shared destroyed, 6 and 1 shared out of control = 10.
*Shared with Capt P.F. Fullard B1553 of 1 Sqn. **Shared with Lt G.K. Cooper B7189, Lt W.H. Sneath B7187.

GIBBONS Frank George Lieutenant 22

After service in the Northumberland Regiment, Gibbons transferred to the RFC where he was commissioned on 25 November 1917. He graduated as a pilot on 2 February 1918, joining 22 Squadron where during the summer he was credited with 14 victories. Of these, three or four fell to his front gun, all the others being claimed by the various gunners with whom he flew. He was awarded a DFC, and in 1919 served with 111 Squadron in the Middle East.

	1918		Bristol					
1*	31 May	Pfalz DIII	A7243	22	S E Armentieres	1915	OOC	CR/SR/?
2**	1 Jun	Pfalz DIII	C961	22	Erquinghem	1915	DES	CR/RAF 1.6
3**	1 Jun	Pfalz DIII	C961	22	Erquinghem	1915	DES	CR/RAF 1.6
4*	2 Jun	Pfalz DIII	C901	22	N E Lens	1050	OOC	CR/SR/?
5†	5 Jun	Pfalz DIII	C929	22	N E La Bassee	1915	OOC	CR/SR/?
6††	28 Jun	Fokker DrI	C989	22	N Estaires	1015	DES	CR/RAF 28.6
7††	10 Jul	Fokker DrI	C989	22	Lille	0945	OOC	CR/SR/?
8†††	27 Aug	Fokker DVII	E2454	22	Douai	1345	OOC	CR/SR/?
9‡	2 Sep	Fokker DVII	D7894	22	Haynecourt	1115	DES	CR/RAF 2.9
10‡	2 Sep	Fokker DVII	D7894	22	Haynecourt	1115	DES	CR/SR/?
11‡	5 Sep	Fokker DVII	E2454	22	Douai	1700	OOC	CR/SR/?
12‡	16 Sep	Fokker DVII	E2454	22	Quesnoy Wood	1530	OOC	CR/SR/?
13‡‡	25 Sep	Fokker DVII	E2477	22	Boulon Wood-Cambrai	1810	DES	CR/RAF 25.9
14‡	27 Sep	Fokker DVII	F6040	22	Sensee Canal-Cambrai	0730	OOC	CR/SR/?

TOTAL: 6 destroyed, 8 out of control = 14.
*Observer: Sgt J.H. Jones. **Observer: 2/Lt J.H. Umney. †Observer: Sgt R.M. Fletcher. ††Observer: Lt V. StB Collins. †††Observer: Lt J. McDonald. ‡Observer: Sgt G. Shannon. ‡‡Observer: 2/Lt J.A. Oliver.

GIBBONS George Everard Captain 20, 62

Joining the RFC in November 1916, Gibbons served first as an observer with 20 Squadron, and later as a pilot. Becoming a flight commander in 62 Squadron during spring and summer of 1918, he usually flew with two of the unit's gunner/observers, Lieutenants S.A.W. Knight and T. Elliott. He claimed eight victories while flying with the former and nine with the latter. He received the MC, followed by a DFC for his 17 victories, becoming yet another high-scoring exponent of the Bristol Fighter. 14 of his victories were claimed with the front gun, the other three falling to that operated by the observer.

	1918		Bristol					
1*	12 Mar	Fokker DrI	----	62	N E Nauroy	1100	OOC	CR/RFC 12.3
2*	17 Mar	EA	----	62	----	----	OOC	RFC 17.3
3*	3 May	Alb. DV	C779	62	N Armentieres	1145	DES(F)	CR/RAF 3.5
4*	3 May	Alb. DV	C779	62	N Armentieres	1145	DES	CR/RAF 3.5
5*	3May	Alb. DV	C779	62	N Armentieres	1200	OOC	CR/SR/?
6*	22 May	LVG. C	C919	62	W Laventie	0805	DES	CR/RAF 22.5
7*	28 May	Fokker DVII	C919	62	Menin-Armentieres	1950	DES(F)	CR/RAF 28.5
8*	28 May	Rumpler C	C919	62	La Creche-Steenwerck	1945	OOC	CR/SR/?
9**	1 Aug	EA	----	62	----	----	OOC	SR/?
10**	3 Aug	EA	----	62	----	----	OOC	SR/?
11**	13 Aug	C	E2457	62	Bullecourt	1025	DES	CR/RAF 13.8
12**	22 Aug	Fokker DVII	E2457	62	W Pronville	0740	DES	CR/RAF 22.8
13***	22 Aug	Fokker DVII	E2457	62	W Pronville	0740	DES(F)	CR/RAF 22.8
14**	3 Sep	Fokker DVII	E2457	62	N Cambrai	1845	OOC	CR/SR/?
15**	3 Sep	Fokker DVII	E2457	62	N Cambrai	1845	OOC	CR/SR/?
16**	4 Sep	Fokker DVII	E2457	62	Abancourt-N Cambrai	0930	DES	CR/RAF 4.9
17**	4 Sep	Fokker DVII	E2457	62	N Cambrai	0930	OOC	CR/RAF 4.9

TOTAL: 8 destroyed, 9 out of control = 17.
*Observer: 2/Lt S.A.W. Knights. **Observer: 2/Lt T. Elliott. ***Observer: 2/Lt T. Elliott. This was probably Uffz Born of Jasta 1, who was killed.

GIBBS Frederick John Captain 23, 64

Gibbs served with 23 Squadron during the summer and autumn of 1917, becoming a flight commander and receiving the MC and Bar; he claimed ten victories before returning to Home Establishment. In late 1918 he joined 64 Squadron, and at 1400 hours on 29 October shot down his 11th and last machine over Estreaux.

	1917		Spad					
1	2 Jun	Alb. DIII	B1661	23	N Lens	1100	OOC	CR/RFC 2.6
2	17 Jun	DFW. C	B1561	23	S E St Julien	0715	DES	CR/RFC 17.6
3	27 Jul	Alb. DV	B3501	23	St Julien	1445	OOC	CR/RFC 27.7
4s*	27 Jul	Aviatik C	B3501	23	Kezelberg	1950	DES	CR/RFC 27.7
5	13 Aug	DFW. C	B3464	23	Comines	1000	DES	CR/RFC 13.8
6	18 Aug	Alb. DV	B3493	23	Comines	0945	OOC	CR/BG Summ
7	22 Aug	DFW. C	B3493	23	Wervicq	0645	DES	CR/RFC 22.8
8	25 Aug	Alb. DV	B3493	23	Langemarck area	1915	OOC	CR/RFC 25.8
9	25 Sep	C	B3575	23	N Wervicq	1115	DES(F)	CR/RFC 25.9
10	2 Oct	Rumpler C	B3575	23	N Wervicq	1115	DES	CR/RFC 2.10
	1918		SE 5A					
11	29 Oct	LVG. C	E5941	64	Estreaux	1400	DES	CR/RAF 29.10

TOTAL: 6 and 1 shared destroyed, 4 out of control = 11.
*Shared with Capt R.H.G. Neville B3519.

GIBBS Gerald Ernest Major 17, 150, 29

Born on 3 September 1896 in Kent, Gerald Gibbs joined the army in 1914 as a private and was sent overseas in October, serving at Suez and on the Turkish border. He was then sent to India, arriving on the North-West Frontier in 1915. He returned to the United Kingdom to receive a commission and then joined the 7th Wiltshire Regiment in Macedonia. He applied for transfer to the RFC and trained at Aboukir in Egypt. Becoming an instructor after training until early 1917, he was then posted to 17 Squadron, again in Macedonia. He first flew BE 2Cs, though on occasions used one of a flight of four Nieuport Scouts borrowed from a French unit. He then operated SE 5As during early 1918, claiming his first victory at the end of January; eight more followed by early May, when the unit's scouts were incorporated into 150 Squadron. After a month with this unit, he returned to the United Kingdom once more. He was ill with malaria during the summer, and on recovery took a refresher course on SEs before going to France just after the Armistice to fly with 29 Squadron as a flight commander. He was awarded an MC and two Bars, the second, in September 1918, crediting him with two victories. In 1919 he brought 70 Squadron home from Germany; he remained in the RAF, serving in the Near East and in Africa, and by 1936 was a Wing Commander. When he retired in 1954 he was an Air Marshal, and had been knighted; he had been the last British AOC in C of the Indian Air Force, and had served with the British Delegation at the United Nations. His autobiography, *Survivor's Story*, was published in 1956. He was still living in Surrey at the time of writing.

	1918		SE 5A					
1s*	28 Jan	DFW. C	B613	17	S Angista	1130	DES	CR/BG Summ
2s**	31 Jan	Rumpler C	B613	17	2m N N E Kayendra	1220	DES	CR/BG Summ
3s**	5 Feb	Alb. DIII	B613	17	Vernak Farm	1510	OOC	CR/BG Summ
4	15 Feb	DFW. C	B690	17	N E Dovista	1530	OOC	CR/BG Summ
5***	13 Mar	Alb. DIII	B613	17	into Lake Doiran	1250	DES	CR/BG Summ
6s†	20 Mar	DFW. CV	B694	17	Cepista	0930	CAPT	CR/BG Summ
7	13 Apr	Alb. DIII	B694	17	Balintse	0730	OOC	CR/BG Summ
8	22 Apr	DFW. C	B694	17	Tumba	0945	OOC?	CR/BG Summ
9	26 Apr	Alb. DIIV	B694	17	Sueti Vrac	0945	OOC	CR/BG Summ
10s††	4 May	DFW. C	B694	17	Marian aerodrome	1040	CAPT	CR/BG Summ

TOTAL: 2 shared captured, 1 and 2 shared destroyed, 4 and 1 shared out of control = 10.
*Shared with Lt A.G. Goulding in Bristol Scout 5574. **Shared with Capt F.G. Saunders B28. ***This was probably Lt Otto Splitgerber the CO of Jasta 38. Gibbs' described the pilot as the leader of the patrol and very skilful. †Shared with Lt A.G. Goulding B690; the crew 'surrendered'. ††Shared with Lt L. Hamilton B691; the crew of this aircraft were killed, one was possibly Lt A. Dannerberg.

GIFFORD Rupert Cyril D'Arcy Lieutenant 208

After joining the RNAS in August 1917, Lieutenant Gifford flew Sopwith Camels with 208 Squadron in 1918, claiming seven victories.

	1918		Camel					
1s*	20 Jul	LVG. C	----	208	N E La Bassee	0730	OOC	CR/AIR 1/1218
2	31 Jul	Pfalz DIII	----	208	1m S Estaires	0930	DES	CR/AIR 1/1218
3s**	14 Aug	DFW.C	----	208	E Oppy	0600	OOC	CR/AIR 1/1218
4s***	25 Aug	C	----	208	Pont a Vendin	1900	DES	CR/AIR 1/1218

5	29 Sep	Fokker DVII	----	208	Lesdins	1230	OOC	CR/AIR 1/1218
6	3 Oct	Fokker DVII	B7177	208	2m N E Brancourt	1830	DES	CR/RAF 3.10

TOTAL: 2 and shared destroyed, 1 and 2 shared out of control = 6.
*Shared with Capt W.L. Jordan, Lt Richards. **Shared with Lt J.B. White, Lt Allison, Lt E.G. Johnstone. ***Shared with Lt W.V. Skall.

GILBERTSON D.H.S. Lieutenant 70

Gilbertson served with 70 Squadron during 1918, flying Sopwith Camels. He was reported missing in E1472 during a combat with JG III near Escaillon, near Douai, on 4 September 1918, when his unit lost eight aircraft.

	1918		Camel					
1	30 May	Alb. DV	C1648	70	S E Albert	1115	OOC	CR/III BG
2	27 Jun	Pfalz DIII	----	70	E Aveluy Wood	2030	OOC	CR/AIR 1/1226
3	1 Jul	Alb. DV	C8268	70	E Bailleul	0700	DES	CR/AIR 1/1226
4	1 Jul	Alb. DV	C8268	70	W Bray	0920	OOC	CR/III BG
5s*	4 Sep	Fokker DVII	E1472	70	Escaillon	0815	DES	CR/RAF 4.9

TOTAL: 1 and 1 shared destroyed, 3 out of control = 5.
*Shared with Lt J.S. Wilson D8175.

GILES Wilfred Bertie Lieutenant 43, 74

Born on 16 April 1896, 'Twist' Giles served with the Somerset Light Infantry from March to September 1916. He was wounded on the Somme Front, and on recovery transferred to the RFC at the start of 1917. After training, he served initially as an observer with 43 Squadron on Sopwith 1½ Strutters, and later trained as a pilot. He returned to France in early 1917 with 74 Squadron, flying SE 5As, where he remained until injured in a crash on 6 August. After the war he became Manager of the Bristol office of the Sun Alliance Insurance company. He later married the widow of Ira Jones and at the time of writing both were still alive.

	1917		Strutter					
1s*	16 Jun	Alb. DIII	A1903	43	Lens	0830	DES	CR/RFC 16.6
	1918		SE 5A					
2	12 May	Alb. DV	C6414	74	N Wulverghem	1830	DES	CR/RAF 12.5
3s**	27 May	Halb. C	----	74	Neuf Berquin	1130	OOC	CR/11 WS
4	29 Jun	Fokker DVII	C6494	74	Bailleul-Kemmel	2015	DES	CR/11 WS
5	7 Jul	LVG. C	C6494	74	Bailleul	1120	DES(F)	CR/RAF 7.7

TOTAL: 2 and 2 shared destroyed, 1 shared out of control = 5
*Pilot: 2/Lt C.G. Moore; shared with 2/Lt S.V.L. Gedge/Pte C.B. Blatherwick A8829, Lt J.H.G. Womersley/1 AM J.M. O'Shea A8244, Sgt A.V. Webb/2/Lt C.E. Day A7798, Capt K.L. Gopsill/2/Lt J.B. Smith A8335. **Shared with Lt J.I.T. Jones C1117.

GILLESPIE William John Lieutenant 41

A Canadian from Dayland, Lieutenant Gillespie joined 41 Squadron on 11 December 1917, serving until summer 1918, by which time he had claimed five victories. He was hospitalized on 18 August, seeing no further action. He was awarded a Croix de Guerre avec Palme by the French, but nothing by the RAF.

	1918		SE 5A					
1	25 Mar	Alb. DV	B8254	41	Sailly	1050	OOC	CR/RFC 25.3
2	27 May	Alb. DV	C5436	41	E Merville	1600	OOC	CR/SR/?
3	27 Jun	Alb. DV	C1895	41	S E Albert	2010	OOC	CR/SR/?
4	3 Jul	Pfalz DIII	C1895	41	E Lamotte	1915	OOC	CR/SR/?
5s*	7 Jul	Alb. C	C1895	41	La Boissiere	1215	OOC	CR/SR/?

TOTAL: 4 and 1 shared out of control = 5
*Shared with Capt F.R.G. McCall D6877.

GILLET Frederick Warrington Captain 79

Born in 1895, although an American by birth, Frederick Gillet joined the RAF, and after training was posted to 79 Squadron on 29 March 1918 to fly Sopwith Dolphins. He sent down a balloon in flames on 3 August, and 15 days later claimed a Fokker DVII destroyed. A pair of two-seaters and another balloon were claimed by 1 September, and he was awarded a DFC which was gazetted on 2 November. During September and October he was continually in action and claimed another 11 victories, nine of them Fokker DVIIs; he twice claimed two of these fighters in a day. He claimed a two-seater on 4 November, and on 10th a Halberstadt two-seater and two DVIIs that collided and were destroyed. This raised his score to 20 destroyed, three of them balloons. After the war Gillet went into a variety of business ventures; he died on 21 December 1969, aged 74. He also received the Belgian Croix de Guerre.

	1918		Dolphin					
1	3 Aug	Balloon	C3887	79	N Estaires	0735	DES	CR/RAF 3.8

2	18 Aug	Fokker DVII	C3887	79	N E Estaires	1240	DES	CR/RAF 18.8
3	24 Aug	DFW. C	C3887	79	2m E Bailleul	1935	DES	CR/RAF 24.8
4	1 Sep	LVG. C	C4059	79	N E Armentieres	1320	DES	CR/RAF 1.9
5	1 Sep	Balloon	C4059	79	Armentieres	1325	DES	CR/RAF 1.9
6	5 Sep	Fokker DVII	C4059	79	E Armentieres	1855	DES	CR/RAF 5.9
7	21 Sep	Fokker DVII	E4859	79	Habourdin-Wavrin	1150	DES	CR/RAF 21.9
8	28 Sep	Alb. C	C4059	79	Bousbecque	1255	DES	CR/RAF 28.9
9	28 Sep	Fokker DVII	C4059	79	1m E Passchendaele	1730	DES	CR/RAF 28.9
10	29 Sep	Fokker DVII	C4059	79	W Roulers	1010	DES(F)	CR/RAF 29.9
11	2 Oct	Balloon	C4059	79	4m E Roulers	0710	DES	CR/RAF 2.10
12	5 Oct	Fokker DVII	C4059	79	Courtrai	0830	DES	CR/RAF 5.10
13	8 Oct	Fokker DVII	C4059	79	N E Menin	1625	DES	CR/RAF 8.10
14	8 Oct	Fokker DVII	C4059	79	Gulleghem	1630	DES	CR/RAF 8.10
15	14 Oct	Fokker DVII	C7244	79	E Inglemunster	1030	DES	CR/RAF 14.10
16*	14 Oct	Fokker DVII	C7244	79	Gits	1425	DES	CR/RAF 14.10
17	4 Nov	Fokker DVII	C3584	79	W Renaix	1306	DES	CR/RAF 4.11
18	10 Nov	Fokker DVII	C3584	79	N Pelceghem	0630	DES	CR/11 WS
19**	10 Nov	Fokker DVII	C3584	79	N W Besseghem	0635	DES	CR/11 WS
20**	10 Nov	Fokker DVII	C3584	79	N W Besseghem	0635	DES	CR/11 WS

TOTAL: 3 balloons, 17 destroyed = 20

*Note: the CR says C7244, but this was a DH 6 serial! Either this aircraft was a rebuild, or the serial was totally incorrect.
**These 2 aircraft collided; all 3 were confirmed by 11 Wing on 13 Nov 1918.

GILMOUR John Ingles Major 27, 65, 28

Transferring from the Argyll and Sutherland Highlanders to the RFC, John Gilmour first flew with 27 Squadron in early and mid 1916, flying Martinsyde G.100 'Elephants'. He was probably the most successful exponent of this aircraft as a fighter, gaining three victories on the type. He was awarded an MC, though this was mainly for his bombing operations with the squadron. Late in 1917 he was posted to 65 Squadron to fly Sopwith Camels as a flight commander, claiming two victories on 18 December and three on 4 January 1918. On 1 July he claimed five scouts in one day, two Fokker DVIIs, two Albatros DVs and a Pfalz DIII. By the middle of the summer his score had risen to 39, and he had received two Bars to his MC and a DSO. After a rest from operations, he was promoted to Major and posted in October to command 28 Squadron in Italy, but he did not have a chance to add further to his score here before the war on this front ended. His score has been listed as 44 for many years, but recent research has shown this to be incorrect.

	1916		Martinsyde					
1s*	15 Sep	Alb. DI?	----	27	Bourlon	0915	DES	CR/RFC 15.9
2	24 Sep	Fokker E	7284	27	Havrincourt Wood	1700	DES	CR/RFC 24.9
3	26 Sep	Fokker E	7284	27	W Havrincourt Wood	1200	OOC	CR/RFC 26.9
	1917		Camel					
4	18 Dec	Alb. DV	B9166	65	Roulers	1425	DES	CR/RFC 18.12
5	18 Dec	C	B9166	65	Roulers	1435	OOC	CR/RFC 18.12
	1918							
6	4 Jan	C	B5612	65	S Roulers	1040	DES(F)	CR/RFC 4.1
7	4 Jan	Alb. DV	B5612	65	S Roulers	1100	OOC	CR/RFC 4.1
8	4 Jan	Alb. DV	B5612	65	S Gheluvelt	1110	DES	CR/RFC 4.1
9	9 Jan	C	B5612	65	Roulers	1255	OOC	CR/RFC 9.1
10	3 Feb	Alb. DV	B5612	65	S Roulers	1035	OOC	CR/RFC 3.2
11	5 Feb	Balloon	B5612	65	N W Menin	1330	DES(F)	CR/RFC 5.2
12	26 Mar	C	C8278	65	N W Lille	1125	OOC	CR/RFC 26.3
13	10 Apr	Alb. DV	C8278	65	1000y E Morcourt	0930	DES	CR/RAF 10.4
14	11 Apr	Rumpler C	B1799	65	N E Moreuil Wood	1325	DES	CR/RAF 11.4
15**	12 Apr	Rumpler C	C8278	65	Morlancourt	1330	DES(F)	CR/RAF 12.4
16	16 Apr	C	C8278	65	N Hangard Wood	1740	DES(F)	CR/RAF 16.4
17	23 Apr	Fokker DrI	C8278	65	Mericourt	1800	DES	CR/RAF 23.4
18	25 Apr	Alb. DV	C8278	65	N Lamotte	1800	DES	CR/RAF 25.4
19	29 Apr	Pfalz DIII	C8278	65	Hamel area	1030	DES	CR/RAF 29.4
20	2 May	C	C8278	65	Miraumont Wood	1150	DES(F)	CR/RAF 2.5
21	2 May	C	C8278	65	Villers Brettoneaux	1205	CAPT	CR/RAF 2.5
22	9 May	C	C8278	65	N E Albert	1300	DES	CR/RAF 9.5
23s***	10 May	Alb. DV	C8278	65	N Villers-Brettoneaux	1930	DES	CR/RAF 10.5
24	18 May	Alb. DV	C8278	65	E Bray	1020	DES	CR/RAF 18.5
25s	18 May	C	C8278	65	E Lamotte	1030	DES	CR/RAF 18.5
26†	20 May	C	D8118	65	Caix-Guillaucourt	1320	DES	CR/RAF 20.5
27s††	20 May	Fokker DrI	D8118	65	S E Albert	2030	DES	CR/RAF 20.5

28	15 Jun	C	D8118	65	S E Guillaucourt	2035	DES	CR/RAF 15.6
29	20 Jun	Pfalz DIII	D8118	65	Morlancourt	1715	OOC	CR/ORB/?
30	29 Jun	Pfalz DIII	D8118	65	S E Morlancourt	1125	OOC	CR/ORB/?
31	29 Jun	Pfalz DIII	D8118	65	S Cayeux	2055	DES	CR/RAF 29.6
32	1 Jul	Fokker DVII	D8118	65	S E Bray	1910	DES(F)	CR/RAF 1.7
33	1 Jul	Fokker DVII	D8118	65	S E Bray	1912	OOC	CR/ORB/?
34	1 Jul	Fokker DVII	D8118	65	Foucaucourt	1945	DES(F)	CR/RAF 1.7
35	1 Jul	Pfalz DIII	D8118	65	Proyart	1950	OOC	CR/ORB/?
36	1 Jul	Alb. DV	D8118	65	S E Lamotte	1955	DES(F)	CR/RAF 1.7
37	2 Jul	Pfalz DIII	D8118	65	Caix-Cayeux	2027	DES	CR/RAF 2.7
38	3 Jul	Pfalz DIII	D8118	65	S W Villers-Brettoneaux	1915	DES(F)	CR/RAF 3.7
39	3 Jul	Pfalz DIII	D8118	65	S Wiencourt	1920	DES	CR/RAF 3.7

TOTAL: 1 balloon, 1 captured, 24 and 3 shared destroyed, 10 out of control = 39.

*Shared with Capt O.T. Boyd, Lt Shirlaw, Lt J.M. McAlery, Lt Dunstan, Lt H.A. Taylor, Lt E.H. Wingfield, 2/Lt C.J. Kennedy, 2/Lt O.C. Godfrey. **Probably Lt J. Hemprich/Lt B. Plesch KIA of FA 17. ***Shared with Lt T. Williams, Lt H.J. Spreadbury, 2/Lt M.A. Newnham, 2/Lt H.E. Browne, Lt W.F. Scott-Kerr. †Shared with 2/Lt H. Browne C8278. ††Shared with Lt E.C. Eaton D6630.

GLEN James Alpheus Captain 3(N), 203

Jimmy Glen was a Canadian from Ontario, born on 30 June 1890, who joined the RNAS early in the war, and served with 'B' Flight of 3 Naval Squadron in 1917. He had a period of illness from August 1917, returning to active duty on 1 January 1918, when he became a Flight Lieutenant and acting flight commander with 203 Squadron. He received the DSC and Bar and the French Croix de Guerre in 1918, and claimed 15 victories before returning to Home Establishment in May 1918. After the war he remained in the RAF and in the 1920s was attached to the RCAF as an instructor at Camp Borden. He retired in 1928.

	1917		Pup					
1	23 May	Alb. DIII	N6183	3N	Bourlon Wood	1340	OOC	CR/RFC 23.5
2	27 May	Alb. DIII	N6183	3N	Ecourt St Quentin	0730	DES	CR/RFC 27.5
3	17 Jun	DFW. C	N6479	3N	N E Ypres	0630	OOC	CR/RFC 17.6
4s*	7 Jul	Seaplane C	N6183	3N	6m N Ostend	1110	DES	CR/RNAS 7.7
5	7 Jul	Seaplane	N6183	3N	12m N W Ostend	1120	DES	CR/RNAS 7.7
			Camel					
6s**	27 Jul	Seaplane	B3782	3N	20m off Ostend	1415	DES	CR/RNAS 27.7
	1918							
7s***	28 Jan	DFW. C	B6408	3N	Houthoulst Forest	1105	OOC	CR/RNAS 28.1
8s†	30 Jan	Alb. DV	B6242	3N	Gheluvelt	1045	OOC	CR/RNAS 30.1
9s†	30 Jan	Alb. DV	B6242	3N	Gheluvelt	1045	OOC	CR/RNAS 30.1
10s††	9 Mar	DFW. C	B7185	3N	Henin-Lietard	1120	DES(F)	CR/ORB/?
11s‡	16 Mar	Hannover C	B7185	3N	Gavrelle	1120	DES(F)	CR/RFC 16.3
12s‡‡	21 Mar	Alb. DV	B7185	3N	Douai	1115	OOC	CR/RFC 21.3
13s‡‡‡	21 Mar	Alb. C	B7185	3N	4m E Bapaume	1645	DES(F)	CR/RFC 21.3
14s§	9 Apr	Alb. C	B7185	203	Givenchy	1610	DES(F)	CR/RAF 9.4
15	11 Apr	Alb. C	B7185	203	Laventie	1830	DES(F)	CR/RAF 11.4

TOTAL: 3 and 6 shared destroyed, 2 and 4 shared out of control = 15.

*Shared with FSL J.S.T. Fall N6364, FSL L.H. Rochford N6163, FSL F.C. Armstrong. **Shared with FSL J.S.T. Fall N6364, FSL L.D. Bawlf B3805, FSL H.F. Beamish N6377, FSL A.B. Ellwood B3781. ***Shared with F/Lt L.H. Rochford B6401, FSL C.S. Devereux B7230. †Shared with F/Lt L.H. Rochford B6401, FSL A.B. Ellwood B6408. ††Shared with FSL W.H. Chisam. ‡Shared with F/Cdr L.H. Richford B7203, FSL A.B. Ellwood B7229. ‡‡Shared with F/Cdr L.H. Rochford B7222. ‡‡‡Shared with F/Cdr L.H. Rochford B7203, FSL O.P. Adam B3798, FSL K.D. Macleod B7222, FSL W.H. Chisam B7223, FSL A.B. Ellwood B7229, FSL C.S. Devereux B7228, FSL L.A. Sands B7216, FSL R.C. Berlyn B7224, FSL E.T. Hayne B7231. §Shared with Capt R.A. Little B7231, Lt A.B. Ellwood B7229.

GLYNN Clive Beverley Captain 56, 74

After serving in the Liverpool Regiment, where he became a Captain, Glynn applied for transfer to the RFC, and was posted to 56 Squadron on 17 June 1917 at the age of 24. He did not remain long, being returned to Home Establishment for further training, on conclusion of which he joined 74 Squadron. Going to France with this unit early in 1918, he first claimed on 29 April when he shot down a Fokker Triplane. During the summer and early autumn he claimed six Fokker DVIIs, two in one day on one occasion, and received a DFC after his fourth victory. While with the squadron he was promoted to flight commander, and ended the war with a score of eight.

	1918		SE 5A					
1*	29 Apr	Fokker DrI	C1078	74	S Dickebusch Lake	1140	DES	CR/RAF 29.4
2	26 May	Pfalz DIII	C6469	74	S E Bailleul	0720	OOC	CR/11 WS

3	23 Aug	Fokker DVII	----	74	Passchendaele	1905	OOC	CR/11 WS
4	25 Aug	Fokker DVII	----	74	Warneton	1845	DES	CR/RAF 25.8
5	21 Sep	Fokker DVII	----	74	Lille	1845	DES	CR/RAF 21.9
6	1 Oct	Fokker DVII	----	74	Courtrai-Roulers	1400	DES	CR/RAF 1.10
7	1 Oct	Fokker DVII	----	74	Courtrai-Roulers	1400	DES(F)	CR/RAF 1.10
8	9 Oct	Fokker DVII	----	74	3m E Roulers	0855	DES(F)	CR/RAF 9.10

TOTAL: 6 destroyed, 2 out of control = 8.
*Probably Lt Heinrich Bongartz, the 34 victory ace and commander of Jasta 36, who was wounded.

GOBLE Stanley James Major 1W, 8(N), 5(N), 205

Born at Croyden in Victoria, Australia, on 21 August 1891, he joined the RNAS in 1915, serving with 1 Naval Wing, flying Nieuport Scouts and Sopwith Pups. He claimed his first victory on 21 July 1916, while on 24 September he shot down one of several enemy machines that had bombed Dunkirk. He then went as a flight commander to 8(N) Squadron and by the end of the year had brought his score to eight. He received the DSO and DSC before he returned to England. In 1918 he took command of 5 Naval Squadron — later 205 Squadron, RAF — which was operating with DH 4s. He flew on several bombing raids in the rear seat and on 16 March he and his pilot, Flight Lieutenant Watkins, were attacked by several enemy scouts, two of which Goble claimed to have shot down with his rear Lewis gun. On 17 June, while bombing Chaulnes, his pilot Captain Gamon was wounded in the head and fainted. Goble regained control of the 'Four', released the bombs and glided towards the lines. Crossing these at 6,000 feet, his pilot then recovered and brought the machine home safely. In 1921 Goble joined the RAAF, rising to the rank of Air Commodore by 1935; he was Air Member for Personnel. In 1936 he took part in an exchange scheme between the RAF and RAAF, coming to England to be AOC No 2 Group, Bomber Command. He then commanded the Australian elements of the Empire Air Training Scheme. Goble died in Melbourne on 24 July 1948 with the rank of Air Vice-Marshal, CBE.

	1916		Nieuport					
1	21 Jul	C	8517	1W	3m E Dixmude	1750	OOC	CR/RNAS 21.7
2	15 Aug	Seaplane C	8517	1W	off Westende	0720	DES	CR/RNAS 15.8
			Pup					
3	24 Sep	LVG. C	3691	1W	Ghistelles	1530	OOC	CR/RNAS 24.9
4	16 Nov	LVG. C	N5194	8N	Gommecourt	1055	OOC	CR/RFC 16.11
5	17 Nov	C	N5194	8N	Bapaume	1535	DES	CR/RFC 17.11
6	27 Nov	C	N5194	8N	S E Bapaume	0950	DES(F)	CR/RFC 27.11
7	4 Dec	Halb. DII	N5194	8N	S E Bapaume	1100	OOC	CR/DOS/?
8	11 Dec	C	N5194	8N	E Bucquoy	1010	OOC	CR/DOS/?
	1918		DH 4					
9*	16 Mar	Alb. DV	N6001	5N	Bohain-Le Catelet	1100	DES	CR/RFC 16.3
10*	16 Mar	Alb. DV	N6001	5N	Bohain-Le Catelet	1100	OOC	CR/RFC 16.3

TOTAL: 4 destroyed, 6 out of control = 10.
*Pilot: F/Lt T. Watkins.

GODFREY Albert Earl Captain 10, 25, 40, 44, 78

A Canadian from Vancouver, British Columbia, Godfrey was born in July 1890. When war was declared he was in the process of building his own aeroplane, and he immediately applied to join the RFC. He was told he could only be accepted if he learned to fly at his own expense, but this was out of the question, so in January 1915 he enlisted in the 11th Mounted Rifles, and later the 1st Pioneer Battalion, arriving in England in November 1915. His CO would not allow him time in which to learn to fly, so he went with his unit to France where he served in the trenches until mid 1916, when he applied to transfer to the RFC as an observer. He was accepted, and flew with 10 and 25 Squadrons from July to December 1916. After pilot training, he eventually got his wish to join a scout squadron, going to 40 which was flying Nieuports. He served throughout the early summer of 1917, receiving an MC and claiming 14 enemy aircraft. Returning to Home Establishment in September, he served with 44 and 78 (Home Defence) Squadrons until April 1918, when he returned to Canada to assist with the Canadian Training Brigade until the end of the war. He joined the RCAF after the war, received an AFC, and by the beginning of World War II had risen to the rank of Group Captain. At that time he was serving in England at the Imperial Defence College. 'Steve' Godfrey attended the World War I Aces' Reunion in Paris in 1981, although terminally ill with cancer. He died soon afterwards on 1 January 1982.

	1916		FE 2B					
1*	16 Oct	Roland D	4847	25	W Douai	1120	OOC	CR/RFC 16.10
	1917		Nieup					
2**	28 May	Alb. DIII	B1684	40	N E Douai	1950	OOC	CR/RFC 29.5
3	1 Jun	LVG. C	B1684	40	Arras	1100	DES	CR/RFC 1.6

4	3 Jun	Alb. DIII	B1684	40	Cambrai-Somme	0940	OOC	CR/RFC 3.6
5	5 Jun	Alb. DIII	B1684	40	N E Vitry	2050	OOC	CR/RFC 6.6
6	7 Jun	Alb. DIII	B1684	40	N Lille	0710	DES	CR/RFC 7.6
7	24 Jun	Alb. DIII	B1684	40	S E Lille	2020	OOC	CR/RFC 24.6
8	2 Jul	Alb. DIII	B1684	40	N Douai	1030	OOC	CR/RFC 2.7
9	21 Jul	Alb. DIII	B1684	40	Vitry	0730	OOC	CR/RFC 21.7
10	27 Jul	Alb. DIII	B1684	40	E Arras	1625	OOC	CR/RFC 27.7
11	12 Aug	Alb. DIII	B1684	40	Lens	1945	OOC	CR/RFC 12.8
12	13 Aug	Alb. DIII	B1684	40	Pont a Vendin area	1940	DES	CR/RFC 13.8
13	14 Aug	DFW. C	B1684	40	Lens	1730	DES	CR/RFC 15.8
14	22 Aug	C	B3601	40	Hulloch	1040	OOC	CR/RFC 22.8

TOTAL: 4 destroyed, 9 and 1 shared out of control = 14.
*Pilot: 2/Lt J.L.N. Bennett-Boggs. **Shared with Lt W.A. Bond B1545.

GONNE Michael Edward Captain 54

Seconded to the RFC from the Royal Fusiliers as a Captain in May 1917, he flew as a pilot, and later as a flight commander, with 54 Squadron on the Western Front during 1917-18. He saw action in both Sopwith Pups and Camels, was awarded the MC and claimed five victories. On 8 August 1918 Gonne was last seen near Brie, on the Somme, at 1315 hours in D6575; he was probably shot down and killed by German aircraft.

	1917		Pup					
1	25 Sep	Alb. DIII	A6215	54	off Middelkerke	1130	DES	CR/RFC 25.9
2s*	18 Oct	Alb. DIII	A6215	54	Leke	1430	DES	CR/RFC 18.10
	1918		Camel					
3	5 Jan	DFW. C	B5422	54	St Quentin-Marty	1555	OOC	CR/RFC 5.1
4	25 Jan	Alb. DV	B6403	54	Grougis	1310	OOC	CR/RFC 25.1
5s**	25 Jan	Rumpler C	B6403	54	Fieulaine	1325	DES(F)	CR/RFC 25.1

TOTAL: 1 and 2 shared destroyed, 2 out of control = 5.
*Shared with Lt G.A. Hyde B1792. **Shared with Lt W.H. Kelley, 2/Lt D.F. Lawson.

GOOD Herbert Barrett Lieutenant 92

Good flew SE 5As with 92 Squadron in the summer of 1918, where in a short period of time he claimed five victories before being killed in action during a fight with several Fokker Biplanes on 5 September 1918; he was shot down by either Leutnant G. Meyer or Vizefeldwebel Himmer of Jasta 37.

	1918		SE 5A					
1	7 Aug	Fokker DVII	D6925	92	S E Steenwerck	0815	DES	CR/RAF 7.8
2	7 Aug	Fokker DVII	D6925	92	N W Armentieres	0850	OOC	CR/ORB/?
3	11 Aug	Fokker DVII	D6925	92	Nesle	1130	DES	CR/RAF 11.8
4	14 Aug	Fokker DVII	D6925	92	S Peronne	1135	DES(F)	CR/RAF 14.8
5	25 Aug	Fokker DVII	D6925	92	N Lille	1415	OOC	CR/ORB/?

TOTAL: 3 destroyed, 2 out of control = 5.

GOODE Harry King Lieutenant 66

Harry Goode was born in Nuneaton, Warwickshire, in 1895. After serving for three years in the ranks with the Royal Engineers, he was commissioned in the RFC in November 1917. He joined 66 Squadron in Italy on 27 May 1918 and in a short space of time claimed 15 victories, seven of these being balloons. In his last action on 29 October, he shot down a balloon, then attacked the airfield at South Gioncomc, shooting it up and claiming three enemy machines destroyed on the ground. He was awarded the DSO and DFC. He remained in the RAF, serving as a Flight Lieutenant at Hendon in 1934, and in December 1935 took command of 24 Squadron. He retired from the service as a Group Captain, AFC, in December 1941. He was employed in a civilian capacity with the Accident Branch of the RAF, but was killed when a passenger in a Liberator of 120 Squadron which crashed on 21 August 1942.

	1918		Camel					
1	25 Jun	C	D9410	66	Vazzena, S Asiago	0735	DES(F)	ORB/SR/14 W
2*	18 Jul	Alb. DIII	B2363	66	Mt Baldo	0805	DES	ORB/SR/14 W
3	1 Aug	C	E1494	66	S Guistina	0930	DES	ORB/SR/14 W
4	5 Aug	Balloon	E1494	66	S E Oderzo	0920	DES	ORB/SR/14 W
5	9 Aug	Brand. C	E1494	66	N Motta	0740	DES	ORB/SR/14 W
6	11 Aug	Alb. DIII	E1494	66	Valpregara	1950	OOC	ORB/SR/14 W
7	22 Aug	Alb. DIII	E1494	66	Conegliano	1110	DES(F)	ORB/SR/14 W
8	30 Sep	LVG. C	E7211	66	N E Conegliano	1815	DES	ORB/SR/14 W
9s**	8 Oct	C	E7211	66	S W Vallo	1120	DES	ORB/SR/14 W
10	16 Oct	Balloon	E7211	66	Oderzo	----	DES	ORB/SR/14 W

11s***	22 Oct	Balloon	E7211	66	S W Vazzolo	1645	DES	ORB/SR/14 W
12	27 Oct	Balloon	E7211	66	38K 55 38	0815	DES	ORB/SR/14 W
13	28 Oct	Balloon	E7211	66	S Oderzo	0810	DES	ORB/SR/14 W
14	28 Oct	Balloon	E7211	66	St Stino	1045	DES	ORB/SR/14 W
15	29 Oct	Balloon	E7211	66	39M 93 24	0730	DES	ORB/SR/14 W

TOTAL: 6 and 1 shared balloons, 6 and 1 shared destroyed, 1 out of control = 15.
*Probably Fw Walter Langthaler of Flik 9j in 153:252, who was killed. **Shared with Capt P. Carpenter C3290. ***Shared with Capt H. Hindle-James E1576.

GOODISON Henry Arthur Frank Lieutenant 23

He served in 23 Squadron in early 1918 and until mid summer, flying Spads and then Dolphins. He later served in 204 Training Depot Squadron as an instructor.

	1918		Spad					
1s*	18 Mar	Alb. DV	B6845	23	Essigny le Grand	0745	CAPT	CR/RFC 18.3
2s**	23 Mar	LVG. C	B6835	23	W Chapien a/d	1125	CAPT	CR/RFC 23.3
			Dolphin					
3s***	31 May	C	C3871	23	S E Wiencourt	0755	DES(F)	CR/RAF 31.5
4	3 Jun	Pfalz DIII	C4150	23	Montdidier	1740	DES	CR/RAF 3.6
5	27 Jun	Fokker DVII	C4150	23	E Bray	0950	OOC	CR/?

TOTAL: 2 shared captured, 1 and 1 shared destroyed, 1 out of control = 5.
*Shared with 2/Lt E.R. Varley B6835; this was an aircraft from Jasta 44. **Shared with Capt L.D. Baker B6842. ***Shared with Lt H.E. Faulkner C4130.

GORDON Frederick Stanley Lieutenant 74

Freddie Gordon from Hillsboro, Auckland, New Zealand, served with 74 Squadron during summer 1918, being credited with nine victories, seven over aircraft and two over balloons. His sister later married his Commanding Officer, Major K. 'Grid' Caldwell. Frederick Gordon died on 27 June 1985.

	1918		SE 5A					
1s*	2 Aug	LVG. C	D3438	74	Dickebusch	0930	CAPT	CR/RAF 2.8
2	16 Aug	Fokker DVII	D3438	74	Messines	0830	DES	CR/11 WS
3	16 Aug	Fokker DVII	D3438	74	Messines	0830	OOC	CR/11 BG Summ
4s**	16 Aug	Rumpler C	D3438	74	E Kemmel Hill	1250	DES(F)	CR/RAF 16.8
5	22 Aug	LVG. C	D3438	74	Estaires	0550	OOC	CR/11 WS
6	4 Sep	Balloon	E1978	74	S Roulers	0805	DES	CR/RAF 4.9
7s***	28 Oct	Fokker DVII	----	74	N W Wortegem	1445	DES	CR/RAF 28.10
8	28 Oct	Fokker DVII	----	74	Wortegem	1450	OOC	CR/11 WS
9	30 Oct	Balloon	----	74	Quaremont	0830	DES	CR/RAF 30.10

TOTAL: 2 balloons, 1 shared captured, 1 and 2 shared destroyed, 3 out of control = 9.
*Shared with Lt G.W.G. Gauld D6468; this was Vzfw Anton Daron/Lt Ludwig Molitar of FAA 268, who were killed. **Shared with 1/Lt H.G. Shoemaker E4685. ***Shared with Capt A.C. Kiddie, Lt R.O. Hobhouse.

GORDON Robert MacIntyre Lieutenant 204

Gordon, from Queen's Park, Glasgow, was born on 30 September 1899. He joined 204 Squadron on 26 May 1918, and first claimed in late June. Between then and early September he claimed eight victories and was awarded a DFC on 10 September, but on 29 September he was hospitalized after a slight wound, returning to the squadron in early October. He was promptly sent on a week's rest at the No 5 Group Rest Home at Wissant. Subsequently on 27 October he claimed a Fokker DVII in flames, but was himself wounded again in this combat and was hospitalized once more, seeing no further action. After the war he became a doctor.

	1918		Camel					
1	30 Jun	C	D1868	204	Zeebrugge	1430	OOC	CR/5 GP Comm
2	30 Jun	Fokker DVII	D1868	204	Zeebrugge	1440	OOC	CR/5 GP Comm
3	31 Jul	Fokker DVII	D8146	204	10m N E Ypres	1930	OOC	CR/5 GP Comm
4	12 Aug	Fokker DVII	D9498	204	Blankenberghe	1055	DES	CR/5 GP Comm
5	12 Aug	Fokker DVII	D9498	204	Blankenberghe	1055	OOC	CR/5 GP Comm
6s*	15 Aug	Fokker DVII	D8145	204	Menin	1900	DES(F)	CR/5 GP Comm
7**	15 Aug	Fokker DVII	D8145	204	Menin	1900	DES(F)	CR/5 GP Comm
8	3 Sep	Fokker DVII	D8146	204	Gheluvelt	1150	OOC	CR/5 GP Comm
9	27 Oct	Fokker DVII	F3929	204	S Ghent	0910	DES(F)	CR/5 GP Comm

TOTAL: 2 and 1 shared destroyed, 5 out of control = 9.
*Shared with Lt C.R.R. Hickey C74. **One of these two was possible Vzfw E. Vitzthum of Jasta 16, who was killed.

GORRINGE Frank Clifford Captain 43, 70, 210

Born on 30 September 1889 in Eastbourne, Sussex, Gorringe was living in Canada in 1914. Trained as an observer, he first flew on operations as a gunner in a Sopwith 1½ Strutter of 43 Squadron in 1917. He then trained as a pilot and late the same year was posted to 70 Squadron which was flying Camels. He claimed his first victory on 7 November, when he sent down a two-seater out of control, and these became his main prey. By February 1918 he had brought his score to 14; he was awarded an MC, gazetted on 4 March. After a period in England he returned to take a flight commander's post with 210 Squadron on 25 October 1918. Here he flew several ground attack sorties in support of the army, actually landing behind advancing troops on 9 November to give them the exact details of enemy positions. For these actions he was awarded a DFC, gazetted on 8 February 1919.

	1917		Camel					
1	7 Nov	C	B5406	70	S E Houthoulst Forest	0720	OOC	CR/RFC 7.11
2	18 Dec	C	B6426	70	N Comines	1245	CAPT	CR/RFC 18.12
3s*	19 Dec	Alb. DV	B6424	70	20 Q 27	0945	DES(F)	CR/RFC 19.12
4	23 Dec	C	B6426	70	N E Hollebeke	1515	DES(F)	CR/RFC 23.12
5	28 Dec	C	B6426	70	Ploegsteert	1150	DES	CR/RFC 28.12
	1918							
6s**	1 Jan	C	B6426	70	E Zandvoorde	0940	DES(F)	CR/RFC 1.1
7	3 Jan	C	B6426	70	N Wervicq	1340	DES(F)	CR/RFC 3.1
8s***	4 Jan	C	B2492	70	E Gheluvelt	0920	DES	CR/RFC 4.1
9	4 Jan	Alb. DV	B6426	70	Passchendaele	1330	DES(F)	CR/RFC 4.1
10s†	6 Jan	Alb. DV	B6426	70	E Passchendaele	1415	DES	CR/RFC 6.1
11	2 Feb	C	B5598	70	Becelaere	1545	DES	CR/RFC 2.2
12s††	17 Feb	C	----	70	Houthoulst Forest	----	OOC	RFC 17.2
13	18 Feb	Alb. DV	B4630	70	Houthoulst	1215	DES(F)	CR/RFC 18.2
14	18 Feb	Alb. DV	B4630	70	Houthoulst	1215	DES	CR/RFC 18.2

TOTAL: 1 captured, 7 and 4 shared destroyed, 1 and 1 shared out of control = 14.
*Shared with 2/Lt F.G. Quigley B2497. **Shared with Lt C. Smith. ***Shared with Lt H. Soulby. †Shared with Capt F.G. Quigley B2447. ††Shared with Capt F.G. Quigley.

GOSSIP George Hatfield Dingley Captain 4(N), 204

Born on 6 January 1897 in Hampstead, North London, he joined the RNAS on 30 April 1916, and was posted to 4 Naval Squadron on 5 July 1917, where he claimed three victories before the end of the year. Promoted to Captain in July 1918 after the unit had become 204 Squadron, RAF, he claimed a further three victories during the early summer; he left the unit on 10 August. George Gossip died in 1922 and was buried in the Military Cemetary at Scutari, Istanbul.

	1917		Camel					
1	1 Oct	Alb. DV	B3856	4N	Zeebrugge	1345	OOC	CR/RNAS 1.10
2	4 Nov	Alb. C	B3856	4N	20m N E Zeebrugge	1445	DES	CR/RNAS 4.11
3	13 Nov	Alb. C	B3856	4N	S E Dixmude	1130	OOC	CR/RNAS 13.11
	1918							
4	20 May	Alb. DV	B3832	204	Ghistelles	1845	OOC	CR/5 GP Comm
5	30 Jun	Fokker DVII	D3353	204	Zeebrugge	1440	OOC	CR/5 GP Comm
6	30 Jul	Fokker DVII	D3342	204	S E Ostend	1055	OOC	CR/5 GP Comm

TOTAL: 1 destroyed, 5 out of control = 6.

GOULDING Acheson Gosford Captain 17, 150

Born in France of Canadian parentage, Goulding was in Canada at the outbreak of war. He transferred from the Canadian Infantry to the RFC after arrival in Europe, and after training was posted to 17 Squadron in Macedonia in February 1917, where he flew BE 12s and Nieuports, being awarded an MC. In 1918 he started flying SE 5As, he and his fellow scout pilots being transferred to form part of the new 150 Squadron in which Goulding became a flight commander. He was awarded a DFC, gazetted on 1 January 1919, his final score being nine.

	1918		Nieuport					
1s*	28 Jan	DFW. CV	5574	17	S Angista	1130	CAPT	CR/BG Summ
			SE 5A					
2s**	20 Mar	DFW. CV	B690	17	Cepista	0930	CAPT	CR/BG Summ
3	24 Mar	Alb. DIII	B690	17	Tolos	0700	OOC	CR/BG Summ
4s***	21 Apr	DFW. C	B690	17	Barakli-Dzuma	1115	OOC	CR/BG Summ
5s†	25 Apr	DFW. C	B690	17	Angista	1000	OOC	CR/BG Summ
6s††	10 May	Pfalz DIII	B28	150	N Livunovo	0800	DES	CR/BG Summ

7s†††	13 May	Alb. DIII	B28	150	Livunovo	0800	OOC	CR/BG/Summ
8s‡	28 May	DFW. C	B690	150	E Vardarhohe	1500	DES(F)	CR/BG Summ
9s‡‡	18 Jun	Alb. DV	B163	150	N Paljorca	0750	DES	CR/BG Summ

TOTAL: 2 shared captured, 3 shared destroyed, 1 and 3 shared out of control = 9.
*Shared with Lt G.E. Gibbs B613. **Shared with Capt G.E. Gibbs B694. ***Shared with Lt L. Hamilton B694. †Shared with Lt A.E. deM Jarvis in Bristol Monoplane C4913. ††Shared with Lt C.B. Green B638. †††Shared with Capt G.G. Bell B695. ‡Shared with Lt F.D. Travers B688. ‡‡Shared with Capt G.G. Bell B692.

GRAHAM Gavin Lynedoch Lieutenant 70, 73

Graham served with the 18th Hussars from April 1915 to August 1916, when he was seconded to the RFC. He flew as an observer in 70 Squadron until March 1917, at which time he was selected for pilot training. On 14 December he joined 73 Squadron and flew with this unit until the late summer of 1918, claiming 13 victories and receiving the DFC. He logged some 200 hours as an observer and over 250 more as a pilot.

	1918		Camel					
1	3 May	Alb. DV	----	73	Ploegsteert	1250	OOC	CR/RAF 3.5
2	21 May	Fokker DrI	----	73	Armentieres	1830	DES	CR/RAF 21.5
3	10 Jun	Alb. DV	B2351	73	Mesnet, E Montdidier	1830	DES	CR/RAF 10.6
4	18 Jul	Fokker DVII	D1958	73	Oulchy le Chateau	1500	DES	CR/RAF 18.7
5	19 Jul	Fokker DVII	D1958	73	Chateau Verses-Feuille	0620	CAPT	CR/RAF 19.7
6s*	21 Jul	Fokker DrI	D1958	73	N E Oulchy le Chateau	2000	DES	CR/RAF 21.7
7	22 Jul	Fokker DVII	D9492	73	Bazoches	1810	OOC	CR/?
8	22 Jul	Fokker DVII	D9492	73	Bazoches	1810	DES	CR/RAF 22.7
9	25 Jul	Fokker DVII	D9492	73	E Courmont	1900	DES	CR/RAF 25.7
10	29 Jul	Fokker DVII	D9492	73	N E Soissons	1945	DES(F)	CR/RAF 29.7
11s**	8 Aug	C	D9492	73	Nesle	1720	DES	CR/RAF 8.8
12	25 Aug	Fokker DVII	E1553	73	N Bapaume	1125	DES	CR/RAF 25.8
13s***	25 Aug	Fokker DVII	E1553	73	N Bapaume	1130	OOC	CR/?

TOTAL: 1 captured, 7 and 2 shared destroyed, 2 and 1 shared out of control = 13.
*Shared with Major R.H. Freeman D1918, Capt M.leB. Smith D8164, Lt W.S. Stephenson C8296, 2/Lt K.S. Laurie B7874, Lt W. Sidebottom D8199, 2/Lt R.N. Chandler D1922, Lt J. Balfour D8114. **Shared with Lt E.J. Lussier B2525, 2/Lt R.W. Chandler D1922. ***Shared with Lt G. Carr-Harris D9448.

GRAHAM Ronald Major SDF, 13(N), 213

Ronnie Graham was born in Japan on 19 July 1896 and became a medical student before the war. In 1915 he joined the RN Division, but in September went into the RNAS as a Flight Sub Lieutenant, serving at the seaplane base at Dover in 1916. The following year the unit moved to Dunkirk, giving cover to the North Sea Fleet. During his service he was forced to ditch in the sea twice. Later the unit became 13(N) Squadron, previously known as the St Pol Seaplane Defence Flight. On 29 December 1917 he had a bad crash whilst stunting for his girlfriend — a nurse — and was away for some months convalescing. He returned to command the unit in 1918 when it became 213 Squadron, RAF. He was awarded the DSO,DSC and Bar, and the DFC, together with the Croix de Guerre and Belgian Order of the Crown. He was also the principal artist in the RNAS, producing a whole series of paintings of events of the Air Service at Dunkirk. He remained in the RAF, becoming chief instructor at the Staff College. He retired with the rank of Air Vice-Marshal, CB,CBE, and died in his Scottish ancestral homeland in 1967.

	1917		Sop Baby					
1	19 Jun	Seaplane	N1016	SDF	10m N N E Nieuport	0530	DES	3W DOS/?
			Pup					
2s**	12 Aug	Seaplane	N6478	SDF	off Ostend	1745	DES	CR/RNAS 12.8
			Camel					
3s***	15 Sep	Seaplane	B3794	13N	12m N E Nieuport	1910	DES(F)	DRO/RNAS 15.9
4†	25 Sep	Seaplane C	B6240	13N	near Ostend	1700	DES	CR/RNAS 25.9
	1918							
5	19 Oct	LVG. C	D8504	213	Somergem	1520	DES(F)	CR/5 GP Comm

TOTAL: 3 and 2 shared destroyed = 5.
*In this action Seeflug II shot down two RNAS seaplanes, but Graham shot down Vzflgm Dyck, who died of wounds. **Shared with FSL L.H. Slatter N6459, F/Lt P.S. Fisher N6437; this was a Friedrichshafen FF 33L 1246, flown by Flgm Paatz/Vzfw Putz of Seeflug 1, who were killed. ***Shared with FSL L.H. Slatter B3793; this was an Albatros W4 1484, flown by Flgm Dauke of Seeflug 1, who was killed. †This was Vzflgm Plattenburg (WIA)/Lt Brettmann of Seeflug 1 in an FF 33L 1582.

GRANGE Edward Rochfort Flight Lieutenant 1W, 8(N)

From Toronto, Canada, Grange graduated from the Curtiss Flying School in the USA, in September 1915 and enlisted in the RNAS. He served in France on the Channel coast from February 1916 with 1 Naval Wing, but in October was posted to 8(N) Squadron. With this unit he was wounded in the shoulder on 7 January 1917. On 16 February he was awarded a DSC for three out of control on 4 January and others driven down on the 5th and 7th of that month. He spent the rest of his service based in England as an instructor. In 1981 he attended the Aces' Reunion in Paris, and at the time of writing was still alive.

	1916		Pup					
1*	25 Sep	Seaplane	N5182	1W	6m off Ostend	c1200	DES	DRO/RNAS 25.9
	1917							
2	4 Jan	Alb. DII	N5194	8N	N Bapaume	1500	DES	CR/RFC 4.1
3	4 Jan	Alb. DII	N5194	8N	N Bapaume	1500	OOC	CR/RFC 4.1?
4	4 Jan	Alb. DII	N5194	8N	N Bapaume	1500	OOC	CR/RFC 4.1?
5**	7 Jan	Alb. DII	N5194	8N	Grevilles area	1100	OOC	SS/?

TOTAL: 2 destroyed, 3 out of control = 5.
*This is a Sablatnig SF 2 No 609 of Seeflug 1; Lt Z.S. Soltenborn/Lt Z.S. Rothig were killed. **Grange was wounded in action in this fight.

GRAY William Edrington Lieutenant 213

Born on 11 October 1898 in Berwick on Tweed, Gray joined the RNAS on 25 July 1917 and flew in 213 Squadron from May 1918. His first claim was made on 19th of that month when he and Captain Pinder shot down in flames an Albatros that had just burned a Belgian balloon. His score had risen to five by the end of the war and he was awarded a DFC, gazetted in 1919.

	1918		Camel					
1s*	19 May	Alb. DV	B6239	213	1m S Woumen	1735	DES(F)	CR/5 GP Comm
2s**	2 Jun	Pfalz DIII	D3409	213	Moorslede	1935	OOC	CR/5 GP Comm
3s***	11 Aug	Alb. C	D8189	213	4m S E Dixmude	1940	DES	CR/5 GP Comm
4†	21 Aug	Fokker DVII	D8189	213	2m N W Zeebrugge	1915	DES	CR/5 GP Comm
5	25 Sep	Fokker DVII	D8189	213	4m W Thorout	1745	OOC	CR/ORB/?

TOTAL: 1 and 2 shared destroyed, 1 and 1 shared out of control = 5.
*Shared with Capt J.W. Pinder C65; this was Vzfw Triebswetter of Jasta 16 who was killed. **Shared with Capt J.W. Pinder C65. ***Shared with Lt A.H. Turner D9964, Lt C.P. Sparkes B7252, 2/Lt E. Toy D3409. †The pilot baled out, but the parachute did not work.

GREEN Charles Bremneri Lieutenant 47, 150

After service with the Canadian infantry, Green transferred to the RFC and joined 47 Squadron in Salonika where he flew SE 5As in early 1918, claiming one victory during April. He then transferred to the new 150 Squadron where during the spring and summer he claimed a further 10 victories, being awarded a DFC.

	1918		SE 5A					
1s*	13 Apr	Alb. DIII	B30	47	1500y S Brajkovic	0730	DES	CR/BG Summ
2s**	6 May	DFW. C	C1587	150	N Cerniste	0950	OOC	CR/BG Summ
3s***	10 May	Pfalz DIII	B688	150	N Livunovo	0800	DES	CR/BG Summ
4	1 Jun	Alb. DIII?	B695	150	Casandale	1507	OOC	CR/BG Summ
5	1 Jun	Alb. DIII?	B695	150	Casandale	1508	OOC	CR/BG Summ
6s†	12 Jun	Alb. DV	B695	150	S S E Parduvica	0800	DES	CR/BG Summ
7††	12 Jun	Alb. DV	B695	150	S S E Parduvica	0805	DES	CR/BG Summ
8	18 Jun	Alb. DV	B695	150	Smokvica	0830	OOC	CR/BG Summ
9†††	20 Jun	DFW. C	B695	150	Palmis	1015	DES(F)	CR/BG Summ
10s‡	28 Jun	DFW. C	B163	150	S W Furka	1200	DES	CR/BG Summ
11	18 Jul	Alb. DV	B163	150	Cernica	0850	OOC	CR/BG Summ

TOTAL: 2 and 4 shared destroyed, 4 and 1 shared out of control = 11.
*Shared with Capt G.G. Bell B692. **Shared with Lt W. Ridley C4963. ***Shared with Capt A.G. Goulding B28. †Shared with Lt G.C. Gardiner C1586. ††150 claimed 4 aircraft; one was Oblt K. Grashoff, the commander of Jasta 38, who was killed. †††The observer jumped out, this was Sgt Donthozarseff/Lt Todorpuchef of Bulgarian Flying Section 2, who were killed. ‡Shared with Lt B. Spackman B30.

GREEN James Hubert Ronald Sergeant 25

Sergeant Green served in 25 Squadron, flying FE 2Bs from the autumn of 1916 until summer 1917, claiming five victories. A former Air Mechanic, he had received Aero Certificate No 2841 on 28 April 1916.

	1916		FE 2					
1*	20 Oct	D	6990	25	E Lille	1515	DES	CR/RFC 20.10
2s**	17 Nov	EA	4877	25	Vitry	1930	DES	CR/RFC 17.11
3***	23 Nov	Alb. DII	7672	25	E Oppy	1545	OOC	CR/RFC 23.11
	1917							
4†	26 Apr	Alb. DIII	5247	25	Drocourt	1720	OOC	CR/RFC 26.4
5s††	6 Jun	Alb. DIII	A6365	25	Sallaumines	1205	OOC	CR/RFC 6.6

TOTAL: 1 and 1 shared destroyed, 2 and 1 shared out of control = 5.

*Observer: Cpl W.P. Gilbert. **Observer: Cpl A.G. Bower: shared with Capt R. Chadwick/Lt W.G. Meggitt 7022, 2/Lt H.L. Chadwick/2/Lt C.J. Butler 7025, 2/Lt D.S. Johnson/2/Lt I. Heald 6990, Lt C. Dunlop/2/Lt H. Scandrett 7024. ***Observer: Cpl A.G. Bower. †Observer: 2/Lt H.E. Freeman-Smith. ††Observer: Pte H. Else; shared with Capt C. Dunlop/2/Lt F. Cornish A6401, Lt D. Maclaurin/2/Lt E.C. Middleton A6500.

GREEN Wilfred Barrat Captain 32

Wilfred Green, a native of Stoke-on-Trent, served with 32 Squadron which he joined in November 1917. He flew during the spring and summer of 1918, becoming a flight commander in May. He also took part in many ground attack sorties. He was awarded a DFC after seven victories, which was gazetted in December 1918. He was also made a Chevalier of the Legion d'Honneur. His elder brother Tom was killed in action whilst serving with 3 Squadron in February 1917.

	1918		SE 5A					
1	2 Apr	Pfalz DIII	B8345	32	N E Moreuil	1500	OOC	CR/ORB/?
2	16 May	Pfalz DIII	C1093	32	Fresnes	1845	DES(F)	CR/RAF 16.5
3	15 Jul	Pfalz DIII	C1093	32	Dormans	1230	OOC	CR/ORB/?
4	16 Jul	Fokker DVII	C1836	32	Treloup	2015	OOC	CR/ORB/?
5	22 Jul	Fokker DVII	C1093	32	Mont Notre Dame	1805	OOC	CR/ORB/?
6	25 Jul	Fokker DVII	C1093	32	Fismes	1915	OOC	CR/ORB/?
7	23 Aug	Fokker DVII	C1097	32	Somain, E Douai	0730	DES	CR/ORB/?

TOTAL: 2 destroyed, 5 out of control = 7.

GREENE John Edmund Captain 13(N), 213

A Canadian from Winnipeg, born on 2 July 1894, John Greene joined the RNAS in 1916, and served with 13(N) Squadron, flying Camels, in 1917. On 4 December he attacked and drove down a balloon, seeing the observer bale out. He shared in shooting down a seaplane on 29 January 1918, and by the end of March had added two more victories. On 1 April, the day on which the RNAS became part of the RAF, and his squadron became 213, he destroyed a seaplane. During the ensuing summer and autumn he claimed a further 11 victories, the last on 14 October, on which day he was himself killed in action in D3409, shot down either by pilots of Jasta 43, who claimed three Camels on this date, or Jasta 63, who claimed one more; he crashed in the Belgian lines and was buried there. He had been awarded the DFC.

	1918		Camel					
1s*	29 Jan	Seaplane	B3909	13N	100y off Blankenberghe	1400	DES	DRO/RNAS 29.1
2s**	12 Mar	Rumpler C	B6407	13N	Ostend-Wenduyne	0905	DES(F)	CR/RNAS 12.3
3	24 Mar	Pfalz DIII	B3999	13N	E Middelkerke	1030	OOC	CR/DRO/?
4***	1 Apr	Seaplane	B3999	213	Zeebrugge	c1430	DES	CR/ORB/?
5	11 May	Alb. DV	D3357	213	4m N Westende	1445	DES	CR/5 GP Comm
6	11 May	Alb. DV	D3357	213	N Westende	1445	OOC	CR/5 GP Comm
7	12 Aug	Fokker DVII	D9659	213	4m S E Ypres	1215	OOC	CR/5 GP Comm
8	13 Aug	Pfalz DIII	D9659	213	3m W Ostend	1340	OOC	CR/5 GP Comm
9	25 Aug	Fokker DVII	E1406	213	10m S Ostend	0730	DES	CR/5 GP Comm
10	5 Sept	Fokker DVII	E1406	213	S Varsenaere a/d	1440	DES	CR/5 GP Comm
11	4 Oct	Fokker DVII	B7270	213	2m E Roulers	0930	DES	CR/5 GP Comm
12	4 Oct	Fokker DVII	B7270	213	N Iseghem	1555	DES(F)	CR/5 GP Comm
13†	4 Oct	Fokker DVII	B7270	213	N Iseghem	1555	OOC	CR/5 GP Comm
14	8 Oct	Fokker DVII	D3409	213	E Aertrycke	1205	DES	CR/5 GP Comm
15s††	14 Oct	Fokker DVII	D3409	213	Ardoye	1015	OOC	CR/5 GP Comm

TOTAL: 6 and 3 shared destroyed, 5 and 1 shared out of control = 15.

*Shared with F/Cdr L.H. Slatter B7186, FSL J.D. Paynter B3782, FSL G.C. Mackay B6407, FSL M.L. Cooper B6410. **Shared with FSL M.L. Cooper B6410, FSL G.C. Mackay B6400, FSL Bell B7226. ***213 claimed 3 seaplanes: Seeflug 1 lost 2; FlObMt M. Behrendt/Lt d R. Hauptvogel and Flgm Fricke/Lt Z S. Tornau were killed. †In this fight 213 claimed 3 Fokkers, Vzfw P. Podbiel of Jasta 40 was killed. ††Shared with 1/Lt K. MacLeish B7270.

GRENFELL Eustace Osborne Major 1, 60, 23

One of the famous names of the RFC, Eustace Grenfell transferred from the Duke of Cornwall's Light Infantry, and served with 1 Squadron in 1915, receiving an MC for an engagement on 17 January 1916. After a spell at the Central Flying School, he became a flight commander in 60 Squadron late in September 1916. He crashed on 11 December whilst circling over his last victim, and broke a leg. Later in the war he commanded 23 Squadron and post-war became a Group Captain, MC, DFC, AFC.

	1915		Morane					
1	13 Sep	Alb. C	----	1	Wytschaete-Menin	0740	DD	RFC 13.9
2	7 Dec	Alb. C	5069	1	Tournai-Lille	----	DD	FRC 7.12
	1916							
3	17 Jan	Fokker E	----	1	Houthoulst Forest	----	OOC	RFC 17.1
4	17 Jan	Fokker E	----	1	Houthoulst Forest	----	FTL	RFC 17.1
5	17 Jan	Alb. C	----	1	N E Houthoulst Forest	----	DD	RFC 17.1
6	17 Jan	Fokker E	----	1	N E Houthoulst Forest	----	DD	RFC 17.1
			Nieuport					
7	20 Oct	Alb. DI	A208	60	Rocquigny	1015	OOC	CR/RFC 20.10
8s*	11 Dec	Alb. CII	A278	60	Dainville	1030	CAPT	CR/RFC 11.12

TOTAL 1 shared captured, 2 out of control, 1 forced to land, 4 driven down = 8.
*Shared with Lt H. Meintjes, Lt A.P.V. Daly, Lt K.L. Caldwell, Lt A.D. Whitehead, Lt L.S. Weedon: Aircraft No. 174/16, pilot died of wounds, observer Lt Baldamus, was captured.

GRIBBEN Edward C. Captain 70, 44, 41,

Born on 11 September 1891 in Hollywood, County Down, Gribben was commissioned on 4 August 1914 in the Royal Irish Rifles; he became a Captain on 1 December. Later transferring to the RFC, he joined 70 Squadron in France in 1917, and flying Camels, he claimed at least five victories and received the MC. He returned to England on 9 September 1917 where he flew night fighter Camels with 44(HD) Squadron. During 1918 he became a test pilot at Farnborough with the rank of Captain. He was posted to 41 Squadron as a flight commander on 2 October 1918, but two days later was shot-up by a Fokker DVII while in F5494 and had to force-land, wounded in one arm.

	1917		Camel					
1	17 Jul	Alb. DV	----	70	S Gheluvelt	2055	OOC	CR/RFC 17.7
2	24 Jul	Alb. DIII	B3813	70	E Polygon Wood	2030	OOC	CR/RFC 24.7
3	10 Aug	Alb. DIII	B3840	70	Roulers-Menin	1945	DES	CR/RFC 10.8
4	10 Aug	Alb. DIII	B3840	70	Roulers-Menin	1945	OOC	CR/RFC 10.8
5	13 Aug	DFW. C	B3840	70	E Dixmude	1930	DES	CR/AIR 1/1226

TOTAL: 2 destroyed, 3 out of control = 5.

GRIFFITH John Sharpe Lieutenant 60

An American from Seattle, Washington born on 26 November 1898, John Griffith joined the RFC in 1917 and after training was posted to 60 Squadron in February 1918. He flew SE 5As with this unit, claiming seven enemy machines shot down. He received the DFC, but was wounded on 18 July when he made a force-landing near Boiry, Notre Dame, after being hit by anti-aircraft fire. He saw no further action. In 1919 he flew in North Russia with the RAF. During World War II he served with the USAAF. He died on 14 October 1974 in Riverhead, Long Island, at the age of 74.

	1918		SE 5A					
1	9 Mar	Alb. DV	C5385	60	N Menin	1110	OOC	CR/RFC 9.3
2	18 Mar	Alb. DV	C1069	60	Roulers	1250	OOC	CR/RFC 18.3
3s*	30 Mar	LVG. C	C1069	60	Becourt	1150	DES	CR/RFC 30.3
4s**	6 May	Alb. DV	D3503	60	Guillaucourt	1115	DES	CR/RAF 6.5
5s***	16 May	LVG. C	D3503	60	Fampoux	0845	DES	CR/RAF 16.5
6†	1 Jul	Alb. DV	D3503	60	Lamotte	0845	DES	CR/RAF 1.7
7	7 Jul	DFW. C	D5992	60	Achiet le Grand	1140	DES	CR/RAF 7.7

TOTAL: 2 and 3 shared destroyed, 2 out of control = 7.
*Shared with Lt W.J.A. Duncan C9536. **Shared with Lt W.J.A. Duncan B567. ***Shared with 2/Lt H.G. Hegarty B190. †This was Vzfw J. Schalk of Jasta 34, who was killed.

GRINNELL-MILNE Duncan Captain 16, 56

Commissioned in the Rifle Brigade (SR) in 1914, Duncan Grinnell-Milne was just 18 when war began. Considered too young for active service in France, he transferred to his brother's regiment, the 7th Royal Fusiliers. He then applied to join the RFC, and after training finally got to France as a pilot with 16 Squadron, flying Short horns and BEs. He flew many reconnaissance sorties and had several fights with enemy machines when air fighting was still in its infancy. His actions led to a victory on 28 November 1915 when he and his observer shot down a two-seater. A few months later he was hit and shot down, and taken prisoner. He spent two and a half years in a POW camp, but finally escaped and found his way back to England, where he received the MC. He eventually wangled his way back to France, joining 56 Squadron. During the last weeks of the war he did much air fighting and ground strafing, and was awarded the DFC and Bar, and promoted to Captain. He claimed five more victories during this period. After the war he remained in the RAF, going to 214 Squadron in Egypt in 1919, and 14 Squadron in 1920. He left the service in 1926 after being assistant Air Attache in Paris, and after flying over 2000 hours on some 60 types of machines. He served again during World War II, and in 1940 flew on several operations in Wellington bombers over Libya. After a short stay in Greece, he became medically unfit for the RAF, and joined the BBC until the end of 1946. He was also known for his writing, perhaps his most famous work being *Wind in the Wires*. He died in November 1973.

	1915		BE 2					
1*	28 Nov	Alb. C	----	16	Sequedin	----	DES	RFC 28.11
	1918		SE 5A					
2	5 Oct	Balloon	F5481	56	S W Busigny	1315	DES	CR/RAF 5.10
3	21 Oct	Fokker DVII	F863	56	N Bousies	1500	DES	CR/RAF 21.10
4	29 Oct	Fokker DVII	F863	56	Mormal Woods	1420	DES	CR/RAF 29.10
5	29 Oct	Fokker DVII	F863	56	S Bois de Levoque	1420	OOC	CR/Auto
6	3 Nov	Fokker DVII	C1149	56	N E Valenciennes	1200	DES	CR/RAF 3.11

TOTAL: 5 destroyed, 1 out of control = 6.
*Observer: Capt Strong.

GROOM Victor Emmanuel Captain 20

Born in London on 4 August 1898, he joined the Artists Rifles and was commissioned in the West Yorkshire Regiment in April 1917. He was then attached to the RFC and officially transferred in September. After training he went to 20 Squadron on 18 March 1918, flying Bristol Fighters. On one of his first patrols, the leader of his formation fired a white Very light which arced up into the sky, fell and landed in Groom's observer's cockpit, setting fire to a pouch containing flares and cartridges. The resulting fire was finally extinguished at the cost of burns to the observer's hands. Groom flew over 350 hours in France, undertaking many fighter reconnaissance patrols during which he and his observer, 2nd Lieutenant Ernest Hardcastle, claimed at least eight victories; both received DFCs. In September he returned home for a rest, went down with influenza, and did not return to operations. In 1919 he went to Egypt with 111 Squadron, then in 1920-21 served with 55 Squadron in Iraq, flying DH 9As. Here he received a Bar to his DFC for landing and picking up a downed crew while under fire from hostile natives. Continuing in the RAF, he reached the rank of Air Marshal, holding posts as AOC in C, Technical Training Command, and C in C, MEAF. For his services he was knighted Sir Victor Groom, KCVO, KBE, CB, DFC, Legion of Honour. He now lives in Putney, West London, since retiring in 1955. On Armistice Day 1987 he appeared in a BBC TV documentary concerning Manfred von Richthofen.

	1918		Bristol					
1*	8 May	Fokker DrI	----	20	N W Wervicq	1645	DES(F)	CR/RAF 8.5
2*	14 May	Alb. DV	C4764	20	3m E Zillebeke Lake	1845	DES	CR/RAF 14.5
3*	14 May	C	C4764	20	S W Polygon Wood	1850	DES	CR/RAF 14.5
4*	19 May	Alb. DV	----	20	S Calonne	1030	OOC	CR/11 WS
5*	1 Jun	Pfalz DIII	C4764	20	N W Comines	0630	DES	CR/RAF 1.6
6*	1 Jun	Pfalz DIII	C4764	20	N W Comines	0630	DES	CR/RAF 1.6
7*	30 Jul	Fokker DVII	D7939	20	Bailleul	1930	DES(F)	CR/RAF 30.7
8*	30 Jul	Fokker DVII	D7939	20	Bailleul	1930	DES(F)	CR/RAF 30.7

TOTAL: 7 destroyed, 1 out of control = 8.
*Observer: 2/Lt E. Hardcastle.

GROSVENOR Robert Arthur Captain 57, 84

The son of Lord Arthur and Lady Grosvenor of Broxton Hall, Chester, The Honourable 'Robin' Grosvenor was born on 25 May 1895 and was educated at Wellington School. Commissioned in the 2nd Dragoon Guards, he was awarded an MC during 1915, but late in 1916 he transferred to the RFC and flew as a pilot with 57 Squadron on FE 2Ds. Converting to single-seaters, he went to 84 Squadron in November 1917, eventually commanding 'A' Flight. He claimed 16 victories and was awarded a Bar to his MC before returning to England. World War II brought brief service back in the RAF, but he was invalided out in 1940; he died on 12 June 1953.

	1917		SE 5A					
1s*	6 Dec	C	----	84	Cambrai	1430	OOC	CR/RFC 6.12
	1918							
2	18 Feb	C	B527	84	5m E St Quentin	1105	OOC	CR/RFC 19.2

3	19 Feb	C	B527	84	St Gobain Wood	1015	DES	CR/RFC 19.2
4	19 Feb	Alb. DV	B527	84	St Gobain Wood	1020	OOC	CR/RFC 19.2
5s**	25 Mar	LVG. C	C1077	84	Flers	0930	DES(F)	CR/RFC 25.3
6	3 Apr	Pfalz DIII	B8408	84	Rosieres a/d	1150	DES	CR/RAF 3.4
7	3 Apr	Pfalz DIII	B8408	84	E Villers Brettonneaux	1151	DES	CR/RAF 3.4
8	10 Apr	Pfalz DIII	B8408	84	E Albert	1100	OOC	CR/RAF 10.4
9	12 Apr	Alb. DV	B8408	84	W Plessier	1805	DES	CR/RAF 12.4
10	12 Apr	Alb. DV	B8408	84	E Hangard Wood	1810	DES	CR/RAF 12.4
11	24 Apr	C	B8408	84	Villers Brettonneaux	1810	OOC	CR/RAF 24.4
12	25 Apr	Pfalz DIII	D8408	84	E Wiencourt	1700	DES	CR/RAF 25.4
13	25 Apr	Pfalz DIII	B8408	84	E Wiencourt	1700	OOC	CR/RAF 25.4
14***	25 Apr	Pfalz DIII	B8408	84	E Wiencourt	1700	OOC	CR/RAF 25.4
15	18 May	Alb. Dv	B8408	84	Chaulnes	1130	OOC	CR/RAF 18.5
16	18 May	C	B8408	84	N E Moreuil	1200	DES	CR/RAF 18.5

TOTAL: 7 and 1 shared destroyed, 7 and 1 shared out of control = 16.
*Shared with Lt J.S. Ralston C5310. **Shared with 2/Lt W.H. Brown C9267. ***84 made 8 claims, Oblt A. Dieterle (WIA), and Lt W. Meyer (KIA) of Jasta 34 were lost.

GURDON John Everard Captain 22

After leaving Tonbridge School in 1916, he joined the army, attending Sandhurst in September. He was later commissioned in the Suffolk Regiment and transferred to the RFC in May 1917. While he was training as a pilot with 67 Reserve Squadron, he had a bad crash due to a failure in his elevator controls, but recovered and finished his training at the CFS. In 1918 he went to 22 Squadron, flying Bristol Fighters. With this unit he received the DFC and Bar, claiming 28 enemy machines, at least 17 of them with the front gun. He was involved in the famous 'Two versus Twenty' fight on 7 May, he and John Thornton, his observer, claiming three of the eight victories (Atkey and Gass getting the other five). On 10 June he was badly shot-up, receiving a bullet through his arm, while his observer, 2nd Lt J.J. Scaramanga, was killed. In August whilst on patrol he suffered concussion from an extra-close 'Archie' burst. With this added to his recent wound, which had been troubling him, he became unfit for further operational flying. He returned home in September and relinquished his commission on 21 December 1918.

	1918		Bristol					
1*	2 Apr	Fokker DrI	B1162	22	W Vauvillers	1645	OOC	CR/RAF 2.4
2*	2 Apr	Fokker DrI	B1162	22	W Vauvillers	1645	OOC	CR/RAF 2.4
3*	7 May	D	B1253	22	E Arras	1845	DES(F)	CR/RAF 7.5
4*	7 May	D	B1253	22	E Arras	1845+	DES	CR/RAF 7.5
5*	7 May	D	B1253	22	E Arras	1850+	DES	CR/RAF 7.5
6**	8 May	DFW. C	B1253	22	Cuincy, N W Douai	1845	DES	CR/RAF 8.5
7*	9 May	D	B1164	22	S E Lille	0940	OOC	CR/RAF 9.5
8***	9 May	Pfalz DIII	B1162	22	N Douai	0840	OOC	CR/RAF 9.5
9***	9 May	Pfalz DIII	B1162	22	N Douai	0840	OOC	CR/RAF 9.5
10***	9 May	Pfalz DIII	B1162	22	N Douai	0840	DES	CR/RAF 9.5
11†	5 Jun	Alb. DV	A7243	22	S Laventie	1030	OOC	CR/SR/?
12†	5 Jun	Pfalz DIII	A7243	22	N E La Bassee	1915	DES(F)	CR/RAF 5.6
13††	19 Jun	Fokker DVII	C989	22	S E Armentieres	2020	DES	CR/RAF 19.6
14††	19 Jun	Fokker DVII	C989	22	S E Armentieres	2020	DES	CR/RAF 19.6
15†††	23 Jun	Fokker DVII	C989	22	E La Bassee	2015	OOC	CR/SR/?
16†††	23 Jun	Fokker DVII	C989	22	E La Bassee	2015	OOC	CR/SR/?
17††	27 Jun	Fokker DrI	C989	22	S E Armentieres	1850	OOC	CR/SR/?
18††	1 Jul	Pfalz DIII	C989	22	Armentieres	1940	OOC	CR/SR/?
19††	4 Jul	Fokker DVII	C989	22	Noyelles, N Seclin	1920	DES	CR/RAF 4.7
20††	9 Jul	DFW. C	C989	22	N La Bassee	1100	DES	CR/SR/?
21††	10 Jul	Pfalz DIII	C989	22	Armentieres-Lille	0930	DES(F)	CR/RAF 10.7
22††	10 Jul	Pfalz DIII	C989	22	Armentieres-Lille	0930	OOC	CR/RAF 10.7
23††	10 Jul	Pfalz DIII	C989	22	Armentieres-Lille	0930	OOC	CR/RAF 10.7
24‡	8 Aug	Alb. DV	E2454	22	Douai	1030	OOC	CR/SR/?
25s‡‡	8 Aug	Pfalz DIII	E2454	22	N E Vitry	1040	DES(F)	CR/RAF 8.8
26‡	10 Aug	Fokker DVII	E2454	22	S W Peronne	1810	DES	CR/RAF 8.8
27‡	10 Aug	Fokker DVII	E2454	22	S W Peronne	1810	DES	CR/RAF 8.8
28‡	13 Aug	Fokker DVII	E2454	22	Auberchicourt	1120	OOC	CR/SR/?

TOTAL: 13 and 1 shared destroyed, 14 out of control = 28.
*Observer: 2/Lt A.J.H. Thornton. **Observer: 2/Lt C.G. Gass. ***Observer: 2/Lt A.V. Bollins. †Observer: Sgt J.H. Hall. ††Observer: 2/Lt J.J. Scaramanga. †††Observer: 2/Lt J. McDonald. ‡Observer: Lt C.G. Gass. ‡‡Observer: Lt C.G. Gass; shared with Capt W.F.J. Harvey/Capt D.E. Waight E2466.

HACKWILL George Henry Captain 22, 44, 54

Transferring to the RFC in 1915 after service in the Somerset Light Infantry, Hackwill flew as an FE 2B pilot with 22 Squadron in 1916, undertaking many varied sorties during which he and his observers accounted for at least two enemy machines. He returned to Home Establishment as an instructor in 1917, and later that year became a flight commander with 44 (Home Defence) Squadron, sharing in the destruction of a night raider in January 1918. In March he returned to France as a flight commander with 54 Squadron and brought his score to nine victories, receiving an MC. On 30 October he destroyed an LVG on the ground with bombs during an airfield strafe; this is not included in his score.

	1916		FE 2B					
1*	21 Jul	Roland C	5214	22	W Beaulencourt	2000	DES	CR/RFC 21.7
2**	20 Oct	Alb. DI	4849	22	Grevillers	0930	OOC	CR/RFC 20.10
	1918		Camel					
3s***	25 Jan	Gotha GV	B2402	44	Wickford	2210	CAPT	Cole & Cheeseman
4	25 Apr	LVG. C	D6517	54	S E Bailleul	0730	OOC	CR/RAF 25.4
5	4 Jul	Hannover C	D6479	54	Harbonnieres	1430	OOC	CR/?
6	5 Jul	Pfalz DIII	D6479	54	Chuignolles	1045	OOC	CR/?
7	25 Jul	Fokker DVII	D9573	54	S Bazoches	1915	DES	CR/RAF 25.7
8s†	7 Sep	Halb. C	F2144	54	N E Marquion	1910	DES	CR/RAF 7.9
9	15 Sep	Fokker DVII	F2144	54	Ferin	1840	OOC	CR/?

TOTAL: 1 shared captured, 2 and 1 shared destroyed, 5 out of control = 9.
*Observer: 2/Lt W.B. Parsons; probably Lt Otto Parschau of AKN who was killed. **Observer: 1 AM Edwards. ***Shared with Lt C.C. Banks B3827; this was Gotha GV 938/16, flown by Uffz Karl Ziegler, Lt Friedrich von Thomsen, Uffz Walter Heiden, who were killed. †Shared with Lt M.G. Burger E5175, Lt J.C. MacLennan F1962, Lt Vandyk F2063, Lt Berrington F2129, Lt Fuller F5932.

HAINES Alfred John Lieutenant 45

Haines served in 45 Squadron, flying Sopwith Camels in Italy in 1918, where he claimed victories over six enemy aircraft and was awarded the DFC. On 20 March, 45 got into a fight with some machines which turned out to be Italian rather than hostile, but Haines got a bullet through his flying helmet from one of these. He was killed in action on 10 August 1918; flying at 10,000 feet, he received a direct hit by anti-aircraft fire over the Asiago Plateau and crashed in 'No Man's Land'. His body was brought to the British lines under a white flag, by arrangement with the Austro-Hungarian Army.

	1918		Camel					
1	4 Feb	Alb. DV	B5182	45	Susegana	1115	DES	CR/7 BG
2	7 Jun	Alb. DIII	D1975	45	Arsiera	0742	DES(F)	CR/14 W
3	7 Jun	Alb. DIII	D1975	45	Arsiera	0742	DES(F)	CR/14 W
4	23 Jul	Aviatik C	D9412	45	Grigno-Rutzu	0715	DES	ORB/14 W
5	29 Jul	Phonix D	D9412	45	Pratta	0900	DES	ORB/14 W
6	29 Jul	Phonix D	D9412	45	Pordenone	0900	DES	ORB/14 W

TOTAL: 6 destroyed = 6.

HALE Frank Lucien Captain 32, 85

Born on 6 August 1895, Frank Hale was an American from Arkansas. Commissioned in September 1917, he was attached to the RAF, serving with 32 Squadron. While with this unit he claimed seven Fokker DVIIs shot down during the summer of 1918, and was awarded a DFC, gazetted on 9 February 1919. He also served briefly with 85 Squadron without scoring, and was promoted to Captain. His score is frequently listed as 18, but this related to an incorrect obituary notice. He remained in the RAF until 1922, serving in 79 Squadron during 1919. During World War II he did some flying with the US 8th Air Force, but retired from this service in 1943 with a heart condition, dying at his home in Buffalo on 7 June 1944.

	1918		SE 5A					
1	25 Aug	Fokker DVII	E4026	32	Hancourt	1900	DES	CR/RAF 25.8
2	4 Sep	Fokker DVII	E4026	32	N Cambrai	0945	DES(F)	CR/RAF 4.9
3	4 Sep	Fokker DVII	E4026	32	S E Arras	0950	OOC	CR/IX Brig
4	16 Sep	Fokker DVII	E4026	32	Brunemont	1810	DES	CR/RAF 16.9
5	27 Sep	Fokker DVII	E4026	32	Cambrai	1720	DES	CR/RAF 27.9
6	27 Sep	Fokker DVII	E4026	32	Cambrai	1720	OOC	CR/RAF 27.9
7	27 Sep	Fokker DVII	E4026	32	Cambrai	1720	OOC	CR/RAF 27.9

TOTAL: 4 destroyed and 3 out of control = 7.

HALES John Playford Captain 9(N), 203

A Canadian from Guelph, Ontario, born on 11 September 1893, 'Jack' Hales was commissioned as a Flight Sub Lieutenant on 12 October 1916, serving with 9(N) Squadron during the summer and autumn of 1917. He was promoted Flight Lieutenant on 30 December 1917 and Captain on 1 April 1918, the day of the formation of the RAF. He joined 203 Squadron in July 1918, but was killed on 23 August when his Camel, D9671, was hit by anti-aircraft fire and spun in near Bray.

	1917		Camel					
1	23 Sep	Alb. DIII	B3832	9N	Ostend-Dixmude	0815	DES	CR/RFC 23.9
2s*	28 Sep	Alb. DIII	B3832	9N	Dixmude	1610	DES	CR/RFC 28.9
3	15 Oct	Alb. DV	B3832	9N	Middelkerke	1215	OOC	CR/DOS/?
4s**	23 Nov	Alb. DV	B3832	9N	S Dixmude	1220	OOC	CR/RNAS 23.11
	1918							
5	11 Aug	Fokker DVII	D9671	203	E Bray	1930	OOC	CR/Rochford

TOTAL: 1 and 1 shared destroyed, 2 and 1 shared out of control = 5.
*Shared with F/Cdr S.T. Edwards B6217, FSL F. Banbury B6230, FSL O.M. Redgate B3818, FSL M.S. Taylor B5652.
**Shared with F/Cdr F.E. Banbury B6330.

HALL Frederick Vincent Lieutenant 4(N), 8(N), 10(N), 210

Born on 20 March 1898 in Muswell Hill, North London, and educated at Highgate School, Hall was commissioned as a Flight Sub Lieutenant on 2 July 1916. Initially he joined 4(N) Squadron on 26 April 1917, but was posted to 8 Naval on 5 May after he had achieved one victory. He was shot down and wounded by scouts of Jasta 7 or 11 on 23 or 24 May (dates differ). On recovery in October, he joined 10(N) Squadron, claiming six further victories by mid May 1918. On 15th of that month Lieutenant Magnus Kelly's Camel was struck by anti-aircraft fire and collided with Hall's aircraft, which crashed, killing the pilot.

	1917		Pup					
1s*	2 May	C	N5196	4N	Dunkirk	1720	CAPT	CR/RNAS 2.5
			Camel					
2	15 Nov	Alb. DV	B6320	10N	N N E Dixmude	1300	OOC	CR/RFC 15.11
3s**	5 Dec	Alb. DV	B6320	10N	Keyem-Leke	1535	DES	CR/RNAS 5.12
	1918							
4	18 Feb	Alb. DV	B6351	10N	S Menin	0950	DES	CR/RNAS 18.2
5	8 May	Pfalz DIII	B6351	210	Bac St Maur	1055	DES	CR/RAF 7.5
6s***	9 May	Alb. C	C62	210	1m N Aubers	1615	DES	CR/RAF 9.5
7	14 May	Pfalz DIII	D3385	210	Ypres-Zillebeke	2015	OOC	CR/ORB/?

TOTAL: 1 shared captured, 2 and 2 shared destroyed, 2 out of control = 7.
*Shared with F/Cdr J.D. Newberry N6462. **Shared with F/Lt W.A. Curtis B5663. ***Shared with Capt A.W. Carter D3364, Capt E.S. Arnold B7227.

HALL Robert Norwood Captain 40, 44

A South African, Hall joined the Royal Field Artillery, later seeing service with the RFC. He was posted to 40 Squadron early in 1917, claiming five victories by mid August, when he was transferred to Home Establishment. Here he served with 44 (Home Defence) Squadron until at least May 1918.

	1917		Nieup					
1	24 Apr	C	----	40	3m E Lens	----	OOC	Citation
2	7 May	Balloon	B1542	40	Quiery la Motte	0935	DES	CR/RFC 7.5
3s*	7 May	Balloon	B1542	40	Quiery la Motte	0935	DES	CR/RFC 7.5
4s*	7 May	Balloon	B1542	40	Quiery la Motte	0935	DES	CR/RFC 7.5
5	15 Aug	Alb. DV	A6733	40	Lens	1250	DES	CR/RFC 15.8

TOTAL: 1 and 2 shared balloons, 1 destroyed, 1 out of control = 5.
*Shared with Lt C.W. Cudemore A6794.

HALLONQUIST Joseph Eskel Captain 28

Formerly a chief clerk in a British Columbia bank in Canada, Joe Hallonquist joined the 19th Reserve Battalion, Canadian Expeditionary Force, before transferring to the RFC. After training with 26 and 73 Training Depot Squadrons, he was posted to 28 Squadron in Italy on 23 January 1918, with the rank of Honorary Captain. It was said of him that he was one of 28's stoutest fighters; he claimed five victories and was awarded the DFC and the Italian Bronze Medal for Military Valour. On 29 October he was shot down by anti-aircraft fire and was taken prisoner, but survived his brief captivity to return to Canada after the war.

	1918		Camel					
1	17 Apr	Alb. DIII	B2362	28	Fontanelle	1330	DES	CR/7 BG
2*	26 May	Alb. DV	B1952	28	1km E Fontanelle	0845	DES	CR/14 W

3	15 Jun	Alb. DIII	B6363	28	Feltre	0800	DES	CR/14 W
4	30 Jun	Alb. DIII	B6363	28	Campolongo	0815	DES	CR/14 W
5s**	13 Jul	Brand. C	B6363	28	Pordenone	0725	DES	CR/14 W
****	28 Jul	Alb. DV	D8244	28	Villaga	0800	OOC	CR/ORB/

TOTAL: 4 and 1 shared destroyed = 5.
*Zgsf Ferdinand Udvardy, of Flik 42j, crash landed. **Shared with Lt J. Mackereth B6344, Lt A.R. Strang D8209. ***This was disallowed by Wing.

HAMERSLEY Harold Alan Captain 60

Born in Guildford, Western Australia, on 6 February 1896, he was commissioned in the AIF and served at Gallipoli in 1915. He transferred to the RFC, and in September 1917 was posted to 60 Squadron. On 23 September he nearly became the 49th victory of Werner Voss; in the early stages of the famous fight in which Voss was killed, Alan Hamersley's SE 5 was hit and damaged by the German's fire. He was promoted to Captain, received an MC, and claimed 13 enemy machines shot down before returning to England in May 1918. In 1920-22 he again flew with 60 Squadron, this time in India, and then for a time was test pilot at Avro's; he held an altitude record in a machine powered by an Austin Seven engine. He became a Squadron Leader in March 1935, and in July went to Worthy Down for engineering duties. In 1938 he was CO of the University of London Air Squadron, and 1940 commanded RAF Hullavington; he later became President of the Aircrew Selection Board in Scotland. He retired from the RAF and died in December 1967.

	1917		SE 5A					
1	16 Sep	Alb. DIII	A8934	60	S Houthem	1835	DES	CR/RFC 16.9
2s*	22 Sep	Alb. DIII	B539	60	S E Zonnebeke	1045	OOC	CR/RFC 22.9
3	21 Oct	Alb. DV	B523	60	Poelcapelle	1305	OOC	CR/RFC 21.10
4	5 Nov	Alb. DV	B626	60	1m N Westroosebeke	1210	DES	CR/RFC 5.11
5	8 Nov	Alb. DV	B4887	60	Westroosebeke	1540	DES	CR/RFC 8.11
6s**	18 Nov	DFW. C	B4887	60	N E Westroosebeke	1105	DES	CR/RFC 18.11
	1918							
7	25 Jan	Alb. DV	C5321	60	N E Staden	----	DES	CR/RFC 25.11
8	18 Feb	Fokker DrI	B4887	60	N Hadzaeme	1240	DES	CR/RFC 18.2
9	9 Mar	Pfalz DIII	B4887	60	Dadizeele	1135	DES	CR/RFC 9.3
10	18 Mar	Alb. DV	C5385	60	Rumbeke	1250	DES	CR/RFC 18.3
11	30 Mar	LVG. C	C5385	60	Mametz Wood	1035	DES	CR/ORB/?
12	30 Mar	Alb. DV	C5385	60	Fricourt	1115	OOC	CR/RFC 30.3
13	30 Mar	Alb. DV	C5385	60	Hem	1115	DES	CR/RFC 30.3

TOTAL: 9 and 1 shared destroyed, 2 and 1 shared out of control = 13.
*Shared with Capt R.L. Chidlaw-Roberts A8932. **Shared with Capt R.L. Chidlaw-Roberts B536.

HAMILTON Herbert James Captain 1, 29

A Londoner, born in 1895, Hamilton transferred to the RFC from the Duke of Cornwall's Light Infantry in early 1916. After a period as an instructor during which he amassed some 500 hours' flying, he joined 1 Squadron at the front in August 1917, flying Nieuport Scouts. He claimed one victory on 2 October, and was then posted to 29 Squadron as a flight commander. After two more victories in Nieuports, he was posted back to 1 Squadron in early March 1918, by which time the unit had converted to SE 5As. During the month he destroyed a balloon and shared in victories over two aircraft to bring his score to six, as well as taking part in many ground attack sorties. On 26 March while flying B32, his SE 5A, he was forced to land by a Fokker Triplane. He was awarded an MC, gazetted on 26 July 1918, by which time he had returned to Home Establishment; here he was killed in a flying accident on 13 June 1918 in Yorkshire.

	1917		Nieuport					
1s*	2 Oct	DFW. C	B6774	1	Comines	1105	OOC	CR/RFC 2.10
2s**	5 Dec	Alb. DV	B3631	29	E Staden	1545	OOC	CR/ORB/?
	1918							
3	16 Feb	C	B3631	29	Moorslede	1026	OOC	CR/RFC 16.2
			SE 5A					
4s***	9 Mar	Balloon	B32	1	Lomme	1435	DES	CR/RFC 9.3
5†	11 Mar	C	B32	1	Ypres	1810	OOC	CR/RFC 11.3
6s††	13 Mar	Pfalz DIII	B32	1	Wieltje	1220	OOC	CR/RFC 13.3

TOTAL: 1 balloon, 1 and 4 shared out of control = 6.
*Shared with 2/Lt G.B. Moore B1508. **Shared with 2/Lt F.J. Williams B6826. ***Shared with Lt J.C. Bateman A8930, 2/Lt A. McN. Denovan B511, 2/Lt I.O. Chantler B4851, 2/Lt E.E. Owen A8932, 2/Lt F.J. Chown B597. †Shared with 2/Lt P.J. Clayson A8908. ††Shared with Capt W.D. Patrick B641, Capt G.B. Moore B511, Lt H.A. Rigby C9624, Lt A. Hollis B520, 2/Lt L.W. Mawbey B632, 2/Lt A.E. Sweeting A8932, 2/Lt W.M.R. Gray A8904.

HAMILTON Leslie Lieutenant 17, 150

He served in 17 Squadron in Salonika in early 1918, flying SE 5As and shared in one victory in April. The scouts from his squadron were then amalgamated with those from 47 Squadron to form 150 Squadron. By early September he had brought his score to five, all of them shared, and he was then awarded a DFC, gazetted on 8 February 1919. On 18 September he claimed one of the first Fokker DVIIs to be identified in the area to bring his final score to six. He was lost in an Atlantic record attempt in 1927, with Colonel F.F. Minchin.

	1918		SE 5A					
1s*	21 Apr	DFW. CV	B694	17	Barakli-Dzuma	1115	OOC	CR/BG Summ
2s**	4 May	DFW. C	B691	150	Marian a/d	1040	CAPT	CR/BG Summ
3s***	15 Jun	Alb. DV	B28	150	Dragotin	0930	OOC	CR/BG Summ
4s†	23 Jun	Alb. DV	B28	150	Hill 5401; Rupel Pass	0745	DES	CR/BG Summ
5s††	4 Sep	C	----	150	N Karusu bridge	1055	DES	CR/BG Summ
6	18 Sep	Fokker DVII	B692	150	Karali	0700	OOC	CR/BG Summ

TOTAL: 1 shared captured, 2 shared destroyed, 1 and 2 shared out of control = 6.
*Shared with Lt A.G. Goulding B690. **Shared with Capt G.E. Gibbs B694; the crew were killed. **Shared with Capt Walmsley/Lt W. Williamson in AW Fk No 3351 of 47. †Shared with Capt G.G. Bell B692. ††Shared with Lt F.D. Travers C6176.

HAMILTON Lloyd Andrews 1st Lieutenant 3, 17US

Born in Troy, New York, on 13 June 1894, the son of the Reverend J.A. Hamilton of Vermont, Lloyd Hamilton attended Harvard University in 1916. In May 1917 he joined the regular US Army and trained as an officer at Plettsburgh, New York. He was transferred to the Massachusetts Institute of Technology, and completed his training in the United Kingdom as a pilot in the US Air Service. Commissioned on 3 March 1918, he was posted to 3 Squadron, RFC, under an arrangement with the British Government to gain experience flying Camels in combat. He first claimed on 11 April, when he shared in the destruction of an LVG two-seater. He was credited with four further victories with 3 Squadron, but in July he returned to the USAS to become a flight commander with the 17th Aero Squadron, which he helped to train, also on Camels. This unit then served in the British 65th Wing on the Western Front, and in early August he began adding to his score. He led a bombing attack on a German airfield on 13th, setting five aircraft on fire on the ground. On 24th of the month he and another pilot shot down a balloon, his tenth victory, but he was hit by machine gun fire from the ground and fatally wounded, crashing near Lagnicourt. He was awarded the American DSC.

	1918		Camel					
1s*	11 Apr	LVG. C	----	3	Ervillers	1600	DES(F)	CR/RAF 11.4
2**	12 Apr	Alb. DV	D6519	3	Ovillers	1200	DES(F)	CR/RAF 12.4
3s***	18 May	Alb. C	D6519	3	57C S17	0800	OOC	CR/RAF 18.5
4s†	27 May	Alb. C	----	3	57D R32	1240	OOC	CR/?
5	3 Jun	Alb. DV	C1631	3	Adinfer Wood	2030	OOC	CR/?
6	7 Aug	Fokker DVII	D9399	17US	Armentieres	1120	DES	CR/RAF 7.8
7s††	14 Aug	Fokker DVII	D1940	17US	S W Bruges	1130	DES	CR/RAF 14.8
8	21 Aug	Fokker DVII	D1940	17US	Beugny-Beaumetz	1255	DES(F)	CR/RAF 21.8
9s†††	21 Aug	Balloon	D1940	17US	57C H17	1845	DES	CR/RAF 21.8
10s‡	24 Aug	Balloon	D1940	17US	Lagnicourt	1415	DES	CR/RAF 24.8

TOTAL: 2 shared balloons, 3 and 2 shared destroyed, 1 and 2 shared out of control = 10.
*Shared with Capt D.J. Bell, Lt C.E. Mayer, Lt A.W. Franklyn. **This was probably Lt Lupp of Jasta 46. ***Shared with 1/Lt W.D. Tipton, Lt Macklin. †Shared with Capt D.J. Bell, Lt W. Hubbard. ††Shared with 2/Lt R.M. Todd D9513, 1/Lt J.F. Campbell D9399 and Lt G.F. Baker/Cpl H. Lindsay B7679, Lt W.D. Gairdner/2/Lt H.M. Moodie B7603 of 211 Sqn in DH 9's. †††Shared with 2/Lt R.M. Todd D9513. ‡Shared with 1/Lt J.F. Campbell D6513.

HAMMERSLEY Reuben Lieutenant 24

Joining the RFC in May 1917, Hammersley served with 24 Squadron during the first half of 1918, claiming eight victories and receiving a French Croix de Guerre.

	1918		SE 5A					
1s*	19 Feb	Rumpler C	B891	24	Servais	0840	DES(F)	CR/RFC 19.2
2s*	19 Feb	DFW. C	B891	24	Bernot	0850	DES	CR/RFC 19.2
3	26 Feb	Alb. DV	B8257	24	E Laon	1605	OOC	CR/RFC 26.2
4	6 Mar	DFW. C	B8257	24	E St Quentin	1635	OOC	CR/SR/ORB/?
5	23 Mar	Alb. DV	C9267	24	St Simon	1600	OOC	CR/RFC W D
6	12 Apr	Alb. DV	C1082	24	Hangard-Moreuil	1615	DES	CR/RAF 12.4
7s**	19 May	Pfalz DIII	C1085	24	Proyart	1200	OOC	CR/SR/ORB/?
8	20 May	Pfalz DIII	C1085	24	Chaulnes-Albert	0835	OOC	CR/SR/ORB/?

TOTAL: 1 and 2 shared destroyed, 4 and 1 shared out of control = 8.
*Shared with Lt A.K. Cowper B664, 2/Lt P.A. MacDougall B120, Lt R.T. Mark B67. **Shared with 2/Lt E.B. Wilson C1600.

HAND Earl McNabb Captain 45

A Canadian who served with 45 Squadron in France and Italy, 1917-18, he was known as 'Handie', and claimed seven victories of which five were confirmed. Leading a three-man patrol on 1 June 1918 he was close to the lines when Lieutenant O'Neill had to return with engine trouble. Hand, whose Captaincy had come through that very day, carried on with Lieutenant Huins; when they sighted an Austrian aircraft, both dived down and Hand engaged it in a tight circle. The Austrian machine was black with a large 'L' on the top centre section, and was flown by the ace Oberleutnant Frank Linke-Crawford. Hand's Camel was hit in the petrol tank and went down in flames, but he was not killed, although he was badly burned; he crashed and was taken prisoner. Lieutenant Huins — later Wing Commander T.P. Huins, OBE, AFC, MD — engaged the Austrian and held a collision course, both pilots opening fire. Linke-Crawford was the first to break off, diving under the Camel, down to ground level. Huins' machine was hit in the engine, struts and leading edge of the starboard lower wing, and could not follow. In 1919 Hand's actions were rewarded by the DFC; he returned to England from Italy in 1919, and then went home to Canada. He helped to form the Toronto Flying Club, and became a magistrate in that city.

	1917		Camel					
1	15 Nov	Alb. DV	B2430	45	Poelcapelle	0940	OOC	CR/RFC 15.11
	1918							
	11 Jan	Alb. DIII	B6238	45	Vittorio	1145	OOC	CR/?
*	11 Jan	Alb. DIII	B6238	45	Vittorio	1145	OOC	CR/?
2	30 Jan	DFW. C	B4609	45	Ormelie	1050	DES	CR/7 BG
3	23 Apr	Alb. DIII	B2430	45	N Levico	0900	DES	CR/7 BG
4	2 May	Alb. DIII	B2430	45	Mt Chiesa	1035	DES	CR/7 BG
5	9 May	Alb. DIII	B2430	45	Vazzolo	1040	DES	CR/14 W

TOTAL: 4 destroyed, 1 out of control = 5.
*Although claimed as out of control, these claims were disallowed by both Wing and Brigade.

HARDMAN James Donald Innes Captain 19

Born in Yorkshire on 21 December 1899, he joined the Artists Rifles on leaving school, and then the RFC in early 1917. He was commissioned in May 1917 but was too young to go to France until February 1918, when he was posted to 19 Squadron which was just converting from Spads to Dolphins. He claimed nine victories, becoming a flight commander later in the year. On 30 October he led 12 Dolphins as an escort to DH 4s of 98 Squadron; several German scouts were claimed shot down during a big dogfight with JG III in which four or five British bombers were also lost, and only three of the Dolphins managed to get back to base. After the war Hardman went back to Oxford University, then returned to the RAF in 1921, becoming a Squadron Leader in 1936. He retired in January 1958 as Air Chief Marshal Sir Donald Hardman, GBE, KCB, DFC, and died on 2 March 1982. Post World War II he commanded the RAAF on exchange from the RAF.

	1918		Dolphin					
1	9 May	Alb. C	C3818	19	Plouvain	1030	OOC	CR/RAF 9.5
2s*	16 May	C	C3818	19	Bucquoy	1110	OOC	CR/RAF 16.5
3s**	31 May	Pfalz DIII	C3818	19	Armentieres	0750	OOC	CR/ORB/?
4	25 Jun	Pfalz DIII	C3818	19	Comines	0715	OOC	CR/ORB/?
5s***	1 Jul	LVG. C	C3818	19	W Steenwerck	1430	DES(F)	CR/RAF 1.7
6s†	16 Sep	Fokker DVII	D3769	19	N Lille	0940	OOC	ORB/?
7	27 Oct	Fokker DVII	D5237	19	Quaroble	1150	DES(F)	ORB/RAF 27.10
8	30 Oct	Fokker DVII	D5237	19	Mons	1130	DES(F)	CR/RAF 30.10
9	30 Oct	Fokker DVII	D5237	19	Mons	1130	DES(F)	CR/RAF 30.10

TOTAL: 3 and 1 shared destroyed, 2 and 3 shared out of control = 9.
*Shared with Major A.D. Carter C4017. **Shared with Lt L.H. Ray C4129. ***Shared with Capt G.B. Irving C3996, Lt J.A. Aldridge C3883. †Shared with Capt C.V. Gardner C3818.

HARLOCK Frederick George Lieutenant 20

Harlock, from Stamford, Lincolnshire, served with 20 Squadron during the summer and autumn of 1918. Born on 27 November 1897, he was a motor driver before the war, and had married. He joined the RASC in August 1916, transferring to a Welsh infantry regiment until July 1917, when he joined the RFC. His final victory was claimed on 3 October 1918 over a Fokker DVII, to bring his score to eight. In June 1919 he was posted to 88 Squadron, after prior service with 57 Squadron.

	1918		Bristol					
1*	17 Jul	Fokker DVII	----	20	N Tourcoing	1850	OOC	CR/?
2**	13 Aug	Fokker DVII	C4718	20	Quesnoy	1915	DES	CR/RAF 13.8
3**	20 Sep	Fokker DVII	E2258	20	Mesnil	1000	DES	CR/RAF 20.9
4**	20 Sep	Fokker DVII	E2258	20	Mesnil	1015	DES(F)	CR/RAF 20.9

5**	25 Sep	Fokker DVII	E2340	20	Magny	1820	DES	CR/RAF 25.9
6**	25 Sep	Fokker DVII	E2340	20	Lehaucourt	1820	DES	CR/RAF 25.9
7**	27 Sep	Fokker DVII	E2338	20	N E Marcy	1030	DES	CR/RAF 27.9
8***	3 Oct	Fokker DVII	E2338	20	Mericourt	1005	DES	CR/RAF 3.10

TOTAL: 7 destroyed, 1 out of control = 8.
*Observer: Pbr A.S. Draisey. **Observer: 2/Lt A.S. Draisey. ***Observer: Lt J.F. Kidd.

HARRIES Thomas Montagu Lieutenant 45, 24

Harries flew as a Corporal observer with 45 Squadron for six months from April 1917, claiming six victories whilst flying in Sopwith 1½ Strutters. Trained as a pilot after the unit was re-equipped with Camels, he was posted to 24 Squadron as a Lieutenant where during the summer of 1918 he claimed a further five victories, three of them shared. He was awarded a DFC, gazetted on 8 February 1919.

	1917		Strutter					
1*	9 May	Alb. DIII	A963	45	W Menin	1755	DES(F)	CR/RFC 9.5
2**	12 May	Alb. C	A963	45	2m E Armentieres	1030	CAPT	CR/RFC 12.5
3***	3 Jun	Alb. DIII	----	45	S E Quesnoy	1815	DES	CR/RFC 3.6
4†	7 Jul	Alb. DV	----	45	1m N Wervicq	1700	DES(F)	CR/RFC 7.7
5†	7 Jul	Alb. DV	----	45	Wervicq	1700	OOC	CR/RFC 7.7
6†	7 Jul	Alb. DV	----	45	Wervicq	1700	OOC	CR/RFC 7.7
	1918		SE 5A					
7	8 Aug	LVG. C	C8844	24	Meharicourt	1945	DES	CR/RAF 8.8
8s††	10 Aug	Fokker DVII	C8844	24	N E Rosieres	0750	OOC	CR/SR/ORB/?
9	19 Aug	Fokker DVII	E6006	24	Fresnoy	1130	OOC	CR/SR/ORB/?
10s†††	30 Aug	Alb. C	E6006	24	Bus	0630	DES	CR/RAF 30.8
11s‡	29 Oct	C	F5459	24	Bois l'Evegne	1500	DES	CR/RAF 29.10

TOTAL: 1 captured, 4 and 2 shared destroyed, 3 and 1 shared out of control = 11.
*Pilot: 2/Lt J. Johnstone. **Pilot: 2/Lt J. Johnstone. The crew were Lt A. Hauboldt/Lt Mohr of FA 18. **Pilot 2/Lt R.S. Watt. †Pilot: Sgt Yeomans. ††Shared with Capt W. Selwyn C8840, Lt W.C. Lambert B8395, 2/Lt H.L. Bair C1945. †††Shared with Lt H.D. Barton C8840, 2/Lt H.L. Bair B8505. ‡Shared with Capt W.H. Longton F5508, Lt H.V. Evans F5791.

HARRIS Arthur Travers Major 70, 51, 45, 44

Born in Cheltenham on 13 April 1892, Arthur Harris spent his early life in Africa. On the outbreak of war he served as a bugler in West Africa with the 1st Rhodesian Regiment. In 1915 he joined the RFC and spent some months in various Home Defence squadrons, being involved in the destruction of the first Zeppelin to be shot down over England, by Leefe Robinson. In 1917 he joined 45 Squadron as a flight commander in France, flying 1½ Strutters and later, Camels; for a time he was acting CO. He claimed five enemy machines, three while flying Strutters and two whilst on Camels. In 1918 he returned to England to command 44(Home Defence) Squadron and was awarded an AFC. He remained in the RAF, rising to high rank, and during World War II was famous as 'Butch' or 'Bomber' Harris, AOC in C of Bomber Command from 1942-1945. He retired as Marshal of the Royal Air Force Sir Arthur Harris, GCB, OBE, AFC, LL D, and died on 6 April 1984.

	1917		Strutter					
1*	5 Jul	Alb. DV	----	45	W Ypres	1720	OOC	CR/RFC 5.7
2*	7 Jul	Alb. DIII	----	45	N W Comines	1315	DES	CR/RFC 7.7
3*	12 Jul	Alb. C	----	45	Kortewilde	1500	OOC	CR/RFC 12.7
			Camel					
4	27 Aug	Alb. DV	B3875	45	Moorslede	1215	OOC	CR/RFC 27.8
5	3 Sep	Alb. DV	----	45	Ledeghem-Dadizeele	1500	DES(F)	CR/RFC 3.9

TOTAL: 2 destroyed, 3 out of control = 5.
*Observer: 2/Lt P.F. Webb.

HARRISON Thomas Sinclair Captain 29

Born on 8 January 1898 and from King William Town, South Africa, Harrison was an ex-artilleryman who had served in German East Africa in 1916-17. Joining the RFC in April 1917, he finally reached the front in May 1918 when he joined 29 Squadron to fly SE 5As. He claimed his first victory, a Halberstadt two-seater in flames, on 27 June, followed by six more claims during July, and a further five in August. These successes gained him the award of a DFC during July. After one victory during September, he claimed six more in October while during November, the month in which he became a flight commander, he added three more to bring his total to 22. A Bar to his DFC was gazetted on 3 December; he also received the Belgian Croix de Guerre.

	1918		SE 5A					
1	27 Jun	Halb. C	C8859	29	E Estaires	0925	DES(F)	CR/RAF 27.6
2	1 Jul	Hannover C	C8859	29	N E Bailleul	0915	DES	CR/RAF 1.7

3	4 Jul	LVG. C	D3915	29	E Neuf Berquin	1250	DES(F)	CR/RAF 4.7
4	4 Jul	Pfalz DIII	D3915	29	W Estaires	1255	DES	CR/RAF 4.7
5	8 Jul	LVG. C	C8859	29	N E Neuf Berquin	1910	OOC	CR/ORB/11 WS
6	13 Jul	Balloon	C8859	29	E Bailleul	0515	DES	CR/RAF 13.7
7	22 Jul	Halb. C	E5947	29	La Gorgue	0910	DES(F)	CR/RAF 22.7
8	9 Aug	Halb. C	E5947	29	E Merville	1830	DES	CR/RAF 9.8
9	12 Aug	Balloon	E5947	29	E Estaires	0930	DES	CR/RAF 12.8
10	13 Aug	Hannover C	E5947	29	Merville	0845	DES	CR/RAF 13.8
11s*	16 Aug	Halb. C	E5947	29	E Steenwerck	1220	DES	CR/RAF 16.8
12	16 Aug	Halb. C	E5947	29	Estaires-Laventie	1235	DES(F)	CR/RAF 16.8
13	6 Sep	Fokker DVII	E5947	29	S E Armentieres	1840	OOC	CR/ORB/11 WS
14	2 Oct	Fokker DVII	B8507	29	W Roulers	1520	DES	CR/RAF 2.10
15	4 Oct	Fokker DVII	B8507	29	E Comines	0920	OOC	CR/ORB/11 WS
16	7 Oct	LVG. C	B8507	29	Staden-Roulers	0845	DES	CR/RAF 7.10
17s**	7 Oct	LVG. C	B8507	29	Staden-Roulers	0850	DES	CR/RAF 7.10
18	14 Oct	Fokker DVII	C9071	29	W Roulers	0855	OOC	CR/ORB/11 WS
19	27 Oct	Fokker DVII	E5999	29	S E Renaix	0950	DES	CR/RAF 27.10
20	1 Nov	Hannover C	C9071	29	Tournai	1215	OOC	CR/ORB/11 WS
21	4 Nov	DFW. C	F5642	29	E Mont St Auber	1045	DES	CR/RAF 4.11
22	10 Nov	Fokker DVII	C9071	29	Moorleghen	1345	DES	CR/RAF 10.11

TOTAL: 2 balloons, 13 and 2 shared destroyed, 5 out of control = 22.
*Shared with Lt R.G. Robertson D6874. **Shared with Capt C.H.R. Lagesse E4084.

HARRISON William Leeming Captain 40, 1

Harrison, a Canadian from Toronto, born in 1898, first served with the Canterbury Mounted Rifles, transferring to the RFC in May 1917. After training, this pilot joined 'C' Flight of 40 Squadron in France in summer 1917. Flying Nieuport Scouts, he claimed two victories. By the new year the squadron was flying SE 5As and in these he quickly built up his score. In April he was promoted to the rank of Captain and posted to command a flight in 1 Squadron, claiming one victory with this unit before being wounded in action. His MC was gazetted in May 1918, followed later by a Bar. He died in 1960.

	1917		Nieuport					
1	9 Aug	Balloon	A6774	40	Arras area	c0945	DES	CR/ORB/OH/?
	1918		SE 5A					
2	19 Jan	DFW. C	B22	40	E N E Arras	1205	DES	CR/RFC 19.1
3	26 Feb	Alb. DV	C1071	40	N Arras-Cambrai Rd	0945	OOC	CR/I BG WD
4	6 Mar	Alb. DV	C1071	40	N E La Bassee	1200	OOC	CR/RFC 6.3
5	6 Mar	Alb. DV	C1071	40	N W Lens	1625	DES	CR/RFC 6.3
6	9 Mar	Alb. DV	C1071	40	Esquerchin	1215	OOC	CR/RFC 9.3
7	11 Mar	C	B4863	40	W La Bassee	1135	DES	CR/RFC 11.3
8	18 Mar	C	C1071	40	Courcelles	1025	DES(F)	CR/RFC 18.3
9	24 Mar	Alb. C	B196	40	St Leger	1025	DES	CR/RFC 24.3
10	26 Mar	Alb. DV	B189	40	Authuille	1740	OOC	CR/RFC 26.3
11	1 Apr	C	D3526	40	W Izel les Esquerchin	1220	DES	CR/RAF 1.4
12	11 Apr	Pfalz DIII	C6405	1	S Armentieres	1900	DES	CR/RAF 12.4

TOTAL: 1 balloon, 7 destroyed, 4 out of control = 12.

HARTLEY Herbert Henry Lieutenant 48

Lieutenant Hartley joined 48 Squadron during the summer of 1917, and claimed his first victory on 15 September. His second followed at the end of October, but he did not claim again until February 1918. On 8 March he drove down two Albatros scouts out of control, while his gunner destroyed a third. His seventh and final victory over a Fokker Triplane was claimed on 11 March. Four of these claims were gained with the front gun, two with the rear, and one was a joint effort. He was killed in action on 14 March, shot through the heart, but his gunner successfully took over the controls and managed to land the aircraft.

	1917		Bristol					
1*	15 Sep	Alb. DV	A7213	48	E Dixmude	1850	DES	CR/RFC 15.9
2s**	29 Oct	Alb. DIII	A7254	48	N E Dixmude	1620	DES(F)	CR/RFC 19.1
	1918							
3***	9 Feb	Alb. DIII	C4628	48	S Guise	1200	OOC	CR/RFC 9.2
4†	8 Mar	Alb. DV	A7114	48	Busigny	1050	OOC	CR/RFC 8.3
5†	8 Mar	Alb. DV	A7114	48	Busigny	1050	OOC	CR/RFC 8.3
6†	8 Mar	Alb. DV	A7114	48	S Bohain	1600	DES	CR/RFC 9.3
7†	11 Mar	Fokker DrI	A7114	48	St Quentin	1255	OOC	CR/RFC 11.3

TOTAL: 3 destroyed, 4 out of control = 7.
*Observer: 2/Lt E.C. Birch. **Observer: 2/Lt E.C. Birch; shared with 2/Lt L.A. Payne/2/Lt V. Bourdillon. ***Observer: Lt R.S. Herring. †Observer: Lt J.H. Robertson.

HARTNEY Harold Evans Lieutenant Colonel 20, 27US, 1PG

Born at Pakeham, Ontario, on 19 April 1888, he served as a Lieutenant in the Saskatoon 105th Fusiliers of the Canadian Militia, after attending Toronto University. He was mobilized in October 1914 after taking up law studies, and was married before being sent to England in May 1915; in October he transferred to the RFC. He was posted to 20 Squadron, flying FE 2Ds in 1916. On 14 February 1917 he was badly shot up by enemy scouts from Jasta 18, and was wounded, although his gunner claimed two of their attackers shot down. After recovery in England he transferred to the US Air Service in September 1917 as a Major, and was posted to the States to take command of the 27th Aero Squadron, to prepare it for the front. Early in 1918 he led this unit to France via England, where it went into action in June, first with Nieuport 28s, later with Spad XIIIs. On 25 June he claimed a two-seater, his seventh victory in air combat. On 21 August he became Commander, 1st Pursuit Group, with the rank of Lieutenant Colonel. In October a night fighter unit was assigned to the Group (the 185th Aero Squadron), and on the night of 22 October Hartney went up in one of the unit's Camels and encountered a Gotha, which he hit and drove down; during the combat he inadvertently knocked off his petrol switch which caused his engine to stop, and he was not able to follow his victim down; thus he was not able to claim a victory. After the war he returned to the USA to the Chief of Air Staff's Office. He left the service in 1921, taking part in air racing and helped to form the National Aeronautical Association. In 1923 he became an American citizen, and later wrote his autobiography, *Up and at'Em*, together with three other books; he died in 1947.

	1916		FE 2D					
1*	1 Jul	Fokker E	A3	20	Lille-Tourcoing	0555	OOC	CR/11 WS
2*	1 Jul	Fokker E	A3	20	Lille-Tourcoing	0555	OOC	CR/11 WS
3**	20 Oct	Fokker D?	A30	20	Lille	0830	OOC	CR/11 WS
	1917							
4***	2 Feb	Halb. DII	A1960	20	Lille	1415	DES	CR/RFC 4.2
5**	14 Feb	Alb. DII	A1960	20	Passchendaele	1700	DES	Hartney
6†	14 Feb	Alb. DII	A1960	20	Passchendaele	1700	OOC	Hartney
	1918		Nieup. 28					
7s††	25 Jun	C	----	27US	Lorry	1840	OOC	C&CUS 24/2

TOTAL: 2 destroyed, 4 and 1 shared out of control = 7.

*Observer: 2AM A. Stanley. **Observer: 2/Lt W. Jourdan. ***Observer: 2/Lt H.R. Wilkinson. †Observer: Lt W. Jourdan. There is no combat report on this fight as Hartney was shot down and wounded. ††Shared with 2/Lt J.K. McArthur: possibly Vzfw Muhlhausen of FA 12, who was wounded.

HARVEY William Frederick James Captain 22

Born on 8 January 1897, Harvey served with the Signal Company of the Royal Engineers(TA) until he transferred to the RFC in December 1916. In December 1917 he was posted as a pilot to 22 Squadron, flying Bristol Fighters. In 1918 he was promoted to Captain and took command of 'B' Flight, he and his observers accounting for no less than 26 aircraft and balloons, 18 with the front gun, eight with the rear. Harvey was awarded the RAF's first DFC and a Bar to this. After the war he served as an instructor with 33 TD Squadron of the Army of the Rhine, before leaving the service to become a farmer. During World War II he again served his country, becoming an MBE for his work. After the war he retired to Kent where he wrote many magazine articles for *Air Pictorial*, and the history of his old squadron — No 22 — under the title *Pi in the Sky*. In 1969 he became the President of the British Section of Cross & Cockade, but died on 21 July 1972.

	1918		Bristol					
1*	16 Mar	Pfalz DIII	A7161	22	Beaumont	1100	OOC	CR/RFC 16.3
2**	18 Mar	Alb. DV	C4808	22	Carvin	1030	DES(F)	CR/RFC 18.3
3***	24 Mar	Alb. DV	A7286	22	S E Arras	1315	DES	CR/RFC 24.3
4***	24 Mar	Alb. DV	A7286	22	S E Arras	1315	OOC	CR/RFC 24.3
5***	25 Mar	Alb. DV	A7286	22	St Ledger	0825	DES	CR/RFC 25.3
6***	30 Mar	Balloon	C4894	22	N E Albert	----	DES	CR/RFC 30.3
7†	20 May	Balloon	B1209	22	Bailleul	1700	DES	CR/RAF 20.5
8†	20 May	Balloon	B1209	22	Bailleul	1700	DES	CR/RAF 20.5
9†	22 May	DFW. C	C776	22	Merville-Estaires	1925	OOC	CR/?
10†	26 May	Pfalz DIII	C842	22	Armentieres-Lille	1945	OOC	CR/?
11†	28 May	C	C4631	22	La Bassee	1100	DES	CR/RAF 28.5
12†	28 May	C	C4631	22	La Bassee	1105	DES	CR/RAF 28.5
13†	10 Jul	Fokker DRI	C1040	22	S E Lille	0915	DES	CR/RAF 10.7
14†	10 Jul	Fokker DRI	C1040	22	S E Lille	0920	DES	CR/RAF 10.7
15†	20 Jul	Fokker DVII	C989	22	S Lille	0900	DES	CR/RAF 20.7
16†	20 Jul	Fokker DVII	C989	22	S Lille	0915	DES	CR/RAF 20.7
17†	20 Jul	Fokker DVII	C989	22	S Lille	0930	OOC	CR/RAF 20.7
18††	8 Aug	Pfalz DIII	E2466	22	N E Vitry	1040	DES	CR/RAF 8.8

19s†††	8 Aug	Pfalz DIII	E2466	22	N E Vitry	1040	DES	CR/RAF 8.8
20††	11 Aug	Fokker DVII	E2466	22	S E Armentieres	1955	OOC	CR/?
21††	13 Aug	Rumpler C	E2466	22	2m N W Cambrai	1100	DES	CR/RAF 13.8
22††	13 Aug	Pfalz DIII	E2466	22	2m N W Cambrai	1101	OOC	CR/?
23††	14 Aug	C	E2466	22	S W Lille	1050	OOC	CR/?
24††	16 Aug	Pfalz DIII	E2466	22	S S E Lille	1045	DES	CR/RAF 16.8
25††	21 Aug	C	E2466	22	Ervillers	1410	OOC	CR/?
26s‡	22 Aug	Halb. C	E2466	22	N E Bailleul	1910	DES	CR/RAF 22.8

TOTAL: 3 balloons, 12 and 2 shared destroyed, 9 out of control = 26.
*Observer: Sgt A. Burton. **Observer: 2/Lt J.L. Morgan. ***Observer: 2/Lt H.F. Moore. †Observer: Lt G. Thomson. ††Observer: Capt D.E. Waight. †††Observer: Capt D.E. Waight; shared with Capt J.E. Gurdon/2/Lt C.G. Gass E2454. ‡Observer: Capt D.E. Waight; shared with Lt I.O. Stead/2/Lt W.A. Cowie, Lt H.H. Beddow/Lt T.J. Birmingham.

HAWKER Lanoe George Major 6, 24

Son of a distinguished military family, Hawker was born on 30 December 1890, and joined the Royal Engineers as an officer cadet on completion of his education. Always a clever inventor, and keen on anything mechanical, he transferred to the RFC before the outbreak of war, already having qualified as a pilot privately at Hendon. He was posted to France with 6 Squadron in October 1914, flying Henry Farmans. The squadron later converted to BE 2Cs and he undertook much reconnaissance work, together with a lone bombing attack on some Zeppelin sheds, receiving the DSO for these operations. During 1915 the squadron began receiving a few scouting aircraft, and some FE 2 two-seater pushers. Hawker designed a special mounting for a Lewis gun to be fitted to a Bristol Scout, so that it could fire forward and outward at an angle, missing the propeller arc. He had frequently attempted without success to attack enemy aircraft with rifle and revolver fire, but now, with this new armament, he can be said to have become the first true fighting scout pilot of the RFC. Following an initial victory in June, he made three flights in a Bristol Scout on 25 July 1915, during which he claimed two enemy aircraft, one in flames and one forced to land; for this feat he was awarded a Victoria Cross. He continued attacking the enemy either in his Bristol, or in an FE, supplementing the observer's Lewis gun fire with his own Lee-Enfield rifle in the latter, and claimed at least three more victories in August, two of these on 11th.

He was posted to England in late 1915, by which time he was credited with at least seven victories; this made him the first British ace and a figure of considerable fame in the RFC. In England he was given the task of forming the first single-seat fighting scout squadron, No 24, with the new DH 2 pusher scouts, and in February 1916, promoted to Major, he led this unit to France, where it quickly made its presence felt. As Commanding Officer he did not get much chance to fly himself, and did not add to his victories. As the year wore on, the Germans introduced new tractor scouts to the front, and the early superiority of the DH 2s was lost. Flying with his squadron whenever he could in order to encourage the pilots, he became involved in a dogfight with an Albatros DII flown by Freiherr Manfred von Richthofen on 23 November 1916. This classic combat was one of the longest on record as each pilot used all his skill to try and outmanoeuvre the other. Finally, short of fuel, Hawker was forced to try and run for home, whereupon he was shot down and killed, becoming Richthofen's 11th victim.

	1915		Bristol Scout					
1*	21 Jun	DFW. C	1609	6	Poelcapelle	----	OOC	
2**	25 Jul	Alb. C	1611	6	Passchendaele	c1845	FTL	RFC 25.7
3***	25 Jul	Alb. C	1611	6	S E Zillebeke	1900	CAPT	RFC 25.7
			FE 2B					
4†	2 Aug	C	4227	6	Wulverghem	----	FTL	RFC 2.8
5††	11 Aug	Aviatik C	4227	6	Houthem	1545	DES	Hawker VC
6†††	11 Aug	Fokker E	4227	6	Lille-Roubaix	1915	DES	Hawker VC
			Bristol Scout					
7	7 Sep	Biplane	1611	6	Bixschoote	----	DES	RFC 7.9

TOTAL: 1 Captured, 3 destroyed, 1 out of control, 2 FTL = 7.
*Noted as 'brought down' in Air 1/758/204/4/119 "Combats in the Air: Summary of Results". **This aircraft was from FA 3. ***Oblt A. Ubelacker ?/ Hptm Roser, both KIA. †Observer: Lt Payze. ††Observer: Lt N. Clifton. 12 Div. reported it destroyed. †††Observer: Lt N. Clifton. 8 Div reported it probably destroyed. Hawker; in a letter dated 16.8.15 says this was number 5 since 25.7.
NB: The *Combats in the Air: Summary of Results* notes all 7 of these claims, as at this early stage of the war 'forced to land' claims were counted. Other Air Forces, such as the Austro Hungarians and the Americans still did until the end of the war. There is a pencilled 'No' written on the 2 and 11 August claims. The origin and meaning of this is not known. Without doubt, Hawker was the first British Commonwealth ace.

HAY Hugh Allport Captain 11

Hay joined 11 Squadron early in 1918 as a Lieutenant already with an MC following service in the Royal Warwickshire Regiment, and by late summer had three victories to his credit. He was promoted to flight commander at the end of August and made two further claims on 6 September to bring his score to five.

	1918		Bristol					
1*	7 Apr	Alb. C	C4861	11	Grevillers	1205	OOC	CR/RAF 7.4
2*	4 May	Pfalz DIII	C4861	11	Marquion	1840	DES(F)	CR/RAF 4.5
3**	11 Aug	Alb. DV	E4276	11	S Peronne	1910	DES(F)	CR/RAF 11.8
4***	6 Sep	Fokker DVII	C937	11	W Cambrai	1030	DES	CR/RAF 6.9
5***	6 Sep	Fokker DVII	C937	11	W Cambrai	1030	OOC	CR/RAF 6.9

TOTAL: 3 destroyed, 2 out of control = 5.
*Observer: Sgt P.A. Sherlock. **Observer: 2/Lt E.J. Norris. ***Obsrver: Lt A.H. Craig.

HAY Roger Bolton Lieutenant 48

Hay served with 48 Squadron from its formation, receiving an MC for four victories in late May 1917. The precise shares he achieved in these is uncertain, but the details listed below are believed to be substantially correct. On 17 July 1917, Hay was shot down in A7166 north-east of Nieuport by Vizefeldwebel Werner of Jasta 17, and was killed; his observer, 2nd Lieutenant O.J. Partington, survived as a prisoner of war.

	1917		Bristol					
1s*	23 Apr	Alb. DIII	----	48	Vimy	----	OOC	SR/RFC 23.4
2s**	24 Apr	Alb. DIII	---	48	Cagnicourt	----	OOC	SR/RFC 24.4
3s***	27 Apr	C	----	48	Vitry	----	DES	SR/RFC 27.4
4†	15 Jun	Alb. DIII	A7146	48	Etaing	1940	DES	CR/RFC 15.6
5	12 Jul	Alb. DIII	A7152	48	Ghistelles	1845	OOC	CR/RFC 12.7

TOTAL: 1 and 1 shared destroyed, 1 and 2 shared out of control = 5.
*Observer: ?, shared with Lt F.P. Holliday/Capt A.H.W. Wall, Lt W.O.B. Winkler/2/Lt E.S. Moore. **Observer: ?, shared with Lt F.P. Holliday/Capt A.H.W. Wall, Lt W.O.B. Winkler/2/Lt E.S. Moore. ***Observer: ?, shared with Lt W.T. Price/Lt M.A. Benjamin. †Observer: Lt V.W.G. Nutkins.

HAYNE Edwin Tufnell Captain 3(N), 203

Born in South Africa on 28 May 1895, he joined the RNAS, becoming a Flight Sub Lieutenant on 5 July 1916. He joined 'A' Flight of 3 Naval Squadron in 1917, receiving the DSC in November 1917 and the DFC in September 1918; altogether he claimed 15 victories. He had several indecisive combats, and after his final victory on 16 June 1918, reported no less than 15 further indecisive engagements before he returned to Home Establishment on 16 July. On 16 August 1917 he had attacked a German aerodrome, strafing and putting out of action several aircraft. He was flying low for over two hours, also attacking transport, troops and railways until all his ammunition was expended. He was later killed in a flying accident at Castle Bromwich in a Bristol Fighter.

	1917		Camel					
1	22 Aug	Alb. DV	B3895	3N	S Middelkerke	1550	OOC	CR/RNAS 22.8
2s*	10 Sep	DFW. CV	B3895	3N	Furnes	1800	CAPT	CR/RNAS 10.9
	1918							
3	18 Mar	Alb. DV	B7231	3N	Haboudin-Seclin	1105	OOC	CR/RFC 18.3
4s**	18 Mar	DFW. C	B7231	3N	1m E Henin-Lietard	1240	DES	CR/RFC 18.3
5s***	21 Mar	Alb. C	B7231	3N	4m E Bapaume	1645	DES(F)	CR/RFC 21.3
6s†	24 Mar	Alb. DV	B7231	3N	Vaux	1655	OOC	CR/RFC 24.3
7	3 May	Fokker DrI	D3376	203	Neuve Eglise Armentieres	1140	OOC	CR/RAF 3.5
8	3 May	Fokker DrI	D3376	203	Neuve Eglise Armentieres	1140	OOC	CR/?
9s††	15 May	LVG. C	D3376	203	Salome	1145	DES	CR/RAF 15.5
10	17 May	DFW. C	D3376	203	Steenwerck	1150	DES	CR/RAF 17.5
11s†††	18 May	Pfalz DIII	D3376	203	Neuf Berquin	0750	OOC	CR/RAF 18.5
12	18 May	Pfalz DIII	D3376	203	Merville-Estaires	1040	DES(F)	CR/RAF 18.5
13	19 May	Pfalz DIII	D3376	203	E Merville	1035	DES	CR/RAF 19.5
14	30 May	Alb. DV	D3376	203	Fournes-en-Weppes	1810	OOC	CR/?
15‡	16 Jun	DFW. C	D3417	203	Estaires	0610	DES	CR/?

TOTAL: 1 shared captured, 3 and 4 shared destroyed, 5 and 2 shared out of control = 15
*Shared with F/Cdr R.F. Redpath B3785, FSL G.S. Harrower B3782, FSL H.F. Beamish N6377, FSL G.B. Anderson B3895. **Shared with FSL R.C. Berlyn B7197. ***Shared with F/Cdr L.H. Rochford B7203, FSL O.P. Adam B3798, FSL J.A. Glen B7185, FSL K.D. Macleod B7222, FSL W.H. Chisam B7223, FL A.B. Ellwood E7229, FSL C.S. Devereux B7228, FSL L.A. Sands B7216, FSL R.C. Berlyn B7224. †Shared with F/Cdr F.C. Armstrong B7218, FSL S. Smith B7274, FSL R.C. Berlyn B7274, FSL L.D. Bawlf B7192, F/Cdr A.T. Whealy B7220, FL E. Pierce B7227, FSL F.J.S. Britnell B7229. ††Shared with Capt H.F. Beamish B3855, 1/Lt W.W. Goodnow B7198, Lt A.N. Webster B3788, Lt J.D. Breakey B3384, Lt H.W. Skinner B7123. †††Shared with Capt R.A. Little B7220. ‡Shared with Lt C.F. Brown D9535, Lt R. Stone D3371, Lt Y. Kirkpatrick D3414, Lt W. Sidebottom B7185.

HAZELL Tom Falcon Major 1, 24, 203

Tom Hazell, from County Galway, Ireland, left Tonbridge School in 1911; he joined the army on the outbreak of war, becoming a 2nd Lieutenant in the 7th Battalion, Royal Inniskilling Fusiliers, in October 1914. He served in France until June 1916, when he transferred to the RFC. Surviving a bad crash in Kent on 30 June, he eventually joined 1 Squadron in France later that year. Serving with this unit, he became a flight commander and received the MC, claiming 20 enemy aircraft. Returning home, he served as an instructor at the CFS until he took command of 'A' Flight of 24 Squadron in June 1918, adding a further 23 victories to his score, including ten kite balloons. Then in October 1918 he took command of 203 Squadron until the Armistice. He was awarded the DSO, DFC and Bar, and granted a Permanent Commission in the RAF in August 1919. On one occasion he was injured in a crash which left him paralysed down one side of his face and body, but he later recovered to fly again. He died in 1946.

	1917		Nieuport					
1	4 Mar	HA	A6604	1	Westhoek	1610	OOC	CR/RFC WD
2	24 Apr	Alb. C	A6738	1	Bois Grenier	1200	DES(F)	CR/RFC 24.4
3	9 May	Alb. C	B1632	1	Houthem	0740	OOC	CR/RFC 9.5
4	4 Jun	Alb. DIII	B1649	1	E Hollebeke	0700	DES	CR/RFC 4.6
5	4 Jun	Alb. DIII	B1649	1	E Hollebeke	0702	DES	CR/RFC 4.6
6	5 Jun	Alb. DIII	B1649	1	E Ypres	0630	DES	CR/RFC 5.6
7	5 Jun	C	B1649	1	Houthem	0900	DES	CR/RFC 6.6
8	8 Jun	Alb. DIII	B1649	1	1m E Becelaere	0640	OOC	CR/RFC 8.6
9	9 Jun	Alb. DIII	B1649	1	Zandvoorde	2000	OOC	CR/RFC 9.6
10	12 Jul	Alb. DIII	B3455	1	Menin	2020	OOC	CR/RFC 12.7
11s*	12 Jul	Alb. DIII	B3455	1	Dadizeele	2030	OOC	CR/RFC 12.7
12	22 Jul	DFW. C	B3455	1	Houthem-Amerika Farm	0820	DES	CR/RFC 22.7
13	22 Jul	Alb. DV	B3455	1	Wervicq	1900	DES	CR/RFC 23.7
14	22 Jul	Alb. DV	B3455	1	Houthem	1920	DES	CR/RFC 23.7
15	10 Aug	Alb. DV	B3455	1	Bousbecque	1420	OOC	CR/RFC 10.8
16	13 Aug	Rumpler C	B3455	1	Becelaere	0710	DES	CR/RFC 13.8
17s**	13 Aug	Alb. C	B3455	1	Houthem	0920	OOC	CR/RFC 13.8
18***	14 Aug	Alb. DV	B3455	1	S Moorslede	1910	DES(F)	CR/RFC 15.8
19	14 Aug	Alb. DV	B3455	1	S Moorslede	1915	OOC	CR/RFC 15.8
20	16 Aug	Alb. DV	B3455	1	Houthoulst	1945	OOC	CR/RFC 17.8
	1918		SE 5A					
21	4 Jul	Fokker DVII	D3444	24	Cerisy	0850	OOC	CR/ORB/?
22	17 Jul	Balloon	E1388	24	Ovillers	1005	DES	CR/RAF 17.7
23	22 Jul	Balloon	E1388	24	S Harbonnieres	0650	DES	CR/ORB/Cit/?
24s†	22 Jul	Balloon	E1388	24	Proyart	0730	DES	CR/RAF 22.7
25	26 Jul	Balloon	E1388	24	Harbonnieres	0715	DES	CR/RAF 26.7
26s††	31 Jul	Hannover C	E1388	24	Caix	1100	DES	CR/RAF 31.7
27†††	1 Aug	Alb. C	E1388	24	Meaulte	1040	DES(F)	CR/RAF 1.8
28	8 Aug	Fokker DVII	E1388	24	Lihon	1850	OOC	CR/ORB/SR/?
29	8 Aug	Fokker DVII	E1388	24	Lihon	1900	DES	CR/RAF 8.8
30	8 Aug	DFW. C	E1388	24	Rosieres	1910	CAPT	CR/RAF 8.8
31s‡	10 Aug	Hannover C.	B8423	24	Meharicourt	1350	OOC	CR/ORB/SR/?
32	10 Aug	Fokker DVII	B8423	24	Foucaucourt	1400	DES(F)	CR/ORB/SR/?
33‡‡	14 Aug	Fokker DVII	B8422	24	Nesle	0800	OOC	CR/ORB/SR/?
34	18 Aug	Rumpler C	B8422	24	Cappy	1940	DES(F)	CR/RAF 18.8
35s‡‡‡	21 Aug	Balloon	B8422	24	Meharicourt	1210	DES	CR/ORB/SR/?
36	21 Aug	Balloon	B8422	24	Meharicourt	1220	DES	CR/RAF 22.8
37	22 Aug	Balloon	B8422	24	Meharicourt	1220	DES	CR/RAF 22.8
38	4 Sep	Balloon	E1269	24	Bernes	1040	DES	CR/RAF 4.9
39	4 Sep	Balloon	E1269	24	Gouzeaucourt	1045	DES	CR/RAF 4.9
40	8 Sep	Fokker DVII	E1269	24	Le Catelet	0815	DES	CR/RAF 8.9
41	2 Oct	Balloon	F5450	24	La Fere	1045	DES	CR/SR/?
42	4 Oct	Fokker DVII	F5450	24	E Beaurevoir	1140	DES	CR/RAF 4.10
43	4 Oct	Fokker DVII	F5450	24	E Beaurevoir	1150	DES	CR/RAF 4.10

TOTAL: 1 captured, 8 and 2 shared balloons, 17 and 1 shared destroyed, 11 and 3 shared out of control = 43.
*Shared with Lt R.E. Money-Kyle B3484. **Shared with 2/Lt H.G. Reeves B1672. ***This was Lt Hubner of Jasta 4, who was killed. †Shared with 2/Lt G.B. Foster D6918. ††Shared with 1/Lt G.B. Foster D6918, 2/Lt E.P. Crossen E1392. †††The observer jumped, or fell out. ‡Shared with 2/Lt J.A. Southey C1813. ‡‡This aircraft was possible Lt H. Kroll of Jasta 24, who was wounded. ‡‡‡Shared with 2/Lt J.A. Southey C1813.

HEADLAM Eustace S. Lieutenant 1 AFC

Born on 26 May 1892, Headlam was an Australian who flew Bristol Fighters in Palestine with 1 AFC Squadron. He claimed victories over five aircraft and drove down a sixth.

	1918		Bristol					
1*	5 Mar	Alb. DIII	A7198	1AFC	5m S E Jiljulieh	1000	OOC	CR/40 WWD
2**	27 Mar	AEG. C	----	1AFC	Amman	0745	FTL/DES	CR/40 WWD
3	27 Mar	AEG. C	----	1AFC	Amman	0745	FTL/DES	CR/40 WWD
4s***	22 Sep	C	B1286	1AFC	Mafrak, E Deraa	1000	DES	CR/40 WWD
5s†	19 Oct	DFW. C	B1295	1AFC	25m S W Aleppo	1030	DES	CR/40 WWD

TOTAL: 2 and 2 shared destroyed, 1 out of control = 5.

*Observer: Lt E.B.S. Beaton. **Observer: Lt W.A. Kirk. ***Observer: Lt W.H. Lilly; shared with Capt R.M. Smith/Lt E.A. Mustard B1229. †Observer: Lt W.H. Lilly; shared with Capt R.M. Smith/Lt A.V. McCann B1229.

HEGARTY Herbert George Captain 60

Posted to 60 Squadron in November 1917, he flew with this unit until July 1918. During this period he accounted for at least eight hostile aircraft and received an MC. He was promoted to Captain, becoming a flight commander.

	1918		SE 5A					
1	28 Jan	Alb. DV	B626	60	Kortemarck	1320	OOC	CR/RFC 28.1
2s*	4 Feb	Alb. DV	B626	60	Zonnebeke	1125	DES(F)	CR/RFC 4.2
3	18 Feb	Alb. DV	C9536	60	Staden	1230	OOC	CR/SR/?
4	30 Mar	Alb. DV	C5381	60	Treux, S Albert	1110	DES	CR/RFC 30.3
5	14 May	Alb. C	B190	60	Moreuil	0730	DES	CR/RAF 14.5
6s**	16 May	LVG. C	B190	60	Fampoux	0845	DES	CR/RAF 16.5
7	30 Jun	Alb. DV	D5992	60	Rainecourt	0510	DES	CR/SR/?
8	1 Jul	Halb. C	D5992	60	Bray	0840	DES	CR/RAF 1.7

TOTAL 4 and 2 shared destroyed, 2 out of control = 8.

*Shared with Lt H.D. Crompton B545. **Shared with 2/Lt J.S. Griffith D3503.

HEMMING Alfred Stewart Captain 41

A South African, Hemming joined 41 Squadron on 24 November 1917 and flew SE 5As, receiving the DFC and being credited with eight victories. He was promoted to Captain in July, but was hospitalized on 29 August 1918.

	1918		SE 5A					
1s	9 Jan	Rumpler C	B639	41	Marcoing	1145	DES	CR/RFC 9.1
2	21 Mar	Alb. DV	B8267	41	Bourlon Wood area	1345	OOC	CR/SR/?
3	24 Mar	Fokker DrI	B8235	41	Vaulx	0845	DES	CR/RFC 24.3
4	24 Mar	Fokker DrI	B8267	41	S W Havrincourt	1455	DES(F)	CR/RFC 24.3
5	15 May	C	C1071	41	Fournes au Werres	1620	OOC	CR/RAF 15.5
6	3 Aug	Alb. C	E1326	41	Bray	1915	OOC	CR/SR/?
7	9 Aug	DFW. C	D8446	41	S Contalmaison	0555	DES	CR/SR/?
8	12 Aug	Fokker DVII	B8493	41	S Morcourt	1840	DES	CR/SR/?

TOTAL: 4 and 1 shared destroyed, 3 out of control = 8.

HEMMING Geoffrey William Flight Sub Lieutenant 4(N), 204

Born in Worcester on 3 April 1898, Flight Sub Lieutenant Hemming was with 4(N) Squadron as it was forming in April 1917, flying Sopwith Pups in the Ostend area. On 12 May he claimed a Siemens Schukert DI, adding in June another SS DI shot down and a second out of control. The squadron then converted to Camels, and on 22 August in one of these he claimed three Albatros Scouts out of a formation of 20, to bring his score to six. These were his last victories, all gained in the Ostende-Zeebrugge-Dixmude area, although he remained with the unit until June 1918 without adding further to his score. He was awarded a DSC and Croix de Guerre.

	1917		Pup					
1	12 May	SS DI?	N6177	4N	5m off Zeebrugge	0720	DES	CR/RNAS 12.5
2	6 Jun	SS DI	N6199	4N	N E Dixmude	1600	DES	CR/SR/Belg
3	6 Jun	SS DI	N6199	4N	N E Dixmude	1600	OOC	CR/SR/Belg
			Camel					
4	22 Aug	Alb. DV	B3841	4N	S E Ostend	0945	OOC	CR/RNAS 22.8
5	22 Aug	Alb. DV	B3841	4N	S E Ostend	0945	OOC	CR/RNAS 22.8
6	22 Aug	Alb. DV	B3841	4N	Ostend-Bruge	0950	OOC	CR/RNAS 22.8

TOTAL: 2 destroyed, 4 out of control = 6.

HENDERSON Ian Henry David Captain 19, 56

A Scot, he was the son of General Sir David Henderson, commanding General of the RFC. He transferred to the Corps from the Argyll and Sutherland Highlanders, and following pilot training was posted to 19 Squadron in 1916. Here he claimed three victories. He gained much experience and received the MC. In 1917 he was promoted to Captain and joined 56 Squadron, to command 'B' Flight — a post which he held until Jimmy McCudden took over in August. He had several fights with hostile aircraft and was credited with four further victories before returning to England. He represented his father at Albert Ball's memorial service, but was himself killed in a flying accident on 21 June 1918.

	1916		BE 12					
1	24 Aug	EA	----	19	----	----	OOC	CR/RFC 24.8
2	31 Aug	D	----	19	Havrincourt Wood	----	DES	RFC WD
			Spad					
3*	10 Nov	C	A263?	19	Guedecourt	----	DES(F)	RFC 10.11
	1917		SE 5A					
4	12 Jul	Alb. DV	A4855	56	Zandvoorde	1400-1500	OOC	CR/RFC 12.7
5	13 Jul	Alb. DV	A4855	56	Moorslede	1930-2110	OOC	CR/9 WWD
6s**	17 Jul	Alb. DV	A8909	56	Roulers-Menin Rd	2015	OOC	CR/RFC 17.7
7	28 Jul	Alb. DV	B504	56	Menin	0830-0930	OOC	CR/RFC 28.7

TOTAL: 2 destroyed, 4 and 1 shared out of control = 7.

*this was the crew of Lt H. Eder/Lt K. Staemm of FA 13, who were killed. **Shared with 2/Lt L.M Barlow A8910, 2/Lt A.P.F. Rhys Davids A4863, 2/Lt K.K. Muspratt A8913, Lt V.P. Cronyn A4856.

HEPBURN Allan Captain 24, 40, 88

Born in Melbourne, Australia, on 11 October 1896, he served in the Artists' Rifles in France during 1916. Joining the RFC, he flew DH 5s with 24 Squadron from June 1917. He was slightly wounded in action on 26 October, but continued to fly until mid-November. He was then posted to 40 Squadron as a flight commander to succeed 'Mick' Mannock, but was involved in an accident soon after arrival and was sent back to England to recuperate. On recovery in April 1918 he joined 88 Squadron, now flying Bristol Fighters, to command 'A' Flight. With this unit he and his gunner/observers claimed 16 victories. He received a DFC at the end of 1918. Returning to Australia after the war, he joined the RAAF in 1921, becoming a Wing Commander in the 1930s. He died on 21 July 1975.

	1918		Bristol					
1*	17 May	Alb. DV	C821	88	E Middelkerke	0745	OOC	CR/RAF 17.5
2**	31 May	Alb. DV	C821	88	Ostend	1950	OOC	CR/SR/?
3**	2 Jun	Alb. DV	C821	88	Middelkerke-Ostend	1935	DES(F)	CR/RAF 2.6
4***	29 Jul	Fokker DVII	C821	88	Bois Grenier	1830	OOC	CR/SR/?
5***	31 Jul	Fokker DVII	C821	88	Zelobes	1200	DES(F)	CR/RAF 31.7
6†	29 Aug	Fokker DVII	C821	88	E Lille	0815	OOC	CR/10 BG
7***	1 Sep	Fokker DVII	C821	88	E Becelaere	1910	DES(F)	CR/RAF 1.9
8†	5 Sep	Fokker DVII	C821	88	N Douai	1900	OOC	CR/SR/?
9†	5 Sep	Fokker DVII	C821	88	Armentieres	1905	DES(F)	CR/RAF 5.9
10†	6 Sep	Fokker DVII	C821	88	N Douai	1845	OOC	CR/SR/?
11†	24 Sep	Fokker DVII	C821	88	Habourdin	1010	DES(F)	CR/SR/?
12†	8 Oct	Fokker DVII	C821	88	S W Cambrai	1245	OOC	CR/SR/?
13†	9 Oct	Fokker DVII	C821	88	Seclin	0845	DES	CR/RAF 9.10
14††	28 Oct	Fokker DVII	C821	88	Leuze-Ath	1445	OOC	CR/SR/?
15†††	4 Nov	Pfalz DXII	C821	88	Faucaumont	1300	DES	CR/RAF 9.10
16†††	4 Nov	Pfalz DXII	C821	88	W Mainvault-Faucaumont	1300	DES	CR/RAF 9.10

TOTAL: 8 destroyed, 8 out of control = 16.

*Observer: 2/Lt G.W. Lambert. **Observer: 2AM Proctor. ***Observer: Sgt E. Antcliffe. †Observer: 2/Lt H.G. Eldon. ††Observer: Lt Marshall. †††Observer: 2/Lt A. Tranter.

HERON Oscar Aloysius Patrick Captain 70

Lieutenant Heron joined 70 Squadron in France in summer 1918, and on 30 June claimed an enemy scout, sending down a second out of control. Success then eluded him until mid-August, when he accounted for a Fokker DVII, claiming another of these during the following month; he was then awarded a DFC. He began October by shooting down an LVG, but the rest of his victories, all claimed during this month, were over the excellent DVIIs. By the end of the month his score had reached 13, and he had been promoted to flight commander, and received the Belgian Croix de Guerre.

	1918		Camel					
1	30 Jun	Alb. DV	D6492	70	E Bray	2035	OOC	CR/?
2	30 Jun	Alb. DV	D6492	70	E Bray	2040	DES(F)	CR/RAF 30.6
3	19 Aug	Fokker DVII	C3306	70	Houthem-Hollebeke	1955	DES	CR/RAF 19.8

1. Major T.F. Hazell, DSO, MC, DFC & Bar, flew with 1 and 24 Squadrons, then commanded 203 Squadron in 1918; he claimed over 40 victories. *(Franks collection)*

2. Captain Oscar Heron, DFC, 70 Squadron, 1918. *(S. St Martin)*

3. Captain W.C. Hilborn, DFC, from Canada, served with all three Camel squadrons in Italy (28, 45 and 66), but died after a crash in August 1918. *(S. St Martin)*

4. Captain L.N. Hollinghurst, DFC, claimed his victories with 87 Squadron in 1918. He remained in the RAF, flying on D-Day and during the Arnhem paratroop landings, becoming Air Chief Marshal Sir Leslie Hollinghurst. *(L.N. Hollinghurst)*

1. Captain S.B. 'Nigger' Horn, MC, (left) 60 and 85 Squadrons, Lieutenant J. Dymond, USAS, (1 victory and Lieutenant W.H. Longton, DFC & 2 Bars, 85 and 24 Squadrons. *(P. Rosie)*

2. Lieutenant T.S. Horry, DFC, 92 Squadron, 1918. *(Bruce & Leslie)*

3. A Canadian, G.R. Howsom, MC, flew with 70 and 43 Squadrons; he later became Air Vice-Marshal with the RCAF. *(S. St Martin)*

4. Captain C.E. 'Spike' Howell, MC, DFC, and Lieutenant E.Mc. Hand, DFC, 45 Squadron. *(G.H. Williams)*

1. Captain Will Hubbard, DFC, commanded 'C' Flight in 3 Squadron in 1918. *(via G. Muir)*

2. Three Camel pilots with 28 Squadron in Italy; (l to r) Lieutenant H.B. Hudson, MC, (Canadian) Lieutenant G.M. McLeod and Lieutenant N.C. Jones, DFC. Hudson and Jones later flew with 45 Squadron. *(J. Mitchell)*

3. Eric 'Taffy' Hughes flew with 45 and 3 Squadrons, 1917-18. *(E.Y. Hughes)*

4. Two Bristol Fighter aces, Captains G.F. Hughes, MC, AFC, (left) (62 Squadron) and W. Beaver, MC, (20 Squadron). Hughes was an Australian, Beaver an American. *(S. St Martin)*

1. Lieutenant D.S. Ingalls, DSM, DFC, a US Navy pilot attached to 213 Squadron, RAF, to fly Camels. He claimed six victories with this unit to become his service's only ace of World War I. *(Franks collection)*

2. Captain L.F. Jenkin, MC & Bar, 1 Squadron, 1917. *(Franks collection)*

3. Captain G.O. Johnson, MC, from Canada, flew with 84 and 24 Squadrons. He later became an Air Marshal in the RCAF. *(S. St Martin)*

4. Captain E.C. Johnston, DFC, from Australia, flew with 24 and then 88 Squadrons. He became Controller of Civil Aviation in Australia in the 1930s.

3

2

4

1. Captain Field E. Kindley, DSC, an American who flew with 65 Squadron and then the 148th Aero Squadron, USAS, in 1918. *(S. St Martin)*

2. Captain J.I.T. Jones, DSO, MC, DFC & Bar, MM, claimed 37 victories with 74 Squadron in 1918. He served as a Group Captain commanding an Operational Training Unit during World War II. *(R.C. Bowyer)*

3. Captains N.C. Jones, DFC, (left) and C.M. MacEwen, MC, DFC, 28 Squadron in Italy. 'Black Mike' MacEwen commanded No 6 RCAF Bomber Group in Bomber Command in World War II and became an Air Vice-Marshal. *(Bruce & Leslie)*

4. Captain A.C. Kiddie, DFC & Bar, from South Africa, flew with 32 and 74 Squadrons. *(Franks collection)*

1. Captain C.F. King, MC, DFC, (left) Lieutenant G.G. Bailey, DFC, and Lieutenant A.C. Dean (1 victory and prisoner of war), 43 Squadron, 1918. *(J. Beedle)*

2. Captain S.M. Kinkead, DSO, DSC, DFC, a South African who flew with 1(Naval)/201 Squadron on the Western Front, and then with 47 Squadron in Russia in 1919. *(R.C. Bowyer)*

3. 1st Lieutenant Duerson Knight, USAS, from Chicago, flew SE 5As with 1 Squadron in 1918 before transferring to a US Air Service unit. *(D. Knight)*

4. 2nd Lieutenant Howard C. Knotts, DSC, DFC, flew with the 17th Aero Squadron, USAS. He was shot down and became a prisoner one month before the war ended. *(S. St Martin)*

. Lieutenant H.A. Kullberg, DFC, an American who flew with 1 quadron until he was wounded during September 1918. *(Franks ›llection)*

. Captain H.P. Lale, DSO, DFC & Bar, (centre) flew with 48 and) Squadrons in 1917-18; he retired from the RAF as a Group aptain. With him are Lieutenants Kirby and Saker. *(S. St Martin)*

. Captain W.C. 'Bill' Lambert, DFC, an American from Ohio, aimed 17 victories with 24 Squadron in 1918. *(W.C. Lambert)*

Captain John Leacroft, MC & Bar, 19 Squadron, who retired om the RAF as a Group Captain. *(J. Leacroft)*

1. Captain K.M. St. C.G. Leask, MC & Bar, 41 and 84 Squadrons, 1917-18. He later became an Air Vice-Marshal and a CB. *(Franks collection)*

2. Major M. LeBlanc-Smith, DFC, served with 18 Squadron in 1915-16, then with 73 Squadron first as a flight commander, then as commanding officer. *(M. LeBlanc-Smith)*

3. Captain O.C. 'Boots' LeBoutillier, an American in the RNAS who flew with 9(Naval)/209 Squadron in 1917-18; he was a participant in von Richthofen's last fight. *(R.C. Bowyer)*

4. Captain A.S.G. Lee, MC, 46 Squadron, 1917-18. He retired from the RAF as an Air Vice-Marshal after World War II. *(A.S. Gould Lee)*

1. Captain A.A. 'Ack-Ack' Leitch, MC, DFC, from Canada, who served in 65 Squadron. *(L. Coombes)*

2. Captain A.T. Loyd flew FE 2Bs with 25 and 22 Squadrons, then DH 5s with 32 Squadron. He was killed in action in September 1917.

3. Lieutenant G.A. 'Flossy' Lingham, DFC, 43 Squadron. *(L.A. Rogers)*

4. Captain Gwilym Lewis, DFC, (left) 32 and 40 Squadrons, 1916-18, with Captain G.E.H. McElroy MC & 2 Bars, DFC & Bar, who served with distinction with 24 and 40 Squadrons, 1917-18, claiming nearly 50 victories before his death in action in July 1918. *(G.H. Lewis)*

1. Lieutenant F.E. Luff, DFC, from Ohio, flew with 74 Squadron before going to the 25th Aero Squadron, USAS. *(Franks collection)*

2. William MacLanachan flew alongside Mannock in 40 Squadron; he later wrote the book *Fighter Pilot* in 1936 under the pen name 'McScotch'. *(Franks collection)*

3. Captain Emile J. Lussier, DFC, a Canadian who served with 73 Squadron in 1918. *(R. Manning)*

4. Captain D.R. Maclaren, DSO, MC & Bar, DFC, (left) claimed over 50 victories with 46 Squadron in 1918. He is seen here with fellow Canadian, Captain A.E. McKeever, DSO, MC, the top scoring Bristol Fighter pilot, who served with 22 Squadron during 1917. *(Public Archive Of Canada)*

1. Captain Norman MacMillan, MC, AFC, 45 Squadron, 1917-18, who later became a famous aviation author. *(N. MacMillan)*

2. Lieutenant J.A. McCudden, MC, younger brother of James McCudden, VC. John flew with 84 Squadron, but was killed in action in March 1918 after gaining 11 victories. *(Franks collection)*

3. Major J.T.B. McCudden, VC, DSO & Bar, MM,CdeG, gained 57 victories before being killed in an accident in July 1918. He achieved fame flying with 56 Squadron in 1917-18, but also flew with 3, 20, 29 and 66 Squadrons. *(R.C. Bowyer)*

4. Captain M.C. McGregor, DFC & Bar, from New Zealand, saw action with 54 and 85 Squadrons, 1917-18. *(P. Sortehaug)*

1. Captain Finley McQuiston, DFC, gained his victories with 19 Squadron in 1918. *(P. Rosie)*

2. Captain R.L. Manuel, DFC & Bar, from Australia, flew with 2 AFC Squadron in 1918. He served in the RAAF during World War II. *(S. St Martin)*

3. Captain Roy Manzer, DFC, from Canada. He flew with 84 Squadron during 1918, but was shot down and taken prisoner in August. *(Franks collection)*

4. Major 'Mick' Mannock, VC, DSO & 2 Bars, MC & Bar, flew Nieuports and SEs with 40, 74 and 85 Squadrons, commanding the latter unit during 1918. He was killed in action in July 1918. *(R.C. Bowyer)*

2

1

3

4

1. Captain C.J. 'Chips' Marchant, MC, 46 Squadron, 1917-18, with his Sopwith Pup during his first period at the front. *(A.S. Gould Lee)*

2. Two pilots of 84 Squadron in 1918; Lieutenant N.W.R. Mawle, DFC, (left) who was later a Group Captain, and Lieutenant C.R. 'Ruggles' Thompson, DFC, from South Africa. *(H.W.L. Saunders via Bruce & Leslie)*

3. Major R.S. Maxwell, MC, DFC & Bar, AFC, (right) who flew with 20, 18 and 54 Squadrons during 1916-18. On the left is Captain V.S. Bennett of 54 Squadron. *(S. St Martin)*

4. Captain W.R. 'Wop' May, DFC, from Canada, nearly became von Richthofen's 81st victim whilst flying with 209 Squadron, but survived to claim 13 victories before the war ended. *(Public Archive of Canada)*

1. Captain R.A. Maybery, MC & Bar, 56 Squadron, 1917. *(Franks collection)*

2. Captain F.H.M. Maynard, AFC, 1(Naval) Squadron, 1917. He subsequently retired as an Air Vice-Marshal after service on Malta and with Coastal Command during World War II. *(via R.C. Bowyer)*

3. Captain J. Mitchell, MC, DFC, (left) and Captain P.Wilson, MC, 28 Squadron, Grossa, Italy, 1918.

4. Captain J.F. Morris, MC & Bar, was observer with 11 Squadron before becoming a pilot. He flew with 23 and 25 Squadrons during 1917-18. *(Franks collection)*

. Major G.W. Murlis-Green, DSO & Bar, MC & 2 Bars saw action ith 17 Squadron in Salonika. He flew against German raiders over ngland with 44 and 151(Home Defence) Squadrons in 1918. *(Franks llection)*

40 Squadron pilots early in 1918; (l to r): Lieutenant C. Usher (3 ctories), Major R.S. Dallas (commanding officer), Captain I.P.R. apier, MC, Ld'H, CdeG, and Lieutenant C.O. Rusden (3 ctories). *(R.C. Bowyer)*

Lieutenant W.J.B. Nel, 84 Squadron, 1918. *(Franks collection)*

Captain M.A. Newnham, DFC & Bar, 65 Squadron, 1918; later a roup Captain in World War II. *(M.A. Newnham)*

1

3

4

2

1. Major E.W. Norton, DSC, served first with 6(Naval) Squadron, 1916-17, then commanded 204 Squadron in 1918. *(R.C. Bowyer)*

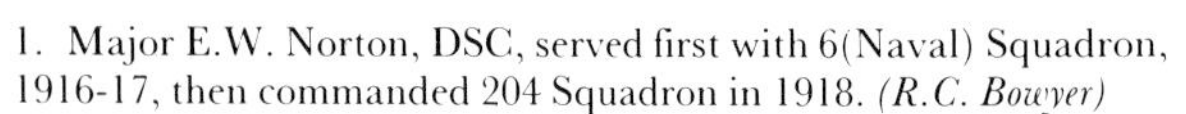

2. 43 Squadron group; front row, (l to r): Captain A.H. Orlebar, who claimed victories with 19, 73 and 43 Squadrons, Major C.C. Miles (commanding officer), Captain C.C. Banks, MC, DFC, who also shot down a night raider with 44(Home Defence) Squadron. *(R.C. Bowyer)*

3. Captain H.A. Patey, DFC, flew with 210 Squadron in 1918. He was shot down and taken prisoner in September; repatriated in December, he died during the influenza epidemic in February 1919, aged 20. This photo was taken whilst he was in captivity. *(G.S. Leslie)*

4. Captain A.A.N.D. 'Jerry' Pentland, MC, DFC, an Australian who flew with 19 and 87 Squadrons, and was wounded twice. He saw service with the RAAF during World War II. *(Franks collection)*

4	28 Sep	Fokker DVII	D6696	70	N E Passchendaele	1145	DES	CR/RAF 28.9
5	1 Oct	LVG. C	E7201	70	S W Ardoye	1630	DES	CR/RAF 1.10
6	7 Oct	Fokker DVII	D6696	70	Lichtervelde	0845	DES(F)	CR/RAF 7.10
7	7 Oct	Fokker DVII	D6696	70	Lichtervelde	0845	DES(F)	CR/RAF 7.10
8	9 Oct	Fokker DVII	E7277	70	E Roulers	0940	DES	CR/RAF 9.10
9	9 Oct	Fokker DVII	E7277	70	Roulers	0941	DES	CR/RAF 9.10
10s*	9 Oct	Fokker DVII	E7277	70	W Mayerneine	0945	CAPT	CR/RAF 9.10
11	26 Oct	Fokker DVII	C8201	70	S Monchau	1515	DES	CR/RAF 26.10
12	26 Oct	Fokker DVII	C8201	70	Montroelau Bois	1515	OOC	CR/11 WS
13	28 Oct	Fokker DVII	B7883	70	Quatres	1140	DES(F)	CR/RAF 28.10

TOTAL: 1 shared captured, 10 destroyed, 2 out of control = 13.
*Shared with Capt S.T. Liversedge E7161, Lt E.A. Copp, Lt A. Webster D6696, Lt K. B. Watson E7173.

HEWAT Richard Alexander Lieutenant 19, 87

'Bill' Hewat, a Canadian, joined the RFC in June 1917 and was posted to 19 Squadron in September. On 26 October he was wounded in the head by machine gun fire from the ground when at an altitude of 200 feet after shooting down a German aircraft. On recovering, he joined 87 Squadron at Hounslow, accompanying this unit to France in April 1918. On 14 August 1918 he took off in Dolphin E4434 on a lone patrol, but did not return; he probably fell victim to JG III.

	1917		Spad					
1s*	30 Sep	C	A6662	19	Gheluwe	0900	OOC	ORB/RFC 30.9
2s**	9 Oct	Alb. C	A6662	19	Moorslede	1040	OOC	CR/RFC WD
3	26 Oct	C	A6662	19	N Gheluwe	1020	OOC	CR/RFC WD
	1918		Dolphin					
4	19 Jul	Alb. DV	E4434	87	S E Arras	0930	OOC	CR/?
5	20 Jul	DFW. C	E4434	87	Tortequesne	1015	DES	CR/RAF 20.7
6	9 Aug	Fokker DVII	C4155	87	Foucaucourt	1800	DES	CR/RAF 9.8

TOTAL: 2 destroyed, 2 and 2 shared out of control = 6.
*Shared with Capt F. Sowrey A6777, Lt Delamere B3489, Lt R.M. Strang B1697, Lt J.G.S. Candy B3615. **Shared with Lt J.G.S. Candy B3615, Capt F. Sowrey A6777.

HICKEY Charles Robert Reeves Captain 4(N), 204

Charles Hickey, a Canadian from Parksville, British Columbia, was born on 10 September 1897. He first served with the Canadian Mounted Rifles. Volunteering for flying duties, he transferred to the RNAS, and after training was posted to 4(N) Squadron on the Channel coast near the Franco-Belgian border in August 1917. He claimed two victories before the end of the year, and two more in March 1918 before the unit was amalgamated into the new RAF as 204 Squadron. Two further victories followed in April and May, and he added another three by 3 August when he was awarded a DFC, followed by a Bar on 5 September. By 1 October he had claimed 15 victories since the beginning of June and been promoted to flight commander on 24 August. Probably his most unusual success occurred on 21 April 1918 when he forced a Rumpler two-seater to land in Allied lines at Wulpen. He landed alongside and tried to keep a crowd of Belgian civilians away from the damaged aircraft, but five minutes after landing it suddenly blew up, killing several of the Belgians and slightly injuring him. On 3 October, after 21 victories, Captain Hickey collided with 2nd Lieutenant S.E. Matthey's Camel in the air and was killed in the subsequent crash. The award of a DSO was announced on 2 November.

	1917		Camel					
1	22 Aug	Alb. DV	N6347	4N	S E Ostend	0945	OOC	CR/RNAS 22.8
2	23 Nov	Alb. DV	B6300	4N	E Dixmude	1400	OOC	CR/DOS/DL/?
	1918							
3	26 Mar	Pfalz DIII	B3892	4N	N E Dixmude	1700	OOC	CR/DOS/DL/?
4	26 Mar	Pfalz DIII	B3892	4N	2m E Dixmude	1700	DES	CR/DOS/DL/?
5s*	21 Apr	Rumpler C	B6350	204	Wulpen	1200	CAPT	CR/ORB/?
6	27 May	Alb. DIII	C74	204	Ostend	1920	OOC	CR/5 GP Comm
7	12 Jun	Pfalz DIII	C74	204	Nieuport Pier	1530	DES(F)	CR/5 GP Comm
8	30 Jun	Fokker DVII	D3359	204	off Blankenberghe	1430	OOC	CR/5 GP Comm
9	31 Jul	Fokker DVII	C74	204	5m N E Thorout	1930	DES(F)	CR/5 GP Comm
10s**	14 Aug	Fokker DVII	C74	204	5m E Dixmude	1100	DES	CR/5 GP Comm
11***	15 Aug	Fokker DVII	C74	204	Menin	1900	DES(F)	CR/5 GP Comm
12	15 Aug	Fokker DVII	C74	204	Menin	1900	OOC	CR/5 GP Comm
13	15 Aug	Fokker DVII	C74	204	Menin	1900	DES	CR/5 GP Comm
14	15 Sep	Fokker DVII	C74	204	Zeebrugge	1400	OOC	CR/5 GP Comm
15s†	16 Sep	Fokker DVII	F3942	204	Blankenburghe-Zeebrugge	1855	DES(F)	CR/5 GP Comm
16	16 Sep	Fokker DVII	F3942	204	Blakenburghe-Zeebrugge	1910	DES(F)	CR/5 GP Comm

17	16 Sep	Fokker DVII	F3942	204	Blakenburghe-Zeebrugge	1910	OOC	CR/5 GP Comm
18	26 Sep	Fokker DVII	D9626	204	Blakenberghe	1050	DES	CR/5 GP Comm
19	26 Sep	Fokker DVII	D9626	204	Blakenberghe	1050	OOC	CR/?
20	28 Sep	Fokker DVII	D9626	204	N W Wercken	1230	DES	CR/5 GP Comm
21	1 Oct	Rumpler C	D9626	204	E Lichtervelde	1630	DES	CR/5 GP Comm

TOTAL: 1 shared captured, 8 and 2 shared destroyed, 9 and 1 shared out of control = 21.
*Shared with Capt R.McK. Kierstead B6389. **Shared with Lt H.H. Blanchard B8187. ***Shared with Lt R.M. Gordon D8145. †Shared with 2/Lt N. Smith D8188, Lt R.M. Bennett D8187, Lt F.G. Bayley, 2/Lt J.R. Chisman.

HICKS George Rensbury Lieutenant 74

Lieutenant 'Bill' Hicks flew in 74 Squadron during the summer of 1918, claiming six victories. His sixth victory, on 24 September, was over one of the rare Siemens Schuckert DIVs, which he shot down out of control.

	1918		SE 5A					
1	15 Jul	Fokker DVII	C6474	74	S E Roulers	0850	OOC	CR/11 WS
2	24 Jul	DFW. C	C6905	74	Lestrem	0625	DES(F)	CR/RAF 24.7
3s*	19 Aug	DFW. C	----	74	Ploegsteert Wood	2010	DES	CR/RAF 19.8
4	5 Sep	Fokker DVII	----	74	S Cambrai	1045	DES	CR/RAF 5.9
5	5 Sep	Fokker DVII	----	74	W Lille	1910	OOC	CR/11 WS
6	24 Sep	SSDIV	----	74	3m E Armentieres	1030	OOC	CR/11 WS
7s**	24 Sep	Rumpler C	----	74	Capinghem	1045	DES	CR/RAF 24.9
8s**	26 Sep	DFW. C	----	74	3m S E Armentieres	1510	DES	CR/RAF 26.9

TOTAL: 2 and 3 shared destroyed, 3 out of control = 8.
*Shared with Lt H.G. Shoemaker. **Shared with Capt B. Roxburgh-Smith.

HIGHWOOD Sidney William Captain 84

Born on 30 December 1896, and from Morden, Kent, Highwood was commissioned in October 1917 and joined 84 Squadron on 20 May 1918. Of the 16 victories claimed by Sid Highwood, nine were kite balloons. On 24 September he claimed three of these formidable targets, adding two more on 29th. For these exploits he was awarded a DFC and Bar.

	1918		SE 5A					
1	8 Aug	Fokker DVII	C8496	84	N Foucaucourt	1830	OOC	CR/?
2	11 Aug	Fokker DVII	C9869	84	Villers Carbonnel	1810	OOC	CR/?
3s*	22 Aug	Rumpler C	C9869	84	S E Villers Carbonnel	1100	DES	CR/RAF 22.8
4s**	4 Sep	Balloon	D6920	84	Douvieux	1330	DES	CR/RAF 4.9
5	5 Sep	Balloon	C9039	84	S Poeuilly	0950	DES	CR/RAF 5.9
6	7 Sep	Balloon	D6920	84	Bellenglise	1130	DES	CR/RAF 7.9
7	14 Sep	Balloon	D6920	84	Bantouzelle	1030	DES	CR/RAF 14.9
8s***	16 Sep	Rumpler C	C6490	84	Selenoy	0630	DES	CR/RAF 16.9
9	24 Sep	Balloon	E4071	84	Gouy	0915	DES	CR/RAF 16.9
10	24 Sep	Balloon	E4071	84	Cambrai	1350	DES	CR/RAF 16.9
11	24 Sep	Balloon	E4071	84	Cambrai	1350	DES	CR/RAF 16.9
12s†	29 Sep	Balloon	E4071	84	Beaurevoir	1010	DES	CR/RAF 29.9
13	29 Sep	Balloon	E4071	84	L'Espagne	1011	DES	CR/RAF 29.9
14	3 Oct	Fokker DVII	E4071	84	Mont d'Origny	1125	DES(F)	CR/RAF 3.10
15s††	3 Oct	Fokker DVII	E4071	84	E Fresnoy	1815	DES	CR/RAF 3.10
16	30 Oct	Fokker DVII	E5073	84	Foret de Le Chelles	0945	DES	CR/RAF 30.10

TOTAL: 7 and 2 shared balloons, 2 and 3 shared destroyed, 2 out of control = 16.
*Shared with Lt G.A. Vaughn E4012. **Shared with 2/Lt C.R. Thompson F6420. ***Shared with Lt C.F.C. Wilson B8420. †Shared with 2/Lt D.C. Rees. ††Shared with Lt J.G. Coots F5489.

HILBORN William Carroll Captain 66, 28, 45

Born in Alexandria, British Columbia in 1899, this Canadian joined the RFC in July 1917. He was posted to 66 Squadron on 10 November and flew in Italy until 2 August 1918, during which time he claimed six enemy aeroplanes. On this latter date he was posted to 28 Squadron where he claimed one further victory. He joined 45 Squadron as a flight commander on 13 August, but was fatally injured in a flying accident on 16th, succumbing to his injuries on 26th. The awarded of a DFC was gazetted in November.

	1918		Camel					
1	1 May	Alb. DIII	B5220	66	Fonzaso	0850	DES	ORB/SR/14 W
2	4 May	Alb. DIII	B5220	66	Conegliano	0945	DES	ORB/SR/14 W
3*	11 May	Alb. DIII	B5220	66	Torre di Mosto	1050	DES	ORB/SR/14 W
4	20 May	Berg DI	B5220	66	Fontane	1200	DES	ORB/SR/14 W
5**	18 Jul	Alb. DIII	D8101	66	Stocareddo	0807	DES	ORB/SR/14 W
6	29 Jul	Alb. DIII	E1496	66	Feltre	0740	DES	ORB/SR/14 W

7	12 Aug	Alb. DIII	E1503	28	Cessalto	1140	DES	CR/14 W

TOTAL: 6 destroyed, 1 out of control = 7.
*66 claimed 2 others destroyed, to Capt W.G. Barker, Lt G.A. Birks; Zgsfhr Slavko Gyurgyev of Flik 61j was killed in 153:145.**This was Fw Walther Langthaler of Flik 9j, who was killed in 153.252.

HILTON D'Arcy Fowlis Lieutenant 29

Lieutenant Hilton, an American from Michigan, was born on 17 October 1889 and joined the RFC in November 1916, serving with 29 Squadron during the summer and autumn of the following year. He claimed eight victories while flying Nieuport Scouts, and was awarded an MC which was gazetted on 23 April 1918. He returned to Home Establishment on 14 November 1917. Hilton died shortly after World War II.

	1917		Nieuport					
1	31 Jul	Alb. DV	B3494	29	Westhoek	1215	DES	CR/RFC 31.7
2	31 Jul	Balloon	B3494	29	Polygon Racecourse	1830	DES	CR/RFC 31.7?
3	9 Aug	Alb. DV	B3494	29	Langemarck	1800	OOC	CR/RFC 10.8
4	11 Aug	Alb. DV	B3494	29	E Houthoulst Forest	1905	OOC	CR/RFC 11.8
5	16 Aug	Alb. DV	B3494	29	1m E Zonnebeke	0700	OOC	CR/RFC 16.8
6	16 Aug	Alb. DV	B3494	29	E Zonnebeke	0730	OOC	CR/RFC 16.8
7	30 Oct	C	D6800	29	E Houthoulst Forest	1030	OOC	CR/RFC 30.10
8	13 Nov	Alb. DV	D6828	29	N W Roulers	1200	OOC	CR/RFC 13.11

TOTAL: 1 balloon, 1 destroyed, 6 out of control = 8.

HINCHLIFFE Walter George Raymond Captain 10(N), 210

Ray Hinchliffe was born in Liverpool on 10 June 1894, serving from 1914-16 with the Royal Artillery, and then joining the RNAS. After pilot training he was retained as an instructor at RNAS Cranwell and clocked-up 1,250 hours flying in 13 months. Finally he was released to an operational unit, and joined 10 Naval, later 210 Squadron, RAF, in January 1918. As a flight commander he claimed six victories and took part in two raids on enemy aerodromes, one at night. On 3 June, while returning from picking up a forced down Camel, he burst a tyre whilst landing in the dark, and crashed. He had severe facial injuries and lost the sight of his left eye; for the rest of his life he wore a patch to cover his disfigurement. For his services he received the DFC and AFC. After the war he flew with KLM, the Royal Dutch airline, and later with Imperial Airways; by the mid 1920s he was one of the most experienced pilots in the world, having completed over 9,000 hours flying. In 1928 he planned to fly the Atlantic from east to west, with Miss Elsie Mackay, the millionairess daughter of Lord Inchcape. They took off from his old airfield at Cranwell on 13 March 1928, but were never seen again. His life has been the subject of a book and a film, *The Ghost of Flight 401*.

	1918		Camel					
1	3 Feb	Alb. DV	B6204	10N	S W Rumbeke	1515	DES	CR/RNAS 3.2
2	10 Mar	C	B7190	10N	Roulers	1545	DES	CR/RNAS 10.3
3	3 Apr	C	B7190	210	Roulers	1130	DES(F)	CR/RNAS 3.4
4	16 May	Alb. C	D3887	210	1m W Kemmel	1145	DES	CR/RAF 16.5
5	18 May	Alb. DV	D3887	210	Neuve-Eglise area	1045	OOC	CR/?
6	19 May	C	D3887	210	N E Armentieres	1045	DES	CR/RAF 19.5

TOTAL: 5 destroyed, 1 out of control = 6.

HIND Ivan Frank Captain 40

Joining the RFC as a cadet on 10 May 1917, Hind joined 40 Squadron, serving from the early spring of 1918 and throughout the summer. He was promoted to flight commander in August and on 8th of that month claimed his final victory. His score included three aircraft destroyed and five out of control. He was killed in action on 12 August, when he and Lieutenant A.M. Wood were shot down over Brie by Leutnant Ernst Udet of Jasta 4 and Leutnant Otto Könnecke of Jasta 5 for their 40th and 29th victories respectively; Hind was flying E3984 at the time.

	1918		SE 5A					
1s*	12 Apr	Alb. DV	B675	40	S Estaires	0650	OOC	CR/RAF 12.4
2	14 May	Pfalz DIII	B675	40	E Lens	1810	OOC	CR/RAF 14.5
3	19 May	Pfalz DIII	B675	40	Provin	1855	OOC	CR/RAF 19.5
4s**	20 May	Pfalz DIII	----	40	Merville	2000	OOC	CR/?
5	27 May	Pfalz DIII	B675	40	E Billy	2010	DES	CR/RAF 27.5
6s***	7 Jul	LVG. C	C5358	40	Lens	0925	CAPT	CR/RAF 7.7
7†	25 Jul	Fokker DVII	C5358	40	S W Lille	1720	DES(F)	CR/RAF 25.7
8	8 Aug	Fokker DVII	E3984	40	Brebieres	1035	OOC	CR/?

TOTAL: 1 shared captured, 2 destroyed, 4 and 1 shared out of control = 8.
*Shared with Capt I.P.R. Napier B157. **Shared with Major R.S. Dallas, Lt H.H. Wood, Lt C.O. Rusden, Capt G.H. Lewis, Lt D.S. Poler. ***Shared with Capt G.H. Lewis B3511; Gefr Weber/? of FA 13 POW. †Certainly Lt Josef Raesch of Jasta 43, who was shot down in flames in this area at this time. Raesch baled out successfully.

HOBSON Frank H Captain 70

Born on 20 November 1893, and from Bungay, Suffolk, Hobson joined the RFC on 10 May 1917, receiving his commission on 21 June and joining 84 Squadron on 27 October. He took part in the spring battles of the German offensive and had been awarded an MC by the end of April for seven victories. He returned to Home Establishment on 11 May 1918.

	1917		Camel					
1	24 Sep	Alb. DV	B2305	70	Houthoulst Forest	1815	OOC	CR/RFC 24.9
2	9 Oct	Alb. DV	B2389	70	Lindeken	1555	DES	CR/RFC 9.10
3s*	27 Oct	Alb. DV	B2389	70	Roulers	1400	OOC	CR/RFC 27.10
4	23 Nov	Alb. DV	B2452	70	Westroosebeke	1350	DES	CR/RFC 23.11
5	19 Dec	C	B5179	70	Stadenberg	1235	DES	CR/RFC 19.12
6	19 Dec	C	B5179	70	Stadenberg	1235	DES(F)	CR/RFC 19.12
7	22 Dec	Alb. DV	B6251	70	Westroosebeke	1350	DES	CR/RFC 22.12
8s**	27 Dec	C	B6251	70	Zarren	1050	DES	CR/RFC 28.12
	1918							
9	7 Jan	C	----	70	----	----	OOC	RFC 7.1
10	19 Jan	C	B6251	70	Warneton	1100	DES(F)	CR/RFC 19.1
11	29 Jan	Alb. DV	B2449	70	W Staden	1410	OOC	CR/RFC 29.1
12	22 Mar	Alb. DV	C8217	70	N W Cambrai	1530	OOC	CR/RFC 22.3
13	22 Mar	Alb. C	C8217	70	Sailly	1550	DES(F)	CR/RFC 22.3
14	23 Mar	Alb. DV	C8217	70	Morchies	1310	DES	CR/RFC 23.3
15	25 Mar	Alb. DV	C8217	70	N Bapaume-Cambrai Rd	1645	DES	CR/RFC 25.3

TOTAL: 9 and 1 shared destroyed, 4 and 1 shared out of control = 15.
*Shared with Maj M.H.B. Nethersole B2449, Capt F.H. Lawrence B2423, 2/Lt E.B. Booth B6366, Lt Goode B2361, 2/Lt C.W. Primeau B2349. **Shared with 2/Lt F.G. Quigley B2447, Lt K.A. Seth-Smith B2438.

HOBSON Percy Kyne Lieutenant 84

Born in Bungay, Suffolk on 20 November 1893, Hobson joined the RFC on 10 May 1917, and graduated on 27 September. He joined 84 Squadron on 22 October 1917, and took part in the spring battles of the German offensive. He was awarded an MC, and by the end of April had claimed three and shared a fourth destroyed, together with three more out of control. He left for Home Establishment on 11 May.

	1918		SE 5A					
1	13 Feb	Alb. DV	D260	84	N E St Quentin	1210	DES	CR/?
2*	18 Feb	Alb. DV	C5313	84	Beaurevoir	1100	OOC	CR/?
3**	13 Mar	Alb. DV	D260	84	N E St Quentin	1010	DES	CR/RFC 13.3
4s***	16 Mar	LVG. C	D260	84	Villers Outreaux	1125	DES	CR/RFC 16.3
5	20 Apr	Alb. DV	B6410	84	S E Marcelcave	0920	OOC	CR/RAF 20.4
6	21 Apr	Alb. C	B6410	84	S W Mezieres	1300	DES	CR/RAF 21.4
7	23 Apr	Fokker DrI	B6410	84	Framerville	1640	OOC	CR/RAF 23.4

TOTAL: 3 and 1 shared destroyed, 3 out of control = 7.
*Probably Lt H.J. von Hippel of Jasta 5, who crash landed. **This was Oblt H. Mettlich, the commander of Jasta 8 who was killed. ***Shared with Lt G.O. Johnson B699.

HODSON George Stacey Lieutenant 73, 213

Born on 2 May 1899 in Belmont, Surrey, and educated at Dulwich College, Hodson joined the RFC in September 1917; in November 1917 he was posted to 73 Squadron. With this unit he claimed five victories and participated in five others. After service as an instructor from April, he was then sent to 213 Squadron in August, where he served until the end of the war, bringing his score to ten, after flying 190 hours over the lines. On 18 September he and two other pilots destroyed a balloon which fell in flames and set fire three aircraft hangars, all of which were destroyed. In March 1919 he went to No 11 Aircraft Park; although recommended for a DFC by his Commanding Officer, he did not receive any decoration for his war services. Remaining in the RAF, he served with the RNZAF from 1938-43 on an exchange scheme. He later commanded RAF Holme, and from 1946-47 was AOC, Coastal Command; later in 1949 he became SASO, Home Command. His final rank was Air Marshal, CB, CBE, AFC; he died in England on 1 October 1976.

	1918		Camel					
1	10 Mar	Fokker DrI	B7291	73	W Bohain	1425	DES(F)	CR/RFC 11.3
2	13 Mar	Alb. DV	B7291	73	Wambaix	1015	DES(F)	CR/RFC 13.3
3	22 Mar	Alb. DV	B7282	73	Marteville	1505	OOC	CR/RFC 22.3
4	31 Mar	Alb. DV	C8292	73	Abancourt-Warfusee	1000	DES(F)	CR/RFC 31.3
5s*	18 Sep	Balloon	D3341	213	La Barriere	1050	DES	CR/5 GP Comm
6	24 Sep	Fokker DVII	D3341	213	S W Thorout	1450	OOC	CR/5 GP Comm
7	24 Sep	Fokker DVII	D3341	213	1m W Mitswaere?	1455	DES	CR/5 GP Comm

8s**	24 Sep	Rumpler C	D3341	213	St Pierre Capelle	1730	DES(F)	CR/5 GP Comm
9	4 Oct	Fokker DVII	F3965	213	S Roulers	1555	DES	CR/5 GP Comm
10	14 Oct	Fokker DVII	D3400	213	Beerst	1430	DES	CR/5 GP Comm

TOTAL: 1 shared balloon, 6 and 1 shared destroyed, 2 out of control = 10.
*Shared with Lt D.S. Ingalls D9649, Lt H.C. Smith D3378. **Shared with lt D.S. Ingalls D9649.

HOIDGE Reginald Theodore Carlos Captain 56, 1

After transferring from the Canadian Royal Garrison Artillery to the RFC and receiving his flying training, Lieutenant Hoidge was posted to the newly-formed 56 Squadron, the first unit to take the SE 5 to the front. He began claiming on 5 May 1917, and by the end of May was recommended for an MC; this was awarded on 18 July for taking part in 24 offensive patrols and gaining seven victories. He remained with the squadron until early November, by which time he was flying SE 5As, and his score had risen to 27. After a year off operations, he was posted in the autumn of 1918 to 1 Squadron as a flight commander, where he shot down one Fokker DVII, the pilot of this being seen to bale out. He died in 1963.

	1917		SE 5					
1	5 May	Alb. DIII	A4862	56	Montigny	1845-1945	OOC	CR/RFC 5.5
2	7 May	Alb. DIII	A4862	56	N E Cambrai	1830	DES	CR/RFC 7.5
3s*	7 May	Alb. DIII	A4862	56	N Cambrai	1830-1900	OOC	CR/RFC 7.5
4	20 May	Halb. D	A4862	56	Bugnicourt	1200	OOC	CR/RFC 20.5
5s**	24 May	Alb. DIII	A4862	56	S Douai	1900-2000	OOC	CR/RFC 24.5
6s***	24 May	C	A4862	56	Gouy sous Bellone	1900-2000	DES(F)	CR/RFC 24.5
7	24 May	Alb. DIII	A4862	56	Sains	1900-2000	OOC	CR/RFC 24.5
8	27 May	Alb. DIII	A4862	56	E Bugnicourt	1900-2000	OOC	CR/RFC 27.5
9	8 Jun	C	A8914	56	Lompret	0830-0945	OOC	CR/RFC 8.6
10	17 Jun	C	A8914	56	La Bassee	0845-0930	DES	CR/RFC 17.6
11	12 Jul	Alb. DV	A8914	56	Polygon Wood	2000	OOC	CR/RFC 12.7
12	12 Jul	Alb. DV	A8914	56	W Menin	2000	OOC	CR/RFC 12.7
13	20 Jul	Alb. DV	A8914	56	Zonnebeke	1915-2015	OOC	CR/RFC 20.7
14	23 Jul	Alb. DV	A8914	56	Zonnebeke	1945-2045	OOC	CR/RFC 23.7
15	27 Jul	Alb. DV	A8914	56	N E Roulers	1930-2045	OOC	CR/RFC 27.7
16	28 Jul	Alb. DV	A8914	56	W Roulers	1930-2030	DES	CR/RFC 28.7
17	28 Jul	Alb. DV	A8914	56	Dadizeele	1930-2030	OOC	CR/RFC 28.7
			SE 5A					
18	22 Aug	Alb. DV	B4851	56	S W Roulers	1845-1920	OOC	CR/RFC 22.8
19	5 Sep	Alb. DV	B528	56	S Houthoulst Forest	1815-1900	OOC	CR/RFC 5.9
20	10 Sep	Alb. DV	B4851	56	W Roulers	1740-1845	OOC	CR/RFC 10.9
21	11 Sep	Alb. DV	B4851	56	N E Houthoulst Forest	1815-1915	OOC	CR/RFC 11.9
22	21 Sep	Alb. DV	B506	56	Gheluwe	1730-1830	DES	CR/RFC 21.9
23	23 Sep	Pfalz DIII	B506	56	N Zonnebeke	1740-1835	OOC	CR/RFC 23.9
24†	28 Sep	Alb. DV	B506	56	E Westroosebeke	1715-1725	DES	CR/RFC 28.9
25	18 Oct	C	B506	56	E Comines	0810-1020	DES	CR/RFC 18.10
26	18 Oct	C	B506	56	E Wervicq	0810-1020	OOC	CR/RFC 18.10
27	31 Oct	Alb. DV	B506	56	Roulers	1440-1620	OOC	CR/9 W W.D.
	1918							
28††	29 Oct	Fokker DVII	E5799	1	Pommereuil	1430	DES	CR/RAF 29.10

TOTAL:7 and 1 shared destroyed, 18 and 2 shared out of control = 28.
*Shared with Capt H. Meintjes A8900, Lt C.A. Lewis A4853, 2/Lt W.B. Melville A4852. **Shared with Capt C.M. Crowe A8910, 2/Lt A.P.F. Rhys Davids A4868, 2/Lt K.K. Muspratt A4861, 2/Lt J.S. Turnbull A8913. ***Shared with 2/Lt A.P.F. Rhys Davids A4868. †This was either Lt Karl Menckhoff, an ace of Jasta 3, who crash landed or Lt Kurt Wissemann who was killed by Hoidge or Bowman. ††The pilot of this aircraft baled out successfully.

HOLLIDAY Fred Parkinson Major 48

An Australian, working in Canada as a mining engineer at the outbreak of war, Holliday flew in 48 Squadron during 1917, with Captain Wall as gunner. Holliday was one of the original Bristol F2A pilots; he claimed five victories during April, the squadron's first month in action, and six more in May, on one occasion claiming four in one day. On 3 June he shot the tail right off an Albatros scout, and later in that month claimed three further victories, with another on 3 July, his last with Captain Wall. Awarded a DSO and MC, he was now promoted to flight commander, and on 27 July, flying with Lieutenant W. O'Toole, claimed his 17th and last victory. He was promoted to the rank of Major later in the war, and toured America in 1920 with a group of RAF aces. He emigrated to Canada in the early twenties.

	1917		Bristol					
1*	6 Apr	Alb. DIII	----	48	N E Arras	----	OOC	RFC 6.4
2*	23 Apr	Alb. DIII	----	48	Vitry	----	DES	RFC 23.4
3s**	23 Apr	Alb. DIII	----	48	Cagnicourt	----	OOC	RFC 23.4

4*	24 Apr	C	----	48	Cagnicourt	----	DES	RFC 24.4
5s†	24 Apr	Alb. DIII	----	48	Cagnicourt	----	OOC	RFC 24.4
6s††	9 May	LVG. C	A7108	48	Vitry-Noyelles	0820	DES	CR/RFC 9.5
7*	9 May	Alb. DIII	A7108	48	E Vitry	1725	OOC	CR/3 BG W.D.
8*	9 May	Alb. DIII	A7108	48	E Vitry	1730	OOC	CR/3 BG W.D.
9*	9 May	Alb. DIII	A7108	48	E Vitry	1730	OOC	CR/3 BG W.D.
10*	11 May	Alb. DIII	A7108	48	S W Izel les Esquerchin	1605	OOC	CR/RFC 11.5
11*	11 May	Alb. DIII	A7108	48	S W Izel les Esquerchin	1605	DES	CR/RFC 11.5
12*	3 Jun	Alb. DIII	A7108	48	Plouvain	1920	DES	CR/RFC 3.6
13*	14 Jun	Alb. DIII	A7108	48	Arleux	2015	DES	CR/RFC 14.6
14*	14 Jun	Alb. DIII	A7108	48	Arleux	2020	OOC	CR/RFC 14.6
15*	15 Jun	Alb. DIII	A7108	48	Etaing	1945	OOC	CR/RFC 15.6
16*	3 Jul	Alb. DIII	A7108	48	Haucourt	1840	OOC	CR/RFC 3.7
17†††	27 Jul	DFW. C	A7108	48	Westende	1645	OOC	CR/RFC 27.7

TOTAL: 5 and 1 shared destroyed, 9 and 2 shared out of control = 17.
*Observer: Capt A.H.W. Wall. **Observer: Capt A.H.W. Wall; shared with Lt W.O.B. Winkler/2/Lt E.S. Moore, Lt R.B. Hay/?, Lt W.T. Price/Lt M.A. Benhamin. †Observer: Capt A.H.W. Wall; shared with Lt R.B. Hay/?, Lt W.O.B. Winkler/2/Lt E.S. Moore. ††Observer: Capt A.H.W. Wall; shared with 2/Lt W.T. Price/2/Lt E.S. Moore E7110. The crew were shot on the ground. †††Observer: Lt W. O'Toole.

HOLLINGHURST Leslie Norman Captain 87

Born on 2 January 1895, he joined the Signal Service of the Royal Engineers in 1914, and was commissioned in the 3rd Battalion, Middlesex Regiment, serving at Gallipoli and Salonika, before transferring to the RFC in 1916. After pilot training he was retained at various bases in England as a test pilot. When he finally received a posting to 87 Squadron which was preparing to go to France, 'Holly' had nearly 400 flying hours in his log books. He flew with 87 from April 1918 until the end of the war, claimed 10 victories and received the DFC, reaching the rank of Captain by the end of the year. In 1919 he flew with 23 and 79 Squadrons as a flight commander, before going to India with 48 Squadron, and later with 5 Squadron. This was, however, only the first step to high rank within the RAF. He received the OBE in 1932, took command of 20 Squadron in India in 1933, and by the outbreak of World War Two was a Group Captain. During the second war he became O.C. Airborne Forces, and although against orders, he flew on operations both on the night of 5/6 June 1944, and during the Arnhem paratroop landings later that year. He was knighted in 1948 and retired from the RAF in 1952 with the rank of Air Chief Marshal, GBE, KCB, DFC. He remained in close contact with the service after his retirement and was associated with the Air Training Corps. He lived in Putney, West London, until his sudden death on 8 June 1971 whilst returning from the D-Day Pilgrimage to Normandy.

	1918		Dolphin					
1	6 Jul	Fokker DVII	C4136	87	Bapaume	1135	OOC	CR/RAF 6.7
2	7 Aug	LVG. C	C4136	87	Bapaume	1000	DES	CR/RAF 7.8
3	9 Aug	Pfalz DIII	C4136	87	Dernicourt	1710	DES(F)	CR/RAF 9.8
4s*	9 Aug	LVG. C	C4136	87	Dernicourt	1710	OOC	CR/RAF 9.8
5	10 Aug	Fokker DVII	C4136	87	Fresnes	0915	DES	CR/RAF 10.8
6	3 Sep	Hannover C	C4239	87	Masnieres	1845	DES(F)	CR/RAF 3.9
7	20 Sep	Fokker DVII	C4136	87	Noyelles	1530	DES	CR/RAF 20.9
8	23 Sep	Fokker DVII	C4230	87	Bourlon Wood	1810	DES	CR/RAF 23.9
9	27 Sep	Fokker DVII	C4136	87	Rumilly	1120	OOC	CR/?
10	29 Sep	Fokker DVII	C4136	87	Estourmel	0730	OOC	CR/?
11s**	4 Oct	Fokker DVII	C4136	87	Desieres	1800	DES(F)	CR/RAF 4.10

TOTAL: 6 and 1 shared destroyed, 3 and 1 shared out of control = 11.
*Shared with Lt C.S. Harvey D3774. **Shared with Lt C.E. Worthington D3590.

HOOPER Geoffrey Herbert Captain 11, 20

Geoffrey Hooper, an Australian, enlisted in the Royal Engineers on 1 November 1915, then transferred to the RFC in August 1916. He joined 11 Squadron on 12 April 1917, becoming a flight commander during the late summer. He accounted for three Albatros scouts, his third victory being gained with Lieutenant L.A. Powell, Andrew McKeever's gunner, in the rear seat. He was awarded an MC on 18 September 1917, being rested from operations from 12 December. After service with 38 Training Squadron, he joined 20 Squadron on 14 September 1918, again as a flight commander, and teamed-up with a very successful gunner, Lieutenant H.L. Edwards. In six days in September they claimed seven Fokker DVIIs shot down. Hooper's 11th and final victory, again a DVII, occurred on 10 November, the day before the end of the war. He also took part in many day and night bombing raids, and was awarded a DFC, gazetted in 1919. He left the RAF in 1923.

	1917		Bristol					
1*	26 Jun	Alb. DIII	A7140	11	Etaing-Dury	1845	DES	CR/RFC 26.6
2**	18 Aug	Alb. DIII	A7121	11	Douai	0615-0645	OOC	CR/RFC 18.8

3***	11 Sep 1918	Alb. DV	----	11	Cagnicourt	1845	OOC	CR/RFC 12.9
4†	24 Sep	Fokker DVII	E2536	20	S E St Quentin	1600	DES	CR/RAF 24.9
5†	25 Sep	Fokker DVII	E2536	20	N E St Quentin	1815	DES	CR/RAF 25.9
6†	25 Sep	Fokker DVII	E2536	20	N E St Quentin	1815	DES	CR/RAF 25.9
7†	25 Sep	Fokker DVII	E2536	20	N E St Quentin	1820	DES(F)	CR/RAF 25.9
8†	29 Sep	Fokker DVII	E2536	20	N St Quentin	1020	OOC	CR/?
9†	29 Sep	Fokker DVII	E2536	20	N St Quentin	1025	OOC	CR/?
10†	29 Sep	Fokker DVII	E2536	20	N St Quentin	1025	DES	CR/RAF 29.9
11††	10 Nov	Fokker DVII	E2407	20	Charleroi	0830	OOC	CR/?

TOTAL: 6 destroyed, 5 out of control = 11.

*Observer: Capt F.J. Carr. **Observer: Lt H.G. Kent. ***Observer: 2/Lt L.A. Powell. †Observer: Lt H.L. Edwards. Observer: Lt M.A. McKenzie.

HORN Spencer Bertram Captain 60, 85

'Nigger' Horn's parents lived in Australia, where his two elder brothers were born. However he was born in England the day after the ship carrying his family there had docked! He served as an officer in the Dragoon Guards early in the war, before he joined the RFC. After training in France and England, he went to 60 Squadron in 1917 flying Nieuport Scouts. He flew with this unit from April to November, received an MC and claimed six victories. When Captain Bishop,VC, left 60 in August, Horn was given command of 'C' Flight, having served under Bishop since joining the squadron. Leaving for a spell on Home Establishment, he instructed at Ayr until the new year. In March 1918 Bishop, who was forming 85 Squadron, asked him to be one of his flight commanders, and Horn quickly agreed. Returning to France with the squadron in May, he brought his score to 13 before the end of the war. He retired from active service with the rank of Lieutenant Colonel, having returned to the Army at the conclusion of hostilities. One of his brothers, Major K.K. Horn, commanded 54 Squadron during 1917.

	1917		Nieup					
1	2 May	Alb. DIII	B1539	60	Vitry-Belonne	1630	DES	CR/C&CB 11/4
2	6 May	Alb. DIII	B1539	60	Cambrai	1800	OOC	CR/C&CB 11/4
			SE 5A					
3s*	5 Aug	Alb. DIII	A8930	60	Hendecourt	2000	DES(F)	CR/RFC 5.8
4	9 Aug	Alb. DV	A8930	60	Cagnicourt	0700	OOC	CR/RFC 9.8
5	26 Aug	C	A8936	60	Gillemont Farm	0715	DES(F)	CR/RFC 26.8
6s**	5 Sep	Alb. DV	A8936	60	Sailly en Ostrevent	1900	OOC	CR/RFC 6.9
	1918							
7	30 May	Pfalz DIII	D6027	85	Nieppe	2040	OOC	CR/?
8	16 Jun	Pfalz DIII	D6027	85	Neuve-Eglise	0750	DES	CR/RAF 16.6
9	7 Jul	Fokker DVII	C1904	85	Doulieu	2020	OOC	CR/?
10	7 Jul	Fokker DVII	C1904	85	Steenwerck	2020	DES	CR/RAF 7.7
11	14 Aug	Fokker DVII	C1904	85	Guyencourt	1530	DES	CR/?
12	22 Aug	Fokker DVII	C1904	85	Suzanne	1650	OOC	CR/?
13	17 Sep	C	C1904	85	Graincourt lez Havrincourt	1410	DES	CR/RAF 17.9

TOTAL: 6 and 1 shared destroyed, 5 and 1 shared out of control = 13.

*Shared with Capt W.E. Molesworth A4851. Probably Lt B. Lehmann of Jasta 12, who was killed. **Shared with Lt J.B. Crompton A8918.

HORRY Thomas Stanley Lieutenant 92

Horry flew to France in 1918 as a pilot with 92 Squadron on SE 5As. He did most of his scoring during the last few weeks of the war, and received a DFC. He claimed four enemy aircraft shot down and assisted in at least four more for a personal score of eight. He remained in the RAF, later being awarded the AFC. In 1936 he was a Flight Lieutenant with 5 FTS.

	1918		SE 5A					
1s*	4 Oct	Hannover C	----	92	S E Bertry	0800	OOC	CR/?
2	14 Oct	Fokker DVII	F858	92	S E Le Cateau	1630	OOC	CR/?
3s**	23 Oct	DFW. C	----	92	S Pont du Nord	1300	DES	CR/RAF 23.10
4s***	27 Oct	Alb. C	F858	92	Mormal Wood	0630	DES	CR/RAF 27.10
5†	27 Oct	C	F858	92	2m E Le Quesnoy	0735	DES	CR/RAF 27.10
6	29 Oct	Fokker DVII	F858	92	Maroilles	0915	OOC	CR/?
7	29 Oct	Halb. C	F858	92	E Le Quesnoy	1030	DES	CR/RAF 29.10
8	30 Oct	DFW. C	F858	92	W Sassegrien	0905	DES(F)	CR/RAF 30.10

TOTAL: 2 and 3 shared destroyed, 2 and 1 shared out of control = 8.

*Shared with Capt J.M. Robb, Capt W.S. Philcox, Lt E. Shapard. **Shared with Capt J.M. Robb, Lt E.S. Robins, Lt C.H.E. Coles, Lt E. Madill, Capt W.E. Reed, Lt E. Shapard, Lt J.V. Gascoyne, Lt J. Daniel. ***Shared with Capt W.S. Philcox, Lt E.F. Crabb. †Shared with Lt J.V. Gascoyne, Lt J. Daniel.

HOWARD Richard Watson Captain 68, 57, 2AFC

Born in Sydney on 9 October 1896, but raised in Newcastle, New South Wales, this Australian studied engineering in Hamilton, NSW, joining the Australian Army Engineers on 13 September 1915. He served in France from March to December 1916 before transferring to the AFC, joining 68 Squadron on 7 April 1917. On 26 May he was posted to 57 Squadron on DH 4s, where he remained until 2 July, when he returned to 68, going back to France with the unit late in the year, flying DH 5s. During November he claimed a victory over Cambrai and took part in much ground attack work, but was forced to land twice, while on a third occasion his aircraft was severely damaged by an enemy machine; he was awarded an MC. Promoted to flight commander on 22 February 1918 in what had now become 2AFC Squadron and had re-equipped with SE 5As, he gained further victories during that month, while during the heavy fighting of March he claimed six. On 22nd however, he was shot down near Vermond in D212 by Leutnant Böhning of Jasta 79, a 17 victory ace, and died of his wounds.

	1917		DH 5					
1s*	22 Nov	DFW. C	A9294	2AFC	Graincourt	1140	CAPT	CR/RFC 22.11
	1918		SE 5A					
2	28 Feb	Alb. DV	D212	2AFC	Carvin	1230	OOC	CR/RFC 18.2
3s**	8 Mar	C	D212	2AFC	Henin-Lietard	1100	OOC	CR/RFC 8.3
4	8 Mar	Alb. DV	D212	2AFC	Brebieres	1120	OOC	CR/RFC 8.3
5	9 Mar	Alb. DV	D212	2AFC	N E La Bassee	0935	OOC	CR/RFC 9.3
6	9 Mar	Alb. DV	D212	2AFC	N E La Bassee	0945	OOC	CR/ORB/OH/?
7	10 Mar	Alb. DV	D212	2AFC	Pont-a-Vendin	1540	OOC	CR/RFC 10.3
8	18 Mar	Rumpler C	D212	2AFC	Habourdin	1255	DES(F)	CR/RFC 18.3

TOTAL: 1 shared captured, 1 destroyed, 6 out of control = 8.
*Shared with Capt J.M. Child B562 of 84 Sqn. Note Child times the combat 10 minutes later, and in a slightly different location. **Shared with Lt A.L. Paxton C9496.

HOWE Percy Frank Charles Lieutenant 74

Commissioned in the RFC in September 1917, Howe was from Swaziland, Africa, which earned him the nickname 'Swazi'. An original member of 74 Squadron in 1918, he served in Mannock's flight until July, claiming five victories.

	1918		SE 5A					
1s*	12 Apr	Alb. DV	----	74	Bois de Phalempin	1440	DES	CR/RAF 12.4
2	21 May	Pfalz DIII	----	74	N E Merville	0840	OOC	CR/11 WS
3	12 Jun	Pfalz DIII	D6854	74	Bailleul-Armentieres	2010	DES	CR/RAF 12.6
4	15 Jun	Pfalz DIII	D6854	74	Menin-Courtrai	0730	OOC	CR/11 WS
5	15 Jun	Pfalz DIII	D6854	74	2m S Zillebeke Lake	0810	DES	CR/RAF 15.6

TOTAL: 2 and 1 shared destroyed, 2 out of control = 5.
*Shared with Capt E.C. Mannock, Lt H.E. Dolan, Lt B. Roxburgh-Smith, Lt H.G. Clements.

HOWELL Cedric Ernest Captain 45

Born on 17 June 1896, 'Spike' Howell was an Australian who served with 46 Battalion of the ANZAC in France as a sniper, before transferring to the RFC with the original batch of 200 Australians recruited from the AIF. He was taught to fly by Captain G.F. Hughes, and in 1917 joined 45 Squadron in France; he subsequently served during the first half of 1918 with this unit in Italy, claiming 19 victories and receiving the DSO, MC and DFC. He and his companions often claimed to have taken on great odds against German and Austrian machines, and on these occasions 'Spike' Howell was in his element. On 8 June he led two other Camels against six Austrian scouts and claimed two shot down. Then on 12 July he and Lieutenant Rice-Oxley fought off ten scouts, Howell claiming five, just as the Italian ace, Silvio Scaroni (26 victories) shot another off his tail. Scaroni was then hit himself and badly wounded (Austrian records indicate no losses actually being suffered during this engagement). Howell survived the dogfights over Northern Italy only to drown off Corfu on 10 December 1919, when the aircraft he was attempting to fly back to Australia crashed into the sea.

	1918		Camel					
1*	14 Jan	Alb. DIII	B4609	45	Cimetta-Cadogne	1500	DES(F)	CR/7 BG
2**	26 Jan	Alb. DIII	B4609	45	Sette Casoni	1335	DES	CR/7 BG
3	23 Apr	Alb. DIII	B5238	45	N Levico	0900	DES	CR/7 BG
4	13 May	Alb. DIII	B5238	45	Coldarco	0615	OOC	CR/14 W
5	13 May	Alb. DIII	B5238	45	Coldarco	0615	DES	CR/14 W
6	13 May	Alb. DIII	B5238	45	Costa	0620	DES	CR/14 W

7	13 May	Alb. DIII	B5238	45	Brenta-Rocca	0640	DES(F)	CR/14 W
8	8 Jun	Phonix DI	D9394	45	Mt Tomba	0800	DES	CR/14 W
9	8 Jun	Berg DI	D9394	45	Mt Tomba	0800	DES	CR/14 W
10	19 Jun	Alb. DV	D9394	45	Camporovere	0935	DES	ORB/14 W
11***	19 Jun	Alb. DV	D9394	45	Mt Meatta	0935	DES	ORB/14 W
12	12 Jul	Alb. DV	D9394	45	Feltre	0800	DES	ORB/14 W
13	12 Jul	Phonix DI	D9394	45	Feltre	c0805	DES(F)	ORB/14 W
14	12 Jul	Berg DI	D9394	45	Feltre	c0805	DES(F)	ORB/14 W
15	12 Jul	Phonix DI	D9394	45	Feltre	c0810	OOC	ORB/14 W
16	12 Jul	Berg DI	D9394	45	Feltre	c0810	OOC	ORB/14 W
17†	14 Jul	Alb. DV	D9394	45	Tresche-Potzo	0800	CAPT	ORB/14 W
18	15 Jul	Phonix DI	D8113	45	Costa Alta	1015	DES(F)	CR/14 w
19	15 Jul	Phonix DI	D8113	45	Mt Forcellona	1020	DES	CR/14 W

TOTAL: 1 captured, 15 destroyed, 2 out of control = 19.
*This was most probably Lt Wrege of Jasta 39, who was killed. **The likely loss was Korp. R. Klemm of Flik 56, who was forced to land in 153:123. ***45 claimed 7 victories in this fight. Flik 9j lost 2 pilots killed, and 1 aircraft damaged. See J.H. Dewhurst for details. †This was Flzfhr Michael Solsky of Flik 3j in 153:249, who died of wounds.

HOWELL Malcolm G. Lieutenant 208

An American member of 208 Squadron during 1918, he accounted for four enemy aircraft and shared in a victory over another whilst flying Camels.

	1918		Camel					
1s*	28 Jul	Rumpler C	----	208	S Estaires	0950	DES	CR/RAF 28.7
2	31 Jul	Pfalz DIII	----	208	Henin-Lietard	1145	DES	CR/RAF 31.7
3	13 Sep	DFW. C	----	208	S Henin-Lietard	0750	OOC	CR/?
4	26 Sep	Fokker DVII	B1535	208	N St Quentin	1825	OOC	CR/?
5	5 Oct	Fokker DVII	E7172	208	Fonsommes-Croix	1250	OOC	CR/?

TOTAL: 1 and 1 shared destroyed, 3 out of control = 5.
*Shared with Lt J.B. White, Lt G.A. Wightman.

HOWSAM George Robert Captain 70, 43

Born on 21 January 1894, Howsam was a Canadian from Toronto, who joined 70 Squadron in autumn 1917 and claimed his first victory on 28 December. During January 1918 he claimed seven more, including four during three sorties on 22nd. By mid-March his score had risen to 12 and he had been awarded an MC on 4th. He left the squadron after being wounded on 24 March, and returned to Home Establishment. He came back to the Western Front in October 1918 as a flight commander in 43 Squadron which had received the new Sopwith Snipes. Flying one of these, he shot down a Fokker DVII in flames on 30 October. He later served in the RCAF, retiring as an Air Vice-Marshal, CBE, in 1945.

	1917		Camel					
1	28 Dec	Alb. C	B2311	70	Zarren	1100	DES	CR/RFC 28.12
	1918							
2	19 Jan	Alb. C	B5598	70	Moorslede	1020	OOC	CR/RFC 19.1
3	22 Jan	Alb. DV	B5598	70	Westroosebeke	1245	DES	CR/RFC 22.1
4	22 Jan	C	B2530	70	N E Houthoulst Wood	1315	DES(F)	CR/RFC 22.1
5s*	22 Jan	Alb. DV	B2530	70	N E Houthoulst Wood	1414	DES(F)	CR/RFC 22.1
6s*	22 Jan	Alb. DV	B2530	70	N E Houthoulst Wood	1414	OOC	CR/RFC 22.1
7	24 Jan	Alb. C	B5598	70	Westroosebeke	1120	DES	CR/RFC 24.1
8	25 Jan	Alb. DV	B2530	70	N Bixschoote	1525	OOC	CR/RFC 25.1
9	27 Feb	Alb. C	B5598	70	Warneton	1105	DES	CR/RFC 27.2
10	8 Mar	Alb. DV	C8204	70	Roulers	1315	OOC	CR/RFC 8.3
11	9 Mar	Alb. DV	C8204	70	Menin-Roulers	0930	DES	CR/RFC 9.3
12	9 Mar	Alb. DV	C8204	70	Menin	0940	OOC	CR/RFC 9.3
			Snipe					
13	30 Oct	Fokker DVII	E8013	43	Aulnoye	1340	DES(F)	CR/RFC 9.3

TOTAL: 7 and 1 shared destroyed, 4 and 1 shared out of control = 13
*Shared with Capt F.G. Quigley B5214.

HOY Ernest Charles Captain 29

Born in Vancouver, Canada, on 6 May 1895, Hoy joined 29 Squadron in January 1918. He was then hospitalized from May to August, but on his return began claiming, and was soon promoted to flight commander. He claimed double victories on three occasions, his last victory on 27 September bringing his personal score to 13. The following day he was shot down south of Menin in C1914, and remained a prisoner for the rest of the war. He was awarded the DFC after his fifth victory, the decoration being gazetted on 3 December 1918. In August 1919 he made the first air-mail flight over the Canadian Rockies in a Curtis JN 4 in 16 hours 42 minutes. He attended the Aces Reunion in Paris in 1981, and died on 22 April 1982.

	1918		SE 5A					
1	12 Aug	Fokker DVII	D6939	29	Comines	0920	DES	CR/RAF 12.8
2s*	14 Aug	Halb. C	----	29	Armentieres	1010	DES(F)	CR/RAF 14.8
3	16 Aug	Pfalz DIII	C9071	29	Poelcapelle	1840	DES	CR/RAF 16.8
4s**	23 Aug	Balloon	D6939	29	S E Kemmel	0630	DES	CR/RAF 23.8
5	23 Aug	DFW. C	D6939	29	S E Kemmel	0635	DES	CR/RAF 23.8
6	24 Aug	Fokker DVII	D6939	29	S Comines	1910	DES	CR/RAF 24.8
7	24 Aug	Fokker DVII	D6939	29	S Comines	1915	OOC	CR/SR/11 WS
8	1 Sep	Balloon	D6939	29	N Armentieres	1025	DES	CR/RAF 1.9
9	1 Sep	Fokker DVII	D6939	29	N E Armentieres	1810	OOC	CR/SR/11 WS
10	3 Sep	Fokker DVII	D6939	29	N Comines	1930	DES	CR/SR/11 WS
11	16 Sep	Fokker DVII	E5974	29	N Quesnoy	0840	DES	CR/RAF 16.9
12	16 Sep	Fokker DVII	E5974	29	E Becelaere	0845	DES	CR/RAF 16.9
13	27 Sep	Fokker DVII	C1914	29	Passchendaele	1815	DES	CR/RAF 27.9

TOTAL: 1 shared balloon, 9 and 1 shared destroyed, 2 out of control = 13.
*Shared with Lt C.J. Venter D6965. **Shared with Lt C.G. Ross C9071, 2/Lt A.F. Diamond C8859.

HUBBARD Will Captain 3

Born on 25 February 1895, Will Hubbard, a native of Leamington Spa, Warwickshire, flew Camels with 3 Squadron in 1918, becoming a flight commander and receiving the DFC. He flew many ground attack sorties and in air combat was credited with ten victories. On 26 August he had just sent down a two-seater in a spin when he had engine failure and was forced to land inside the enemy lines. A German soldier fired at him with a pistol from a distance of about 15 yards and holed the Camel's petrol tank. Hubbard, however, managed to get his engine going and took off, his remaining petrol being just sufficient to carry him to the Allied side of the lines where he crash-landed. On 29 October 1918 he claimed 3 Squadron's last victory of the war.

	1918		Camel					
1s*	2 May	DFW. C	D9297	3	Arras	1615	OOC	CR/RAF 2.5
2	14 May	DFW. C	D9297	3	Vaux	1735	DES(F)	CR/RAF 14.5
3	14 May	DFW. C	D9297	3	Vaux	1736	DES	CR/RAF 14.5
4s**	27 May	Alb. C	----	3	57 D R 32	1240	OOC	CR/ORB/?
5s***	9 Jun	Alb. C	B2491	3	57 D R 3	1100	DES	CR/RAF 9.6
6	21 Aug	Halb. C	D6627	3	St Ledger	1155	DES	CR/RAF 21.8
7	26 Aug	Alb. C	D6627	3	57 C N 18	1255	OOC	CR/ORB/?
8	4 Sep	Fokker DVII	F6032	3	51 B W 21	1010	DES	CR/RAF 4.9
9	5 Sep	Alb. C	F6032	3	Peronne	1205	DES	CR/RAF 5.9
10	29 Oct	Fokker DVII	F6032	3	51 M ? 21	1005	OOC	CR/ORB/?

TOTAL: 5 and 1 shared destroyed, 2 and 2 shared out of control = 10.
*Shared with 1/Lt W.D. Tipton D6519. **Shared with Capt D.J. Bell, Lt L.A. Hamilton. ***Shared with Lt A.W. Franklyn D6431.

HUBBARD William Henry Captain 7, 5, 73

A Canadian, he joined the RFC in 1916, serving with 7 and 5 Squadron, flying BE 2Cs. On 8 September he and his observer, Lieutenant H.B. Rickards, were attacked by a Fokker monoplane but they sent the German down to crash. Hubbard was wounded on 26 December 1916 and returned to Home Establishment. In 1918 he was posted from his instructor's position in England to become a flight commander with 73 Squadron, claiming 11 further victories and receiving the DFC and Bar. He also flew many ground attack missions, inflicting a great deal of damage.

	1916		BE 2C					
1*	8 Sep	Fokker E	----	5	St Julien	P.M.	DES	RFC 9.9
	1918		Camel					
2	11 Apr	Alb. DV	C8269	73	5m S E Villers-Brettoneaux	1910	OOC	CR/RAF 12.4
3	21 May	Alb. DV	----	73	Armentieres	1830	DES	CR/RAF 21.5
4	6 Jun	Fokker DVII	D1841	73	Champien	1710	OOC	CR/Air I/1226
5	9 Jun	Fokker DVII	D1841	73	Conchy	1410	OOC	CR/Air I/1226

6	10 Jun	Fokker DVII	D8141	73	S W Rollot	0705	OOC	CR/Air I/2215
7	11 Jun	Fokker DVII	D8141	73	3m N E Rollot	1600	DES	CR/RAF 11.6
8	8 Jul	Fokker DVII	D1958	73	Seclin	0720	DES(F)	CR/RAF 8.7
9	29 Aug	Fokker DVII	D1958	73	N E Monchy	1030	OOC	CR/AIR I/1226
10	29 Aug	Fokker DVII	D1958	73	E Hendecourt	1040	CAPT	CR/RAF 29.8
11	15 Sep	Fokker DVII	F1917	73	Gouy sous Bellone	1810	DES	CR/RAF 15.9
12	8 Oct	Fokker DVII	F6351	73	Maretz	0815	OOC	CR/AIR I/1226

TOTAL: 1 captured, 5 destroyed, 6 out of control = 12.
*Observer: Lt H.B. Rickards.

HUDSON Frank Neville Captain 15, 54

Seconded to the RFC from the East Kent Regiment early in the war, he first flew with 15 Squadron during 1916. He remained in action throughout most of the year, bombing and strafing enemy positions, but during one sortie was wounded in the head, although he continued to complete the mission. For this work he was awarded an MC. In 1917 he went to 54 Squadron as a flight commander and with this unit he claimed at least six victories before he was shot down on 13 July in A6240 between Bruges and Ostend by Leutnant Fleckern of Jasta 20; wounded, he came down inside German lines where he was taken prisoner. All his claims with 54 Squadron were made whilst flying Pups.

	1917		Pup					
1	27 Jan	C	A652	54	Courcelette	1410	DES(F)	CR/RFC 27.1
2	13 Feb	C	----	54	Le Transloy	1045	OOC	CR/RFC 27.1
3s*	5 Apr	Balloon	----	54	Gouy	----	DES	SR/RFC 5.4
4	6 Apr	C	A6166	54	Le Catelet	0730	OOC	CR/RFC 6.4
5	26 Apr	Alb. DIII	----	54	Premont	1910	OOC	CR/RFC 26.4
6	11 Jul	Alb. C	A6246	54	N W Nieuport	0410	DES	CR/RFC 11.7

TOTAL: 1 shared balloon, 2 destroyed, 3 out of control = 6.
*Shared with Capt R.G.H. Pixley, Lt M.D.G. Scott, 2/Lt R.M. Charley.

HUDSON Harold Byron Lieutenant 28, 45

From Victoria, British Columbia, this Canadian joined the RFC and was sent to Italy, serving with 28 Squadron, where he was known as 'Steve'. He flew in Captain Barker's flight, and on 24 January and 12 February 1918 went on balloon strafes with Barker, sharing in the destruction of seven balloons. In addition, he accounted for a further six German and Austrian machines while with 28, and received an MC. He was posted briefly to 45 Squadron, but did not add to his victories whilst with this unit.

	1918		Camel					
1s*	24 Jan	Balloon	B6356	28	2km E Conegliano	1620	DES	CR/7 BG
2s*	24 Jan	Balloon	B6356	28	E Conegliano	1621	DES	CR/7 BG
3**	5 Feb	Alb. DV	B6356	28	Portobuffole	1210	DES	CR/7 BG
4s*	12 Feb	Balloon	B6356	28	Fossamerlo	1445	DES	CR/7 BG
5s*	12 Feb	Balloon	B6356	28	Fossamerlo	1445	DES	CR/7 BG
6s*	12 Feb	Balloon	B6356	28	Fossamerlo	1445	DES	CR/ORB/?
7s*	12 Feb	Balloon	B6356	28	Fossamerlo	1445	DES	CR/ORB/?
8s*	12 Feb	Balloon	B6356	28	Fossamerlo	1445	DES	CR/14 W
9	20 Feb	Alb. DV	B6356	28	Conegliano	1000	OOC	CR/14 W
10	20 Feb	Alb. DV	B6356	28	Conegliano	1000	OOC	CR/14 W
11	13 May	Rumpler C	B6356	28	E Quero	0845	DES(F)	CR/14 W
12	23 May	Alb. DIII	B6356	28	1k S Grigno	0725	DES	CR/14 W
13	26 May	Alb. DIII	B2362	28	Fontanella	0845	DES	CR/14 W

TOTAL: 7 shared balloons, 4 destroyed, 2 out of control = 13.
*Shared with Capt W.G. Barker B6313. **Probably FwP Karl Semmelrock of Flik 51j, who was killed in 153:126.

HUGHES David James Captain 3

Born in Wales on 16 April 1899, Hughes served as an instructor on completion of training. He then flew Camels with 3 Squadron during the late summer and autumn of 1918, becoming a flight commander. He claimed five victories including a Fokker DVII forced to land in Allied lines on 4 September, and was awarded a DFC, gazetted on 3 December 1918.

	1918		Camel					
1	8 Aug	Alb. C	D6603	3	N Chaulnes	1800	DES(F)	CR/RAF 8.8
2	10 Aug	Fokker DVII	D6603	3	62 ? C54	1040	OOC	CR/ORB/?
3s*	26 Aug	Alb. C	F1972	3	S W Bapaume	0700	DES	CR/RAF 26.8
4**	4 Sep	Fokker DVII	F1972	3	51B W21	1010	CAPT	CR/RAF 4.9
5	23 Oct	C	H829	3	57S ?4	1210	OOC	CR/ORB/?

TOTAL: 1 captured, 2 destroyed, 2 out of control = 5.
*Shared with Lt V.H. McElroy C8344. **This was Flgr Otto Wagner of Jasta 79b, who was captured.

HUGHES Eric Yorath Captain 46, 3

'Taffy' Hughes was born in Brigend, South Wales, on 6 July 1894. He enlisted as a gunner in the Welsh Brigade, Royal Field Artillery, in November 1914, serving in France in 1915 and later in Egypt with the 52nd Division in 1916. Volunteering for the RFC in August 1916, he returned to England. While doing an engines' course at Oxford his room-mate was W.A. Bishop, who was later to win the VC. Finishing his training, he was posted to France and joined 46 Squadron on 16 June 1917 with a total of 18 hours flying time. He claimed at least four victories before being promoted to Captain and posted to 3 Squadron as a flight commander on 30 November. Here he shot down one enemy aircraft, but was rested in February 1918 after eight months active flying. During World War Two he served in Training Command, receiving an AFC and becoming a Wing Commander; he retired from the service in 1947, settling at Hove in Sussex.

	1917		Pup					
1s*	4 Sep	Alb. C	A6188	46	S Scarpe	0930	OOC	CR/11 WS
2s**	11 Sep	C	A6188	46	S Scarpe	1055	OOC	CR/RFC 11.9
3s***	21 Sep	C	A6188	46	S Scarpe	0820	OOC	CR/RFC 21.9
4	1 Dec	Alb. DIII	B2191	46	Cambrai	0910	DES	CR/RFC 1.12
			Camel					
5	12 Dec	Alb. DV	B5238	3	Cambrai	1020	OOC	CR/RFC 12.12

TOTAL: 1 destroyed, 1 and 3 shared out of control = 5.

*Shared with Capt M.D.G. Scott B1843, Lt C.W. Odell B1842, Lt C. Courtneidge B1802, Lt E. Armitage B1837. **Shared with Capt M.D.G. Scott B1843, Lt A.G. Lee B1777, Lt E. Armitage. ***Shared with Capt M.D.G. Scott B2191, Lt A.G. Lee B1777.

HUGHES Geoffrey Forrest Captain 62

Born in Sydney, New South Wales, on 12 July 1895, this Australian flew with 62 Squadron in the spring of 1918, his usual observer being Captain H. Claye. During one of his early combats on 10 March, he claimed two enemy aircraft shot down, while his next combat the following day brought claims for one Triplane shot down and three more driven down and forced to land, although these latter were not added to his score. For this particular action he received the MC, as did his observer; these awards were gazetted in May, by which time his victories totalled 11. After the war he received the AFC before going into civil aviation in Australia. He died of pneumonia on 13 September 1951.

	1918		Bristol					
1*	21 Feb	C	C4630	62	Armentieres area	----	DES	SR/RFC 21.2
2*	10 Mar	Alb. DV	----	62	----	----	DES	RFC 10.3
3*	10 Mar	Alb. DV	----	62	----	----	OOC	RDC 10.3
4*	11 Mar	Fokker DrI	----	62	----	----	OOC	RFC 11.3
5*	13 Mar	Fokker DrI	C4630	62	E Cambrai	1030	OOC	CR/RFC 13.3
6s**	13 Mar	Fokker DrI	C4630	62	E Cambrai	1030	DES	CR/RFC 13.3
7*	12 Apr	Alb. DV	----	62	S Bois du Biez	1420	OOC	SR/RAF 12.4
8*	12 Apr	LVG. C	----	62	Auchy les La Bassee	1500	DES(F)	SR/RAF 12.4
9*	22 Apr	Fokker DVI?	----	62	Nieppe Forest	1030	OOC	SR/RAF 22.4
10*	22 Apr	Fokker DVI?	----	62	Nieppe Forest	1030	OOC	SR/RAF 22.4
11*	10 May	Rumpler C	----	62	Combles-Peronne	1835	OOC	SR/RAF 10.5

TOTAL: 4 destroyed, 7 out of control = 11.

*Observer: Capt H Claye. **Observer: Capt H. Claye; this was Lt L. von Richthofen of Jasta 11, who crashed landed after combat with Hughes/Claye and Capt A.H. Orlebar in Camel B7282 of 73 Sqn.

HUNT Frederick John Lieutenant 74

'Jack' Hunt, from Whitchurch, Hampshire, joined 74 Squadron in late July 1918, and on 1 September shot down a kite balloon. Between then and 27 October he claimed three Fokker DVIIs destroyed and two out of control, adding another balloon to these on the latter date. He was awarded a DFC, gazetted on 8 February 1919, and on 30 October claimed two more DVIIs to bring his score to nine.

	1918		SE 5A					
1	1 Sep	Balloon	E5967	74	N E Armentieres	1350	DES	CR/RAF 1.9
2	4 Sep	Fokker DVII	----	74	.5m S Lille	1930	OOC	CR/11 WS
3	17 Sep	Fokker DVII	D6967	74	N Courtrai	1845	DES(F)	CR/RAF 17.9
4	21 Sep	Fokker DVII	----	74	Lille	1840	DES	CR/RAF 21.9
5	26 Oct	Fokker DVII	----	74	Cordes	1455	DES	CR/RAF 26.10
6	26 Oct	Fokker DVII	----	74	Cordes	1455	OOC	CR/11 WS
7	27 Oct	Balloon	C1137	74	Molenbaix	0940	DES	CR/RAF 27.10
8	30 Oct	Fokker DVII	----	74	De Klype	0820	DES	CR/RAF 30.10
9	30 Oct	Fokker DVII	----	74	Quaremont	0825	DES(F)	CR/RAF 30.10

TOTAL: 2 balloons, 5 destroyed, 2 out of control = 9.

HUNTER John Ellis Langford Captain 4(N), 204

Born on 31 July 1896 and joining 4(N) Squadron in July 1917, Hunter claimed three victories in September of that year and two more in March 1918, by which time he had become a Flight Lieutenant and had received a DSC. He continued flying with the unit when it became 204 Squadron, RAF, and on 31 July claimed two Fokker DVIIs. Now a flight commander, he was again in combat with DVIIs on 12 August when he sent down two in flames and another out of control, but he was himself wounded in the leg. The award of a DFC was promulgated on 10 September.

	1917		Camel					
1s*	3 Sep	C	B3879	4N	1m S W Ghistelles	1650	OOC	CR/RNAS 3.9
2s**	22 Sep	Seaplane	B3879	4N	22m N E Ostend	0815	DES	CR/RNAS 22.9
3	22 Sep	Seaplane	B3879	4N	22m N E Ostend	0815	DES	CR/RNAS 22.9
	1918							
4	21 Mar	Pfalz DIII	B3879	4N	5m off Middelkerke	0825	DES	CR/RNAS 21.3
5	26 Mar	Pfalz DIII	B3879	4N	1.5m N E Dixmude	1700	DES	CR/RNAS 27.3
6	2 May	Rumpler C	B3879	204	S Dixmude	1815	OOC	CR/ORB/DL
7	30 Jun	Fokker DVII	B3895	204	Blankerberghe	1445	OOC	CR/5 GP Comm
8	31 Jul	Fokker DVII	B3894	204	Roulers	1930	DES	CR/5 GP Comm
9	31 Jul	Fokker DVII	B3894	204	Roulers	1930	DES	CR/5 GP Comm
10	12 Aug	Fokker DVII	B3894	204	Blankenberghe	1055	DES(F)	CR/5 GP Comm
11	12 Aug	Fokker DVII	B3894	204	Blankenberghe	1055	DES	CR/5 GP Comm
12	12 Aug	Fokker DVII	B3894	204	Blakenberghe	1055	OOC	CR/ORB/?

TOTAL: 7 and 1 shared destroyed, 3 and 1 shared out of control = 12.
*Shared with FSL K.V. Turney B3867. **Shared with FSL K.V. Turney B3867, FSL A.C. Burt B6213.

HUNTER Thomas Vicars Captain 66

Educated at Eton and Sandhurst, Tom Hunter joined the Rifle Brigade and was commissioned in December 1914. Going to France, he was badly wounded in January 1915, resulting in the loss of a leg. He joined the RFC early in 1917 and became known as 'Sticky' because of his false leg. After training, he went to 66 Squadron flying Pups, becoming a flight commander in September. He accounted for five hostile machines by mid-November. Whenever a mess party got too hectic, he would take off his wooden leg to avoid it being broken. This gallant flyer was killed on 5 December 1917 in a flying accident immediately after the squadron had arrived in Italy.

	1917		Pup					
1	12 Jul	Alb. DIII	B1760	66	N E Ypres	2000	OOC	CR/RFC 12.7
2	27 Jul	Alb. DIII	B1760	66	Ardoye	1425-1730	DES	ORB/RFC 27.7
3	28 Jul	Alb. DIII	B1760	66	E Roulers	1835-2130	OOC	ORB/RFC 28.7
4	3 Sep	Alb. DV	B1760	66	N E Menin	1135	OOC	CR/RFC 3.9
			Camel					
5	8 Nov	Alb. DV	B5173	66	----	0830-1050	OOC	ORB/RFC 8.11

TOTAL: 1 destroyed, 4 out of control = 5.

HURST Cyril Edward Lieutenant 22

Joining the RFC as a cadet on 8 November 1917, he flew with 22 Squadron from summer 1918, making his first claim on 16 August while flying with Sgt H.C. Hunt, his usual observer. His fifth and last claim was made two weeks later on 31 August.

	1918		Bristol					
1*	16 Aug	C	F5824	22	Fresnoy	1100	DES	CR/RAF 16.8
2*	25 Aug	Pfalz DIII	C1035	22	W Peronne	1830	DES	CR/RAF 25.8
3*	25 Aug	Fokker DrI	C1035	22	Maricourt	1835	DES	CR/RAF 25.8
4*	25 Aug	Pfalz DIII	C1035	22	W Maricourt	1835	OOC	CR/ORB/?
5*	31 Aug	Fokker DVII	F5824	22	S E Vitry	1710	OOC	CR/ORB/?

TOTAL: 3 destroyed, 2 out of control = 5.
*Observer: Sgt H.C. Hunt.

HUSKINSON Patrick Major 2, 19

Born 17 March 1896, Huskinson left Harrow School to enter the Royal Military College at Sandhurst; he was commissioned in the Sherwood Foresters, then serving with the Notts and Derby Regiment. Transferring to the RFC in 1915, he flew with 2 Squadron in 1916, receiving the MC. The following year he was posted to 19 Squadron and flew Spads, and in 1918, Dolphins, claiming 11 victories and adding a Bar to his MC. In 1919 he took command of 70 Squadron in Germany. Remaining in the RAF, he became a Wing Commander in 1933 and in 1936 was OC, RAF North Coates. Early in World War Two he was blinded in an air raid, but remained in the Air Force, and in spite of his handicap designed the 'block-buster' 4,000 lb bomb. He was appointed a

CBE in 1942, and awarded the American Legion of Merit in 1945, attaining the rank of Air Commodore. He died on 24 November 1966. He wrote *Vision Ahead* in 1949.

	1917		Spad					
1	24 Oct	Alb. DV	A6777	19	Menin	0845	OOC	CR/RFC 24.10
2	27 Oct	Alb. C	A6777	19	Oosthoek	1050	OOC	CR/RFC 27.10
3	13 Nov	C	A6773	19	Mooorslede	1035	DES	CR/RFC 13.11
4	3 Dec	Alb. DIII	B1593	19	Menin	1215	OOC	CR/RFC 3.12
5	29 Dec	Alb. DV	B1593	19	Houthoulst Forest	1020	OOC	CR/RFC 29.12
6	29 Dec	Alb. DV	B1593	19	Houthoulst Forest	1025	OOC	CR/RFC 29.12
	1918							
7	6 Jan	Alb. DV	B1593	19	Houthoulst Forest	0700	OOC	ORB/RFC 6.1
			Dolphin					
8	8 Mar	Alb. DV	C3792	19	Gheluwe	1105	OOC	ORB/RFC 8.3
9	9 Mar	Pfalz DIII	C3792	19	S E Wervicq	1305	DES	ORB/RFC 9.3
10	15 Mar	Alb. DV	C3792	19	S E Comines	1140	OOC	ORB/RFC 15.3
11	17 Mar	Pfalz DIII	C3792	19	Roulers	1225	DES	ORB/RFC 17.3

TOTAL: 3 destroyed, 8 out of control = 11.

HUSTINGS Norman William Lieutenant 19

Hustings received his commission in the RFC in September 1917 and joined 19 Squadron early the following year. Flying Sopwith Dolphins with this unit, he claimed seven enemy scouts during the early months of 1918.

	1917		Spad					
1s*	29 Nov	Alb. DV	B1660	19	E Becelaere	1245	OOC	ORB/SR/?
	1918		Dolphin					
2	15 Mar	Alb. DV	C3899	19	S E Comines	1140	OOC	ORB/RFC 15.3
3	21 Apr	Pfalz DIII	C3899	19	Steenwerck	1915	OOC	CR/RAF 21.4
4**	2 May	Fokker DrI	C3899	19	S Armentieres	1745	OOC	CR/RAF 2.5
5	17 May	Pfalz DIII	C4043	19	Armentieres	1045	OOC	CR/RFC 17.5
6	20 May	Pfalz DIII	C3899	19	N W Armentieres	1830	OOC	CR/ORB/?
7	7 Jun	Alb. DV	C3899	19	E Henin-Lietard	1015	DES	CR/RAF 7.6

TOTAL: 2 destroyed, 5 out of control = 7.

*Shared with Capt O.C. Bryson A6780, Capt G.W. Taylor A6805. **Major A.D. Carter also claimed a Triplane: Uffz Meersdorff of Jasta 26 was killed at this location in a Triplane.

HUSTON Victor Henry Major 18

An Irishman living in Vancouver, Canada, in 1914, Huston joined the Canadian Expeditionary Force, arriving in France in 1915. In 1916 he joined the RFC and became an FE 2B pilot with 18 Squadron from December of that year. He and his observers had claimed five victories by 27 May 1917, when he and Lieutenant E.A. Ford shared an Albatros Scout destroyed with Flight Sub Lieutenant H.S. Kerby of 3(Naval) Squadron; this was to be Huston's last claim, and an MC was awarded to him on 16 June. In August 1918 he departed for Chile as Chief Instructor in the new Chilean Air Force, but he left the RAF in November 1919.

	1917		FE 2B					
1*	15 Feb	C	A5445	18	Grevillers	1015	DES	CR/RFC 15.2
2**	5 Apr	Alb. DII	4969	18	Inchy	1200	OOC	CR/RFC 5.4
3**	5 Apr	Alb. DII	4969	18	Inchy	1200	OOC	CR/RFC 5.4
4***	24 Apr	Alb. DIII	----	18	----	----	DES	RFC 24.4
5***	13 May	Halb. D	4998	18	N W Cambrai	1745	DES	CR/RFC 13.5
6†	27 May	Alb. DV	4998	18	N Havrincourt	0745	DES	CR/RFC 27.5

TOTAL: 3 and 1 shared destroyed, 2 out of control = 6.

*Observer: 2/Lt P.S. Taylor. **Observer: 2/Lt G.N. Blennerhasset. ***Observer: Lt E.A. Foord. †Observer: Lt E.A. Foord; shared with FSL H.S. Kerby in Pup N6465, of 3N.

HYDE G.A. Captain 54

Hyde joined the RFC from the King's Rifle Corps, with which he had been awarded an MC. After his training, he was posted to 54 Squadron based at Chipilly, in February 1917. He flew Pups throughout that year, becoming 'A' Flight commander in October. Just after the squadron re-equipped with Camels, and after 10 months' active service in France, he returned to England to end the war as an instructor. He was known as 'Milford'.

	1917		Pup					
1s*	17 Mar	C	----	54	3m E Roye	1135	OOC	CR/RFC 17.3?
2	30 Apr	Alb. DIII	A649	54	Walincourt	0630	OOC	CR/RFC 30.4
3s**	12 Aug	Alb. DIII	----	54	----	----	OOC	RFC 12.8

4s***	24 Sep	Alb. DV	A6156	54	Mannekensvere	1240	OOC	CR/RFC 24.9
5s†	18 Oct	Alb. DV	B1792	54	Leke	1430	DES	CR/RFC 18.10

TOTAL: 1 shared destroyed, 1 and 3 shared out of control = 5.
*Shared with 2/Lt N.A. Phillips, Cap A.G. Pixley, 2/Lt J.W. Sheridan. **Shared with 2/Lt Gibbes. ***Shared with Capt F.J Morse B1792. †Shared with 2/Lt M.E. Gonne A6215.

IACCACI August Thayer Captain 20, 48

An American from New York, August Iaccaci and his brother Paul both joined the RFC and after training were both posted to 20 Squadron to fly Bristol Fighters, August arriving with this unit on 25 April 1918. He claimed his first victories in May, flying with 1st Air Mechanic (later Sergeant) A. Newlands as his gunner. He received the DFC in July and with his gunner was credited with 17 victories by October, by which time he had been posted to 48 Squadron as a flight commander. He returned to England on 2 October after receiving a slight eye wound.

	1918		Bristol					
1*	19 May	Pfalz DIII	C859	20	S Vieux Berquin	1040	DES	CR/RAF 19.5
2*	22 May	C	----	20	Bailleul	----	DES	SR/Per Rec
3*	27 May	Pfalz DIII	B1114	20	3km S Neuve Eglise	1215	DES	CR/RAF 27.5
4**	31 May	Alb. DV	C4762	20	S W Armentieres	0800	OOC	CR/11 WS
5***	31 May	Pfalz DIII	----	20	N Comines	1850	OOC	SR/?
6†	1 Jun	Pfalz DIII	C976	20	N Merville	1200	OOC	CR/11 WS
7††	8 Jun	Pfalz DIII	C892	20	N E Wervicq	1720	DES	CR/RAF 8.6
8††	17 Jun	Pfalz DIII	C892	20	Houthem	0715	DES	CR/RAF 17.6
9†††	30 Jun	Pfalz DIII	C892	20	W Halluin	0730	DES	CR/RAF 30.6
10s‡	14 Jul	Fokker DVII	----	20	S E Ypres	0900	OOC	CR/SR/?/11 WS
11†††	6 Sep	Fokker DVII	E2213	20	Cambrai-St Quentin	0830	OOC	CR/ORB/?
12†††	6 Sep	Fokker DVII	E2213	20	N E St Quentin	0855	DES	CR/RAF 6.9
13†††	15 Sep	Fokker DVII	E2213	20	S Lesdin	1115	DES	CR/RAF 15.9
14†††	15 Sep	Fokker DVII	E2213	20	S Morcourt	1120	DES	CR/RAF 15.9
15†††	16 Sep	Fokker DVII	E2213	20	W Lesdin	0825	DES	CR/RAF 16.9
16†††	27 Sep	Fokker DVII	E2213	20	S Fontaine	1030	DES	CR/RAF 27.9
17†††	27 Sep	Fokker DVII	E2213	20	N Bernot	1030	OOC	CR/ORB/?

TOTAL: 11 destroyed, 5 and 1 shared out of control = 17.
*Observer: 1 AM A. Newlands. **Observer: Sgt D.A. Malpas. ***Observer: 2/Lt E. Hardcastle. †Observer: Sgt W. O'Neill. ††Observer: Cpl A. Newlands. †††Observer: Sgt A. Newlands. ‡Observer: Lt R.W. Turner; shared Capt D. Latimer/Lt T.C. Noel C987.

IACCACI Paul Thayer Lieutenant 20

An American from New York, brother of August Iaccaci, Paul arrived in France with his brother in April 1918 to join 20 Squadron. Flying with various gunners, Paul was awarded the DFC in September; when he returned home he had been credited with 17 victories, three being gained in one action on 4 July — an auspicious date for an American! He returned to the USA after the war and died in the mid 1960s.

	1918		Bristol					
1*	18 May	Fokker DrI	----	20	S W Nieppe	c1140	OOC	SR/?
2**	19 May	Fokker DrI	C4604	20	Merville	1055	DES	CR/RAF 19.5
3*	31 May	Pfalz DIII	B1122	201E	Merville	07450	DES(F)	CR/RAF 31.5
4*	31 May	Alb. DV	B1122	20	S Merville	0800	DES	CR/RAF 31.5
5***	31 May	Alb. DV	C4699	20	N W Armentieres	1855	OOC	CR/11 WS
6†	13 Jun	Alb. DV	B1122	20	N N W Armentieres	0800	OOC	CR/11 WS
7†	17 Jun	Pfalz DIII	B1122	20	Houthem	0725	DES	CR/RAF 17.6
8††	26 Jun	Pfalz DIII	D8090	20	Armentieres	1900	OOC	CR/11 WS
9†††	4 Jul	Alb. DV	C951	20	W Veldhoek	1620	DES	CR/RAF 4.7
10†††	4 Jul	Alb. DV	C951	20	W Veldhoek	1630	OOC	CR/SR/11 WS
11†††	4 Jul	Alb. DV	C951	20	N E Zillebeke Lake	1640	DES	CR/RAF 4.7
12†††	10 Jul	Fokker DVII	D7919	20E	Z Zillebeke Lake	0920	DES	CR/RAF 10.7
13†††	10 Jul	Fokker DVII	D7919	20	E Zillebeke Lake	0920	OOC	CR/RAF 10.7
14‡	30 Jul	Fokker DVII	D7915	20	N E Bailleul	1930	DES(F)	CR/RAF 30.7
15‡‡	3 Sep	Fokker DVII	E2470	20	Havrincourt Wood	1745	DES	CR/RAF 3.9
16‡‡	6 Sep	Fokker DVII	E2470	20	Cambrai-Peronne Rd	0830	DES	CR/RAF 6.9
17‡‡	6 Sep	Fokker DVII	E2470	20	St Quentin	0850	OOC	CR/ORB/SR/?

TOTAL: 10 destroyed, 7 out of control = 17.
*Observer: 1 AM A. Newlands. **Observer: Sgt W. Sansome. ***Observer: 1 AM S.W. Melbourne. †Observer: Lt W. Noble. ††Observer: 2/Lt F.J. Ralphs. †††Observer: 2/Lt R.W. Turner. ‡Observer: 2/Lt H.L. Edwards. ‡‡Observer: Lt A. Mills.

INGALLS David Sinton Lieutenant 213, 217

An American, David Ingalls was born on 28 January 1899 in Cleveland, Ohio. He attended Yale University where he joined the flying club, and at 18 was accepted for duty with the US Navy as Naval Aviator No 85. Late in 1917 he was posted to France with a coastal patrol squadron, but finding this dull, flew Camels with 213 Squadron, RAF, from 29 March until 20 April 1918. He then flew DH 4s before rejoining 213 on 9 August. From 11 August to 24 September 1918 he was credited with six victories, five of them shared. He was awarded a DFC and an American DSC as the only US Navy ace of World War One. After the war he became a lawyer, but he was recalled to duty in World War II as a Commander; serving for three years, he retired as a Rear Admiral, USNR. He then worked as a vice-president of Pan American World Airways, and then as president and publisher of the Cincinnati *Times-Star* newspaper. David Ingalls died on 26 April 1985.

	1918		Camel					
1s*	11 Aug	Alb. C	C73	213	7m N E Dixmude	0955	DES	CR/5 GP Comm
2s**	21 Aug	LVG. C	N6376	213	S Zevecote	1650	DES	CR/5 GP Comm
3s***	15 Sep	Rumpler C	D9649	213	Ostend	1400	DES(F)	CR/5 GP Comm
4s†	18 Sep	Balloon	D9649	213	La Barriere	1050	DES	CR/5 GP Comm
5	20 Sep	Fokker DVII	D8177	213	Vlisseghem	1045	DES	CR/5 GP Comm
6s††	24 Sep	Rumpler C	D9649	213	St Pierre Cappele	1730	DES(F)	CR/5 GP Comm

TOTAL: 1 shared balloon, 1 and 4 shared destroyed = 6.
*Shared with Lt C.P. Brown D9490. **Shared with Capt C.P. Brown D9649, Lt H.C. Smith D3341. ***Shared with Lt H.C. Smith D3378. †Shared with Lt H.C. Smith D3378, Lt G.S. Hodson D3341. ††Shared with Lt G.S. Hodson D3341.

IRVING Gordon Budd Captain 19

A Canadian who joined the RFC in 1917, he was posted after training to 19 Squadron in November of that year. Flying Sopwith Dolphins, he claimed at least 12 victories, being awarded the DFC which was gazetted in August. He was promoted to Captain and flight commander in May. During a patrol on 11 August Irving, in F3342, was shot down in flames, while two of his pilots were also brought down, one being killed and one captured during a hectic dogfight with Jastas 10 and 37 near Albert. The three Dolphins were claimed by Leutnants A. Heldmann (10 victories), J. Grassmann (five victories) and G. Meyer of Jasta 37.

	1918		Dolphin					
1s*	24 Mar	C	C3838	19	W Roulers	1040	OOC	ORB/RFC 24.3
2	21 Apr	Pfalz DIII	C3799	19	Steenwerck	1915	DES(F)	CR/RAF 21.4
3s*	23 Apr	Pfalz DIII	C3799	19	N La Bassee	1820	OOC	CR/RFC 23.4
4s*	8 May	Alb. DV	C3799	19	S E Bailleul	1020	DES	CR/RAF/8.8?
5	31 May	Pfalz DIII	C3799	19	S E Estaires	0700	OOC	CR/ORB/?
6	31 May	Alb. DV	C3799	19	S W Armentieres	0800	OOC	CR/ORB/?
7s**	6 Jun	DFW. C	C3799	19	Vieux Berquin	0715	OOC	ORB/SR/?
8	17 Jun	Pfalz DIII	C3799	19	S Armentieres	0915	OOC	ORB/SR/?
9	27 Jun	Pfalz DIII	D3696	19	Estaires	1800	OOC	CR/ORB/SR/?
10s***	1 Jul	LVG. C	C3996	19	W Steenwerck	1430	DES(F)	CR/RAF 1.7
11	2 Jul	Fokker DrI	C3996	19	Estaires	0530	OOC	CR/ORB/SR/?
12	11 Aug	Pfalz DIII	E4432	19	E Albert	1700	OOC	CR/ORB/SR/?

TOTAL: 1 and 3 shared destroyed, 6 and 2 shared out of control = 12.
*Shared with Major A.D. Carter C4017. **Shared with Lt F. McQuistan C3902, Capt J.D. de Pencier C3829, Lt C.V. Gardner C4129. ***Shared with Lt J.D. Hardman C3818, Lt J.A. Aldridge C3833.

IRWIN William Roy Captain 56

A Canadian from Ripley, Ontario, he was born on 7 June 1898, and was posted to 56 Squadron in January 1918. He received the DFC and Bar for actions fought on 10 August and 3 September. On the first date he and 'Hank' Burden fought several Fokker Biplanes, Irwin claiming two and Burden three. That afternoon they had another fight, Burden getting two more and Irwin one. On 3 September he led a patrol which claimed four Fokkers shot down, accounting for two himself. The squadron gave him credit for 11 victories by the end of the war, during which he had flown over 70 operational patrols and six special missions. He died on 14 January 1969.

	1918		SE 5A					
1s*	3 May	Rumpler C	C5435	56	Montauban	0955	DES	CR/RAF 3.5
2s*	3 May	Rumpler C	C5435	56	S E Bapaume	1015	OOC	CR/RAF 3.5
3	28 Jun	Alb. DIII	B179	56	Dompierre	2020	DES	CR/RAF 28.6

4	8 Aug	Fokker DVII	D6121	56	N E Chaulnes	1905	DES	CR/RAF 8.8?
5	10 Aug	Fokker DVII	D6121	56	Marchelpot	1150	DES	CR/RAF 10.8?
6	10 Aug	Fokker DVII	D6121	56	Marchelpot	1150	DES	CR/RAF 10.8?
7	10 Aug	Fokker DVII	D6121	56	E Roye	2010	OOC	CR/?
8	12 Aug	Fokker DVII	D6121	56	Ham	1645	DES	CR/RAF 12.8
9	12 Aug	Fokker DVII	D6121	56	Ham	1645	DES	CR/RAF 12.8
10	3 Sep	Fokker DVII	D338	56	Etaing	0710	DES	CR/RAF 3.9
11	3 Sep	Fokker DVII	D338	56	Haynecourt	0710	DES	CR/RAF 3.9

TOTAL: 8 and 1 shared destroyed, 1 and 1 shared out of control = 11.
*Shared with Capt E.D. Atkinson B8494, Lt T Durrant B183.

JAMES Mansell Richard Captain 45

This Canadian flew with 45 Squadron in Italy in 1918, claiming 11 victories including nine destroyed. His award of the DFC was gazetted in November and he was promoted to Captain.

	1918		Camel					
1	3 Jun	Alb. DV	B3872	45	Feltre	0905	DES	CR/14 W
2	7 Jun	Alb. DIII	D8102	45	San Marino	0930	DES	CR/14 W
3	7 Jun	Alb. DIII	D8102	45	Collicella	0935	DES	CR/14 W
4*	20 Jul	Alb. DV	D8211	45	E Feltre	0720	DES	ORB/14 W
5*	20 Jul	Alb. DV	D8211	45	E Feltre	0720	DES	ORB/14 W
6	5 Aug	AEG. C	D8211	45	Porteghetti	0630	DES	ORB/14 W
7	6 Aug	Alb. DV	D8211	45	Segusino	1050	OOC	ORB/14 W
8	6 Aug	Alb. DV	D8211	45	Segusino	1050	OOC	ORB/14 W
9**	6 Aug	Alb. DV	D8211	45	Segusino	1050	DES	ORB/14 W
10***	31 Aug	Alb. DIII	D8211	45	Mt Segugio	0945	DES	CR/14 W
11†	31 Aug	Alb. DIII	D8211	45	Arsiero	0945	DES	CR/14 W

TOTAL: 9 destroyed, 2 out of control = 11.
*45 squadron made two other claims in this fight. Fwp H. Mayerbaurl of Flik 41j was killed in Phonix D1 122:18. **Possibly Flp R. Ax of Flik 30j, who was wounded and crash landed 153:194. ***This was Lt J. Kubelik of Flik 3j, who was killed in 153:271. †This was Lt Stanislaw M. Tomice von Tomicki of Flik 3j, who was killed in 153:173.

JARVIS Arthur Eyguem De Montainge Lieutenant 17, 150

A Canadian, 'Jacko' Jarvis served in the East Ontario Regiment before joining the RFC. Posted to 17 Squadron in Macedonia in early 1918, he initially flew one of the rare Bristol M 1C monoplanes in action. On 25 April he claimed a DFW shared with Lieutenant A.G. Goulding who was flying an SE 5A. Next day he shared another DFW with a Nieuport Scout, but shortly after this the scout pilots of the squadron joined those of 47 Squadron to form 150 Squadron. On 20 May, now flying a Camel, he attacked an LVG and shot it down out of control, the observer falling out. This aircraft had very odd markings and may have been Bulgarian. The rest of his combats with the squadron were all fought in SE 5As, and were mainly shared with other pilots, his final score being seven. Jarvis died on 20 January 1969.

	1918		Bristol M1C					
1s*	25 Apr	DFW. CV	C4913	17	Angista	1000	OOC	CR/BG Summ
2s**	26 Apr	DFW. CV	C4913	17	Kuakli	1045	DES	CR/BG Summ
			Camel					
3	20 May	LVG. C	----	150	Hudova	1215	OOC	CR/BG Summ
			SE 5A					
4s***	11 Jul	Alb. DV	----	150	1m N W Furka	0700	OOC	CR/BG Summ
5s†	19 Jul	Alb. DV	B30	150	W Livunovo	0800	DES	CR/BG Summ
6	26 Jul	Rumpler C	B163	150	S E Cerniste	0910	DES	CR/BG Summ
7s††	26 Jul	DFW. CV	B30	150	Elisan	1220	CAPT	CR/BG Summ

TOTAL: 1 shared captured, 1 and 2 shared destroyed, 1 and 2 shared out of control = 7.
*Shared with Lt A.G. Goulding in SE 5A B690. **Shared with Lt J.J. Boyd Harvey in Nieuport 5177. ***Shared with Lt J.A. Beeny B695, Lt W. Ridley B30. †Shared with Capt G.G. Bell B692, Capt G.M. Brawley B694, Lt W. Ridley C9501. ††Shared with Lt C.B. Spackman C9501. The crew were captured.

JARVIS Arthur Gordon Lieutenant 28

From London, the son of the Rev C. Jarvis, he joined the RFC in 1916, and after training was posted to France where he joined 28 Squadron. He took part in attacks on Roulers aerodrome which took place on three successive weekends, after which a sweep was made far behind the enemy lines. His first victory was claimed in December, by which time 28 Squadron had moved to Italy. In addition to air fighting in which he claimed five victories, he was engaged on many low bombing and strafing attacks, flying at times as far as the Alps and also along the Asiago Valley and the Piave river. He remained in the RAF after the war, retiring as a Group Captain, OBE, DFC.

	1917		Camel					
1s*	26 Dec	DFW. C	B2303	28	2km N W Pevegliano	0920	CAPT	CR/7 BG
	1918							
2	4 Feb	Alb. DIII	B6285	28	600y N Ponte Priula	1120	DES	CR/7 BG
3	15 Jun	Balloon	B7354	28	Comba	0745	DES	CR/14 W
	1918							
4s**	25 Jun	Berg DI	D8170	28	Udine	1010	OOC	CR/ORB/?
5s***	23 Jul	Alb. DV	D8170	28	2km N E S Polo di Piave	0830	DES	CR/14 W

TOTAL: 1 balloon, 1 shared captured, 1 and 1 shared destroyed, 1 shared out of control = 5.
*Shared with 2/Lt P.G. Mulholland B5183, Lt O.W. Frayne B6345 and several Italian fighters: The crew of two from FA 2 were both killed. They are believed to have been Uffz Pethzold and Lt Voight. **Shared with Capt T.F. Williams D8208, Lt G.G. Constanduros D8206. ***Shared with Capt T.F. Williams D6342; This was probably? Salm of Flik 74j, who was killed in Aviatik DI, 38:61.

JARVIS Louis William Captain 56, 1

Born on 2 September 1892, Jarvis was a Londoner who had been commissioned in the Army in August 1914 and had seen service at Gallipoli before transferring to the RFC. He joined 56 Squadron on 14 October 1917 as a flight commander, and gained three individual and four shared victories. On 23 March he was one of a patrol of six pilots who brought down an enemy two-seater. Subsequently he was posted to 1 Squadron late in the war, and in December 1918 he served with 29 Squadron.

	1918		SE 5A					
1s*	19 Feb	Alb. C	B53	56	S W Rumaucourt	1240	OOC	CR/RFC 19.2
2	16 Mar	Alb. DV	C5430	56	E Sancourt	1200	OOC	CR/RFC 16.3
3s**	23 Mar	C	C5430	56	Moreuil	0740	OOC	CR/RFC 23.3
4s***	27 Mar	Alb. DV	C5430	56	S E Bray	1315	DES	CR/RFC 27.3
5†	11 Apr	Pfalz DIII	C5430	56	Becourt	1830	DES	CR/RAF 11.4
6s††	2 May	Fokker DrI	D257	56	S E Martinpuich	1125	OOC	CR/RAF 2.5
7†††	2 May	Fokker DrI	D257	56	S E Martinpuich	1125	DES	CR/RAF 2.5

TOTAL: 2 and 1 shared destroyed, 1 and 3 shared out of control = 7.
*Shared with Capt F. Billings B4880. **Shared with Lt M.E. Mealing C5389, 2/Lt H.J. Walkerdine B8266, Lt E.D.G. Galley B59, Lt H.J. Burden D283, 2/Lt W.S. Maxwell B119. ***Shared with 2/Lt H.J. Walkerdine B8266. †This was Lt Beyschlag of Jasta 35, who crash landed. ††Shared with 2/Lt C. Parry B144. †††Probably Lt M. Stoy, of Jasta 10 who was wounded.

JEFFS Charles Hugh Lieutenant 56

Jeffs, from Grimsby, Lincolnshire, transferred to the RFC from the Border Regiment, and after training was posted to 56 Squadron on 18 August 1917, aged 22. He was credited with five victories before he was shot down whilst flying B524 by Oberleutnant Bruno Loerzer, Commander of Jasta 26, on 5 October. Jeffs, who was Loerzer's 11th victory, was taken prisoner.

	1917		SE 5A					
1	22 Aug	Alb. DV	B524	56	Gheluvelt	0615-0715	DES	CR/RFC 22.8
2	6 Sep	Alb. DIII	B524	56	E Poelcapelle	0700-0730	DES	CR/RFC 6.9
3	10 Sep	Alb. DIII	B524	56	Gheluvelt	1740-1845	OOC	CR/RFC 10.9
4	14 Sep	Alb. DV	B524	56	S Houthoulst Forest	0845-0915	OOC	CR/RFC 14.9
5s*	29 Sep	Alb. DV	B524	56	Staden	1750-1810	OOC	CR/RFC 29.9

TOTAL: 2 destroyed, 2 and 1 shared out of control = 5.
*Shared with Capt G.C. Maxwell B502, Lt R.H. Sloley A8928, Lt H.A. Johnston B12, Lt R.W. Young A8946, Lt R.J. Preston Cobb B527.

JENKIN Louis Fleeming Captain 1

Born in London in 1895, Louis Jenkin transferred to the RFC from the 9th Loyal North Lancs Regiment, and after training joined 1 Squadron on 15 May 1917, flying Nieuport Scouts. He claimed his first victory, an Albatros Scout, on 23 May, and by 31 July had brought his score to 20. On this latter day he strafed Herseaux aerodrome, setting fire to one scout in a line of six. He was awarded an MC on 16 August and on 4 September claimed another victory. He added an Albatros Scout on 11 September, but was reported missing later this day, the same as that on which the great French ace, Georges Guynemer, was lost. Jenkin was shot down in B3635, probably by Oberleutnant Schmidt of Jasta 29. The award of a Bar to his MC was announced on 17 September.

	1917		Nieuport					
1	23 May	Alb. DIII	B1554	1	S Becelaere	1800	OOC	CR/RFC 23.5
2	25 May	Alb. DIII	B1638	1	Tenbrielen	1000	OOC	CR/RFC 25.5
3	2 Jun	Alb. DIII	B1690	1	Wervicq	0915	OOC	CR/RFC 2.6
4s*	7 Jun	Alb. DIII	B1547	1	Zandvoorde	0940	DES	CR/RFC 7.6
5	8 Jun	Alb. DIII	B1547	1	Becelaere	1245	OOC	CR/RFC 8.6
6	9 Jun	Alb. DIII	B1547	1	E Houthem	1400	DES	CR/RFC 9.6
7	9 Jun	Alb. DIII	B1547	1	Dadizeele	1510	DES(F)	CR/RFC 9.6
8	14 Jun	Alb. DIII	B1547	1	Messines-Wervicq	2050	OOC	CR/RFC 14.6
9	17 Jun	Alb. DV	B1649	1	Roulers	0815	OOC	CR/RFC 17.6
10s**	18 Jun	Alb. DV	B1681	1	Oostaverne	1145	DES	CR/RFC 18.6
11	20 Jun	Alb. C	B1547	1	S Houthem	1815	OOC	CR/RFC 20.6
12***	2 Jul	DFW. C	B1547	1	Houthem	0925	DES(F)	CR/RFC 2.7
13	7 Jul	Alb. DV	B1547	1	Roulers	2040	OOC	CR/RFC 7.7
14	12 Jul	Alb. DV	B1547	1	Menin	2020	OOC	CR/RFC 12.7
15	13 Jul	DFW. C	B1547	1	Houthem	0845	DES	CR/RFC 13.7
16	16 Jul	Alb. DV	B1547	1	Tenbrielen	1935	OOC	CR/RFC 16.7
17	22 Jul	Alb. DIII	B1547	1	Kortewilde	1930	DES	CR/RFC 22.7
18	22 Jul	Alb. DIII	B1547	1	Wervicq	1945	DES	CR/RFC 22.7
19	28 Jul	Alb. DIII	B1547	1	N Wervicq	1000	DES	CR/RFC 28.7
20	28 Jul	C	B1547	1	Zandvoorde	1010	DES	CR/RFC 28.7
21	4 Sep	DFW. C	B3474	1	Polygon Wood	1600	OOC	CR/RFC 4.9
22	11 Sep	Alb. DV	B3635	1	Gheluwe	0835	OOC	CR/RFC 11.9

TOTAL: 8 and 2 shared destroyed, 11 and 1 shared out of control = 22.
*Shared with Lt F. Sharpe B3481. **Shared with Lt C.S.T. Lavers B3495, 2/Lt H.G. Reeves B1630. ***Both crew members jumped out.

JENKINS William Edwin Lieutenant 60

Bill Jenkins joined 60 Squadron in April 1917, serving in Caldwell's 'B' Flight. Whilst flying Nieuport Scouts with this unit he claimed five victories and drove down six more. An Albatros which he claimed out of control on 29 June was flown by the German ace, Oberleutnant Adolf von Tutschek of Jasta 12, who was forced to land. Converting to SE 5A aircraft, he added five more victories by 19 November. On 23 November however, whilst flying B608 over Poperinghe, he collided with the aircraft flown by 2nd Lieutenant M. West-Thompson, both pilots being killed in the resultant crash.

	1917		Nieuport					
1	11 May	Alb. DIII	B1566	60	Brebieres	1400	OOC	CR/RFC 11.5
2s*	21 Jun	Alb. C	B1629	60	Brebieres	0700	OOC	CR/SR/?
3**	29 Jun	Alb. DIII	B1629	60	E Lens	1830	OOC	CR/SR/?
4s***	3 Jul	Alb. DIII	B1629	60	Graincourt	1830	OOC	CR/RFC 4.7
5s†	15 Jul	Alb. DV	B1629	60	Vitry	1950	DES	CR/RFC 15.7
			SE 5A					
6s††	20 Sep	Alb. DV	B523	60	Zonnebeke	1655	OOC	CR/RFC WD
7	25 Sep	C	B523	60	1m E Ypres lines	1540	DES	CR/RFC 25.9
8	11 Nov	Balloon	B608	60	Ypres	1530	DES	CR/SR/?
9s†††	19 Nov	DFW. C	B623	60	S W Becelaere	1520	OOC	CR/RFC 19.11
10s†	19 Nov	DFW. C	B623	60	S W Becelaere	1520	OOC	CR/RFC 19.11

TOTAL: 1 balloon, 1 and 2 shared destroyed, 2 and 4 shared out of control = 10.
*Shared with 2/Lt J. Collier B1618, 2/Lt R.B. Steele B1605. **Probably Oblt A. v Tutshek of Jasta 12, who force-landed. ***Shared with 2/Lt A.R. Adam B1585. †Shared with Capt K.L. Caldwell B1654, W.W.B. Sherwood B1605. ††Shared with Lt I.C. Macgregor A8914, Lt G.F. Elliott B4860. †††Shared with Lt W.J.A. Duncan B608.

JENKINS William Stanley Captain 210

Born in Montreal, Canada, on 26 May 1890, he served in France with the 87th Battalion, Canadian Infantry, becoming a Corporal. He transferred to the RFC in July 1917, and trained with 87 and 40 Squadrons in England, finally joining 210 Squadron in France in May 1918. Almost at once he went into hospital, but was soon back and began to claim heavily. By the end of the war he had claimed 12 enemy machines and had received the DFC and Bar.

	1918		Camel					
1	27 May	Alb. DV	D3404	210	E Ypres	1920	DES	CR/RAF 28.5
2s*	6 Jun	C	D9590	210	Doulieu	0825	DES	CR/RAF 6.6
3	21 Aug	Alb. DV	E4407	210	W Warneton	1220	DES	CR/5 GP Comm
4	31 Aug	Fokker DVII	E4407	210	Wijnendaele Wood	1625	OOC	CR/5 GP Comm
5	3 Sep	Fokker DVII	E4407	210	Lille	1810	OOC	CR/5 GP Comm
6	17 Sep	Fokker DVII	E4407	210	S Ostend	1830	DES(F)	CR/5 GP Comm
7	17 Sep	Fokker DVII	E4407	210	S Ostend	1830	DES(F)	CR/5 GP Comm
8	24 Sep	Fokker DVII	E4407	210	Schooze-Keyem	1440	DES	CR/5 GP Comm
9	29 Sep	Fokker DVII	D8147	210	1m W Lichtervelde	0755	DES	CR/5 GP Comm
10	1 Oct	Fokker DVII	D8147	210	Roulers	1710	OOC	CR/5 GP Comm
11	10 Nov	DFW. C	D8219	210	Merbes le Chateau	0840	DES	CR/RAF 10.11
12	10 Nov	Fokker DVII	D8219	210	E Binche	1315	DES	CR/RAF 10.11

TOTAL: 8 and 1 shared destroyed, 3 out of control = 12.
*Shared with Capt J.G. Manuel D3410.

JERRARD Alan Lieutenant 19, 66

Born on 3 December 1897, Jerrard transferred from the 5th South Staffordshire Regiment to the RFC in 1915 and in 1917 joined 19 Squadron flying Spads, but was injured in a crash on 5 August. On recovery he was posted to 66 Squadron in Italy on 22 February 1918, where he claimed four victories in one month. On 30 March he took off in company with Captain P. Carpenter and Lieutenant Eycott-Martin and engaged four Albatros Scouts and a Rumpler two-seater. A fight developed and several more Austrian single-seaters joined in — reportedly as many as 19, but now known only to number five or six. In what now appears to be some confused fighting, Carpenter claimed one shot down and Eycott-Martin two. From this fight Jerrard failed to return and was later reported a prisoner. The two survivors lodged a report indicating that Jerrard had fought a gallant fight against several enemy machines, shooting down three of them before he himself was brought down. For this action he was awarded the Victoria Cross, the only one granted in Italy to the RFC or RAF, and the only such decoration to be given to a Camel pilot. In fact the action was far from what the report indicated, Jerrard later stating that he had dived down and shot-up the Austrian aerodrome at Mansue, shooting up the hangars and firing into several aircraft which either took off or tried to land. Finally running out of ammunition, he hedge-hopped away, but was attacked and shot down, crashing into a tree. He was the victim of the Austrian ace Benno Fiala von Fernbrugg (29 victories), who commanded Flik 51J. He was unable to confirm whether he had brought down any of the Austrian machines. Official records credited Jerrard with three victories for this date, bringing his score to eight, although he never claimed these himself. He also received the Italian Bronze Medal for Military Valour. He remained a prisoner until the end of 1918 when he managed to effect an escape at the close of the war, gaining Allied lines. He returned to England in November and then served in Russia in 1919. He remained in the RAF, holding various minor posts as a Flight Lieutenant before he retired. He ended his days in Weston-super-Mare, where he died on 14 May 1968.

	1918		Camel					
1	27 Feb	Berg DI	B3840	66	Vittorio	1245	OOC	ORB/SR/14 W
2	7 Mar	Balloon	B5648	66	Chiarano	1015	DES	ORB/SR/7 BG
3	11 Mar	Berg DI	B5648	66	N Valstagna	1140	DES	ORB/SR/7 BG
4	21 Mar	Alb. DIII	B5648	66	E Vazzola	1245	DES	ORB/SR/7 BG
5	30 Mar	Alb. DIII	B5648	66	3m S Mansue	1141	DES	CR/ORB/7 BG
6	30 Mar	Alb. DIII	B5648	66	Mansue	1145	DES	CR/ORB/7 BG
7	30 Mar	Alb. DIII	B5648	66	.5m N Mansue	1150	DES	CR/ORB/7 BG

TOTAL: 1 balloon, 5 destroyed, 1 out of control = 7.

JOHNS Reginald Leach Lieutenant 8(N), 208

From Kilburn, north-west London, Johns was born on 13 November 1894. He joined the RNAS in June 1917 and was posted to 8(N) Squadron in December of that year. By June 1918, by which time the unit had become 208 Squadron, RAF, he had claimed nine victories, six of them shared. He was killed in a flying accident on 11 July 1918.

	1918		Camel					
1s*	24 Jan	Alb. DV	B6356	8N	Neuvireuil	1135	OOC	CR/RFC 24.1

2	29 Jan	Alb. DV	B6328	8N	Henin-Lietard	1525	OOC	CR/RFC 29.1
3s**	2 Feb	C	----	8N	Douai-Ostricourt	1130	DES	CR/RFC 2.2
4s**	2 Feb	Alb. DV	----	8N	Carvin	1215	OOC	CR/RFC 2.2
5s***	22 May	C	----	208	2m N E Lens	0800	OOC	CR/ORB/?
6s†	31 May	Fokker DrI	----	208	Merville	1110	OOC	CR/ORB/?
7	1 Jun	Alb. DV	----	208	N E Lens	1110	OOC	CR/ORB/?
8s††	2 Jun	Alb. DV	----	208	N Lestrem	1215	DES	CR/RAF 2.6
9	2 Jun	Alb. DV	----	208	Merville-Estaires	1220	OOC	CR/ORB/?

TOTAL: 2 shared destroyed, 3 and 4 shared out of control = 9.
*Shared with FSL E.G. Johnstone B6377, FSL W.L. Jordan B6369. **Shared with F/Cdr R.J.O. Compston, FSL W.F. Crundall, FSL H. Day. ***Shared with Capt W.L. Jordan, Lt J.S. Macdonald, Lt E.G. Johnstone, Lt P.M. Dennett, Capt G.K. Cooper, Lt H.H.S. Fowler. †Shared with Capt W.L. Jordon, Lt P.M. Dennett, Lt J.S. Macdonald. This was Lt W. Grabe of Jasta 14, who was fatally wounded. ††Shared with Capt W.L. Jordan, Lt P.M. Dennett, Lt J.S. Macdonald.

JOHNSON Frank Sergeant 22, 20, 62

Johnson first flew as an observer in 22 Squadron in 1916, participating in four victories and receiving a DCM. Trained as a pilot, he was then posted to 20 Squadron in November 1917. Here he flew with a number of different observers, although his most frequent partner was the 'ace' gunner, Captain J.H. Hedley. During his time with the unit Johnson was credited with a further nine victories, but received no additional decorations until 5 May 1918, when he was awarded a Bar to his DCM. By this time he had already moved to 62 Squadron, and had claimed a further three victories to bring his total to 16.

	1916		FE 2B					
1s*	24 Sep	Halb. D?	4924	22	Epehy	1635	OOC	CR/IV BG WD
2**	16 Oct	Alb. DI	4855	22	Guedecourt	1440	OOC	CR/IV BG WD
3***	22 Nov	Alb. DI	7706	22	Bancourt	1330	OOC	CR/RFC 22.11
	1917							
4†	4 Feb	Alb. DII	7697	22	Haplincourt	1345	DES	CR/RFC 4.2
			Bristol					
5††	11 Oct	Alb. DIII	B1130	20	Moorslede	0715	OOC	CR/RFC 11.10
6†††	3 Dec	Alb. DV	A7214	20	Wervicq	1215	OOC	CR/RFC 3.12
7‡	5 Dec	Alb. DV	A7144	20	Dadizeele	0925	OOC	CR/RFC 5.12
8‡	10 Dec	Alb. DV	A7144	20	E Staden	0915	DES	CR/RFC 10.12
9‡	22 Dec	Alb. DV	A7144	20	Roulers	1400	DES	CR/RFC 22.12
10‡	22 Dec	Alb. DV	A7144	20	Roulers	1420	OOC	CR/RFC 22.12
	1918							
11‡‡	25 Jan	Alb. DIII	C4604	20	Staden	1230	OOC	CR/RFC 25.1
12‡	17 Feb	Pfalz DIII	B1177	20	Mooslede	1120	OOC	CR/RFC 17.2
13‡	17 Feb	Pfalz DIII	B1177	20	W Moorslede	1130	DES	CR/RFC 17.2
14‡‡‡	27 Mar	----	----	62	----	----	OOC	SR/C&CU 17.4
15§	12 Apr	Alb. DV	B1136	62	Allennes	1420	DES	CR/RAF 12.4
16§	12 Apr	Alb. DV	B1136	62	1m N Chemy	1425	DES	CR/RAF 12.4

TOTAL: 7 destroyed, 8 and 1 shared out of control = 16.
*Pilot: 2/Lt A. Cropper; shared with Capt J.H.S. Tyssen/2/Lt S.H. Clarke 6372, 2/Lt W.E. Knowlden/2/Lt B.W.A. Ordish 6374, 2/Lt J.F.A. Day/Major R.B. Martyn 4935. **Pilot: 2/Lt C.S. Duffus. ***Pilot: 2/Lt N.H. Tolhurst. †Pilot: Capt H.R. Hawkins. ††Observer: Lt N.M. Sanders. †††Observer: 2/Lt S.H.P. Masding. ‡Observer: Capt J.H. Hedley. ‡‡Observer: 2/Lt D.H. Prosser. ‡‡‡Observer: Sgt C. Brammer. §Observer: Sgt W.N. Holmes.

JOHNSON George Owen Captain 84, 24

Born in Woodstock, Ontario, Canada on 24 January 1896, George Johnson served as a 2nd Lieutenant in the CSCI from 1913 to 1916, when he transferred to the RFC. Joining 84 Squadron early in 1918, he claimed several victories before he was sent to 24 Squadron as a flight commander on 18 April. With this latter unit he claimed five more, bringing his total to 11; he was awarded the MC and French Croix de Guerre with Palm. In action on 17 June, he and two others were credited with forcing down the German pilot, Kurt Wusthoff, who was taken prisoner. Returning to Canada after the war, Johnson joined the RCAF and rose to the rank of Air Marshal before he retired after World War II. In 1944-5 he was head of the RCAF in England, and was made a CB in 1947. He retired to Florida where he died on 24 March 1980.

	1918		SE 5A					
1	16 Feb	Alb. DV	----	84	S E St Quentin	1115	DES	CR/RFC 16.2
2*	18 Feb	Alb. DV	C5436	84	S E Beaurevoir	1100	OOC	CR/?
3s**	11 Mar	Alb. DV	B699	84	Lavergies	1040	DES	CR/RFC 11.3
4s***	16 Mar	LVG. C	B699	84	Villers-Outreaux	1125	DES	CR/RFC 16.3
5	18 Mar	Alb. DV	B699	84	Sesquehart	1140	OOC	CR/RFC 18.3
6	12 Apr	DFW. C	C1097	84	E Albert	1130	OOC	CR/RAF 12.4

7s†	21 Apr	Balloon	C1084	24	La Quesnel	1100	DES	CR/RAF 21.4
8	23 Apr	Pfalz DIII	C1084	24	S Warfusee	1445	DES	CR/RAF 23.4
9	4 May	Fokker DrI	C1084	24	Bray-Dompierre	1900	OOC	CR/ORB/SR/?
10	12 Jun	Fokker DVII	C1084	24	Hangest	1200	OOC	CR/ORB/SR/?
11s††	17 Jun	Fokker DVII	C1084	24	Cachy	1200	CAPT	CR/RAF 17.6

TOTAL: 1 shared balloon, 1 shared captured, 2 and 2 shared destroyed, 5 out of control = 11.
*Probably Vfzw Martin Klein of Jasta 5, who was killed. **Shared with Capt F.E. Brown C5346. ***Shared with 2/Lt P.K. Hobson D260. †Shared with Lt W.C. Lambert C1082. ††Shared with Capt I.D.R. MacDonald D3444, Lt H.D. Barton C6481, and Lt C.E. Walton of 23 Sqn in Dophin C4185. This was Lt Kurt Wusthoff, a 27 victory ace, formerly of Jasta 4, on his first flight with Jasta 15.

JOHNSTON Edgar Charles Captain 24, 88

Born in Perth, Australia, on 30 April 1896, he served with the Australian Imperial Forces from 1915-16, at which time he transferred to the RFC. Initially he flew with 24 Squadron late in 1917, and claimed one victory. He then went to 88 Squadron, which was forming in England, and returned to France with this unit, commanding 'B' Flight. He and his observers claimed 20 victories, and Johnston was awarded the DFC. He took part in many ground attack and bombing missions, and was a most capable leader and fighter pilot. After the war he returned to Australia, and with the civil rank of Captain became controller of civil aviation in that country, from 1933-6. He then became Assistant Director General of the Department of Civil Aviation, 1939-55, and advisor to Qantas 1955-67. Johnston celebrated his 90th birthday in Melbourne in 1986, but died on 22 May 1988.

	1917		DH 5					
1	10 Dec	Alb. DV	A9239	24	Honnecourt	1200	OOC	CR/SR/?
	1918		Bristol					
2*	18 May	Alb. DV	C4867	88	N Langemarck	0730	OOC	CR/RAF 18.5
3*	18 May	Alb. DV	C4867	88	N Langemarck	0735	DES(F)	CR/RAF 18.5
4*	8 Jun	Alb. DIII	----	88	E Couckelaere	----	DES	SR/RAF Comm?
5*	1 Jul	Fokker DVII	C4867	88	W Westroosebeke	1945	DES(F)	CR/SR/10 BG/?
6*	8 Aug	Fokker DrI	E2458	88	Provin	1030	DES	CR/RAF 8.8
7*	8 Aug	Fokker DrI	E2458	88	Provin	1030	OOC	CR/SR/?
8*	11 Aug	Fokker DVII	E2458	88	Rancourt	1130	DES	CR/RAF 11.8
9*	11 Aug	Fokker DVII	E2458	88	Rancourt	1135	OOC	CR/SR/?
10*	13 Aug	Fokker DVII	D8064	88	Provin	1610	OOC	CR/SR/?
11s**	19 Aug	Fokker DVII	C4867	88	Oignies	1030	OOC	CR/SR/?
12***	4 Sep	Fokker DVII	C4867	88	Seclin	0900	DES(F)	CR/RAF 4.9
13***	4 Sep	Fokker DVII	C4867	88	Phalempin	0915	OOC	CR/SR/?
14***	4 Sep	Fokker DrI	C4867	88	Provin	0930	OOC	CR/SR/?
15†	20 Sep	Fokker DVII	----	88	S E Quesnoy	0755	DES	CR/RAF 20.9
16***	22 Sep	LVG. C	----	88	----	----	OOC	SR/?
17††	27 Sep	Fokker DVII	E2533	88	Abancourt	1410	OOC	CR/SR/?
18†††	2 Oct	Fokker DVII	E2533	88	Wavrin-Berclaw	0815	DES(F)	CR/SR/?
19†††	2 Oct	Fokker DVII	E2533	88	Wavrin-Berclaw	0815	OOC	CR/SR/?
20	3 Oct	Fokker DVII	E2533	88	Meurchin	1730	DES	CR/SR/?

TOTAL: 7 and 1 shared destroyed, 11 and 1 shared out of control = 20.
*Observer: 2/Lt J. Rudkin. **Observer: 2/Lt J. Rudkin; shared with Lt K.B. Conn/Lt B.H. Smyth E2216. ***Observer: Lt W.J.N. Grant. †Observer: 2/Lt W.J.N. Grant; shared with Lt K.B. Conn/Lt B. Digby Worsley E2216, Lt C.R. Poole/Sgt C. Hill C922. ††Observer: 2/Lt H.R. Goss. †††Observer: Sgt C.M. Maxwell.

JOHNSTON Phillip Andrew Flight Commander 8(N)

After flying on Home Defence duties during 1915, Johnston, a Londoner, joined 8 Naval Squadron on 27 April 1917. He claimed six victories flying both Triplanes and camels, and became a flight commander. He was killed on 17 August 1917 when his Camel, B3757, collided with that of Flight Sub Lieutenant B.A. Bennetts (B3877) whilst in combat over Wingles, the two aircraft being claimed by Oberleutnant Hans Bethge, Commander of Jasta 30, as his 12th and 13th victories.

	1917		Triplane					
1	3 May	Alb. DIII	N5449	8N	Henin-Lietard	1810	OOC	CR/RFC 3.5
2	27 May	Alb. DIII	N6295	8N	Neuvireuil	1820	OOC	CR/RFC 28.5
3s*	16 Jun	Aviatik C	N6295	8N	Wingles	0930	DES	CR/RFC 16.6
			Camel					
4	13 Jul	Aviatik C	N3757	8N	Cuincy	0940	OOC	CR/RFC 13.7
5s**	13 Jul	Aviatik C	N5757	8N	2-3m E Lens	1040	OOC	CR/RFC 13.7
6***	22 Jul	Alb. DIII	N3757	8N	Hamblain	0625	DES	CR/RFC 22.7

TOTAL: 1 and 1 shared destroyed, 3 and 1 shared out of control = 6.
*Shared with F/Lt R.A. Little N5493. **Shared with FSL W.L. Jordon N6392. ***Probably Vzfw G. Oefele of Jasta 12, who was killed.

JOHNSTONE Edward Grahame Lieutenant 8(N), 208

Born on 6 May 1899 in London, he enlisted in the RNAS on 6 May 1917, and after operational training with 12(N) Squadron during November, he was posted to 8(N) Squadron late in the year. With this unit — 208 Squadron,RAF, from April 1918 — he was to claim 17 victories and receive a DSC. It is likely that his extreme youth prevented his promotion to flight commander whilst with the unit.

	1917		Camel					
1s*	6 Dec	DFW. C	----	8N	Henin-Lietard	0900	OOC	RFC 6.12
	1918							
2s**	1 Jan	Alb. DV	N6376	8N	Bailleul	1500	OOC	CR/RFC 1.1
3s***	4 Jan	DFW. C	N6376	8N	Oppy-Monchy	1130	DES	CR/RFC 4.1
4s†	19 Jan	Alb. DV	N6377	8N	Wingles	1125	OOC	CR/RFC 19.1
5	19 Jan	Alb. DV	N6377	8N	Henin-Lietard	1500	OOC	CR/RFC 19.1
6s††	24 Jan	Alb. DV	N6377	8N	Neuvreuil	1130	OOC	CR/RFC 24.1
7s†††	24 Jan	Alb. DV	N6377	8N	Neuivireuil	1130	OOC	CR/RFC 24.1
8s††	25 Jan	Pfalz DIII	N6377	8N	Beaumont	1315	DES	CR/RFC 25.1
9s‡	3 Feb	DFW. C	N6377	8N	Sallaumines	1225	DES	CR/RFC 3.2
10	18 Feb	Alb. DV	B7218	8N	2m N E Vitry	1115	OOC	CR/RFC 18.2
11	8 May	Alb. DV	D1813	208	Meurchin	1115	DES	CR/RFC 8.5
12‡‡	22 May	C	----	208	2m N E Lens	0800	OOC	CR/ORB/?
13s‡‡‡	4 Jun	Alb. DV	----	208	2m E Merville	1820	OOC	CR/?
14	28 Jul	DFW. C	----	208	Merville	0915	OOC	CR/?
15	31 Jul	Pfalz DIII	----	208	Estaires	0930	OOC	CR/?
16	7 Aug	Pfalz DIII	----	208	Meurchin	1150	OOC	CR/?
17s§	14 Aug	DFW. C	----	208	E Oppy	0600	OOC	CR/?

TOTAL: 1 and 3 shared destroyed, 5 and 8 shared out of control = 17.
*Shared with F/Cdr R.J.O. Compston, FSL W.L. Jordon, FSL P.M. Dennett. **Shared with FSL W.L. Jordon B6447, FSL Reid N6448. ***Shared with FSL W.L. Jordon B6447, FSL P.M. Dennett N6319, FSL A.J. Dixon N6278. †Shared with FSL W.L. Jordon N6369, FSL P.M. Dennett B6447. ††Shared with FSL W.L. Jordon N6369. †††Shared with FSL W.L. Jordon N6369, FSL R.L. Johns N6356. ‡Shared with F/Cdr R.J.O. Compston N6340, FSL W.L. Crundall N6356. ‡‡Shared with Capt W.L. Jordon, Lt R.L. Johns, Lt J.S. Macdonald, Lt P.M. Dennett, Capt G.K. Cooper, Lt H.H.S. Fowler. ‡‡‡Shared with Capt W.L. Jordon. §Lt J.B. White, Lt Allison, Lt R.G. Gifford.

JONES Albert Leslie Lieutenant 10(N), 210

Born in Warwickshire on 19 December 1897, Jones joined the RNAS in March 1916, but did not become a pilot until October 1917. On completion of flying training he was posted to 210 Squadron,RAF, on 29 January 1918, where he claimed seven victories and badly damaged an eighth aircraft. He left for Home Establishment on 13 August.

	1918		Camel					
1	14 May	Halb. C	B7227	210	Ypres	1945	OOC	CR/?
2	14 May	Halb. C	B7227	210	Ypres-Roulers	2000	OOC	CR/?
3s*	17 May	Rumpler C	D3365	210	N E Bailleul	1105	DES	CR/RAF 17.5
4s**	21 May	Balloon	B7227	210	Pont Ricquen	1710	DES	CR/RFC 21.5
5	5 Jun	Balloon	D3381	210	Estaires	1000	DES	CR/RAF 5.6
6	28 Jun	Pfalz DIII	D3381	210	Estaires	1640	DES	CR/?
7	1 Aug	Fokker DVII	C200	210	S E Ostend	1640	OOC	CR5 GP Comm

TOTAL: 1 and 1 shared balloons, 1 and 1 shared destroyed, 3 out of control = 7.
*Shared with Lt H.A. Patey D3391. **Shared with Lt S.C. Joseph D3401, Lt C.W. Payton C62.

JONES George Captain 4 AFC

George Jones was born in Rushworth, Victoria, on 22 November 1896, and was a motor mechanic before the war. Joining the Australian Light Horse in June 1915, he served at Gallipoli and in Palestine before transferring to the AFC. He was posted to 4 AFC Squadron in France at the beginning of 1918. He gained his first victory in February, but on 24 March while bombing enemy troops, was wounded in the back. As a result he was off operations for some months. Returning to the squadron in the late summer, he claimed three more victories before the unit exchanged their Camels for Snipes. With these, he shot down two Fokker DVIIs on 29 October and one on 4 November to bring his score to seven. He was then promoted to flight commander and was awarded a DFC. He remained in the Royal Australian Air Force after the war, and in World War II undertook a number of very senior training and staff jobs, becoming Chief of Air Staff. By 1953 he had been knighted and had reached the rank of Air Marshal by 1948, receiving a KBE and CB. At the time of writing he was living in Melbourne in retirement, the last surviving Australian ace.

	1918		Camel					
1*	21 Feb	Alb. DV	B2551	4AFC	Habourdin	1050	DES(F)	CR/RFC 21.2
2	6 Sep	Fokker DVII	F1548	2AFC	Douai	1855	OOC	CR/ORB/OH/?
3	16 Sep	Fokker DVII	C3324	4AFC	Frelinghien	0820	DES	CR/RAF 16.9

4	24 Sep	Halb. C	C3324	4AFC	Lens	0645	DES	CR/RAF 24.9
			Snipe					
5	29 Oct	Fokker DVII	E8052	4AFC	N E Tournai	1610	DES	CR/RAF 29.10
6	29 Oct	Fokker DVII	E8052	4AFC	N E Tournai	1610	DES(F)	CR/RAF 29.10
7	4 Nov	Fokker DVII	E8052	4AFC	Buissenel	1315	DES(F)	CR/RAF 4.11

TOTAL: 6 destroyed, 1 out of control = 7.
*This was Vzfw G. Weber, of Jasta 46, who was killed.

JONES Hubert Wilson Godfrey Major 32, 24, 19

Following previous service with the Welsh Regiment during which he was awarded the MC, Jones transferred to the RFC as a Captain, joining 32 Squadron in 1916. He took command of 'C' Flight, 24 Squadron, on 11 March 1917. During the evening of 21 March his DH 2, A305, was shot down by Leutnant W. Olsen/Leutnant W. Hilf of Fliegerabteilung 23, coming down in Allied lines near Roupy (this claim was incorrectly listed as occurring on 22nd in German records). Upon recovery from the wounds he had suffered, Jones served at the Central Flying School until November 1918, when he became Commanding Officer of 19 Squadron, a post he was to hold until December 1919, and again in 1925-28.

	1916		DH 2					
1	11 Aug	Fokker E	7859	32	Rancourt	1330	OOC	CR/RFC 11.8
2	23 Sep	LVG. C	A2533	32	Eaucourt l'Abbaye	1530	DES	ORB/RFC 23.9
3	1 Oct	C	A2533	32	Bihaucourt	2130	OOC	CR/ORB/SD/?
4s*	16 Nov	C	7882	32	Loupart Wood	0900	OOC	ORB/SD/RFC 16.1
5s*	16 Nov	C	7882	32	Loupart Wood	0900	OOC	ORB/SD/RFC 16.1
	1917							
6	5 Feb	Alb. DI	7897	32	Grevillers	1515	OOC	ORB/RFC 5.2
7	15 Feb	Alb. DI	A2548	32	Grevillers	0915	OOC	ORB/RFC 15.2

TOTAL: 1 destroyed, 4 and 2 shared out of control = 7.
*Shared with Lt M.J.J.G. Mare-Montembault 7899, Lt P.B.G. Hunt 7938.

JONES James Ira Thomas Captain 10, 74

An aggressive Welshman of small stature, 'Taffy' Jones joined the Territorial Army in 1913 to give some excitement to his life as a clerk. At the outbreak of war, while awaiting call-up, he trained as a civilian wireless operator, and then joined the RFC, being posted to 10 Squadron as a 1st Class Air Mechanic on wireless duties. He was posted to France in July 1915, and the following January began flying over the lines as an observer. In May, while with a ground wireless receiving station at the front, he rescued two wounded gunners whilst their battery was under fire, and was awarded an MM and the Russian Medal of St.George. He won his observer's brevet in October 1916 on BE 2Cs, Ds and Es, and on 27 May 1917 was sent home for a commission and pilot training. He joined 74 Squadron early in 1918 as it was forming, and at once began a close friendship with his flight commander, Captain E. 'Mick' Mannock. He also made a name for himself for the number of aircraft he crashed while landing, an exercise which he admitted he never fully mastered! Back in France on 30 March, he quickly put his aggressive spirit to work, and by 31 May was awarded an MC. The following month he was promoted to flight commander; the award of a DFC was gazetted on 3 August for destroying six aircraft in 11 days, and on 30 July he shot down an LVG while flying a badly damaged SE 5A, which collapsed when he landed it. On 25 August he was awarded a DSO, and the following month a Bar to his DFC was gazetted for 21 victories in three months. Serving right to the end of the war, he had brought his score to 37 by early August, but he did not claim again before the close of hostilities, and after the Armistice he became Commanding Officer of 74 Squadron until it disbanded in 1919.

He then volunteered to join the British forces fighting the Bolsheviks in Russia and was posted to the Archangel front in the north, but was disappointed to see no action in the air there. He received a permanent commission in the RAF and served until June 1936. In August 1939 he was recalled as a Group Captain and was put in charge of the operational training of fighter pilots. He took part unofficially in several offensive sweeps over Europe, flying Spitfires, and during the Battle of Britain he attacked a Junkers Ju 88 bomber while flying in an unarmed Hawker Henley target tug, firing his Very pistol at it. He wrote three books, two of them between the wars; one of these was about Mannock, under the title of *King of Air Fighters*, and one entitled *An Air Fighter's Scrapbook*. After World War II he wrote of his own experiences and the history of 74 Squadron in two wars under the title *Tiger Squadron* . He died on 30 August 1960, aged 65, after falling off a ladder.

	1918		SE 5A					
1	8 May	C	C6406	74	Bailleul-Nieppe	1825	DES(F)	CR/RAF 8.5
2	12 May	Alb. DV	C6406	74	N Wulverghem	1822	OOC	CR/RAF 12.5
3	17 May	Hannover C	C1117	74	Merville-Estaires	0930	DES(F)	CR/RAF 17.5
4	17 May	Alb. C	C1117	74	Merville	0930	OOC	CR/RAF 17.5
5	18 May	Alb. C	C1117	74	Nieppe	1250	DES(F)	CR/RAF 18.5
6	19 May	Balloon	C1117	74	N W Armentieres	1655	DES	CR/RAF 19.5
7	22 May	Pfalz DIII	C1117	74	Quesnoy	1245	DES(F)	CR/RAF 22.5

8	22 May	Pfalz DIII	C1117	74	Fromelles	1815	OOC	CR/11 WS
9	26 May	Pfalz DIII	C1117	74	N Armentires	1955	DES	CR/11 WS
10	27 May	Alb. C	C1117	74	N E Nieppe Forest	1100	DES	CR/RAF 27.5
11s*	27 May	Halb. C	C1117	74	Neuf Berquin	1130	OOC	CR/11 WS
12	30 May	LVG. C	C1117	74	E Bailleul	1505	DES	CR/RAF 30.5
13	30 May	Halb. C	C1117	74	S E Bois du Biez	2035	DES	CR/RAF 30.5
14	31 May	Pfalz DIII	C1117	74	Ploegsteert Wood	1910	DES	CR/RAF 31.5
15	31 May	Pfalz DIII	C1117	74	Comines	1945	OOC	CR/11 WS
16	1 Jun	Pfalz DIII	C1117	74	E Dickebusch Lake	0740	DES	CR/RAF 1.6
17	18 Jun	DFW. C	C1117	74	N Bailleul	1230	DES	CR/RAF 18.6
18	21 Jun	LVG. C	D6895	74	Ploegsteert Wood	2015	DES(F)	CR/RAF 21.6
19	25 Jun	Halb. C	D6895	74	Steenwerck	1215	DES(F)	CR/RAF 25.6
20	25 Jun	Fokker DVII	D6895	74	Estaires	1230	DES	CR/RAF 25.6
21**	27 Jun	Hannover C	D6895	74	La Couture	1130	DES(F)	CR/RAF 27.6
22	29 Jun	Fokker DVII	D6895	74	Comines	1945	DES	CR/RAF 29.6
23	1 Jul	Rumpler C	D6895	74	Tourcoing	1350	DES	CR/RAf 1.7
24	24 Jul	DFW. C	D6895	74	Merville	0720	DES	CR/RAF 24.7
25	24 Jul	DFW. C	D6895	74	Merville	1720	DES(F)	CR/RAF 24.7
26	24 Jul	DFW. C	D6895	74	E Kemmel	1730	OOC	CR/11 WS
27	25 Jul	DFW. C	D6895	74	S E Neuve Eglise	1105	DES(F)	CR/RAF 25.7
28***	26 Jul	DFW. C	D6895	74	W Bailleul	0515	DES	CR/RAF 26.7
29s†	30 Jul	Rumpler C	D6895	74	Cassell-Ypres	1210	DES(F)	CR/RAF 30.7
30	30 Jul	LVG. C	D6895	74	Merville	1230	DES	CR/RAF 30.7
31	30 Jul	Fokker DVII	D6938	74	E Armentieres	1750	OOC	CR/11 WS
32	3 Aug	LVG. C	E5967	74	S E Merville	1940	DES	CR/RAF 3.8
33	4 Aug	Hannover C	D6958	74	W Estaires	1710	DES	CR/RAF 4.8
34	6 Aug	Fokker DVII	D6958	74	Sailly sur la Lys	0750	DES(F)	CR/RAF 6.8
35	6 Aug	Fokker DVII	D6958	74	Sailly sur la Lys	0750	DES(F)	CR/RAF 6.8
36	7 Aug	LVG. C	D6958	74	.5m S E Estaires	1225	DES	CR/RAF 7.8
37	7 Aug	C	D6958	74	E Houthoulst Forest	1715	DES	CR/RAF 7.8

TOTAL: 1 balloon, 28 and 1 shared destroyed, 6 and 1 shared out of control = 37.
*Shared with Lt W.B. Giles. **This was Uffz H. Dippon/Lt A. Graebe of FA 32, who were killed. ***This was Uffz G. Liefering/Lt P Jahnert of FAA 204, who were killed. †Shared with Lt G.W.G. Gauld, Lt H.G. Shoemaker E1389.

JONES Norman Cyril Captain 28, 45

From Cheshire, he joined the Royal Field Artillery (TF) before transferring to the RFC. He went to Italy in late 1917, joining 28 Squadron, where he shot down his first enemy aircraft on 25 January 1918. Shortly afterwards, he was promoted to Captain and became a flight commander with 45 Squadron, where he claimed a further eight victories and was awarded the DFC.

	1918		Camel					
1*	25 Jan	Aviatik C	B6344	28	Sernaglia-San Pietro	1045	DES	CR/7 BG
2s**	19 May	C	B6372	45	Mel	0625	DES(F)	CR/14 W
3	20 May	Alb. DIII	B6372	45	N E Asiago	1040	DES	CR/14 W
4	1 Jun	Alb. DV	B6372	45	Feltre	0945	DES(F)	CR/14 W
5	7 Jun	DFW. C	B6372	45	Arsiera	1740	DES	CR/14 W
6	28 Jun	Alb. DIII	D8169	45	1m W Pedavena	0835	DES	ORB/14 W
7	29 Jul	Alb. DIII	D8169	45	Brugnera	c0900	DES	ORB/14 W
8	21 Aug	Alb. DV	D8234	45	Ghiarona	0815	DES	ORB/14 W
9	21 Aug	Alb. DV	D8234	45	Ghiarona	0815	OOC	ORB/14 W

TOTAL: 7 and 1 shared destroyed, 1 out of control = 9.
*Probably Vzfw K. Preuss/Lt H. Meissner of FA 17, who were killed. **Shared with 2/Lt C.G. Catto B6412.

JONES-WILLIAMS Arthur Gordon Captain 29, 65

A Welshman born on 6 October 1898, he first saw service with the Welsh Regiment before he was seconded to the RFC in August 1916. After training with 66 Squadron, he joined 29 Squadron on 22 March 1917, flying Nieuports and becoming a flight commander during May. He was awarded an MC during that month and a Bar in July, when he went into hospital prior to a posting to Home Establishment. He returned to France to command a flight of 65 Squadron in 1918, where he raised his score to 11. He remained in the RAF, and in 1923 served in Kurdistan, flying DH 9As. In April 1929, now a Squadron Leader, he flew with Flight Lieutenant N.H. Jenkins on a non-stop flight from Cranwell to India, covering the 4,130 miles in 50 hours. Later that year, again flying a Fairey monoplane, they planned a flight to South Africa, but crashed in Tunisia and were both killed on 17 December .

	1917		Nieup					
1	14 Apr	Alb. DIII	A6721	29	Neuvireuil-Vitry	0950	OOC	CR/ORB/SR/?
2	23 Apr	Alb. DIII	A6721	29	Vitry	1630	OOC	CR/RFC 23.4

3	23 Apr	Alb. DIII	A6721	29	Vitry	1630	OOC	CR/RFC 23.4
4	25 Jun	Alb. DIII	B1577	29	Douai	1915	OOC	CR/RFC 25.6
5	29 Jun	Alb. DIII	B1577	29	Saudemont	0720	OOC	CR/RFC 29.6
6	12 Jul	Alb. DV	B3656	29	Zonnebeke-Roulers	1020	OOC	CR/RFC 12.7
7	20 Sep	Alb. DIII	B3647	29	Westroosebeke	1115	OOC	CR/RFC 20.9
8	23 Sep	Alb. DIII	B3647	29	Zonnebeke-Langemarck	1245	OOC	CR/RFC 23.9
	1918		Camel					
9	5 Sep	Fokker DVII	B1887	65	E Ostend	1345	OOC	CR/ORB/?
10	1 Oct	Fokker DVII	E7217	65	E Roulers	1000	DES	CR/RAF 1.10
11	4 Oct	Fokker DVII	E7217	65	Lendelede	1750	DES	CR/RAF 4.10

TOTAL: 2 destroyed, 9 out of control = 11.

JORDAN William Lancelot Captain 8(N), 208

A Londoner, born on 3 December 1895, Jordan joined the RNAS as an air mechanic, subsequently flying as an air gunner. He later received pilot training and was posted to 8(N) Squadron to fly Sopwith Triplanes. In the summer of 1917 the unit received Camels to replace the former aircraft, and it was in one of these that he claimed his first victory on 13 July. By the end of February 1918 he had claimed 18 victories, and received a DSC, gazetted on 22 February, and a Bar awarded later the same month. In mid April he was promoted to Captain (RAF), and during the early summer of 1918 made many more claims. He was awarded a DFC after his 25th, and by mid August when he was rested from operations, his score had reached 39; 20 of these were shared victories. He was killed in a car accident during the 1930s.

	1917		Camel					
1s*	13 Jul	Rumpler C	N6372	8N	2-3m E Lens	1040	OOC	CR/RFC 13.7
2	28 Jul	Alb. DV	N6372	8N	Lens-La Bassee	0915	OOC	CR/ORB/DL/?
3s**	9 Aug	Alb. DV	N6372	8N	E Henin-Lietard	0935	OOC	CR/ORB/DL/?
4s***	11 Aug	Alb. DV	N6372	8N	Acheville	1930	OOC	CR/ORB/DL/?
5s†	19 Aug	DFW. C	B3921	8N	E Lens	0850	OOC	CR/ORB/DL/?
6s††	6 Dec	DFW. C	----	8N	Henin-Lietard	0900	OOC	CR/RFC 6.12
7s†††	6 Dec	DFW. C	----	8N	Drocourt-Douai	1125	OOC	CR/RFC 6.12
8	28 Dec	Alb. DV	B6447	8N	Mericourt	1125	OOC	CR/RFC 28.12
	1918							
9s‡	1 Jan	Alb. DV	B6447	8N	Bailleul	1500	OOC	CR/RFC 1.1
10s‡‡	3 Jan	Hannover C	B6447	8N	Arras	1005	DES	CR/RFC 3.1
11s‡‡‡	4 Jan	DFW. C	B6447	8N	Oppy-Monchy	1130	DES	CR/RFC 4.1
12s§	6 Jan	Alb. DV	B6447	8N	Quiery la Motte	1150	DES	CR/RFC 6.1
13s§§	19 Jan	Alb. DV	N6369	8N	Wingles	1125	OOC	CR/RFC 19.1
14s§§§	24 Jan	Alb. DV	N6369	8N	Neuvireuil	1130	OOC	CR/RFC 24.1
15s#	24 Jan	Alb. DV	N6369	8N	Neuvireuil	1135	OOC	CR/RFC 24.1
16s§§§	25 Jan	Pfalz DIII	N6369	8N	Beaumont	1315	DES	CR/RFC 25.1
17	28 Jan	Alb. DV	N6369	8N	Beaumont-Drocourt	1133	OOC	CR/RFC 28.1
18	18 Feb	Alb. DV	B7198	8N	2m N E Vitry	1115	OOC	CR/RFC 18.2
19	6 Apr	Alb. DV	D3335	208	1m E Oppy	1110	DES	CR/RAF 6.4
20	12 Apr	C	D1869	208	1m N W La Bassee	1740	DES	CR/RAF 12.4
21	4 May	Pfalz DIII	----	208	1m S E La Bassee	1930	OOC	CR/RAF 4.5
22	12 May	C	D1906	208	1.5m ESE Calonne	2000	DES	CR/RAF 12.5
23s##	22 May	C	----	208	2m N E Lens	1110	OOC	CR/?
24	23 May	Fokker DrI	----	208	E Lens	0645	OOC	CR/?
25s###	31 May	Fokker DrI	----	208	Merville	1110	OOC	CR/?
26	1 Jun	Alb. DV	B1889	208	2m N E Lens	1110	OOC	CR/?
27s¶	2 Jun	Alb. DV	----	208	N Lestrem	1215	DES	CR/RAF 2.6
28s¶¶	4 Jun	Alb. DV	----	208	2m E Merville	1820	OOC	CR/?
29	7 Jul	Fokker DrI	----	208	2m E La Bassee	1940	OOC	CR/?
30	8 Jul	Fokker DrI	----	208	Meurchin-Epinoy	0750	OOC	CR/?
31	8 Jul	Pfalz DIII	----	208	Mettalergique Works	0800	OOC	CR/?
32	9 Jul	DFW. C	----	208	Richebourg St Vaast	1150	DES	CR/RAF 9.7
33	16 Jul	LVG. C	----	208	Laventie	1125	DES	CR/RAF 16.7
34s¶¶¶	16 Jul	LVG. C	----	208	Merville	c1145	DES	CR/?
35s○	20 Jul	C	----	208	N E La Bassee	0730	OOC	CR/?
36	31 Jul	Pfalz DIII	----	208	Estaires	0930	OOC	CR/?
37	31 Jul	Pfalz DIII	----	208	Estaires	0930	OOC	CR/?

38	7 Aug	Fokker DrI	----	208	Meurchin	1150	OOC	CR/?
39	12 Aug	LVG. C	----	208	1.5m N E Pacaut Wood	1220	OOC	CR/?

TOTAL: 6 and 5 shared destroyed, 14 and 14 shared out of control = 39.
*Shared with FSL P.A. Johnston in Triplane N3757. **Shared with F/Lt R.R. Thornely B3945. ***Shared with F/Cdr C.D. Booker in Triplane N5482; this was Oblt Adolf von Tutschek, the commander of Jasta 12, at that time with 23 of his 27 victories. †Shared with F/Lt R.R. Thornely B3845, FSL R. Macdonald N6375, FSL J.A. Thompson B6378. ††Shared with F/Cdr R.J.O. Compston, FSL E.G. Johnstone, FSL P.M. Dennett. †††Shared with F/Cdr R.J.O. Compston, FSL Reid. ‡Shared with FSL E.G. Johnstone N6376, FSL Reid B6448. ‡‡Shared with F/Cdr R.J.O. Compston N6340, FSL P.M. Dennett N6319. ‡‡‡Shared with FSL E.G. Johnstone N6376, FSL A.J. Dixon B6278, FSL P.M. Dennett B6319. §Shared with F/Cdr R.J.O. Compston N6340. §§Shared with Lt E.G. Johnstone N6377, Lt P.M. Dennett B6447. §§§Shared with Lt E.G. Johnstone N6377. #Shared with Lt E.G. Johnstone N6377, FSL R.B. Johns N6356. ##Shared with Lt R.L. Johns, Lt J.S. McDonald, Lt E.G. Johnstone, Lt P.M. Dennett, Capt G.K. Cooper, Lt H.H.S. Fowler. ###Shared with Lt R.L. Johns, Lt P.M. Dennett, Lt J.S. McDonald. This was probably Lt W. Grabe, of Jasta 14, who was shot down and died of wounds. ¶Shared with Lt R.L. Johns, Lt P.M. Dennett, Lt J.S. McDonald. ¶¶Shared with Lt E.G. Johnstone. ¶¶¶Shared with Lt W.E. Carveth, Lt Richards. ○Shared with Lt Richards, Lt R.G. Gifford.

JOSEPH Solomon Clifford Captain 10(N), 210

Born in Birmingham on 29 April 1893, he joined the RNAS in August 1917. After training and a brief stay with 12 Naval Squadron, he was posted to 10(N) — later 210 Squadron, RAF — in February 1918. He subsequently commanded a flight and received the DSO and DFC. He claimed a total of 13 victories before being wounded.

	1918		Camel					
1	7 May	Alb. DV	B6228	210	Armentieres	1055	OOC	CR/ORB/?
2s*	9 May	Alb. C	B6228	210	Bailleul	1145	OOC	CR/ORB/?
3	14 May	Alb. DV	D3406	210	Ypres-Zillebeke	2015	OOC	CR/ORB/?
4s**	21 May	Balloon	D3401	210	Pont Ricquen	1710	DES	CR/RAF 21.5
5	6 Jun	C	D3401	210	Neuf Berquin	0750	DES	CR/RAF 6.6
6s***	6 Jun	C	D3401	210	Vieux Berquin	0825	DES	CR/RAF 6.6
7	9 Jun	Pfalz DIII	D7155	210	Ploegsteert Wood	0830	OOC	CR/?
8	26 Jun	LVG. C	D9616	210	2m N Armentieres	1925	DES(F)	CR/RAF 26.6
9	29 Jun	Fokker DVII	D9616	210	Armentieres	1930	DES	CR/RAF 29.6
10	30 Jul	Fokker DVII	F1405	210	E Dixmude	0955	OOC	CR/5 GP Comm
11	6 Aug	Fokker DVII	D9615	210	1-2m W Ostend	1920	DES	CR/5 GP Comm
12s†	3 Sep	Fokker DVII	D3374	210	Menin-Courtrai	1830	DES	CR/5 GP Comm
13	30 Oct	Fokker DVII	D3336	210	Rombies-Estreaux	1115	DES	CR/RAF 30.10

TOTAL: 1 shared balloon, 5 and 2 shared destroyed, 4 and 1 shared out of control = 13.
*Shared with Capt A.W. Carter D3364, Capt E.S. Arnold B7227. **Shared with Lt A.L. Jones B7227, Lt C.W. Payton C62. ***Shared with Lt K.T. Campbell D3391. †Shared with Lt C.W. Payton D9655, 2/Lt J.A. Lewis E4405, Lt I.C. Sanderson D3357, Lt H.R. Hughes B7222.

JOSLYN, Harold Waddell Lieutenant 20

A Canadian from Sintaluta, Saskatchewan, born on 9 October 1893, Joslyn served in the 68th Battalion of the Canadian Expeditionary Force. He transferred to the RFC, becoming a pilot in 1917 and joining 20 Squadron where he flew FE 2Ds with either 2nd Air Mechanic Potter or 2nd Lieutenant J.P. Adams as gunner. In the three months of June-August, he claimed seven Albatros Scouts, three of them destroyed and three out of control, one of the latter pouring smoke. He was lost in action on 17 August 1917, flying with 2nd Lieutenant A. Urquhart (Australian) in B1891; he was shot down in the Halluin area at 1015, one of two FE 2s lost when four were claimed by Jastas 6 and 26.

	1917		FE 2D					
1*	29 Jun	Alb. DV	A6415	20	Houthem	1315	DES(F)	CR/RFC 29.6
2*	2 Jul	Alb. DV	A6415	20	Comines-Houthem	1245	OOC	CR/ORB/?
3*	7 Jul	Alb. DV	A6415	20	Wervicq	1900	OOC	CR/RFC 8.7
4	22 Jul	Alb. DV	A6458	20	Menin-Wervicq	1645	DES(F)	CR/RFC 22.7
5*	27 Jul	Alb. DV	A6415	20	Menin	1945-2045	OOC	CR/RFC 27.7
6*	28 Jul	Alb. DV	A6429	20	Kezelbars	0915	OOC	CR/RFC 28.7
7**	15 Aug	Alb. DV	A6359	20	S E Poelcapelle	1810	DES	CR/RFC 15.8

TOTAL: 3 destroyed, 4 out of control = 7.
*Observer: Pte F.A. Potter. **Observer: 2/Lt J.P. Adams.

JUNOR Kenneth William Captain 56

Ken Junor was born in Toronto, Canada, on 3 August 1894, and attended Toronto University until 1915; he then joined the 4th Canadian Mounted Rifles. In March 1916 he was posted to England, now with the 11th Machine Gun Company, and arrived in France four months later. He transferred to the RFC in 1917 and in December of that year was posted to 56 Squadron. He claimed four aircraft by the end of February and was awarded an MC, gazetted on 23 April. On this latter date he was killed, having brought his score to eight in the intervening weeks. He fell victim to Leutnant Egon Koepsch of Jasta 4, crashing at Bray sur Somme.

	1918		SE 5A					
1	29 Jan	Alb. DV	B591	56	Beaurevoir	1140	OOC	CR/SR/?
2*	30 Jan	Alb. DV	C9532	56	N W Wambaix	1410	DES(F)	CR/RFC 30.1
3	17 Feb	Alb. DV	C9532	56	Moeuvres	1145	DES(F)	CR/RFC 17.2
4	26 Feb	Alb. DV	B536	56	Sains les Marquion	1320	OOC	CR/RFC 26.2
5	22 Mar	Alb. DV	B536	56	Havrincourt Wood	1550	DES	CR/RFC 22.3
6	1 Apr	Fokker DrI	C1086	56	Guillemont	1235	OOC	CR/RAF 1.4
7**	11 Apr	Alb. DV	C1086	56	W Aveluy	1830	DES	CR/RAF 11.4
8	20 Apr	Rumpler C	C1086	56	S W Paisieux	1015	DES	CR/RAF 20.4

TOTAL: 5 destroyed, 3 out of control = 8.
*This was Oblt Bruno Justinus, of Jasta 35, who was killed. **This was Pnr A Kohler, of Jasta 35, who was forced to land.

KEEBLE Noel Captain 1W,202

Born 6 April 1892, Keeble joined the RNAS and was with 1 Wing at Dunkirk in late 1915. On 25 January 1916 while flying a Nieuport, he forced a seaplane to land in the sea off Nieuport. Continuing to fly scouts throughout 1916, he claimed one further victory in October. Subsequently in 1918 he was flight commander in 202 Squadron flying DH 4s on reconnaissance and artillery observation duties for the Navy along the coast of Belgium. With this unit he claimed a further four victories, all with Capt. E.C.B. Betts as his observer/gunner. He was awarded a DSO, DFC and Bar.

	1916		Nieuport					
1*	25 Jan	Seaplane	3178	1W	7m off Nieuport	0800	FTL	CR/DRO/?
			Pup					
2	23 Oct	Seaplane	5183	1W	10m off Ostend	----	DES	RNAS 23.10
	1918		DH 4					
3**	5 Jun	Pfalz DIII	A7446	202	N Eesen	1200	DES	CR/5 GP Comm
4**	10 Aug	Fokker DVII	A7446	202	Bruges	1425	OOC	CR/5 GP Comm
5**	16 Sep	Pfalz DIII	A7446	202	Lissewerghe	1100	DES	CR/5 GP Comm
6**	16 Sep	Fokker DVII	A7446	202	Dudzeele	1125	DES(F)	CR/5 GP Comm

TOTAL: 4 destroyed, 1 out of control 1 forced to land = 6.
*FTL on sea. **Observer: Capt E.C.B. Betts.

KEEN Arthur William Major 70, 40

He served initially with 70 Squadron in 1916, flying Sopwith 1½ Strutters and claiming one victory. In 1917 he went to 40 Squadron as a flight commander. He was awarded the MC and claimed at least 12 victories before he returned to England. In 1918 he rejoined 40 as its Commanding Officer following the death in action of Major Dallas. He added two further victories to his tally, before being involved in a flying accident on 15 August 1918 during which he suffered severe burns. He died of these on 12 September.

	1916		Strutter					
1*	28 Aug	Fokker DII	A3432	70	Bapaume	1800	OOC	CR/RFC 28.8
	1917		Nieup					
2s**	1 May	Alb. DIII	B1633	40	E Douai	1245	DES	CR/?
3	12 May	Alb. C	B1633	40	Oignies	1840	OOC	CR/RFC 12.5
4	15 Jun	Alb. DIII	A6771	40	Vitry	2015	DES(F)	CR/RFC 15.6
5	25 Jun	Alb. DIII	B1686	40	N E Douai	1855	OOC	CR/RFC 25.6
6	2 Jul	Alb. DV	B1686	40	S E Lens	1155	OOC	CR/RFC 2.7
7	9 Aug	DFW. C	B3465	40	Beaumont	1000	OOC	CR/?
8	9 Aug	Alb. DV	B3465	40	Oppy	1950	OOC	CR/RFC 10.8
9	12 Aug	DFW. C	B3465	40	N Douai	1030	DES	CR/RFC 12.8
10	12 Aug	Alb. DV	B3465	40	Lens	1945	DES	CR/RFC 13.8
11	15 Aug	Alb. DV	B3465	40	4m N E Lens	0930	DES(F)	CR/RFC 15.8
12	15 Aug	Alb. DV	B3465	40	N E Lens	0930	OOC	CR/RFC 15.8
	1918		SE 5A					
13	30 Jun	Fokker DrI	D6122	40	Beauchamps	1240	DES(F)	CR/RAF 30.6
14	9 Aug	Alb. DV	D6122	40	Brie	1650	DES(F)	CR/RAF 9.8

TOTAL: 6 and 1 shared destroyed, 7 out of control = 14.
*Observer: Capt F.G. Glenday. **Shared with Capt D.C. Rutter/1 AM A.W. Cant, in Strutter A8221 of 43 Sqn.

KEIRSTEAD Ronald McNeill Captain 4(N), 204

Born on 20 June 1895, this Canadian from Wolfeville, Nova Scotia, flew with 4(N) Squadron from 15 June 1917 to July 1918. During his year with the unit he claimed victories over 13 aircraft, including two Albatros Scouts on 24 September 1917 and two more Scouts on 21 October. On 26 March 1918, by which time he had been promoted to the rank of Flight Commander, he shared in shooting down a Pfalz DIII in Allied lines with a Belgian Spad, and claimed two more single-handed. He was awarded a DSC, gazetted on 22 February 1918. During World War II he was in the Ministry of Munitions in the Canadian Government, but during a demonstration of a new device to actuate a striker, a shell accidentally discharged, seriously impairing his sight.

	1917		Camel					
1s*	10 Jul	Alb. DV	N6362	4N	S E Nieuport	1950	DES(F)	CR/RNAS 10.7
2s**	25 Jul	Seaplane	N6370	4N	30m N N E Ostend	1930	DES	CR/RNAS 25.7
3	18 Aug	Alb. DV	N6370	4N	E Dixmude	0910	OOC	CR/RNAS 18.8
4	24 Sep	Alb. DV	N6370	4N	S E St Pierre Capelle	1809	OOC	CR/RNAS 24.9
5***	24 Sep	Alb. DV	N6370	4N	St Pierre Capelle	1810	DES(F)	CR/RNAS 24.9
6	21 Oct	Alb. DV	N6370	4N	Ghistelles	1025	DES	CR/RNAS 21.10
7	21 Oct	Fokker DV	N6370	4N	S Ghistelles	1030	OOC	CR/RNAS 21.10
8	6 Dec	DFW. C	B6389	4N	N La Panne	1330	OOC	CR/DRO/DL/?
	1918							
9	26 Mar	Pfalz DIII	B6389	4N	W Dixmude	1700	DES	CR/RNAS 27.3
10	26 Mar	Pfalz DIII	B6389	4N	Pervyse-Dixmude	1700	OOC	CR/RNAS 27.3
11s†	26 Mar	Pfalz DIII	B6389	4N	Dixmude	1700	DES	CR/RNAS 27.3
12††	21 Apr	Rumpler C	B6389	204	Wulpen	1200	CAPT	CR/5 GP Comm
13	12 Jun	Pfalz DIII	B6389	204	N Middelkerke	1530	OOC	CR/5 GPComm

TOTAL: 1 shared captured, 3 and 3 shared destroyed, 6 out of control = 13.
*Shared with F/Cdr A.J. Chadwick N6369. **Shared with F/Cdr A.J. Chadwick N6369, FSL A.J. Enstone B3841. ***This was Oblt Jahn, of Jasta 28, who was killed. †Shared with a Belgian Spad. ††Shared with FSL C.R.R. Hickey B6350. Possible Sgt Iredi/Lt. Hachmer, both prisoners.

KELLY Ernest Tilton Sumpter 2nd Lieutenant 1

A Canadian from Picton, Ontario, Kelly was born in 1898 and joined the RFC on 6 July 1917. He was posted to 1 Squadron early in 1918, claiming six victories. On 13 June he was shot down south of Laventie in SE 5A B8508 by Fokker Dr Is, probably of Jasta 14; he did not survive.

	1918		SE 5A					
1s*	27 May	C	B130	1	1m S Bailleul	1425	DES(F)	CR/RAF 27.5
2s*	27 May	C	B130	1	Kemmel	1450	DES	CR/RAF 27.5
3s**	28 May	C	B130	1	Meteren-Bailleul	0635	OOC	CR/ORB/?
4s***	28 May	DFW. C	B130	1	Meteren-Bailleul	0700	DES	CR/RAF 28.5
5	30 May	Alb. DV	B1301	1	N La Gorgue	1430	OOC	CR/RAF 30.5
6s†	1 Jun	Pfalz DIII	B733	1	Armentieres	1940	OOC	CR/ORB/?

TOTAL: 3 shared destroyed, 1 and 2 shared out of control = 6.
*Shared with Capt P.J. Clayson C1114, Lt D. Knight C6479, Lt B.H. Moody C1092, Lt H.A. Kullberg D337. **Shared with Lt E.M. Forsyth B733, Lt B.H. Moody C1092, Lt E.E. Owen B8512, Lt A.F. Scroggs C6416, Capt K.S. Henderson C1112, Lt K.J.P. Laing B8504, Lt H.B. Bradley C1102, Lt H.A. Kullberg B8254, Lt D. Knight C6479, Capt P.J. Clayson C1849. ***Shared with Lt E.M. Forsyth B733, Lt B.H. Moody C1092, Lt E.E. Owen B8512, Lt A.F. Scroggs C6416, Capt K.S. Henderson C1112, Lt K.J.P. Laing B8504, Lt H.B. Bradley C1102, Lt H.A. Kullberg B8254, Lt D. Knight C6479, Capt P.J. Clayson C1849. †Shared with Capt C.S.T. Lavers C1110, Lt D. Knight C1106, Lt L.W. Mawbey B130, Lt E.M. Newman C1101, Capt P.J. Clayson C1114, Lt H.A. Kullberg B8512, Lt C.B. Henderson C1849, 2/Lt H.S. Hennessy D337, Lt W.A. Smart C1092.

KENNEY Edward Patrick Lieutenant 1 AFC

An Australian from Trafalgar, Victoria, where he was born in January 1888, Kenney was an accountant before the war. After service with the Australian Light Horse, he transferred to the AFC and served with 1 AFC Squadron in Egypt, flying Bristol Fighters. On 28 April 1918 he and another pilot forced three Albatros Scouts to land, and machine-gunned them; he was awarded an MC, gazetted on 16 September. On 3 August he and his gunner attacked two Albatros two-seaters, forcing one to land and attacking it on the ground; they also shot down two more Albatroses. In late September he was sent on detachment with two other aircraft from the unit to the Deraa area, and here on 23rd he attacked an airfield with bombs, destroying or damaging several two-seaters on the ground. Later in the day he shot down a DFW. He was awarded a DFC, and the citation — gazetted on 8 February, 1919 — credited him with one destroyed, two out of control and four forced to land.

	1918		Bristol					
1*	28 Apr	Alb. DIII	C4626	1AFC	S Nablus	1745	OOC	CR/40 W WD
2**	30 Jul	DFW. C	C4626	1AFC	Wadi Aujah	0710	FTL/DES	CR/40 W WD

3**	3 Aug	Alb. C	C4626	1AFC	N W Afuleh	1130	FTL/DES	CR/40 W WD
4***	3 Aug	Alb. C	C4626	1AFC	Leijun	1145	OOC	CR/40 W WD
5s†	3 Aug	Alb. C	C4626	1AFC	2m N E Ez Buba	1210	DES	CR/40 W WD
6††	23 Sep	DFW. C	C4626	1AFC	1.5m N W Deraa	0715	FTL/DES	CR/40 W WD
7***	28 Sep	DFW. C	C4626	1AFC	Damascus a/d	0815	FTL/DES	CR/40 W WD

TOTAL: 1 shared destroyed, 4 forced to land and destroyed, 2 out of control = 7.

*Observer: Lt F.C. Hawley; 2 more were driven down by Kenny/Hawley and Lt E.C. Stooke/Lt H.B. Fletcher. Lt Botzow of Jasta 1F/ or 55 was killed in action. **Observer: Lt L.W. Sutherland; the observer was shot on the ground and the aircraft shot up. ***Observer: Lt L.W. Sutherland. †Observer: Lt L.W. Sutherland; shared with Lt P.J. McGinness/Lt Fysh B1223. ††Observer: Lt L.W. Sutherland; This aircraft was forced to land, strafed and bombed and the crew killed.

KERBY Harold Spencer Captain 3W, 9(N), 3(N), Walmer

Born on 14 May 1893, he joined the RNAS and trained as a pilot with the Graham White School at Hendon, receiving Certificate No.1214 in May 1915. In June he was posted to the Dardanelles with 3 Naval Wing, being invalided home to England in March 1916. On recovery, he was posted to Dover in January 1917; in March he joined 9 Naval Squadron and brought down his first enemy aircraft on 24 March. He was then posted to 3 Naval. By July, when he again returned to the United Kingdom, he had brought his score to seven. Based at Walmer as CO of the defence flight there, he was involved in home defence sorties during two daylight Gotha raids in August. He caused one Gotha to crash on 12th., and another on 22nd. He received the DSC, and in 1918 took command of No.4 FTS, where he was also awarded the AFC. He remained in the RAF, and in 1936 was Air Attache in Peking, and later in Shanghai, with the rank of Wing Commander. In January 1939 he became a Group Captain.

	1917		Pup					
1s*	24 Mar	Seaplane	N6177	9N	Wenduyne	c1100	DES	CR/DRO/DL
2	22 Apr	Alb. C	N6160	3N	Cambrai	1910	OOC	CR/ORB/?
3	23 Apr	Alb. DIII	N6160	3N	Le Pave	1730	DES	CR/ORB/?
4**	23 Apr	Alb. DIII	N6160	3N	Le Pave	1730	DES	CR/ORB/?
5s***	6 May	Alb. DIII	N6465	3N	Bourlon Wood	1905	OOC	CR/RFC 6.5
6	6 May	Alb. DIII	N6465	3N	Lagnicourt	1905	OOC	CR/RFC 6.5
7	27 May	Alb. DIII	N6465	3N	Villers	0745	DES	CR/RFC 27.5
8†	12 Aug	Gotha GIV	N6440	WAL.	off Southend	c2000	DES	Cole & Cheeseman
9††	22 Aug	Gotha GIV	N6440	WAL.	.5m off Margate	c1045	DES	Cole&Cheeseman

TOTAL: 5 and 1 shared destroyed, 2 and 1 shared out of control = 9.

*Shared with FSL Bromford N6164. **These two aircraft collided. ***Shared with FSL F.C. Armstrong N6178. †This was Gotha GIV 656/16; Lt Kurl Rolin/Uffz Rudi Stolle/Uffz Otto Rosinsky, 16 Staffel, Kampfgeschwader 3, all killed in action. ††This was Gotha GIV 663/16; Lt Werner Joschkowitz/Lt Walter Latowski/Uffz Bruno Schneider of KG 3. Schneider became a prisonter, the other two were killed. This aircraft was also claimed by F/Lt G.E. Hervey.

KIDDIE Andrew Cameron Captain 74

Andrew Kiddie, a South African from Kimberley, served with the army in West Africa early in the war before coming to England to join the RFC. After flying with 32 Squadron where he gained one victory, he served on Home Establishment as an instructor, proving very good at this job, and among the pilots trained by him was Ira 'Taffy' Jones. In the spring of 1918 he was posted to the newly-formed 74 Squadron, going to France with this unit, where he claimed his first victory on 3 May, sharing in the destruction of a two-seater. Five days later the flight of six SE 5As in which he was flying was attacked by surprise by ten Fokker Triplanes, and Kiddie was the only member of the flight to land back at base, his aircraft having been heavily damaged. Undaunted by this, he shot down a balloon on 19 May, and two more aircraft by the end of the month. 'Old Man' as he was known in the squadron due to his staid and unruffled demeanour, was promoted to flight commander during the summer and by the end of the war had added victories over seven enemy scouts to his score to give him a total of 15. He was awarded a DFC after his seventh victory, and this was followed by the award of a Bar and a Belgian Croix de Guerre.

	1917		DH5					
1	20 Jul	EA	----	32	----	----	OOC	CR
	1918		SE 5A					
2s*	3 May	LVG. C	----	74	S Merville	1855	DES	CR/RAF 3.5
3	19 May	Balloon	C6450	74	W Armentieres	1700	DES	CR/11 WS
4	21 May	Pfalz DIII	C6450	74	N E Merville	0750	OOC	CR/11 WS
5	30 May	Alb. DV	C6491	74	Steenwerck	1540	OOC	CR/11 WS
6s**	6 Jun	Pfalz DIII	----	74	2m W Roulers	1935	DES	CR/RAF 6.6
7s***	9 Jun	Alb. C	----	74	S Mt Kemmel	0805	DES	CR/RAF 9.6
8	30 Jul	Pfalz DIII	E1400	74	Merville	1145	DES	CR/RAF 30.7
9	5 Sep	Fokker DVII	----	74	S Cambrai	1045	DES	CR/RAF 5.9

10	5 Sep	Fokker DVII	----	74	W Lille	1910	OOC	CR/11 WS
11	26 Oct	Fokker DVII	----	74	Cordes	1455	DES	CR/RAF 26.10
12s†	28 Oct	Fokker DVII	----	74	N W Wortegem	1440	DES	CR/RAF 28.10
13	30 Oct	Fokker DVII	----	74	Quaremont-Wortegem	0820	DES	CR/RAF 30.10
14	1 Nov	Fokker DVII	----	74	W Audenarde	1550	DES	CR/RAF 1.11
15	4 Nov	Fokker DVII	----	74	Cordes	1015	DES	CR/RAF 4.11

TOTAL: 1 balloon, 7 and 3 shared destroyed, 4 out of control = 15.
*Shared with Capt E.C. Mannock D278, Lt H.E. Dolan B173, Lt H.G. Clements; this was Uffz Schoning/Lt Beuttler of FA 32, who was killed. **Shared with Capt E.C. Mannock, Capt W.E. Young, Lt H.G. Clements. ***Shared with Capt E.C. Mannock, Lt H.G. Clements. †Shared with LT F.S. Gordon, Lt R.O. Hobhouse.

KINDLEY Field Eugene Captain 65, 148US

An American from Gravette, Arkansas, Field Kindley was born on 13 March 1896, and was a motion picture operator before the war. In May 1917 he joined the Aviation Section of the US Signal Corps, later the USAS, and in September 1917 was posted to England for advanced training with the RFC. Commissioned on 22 March 1918, he was posted during the spring to 65 Squadron, RAF, to fly Camels operationally. After one victory in June, he was posted the following month to the 148th Aero Squadron, USAS, which was under RAF command, and claimed 11 more victories with this unit, six destroyed and five out of control. He was awarded a DSC, becoming a Captain in February 1919. A year later on 3 February 1920, still with the service, he was killed in a flying accident in Texas.

	1918		Camel					
1*	26 Jun	Pfalz DIII	D1878	65	E Albert	2035	DES	CR/BG WD
2	13 Jul	Alb. DV	D8245	148US	Poperinghe	0857	DES	CR/RAF 13.7
3	3 Aug	Fokker DVII	D8245	148US	S E Ostend	0930	DES	CR/USAF/133
4**	13 Aug	Fokker DVII	D8245	148US	N Roye	1352	OOC	CR/USAF/133
5	2 Sep	Fokker DVII	D8245	148US	S Rumaucourt	1150	DES	CR/RAF 2.9
6	5 Sep	Fokker DVII	E1539	148US	St Quentin Lake	1720	OOC	CR/USAF/133
7	15 Sep	Fokker DVII	E1539	148US	Epinoy	1050	OOC	CR/USAF/133
8s***	17 Sep	Fokker DVII	E1539	148US	Epinoy	1300	DES	CR/RAF 17.9
9	24 Sep	Fokker DVII	E1539	148US	W Cambrai	0728	DES	CR/RAF 24.9
10	26 Sep	Fokker DVII	E1539	148US	E Bourlon Wood	1325	DES	CR/USAF/133
11	27 Sep	Halb. C	E1539	148US	Noyelles l'Escaut	0920	DES	CR/RAF 27.9
12s***	28 Oct	Fokker DVII	E1539	148US	Villers Pol	1205	DES	CR/RAF 28.10

TOTAL: 7 and 2 shared destroyed, 3 out of control = 12.
*Probably Lt W. Lehmann, the commander of Jasta 5. **148 made one other claim; possibly Lt Lothar von Richthofen, the commander of Jasta 11, who was wounded in action. ***Shared with 1/Lt J.O. Creech F6176.

KING Cecil Frederick Captain 43

Joining 43 Squadron late in 1917, Lieutenant King was awarded an MC early in 1918 for having destroyed one enemy aircraft and sent down four out of control, as well as taking part in many ground attack missions. His score continued to mount, and although slightly wounded during a combat on 28 March, he was back in action on 3 April. He was promoted to command 'B' Flight after Captain John Trollope was shot down, and in September converted to the new Snipe fighter, gaining three victories in one of these to bring his score to 22. He was awarded a DFC, but was killed in a flying accident on 24 January 1919. He received the French Croix de Guerre.

	1917		Camel					
1s*	12 Nov	Alb. DIII	B6210	43	E Annay	1215	OOC	CR/RFC 12.11
	1918							
2	16 Feb	Pfalz DIII	B2432	43	S Courrieres	1115	OOC	CR/RFC 16.2
3s**	17 Feb	C	B5608	43	Pont a Vendin	0920	OOC	CR/RFC 17.2
4s***	18 Feb	C	B5608	43	E Henin-Lietard	1010	OOC	ORB/RFC 18.2
5	26 Feb	Alb. DV	B5608	43	Fresnoy	1015	DES	CR/RFC 26.2
6	13 Mar	Alb. DV	B5608	43	La Bassee	1300	DES	CR/RFC 13.3
7s†	24 Mar	DFW. C	C8262	43	S E Mercatel	1100	DES	CR/RFC 24.3
8	28 Mar	Alb. DV	D1777	43	4m E Albert Bray Rd	0935	DES	CR/RFC 28.3
9s††	3 Apr	Fokker DrI	D1777	43	Morlancourt	0920	DES	CR/Brig Summ
10	6 Apr	Fokker DrI	D1782	43	Guillancourt	1735	OOC	CR/ORB/?
11	12 Apr	Pfalz DIII	D1792	43	Bois du Biez	1115	DES	CR/RFC 12.4
12	8 May	Fokker DrI	D1864	43	S E Bailleul	1315	OOC	CR/RAF 8.5
13	30 May	Alb. DV	D1864	43	Flers	1445	OOC	ORB/?
14	7 Jun	Alb. DV	D1864	43	S E Roye	0910	DES	CR/RAF 7.6
15	10 Jun	Alb. DV	D1864	43	W Ressons	1915	DES	CR/RAF 10.6
16	13 Jun	Pfalz DIII	D1864	43	N E St Amand	0840	DES	CR/RAF 13.6

17	18 Jul	Pfalz DIII	D1864	43	Neuilly St Front	1515	DES(F)	CR/RAF 18.7
18	30 Jul	Fokker DVII	D1864	43	Fere en Tardenois	1910	OOC	ORB/?
19	8 Aug	Fokker DVII	D1864	43	W Peronne	1645	OOC	CR/?
			Snipe					
20s†††	27 Sep	Fokker DVII	E8031	43	Cambrai	0925	OOC	CR/Wing
21s‡	1 Oct	Fokker DVII	E8031	43	Quievy	1030	OOC	CR/Wing
22	30 Sep	Fokker DVII	E8031	43	Aulnoye	1335	OOC	CR/Wing

TOTAL: 8 and 2 shared destroyed, 7 and 5 shared out of control = 22.
*Shared with Lt W. MacLanachan in Nieup. B8913 of 40 Sqn. **Shared with Capt H.H. Balfour B5620, 2/Lt Grandy B6272. ***Shared with Capt H.H. Balfour B5620, 2/Lt Grandy B6272, 2/Lt C.R. Maasdorp B5409, 2/Lt N. Orcutt B5628. †Shared with 2/Lt R.J. Owen C8259. ††Shared with Lt L.G. Loudon C8215, Capt T. O'Neil C8298. †††Shared with Lt C.C. Banks E8028. ‡Shared with Lt A.C. Macauley.

KING Leslie Walter Lieutenant 22

After joining the RFC in October 1917, Lieutenant King served in 22 Squadron during the spring and summer of 1918, flying Bristol Fighters with various gunners in the rear seat. Between May and August he claimed nine victories, twice claiming two in a day.

	1918		Bristol					
1*	9 May	Pfalz DIII	C840	22	N Douai	1845	OOC	CR/RAF 9.5
2**	31 May	Alb. DV	C4835	22	Neuve Chapelle	1030	DES(F)	CR/RAF 31.5
3**	2 Jun	Alb. DV	C4835	22	S E La Bassee	1015	OOC	CR/ORB/?
4**	2 Jun	C	C4835	22	S E La Bassee	1015	OOC	CR/ORB/?
5***	8 Aug	Pfalz DIII	D7894	22	S Douai	1030	OOC	CR/ORB/?
6***	10 Aug	Fokker DVII	D7894	22	S W Peronne	1810	DES	CR/RAF 10.8
7***	10 Aug	Fokker DVII	D7894	22	S W Peronne	1810	DES	CR/RAF 10.8
8***	21 Aug	Fokker DVII	E2454	22	Albert-Cambrai	1945	OOC	CR/ORB/?
9***	27 Aug	Fokker DVII	----	22	Senlemont	1400	OOC	CR/?

TOTAL: 3 destroyed, 6 out of control = 9.
*Observer: Lt H.E. Elsworth. **Observer: Lt J. McDonald. ***Observer: Lt V. StB Collins.

KING Elwyn Roy Captain 4 AFC

'Bow' King was born on 13 May 1894 in Bathurst, New South Wales, and in 1914 was head of a motor engineering business. He volunteered for the Australian Light Horse, but transferred to the AFC, and was posted to 4 AFC Squadron. He first claimed on 20 May 1918, and during June shot down two aircraft and a balloon. In action throughout the summer, he was promoted to flight commander in mid-September, and by the end of that month his score stood at 18. On 2 October he destroyed his fourth balloon by dropping bombs on it in the air, but this was his last victory with the Camel, as the squadron now received the newer Sopwith Snipe. During the last days of the war he claimed seven more aircraft, the highest number gained with the Snipe by any pilot, and this included three Fokker DVIIs on 30 October, plus two more on 4 November. He received the DSO and DFC, his final total having reached 26. Returning to Australia, he resumed his involvement in engineering. During World War II he rejoined the RAAF, but died while station commander of Point Cook airbase.

	1918		Camel					
1	20 May	Pfalz DIII	D6506	4AFC	Kemmel-Neuve Eglise	0755	OOC	CR/ORB/?
2	19 Jun	Balloon	D1895	4AFC	E Estaires	1455	DES	CR/ORB/?
3	26 Jun	Pfalz DIII	D1895	4AFC	Armentieres area	1805	DES	CR/RAF 26.6
4	28 Jun	LVG. C	D1895	4AFC	Wytschaete	1840	DES	CR/RAF 28.6
5	25 Jul	LVG. C	E1416	4AFC	N Armentieres	0415	DES	CR/RAF 25.7
6	30 Jul	Fokker DVII	E1416	4AFC	N Armentieres	2005	OOC	CR/ORB/?
7	3 Aug	Hannover C	E1416	4AFC	N E Merville	0530	DES	CR/ORB/?
8s*	4 Aug	AGO. C	E1416	4AFC	S Laventie	2015	DES	CR/RAF 4.8
9	10 Aug	Balloon	D1895	4AFC	E Estaires	0745	DES	CR/RAF 10.8
10	10 Aug	LVG. C	D1895	4AFC	Estaires-Laventie	0815	DES	CR/RAF 10.8
11s**	13 Aug	C	----	2AFC	Cartigny	1700	DES	CR/ORB/?
12s***	16 Aug	Fokker DVII	----	4AFC	Wavrin	1315	DES	CR/ORB/?
13	30 Aug	DFW. C	D1895	4AFC	Marquillies	0615	DES	CR/RAF 30.8
14	1 Sep	Balloon	D1895	4AFC	Le Grand Riez	0745	DES	CR/RAF 1.9
15	4 Sep	LVG. C	D1895	4AFC	Erquinghem le Sec	0710	DES	CR/RAF 4.9
16	6 Sep	DFW. C	E1416	4AFC	E Wavrin	0630	OOC	CR/ORB/?
17†	16 Sep	Fokker DVII	E7202	4AFC	Le Quesnoy	0625	DES	CR/RAF 16.9
18	24 Sep	Alb. C	E7202	4AFC	E Ploegsteert	1720	DES	CR/RAF 24.9
19	2 Oct	Balloon	E7202	4AFC	S E Don	0635	DES	CR/ORB/?
			Snipe					

20	28 Oct	Fokker DVII	E8050	4AFC	Ath	1455	OOC	CR/ORB/?
21	29 Oct	LVG. C	E8050	4AFC	La Tombe	1545	DES	CR/RAF 29.10
22	30 Oct	Fokker DVII	E8050	4AFC	Leuze	1455	OOC	CR/ORB/?
23††	30 Oct	Fokker DVII	E8050	4AFC	Leuze	1456	DES	CR/RAF 30.10
24††	30 Oct	Fokker DVII	E8050	4AFC	Leuze	1456	DES	CR/RAF 30.10
25	4 Nov	Fokker DVII	E8050	4AFC	E Buissenal	1315	DES	CR/ORB/?
26	4 Nov	Fokker DVII	E8050	4AFC	E Buissenal	1320	DES(F)	CR/RAF 4.11

TOTAL: 4 balloons, 13 and 3 shared destroyed, 6 out of control = 26.

*Shared with Lt H.G. Watson D1859. **Shared with Lt C. Carter, Lt N.C. Trescowthick, Lt R.G. Smallwood. *** Shared with Capt A.H. Cobby, Lt D.C. Carter, Lt T.R. Edols, Lt M.H. Eddie, Lt N.C. Trescowthick. †Probably Gefr K. Brandt of Jasta 51, who was killed. ††These two aircraft collided.

KINKEAD Samuel Marcus Captain 3W, 1(N), 201, 47

'Kink' was a South African from Johannesburg, born on 25 February 1897, who joined the RNAS in September 1915. As a pilot he served in the Dardanelles with 3 Naval Wing, being credited with three victories. Returning to England, he was posted to the base at Dunkirk at the end of 1916, and later joined 1 Naval Squadron, flying with this unit on the Somme front in June 1917. From here the squadron moved to the Ypres front and was engaged in heavy fighting. By the end of 1917 he returned to Home Establishment with a total of 15 victories, but in 1918 he rejoined 1(N) Squadron, which soon became 201 Squadron, RAF. By the end of August he had brought his score to 32 and had been awarded the DSC and Bar, together with the DFC and Bar. In 1919 he went to Russia with 47 Squadron and flying with that unit's Camel flight against the Bolsheviks, he gained several victories — perhaps as many as ten. In Russia he was awarded the DSO. In 1921 he became a flight commander with 30 Squadron under his old CO, Ray Collishaw, and took part in several small wars in Mesopotamia and Kurdistan. Later he was chosen to be a member of the RAF Schneider Trophy team, but while in practice was killed flying the Supermarine S 5 on 12 March 1928.

	1916		Bristol Scout					
1	11 Aug	Fokker E	----	3W	Xanthi	----	DD?	AIR I/2314
			Nieuport					
2	28 Aug	C	----	3W	2m N E Zinelli	----	FTL?	AIR I/2214
3	----	----	----	3W		----	??	????
	1917							
4	17 Sep	DFW CV	N5465	1N	Comines	1145	OOC	CR/DOS/DL?
5	17 Oct	DFW. CV	N5465	1N	Comines	1100-1130	OOC	CR/RFC 17.10
6s*	18 Oct	C	N5465	1N	E Poelcapelle	1030	OOC	CR/RFC 18.10
7	24 Oct	C	N5465	1N	Comines-Wervicq	1330	DES	CR/RFC 24.10?
8	29 Oct	Alb. DIII	N5465	1N	Gheluveldt	1715	OOC	CR/RFC 29.10
9s**	12 Nov	Pfalz DIII	N5465	1N	Dixmude	1545	DES(F)	CR/RNAS 12.11
	1917		Camel					
10	15 Nov	Alb. DV	B6398	1N	Beerst	1315	OOC	CR/RNAS 15.11
11	15 Nov	Alb. DV	B6398	1N	N Dixmude	1355	DES	CR/RNAS 15.11
12	4 Dec	DFW. CV	B6398	1N	S E Dixmude	1600	OOC	CR/RNAS 4.12
13	6 Dec	C	B6398	1N	Houthoulst	0700-0800	OOC	CR/RNAS 6.12
14	6 Dec	Alb. DV	B6398	1N	Passchendaele	1100	OOC	CR/DOS/DL?
	1918							
15	10 Mar	Alb. DV	B6398	1N	2m N W Menin	1530	OOC	CR/RNAS 10.3
16	16 Mar	Alb. DV	B6211	1N	Roulers	1625	OOC	CR/RNAS 17.3
17	21 Mar	Alb. DV	B6409	1N	Nieuport	1550	OOC	CR/RNAS 21.3
18	22 Mar	Alb. DV	B6211	1N	Slype	1410	OOC	CR/Citation
19	6 Apr	Fokker DrI	B6409	201	Mericourt	1315	OOC	CR/RAF 6.4
20s***	2 May	C	----	201	N Albert	1010	OOC	CR/RAF 2.5
21	10 May	Alb. DV	B6297	201	N E Villers Brettoneaux	1950	DES	CR/RAF 10.5
22s†	15 May	Alb. DV	----	201	Bapaume	0645	DES	CR/RAF 15.5
23	15 May	Alb. DV	B6297	201	E Albert	1745	OOC	CR/RAF 15.5
24s††	23 May	Alb. DV	B7190	201	Arras-Cambrai	0740	OOC	CR/?
25	30 May	Alb. DV	B7190	201	S E Albert	1055	OOC	CR/?
26	30 May	Alb. DV	B7190	201	Achiet le Grand	1955	OOC	CR/?
27	29 Jul	Fokker DVII	D3343	201	Armentieres	1120	OOC	CR/?
28	30 Jul	Fokker DVII	D3343	201	S W Armentieres	1015	OOC	CR/?
29	10 Aug	Fokker DVII	B7190	201	Foucaucourt	0900	OOC	CR/?
30	11 Aug	Fokker DVII	B7190	201	Fouquescourt	c1915	DES	CR/RAF 11.8
31	12 Aug	Fokker DVII	C64	201	Lihons	1915	OOC	CR/?
32	12 Aug	Fokker DVII	C64	201	Bayonvillers	c1710	CAPT	CR/RAF 13.8
	1919							
33	30 Sep	Nieuport	F1955	47	N Tcherni Yar	----	DES	AIR I/2375

34	7 Oct	Nieuport	F1955	47	Dubouka	----	OOC?	AIR I/1956
35	18 Oct	Nieuport	----	47	Feskouatka	----	OOC?	AIR I/1956

TOTAL: 1 captured, 5 and 2 shared destroyed, 21 and 3 shared out of control, +3/8? = 35/40.
*Shared with FSL J.H. Forman N5479. **FSL J.H. Forman Camel B5651. ***Shared with Lt H.L. Wallace, Lt R.E. Bright, 2/Lt H. Riddell, Lt R.C.B. Brading, Lt A.G.A. Spence. †Shared with Major C.D. Booker, Lt H.L. Wallace, Lt R.S.S. Orr, Lt R. Hemmens, Lt M.H. Findlay, Lt J.H. Forman, Lt R. McLaughlin, Lt R.C.B. Brading. ††Shared with Major C.D. Booker D1852.
NB: Kinkead apparently made 3 claims in the Mediterranean in 1916, as well as up to 10 in Russia. Ths could raise his score to 40 or more.

KIRKMAN Robert Kirby Captain 20

Having served in the Leicester Regiment, Kirkman transferred to the RFC and in summer 1917 was posted to 20 Squadron. Flying with a number of different gunners he claimed four victories before the end of the year, and two more in January 1918. On 23 March, flying with the 'ace' gunner, Captain J.H. Hedley, they shot down two Albatros Scouts, one out of control, one on fire. Kirkman was awarded an MC and promoted Flight Commander. However on 27 March he and Hedley became prisoners when their Bristol, B1156, was shot down south of Albert around midday by Leutnant Karl Gallwitz of Jasta Boelcke. They have often been listed as victims of Manfred von Richthofen, but in fact the latter's claims on this date were made some five and a half hours later.

	1917		Bristol					
1*	11 Sep	Alb. DV	A7234	20	E Menin	1400	DES(F)	CR/RFC 11.9
2*	21 Sep	Alb. DV	A7141	20	Becelaere	1100	OOC	CR/RFC 21.9
3**	13 Nov	Alb. DV	A7253	20	Becelaere	1500	OOC	CR/RFC 13.11
4**	5 Dec	Alb. DV	A7298	20	Oostnieuwkerke	1250	OOC	CR/RFC 5.12
	1918							
5	22 Jan	Alb. DV	B1156	20	Moorslede	1115	OOC	CR/RFC 22.1
6†	25 Jan	Alb. DV	B1156	20	Courtemarck	1235	DES(F)	CR/RFC 25.1
7††	23 Mar	Alb. DV	B1156	20	E Wervicq	1210	DES(F)	CR/RFC 23.3
8††	23 Mar	Alb. DV	B1156	20	E Menin	1245	OOC	CR/RFC 23.3

TOTAL: 3 destroyed, 5 out of control = 8.
*Observer: 2/Lt J.P. Flynn. **Observer: Capt L.W. Burbidge. ***Observer: 2AM J. McMechan. †Observer: Lt A.D. Keith. ††Observer: Capt J.H. Hedley.

KITTO Francis Mansel Captain 43, 54

Joining 43 Squadron on formation, Kitto went to France with the unit early in 1917, flying Sopwith 1½ Strutters. Here he gained two victories before he was wounded and returned to England. He was back with the squadron late in the summer, and with his gunner, 1st Air Mechanic Cant, claimed the unit's last 1½ Strutter victory, sending down an Albatros Scout, but being attacked by four others which were driven off by six Nieuports of 40 Squadron. He converted to Camels and early in 1918 joined 54 Squadron as a flight commander, claiming six enemy scouts shot down while with that unit. He was awarded an MC, gazetted on 22 June 1918.

	1917		Strutter					
1*	17 Mar	Alb. DII	A967	43	E Arras	1030	OOC	CR/?
2**	8 Apr	Alb. DIII	A7804	43	N E Vimy	1130	OOC	CR/RFC 8.4
3**	17 Aug	Alb. DV	A8244	43	La Bassee-Lens	0740	OOC	CR/RFC 17.8
	1918		Camel					
4	15 Mar	Alb. DV	C1603	54	Sequehart	1250	OOC	CR/RFC 15.3
5	24 Mar	Alb. DV	C1603	54	Mons	1025	DES	CR/RFC 24.3
6	24 Mar	Alb. DV	C1603	54	W St Quentin	1045	DES	CR/RFC 24.3
7	4 Apr	Alb. DV	C1603	54	S E Hamel	1530	DES	CR/RAF 4.4
8	17 Jun	Pfalz DIII	D6575	54	S Ploegsteert Wood	1000	DES	CR/RAF 17.6
9	4 Jul	Fokker DVII	D6575	54	Estrees	1855	OOC	CR/?

TOTAL: 4 destroyed, 5 out of control = 9.
*Observer: 2/Lt H.E. Ward. **Observer: 1 AM A.W. Cant.

KNIGHT Arthur Gerald Captain 4, 24, 29

Born in England on 30 July 1895, 'Jerry' Knight went to Canada in his early years, finishing his education at Toronto University. Early in the war he returned to his native country and joined the RFC; after pilot training he was posted to 4 Squadron in February 1916. In June he joined 24 Squadron, flying DH 2s under Major Hawker, VC, and soon proving to be a very capable fighting pilot. He flew throughout the Battle of the Somme, claiming at least seven victories and driving down two others damaged, for which he was awarded the DSO and MC. He was promoted to Captain and sent as a flight commander to 29 Squadron in November, gaining one more victory. He was then shot down and killed in combat with Manfred von Richthofen on 20 December, the German's 13th victory. He was Mentioned in Despatches during January 1917.

	1916		DH 2					
1	22 Jun	LVG. C	6011	24	Courcelette	1915	DES	CR/AIR I/1557
2	19 Jul	Fokker E	5931	24	Bapaume-Peronne Rd	1030	OOC	ORB/RFC 19.7?
3	2 Sep	D	5931	24	Warlencourt	1805	OOC	CR/RFC 3.9
4s*	14 Sep	Fokker D	5931	24	Manancourt	2045	DES(F)	CR/RFC 14.9
5	15 Sep	D	7930	24	Flers	1440	DES(F)	CR/RFC 15.9
6	17 Oct	Roland CII	5931	24	Beaumetz	1000	OOC	CR/RFC 17.10
7s**	9 Nov	D	A305	24	Le Transloy	1345	DES	CR/RFC 9.11
8	16 Dec	D	A2614	29	----	----	OOC	CR/RFC 16.12

TOTAL: 2 and 2 shared destroyed, 4 out of control = 8.
*Shared with Sgt S. Cockerell 7873. **Shared with 2/Lt E.C. Pashley 7930, 2/Lt A.E. McKay 7884.

KNIGHT Duerson 1st Lieutenant 1

Lieutenant Knight, a pilot of the USAS, born on 21 January 1893 in Chicago, was attached to the RAF for combat experience in spring and summer 1918, flying SE 5As with 1 Squadron. During May – June period he shared in eight victories, one of which was a Fokker Triplane which was forced to land and was captured, and claimed one individual success. On 22 August he shot down a Fokker DVII in flames, and was then posted to an American squadron.

	1918		SE 5A					
1s*	27 May	C	C6479	1	1m S Bailleul	1425	DES(F)	CR/RAF 27.5
2s*	27 May	C	C6479	1	Kemmel	1450	DES	CR/RAF 27.5
3s**	28 May	C	C6479	1	Meteren-Bailluel	0635	OOC	CR/ORB/?
4s**	28 May	DFW. C	C6479	1	Meteren-Vieux Berquin	0700	DES	CR/RAF 28.5
5s***	1 Jun	Pfalz DIII	C1106	1	Armentieres	1940	OOC	CR/ORB
6s†	9 Jun	Fokker DrI	C1106	1	Dickebusch	0630	CAPT	CR/RAF WD
7	9 Jun	Pfalz DIII	C1106	1	Estaires	0720	OOC	CR/ORB/?
8s††	23 Jun	C	C1894	1	.5m N W Lestrem	0600	DES	CR/ORB/?
9s†††	27 Jun	LVG. C	C1894	1	.5 E Meteren	0427	DES(F)	CR/RAF 27.6
10	22 Aug	Fokker DVII	C1812	1	Archiet le Grand	0720	CAPT	CR/RAF 22.8

TOTAL: 1 and 1 shared captured, 5 shared destroyed, 1 and 2 shared out of control = 10.
*Shared with Capt P.J. Clayson C1114, Lt H.A. Kullberg D337, Lt B.H. Moody C1092, Lt E.T.S. Kelly B130. **Shared with Lt E.M. Forsyth B733, Lt B.H. Moody C1092, Lt E.E. Owen B8512, Lt A.F. Scroggs C6416, Capt K.S. Henderson C1112, Lt H.B. Bradley C1102, Lt E.T.S. Kelly B130, Lt H.A. Kullberg B8254, Lt K.J.P. Laing B8504, Capt P.J. Clayson C1849. ***Shared with Capt C.S.I. Lavers C1110, Lt W.A. Smart C1092, Lt L.W. Mawbey B130, Lt E.M. Newman C1101, Capt P.J. Clayson C1114, Lt H.A. Kullberg B8512, Lt C.B. Henderson C1849, 2/Lt H.S. Hennessy D337, Lt E.T.S. Kelly B733. †Shared with Lt H.B. Bradley C1102, 2/Lt H.B. Parkinson C6458, Lt E.E. Owen B8512, Lt H.A. Kullberg C8842, Lt K.J.P. Laing C1898, Lt E.S. Crossley D6881, Lt J.C. Bateman B8254, Capt P.J. Clayson C1114, Lt C.B. Henderson. This was Gefr Preiss of Jasta 14 who was captured. ††Shared with Capt P.J. Clayson C1114, Lt H.A. Kullberg C1835, Lt J.C. Bateman B8254, Lt C.B. Henderson C1849. †††Shared with Capt P.J. Clayson C1114, Lt H.A. Kullberg C1835. Probably Lt G. Kuter/Lt J. Frankenstein of FAA 213, who were killed.

KNOTTS Howard Clayton 2nd Lieutenant 17US

An American from Carlinsville, Illinois, where he was born on 25 August 1895, Howard Knotts graduated in 1915 and joined the aviation section of the Signal Corps, being sent to Toronto, Canada, for training by the RFC. In 1917 and early 1918 he served in the States with the 182nd Aero Squadron, but in August was posted to France to join the 17th Aero Squadron which was operating Camels under RAF command. With this unit he claimed six victories, all being Fokker DVIIs. His last combat occurred on 24 September 1918, when he sent down two DVIIs, one in flames and one to crash, before being shot down himself, and becoming a prisoner of war. While being taken to the rear in a train, he managed to set fire to seven DVIIs which were being carried on the same train, an act of sabotage for which he was nearly shot. He left the air service in 1919 and entered the legal profession, becoming a noted aviation lawyer. He died on 23 November 1942, aged 47.

	1918		Camel					
1	25 Aug	Fokker DVII	B5428	17US	E Bapaume	1750	DES(F)	CR/RAF 25.8
2	13 Sep	Fokker DVII	B7896	17US	57 C E 21d	1850	DES	CR/RAF 13.9
3s*	17 Sep	Fokker DVII	F6308	17US	Arleux	1845	DES	CR/RAF 17.9
4	22 Sep	Fokker DVII	B7896	17US	S W Cambrai	0910	DES	CR/RAF 22.9
5	24 Sep	Fokker DVII	B7896	17US	N W Havrincourt	1040	DES	CR/RAF 24.9
6	24 Sep	Fokker DVII	B7896	17US	N W Havrincourt	1042	DES(F)	CR/RAF 24.9

TOTAL: 6 destroyed = 6.
*Shared with Lt W.T. Clements F5993.

KOCH Alfred Lieutenant 1, 6, 70

Alfred Koch, a Canadian, first flew as an observer with 1 Squadron, and then with 6 Squadron in 1916, but was wounded on 22 October and returned to England to recuperate. Training as a pilot, he joined 70 Squadron, flying his first patrol in a Camel on 9 October 1917. With the unit he was to claim 10 victories, and was awarded an MC. He also carried out many ground attack missions and a valuable reconnaissance sortie. He received a second slight wound on 7 March. In 1984 Koch attended a reunion at the age of 99.

	Date	Type	Aircraft	Sqn	Location	Time	Result	Source
	1917		Camel					
1*	18 Oct	Alb. DV	B2399	70	Westroosebeke	0900	DES	CR/SR/
2	20 Oct	Alb. DV	B2399	70	Abeele	1130	OOc	CR/RFC 20.10
3	8 Nov	Alb. DV	B2444	70	Westroosebeke	1145	OOC	CR/RFC 8.11
	1918							
4	24 Jan	Alb. C	B9138	70	Westroosebeke	1130	OOC	CR/RFC 24.1
5	29 Jan	C	B9138	70	Dadizeele	1600	OOC	CR/RFC 29.1
6s**	11 Mar	Balloon	----	70	Menin	1230	DES(F)	CR/RFC 11.3
7s***	11 Mar	Pfalz DIII	----	70	Passchendaele	1700	DES	CR/RFC 12.3
8	22 Mar	Alb. C	C1672	70	200y S E Cagnicourt	1525	OOC	CR/RFC 22.3
9	22 Mar	Alb. DV	C1672	70	S E Lagnicourt	1535	DES	CR/RFC 22.3
10	23 Mar	Alb. DV	C1672	70	N W Cambrai	0835	OOC	CR/RFC 23.3

TOTAL: 1 shared balloon, 2 and 1 shared destroyed, 6 out of control = 10.
*This claim was confirmed by the RFA on 21 October. **Shared with Capt F.G. Quigley, Lt K.A. Seth-Smith, Lt W.M. Carlaw. ***Shared with Capt F.G. Quigley.

KULLBERG Howard Albert Captain 1

An American pilot, born in Somerville, Massachusetts, on 10 September 1896, attached to the RAF, Kullberg was posted to 1 Squadron in the spring of 1918 and first claimed on 27 May and was then awarded a DFC, on 30 August which was gazetted on 2 November. The day after being recommended for the award he was arrested for being in possession of a camera! On 16 September he again claimed a DVII shot down, but was chased at low level by five others and was wounded in the leg in three places, being taken to hospital on landing and not returning to operations. He was promoted to flight commander whilst with the squadron .

	Date	Type	Aircraft	Sqn	Location	Time	Result	Source
	1918		SE 5A					
1s*	27 May	C	D337	1	1m S Bailleul	1425	DES(F)	CR/RAF 27.5
2s*	27 May	C	D337	1	Kemmel	1450	DES	CR/RAF 27.5
3s**	28 May	C	B8254	1	Meteren-Bailluel	0635	OOC	CR/ORB/?
4s**	28 May	DFW. C	B8254	1	Meteren-Vieux Berquin	0700	DES	CR/RAF 28.5
5	1 Jun	Pfalz DIII	B8512	1	Armentieres	1940	DES	CR/RAF 1.6
6s***	1 Jun	Pfalz DIII	B8512	1	Ploegsteert Wood	1940	OOC	CR/ORB/?
7s†	9 Jun	Fokker DrI	C8842	1	Dickebusch	0630	CAPT	CR/RAF 9.6
8	9 Jun	C	C8842	1	N Merville	0730	OOC	CR/ORB/?
9s††	15 Jun	Balloon	C1835	1	S Estaires	1315	DES	CR/RAF 15.6
10s†††	23 Jun	C	C1835	1	.5m N W Lestrem	0600	DES	CR/ORB/?
11s‡	27 Jun	LVG. C	C1835	1	.5m E Meteren	0427	DES(F)	CR/RAF 27.6
12s‡‡	1 Jul	Halb. C	C1835	1	Messines	0805	DES(F)	CR/RAF 1.7
13	9 Jul	Fokker DVII	C1835	1	Oostnieuwkerke	2050	DES	CR/RAF 9.7
14	29 Jul	Alb. C	C1835	1	N Steenwerck	1745	DES	CR/RAF 29.7
15	9 Aug	Fokker DVII	C1835	1	Proyart	1025	DES	CR/RAF 9.8
16	30 Aug	Fokker DVII	B8427	1	Bourlon	1830	DES	CR/RAF 30.8
17	30 Aug	Fokker DVII	B8427	1	Bourlon	1830	DES	CR/RAF 30.8
18	3 Sep	Fokker DVII	B8427	1	Avesnes le Sec	1820	DES	CR/RAF 3.9
19	16 Sep	Fokker DVII	B8427	1	Valenciennes	1030	DES(F)	CR/RAF 16.9

TOTAL: 1 shared balloon, 1 shared captured, 8 and 6 shared destroyed, 1 and 2 shared out of control = 19.
*Shared with Capt P.J. Clayson C1114, Lt D. Knight C6479, Lt B.H. Moody C1092, Lt E.T.S. Kelly B130. **Shared with Lt E.M. Forsyth B733, Lt B.H. Moody C1092, Lt E.E. Owen B8512, Lt A.F. Scroggs C6416, Capt K.S. Henderson C1112, Lt H.B. Bradley C1102, Lt E.T.S. Kelly B130, Lt D. Knight C6479, Lt K.J.P. Laing B8504, Capt P.J. Clayson C1849. ***Shared with Capt C.S.T. Lavers C1110, Lt W.A. Smart C1092, Lt L.W. Mawbey B130, Lt E.M. Newman C1101, Capt P.J. Clayson C1114, Lt D. Knight C1106, Lt C.B. Henderson C1849, 2/Lt H.S. Hennessy D337, Lt E.T.S. Kelly B733. †Shared with Lt H.B. Bradley C1102, 2/Lt H.B. Parkinson C6458, Lt E.E. Owen B8512, Lt D. Knight C1106, Lt K.J.P. Laing C1898, Lt E.S. Crossley D6881, Lt J.C. Bateman B8254, Capt P.J. Clayson C1114, Lt C.B. Henderson. this was Gefr Preiss of Jasta 14 who was captured. ††Shared with Capt P.J. Clayson C1114, 2/Lt G.W. Bellin B6881. †††Shared with Capt P.J. Clayson C1114, Lt D. Knight C1894, Lt J.C. Bateman N8254, Lt C.B. Henderson C1849. ‡Shared with Capt P.J. Clayson C1114, Lt D. Knight C1894, Probably Lt G. Kuter/Lt J. Frankenstein of FAA 213. ‡‡Shared with Lt J.C. Bateman B8254, Lt W.A. Smart C1092.

LAGESSE Camille Henri Raoul Captain 29

Born on 10 January 1893, Lagesse joined the RFC in July 1917, being posted to 29 Squadron on 20 March 1918; he claimed his first victories during May. On 6 June he forced a German pilot to land his Fokker DVII inside Allied territory, the pilot being Leutnant Hans Schultz of Jasta 18, who was taken prisoner (his aircraft is now in the RAF Museum Collection). Lagesse — his friends on the squadron somewhat unkindly corrupted his name to 'Large Arse' — was promoted to Captain during June, and by mid October had claimed at least 20 victories and received the DFC and Bar. He was then rested since he had become physically exhausted after 426 hours' war flying. He also received a Belgian Croix de Guerre.

	1918		SE 5A					
1*	22 May	DFW. C	D5969	29	N Steenwerck	0525	DES(F)	CR/RAF 22.5
2	28 May	Pfalz DIII	D5969	29	Neuf Berquin	1120	DES	CR/RAF 28.5
3	29 May	Alb. DV	D5969	29	W Armentieres	1940	OOC	ORB/SR/?
4s**	2 Jun	C	D5969	29	Bailleul-Armentieres	0815	OOC	ORB/SR/?
5***	6 Jun	Fokker DVII	D5969	29	N Hazebrouck	1810	CAPT	CR/RAF 6.6
6	19 Jun	Balloon	E1263	29	N E Estaires	1935	DES	CR/RAF 19.6
7	4 Aug	DFW. C	E1263	29	S Wulverghem	0730	DES	CR/RAF 4.8
8	12 Aug	Fokker DVII	E1263	29	S E Bailleul	1940	DES	CR/RAF 12.8
9	18 Aug	Pfalz DIII	C1942	29	Bailleul	1750	DES(F)	ORB/RAF 18.8
10	14 Sep	Balloon	E4084	29	W Quesnoy	1010	DES	CR/RAF 14.9
11	16 Sep	Fokker DVII	E4084	29	E Linselles	0835	DES	CR/RAF 16.9
12	2 Oct	Fokker DVII	E5999	29	Roulers	1520	DES	CR/RAF 2.10
13s†	5 Oct	Balloon	E4084	29	E N E Menin	0800	DES	CR/RAF 5.10
14††	7 Oct	Fokker DVII	E4084	29	Staden	0850	DES(F)	CR/RAF 7.10
15s†††	7 Oct	LVG. C	E4084	29	Staden-Roulers	0845	DES	CR/RAF 7.10
16‡	7 Oct	Rumpler C	E4084	29	S E Houthoulst Forest	0850	CAPT	CR/RAF 7.10
17	8 Oct	Fokker DVII	E4084	29	S E Roulers	1330	DES	CR/RAF 8.10
18	8 Oct	Fokker DVII	E4084	29	N Roulers	1425	DES	CR/RAF 8.10
19	14 Oct	Fokker DVII	E4084	29	Roulers	0835	DES	CR/RAF 14.10
20	14 Oct	Fokker DVII	E4084	29	W Roulers	0850	CAPT	CR/RAF 14.10

TOTAL: 2 and 1 shared balloons, 3 captured, 10 and 2 shared destroyed, 1 and 1 shared out of control = 20.
*Shared with Lt L.C. Tims D5963. **Shared with Lt C.J. Venter B8240. ***This was Lt Hans Schulz of Jasta 18, who was taken prisoner. †Shared with Lt D.M. Layton E5543, Lt D.M. Murray C1141. ††The pilot baled out, but burnt on the way to the ground and was apparently killed. †††Shared with Lt T.S. Harrison E8507. ‡Both crew members of this aircraft were killed.

LAING Kenneth Joseph Price Lieutenant 1

Born in 1890 in Hawick, Scotland, Laing was commissioned in the RFC on 21 June 1917. He joined 1 Squadron on 13 April 1918, claiming five victories. Whilst on leave in July, he was injured in a motorcycle accident, and did not return to the unit.

	1918		SE 5A					
1s*	21 May	Rumpler C	C9261	1	Merville	0950	DES	CR/RAF 21.5
2s**	28 May	C	B8504	1	Meteren-Bailleul	0635	OOC	CR/ORB/?
3s**	28 May	DFW. C	B8504	1	Meteren-Bailleul	0700	DES	CR/RAF 28.5
4	5 Jun	C	C1898	1	S W Bailleul	0845	DES	CR/ORB/?
5s***	9 Jun	Fokker DrI	C1898	1	Dickebusch	0630	CAPT	CR/RAF WD

TOTAL: 1 shared captured, 1 and 2 shared destroyed, 1 shared out of control = 5.
*Shared with Lt E.M. Forsyth B733. **Shared with Lt E.M. Forsyth B733, Lt B.H. Moody C1092, Lt E.E. Owen B8512, Lt A.F. Scroggs C6416, Capt K.S. Henderson C1112, Lt E.T.S. Kelly B130, Lt H.B. Bradley C1102, Lt H.A. Kullberg B8254, Lt D. Knight C6479, Capt P.J. Clayson C1849. ***Shared with Lt H.B. Bradley C1102, 2/Lt H.B. Parkinson C6458, Lt E.E. Owen B8512, t H.A. Kullberg C8842, Lt D. Knight C1106, Lt E.S. Crossley D6681, Lt J.C. Bateman B8254, Capt P.J. Clayson C1114, Lt C.B. Henderson C1849. Gefr Preiss of Jasta 14 was captured.

LALE Horace Percy Captain 48, 39, 20

Born on 8 April 1896, he joined the RFC in 1916 and soon became a most successful exponent of the Bristol Fighter, flying with both 48, and later 20 Squadrons. With 48 he and his observer gained at least four victories during the summer of 1917. Then followed a period on home defence with 39 Squadron before he was posted to 20 Squadron as a flight commander in 1918. Here he brought his score to 23 by the war's end and received a DFC. On 3 September 1918 during one fight, his observer, Lieutenant F.J. Ralphs, DFC, sent down one enemy aircraft, but was then himself hit and killed. After the war Lale served in Wurzistan, where he was awarded the

DSO. In 1924 he took command of 32 Squadron. From 1928 to 1930 he led 30 Squadron before being promoted Wing Commander. He was made Group Captain in 1936, and later served for several years on the Grant's Committee of the RAF Benevolent Fund. He died in the 1950s after suffering from arthritis for several years.

	1917		Bristol					
1*	24 Jun	Alb. DIII	A7119	48	Douai	2015	OOC	CR/RFC 25.6
2**	22 Jul	Alb. DIII	A7117	48	2m E Ostend	1330	OOC	CR/4 BG WD
3**	19 Aug	Alb. DV	A7176	48	5m S Nieuport	1700	OOC	CR/RFC 20.8
4**	14 Sep	Alb. DV	A7219	48	Slype	1845	OOC	CR/?
	1918							
5***	30 Jun	Fokker DVII	A8716	20	N W Menin	0730	DES	CR/RAF 30.6
6†	25 Jul	Fokker DVII	C4718	20	N Comines	0850	DES	CR/RAF 25.7
7s††	25 Jul	Fokker DVII	C4718	20	Comines	0855	DES(F)	CR/RAF 25.7
8†††	11 Aug	Balloon	E2467	20	W Courtrai	1740	DES	CR/RAF 11.8
9†	14 Aug	Fokker DVII	E2467	20	Dadizeele	c1830	OOC	CR/?
10†	21 Aug	Pfalz DIII	E2467	20	N E Gheluwe	1910	DES	CR/RAF 21.8
11s‡	21 Aug	Fokker DVII	E2467	20	Gheluwe	1915	DES(F)	CR/RAF 21.8
12†	21 Aug	Alb. DV	E2467	20	Gheluwe	1915	OOC	CR/?
13†	21 Aug	Fokker DVII	E2467	20	W Menin-Roulers Rwy	1917	DES	CR/RAF 21.8
14†	3 Sep	Fokker DVII	E2181	20	S Havrincourt Wood	1745	OOC	CR/?
15‡‡	5 Sep	Fokker DVII	E2467	20	S E Cambrai	1520	DES	CR/RAF 5.9
16‡‡	6 Sep	Fokker DVII	E2181	20	St Quentin	0845	DES(F)	CR/RAF 6.9
17‡‡	6 Sep	Fokker DVII	E2181	20	St Quentin	0845	DES(F)	CR/RAF 6.9
18‡‡	7 Sep	Fokker DVII	E2181	20	N E St Quentin	1810	DES	CR/RAF 7.9
19‡‡‡	3 Oct	Fokker DVII	E2588	20	E Mericourt	1005	OOC	CR/RAF 3.10
20§	23 Oct	Fokker DVII	E2407	20	S W Noyelles	1510	DES	CR/RAF 23.10
21§	23 Oct	Fokker DVII	E2407	20	E Preux	1515	DES	CR/RAF 23.10
22§	30 Oct	Fokker DVII	E2407	20	S Avesnes	1205	DES	CR/RAF 30.10
23§	30 Oct	Fokker DVII	E2407	20	S Avesnes	1205	DES	CR/RAF 30.10

TOTAL: 1 balloon, 12 and 2 shared destroyed, 8 out of control = 23.
*Observer: 2/Lt R.N.W. Jeff. **Observer: 2/Lt G.R. Waters. ***Observer: Lt E Hardcastle. †Observer: 2/Lt F.J. Ralphs. ††Observer: 2/Lt F.J. Ralphs; shared with Lt D.E. Smith/Pbr J. Hills C4672, Lt W.M. Thomson/Sgt J.D.C. Summers C843. †††Observer: 2/Lt J. Hills. ‡Observer: 2/Lt F.J. Ralphs; shared with patrol. ‡‡Observer: Lt H.L. Edwards. ‡‡‡Observer: Lt W. Learmond. §Observer: Lt C.G. Boothroyd.

LAMBERT William Carpenter Captain 24

Born on 18 August 1894, Bill Lambert was an American from Irontown, Ohio. He joined 24 Squadron in March 1918 and first claimed during April. On 2 June he claimed one of the rare Siemens Schukert DIII fighters shot down, and by the end of the month had 11 victories, seven destroyed and four out of control, for which he was awarded a DFC, gazetted on 3 August. He became a flight commander, and by mid August had brought his score to 18. He subsequently wrote a very evocative book about his wartime flying, *Combat Report*, followed by a second covering his post war flying experiences. He died on 19 March 1982.

	1918		SE 5A					
1	7 Apr	Alb. DV	B79	24	Moreuil Wood	1550	OOC	CR/RAF 7.4
2	12 Apr	Alb. DV	C1084	24	Hangard-Moreuil	1615	DES	CR/RAF 12.4
3s*	21 Apr	Balloon	C1082	24	La Quesnil	1100	DES	CR/RAF 21.4
4	4 May	Pfalz DIII	C1082	24	Bray-Dompierre	1845	OOC	CR/ORB/?
5s**	9 May	Alb. DV	C1082	24	Hangard Wood	1945	DES	CR/RAF 9.5
6	20 May	Pfalz DIII	C1870	24	Chaulnes-Albert	0835	OOC	CR/ORB/?
7	2 Jun	S.S. DIII	C1870	24	Davenescourt	1115	DES	CR/RAF 2.6
8	17 Jun	Fokker DVII	C1870	24	Villers-Brettoneaux	1200	DES	CR/RAF 17.6
9	17 Jun	Fokker DVII	C1870	24	Villers-Brettoneaux	1200	DES(F)	CR/RAF 17.6
10	27 Jun	Pfalz DIII	C1084	24	Chipilly	1925	OOC	CR/ORB/?
11	29 Jun	Alb. DV	C1084	24	N La Quesnel	1850	DES	CR/RAF 29.6
12	4 Jul	Fokker DVII	C1084	24	Bayonvillers	0900	DES	CR/RAF 4.7
13	4 Jul	Fokker DVII	C1084	24	Bayonvillers	0901	DES	CR/RAF 4.7
14s***	4 Aug	LVG. C	C1084	24	E Morlancourt	0920	DES	CR/RAF 4.8
15s†	10 Aug	LVG. C	B8395	24	N E Rosieres	0750	OOC	CR/ORB/?
16	10 Aug	Fokker DVII	B8395	24	Fouquescourt	1400	OOC	CR/ORB/?
17	10 Aug	Hannover C	B8395	24	N E Parvillers	1405	DES	CR/RAF 10.8
18††	19 Aug	Fokker DVII	B8395	24	W Nesle	1159	DES	ORB/SR/Lamb

TOTAL: 1 shared balloon, 9 and 2 shared destroyed, 5 and 1 shared out of control = 18.
*Shared with Lt G.O. Johnson C1084. **Shared with 2/Lt T.B. Hellett C1845. ***Shared with 2/Lt T.B. Hellett C1085; Lt Otto Kiehn/Lt Peter Martini of FAA 207, were killed. 24 claimed one more destroyed and 1 more out of control. †Shared with Capt W. Selwyn C8840, Lt T.M. Harries C8844, 2/Lt H.L. Bair C1945. ††The ORB only mentions that Lambert was on this patrol. He collapsed that night after a bombing raid on 48 Sqn., and nothing was done to confirm this claim. However, all other claims here are also correctly listed in his autobiography.

LANDIS Reed Gresham Major 40, 25US, 4PG

An American citizen, Reed Landis was born on 17 July 1896, in Ottawa, Illinois. He joined the Illinois Cavalry on reaching military age, and in 1916 served as a private on the Mexican border. In 1917 he transferred to the aviation section of the Signal Corps and was later sent to England for flying training, then being posted to 40 Squadron, RAF, in early summer 1918 to gain combat experience. By 19 August he had claimed victories over 11 aircraft and a balloon; his best day was 8 August when he claimed two aircraft and the balloon. He then returned to England and was posted to the 25th Aero Squadron, USAS, as a flight commander. When this unit moved to France shortly afterwards, to become part of the 4th Pursuit Group, he was promoted to command. He was awarded a DFC and a US DSC. After the war he left the air service, and in 1940 was a regional vice-president of American Airlines. In 1942 he was recalled to the USAAF, where he worked at a staff post in Washington, reaching the rank of Colonel. He retired shortly after the war, and died in 1974.

	1918		SE 5A					
1	8 May	Pfalz DIII	B189	40	Vitry en Artois	1745	OOC	CR/RAF 8.5
2*	19 May	Pfalz DIII	B178	40	Provin	1855	DES	CR/RAF 19.5
3	14 Jul	Pfalz DIII	D6122	40	Epinoy	0730	DES	CR/RAF 14.7
4	22 Jul	Fokker DVII	E1318	40	Carvin	0850	DES	CR/RAF 22.7
5	7 Aug	LVG. C	E1318	40	N Pont a Vendin	1015	OOC	CR/?
6	8 Aug	Fokker DrI	E1318	40	W Douai	1035	DES(F)	CR/RAF 8.8
7	8 Aug	DFW. C	E1318	40	S Vitry	1045	DES	CR/RAF 8.8
8	8 Aug	Balloon	E1318	40	Vitry	1047	DES	CR/RAF 8.8
9	12 Aug	Fokker DVII	E1318	40	W Mons	1000	DES	CR/RAF 12.8
10	13 Aug	Fokker DVII	E1318	40	S Lens	1205	OOC	CR/?
11	19 Aug	Fokker DVII	E1318	40	Seclin-La Bassee	1005	DES	CR/RAF 19.8
12	19 Aug	Fokker DrI	E1318	40	W Seclin	1025	DES	CR/RAF 19.8

TOTAL: 1 balloon, 8 destroyed, 3 out of control = 12.
*40 made 3 claims; Vzfw Julius Trotsky of Jasta 43 was killed.

LANGAN-BYRNE Patrick Anthony Lieutenant 24

An Irishman, Patrick Langan-Byrne transferred to the RFC from the Royal Artillery. He flew DH 2s with 24 Squadron in the late summer of 1916, and was awarded the DSO for exceptional gallantry; he claimed three enemy machines shot down and compelled seven others to land — typical of the type of essentially moral victories which were frequently credited to pilots during 1916, but not thereafter. On 23 September he was shot down by four enemy scouts and was feared lost, but he turned up safely and the next day was out again attacking enemy troops and transports. In October he took command of 'B' Flight, but on 16th of that month during a fight with 12 Albatros Scouts of Jasta 2, he was shot down and killed by the German ace Oswald Boelke for the latter's 34th victory.

	1916		DH 2					
1	31 Aug	HA	6010	24	N Bapaume	c1800	FTL	CR/RFC 31.8
2	2 Sep	D	6010	24	Beaulencourt	1935	OOC	CR/ORB/?
3	15 Sep	D	7911	24	N E Morval	0830	DES(F)	CR/RFC 15.9
4	16 Sep	Fokker DII	7911	24	Achiet	1900	DES	CR/RFC 15.9
5	21 Sep	LVG. C	7911	24	N Miraumont	1745	FTL	CR/RFC 21.9
6	22 Sep	EA	7911	24	Velu	1140	FTL	CR/ORB/?
7	22 Sep	Rumpler C	7911	24	Grandcourt	1800	FTL	CR/ORB/?
8	23 Sep	Rumpler C	7911	24	E Combles	0815	FTL	CR/ORB/?
9	28 Sep	LVG. C	A2538	24	Rocquigny	1710	FTL	CR/ORB/?
10	16 Oct	Alb. DI	5925	24	Biefvillers	1030	FTL	CR/ORB/?

TOTAL: 2 destroyed, 1 out of control, 7 forced to land = 10.

LANGLANDS David Lieutenant 23

After service as an observer, Langlands trained as a pilot and enjoyed a brief career with 23 Squadron during the early summer of 1917, although quite an eventful one. Flying Spads, his first victory was claimed on 6 July. Six days later he was ordered to attack a German two-seater which was over the front line directing artillery fire on British positions. Attacking this aircraft, he sent it down to crash. Four days later he went after a scout which was attacking the British balloon line; pursuing the German, Langlands forced him back to the Allied side and compelled him to land near Poperinge, where the luckless pilot, VzFw Ernst Clausnitzer of Jasta 4, was taken prisoner.

	1917		Spad					
1	6 Jul	Alb. DV	B3501	23	S E Houthoulst	1140	OOC	CR/RFC 6.7
2	11 Jul	Alb. DV	B3501	23	Tenbrielen	1745	DES(F)	CR/RFC 11.7
3	11 Jul	Alb. DV	B3501	23	Tenbrielen	1745	OOC	CR/RFC 11.7
4	12 Jul	C	A6709	23	E Polygon Wood	1320	DES	CR/RFC 12.7
5*	16 Jul	Alb. DV	----	23	S E Poperinghe	----	CAPT	RFC 16.7

TOTAL: 1 captured, 2 destroyed, 2 out of control = 5.
*This was Vzfw Ernst Clausnitzer of Jasta 4, who became a prisoner.

LARKIN Herbert Joseph Captain 5, 87

'Jimmy' Larkin was born in Brisbane, Australia, on 8 October 1894. In 1914 he served in the Royal Engineers in Egypt and Gallipoli as a Sergeant, but was wounded. Transferring to the RFC on recovery, he served as a pilot with 5 Squadron, flying RE 8s; he was awarded a French Croix de Guerre for this service. In 1918 he became 'A' Flight commander with 87 Squadron, returning to France in April of that year. He claimed 11 victories and was awarded the DFC. It was said of him that he was a cool, calculating killer, and an excellent pilot. Returning to Australia, he was Managing Director of the Larkin Aircraft Supply Company in Melbourne in the 1930s. Following the failure of his business, he returned to the Old World, settling in the Channel Islands where he became a noted horticulturalist until his death in 1972.

	1918		Dolphin					
1	3 Jun	Alb. DV	C4173	87	Peronne	1835	OOC	CR/?
2	3 Jun	Fokker DrI	C4173	87	Peronne	1835	OOC	CR/?
3	21 Aug	Fokker DVII	C8163	87	Peronne	1240	DES	CR/RAF 21.8
4	21 Aug	Fokker DVII	C8163	87	Peronne	1240	OOC	CR/?
5	21 Aug	Fokker DVII	C8163	87	Fremicourt	1815	DES	CR/RAF 21.8
6	25 Aug	Fokker DVII	C8163	87	Haplincourt	1800	DES	CR/RAF 25.8
7	30 Aug	Fokker DVII	C8163	87	Velu Wood	1810	DES(F)	CR/RAF 30.8
8	30 Aug	Fokker DVII	C8163	87	Velu Wood	1815	OOC	CR/?
9	3 Sep	Fokker DVII	C8163	87	Epinoy	1830	OOC	CR/?
10	3 Sep	Fokker DVII	C8163	87	Epinoy	1830	OOC	CR/?
11	16 Sep	Fokker DVII	C8163	87	W Abancourt	1730	DES	CR/RAF 16.9

TOTAL: 5 destroyed, 6 out control = 11.

LARSEN Jens Frederick Lieutenant 84

An American from Waltham, Massachusetts, 'Swede' Larson was born on 10 August 1891. He joined the Canadian Army, serving with the Field Artillery, but transferred to the RFC on 19 October 1916, subsequently becoming one of the original members of 84 Squadron, with which unit he claimed nine victories. On 6 April 1918 he was instrumental in bringing down an LVG two-seater after he had first silenced the rear gunner, the machine crashing inside the British lines. He went into hospital on 11 April, and did not fly again with 84.

	1917		SE 5A					
1	26 Nov	Alb. DV	B612	84	Fonsomme-Mont d'Origny	0800	OOC	CR/RFC 26.11
	1918							
2	3 Jan	C	A8342	84	3m N E St Quentin	1500	DES(F)	CR/RFC 3.1
3	16 Feb	Alb. DV	A8942	84	La Fere	1020	OOC	CR/RFC 16.2
4s*	19 Feb	Alb. DV	----	84	St Gobain Wood	1020	OOC	CR/RFC 19.2
5	15 Mar	Pfalz DIII	C1077	84	N E Ribemont	0920	OOC	CR/RFC 15.3
6	18 Mar	Fokker DrI	C1077	84	Le Cateau	1130	OOC	CR/RFC 18.3
7	3 Apr	Alb. DV	C1772	84	Rosieres	1150	OOC	CR/RAF 3.4
8	3 Apr	Alb. DV	C1772	84	1m E Rosieres	1150	DES	CR/RAF 3.4
9s**	6 Apr	LVG. C	C1772	84	N Hangard	1120	CAPT	CR/RAF 6.4

TOTAL: 1 shared captured, 2 destroyed, 6 out of control = 9.
*Shared with 2/Lt J.A. McCudden C5310. **Shared with Lt C.L. Stubbs C9519, Lt H.W.L. Saunders C1794, Lt H.O. MacDonald C6410; this was Uffz Drexler/Lt Kalfeken of FAA 205.

LATIMER Dennis Captain 20

Dublin-born, this pilot joined 20 Squadron early in 1918, and gained his first victory in March. In May he teamed-up with Lieutenant T.C. Noel and during the month they claimed nine enemy machines destroyed plus four more out of control. For this they were both awarded the MC and Latimer became a flight commander. The successful partnership continued through June and July by which time they had brought their score to 23. In August Latimer flew with another successful observer, Sergeant Newland, DFM, and with him gained five further victories to bring his total to 28, which gained him the DFC. On 22 August he and Noel were shot down in D7993 near Westroosebeke by Lt Willi Nebgen of Jasta 7; Latimer became a prisoner, but Noel was killed.

	1918		Bristol					
1*	13 Mar	Alb. DV	C4615	20	Comines-Wervicq	1255	OOC	CR/RFC 13.3
2**	21 Apr	Alb. DV	B1232	20	N Wervicq	1110	OOC	CR/I BG Summ
3**	8 May	Alb. DV	C856	20	S E Wervicq	1320	DES(F)	CR/RAF 8.5
4**	8 May	Fokker DrI	C856	20	Comines-Wervicq	1640	DES(F)	CR/RAF 8.5
5**	8 May	Fokker DrI	C856	20	Comines-Wervicq	1640	OOC	CR/RAF 8.5
6**	8 May	Fokker DrI	C856	20	Comines-Wervicq	1641	OOC	CR/RAF 8.5
7**	14 May	Alb. DV	C856	20	Wervicq	1845	DES	CR/RAF 14.5
8***	14 May	Alb. DV	C856	20	Zillebeke	1850	CAPT	CR/RAF 14.5
9**	15 May	Pfalz DIII	C856	20	N W Lille	1045	OOC	CR/RAF 15.5
10**	15 May	Fokker DrI	C856	20	Comines-Ypres	1115	DES	CR/RAF 15.5
11**	18 May	Pfalz DIII	C856	20	Comines	0700	DES	CR/RAF 18.5
12**	18 May	Pfalz DIII	C856	20	N E Nieppe Forest	1140	DES	CR/RAF 18.5
13**	18 May	Pfalz DIII	C856	20	Merville	1145	OOC	CR/SR/?
14**	20 May	Alb. DV	C856	20	N E Merville	1130	DES(F)	CR/RAF 20.5
15**	20 May	Alb. DV	C856	20	Coucou airfield	1135	DES	CR/RAF 20.5
16**	1 Jun	Pfalz DIII	C892	20	Comines	0630	DES	CR/RAF 1.6
17**	9 Jun	Pfalz DIII	C892	20	Comines	0915	DES	CR/RAF 9.6
18s†	17 Jun	Fokker DVII	C987	20	Boesinghe	0745	OOC	CR/SR/11 WS
19**	30 Jun	Pfalz DIII	C987	20	Comines	0730	DES	CR/RAF 30.6
20**	1 Jul	Fokker DrI	C987	20	Menin	1845	OOC	CR/SR/11 WS
21**	14 Jul	Fokker DVII	C987	20	S E Ypres	0900	OOC	CR/SR/11 WS
22s††	14 Jul	Fokker DVII	C987	20	S E Ypres	0900	OOC	CR/SR/11 WS
23**	19 Jul	Fokker DVII	C987	20	N Comines	0845	DES	CR/RAF 19.7
24†††	14 Aug	Pfalz DIII	D7993	20	Dadizeele	1800-1830	DES	CR/RAF 14.8
25†††	14 Aug	Pfalz DIII	D7993	20	Dadizeele	1800-1830	DES	CR/RAF 14.8
26†††	21 Aug	Pfalz DIII	D7993	20	Menin	1910	DES	CR/RAF 21.8
27†††	21 Aug	Pfalz DIII	D7993	20	Dadizeele	1915	DES	CR/RAF 21.8
28s‡	21 Aug	Pfalz DIII	D7993	20	Gheluwe	1915	DES	CR/RAF 21.8

TOTAL: 1 captured, 16 and 1 shared destroyed, 8 and 2 shared out of control = 28.
*Observer: 2/Lt J.J. Scaramanga. **Observer: Lt T.C. Noel. ***Observer: Lt T.C. Noel; Uffz Florian of Jasta 51 was taken prisoner. †Observer: Lt T.C. Noel; shared with W.M. Thomson/Pbr F.J. Ralphs C843. ††Observer: Lt T.C. Noel; shared with Lt A.T. Iaccaci/2/Lt R.W. Turner. †††Observer: Sgt. A. Newland. ‡Observer: Sgt A. Newland; shared with Capt H.P. Lale/2/Lt F.J. Ralph E2467, Lt J.H. Colbert/2/Lt H.L. Edwards E2158.

LATTA James Douglas Captain 5, 1, 60, 66

After service as a Corps pilot in 5 Squadron, Latta was posted to 1 Squadron in February 1916 to become a scout pilot. He was awarded an MC on 27 July of that year, and on 11 October went to 60 Squadron as a flight commander until rested on 23 November. In May 1917 he joined 66 Squadron as a flight commander flying Pups, but was wounded in action on 8 June of that year when he was shot down in B1726 near Varmezelle by Oberleutnant von Voight of Jasta 8. He did not see further active service.

	1916		Nieuport					
1*	1 Jun	EA	----	1	Wezmacquart	1530	DES	RFC WD
2	25 Jun	Balloon	----	1	N Le Sars	1600	DES	SR/RFC WD
3	26 Jun	Balloon	----	1	S Wervicq	2030	DES	SR/RFC WD
4	31 Aug	LVG. C	A135	60	Bapaume	1845	OOC	CR/RFC 31.8
5	19 Sep	Fokker DII	A135	60	Achiet le Grand	1830	OOC	CR/RFC 19.9

TOTAL: 2 balloons, 1 destroyed, 2 out of control = 5.
*This claim was confirmed late by 1 ANZAC Corps.

LAURENCE Frederic Hope Captain 70

Captain Laurence was a flight Commander in 70 Squadron when the first Camels were received by the unit in summer 1917. He claimed his first victory on 28 July. He remained with the squadron through the rest of the summer and autumn, claiming four more victories and being awarded an MC on 26 November.

	1917		Camel					
1s*	28 Jul	C	----	70	Ypres	----	OOC	RFC 28.7
2	20 Oct	Alb. DV	B2423	70	Roulers-Menin Rd.	1115	OOC	CR/RFC 20.10
3	21 Oct	Alb. DV	B2423	70	W Roulers	1015	OOC	CR/RFC 21.10
4	27 Oct	Alb. DV	B2423	70	Roulers	1400	OOC	CR/RFC 27.10
5s**	27 Oct	Alb. DV	B2423	70	Roulers	1400	OOC	CR/RFC 27.10

TOTAL: 2 and 3 shared out of control = 5.
*Shared with Patrol. **Shared with Major Nethersole, 2/Lt C.W. Primeau, 2/Lt E.B. Booth, Lt Goode, 2/Lt F.H. Hobson.

LAVERS Charles Stewart Iouzeau Captain 23, 1

Born in St Albans on 17 August 1896, Lavers served with the West Yorkshire Regiment in England from September 1915 to May 1916, when he was posted to the 1st Battalion in France. He transferred to the RFC in September, becoming an observer in 23 Squadron. He was slightly wounded in the head on 23 November. In March 1917 when the squadron converted to Spad single-seaters, he was sent back to England to train as a pilot. He then joined 1 Squadron on 1 June 1917. He was forced to land near Menin on 15 July after suffering slight wounds. In November he was posted to Home Establishment, where he served with 44 (Home Defence) Squadron, becoming a Captain on 1 February 1918. He rejoined 1 Squadron on 4 May and shared in four further victories before the end of the war, including a Pfalz DXII of Jasta 23 on 15 September, which was forced to land in Allied lines, the pilot dying of his wounds. Lavers was awarded a DFC. Postwar he joined the family timber merchant's business.

	1917		Nieuport					
1s*	18 Jun	Alb. DV	B3495	1	Oostaverne	1145	DES	CR/RFC 18.6
2	7 Jul	Alb. DV	B3485	1	Roulers	2040	OOC	CR/RFC 8.7
3	11 Jul	Alb. DV	B3485	1	E Comines	2015	OOC	CR/RFC 11.7
4	14 Aug	Alb. DV	B1692	1	S Moorslede	1910	OOC	CR/RFC 14.8
5s**	17 Aug	DFW. C	B1692	1	Tenbrielen	1015	OOC	CR/RFC 17.8
	1918		SE 5A					
6s***	1 Jun	Pfalz DIII	C1110	1	Armentieres	1940	DES	CR/RAF 1.6
7s†	17 Jun	Fokker DVII	B733	1	Ploegsteert	1030	OOC	CR/ORB/?
8s††	15 Sep	Pfalz DXII	E5969	1	Marquion-Recourt	1705	CAPT	CR/RAF 15.9
9s†††	1 Oct	Fokker DVII	C9292	1	N E St Quentin	1710	OOC	CR/ORB/?

TOTAL: 1 shared captured, 2 shared destroyed, 3 and 3 shared out of control = 8.
*Shared with Lt L.F. Jenkin B1681, 2/Lt H.G. Reeves, B1630. **Shared with Lt W.V.T. Rooper B1675. ***Shared with Lt W.A. Smart C1092, Lt L.W. Mawbey B130, Lt E.M. Newman C1101, Lt E.T.S. Kelly B733, Lt H.A. Kullberg B8512, Capt P.J. Clayson C1114, Lt C.B. Henderson C1849, Lt D. Knight C1106, 2/Lt H.S. Hennessey D377. †Shared with Lt E.M. Newman D6878, Lt F.A.S. Nesbitt B7881, Lt H.B. Bradley C1102. ††Shared with Capt G.W.D. Allen F5912, Lt B.H. Moody B8501, Lt D.E. Cameron F6429 and Capt W.E. Staton/Lt L.E. Mitchell of 62 Sqn Lt P. Vogel of Jasta 23 died of wounds. †††Shared with Lt B.H. Moody B8501, Lt W.A. Smart D6973, Lt F.M. Squires E6009, Lt F.A.S. Nesbitt B7881, Lt Boyd C9065, Lt D.E. Cameron H7257, Lt L.H. Phinney D6951, Capt W. Pallister F5473, Lt W. Newby E1353, Lt C.W. Arning E4023, 2/Lt W. Joffe B8427, Lt Dickinson C1812.

LAWSON George Edgar Bruce Lieutenant 32

Served in 32 Squadron from April 1918, flying SE 5As. He was awarded the DFC and claimed six enemy machines. On 27 September he claimed two Fokker Biplanes, one of which was flown by Oberleutnant Fritz Rumey (45 victories) of Jasta 5. After the war this native of South Africa joined the SAAF in 1922, but was killed flying as a passenger in a DH 9 on 19 November of that year.

	1918		SE 5A					
1	7 Jun	Alb. DV	C1881	32	Lagny	1130	OOC	CR/ORB/SR/?
2	6 Sep	Fokker DVII	E1399	32	Holnon	1700	DES	CR/RAF 6.9
3	16 Sep	Fokker DVII	E1399	32	Marquion	1800	OOC	CR/RAF 16.9
4	24 Sep	Fokker DVII	E1399	32	N Cambrai	1710	OOC	ORB/SR/?
5	27 Sep	Fokker DVII	E1399	32	Emerchicourt	0930	DES	CR/RAF 27.9
6	27 Sep	Fokker DVII	E1399	32	Emerchicourt	0930	DES(F)	CR/RAF 27.9

TOTAL: 3 destroyed, 3 out of control = 6.
*This was Lt Fritz Rumey, a 45 victory ace of Jasta 45, who was killed.

LEACROFT John Captain 14, 19

Born on 4 November 1888, John Leacroft served as an observer with 14 Squadron in Egypt early in the war. After pilot training, he joined 19 Squadron in France and completed two successful tours with the unit, one in 1917, the other in 1918. He received the MC and Bar, and claimed 22 victories. He was twice shot down, once when a Fokker holed his petrol tank and forced him down upside down near Passchendaele, and once when he came down in the Australian lines, cutting their telephone wires, to their great annoyance. He remained in the RAF, becoming a Wing Commander in 1933 and Group Captain in 1937, retiring in December of that year. He again served as a Group Captain in World War II, before retiring to Bexhill, where he died in 1971.

	1917		Spad					
1	17 Jun	C	B1535	19	E La Bassee	1130	OOC	CR/RFC 17.6
2	6 Jul	Alb. DV	B3520	19	Houthoulst Forest	1435-1639	OOC	ORB/RFC 6.7
3	26 Aug	Alb. DV	B3559	19	Bisseghem	0540	DES	CR/RFC 26.8
4	1 Sep	Alb. DV	B3559	19	E Polygon Wood	0655	DES	CR/RFC 1.9
5	1 Sep	Alb. DV	B3559	19	S E Comines	0815	OOC	ORB/RFC 1.9
6	3 Sep	Alb. DV	B3559	19	S E Comines	0830	OOC	CR/RFC 3.9
7s*	19 Sep	Alb. DV	B3559	19	N Roubaix	1535	OOC	CR/RFC 19.9
8	19 Sep	Alb. DV	B3559	19	W Moorslede	1600	OOC	CR/RFC 19.9
9	21 Sep	Alb. DV	B3559	19	Dadizeele	0950	OOC	CR/RFC 21.9
10	25 Sep	C	B3559	19	Menin	1000	OOC	CR/RFC 26.9
11	14 Oct	Alb. DV	B3646	19	Becelaere	1620	DES	CR/RFC 14.10
12	21 Oct	Alb. DV	A6805	19	Oude-Menin	1020	DES	CR/RFC 21.10
13	24 Oct	Alb. DV	A6802	19	N E Menin	0845	OOC	CR/RFC 24.10
14	24 Oct	Alb. DV	A6802	19	N Menin	0845	OOC	CR/ORB/?
	1918		Dolphin					
15	15 Mar	Alb. DV	C3843	19	E Tourcoing	1115	OOC	CR/RFC 15.3
16	15 Mar	Alb. DV	C3843	19	E Wervicq	1150	OOC	CR/RFC 15.3
17**	17 Mar	Pfalz DIII	C3829	19	De Ruiter	1225	DES(F)	CR/RFC 17.3
18s***	23 Mar	C	C3829	19	Lille	1540	DES(F)	CR/RFC 23.3
19	24 Mar	Alb. DV	C3829	19	W Menin	1050	OOC	CR/RFC 24.3
20	24 Mar	Alb. DV	C3829	19	W Menin	1055	DES	CR/RFC 24.3
21	12 Apr	Pfalz DIII	C3829	19	Estaires	1400	DES(F)	CR/RAF 12.4
22	2 May	Pfalz DIII	C3829	19	S Armentieres	1745	DES	CR/RAF 2.5

TOTAL: 8 and 1 shared destroyed, 12 and 1 shared out of control = 22.

*Shared with 2/Lt F.W. Kirby B3574. **In this area 19 claimed 5 destroyed and 1 out of control; Lt Jahnsen of Jasta 28 was killed. ***Shared with Lt A.B. Fairclough C3940.

LEASK Kenneth Malice St Clair Graeme Captain 42, 41, 84

Born on 30 October 1896, in Southsea, Hampshire, Leask was in the Devonshire Regiment when he received his commission; at the age of 18 he then served with the Machine Gun Corps as an instructor until transferring to the RFC in May 1916. After pilot training he went to 42 Squadron, flying BEs in France until December when he transferred to 41 Squadron on FE 8s, becoming a flight commander. He flew with 41 until May 1917, when he was posted home as an instructor. He applied to join 84 Squadron which was just forming, and took command of 'A' Flight, returning to France in September. Now flying the SE 5A, his previous experience proved useful in introducing the unit's new young pilots to operational flying. He received the MC and Bar and took part in many ground attacks during the German offensive in March 1918. His last day with the squadron was on 1 April, when he had to make three forced landings. During his period with 84 he flew well over 100 patrols and accounted for eight enemy aircraft. After the war he flew with 28 Squadron and later commanded 60 Squadron in India; by 1933 he was a Wing Commander. Later he was Director General of the Air Ministry before retiring as an Air Vice-Marshal, CB, to live in Buckinghamshire. He died with his wife in a car accident on 24 April 1974.

	1917		SE 5A					
1s*	21 Oct	C	B4874	84	E Roulers-Menin Rd.	1440	OOC	CR/RFC 21.10
2	21 Oct	Alb. DV	B4874	84	Roulers	1500	OOC	CR/RFC 21.10
3	31 Oct	Alb. DV	B579	84	Menin	1540	OOC	CR/RFC 31.10
4	30 Nov	C	----	84	S E Gouzeaucourt	----	DES	RFC 30.11
	1918							
5	30 Jan	Alb. DV	B637	84	Villers Outreaux	1145	OOC	CR/RFC 30.1
6	6 Mar	Alb. DV	B637	84	Renansart	0940	DES	CR/RFC 6.3
7	18 Mar	Alb. DV	B637	84	Wassigny	1130	OOC	CR/RFC 18.3
8	23 Mar	Alb. DV	B637	84	N E Ham	1655	DES	CR/RFC 24.3

TOTAL: 3 destroyed, 4 and 1 shared out of control = 8.

*Shared with Lt J.S. Ralston B564.

LEBLANC-SMITH Maurice Major 18, 73

Born on 23 February 1896, at Leatherhead, Surrey, he joined the RFC early in the war and was a pilot in 18 Squadron during 1915-16, flying Vickers FB 5s and DH 2s. During his service with the squadron he flew many bombing and reconnaissance missions. After a period as an instructor, he became a flight commander with 73 Squadron in 1918, later becoming the unit's commanding officer. He claimed six more enemy machines and received the DFC in August. In February 1919 he commanded 11 Squadron. Leblanc-Smith died in England on 29 October 1986.

	1918		Camel					
1	10 Mar	Fokker DrI	B5572	73	W Bohain	1415	DES	CR/RFC 10.3
2	16 May	D	----	73	S Arras-Cambrai Rd.	----	DES	RAF 16.5
3	6 Jun	Fokker DVII	D1794	73	S Roye	1035	DES	CR/RAF 6.6
4	12 Jun	Alb. DV	D1794	73	1000y N Courcelles	1000	DES	CR/RAF 12.6
5	12 Jun	Fokker DVII	D1794	73	W Tricot	1915	CAPT	CR/RAF 12.6
6*	12 Jun	Alb. DV	D1794	73	W Tricot	1950	CAPT	CR/RAF 12.6

TOTAL: 2 captured, 4 destroyed = 6.
*One of these was probably Lt Rudolf Croissant of Jasta 68, the other was possible Lt Erich of Jasta 36.

LE BOUTILLIER, Oliver Colin Captain 9(N), 209

Born in 1895, 'Boots' was an American from New Jersey, who joined the RNAS in Canada, eventually becoming a pilot and going to France to join 9 Naval Squadron in 1917. Flying Sopwith Triplanes he gained at least four victories. In 1918, by which time 209 Squadron as the unit had become, had re-equipped with Camels, he became a flight commander. He was involved in the air fight in which Manfred von Richthofen was killed, and by mid year had brought his score to ten. When the war ended he had more than 600 hours flying time and he returned to America to become a skywriter. He was later an official of the Skywriting Corporation of America, and became a stunt pilot in Hollywood, flying in 18 films including the classic *Hell's Angels*. He flew in National Air Races and even gave Amelia Earhart her first dual instruction on a twin-engined aeroplane. In 1937 he joined the Civil Aeronautics Administration and during World War II was Inspector in charge of Colorado and Wyoming. After a flying life of 19,000 hours, he retired to Las Vegas where he died on 12 May 1983.

	1917		Triplane					
1	25 May	LVG. C	N5459	9N	off Ostend	1630	OOC	CR/DOS/?
2	5 Jun	Alb. DIII	N5459	9N	off Ostend	1930	OOC	CR/DOS/DL?
3s*	17 Jul	Alb. DV	N5459	9N	Nieuport	0510	OOC	CR/RFC 17.7
4	29 Jul	Alb. DIII	N5484	9N	Leke	0530	OOC	CR/RFC 29.7
	1918		Camel					
5s**	21 Apr	Alb. C	D3338	209	Beaucourt	1025	DES(F)	CR/RAF 21.4
6s***	22 Apr	Alb. C	D3338	209	Albert	0610	CAPT	CR/RAF 22.4
7	4 May	Pfalz DIII	D3338	209	E Villers-Brettoneaux	1555	OOC	CR/?
8†	9 May	Fokker DrI	D3338	209	S Bray	1145	DES	CR/RAF 9.5
9s††	16 May	LVG. C	D3338	209	Bayonvillers	0940	DES(F)	CR/RAF 16.5
10	31 May	Alb. DV	D3338	209	Vauvillers	1920	OOC	CR/?

TOTAL: 1 shared captured, 1 and 2 shared destroyed, 5 and 1 shared out of control = 10.
*Shared with F/Lt E. Pierce N5377, FSL MacDonald N5378, FSL R.B. Freeland N5489, FSL W.E.B. Oakley N5475. **Shared with Lt R.M. Foster B3858, Lt M.S. Taylor B7200; probably Lt K. Fischer/Lt Robinius of FAA 203. ***Shared with Lt M.S. Taylor, Lt M.A. Harker, Lt R.M. Foster, Lt C.G. Brock; this was DFW. CV 7752/17 of Flgr O. Raschke/Lt K. Schneider of FAA 209, who were killed. †Certainly Lt Johann Janzen, the acting commander of Jasta 6, who crashed unhurt. ††Shared with Capt R.M. Foster B3858.

LEE Arthur Stanley Gould Captain 46

Born on 31 August 1894, Arthur Gould Lee joined the Sherwood Foresters early in the war and later transferred to the RFC. During training he crashed and broke his leg. Forced to remain in England until he had fully recovered, he was enabled to amass a considerably greater then average number of flying hours before being posted to France, which was to stand him in good stead. He joined 46 Squadron in May 1917, flying Sopwith Pups. He served throughout the rest of the year, becoming a flight commander in November, and being awarded an MC in December. During the Battle of Cambrai he was shot down by ground fire on three occasions, on 22, 26 and 30 November, while engaged in low bombing and strafing attacks. He returned to Home Establishment in January 1918, having flown some 222 hours over the lines during 118 patrols. He had been reported missing four times, had 56 combats and claimed seven victories, plus three others driven down and one forced to land. Remaining in the RAF after the war, he attained the rank of Air Vice-Marshal before he retired in 1946. He subsequently wrote a book on his experiences in 1917 entitled *No Parachute*, followed by a second called *Open Cockpit* and a third *Flypast*. He succeeded W.J.F. Harvey as President of Cross & Cockade, Great Britain, an office he held until his death on 21 May 1975.

	1917		Pup					
1	4 Sep	Alb. DV	B1777	46	N E Polygon Wood	1700	OOC	CR/RFC 4.9
2s*	11 Sep	C	B1777	46	S Scarpe River	1055	OOC	CR/RFC 11.9
3s**	21 Sep	C	B1777	46	S Scrape River	0820	OOC	CR/RFC 21.9
4	22 Sep	Alb. DV	B1777	46	Sailly-en-Ostrevent	1030	OOC	CR/11 Sq NP
5	30 Sep	DFW. C	B1777	46	Vitry	1635	OOC	CR/RFC 30.9
			Camel					
6	30 Nov	DFW. C	B2501	46	Havrincourt-Flesquires	0900	DES	CR/RFC 30.11
7	30 Nov	Alb. DV	B2501	46	W Bourlon	1500	DES	CR/2 BG WD

TOTAL: 2 destroyed, 3 and 2 shared out of control = 7.
*Shared with Capt M.D.G. Scott B1843, Lt E.Y. Hughes, Lt E. Armitage. **Shared with Capt M.D.G. Scott B2191, Lt E.Y. Hughes A6188.

LEITCH Alfred Alexander Captain 43, 65

A Canadian from Ontario, he was known as 'Ack-Ack'. He joined 1 ASD in 1917, and was then posted to 43 Squadron in December, serving until January 1918. He then went to 65 Squadron, flying Camels and receiving awards of the MC and DFC; he was credited with seven victories. On 25 May he forced down an Albatros Scout inside Allied lines, the pilot, VzFw Karl Keller of Jasta 76, being taken prisoner. Tall in stature, Leitch was an excellent pilot in spite of having a deformed foot. However, before he was due to return home, he crashed a Sopwith Salamander which he was testing and was slightly injured. He served in the RCAF during the 1920s.

	1918		Camel					
1	5 Feb	Alb. DV	B2411	65	Dadizeele	1330	OOC	CR/RFC 5.2
2	9 May	Pfalz DIII	C8280	65	Wiencourt	1950	OOC	CR/ORB/?
3	15 May	Fokker DrI	C8280	65	S E Albert	2010	DES	CR/RAF 15.5
4*	25 May	Alb. DV	D1903	65	Senlis	1950	CAPT	CR/ORB/?
5	29 May	Alb. DV	D1903	65	S W Albert	0850	DES	CR/ORB/?
6	26 Jun	Pfalz DIII	D1903	65	E Albert	2030	DES	CR/ORB/?
7	26 Jun	Pfalz DIII	D1903	65	E Albert	2030	OOC	CR/ORB/?

TOTAL: 1 captured, 3 destroyed, 3 out of control = 7.
*This was Vzfw K. Koller of Jasta 76b, who became a prisoner.

LEITH James Leith Captain 25, 46

Born on 20 December 1896, he joined the Hampshire Regiment at the outbreak of war, being attached to the RFC in January 1915. This Londoner had become a 25 Squadron FE 2B pilot by late 1916, he and his gunner claiming five victories by March 1917. He had become a flight commander during February, subsequently adding three more victories before he was rested in May. In September 1918 Leith joined 46 Squadron as a flight commander on Camels; here he shared one out of control claim on 2 October.

	1916		FE 2B					
1*	22 Oct	D	7693	25	Seclin	0904	DES	CR/RFC 22.10
2**	9 Nov	Fokker D	7693	25	Henin-Lietard	0830	OOC	CR/RFC 9.11
	1917							
3***	24 Jan	Alb. DII	4946	25	Lieven-Lens	1500	DES	CR/RFC 24.1
4†	29 Jan	Alb. DII	7693	25	Harnes	1050	OOC	CR/RFC 29.1
5††	1 Mar	Alb. DII	A782	25	Mericourt	1500	OOC	CR/RFC 1.3?
6†††	17 Mar	Alb. DII	7693	25	Arras	1725	OOC	CR/RFC 17.3
7s‡	13 Apr	Alb. DIII	A782	25	Sallaumines	1930	DES	CR/RFC 14.4
			Fe 2D					
8††	21 Apr	Alb. DIII	A6383	25	Rouvroy-Oppy	1855	OOC	CR/8N/?
	1918		Camel					
9s‡‡	2 Oct	Fokker DVII	H7279	46	Morcourt	1030	OOC	CR/V BG WD

TOTAL: 2 and 1 shared destroyed, 5 and 1 shared out of control = 9.
*Observer: Sgt L.S. Court. **Observer: 2/Lt E.L. Chadwick. ***Observer: 2/Lt A.G. Severs. †Observer: 2/Lt D.C. Woollen. ††Observer: Lt G.M.A. Hobart-Hampden. †††Observer: 2 AM L. Emsden. ‡Observer: Lt G.M.A. Hobart-Hampden; shared with Sgt W.J. Burtenshaw/Sgt J.H. Brown 7003. ‡‡Shared with Capt D.R. Maclaren F2137, Lt C.H. Sawyer F1974.

LENNOX James Scott Lieutenant 66

Born in Glasgow in 1898, Lennox was commissioned in the RFC on 4 August 1917 and joined 66 Squadron in Italy on 12 March 1918. He opened his scoring with two claims in May, adding one more in July, one in August and one on 27 October. He was awarded the Italian Crocce de Guerra in March 1919.

	1918		Camel					
1	20 May	Alb. DV	B7350	66	Alano di Piave	1820	OOC	ORB/SR/?
2	21 May	Alb. DV	B7350	66	Moriago	0805	DES	ORB/SR/14 W
3	15 Jul	Alb. DIII	D9388	66	Levico-Marter	1005	DES	ORB/SR/14 W
4	26 Aug	Alb. DV	D8215	66	S Biago	c0900	DES	ORB/SR/14 W
5	27 Oct	C	E1582	66	S Polo di Piave	1010	OOC	ORB/SR/14 W

TOTAL: 3 destroyed, 2 out of control = 5.

LETTS John Herbert Towne Captain 27, 48, 64, 87

John Letts from Lincoln, born in mid 1897, entered Sandhurst before he served in the Lincolnshire Regiment before transferring to the RFC. Here he flew with 27 Squadron in 1916, then joining 48 Squadron as it was about to move to France with the first Bristol Fighters. When Captain W. Leefe-Robinson, VC, was shot down during the unit's first patrol, Letts replaced him as flight commander, but on 11 May 1917 he and his observer, 2nd Lieutenant J. Jameson, were shot down near Gavrelle in A7104 by Leutnant Maashoff of Jasta 11, and Letts was slightly wounded. Recovering, he was awarded an MC on 16 August and next day shared in the destruction of an Albatros Scout. In September he claimed three more victories to bring his score to 13. In 1918 he returned to France as a flight commander in 64 Squadron, but was attached to 87 Squadron. On 11 October he took off in an SE 5A of 32 Squadron (C6484) and tried to roll immediately the aircraft had got off the ground; it crashed and he was killed instantly.

	1917		Bristol					
1s*	9 Apr	Alb. DIII	----	48	E Arras	PM	OOC	RFC 9.4
2s*	9 Apr	Alb. DIII	----	48	E Arras	PM	OOC	RFC 9.4
3s**	4 May	C	A3350	48	Pelves	1615	DES	CR/RFC 4.5
4s***	11 May	Alb. DIII	A7104	84	Biache-Dury	1245	OOC	CR/RFC 11.5
5†	12 May	Alb. DIII	A7106	48	Beaumont	0830	OOC	CR/RFC 12.5
6††	12 May	Alb. DIII	A7106	48	Izel	1430	OOC	CR/RFC 12.5
7††	24 May	C	A3350	48	Vitry	1540	OOC	CR/RFC 24.5
8s†††	26 May	Alb. DIII	A7106	48	Cantin Palleul	1945	OOC	CR/RFC 26.5
9†	5 Jun	C	A7106	48	Riencourt-Cagnicourt	0725	OOC	CR/RFC 5.6
10s‡	17 Aug	Alb. DV	A7219	48	E Nieuport	1100	DES	CR/RFC 17.8
11‡‡	4 Sep	Alb. DV	A7219	48	Ghistelles	1900	DES	CR/RFC 4.9
12‡‡	4 Sep	Alb. DV	A7219	48	Ghistelles	1900	DES	CR/RFC 4.9
13‡‡	15 Sep	C	B1117	48	N E Dixmude	1915	DES	CR/RFC 15.9

TOTAL: 3 and 2 shared destroyed, 4 and 4 shared out of control = 13.

*Observer: Lt H.G. Collins; shared with Capt A.M. Wilkenson/2/Lt L.W. Allen. **Observer: 2/Lt L. Speller; shared with 2/Lt H. Smither/2 AM V. Reed A3347. ***Observer: 2/Lt J. Jameson; shared with 2/Lt H. Smither/2 AM Rutherford A3350. †Observer: 2/Lt J. Jameson. ††Observer: Lt L.G. Allen. †††Observer: Lt C.A. Malcomson; shared with 2/Lt H. Smither/2/Lt J. Jameson A7109. ‡Observer: Lt J. Jameson; shared with 2/Lt A.C. Simpson/2/Lt L.H. Tanner A7150. ‡‡Observer: 2/Lt J. Frost.

LEWIS Cecil Arthur Captain 3, 56, 44, 61, 152

Born on 29 March 1898, Cecil Lewis joined the RFC in 1915. The following year he was at the aircraft depot at St Omer prior to a posting to 3 Squadron. He then served with the latter unit from May until September, flying Morane Parasols throughout the Battle of the Somme, for which he received an MC. After a period in England, he was posted to 56 Squadron and returned to France with this unit in April 1917. Again in England, he flew with 44 and 61 (Home Defence) Squadrons until late 1918, when he once more went back to France with 152 Night-fighter Squadron, but the war ended before this unit got into action. He wrote a famous book on his experiences called *Sagittarious Rising* which ended with his time with the Chinese Air Force in the early 1920s. He was one of the four founder members of BBC Radio; after service in the RAF during World War II, he flew to South Africa in a light aircraft, and continued to write. His latest book *Pathfinder*, was published in 1986. In 1987, to celebrate the 70th anniversary of 56 Squadron's formation, Lewis, the last survivor of the original pilots, wrote an article about his old unit.

	1917		SE 5					
1	5 May	Alb. DIII	A4853	56	Montigny	1845-1945	OOC	CR/RFC 5.5
2	7 May	C	A4853	56	S Lens	0930	OOC	CR/RFC 7.5
3s*	7 May	Alb. DIII	A4853	56	N Cambrai	1830-1900	OOC	CR/RFC 7.5
4s**	11 May	Alb. DIII	A4853	56	Pont a Vendin	0600-0810	OOC	CR/RFC 11.5
5	23 May	Alb. C	A4853	56	Beaumont	1555-1810	OOC	CR/RFC 23.5

6	27 May	Alb. DIII	A4853	56	E Bugnicourt	1900-2000	OOC	CR/RFC 27.5
7	7 Jun	Alb. DIII	A4853	56	Wervicq	1200-1230	OOC	CR/?/Revell
8	17 Jun	Alb. DIII	A4853	56	Haubourdin	0845-0930	OOC	CR/RFC 17.6

TOTAL: 6 and 2 shared out of control = 8.
*Shared with Capt H. Meintjes A8900, 2/Lt R.T.C. Hoidge A4862, 2/Lt W.B. Melville A4852. **Shared with Lt G.C Maxwell A8902.

LEWIS Gwilym Hugh Captain 32, 40

Born at Moseley, Birmingham, on 5 August 1897, he was educated at Marlborough and Kings College. Commissioned in the 2/4th Northampton Regiment in September 1915, he then transferred to the RFC, having been taught to fly privately at Hendon. In 1916 he was an original member of 32 Squadron flying DH 2s, and claimed at least two victories before returning to England. Promoted to Captain, he returned to France in late 1917 as a flight commander with 40 Squadron. Here he brought his score to 12 and was awarded the DFC, before being posted home on 20 July 1918. After the war he became the Recorder of Chesterfield, and later a successful businessman. His autobiography, *Wings of the Somme*, was published in 1976, and at the time of writing he was still an active member of Cross & Cockade, Great Britain.

	1916		DH 2					
1s*	15 Jul	Fokker E	7859	32	E La Bassee	0500	DES	CR/RFC 15.7
2	22 Sep	Roland CII	7888	32	Bancourt	1115	DES	ORB/19 Sqn
	1917		SE 5A					
3	19 Dec	Alb. DIII	B24	40	Lens-Pont a Vendin	1300	OOC	CR/RFC 19.12
	1918							
4	19 Jan	Alb. DV	C9534	40	Henin-Lietard	1115	OOC	CR/I BG WD
5s**	16 Feb	Pfalz DIII	C9534	40	Lille	1005	OOC	CR/RFC 16.2
6	11 Apr	Fokker DrI	D3540	40	E Lens	1655	DES	CR/RAF 11.4
7	12 Apr	Pfalz DIII	D3540	40	Croix Barbee	1730	OOC	CR/SR/?
8s***	20 May	Pfalz DIII	----	40	Merville	2000	OOC	CR/SR/?
9	21 May	Pfalz DIII	D3540	40	Douai	0840	DES	CR/RAF 21.5
10†	27 May	Pfalz DIII	D3540	40	E Hulloch	2025	DES(F)	CR/RAF 27.5
11	2 Jul	Fokker DVII	D3511	40	N E Lens	1220	OOC	CR/?
12s††	7 Jul	LVG. C	D3511	40	Lens	0925	CAPT	CR/RAF 8.7

TOTAL: 1 shared captured, 3 and 1 shared destroyed, 5 and 2 shared out of control = 12.
*Shared with 2/Lt K. Mathewson/1 AM J. Booth in FE 2 4272 of 25 Sqn. **Shared with Lt C.W. Usher. ***Shared with Major R.S. Dallas, Lt I.F. Hind, Lt H.H. Wood, Lt C.O. Rusden, Lt D.S. Poler. †40 made three claims; Vzfw Scheibler of Jasta 30 was wounded. ††Shared with Lt I.F. Hind C5358; This was Gefr Weber/? of FA 13.

LIBBY Frederick Captain 23, 11, 43, 25

An American cowboy from Sterling, Colorado, Libby was born on 15 July 1891. When war broke out in Europe, he travelled to Canada in search of adventure, joining the army there and arriving in France in 1915. After some months in the trenches he transferred to the RFC, and was posted to 23 Squadron as an observer on FE 2Bs. On his first operational flight with Lieutenant Hicks piloting the aircraft, he shot down an enemy aircraft in flames. By August he had been posted to 11 Squadron, where he flew with Captain Stephen Price. On 25 August 1916 he claimed his fifth victory, the first American to reach this total. For this he was awarded an MC, gazetted on 14 November. By this time he had around ten victories as a gunner, but then undertook pilot training and on 7 March 1917 joined 43 Squadron to fly Sopwith 1½ Strutters. He claimed two further victories with this unit before being posted to 25 Squadron on DH 4 bombers, where he claimed a further two victories to raise his total to 14. On 15 September he transferred to the USAS following the entry of the United States into the war, and with his national force did not see any further active service. He died in Los Angeles on 9 January 1970.

	1916		FE 2					
1s*	15 Jul	AGO. C	----	23	Bapaume	1530	DES(F)	CR/RFC 15.7
2s**	22 Aug	Roland CII	6994	11	S Bapaume	1910	OOC	CR/RFC 22.8
3s**	22 Aug	Roland CII	6994	11	S Bapaume	1910	OOC	CR/RFC 22.8
4***	22 Aug	Roland CII	6994	11	S Bapaume	1910	OOC	CR/RFC 22.8
5***	25 Aug	Aviatik C	6994	11	Bapaume	1300	OOC	CR/RFC 25.8
6***	14 Sep	C	6994	11	S E Bapaume	0930	OOC	CR/RFC 14.9
7†	22 Sep	D	----	11	Logeast	----	OOC	RFC WD
8††	10 Oct	D	7678	11	Bapaume	1600	OOC	CR/RFC 10.10
9***	17 Oct	Alb. DI	7027	11	Mory	1115	OOC	CR/RFC 17.10
10s†††	20 Oct	Alb. DI	7027	11	Douxcette-Ayette	1130	OOC	CR/RFC 20.10
	1917		Strutter					
11‡	6 May	C	A1010	43	S Avion	1630	DES	CR/RFC 6.5

12‡‡	23 Jul	Alb. DIII	A8785 DH4	43	N E Lens	1745	OOC	CR/RFC 23.7
13‡‡‡	8 Aug	Alb. DV	A7543	25	Henin-Lietard	2130	OOC	CR/RFC 9.8
14‡‡‡	14 Aug	C	A7543	25	Lens	0520	OOC	CR/RFC 14.8

TOTAL: 1 and 1 shared destroyed, 8 and 4 shared out of control = 14.
*Pilot: Lt E.D. Hicks; shared with Lt Tyler/2/Lt J.A. Turnbull. **Pilot: Capt S.W. Price; shared with 2/Lt L.B.F. Morris/Lt L. Rees 6983. ***Pilot: Capt S.W. Price. †Pilot: Sgt Thompson. ††Pilot: 2/Lt R.P. Harvey. †††Pilot: Capt S.W. Price; shared with Lt Dowling/Lt A.L. Harrow-Bunn. ‡Observer: Lt J.L. Dickson. ‡‡Observer 2/Lt E.W. Pritchard. ‡‡‡Observer: 2/Lt D.M. Hills.

LIGHTBODY John Douglas Lieutenant 204

Born on 30 October 1899 in Hamilton, Scotland, Lightbody flew with 204 Squadron from 16 September 1918, claiming five victories during October. On 23rd three Fokker DVIIs attacked him and forced him down to 100 feet above the ground. At this level he put his Camel into a steep and sharp turn at which point two of his attackers collided and fell to pieces. He was reported missing on 4 November 1918 in F6257 near Melle, shot down by another DVII.

	1918		Camel					
1	9 Oct	Fokker DVII	F3109	204	Courtrai	1120	OOC	CR/5 GP Comm
2*	23 Oct	Fokker DVII	F3109	204	Termonde	1105	DES	CR/RAF 23.10
3*	23 Oct	Fokker DVII	F3109	204	Termonde	1105	DES	CR/RAF 23.10
4	27 Oct	Fokker DVII	F3109	204	Ghent	0910	OOC	CR/SR/?
5	30 Oct	Fokker DVII	F3109	204	Nazereth	1315	OOC	CR/SR/?

TOTAL: 3 destroyed, 2 out of control = 5.
*These two Fokkers collided whilst shooting up Lightbody!

LINDUP Ernest Lieutenant 20

Lindup served in 20 Squadron during the first half of 1918, claiming five victories in company with his various observers in the Bristol Fighter. He received an MC.

	1918		Bristol					
1*	4 Feb	Alb. DV	----	20	Menin-Roulers Rd.	c1415	OOC	SR/RFC 4.2
2**	17 Feb	Pfalz DIII	C4641	20	Westroosebeke	1130	DES(F)	CR/RFC 17.2
3***	13 Mar	Pfalz DIII	B1191	20	Houthem	1220	OOC	CR/RFC 13.3
4†	28 Mar	Fokker DrI	B1191	20	Albert	0830	OOC	CR/RFC 28.3
5††	31 May	Pfalz DIII	C850	20	S Armentieres	1850	DES	CR/RAF 31.5

TOTAL: 2 destroyed, 3 out of control = 5.
*Observer: 2/Lt N.S. Dougall. **Observer: Cpl M. Mather. ***Observer: Cpl F. Archer. †Observer: 2/Lt H.G. Crowe. ††Observer: Sgt E.A. Deighton.

LINGHAM George Alexander Lieutenant 43

Born in Melbourne, Australia on 30 November 1898, 'Flossy' Lingham joined the RFC in 1916. He was posted to 43 Squadron late in 1917 and served with the unit throughout 1918, receiving a DFC. After the war he went into civil aviation, and during the 1930s was a Director of the Heston Aircraft Company.

	1918		Camel					
1	9 Mar	DFW. C	B5631	43	N E Pont a Vendin	1015	OOC	CR/RFC 9.3
2	13 Mar	Alb. DV	B5631	43	La Bassee	1300	DES	CR/RFC 13.3
3	6 Apr	Fokker DrI	D1785	43	Abancourt	1435	DES	CR/RAF 6.4
4	12 Apr	Alb. DV	D1785	43	N E La Gorgue	1700	OOC	CR/RAF 12.4
5	3 May	Pfalz DIII	D1785	43	Vieux Berquin	1135	OOC	CR/RAF 3.5
6	10 Jun	Alb. DV	D1785	43	Cuvilly, W Ressons	1925	OOC	CR/ORB/?

TOTAL: 2 destroyed, 4 out of control = 6.

LITTLE Robert Alexander Captain 1W, 8(N), 203

Born on 19 July 1895 in Melbourne, Australia, Bob Little joined the RNAS in 1915 and was trained as a pilot at Hendon, qualifying on 27 October of that year, following which he was commissioned. Late in January 1916 he was posted to Eastchurch to begin operational flying, and at the end of June he arrived in France, being based at Dunkirk, where he flew a Bristol Scout. He then took part in several bombing raids, flying Sopwith 1½ Strutters, but on 26 October 1916, 8 Naval Squadron arrived in France and he was posted to this unit to fly Sopwith Pups. The unit went into action on the Western Front on 9 November, and Little had claimed four victories by the following March, for which he received a DSC. The unit then converted to Sopwith Triplanes, and in April rejoined the RFC at the front, where on 7th April Little became involved in a lone fight with Albatros Scouts, escaping unscathed. On 30 April he and three other pilots dived on 12 Albatros DIIs which were attacking two RE 8s, and claimed five of them shot down, Little personally accounting for two to bring his own score to 12. He claimed his last victory with the Triplane on 10 July, and then flew Camels briefly for the rest of the month, but was then rested with his total at 38, 24 of these whilst flying Triplanes.

He received a DSO, and Bar to his DSC in August, and a Bar to the DSO in September , but did not see any further combat until March 1918, by which time he had joined Collishaw's unit, 3 (N) Squadron, as a flight commander, to fly Camels again. On 1 April he shot down a Fokker Triplane and over the next two months claimed at least eight more victories, culminating with two two-seaters on 22 May. Five days later he took off at night to try and intercept a Gotha bomber, and was on its tail when it was caught in a searchlight beam. A bullet, either from one of the defending gunners in the bomber, or from the ground, hit him and passed through both thighs, causing him to crash-land near Noeux, where he bled to death. Little's score is at least 47 destroyed and out of control, plus many forced to land or driven down, making him the most successful Australian fighter pilot of the war. He had married in September 1916, and left a son.

	1916		Pup					
1	23 Nov	C	N5182	8N	1m N E La Bassee	0950	DES(F)	CR/RFC 23.11
2	4 Dec	Halb. DII	N5182	8N	N E Bapaume	1130	OOC	CR/RFC 4.12
3	20 Dec	C	N5182	8N	Fontaine	1115	OOC	CR/ORB/DL/SR
	1917							
4	7 Jan	Alb. DII	N5194	8N	Grevillers	1100	OOC	CR/RFC 7.1
			Triplane					
5	7 Apr	Alb. DIII	N5469	8N	S E Lens	1930	DES	CR/RFC 8.4
6	9 Apr	Halb. DII	N5469	8N	Noyelles-Lens	1200	OOC	CR/RFC 9.4
7	21 Apr	Alb. DIII	N5469	8N	N E Oppy	1855	DES	CR/RFC 21.4
8s*	24 Apr	Aviatik C	N5469	8N	Auchel	1230	CAPT	CR/RFC 24.4
9	28 Apr	C	N5493	8N	Oppy	1225	DES	CR/RFC 29.4
10s**	29 Apr	Alb. DIII	N5493	8N	Douai	1915	DES	CR/RFC 29.4
11	30 Apr	Alb. DIII	N5493	8N	E Arras	0710	OOC	CR/RFC 30.4
12	30 Apr	Alb. DIII	N5493	8N	E Arras	0725	OOC	CR/RFC 30.4
13	2 May	Alb. DIII	N5493	8N	Vitry	1930	OOC	CR/RFC 3.5
14	9 May	LVG. C	N5493	8N	S E Lens	1010	OOC	CR/RFC 9.5
15	9 May	Alb. DIII	N5493	8N	S E Lens	1015	OOC	CR/RFC 9.5
16	10 May	Alb. DIII	N5493	8N	Lens	----	OOC	SR/RFC 10.5
17	18 May	DFW. C	N5493	8N	N E Lens	1100	DES	CR/RFC 18.5
18	18 May	Alb. DIII	N5493	8N	N E Lens	1115	DES	CR/RFC 18.5
19s***	23 May	Alb. DIII	N5493	8N	W Douai	1545	OOC	CR/RFC 23.5
20	25 May	Alb. DIII	N5493	8N	Quiery la Motte	0810	OOC	CR/RFC 25.5
21s†	16 Jun	C	N5493	8N	Wingles	0930	DES	CR/RFC 16.6
22	21 Jun	Alb. DV	N5493	8N	E Henin-Lietard	1025	DES	CR/RFC 21.6
23††	26 Jun	C	N5493	8N	1m E Acheville	1835	DES(F)	CR/RFC 26.6
24s†††	29 Jun	Alb. DV	N5493	8N	E Lens	0655	OOC	CR/RFC 29.6
25	3 Jul	Alb. DV	N5493	8N	Lens	1100	OOC	CR/RFC 3.7
26	3 Jul	Alb. DV	B5493	8N	Lens-La Bassee	1130	OOC	CR/RFC 3.7
27	6 Jul	C	N5493	8N	N Izel	1115	DES	CR/RFC 6.7
28	10 Jul	Alb. DV	N5493	8N	Fampoux	1445	OOC	CR/RFC 10.7
			Camel					
29	12 Jul	Alb. DV	N6378	8N	Vitry-Drocourt-Queant	1300	OOC	CR/RFC 12.7
30s‡	13 Jul	C	N6378	8N	Lens	1015	OOC	CR/RFC 13.7
31	13 Jul	Alb. DV	N6378	8N	Croiselles	1130	CAPT	CR/RFC 13.7
32	15 Jul	Alb. DV	N6378	8N	Lens	2045	OOC	CR/RFC 15.7
33	16 Jul	C	N6378	8N	Gavrelle	0830	OOC	CR/RFC 16.7
34s‡‡	20 Jul	DFW. CV	N6378	8N	Lens	1840	DES	CR/RFC 21.7
35	21 Jul	Alb. DV	N6378	8N	E Oppy	1930	OOC	CR/RFC 21.7
36	22 Jul	C	N6378	8N	Rouvroy	0620	OOC	CR/RFC 22.7
37	22 Jul	Alb. DV	N6378	8N	Lens	1945	OOC	CR/ORB/?
38s‡‡‡	27 Jul	C	B3877	8N	Loos	1600	DES	CR/RFC 27.7
	1918							
39	1 Apr	Fokker DrI	B7198	203	3m E Oppy	1400	DES	CR/RAF 1.4
40§	6 Apr	DFW. CV	B7231	203	N E Lens	1230	DES(F)	CR/RAF 6.4
41	7 Apr	Fokker DrI	B7231	203	1m S E Violanes	1300	DES	CR/RAF 7.4
42s§§	9 Apr	Alb. C	B7231	203	Givenchy	1610	DES(F)	CR/RAF 9.4
43	11 Apr	Alb. DV	B7231	203	Bac St Maur	1430	DES	CR/RAF 11.4
44§§§	21 Apr	Pfalz DIII	B6319	203	W Bailleul	1500	OOC	CR/RAF 21.4

45s#	18 May	Pfalz DIII	B7220	203	Neuf Berquin	0750	OOC	CR/RAF 18.5
46	22 May	Alb. C	D3416	203	Mory-St Leger	1140	DES	CR/RAF 22.5
47	22 May	DFW. C	D3416	203	Morchies	1145	DES	CR/RAF 22.5

TOTAL: 1 and 1 shared captured, 17 and 5 shared destroyed, 21 and 2 shared out of control = 47.
*Shared with Lt I.P.R. Napier in Nieuport A6778 of 40 Sqn: Lt Huppertz/Lt Neumuller of FA 18 were taken prisoner. **Shared with FSL R.P. Minifie N5446, a Triplane of Naval 1. ***Shared with F/Cdr C.D. Booker N5482. †Shared with FSL P.A. Johnston N6295. ††Possibly Gefr E. Bittorf/Lt P. Schweizer, who were killed near here. †††Shared with FSL R.R. Soar N6292. ‡Shared with FSL R.R. Soar N6376. ‡‡Shared with FSL J.H. Thompson, FSL R. Macdonald N6375, FSL W.M. Davidson N6376. ‡‡‡Shared with FSL R. Macdonald N6375; probably Uffz H. Jourgens/Lt A. Kochler, who were killed near here. §Probably Flgr K. Ankele/Lt Born of FAA 268, who were killed. §§Shared with Lt A.B. Ellwood B7229, Lt J.A. Glen B7185. §§§This was Uffz Kauffmann of Jasta 47, who was wounded; straight afterwards Little was shot down by Vzfw Ehmann, also of Jasta 47, and crashed in Allied lines. #Shared with Lt E.T. Hayne D3376.

LITTLE Robert Hazen Lieutenant 20, 48

A Canadian, Little served with 20 Squadron late in 1917, transferring to 48 Squadron on 31 January 1918. Here he remained until 8 August, flying Bristol Fighters; he and his observers claimed five victories.

	1918		Bristol					
1*	6 Mar	Pfalz DIII	B1265	48	La Fere-Hanegicourt	0950	DES	CR/SR/?
2**	25 Apr	Rumpler C	C814	48	1m E Harbonnieres	1705	DES	CR/RAF 25.4
3***	10 May	Fokker DrI	C841	48	Suzanne	1540	DES(F)	CR/RAF 10.5
4***	10 May	Fokker DrI	C841	48	Maricourt	1555	OOC	CR/RAF 10.5
5†	27 Jun	Fokker DVII	C841	48	E Lamotte	1800	OOC	CR/SR/?

TOTAL: 3 destroyed, 2 out of control = 5.
*Observer: Lt L.N. Jones. **Observer: Cpl W. Beales. ***Observer: Lt H.F. Lumb. †Observer: 2/Lt E. Vickers.

LIVERSEDGE Sydney Tyndall Captain 70

Liversedge joined 70 Squadron early in 1918 and remained with the unit throughout the year, becoming a flight commander in September. By this time he had claimed 11 victories to which he added two more before the close of hostilities.

	1918		Camel					
1s*	6 Apr	Alb. C	C8220	70	Bray	1545	OOC	CR/RAF 6.4
2s**	15 May	Pfalz DIII	C8266	70	Achiet le Petit	0730	OOC	CR/RAF 15.5
3	27 May	LVG. C	C1602	70	Ribemont	1155	DES(F)	CR/RAF 27.5
4	27 Jun	Alb. DV	C8268	70	E Albert	2030	OOC	CR/?
5	27 Jun	Pfalz DIII	C8268	70	E Albert	2040	OOC	CR/?
6	1 Jul	Alb. DV	C8237	70	Bray	0920	OOC	CR/?
7	14 Jul	Alb. C	C8268	70	E Bailleul	0700	DES	CR/RAF 14.7
8	29 Jul	Fokker DVII	C8265	70	E Armentieres	1915	OOC	CR/?
9	2 Aug	Alb. C	C8268	70	S Armentieres	0710	DES	CR/RAF 2.8
10	3 Sep	Fokker DVII	E7167	70	S Roulers	0910	DES	CR/RAF 3.9
11	15 Sep	Fokker DVII	E7167	70	Houthoulst	1815	OOC	CR/11 WS/?
12	9 Oct	LVG. C	E7161	70	Inglemunster	0930	DES	CR/RAF 12.10
13s***	9 Oct	Fokker DVII	E7161	70	W Mayerneine	0945	CAPT	CR/RAF 12.10

TOTAL: 1 shared captured, 5 destroyed, 5 and 2 shared out of control = 13.
*Shared with Capt H.N.C. Robinson C8217. **Shared with Lt G.C. Morris C8204. ***Shared with Lt O.A. Heron. Lt E.A. Copp, Lt A. Webster, Lt K.B. Watson.

LLOYD George Lawrence Major 60,40

After service with the Staffordshire Yeomanry, 'Zulu' Lloyd, a South African, transferred to the RFC and joined 60 Squadron in April 1917, flying Nieuport Scouts. He claimed four victories before he was posted as a flight commander to 40 Squadron. Here he claimed four more and was awarded an MC, and later an AFC.

	1917		Nieup					
1	22 Apr	Balloon	A6776	60	N E Boiry Notre Dame	0705	DES	CR/RFC 22.4
2	29 Jun	Alb. DIII	B1606	60	Douai-Estrees	1800	DES	CR/RFC 29.6
3	29 Jun	Alb. DIII	B1606	60	Douai-Estrees	1815	OOC	CR/RFC 29.6
4	7 Jul	Alb. DIII	B1606	60	Wancourt	1145	OOC	CR/C&CB 11.4
5	14 Jul	Alb. DIII	B1645	40	E Douai	0645	OOC	CR/I BG WD
6	12 Aug	Alb. DV	B1693	40	3m E Lens	2010	OOC	CR/RFC 13.8
7	18 Aug	Alb. C	B1645	40	Fromelles	0815	DES	CR/RFC 18.8
8	7 Oct	Alb. DV	B3612	40	La Bassee	0745	DES	CR/RFC 7.10

TOTAL: 4 destroyed, 4 out of control = 8.

LLOYD-EVANS Dudley Captain 64

He served and was commissioned in the South Wales Borderers in the early war years, being awarded an MC. In 1917 he transferred to the RFC, and after completing his training, was posted to 64 Squadron. He claimed eight victories during the summer, being promoted to flight commander and awarded a DFC in September. After the war he remained in the RAF and in 1920 flew DH 9As with 55 Squadron in Mesopotamia. In attacks against hostile tribesmen he flew many operations attacks with this squadron. On 1 November he showed considerable skill when he landed under fire to pick up another DH crew which had been compelled to force-land. For this action he received a Bar to his DFC.

	1918		SE 5A					
1	31 May	Alb. DV	----	64	La Bassee	1940	DES	CR/RAF 31.5
2	25 Jul	Fokker DVII	----	64	W Aubers	0810	DES	CR/RAF 25.7
3	21 Aug	Fokker DVII	D6988	64	N E Douai	1630	DES	CR/RAF 21.8
4	23 Aug	LVG. C	E4002	64	Cantin	----	DES	ORB/C&CB 2.2
5	3 Sep	Fokker DVII	E4100	64	Brebieres	0730	OOC	ORB/C&CB 2.2
6	5 Sep	Fokker DVII	E4100	64	N E Cambrai	1015	OOC	ORB/C&CB 2.2
7	18 Sep	Fokker DVII	E4100	64	E Havrincourt	1730	OOC	CR/ORB 2.2
8	18 Sep	Fokker DVII	E4100	64	E Havrincourt	1730	DES	CR/RAF 18.9

TOTAL: 5 destroyed, 3 out of control = 8.

LONG Selden Herbert Major 29, 24, 46,111

Transferred to the RFC from the Durham Light Infantry, Long was known as 'Tubby' which suited his general appearance. He flew with 29 Squadron during 1916, before becoming 'C' Flight commander in 24 Squadron early in 1917; with both units he flew DH 2s. Awarded the DSO and MC, he claimed ten victories and many driven down. Returning for a spell on Home Establishment as a squadron commander, he managed to obtain an early posting back to France where he joined 46 Squadron as a flight commander on 5 July 1917, thus dropping rank to resume operational flying. Now on Pups, he did not add to his score, but was made acting CO in August. However, before the month was out he was posted to 28 Training Squadron, from where he later went to Palestine to command 111 Squadron. He wrote a book about his experiences which was published in 1920 entitled *In the Blue*.

	1916		DH 2					
1	6 Aug	Fokker E	7915	29	Ypres Salient	1945	OOC	CR/SR/?
2	16 Nov	Roland CII	A305	24	Beaulencourt	1215	CAPT	CR/RFC 16.11
3s**	11 Dec	Alb. DI	A305	24	Bapaume	1000	DES	CR/RFC 11.12
4s***	20 Dec	Alb. DII	A305	24	Velu	1200	DES(F)	CR/IV BG WD
5s†	26 Dec	C	A3059	24	Le Transloy	1230	OOC	CR/IV BG WD
6	27 Dec	Alb. DII	7930	24	Bois de Vaux	1225	OOC	CR/RFC 27.12
	1917							
7††	25 Jan	LVG. C	A305	24	Bapaume-Clery	1005	DES	CR/RFC 25.1
8†††	27 Jan	C	A305	24	Bapaume	1005	DES	CR/RFC 27.1
9‡	6 Mar	C	A305	24	----	----	DES	SR/RFC 6.3

TOTAL: 1 captured, 2 and 3 shared destroyed, 2 and 1 shared out of control = 9.

**Shared with 2/Lt E.C. Pashley 7930. and Capt C.S. Duffus/2/Lt G.O. McEntee in FE 2b 7697 of 22 Sqn. ***Shared with Lt K. Crawford 6008. †Shared with 2/Lt F.B. Sedgwick. ††Probably Lt E. Erdmann/Lt G. Kallenbach, who were killed. Long reported that they jumped out. †††Probably Vzfw K. Lang/Lt M. Brandt, who were killed. ‡Shared with 2/Lt E.C. Pashley.

LONGTON Walter Hunt Captain 85,24

'Scruffy' Longton was a car tester before World War I with the Sunbeam Motor Company, as well as a well-known motorcyclist. Joining the RFC, he qualified as a pilot and became a test pilot in England. For his valuable work he was awarded the AFC in June 1918. He was then posted to France to serve with 85 Squadron, claiming six victories and receiving the DFC. He then joined 24 Squadron as 'B' Flight commander on 27 September. Here he brought his tally to 11 and was one of the very few pilots to receive two Bars to his DFC, awarded for air combat and ground attacks. He remained in the RAF after the war, rising to Squadron Leader in January 1924; later that year he took command of 58 Squadron. In October 1926 he was posted to No 1 FTS at Netheravon, but was killed in a collision in June 1927 when taking part in an air race at Bournemouth.

	1918		SE 5A					
1	7 Jul	Fokker DVII	D6026	85	Doulieu	2015	DES	CR/RAF 8.7
2	10 Jul	Hannover C	D6026	85	36A K 29	0650	DES	CR/RAF 10.7
3	14 Jul	Alb. C	D6927	85	N E Estaires	0855	DES	CR/RAF 14.7
4	24 Jul	Pfalz DIII	C1904	85	S E Kemmel	1045	DES	CR/RAF 24.7
5	9 Aug	Alb. C	D6963	85	Ploegsteert-Bailleul	0740	DES(F)	CR/RAF 9.8

6	22 Aug	Fokker DVII	D6963	85	Haut Allaines	1650	DES	CR/RAF 22.8
7	8 Oct	Balloon	F5508	24	S Busigny	0730	DES	CR/RAF 8.10
8	14 Oct	Fokker DVII	F5508	24	Wassigny	1550	DES	CR/RAF 14.10
9	29 Oct	Fokker DVII	F5508	24	Favril	1430	DES	CR/RAF 29.10
10s*	29 Oct	C	F5508	24	Bois l'Evegne	1500	DES	CR/RAF 29.10
11	30 Oct	Fokker DVII	F5508	24	Marvilles	1220	DES	CR/RAF 30.10

TOTAL: 1 balloon, 9 and 1 shared destroyed = 11.
*Shared with Lt T.M. Harries F5459, 2/Lt H.V. Evans F5791.

LORD Frederick Ivery Captain 79

Born in Wisconsin, USA, on 18 April 1900, Fred Lord served in the 3rd Texas Infantry before being discovered to be under age. He then made his way to Canada and with a 'doctored' birth certificate, joined the RFC. After completing his training in England, he went to France flying Dolphins with 79 Squadron in March 1918, just one month before his 18th birthday. He claimed a total of 12 victories, received the DFC and became a flight commander before being wounded on 17 October. In 1919 he served in Russia as CO of the RAF base at Pinega, flying RE 8s. For operations here he added a Bar to his DFC and received two Russian decorations, before leaving the service and returning to the US in November. During the 1920s he spent a good deal of time 'barnstorming'; started a flying service between Texas and Mexico, and it is believed that he gave instruction to the Mexican Air Force. In 1936 he went to Spain and flew during the Civil War with the Republican Air Force on Breguet 19 two-seaters; later he returned home again after becoming ill. During World War II he is reported to have again used a forged birth certificate to join the RAF, and was reputed to have actually been posted to his old unit — 79 Squadron — which was now flying Hurricanes, before the authorities caught up with him. He was then sent to fly non-operationally with the Air Traffic Authority on trans-Atlantic ferry work.

	1918		Dolphin					
1	28 May	Balloon	C4182	79	Comines	0730	DES	CR/RAF 28.5
2	7 Jun	Alb. DV	C4131	79	La Bassee	0900	DES	CR/RAF 7.6
3	27 Jun	Alb. DV	C4131	79	Neuve Eglise	1930	DES	CR/RAF 27.6
4	27 Jun	Fokker DrI	C4131	79	Neuve Eglise	1945	DES	CR/RAF 27.6
5	27 Jun	Alb. DV	C4131	79	Neuve Eglise	1945	OOC	CR/11 WS
6	21 Aug	C	D3771	79	N W Armentieres	2020	DES	CR/RAF 21.8
7*	3 Sep	Fokker DVII	C4127	79	Armentieres	1150	DES(F)	CR/11 WS
8	5 Sep	Fokker DVII	----	79	E Ploegsteert	1900	OOC	CR/RAF 5.9
9	16 Sep	Fokker DVII	C4127	79	Messines	0945	OOC	CR/11 WS
10	17 Sep	Fokker DVII	C4127	79	Comines	1010	DES	CR/RAF 17.9
11	20 Sep	Hannover C	C4127	79	N Habourdin	0635	DES	CR/RAF 20.9
12	28 Sep	Pfalz DIII	C4127	79	Wereken	1315	DES	CR/RAF 28.9

TOTAL: 1 ballon, 8 destroyed, 3 out of control = 12.
*This pilot baled out, but his parachute burnt, and he was killed.

LOWE Cyril Nelson Captain 11, 24

Born on 7 October 1891 in Lincolnshire, and educated at Cambridge, Lowe served with the Army Service Corps in France from 1914-16, then transferring to the RFC. He served with 11 Squadron from 1916-17, and in 1918 was promoted Captain and posted as a flight commander to 24 Squadron. He was awarded the MC and DFC, claiming nine victories. After the war he commanded 1 and 6 Squadrons in Iraq during 1926-27, and then from 1927 to 1930 was CO 43 Squadron, which took part in the early Hendon Air Pageants. He played rugby for England as a wing three-quarter during this period. From 1930 he was CFI, No 2 FTS, becoming a Wing Commander in 1933 and a Group Captain in 1938. He retired in October 1944, and died in 1985.

	1917		FE 2B					
1*	15 Mar	C	----	11	Bailleul	----	DES	RFC 15.3
2*	24Mar	Alb. DIII	A5442	11	Fontaine les Croisilles	0945	OOC	CR/C&CA 18.4
	1918		SE 5A					
3	23 Apr	Pfalz DIII	D275	24	S Warfusee	1415	OOC	CR/RAF 23.4
4s**	3 May	Fokker DrI	D275	24	Marcelcave	1145	OOC	CR/RAF 3.5
5	9 May	Alb. DV	D275	24	Hangard Wood	1845	OOC	CR/RAF 9.5
6	6 Jun	Fokker DrI	C6452	24	Mezieres	1130	DES	CR/RAF 10.6
7	7 Jun	Fokker DrI	C6452	24	Rosieres	1145	DES(F)	CR/RAF 7.6
8	25 Jun	Fokker DVII	C6452	24	Contalmaison	1110	DES(F)	CR/RAF 25.6
9	1 Jul	LVG. C	E1293	24	Meaulte	0850	OOC	CR/ORB/SR/?

TOTAL: 4 destroyed, 4 and 1 shared out of control = 9.
*Observer: 2/Lt G. Masters. **Shared with Lt R.T. Mark C5367.

LOYD Alwyne Travers Captain 25, 22, 32

Born in Hawkhurst, Kent, of Welsh parents, he was educated at Eton. He joined the 5th Buffs on the outbreak of war, transferring to the RFC and joined 25 Squadron on 22 June 1916, aged 21. He subsequently served in 22 Squadron, and after a rest, joined 32 Squadron in mid 1917, where he claimed his four final victories. He was killed in action east of Ypres on 28 September 1917 when A9211 was shot down, either by Flak or by Oberleutnant Rudolph Berthold of Jasta 18.

	1916		FE 2B					
1s*	7 Sep	Fokker E	6993	25	Pont a Vendin	1750	OOC	CR/RFC 8.9
2**	4 Dec	EA	4855	22	Beaulencourt	1010	OOC	CR/11 W
	1917		DH 5					
3	13 Aug	Alb. DV	A9211	32	N E Polygon Wood	1945	DES	CR/RFC 14.8
4	22 Aug	C	A9211	32	Bellewaarde Lake	0530	OOC	CR/RFC WD
5s***	20 Sep	Alb. DV	A9211	32	S Becelaere	1405	DES	CR/RFC 20.9
6s†	20 Sep	C	A9211	32	Becelaere	1745	OOC	CR/RFC 20.9

TOTAL: 1 and 1 shared destroyed, 2 and 2 shared out of control = 6.
*Observer: 2/Lt C.S. Workman; shared with Capt C.H. Dixon/AM J.H. Booth 6997, 2/Lt N.W. Webb/Cpl H. Brown. **Observer: 2/Lt L.C. Welford. ***Shared with 2/Lt P.E. Woods A9280. †Shared with Lt E.A. Packe A9219.

LUCHFORD Henry George Ernest Lieutenant 20

Harry Luchford came from Bromley, Kent, and before the war worked as a bank clerk. He joined the Norfolk Regiment in 1914, and was later commissioned in the Army Service Corps, going to France in September of that year. He served with the Indian Cavalry Division until January 1916, when he transferred to the RFC after a period in England. He qualified as a pilot on 19 May 1917, and later that month went to France to join 20 Squadron, flying FE 2Bs and Ds. He flew in action with several observers, but particularly with Lieutenant V.R.S. White, who like Luchford, was to receive both the MC and Bar for their joint actions. Subsequently Luchford successfully made the transition to Bristol Fighters in late August 1917, claiming 13 more victories on these before, on 2 December, he was shot down and killed in A7292 by Leutnant Walter von Bulow of Jasta 36 as the German's 28th victory. The Bristol fell near Becelaere where Luchford's gunner on this occasion, Captain J.E. Johnston, survived and became a prisoner.

	1917		FE 2D					
1*	13 Jun	Alb. DIII	A6516	20	Houthem	0845	OOC	CR/RFC 13.6
2**	29 Jun	Alb. DIII	A6516	20	Zonnebeke	1320	DES(F)	CR/RFC 29.6
3*	3 Jul	Alb. DIII	A6547	20	Becelaere	1500	DES	CR/RFC 3.7
4*	6 Jul	Alb. DIII	A6512	20	Comines	1830	OOC	CR/SR 11 WS
5*	6 Jul	Alb. DIII	A6512	20	Comines	1830	OOC	CR/SR/11 WS
6***	17 Jul	Alb. DIII	A6548	20	Polygon Wood	1955	OOC	CR/RFC 17.7
7***	21 Jul	Alb. DIII	A6548	20	Menin	1850	OOC	CR/RFC 22.7
8***	27 Jul	Alb. DIII	A1956	20	N Menin	1945-2040	DES(F)	CR/RFC 27.7
9***	27 Jul	Alb. DIII	A1956	20	N Menin	1945-2040	OOC	CR/RFC 27.7
10*	16 Aug	Alb. C	A6448	20	Menin	1145	OOC	CR/RFC 16.8
11*	17 Aug	Alb. DV	B1897	20	Houthem	1445	DES	CR/RFC 17.8
			Bristol					
12†	9 Sep	Alb. DV	A7215	20	Becelaere	1315	OOC	CR/RFC 9.9
13†	11 Sep	Alb. DV	A7215	20	E Menin	1400	OOC	CR/RFC 11.9
14†	21 Sep	Alb. DV	A7428	20	Becelaere	1700	OOC	CR/RFC 21.9
15†	25 Sep	Alb. DV	B1128	20	E Gheluvelt	1830	DES	CR/RFC 25.9
16†	28 Sep	Alb. DV	B1122	20	Menin	1230	DES(F)	CR/RFC 28.9
17†	28 Sep	Alb. DV	B1122	20	Menin	1230	DES	CR/RFC 28.9
18†	1 Oct	Alb. DV	B1122	20	S E Roulers	1445	DES	CR/RFC 1.10
19††	11 Oct	Alb. DV	B1122	20	Moorslede	0715	DES(F)	CR/RFC 11.10
20†††	11 Oct	Alb. DV	B1122	20	Moorslede	0715	OOC	CR/RFC 11.10
21‡	17 Oct	Alb. DV	B1138	20	Dadizeele	1000	DES	CR/RFC 17.10
22‡	18 Oct	Alb. DV	B1138	20	Houthem-Tenbrielen	0845	DES	CR/RFC 18.10
23‡	18 Oct	DFW. C	B1138	20	W Dadizeele	0900	DES	CR/RFC 18.10
24‡	21 Oct	LVG. C	B1138	20	Menin	1520	DES	CR/RFC 21.10

TOTAL: 13 destroyed, 11 out of control = 24.
*Observer: 2/Lt J. Tennant. **Observer: 2/Lt W.D. Kennard. ***Observer: Lt M.W. Waddington. †Observer: Lt R.F. Hill. ††Observer: Sgt W.J. Benger. †††Observer: Sgt W.J. Benger. ‡Observer: Lt V.R.S. White.

LUFF Frederick Ernest 1st Lieutenant 74, 25US

An American from Cleveland, Ohio, Luff joined the USAS, and after training was attached to the RAF to gain operational experience. In July 1918 he was posted to 74 Squadron to fly SE 5As, and in one month claimed three Fokker DVIIs and two balloons. He received the DFC and was then posted to the 25th Aero Squadron of the USAS, but did not gain any further victories. Injured in a crash in 1919, he never regained full health, and died in Queensland Ohio on 27 April 1931.

	1918		SE 5A					
1	19 Aug	Fokker DVII	----	74	Gheluvelt	1935	DES	CR/RAF 19.8
2	29 Aug	Balloon	D5978	74	Armentieres	0750	DES	CR/RAF 29.8
3	1 Sep	Balloon	E5976	74	Menin	0830	DES	CR/RAF 1.9
4	5 Sep	Fokker DVII	----	74	S Cambrai	1045	DES	CR/RAF 5.9
5	15 Sep	Fokker DVII	----	74	N E Armentieres	1850	DES	CR/RAF 15.9

TOTAL: 2 balloons, 3 destroyed = 5.

LUKE Thomas Carlyon Captain 66, 209

'Sammy' Luke transfered to the RFC from the Royal Engineers early in 1917, and became a pilot in 66 Squadron later that year. He claimed at least four enemy machines shot down and received the MC before being himself shot down and wounded on 28 July. In the summer of 1918 he went as a flight commander to 209 Squadron where he claimed two more victories. Remaining in the RAF after the war, he commanded 18 Squadron in 1934 and was awarded the AFC shortly before his death in 1935.

	1917		Pup					
1	23 May	C	B1703	66	----	1825-2050	OOC	ORB/?
2	28 May	C	B1703	66	----	0600-0830	OOC	ORB/?
3	15 Jun	Alb. DIII	B1724	66	W Houthem	0900	DES	CR/RFC 15.6
4	28 Jul	Alb. DIII	B1724	66	E Roulers	1845-2055	DES(F)	ORB/RFC 28.7
	1918		Camel					
5s*	8 Aug	Halb. C	C142	209	Harbonnieres	1905	DES(F)	CR/RAF 8.8
6	25 Aug	Fokker DVII	D9637	209	Baissy	1430	DES	CR/RAF 25.8

TOTAL: 3 and 1 shared destroyed, 2 out of control = 6.
*Shared with Capt R.M. Foster C61, Lt C.G. Edwards D9588, Lt K.M. Walker C199, Lt M.A. Harker D9625.

LUSSIER Emile John Captain 73

A French-Canadian who was born in the United States in Chicago on 10 October 1895, and later settled there, Lussier flew Sopwith Camels with 73 Squadron from March 1918. He claimed 11 victories with this unit and received the DFC for an action he fought on 25 August, when he claimed three aircraft shot down; this award was gazetted on 2 November 1918. He was promoted to Captain during October of that year. Lussier died on 11 December 1974.

	1918		Camel					
1	25 Jul	Fokker DVII	D9438	73	S Villers	1900	DES	CR/RAF 25.7
2	25 Jul	Fokker DVII	D9438	73	S Villers	1900	OOC	CR/?
3*	30 Jul	LVG. C	----	73	N Vezilly	1400	DES	CR/RAF 30.7
4**	8 Aug	C	B2525	73	Nesle	1720	DES	CR/RAF 8.8
5	19 Aug	Fokker DVII	D9438	73	Combles	0810	OOC	CR/?
6	25 Aug	Fokker DVII	E1551	73	Sapignies	1125	DES	CR/RAF 25.8
7	25 Aug	Fokker DVII	E1551	73	N E Bapaume	1830	OOC	CR/RAF 25.8
8	25 Aug	Fokker DVII	E1551	73	N E Bapaume	1830	OOC	CR/?
9	29 Aug	Fokker DVII	E1551	73	N E Arras	1030	OOC	CR/?
10	15 Sep	Fokker DVII	E1551	73	Aubigny au Bac	1745	DES	CR/RAF 15.9
11	18 Oct	Fokker DVII	E7184	73	N Le Cateau	1500	OOC	CR/?

TOTAL: 3 and 2 shared destroyed, 6 out of control = 11.
*Shared with 2/Lt N. Cooper F6663, Lt A. McConnell-Wood B5568. **Shared with Lt G.L. Graham, 2/Lt R.W. Chandler D1822.

MACANDREW Colin Glen Orr 2nd Lieutenant 11, 57

An ex-member of the Ayrshire Yeomanry Territorial Force, MacAndrew served in 11 Squadron in summer 1917. Flying Bristol Fighters, he claimed his first two victories on 28 June, followed by two more on 9 August. His fifth and final victory was claimed on 18 August, but he was killed on 2 October 1917 in a DH 4 after being posted to 57 Squadron when three of the unit's bombers were shot down by pilots of Jasta 18.

	1917		Bristol					
1*	28 Jun	Alb. DV	A7127	11	Fresnes	1520	OOC	CR/RFC 28.6
2*	28 Jun	Alb. DV	A7127	11	Fresnes	1520	OOC	CR/RFC 28.6

3**	9 Aug	Alb. DV	A7143	11	Quierry la Motte	0900	DES	CR/RFC 9.8
4**	9 Aug	Alb. DV	A7143	11	Quierry la Motte	0900	DES	CR/RFC 9.8
5***	18 Aug	Alb. DV	----	11	S W Douai	c0645	DES	CR/RFC 18.8

TOTAL: 3 destroyed, 2 out of control = 5.
*Observer: 2/Lt A.M. West. **Observer: Lt H.C. McKinney. ***Observer: Pte Long.

MACDONALD Hector Omdurman Lieutenant 84

A South African from Capetown, born on 29 June 1899, Hector Macdonald was commissioned in the RFC on 20 July 1917, and joined 84 Squadron on 3 February 1918. With this unit he was credited with four victories individually plus another three shared. After the war he became a successful sugar planter, but during World War II he joined the SAAF as an armaments officer. Here he was killed in an aircraft accident.

	1918		SE 5A					
1s*	6 Apr	C	C6465	84	N Hangard	1120	CAPT	CR/RAF 6.4
2	17 May	Alb. DV	C6465	84	Hangest	1330	OOC	CR/RAF 17.5
3	19 May	Alb. DV	C9519	84	S E Villers Brettoneaux	1330	OOC	CR/RAF 19.5
4s**	19 May	Alb. DV	C9519	84	S E Villers Brettoneaux	1835	DES	CR/RAF 19.5
5s**	19 May	Alb. DV	C9519	84	S E Villers Brettoneaux	1835	DES	CR/RAF 19.5
6	28 May	Alb. DV	C6455	84	S Villers Brettoneaux	1330	OOC	CR/?
7	30 Oct	Fokker DVII	E6008	84	2m W Leunelle	0930	DES	CR/RAF 30.10

TOTAL: 1 shared captured, 1 and 2 shared destroyed, 3 out of control = 7.
*Shared with Lt J.F. Larson C1772, Lt C.L. Stubbs C9519, Lt H.W.L. Saunders C1794; this was Uffz Drexler/Lt Kalfaken of FAA 205. **Shared with Capt A.W. Beauchamp Proctor C1772, Lt B. Oliver C9519, 2/Lt E.E. Biccard C6442.

MACDONALD Ross Morrison Lieutenant 15, 87

MacDonald enlisted in the 79th Battalion, Cameron Highlanders of Canada (Winnipeg), and was commissioned on 1 September 1916. He arrived in England in October 1916 and was seconded to the RFC the following February. In March he joined 15 Squadron in France as an observer, and during the next few months was frequently mentioned, with his pilot Lieutenant F.M. Carter, for their good work in artillery observation duties. After pilot training during the winter of 1917-18, he was posted to 87 Squadron, flying Sopwith Dolphins, and went back to France with this unit in April. In action with the squadron, he claimed five victories before being shot down on 29 September, to become a prisoner. Repatriated in November 1918, he returned to Canada in December and in July 1919 joined the Queen's Own Cameron Highlanders. He died in August 1960 after a career with the Canadian Railways.

	1918		Dolphin					
1	16 Jul	Rumpler C	C4155	87	E Biefvillers	1215	DES	CR/RAF 16.7
2	20 Jul	Rumpler C	----	87	----	----	OOC	SR/?
3s*	22 Sep	Rumpler C	C4156	87	N E Bapaume	0910	OOC	CR/SR/?
4	23 Sep	Fokker DVII	C4156	87	N E Cambrai	1748	DES	CR/RAF 23.9
5	23 Sep	Fokker DVII	C4156	87	Bourlon Wood	1810	OOC	CR/SR/?

TOTAL: 2 destroyed, 2 and 1 shared out of control = 5.
*Shared with Capt A.W. Vigers C4159.

MACDONALD William Myron Lieutenant 66

A Canadian from Vancouver, born in 1889, he served with the Army Service Corps (MT) for over two years, most of that time being overseas. Commissioned in the RFC in August 1917, he was posted to 66 Squadron in March 1918. Flying in Italy, he claimed eight hostile aircraft destroyed and received the DFC on 20 August.

	1918		Camel					
1	24 May	LVG. C	B7358	66	Stradatta airfield	1905	DES	ORB/SR/14 W
2	31 May	Berg DI	B6424	66	S E Nerversa	0930	DES	ORB/SR/14 W
3	10 Jun	Berg DI	D1913	66	Giaron-Cismon	0610	DES	ORB/SR/14 W
4	10 Jun	Alb. DIII	D1913	66	Seren	0625	DES	ORB/SR/14 W
5	5 Aug	C	E1496	66	Maria	1310	DES	ORB/SR/14 W
6	11 Aug	C	E1499	66	E Cassotto	1945	DES(F)	ORB/SR/14 W
7	15 Aug	Alb. DIII	E1499	66	S Fonzaso	1010	DES(F)	ORB/SR/14 W
8	15 Aug	Alb. DIII	E1499	66	S W Fonzaso	1015	DES	ORB/SR/14 W

TOTAL: 8 destroyed = 8.

MACGREGOR Norman Miers Flight Lieutenant 6(N), 10(N)

Flew with the RNAS in 1917, initially with 6 Naval Squadron, where he claimed four victories flying both Nieuport Scouts and Sopwith Camels. In September he was posted to 10 Naval Squadron and added a further three to his score. His first victory with this unit was over Oberleutnant Kurt Wolff, commander of Jasta 11, (von Richthofen's old unit) who had victories over 33 Allied aircraft to his credit at this time. Although MacGregor initially claimed the Triplane as out of control, Wolff's machine was known to have spun down and exploded on impact with the ground. It was also the first Triplane actually to be lost in combat by the Germans. When MacGregor returned to England at the end of the year, he had flown 325 operational hours; the award of a DSC was gazetted in February 1918. Macgregor was born on 29 May 1896.

	1917		Camel					
1s*	28 Jul	DFW. C	B3833	6N	N5 central	1600	DES	CR/RFC 28.7
2s**	17 Aug	C	B3833	6N	1m E Westende	1815	OOC	CR/ORB/DL
3s***	20 Aug	Alb. DV	B3833	6N	Moere	1050	OOC	CR/ORB/DL
4	22 Aug	Alb. DIII	B3833	6N	N St Pierre Capelle	0945	DES	CR/RFC 22.8
5†	15 Sep	Fokker DrI	B3833	10N	Moorslede	1650	OOC	CR/RFC 15.9
6s††	10 Dec	Alb. DV	B6299	10N	Oostnieuwkerke	1120	DES(F)	CR/RFC 10.12
7	12 Aug	Alb. DV	B6299	10N	E Dixmude	1540	OOC	CR/RFC 12.12

TOTAL: 1 and 2 shared destroyed, 2 and 2 shared out of control = 7.

*Shared with FSL F.C. Winter B3821. **Shared with F/Cdr B.P.H. de Roeper B3882. FSL R.E. Carroll N6351. ***Shared with F/Cdr B.P.H. de Roeper B3882. †This was Oblt Kurt Wolff, a 33 victory ace, and commander of Jasta 11, who was killed. ††Shared with FSL J.G. Clark B5658.

MACKAY George Chisholme Captain 13(N), 213

A Canadian from Toronto, born on 17 May 1898, who served in the RNAS and RAF during 1917-18, MacKay flew initially with the Seaplane Defence Flight, remaining with this unit when it became 13(N) — and subsequently 213 Squadron. Promoted flight commander, he flew over 300 hours on operations, and claimed 18 victories. A two-seater that he attacked on 19 December 1917 went spinning down out of control, throwing out the unfortunate observer. At the end of the war he was posted to 233 Squadron at Dover. His DFC was gazetted in June 1918. He also received the Belgian Order of Leopold and Croix de Guerre.

	1917		Camel					
1s*	4 Dec	C	B6357	13N	Houthoulst Forest-Zarren	1535	DES	CR/RNAS 5.12
2s**	5 Dec	Alb. C	N6335	13N	4m N W Wenduyne	1505	DES	CR/RNAS 6.12
3	19 Dec	Alb. C	B6407	13N	Ostend-Zeebrugge	1445	OOC	CR/RNAS 19.12
	1918							
4s***	29 Jan	Seaplane	B6407	13N	100y off Blankenberghe Pier	1400	DES	CR/RNAS 29.1
5s†	12 Mar	Rumpler C	B6400	13N	Ostend-Wenduyne	0905	DES(F)	CR/RNAS 12.3
6	24 Mar	Pfalz DIII	B7186	13N	2m N Ostend	1100	DES	CR/RNAS 24.3
7††	1 Apr	Seaplane	N6340	213	Zeebrugge	c1430	DES	CR/RNAS 1.4
8s†††	11 May	Alb. DV	D3351	213	4m N Westende	1445	DES	CR/5 GP Comm
9	1 Jun	Rumpler C	D3400	213	Steene	1415	DES	CR/5 GP Comm
10	12 Aug	Fokker DVII	B6401	213	4m S E Ypres	1215	OOC	CR/5 GP Comm
11	13 Aug	Pfalz DIII	D8216	213	Dixmude	1050	OOC	CR/SR/?
12	25 Aug	Fokker DVII	F5913	213	10m S Ostend	0730	OOC	CR/SR/?
13	5 Sep	Fokker DVII	F5913	213	2.5m S Varsenaere	1440	DES	CR/5 GP Comm
14s‡	6 Sep	Rumpler C	F5913	213	1m N Zevecote	1500	DES	CR/5 GP Comm
15	1 Nov	Fokker DVII	F3944	213	7m S Ghent	1415	OOC	CR/5 GP Comm
16s‡‡	1 Nov	C	F3944	213	S Ghent	1430	DES	CR/5 GP Comm
17	9 Nov	Fokker DVII	D9648	213	10m S E Ghent	1515	OOC	CR/5 GP Comm
18s‡‡	10 Nov	LVG. C	D9648	213	7m S E Ghent	1040	DES	CR/5 GP Comm

TOTAL: 4 and 8 shared destroyed, 6 out of control = 18.

*Shared with FSL J.W. Pinder N6335. **Shared with FSL J.W. Pinder B6357, FSL M.L. Cooper B6407, FSL J.dC. Paynter B6391. ***Shared with F/Cdr L.H. Slatter B7186. FSL J.dC. Paynter B3782, FSL J.E. Greene B3909, FSL M.L. Cooper B6410. †Shared with FSL J.E. Greene B6407, FSL M.L. Cooper B6401, FSL E.V. Bell B7226. ††Three seaplanes were claimed by 213. At least two were lost. †††Shared with Lt J.E. Greene D3357. ‡Shared with Lt A.H. Turner D3349. ‡‡Shared with Lt M.N. Hancocks F5913, Lt A.H. Turner F3966. ‡‡‡Shared with Lt A.B. Rosevear D8218, Lt A.F. Chick D9675, Lt H.H. Gilbert F8505.

MACKERETH John Captain 28

After service in the Royal Sussex Regiment, Mackereth transferred to the RFC on 21 June 1917 and served as a Lieutenant with 28 Squadron in Italy in 1918, claiming six victories, including a balloon. On 7 July he encountered an Albatros Scout which he shot down in flames; somewhat embarrassingly this proved to have been flown by Stabsfeldwebel Zeilburger of Flik 30J, who had been dropping messages concerning the fate of two Allied pilots who had been lost earlier. Promoted to Captain, Mackereth was posted to 66 Squadron where he shot down another balloon on 31 August, bringing his score to seven; in gaining this victory his Camel, E1496, was hit and he himself was wounded in the leg. He crash-landed and was taken prisoner.

	1918		Camel					
1	19 May	Balloon	B7351	28	Piave de Soligo	1625	DES	CR/14 W
2	1 Jun	Alb. DV	B7351	28	Susegana-Sarano	0745	DES(F)	CR/14 W
3	15 Jun	Alb. DV	D8111	28	5km W Feltre	0805	DES(F)	CR/14 W
4	30 Jun	Alb. DV	D8209	28	Campolongo	0815	DES	CR/14 W
5*	7 Jul	Alb. DV	D8209	28	Pederiva	1045	DES(F)	CR/14 W
6s**	13 Jul	C	B6349	28	Pordenone	0725	DES	CR/14 W
7	31 Aug	Balloon	E1496	66	Conegliano	0835	DES	ORB/SR/14 W

TOTAL: 2 balloons, 4 and 1 shared destroyed = 7.
*This was Stfwp H. Zeilburger of Flik 30j, who was killed in 153:257. **Shared with Capt J.E. Hallonquist B6363, Lt A.R. Strang D8209.

MACLAREN Donald Roderick Major 46

MacLaren, a Scots-Canadian, was born in Ottawa on 28 May 1893, and moved with his family to Calgary six years later. He became an expert marksman early in life, and managed to gain a place at university. Unfortunately ill health forced him to leave early in 1914, and he then worked with his family in a fur-trading post. On 8 May 1917 he joined the RFC, and after training became an instructor at Camp Borden, Ontario. In autumn 1917 he was posted to England, and arrived in France on 23 November to join 46 Squadron on the Western Front. On 21 March 1918 he bombed a German long-range gun, then claiming two LVG two-seaters and a kite balloon shot down; the following month he was promoted to flight commander on 6th. He was awarded an MC in April, and a Bar to this the following month; a DFC followed in August, in which month he was on leave for three weeks. On 9 October he shared in shooting down a Hannoveraner to bring his score to 54, which included six balloons and a high proportion of shared victories. Next day he broke his leg whilst wrestling with a friend — a very similar occurrence to that which had befallen Philip Fullard a year earlier, soon after his score had topped 40; on 6 November 1918 MacLaren was sent back to England. A DSO was gazetted on 8 February 1919, and the French awarded him a Croix de Guerre and made him a Companion of the Legion D'Honneur. By the end of the war he had been promoted to the rank of Major, and after the close of hostilities he assisted in the formation of the Canadian Air Force until the late twenties, when he resigned his commission to go into commercial aviation. He died in July 1989.

	1918		Camel					
1	6 Mar	Hannover C	B9153	46	E Douai	1345	OOC	CR/RFC 6.3
2	10 Mar	Alb. DV	B9153	46	W Graincourt	0730	DES	CR/RFC 10.3
3	21 Mar	Balloon	B9153	46	Biache St Vaast	1615	DES	CR/RFC 21.3
4	21 Mar	LVG. C	B9153	46	W Douai	1630	DES	CR/RFC 21.3
5	21 Mar	LVG. C	B9153	46	E Marquion	1645	DES	CR/RFC 21.3
6	22 Mar	C	B9153	46	Bullecourt	1400	OOC	CR/RFC 22.3
7s*	22 Mar	C	B9153	46	Bullecourt	1500	OOC	CR/RFC 22.3
8	23 Mar	Alb. C	B9153	46	N Croisilles	0900	OOC	CR/RFC 23.3
9s**	23 Mar	Alb. C	B9153	46	N Croisilles	0900	OOC	CR/RFC 23.3
10	23 Mar	C	B9153	46	Bullecourt	1300	DES	CR/RFC 23.3
11	24 Mar	Balloon	----	46	----	----	DES	OH/?
12	25 Mar	C	B9153	46	----	1715	DES	CR/RFC 25.3
13	27 Mar	Junkers JI	B9153	46	57 D Q 12	1530	OOC	CR/RFC 27.3
14s***	2 Apr	C	B9153	46	Courcelles	1245	DES	CR/RAF 2.4
15s†	2 Apr	Balloon	B9153	46	----	1315	DES	CR/RAF 2.4
16	21 Apr	Alb. DV	B9153	46	Acheville	1100	OOC	CR/RAF 21.4
17	3 May	LVG. C	B9153	46	S Bailleul	1230	DES	CR/RAF 3.5
18s††	3 May	Halb. C	B9153	46	N W Don	1300	DES	CR/RAF 3.5
19s●	4 May	Alb. DV	B9153	46	N Bullecourt	1800	OOC	CR/RAF 4.5
20s†††	6 May	DFW. C	----	46	St Venant	1800	CAPT	CR/RAF 6.5
21	8 May	Alb. DV	D6418	46	N Laventie	1900	OOC	CR/RAF 8.5
22	9 May	Pfalz DIII	D6418	46	Neuf Berquin	1915	OOC	CR/RAF 9.5
23	15 May	Pfalz DIII	D6418	46	Armentieres	1245	OOC	CR/RAF 15.5
24	15 May	Pfalz DIII	D6418	46	Armentieres	1245	OOC	CR/RAF 15.5
25s‡	20 May	DFW. C	D6418	46	N La Bassee	1700	DES	CR/RAF 20.5
26	20 May	Balloon	D6418	46	S Steenwerck	1705	DES	CR/RAF 20.5
27	20 May	Balloon	D6418	46	S Steenwerck	1705	DES	CR/RAF 20.5

28‡‡	23 May	Pfalz DIII	D6418	46	S Armentieres	0745	OOC	CR/?
29	26 May	C	D6418	46	Laventie	1745	DES	CR/?
30	28 May	Alb. DV	D6418	46	N Laventie	0650	OOC	CR/?
31	30 May	Pfalz DIII	D6418	46	Estaires	1930	OOC	CR/RAF 30.5
32	31 May	Pfalz DIII	D6418	46	N Estaires	2030	OOC	CR/I BG WD
33	2 Jun	Alb. DV	D6418	46	E Laventie	1730	OOC	CR/?
34	7 Jun	Pfalz DIII	D6418	46	S Armentieres	1115	DES	CR/RAF 7.6
35	1 Jul	C	D6418	46	E Neuve Chapelle	0945	DES	CR/RAF 1.7
36s‡‡‡	8 Jul	Fokker DVII	D6418	46	Fromelles	0530	OOC	CR/?
37	8 Jul	Fokker DVII	D6418	46	S E Merville	2030	OOC	CR/?
38	15 Jul	DFW. C	D6603	46	W Neuve Chapelle	1445	DES	CR/RAF 15.7
39	19 Jul	Balloon	D6603	46	S Estaires	1520	DES	CR/RAF 19.7
40	22 Jul	Alb. DV	D6603	46	Bailleul	1930	DES	CR/RAF 22.7
41	22 Jul	Alb. DV	D6603	46	Bailleul	1930	DES	CR/RAF 22.7
42s§	1 Aug	C	D6603	46	Armentieres	1200	DES	CR/RAF 1.8
43	24 Aug	DFW. C	D6603	46	E Bray	1930	OOC	CR/V BG WD
44s§§	25 Aug	DFW. C	D6603	46	E Delville Wood	1845	DES	CR/RAF 25.8
45	26 Aug	Fokker DVII	D6603	46	Hendecourt	0700	DES	CR/RAF 26.8
46	15 Sep	Fokker DVII	F2137	46	N Gouzeaucourt	1415	OOC	CR/V BG WD
47s§§§	16 Sep	Fokker DVII	F2137	46	Cambrai	1815	DES(F)	CR/RAF 16.9
48	16 Sep	Fokker DVII	F2137	46	Cambrai	1815	OOC	CR/V BG WD
49s#	17 Sep	Fokker DVII	F2137	46	Cambrai	1200	OOC	CR/V BG WD
50s##	17 Sep	Fokker DVII	F2137	46	Cambrai	1200	OOC	CR/V BG WD
51	26 Sep	Fokker DVII	F2137	46	Havrincourt	1815	DES	CR/RAF 26.9
52s###	29 Sep	Fokker DVII	F2137	46	near Le Cateau	1640	OOC	CR/V BG WD
53s¶	2 Oct	Fokker DVII	F2137	46	Morcourt	1030	OOC	CR/V BG WD
54	9 Oct	C	F2137	46	W Ricqueval Wood	1430	DES	CR/RAF 9.10

TOTAL: 1 shared captured, 5 and 1 shared balloons, 15 and 6 shared destroyed, 18 and 8 shared out of control = 54.
*Shared with Capt C.J. Marchant C1554. **Shared with 2/Lt H.P. Blakely B5435, 2/Lt J.H. Smith C1685. ***Shared with Capt S.P. Smith, Lt A.G. Vlasto, Lt H.G.W. Debenham, 2/Lt R.K. McConnell. †Shared with 2/Lt J.H. Smith C1617. ††Shared with 2/Lt V.M. Yeates C1637. •Shared with Lt R.K. McConnell C1637, Lt H.L.M. Dodson C1643. †††Shared with Capt C.H. Marchant, 2/Lt J.H. Smith, 2/Lt V.M. Yeates, 2/Lt H.T.W. Manwaring. This was Lt Junemann/Lt Barth of FA 14. ‡Shared with Lt C.R. Chapman B9253. ‡‡Probably Lt Hans Oberlander, of Jasta 30, who was wounded. ‡‡‡Shared with Lt R.K. McConnell. §Shared with Major A.H. O'Hara Wood F5950, Lt R.K. McConnell D6693, 2/Lt L.S. Skerrington. §§Shared with Lt P.F. Paton D1942. §§§Shared with Lt R. Viall F1971, Lt C.H. Sawyer D6693. #Shared with 2/Lt R.D. Gilpin Brown F5950, Lt P.M. Tudhope F1966, Lt C.H. Sawyer D6693, Capt C.W. Odell D1942, 2/Lt L.S. Skerrington F6330. ##Shared with 2/Lt R.D. Gilpin Brown F5950, Lt P.M. Tudhope F1966, Lt C.H. Sawyer D6693, Capt C.W. Odell D1942, 2/Lt L.S. Skerrington F6330. ###Shared with Lt C.H. Sawyer D9457. ¶Shared with Capt J.L. Leith H7279, Lt C.H. Sawyer F1974.

MACLANACHAN William Lieutenant 40

After two uneventful years in the army, he transferred to the RFC and after his final training at Gosport, was sent to France to join 40 Squadron. Here he became a close friend of 'Mick' Mannock, with whom he often flew. He was credited with at least seven victories, but strangely received no decoration for his work, although a competent patrol leader. He finally returned to England in January 1918. After the war he wrote several articles on his flying days and a book entitled *Fighter Pilot*, all under the name 'McScotch'. For many years he was aviation correspondent for *The Times*, and died in the early 1960s.

	1917		Nieuport					
1	12 Jul	C	B1693	40	Brebieres	1215	OOC	CR/RAF 12.7
2	16 Aug	DFW. C	B1693	40	Sallaumines	0815	OOC	CR/RFC 16.8
3	20 Aug	DFW. C	B1693	40	E La Bassee	0930	OOC	CR/RFC 20.8
4	22 Aug	Alb. DV	B1693	40	Douai-Henin-Lietard	1010	OOC	CR/RFC 22.8
5	15 Sep	Alb. DV	B3608	40	S E Vimy	1405	OOC	CR/RFC 15.9
6	23 Sep	Alb. DV	B3608	40	S W Henin-Lietard	1530	DES	CR/RFC 23.9
			SE 5A					
7s*	12 Nov	Alb. DIII	A8913	40	Annay	1220	OOC	CR/RFC 12.11

TOTAL: 1 destroyed, 5 and 1 shared out of control = 7.
*Shared with 2/Lt C.F. King B6210, a Camel of 43 Squadron.

MACLEAN Loudoun James Captain 41

Born in Ealing, West London, on 1 February 1893, he was commissioned on 1 April 1914 and served in the 57th Company of the Royal Engineers. Following action for which he received an MC in September 1915, he was attached to the RFC in May 1917, and was posted to 41 Squadron, flying FE 8s and then DH 5s. Following the unit's conversion to SE 5As, MacLean became a flight commander in November 1917, during which month he was awarded a Bar to his MC. He returned to Home Establishment in February 1918 and after the war remained in the RAF, serving with 85 Squadron in December of that year, 70 Squadron in February 1919, and subsequently in 43 Squadron.

	1917		SE 5A					
1s*	29 Nov	Alb. DV	B642	41	Douai	1050	OOC	CR/RFC 29.11
2s**	30 Nov	Alb. DV	B38	41	Inchy en Artois	1330	DES	CR/RFC 30.11
3s***	30 Nov	C	B633	41	Rumily	1400	DES	CR/RFC 30.11
	1918							
4s†	9 Jan	Rumpler C	B38	41	E Marcoing	1145	OOC	CR/RFC 9.1
5s††	3 Feb	C	B38	41	N W Douai	1010	OOC	CR/RFC 3.2

TOTAL: 2 shared destroyed, 3 shared out of control = 5.
*Shared with Lt R. Winnicott B667, Lt D.V.D. MacGregor B644, Lt Essell B65. **Shared with Lt D.V.D. MacGregor B644. ***Shared with Capt M. Thomas B38, Lt R. Winnicott B569, Lt F.H. Taylor B667. †Shared with 2/Lt A.T. Isbell B698, 2/Lt A.S. Hemming B639. ††Shared with 2/Lt G.A. Lippsett B60.

MACLEOD Malcolm Plaw Lieutenant 41

Born in Winnipeg, Canada, on 24 January 1897, Malcolm MacLeod was commissioned in the RFC on 13 August 1917 and was posted to France next day, joining 41 Squadron on 17th. Here he claimed seven victories during the last weeks of the war, being awarded the DFC and Belgian Croix de Guerre. During World War II he served in the RCAF as a Flight Lieutenant.

	1918		SE 5A					
1	30 Aug	Fokker DVII	E3971	41	S W Armentieres	1730	OOC	CR/SR/?
2	7 Oct	Fokker DVII	E6027	41	S Lille	0725	OOC	CR/SR/?
3	30 Oct	Halb. C	H683	41	N W Beclers	1145	DES	CR/RAF 30.10
4	30 Oct	Fokker DVII	H683	41	N Roulers	1600	DES	CR/RAF 30.10
5s*	4 Nov	Balloon	H683	41	Pipaix	1125	DES	CR/RAF 4.11
6	4 Nov	Balloon	H683	41	Baugnies	1125+	DES	CR/RAF 4.11
7	9 Nov	Fokker DVII	H683	41	Renaix	0900	OOC	CR/SR/?

TOTAL: 1 and 1 shared balloons, 2 destroyed, 3 out of control = 7.
*Shared with Capt W.E. Shields C1912.

MACMILLAN Norman Captain 45

Born on 9 August 1892 in Scotland, he served in France with the Highland Light Infantry for some 16 months before joining the RFC in 1916. He learned to fly at Netheravon, then in 1917 went to 45 Squadron on 1½ Strutters. He flew many missions on this type and claimed two victories before 45 was re-equipped with Camels during August 1917. He then gained the unit's first Camel victory on 25 August. On 11 September he twice claimed Fokker Triplanes out of control during two separate engagements in the space of a few minutes. However it is now clear that on each occasion he had encountered Leutnant Werner Voss in the prototype Triplane, who was not in fact shot down on either occasion, but escaped by violent diving manoeuvres. MacMillan was to claim nine victories in all, the last in Italy after 45 Squadron had moved there. He was then injured in an unfortunate accident on 6 January 1918, and did not see further combat. Returning to England, he became an instructor and was awarded the MC, and later the AFC. He was closely associated with flying for many years and also became a keen writer on aviation subjects; his book *Into the Blue* is regarded as a classic. During World War II he became a Wing Commander war correspondent, and then retired to Cornwall, becoming Deputy Lord Lieutenant of that country; he also received the OBE. Norman MacMillan died on 5 August 1976.

	1917		Strutter					
1*	5 Jun	Alb. DIII	----	45	Menin	1015	OOC	CR/RFC 5.6
2**	21 Aug	DFW. C	B2583	45	E Ploegsteert Wood	1025	DES(F)	CR/RFC 21.8
			Camel					
3	25 Aug	Alb. DIII	B3917	45	Polygon Wood	1930	OOC	CR/RFC 25.8
4	3 Sep	Alb. DIII	B6236	45	Tenbrielen	0935	DES(F)	CR/RFC 3.9
5	10 Sep	DFW. C	B6236	45	Houthoulst Forest	1720	OOC	CR/RFC 10.9
6	11 Sep	Fokker DrI	----	45	E Langemarck	1525	OOC	CR/RFC 12.9
7	11 Sep	Fokker DrI	----	45	E Langemarck	1525	OOC	CR/RFC 12.9
8	15 Oct	C	----	45	Houthoulst Forest	1150	OOC	CR/RFC 15.10
9	20 Oct	Alb. DV	----	45	Kastelhoek	1240	DES(F)	CR/RFC 20.10

TOTAL: 3 destroyed, 6 out of control = 9.
*Observer: 2/Lt P.F. Webb. **Observer: 2/Lt R.S.V. Morris.

MACRAE John Finlay Noel Lieutenant 23

Born on 5 December 1895 in Beaverton, Ontario, MacRae transferred to the RFC from the Royal Highlanders in 1915 and served with 23 Squadron from the autumn of 1917, flying Spad XIIIs. His last two victories were claimed on 21 March 1918, the first day of the German Spring Offensive.

	1917		Spad					
1	18 Nov	C	B3640	23	S Westroosebeke	0700	OOC	CR/RFC 18.11
2	5 Dec	Alb. DV	B3646	23	Westroosebeke	1425	OOC	CR/RFC 5.12
	1918							
3s*	9 Mar	C	B6847	23	S Masnieres	0915	DES	CR/V BG WD
4	21 Mar	C	B6854	23	Holnon Wood	1800	OOC	CR/V BG WD
5	21 Mar	Alb. DV	B6854	23	Holnon Wood	1855	DES	CR/V BG WD

TOTAL: 1 and 1 shared destroyed, 3 out of control = 5.
*Shared with Capt J.F. Morris B6856, Lt G.W.R. Pidsley B3479.

MADDOCKS Henry Hollingrake Captain 54

Joining 54 Squadron in 1917, Lieutenant Maddocks flew Sopwith Pups during the late summer and autumn, claiming four victories. During the winter the squadron converted to Camels and he was promoted to flight commander; on 3 January 1918 he gained the unit's first victory on the new type. He was awarded an MC, and had brought his score to seven by early February, including the Commanding Officer of Jasta 48, Leutnant Karl Stock, an ex-member of von Richthofen's Circus, on 3 February.

	1917		Pup					
1	12 Aug	Alb. DV	----	54	----	----	OOC	CR/RFC 12.8
2	16 Sep	Alb. DIII	A6238	54	E Slype	1815	DES(F)	CR/RFC 16.9
3	25 Sep	Alb. DV	A6238	54	N Middelkerke	1130	DES(F)	CR/RFC 25.9
4s*	4 Nov	Alb. DV	----	54	N Dixmude	1350	DES	CR/RFC 4.11
	1918		Camel					
5	3 Jan	DFW. C	B9143	54	E St Quentin	0825	DES(F)	CR/RFC 3.1
6**	3 Feb	Alb. DV	B5245	54	Honnecourt	1045	DES(F)	CR/RFC 3.2
7**	3 Feb	Alb. DV	B5243	54	Honnecourt	1045	DES(F)	CR/RFC 3.2

TOTAL: 6 destroyed, 1 out of control = 7.
*Shared with 2/Lt S.J. Schooley. **These were Lt Karl Stock and Lt M. Kersting, of Jasta 48, who were both killed.

MAGOUN Francis Peabody Lieutenant 1

Born 6 January 1895, Magoun was an American citizen who joined the RFC on 4 July 1917. After training he was posted to 1 Squadron on 15 November. He first claimed on 28 February 1918, when he shared in sending down an Albatros Scout out of control. During the next month he shot down another Albatros and shared in two more victories, but on 10 April he was wounded, spending some time in hospital. He rejoined the squadron on 9 October, and during the final month of the war claimed one further victory. He was awarded an MC, gazetted on 22 June 1918. After the war Magoun became a noted academic, writing several books and becoming a Professor of English at Harvard University. He died on 5 June 1979.

	1918		SE 5A					
1s*	28 Feb	Alb. DV	A8904	1	Gheluvelt	1710	OOC	CR/RFC 1.3
2s**	15 Mar	DFW. C	A8904	1	Dadizeele-S Ledgehem	1035	DES	CR/RFC 15.3
3s***	28 Mar	LVG. C	C5306	1	Gavrelle, N Oppy	0840	DES	CR/RFC 28.3
4	28 Mar	Alb. DV	C5306	1	Quiery	0855	DES	CR/ORB/?
5	28 Oct	Fokker DVII	E5578	1	Anor	1340	OOC	CR/ORB/?

TOTAL: 1 and 2 shared destroyed, 1 and 1 shared out of control = 5.
*Shared with Capt W.D. Patrick B641. **Shared with 2/Lt L.W. Mawbey B632. ***Shared with Capt G.B. Moore C1083.

MAKEPEACE Reginald Milburn Captain 20, 11

Although born in Liverpool on 27 December 1887, Makepeace was resident in Canada in 1914. Joining the RFC, he was posted to 20 Squadron on 8 June 1917, flying FE 2Ds, claiming his first victory in June. On 27 July he and his observer, Private Pilbrow, claimed three Albatros Scouts shot down; Makepeace was then awarded the MC. After he had claimed eight victories, 20 Squadron converted to Bristol Fighters, and in the next few months Makepeace raised his score to 16 by 4 January 1918. Promoted to Captain, he went to 11 Squadron on 23 January 1918, where he gained his 17th and last victory while flying as observer to Lieutenant John Chick.

	1917		FE 2D					
1*	29 Jun	Alb. DIII	A6498	20	Houthem	1330	OOC	CR/RFC 29.6
2**	6 Jul	Alb. DIII	A6457	20	Comines	1830	OOC	CR/RFC 6.7
3***	27 Jul	Alb. DIII	A6458	20	Menin	1945-2040	DES(F)	CR/RFC 27.7
4***	27 Jul	Alb. DIII	A6458	20	Polygon Wood	1945-2040	DES	CR/RFC 27.7
5***	27 Jul	Alb. DIII	A6458	20	S Polygon Wood	1945-2040	OOC	CR/RFC 27.7
6***	28 Jul	Alb. DIII	A1956	20	Kezelbars	0920	OOC	CR/RFC 28.7
7*	16 Aug	Alb. DV	A3	20	Zonnebeke	0905	OOC	CR/RFC 16.8
8s†	17 Aug	Alb. DV	B1897	20	E Polygon Wood	2000	OOC	CR/RFC 17.8
			Bristol					
9*	3 Sep	Alb. DV	A7214	20	Menin-Wervicq	1010	DES(F)	CR/RFC 3.9
10*	5 Sep	Alb. DV	A7203	20	W Lille	1117	OOC	CR/RFC 5.9
11*	11 Sep	Alb. DV	A7214	20	E Menin	1400	OOC	CR/RFC 11.9
12*	17 Oct	Alb. DV	A7255	20	Zonnebeke	0840	OOC	CR/RFC 17.10
13*	17 Oct	Alb. DV	A7255	20	N E Zonnebeke	0905	OOC	CR/ORB/?
14††	15 Nov	Alb. DV	A7193	20	Moorslede	1500	OOC	CR/RFC 15.11
15†††	22 Dec	Alb. DV	A7255	20	Moorslede	1415	DES	CR/RFC 22.12
	1918							
16‡	4 Jan	Alb. DV	A7255	20	Menin	1200	OOC	CR/RFC 4.1
17‡‡	28 Jan	DFW. C	----	11	N Bourlon Wood	1715	OOC	CR/RFC 28.1

TOTAL: 4 destroyed, 12 and 1 shared out of control = 17.
*Observer: Lt M.W. Waddington. **Observer: 2/Lt W.D. Kennard. ***Observer: Pte S. Pilbrow. †Observer: Gnr J. McMechan. Shared with 2/Lt W. Durrand/2/Lt J.P. Flynn A6456. ††Observer: 2/Lt W.T.V. Harmer. †††Observer: Lt G.A. Brooke. ‡Observer: Capt J.H. Hedley. ‡‡Pilot: 2/Lt J.S. Chick.

MALCOLM Reginald George Lieutenant 25

A Canadian, born in Manitoba in 1890, Malcolm flew FE 2s with 25 Squadron in the early months of 1917, claiming eight victories in company with his various gunners. The award of the MC was gazetted in July of that year.

	1917		FE 2D					
1s*	4 Mar	LVG. C	7693	25	Courrieres	1115	DES	CR/RFC 4.3
2**	17 Mar	Alb. DII	A782	25	Oppy-Beaumont	c1130	DES	CR/RFC 17.3
3***	13 Apr	Alb. DIII	A6385	25	Henin-Lietard	1930	DES	CR/RFC 13.4
4s†	14 Apr	Alb. DIII	A6383	25	Henin-Lietard	1930	DES	CR/RFC 14.4
5s††	21 Apr	Alb. DIII	A8375	25	Thelus-Vimy	1845	CAPT	CR/RFC 21.4
6***	1 May	Alb. DIII	7672	25	Izel	0620	DES	CR/RFC 1.5
7***	1 May	Alb. DIII	7672	25	W Lens	0645	CAPT	CR/RFC 1.5?
8***	1 May	Alb. DII	4839	25	Bois Bernard	1800	DES(F)	CR/RFC 2.5

TOTAL: 1 and 1 shared captured, 4 and 2 shared destroyed = 8.
*Observer: Cpl L. Emsden; shared with Lt A.E. Boultbee/Sgt J. Brown A5439, 2/Lt R.N.L. Munro/Sgt G. Goodburn 7025, 2/Lt W.D. Matheson/Sgt W.A. Barnes A780. **Observer: Lt C.W. Wilson. ***Observer: Cpl L. Emsden. †Observer: 2/Lt J.B. Weir; shared with Sgt W.J. Burkenshaw/Sgt J.H. Brown A7003. ††Observer: 2/Lt J.B. Weir; shared with F/Cdr A.R. Arnold of 8N in Triplane N5458.

MALLEY Garnet Francis Captain 4 AFC

A mechanic in Sydney, New South Wales, before the war, Malley, who had been born in November 1892, joined the Australian Artillery and later transferred to the AFC. He went to France with 4 AFC Squadron early in 1918, and claimed three victories during March. Two more followed in May, during which month he was promoted to flight commander and awarded an MC. His final victory was claimed on 1 June, bringing his score to six.

	1918		Camel					
1	16 Mar	Pfalz DIII	B2488	4AFC	Annoeullin	1000	OOC	CR/RFC 16.3
2	23 Mar	Alb. DV	B2488	4AFC	Vaulx	1630	DES	CR/RFC 23.3
3	23 Mar	Alb. DV	B2488	4AFC	Vaulx	1630	DES	CR/RFC 23.3
4	15 May	C	C8261	4AFC	Bac St Maur	1700	DES	CR/RAF 15.5
5	30 May	Balloon	D6806	4AFC	Estaires	1657	DES	CR/RAF 30.5
6	1 Jun	Pfalz DIII	D6600	4AFC	Bac St Maur	1530	DES	CR/RAF 1.6

TOTAL: 1 balloon, 4 destroyed, 1 out of control = 6.

MALONE John Joseph Flight Sub-Lieutenant 3W, 3(N)

Born in America of Canadian parentage on 20 December 1894, he signed on in Canada early in the war for service in the RNAS. In 1916 he joined 3 Naval Wing on Sopwith 1½ Strutters, but was soon posted as a scout pilot to 3(N) Squadron as it was forming, due to his excellent piloting skill. Over the Western Front in March-April 1917 he achieved considerable success, receiving the DSO. When, on 24 April he forced a DFW down to land inside the Allied lines, Malone landed beside the German machine to find the pilot wounded and the observer dead. Two days later Malone raised his score to ten, but on 30 April was shot down and killed in Sopwith Pup N6175 by Leutnant Paul Billik of Jasta 12, the first victory for the later great ace.

	1917		Pup					
1	4 Mar	Halb. DII	9898	3N	Manancourt	1145	OOC	CR/ORB/DL
2*	17 Mar	C	9898	3N	N E Bapaume	1025	OOC	CR/RFC 19.3
3	17 Mar	Alb. DII	9898	3N	Ervillers	1100	DES(F)	CR/RFC 17.3
4	17 Mar	Alb. DII	9898	3N	Arras	1450	DES(F)	CR/RFC 17.3
5	21 Apr	C	N6208	3N	5m N Queant	1740	OOC	CR/RFC 21.4
6	23 Apr	Alb. DIII	N6208	3N	Croisilles	0630	DES	CR/RFC 23.4
7	23 Apr	Alb. DIII	N6208	3N	Croisilles	0715	OOC	CR/RFC 23.4
8	23 Apr	Alb. DIII	N6208	3N	Croisilles-Havrincourt	0745	OOC	CR/RFC 23.4
9s**	24 Apr	DFW. C	N6208	3N	Morchies-Louverval	1650	CAPT	CR/RFC 24.4
10***	26 Apr	Alb. DIII	N6202	3N	N Cambrai	1915	DES	CR/RFC 26.4

TOTAL: 1 shared captured, 4 destroyed, 5 out of control = 10.
*Although claimed as "driven down", this aircraft was confirmed as out of control next day. **Shared with F/L H.G. Travers N6169, FSL F.D. Casey N6182. This was Uffz Max Haase/Lt Karl Keim FA 26. Keim was killed. ***Probably Vzfw Emil Eisenhuth of Jasta 3, who was killed.

MANLEY Patrick Scarsfield 2nd Lieutenant 62

A Canadian, Manley joined 62 Squadron in late summer 1918, making all his claims in the space of two weeks during September. On 27th of that month he and his observer, Sergeant G.F. Hines, were shot down in C994, and became prisoners.

	1918		Bristol					
1*	15 Sep	EA	----	62	Marquion	1705	OOC	SR/C&CA 17.4
2*	16 Sep	Fokker DVII	----	62	----	----	OOC	SR/C&CA 17.4
3*	17 Sep	Fokker DVII	----	62	----	----	OOC	SR/C&CA 17.4
4*	24 Sep	Fokker DVII	----	62	E Cambrai	----	DES	SR/C&CA 17.4
5*	24 Sep	Fokker DVII	----	62	E Cambrai	----	DES(F)	SR/C&CA 17.4

TOTAL: 2 destroyed, 3 out of control = 5.
*Observer: Sgt G.F. Hines.

MANN William Edward George Captain 208

Born on 20 April 1899, he flew with 208 Squadron throughout 1918, becoming a flight commander, receiving the DFC, and claiming 13 victories. Known as 'Pedro', he remained in the RAF, and in the early 1920s was an instructor at the Central Flying School. In July 1921 he took part in the second Hendon Air Pageant, flying a Snipe; he again participated in the show in 1924. In December 1934 he was promoted Squadron Leader, and two years later attended the 14th Course at the Staff College at Andover. He eventually reached the rank of Air Commodore, CB, CBE, and in 1962 was with Decca Navigation Company in Beirut.

	1918		Camel					
1	8 May	Alb. DV	D1845	208	Provin	1115	OOC	CR/RAF 8.5
2	9 May	Alb. DV	D1845	208	Phalempin	1345	OOC	CR/RAF 9.5
3s*	8 Jul	Rumpler C	----	208	1m S W Estaires	0810	DES	CR/RAF 8.7
4s**	31 Jul	Alb. DV	----	208	S W Douai	2020	DES	CR/RAF 31.7
5	9 Aug	Fokker DVII	D1834	208	Nesle	1125	OOC	CR/?
6	16 Aug	Hannover C	D6634	208	Oppy	0905	DES	CR/RAF 16.8
7	27 Aug	Fokker DVII	F1588	208	S Scarpe River	0750	DES(F)	CR/RAF 27.8
8	1 Sep	DFW. C	F1588	208	N Gloster Wood	1000	OOC	CR/?
9	3 Sep	Fokker DVII	F1588	208	Marquion	1425	OOC	CR/?
10	6 Sep	Fokker DVII	----	208	Canal du Nord	1830	DES(F)	CR/RAF 6.9
11	6 Sep	Fokker DVII	----	208	Canal du Nord	1830	OOC	CR/RAF 6.9
12	25 Sep	Halb. C	----	208	Gouy	1750	DES	CR/RAF 25.9
13	26 Sep	Fokker DVII	----	208	S E St Quentin	1840	OOC	CR/?

TOTAL: 4 and 2 shared destroyed, 7 out of control = 13.
*Shared with Lt J. Mollison. **Shared with Lt L.E.A. Green.

MANNOCK Edward Major 40, 74, 85

Born at Aldershot on 24 May 1887, the son of a serving army NCO, Mannock was working with a British telephone company in Turkey at the outbreak of war, and was interned. Due to poor health, he was repatriated on 1 April 1915, but on his return to England joined the RAMC. He was commissioned in the Royal Engineers a year later, and then in August 1916 transferred to the RFC. Following training, during which one of his instructors was James McCudden, he was posted in April 1917 to 40 Squadron which was equipped with Nieuport Scouts. At first, due to his highly-strung and sensitive nature, success eluded him. This caused some members of the squadron to doubt his fighting spirit. However after a month he managed to shoot down a balloon, and within a further month had achieved a victory over an Albatros Scout of Jasta 33. During the summer he found his form, and by the end of July he had received an MC and become a flight commander. In October he was awarded a Bar to his MC, his score having reached 15. 40 Squadron then converted to SE 5s, and he gained one further victory on 1 January 1918 before returning to Home Establishment.

In February he was posted as a flight commander to 74 Squadron which was forming on SE 5As, and on 30 March returned to France with this unit. Here he was to claim a further 36 victories. On 24 May he was awarded the DSO, followed by a Bar to this prestigious decoration only two weeks later. On 18 June he was given command of 85 Squadron which had been under the command of 'Billy' Bishop, VC. Mannock's skill as a leader turned this into an extremely efficient unit, rather than a collection of individuals. Prior to his arrival the vast majority of the unit's claims had been made only by Bishop personally. While leading the unit, Mannock was to add a further eight claims to his total, plus one driven down and forced to land, and two which collided in a fight in which he was involved, none of these latter three being claimed by him. At dawn on 26 July, he and a pilot who had yet to score — Lieutenant D.C. Inglis — shot down an LVG at extremely low altitude near the German front lines. Immediately after this victory, his 61st, Mannock was shot down by machine gun fire from Infantry Regiment 100, and crashed to his death behind German lines. Inglis was also shot down, but survived a crash in British lines.

Like most British aces, Mannock was virtually unknown to the British public during the war, but was revered by the men who served with him as a great leader and tactician. On 18 July 1919 the award of the Victoria Cross was announced, crediting him with 59 destroyed. Subsequently in books written by Ira T. Jones, who had been his protege in 74 Squadron, and who was not only a great admirer of Mannock, but also a detractor of Bishop, a score of 73 (one above the Canadian's stated total) was claimed for him, and this became established wisdom for many years. Several books have been written about the life of this great pilot, the most recent being *Mick: The Story of Major Edward Mannock*, by J. Dudgeon, published in 1981. Exhaustive research has provided details of all the claims made by Mannock, and these are set out in more than usual detail herewith, together with an explanation of where it is believed errors have occurred in previous efforts to produce such a list. Mannock's claims generally have proved verifiable to an above average extent from German records.

	1917		Nieuport					
1	7 May	Balloon	A6733	40	Quierry la Motte	0935	DES	CR/RFC 7.5
2s*	7 Jun	Alb. DIII	B1552	40	N Lille	0715	OOC	CR/RFC 5.6
3**	12 Jul	DFW. C	B1682	40	Avion	1010	CAPT	CR/RFC 12.7
4***	13 Jul	DFW. C	B1682	40	Sallaumines	0920	OOC	CR/RFC 13.7
5	5 Aug	Alb. DV	B3554	40	Avoin	1610	OOC	CR/RFC 5.8
6†	12 Aug	Alb. DV	B3554	40	S E Petit-Vimy	1515	CAPT	CR/RFC 12.8
7	15 Aug	Alb. DV	B3554	40	Lens	1215	OOC	CR/RFC 15.8
8††	15 Aug	Alb. DV	B3554	40	N Lens	1930	OOC	CR/RFC 16.8
9	17 Aug	DFW. C	B3554	40	N E Sallaumines	1050	DES	CR/RFC 17.8
10s†††	4 Sep	DFW. C	B3607	40	E Lens-Lievin	1130	OOC	CR/RFC 4.9
11‡	4 Sep	DFW. C	B3607	40	Petit-Vimy	1630	CAPT	CR/RFC 4.9
12	11 Sep	DFW. C	B3607	40	Thelus-Oppy	1115	OOC	CR/RFC 11.9
13‡‡	20 Sep	DFW. C	B3607	40	Hulloch	1735	OOC	CR/RFC 20.9
14	23 Sep	C	B3541	40	Oppy	1645	DES(F)	CR/RFC 23.9
15‡‡‡	25 Sep	Rumpler C	B3607	40	Sallaumines	1510	OOC	CR/RFC 25.9
	1918		SE 5A					
16s§	1 Jan	DFW. C	B665	40	Fampoux	1135	CAPT	CR/RFC 1.1
17	12 Apr	Alb. DV	D278	74	E Merville	0900	DES	CR/RAF 12.4
18s§§	12 Apr	Alb. DV	D278	74	Bois de Phalempin	1440	DES	CR/RAF 12.4
19	23 Apr	Pfalz DIII	D278	74	E Merville	1810	DES(F)	CR/RAF 23.4
20§§§	29 Apr	Fokker DVI?	D278	74	S Dickebusch Lake	1140	DES(F)	CR/RAF 29.4
21s#	30 Apr	Alb. C	D278	74	S E Dickebusch Lake	1140	CAPT	CR/RAF 30.4
22##	3 May	LVG. C	D278	74	S Merville	1875	DES	CR/RAF 3.5
23###	6 May	Fokker DrI	D278	74	Gheluvelt	0920	DES	CR/RAF 6.5
24¶	11 May	Pfalz DIII	C1112	74	N E Armentieres	1740	DES(F)	CR/RAF 11.5

25	12 May	Alb. DV	C1112	74	N Wulverghem	1820	DES	CR/RAF 12.5
26	12 May	Alb. DV	C1112	74	N Wulverghem	1820	DES	CR/RAF 12.5
27	12 May	Pfalz DIII	C1112	74	N Wulverghem	1820	DES	CR/RAF 12.5
28	16 May	Pfalz DIII	C1112	74	S W Houthoulst Forest	1100	DES	CR/RAF 16.5
29	17 May	Pfalz DIII	D278	74	S Bailleul	1120	DES(F)	CR/RAF 17.5
30	17 May	Alb. C	D278	74	N E Ypres	1430	DES(F)	CR/RAF 17.5
31¶¶	18 May	Alb. C	D278	74	Steenwerck	0825	DES(F)	CR/RAF 18.5
32¶¶¶	21 May	Hannover C	D278	74	La Courenne	0928	DES	CR/RAF 21.5
33	21 May	Pfalz DIII	D278	74	Hollebeke	1900	DES	CR/RAF 21.5
34	21 May	Pfalz DIII	D278	74	Hollebeke	1900	DES	CR/RAF 21.5
35○	21 May	Pfalz DIII	D278	74	S Hollebeke	1905	DES	CR/RAF 21.5
36	22 May	Pfalz DIII	D278	74	Fromelles	c1815?	OOC	11 WS/JD
37	26 May	Pfalz DIII	D278	74	.5m S Balleul	1940	DES(F)	CR/RAF 26.5
38	26 May	Alb. DV	D278	74	S Bailleul	1940	OOC	CR/11 WS
39	29 May	Alb. DV	C6468	74	N E Armentieres	1925	DES(F)	CR/RAF 29.5
40	29 May	Alb. DV	C6468	74	N E Armentieres	2005	OOC	CR/11 WS
41	31 May	Pfalz DIII	C6468	74	N Wytschaete	1940	OOC	CR/11 WS
42	1 Jun	Pfalz DIII	C6468	74	Estaires	1630	DES	CR/RAF 1.6
43	1 Jun	Pfalz DIII	C6468	74	Estaires	1630	DES	CR/RAF 1.6
44○○	1 Jun	Pfalz DIII	C6468	74	Estaires	1630	OOC	CR/RAF 1.6
45○○○	2 Jun	Pfalz DIII	C6468	74	2m S Mt Kemmel	1540	OOC	CR/11 WS
46	6 Jun	Fokker DVII	C6468	74	E Ypres	1540	DES	CR/11 WS
47s●	6 Jun	Pfalz DIII	C6468	74	2m W Roulers	1945	DES	CR/RAF 7.6
48s●●	9 Jun	Alb. C	----	74	S Mt Kemmel	0805	OOC	CR/11 WS
49s●●●	9 Jun	Alb. C	----	74	S Mt Kemmel	0810	DES	CR/11 WS
50	16 Jun	Pfalz DIII	C5845	74	3m S Zillebeke Lake	0745	DES	CR/RAF 16.6
51	16 Jun	Pfalz DIII	C5845	74	3m S Zillebeke Lake	0745	OOC	CR/11 WS
52	17 Jun	Hannover C	C5845	74	Armentieres	0945	DES	CR/RAF 17.6
53	7 Jul	Fokker DVII	E1295	85	Doulieu	2020	DES	CR/RAF 7.7
54	7 Jul	Fokker DVII	E1295	85	Doulieu	2020	OOC	CR/11 WS
55	14 Jul	Fokker DVII	E1295	85	N Merville	0835	DES	CR/RAF 14.7
56☆	19 Jul	Alb. C	E1295	85	Merville	0823	DES	CR/RAF 19.7
57☆☆	20 Jul	C	E1295	85	N E La Bassee	1117	DES	CR/RAF 20.7
58	20 Jul	Fokker DVII	E1295	85	S Steenwerck	1215	OOC	CR/11 WS
60	22 Jul	Fokker DrI	E1295	85	Armentieres	0952	DES	CR/RAF 22.7
61s☆☆☆	26 Jul	C	E1295	85	Lestrem	0530	DES	CR/RAF 26.7

TOTAL: 1 balloon, 3 and 2 shared captured, 30 and 5 shared destroyed, 17 and 3 shared out of control = 61.
*Shared with 2/Lt C.J. Lally/2/Lt L.F. Williams in FE 2D A6417, of 25 Squadron. Possibly Vzfw Eberlein of Jasta 33, who was wounded. **Vzfw Reubelt (KIA)/Lt H Bottcher (POW) of Schlasta 12. ***Possibly Lt Walkermann, an observer of FAA 240, who was wounded. †This was Lt Joachim von Bertrab of Jasta 30, who was captured. ††Possibly Lt Brugmann of Jasta 30 who was killed. †††Shared with Sgt L.A. Herbert A6646; probably Vzfw Eddelbuttel (WIA)/Lt Kuhn of FAA 240. ‡This was Vzfw G. Frischkorn/Lt F. Frech KIA of FA 235. ‡‡Possibly Uffz Halbreiter/Lt Beauchamp of FAA 240. ‡‡‡Possibly Vzfw Meckes/Lt H. Otto of FAA 224, who were wounded. §Shared with F/Cdr R.J.O. Compston B6340/FSL G.K. Cooper B6321 of 8N Squadron. Vzfw F. Korbacher/Lt W. Klein of FAA 258, who were killed. §§Shared with Lt H.E. Dolan, Lt B. Roxburgh-Smith, Lt P.F.C. Howe, Lt H.G. Clements. §§§This was Lt L. Vortmann of Jasta B, who was killed. #Shared with Lt H.E. Dolan B173; this crew was Flgr Zimmermann/Vzfw Speer of Sch 10, who were killed. ##Shared with Lt H.E. Dolan, Lt H.G. Clements, Lt A.C. Kiddie; Uffz Schoning/Lt Beuttler of FA 32 were killed. ###This was Lt G. Derlin of Jasta 20, who was killed. ¶This was Lt Oskar Aeckerle, of Jasta 47, who was killed. ¶¶This crew was Lt Fischer/Lt Pietz of FA 19. ¶¶¶This crew was Gerf Menzel/Lt Steinmeyer of FA 9, who were killed. ○One known loss was Vzfw H. Schorn of Jasta 16, who was killed. ○○One known loss was Lt Saint Mont of Jasta 52, who was killed. ○○○Possibly Lt Dunkelberg of Jasta 58, who was killed. ●Shared with Lt H.G. Clements, Capt W.E. Young, Lt A.C. Kiddie, and possibly 5 others. ●●Shared with Lt A.C. Kiddie, Lt H.G. Clements. ●●●Shared with Capt W.E. Young. ☆This crew was Uffz A. Hartmann/Lt E. von Sydow of FA 7, who were killed. ☆☆Possibly Uffz Rath/Lt Gros of FA 7, who were killed. ☆☆☆Shared with Lt D.C. Inglis E1294. This crew was Vzfw Josef Hein/Lt Ludwig Schopf of FAA 292, who were killed.
NB: Mannock is often credited with 73 victories, with one of the most complete lists published being in "Mick": The Story of Major Edward Mannock VC, DSO, MC. RAF" by Jim Dudgeon. The following are comments on possible claims listed in Dudgeon's book.

1&2	9 Jun 1917	2 Alb DV claimed as out of control "unconfirmed". This is correct, they were not credited, and can be counted as driven down.
3	13 Jul 1917	A C type credited as driven down.
4	28 Jul 1917	Alb. DV as OOC. this was not credited, and should be regarded as driven down. It is not in the RFC Communiques.

5&6	28 Jul 1917	2 balloons destroyed with no details. The authors cannot find any evidence either.
7	16 Aug 1917	C Type destroyed. This is an error, as the RFC Communique appears to have put the 15 Aug claim at 1930 (for which a combat report exists) in on the 16th.
8	22 Aug 1917	Alb. DV; claimed as out as control. This was not allowed and given as driven down.
9	22 Apr 1918	No records have been found for this claim. It is probably a misdating of the 23 April claim.
10	23 Apr 1918	Dudgeon lists two claims, but only one was made.
11	29 Apr 1918	The second claim is a mistake from the RAF Communique, where the claim by Capt Manuel is printed as being by Mannock.
12	30 Apr 1918	There are no records showing the Alb. DV listed with no details by Dudgeon. It is certainly a repeat of the 29 April 1918 claim.
13	4 May 1918	This is the 7 May claims misdated in "Taffy" Jones' diary.
14	14 May 1918	There are no records for this claim. It is possibly a misdate for the 9 Jun 1918 claim by the same pilots.
15	29 May 1918	The third OOC claim was claimed as a driven down and given as such.
16	7 June 1918	This is the 9 Jun claim shared with Young misdated.
17	8 Jul 1918	This is the 7 Jul claim entered a day late in the RAF Communique because it was made late in the evening.
18	10 Jul 1918	There are no records of any claim on this date.

From this it appears that Mannock regarded the 4 claimed as out of control (but disallowed) victories, as in a letter dated 6 Jun 1918 he claims 51, with 47 official. The list above tallies with the 47 official. The ORB for 40 Squadron lists all the 200 operational sorties Mannock flew with the unit, and the claims listed above agree with the ORB.

MANSBRIDGE Leslie Morton Captain 1, 23

A native of Queensborough Terrace, Wales, Mansbridge joined the RFC on 16 August 1916 shortly after his 19th brithday, and was posted to 1 Squadron on 25 February 1917. On 3 June he was promoted to command a flight but that same day he and Lieutenant L.F. Jenkin were forced to land near Gheluwe (in B1639 and B1690 respectively) by Flugmeistern Kunstler and B. Heinrich of Marinefeldjasta 1, Mansbridge suffering wounds. On recovery in 1918 he joined 23 Squadron as a flight commander to fly Dolphins, gaining his fifth victory with this unit.

	1917		Nieuport					
1s*	1 May	Alb. C	A6670	1	Ploegsteert	1000	DES	CR/RFC 1.5
2	24 May	Alb. DIII	A6670	1	Zandvoorde	2005	OOC	CR/RFC 25.5
3	28 May	Alb. DIII	B1639	1	Wervicq	0930	OOC	CR/ORB/11 WS
4	2 Jun	Alb. DIII	B1639	1	Wervicq	0915	OOC	CR/RFC 2.6
	1918		Dolphin					
5	22 Apr	Fokker DrI	D3769	23	E Warfusee-Abancourt	1140	OOC	CR/RAF 22.4

TOTAL: 1 shared destroyed, 4 out of control = 5.
*Shared with Capt C.J.Q. Brand A6668.

MANSELL William Stanley Lieutenant 22, 1

Born in Wimbledon, South London on 25 September 1896, Mansell was commissioned in the 3rd E. Surrey Regt on 8 April 1915, going to France in February 1916. He transferred to the RFC as an observer in 1916, serving with 22 Squadron until wounded in action on 6 August. Training as a pilot upon his recovery, he graduated on 20 June and on 14 July 1917 joined 1 Squadron. He was killed on 11 September 1917 at the age of 20, when his Nieuport B3648 was shot down South of Houthem by anti-aircraft fire from Oberleutnant Sturm's KFlak 91. He had four brothers and one step brother who also served in the forces during the war.

	1916		FE 2B					
1*	21 Jul	Roland D	4267	22	Leuze Wood	1000	DES	CR/RFC 21.7
	1917		Nieup					
2	21 Jul	Alb. DV	A6680	1	N Polygon Wood	1950	OOC	CR/RFC 22.7
3	21 Aug	Alb. DV	B3558	1	Houthoulst	1910	OOC	CR/RFC 22.8
4	3 Sep	Alb. DV	B3558	1	Gheluwe	1850	DES	CR/RFC 3.9
5	9 Sep	Alb. DV	B3468	1	Becelaere	1440	DES	CR/RFC 9.9

TOTAL: 3 destroyed, 2 out of control = 5.
*Pilot: 2/Lt E.G.A. Bowen.

MANUEL John Gerald Captain 10(N), 210

Born on 29 March 1893 in Edmonton, Alberta, Canada he joined the Canadian Field Artillery in October 1914, then transferred to the RNAS in March 1917. After training and a brief stay with 12(N) Squadron, he was posted to 10(N) on 12 August 1917. He received the DSC, and when the unit became 210 Squadron, RAF, added a DFC, claiming a total of 13 victories. On 9 May 1918, while on a patrol, he fired a white Very signal, but the pistol exploded, causing injuries to his hand and blowing out the left side of the cockpit. After a short stay in hospital he returned to operations, but on 10 June was killed in B7249 when he collided with 2nd Lieutenant F.C. Dodd in D9590, a new pilot, and went down behind enemy lines. During the period 9-17 April, he flew many ground attack sorties, dropping 32 bombs and firing 3,550 rounds of ammunition at ground targets.

	1917		Camel					
1	21 Aug	Alb. DV	N5380	10N	E Menin	1830	OOC	CR/RFC 21.8
2	21 Aug	Alb. DV	N5380	10N	E Menin	1835	DES	CR/RFC 21.8
3	20 Sep	C	B3950	10N	Houthoust Forest	1115	DES	CR/RFC 20.9
4	15 Nov	Alb. DV	B3864	10N	Keyem	1245	DES	CR/RFC 15.11
	1918							
5	18 Feb	Alb. DV	B7195	10N	S Menin	0950	DES	CR/RNAS 18.2
6	19 Feb	Alb. DV	----	10N	10m N E Roulers	----	OOC	RNAS 19.2
7	10 Mar	Alb. DV	B5749	10N	S E Dixmude	1600	DES	CR/DOR/DL/?
8	11 Apr	C	B7195	210	Fleurbaix	1430	DES	CR/RAF 11.4
9	11 Apr	Alb. C	B7195	210	Fleurbaix	1435	DES	CR/RAF 11.4
10	29 Apr	Alb. DV	D3366	210	N E Hollebeke	1445	DES	CR/RAF 29.4
11s*	6 Jun	C	D3410	210	Doulieu	0825	DES	CR/RAF 6.6
12	9 Jun	Pfalz DIII	D3410	210	N E Ploegsteert Wood	0820	OOC	CR/?
13	9 Jun	Pfalz DIII	D3410	210	N E Ploegsteert Wood	0835	DES	CR/RAF 9.6

TOTAL: 9 and 1 shared destroyed, 3 out of control = 13.
*Shared with Lt W.S. Jenkins D9590.

MANUEL Roby Lewis Captain 2AFC

Born on 7 October 1895 in Kerang, Victoria, Manuel was a farmer before the war. After service with the Australian Infantry, he transferred to the AFC and was posted to 2AFC Squadron in France on completion of training. He claimed his first victory on 2 April, and in June added four more; he was awarded a DFC in July and was promoted to flight commander. On 16 September he shot down one Fokker DVII which crashed, and claimed a second out of control; he then landed beside his first victim, an unknown Vizefeldwebel, who died as a result of the wounds he had sustained in this combat, as Manuel stood by helpless. Manuel served in the RAAF during World War II, and as late as 1968 was still piloting his own light aircraft on occasions. He died on 18 October 1975.

	1918		SE 5A					
1s*	2 Apr	C	B184	2AFC	Demuin	0700	DES	CR/RAF 2.4
2	2 Jun	Pfalz DIII	B184	2AFC	15m E Villers Brettoneaux	0805	DES	CR/RAF 2.6
3	2 Jun	Pfalz DIII	B184	2AFC	15m E Villers Brettoneaux	0805	DES	CR/ORB/OH
4**	2 Jun	Pfalz DIII	B184	2AFC	10m E Villers Brettoneaux	0830	OOC	CR/ORB/OH
5	12 Jun	Pfalz DIII	B184	2AFC	N Bussy	1045	DES(F)	CR/RAF 12.6
6	22 Jul	Pfalz DIII	C1948	2AFC	1m E Lens	0920	OOC	CR/ORB/OH
7	22 Jul	Fokker DVII	C1948	2AFC	1m E Lens	0920	OOC	CR/ORB/OH
8	31 Jul	Alb. DV	C1948	2AFC	Estaires	0955	OOC	CR/ORB/OH
9	14 Aug	Fokker DVII	C1948	2AFC	1m W Perenchies	1800	DES	CR/RAF 14.8
10	16 Sep	Fokker DVII	C1948	2AFC	Habourdin	0730	OOC	CR/ORB/OH
11***	16 Sep	Fokker DVII	C1948	2AFC	1.5m S Droglandt	0800	CAPT	CR/RAF 16.9
12s†	24 Sep	Alb. C	C1948	2AFC	La Bassee-Bethune	1030	OOC	CR/ORB/?

TOTAL: 1 captured, 4 and 1 shared destroyed, 5 and 1 shared out of control = 12.
*Shared with Capt H.G. Forrest C9539. **The Australian Official History, gets the dates wrong for 2AFC's combats on 1 and 2 June. This claim is wrongly dated in the Official History as being on June 1. ***Manuel landed alongside this aircraft, and burind the pilot. †Shared with Lt F.R. Smith C6403.

MANZER Roy Captain 84

Born in Medicine Hat, Alberta, Canada, on 31 August 1896, and commissioned in the RFC in October 1917, Manzer served with 84 Squadron during the spring and summer of 1918, claiming at least 11 victories; he was awarded a DFC early in August of that year. On 28 May he had driven one scout down out of control, when he collided with another, the undercarriage of his SE 5A striking the top wing and causing the enemy aircraft to crash. On 10 July he drove down two balloons in a damaged condition, and on 19th flamed another, forced a two-seater to land, and drove down an enemy scout damaged. He then took command of 'C' Flight on 6 August, but two days later was shot down during a ground-strafing attack and was taken prisoner.

	1918		SE 5A					
1	25 Apr	Alb. DV	D259	84	E Abancourt	1700	DES	CR/RAF 25.4
2*	16 May	Fokker DrI	D259	84	S Herleville	1805	DES	CR/RAF 16.5
3**	28 May	Alb. DV	D259	84	S E Warfusee	0920	OOC	CR/RAF 28.5
4**	28 May	Alb. DV	D259	84	S E Warfusee	0920	DES	CR/RAF 28.5
5	18 Jun	Fokker DrI	C1871	84	S E Warfusee	1055	DES	CR/RAF 12.6
6	29 Jun	Fokker DVII	C8732	84	S E Wiencourt	2045	OOC	CR/?
7	19 Jul	Balloon	C8732	84	E Le Quesnel	1815	DES	CR/RAF 19.7
8s***	28 Jul	Rumpler C	C8732	84	Harbonnieres	0940	DES	CR/RAF 28.7
9s***	29 Jul	Rumpler C	C8732	84	1m E Bois de Tailles	0800	DES	CR/RAF 29.7
10	3 Aug	Fokker DVII	C8732	84	Bray	0650	DES(F)	CR/RAF 3.8
11	7 Aug	Pfalz DIII	C8732	84	E Le Quesnel	0910	DES	CR/RAF 7.8

TOTAL: 1 balloon, 6 and 2 shared destroyed, 2 out of control = 11.
*84 made 2 claims, one was probably Vzfw Schmutzler of Jasta 4, who was killed. **These aircraft collided. ***Shared with Lt G.A. Vaughn C6457.

MARCHANT Cecil James Captain 46, 78, 44

Born on 15 July 1895, Londoner 'Chips' Marchant enlisted in the army when he was 18 and spent a year and a half in the trenches before transferring to the RFC. He was posted to 46 Squadron in 1917 flying Pups, but did not make any claims during his first tour, which ended in June. In January 1918 he was promoted to Captain and returned to the unit the following month, claiming at least nine victories in just over two months; he was awarded the MC, gazetted on 22 June. He was wounded on 2 July and hospitalization ended his front-line career. After the war he went into the family business, helping to organise squadron reunions in his spare time. He died during the 1960s.

	1918		Camel					
1s*	22 Mar	LVG. C	C1554	46	Bullecourt	1500	OOC	CR/RFC 22.3
2	23 Mar	C	B9211	46	Croisilles	1015	OOC	CR/SR/?
3	23 Mar	C	B9211	46	Mory	1030	DES(F)	CR/RFC 23.3
4	23 Mar	Alb. DV	----	46	Morchies	1410	OOC	CR/RFC 23.3
5s**	3 Apr	Alb. C	B9211	46	57 D L32	1245	DES	CR/RAF 3.4
6s**	20 Apr	Alb. C	B9211	46	Harnes	1000	DES	CR/RAF 20.4
7s***	25 Apr	LVG. C	----	46	W Lens	----	DES	CR/I BG WD
8s†	2 May	Pfalz DIII	B9211	46	Estaires	1700	OOC	CR/RAF 2.5
9s††	6 May	DFW. C	----	46	St Venant	1800	CAPT	CR/RAF 6.5

TOTAL: 1 shared captured, 1 and 3 shared destroyed, 2 and 2 shared out of control = 9.
*Shared with 2/Lt D.R. MacLaren B9153. **Shared with 2/Lt M.M. Freehill B5636. ***Shared with 2/Lt E. Smith, 2/Lt P.M. Tudhope. †Shared with 2/Lt J.H. Smith C1575. ††Shared with Capt D.R. MacLaren, 2/Lt J.H. Smith, Lt V.M. Yeates, 2/Lt H.T.W. Manwaring; this was Lt Junemann/Lt Barth of FA 14.

MARE-MONTEMBAULT Maximillian John Jules Gabriel Lieutenant 32

'Monty' Mare-Montembault joined 32 Squadron on 10 August 1916, becoming part of the 'backbone' of the unit. He survived encounters with two of the leading German pilots of the day. The first occurred on 10 October 1916 when he was chased along the Bapaume-Albert road and shot down into British lines by Hauptmann Oswald Boelcke as his 34th victory. Subsequently on 6 March 1917 he was again shot down, this time near Beugnatre, by Oberleutnant Adolf von Tutschek of Jasta B — the first of the German's 27 victories. This time Mare-Montembault fell in German territory, and although unhurt, he became a prisoner of war for the duration. He was awarded an MC, and recommended for a DSO which he did not receive.

	1916		DH 2					
1	15 Sep	Roland C	A2539	32	S Bapaume	1150	DES(F)	CR/RFC 15.9
2	22 Oct	Alb. DI	7882	32	Irles	1005	OOC	ORB/SD/RC/?
3s*	16 Nov	C	7899	32	Loupart Wood	0900	OOC	ORB/SD/RFC 16.11
4s*	16 Nov	C	7899	32	Loupart Wood	0900	OOC	ORB/SD/RFC 16.11
5	17 Nov	C	7899	32	Bucquoy	c1400	OOC	ORB/RFC 17.11
	1917							
6s**	6 Mar	Alb. DI	7882	32	E Bapaume	c1500	DES	ORB/RFC 6.3

TOTAL: 1 and 1 shared destroyed, 2 and 2 shared out of control = 6.
*Shared with Capt H.W.G. Jones 7882, Lt P.B.G. Hunt 7938. **Shared with Lt H.G. Southon 7941.

MARK Ronald Turnbull Lieutenant 24

Mark flew with 24 Squadron from 10 January to 28 May 1918. He was awarded an MC and Bar, and was credited with a final score of 14, eight of these being shared. On 21 May he dived on an enemy aircraft but his SE 5A began to break up, the top plane cracking under the strain of the dive. With a German scout on his tail, he made for Allied lines, but while doing so, saw a scout on the tail of Captain C.N. Lowe's aircraft and attacked this. This also turned on him, but Lowe came to his aid and shot this aircraft down. On landing his damaged SE, Mark crashed and the aircraft burst into flames, but he was able to scramble out unhurt.

	1918		SE 5A					
1s*	18 Feb	DFW. C	B67	24	La Fere	0830	OOC	CR/SR/5 BG
2	18 Feb	Pfalz DIII	B67	24	E St Quentin	1430	OOC	CR/RFC 18.2
3s**	19 Feb	DFW. C	B67	24	Servais	0840	DES(F)	CR/RFC 19.2
4s**	19 Feb	Rumpler C	B67	24	Bernot	0850	DES	CR/RFC 19.2
5s***	26 Feb	Fokker DrI	B67	24	E Samoussy	0900	DES	CR/RFC 26.2
6s†	11 Mar	C	C6397	24	E Bellenglise	1315	OOC	CR/RFC 11.3
7	13 Mar	C	C6397	24	Bellicourt	1245	OOC	CR/RFC 13.3
8s††	15 Mar	Rumpler C	C9494	24	N Premonte	1020	DES	CR/RFC 15.3
9	17 Mar	Pfalz DIII	B8411	24	S W Ramicourt	1825	OOC	CR/RFC 17.3
10	22 Mar	Alb. DV	B8411	24	E Matigny	1540	DES(F)	CR/RFC 22.3
11	26 Mar	C	B8411	24	Guyencourt	1700	DES	CR/RFC 26.3
12s†††	4 Apr	Rumpler C	B8411	24	St Nicholas	1730	CAPT	CR/RAF 4.4
13	23 Apr	Pfalz DIII	C6417	24	S Warfusee	1415	DES	CR/RAF 23.4
14s‡	3 May	Fokker DrI	C5367	24	Marcelcave	1145	OOC	CR/SR/?

TOTAL: 1 shared captured, 3 and 4 shared destroyed, 3 and 3 shared out of control = 14.
*Shared with 2/Lt H.D. Barton B120, Lt A.K. Cowper B664. **Shared with Lt A.K. Cowper B664, Lt P.A. MacDougall B120, Lt R.G. Hammersley B891. ***Shared with Lt I.D.R. MacDonald C1087, 2/Lt J.J. Dawe B85, 2/Lt W.F. Poulter C9494, 2/Lt H.V.L. Tubbs C9542, 2/Lt H.B. Richardson B124. †Shared with Capt A.J. Brown C9494, 2/Lt P.J. Nolan C5301, 2/Lt H.B. Richardson C1070, Lt E.W. Lindeburgh B125. ††Shared with Lt A.K. Cowper C5428, Lt H.B. Richardson B8257. †††Shared with 2/Lt C.M.G. Farrell C1099; probably Uffz Brocklebenck/Lt Behnecke of FA 33 who were captured. ‡Shared with Capt C.N. Lowe D275.

MARKS George Ivan Douglas Lieutenant 23

This Canadian flew Spads with 23 Squadron in the summer of 1917. He claimed eight victories, three of them shared, before being taken ill on 5 September. He then saw no further action. He died during the late 1940s.

	1917		Spad					
1s*	24 Jun	Alb. DV	B1698	23	St Jean	1630	DES(F)	CR/RFC 25.6
2s**	6 Jul	C	----	23	Zandvoorde	1430	DES	CR/RFC 6.7
3	6 Jul	Alb. DV	B3529	23	Polygon Wood	2025	DES	CR/RFC 6.7
4	17 Jul	Alb. DV	B3529	23	Becelaere	1030	DES	CR/RFC 17.7
5	10 Aug	Alb. DV	B3490	23	Wervicq	0930	DES	CR/RFC 10.8
6	10 Aug	Alb. DV	B3490	23	S Comines	0945	OOC	CR/RFC 10.8
7	14 Aug	Alb. DIII	B3539	23	Passchendaele	1900	OOC	CR/V BG WD
8s***	14 Aug	DFW. C	B3539	23	E St Julien	1915	DES	CR/V BG WD

TOTAL: 3 and 3 shared destroyed, 2 out of control = 8.
*Shared with Capt C.K.C. Patrick B1580, 2/Lt S.C. O'Grady B3464. **Shared with Capt C.K.C. Patrick, Lt D. MacGregor. ***Shared with 2/Lt S.C. O'Grady, 2/Lt C.F. Briggs, 2/Lt T.A. Doran.

MARTIN T.W. Lieutenant 22

Martin flew Bristol Fighters with 22 Squadron during the summer of 1918, claiming six victories.

	1918		Bristol					
1*	9 Jul	Alb. DV	D7896	22	N La Bassee	1100	DES	CR/RAF 9.7
2*	9 Jul	Alb. DV	D7896	22	W Steenwerck	1130	DES	CR/ORB/?
3**	10 Jul	Pfalz DIII	D7896	22	Lille	1000	OOC	CR/RAF 10.7
4***	21 Aug	Fokker DVII	C1040	22	N Cambrai	1945	OOC	CR/ORB/?
5*	27 Aug	Fokker DVII	----	22	Senlemont	1400	OOC	SR/ORB/?
6†	16 Sep	Fokker DVII	D8089	22	Quesnoy Wood	1530	DES	CR/RAF 16.9

TOTAL: 3 destroyed, 3 out of control = 6.
*Observer: Sgt J.H. Hall. **Observer: Capt D.E. Waight. ***Observer: Sgt G. Shannon. †Observer: Sgt M. Jones.

MASTERS Ernest Harold Lieutenant 45

Born in Coventry, Masters flew Sopwith Camels with 45 Squadron in France and Italy in 1918. He fought throughout the summer, claiming seven German and Austro-Hungarian machines and when the squadron returned to France late in the war, he claimed his eighth and last victory on 23 October. He was killed in a flying accident on 24 December 1918 in C54 due to an aerial collision. He had received the Croix de Guerre.

	1918		Camel						
1	13 May	Alb. DIII	B2379	45	Costa	0620	DES	CR/14	WS
2s*	13 May	LVG. C	B2379	45	Frison	0630	DES	CR/14	WS
3**	19 Jun	Alb. DV	D1974	45	Mt Meatta	0933	DES	ORB/14	WS
4**	19 Jun	Alb. DV	D1974	45	Asiago	0935	OOC	ORB/14	WS
5	14 Jul	D	D1974	45	Mt Cismon	0945	DES	ORB/14	WS
6	10 Aug	LVG. C	C54	45	Foclatti	0650	DES	CR/14	WS
7	20 Aug	C	C54	45	S Asiago	1910	DES	CR/14	WS
8	23 Oct	Rumpler C	F7212	45	Coincourt	1200	OOC	CR/ORB/?	

TOTAL: 5 and 1 shared destroyed, 2 out of control = 8.

*Shared with 2/Lt F.S. Bowles B2426. **In this combat 45 Sqn claimed a total of 6 destroyed and 1 out of control. Flik 9j lost 2 and 1 damaged. See C.E. Howell entry for details.

MAUD Charles Midgley Captain 66

Maud, a Yorkshireman from Leeds, served in the Royal Field Artillery from May 1915 to July 1917, when he transferred to the RFC. On 8 March 1918 he joined 66 Squadron, aged 21, and later became a flight commander. Flying in Italy, he claimed ten enemy machines between May and August. He was awarded the DFC on 2 September, and the French Croix de Guerre.

	1918		Camel					
1	1 May	Alb. DIII	B7283	66	S W Conegliano	1115	DES	ORB/SR/14 WS
2	2 May	LVG. C	B7283	66	S Oderzo	1105	DES	ORB/SR/14 WS
3	10 May	Alb. DV	B5623	66	S W Caldonazzo	1050	OOC	ORB/SR/14 WS
4	18 May	Alb. DIII	B5623	66	Centa Valley	1010	DES	ORB/SR/14 WS
5	20 May	Alb. DV	B5623	66	Alano di Piave	1825	OOC	ORB/SR/?
6	8 Jun	Alb. DIII	D9390	66	S St Stino di Livenza	1220	DES	ORB/SR/14 WS
7	10 Jul	LVG. C	D9408	66	S W Belluno	0840	DES	ORB/14 WS
8*	5 Aug	LVG. C	C46	66	W Forca, Feltre	0820	DES	ORB/14 WS
9	22 Aug	LVG. C	C46	66	Vittorio	1220	DES	ORB/14 WS
10	23 Aug	DFW. C	C46	66	Vidor	0645	DES	ORB/14 WS
11	7 Oct	Alb. DV	C46	66	Oderzo	c1030	OOC	ORB/14 WS

TOTAL: 8 destroyed, 3 out of control = 11.

*This was probably 369:37 of Flik 57.

MAUDUIT Ronald Frank Strickland Lieutenant 11

Born on 30 October 1894, Mauduit was commissioned in the 7th Dragoon Guards on 4 August 1914. Transferring to the RFC, he joined 11 Squadron on 3 June 1917, flying with various gunners. On 21 October he shot down one in flames and another out of control with the front gun, while a third was hit by the rear gun, manned by Corporal Mason, and seen to crash. Mauduit was awarded an MC.

	1917		Bristol					
1*	12 Jul	Alb. DV	----	11	Pelves	2015	OOC	CR/RFC 12.7
2*	20 Jul	Alb. DV	A7128	11	Novelles	1845	OOC	CR/RAF 20.7
3**	14 Aug	Alb. DV	A7124	11	Bresbieres	1315	OOC	CR/RFC 14.8
4***	10 Sep	Alb. DV	----	11	Dury	1830	OOC	CR/RFC 10.9
5†	17 Oct	Alb. DV	A7275	11	Sensee Canal-Cambrai	c1030	OOC	CR/RFC WD
6†	17 Oct	Alb. DV	A7275	11	Sensee Canal-Cambrai	c1030	OOC	CR/RFC WD
7††	21 Oct	Alb. DV	----	11	Boiry	1045	DES(F)	CR/RFC 21.10
8††	21 Oct	Alb. DV	----	11	Lecluse	1048	OOC	CR/RFC 21.10
9††	21 Oct	Alb. DV	----	11	Lecluse	1048	DES	CR/RFC 21.10

TOTAL: 2 destroyed, 7 out of control = 9.

*Observer: Lt E.R. Dibbs. **Observer: Pte J. Mason. ***Observer: Lt C.C. Dennis. †Observer: Lt L.H. McRobert. ††Observer: Cpl J. Mason.

MAUND Hugh Bingham Captain 10(N), 210, 204

Born on 30 May 1896 in Hampstead, London, Maund joined 6(N) Squadron in summer 1917, but when this unit was disbanded he was posted to 10(N) on 30 August as a Flight Sub Lieutenant, claiming two victories before the end of the year. In April 1918 the unit became 210 Squadron, RAF, and during May he claimed five aircraft and a share in a balloon to raise his score to eight before he was wounded on 28th of the month. In January 1919 he joined 204 Squadron, becoming Commanding Officer on 23rd.

	1917		Camel					
1	19 Sep	Alb. DV	B6211	10N	E Hooge	1000	OOC	CR/RFC 19.9
2s*	15 Nov	C	B6351	10N	W Dixmude	1300	OOC	CR/RFC 15.11
	1918							

3	11 May	Hannover C	D3354	210	Armentieres	1925	OOC	CR/ORB/?
4	16 May	Pfalz DIII	D3410	210	3m E Ypres	1945	OOC	CR/ORB/?
5	18 May	Pfalz DIII	D3410	210	Bac St Maur	2005	DES	CR/RAF 18.5
6	20 May	Pfalz DIII	D3410	210	E Estaires	1210	OOC	CR/ORB/?
7s**	21 May	Balloon	D3410	210	Ploegsteert Wood	1120	DES	CR/RAF 21.5
8	27 May	Pfalz DIII	D3410	210	Bailleul	0810	OOC	CR/ORB/?

TOTAL: 1 shared balloon, 1 destroyed, 5 and 1 shared out of control = 8.
*Shared with FSL A.M. Alexander B6341. **Shared with Lt H.A. Patey B7849, Lt G.B. Wootten B7227.

MAWLE Norman William Reginald Lieutenant 7, 84

Born on 27 February 1897 in Banbury, he transferred to the RFC from the London Regiment and was attached to 7 Squadron for five weeks. As a pilot he was posted to 84 Squadron in June 1918 flying SE 5As, claiming 12 victories including four kite balloons in a period of three weeks. He was awarded the DFC before being wounded during August. On 30 July he sent one Fokker spinning down, then caused two others to collide and crash. His last combat took place on 8 August when he carried out a strafing attack on two balloons being towed by horses. He set one balloon on fire, but was hit by ground fire and wounded in the stomach and arm. In later years he became a Group Captain.

	1918		SE 5A					
1	17 Jul	Balloon	D6917	84	Proyart	1035	DES	CR/RAF 17.7
2	20 Jul	Balloon	D6917	84	S W Proyart	0910	DES	CR/RAF 20.7
3	20 Jul	Fokker DVII	D6917	84	N E Morcourt	0915	DES	CR/RAF 20.7
4s*	24 Jul	Fokker DVII	C1868	84	Warfusee	1115	DES	CR/RAF 24.7
5s**	29 Jul	LVG. C	D6917	84	S E Proyart	0715	DES	CR/RAF 29.7
6	30 Jul	Fokker DVII	D6917	84	S Warvillers	1015	OOC	CR/RAF 30.7
7***	30 Jul	Fokker DVII	D6917	84	S Warvillers	1020	DES	CR/RAF 30.7
8***	30 Jul	Fokker DVII	D6917	84	S Warvillers	1020	DES	CR/RAF 30.7
9	4 Aug	Balloon	D6917	84	S E Proyart	0550	DES	CR/RAF 4.8
10	7 Aug	Fokker DVII	D6917	84	N E Le Quesnel	0850	OOC	CR/?
11	7 Aug	Fokker DVII	D6917	84	S E Villers Brettoneaux	0910	DES(F)	CR/RAF 7.8
12	8 Aug	Balloon	D6917	84	E Harbonnieres	1000	DES	CR/RAF 8.8

TOTAL: 4 balloons, 4 and 2 shared destroyed, 2 out of control = 12.
*Shared with Capt J.S. Ralston D6914. **Shared with Lt A.C. Lobley C8693. ***These two aircraft collided.

MAXTED William Henry 2nd Lieutenant 3

Born in Hemel Hempstead, Hertfordshire, on 2 July 1899, Maxted was commissioned in the RFC on 21 October 1917 and joined 3 Squadron on 16 August 1918, making his first claim on 16 September. Two more and a share in a balloon followed on 27th, his final score being five. He was killed in a flying accident on 17 December 1918, when his Camel, H809, broke up when diving at a ground target at Berck-sur-Mer.

	1918		Camel					
1	16 Sep	Fokker DVII	B7905	3	Bourlon Wood	1810	OOC	CR/WD/?
2	27 Sep	LVG. C	B7903	3	57 C L 27	0805	DES(F)	CR/RAF 27.9
3	27 Sep	LVG. C	B7905	3	57 C L 27	0805	DES	CR/WD/?
4s*	27 Sep	Balloon	B7905	3	57 B M 14	0820	DES	CR/RAF 27.9
5	1 Oct	Fokker DVII	B7905	3	57 B M 6	1610	OOC	CR/WD/?

TOTAL: 1 shared balloon, 2 destroyed, 2 out of control = 5.
*Shared with Lt G.R. Riley F2153.

MAXWELL Gerald Joseph Constable Major 56

Born in Inverness on 8 September 1895, and a nephew of Lord Lovat who had gained fame for his Scouts during the Boer War, Gerald Maxwell was commissioned on the outbreak of war and fought at Gallipoli. He then served in Egypt before returning to the United Kingdom, where he transferred to the RFC in September 1916. He went solo on 11 December after only 22 minutes dual instruction, and after advanced training at CFS, joined 56 Squadron which was forming on the first SE 5s at London Colney in March 1917, serving in Captain Albert Ball's 'A' Flight. Arriving in France in April, he shared a victory on his first patrol, but four days later was hit by anti-aircraft fire and crashed, fortunately unhurt. He was promoted to flight commander on 26 July, and by this time had eight victories. By 30 September he had claimed his 20th, and was awarded an MC on 18 October, being posted home three days later. He became an instructor at the School of Aerial Fighting at Turnberry, where he was soon requesting a 'refresher' course on operations, and after much trying he finally got back to 56 Squadron for a period of five weeks in the summer of 1918. Here he gained six more victories and was awarded a DFC. He left the RAF after the war with the rank of Major, and entered the Stock Exchange. During the 1930s he joined the Royal Auxilliary Air Force and was called up in World War II, becoming station commander at Ford. Ultimately he flew 167 different aircraft types including a Meteor jet fighter, and left the RAF finally with the rank of Wing Commander. He died on 18 December 1959. His younger brother, Michael, was to become an ace during the second war.

	1917		SE 5					
1s*	24 Apr	Alb. DII	A4863	56	Hamel	1515	OOC	CR/SR/TVA
2	4 May	Alb. DII	A8902	56	Souchy Lestree	1850-2000	OOC	CR/SR/TVA
3s**	11 May	Alb. DIII	A8902	56	Pont a Vendin	0600-0810	OOC	CR/RFC 11.5
4s***	12 May	Alb. DIII	A8902	56	E Lens	0845	OOC	CR/RFC 12.5
5s†	15 Jun	Alb. C	A8921	56	Fort Carnot	1315	DES	CR/RFC 15.6
			SE 5A					
6	20 Jul	Alb. DV	B502	56	Houthoulst Forest-Roulers	1915-1945	OOC	CR/RFC 20.7
7	20 Jul	Alb. DV	B502	56	Houthoulst Forest-Roulers	1915-1945	OOC	CR/RFC 20.7
8	26 Jul	C	B502	56	N E Ypres	1930-2030	OOC	CR/RFC 26.7
9s††	14 Aug	C	B502	56	E Westroosebeke	1730-1830	OOC	CR/RFC 14.8
10	18 Aug	Alb. DV	B502	56	Menin	0630-0710	OOC	CR/RFC 18.8
11s†††	18 Aug	Alb. DV	B502	56	Menin	0630-0710	OOC	CR/RFC 18.8
12	21 Aug	Alb. DV	B502	56	N Thorout	1830-1900	DES	CR/RFC 21.8
13	22 Aug	Alb. DV	B502	56	E Houthoulst Forest	0615-0715	DES	CR/RFC 22.8
14	22 Aug	Alb. DV	B502	56	E Houthoulst Forest	0615-0715	DES	CR/RFC 22.8
15	11 Sep	C	B527	56	E Houthoulst Forest	0700-0815	OOC	CR/RFC 11.9
16	20 Sep	C	B502	56	E Ypres	1115-1200	OOC	CR/RFC 20.9
17	21 Sep	C	B502	56	Verlinghem	0845-0900	DES	CR/RFC 21.9
18	29 Sep	Alb. DV	B2	56	Staden	1750-1810	DES	CR/RFC 29.9
19s‡	26 Sep	Alb. DV	B2	56	Staden	1750-1810	OOC	CR/RFC 29.9
20	30 Sep	Alb. DV	B502	56	Comines	1730-1800	OOC	CR/RFC 30.9
	1918							
21	16 Jun	C	B8402	56	Hamlincourt	0520	DES	CR/RAF 16.6
22	16 Jun	C	B8402	56	Wancourt	0730	DES	CR/RAF 16.6
23	27 Jun	Fokker DrI	D6126	56	Peronne	1945	OOC	CR/RAF 27.6
24	28 Jun	Fokker DVII	D6126	56	Dompierre	2010	DES	CR/RAF 28.6
25s‡‡	1 Jul	Fokker DrI	D6126	56	N E Albert	0540	DES	CR/RAF 1.7
26	5 Jul	Fokker DVII	D6126	56	Dompierre	2030	DES	CR/SR/TVA

TOTAL: 10 and 2 shared destroyed, 8 and 6 shared out of control = 26.
*Shared with Lt C.R.W. Knight A4855. **Shared with Lt C.A. Lewis A4853. ***Shared with Capt E.W. Broadberry A8903, Lt E.A. Lloyd. †Shared with Capt P.B. Prothero A8909. ††Shared with 2/Lt R.H. Sloley A4868. †††Shared with Lt J.S. Turnbull A8946, Lt D.S. Wilkinson B521, 2/Lt R.H. Sloley A4868, 2/Lt W.J. Potts B4857, Capt H.M. Rushworth B517. ‡Shared with Lt R.H. Sloley A8928, Lt H.A. Johnston B12, Lt C.H. Jeffs B524, Lt R.W. Young A8946, Lt R.J. Preston-Cobb B527. ‡‡Shared with Capt C.M. Crowe C1848.

MAXWELL Reginald Stuart Major 25, 20, 18, 54

Born on 20 July 1894, 'George' Maxwell as he was known, joined the RFC in 1915, flying home defence sorties with 17(Reserve) Squadron before joining 25 and then 20 Squadrons on FE 2Bs and Ds during the summer of 1916. He was promoted to flight commander while with the unit, and in December was posted to command 18 Squadron on FE 2Bs, remaining with this unit for three months. He was awarded an MC, gazetted on 1 January 1917. His second tour began about a year later, this time commanding 54 Squadron on Sopwith Camels. He claimed two victories with this unit early in 1918, and three more in the closing months of the war, being awarded a DFC which was gazetted on 8 February 1919. He remained in the RAF after the war, and served in the Middle East, in Iraq and Mesopotamia with 55 Squadron, receiving a Bar to his DFC on 28 October 1921 for operations here against the Turks. From 1925-27 he commanded 47 Squadron in Egypt, and in 1931 was promoted to Wing Commander. Five years later he became an Air Commodore and commanded RAF Mildenhall in England.

	1916		FE 2B					
1*	27 Apr	Aviatik C	----	25	Herlies	0700	FTL	SR/RFC 27.4
2**	21 Jul	Rumpler C	A13	20	W Lille	0945	OOC	CR/11 WS
3***	3 Aug	Roland CII	A23	20	Gheluwe	1010	DES	CR/RFC 3.8
4†	17 Sep	D	A29	20	Wervicq	1045	DES	CR/RFC 17.9
	1918		Camel					
5††	18 Jan	Alb. DV	B6403	54	Beaurevoir	0920	DES	CR/RFC 18.1
6	21 Apr	Alb. DV	D6587	54	Becelaere	0715	OOC	CR/?
7†††	19 Sep	DFW. CV	C3380	54	E Havrincourt Wood	1810	OOC	CR/?
8	1 Oct	DFW. CV	C8336	54	1200y W Abancourt	1715	DES	CR/RAF 1.10
9	9 Nov	Alb. C	C8836	54	Croisette	1435	DES	CR/RAF 9.11

TOTAL: 5 destroyed, 3 out of control, 1 forced to land = 9.
*Observer: 2/Lt S.A. Sharpe. **Observer: 2/Lt H.J. Hamilton. ***Observer: 1 AM D.A. Stewart. †Observer: 2 AM A. Stanley. ††54 made two claims: Flgr Reinsberg of Jasta 10 was killed. †††Probably Gefr Paul Milkowski/Lt Robert Muller of FAA 224, who were killed.

MAY Wilfred Reid Captain 209

Whatever doubt still exists as to who shot down Baron von Richthofen over the Somme Valley on the morning of 21 April 1918, one thing is not in doubt; Lieutenant 'Wop' May was almost Richthofen's 81st victim! Born in Edmonton, Alberta, Canada, on 20 March 1896, he served with the Canadian Infantry during 1915-16 before transferring to the RFC in 1917. Posted to 209 Squadron in April 1918, his flight commander proved to be his old school friend, Roy Brown. Surviving his first combat on that fateful 21 April, 'Wop' claimed his initial victory on 15 May and went on to claim 12 more. He was awarded the DFC and promoted to Captain in September. After the war he returned to Canada and in 1935 was chief test pilot for Canadian Airways; he also held the rank of Flight Lieutenant in the RCAF Reserve of Officers. He received the OBE in 1934 and died in 1952.

	1918		Camel					
1	15 May	Alb. DV	B6398	209	Belloy-Pozieres	1015	OOC	CR/?
2s*	16 May	Fokker DrI	----	209	Corbie	1615	CAPT	CR/RAF 16.5
3**	27 May	LVG. C	B6379	209	S Albert	1200	CAPT	CR/RAF 27.5
4	5 Jun	LVG. C	B6379	209	S E Villers Brettoneaux	0800	DES(F)	CR/RAF 5.6
5	1 Jul	Fokker DrI	B6379	209	E Albert	2020	DES(F)	CR/RAF 1.7
6s***	1 Aug	Fokker DVII	F5925	209	Bailleul	0945	DES	CR/RAF 1.8
7	12 Aug	Fokker DVII	F5944	209	W Proyart	0900	OOC	CR/?
8	25 Aug	Fokker DVII	D9594	209	Baissy	1430	DES	CR/RAF 25.8
9	27 Aug	Halb. C	D9594	209	Monchy	1305	DES	CR/RAF 27.8
10	27 Aug	Hannover C	D9594	209	E Remy	1310	DES	CR/RAF 27.8
11	15 Sep	Fokker DVII	D9594	209	E Epinoy	1715	DES	CR/RAF 15.9
12s†	20 Sep	Fokker DVII	D9594	209	Sauchy Lestree	1645	OOC	CR/?
13	21 Sep	Fokker DVII	D9594	209	Ecoust St Quentin	1835	OOC	CR/?

TOTAL: 1 and 1 shared captured, 6 and 1 shared destroyed, 3 and 1 shared out control = 13.
*Shared with Capt S.T. Edwards, Lt M.S. Taylor. Lt Hubner of Jasta 4 was captured. **This was the crew Vzfw Jodicke/Uffz Jakobs of Schl 1. ***Shared with Capt R.M. Foster C61. †Shared with Lt C. Knight F3233.

MAYBERY Richard Aveline Captain 56

Born in Brecon, Wales, in 1895, the only son of the late Major A. Maybery and Mrs Maybery, MBE, he served with the 21st Lancers before joining the RFC. He flew with 56 Squadron from June 1917, being awarded an MC and Bar, and becoming 'A' Flight commander on 19 November. He was killed in action exactly one month later during a fight over Bourlon Wood, shot down by VzFw Artur Weber of Jasta 5; Maybery was reported to have shot down his 21st enemy machine during this combat; a note dropped by a German airman a few days later confirmed his death. Extremely aggressive and rather headstrong, Maybery was considered one of the bravest pilots in the unit, his name being bracketed with those of Albert Ball and Rhys-Davids. However, like them he built up a sizeable score rapidly, but then died in combat.

	1917		SE 5A					
1	7 Jul	Alb. DV	A8934	56	Henin-Lietard	0830-0915	OOC	CR/RFC 7.7
2	12 Jul	Alb. DV	A8934	56	Dadizeele	2000-2030	DES	CR/RFC 12.7
3	16 Jul	Alb. DV	A8934	56	Polygon Wood	1815-1915	OOC	CR/RFC 16.7
4	23 Jul	Alb. DV	A8934	56	Moorslede	1945-2045	DES	CR/RFC 23.7
5	27 Jul	Alb. DIII	A8934	56	N E Roulers	1930-2045	OOC	CR/RFC 27.7
6	31 Jul	C	A8934	56	Welveghem	0445-0615	DES	CR/RFC 31.7
7	10 Aug	Alb. DIII	B502	56	S Roulers	1845-2015	DES	CR/RFC 10.8
8s*	10 Aug	Alb. DIII	B502	56	N Houthoulst Forest	1845-2015	DES	CR/RFC 10.8
9	22 Aug	Alb. DV	B4859	56	Clerkavenhoek	1845-1930	DES	CR/RFC 22.8
10s**	3 Sep	Alb. DV	B508	56	Houthem	1845-1915	DES	CR/RFC 3.9
11	5 Sep	Alb. DV	B508	56	Moorslede	1815-1915	DES	CR/RFC 5.9
12	10 Sep	Alb. DV	B508	56	S E Houthoulst Forest	1740-1845	DES	CR/RFC 10.9
13	10 Sep	Alb. DV	B508	56	Zonnebeke-Moorslede	1740-1845	OOC	CR/RFC 10.9
14	30 Sep	Pfalz DIII?	B528	56	W Roulers	1700-1800	DES	CR/RFC 30.9
15	2 Oct	Alb. DV	B542	56	Rollechemcapelle	1030-1145	DES	CR/RFC 2.10
16	28 Oct	Alb. DV	B511	56	Dadizeele	0830-0855	DES	CR/RFC 28.10
17	31 Oct	Alb. DV	B595	56	E Ledeghem	0855-1115	OOC	CR/RFC 31.10
18	31 Oct	Alb. DV	B595	56	S W Roulers	1445	DES	CR/9 W WD
19	30 Nov	Alb. DV	B501	56	Bourlon Wood	----	DES	CR/RFC 30.11
20	30 Nov	Alb. DV	B501	56	Bourlon Wood	----	DES	CR/RFC 30.11
21	19 Dec	Alb. DV	B506	56	Bourlon Wood	1250	DES(F)	CR/RFC 19.12

TOTAL: 14 and 2 shared destroyed, 5 out of control = 21.
*Shared with Lt V.P. Cronyn B504. **Shared with 2/Lt A.P.F. Rhys Davids B511.

MAYNARD Forster Herbert Martin Captain 1(N)

He joined the RN Division in England in 1914, and transferred to the RNAS the following year. After training, he became an instructor until 1916, when he flew with several Home Defence units before going to 1 Naval Squadron in January 1917. Here he claimed six victories, but in September was posted to the Aircraft Depot at Dunkirk. Later, in England he was injured in a crash, and then became CO of a training depot. He remained in the RAF after the war, commanding 12 Squadron from 1929-30. In 1940-41 he was AOC, Malta; he went on to become AOC Adminstration, Coastal Command until 1944, when he was appointed AOC, 19 Group. He retired as Air Vice-Marshal, CB, AFC, US Legion of Merit.

	1917		Triplane					
1	29 Apr	Alb. DIII	N5427	1N	Fresnoy	1900	OOC	CR/RFC 30.4
2	14 Jun	Alb. DIII	N5479	1N	N E Ypres	2056	DES(F)	CR/RFC 14.6
3s*	13 Jul	C	N5479	1N	E Warneton	1025	DES	CR/ORB/DL
4s**	17 Jul	Alb. DV	N5479	1N	4m E Messines	1805	OOC	CR/ORB/11 WS
5	9 Aug	Alb. DV	N6301	1N	Moorslede	0740	OOC	ORB/RFC 9.8
6	10 Aug	Alb. DV	N534	1N	Comines	0740	OOC	CR/RFC 10.8

TOTAL: 1 and 1 shared destroyed, 3 and 1 shared out of control = 6.
*Shared with FSL A.G.A. Spence N5454, FSL H.V. Rowley N6308. **Shared with FSL E. Anthony N6296, FSL C.B. Ridley N6304, FSL H.V. Rowley N5373, FSL C.G. Brock N5485, FSL G.B.G. Scott N5455, FSL H.L. Everitt N6306, FSL A.G.A. Spence N6300.

McCALL Frederick Robert Gordon Captain 13, 41

Born in Vernon, British Columbia, on 4 December 1896, McCall was to become another outstanding Canadian fighter pilot. Initially he joined the 175th Battalion of the Alberta Regiment in February 1916 and in eight months had become a Sergeant, when the unit was posted to the United Kingdom. He was then commissioned, and in March 1917 transferred to the RFC. He was posted to France the following December to join 13 Squadron, flying RE 8s, and teamed up with Lieutenant F.C. Farrington, quickly showing that even on these reconnaissance machines he was a most aggressive pilot. In January 1918 he and Farrington claimed an enemy scout shot down, and on 4 March he received an MC. He claimed a further two victories before 15 April, when he was awarded a Bar to his decoration, and went on leave. Two weeks later he joined 41 Squadron to fly SE 5As, and by 1 June had claimed three more aircraft, receiving a DFC. 14 more victories followed in June, including five in one day and four in another; he claimed a further eight in July. He was awarded a DSO after his 24th victory, his score continuing to mount through the first half of August. On 17th he and fellow Canadian ace and squadron-mate, W.G. Claxton, were involved in a fight with a large number of German scouts, Claxton being shot down. The reports in some accounts published post war that each pilot had claimed three victories during this engagement are not accurate, and cannot be verified. Immediately after this combat, McCall was taken ill, and was sent back to England. He returned to Canada on sick leave, and was there when the war ended. He then left the RAF, and established an air transport business in his home country. McCall died on 2 January 1949.

	1918		RE 8					
1*	6 Jan	Alb. DV	B6523	13	Jigsaw Wood	1340	DES	CR/RFC 6.1
2**	6 Mar	Alb. DV	B6365	13	Monchy le Preux	1115	OOC	CR/RFC 6.3
3***	27 Mar	Rumpler C	B5090	13	S Tilloy	1330	DES	CR/RFC 27.3
			SE 5A					
4	25 May	C	D3927	41	S Estaires	1415	OOC	CR/SR/?
5†	29 May	DFW. C	D3927	41	Estaires-La Gorgue	1305	DES(F)	CR/RAF 29.5
6	30 May	C	D3927	41	Beaucamp	1320	OOC	CR/SR/?
7	9 Jun	DFW. C	D5959	41	Mezieres	0625	DES	CR/RAF 9.6
8s††	13 Jun	DFW. C	D3927	41	Orvillers	1035	DES	CR/RAF 13.6
9	16 Jun	Fokker DVII	D3927	41	S W Combles	2000	DES	CR/RAF 16.6
10	27 Jun	Halb. C	D3927	41	Goyencourt	2015	DES	CR/RAF 27.6
11	27 Jun	Pfalz DIII	D3927	41	Bray	2040	OOC	CR/SR/?
12s†††	28 Jun	Rumpler C	D3927	41	Belloy en Santerre	1150	DES	CR/RAF 28.6
13	28 Jun	Halb. C	D3927	41	Bray-Peronne	2010	DES	CR/RAF 28.6
14	28 Jun	Pfalz DIII	D3927	41	Bray-Peronne	2010	OOC	CR/SR/RAF WD
15	28 Jun	Alb. DV	D3927	41	Bray-Peronne	2010	OOC	CR/SR/RAF WD
16	30 Jun	Alb. DV	D3927	41	Bray	0815	DES(F)	CR/RAF 30.6
17	30 Jun	Alb. DV	D3927	41	Cappy	0820	DES	CR/RAF 30.6
18	30 Jun	Alb. DV	D3927	41	Caix	0845	DES	CR/RAF 30.6
19	30 Jun	Fokker DVII	D3927	41	W Roye	0940	OOC	CR/SR/RAF WD
20	30 Jun	Alb. DV	D3927	41	E Albert	1745	OOC	CR/SR/?
21	1 Jul	Alb. DV	D3927	41	E Lamotte	1920	OOC	CR/SR/?
22	3 Jul	Fokker DVII	D3927	41	E Bayonvillers	1915	DES	CR/RAF 3.7

23	3 Jul	Fokker DVII	D3927	41	N Bayonvillers	1910	DES(F)	CR/RAF 3.7
24s‡	4 Jul	Fokker DVII	D6154	41	Proyart	1330	OOC	CR/SR/?
25s‡	4 Jul	Fokker DVII	D6154	41	Proyart	1330	OOC	CR/SR/?
26s‡‡	7 Jul	Alb. C	D6877	41	W Montdidier	1215	OOC	CR/SR/?
27s‡‡‡	30 Jul	Alb. C	E1289	41	Guillaucourt	1200	DES	CR/RAF 30.7
28s‡‡‡	31 Jul	Alb. C	E1289	41	Pozieres	1210	DES	CR/RAF 31.7
29	1 Aug	Alb. C	E1289	41	Contalmaison	0900	OOC	CR/SR/RAF WD
30	9 Aug	Fokker DVII	F3966	41	N Bray	1815	DES	CR/SR/RAF WD
31	9 Aug	Fokker DVII	F3966	41	Carnoy-Suzanne	1830	DES(F)	CR/RAF 9.8
32§	11 Aug	Fokker DVII	E4018	41	Estrees	0830	DES	CR/RAF 11.8
33	12 Aug	Fokker DVII	E4018	41	N Bayonvillers	0915	CAPT	CR/RAF 12.8
34	12 Aug	Fokker DVII	E4018	41	N E Foucaucourt	0925	DES	CR/SR/?
35	17 Aug	LVG. C	E4018	41	Outtersteene	0920	OOC	CR/SR/?

TOTAL: 1 captured, 16 and 4 shared destroyed, 11 and 3 shared out of control = 35.

*Obsever: 2/Lt F.C. Farrington. **Observer: 2/Lt F.C. Farrington. Possibly Lt R. Schonger of Jasta 23 who was wounded. ***Observer: Lt B.S.B. Andrews. †The crew Uffz H. Tatarka/Lt F. Gesell of FA 7, were killed. ††Shared with Lt J.S. Turnbull D3955. †††Shared with Lt E.J. Stephens D5961. ‡Shared with Lt E.F.H. Davis D6023. ‡‡Shared with Lt W.J. Gillespie C1895. ‡‡‡Shared with Lt W.G. Claxton E1309. §This was Offstvtr Blumenthal of Jasta 53, who was captured. Blumenthal confirmed the report for McCall.

McCALL Malcolm Lieutenant 20

Lieutenant McCall served with 20 Squadron in 1917, claiming his first victory on 6 July. He was shot down in his FE 2D (A1865) on 21 July, and was wounded, his observer, Lieutenant Mauduit, being killed. He returned to the unit in the late summer of 1918, now flying Bristol Fighters, and claimed five victories during September. All were Fokker DVIIs, and in fact all were credited to the rear gun, manned by Lieutenant C.G. Boothroyd.

	1917		FE 2D					
1*	6 Jul	Alb. DV	A6498	20	Comines	1830	DES(F)	CR/RFC 6.7
	1918		Bristol					
2**	20 Sep	Fokker DVII	D7915	20	E Longchamps	1020	DES	CR/RAF 20.9
3**	20 Sep	Fokker DVII	D7915	20	N Longchamps	1025	OOC	CR/ORB/SR/?
4**	25 Sep	Fokker DVII	E2568	20	Estrees	1830	DES(F)	CR/RAF 25.9
5**	27 Sep	Fokker DVII	E2470	20	W Bernot	1030	DES	CR/RAF 27.9
6**	29 Sep	Fokker DVII	E2470	20	Lehancourt	1030	DES	CR/ORB/SR/?

TOTAL: 5 destroyed, 1 out of control = 6.

*Observer: Lt M.W. Waddington. **Observer: Lt C.G. Boothroyd.

McCLINTOCK Ronald St Clair Major 2, 64, 3

Born on 13 July 1898, he served initially with the West Lancashire Brigade of the Royal Field Artillery as a 2nd Lieutenant, later joining the RFC. He then flew as an observer with 2 Squadron from December 1915, before becoming a pilot. In July 1917 he was posted as a flight commander to 64 Squadron, flying DH 5s and SE 5As, and in April was awarded an MC. When he left the squadron that same month to take command of 3 Squadron, he had flown over 40 offensive patrols and claimed five victories.

	1918		SE 5A					
1	10 Mar	LVG. C	C9603	64	Marquion	1350	OOC	CR/RFC 10.3
2	23 Mar	Pfalz DIII	C9603	64	Pronville	1440	DES	CR/RFC 23.3
3	23 Mar	Alb. DV	C9603	64	Biache	1515	DES	CR/RFC 23.3
4	24 Mar	C	C9603	64	Le Transloy	1835	DES	CR/RFC 24.3
5	2 Apr	Alb. DV	B124	64	Fricourt	1810	DES	CR/RAF 2.4

Total: 4 destroyed, 1 out of control = 5.

McCLOUGHRY Edgar James Kingston Captain 23, 4 AFC

An Australian from Adelaide, McCloughry was born on 10 September 1896 and was a student when war broke out in 1914. He joined the Australian Engineers, but transferred to the flying service in December 1916, serving initially with 23 Squadron on Spads. Injured in a flying accident, he was hospitalized in England, becoming an instructor on recovery. He was then posted as a flight commander to 4 AFC Squadron which was in France under the command of his brother Wilfred, equipped with Camels. On 12 June he claimed a balloon and a Pfalz Scout shot down, while on 1 July he was attacked by two Pfalz which collided during the chase; one crashed and he shot down the second in flames. By mid July he had claimed nine with the squadron, and was awarded a DFC which was gazetted on 21 September, together with a Bar, awarded late in July. He was then awarded a DSO, gazetted on 3 December. Meanwhile on 24 September he claimed a DFW and a Fokker DVII, following which he bombed and strafed a train, but was hit by return fire and wounded in the thigh. He returned to base and was taken to hospital, not being able to fly again before the Armistice. So far as can definitely be ascertained, his final score appears to be 21, although fellow pilots considered that some of his claims were "over-enthusiastic". He served in the RAF after the war, attending the Staff College at Camberley as a Squadron Leader in 1936, then commanding 4 (Army Co-operation) Squadron. He held various senior staff positions during World War II, and in 1947 was appointed Air Vice-Marshal. He retired from the air force in 1953 and died on 15 November 1972, having written five books on aerial strategy.

	1918		Camel					
1	12 Jun	Balloon	D1961	4AFC	N E Estaires	1150	DES	CR/RAF 12.6
2*	12 Jun	Pfalz DIII	D1961	4AFC	N Estaires	1200	DES	CR/RAF 12.6
3	18 Jun	Fokker DrI	D1961	4AFC	Neuve-Chapelle Laventie	1040	DES	CR/RAF 18.6
4	27 Jun	LVG. C	D1961	4AFC	W Sailly sur la Lys	1620	DES	CR/RAF 27.6
5	28 Jun	Fokker DVII	D1961	4AFC	Merville	1612	OOC	CR/ORB/?
6**	1 Jul	Pfalz DIII	D1961	4AFC	S Neuve Chapelle	1645	DES	CR/RAF 1.7
7**	1 Jul	Pfalz DIII	D1961	4AFC	S Estaires	1645	DES	CR/RAF 1.7
8	11 Jul	Rumpler C	D1961	4AFC	S E Estaires	0415	DES	CR/RAF 11.7
9	11 Jul	Pfalz DIII	D1961	4AFC	N Estaires	0420	DES	CR/RAF 11.7
10	13 Jul	Alb. C	D1961	4AFC	W Merville	2115	DES	CR/RAF 13.7
11	16 Jul	Balloon	D1961	4AFC	Bac St Maur	0409	DES	CR/RAF 16.7
12	19 Jul	Pfalz DIII	D1961	4AFC	Erquinghem	0405	DES(F)	CR/RAF 19.7
13	22 Jul	Fokker DVII	D1961	4AFC	E Sailly	0540	DES	CR/RAF 22.7
14	24 Jul	Rumpler C	D1961	4AFC	Pont Ricquen	2055	DES	CR/RAF 24.7
15	28 Jul	Balloon	D1961	4AFC	S E La Gorque	0420	DES	CR/RAF 28.7
16	31 Jul	LVG. C	D1961	4AFC	Wavrin	0920	DES	CR/RAF 31.7
17	31 Jul	Fokker DVII	D1961	4AFC	E Estaires	2035	DES	CR/RAF 31.7
18	4 Sep	Balloon	E7160	4AFC	Erquinghem	0555	DES	CR/RAF 4.9
19	6 Sep	LVG. C	E7160	4AFC	N Don	1845	OOC	CR/ORB/?
20	24 Sep	DFW. C	E7160	4AFC	E Lille	0625	DES	CR/RAF 24.9
21	24 Sep	Fokker DVII	E7160	4AFC	Lille	0635	DES	CR/RAF 24.9

TOTAL: 4 balloons, 16 destroyed, 1 out of control = 21.
*This was Lt Helten, of Jasta 20, who was killed. **These two aircraft collided.

McCONNELL Roy Kirkwood Lieutenant 46

Lieutenant McConnell, a Canadian, was born on 19 December 1898 and joined the RFC in May 1917. He was posted to 46 Squadron on 13 October of that year, and claimed his first victory on 23 March 1918. By mid-September he had accounted for three more aircraft individually and shared in three other victories, but on 16th was posted to Home Establishment. The award of a DFC was announced on 28 September.

	1918		Camel					
1	23 Mar	Alb. DV	C1572	46	Morchies	1410	OOC	CR/RFC 23.3
2s*	2 Apr	C	----	46	Courcelles	1245	DES	CR/RAF 2.4
3s**	4 May	Alb. DV	C1643	46	N Bullecourt	1800	OOC	CR/RAF 4.5
4s***	8 Jul	Fokker DVII	D9407	46	Fromelles	0530	OOC	CR/?
5s†	1 Aug	C	D6693	46	Armentieres	1200	DES	CR/80 W
6	3 Aug	Fokker DVII	D9411	46	E Lens	1835	DES	CR/RAF 3.8
7	8 Sep	Rumpler C	D6693	46	S Peronne	0700	DES(F)	CR/RAF 8.9

TOTAL: 2 and 2 shared destroyed, 1 and 2 shared out of control = 7.
*Shared with Capt S.P. Smith, Lt A.G. Vlasto, Lt H.G.W. Debenham, 2/Lt D.R. MacLaren. **Shared with Capt D.R. MacLaren B9153, Lt H.L.M. Dodson C1637. ***Shared with Capt D.R. MacLaren D6418. †Shared with Capt D.R. MacLaren D6603, Major A.H. O'Hara-Wood F5950, Lt L.S. Skerrington B5247.

McCUDDEN John Anthony Lieutenant 25, 84

Brother of James McCudden,VC, John was born on 14 June 1897 and joined the Royal Engineers in 1912. He went to France in May 1916 as a dispatch rider, then transferred to the RFC in August. After pilot training he joined 25 Squadron, flying DH 4 bombers with this unit in September 1917. He was credited with two victories, one with his front gun, the other claimed by his gunner, and he carried out many sorties. In 1918 he converted to single-seaters, going to 84 Squadron flying SE 5As with the rank of 2nd Lieutenant. With this unit he claimed six more enemy machines, receiving the MC. He lived under the shadow of his elder, successful, brother, who he tried to emulate. Probably because of this he became far too impetuous and aggressive to live long in combat. On 18 March he got into a fight with a patrol from the Richthofen Circus (JG I), and was shot down and killed by Leutnant Hans Wolff of Jasta 11. He was buried at St Souplet next day.

	1917		DH 4					
1*	27 Oct	Alb. DV	A7487	25	Roulers	0950	OOC	CR/RFC 27.10
2**	26 Nov	Alb. C	A7535	25	Denain-Neuville	1230	OOC	CR/SR/9 WS
	1918		SE 5A					

3	30 Jan	Alb. DV	C5310	84	Villers Outreaux	1145	OOC	CR/RFC 30.1
4s***	15 Feb	Rumpler C	C5310	84	Mont St Martin	1545	OOC	CR/?
5	16 Feb	Rumpler C	C5310	84	St Quentin	0940	DES	CR/RFC 16.2
6†	17 Feb	Fokker DrI	C5310	84	7-8m N E St Quentin	1115	DES	CR/RFC 17.2
7	19 Feb	Alb. DV	C5310	84	N La Fere	1015	DES	CR/RFC 19.2
8s††	19 Feb	Alb. DV	C5310	84	St Gobain Wood	1020	OOC	CR/RFC 19.2

TOTAL: 3 destroyed, 3 and 2 shared out of control = 8.

*Observer: AM J. Harris. **Observer: 2/Lt C. Critchley. ***Shared with Lt A.W. Beauchamp Proctor B539. †This was Lt F. Lubbert of Jasta 11, who was wounded. ††Shared with 2/Lt J.F. Larson.

McCUDDEN James Thomas Byford Major 3, 20, 29, 66, 56

Born in Gillingham, Kent, on 28 March 1895, one of six children, three of whom were to fly with the RFC. He joined the Royal Engineers as a bugler in 1910 and transferred to the RFC as a mechanic in 1913. In August 1914 he went to France with 3 Squadron and flew occasionally as an observer, receiving the MM and Croix de Guerre. In January 1916 he returned to England, learned to fly and was posted to 20 Squadron in July, flying FE 2s. The next month he went to 29 Squadron which flew DH 2s, and with this unit he was credited with five victories plus another unconfirmed, for which he received the MC. After a period of instructing, he joined 66 Squadron on attachment for a fighting instructors' course. He was loaned an SE 5 on 21 July by Major Blomfield, CO of 56 Squadron, accompanying a patrol during which he got into a fight with an Albatros Scout and drove it down. Five days later, flying a Pup of 66 Squadron, he gained a similar success; both of these are included in his score. He then went to 56 Squadron as a flight commander, where he was to become a most proficient and highly-regarded officer. Described by Geoffrey Bowman as 'a shooting genius', McCudden was one of the first RFC pilots to employ a scientific approach to his task, which he studied assiduously. He took great pains over the alignment of his guns and their sights. By the end of the year his total had risen to 37, of which no less than 27 were two-seaters, 15 of which crashed in Allied lines. He started 1918 by gaining four more such successes, bringing his score to 57 on 26 February. Of these, 21 had fallen in Allied lines. The vast majority of his claims are confirmed from German records. He was awarded the VC, DSO and Bar, and a Bar to his MC. One of his SE 5As (B4891) became a top-scoring RFC machine, accounting for 34 victims, 31 by McCudden and three by Captain C.M. Crowe, before it was damaged in a crash on 21 March 1918.

Leaving 56 Squadron in March, McCudden returned to Britain where in April he became an instructor at Ayr. He remained in this role until July when he was given command of 60 Squadron. It was while flying to take over this new post that he crashed and was killed. Taking off from Auxi-le-Chateau, he appeared to stall during a steep turn, probably as a result of the engine choking due to an incorrect carburetter being fitted, and dived into the ground. He was taken to a casualty clearing station, but died that evening and was buried at Wavans. His book, *Five Years in the RFC*, which had just been finished, became a classic in the aviation field. A splendid biography, *McCudden VC*, was written by Christopher Cole and was published in the 1960s, while another, *James McCudden VC*, by Alex Revell, was published in 1987.

	1916		DH 2					
1	6 Sep	C	5985	29	Houthem-Gheluwe	1315	DES	CR/RFC 6.9
	1917							
2	26 Jan	C	7858	29	Ficheaux	1005	DES	CR/RFC 26.1
3s*	2 Feb	C	7858	29	S E Adinfer Wood	1450	DES	CR/RFC 2.2
4	6 Feb	Alb. CIII	7858	29	Adinfer Wood	1400	DES	CR/RFC 6.2
5	15 Feb	Roland CII	6002	29	Monchy	1200	DES	CR/RFC 15.2
6**	21 Jul	Alb. DV	A8946	56	Polygon Wood	1930-2030	OOC	ORB/?
7**	26 Jul	Alb. DV	B1756	66	Gheluwe	2015	OOC	ORB/?
			SE 5A					
8	18 Aug	Alb. DV	B519	56	E Houthem	0630-0730	OOC	CR/RFC 18.8
9	19 Aug	Alb. DV	B519	56	Gheluvelt	1630-1730	OOC	CR/RFC 19.8
10***	20 Aug	Alb. DV	B519	56	S E Polygon Wood	1850	DES(F)	CR/RFC 20.8
11	20 Aug	Alb. DV	B519	56	Polygon Wood	c1900	OOC	CR/RFC 20.8
—†	14 Sep	Alb. DV	B4865	56	Roulers	1800	DD	CR/AR/CC/?
12	19 Sep	Rumpler C	B4863	56	Redinghem	1215	DES	CR/RFC 19.9
—††	21 Sep	C	B4863	56	Gheluwe	1300	DD	CR/AR/CC/?
13†††	23 Sep	DFW. CV	B4863	56	N E Houthem	1800-1830	DES	CR/RFC 23.9
14‡	27 Sep	LVG. CV	B4863	56	S W Langemarck	1555-1750	CAPT	CR/RFC 27.9
15‡‡	28 Sep	Alb. DV	B4863	56	S Houthoulst Forest	0800	DES	CR/RFC 28.9
—‡‡‡	1 Oct	Rumpler C	B4863	56	Herlies	1450	OOC	CR/SR/AR/CC/?
16s§	1 Oct	Alb. DV	B4863	56	Westroosebeke	1750	OOC	CR/RFC 1.10
17§§	17 Oct	LVG. CV	B4863	56	S Vlammertinghe	1025	CAPT	CR/RFC 17.10
18§§§	21 Oct	Rumpler C	B4863	56	Marzingarbe	c1300	CAPT	CR/RFC 21.10
19	18 Nov	DFW. CV	B35	56	Bellicourt	0940	DES	CR/RFC 18.11
20#	23 Nov	Alb. DV	B35	56	1m E Noyelles	1200	DES	CR/RFC 23.11

21[##]	29 Nov	DFW. CV	B35	56	S Bellicourt	0730	DES	CR/RFC 29.11
22[###]	29 Nov	DFW. CV	B35	56	Rouvroy	1315	DES	CR/RFC 29.11
23[¶]	30 Nov	LVG. CV	B35	56	S E Havrincourt	1115	CAPT	CR/RFC 30.11
24[¶¶]	5 Dec	Rumpler C	B4891	56	Hermies	1240	CAPT	CR/RFC 5.12
25[¶¶¶]	6 Dec	Rumpler C	B35	56	N W St Quentin	1025	DES	CR/RFC 6.12
26	6 Dec	Alb. DV	B4891	56	Fontaine	1500	OOC	CR/SR/AR/?
27	15 Dec	Rumpler C	B4891	56	E Bois de Vaucelles	1105	DES	CR/RFC 15.12
28[○]	22 Dec	DFW. CV	B4891	56	S W St Quentin	1205	DES	CR/RFC 22.12
29	23 Dec	LVG. C	B4891	56	Anguilcourt	1125	DES	CR/RFC 23.12
30[○○]	23 Dec	Rumpler C	B4891	56	Contescourt	1220	CAPT	CR/RFC 23.12
31[○○○]	23 Dec	Rumpler C	B4891	56	Gouzeaucourt	1440	CAPT	CR/RFC 23.12
32[●]	23 Dec	LVG. CV	B4891	56	Metz-en-Couture	1530	CAPT	CR/RFC 23.12
33[●●]	28 Dec	Rumpler C	B4891	56	Velu Wood	1215	CAPT	CR/RFC 28.12
34[●●●]	28 Dec	Rumpler C	B4891	56	Flers	1230	CAPT	CR/RFC 28.12
35[☆]	28 Dec	LVG. C	B4891	56	Havrincourt Wood	1255	CAPT	CR/RFC 28.12
36[☆☆]	29 Dec	LVG. C	B4891	56	Havrincourt	0855	CAPT	CR/RFC 29.12
37[☆☆☆]	29 Dec	LVG. C	B4891	56	N E Epehy	1400	CAPT	CR/RFC 29.12
	1918							
38	9 Jan	LVG. C	B4891	56	Graincourt	1130	CAPT	CR/RFC 9.1
39[★]	13 Jan	LVG. C	B4891	56	E of Le Haucourt	0940	CAPT	CR/RFC 13.1
40[★★]	13 Jan	DFW. CV	B4891	56	N Vendhuile	0950	CAPT	CR/RFC 13.1
41[★★★]	13 Jan	LVG. C	B4891	56	Lempire	1005	CAPT	CR/RFC 13.1
42[◇]	20 Jan	LVG. C	B35	56	N W Cambrai	1030	DES	CR/RFC 20.1
43[◇◇]	24 Jan	DFW. C	B4891	56	Vitry	1355	DES	CR/RFC 24.1
44	25 Jan	Rumpler C	B4891	56	Itancourt	1445	DES	CR/RFC 25.1
45[◇◇◇]	30 Jan	Alb. DV	B4891	56	Anneux	1115	OOC	CR/RFC 30.1
46	30 Jan	Pfalz DIII	B4891	56	Anneux	1115	OOC	CR/RFC 30.1
47[◆]	2 Feb	LVG. CV	B4891	56	E Velu	1040	CAPT	CR/RFC 2.2
48	16 Feb	Rumpler C	B4891	56	S W Caudry	1035	DES	CR/RFC 16.2
49[◆◆]	16 Feb	DFW. CV	B4891	56	N E Le Catelet	1045	DES	CR/RFC 16.2
50	16 Feb	Rumpler C	B4891	56	Hargicourt	1110	DES	CR/RFC 16.2
51[◆◆◆]	16 Feb	Rumpler C	B4891	56	Lagnicourt	1230	CAPT	CR/RFC 16.2
52[□]	17 Feb	LVG. CV	B4891	56	Guemappe	1025	OOC	CR/RFC 17.2
53[□□]	18 Feb	Alb. DV	B4891	56	Vitry	0940	DES	CR/RFC 18.2
54[□□□]	18 Feb	Alb. DV	B4891	56	Quiery la Motte	0945	DES	CR/RFC 18.2
55[■]	21 Feb	DFW. CV	B4891	56	S Maricourt	1347	DES	CR/RFC 21.2
56[■■]	26 Feb	Rumpler C	B4891	56	Oppy	1120	DES	CR/RFC 26.2
57[■■■]	26 Feb	Hannover C	B4891	56	Cherisy	1130	DES	CR/RFC 26.2

TOTAL: 19 captured, 27 and 1 shared destroyed, 8 and 2 shared out of control = 57.

*Shared with Major A.W. Gratten-Bellew. **McCudden claimed the above two victories in a list of his claims that he prepared and signed at the end of December 1917. He said they were confirmed by Lt A.P.F. Rhys-Davids and Major G.L.P. Henderson the C.O. of 66 Squadron, respectively. Neither appear to have been accepted by higher authority and were only credited as driven down. ***This was Vzfw Josef Oehler of Jasta 24, who was killed. †This was claimed, and allowed by the ORB, Wing and Brigade as driven down. McCudden's list does not mention this claim. It may have been confirmed late. Otherwise, the unit total will not add up to 200 on 30 Sep. If so then McCudden's claim on 21 July can be discounted, as if it was included the until total will not add up to the 100 when it should. Oblt Weigand of Jasta 10, was forced to land slightly wounded. ††This aircraft is also often credited to McCudden. It was also disallowed and does not appear in the communique. If it was counted as well as the 14 September claim, then 56 Squadrons score will not add up to 200 when it should on 30 September. †††This was the crew Uffz Rudolf Francke/Lt Gustav Rudoplh of FA 6, who were killed. ‡This was the crew Uffz Hans Gossler/Uffz Bruno Wiedemann of Schstfl 27, who were killed. ‡‡Lt Gunther Pastor of Jasta 29, was killed. ‡‡‡This claim was apparently a late confirmation, being included in the Squadron Victory log, although marked indecisive on the combat report. It is not in McCudden's own listing. §Shared with Lt L.M. Barlow B511, Lt A.P.F. Rhys-Davids B525, Lt M.H. Coote B1, Lt D.J. Reason A8961. §§The crew of Flgr Horstmann/Oblt Ernst Hadrich of FA 8 were killed. §§§This was the crew Uffz Richard Hiltweis/Lt Hans Laitlo of FA 5, who were killed. #Probably Vzfw Karl Bey of Jasta 5, who was killed. ##The crew of Lt Kurt Dittrich/Lt Manfred Hoettger of FAA 202 were killed. ###This was the crew Lt Georg Deitrich/Lt Dietrich Schenk of FA 268. ¶The crew Vzfw Flohrig, who died of wounds, and Gefr Eckerle, who was captured, were from FA 19. ¶¶The crew were Lt Fritz Pauly/Lt Ernst Sauter of FA 45. ¶¶¶This was the crew Uffz Karl Pohlisch/Lt Martin Becker of FA 255. ○This was Uffz Anton Bode, apparently alone, of Schstfl 5, who was killed. ○○This was the crew Lt Otto Horing/Lt Emil Tibussek of FA 23, who were killed. ○○○The crew, names unknown, from Bogohl 7, were captured. ●The crew of Vzfw Kurt Boje/Vzfw Friedrich Neimann of Schstfl 12 were killed. ●●This was the crew Uffz Munz/Lt Rucker of FA 7, who were killed. ●●●This was Uffz Oskar Guntert/Lt Hans Mittag, a crew of FAA 40, who were killed. ☆This was the crew Lt Albert Weinrich/Lt Walter Bergmann of FAA 210, who were killed. ☆☆The pilot Vzfw Gershel died of wounds, the observer Uffz Lehnert was captured. They were from Schstfl 10. ☆☆☆This was Lt Walter Dern/Lt Georg Muller of FA 33. ★The pilot Notler was killed. The obsever Max Pappenheimer landed the aeroplane, from FAA 264. ★★This was the crew Vzfw Hans Rautenberg/Lt Gerhard Besser of Bogohl 7, who were killed. ★★★Possibly Lt M. Rittermann, reported killed at Gonnelieu. ◇Probably Uffz Gustav Mosch/

Lt Friedrich Bracksiek of FAA 202, who were killed. ◇◇Probably Lt Pallocks, of FAA 240, who died of wounds. ◇◇◇This was Vzfw Adam Barth of Jasta 10, who was killed.◆This was the crew Vzfw Erich Szafranek/Lt Werner Kuczowski of Bogohl 7, who were killed. ◆◆This was Uffz Max Hanicke/Lt F. Dasterbieck, unit unknown, who were killed. ◆◆◆This was the crew Gefr Heinrich Lechleiter/Vzfw Lorenz Zeuch of Schstfl 29, who were killed. □Possibly Uffz Josef Klanke/Lt Otto Jablonski of FAA 263. □□This was Uffz Julius Kaiser of Jasta 35 who was killed. □□□This was Uffz von Stein of Jasta 35, who was wounded. ■This was the crew Vzfw Erich Klingenberg/Lt Karl Heger of FAA 235, who were killed. ■■This was the crew Vzfw Otto Kresse/Lt Rudolf Binting of FA 7, who were killed. ■■■This was the crew Uffz Max Schwaier/Lt Walter Jager of FA 293.
NB: Study the comments on McCullen's claims above. His list, contained in AIR I/479/15/312/240, was prepared in response to the Brigade Commander wishing to know his score. It includes a claim on 23 January 1917 with 29 Squadron. With the above complications there is no doubt that McCudden's confirmed claims totalled at least 55. As can be seen most can be verified. Indeed, the Nachrichtenblatt, the German equivalent of the communiques, translated his book *Flying Fury* and confirmed that on 16th February 1918 he got three destroyed and one forced to land!

McDONALD Ian Donald Roy Captain 39, 24

The son of Donald McDonald, a member of the Legislative Council of the Leeward Islands, Ian joined the RFC, becoming a scout pilot in 1916. After a period with 39(Home Defence) Squadron, he went to France on 11 July 1917, being posted to 'A' Flight of 24 Squadron, flying DH 5s. He claimed three victories on the DH 5, but when SE 5As re-equipped the unit, he achieved more success, taking command of the Flight in March. He was awarded an MC early in 1918. Before he left the squadron in June, he had brought his total victories to 20 and received the DFC. McDonald's last combat was with Leutnant Kurt Wusthoff, when he and two other pilots were credited with shooting down the German inside Allied lines. He was rested from 21 June. After the war he returned to Antigua, but could not settle and so returned to the RAF, becoming an instructor at Cranwell. In 1920 he went out to fly in Mesopotamia where on 21 September 1921 he was hit by ground fire from hostile natives and forced down, being captured. It was later reported that he had been found shot dead at Dangatora; he was 21 years old.

	1917		DH 5					
1	15 Nov	Alb. DIII	A9471	24	S E Dixmude	1330	OOC	CR/RFC 15.11
2	30 Nov	C	A9339	24	Fontaine	1235	OOC	CR/SR/?
3	10 Dec	Alb. DV	A9257	24	S Honnecourt	1200	DES	CR/RFC 10.12
	1918		SE 5A					
4	26 Feb	Fokker DrI	C1057	24	E Laon	0840	DES	CR/RFC 26.2
5s*	26 Feb	Fokker DrI	C1057	24	E Samoussy	0900	DES	CR/RFC 26.2
6	7 Apr	Alb. DV	C9613	24	Moreuil Wood	1550	DES	CR/RAF 7.4
7	11 Apr	LVG. C	C9613	24	Villers-Brettoneaux	1655	OOC	CR/RAF 11.4
8	12 Apr	Alb. DV	C9613	24	Hangard-Moreuil	1615	DES	CR/RAF 12.4
9	12 Apr	Alb. DV	C9613	24	Hangard-Moreuil	1615	OOC	CR/RAF 12.4
10	20 Apr	Pfalz DIII	C9613	24	S Morcourt	0955	DES	CR/RAF 20.4
11	23 Apr	Pfalz DIII	C9613	24	S Warfusee	1445	DES	CR/RAF 23.4
12	3 May	Fokker DrI	C9613	24	Le Quesnel	1835	DES	CR/RAF 3.5
13	16 May	Alb. DV	D279	24	Foucaucourt	0615	OOC	CR/RAF 16.5
14	28 May	Fokker DVII	D3444	24	Maricourt	0600	OOC	CR/5 BG WD
15	31 May	Alb. DV	D3444	24	Becquigny	1730	DES	CR/RAF 31.5
16	2 Jun	S.S. DIII	D3444	24	Contoire	1115	DES	CR/RAF 2.6
17s**	3 Jun	Alb. C	D3444	24	S E Marcelcave	1120	DES	CR/RAF 3.6
18	5 Jun	Balloon	D3444	24	Moreuil	0805	DES	CR/SR/?
19	7 Jun	Fokker DrI	D3444	24	Rosieres	1145	DES	CR/RAF 7.6
20s***	17 Jun	Fokker DVII	D3444	24	Cachy	1200	CAPT	CR/RAF 17.6

TOTAL: 1 balloon, 1 shared captured, 10 and 2 shared destroyed, 6 out of control = 20.
*Shared with 2/Lt J.J. Dawe B85, 2/Lt H.V.L. Tubbs C9542, Lt R.T. Mark B67, 2/Lt H.B. Richardson B124, 2/Lt W.F. Poulter C9494. **Shared with 2/Lt J.J. Dawe B611. ***Shared with Capt G.O. Johnson C1084, 2/Lt H.D. Barton C6481, Lt C.E. Walton in Dolphin C4185, of 23 Sqn. The pilot, Lt Kurt Wusthoff, of Jasta 15, was captured.

McDONALD John Sutholand Captain 208

The first RFC pilot to join the ex-Naval 210 Squadron, RAF, McDonald first claimed in July, bringing his total to nine by the end of the war. By the close of hostilities he had been promoted to the rank of Captain.

	1917		Camel					
1s*	22 May	C	----	208	2m N E Lens	0800	OOC	CR/I BG WD
2s**	31 May	Fokker DrI	----	208	Merville	1110	OOC	CR/I BG WD
3s**	2 Jun	Alb. DV	----	208	N Lestrem	1215	DES	CR/RAF 2.6
4	8 Jul	Fokker DrI	----	208	Meurchin-Epinoy	0750	OOC	CR/?
5	16 Jul	Alb. DV	----	208	Neuve Chapelle	1125	OOC	CR/?
6	31 Jul	Pfalz DIII	----	208	Estaires	0930	OOC	CR/?

7	6 Sep	Fokker DVII	----	208	E canal on Arras-Cambrai Rd.	1830	DES(F)	CR/?
8	2 Oct	Fokker DVII	E7166	208	N E Fresnoy	1145	OOC	CR/?
9	5 Oct	Fokker DVII	----	208	N E Morcourt	1600	OOC	CR/?

TOTAL: 1 and 1 shared destroyed, 5 and 2 shared out of control = 9.
*Shared with Capt W.L. Jordan, Lt R.L. Johns, Lt E.G. Johnstone, Lt P.M. Dennett, Capt G.K. Cooper, Lt H.H.S. Fowler. **Shared with Capt W.L. Jordan, Lt P.M. Dennett, Lt R.L. Johns.

McDONALD Roderick Captain 8(N), 208

A Canadian who flew with 8 Naval Squadron from June 1917, McDonald's first victories were claimed while flying Sopwith Triplanes. After a period of home leave in late 1917, he returned as a flight commander in January 1918. His eighth and last claim on 21 April 1918 was a two-seater of FlgAbt A268, but at 1115 on 8 May McDonald was shot down and killed over Provin by VzFw Julius Trotsky of Jasta 43.

	1917		Triplane					
1s*	24 May	Alb. DIII	N5472	8N	Douai	0750	DES	CR/RFC 24.5
2s*	24 May	Alb. DV	N5472	8N	Willerval	0835	OOC	CR/RFC 24.5
3	28 May	Alb. DIII	N6301	8N	W Douai	2030	OOC	CR/ORB/DL/?
			Camel					
4s**	20 Jul	DFW. C	N6375	8N	Lens	1840	DES	CR/RFC 21.7
5s***	27 Jul	C	N6375	8N	Loos	1600	DES	CR/RFC 27.7
6s†	19 Aug	DFW. C	N6375	8N	E Lens	0850	OOC	CR/RFC 19.8
	1918							
7s††	5 Feb	Alb. DV	N6387	8N	S Pont a Vendin	1245	DES	CR/RFC 5.2
8†††	21 Apr	C	D1852	208	S W Henin-Lietard	0935	DES	CR/RAF 21.4

TOTAL: 1 and 4 shared destroyed, 1 and 2 shared out of control = 8.
*Shared with F/Lt C.D. Booker N5482. **Shared with F/Cdr R.A. Little, FSL J.H. Thompson, FSL W.M. Davidson N6376. ***Shared with F/Cdr R.A. Little B3877. †Shared with F/Lt R.B. Thornely B3845, FSL W.L. Jordan B3921. FSL J.H. Thompson N6378. ††Shared with FSL H. Day N6379, FSL W.H. Sneath N6356, FSL H.H.S. Fowler B3832. †††This was Lt H. Grabhorn/Lt O. Baltzer of FAA 268, who were killed.

McDOUGALL Peter Aitken Lieutenant 24

McDougall was a pilot with 24 Squadron, flying SE 5As from late 1917 to March 1918. He was credited with seven victories before being wounded on 12 March.

	1917		DH 5					
1	15 Nov	Alb. DIII	B362	24	Dixmude	1250	OOC	CR/RFC 15.11
	1918		SE 5A					
2s*	19 Feb	Rumpler C	B120	24	Servais	0840	DES(F)	CR/RFC 19.2
3s*	19 Feb	DFW. C	B120	24	Bernot	0850	OOC	CR/RFC 19.2
4	21 Feb	Alb. DV	B8257	24	S Honnecourt	1015	OOC	CR/SR/Cit.
5	26 Feb	Fokker DrI	B120	24	E Laon	1615	DES	CR/RFC 26.2
6	6 Mar	Alb. DV	B146	24	E St Quentin	1635	OOC	CR/RFC 6.3
7	12 Mar	C	B891	24	S E St Quentin	1015	DES	CR/RFC 12.3

TOTAL: 2 and 1 shared destroyed, 3 and 1 shared out of control = 7.
*Shared with Lt A.K. Cowper B664, Lt R.T. Mark B67, Lt R.G. Hammersley B891.

McELROY George Edward Henry Captain 40, 24

Born on 14 May 1893 at Donnybrook, near Dublin, George McElroy joined the Royal Irish Regiment on the outbreak of war and in October 1914 was posted to France, where he was commissioned in May 1915. He was badly gassed in subsequent service and posted to garrison duty in Ireland. Eager to return to action, he transferred to the RFC in February 1917, and after training, joined 40 Squadron in France to fly Nieuport Scouts. It was not until the squadron had received SE 5As that he gained his first victory, claiming a two-seater on 28 December; all his other victories were to be achieved in 1918. During the next two months he claimed 10 more, and was then posted as a flight commander to 24 Squadron, claiming a further 16 victories by early April. This string of successes brought an MC in February, a Bar in March and a second Bar in April. While landing on 7 April after shooting down three enemy aircraft, he crashed into a tree and was badly shaken. On recovery late in June, he rejoined his old squadron, 40, and once again showed his virtuosity; three victories in quick succession during the last four days of June were followed by 17 more during July, the awards of both a DFC and Bar being made that month. On 20 July his aircraft suffered engine trouble while he was engaging two two-seaters and he crash-landed unhurt. That evening at a farewell party for Captain G.H. Lewis, who had been posted to Home Establishment, he and Mick Mannock admonished each other for being too aggressive and for going too low in pursuit of German aircraft. Six days later Mannock was to die doing just that, while on 31 July, only five days after the loss of Mannock, the man who had been his star pupil in 40 Squadron was to be lost in the same way. 'McIrish' as he was known, took off in SE 5A E1310 and did not return; he had shot down a two-seater at low altitude over Laventie, but had then been hit by anti-aircraft fire and crashed to his death. The Germans reported this when they dropped a message to the RAF to this effect.

	1917		SE 5A					
1	28 Dec	LVG. C	B598	40	Drocourt-Vitry	1120	DES	CR/RFC 28.12
	1918							
2	13 Jan	Rumpler C	B598	40	Pont a Vendin	0920	OOC	CR/RFC 13.1
3	19 Jan	DFW. C	B598	40	Vitry	1205	DES	CR/RFC 19.1
4	24 Jan	DFW. C	B598	40	Oppy-Henin-Lietard	1250	OOC	CR/RFC 24.1
5	2 Feb	C	B598	40	S E Habourdin	1330	OOC	CR/RFC 2.2
6	5 Feb	DFW. C	B22	40	Wingles	1240	DES	CR/RFC 5.2
7	5 Feb	DFW. C	B22	40	N La Bassee	1300	DES(F)	CR/RFC 5.2
8	16 Feb	DFW. C	B598	40	W Henin-Lietard	1130	OOC	CR/RFC 16.2
9	17 Feb	Pfalz DIII	B22	40	Marquain	1125	DES	CR/RFC 17.2
10	17 Feb	C	B22	40	4m S E Lens	1155	DES(F)	CR/RFC 17.2
11	18 Feb	Alb. DV	B598	40	Douvrin	1200	OOC	CR/C&CB 5.1
12	21 Feb	Alb. DV	B664	24	S Honnecourt	1000	OOC	CR/RFC 21.2
13	26 Feb	Fokker DrI	B891	24	4m E Laon	1605	DES(F)	CR/RFC 26.2
14	1 Mar	DFW. C	B891	24	Beaurevoir	1045	OOC	CR/RFC 1.3
15	6 Mar	Alb. DV	C1751	24	N E Bullecourt	0705	DES	CR/RFC 6.3
16	8 Mar	DFW. C	B891	24	E St Quentin	0755	OOC	CR/RFC 8.3
17	8 Mar	Fokker DrI	B891	24	S E La Fere	1455	DES	CR/RFC 8.3
18	9 Mar	Alb. DV	B891	24	N E La Fere	0930	OOC	CR/RFC 9.3
19	27 Mar	Alb. DV	A8900	24	Chipilly	1520	DES(F)	CR/RFC 27.3
20	29 Mar	Alb. DV	C1800	24	Foucaucourt	1530	DES	CR/RFC 29.3
21	29 Mar	DFW. C	C1800	24	E Warfusee	1545	OOC	CR/RFC 29.3
22	1 Apr	Alb. DV	C1084	24	N Ignaucourt	1215	DES	CR/RAF 1.4
23	2 Apr	Alb. DV	C1084	24	E Moreuil	1430	OOC	CR/RAF 2.4
24	4 Apr	Pfalz DIII	C1084	24	N Warfusee	1505	DES	CR/RAF 4.4
25	7 Apr	Alb. DV	C1800	24	Warfusee	1040	OOC	CR/RAF 7.4
26	7 Apr	Alb. DV	C1800	24	3m E Marcelcave	1100	DES	CR/RAF 7.4
27	7 Apr	Fokker DrI	C1800	24	N Moreuil Wood	1115	OOC	CR/RAF 7.4
28	26 Jun	DFW. C	C8869	40	500y S E Annay	0655	DES	CR/RAF 26.6
29	28 Jun	Balloon	C8869	40	Provin	1255	DES	CR/RAF 28.6
30s*	30 Jun	Balloon	C8869	40	Annay	1045	DES	CR/RAF 30.6
31	1 Jul	Balloon	C8869	40	Harnes	1225	DES	CR/RAF 1.7
32	2 Jul	DFW. C	D6122	40	N La Bassee	1022	DES	CR/RAF 2.7
33	2 Jul	DFW. C	E1318	40	N W Pacaut Wood	2100	DES	CR/RAF 2.7
34	5 Jul	DFW. C	C8869	40	Lestrem	1150	OOC	CR/ORB/?
35	6 Jul	Hannover C	C8869	40	N E Arras	0540	DES	CR/RAF 6.7
36s**	8 Jul	Hannover C	C8869	40	E Monchy	0925	OOC	CR/ORB/?
37	8 Jul	Hannover C	C8869	40	3m E La Bassee	1045	DES	CR/RAF 8.7
38	11 Jul	Hannover C	C8869	40	W Vitry	0550	DES	CR/RAF 11.7
39s***	13 Jul	Hannover C	C8869	40	W Estaires	0645	DES	CR/RAF 13.7
40	13 Jul	Pfalz DIII	C8869	40	Vitry	2005	DES	CR/RAF 13.7
41	14 Jul	Hannover C	C8869	40	N Drocourt	0730	DES	CR/RAF 14.7
42	15 Jul	Fokker DVII	C8869	40	N E Hill 70, Lens	2015	DES	CR/RAF 15.7
43	15 Jul	Fokker DVII	C8869	40	N E Hill 70, Lens	2015	OOC	CR/ORB/?
44	19 Jul	Alb. DV	C8869	40	2m N Estaires	1245	DES	CR/RAF 19.7
45	25 Jul	Hannover C	C8869	40	N Neuve Chapelle	0615	DES	CR/RAF 25.7
46	25 Jul	Hannover C	C8869	40	W Bois d'Epinoy	0715	DES	CR/RAF 25.7
†	31 Jul	Hannover C	E1310	40	Laventie	c0930	DES	

TOTAL: 2 and 1 shared balloons, 26 and 2 shared destroyed, 15 out of control = 46.
*Shared with Lt A.R. Whitten D8197, Lt G.J. Strange B191. **Shared with Lt I.L. Roy B180, Lt G.J. Strange B191. ***Shared with Lt F.H. Knobel D3528, Lt I.L. Roy B180, Lt G.J. Strange B191. †The German Air Force, dropped a note saying McElroy had been shot down by anti-aircraft fire, after shooting down a two-seater. Probably this was the crew Sgt Kracht/Vzfw Schuldt of Schl. 19.

McEVOY Christopher Lieutenant 66, 39

Born on 2 January 1899 at Cricklewood, North London, he was the eldest son of the Reverend C. McEvoy, MA. He joined the RFC and in January 1918 was posted to 66 Squadron in Italy. Flying Camels, he claimed nine victories and was awarded a DFC. He had a lucky escape during one of his first combats in February when he was slightly wounded; he remained in hospital for only a short while. In August he went down with dysentry and returned to England, joining 39(Home Defence) Squadron. During World War II he served as a cypher officer with the rank of Flight Lieutenant with Coastal Command. He died on 12 October 1953. His younger brother was Air Chief Marshal Sir Theodore McEvoy, KCB, CBE.

	1918		Camel					
1	30 Mar	Alb. DIII	B7389	66	Mt Melatta	1315	OOC	ORB/SR/7 BG
2*	4 Apr	Alb. DIII	B7389	66	Cismon	0920	DES(F)	ORB/SR/7 BG
3**	17 Apr	Alb. DIII	B7389	66	S Giacomo	1420	DES	ORB/SR/14 W
4s***	26 May	C	B7353	66	Salina	0615	DES	ORB/SR/14 W
5†	21 Jun	Alb. DV	B5180	66	Feltre	0805	OOC	ORB/SR/?
6	4 Jul	Pfalz DIII	D8235	66	N W Asiago	0815	DES(F)	ORB/SR/14 W
7	21 Jul	Alb. DV	B2433	66	Motta	1915	DES	ORB/SR/14 W
8††	1 Aug	Alb. DV	B2433	66	S Mareno-C Tron	1155	DES	ORB/SR/14 W
9††	1 Aug	Alb. DV	B2433	66	Fontaneletto	1210	DES	ORB/SR/14 W

TOTAL: 6 and 1 shared destroyed, 2 out of control = 9.
*Three claims by 66; one loss was a Phonix D1 No 228:24 of Flik 60j. The pilot, Offstell Kurt Gruber an 11 victory ace was killed. **66 made 5 claims; one two seater was lost, as was Oblt Michael Gasser-Norden of Flik 42j in Alb.DIII 153:152, who was killed. ***Shared with Lt H.K. Boysen B5180. †McEvoy was shot down and force landed after this combat. ††One was Oblt Vuk von Hreljanovic of Flik 56j in Alb.D 253:40, who was killed.

McEWAN Clifford Mackay Lieutenant 28

Born on 2 July 1897 in Griswold, Manitoba, Canada, he was a graduate of the University of Saskatchewan. He joined the Canadian Army in March 1916, transferring to the RFC in June 1917 and becoming an original member of 28 Squadron. 'Black Mike', as he was called, went with 28 to Italy and proved a most aggressive fighter, being awarded the MC, DFC and the Italian Bronze Medal for Military Valour. He claimed 27 victories. One claim on 18 February 1918 was only credited as an out of control, but many years later it was confirmed as destroyed when the wreck was found in the Italian mountains. After the war he joined the RCAF, rising to the rank of Air Vice-Marshal. During World War II he was AOC, 6(Canadian) Bomber Group in England from January 1944. He died on 6 August 1967 in Toronto.

	1917		Camel					
1s*	30 Dec	Alb. DIII	B2461	28	2km N E Conegliano	1500	DES(F)	CR/7 BG
	1918							
2	2 Feb	C	B2461	28	N Conegliano	1050	DES(F)	CR/7 BG
3	2 Feb	C	B2461	28	N Conegliano	1050	DES	CR/7 BG
4	18 Feb	Alb. DIII	B5169	28	Rustigne	1200	OOC	CR/7 BG
5	27 Feb	Alb. DV	B5169	28	10 km N Conegliano	1020	DES	CR/7 BG
6	27 Feb	Alb. DV	B5169	28	10 km N Conegliano	1020	DES	CR/7 BG
7	2 May	Alb. DV	B7383	28	Valdobbiadene	1040	DES(F)	CR/14 W
8	3 May	Alb. DIII	B7383	28	2 km S E Mansue	1610	DES	CR/14 W
9	9 May	Alb. DV	B7383	28	S Caldonazzo	0800	DES	CR/14 W
10	21 May	Alb. DV	B7383	28	Motta	1230	DES	CR/14 W
11	24 May	Alb. DIII	B7383	28	Tezze	0645	DES	CR/14 W
12	31 May	C	B7383	28	Folline	1830	DES	CR/14 W
13	3 Jun	Alb. DIII	D1911	28	5 km E Motta a/d	1500	DES	CR/14 W
14**	7 Jun	C	D1911	28	12 km S E Motta	0815	DES	CR/14 W
15	19 Jun	Berg DI	D8112	28	Caldonazzo	0845	DES(F)	CR/14 W
16	19 Jun	Berg DI	D8112	28	Caldonazzo	0845	OOC	CR/ORB
17	21 Jun	Berg DI	D8112	28	Villa Canton	1210	DES	CR/14 W
18	23 Jun	Alb. DIII	D8112	28	N Nerversa	1145	DES	CR/14 W
19	25 Jun	Alb. DV	D8112	28	Godega	0900	OOC	CR/14 W
20	27 Jun	C	D8112	28	Piazza	2045	DES(F)	CR/14 W
21	1 Jul	Berg DI	D8112	28	S Pordenone	1030	DES	CR/?
22	9 Jul	Alb. DIII	D8239	28	Calliano	1450	DES(F)	CR/14 W
23	9 Jul	C	D8239	28	Calliano	1455	DES(F)	CR/14 W
24	20 Jul	Branden. C	D8239	28	Lavarone	0635	DES	CR/14 W
25	11 Aug	Alb. DV	D8208	28	Tontanello	1015	OOC	CR/14 W
26s***	26 Sep	Alb. DV	D8239	28	10 km S W Belluna	1100	DES(F)	CR/14 W
27	4 Oct	Alb. DV	D8241	28	Tagliamento River	1345	DES	CR/14 W

TOTAL: 21 and 2 shared destroyed, 4 out of control = 27.
*Shared with Lt A.G. Cooper B6362. **Possibly an aircraft from Flik 17. ***Shared with Capt S. Stanger.

McGINNESS Paul Joseph Lieutenant 1 AFC

Born in Framlingham, Victoria, on 14 February 1896, 'Ginty', as this Australian was known, received the DCM with the Australian Light Horse in Gallipoli before joining the AFC. As a pilot he flew BEs and Bristol Fighters with 1 AFC Squadron in Palestine, his usual observer being Lieutenant Wilmot Hudson Fysh (later Sir Hudson Fysh). McGinness and Fysh were both awarded DFCs, and 'Ginty' was credited with seven victories. After the war these two airmen formed the now-famous QANTAS Airline in Australia. McGinness died on 25 January 1955.

	1918		Bristol					
1*	2 May	C	C4840	1AFC	Ras Momsar	0740	OOC	CR/40 W WD
2s**	3 Aug	Alb. DIII	B1223	1AFC	2m N E Ez Duba	1210	DES	CR/40 W WD
3***	24 Aug	Pfalz DIII	C4623	1AFC	Kalkilieh	0830	DES(F)	CR/40 W WD
4†	24 Aug	Pfalz DIII	C4623	1AFC	Kalkilieh	0830	FTL/DES	CR/40 W WD
5††	31 Aug	LVG. C	C4623	1AFC	Rantieh	1430	CAPT	CR/40 W WD
6†††	31 Aug	LVG. C	C4623	1AFC	1.5m E Kalkilieh	1430	DES	CR/40 W WD
7s‡	14 Sep	Rumpler C	C4623	1AFC	3m E Jenin	1130	FTL/DES	CR/40 W WD

TOTAL: 1 captured, 3 destroyed, 2 force landed and destroyed, and 1 out of control = 7.
*Observer: LT F.C. Hawley. **Observer: Lt H. Fysh; shared with Lt E.P. Kenny/Lt L.W. Sutherland C4626. ***Observer: Lt H.B. Fletcher. †Observer: Lt H.B. Fletcher. The pilot of this aircraft was shot on the ground. Possibly Vzfw Kruger of Jasta 1(F). ††Observer: Lt H. Fysh. This was Uffz H. Vesper/Lt A. Haendly of FA 301, who were killed. †††Observer: Lt H. Fysh. ‡Observer: Lt H. Fysh; shared with Lt D.R. Dowling/Lt E.A. Mulford B1223. This aircraft was strafed.

McGOUN David Mackay Captain 20, 22

McGoun, from Montreal, Canada, flew Bristol Fighters with 20 Squadron from late 1917 to early 1918. With his observers he claimed at least five victories, then being posted to 22 Squadron as a flight commander. Here he added four more to his score and was awarded the MC.

	1917		Bristol					
1*	27 Oct	Alb. DIII	A7250	20	S W Roulers	1310	OOC	CR/RFC 27.10
	1918							
2**	25 Jan	Alb. DV	C4836	20	Stadenberg	1240	DES	CR/RFC 25.1
3**	25 Jan	Alb. DV	C4836	20	Stadenberg	1240	OOC	CR/RFC 25.1
4**	30 Jan	Alb. DV	C4828	20	W Zedelghem	1425	DES	CR/RFC 30.1
5***	17 Feb	Pfalz DIII	C4826	20	Moorslede	1130	OOC	CR/RFC 17.2
6†	23 Mar	Alb. DV	C4828	22	Auchy en Artois	1100	OOC	CR/RFC 23.3
7†	25 Mar	Alb. DV	C4828	22	St Ledger	0825	DES	CR/RFC 25.3
8†	25 Mar	Alb. DV	C4828	22	St Ledger	0825	OOC	CR/SR/?
9†	12 Apr	C	B1253	22	Laventie	0900	DES	CR/RAF 12.4

TOTAL: 4 destroyed, 5 out of control = 9.
*Observer: 2/Lt N. Couve. **Observer: 2/Lt C.J. Agelasto. ***Observer: 2/Lt S.H.P. Masding. †Observer: 2/Lt F.N. Harrison.

McGREGOR Douglas Urchant Captain 23

Joining the RFC early in 1917, this Canadian was posted to 23 Squadron in April, flying Spads. He was to the fore when attacking ground targets, notably on 6 June, when he made a dawn attack on the German airfield at Chateau du Sart. The award of an MC was made in August and he was promoted to Captain in September. His tour ended with his return to England on 5 October. During 1918 he served as an instructor in Canada.

	1917		Spad					
1s*	13 May	Alb. DIII	B1524	23	Vis en Artois-Vitry	1900	DES(F)	CR/RFC 13.5
2s**	6 Jul	C	B3529	23	Zandvoorde	1430	DES	CR/RFC 6.7
3s***	7 Jul	C	B3488	23	Houthoulst Forest	1940	DES(F)	CR/RFC/8.7
4	7 Jul	C	B3488	23	Houthoulst Forest	1945	DES(F)	CR/RFC 8.7
5	13 Jul	Alb. DIII	B3488	23	Menin	0720	OOC	CR/RFC 13.7
6	15 Jul	Alb. DIII	----	23	Roulers	----	OOC	RFC/15.7
7	7 Aug	Alb. DIII	B3579	23	Dadizeele	1815	OOC	CR/RFC 8.8
8	16 Aug	Alb. DIII	B3579	23	Zonnebeke	0615	DES	CR/RFC 16.8
9	16 Aug	Alb. DIII	B3579	23	Veldhoek	0640	DES(F)	CR/RFC 16.8
10	26 Aug	Alb. DIII	B3572	23	Comines-Polygon Wood	0700	DES	CR/RFC 26.8
11	26 Aug	Alb. DIII	B3572	23	Comines-Polygon Wood	0715	OOC	CR/RFC 26.8
12	26 Sep	Alb. DV	B6762	23	W St Julien	1630	DES	CR/RFC 26.9

TOTAL: 5 and 2 shared destroyed, 4 and 1 shared out of control = 12.
*Shared with 2/Lt S.C. O'Grady. **Shared with Capt C.K.C. Patrick B1580, 2/Lt G.I.D. Marks. ***Shared with Capt C.K.C. Patrick.

McGREGOR Malcolm Charles Captain 54, 91, 85

Born near Hunterville, New Zealand, on 4 March 1896, he qualified for his Aero Certificate in September 1916, and then applied for a commission in the RFC, which was duly granted. He arrived in England and graduated in April 1917 with a total of 28 hours flying. This tall (six feet three inches) pilot was then sent to France, joining 54 Squadron to fly Pups, but was injured in a force-landing after seeing some action and claiming at least one victory. He served briefly with 91 Squadron in England, and then joined 85 Squadron in 1918, being promoted to Captain and returning to France as a flight commander. Here he claimed another ten victories, receiving the DFC and Bar, but on 10 August he was shot down and forced to land. After the war he returned to New Zealand to take up farming, but resumed flying as a Squadron Leader with the RNZAF in 1923. He later turned to commercial aviation, taking a post with Union Airways, but broke his back in a crash in 1932. After recovery, he returned to flying duties, but was killed in a crash on 19 February 1936 while landing at Wellington, North Island, during a heavy rainstorm. His biography, *Mac's Memoirs* was published in 1937.

	1917		Pup					
1	6 Jun	Alb. DIII	A6192	54	S W Cambrai	1200	DES	CR/RFC 6.6
	1918		SE 5A					
2	29 May	C	----	85	Armentieres	2030	OOC	Cit/Biog
3	1 Jun	Pfalz DIII	C6472	85	La Gorgue	2010	OOC	CR/Cit/?
4	1 Jun	Pfalz DIII	C6472	85	La Gorgue	2010	OOC	CR/Cit/?
5	27 Jun	C	C1931	85	Erquinghem	0915	DES	CR/RAF 27.6
6	24 Jul	Fokker DVII	D6923	85	S E Kemmel	1045	OOC	CR/?
7*	24 Jul	Fokker DVII	D6923	85	S E Kemmel	1050	DES	CR/RAF 24.7
8	3 Aug	Fokker DVII	E3922	85	E Bailleul	0810	DES(F)	CR/RAF 3.8
9	22 Aug	Fokker DVII	D6955	85	N W Peronne	1650	DES	CR/RAF 22.8
10s**	8 Oct	Balloon	C1143	85	E Maretz	1300	DES	CR/RAF 8.10
11	23 Oct	C	C1143	85	Foret Englefontaine	0945	DES	CR/RAF 23.10

TOTAL: 1 shared balloon, 6 destroyed, 4 out of control = 11.
*In this fight 85 made 6 claims; Jasta 43 was shot up, with 3 pilots force landing and other aircraft damaged. **Shared with Lt P.D. d'Albenas E5695.

McKAY Alfred Edwin Captain 24, 23

McKay flew DH 2s with 24 Squadron in 1916-17, receiving the MC and claiming four victories, one of which he forced down inside Allied lines. Promoted to Captain, he went to 23 Squadron later in 1917, flying Spads. He claimed six more enemy machines, but was reported missing on 28 December, having become a prisoner of war after being shot down by Leutnant Karl Menckhoff of Jasta 3.

	1916		DH 2					
1	20 Jul	Roland C	6010	24	High Wood	2045	OOC	CR/RFC 20.7
2s*	9 Nov	D	7884	24	Le Transloy	1345	DES	CR/RFC 10.11
	1917							
3s**	24 Jan	Alb. C	7884	24	Flers	1215	CAPT	CR/RFC 24.1
4***	25 Jan	Alb. DII	7884	24	S Bapaume	1035	CAPT?	CR/RFC 25.1
			Spad					
5	19 Nov	C	B3560	23	N E Oostnieuwkerke	1210	DES	CR/RFC 19.11
6	19 Nov	C	B3560	23	Passchendaele	1230	DES	CR/RFC 19.11
7	23 Nov	DFW. C	B3560	23	N Wervicq-Becelaere	1120	OOC	CR/RFC 23.11
8	12 Dec	Alb. DV	B3560	23	Houthoulst Forest	1420	OOC	CR/WD 12.12
9	18 Dec	DFW. C	B3560	23	Gheluvelt	1040	DES	CR/RFC 18.12
10	18 Dec	DFW. C	B3560	23	S Gheluvelt	1015	OOC	CR/RFC 18.12

TOTAL: 1 and 1 shared captured, 3 and 1 shared destroyed, 4 out of control = 10.
*Shared with 2/Lt E.C. Pashley 7930, Lt A.G. Knight A305. **Shared with Capt H.A. Wood 7918; Uffz M. Delkock/Lt E.Burg captured. ***Flgr Kinkel of Jasta Boelcke was captured.

McKEEVER Andrew Edward Lieutenant Colonel 11, 1CAN

Born in Listowel, Ontario, on 21 August 1895, Andrew McKeever was posted to England with the Canadian Expeditionary Force on the outbreak of war. He served in France during 1915-16, gaining a reputation as a marksman, but in December 1916 he transferred to the RFC, joining 11 Squadron on 28 May 1917 as the unit was converting from FE 2s to Bristol Fighters. Here he flew with several gunners, but his most regular companion was Sergeant L.F.Powell, with whom he fought most of his successful combats. His first two claims were submitted on 26 June, while on 7 July he and Powell claimed three victories in one flight, and on 5 August they claimed three more. By early September McKeever had 12 victories to his credit, and was awarded an MC on 17th. Victories continued to come in groups, six more being claimed during the latter part of September, and eight in October. He was recommended for a Bar to his MC after his 20th victory, and this was awarded on 17 October. His final combat occurred on 30 November over Cambrai when he and Powell fought two two-seaters and seven black Albatros Scouts. He was then awarded a DSO, and Powell (who had been commissioned) a DCM. The latter gained one other victory with another pilot, bringing his personal score as a gunner to eight. On 25 January 1918 McKeever returned to the United Kingdom, his score of 31 aircraft remaining the highest for any Bristol Fighter pilot throughout the war. He did not return to the front, but had formed and commanded 1 Squadron, Canadian Air Force on Sopwith Dolphins when the fighting ended; he then returned to Canada. In 1919 he took up a post as aerodrome manager at Mineola Field in the USA, but was injured in a motor accident on 3 September. He lingered for some weeks, but finally died from his injuries on Christmas Day 1919.

	1917		Bristol					
1*	26 Jun	Alb. DV	A7144	11	Etaing-Dury	1845	OOC	CR/RFC 26.6
2*	26 Jun	Alb. DV	A7144	11	E Cambrai	1845+	DES	CR/RFC 26.6
3**	7 Jul	Alb. DV	A7144	11	S Vitry	2030	DES	CR/RFC 8.7
4**	7 Jul	Alb. DV	A7144	11	Vitry	2031	OOC	CR/RFC 8.7
5**	7 Jul	Alb. DV	A7144	11	S Monchy	2040	OOC	CR/RFC 8.7
6***	10 Jul	Alb. DV	A7140	11	Sailly	2030	OOC	CR/RFC 10.7
7***	13 Jul	Alb. DV	A7140	11	Haynecourt	2010	OOC	CR/RFC 13.7
8***	13 Jul	Alb. DV	A7140	11	Haynecourt	2010	OOC	CR/RFC 13.7
9**	5 Aug	Alb. DV	A7159	11	Queant	1950	OOC	CR/RFC 5.8
10**	5 Aug	Alb. DV	A7159	11	Queant	1950	DES(F)	CR/RFC 5.8
11**	5 Aug	Alb. DV	A7159	11	Queant	1950	OOC	CR/RFC 5.8
12†	22 Aug	Alb. DV	A7159	11	Auby-Douai	1845	DES	CR/RFC 23.8
13**	23 Sep	Alb. DV	A7159	11	Vitry	1625	OOC	CR/RFC 23.9
14**	23 Sep	Alb. DV	A7159	11	Vitry	1625	OOC	CR/RFC 23.9
15***	25 Sep	Alb. DV	A7159	11	Le Catelet	1110	DES	CR/RFC 25.9
16††	28 Sep	Alb. DV	----	11	Bugnicourt	1805	DES(F)	CR/RFC 28.9
17††	28 Sep	Alb. DV	----	11	Bugnicourt	1805	OOC	CR/RFC 28.9
18††	28 Sep	Alb. DV	----	11	Bugnicourt	1805	DES(F)	CR/RFC 28.9
19†††	1 Oct	C	A7167	11	Brebieres	1150	DES	CR/RFC 1.10
20**	2 Oct	Alb. DV	----	11	Douai-Cambrai	1800-1820	DES(F)	CR/RFC 2.10
21**	16 Oct	Alb. DV	A7159	11	Brebieres	1020	DES	CR/RFC 16.10
22**	16 Oct	Alb. DV	A7159	11	Douai	1025	DES	CR/RFC 16.10
23†††	20 Oct	Alb. DV	----	11	N W Cambrai	1640	DES(F)	CR/RFC 20.10
24**	31 Oct	Alb. DV	A7153	11	Fresse	1600	DES	CR/RFC 31.10
25**	31 Oct	Alb. DV	A7153	11	Fresse	1600	OOC	CR/RFC 31.10
26**	31 Oct	Alb. DV	A7153	11	Fresse	1600	OOC	CR/RFC 31.10
27‡	11 Nov	DFW. C	A7288	11	Brebieres	1130	DES	CR/RFC 11.11
28**	30 Nov	Alb. DV	A7288	11	S Cambrai	1150	DES(F)	CR/RFC 30.11
29**	30 Nov	Alb. DV	A7288	11	S Cambrai	1150	DES	CR/RFC 30.11
30**	30 Nov	Alb. DV	A7288	11	S Cambrai	1155	DES	CR/RFC 30.11
31**	30 Nov	Alb. DV	A7288	11	S Cambrai	1155	DES	CR/RFC 30.11

TOTAL: 18 destroyed, 13 out of control = 31..
*Observer: 2/Lt E. Oake. **Observer: 2/Lt L.A. Powell. ***Observer: 2/Lt E.V. De G. Dodd. †Observer: 2/Lt L.F. Ebbutt. ††Observer: AM Hewitt. †††Observer: Lt H.G. Kent. ‡Observer: Lt L.V. Pogson.

McKENZIE Robert William Lieutenant 2AFC

McKenzie was born in June 1895 in Adelaide, South Australia, where he worked as a chemist until he joined the Australian Army Medical Corps after the start of the war. He later transferred to the AFC to train as a pilot, and was posted to 68 Squadron in England in September 1917. He first went into action during the Cambrai offensive of November that year, flying DH 5s; on 1 December he hit an Albatros Scout which dived, landed hard and crashed into a shell hole. At the new year the unit was re-numbered 2AFC and was re-equipped with SE 5As, and he next claimed in February 1918. During March he was credited with shooting down four more aircraft and was awarded an MC, but was then posted to Home Establishment.

	1917		DH 5					
1	1 Dec	Alb. DV	A9451	2AFC	N W Villers-Guislain	1215	DES	CR/RFC 1.12
	1918		SE 5A					
2	19 Feb	Alb. DV	C9539	2AFC	Pont a Vendin	1148	DES	CR/RFC 19.2
3	12 Mar	C	B579	2AFC	Wingles	1305	DES	CR/RFC 12.3
4	4 Mar	Alb. DV	B579	2AFC	Wingles	1005	DES	CR/RFC 13.3
5	22 Mar	Alb. DV	C5382	2AFC	Omissy	1510	OOC	CR/RFC 22.3
6	23 Mar	C	C5382	2AFC	Brebieres-Vitry	0955	DES(F)	CR/RFC 23.3

TOTAL: 5 destroyed, 1 out of control = 6.

McLAUGHLIN Robert Captain 201

Served with 201 Squadron throughout 1918, claiming six victories.

	1918		Camel					
1	9 May	Alb. DV	B3884	201	Bapaume	1315	DES	CR/RAF 9.5
2s*	15 May	Alb. DV	----	201	Bapaume	0645	DES	CR/RAF 15.5
3	30 May	Alb. DV	B7191	201	Achiet le Grand	1955	OOC	CR/ORB/?
4s**	12 Aug	Fokker DVII	B6398	201	St Christ	1100	DES	CR/RAF 12.8
5s**	12 Aug	Fokker DVII	B6398	201	St Christ	1100	DES	CR/RAF 12.8
6	16 Sep	Fokker DVII	C195	201	S E Cambrai	1735	OOC	CR/?

TOTAL: 1 and 3 shared destroyed, 2 out of control = 6.

*Shared with Major C.D. Booker, Capt S.M. Kinkhead, Lt M.H. Findlay, Lt R. Hemmens, Lt J.H. Forman, Lt H.L. Wallace, Lt R.C.B. Brading, Lt R.S.S. Orr. **Shared with Capt H.R. de Wilde C143, Lt R. Sykes B7190.

McMAKING Oscar Lennox Lieutenant 45

From Southsea, Hampshire, he flew Sopwith 1½ Strutters with 45 Squadron in 1917. Converting to Camels later in the year, this officer brought his score to six before he was killed in combat on 11 September. His victor was Leutnant Werner Voss of Jasta 10, and he was the German's 47th victory.

	1917		Strutter					
1*	12 Jul	Alb. DIII	----	45	E Messines	1315	OOC	CR/RFC 12.7
2*	12 Jul	Alb. DIII	----	45	Kortewilde	1515	OOC	SR/RFC 12.7
3**	10 Aug	Alb. DIII	B2656	45	Zandvoorde	1830	OOC	CR/SR/?
4**	11 Aug	Alb. DIII	----	45	Deulemont	1845	DES(F)	CR/RFC 11.8
			Camel					
5	3 Sep	Alb. DIII	----	45	Ledeghem-Dadizeele	1500	OOC	CR/RFC 3.9
6	5 Sep	Alb. DIII	----	45	Comines	0800	OOC	CR/RFC 5.9

TOTAL: 2 destroyed, 4 out of control = 6.

*Observer: 2/Lt L.M. Copeland. **Observer: Cpl A. Jex.

McNEANEY John Harry Captain 79

A Canadian from Hamilton, Ontario, McNeaney was commissioned in August 1917 and joined 79 Squadron to fly Sopwith Dolphins during 1918. The squadron flew many ground strafing missions and he was wounded during one of these in June. Returning to action, he claimed five victories during the last three months of the war and was awarded the DFC for an action on 28 September, when he claimed two Fokkers shot down. Taken ill after the war, he died on 1 March 1919.

	1918		Dolphin					
1	16 Sep	Fokker DVII	E4425	79	N W Tourcoing	1615	DES	CR/RAF 16.9
2	28 Sep	Fokker DVII	E4712	79	Passchendaele area	1750	DES	CR/RAF 28.9
3	28 Sep	Fokker DVII	E4712	79	Passchendaele area	1755	DES	CR/RAF 28.9
4	2 Oct	Halb. C	E4712	79	1m S E Roulers	0735	DES	CR/RAF 2.10
5	14 Oct	Fokker DVII	E4712	79	N Roulers	1410	DES	CR/RAF 14.10

TOTAL: 5 destroyed = 5.

McQUISTON Finley Captain 12, 55, 19

McQuiston served with the Royal Field Artillery (TF) before joining the RFC. He was posted to 12 Squadron in June 1916, but was badly wounded in September. In March 1917 he returned to active duty, this time with 55 Squadron, but was again wounded during May, although he claimed to have shot down his attacker on this occasion. After leaving hospital, he converted to single-seaters, and in 1918 was posted to 19 Squadron, flying Sopwith Dolphins. In September he was promoted to Captain, and took part in the Somme and Cambrai offensives. By the end of the war he had claimed ten victories and been awarded a DFC.

	1917		DH 4					
1*	9 May	Alb. DIII	A7420	55	Le Cateau	1400	OOC	CR/RFC 9.5
	1918		Dolphin					
2	17 May	Alb. DV	C3902	19	Armentieres	1045	OOC	CR/RAF 17.5
3	27 Jun	Pfalz DIII	C3829	19	Estaires	1800	OOC	CR/ORB/?
4	7 Aug	Pfalz DIII	C3902	19	E Arras	1110	OOC	CR/ORB/?
5	11 Aug	Pfalz DIII	C3829	19	E Albert	1750	DES(F)	CR/RAF 11.8
6	21 Sep	Fokker DVII	C3829	19	E Thorout	1155	OOC	CR/ORB/?
7	27 Sep	Pfalz DIII	C3829	19	E Aubigny	1240	OOC	CR/ORB/?
8	4 Oct	Pfalz DIII	C3829	19	Cambrai-Le Cateau	1115	DES	CR/ORB/?
9	4 Oct	Alb. DV	C3829	19	Cambrai	1115	OOC	CR/ORB/?
10	5 Oct	Fokker DVII	C3829	19	E Cambrai	0805	DES(F)	CR/RAF 5.10

TOTAL: 3 destroyed, 7 out of control = 10.

*Observer: 2 AM F.G. Ellis.

McRAE Russell Fern Lieutenant 4 AFC, 46

Born on 5 December 1896, in Niagara Falls, Canada, Russell McRae joined the RFC in 1917, receiving a commission in October. After completing his training he was posted to France in May 1918 and served with 4 AFC Squadron, which was seriously understrength in Australian personnel due to the influenza epidemic. Here he gained his first victory. When sufficient Australians were again available, he was posted to 46 Squadron in the same Wing on 9 August, where he gained a further four victories. He returned to Home Establishment on 1 November. McRae attended a Canadian World War I Fliers Association meeting in the early eighties, and is believed still to be alive at the time of writing.

	1918		Camel					
1	29 Jul	LVG. C	B778	4AFC	E Armentieres	0505	OOC	CR/ORB/OH
2	12 Aug	Pfalz DIII	D6867	46	Armentieres	1945	DES(F)	CR/RAF 12.8
3	15 Aug	Fokker DVII	D6867	46	S E Peronne	1810	OOC	CR/SR/?
4	1 Sep	Fokker DVII	F6210	46	E Brie Bridges	1125	OOC	CR/V BG WD
5s*	29 Oct	DFW. C	F6322	46	N Esquerchies	1440	DES	CR/V BG WD

TOTAL: 1 and 1 shared destroyed, 3 out of control = 5.
*Observer: 2/Lt T.L. Jones F6219.

MEALING Maurice Edmund Lieutenant 15, 56

Born on 21 July 1893, Mealing served with the King's Shropshire Light Infantry before transferring to the RFC, where he was commissioned on 16 May 1916. He was posted to 15 Squadron as an observer on 7 August, remaining with this unit until May 1917. He then received pilot training, and was posted to 56 Squadron on 18 October of that same year. His score began to rise early in 1918, and in March, when the German build-up began prior to the big offensive of that month, he achieved considerable success. On 24 March however, he was last seen chasing a pair of two-seaters, but another member of the squadron was certain that he had seen Mealing standing beside his SE 5A (B182) and waving at him. It seems likely that he had been shot down by one of the aircraft he had been pursuing, flown by Unteroffizier Zetter and Leutnant Tegeder of FlgAbt 245; he may then have been shot by hostile troops. The award of an MC was gazetted in May 1918.

	1917		SE 5A					
1	30 Nov	Alb. DV	B595	56	Lesdain	1445	DES	CR/RFC 30.11
2	10 Dec	Balloon	B595	56	N Bois de Vaucelles	1520	DES	CR/RFC 10.12
	1918							
3	25 Jan	C	C5303	56	Fontaine-Notre-Dame	1410	DES	CR/RFC 25.1
4	17 Feb	Alb. DV	B595	56	Brancourt	1445	DES	CR/RFC 17.2
5	8 Mar	C	B595	56	Villers Outreaux	1050	OOC	CR/RFC 8.3
6	8 Mar	C	B595	56	Hamblieres	1125	OOC	CR/SR/?
7*	12 Mar	C	B595	56	N Beaucamp	1120	CAPT	CR/RFC 12.3
8	15 Mar	Alb. DV	B595	56	N Bourlon Wood	1050	OOC	CR/RFC 15.3
9	15 Mar	Alb. DV	B595	56	N Bourlon Wood	1050	DES	CR/RFC 15.3
10s**	15 Mar	C	B595	56	N Bourlon Wood	1150	DES	CR/RFC 15.3
11	21 Mar	Fokker DrI	C5389	56	Inchy	1315-1345	OOC	CR/RFC 21.3
12	23 Mar	Balloon	C5389	56	S Pronville	0730	DES	CR/RFC 23.3
13s***	23 Mar	C	C5389	56	Moreuil	0740	DES	CR/RFC 23.3
14	24 Mar	Pfalz DIII	B182	56	W Tincourt	1315	DES	CR/RFC 24.3

TOTAL: 2 balloons, 1 captured, 4 and 2 shared destroyed and 4 out of control = 14.
*Observer was Lt P. Heinemann of FAA 259. **Shared with Capt W.S. Fielding-Johnson B37. Probably Uffz W. Stein/Lt Somme FAA 293b. ***Shared with 2/Lt H.J. Walkerdine B8266, Capt L.W. Jarvis C5430, Lt E.D.G. Galley B59, Lt H.J. Burden D283, 2/Lt W.S. Maxwell B119.

MEDLICOTT Harold William Lieutenant 2

Transferring from the Royal Field Artillery, 'John' Medlicott served with 2 Squadron in 1915. One of the earliest British aces, he was however, forced to land during a snowstorm whilst on a reconnaissance to Valenciennes on 10 November 1915. He and his observer, Lieutenant A. Whitten Brown (later famous as the navigator for the first trans-Atlantic flight with Alcock in 1919), were captured. Determined not to remain in captivity, Medlicott made several escape attempts, but was shot and killed during the last of these from Bad Colberg POW Camp on 21 May 1918.

	1915		BE 2C					
1*	19 Sep	Alb. C	----	2	4m N E Vitry	----	DES(F)	RFC 20.9
			Bristol Scout					
2	10 Oct	Alb. C	----	2	2m E Lens	----	OOC	RFC 10.10
3**	11 Oct	C	----	2	S Rouvroy	----	DES	RFC WD

			BE 2C					
4s***	11 Oct	Alb. C	----	2	Sailly sur la Lys	c1500	CAPT	RFC 11.10
			Bristol Scout					
5	7 Nov	LVG. C	----	2	Lens	----	OOC	RFC 7.11

TOTAL: 1 shared captured, 2 destroyed, 2 out of control = 5.
*Observer: Lt Gilbert. **Confirmed by intelligence: a crew of FA 62 were reported killed. ***Observer: Lt Russell; shared with Capt W.G.S. Mitchell/Lt Shepherd 10 Sqn. This was a crew from FA 202.

MEEK Earl Stanley Captain 29

Born in Sandford, Ontario, Canada, on 11 July 1895, Meek enlisted in the RFC in December 1916 and was posted to 29 Squadron on 14 July 1917. He first claimed on 27 July, but did not gain any further success until December 1917, when he claimed three further victories. In January he was promoted to flight commander, and had brought his score to six by the end of the month. After the war he became a school teacher, subsequently becoming President of a girls' school.

	1917		Nieuport					
1	27 Jul	Alb. DV	B1551	29	St Julien	0650	OOC	CR/RFC 27.7
2	6 Dec	Alb. DV	B6807	29	Westroosebeke	1350	DES(F)	CR/RFC 6.12
3s*	15 Dec	Alb. DV	B6812	29	Westroosebeke	1400	OOC	CR/RFC 15.12
4	16 Dec	Alb. DV	----	29	Roulers	1035	OOC	CR/RFC 16.12
	1918							
5	28 Jan	Fokker DrI	B3637	29	S Roulers	1220	OOC	CR/RFC 28.1
6	29 Jan	Alb. DV	B3637	29	E Moorslede	1256	DES(F)	CR/RFC 29.1

TOTAL: 2 destroyed, 3 and 1 shared out of control = 6.
*Shared with 2/Lt P. de Fontenay B3625.

MEGGITT William Geoffrey Lieutenant 25, 22

Meggitt from Newport, Monmouthshire, was born in 1894 and was an ex-member of the Welsh Regiment; he served as an observer in 25 Squadron on FE 2s from 26 August 1916, claiming three victories by the end of that year, and one more in February 1917. Posted home, he trained as a pilot, subsequently joining 22 Squadron in September 1917, flying Bristol Fighters. His only claims as a pilot were made on 10 and 11 October, during which month he was awarded an MC. He was reported missing in action on 8 November at 1330 whilst with Captain F.A. Durrad in B1125. His and another 22 Squadron Bristol were shot down north of Moorslede by Leutnant H. Bongartz of Jasta 36 as his 21st victory and Leutnant Dahm of Jasta 26 as his second.

	1916		FE 2B					
1*	22 Oct	D	7007	25	S W Seclin	0900	DES	CR/RFC 22.10
2**	22 Oct	D	4877	25	N W Lille	1620	DES	CR/I BG WD
3s***	17 Nov	EA	7022	25	Vitry	1300	DES(F)	CR/RFC 17.11
	1917							
4†	15 Feb	C	7686	25	Avion	1630	OOC	CR/RFC 15.2
			Bristol					
5††	10 Oct	Alb. DV	B1123	22	Moorslede	1650	DES	CR/SR/9 WS
6†††	11 Oct	Alb. DV	----	22	----	----	OOC	9WS/RFC 11.10

TOTAL: 3 and 1 shared destroyed, 2 out of control = 6.
*Pilot: Sgt W.D. Matheson. **Pilot: 2/Lt D.S. Johnston. ***Pilot: Capt R. Chadwick; shared with 2/Lt H.Dunlop/Lt H. Scandrett 7024. 2/Lt D.S. Johnston/Lt I. Heald 6990, 2/Lt H.L. Chadwick/2/Lt C.J. Butler 7025, Sgt J.H.R. Green/Cpl A.G. Bower 4877. †Pilot Capt L.L. Richardson. ††Observer: 1 AM A. Whitehouse. †††Observer: Capt F.A. Durrad.

MEINTJES Henry Captain 60, 56

'Duke' Meintjes, from Springfontein, South Africa, joined the RFC and flew with 60 Squadron from 1916 to February 1917. Here he became a flight commander, receiving the MC and claiming four victories. In April he went to 56 Squadron, where he added four more victories to his score, but was then wounded in the wrist on the evening patrol during which Albert Ball was lost; Meintjes had been hit by bullets from an Albatros of Jasta 11. Recovering from his injuries, he went to the CFS under his old 60 Squadron CO, Jack Scott, as an instructor, and received the AFC. In 1921 he joined the SAAF, becoming a Major in 1925.

	1916		Nieuport					
1	22 Oct	Roland C	A214	60	Bapaume	0815	OOC	CR/C&CB V11 N3
2s*	11 Dec	Alb. CIII	A214	60	Dainville	1030	CAPT	CR/RFC 11.12
	1917							
3	29 Jan	C	A311	60	Bois du Biez	1030	DES	CR/RFC 29.1
4	29 Jan	Alb. DIII	A311	60	Bois du Biez	1045	DES	CR/C&CB V11 N3
			SE 5					
5	29 Apr	Alb. DIII	A4848	56	Hamel-Recourt	1000	OOC	CR/RFC 29.4

6	2 May	Alb. C	A4848	56	W Corbehem	0730	DES	CR/RFC 2.5
7s**	7 May	Alb. DIII	A8900	56	N Cambrai	1830-1900	OOC	CR/RFC 7.5
8***	7 May	Alb. DIII	A8900	56	E Gouy	1830-1945	DES	CR/RFC 7.5

TOTAL: 1 shared captured, 4 destroyed, 2 and 1 shared out of control = 8.
*Shared with Cap E.O. Grenfell, Lt Daly, Lt Whitehead Lt Weedon, Lt K.L. Caldwell: Albatros No 174/16, pilot died of wounds, Lt Baldamus POW. **Shared with Lt C.A. Lewis A4853, 2/Lt R.T.C. Hoidge A4862, 2/Lt W.B. Melville A4852. ***Probably Lt W. Pluschow of Jasta 11, who was wounded.

MELLERSH Francis John William Captain 9(N), 209

Born on 22 September 1898, he joined the RNAS in 1916. After pilot training he was sent to France and later joined 9 Naval Squadron in 1917. On 12 August, with his flight commander and one other pilot, he chased several enemy bombers from Ostend to London, but lost them over the city. In 1918 he became a flight commander, and figured in the action of 21 April, when von Richthofen was shot down over the Somme Valley. He claimed some five victories. Remaining in the RAF, he served in Iraq and the Middle East, and by 1939 had become a Wing Commander. During World War II he was SASO, 222 Group in Ceylon, 1942-43, and AOC, 237 Group, 1943-45. After the war he was Senior Administrative Officer at Bomber Command from 1949-51, and was knighted Sir Francis Mellersh, KBE, AFC, MA. He was killed in a helicopter crash in the mid 1950s.

	1917		Triplane					
1s*	28 Jul	Aviatik C	N5377	9N	Middelkerke	1735	OOC	CR/RFC 28.7
			Camel					
2s**	15 Oct	Alb. DV	B3830	9N	S Ostend	1230	OOC	CR/DRO/DL
	1918							
3s***	12 Apr	Fokker DrI	D3326	209	Warfusee	0830	OOC	CR/RAF 12.4
4	21 Apr	Fokker DrI	B6257	209	Cerisy	1100	DES	CR/RAF 21.4
5	23 Apr	DFW. C	D3329	209	S W Cerisy	1355	DES	CR/RAF 23.4

TOTAL: 2 destroyed, 3 shared out of control = 5.
*Shared with F/Cdr G.G. Simpson N5462. **Shared with FSL O.M. Redgate B3818. ***Shared with Capt A.R. Brown B7270.

MELLINGS Harold Thomas Captain 2W, 10(N), 210

Born in Shropshire on 5 August 1897, he joined the RNAS in the early months of the war. He first flew in action with 2 Naval Wing in the Eastern Mediterranean from October 1916 to late 1917, during which time he claimed the destruction of at least four enemy aeroplanes whilst flying the Wing's only Triplane; he was awarded the DSC and the Greek War Medal. After a period in England, he went to 10(N) Squadron, later 210 Squadron, RAF, in January 1918. He was slightly wounded by machine gun fire from the ground on 15 April, but during his service with the unit was able to increase his score to 15 before being killed in action on 22 July by Leutnant Lutz Beckmann of Jasta 56. He had received a Bar to his DSC and a DFC before his death.

	1916		Bristol Scout					
1	30 Sep	LVG. C	----	2W	Chakli, near Smyrna	----	OOC	2W DRO
	1917		Triplane					
2	30 Sep	Alb. W4	N5431	2W	Mudros	c0800	DES	2W/TFT
3	19 Nov	Alb. DIII	N5431	2W	----	----	DES	Citation
4	25 Nov	Rumpler C	N5431	2W	----	----	DES(F)	Citation
5	29 Nov	Alb. DIII	N5431	2W	----	----	DES	Citation
	1918		Camel					
6	28 Feb	Alb. DV	B6357	10N	N E Ypres	1715	OOC	CR/DRO/DL
7	10 Mar	Alb. DV	N6357	10N	S E Dixmude	1600	DES	CR/DRO/DL
8	16 Mar	Pfalz DIII	N6376	10N	Roulers	0930	OOC	CR/RNAS 16.3
9	24 Mar	Pfalz DIII	N6376	10N	Menin-Roulers	0920	DES(F)	CR/RNAS 24.3
10	24 Mar	Pfalz DIII	N6376	10N	Menin-Roulers	0920	OOC	CR/RNAS 24.3
11	9 Apr	Alb. C	B6208	210	La Bassee	1515	DES	CR/RAF 9.4
12	20 Jul	Fokker DVII	F5914	210	S E Ostend	0945	DES	CR/5 GP Comm
13s*	20 Jul	Fokker DVII	F5914	210	S E Ostend	0945	OOC	CR/5 GP Comm
14	22 Jul	C	F5914	210	S E Ostend	0830	DES	CR/5 GP Comm
15	22 Jul	Fokker DVII	F5914	210	1m E Ypres	0845	DES	CR/5 GP Comm

TOTAL: 10 destroyed, 4 and 1 shared out of control = 15.
*Shared with Lt A. Buchanan D6909.

MIDDLETON Thomas Percy Captain 48, 20

Lieutenant Middleton went to France in spring 1917 as one of the first Bristol F2A Fighter pilots with 48 Squadron, claiming seven victories. After several months at the front he was rested, returning to France in April 1918 as a flight commander in 20 Squadron on F2Bs. Here he raised his score to 27, being awarded a

DFC, gazetted on 2 July, for his part in the heavy fighting of the spring and early summer. At the time of the recommendation for the award he had claimed six aircraft, including two Triplanes, in two months. He flew mainly with Captain F. Godfrey and Lieutenant A. Mills, both of whom were also awarded DFCs. In later life he lived in Argentina.

	1917		Bristol					
1*	30 Apr	Alb. DIII	----	48	----	----	OOC	RFC 30.4
2s**	2 May	Alb. C	A3325	48	E Adinfer Wood	1000	OOC	CR/RFC 2.5
3***	10 May	Alb. DIII	A3350	48	Brebieres-Douai	0655	DES	CR/RFC 10.5
4†	27 May	Alb. DIII	A7119	48	S W Douai	1945	DES	CR/RFC 27.5
5†	27 May	C	A7119	48	S W Douai	1945	OOC	CR/RFC 27.5
6†	3 Jun	Alb. DIII	A7112	48	E Douai	1050	OOC	CR/SR/?
7†	18 Jun	Alb. DV	A7102	48	S Rumaucourt	1430	DES	CR/RFC 18.6
	1918							
8††	17 Apr	Alb. DV	C4699	20	S E Hazebrouck	1400	DES	CR/11 WS/BGS
9††	17 Apr	Alb. DV	C4699	20	S E Hazebrouck	1400	OOC	CR/11 WS/BGS
10††	3 May	Alb. DV	C4699	20	S Ploegsteert Wood	1055	DES	CR/RAF 3.5
11††	3 May	Alb. DV	C4699	20	La Touquet	1055	OOC	CR/SR/?
12††	8 May	Alb. DV	C4699	20	S E Bailleul	0845	DES	CR/RAF 8.5
13††	8 May	Fokker DrI	C4699	20	E Dranoutre	0930	DES	CR/RAF 8.5
14†††	22 May	C	C856	20	Wytschaete-St Eloi	0705	DES	CR/RAF 22.5
15†††	29 May	Alb. DV	C951	20	Bac St Maur	1830	OOC	CR/11 WS
16†††	30 May	Alb. DV	C951	20	N E Lille	1720	DES	CR/RAF 30.5
17†††	30 May	Pfalz DIII	C951	20	Wez Macquart	1720	DES	CR/RAF 30.5
18†††	31 May	Pfalz DIII	C951	20	S W Armentieres	0740	DES	CR/RAF 31.5
19††	8 Jun	Pfalz DIII	C951	20	S E Comines	1720	DES	CR/RAF 8.6
20††	8 Jun	Pfalz DIII	C951	20	S E Comines	1725	DES	CR/RAF 8.6
21††	12 Jun	Pfalz DIII	C951	20	E Zillebeke Lake	1910	DES	CR/RAF 12.6
22††	30 Jun	Fokker DrI	C951	20	E Comines	0730	DES	CR/RAF 30.6
23††	30 Jun	Pfalz DIII	C951	20	W Wervicq	0750	DES	CR/RAF 30.6
24††	29 Jul	Fokker DVII	C951	20	S Gheluwe	1950	DES	CR/RAF 29.7
25†††	15 Sep	Hannover C	E2470	20	S E St Quentin	1750	DES(F)	CR/RAF 15.9
26†††	20 Sep	Fokker DVII	E2246	20	Rouvroy	1030	DES	CR/RAF 20.9
27†††	20 Sep	Fokker DVII	E2246	20	Neuville	1031	DES	CR/RAF 20.9

TOTAL: 20 destroyed, 6 and 1 shared out of control = 27.
*Observer: 2/Lt C.G. Claye **Observer: 2/Lt C.G. Claye; shared with 2/Lt H.C. Farnes/2/Lt Davis A3349 ***Observer: 2/Lt C.A. Malcomsen †Observer: 2/Lt A.W. Merchant ††Observer: Capt F. Godfrey †††Observer: Lt A. Mills.

MILLER Archibald William Buchanan Lieutenant 1, 29

Born in Staffordshire in 1897, Miller served as an observer in 1 Squadron from November 1915, returning to Home Establishment for pilot training during 1916. He returned to France joining 29 Squadron on 4 May 1917; flying Nieuport Scouts he was credited with six victories before he was killed in action on 13 July at the age of 20, shot down in B1506 by Leutnant Hans Adam of Jasta 6 for the latter's fifth victory.

	1917		Nieuport					
1	1 Jun	Alb. DIII	B1506	29	Brebieres	0515	OOC	CR/RFC 1.6
2	19 Jun	Alb. DIII	B1506	29	Douai	1945	DES	CR/RFC 20.6
3	29 Jun	Alb. DIII	B1506	29	Douai	0745	DES	CR/RFC 29.6
4	29 Jun	Alb. DIII	B1506	29	E Brebieres	0754	OOC	CR/RFC 29.6
5	12 Jul	Alb. DIII	B1506	29	Zonnebeke-Roulers	2015	OOC	CR/RFC 12.7
6	12 Jul	Alb. DIII	B1506	29	Zonnebeke-Roulers	2015	OOC	CR/RFC 12.7

TOTAL: 2 destroyed and 4 out of control = 6.

MILLMAN Norman Craig Captain 48

After joining the RFC in May 1916, this Canadian served in 48 Squadron from 20 August 1917, becoming a flight commander. He left the unit in May 1918.

	1917		Bristol					
1*	11 Nov	Alb. DV	B1134	48	E St Georges	1510	OOC	CR/RFC 11.11
	1918							
2**	3 Jan	Alb. C	B1187	48	Le Catelet	1130	OOC	CR/SR/?
3**	1 Mar	C	B1190	48	Joncourt	1010	OOC	CR/RFC 1.3
4**	1 Mar	Alb. DIII	B1190	48	S St Quentin	1030	OOC	CR/RFC 1.3
5**	8 Mar	Alb. DV	B1190	48	Bohain	1040	OOC	CR/RFC 8.3
6**	8 Mar	Alb. DV	B1190	48	Bohain	1555	OOC	CR/RFC 8.3

TOTAL: 6 out of control = 6.
*Observer: Lt T.C.S. Tuffield. **Observer: 2/Lt H.A. Cooper.

MILLS Kenneth Charles Lieutenant 1

Born in London on 26 March 1899, Mills joined the RFC in June 1917 and served with 1 Squadron during spring 1918. He was killed by ground fire on 8 August of that year whilst flying D6962.

	1918		SE 5A					
1s*	21 Apr	Pfalz DIII	C5374	1	Lompret	1210	OOC	CR/RAF 21.4
2	25 Apr	Fokker DrI	C5374	1	Becelaere-Dadizeele	1845	DES	CR/RAF 25.4
3s**	2 May	LVG. C	C5374	1	Houthoulst	1325	OOC	CR/ORB/?
4s***	3 May	Pfalz DIII	C5374	1	Steenwerck	0730	OOC	CR/ORB/?
5	7 May	C	C1849	1	1m E Kemmel	1645	DES	CR/RAF 7.5

TOTAL: 2 destroyed and 3 shared out of control = 5.
*Shared with Capt C.C. Clark B4810. **Shared with Lt J.C. Bateman B8254. ***Shared with Lt E.E. Owen B504.

MILNE John Theobald Captain 48

Flying with 48 Squadron during the summer of 1917, Milne first claimed in early July, and was promoted flight commander during that month. His final victory was claimed on 28 September, bringing his score to nine, and he was awarded an MC. During September he was wounded, but returned to action. He was reported missing on 24 October, shot down in B1117 by Leutnant Fritz Kieckhafer of Jasta 29 near Merken; his observer, Lieutenant J. Wright, was lost with him. Milne had been highly-regarded in 48 Squadron; after his death his fellow flight commander, Captain Keith Park, delivered his personal effects to his wife. He was introduced to her cousin, who he subsequently married.

	1917		Bristol					
1*	6 Jul	Alb. DIII	A7129	48	E Cambrai	0900	OOC	CR/RFC 6.7
2**	7 Jul	Alb. DV	A7129	48	S Vitry	0550	DES	CR/RFC 7.7
3*	12 Jul	Alb. DV	A7129	48	Leffinghe	1815	DES	CR/RFC 12.7
4***	20 Aug	Alb. DV	A7216	48	Ghistelles	1915	DES	CR/RFC 20.8
5***	20 Aug	Alb. DV	A7216	48	Ghistelles	1915	OOC	CR/RFC 20.8
6***	21 Aug	Alb. DV	A7216	48	E Westende	1945	DES	CR/RFC 21.8
7***	25 Aug	Alb. DV	A7216	48	Westkerke	1210	OOC	CR/RFC 25.8
8**	9 Sep	Alb. DV	A7216	48	Middelkerke	1615	OOC	CR/RFC 9.9
9*	28 Sep	Alb. DV	B1124	48	Slype	0930	OOC	CR/SR/?

TOTAL: 4 destroyed and 5 out of control = 9.
*Observer: 2/Lt L.H. Tanner. **Observer: Lt A.D. Light. ***Observer: 2/Lt W. O'Toole.

MINIFIE Richard Pearman Flight Lieutenant 1W, 1(N)

Born on 2 February 1898, in Melbourne, Australia, he joined the RNAS as a probationary Flight Sub Lieutenant in June 1915. He was posted to 'A' Squadron of 1 Wing late in the year, remaining with the unit until 1(N) Squadron was formed with Sopwith Triplanes early in 1917. He claimed several victories during the spring and early summer of that year, but from August to October claimed 11 victories when the unit was the last equipped with Triplanes still at the front. He was by this time a flight commander. He was awarded a DSC on 2 November and a Bar to this on 30th of the same month. The unit later converted to Camels and he flew these early in 1918, gaining his last four victories in one of these machines. Following the posting of Roderic Dallas for a rest, Minifie became acting Squadron Commander pending the arrival of his great friend and fellow Australian, Charlie Booker. However on 17 March 1918 he was either shot down or suffered engine failure during a fight with Jasta 47, and came down behind German lines, becoming a prisoner. He subsequently received a second Bar to his DSC, awarded on 17 April 1918. In 1919 he returned to Australia and eventually joined the family flour milling business. During World War II he was a Squadron Leader in the Air Training Corps. He died in Melbourne on 31 March 1969.

	1917		Triplane					
1	29 Apr	Alb. DIII	N5446	1N	Epinoy	1110	DES	CR/RFC 29.4
2s*	29 Apr	Alb. DIII	N5446	1N	Douai	1915	DES	CR/RFC 29.4
3s**	11 May	Alb. DII	N5446	1N	Vitry	1940	OOC	CR/ORB/?
4	19 May	Alb. DIII	N5446	1N	Henin-Lietard	1915	OOC	CR/RFC 19.5
5	12 Jun	Alb. DV	N5446	1N	Deulemont	0615	OOC	CR/RFC 12.6
6	12 Jul	Alb. DV	N6303	1N	Quesnoy	0910	OOC	CR/RFC 12.7
7	8 Aug	Alb. DV	N6303	1N	Houthoulst Forest	1600	DES(F)	CR/RFC 8.8
8	15 Aug	Alb. DV	N5454	1N	E Ypres	0915	OOC	CR/RFC 15.8
9	16 Aug	Alb. DV	N5454	1N	Roubaix a/d	0440	DES	CR/RFC 16.8
10	16 Sep	Alb. DV	N5454	1N	N E Messines	1825	DES	CR/RFC 16.9
11	19 Sep	Alb. DV	N5454	1N	Westroosebeke	1800	DES	CR/RFC 19.9
12	26 Sep	C	N5454	1N	E St Julien	1220	DES	CR/RFC 27.9
13	17 Oct	DFW. C	N5454	1N	S Polygon Wood	1045	CAPT	CR/RFC 17.10
14	18 Oct	Gotha	N5454	1N	N Passchendaele	1430	OOC	CR/RFC 18.10

15	20 Oct	Alb. DV	N5454	1N	S Comines	1100	OOC	CR/RFC 20.10
16	27 Oct	Fokker DV	N5454	1N	Westroosebeke	0845	DES	CR/RFC 27.10
17	31 Oct	C	N5454	1N	E Gheluveldt	1855	DES	CR/RFC 31.10
			Camel					
18	29 Nov	Alb. DV	B6420	1N	Middelkerke	1415	OOC	CR/RNAS 29.11
19	8 Dec	DFW. C	B6420	1N	E Dixmude	1120	DES	CR/RNAS 8.12
	1918							
20	13 Mar	Alb. DV	B6420	1N	S E Dixmude	0725	DES	CR/RNAS 13.3
21	13 Mar	Alb. DV	B6420	1N	S E Dixmude	0725	OOC	CR/RNAS 13.3

TOTAL: 1 captured, 10 and 1 shared destroyed, 8 and 1 shared out of control = 21.
*Shared with FSL R.A. Little N5493, of 8N. **Shared with FSL O.B. Ellis N5488.

MITCHELL James Hart Captain 28

A Yorkshireman, Mitchell received the MC while serving with the Royal Artillery, before transferring to the RFC during 1917. He joined 28 Squadron and went to France in October of that year. Here on 20th of that month whilst engaged in escorting Camels of 70 Squadron on an aerodrome strafe, he shot down an Albatros Scout that was attacking a fellow pilot, W.G. Barker, who was later to be awarded the Victoria Cross. In November the unit went to Italy and soon 'Mitch' was made a flight commander and promoted to Captain. Before returning to Home Establishment in July 1918 he had claimed 11 enemy machines, including an AEG bomber, and had been awarded the DFC and the Italian Medal for Military Valour.

	1917		Camel					
1	20 Oct	Alb. DIII	B6344	28	Roulers	1215	DES	CR/RFC 20.10
2	27 Oct	Alb. DV	B6362	28	E Roulers	1343	OOC	CR/RFC 27.10
3	27 Oct	Alb. DV	B6362	28	E Roulers	1345	DES(F)	CR/RFC 27.10
4*	8 Dec	C	B6406	28	4-5 N W Asiago	1110	DES	CR/7 BG
5	10 Dec	Alb. DIII	B6406	28	2m N W Fontane	1115	DES(F)	CR/7 BG
6s**	26 Dec	AEG. C	B6344	28	Montebelluna	1215	CAPT	CR/7 BG
	1918							
7***	4 Feb	Alb. DIII	B6344	28	1km S Motta	1005	DES	CR/7 BG
8†	18 Mar	Alb. DIII	B6344	28	Cordigano	1530	DES(F)	CR/ORB/?
9	17 Apr	Alb. DIII	B6344	28	2m S W Motta	1315	DES(F)	CR/7 BG
10††	26 May	Alb. DIII	B6344	28	2km N Arcade	0845	DES(F)	CR/14 WS
11	7 Jun	Berg DI	D8110	28	6km S W Motta	0520	DES	CR/14 WS

TOTAL: 1 shared captured, 9 destroyed, 1 out of control = 11.
*This was Uffz Bantz/Oblt Kanitz of Flik 58d, who were killed. **Shared with Ten S. Scaroni, Sgt Brenta, 76a Sq. BG IV crew. ***Probably Oblt Loeser, CO of Jasta 39, who was wounded. †This was an all red aircraft with a skull and crossbones — the marking of Oblt Godwin Brumowski. Mitchell was then shot-up and forced to land by Korp F. Schwarzmann 153:134 and Fw S. Fejes 153:132, both from Flik 51j. ††This was FwP F. Hofstadter of Flik 42j, in 153:230.

MOLESWORTH William Earle Major 60, 29

'Moley' Molesworth was born on 14 March 1894 in Ireland, and served with the Royal Munster Regiment before transferring to the RFC. He served with 60 Squadron from March to August 1917, commanding 'A' Flight from May and receiving the MC. With 60 he claimed six victories, and had several fights with the red Albatroses of von Richthofen's Circus. He then went to 29 Squadron in October, adding a Bar to his MC and bringing his total of victories to 18 before being posted to Home Establishment in March 1918. He was later promoted to Major, and also received the Italian Medal for Military Valour. A selection of his letters home were published in *Flypast* magazine during 1979-80.

	1917		Nieuport					
1	22 Apr	Alb. DIII	B1569	60	Vitry	1720	OOC	CR/RFC 22.4
2	24 Apr	Balloon	B1569	60	Boiry Notre Dame	1040	DES	CR/RFC 24.4
3	29 Jun	Alb. DIII	B1652	60	Douai-Estrees	1800	DES	CR/RFC 30.6
4	11 Jul	Alb. DIII	B1652	60	Queant	1410	OOC	CR/C&C V11
			SE 5A					
5s*	5 Aug	Alb. DIII	A4851	60	Hendecourt	2000	DES(F)	CR/RFC 5.8
6	9 Aug	Alb. DV	A8932	60	Cagnicourt	0700	DES	CR/RFC 9.8
			Nieuport					
7	8 Nov	Alb. DV	B6812	29	E Westroosebeke	1515	DES(F)	CR/RFC 8.11
8	8 Nov	C	B6812	29	Houthoulst Forest	1600	DES(F)	CR/RFC 8.11
9	26 Nov	Alb. DV	B6820	29	S E Houthoulst	1450	OOC	CR/RFC 26.11
	1918							
10	3 Jan	Alb. DV	B6812	29	S Moorslede	1530	OOC	CR/RFC 3.1
11	22 Jan	Alb. DV	B6812	29	N E Staden	1235	DES	CR/RFC 22.1
12	24 Jan	C	B6812	29	N E Roulers	1200	DES	CR/RFC 24.1

13	24 Jan	C	B6812	29	N Roulers	1310	DES	CR/RFC 24.1
14	29 Jan	Alb. DV	B6797	29	E Moorslede	1255	DES(F)	CR/RFC 29.1
15	5 Feb	C	B6812	29	Moorslede-Roulers	1020	OOC	CR/RFC 5.2
16	21 Feb	C	B6812	29	Ypres-Zonnebeke	1410	CAPT	CR/RFC 21.2
17	26 Feb	C	B6812	29	S E Becelaere	1100	DES	CR/RFC 26.2
18	18 Mar	Pfalz DIII	B6812	29	S E Rumbeke	1145	DES	CR/RFC 18.3

TOTAL: 1 balloon, 1 captured, 10 and 1 destroyed, 5 out of control = 18.
*Shared with Lt S.B. Horn A8930. This was Lt B. Lehmann of Jasta 12, who was killed.

MOLYNEAUX Harold Arthur Sydney Lieutenant 56

Following service with the 75th Canadian Division, this Canadian joined the RFC and was posted to 56 Squadron on 4 April, 1918. He flew more than 70 offensive patrols, plus five special missions, and was credited with five victories in air combat, receiving the DFC. He was posted to Home Establishment on 8 November.

	1918		SE 5A					
1	12 Aug	Fokker DVII	D6127	56	Ham	1645	DES	CR/RAF 12.8
2	1 Sep	Fokker DVII	D6127	56	S Riencourt	1900	OOC	CR/?
3	3 Sep	Fokker DVII	D6127	56	Etaing	0710	OOC	CR/?
4	16 Sep	Fokker DVII	D338	56	Havrincourt Wood	1755	DES	CR/RAF 16.9
5	24 Sep	Fokker DVII	F5504	56	Haynecourt	0830	DES	CR/?

TOTAL: 3 destroyed, 2 out of control = 5.

MONTGOMERY Kenneth Barbour Captain 45, 66

From Oxton, Cheshire, born in October 1897, Montgomery was commissioned in April 1917 and flew Sopwith 1½ Strutters and later Camels, with 45 Squadron in France during the summer of that year. He was credited with 12 victories and received the MC on 3 January 1918, during which month he was promoted to Captain and posted as a flight commander to 66 Squadron, both units now being in Italy. He was shot down and wounded by anti-aircraft fire on 22 February, becoming a prisoner. The award of a French Croix de Guerre followed on 23 November 1918.

	1917		Strutter					
1*	13 Jul	Alb. DIII	----	45	E Polygon Wood	1515	OOC	CR/RFC 13.7
2**	15 Jul	Alb. DIII	----	45	Polygon Wood	1610	DES(F)	CR/RFC 15.7
3**	11 Aug	Alb. DIII	----	45	Comines	1915	OOC	CR/SR/?
4**	23 Aug	Alb. DV	A1053	45	Bellewaarde Lake	0915	OOC	CR/SR/?
			Camel					
5	20 Sep	Alb. DV	B3811	45	Westroosebeke	1105	OOC	CR/RFC 20.9
6	22 Sep	Alb. DV	----	45	Tenbrielen	0855	OOC	CR/RFC 22.9
7	15 Oct	C	----	45	Houthoulst Forest	1650	DES	CR/RFC 15.10
8s***	26 Oct	C	----	45	Houthoulst Forest	1025	DES	CR/RFC 26.10
9	9 Nov	C	----	45	S Becelaere	1250	OOC	CR/RFC 9.11
10†	15 Nov	Alb. DV	B3929	45	Langemarck	0935	DES(F)	CR/RFC 15.11
	1918							
11††	3 Jan	Alb. DIII	B3929	45	Corbelone	1340	DES	CR/7 BG
12s†††	12 Jan	Alb. DV	B4628	66	S E Fonzaszo	1235	DES	CR/7 BG

TOTAL: 4 and 2 shared destroyed, 6 out of control = 12.
*Observer: Sgt Wickham. **Observer: Lt R.C. Purvis. ***Shared with 2/Lt M.B. Frew. †This aircraft was also claimed by 29 Sqn. The pilot Lt Hans Adam was a 21 victory ace, and commander of Jasta 6. ††Probably, Zgsfr E. Bonsch of Flik 51j, who force-landed 153:31. †††Shared with 2/Lt A.F. Lingard B5244.

MOODY Basil Henry Lieutenant 1

Born in Capetown, South Africa, on 19 January 1898, Moody was commissioned in the RFC on 11 October 1917 and joined 1 Squadron in France on 23 April 1918. He remained with this unit until February 1919, claiming nine victories prior to the close of hostilities.

	1918		SE 5A					
1s*	27 May	C	C1092	1	1m S Bailleul	1425	DES(F)	CR/RAF 27.5
2s*	27 May	C	C1092	1	Kemmel	1450	DES	CR/RAF 27.5
3s**	28 May	C	C1092	1	Meteren-Bailleul	0635	OOC	CR/ORB/?
4s**	28 May	C	C1092	1	Meteren-Vieux Berquin	0700	DES	CR/RAF 28.5
5s***	15 Sep	Pfalz DXII	B8501	1	Recourt	1705	CAPT	CR/RAF 15.9
6	27 Sep	Fokker DVII	B8501	1	Bertry	0915	DES(F)	CR/RAF 27.9

7s†	1 Oct	Fokker DVII	B8501	1	N E St Quentin	1710	OOC	CR/ORB/?
8s††	28 Oct	Fokker DVII	B8501	1	Trelon	1530	DES(F)	CR/RAF 28.10
9s††	28 Oct	Fokker DVII	B8501	1	Trelon	1530	OOC	CR/RAF 28.10

TOTAL: 1 shared captured, 1 and 4 shared destroyed, 3 shared out of control = 9.
*Shared with Capt P.J. Clayson C1114, Lt D. Knight C6479, Lt H.A. Kullberg B8254, Lt E.T.S. Kelly B130. **Shared with Lt E.M. Forsyth B733, Lt E.T.S. Kelly B130, Lt E.E. Owen B8512, LT A.F. Scroggs C6416, Capt K.S. Henderson C1112, Lt K.J.P. Laing B8504, Lt H.B. Bradley C1102, Lt H.A. Kullberg B8254, Lt D. Knight C6479, Capt P.J. Clayson C1849. ***Shared with Capt C.S.I. Lavers E5969, Capt G.W.D. Allen F5912, Lt D.E. Cameron F6429, and Capt W.E. Staton/Lt L.E. Mitchell of 62 Sqn. Lt P. Vogel of Jasta 23 died of wounds. †Shared with Capt C.S.I. Lavers C9292, Lt W.A. Smart D6973, Lt F.M. Squires E6009, 2/Lt F.A. Nesbit B7881, 2/Lt C.R. Boyd C9065, Lt D.E. Cameron H7257. ††Shared with Lt D.E. Cameron H7257.

MOODY Henry Michael Captain 45

Born in the county of Shropshire in 1898, he joined the RFC as a mechanic in December 1916. Later he became a pilot and was commissioned in June 1917. He was posted to 45 Squadron, going to 'A' Flight under Captain Macmillan, and flew many sorties, claiming four enemy aircraft, one of which was an armoured Junkers J1. Going to Italy with the unit in November, he claimed two enemy scouts on 31 December; one of these as it was attacking a French balloon. He was later promoted to Captain, received an MC, and was returned to Home Establishment in June 1918. With the rank of Flight Lieutenant he served in India and England with the RAF until he was killed in a flying accident on 23 April 1931.

	1917		Camel					
1	4 Sep	C	----	45	N E Comines	1450	OOC	CR/SR/?
2	11 Sep	DFW. C	----	45	Westroosebeke	0920	OOC	CR/RFC 11.9
3s*	20 Sep	C	----	45	Passchendaele	1825	DES(F)	CR/RFC 20.9
4	13 Nov	Junkers J1	B6238	45	N E Comines	1610	OOC	CR/RFC 13.11
5	31 Dec	Alb. DIII	B6238	45	Piave de Soligo	0945	OOC	CR/7 BG
6s**	31 Dec	Alb. DV	B6238	45	Parderno	1030	CAPT	CR/7 BG
	1918							
7	11 Jan	Alb. DIII	B6383	45	Corbelone	1530	DES	CR/7 BG
8	30 Jan	Alb. DIII	B4609	45	Susegana	1300	DES	CR/ORB/?

TOTAL: 1 shared captured, 2 and 1 shared destroyed, 4 out of control = 8.
*Shared with 2/Lt E.A.L.F. Smith, 2/Lt R.J. Brownell. **Shared with 2/Lt R.J. Brownell B2430. This was Lt A. Thurm of Jasta 31 who was killed.

MOORE Guy Borthwick Captain 1

Guy Moore, a Canadian from Vancouver, born in 1895, joined 1 Squadron on 16 August 1917, gaining his first victory on 2 October. After he had claimed six more while flying Nieuport Scouts, the squadron converted to SE 5As early in 1918, and he was promoted to flight commander. Early in the year he received an MC for three destroyed, three out of control and a balloon, which was gazetted on 13 May. He had gained several more victories in March, but he was then shot down and killed on 7 April in C1083 at Hollebeke, his aircraft exploding in mid air. He has often been listed as one of Manfred von Richthofen's victims, but this is patently incorrect, as the German's claims were made far away from this location at a different time of day. In fact it seems likely that the SE received a direct hit by an anti-aircraft shell.

	1917		Nieuport					
1s*	2 Oct	DFW. C	B1508	1	Comines	1105	OOC	CR/RFC 2.10
2	5 Oct	C	B1508	1	Houthoulst	1635	DES(F)	CR/RFC 5.10
3	7 Oct	Alb. DV	B1508	1	N Menin	0800	OOC	CR/RFC 7.10
4	8 Oct	Alb. DV	B1508	1	E Polygon Wood	1430	OOC	CR/RFC 8.10
5	9 Oct	Alb. DV	B1508	1	Gheluwe	1330	DES	CR/RFC 9.10
6	17 Dec	Alb. DV	B3629	1	S W Moorslede	1423	OOC	CR/RFC 17.12
	1918							
7	4 Jan	Alb. DV	B3629	1	S Terhand	1105	DES	CR/RFC 4.1
			SE 5A					
8s**	13 Mar	Pfalz DIII	B511	1	Wieltje	1220	OOC	CR/ORB/?
9s***	28 Mar	LVG. C	C1083	1	Gavrelle	0840	DES	CR/ORB/?
10	28 Mar	DFW. C	C1083	1	Bazentin	1405	DES	CR/RFC 28.3

TOTAL: 4 and 1 shared destroyed, 4 and 1 shared out of control = 10.
*Shared with 2/Lt H.J. Hamilton B3474. **Shared with Capt W.D. Patrick B641, Capt H.J. Hamilton B32, Lt H.A. Rigby C9624, 2/Lt L.W. Mawbey B632, 2/Lt P.J. Clayson A8908, 2/Lt A. Hollis B520, 2/Lt W.M.R. Gray A8904. ***Shared with Lt F.P. Magoun C5306.

MORGAN John Towlson Captain 70

Morgan served with the Royal Welsh Fusiliers, reaching the rank of Captain. Transferring to the RFC, he was posted to 70 Squadron in June 1918, claiming five victories with this unit by early September.

	1918		Camel					
1s*	27 Jun	Alb. DV	----	70	Beaumont-Hamel	0915	OOC	CR/III BG
2	29 Jun	Alb. DV	D6642	70	Irles	0920	OOC	CR/III BG
3	30 Jun	Alb. DV	C1908	70	E Bray	2035	OOC	CR/III BG
4	13 Aug	Pfalz DIII	C8201	70	N Tourcoing	0815	OOC	CR/11 WS
5	3 Sep	Fokker DVII	----	70	S Roulers	0910	OOC	CR/11 WS

TOTAL: 4 and 1 shared out of control = 5.
*Shared with 3 other Camel pilots.

MORRIS James Fitz- Captain (see FITZ-MORRIS James)

MORROW Ernest Theophilus Captain 62

A Canadian from Toronto, Morrow joined 62 Squadron on 31 August 1917 and served throughout the spring and summer of 1918. Flying with various gunners, he claimed two destroyed and three out of control, before being promoted to flight commander. On 22 August he claimed two more victories but was himself shot down and severely wounded, probably by pilots of Jasta 1. He was awarded a DFC, gazetted on 2 November.

	1918		Bristol					
1*	26 Mar	EA	----	62	----	----	DES	SR/C&C V16/4
2*	3 May	Alb. DV	C796	62	S Armentieres	1120	DES	CR/RAF 3.5
3*	3 May	Alb. DV	C796	62	S Armentieres	1120	OOC	CR/RAF 3.5
4**	10 Aug	EA	----	62	----	----	OOC	SR/C&C V16/4
5**	10 Aug	EA	----	62	----	----	OOC	SR/C&C V16/4
6**	22 Aug	Fokker DVII	C895	62	Pronville	0745	OOC	CR/RAF 22.8
7***	22 Aug	Fokker DVII	C895	62	Pronville	0745	DES(F)	CR/RAF 22.8

TOTAL: 3 destroyed, 4 out of control = 7.
*Observer: Lt H.E. Merritt. **Observer: 2/Lt L.M. Thompson. ***Observer: Lt L.M. Thompson. This was probably Uffz Born of Jasta 1, who was killed in a fight with Bristols.

MOSTYN W.J. Captain 22

After transferring from the Lincoln Regiment, Mostyn served in 22 Squadron in spring 1918, gaining all his victories in a period of one week. Three of these were accounted for by his front gun, one by the rear gun, manned by Sergeant J.H. Jones, and a fifth shared by both.

	1918		Bristol					
1*	20 May	Pfalz DIII	C901	22	N W Estaires	1850	DES	CR/RAF 20.5
2*	21 May	LVG. C	C901	22	S W Vitry	1015	OOC	CR/SR/?
3*	21 May	LVG. C	C901	22	S W Vitry	1015	OOC	CR/SR/?
4*	22 May	Alb. DV	C901	22	S E Arras	1030	OOC	CR/SR/?
5*	26 May	Alb. DV	C901	22	S E Armentieres	1945	OOC	CR/SR/?

TOTAL: 1 destroyed, 4 out of control = 5.
*Observer: Sgt J.H. Jones.

MOTT Harold Edgar Captain 9(N)

A Canadian from Winnipeg, Manitoba, born 4 December 1897, Mott graduated from the Wright Flying School at Mineola, New York, on 2 August 1916 and became an original member of 9(N) Squadron. He claimed two individual and three shared victories by the end of 1917.

	1917		Pup					
1s*	2 May	C	N5188	9N	Middelkerke	2030	DES	CR/RNAS 3.5
2	12 May	C	N6193	9N	Zeebrugge	0715	OOC	CR/RNAS 12.5
3	5 Jun	C	N6193	9N	off Ostend	1700	DES(F)	CR/DRO/DL
4s**	7 Jul	Alb. DV	N6469	9N	S W Haynecourt	c1730	OOC	CR/ORB/?
			Camel					
5s***	25 Jul	C	B3832	9N	off Westende	1730	OOC	CR/DRO/?

TOTAL: 1 and 1 shared destroyed, 1 and 2 shared out of control = 5.
*Shared with FSL H.F. Stackard 9916. **Shared with F/Cdr H.E. Hervey N6462, FSL J.W. Pinder N6475. ***Shared with F/Lt F.E. Banbury B3820, FSL J.W. Pinder B3870, FSL Snell, FSL O.M. Redgate B3813.

MULOCK Redford Henry Colonel 1W, 3(N), 82W

It is questionable whether Red Mulock qualifies as an ace; he was, however, a great leader and fighter pilot of the early days, and is included because of the particular interest of his career. Born in Winnipeg, Canada, on 11 August 1886, he joined the Canadian Field Artillery in 1911 and served with this formation until 1915 when he transferred to the RNAS. After training, he joined 1 Naval Wing at Dunkirk, first seeing action in July 1915. Flying along the coast and over the Channel in early Nieuport Scouts, he was involved in a number of combats which, although not always conclusive by the standards of even a year later, were nonetheless claimed as victories at that early date. Consequently by early 1916 he had become the first Canadian to claim five successes, and also the first RNAS pilot to achieve this. He was awarded a DSO, gazetted in June 1916, for attacking aircraft, submarine and shipping, and for reconnaissance operations. He later commanded 3(N) Squadron in 1917, receiving the French Legion d'Honneur on 14 September of that year; he also received a Bar to his DSO and was Mentioned in Despatches. By early 1918 he was a Wing Commander, and was later to serve with the RCAF in the inter-war period, rising to the rank of Air Commodore by 1935, when he left to join Canadian Airways.

	1915		Nieuport					
1	30 Dec	C	----	1W	Dixmude	----	OOC	TBYW/
	1916							
2	24 Jan	C	----	1W	----	----	FTL	OH/?
3	26 Jan	C	3977	1W	Nieuport	1500	OOC	CR/DL/
4	21 May	C	3992	1W	off Nieuport	1400	OOC	CR/DL/?
5	21 May	C	3992	1W	off Nieuport	1400	OOC	CR/DL/?

TOTAL: 4 out of control, 1 forced to land = 5.

MUNDAY Richard Burnard Major 8(N)

Believed to be an Australian who joined the RNAS in 1915, Munday became a Flight Sub Lieutenant in May of that year and became an instructor at Cranwell in 1916, where one of his pupils was 'Titch' Rochford, later to become a great ace. He later served with 8(N) Squadron as a flight commander in autumn 1917, specializing in hunting balloons at night! By the end of January 1918 he had claimed five of these, four of them in the dark, including one in its shed on 29 September. During early 1918 he added three victories over aircraft to raise his total to nine. He was awarded a DSC, and after the formation of the RAF, was promoted to Major.

	1917		Camel					
1s*	19 Aug	Alb. DV	N5421	8N	Henin-Lietard	1830	OOC	CR/RFC 19.8
2	2 Sep	Balloon	B3921	8N	Quiery la Motte	2000	DES	CR/ORB/?
3	29 Sep	Balloon	B3921	8N	Brebieres	2200	DES	CR/RFC 29.9
4s**	3 Oct	Balloon	----	8N	Douai	c2300	DES	CR/ORB/MM
5	7 Nov	Balloon	B3921	8N	N Meurchin	0610	DES	CR/RFC 7.11
	1918							
6	21 Jan	Balloon	B6378	8N	Godault Farm	1900	DES	CR/RFC 22.1
7	29 Jan	Alb. DV	B6378	8N	Beaumont-Auby	1510	OOC	CR/RFC 29.1
8	3 Feb	Alb. DV	B6378	8N	Vitry	1230	OOC	CR/RFC 3.2
9	21 Feb	C	B7197	8N	Drocourt	1130	OOC	CR/RFC 21.2

TOTAL: 4 and 1 shared balloons, 4 out of control = 9.
*Shared with F/Cdr C.D. Booker N5460, FSL E.D. Crundall N5465. **Shared with Sqn Cdr C. Draper.

MURLIS-GREEN Gilbert Ware Major 5, 17, 47, 44, 151, 70

Gilbert Murlis-Green joined the Suffolk Regiment in 1914, but the following year transferred to the RFC. He first flew as an observer with 5 Squadron in France late in 1915, but after a short spell on operations was selected for pilot training. In the latter part of 1916 he was posted to 17 Squadron on the Salonica front, first flying BE 2Ds during November. A month later he began flying BE 12 single-seat scouts in which he engaged in several indecisive combats; he had already been recommended for an MC when on 13 December he claimed a victory over a two two-seater, and was at once also recommended for a Bar to this award. The MC was eventually gazetted on New Year's Day 1917, and the Bar on 13 February. By mid-March his score had risen to three and he had become a Captain; he then shot down two twin-engined Friederickshafen aircraft in one sortie, getting another victory next day. This feat led to the award of a DSO, gazetted on 18 June, but it was to be July before he again scored. Then, in a borrowed French Spad armed with two Vickers guns, he shot down a two-seater in flames. Shortly after this, having received a second Bar to his MC, he was posted to Home Establishment where he took command of 44(Home Defence) Squadron, flying Sopwith Camels modified for night fighting, fitted with twin Lewis guns above the top wing instead of the usual twin Vickers on the nose. On 18 December 1917, in one of these aircraft, he shot down the first German aircraft to fall on British soil at night, for which he received a Bar to his DSO. In June 1918 he was posted to 151 Squadron and took this to France as the first specialised night fighter unit on the Western Front. Late in the year he returned to day fighting, leading

70 Squadron — also on Camels. Apart from his British decorations he received both French and Belgian Croix de Guerre, and the Karageorge (Serbian Order of the White Eagle). He remained in the RAF after the war, and was a Group Captain in 1934. His score has been quoted as anything up to 31 in the past, but this is incorrect; it is thought that the larger numbers listed relate to the total number of engagements he fought with enemy aircraft, rather than the number of victories.

	1916		BE 12					
1	13 Dec	DFW. C	6601	17	1m S E Virikleri	1000	DES	CR/OH/?
	1917							
2	4 Jan	Alb. DV	6601	17	1m N Mekes	1100	CAPT	CR/OH/?
3s*	14 Jan	Alb. C	6601	17	Lahana	1115	CAPT	CR/?
4	18 Mar	Fried. G	A4007	17	White Scar Hill	1715	DES	CR/?
5	18 Mar	Fried. G	A4007	17	Volovan	1745	OOC	CR/?
6	19 Mar	Alb. C	A4007	17	Lake Doiran	0830	DES(F)	CR/?
			Spad					
7	13 Jul	Alb. C	S1073	17	6m N W Angista Station	1950	DES(F)	CR/?
			Camel					
8**	18 Dec	Gotha GIII	B5192	44	S E England	1950-2000	CAPT	CR/ADOB

TOTAL: 2 and 1 shared captured, 4 destroyed, 1 out of control = 8.
*Shared with Lt F.G. Saunders 6603. **This was Lt F. Ketelsen/Oblt G. Von Stachelsky/Gefr A. Weissmann of Bogohl III, who were captured.

MURMAN Donald Frederick 1st Lieutenant 40, 25US

Don Murman was posted to 40 Squadron in early May 1918. After making two claims in May, he claimed one and one shared on 25 July; the latter has generally not been included in his score in the past. His fifth and last claim was made on 5 August.

	1918		SE 5A					
1	14 May	DFW. C	D5968	40	Biily-Berclau	1815	OOC	CR/RAF 14.5
2	21 May	Alb. DV	D5968	40	E Lens	0830	OOC	CR/A I/1789
3s*	25 Jul	Fokker DVII	C5357	40	S W Lille	1520	DES	CR/RAF 25.7
4	25 Jul	Fokker DVII	C5357	40	S W Lille	1720	OOC	CR/A I/1789
5	8 Aug	Fokker DVII	B875	40	Don	1030	DES	CR/RAF 8.8

TOTAL: 1 and 1 shared destroyed, 3 out of control = 5.
*Shared with 1/Lt P.V. Burwell D3527.

MUSPRATT Keith Knox Lieutenant 56

A doctor's son from Bournemouth, he learned to fly while still at Sherbourne School when he was 16. When he later joined the RFC, he became an instructor and among his pupils was Arthur Rhys-Davids, who was later to be one of the most successful pilots in 56 Squadron. Muspratt himself subsequently joined 56 Squadron in France, and during his tour accounted for eight enemy machines, being awarded an MC. He returned home in November 1917 and became a test pilot at Martlesham Heath, where he was killed in an aircraft crash on 19 March 1918.

	1917		SE 5					
1s*	24 May	Alb. DIII	A4861	56	S Douai	1900-2000	OOC	CR/RFC 24.5
2	28 May	Alb. DIII	A8913	56	Lecluse	0630-0730	OOC	CR/RFC 28.5
3s**	17 Jul	Alb. DV	A8913	56	Roulers-Menin Rd.	2015	OOC	CR/RFC 17.7
4	14 Aug	C	A8944	56	Houthoulst Wood	c1000	DES	CR/RFC 14.8
5	18 Aug	C	A8944	56	Becelaere	0630-0730	DES	CR/RFC 18.8
6***	22 Aug	C	A8944	56	S St Julian	1830-1950	CAPT	CR/RFC 22.8
7	29 Oct	Alb. DV	A8944	56	Roulers-Menin Rd.	c0900	DES	CR/RFC 29.10
8	31 Oct	C	A8944	56	Stadenberg	0905-1115	DES	CR/RFC 31.10

TOTAL: 1 captured, 4 destroyed, 1 and 2 shared out of control = 8.
*Shared with Capt C.M. Crowe A8910, 2/Lt R.T.C. Hoidge A4862, 2/Lt A.P.F. Rhys-Davids A4868, 2/Lt J.S. Turnbull A8913. **Shared with Capt I.H.D. Henderson A8909, 2/Lt L.M. Barlow A8910, 2/Lt A.P.F. Rhys-Davids A4863, Lt V.P. Cronyn A4856. ***This was Lt Koch/Lt Wolluhn of FAA 210.

NAPIER Charles Georges Douglas Captain 20, 48

After service with 20 Squadron late in 1917, Napier joined 48 Squadron early in the following year, becoming a flight commander. The award of an MC was gazetted on 22 June 1918, but already he and his observer, Sergeant Pat Murphy, had been shot down in flames over Lamotte on 15 May in B1337, during a fight with JG I and Jasta 5; the Germans confirmed their deaths on 12 June.

	1918		Bristol					
1*	7 Feb	LVG. C	----	48	Le Catelet	c0600	DES	Citation
2*	8 Mar	DFW. C	----	48	St Quentin	c0600	DES(F)	Citation
3*	16 Mar	LVG. C	----	48	----	c0600	OOC	Citation
4**	16 Mar	Alb. DIII	----	48	----	c0600	OOC	Citation
5*	27 Mar	C	C4886	48	S W Roye	1120	DES	CR/RFC 27.3
6*	27 Mar	Pfalz DIII	C4886	48	S W Roye	1120	OOC	CR/RFC 27.3
7***	9 May	Fokker DrI	C4750	48	Wiencourt-Mericourt	1540	OOC	CR/V BG WD
8***	9 May	Fokker DrI	C4750	48	Wiencourt-Mericourt	1540	OOC	CR/V BG WD
9***	9 May	Fokker DrI	C4750	48	Wiencourt-Mericourt	1540	OOC	CR/V BG WD

TOTAL: 3 destroyed, 6 out of control = 9.
*Observer: 2/Lt J.M.J. Moore. **Observer: 2/Lt J.M.J. Moore. Note: This citation was written on 31 March 1918, noting Napier's score as 6. Apparently 48 Squadron lost records during the retreat as the citation has a penciled note that the Combat Reports were missing. That the claims were accepted is evidenced by the MC being awarded in April. ***Observer: Sgt W. Beales.

NAPIER Ian Patrick Robert Captain 40

Born on 24 July 1895, Ian Napier was educated at Eton. He joined the RFC from the Argyll and Sutherland Highlanders, and after pilot training went to 40 Squadron, where he was known as 'Old Naps'. Always in the thick of combat, he was credited with 12 victories and was awarded the MC. On 29 April 1918 he forced down a German two-seater of FltAbt 7 in British lines, the crew being taken prisoner. He also took part in many low level strafing and bombing raids. With his knowledge of French, he was on occasions attached to 1st French Army as liaison officer, and for this work he received the Legion d'Honneur and Croix de Guerre. After the war he went into the family shipbuilding and ship-owning business, and from 1951-63 was a member of the Scottish Transport Council. He was a member of the Royal Company of Archers, and held the Order of St.John; he died on 9 May 1977.

	1917		Nieuport					
1s*	14 Apr	Alb. DIII	A6778	40	Mericourt-La Coulette	1610	DES	CR/RFC 14.4
2s**	24 Apr	DFW. CV	A6778	40	Lens	1200	CAPT	CR/RFC 24.4
	1918		SE 5A					
3	6 Mar	Alb. DV	B4888	40	N E Lens	1625	DES	CR/RFC 6.3
4	6 Apr	C	B157	40	Brebieres	1035	DES	CR/RAF 6.4
5s***	12 Apr	Alb. DV	B157	40	S Estaires	0650	OOC	CR/RAF 12.4
6	12 Apr	Alb. DV	B157	40	S Estaires	0650	OOC	CR/RAF 12.4
7s†	29 Apr	DFW. CV	B157	40	W Bethune	0720	CAPT	CR/RAF 29.4
8	3 May	DFW. CV	B157	40	Merville	1850	DES	CR/RAF 3.5
9s††	13 May	DFW. CV	D213	40	Lacouture	0615	DES	CR/RAF 13.5
10	1 Jul	Pfalz DIII	D6180	40	Armentieres	2010	DES	CR/RAF 1.7
11	1 Jul	Rumpler C	D6180	40	La Gorgue	2035	DES	CR/RAF 1.7
12	4 Jul	Fokker DVII	D6180	40	Bois du Biez	1525	OOC	CR/A I/1789

TOTAL: 2 shared captured, 5 and 2 shared destroyed, 2 and 1 shared out of control = 12.
*Shared with Lt D. de Burgh A6781. **Shared with Lt Brevis and FSL R.A. Little N5469 of 8N. ***Shared with 2/Lt I.F. Hind B675. †Shared with Lt P.D. Learoyd D213, Lt L.H. Sutton D3509; this crew were an unnamed pilot and Lt Heidelmeyer of FA 7. ††Shared with Lt J.H. Jennings/2/Lt J.H. Hay of 2 Sqn.

NASH Gerald Ewart Flight Lieutenant 10(N)

A Canadian from Stoney Creek, born on 12 May 1896, Nash joined the RNAS in April 1916. He was posted to 10(N) Squadron in April 1917 to fly Sopwith Triplanes in Collishaw's 'Black Flight', having previously flown 1½ Strutters in 3 Wing. During late May and early June he claimed six victories, but on 26 June he was shot down by Karl Allmenröder of Jasta 11, becoming the latter's 30th victory. Nash became a prisoner, and was repatriated after the war. He served in the RCAF in World War II, retiring in 1945 as a Group Captain. He died on 10 April 1976.

	1917		Triplane					
1	21 May	Alb. DIII	N5492	10N	Ypres-Staden	1030	DES	CR/RFC 21.5
2s*	2 Jun	C	N5492	10N	St Julien	0700-0900	OOC	CR/ORB/AC
3s**	5 Jun	Alb. C	N6302	10N	Wervicq	0850	DES(F)	CR/RFC 5.6
4	6 Jun	Alb. C	N5492	10N	Polygon Wood	1100	DES	CR/RFC 6.6
5	6 Jun	Alb. DIII	N5492	10N	Polygon Wood	1115	OOC	CR/RFC 6.6
6	7 Jun	Alb. DIII	N5492	10N	St Julien	0900	OOC	CR/RFC 7.6

TOTAL: 2 and 1 shared destroyed, 2 and 1 shared out of control = 6.
*Shared with F/Lt R. Collishaw N5490, FSL E.V. Reid N5483, FSL W.M. Alexander N5487. **Shared with F/Lt R. Collishaw N5490, FSL K.G. Boyd N5478, FSL D.F. Fitzgibbon N5466, FSL E.V. Reid.

NASH Thomas Walter Captain 204

Born on 25 November 1891, Tom Nash from Littlehampton, Sussex, joined 204 Squadron on 3 March 1918 (when it was still 4(N) Squadron). He claimed two victories in July, while on 14 August he became a flight commander, claiming two Fokker DVIIs in one sortie next day. He was then awarded a DFC, while during September he claimed a balloon and again, two DVIIs in one day. His final victory on 9 October brought his score to eight, but on 23rd of that month he was reported missing in action over Termonde in D9608 when he and four other members of his flight were shot down by Fokker DVIIs.

	1918		Camel					
1	22 Jul	Rumpler C	B7176	204	5m S Ypres	1530	DES	CR/5 GP Comm
2	31 Jul	Pfalz DIII	B7176	204	Roulers	1130	DES	CR/5 GP Comm
3	15 Aug	Fokker DVII	C72	204	Menin	1905	DES	CR/5 GP Comm
4	15 Aug	Fokker DVII	C72	204	Menin	1905	DES	CR/5 GP Comm
5	16 Sep	Balloon	F3240	204	5m S E Ostend	1135	DES	CR/5 GP Comm
6	24 Sep	Fokker DVII	F3240	204	Pervyse	1850	DES	CR/5 GP Comm
7	24 Sep	Fokker DVII	F3240	204	Pervyse	1850	OOC	CR/5 Gp Comm
8	9 Oct	Fokker DVII	D9608	204	Lichtervelde	1105	DES(F)	CR/5 GP Comm

TOTAL: 1 balloon, 6 destroyed, 1 out of control = 8.

NEL William Joseph Baynes Lieutenant 84

Born on 4 August 1891, and commissioned into the RFC in July 1917, Bill Nel was a South African from the Transvaal who flew with 84 Squadron during the summer of 1918 and was credited with seven victories, over Fokker DVIIs — three destroyed and four out of control. He returned to Home Establishment on 27 September after a total of seven months with the unit. Nel was still active in 1981, having retired from the RAF as a Group Captain.

	1918		SE 5A					
1	27 Jun	Fokker DVII	D6857	84	2m E Villers Brettoneaux	0945	OOC	CR/?
2	24 Jul	Fokker DVII	D6926	84	S E Warfusee-Abancourt	1115	DES	CR/RAF 24.7
3	30 Jul	Fokker DVII	D6926	84	Wiencourt-Caix	1015	OOC	CR/?
4	7 Aug	Fokker DVII	D6926	84	N E Le Quesnel	0910	OOC	CR/?
5	25 Aug	Fokker DVII	E5957	84	S Tempeux	1020	OOC	CR/?
6	20 Sep	Fokker DVII	E6429	84	Mont d'Origny	1000	DES	CR/RAF 20.9
7	24 Sep	Fokker DVII	B8491	84	Estrees-Gouy	0910	DES	CR/RAF 24.9

TOTAL: 3 destroyed, 4 out of control = 7.

NEVILLE Roger Henry Gartside Captain 21, 23

Commissioned in the Duke of Cornwall's Light Infantry on 14 July 1915, Neville transferred to the RFC on 5 December that year and joined 21 Squadron early in 1916. After nearly a year of service, he claimed one victory while flying a BE 12, but was then wounded on 22 September 1916. On recovery, he joined 23 Squadron to fly Spads as a flight commander, and here added four further victories to his total.

	1916		BE 12					
1	14 Sep	LVG. C	6563	21	S W Velu a/d	----	DES	RFC 14.9
	1917		Spad					
2	6 Jul	Alb. DV	B3519	23	Tourcoing	1235	DES	CR/RFC 6.7
3	6 Jul	Alb. DV	B3519	23	Tourcoing	1235	OOC	CR/RFC 6.7
4	11 Jul	Alb. DV	B3519	23	Westroosebeke	1855	OOC	CR/RFC 12.7
5s*	27 Jul	Aviatik C	B3519	23	Kezelberg	1950	DES	CR/RFC 27.7

TOTAL: 2 and 1 shared destroyed, 2 out of control = 5.
*Shared with 2/Lt F.J. Gibbs B3501.

NEWNHAM Maurice Ashdown Captain 4, 65

Born in 1897, Newnham joined the RFC in January 1915 at the age of 17½ as a dispatch rider. He went to France in the autumn of 1915, where he was attached to 4 Squadron. After 18 months he returned to England for training as a pilot, and was commissioned. In March 1918 he returned to active duty, this time as a pilot flying Sopwith Camels with 65 Squadron. He served with this unit until the end of the war, becoming 'B' Flight commander. The citation to the DFC which he was awarded stated that he had taken part in 102 offensive patrols. Many of these were on escort duty for bombing raids on the German submarine pens at Bruges. He also took part in several ground level night bombing attacks on such targets as Zeebrugge mole and a Zeppelin hangar at Gontrode. His total score included five aircraft and three balloons destroyed, and 10 aircraft out of control. Leaving the RAF at the end of the war, he joined the Reserve of Air Force Officers.

Subsequently he served with the RAFVR during the Second World War from 1939-45. For most of this period he was engaged in forming and commanding the RAF Parachute Training School at Ringway, and associated schools in India and the Middle East. During his time at Ringway, Newnham was responsible for training 60,000 British and Allied military paratroops as well as several thousand special agents who were dropped behind enemy lines. He extended the usefulness of parachuting for military purposes by personally making experimental descents at night in fog, into water, and laden with equipment. His experiences were described in his book *Prelude to Glory*, published in 1947. During World War I, in addition to the DFC, he was awarded the French Croix de Guerre avec Palme, and was Mentioned in Despatches. In World War II he was awarded the OBE(Military), the Order of Polonia Restituta (Polish) and the Haakon VII Liberty Cross (Norwegian). Maurice Newham attained the rank of Group Captain on 20 May 1944, and left the service in October 1945. He died in 1974.

	1918		Camel					
1s*	10 May	Alb. DV	----	65	N Villers Brettoneaux	1930	DES	RAF 10.5
2	15 Jun	DFW. C	D1960	65	Brache	2100	OOC	CR/ORB/?
3	20 Jun	Pfalz DIII	D1960	65	S E Bray	1245	DES	CR/RAF 20.6
4	29 Jun	Pfalz DIII	D1962	65	S E Bray	1735	DES	CR/ORB/?
5	29 Jun	Fokker DrI	D1962	65	S E Bray	1735	OOC	CR/ORB/?
6	30 Aug	Fokker DVII	E1481	65	Ghistelles-Snelleghem	1340	OOC	CR/?
7	31 Aug	Fokker DVII	E1481	65	Varssenaere	1615	OOC	CR/?
8	20 Sep	Fokker DVII	E1481	65	Jabbeke	1015	DES	CR/RAF 20.9
9	27 Sep	Fokker DVII	E1481	65	Ghistelles	1150	OOC	CR/ORB/?
10	2 Oct	Balloon	E7279	65	N W Courtrai	0920	DES	CR/RAF 2.10
11	3 Oct	Fokker DVII	E7279	65	S E Moorslede	1530	OOC	CR/ORB/?
12	4 Oct	Fokker DVII	E7279	65	Lendelede	1750	OOC	CR/ORB/?
13	30 Oct	Fokker DVII	E7279	65	W Mullem	1320	OOC	CR/ORB/?
14	30 Oct	Fokker DVII	E7279	65	W Mullem	1322	DES	CR/RAF 30.10
15s**	1 Nov	Balloon	----	65	W Renaix	1025	DES	CR/ORB/?
16	4 Nov	Fokker DVII	E7189	65	S E Ghent	0850	OOC	CR/ORB/SR/?
17	4 Nov	Fokker DVII	E7189	65	S E Ghent	0855	OOC	CR/ORB/SR/?
18	9 Nov	Balloon	E7279	65	N E Gontrode	1345	DES	CR/RAF 9.11

TOTAL: 2 and 1 shared balloons, 5 and 1 shared dstroyed, 9 out of control = 18.
*Shared with Capt J. Gilmour, 2/Lt T. Williams, 2/Lt H. Brown, 2/Lt W.F. Scott-Kerr, 2/Lt H. Spredbury. **Shared with Lt G. Richardson, 2/Lt A.J. Cleare, 2/Lt A.R. Deans, Lt F.J. Wolno, 2/Lt H.G. Luther, 2/Lt R.C. Stiven.

NEWSOME Thomas Henry Lieutenant 22

Lieutenant Newsome served with 22 Squadron during the summer of 1918, claiming four aircraft and a balloon. The balloon and two of the aircraft were credited to the various gunners he flew with.

	1918		Bristol					
1*	8 Aug	Fokker DVII	E7406	22	Brebieres	1045	DES	CR/RAF 8.8
2*	8 Aug	Fokker DVII	E7406	22	Brebieres	1045	DES(F)	CR/RAF 8.8
3**	27 Aug	Balloon	----	22	Lietard-Douai	1730	DES	CR/RAF 27.8
4***	28 Sep	Pfalz DXII	E2263	22	E Bugnicourt	1755	DES	CR/RAF 28.9
5***	3 Oct	Fokker DVII	E2263	22	N E Cambrai	1745	DES	CR/SR/?

TOTAL: 1 balloon, 4 destroyed = 5.
*Observer: Sgt H.C. Hunt. **Observer: Lt C. Partington. ***Observer: Lt R.S.E. Walshe.

NORTON Ernest William Major 1W, 6(N), 204

Born in Scotland on 14 May 1893, Norton joined the RNAS in 1915. As a pilot he flew with 1 Naval Wing and then with 6 Naval Squadron during 1916-17 on Nieuport Scouts, being promoted Flight Lieutenant in July 1916. He was perhaps the most successful pilot with the latter unit during the period and had at least nine victories by the end of April 1917. His first victory was claimed on 20 October 1916, when he destroyed a kite balloon over Ostende using Le Prieur rockets, an action for which he was awarded a DSC. During the war he also received the Belgian Order of the Crown and both Belgian and French Croix de Guerre. In 1918 he commanded 204 Squadron, RAF, until December. Remaining in the service after the war, he served in Iraq during 1924-26, and as a Group Captain in 1932 commanded No 5 Flying Training School.

	1916		Nieup					
1	20 Oct	Balloon	3994	1W	Ostend	1135	DES	DRO/RNAS 20.10
	1917							
2	8 Feb	Aviatik C	N3184	6N	Houthoulst Forest	----	OOC	DRO/RNAS 8.2
3	5 Apr	Alb. DII	N3187	6N	W Douai	1700	DES	ORB/RFC 5.4
4	5 Apr	Alb. DII	N3187	6N	W Douai	1700	OOC	ORB/?

5s*	9 Apr	Alb. DIII	N3187	6N	Cambrai	1145	DES	ORB/RFC 9.4
6	9 Apr	Alb. DIII	N3187	6N	Cambrai	1200	OOC	ORB/RFC 9.4
7s**	29 Apr	Alb. DIII	N3208	6N	E Honnecourt	1315	OOC	ORB/RFC 29.4
8	29 Apr	Alb. DIII	N3208	6N	Guise	1855	DES(F)	ORB/RFC 29.4
9	29 Apr	Alb. DIII	N3208	6N	Guise	1855	OOC	ORB/RFC 29.4

TOTAL: 1 balloon, 2 and 1 shared destroyed, 4 and 1 shared out of control = 9.
*Shared with FSL A.L. Thorne. **Shared with FSL A.H.V. Fletcher N3192.

OADES Sydney Arthur Lieutenant 22

After service as a sapper with the Royal Engineers, he was commissioned in the RFC in July 1917 (backdated to 15 May), and flew with 22 Squadron from late 1917 to early 1918, during which period he was credited with 11 victories and awarded an MC. Flying with various gunners, the majority of his victories were gained with the front gun. He was injured in a crash on 13 March 1918, and this put an end to his combat flying.

	1917		Bristol					
1*	27 Oct	Rumpler C	B7281	22	N Roulers	1015	OOC	CR/RFC 27.10
2**	5 Dec	C	B1164	22	N Roulers	1520	DES	CR/RFC 5.12
3**	6 Dec	C	B1164	22	Habourdin	1115	DES	CR/RFC 6.12
	1918							
4***	6 Jan	Alb. DV	A7300	22	N Roulers	1450	OOC	CR/SR/?
5†	30 Jan	C	B1152	22	E La Bassee	1140	OOC	CR/RFC 30.1
6†	17 Feb	Alb. DV	B1152	22	N Douai	1445	DES	CR/SR/?
7†	18 Feb	Alb. DV	B1152	22	E La Bassee	1140	OOC	CR/RFC 18.2
8†	26 Feb	Alb. DV	B1152	22	Douai	1030	DES(F)	CR/RFC 26.2
9†	26 Feb	Alb. DV	B1152	22	E Lens	1130	OOC	CR/RFC 26.2
10†	5 Mar	C	B1168	22	Lens	1535	DES	CR/RFC 5.3
11†	5 Mar	D	B1168	22	Lens	1545	OOC	CR/RFC 5.3

TOTAL: 5 destroyed, 6 out of control = 11.
*Obsever: 2/Lt H.V.R. Hill. **Observer: 2 AM J.H. Jones. ***Observer: Lt D.N.G. Brampton. †Observer: 2/Lt S.W. Bunting.

OAKS Harold Anthony Captain 48

Born in Ontario, Canada, on 12 November 1896, 'Doc' Oaks joined the Canadian Engineers in 1915, transferring to the RFC in November 1917. He then flew Bristol Fighters with 48 Squadron from 28 March 1918. On 25 June he shot down a Fokker Biplane marked with a skull and crossbone on the fuselage sides, although it was only credited as having gone down out of control. He was promoted to flight commander in July, and was awarded the DFC after bringing his score to 11. He left for Home Establishment on 28 September. After the war he served in the RCAF, later becoming a well-known bush pilot; he ended up as a mining engineer in Toronto. Later he became President of Oaks Airways Ltd, and died in July 1968.

	1918		Bristol					
1*	21 May	Fokker DrI	C883	48	Carnoy	1815	OOC	CR/?
2*	21 May	Fokker DrI	C883	48	1m N Mericourt	1853	DES	CR/RAF 21.5
3s**	10 Jun	Alb. DV	----	48	Roye	1745	DES(F)	CR/RAF 10.6
4***	25 Jun	Fokker DVII	C883	48	Foucaucourt-Rosieres	1145	OOC	CR/V BG WD
5†	2 Jul	Pfalz DIII	C883	48	Foucaucourt	0745	DES	CR/RAF 2.7
6s††	2 Jul	Pfalz DIII	C883	48	Soyecourt	0840	DES	CR/RAF 2.7
7†††	24 Jul	Fokker DVII	F6094	48	Foucaucourt	0730	OOC	CR/V BG WD
8†††	24 Jul	Fokker DVII	F6094	48	Foucaucourt	0730	OOC	CR/V BG WD
9‡	3 Aug	Alb. C	F6094	48	Aveluy	0640	CAPT	CR/RAF 3.8
10‡‡	5 Sep	Fokker DVII	D7984	48	Courtrai-Roulers	1240	DES(F)	CR/RAF 5.9
11‡‡	5 Sep	Fokker DVII	D7984	48	Courtrai-Roulers	1240	OOC	CR/11 WS

TOTAL: 1 captured, 3 and 2 shared destroyed, 5 out of control = 11.
*Observer: 2/Lt C.S. Bissett. **Shared with Capt C.R. Steele, Capt F.C. Ransley, Lt J.E. Drummond. ***Observer: 2/Lt G.J. Maynard. †Observer: Lt G.J. Maynard. ††Observer: Lt G.J. Maynard: shared with Lt N.Y. Lewis/2/Lt H. Buckner and Lt E.D. Shaw/?. †††Observer: 2/Lt C.W. Davies. ‡Observer: 2/Lt H. Knowles; probably Vzfw K. Beckehaufer/Oblt J. Philipp, both KIA, of FAA 263. ‡‡Observer: Lt T. Beck.

ODELL Charles Walter Captain 46

Born on 25 November 1898, Odell joined the RFC in August 1916 after service with the Iniskilling Fusiliers, and was posted to 46 Squadron in June 1917, flying with this unit until late in the year, by which time he had claimed two victories. Posted to Home Establishment on 27 November, he was promoted to Captain in 1918 and returned to 46 as a flight commander on 20 August. Here he brought his score to seven before again being posted home on 5 October.

	1917		Pup					
1s*	4 Sep	Alb. C	B1842	46	S Scarpe	0930	OOC	CR/11 WS
2s**	24 Sep	DFW. C	B1802	46	S E Honnecourt	1030	DES	CR/RFC 24.9
	1918		Camel					
3s***	14 Sep	C	D9457	46	N E Vermand	0800	DES	CR/RAF 14.9
4s†	14 Sep	Balloon	D9457	46	N E Vermand	0815	DES	CR/V BG WD
5s††	17 Sep	Fokker DVII	D1942	46	Cambrai	1200	OOC	CR/V BG WD
6s††	17 Sep	Fokker DVII	D1942	46	Cambrai	1200	OOC	CR/V BG WD
7	29 Sep	Fokker DVII	F2166	46	Le Cateau	1640	OOC	CR/V BG WD

TOTAL: 1 shared balloon, 2 shared destroyed, 1 and 3 shared out of control = 7.
*Shared with Capt M.D.G. Scott B1843, Lt E. Armitage B1837, Lt C. Courtneidge B1802, Lt E.Y. Hughes A6188. **Shared with Capt M.D.G. Scott B2191, Lt E. Armitage B1829, Lt C. Courtneidge B1837. ***Shared with Lt N Bruce F2172, Lt P.F. Paton C8338. †Shared with Lt P.F. Paton C8338. ††Shared with Capt D.R. MacLaren F2137, 2/Lt R.D. Gilpin-Brown F5950 Lt P.M. Tudhope F1966, Lt C.H. Sawyer D6693, 2/Lt L.S. Skerrington F6360. These two aircraft collided.

O'GRADY Standish Conn Captain 23

An Irishman, O'Grady flew Spads with 23 Squadron in 1917. He received the MC and was promoted to Captain, claiming nine victories before being posted to Home Establishment on 15 September 1917. By the late 1930s he had become a professor, but was also a keen glider pilot, and member of the Newcastle Gliding Club. He remained active in gliding until the 1950s; he died during the 1970s.

	1917		Spad					
1	30 Apr	Alb. DIII	A262	23	Inchy-en-Artois	1640	OOC	CR/RFC 30.4
2s*	13 May	Alb. DIII	----	23	Vitry	1900	DES(F)	CR/RFC 13.5
3s**	24 Jun	Alb. DIII	B3464	23	St Jean	1610	DES(F)	CR/RFC 24.6
4s***	12 Aug	Alb. DIII	B3556	23	Gheluvelt	0620	DES	CR/RFC 12.8
5	14 Aug	Alb. DIII	B3556	23	E St Julien	1905	DES	CR/V BG WD
6s†	14 Aug	C	B3556	23	E St Julien	1915	DES	CR/V BG WD
7	20 Aug	Alb. DV	B3556	23	Poelcapelle	1945	DES(F)	CR/RFC 20.8
8	26 Aug	Alb. DV	B3556	23	N Passchendaele	0650	OOC	CR/RFC 26.8
9	26 Aug	Alb. DV	B3556	23	N Comines	0700	OOC	CR/RFC 26.8

TOTAL: 2 and 4 shared destroyed, 3 out of control = 9.
*Shared with 2/Lt D.U. MacGregor B1524. **Shared with Capt W.J.C.K.C. Patrick B1580, 2/Lt G.I.D. Marks B1698. ***Shared with 2/Lt C.T. Warman B1561. †Shared with 2/Lt G.I.D. Marks, 2/Lt C.F. Briggs, 2/Lt T.A. Doran.

OLIVER Thomas Alfred Captain 1, 29

Born in 1895 at Capel Earig, North Wales, Oliver graduated as a pilot in December 1915 and was posted to 1 Squadron the following month. A year later on 11 January 1917 he was rested, subsequently joining 29 Squadron as a flight commander on 10 August 1917. Four days later, after three victories with this unit, he was shot down and killed in B1557 by Oberleutnant Wiegand of Jasta 10.

	1916		Morane					
1*	3 Jul	EA	----	1	Houthoulst Forest	----	DES	SR/RFC 3.7
			Nieuport					
2	6 Aug	C	----	1	Kemmel	----	OOC	SR/RFC 6.8
	1917							
3	11 Aug	Alb. DV	A6784	29	5m N Roulers	1845	OOC	CR/RFC 11.8
4	11 Aug	C	A6784	29	N Roulers	c1845	DES	CR/SR/?
5	12 Aug	C	B1557	29	Polinchove	1545	OOC	CR/RFC 12.8

TOTAL: 2 destroyed, 3 out of control = 5.
*Observer: Sgt Mumford.

OLIVIER Eric Captain 19

Eric Oliver flew with 19 Squadron in the latter months of 1917 and early 1918, flying both Spads and Dolphins. He claimed at least eight victories and was promoted Captain.

	1917		Spad					
1	26 Oct	C	B6776	19	S W Gheluwe	1020	OOC	CR/RFC 26.10
2	31 Oct	Alb. DV	A6714	19	Gheluwe	1000	OOC	CR/RFC 31.10
3s*	15 Nov	C	A6714	19	Zandvoorde	1015	DES	CR/RFC 15.11
4s**	18 Nov	C	A6714	19	Passchendaele	1045	OOC	CR/RFC 18.11
5s***	6 Dec	C	A6714	19	E Roulers	1542	OOC	CR/RFC WD
6s†	22 Dec	Alb. DV	A6714	19	S Quesnoy	1420	DES(F)	CR/RFC 22.12

	1918		Dolphin					
7s††	17 Mar	Alb. DV	C3902	19	N E Menin	1215	DES(F)	CR/RFC 17.3
8	17 Mar	Pfalz DIII	C3902	19	Roulers	1225	DES	CR/RFC WD

TOTAL: 3 shared destroyed, 3 and 2 shared out of control = 8.
*Shared with Major A.D. Carter A8834. **Shared with Major A.D. Carter A8834, Lt A. Reid-Walker A6817. ***Shared with Capt O.C. Bryson A6780, Lt A.B. Fairclough B6802, Lt R.G. Holt B6836. †Shared with Capt O.C. Bryson A6780, 2/Lt E.J. Blyth B3563, Lt A.B. Fairclough B6802, Capt G.W. Taylor B6805, Major A.D. Carter A8834, 2/Lt H.E. Galer B3506. ††Shared with Lt A.B. Fairclough C3940.

OLLEY Gordon Percy Sergeant 1

Born on 29 May 1893, Olley joined the Queen Victoria Rifles, then the Royal Fusiliers, serving as a motor cyclist in London. Transferring to the RFC, he went to France to join 1 Squadron as a dispatch rider. His willingness to fly resulted in him becoming a Corporal observer, and he flew on many sorties with the Canadian pilot, Lieutenant Dore, before returning to England to train as a pilot. 6313 Sergeant Olley rejoined 1 Squadron in 1917 when it was flying Nieuport Scouts, and during the latter months of that year claimed 10 victories and received an MM. At the end of 1917 he again returned home to become a ferry pilot. After the war he flew with Handley Page and KLM, then with Imperial Airways — in spite of a rather high personal record of crashes. During the 1920s and 1930s he did much to develop civil aviation, flying over 13,000 hours as a pilot. Once in the early twenties he flew a passenger aeroplane from Croydon to Le Bourget, and force-landed 17 times; on his final take-off he was grieved to find that the last of his passengers had deserted him! In 1934 he formed Olley Air Services Ltd, and in the same year his book *A Million Miles in the Air* was published. He died in 1954.

	1917		Nieuport					
1	1 Jun	C	B1691	1	Messines	0750	OOC	CR/RFC 12.6
2s*	23 Jun	LVG. C	B1681	1	Wulverghem Houthem	1520	OOC	CR/RFC 23.6
3	26 Jun	Alb. DV	B1681	1	Becelaere	2100	OOC	CR/RFC 26.6
4	16 Jul	Alb. DV	B1681	1	S Poelcapelle	0730	DES	CR/RFC 16.7
5	12 Aug	Alb. C	B1681	1	E Tenbrielen	0800	OOC	CR/RFC 12.8
6	11 Sep	Alb. DIII	B3628	1	Houthoulst	1815	OOC	CR/RFC 12.9
7	21 Sep	DFW. C	B3628	1	Wervicq	0950	DES	CR/RFC 21.9
8s**	2 Oct	DFW. C	B3628	1	E Becelaere	1210	OOC	CR/RFC 2.10
9	5 Oct	C	B6768	1	W Roulers	1635	DES	CR/RFC 5.10
10	14 Oct	DFW. C	B3628	1	Wervicq	1445	OOC	CR/RFC 14.10

TOTAL: 3 destroyed, 5 and 2 shared out of control = 10.
*Shared with 2/Lt W.C. Campbell B1700 **Shared with 2/Lt R.C. Sotham B3589.

ORLEBAR Augustus Henry Captain 19, 44, 73, 43

Born on 17 February 1897, he joined the 1st/5th Bedfordshire Regiment (TF) in January 1915, where he was commissioned 2nd Lieutenant. In September he went to Gallipoli, but in October, while out in No-Man's Land on a reconnaissance, he was hit and wounded by a Turkish sniper. He returned to England, and after recovery, transferred to the RFC. In 1916 he was posted to 19 Squadron, where he flew BE 12s and later, Spads; before he returned to Home Establishment in July he had claimed two victories. After a period with 44(Home Defence) Squadron, he returned to France in December as a flight commander with 73 Squadron. Here he added four more victories before being wounded in action on 23 March 1918. Ten days earlier he had shot down a Fokker Triplane flown by Leutnant Lothar von Richthofen, which had also been fired on by Captain Hughes of 62 Squadron; the pilot was wounded in the crash. Recovering from his second wound of the war, Orlebar remained in England as an instructor until August, when he was given a flight in 43 Squadron which was just converting to the new Snipes. In September he gained his last victory, bringing his total to seven. In spite of all his service, he received no decorations for his work during the war. He remained in the RAF after the war and from 1919-25 flew at the Aeroplane Experimental Establishment, gaining an AFC. In 1934 he was SASO in Aden, after being a part of the Schneider Trophy Team in 1929-31. Becoming a Group Captain in 1937, he commanded RAF Northolt at the start of World War II.

	1917		Spad					
1	23 May	Alb. DIII	A6663	19	E Douai	1915	DES(F)	CR/RFC 23.5
2	5 Jun	Alb. DIII	A6663	19	S E Zonnebeke	1115	OOC	CR/RFC 5.6
	1918		Camel					
3*	13 Mar	Fokker DrI	B7282	73	S E Cambrai	1030	DES	CR/RFC 13.3
4	13 Mar	Alb. DV	B7282	73	S E Cambrai	1030	OOC	CR/RFC 13.3
5	22 Mar	Alb. DV	B7282	73	Ham	1430	DES(F)	CR/RFC 22.3
6	22 Mar	Alb. DV	B7282	73	Ham	1510	OOC	CR/RFC 22.3

			Snipe					
7	29 Sep	Fokker DVII	E8024	43	Remaucourt	1015	OOC	CR/ORB/?

TOTAL: 3 destroyed, 5 out of control = 7.
*This was Lt Lothar von Richthofen of Jasta 11, who crash-landed and was severely wounded.

ORR Osborne John Lieutenant 204

Orr was born in Cleveland, Ohio, in the USA on 15 July 1895. He joined the RAF and was posted to 204 Squadron on 1 August 1918, claiming five victories before being shot down in a Camel D9613 near Termonde on 23 October.

	1918		Camel					
1	12 Aug	Fokker DVII	D3354	204	Blankenberghe	1055	OOC	CR/Air I/59
2	12 Aug	Fokker DVII	D3354	204	Zeebrugge-Ostend	1055	OOC	CR/5 GP Comm
3	14 Aug	Fokker DVII	B7232	204	Roulers	1755	OOC	CR/5 GP Comm
4	15 Aug	Fokker DVII	B7232	204	Menin	1905	OOC	CR/5 GP Comm
5	14 Oct	C	D9613	204	Westende-Nieuport	1315	OOC	CR/5 GP Comm

TOTAL: 5 out of control = 5.

OWEN Ernest Edward Lieutenant 1

Ernest Owen from Ham, Surrey, was born on 23 March 1896 and was a member of the RNVR at the outbreak of war, seeing early service at Antwerp and Gallipoli, and in Egypt. On 17 February 1916, having transferred to the Army, he was commissioned into the Royal Fusiliers, but in 1917 he transferred again, this time to the RFC, gaining his wings on 28 May 1917, and joining 1 Squadron in France on 10 October. Within a week he was hospitalized, not returning until 13 January 1918. Between then and 18 August, when he returned to Home Establishment, he claimed five victories.

	1918		SE 5A					
1s*	3 May	Pfalz DIII	B504	1	Steenwerck	0730	OOC	CR/ORB/SR/?
2s**	28 May	DFW. C	B8512	1	Meteren-Vieux Berquin	0700	DES	CR/RAF 28.5
3***	6 Jun	Pfalz DIII	B8512	1	Armentieres	0745	DES(F)	CR/RAF 6.6
4s†	9 Jun	Fokker DrI	B8512	1	Dickebusch	0640	CAPT	CR/ORB/SR/?
5	8 Aug	Alb. DV	C8846	1	Dompierre	1310	DES	CR/RAF 8.8

TOTAL: 1 shared captured, 2 and 1 shared destroyed, 1 shared out of control = 5.
*Shared with Lt K.C. Mills C5374. **Shared with Capt K.S. Henderson C1112, Capt P.J. Clayson C1849, Lt A.F. Scroggs C6416, Lt D. Knight B6479, Lt H.A. Kullberg B8254, Lt B.H. Moody C1092, Lt W.A. Forsyth B733, Lt E.T.S. Kelly B130, Lt K.J.P. Laing B8504, Lt H.B. Bradley C1102. ***The squadron made 3 claims, Vzfw O. Heller of Jasta 40 was killed. †Shared with Capt P.J. Clayson C1114, Lt K.J.P. Laing C1898, Lt H.A. Kullberg C8842, Lt D. Knight C1106, Lt J.C. Bateman D8254, Lt H.B. Bradley C1102, Lt C.B. Henderson C1849, Lt F.S. Crossley D6881. Gefr Preiss of Jasta 14, was captured.

OWEN Robert Johnstone Lieutenant 43

Commissioned in August 1917, Lieutenant Owen was credited with seven victories while flying Camels with 43 Squadron in the early months of 1918. On 28 March he was a member of a nine man patrol which was surprised by German scouts, and was one of five not to return. Of the five, two were killed and three taken prisoner, Owen being one of the latter. Records seem to indicate that Owen destroyed one enemy machine on this last patrol, but he did not make any claim for this personally on his subsequent release. However Captain Trollope, who had been leading the patrol, did so on his behalf, and this was recorded as such in the RAF Communiques.

	1918		Camel					
1*	19 Feb	Alb. DV	B6210	43	2m E Bois du Biez	1245	DES(F)	CR/RFC 19.2
2	6 Mar	C	B7349	43	E Bois du Biez	1200	DES	CR/RFC 6.3
3	11 Mar	Alb. DV	B7288	43	Sainghin	1350	OOC	CR/RFC 11.3
4s**	24 Mar	DFW. C	C8259	43	S E Mercatel	1100	DES(F)	CR/RFC 24.3
5s***	24 Mar	DFW. C	C8259	43	S E Mercatel	1100	DES	CR/RFC 24.3
6	24 Mar	C	C8259	43	Sailly-Saillisel	1520	DES	CR/RFC 24.3
7	28 Mar	Alb. DV	C8259	43	E Albert	0930	DES	CR/RAF/? 10.8

TOTAL: 4 and 2 shared destroyed, 1 out of control = 7.
*Possibly Lt H. Klein of Jasta 10, who was wounded. **Shared with Capt J.L. Trollope C8270. ***Shared with 2/Lt C.F. King C8262.

PAGE John Albert Flight Lieutenant 10(N)

Page, a Canadian born in Brockville, Ontario, on 11 July 1893, served with home defence units in England during 1916 before joining 3(N) Squadron. He then served with 10(N) Squadron from 26 April 1917, claiming four victories in June and one more in July. On 22 July he was involved in a combat where two enemy scouts were seen to go down, one out of control and the other to hit the ground. A Triplane was also seen to fall, and Page did not return; Flight Commander J.E. Sharman was also lost. No other pilots in the squadron made any claims, so these two victories were credited to Page, bringing his score to seven. The two missing Triplanes had been shot down by Hauptmann Otto Hartmann of Jasta 28 and Leutnant Otto Brauneck of Jasta 11.

	1917		Triplane					
1s*	1 Jun	Aviatik C	N5359	10N	3m S E Ypres	0715	DES	CR/RFC 1.6
2	6 Jun	Alb. DIII	N5359	10N	Polygon Wood	1115	DES	CR/RFC 6.6
3	14 Jun	Alb. DIII	N5359	10N	Zonnebeke	1920	OOC	CR/RFC 14.6
4	15 Jun	Alb. DIII	N5359	10N	Houthem	0940	OOC	CR/RFC 15.6
5	7 Jul	Alb. DV	N5379	10N	Lille	0940	OOC	CR/RFC 7.7
6	22 Jul	Alb. DV	N5478	10N	Becelaere	1100	DES	CR/RFC 22.7
7	22 Jul	Alb. DV	N5478	10N	Becelaere	1100	OOC	CR/RFC 22.7

TOTAL: 2 and 1 shared destroyed, 4 out of control = 7.
*Shared with FSL A.C. Dissette N6294.

PAGET Augustus Lieutenant 66

A native of Wiltshire, Paget joined the RFC in 1917 after service with the 27th Territorial Reserve Battalion. He claimed six victories flying Sopwith Camels in Italy with 66 Squadron during 1918, including the last two successes to be claimed on this front on 28 October. Two days later he was shot down by anti-aircraft fire in E7215 and became a prisoner. The award of a DFC was gazetted on 1 January 1919.

	1918		Camel					
1	15 Sep	Berg DI	B5182	66	5km N E Feltre	0830	DES	ORB/SR/14 W
2s*	25 Oct	Brand C	C135	66	W Feltre	0715	OOC	ORB/SR 14 W
3	25 Oct	Brand C	C135	66	W Feltre	0715	OOC	ORB/SR/14 W
4	27 Oct	Balloon	E7214	66	38 P 8692	1300	DES	ORB/SR/14 W
5**	28 Oct	Alb. DV	E7215	66	Godega a/d	0850	DES(F)	ORB/SR/14 W
6**	28 Oct	Alb. DV	E7215	66	Godega a/d	0855	DES(F)	ORB/SR/14 W

TOTAL: 1 balloon, 3 destroyed, 1 and 1 shared out of control = 6.
*Shared with Lt D.J. Teeporten E1495. **Possible two Albatros of Flik 56, reported lost the day before.

PALLISER A.J. Lieutenant 4 AFC

Born on 2 March 1890, in Launceston, Tasmania, Palliser was a motor mechanic when war broke out, and joined the Australian Army Service Corps. He later transferred to the AFC, and was posted to 4 AFC Squadron in the summer of 1918, flying Camels. He claimed a Fokker DVII in mid-September and a balloon in early October, the squadron then converting to Sopwith Snipes. With the new aircraft he was to claim two DVIIs on 28 October, adding two more destroyed and one out of control next day. On 4 November he was piloting one of four Snipes to be shot down by Jasta Boelcke, and was killed in E8064.

	1918		Camel					
1	16 Sep	Fokker DVII	F1403	4AFC	Frelinghien	0820	DES	CR/RAF 16.9
2	5 Oct	Balloon	E7180	4AFC	N E Quesnoy	0645	DES	CR/RAF 5.10
			Snipe					
3	28 Oct	Fokker DVII	E8064	4AFC	Ath	1455	DES	CR/RAF 28.10
4	28 Oct	Fokker DVII	E8064	4AFC	Ath	1455	DES	CR/RAF 28.10
5	29 Oct	Fokker DVII	E8064	4AFC	N E Tournai	1610	DES(F)	CR/RAF 29.10
6	29 Oct	Fokker DVII	E8064	4AFC	N E Tournia	1610	DES	CR/RAF 29.10
7	29 Oct	Fokker DVII	E8064	4AFC	N E Tournai	1610	OOC	CR/ORB/OH

TOTAL: 1 balloon, 5 destroyed, 1 out of control = 7.

PARK Keith Rodney Major 48

Born at Thames near Auckland, New Zealand, on 15 June 1892, Keith Park served in Egypt and Gallipoli with the New Zealand Artillery, being commissioned in July 1915. The following month he joined the Royal Artillery, being posted to 29th Division in September. He served in France in 1916, but was wounded on 21 October of that year, and was invalided out of the army. He therefore joined the RFC in December 1916, and on completion of his training was immediately made an instructor. This enabled him to raise his flying experience from 35 to 100 hours before joining 48 Squadron on 7 July 1917 to fly Bristol Fighters. Here he became a flight commander on 11 September, receiving the MC and Bar, together with a French Croix de

Guerre. He was shot down twice during this period, once by AA and once on 3 January 1918 by Unteroffizier Ungewitter of SchlachtStaffel 5, crash-landing A7229 unhurt; his victor was later to become an ace. In 1918, after a brief rest, he returned to take command of 48 Squadron on 10 April, by which time he had accounted for 17 enemy machines; he was to add three more by the end of the war. Remaining in the RAF, he reached high rank; he initially commanded 25, and then 111 Squadrons during the twenties, and by 1935 was a Group Captain as Air Attache in Buenos Aires. During World War II he held very important posts, being AOC of 11 Group, Fighter Command, during the critical days of the Battle of Britain; in 1942 he commanded the fighter defences of Malta, later serving as AOC in Burma. He retired as Air Chief Marshal Sir Keith Park, GCB, KBE, MC, DFC, DCL, and returned to his native New Zealand where he died on 6 February 1975. His biography, *Sir Keith Park*, by Vincent Orange, was published in 1984.

	1917		Bristol					
1*	24 Jul	Alb. DIII	A7176	48	off Ravensyde	1740	OOC	CR/RFC 25.7
2**	12 Aug	Alb. DIII	A7176	48	S Slype	1045	OOC	CR/RFC 12.8
3**	16 Aug	DFW. C	A7182	48	Slype	1130	OOC	CR/SR/?
4**	17 Aug	Alb. DIII	A7182	48	3m W Slype	0655	OOC	CR/RFC 17.8
5***	17 Aug	Alb. DIII	A7182	48	3m W Slype	0655	DES	CR/RFC 17.8
6***	17 Aug	Alb. DIII	A7182	48	off Slype	0715	OOC	CR/RFC 17.8
7***	17 Aug	Alb. DIII	A7182	48	Slype	0725	OOC	CR/RFC 17.8
8†	21 Aug	Alb. DV	A7216	48	2m E Westende	0745	OOC	CR/RFC 21.8
9†	21 Aug	Alb. DV	A7216	48	E Westende	0745	OOC	CR/RFC 21.8
10**	25 Aug	Alb. DV	A7213	48	S Slype	2000	DES(F)	CR/RFC 25.8
11s††	2 Sep	Alb. DV	A7170	48	5m E Dixmude	0930	OOC	CR/RFC 2.9
12†††	2 Sep	Alb. DV	A7170	48	S E Dixmude	0935	OOC	CR/RFC 2.9
13‡	5 Sep	Alb. DV	A7182	48	4m off Ostend	1200	DES	CR/RFC 5.9
14‡‡	9 Sep	Alb. DV	A7220	48	Midelkerke-Slype	1615	OOC	CR/RFC 9.9
15‡‡‡	14 Sep	Alb. DV	A7227	48	N Dixmude	1845	OOC	CR/RFC 14.9
16§	14 Sep	Alb. DV	A7227	48	N Dixmude	1845	DES(F)	CR/RFC 14.9
	1918							
17§§	3 Jan	Alb. DIII	A7229	48	St Quentin	1210	OOC	CR/RFC 3.1
18§§§	18 May	Pfalz DIII	C808	48	Bray	1840	OOC	CR/V BG WD
19#	25 Jun	Rumpler C	C940	48	Wiencourt	1125	DES	CR/RAF 25.6
20#	25 Jun	DFW. C	C940	48	Bayonvillers	1130	OOC	CR/V BG WD

TOTAL: 5 destroyed, 14 and 1 shared out of control = 20.

*Observer: 2/Lt A.W. Merchant. **Observer: 2/Lt A.R. Noss. ***Observer: 2/Lt A.R. Noss. One of these was probably Lt Gotte of Jasta 20, who was killed. †Observer: 2/Lt W. O'Toole. ††Observer: 2/Lt A.D. Light, shared with 2/Lt R.L. Curtis/2/Lt D.P.F. Uniacke A7224. †††Observer: 2/Lt A.D. Light. ‡Observer: 2 AM H. Lindfield; this was Lt O. Pernet of Jasta B, who was killed. ‡‡Observer: 2 AM H. Lindfield. ‡‡‡Observer: 2/Lt H. Owen. §Observer: 2/Lt H. Owen; this was Lt M. von Chelius, of Jasta B, who was killed. §§Observer: Lt J.H. Robertson. §§§Observer: 2/Lt G.J. Maynard. #Observer: 2/Lt H. Knowles.

PASHLEY Eric Clowes Lieutenant 24

A Londoner, Pashley obtained his pilot's certificate at Brooklands in September 1911. He opened a flying school at Shoreham in 1913, and after the outbreak of the war was initially employed in testing new aeroplanes. He later joined the RFC and flew DH 2s with 24 Squadron in 1916-17, claiming eight victories (including three members of Jasta Boelcke), also severely damaging another enemy machine. On 23 January 1917 he engaged an Albatros in a combat which ended when his opponent fell out of his machine! Lieutenant Pashley was killed in a flying accident on 17 March 1917, aged 24. His brother, another pre-war pilot, had also been killed in an accident on Christmas Day 1916.

	1916		DH 2					
1	3 Nov	Halb. DII	5925	24	Bapaume	1500-1600	OOC	CR/RFC 3.11
2s*	9 Nov	D	7930	24	Le Transloy	1345	DES	CR/RFC 9.11
3	16 Nov	D	7930	24	Delville Wood	1200	OOC	CR/RFC 16.11
4	22 Nov	D	A2553	24	Ligny	1435	DES	CR/RFC 22.11
5s**	11 Dec	C	7930	24	Bapaume	1000	DES(F)	CR/RFC 11.12
	1917							
6***	23 Jan	Alb. DII	7930	24	Grandcourt	1330	CAPT	CR/RFC 23.1
7†	4 Feb	Alb. DII	7930	24	Fricourt-Maricourt	1400	DES	CR/RFC 4.2
8s††	6 Mar	C	----	24	----	----	DES	RFC 6.3

TOTAL: 1 captured, 2 and 3 shared destroyed, 2 out of control = 8.

*Shared with 2/Lt A.E. McKay 7884, Lt A.G. Knight A305. **Shared with Capt S.H. Long A305. ***This was Vzfw P. Ostrop from Jasta B. †This was Lt von Scheele of Jasta B, who was killed. ††Shared with Capt S.H. Long.

PATEY Herbert Andrew Captain 10(N), 210

Born in London on 25 September 1898, Patey joined the RN Division in September 1914 and served in Egypt and Gallipoli before being invalided home in September 1915 due to dysentry. In November 1915 he was demobilised as being under age, but was called up again in March 1917 when he applied for a commission in the RNAS: this was granted in July. He joined 10(N) Squadron in January 1918, becoming a flight commander of what became 210 Squadron, in June. He claimed 11 victories for which he was awarded a DFC, but was shot down on 5 September by Leutnant Beckmann of Jasta 56, and became a prisoner. He was released after the Armistice, arriving home on Christmas Eve, 1918. Unfortunately, he was to die of influenza on 18 February 1919.

	1918		Camel					
1s*	17 May	Rumpler C	D3391	210	N E Bailleul	1105	DES	CR/RAF 17.5
2s**	21 May	Balloon	B7849	210	Ploegsteert Wood	1120	DES	CR/RAF 21.5
3	17 Jun	Fokker DVII	D3410	210	S E Zillebeke Lake	1500	DES	CR/RAF 17.6
4	26 Jun	Halb. C	D9622	210	W Armentieres	1920	DES(F)	CR/RAF 26.6
5s***	29 Jun	Fokker DVII	D9622	210	Armentieres	1930	DES(F)	CR/RAF 29.6
6	16 Jul	Fokker DVII	B7280	210	Zeebrugge	1155	OOC	CR/5 GP Comm
7	20 Jul	Fokker DVII	B7280	210	S E Ostend	0950	OOC	CR/5 GP Comm
8	31 Jul	Fokker DVII	B7280	210	S W Ghistelles	1115	DES	CR/5 GP Comm
9	1 Aug	Fokker DVII	B7280	210	N Lille	1925	DES(F)	CR/5 GP Comm
10	6 Aug	Fokker DVII	B7280	210	S W Ghistelles	1915	DES	CR/5 GP Comm
11	3 Sep	Fokker DVII	B7280	210	N E Roulers	1830	DES(F)	CR/5 GP Comm

TOTAL: 1 shared balloon, 6 and 2 shared destroyed, 2 out of control = 11.

*Shared with Lt A.L. Jones D3365. **Shared with Lt H.B. Maund D3410, Lt G.B. Wootten B7227. ***Shared with Lt W.W. Gyles D9616. 210 made 2 claims, Uffz Reechendrees of Jasta 56, was killed at this time in this area.

PATRICK William Donald Captain 1

A Scot, born in Ayrshire in 1890, Patrick transferred to the RFC in July 1916, and joined 1 Squadron on 18 September 1917, claiming his first victory a month later. After two more victories he was promoted in December to flight commander, and on 9 January 1918 gained his last victory in a Nieuport Scout. The following month the squadron began operating SE 5As and on the last day of the month he shared in sending an Albatros Scout down out of control. Two more claims followed in March to bring his score to seven, but on 10 April he was shot down over Messines by ground fire in B8371, becoming a prisoner.

	1917		Nieuport					
1s*	24 Oct	C	B6768	1	Moorslede	0625	OOC	CR/RFC 24.10
2**	17 Dec	C	B6830	1	S W Moorslede	1420	OOC	CR/RFC 17.12
3	18 Dec	Alb. DV	B6830	1	N Wervicq	1150	DES	CR/RFC 18.12
	1918							
4	9 Jan	DFW. C	B6830	1	Comines	1025	OOC	CR/RFC 9.1
			SE 5A					
5s***	28 Feb	Alb. DV	B641	1	Gheluvelt	1710	OOC	CR/RFC 1.3
6s†	13 Mar	Pfalz DIII	B641	1	Wieltje	1220	OOC	CR/ORB/?
7	15 Mar	Alb. DV	B520	1	Stadenberg	1010	DES	CR/RFC 15.3

TOTAL: 2 destroyed, 1 and 4 shared out of control = 7.

*Shared with Capt P.F. Fullard B6789. **Shared with Capt W.W. Rogers B6789, Lt R.C. Sotham B6768. ***Shared with 2/Lt F.P. Magoun A8904. †Shared with Capt G.B. Moore B511, Capt H.J. Hamilton B32, Lt H.A. Rigby C9624, Lt A. Hollis B520, 2/Lt L.W. Mawbey B632, 2/Lt P.J. Clayson A8908. 2/Lt A.E. Sweeting A8932, 2/Lt W.M.R. Gray A8904.

PAUL Carrick Stewart Lieutenant 1AFC

Born in New Zealand in 1893, Paul flew Bristol Fighters with 1AFC Squadron in Palestine during 1918, receiving the DFC for claiming four individual and one shared victories. He was drowned whilst on his way home to New Zealand on 22 January 1919.

	1918		Bristol					
1*	23 May	Alb. DV	C4627	1AFC	Nablus	0700	OOC	CR/40 W WD
2**	23 May	Alb. DV	C4627	1AFC	Nablus	0715	DES	CR/40 W WD
3*	13 Jun	Rumpler C	C4627	1AFC	8m N Nablus	0430	DES	CR/40 W WD
4s***	28 Jul	Rumpler C	C4627	1AFC	N W Wadi Farah	1200	DES	CR/40 W WD
5*	16 Aug	Rumpler C	C4627	1AFC	Kefr Kaddum	0830	DES	CR/40 W WD

TOTAL: 3 and 1 shared destroyed, 1 out of control = 5.

*Observer: Lt W.J.A. Weir. **Observer: Lt W.J.A. Weir. This aircraft was forced to land and shot up and destroyed. Probably Vzfw Schniedewind of Jasta 1F, an ace, who was wounded. ***Observer: Lt W.J.A. Weir. Shared with Capt A.R. Brown/Lt G. Findlay B1284. This aircraft was forced down, shot up and the crew machine gunned.

PAYNE James Dennis Captain 41,29

Born on 22 July 1887, Payne learnt to fly as an NCO in 1915. He joined 41 Squadron on 12 June 1917, but was posted out on 16 July, joining 29 Squadron on 6 August. He made his first claim on 12 August, while on 21 October he claimed two two-seaters to bring his total to six. He claimed a further victory next day, and was awarded an MC on 23rd. In November he was promoted to flight commander, and by the end of the year had brought his score to 12. He added two more in early January 1918 before being posted to Home Establishment on 10th.

	1917		Nieup					
1	12 Aug	Alb. DV	A6784	29	N E Houthoulst Forest	0845	DES	CR/RFC 12.8
2	15 Sep	Alb. DV	B3626	29	S E Zillebeke	1710	DES	CR/RFC 15.9
3	20 Sep	Alb. DV	B3626	29	Roulers	1155	OOC	CR/SR/?
4	18 Oct	Alb. C	B6814	29	2m N W Menin	1105	OOC	CR/RFC 18.10
5	21 Oct	C	B6814	29	Houthoulst Forest	1615	DES	CR/RFC 22.10
6	21 Oct	C	B6814	29	Houthoulst Forest	1615	OOC	CR/RFC 22.10
7	22 Oct	Alb. DV	B6814	29	2m W Menin	1635	OOC	CR/RFC 22.10
8	24 Oct	Alb. DV	B6814	29	2m W Roulers	1600	OOC	CR/RFC 24.10
9*	9 Nov	Alb. DV	B6826	29	Dadizeele	0940	OOC	CR/RFC 9.11
10	26 Nov	Alb. DV	B6832	29	Gulleghem	1420	OOC	CR/RFC 26.11
11	26 Nov	Alb. DV	B6832	29	Gulleghem	1420	OOC	CR/RFC 26.11
12	22 Dec	Alb. DV	B6820	29	Staden	1050	OOC	CR/RFC 22.12
	1918							
13	6 Jan	Alb. DV	B3622	29	N E Staden	1525	DES	CR/RFC 6.1
14	9 Jan	C	----	29	----	----	OOC	RFC 9.1

TOTAL: 4 destroyed, 10 out of control = 14.
*This was Lt Walter Gottsch, an ace from Jasta 8, who was wounded.

PAYNE Leonard Allen Captain 48

Joining the RFC in June 1917, Payne was posted to 48 Squadron on 30 September 1917. He became a flight commander during May 1918, when he claimed his tenth victory. His 11th and last, claimed on 4 November, was one of the final three to be recorded by the unit.

	1917		Bristol					
1s*	29 Oct	Pfalz DIII	----	48	N E Dixmude	1620	DES	Citation
	1918							
2**	3 Jan	LVG. C	----	48	----	----	OOC	Citation
3***	26 Feb	LVG. C	----	48	----	----	DES(F)	Citation
4***	8 Mar	Alb. DV	A7298	48	Mont d'Origny	0800	OOC	CR/RFC 8.3
5***	8 Mar	Alb. DV	A7298	48	Mont d'Origny	0800	OOC	Citation
6***	12 Mar	Fokker DrI	----	48	N E St Quentin	1200	OOC	Citation
7†	21 Mar	LVG. C	----	48	----	----	OOC	Citation
8††	19 May	Alb. DV	C793	48	E Proyart	1115	OOC	CR/RAF 19.5
9††	27 May	Alb. DV	C877	48	S Albert	1815	OOC	CR/IV BG WD
10†††	30 May	Alb. DV	C877	48	Bray	1745	DES	CR/RAF 30.5
11‡	4 Nov	Fokker DVII	D6041	48	Lessines-Gramont	1515	DES	CR/RAF 4.11

TOTAL: 4 destroyed, 7 out of control = 11.
*Observer: 2/Lt V. Bourdillon; shared with 2/Lt H.H. Hartley/2/Lt E.C. Birch. **Observer:?. ***Observer: Lt G.H.H. Scutt. †Observer: Lt G.H.H. Scutt. On 30 March, Lt George Howard Homer Scutt and Payne were put in for M.C.'s. Scutt's citation noted 1 destroyed and 3 out of control since 20 February, and Payne's noted 84 ops with 1 destroyed and 2 out of control since 13 September 1917. ††Observer: Lt C.J.R. Gibson. †††Observer: Lt A.E. Ansell. ‡Observer: 2/Lt R.L. Ford.

PAYNTER John de Campbourne Captain 6(N), 9(N), 10(N), 13(N), 213

Born 17 May 1898, in Southsea, Hampshire, Paynter initially saw service with 6(N) Squadron during early 1917. He crashed at Hinges on 9 April and was hospitalized; on recovery he joined 9(N) Squadron, where he shared one victory on 27 October. Shortly thereafter he was posted to 13(N) Squadron, where he remained, becoming a flight commander in spring 1918. He raised his score to 10 on 1 June, and received a DSC, but he had twice been wounded in action. During the night of 18 June the squadron's airfield was raided by German bombers, but Paynter decided not to take shelter. He was fatally wounded by bomb fragments.

	1917		Camel					
1s*	27 Oct	Alb. DV	B3830	9N	Slype	1040	OOC	CR/RNAS 27.10
2s**	5 Dec	Alb. C	B6391	13N	4m N W Wenduyne	1505	DES	CR/RNAS 5.12
	1918							

3s***	29 Jan	Seaplane	B3782	13N	100y off Blankenberghe Pier	1400	DES	CR/RNAS 29.1
4s†	30 Jan	Alb. C	B3782	13N	2m N Ostend	1420	DES	CR/RNAS 30.1
5s††	19 Feb	Seaplane	B3782	13N	E Ostend	1355	DES(F)	CR/RNAS 19.2
6	6 May	Alb. DV	B7254	213	Wenduyne	1950	DES	CR/5 GP Comm
7	8 May	Alb. DV	B7254	213	Wenduyne	1950	DES	CR/5 GP Comm
8	8 May	Alb. DV	B7254	213	Wenduyne	1950	OOC	CR/5 GP Comm
9s†††	1 Jun	Pfalz DIII	B7254	213	Bruge	1420	OOC	CR/5 GP Comm
10s‡	1 Jun	Pfalz DIII	B7254	213	Bruge	1420	OOC	CR/5 GP Comm

TOTAL: 2 and 3 shared destroyed, 1 and 4 shared out of control = 10.

*Shared with Capt S.T. Edwards B6217, FSL F.J.W. Mellersh B6204, FSL J.P. Hales N6342, F/Lt F.E. Banbury B6230, FSL C.A. Narbeth B3883, FSL A.V. Wood B3884, FSL M.S. Taylor B3892, F/Cdr H.F. Stackard B6327. **Shared with FSL J.W. Pinder B6357, FSL G.C. MacKay N6335, FSL M.L. Cooper B6407. ***Shared with F/Cdr L.H. Slatter B7186, FSL J.E. Greene B3919, FSL G.C. MacKay B6407, FSL M.L. Cooper B6410. †Shared with F/Cdr M.J.G. Day N6363. ††Shared with F/Cdr M.J.G. Day N6363, FSL J.C. Stovin N6349, FSL E.V. Bell B3773, FSL G.D. Smith N6345. †††Shared with Lt G.D. Smith C66, Lt C.H Denny D3333, Lt F.L. Cuttle C73, Lt P.L. Jenner D8164. ‡Shared with Lt G.D. Smith C66.

PAYTON Clement Wattson Lieutenant 210

Born in Ashbourne, Derbyshire, on 13 April 1897, he joined the RNAS in November 1917, and went to France in 1918 to join 210 Squadron, on 31 March 1918. He was awarded a DFC, which was gazetted in December, and claimed 11 victories, also taking part in many ground attacks. He was reported missing in action on 2 October 1918 when his Camel (D9658) suffered a direct hit from AA whilst bombing a train near Courtrai.

	1918		Camel					
1	20 May	Alb. DV	C62	210	Menin	0710	OOC	CR/?
2s*	21 May	Balloon	C62	210	Pont Riquen	1710	DES	CR/RAF 21.5
3	26 May	Alb. DV	C62	210	E Bailleul	1700	DES	CR/RAF 26.5
4s**	27 May	Pfalz DIII	C62	210	Bailleul	0810	OOC	CR/?
5s**	1 Jun	C	B7148	210	3m S Bailleul	1745	DES	CR/RAF 1.6
6	15 Jun	Alb. DV	B7148	210	S E Kemmel	1830	OOC	CR/?
7	11 Aug	Fokker DVII	D9655	210	S Slype	1845	DES	CR/5 GP Comm
8s***	3 Sep	Fokker DVII	D9655	210	Menin-Courtrai	1830	DES	CR/5 GP Comm
9	29 Sep	Fokker DVII	E4421	210	Wijnendaele Wood	0800	DES	CR/5 GP Comm
10	1 Oct	Fokker DVII	D9658	210	Houthoulst Forest	0955	DES	CR/5 GP Comm
11	1 Oct	Fokker DVII	E4421	210	S E Roulers	1710	DES	CR/5 GP Comm

TOTAL: 1 shared balloon, 5 and 2 shared destroyed, 2 and 1 shared out of control = 11.

*Shared with Lt S.C. Joseph D3401, Lt A.L. Jones B7227. **Shared with Lt L.P. Coombes B7153. ***Shared with Lt S.C. Joseph D3374, Lt I.C. Sanderson E4405, Lt J.A. Lewis B7222, Lt H.R. Hughes D3357.

PEARSON James William Captain 23

Posted to 23 Squadron in early 1918, just as the unit was changing its Spads for Dolphins, Pearson, an American, served from April to August claiming 12 victories, and being promoted to Captain. The award of a DFC was gazetted in February 1919.

	1918		Dolphin					
1s*	30 May	Alb. C	C3824	23	S Albert	1045	OOC	CR/V BG WD
2	3 Jun	Pfalz DIII	C3824	23	Montdidier	1740	DES(F)	CR/RAF 3.6
3	1 Jul	Alb. DV	C3824	23	Hangest	1135	DES	CR/RAF 1.7
4	1 Jul	Alb. DV	C3824	23	Hangest	1140	OOC	CR/V BG WD
5	1 Aug	Halb. C	D3749	23	Caix-Harbonnieres	0720	DES(F)	CR/RAF 1.8
6	1 Aug	Pfalz DIII	D3749	23	Warfusee	0740	OOC	CR/V BG WD
7	18 Sep	Fokker DVII	E4492	23	Lihaucourt	1215	DES(F)	CR/?
8	18 Sep	Fokker DVII	E4492	23	Lihaucourt	1215	OOC	CR/?
9	28 Oct	Fokker DVII	F5961	23	Bois de Nouvion	1130	OOC	CR/?
10**	28 Oct	Fokker DVII	F5961	23	Bois de Nouvion	1130	DES	CR/RAF 28.10
11	29 Oct	Halb. C	E4588	23	N E Landrecies	1300	OOC	CR/?
12s***	1 Nov	DFW. C	F5961	23	Petit Bart	1210	DES	CR/RAF 1.11

TOTAL: 5 and 1 shared destroyed, 5 and 1 shared out of control = 12.

*Shared with Lt H.E. Faulkner C3871. **Probably Vzfw A. Schyk of Jasta 24, who was killed by a Dolphin. ***Shared with Lt H.N. Compton C4130, 2/Lt E.J. Taylor E4319.

PEARSON William Reginald Guy Captain 32

From South London, the son of Dr Spencer Pearson, he joined the RFC from the Army Service Corps, and became an observer with 2 Squadron from May until December 1916. After pilot training, he was promoted to Captain and flew with 32 Squadron from July 1917 until he returned to Home Establishment on 5 March 1918.

During this period he claimed seven victories; one of these was over a two-seater which he helped force down inside Allied lines. After his return to England, he was killed in a flying accident in July 1918.

	1917		DH 5						
1s*	27 Jul	C	A9399	32	Gheluvelt	1445	DES	ORB/RFC 27.7
2s**	28 Jul	Alb. C	A9207	32	Pilkem	0530	DES	ORB/RFC 28.7
3s***	29 Jul	AGO CIV	A9424	32	Langemarck	0800	CAPT	ORB/RFC 29.7
4	21 Aug	C	A9424	32	S Shrewsbury Wood	0550	OOC	ORB/RFC WD?
5	22 Aug	Alb. DV	A9424	32	Bellewarde Lake	0530	OOC	ORB/RFC 22.8
6s†	4 Dec	C	A9300	32	Becelaere	0855	OOC	ORB/RFC 4.12
7s	5 Dec	C	A9300	32	Becelaere	0855	OOC	ORB/RFC 5.12

TOTAL: 1 shared captured, 2 shared destroyed, 2 and 2 shared out of control = 7.
*Shared with Lt St C.C. Tayler, 2/Lt E. Pownall, 2/Lt R.G. Ottey. **Shared with Capt R.M. Williams B353, Lt St C.C. Tayler A9213, 2/Lt T.E. Salt A9421. ***Shared with Capt R.M. Williams A9398, Lt St C.C. Tayler A9213, 2/Lt C. Turner A9207. This was an aircraft from FAA 202. †Shared with 2/Lt C.J. Howson A9315. ††Shared with 2/Lt W.A. Tyrrell B4916.

PECK Arthur Hicks Captain 111

Born in India on 25 April 1889, Peck was educated at Cambridge. He joined the RFC in 1916 and when he later became a pilot, served as an instructor with the 22nd Training Squadron in the Middle East. In 1917 he was posted to 111 Squadron as 'C' Flight commander and flew in Palestine. Here he claimed eight enemy aircraft shot down and was awarded the DSO, MC and Bar. His first three victories were gained whilst flying Bristol Fighters, and his next five on SE 5As. In 1923 he commanded 25 Squadron, and in 1928 served in Iraq. He became a Group Captain in 1935.

	1917		Bristol					
1*	30 Oct	C	A7194	111	N W Khalasa	0950	CAPT	CR/40 W WD
2*	6 Nov	Rumpler C	A7194	111	Um Dabkal	1045	FTL/DES	CR/40 W WD
3*	8 Nov	Alb. DIII	A7194	111	Huleikat	1300	DES(F)	CR/40 W WD
			SE 5A					
4	4 Dec	Alb. DIII	B26	111	Junction Station	1200	OOC	CR/40 W WD
	1918							
5s**	3 Mar	C	B26	111	S E Yehudieh	0750	DES	CR/40 W WD
6	23 Mar	Alb. DIII	B52	111	N Jericho	0930	OOC	CR/40 W WD
7	23 Mar	Alb. DIII	B52	111	N Jericho	0932	OOC	CR/40 W WD
8	23 Mar	C	B52	111	N Jericho	0935	OOC	CR/40 W WD

TOTAL: 1 caprtured, 3 destroyed, 4 out of control = 8.
*Observer: Capt J.J. Lloyd-Williams. **Shared with Major F.W. Stent B678.

PENNELL Edward Robert Captain 27, 84

Born on 23 May 1894 in London, Pennell served as a Corporal in the Honourable Artillery Company early in the war; he joined the RFC in 1916 and gained his wings on 28 November of that year. He served with 27 Squadron for the first six months of 1917, but was then posted to become one of the original flight commanders in the new 84 Squadron on 23 July. His second tour at the front ended on 6 February 1918, when he was hospitalized.

	1917		Martinsyde					
1	19 Mar	Halb. DII	7500	27	Havrincourt Wood	0820	OOC	CR/RFC 19.3
			SE 5A					
2	22 Nov	Balloon	B4886	84	Raillencourt	0850	DES	CR/ORB/?
3	30 Nov	DFW. C	B4886	84	Honnecourt	1000	DES	CR/RFC WD
4s*	23 Dec	C	B4886	84	N St Quentin	1300	OOC	CR/RFC WD
	1918							
5	13 Jan	C	B4886	84	Villers-Outreaux	1025	OOC	CR/RFC 13.1

TOTAL: 1 balloon, 1 destroyed, 2 and 1 shared out of control = 5.
*Shared with 2/Lt H.W. Brown B559.

PENTLAND Alexander Augustus Norman Dudley Captain 16, 29, 19, 87

Born in Queensland on 5 August 1894, 'Jerry' Pentland served with the 12th Australian Light Horse Regiment in Egypt and Gallipoli from 1914-1916. Transferring to the RFC on 21 February 1916, he trained in England and went to France as a pilot with 16 Squadron in June, flying BE 2Cs. Only a few days after his arrival he and his observer, Captain Waller, encountered and shot down a Fokker. Later in the year he transferred to 29 Squadron where he was taught to fly DH 2s effectively by Sergeant Jack Noakes, but before he could gain any victories on this type, he broke his leg whilst playing rugby. On recovery he became an instructor until July 1917, when he joined 19 Squadron to fly Spads. On one occasion with this unit he took on ten Albatros Scouts single-handed and fought them off, but his machine was so shot about that it was a complete write-off. In addition he found that four bullets had gone through his flying overalls without inflicting any injury! On 26 September however, he crashed after his aircraft had been hit by an artillery shell, and was injured. He soon received an MC, claiming ten victories prior to his crash. On recovery another period of instructing followed before he went to 87 Squadron as a flight commander, accompanying this new unit to France in April 1918. He maintained his somewhat 'lone wolf' tactics with the Dolphins he was now flying, and was always seeking out enemy two-seaters, or leading his patrol in dogfights with German scouts. By late August he had raised his total score to 23 and been awarded a DFC, but on 25 August, after making his last two claims, he was shot down by Jasta 57, and was wounded in the foot. After the war he served with the RAAF, then left to fly in the New Guinea goldfields. In 1930 he became a pilot with the Australian National Airways, while during World War II he ran an air-sea rescue unit in the Pacific with the RAAF rank of Squadron Leader, being awarded the AFC. He retired to Bayview, New South Wales, where he died in 1983. His biography, *Australian Air Ace* by Charles Schaedel, was published in 1979.

	1916		BE 2C					
1*	9 Jun	Fokker E	4077	16	Habourdin	----	DES	CR/RFC 10.6
	1917		Spad					
2s**	20 Jul	Alb. C	----	19	Houthoulst Forest	0625	DES	ORB/?
3	12 Aug	Alb. DIII	B1660	19	Menin	1500	OOC	CR/RFC 12.8
4s***	20 Aug	Alb. C	B3620	19	S E Houthoulst Forest	0625	OOC	CR/RFC 3.9
5s†	26 Aug	DFW. C	B3620	19	Moorseele	0540	DES	CR/RFC 26.8
6	31 Aug	Alb. DV	B3620	19	E Moorslede	1810	OOC	CR/RFC 31.8
7	11 Sep	Rumpler C	B3520	19	S Bousbecque	1315	DES	CR/RFC 11.9
8	15 Sep	Rumpler C	B3620	19	S W Zillebeke Lake	1225	OOC	CR/RFC WD
9	16 Sep	Alb. DV	B3620	19	Wervicq-Quesnoy	1610	OOC	CR/RFC 16.9
10	23 Sep	Scout	B3620	19	Passchendaele	1200	OOC	CR/RFC 23.9
	1918		Dolphin					
11s††	7 May	Rumpler C	C4157	87	Gheluvelt	1740	OOC	CR/SR/?
12	30 May	C	C3827	87	Achiet le Petit	1210	DES	CR/RAF 30.5
13	6 Jun	Rumpler C	C3827	87	Amiens-Clery	0950	OOC	CR/?
14	18 Jun	Rumpler C	C3827	87	Donville	0840	OOC	CR/RAF 18.6
15	18 Jun	Rumpler C	C3827	87	S S W Arras	0840	OOC	CR/RAF 18.6
16	28 Jun	Alb. DV	D3718	87	N Bapaume	0915	OOC	CR/?
17	1 Jul	Rumpler C	D3718	87	Loupart Wood	1025	DES	CR/RAF 14.7
18	9 Aug	Fokker DVII	C4162	87	Dernicourt	1800	DES	CR/RAF 9.8
19	10 Aug	Fokker DVII	C4162	87	Misery	0930	DES	CR/RAF 10.8
20	12 Aug	Rumpler C	D3718	87	Arras-Thelus	1135	DES	CR/RAF 12.8
21s†††	14 Aug	Rumpler C	C4158	87	Aveluy Wood	0840	OOC	CR/?
22	25 Aug	DFW. C	D3718	87	Le Sars	0900	DES	CR/RAF 25.8
23	25 Aug	Fokker DVII	D3718	87	S Guedecourt	0925	DES	CR/RAF 25.8

TOTAL: 10 and 1 shared destroyed, 9 and 3 shared out of control = 23.

*Observer: Capt W.H. Walker. **Shared with Capt F. Sowrey B3616. ***Shared with Lt H.C. Ainger B3564, Capt F. Sowrey B3616. †Shared with Lt H.C. Ainger B3616, Lt A.E. Boeree B3520, Lt R.L. Graham B3618, Lt J.G.S. Candy B3552. ††Shared with Lt L. Murray-Stewart C4156, Lt C.K. Oliver C4163. †††Shared with Lt D.C. Mangan C8109.

PETERS George Clifton Lieutenant 1AFC

An Australian from Adelaide, Peters was born on 6 May 1894 and flew with 1AFC Squadron in Palestine during 1918. With his usual observer, Lieutenant J.H. Traill, he was credited with seven victories and another driven down. Both he and Traill were awarded the DFC, gazetted in February 1919. On 24 August 1918 Peters and Traill, in company with another Bristol Fighter crewed by Lieutenant P.J. McGinness and Lieutenant H.B. Fletcher, engaged seven LVGs and Pfalz Scouts. Information from German sources later confirmed that only one of their machines had returned from this engagement over Bir el Hanuta. Peters later became a Lieutenant Colonel in the Australian Army.

	1918		Bristol					
1*	15 Apr	Alb. DV	C4623	1AFC	Kalkilieh	1150	OOC	CR/40 W WD
2**	9 May	C	C4623	1AFC	Jenin a/d	1515	FTL/DES	CR/40 W WD
3s***	29 May	Rumpler C	C4623	1AFC	N E Nablus	0815	DES(F)	CR/40 W WD
4s†	24 Jul	Rumpler C	B1278	1AFC	Tanturah	0530	DES	CR/40 W WD
5*	24 Aug	LVG. C	B1278	1AFC	E Hanuteh	0815	DES	CR/40 W WD
6*	24 Aug	Pfalz DIII	B1278	1AFC	E Hanuteh	0815	DES	CR/40 W WD
7*	22 Sep	DFW. C	B1278	1AFC	8m N Deraa	1700	DES	CR/40 W WD

TOTAL: 4 and 2 shared destroyed, 1 out of control = 7.

*Observer: Lt J.H. Traill. **Observer: Lt G. Finlay. ***Observer: Lt J.H. Traill; shared with Lt E.C. Stooke/Lt W.J.A. Weir B1280. †Observer: Lt J.H. Traill; shared with Lt J.M. Walker/Lt H.A. Letch B1222.

PEVERELL E.H. Lieutenant 70

Lt Peverell, an ex-Indian Army officer, transferred to the RFC on 30 April 1917. He flew Camels with 70 Squadron in early 1918, claiming five victories.

	1918		Camel					
1	9 Jan	C	----	70	----	----	DES	RFC 9.1
2	29 Jan	Alb. DV	B5640	70	Staden	1110	OOC	CR/RFC 29.1
3	5 Feb	C	B5640	70	Gheluwe-Menin	1350	OOC	CR/RFC 5.2
4	23 Mar	C	C8205	70	Vitry	1700	DES	CR/RFC 23.3
5	11 Apr	C	C1700	70	Etain-Noyelle	1900	OOC	CR/RAF 11.4

TOTAL: 2 destroyed, 3 out of control = 5.

PHILLIPPS Roy Cecil Major 32, 2AFC

Roy Phillipps was born in Sydney, New South Wales, on 1 March 1892, but was raised in Western Australia; he was practising as an accountant in Perth at the outbreak of war. Joining the Australian infantry, he quickly rose to the rank of Captain in the 28th Battalion. Posted to France, he was wounded in the first Australian infantry raid, and was invalided from the front with a partially paralysed leg. Transferring to the AFC, he went to England in early 1917 with the nucleus of the second AFC squadron as adjutant. In England this unit became 68 Squadron, and was to equip with DH 5s. After some flights as a passenger, Phillipps applied and was accepted for pilot training on 24 May, and on qualifying was attached to 32 Squadron in France on 3 August 1917 to gain experience of operational flying on the DH 5; three days later he was hit by AA fire and obliged to crash near Ypres. Unharmed, he rejoined 68 Squadron in September as a flight commander, and was in action over Cambrai in November, forcing an enemy scout to land on 22nd. At the turn of the year the squadron was renumbered 2AFC, and received SE 5As, and during March 1918 he claimed five victories, receiving a Bar to the MC he had already been awarded. Another victory followed in May, and on 12 June he shot down two Fokker Triplanes, an LVG two-seater and a Fokker DVII. Another victory followed in July and three in August to bring his score to 15. He was awarded a DFC and was rested, being promoted to Major to take command of 6 Training Squadron. Between the wars Phillipps farmed in Eastern Australia, but returned to the RAAF in World War II, commanding No 2 Elementary Flying Training School at Archerfield in May 1940. He was subsequently killed in a flying accident having achieved the rank of Wing Commander.

	1917		DH 5					
1	22 Nov	DFW. C	A9288	2AFC	Cambrai	----	CAPT	CR/ORB/OH
	1918		SE 5A					
2	22 Mar	Fokker DrI	C9541	2AFC	Sains les Marquion	1515	DES(F)	CR/RAF 22.3
3	23 Mar	Alb. DV	C9541	2AFC	N Bourlon Wood	0945	DES	CR/RAF 23.3
4	24 Mar	Alb. DV	C9541	2AFC	N E Bapaume	1255	DES	CR/RAF 24.3
5	27 Mar	Fokker DrI	C9541	2AFC	Suzanne	1200	DES(F)	CR/RAF 27.3
6	27 Mar	New Type D	C9541	2AFC	Meaulte	1225	CAPT	CR/RAF 27.3
7	16 May	Pfalz DIII	C5441	2AFC	Bapaume area	1815	DES	CR/RAF 16.5
8	12 Jun	Fokker DrI	D6860	2AFC	Gury	1040	DES	CR/RAF 12.6
9	12 Jun	Fokker DrI	D6860	2AFC	S Connectencourt	1040	DES	CR/RAF 12.6
10	12 Jun	LVG. C	D6860	2AFC	S Marqueglise	1130	CAPT	CR/RAF 12.6
11*	12 Jun	Fokker DVII	D6860	2AFC	Gumay	1145	CAPT	CR/RAF 12.6
12	25 Jul	Fokker DVII	D6860	2AFC	Houplines	0910	DES	CR/RAF 25.7
13	1 Aug	DFW. C	D6860	2AFC	La Bassee	1500	DES	CR/RAF 1.8
14	1 Aug	Fokker DVII	D6860	2AFC	La Bassee	1500	OOC	CR/ORB/OH
15	12 Aug	Fokker DVII	D6860	2AFC	Licourt	1110	DES	CR/RAF 12.8

TOTAL: 4 captured, 10 destroyed, 1 out of control = 15.
*Possibly Oblt F. Loerzer, commander of Jasta 26, who was captured.

PICKTHORNE Charles Edward Murrey Major 8, 32, 84

Born on 20 September 1894, he served with the Army Service Corps from September to December 1915. Seconded to the RFC, he flew as an observer with 8 Squadron in 1916, undertaking many sorties. On 29 June while over enemy lines, his machine was attacked by a Fokker and his pilot, Lieutenant Vaisey, was wounded and lost consciousness. Pickthorne managed to fly the machine back to base and landed safely, even sending a message with his morse-key to have a doctor standing by for his injured companion. When later he trained as a pilot, he was first posted to 32 Squadron at the end of 1916 flying DH 2s. He was slightly wounded on 6 March 1917 during a fight, but he pursued his adversary and brought him down. On 11 March he engaged an Albatros Scout which had a skull and crossbones motif painted on the fuselage sides; he eventually forced the enemy pilot down to land inside the British lines, where it was discovered that the pilot was none other than Crown Prince Frederich of Prussia. After claiming at least four victories he was awarded the MC, and returned to England where he held various posts until late 1918. On 8 November he took command of 84 Squadron, and on 10th led a patrol during which he claimed his fifth and last victory.

	1917		DH 2					
1s*	27 Jan	C	A2545	32	Courcelles-Achiet	0945	DES(F)	ORB/RFC 27.1
2	26 Feb	D	7938	32	Bucquouy	1335	OOC	ORB/RFC 26.2
3	6 Mar	Alb. DI	7898	32	E Bapaume	1005	DES	CR/RFC 6.3
4**	11 Mar	Alb. DI	7938	32	Lagnicourt	1600	CAPT	ORB/RFC 21.3
	1918		SE 5A					
5	10 Nov	Fokker DVII	F904	84	E Mutagne	1000	DES	CR/RAF 10.11

TOTAL: 1 captured, 2 and 1 shared destroyed, 1 out of control = 5.
*Shared with Capt J.M. Robb 7937, Lt F. Billinge 7897, Lt T.A. Gooch 7941, Lt C.G. Eccles A2535, 2/Lt H.D. Davies A2534. **This was Lt Prince Friedrich of Prussia, of FAA 258, who force landed just in front of Australian infantry lines, and tried to get back to his lines. He was shot by the Australians and captured, but died of his wounds.

PIDCOCK Geoffrey Arthur Henzell Captain 60, 44, 1, 73

Born on 6 November 1897, he joined the RFC in April 1916, joining 60 Squadron in August. He flew many operations, claiming at least one victory and driving down two more before he left in May 1917. After a period flying home defence sorties with 44 Squadron, he was posted to 1 Squadron for a six week fighter instructors' refresher course in October and November, before going to 73 Squadron as a flight commander from March to July 1918. With 73 he claimed a further five victories, bringing his total to at least six. In 1920 he went back to 1 Squadron, then in India, and then flew Snipes in Iraq, 1921-23. He retired from the RAF with the rank of Air Vice-Marshal, CB, CBE, Legion d'Honneur, Croix de Guerre (France), and died in February 1976.

	1917		Nieuport					
1s*	5 Apr	Alb. DIII	A6770	60	Riencourt	1845	OOC	CR/RFC 5.4
	1918		Camel					
2	7 Apr	Fokker DrI	D1812	73	N Lamotte	1200	OOC	CR/RAF 7.4
3	12 Apr	Alb. DV	D1812	73	Lestrem	1245	DES	CR/RAF 12.4
4	3 May	Alb. DV	----	73	Ploegsteert	1250	OOC	CR/RAF 3.5
5	11 Jun	Alb. DV	D8106	73	N E Courcelles	1430	DES	CR/RAF 11.6
6s**	13 Jun	C	B8106	73	S Thiescourt	0730	DES	CR/RAF 13.6

TOTAL: 2 and 1 shared destroyed, 2 and 1 shared out of control = 6.
*Shared with with Lt T. Langwill, 2/Lt C.S. Hall, 2/Lt D.N. Robertson, Maj H.E. Hervey, Lt J.M. Elliott. **Shared with Lt E.R. Trendall C8269.

PIERCE Edmond Flight Lieutenant 3(N), 9(N), 203

Born on 22 October 1893, Edmond Pierce was commissioned as a Flight Sub Lieutenant in June 1916, flying Sopwith Pups with 3(N) Squadron from early 1917 where he claimed three solo and two shared victories during April and May. On 4 May he was posted to 9(N) Squadron where he remained until early November, being promoted to Flight Lieutenant on 1 October; however in November he rejoined 3(N), now flying Camels. He claimed two more victories with this unit, to bring his score to nine. He was posted to Home Establishment on 3 May, and was still alive in retirement in Zimbabwe (Rhodesia) at the time of writing.

	1917		Pup					
1s*	12 Apr	Alb. DII	N6171	3N	Pronville	1030	OOC	CR/RFC 12.4
2	12 Apr	Alb. DII	N6171	3N	Pronville	1030	OOC	CR/ORB/DL
3	22 Apr	Alb. DIII	N6171	3N	Cambrai	1915	OOC	CR/RFC 22.4
4	23 Apr	Alb. DIII	N6171	3N	Croisilles	0630	OOC	CR/RFC 23.4
5s**	2 May	Alb. C	N6171	3N	Bourlon Wood	0700	DES(F)	CR/ORB/DL
6	11 May	C	9928	9N	Noordschoote	1200	DES	CR/RNAS 11.5
			Triplane					
7s***	17 Jul	Alb. DV	N5377	9N	Nieuport	0510	OOC	CR/RFC 17.7
	1918		Camel					
8	22 Mar	Alb. DV	B7227	3N	Boursies	1300	DES	CR/RFC 22.3
9s†	24 Mar	Alb. DV	B7227	3N	Vaux	1530	OOC	CR/RFC 24.3

TOTAL: 2 and 1 shared destroyed, 3 and 3 shared out of control = 9.
*Shared with FSL F.C. Armstrong N6178. **Shared with FSL F.C. Armstrong N6178, FSL A.T. Whealy N6194. ***Shared with FSL Macdonald N5378, FSL O.C. Le Boutillier B5459, FSL W.E.B. Oakley N5475, FSL R.B. Freeland N5489. †Shared with FSL S. Smith B7214, FSL R.C. Berlyn B7274, FSL E.T. Hayne B7231, FSL L.D. Bawlf B7192, F/Cdr A.T. Whealy B7220, FSL F.J.S. Britnell B7229.

1. Captain D.H. DeBurgh, AFC, 40 Squadron (left) with Captain G.A.H. Pidcock who flew with 60, 1 and 73 Squadrons between 1916-18. Pidcock later became an Air Vice-Marshal. *(Franks collection)*

2. Lieutenant W.A. Pritt, MC, who despite his boyish appearance flew Pups with 66 Squadron in 1917.

3. Captain R.C. Phillips, MC & Bar, DFC, an Australian pilot with 2 AFC, Squadron, 1918. *(S. St Martin)*

4. Major C.J. Quintin-Brand, DSO, MC, DFC, saw action with 1 Squadron in 1917; he then served with 112 and 151 Squadrons in 1918, commanding the latter. He was subsequently knighted and became an Air Vice-Marshal, commanding No 10 Group, Fighter Command during the Battle of Britain. *(R.C. Bowyer)*

1

3

2

1. Captain A.C. 'Snowy' Randall, DFC, 32 and 85 Squadrons. *(R.C. Bowyer)*

2. Captain O.W. Redgate, DFC, 9(Naval)/ 209 Squadron, 1917-18. *(Franks collection)*

3. 40 Squadron group; (l to r): Lieutenant H.B. Redler, MC, who was later with 24 Squadron, Captain R.N. Hall, MC, Lieutenant C.L. Bath and Captain W.A. Bond, DSO, MC & Bar, who was killed in action in July 1917. *(J.H. Tudhope)*

4. Captain A.E. Reed, DFC & Bar, from South Africa, flew with 29 Squadron. *(Franks collection)*

1. Lieutenant A.P.F. Rhys-David, DSO, MC, (centre), 56 Squadron, 1917; he is flanked by Lieutenant K.K. Muspratt, MC and Lieutenant V.P. Cronyn (3 victories). *(Franks collection)*

2. Lieutenant C.R. Richards, MC, an Australian who served with 20 Squadron in 1917, until shot down and taken prisoner during August. *(C. Schaedel)*

3. Lieutenant H.A. Rigby (Australian), 1 Squadron, 1918. *(Franks collection)*

4. Lieutenant G.R. Riley, MC, joined 3 Squadron on his 19th birthday in February 1918. *(G. Muir)*

1. Captain J.M. Robb, DFC, first saw action with 32 Squadron in 1916. By 1918 he had become a flight commander with 92 Squadron. He retired as Air Chief Marshal Sir James Robb, GCB, KBE, DSO, DFC. *(Franks collection)*

2. Captain L.H. 'Titch' Rochford, DSO & Bar, DFC, served in 3(Naval)/203 Squadron during 1917-18, with Ray Collishaw. *(R.C. Bowyer)*

3. Captain W.W. Rogers, MC, (Canadian) seated in his 1 Squadron Nieuport Scout in 1917. *(IWM)*

4. 92 Squadron group; front (l to r) — Lieutenant Haddon-Smith, Captain O.J. Rose, DFC & Bar (American — 16 victories), Lieutenant T.S. Horry, DFC, (8 victories); back — Lieutenant E.F. Crabb, DFC, (Canadian — 6 victories), Lieutenan E. Shappard (3 victories), Lieutenant Millar. *(Franks collection)*

1. Captain C.G. Ross, DFC & Bar, a South African in 29 Squadron, 1918. *(Franks ollection)*

2. 29 Squadron group; (l to r): Lieutenant :.H.R. Lagesse, DFC & Bar, Lieutenant Humphries, Lieutenant C.G. Ross, DFC, ieutenant J.G. Coombe (holding map), ieutenant H.A. Whittaker (far rear), ieutenant Walker, Lieutenant R.H. Rusby, MC (front centre), Lieutenant Prior behind Rusby), Lieutenant Reid, Lieutenant T.C. Tims, Lieutenant Beavan, Lieutenant MacLoughlin (front, smoking), Lieutenant Durrant, Captain C.J. Venter, DFC & Bar. *(Franks collection)*

3. Captain Ben Roxburgh-Smith, DFC, 74 Squadron. *(Franks collection)*

4. Lieutenant Indra Lal Roy, DFC, the only Indian pilot ever to become an ace, flew with 56 and then 40 Squadrons in 1917. *(Franks collection)*

1. Captain H.J.T. Saint, DSO, joined the RNAS in 1915 and saw action with 10(Naval) Squadron in 1917. He was later Chief Test Pilot for the Gloster Aircraft Company. *(R.C. Bowyer)*

2. Captain H.W.L.'Dingbat' Saunders, MC, DFC, MM, a South African who flew with 84 Squadron. He later became Air Chief Marshal Sir Hugh Saunders. *(H.W.L. Saunders)*

3. Captain O.J.F. Scholte, MC, 48 and 60 Squadrons. *(Franks collection)*

4. Lieutenant D.A. Savage, MC, 62 Squadron and Lieutenant W.R. McMichael, 48 Squadron (two victories), in 1919. *(Bruce & Leslie)*

. William Barker, DSO, MC, (seated ›entre) with men of his 139 Squadron, Italy, 918. To the right of Barker is Captain S. Dalrymple, DFC, who had previously ›erved with 27 and 24 Squadrons in France; ›ext is Lieutenant C.W. Curtis (4 victories) ›nd extreme right is Lieutenant W.C. ›imon, DFC, an American with 8 victories. *via C.F. Geyto)*

. Pilots of 3(Naval) Squadron; (l to r) Commander R. Bell Davies, VC, DSO, Lieutenant Downes, Lieutenant F.C. Armstrong (15 victories), Lieutenant J.A. Glen (16 victories), unknown, Lieutenant J.E. Sharman (9 victories). *(S. St Martin)*

3. Captain E.L. Simonson (right) and Lieutenant McMurtie, 2 AFC Squadron, 1918. *(Franks collection)*

4 Major A.M. Shook, DSO, DSC, AFC, CdeG, from Ontario, saw action with 4(Naval) Squadron, 1917-18. *(S. St Martin)*

1. Captain C.J. Sims, DFC, claimed his victories with 213 Squadron, 1918 (note Aldis sight and windscreen). *(F.T. Sargent)*

2. Captain J.A. Slater, MC & Bar, DFC, served as an observer before becoming a pilot then flew with 1 and 64 Squadrons, 1917-18. *(Bruce & Leslie)*

3. Captain L.H. Slatter, OBE, DSC & Bar, DFC, flew Pups and Camels with 13(Naval)/213 Squadron, 1917-18, and then served in Russia in 1919. *(Franks collection)*

4. Captain J.V. Sorsoleil, MC, from Toronto, flew with 84 Squadron in 1917-18; he was a Squadron Leader in World War II. *(S. St Martin)*

1

2

3

4

Lieutenant H.F. Stackard, 9(Naval) Squadron, 1917. *(S. St Martin)*

Major F. Sowrey, DSO, MC, AFC, shot down Zeppelin L.32 in September 1916. He then became a successful Spad pilot with 19 Squadron, before commanding 143(Home Defence) Squadron in 1918. Note twin Lewis guns on the top wing of his Home Defence BE. *(Sowrey family)*

3. Captain Stanley Stanger, MC, DFC, from Montreal, flew with 66 and 28 Squadrons in Italy, 1917-18. *(S. St Martin)*

4. Captain E.W. Springs, DSC, DFC, from South Carolina, flew with 85 Squadron and then with the 148th Aero Squadron, USAS, in 1918. He was later famous as an author of World War I aviation books, and became a multi-millionaire industrialist. *(S. St Martin)*

1. Captain W.S. Stephenson, MC, DFC, a Canadian with 73 Squadron in 1918. Later knighted, he became head of Canadian Intelligence in World War II. *(via R. Manning)*

2. Captain C.R. Steele, DFC, 20 and 48 Squadrons. He became an Air Marshal and was knighted later in life. *(Franks collection)*

3. Captain W.E. 'Bull' Staton, MC, DFC & Bar, 62 Squadron, 1917-18. He was to be awarded the DSO in 1940 for leading a bomber squadron, and then saw service in the Far East, becoming a prisoner of the Japanese. *(Franks collection)*

4. Major W.V. Strugnell, MC & Bar, of 1 and 54 Squadrons, 1917. He had learned to fly in 1912 and had first gone to France in 1914. He retired as a Group Captain. *(P. Strugnell)*

1. Major the Honourable R.N. Stuart-Wortley, MC, served with 22 Squadron, then commanded 88 Squadron in 1918. *(Franks collection)*

2. Captain J.K. Summers, MC, served with 209 Squadron in 1918, but had received his MC whilst flying artillery observation sorties with 3 Squadron during 1917. *(J.K. Summers)*

3. Captain R. Sykes, DFC, 9(Naval) Squadron, 203 and 201 Squadrons; he later served in Russia in 1919. *(R. Sykes)*

4. Captain E.R. Tempest, MC, DFC, flew with 64 Squadron following service with 6 and 15 Corps Squadrons. *(S. St Martin)*

1. Captain W. Mc. Thomson, MC, DFC, (left) a Canadian, and Lieutenant V.E. Groom, DFC, both of 20 Squadron, 1918. *(S. St Martin)*

2. Captain J. Todd, MC, DFC, 70 Squadron, 1918. *(S. St Martin)*

3. 47 Squadron group, Macedonia, 1918; standing: Lieutenant A.E. deM. Jarvis, DFC, (Canadian — 7 victories); seated (l to r): Lieutenant W. Ridley, (4 victories), Lieutenant C.B.S. Spackman, (3 victories), Captain A.G. Goulding, MC, (9 victories), Captain F.D. Travers, DFC, (9 victories) and Lieutenant J.A. Beeney, (2 victories). *(F.D. Travers)*

4. Captain J.T. Trollope, MC & Bar, flew with 70 and 43 Squadrons during 1917-18; he claimed six enemy aircraft in one day in March 1918. Trollope served as a Wing Commander in World War II. *(via R.C. Bowyer)*

. Captain W.A. Tyrrell, MC, 32 Squadron, 1917-18, who was
cilled in action in June 1918, aged 19. *(Franks collection)*

. Captain C.J. 'Boetie' Venter, DFC & Bar, a South African who
erved with 29 Squadron in 1918, and rose to the rank of Major
General in the SAAF. *(R.C. Bowyer)*

. Captain A.W. Vigers, MC, DFC, 87 Squadron, 1918, flew with
QANTAS in the 1920s. *(Franks collection)*

. Lieutenant K.B. Watson, DFC, from Ontario, 70 Squadron, 1918.
S. St Martin)

1. Captain F.G.C. Weare, MC, 22 Squadron, 1918. *(S. St Martin)*

2. Three pilots of 2 AFC Squadron; (l to r): Lieutenant J.A. Egan, Lieutenant E.E. Davies, DFC, and Lieutenant J.J. Wellwood, DFC. *(R. Guest)*

3. Three pilots of 3(Naval) Squadron; (l to r): Lieutenant E.T. Hayne, DSC, DFC, (South African), Captain A.T. 'Art' Whealy, DSC & Bar, DFC, (Canadian) and Captain H.F. 'Kiwi' Beamish, DSC, (New Zealander). *(R.C. Bowyer)*

4. Major H.G. White, 20 and 29 Squadrons, 1917-18, retired as an Air Vice-Marshal, CB, CBE. *(H.G. White)*

1. Captain J.L.M. White, DFC & Bar, a Canadian in 65 Squadron in 1918, who was subsequently killed in a flying accident whilst with the RCAF in 1925. *(Public Archive of Canada)*

2. Major A.M. Wilkinson, DSO & Bar, who flew with 24 and 48 Squadrons; he later commanded 23 Squadron. *(Franks collection)*

3. Captain T.F. Williams, MC, from Ontario, flew with 45 and 28 Squadrons in Italy. *(S. St Martin)*

4. Lieutenant T.M. Williams, MC, DFC, a South African, served with 65 Squadron during 1917-18. He later flew in Russia in 1919, where he received a Bar to his DFC. In World War II he held commands in India and Burma, becoming an Air Marshal and being knighted. *(T.M. Williams)*

5. Group of 28 Squadron pilots in Italy; second from left, Lieutenant J. Mackereth (later with 66 Squadron); 4th, Captain P. Wilson, MC; 5th, Lieutenant G.F.M. Apps, DFC (66 Squadron) 6th, Lieutenant H.B. Hudson, MC; 7th, Captain S. Stanger, MC, DFC. The others are unknown. *(Bruce & Leslie)*

1. Captain H.A. Whistler, DSO, DFC & 2 Bars, was the top-scoring pilot in 80 Squadron in 1918 (3rd from right, standing). *(S. St Martin)*

2. Captain H.A. Wood MC, from Toronto, served with 24 Squadron in 1917. *(S. St Martin)*

3. Lieutenant R. Winnicott, MC, flew DH 5s and SE 5As with 41 Squadron until his death in December 1917. *(Franks collection)*

4. Lieutenant W.B. Wood, MC & Bar, 29 Squadron, 1917. *(via J. Wales)*

5. Captain H.W. Woollett, DSO, MC & Bar, claimed over 30 victories whilst serving with 24 and 43 Squadrons during 1917-18. *(J. Beedle)*

PINDER John William Captain 9(N), 13(N), 213, 45

An RNAS pilot born in Deal, Kent, on 14 February 1898, who flew with 9(N) Squadron in 1917, he claimed three victories whilst with this unit. He was then posted to 13(N) Squadron as a flight commander, and by the end of April 1918 had claimed six victories during 166 hours of war flying. Continuing in action with what had now become 213 Squadron, RAF, he brought his score to 12 and was awarded a DFC. On 19 May he and another pilot shot down a German scout that had just destroyed a Belgian balloon, and on 27 June he went after a Fokker that had just shot down a DH 9 of 218 Squadron; following his attack, this spun down and crashed into the sea. He left the squadron at the end of August to take a post at the Air Ministry for an appointment with the Grand Fleet, but in October he was posted back to France to join 45 Squadron, which had just returned from Italy to become a part of the Independent Air Force. With this unit he claimed five more enemy machines to bring his total victories to 17; he also received a Bar to his DFC.

	1917		Triplane					
1	5 Jun	Alb. DIII	N5462	9N	Ostend	1930	OOC	CR/DL
2s*	7 Jul	Alb. DIII	N6475	9N	S W Haynecourt	1730	OOC	CR/RFC 7.7
			Camel					
3s**	25 Jul	C	B3870	9N	off Westende	1730	OOC	CR/DL
4	17 Oct	Seaplane	N6439	13N	3m N Zeebrugge	0730	DES	CR/RNAS 17.10
5s***	4 Dec	Aviatik C	N6335	13N	Houthoulst-Zarren	1535	OOC	CR/RNAS 4.12
6s†	5 Dec	Alb. C	B6357	13N	4m N W Wenduyne	1505	DES	CR/RNAS 5.12
	1918							
7s††	19 May	Alb. DV	C65	213	1m S Woumen	1735	DES(F)	CR/5 GP Comm
8s†††	2 Jun	Pfalz DIII	C65	213	Moorslede	1935	OOC	CR/5 GP Comm
9	7 Jun	Alb. DV	C65	213	4m S Dixmude	1805	OOC	CR/5 GP Comm
10s‡	15 Jun	Hannover C	C65	213	Poperinghe	1745	OOC	CR/5 GP Comm
11	27 Jun	Fokker DVII	C65	213	off Blankenberghe	1020	DES(F)	CR/5 GP Comm
12	30 Jul	Alb. DV	D8216	213	3m S W Ostend	1205	OOC	CR/5 GP Comm
13	9 Oct	Rumpler C	D8240	45	Xaffevillers	1500	OOC	CR/ORB/?
14	23 Oct	Alb. C	E7244	45	S St Die	1220	OOC	CR/ORB/?
15	23 Oct	Rumpler C	E7244	45	Fruize	1240	CAPT	CR/8 BG Summ
16	28 Oct	Rumpler C	E7244	45	Corcieux	1050	CAPT	CR/8 BG Summ
17	5 Nov	Rumpler C	E7244	45	N Parroy	1550	DES	CR/8 BG Summ

TOTAL: 2 captured, 3 and 2 shared destroyed, 5 and 5 shared out of control = 17.
*Shared with F/Cdr G.E. Hervey N6174, FSL A.T. Whealy N6472, FSL H.G. Mott N6469, FSL J.C. Tanner N6166. **Shared with F/Lt F.E. Banbury B3820, FSL Snell B3813, FSL O.M. Redgate B3832, FSL H.G. Mott. ***Shared with FSL G.C. Mackay B6357. †Shared with FSL G.C. Mackay N6335, FSL M.L. Cooper B6407, FSL J. deC Paynter B6391. ††Shared with Lt W.E. Gray B6234: Vzfw Triebswetter of Jasta 16 was killed. †††Shared with Lt W.E. Gray D3409. ‡Shared with Lt A.R. Talbot B7154, Lt C.P. Sparkes B7229.

PINEAU Cleo Francis Lieutenant 210

Pineau was an American from Alberquerque, New Mexico, who was born on 23 July 1893. He joined the RFC in December 1917 and after training was posted to 210 Squadron on 2 June 1918, flying Camels. He claimed six victories and was awarded the DFC, but was shot down four miles north-east of Roulers in D8168 by a Fokker Triplane early on 8 October, and was taken prisoner. He died in Williamsport, Pennsylvania.

	1918		Camel					
1	6 Sep	Fokker DVII	F3238	210	W Ostend	1835	OOC	CR/5 GP Comm
2	16 Sep	Fokker DVII	F3238	210	N W Zeebrugge	1110	DES	CR/5 GP Comm
3	24 Sep	Fokker DVII	F3238	210	N St Pierre Capelle	1440	DES	CR/5 GP Comm
4	24 Sep	Fokker DVII	F3238	210	3m S E Nieuport	1445	OOC	CR/5 GP Comm
5	1 Oct	Fokker DVII	F3238	210	S E Roulers	1710	DES(F)	CR/5 GP Comm
6	8 Oct	Fokker DVII	D1868	210	4m N E Roulers	0923	DES	CR/5 GP Comm

TOTAL: 4 destroyed and 2 out of control = 6.

PITHEY Croye Rothes
RHODES Hervey Lieutenants 12

Pithey, and his observer, Rhodes, were not members of a fighter squadron, but they are included here because of their position as top-scoring Corps aircrew. Pithey was a South African, and Rhodes had served with the Yorkshire Regiment before joining the RFC, but they came together in March 1918 as an RE 8 crew in 12 Squadron. The RE 8 was one of the most unlikely aircraft in which to do combat with enemy machines, but these two flyers not only fought off attacks while engaged on line patrols and artillery observation missions, but they also attacked other German aircraft and balloons in the air. Both received the DFC and Bar, and between them they accounted for two balloons and eight hostile aircraft. They were both wounded on 27 September, bringing their partnership to an end. Subsequently Pithey was killed in Ireland in 1919, but Rhodes went back to his trade, going into business on his gratuity. He was later a Labour Member of Parliament for Ashton, and held Government appointments. He subsequently became Lord Rhodes, and was appointed Lord Lieutenant of Lancashire. He died on 11 September 1987.

	1918		RE 8					
1	7 May	Balloon	----	12	----	----	DES	RAF 7.5
2	4 Jun	Balloon	----	12	----	----	DES	Air I/1004
3	7 Jun	Pfalz DIII	B7715	12	Sheet 57c B8	0920	DES	CR/RAF 7.6
4	7 Jun	Pfalz DIII	B7715	12	Sheet 57c B8	0920	OOC	CR/RAF 7.6
5	7 Jun	Pfalz DIII	B7715	12	Sheet 57c B8	0920	OOC	CR/RAF 7.6
6	21 Aug	Fokker DVII	E47	12	Behaignies	1130	OOC	CR/RAF 21.8
7	23 Aug	LVG. C	----	12	Boyelles	1740	DES(F)	CR/RAF 23.8
8	28 Aug	DFW. C	F6097	12	E St Leger	0945	DES	CR/RAF 28.8
9	30 Aug	Fokker DVII	F6097	12	Bullecourt	1650	DES(F)	CR/RAF 30.8
10	3 Sep	LVG. C	F6097	12	Lagnicourt	1715	DES	CR/RAF 3.9

TOTAL: 2 balloons, 5 destroyed, 3 out of control = 10.
NB: On May 8 1918, whilst flying with 2/Lt N. Garland, 2/Lt H. Rhodes shot down an enemy aircraft out of control.

POOLE George Ramsden Lieutenant 88

Born on 16 April 1896, in Bradford, West Yorkshire, Poole joined the 6th West Yorkshire Regiment in 1913, serving in the ranks until 1917. He transferred to the RFC in September of that year and joined 88 Squadron on 15 June 1918. His usual gunners were Sergeants C. Hill and E. Antcliffe.

	1918		Bristol					
1*	31 Jul	Fokker DVII	D8064	88	Estaires-Merville	0945	OOC	CR/SR/?
2**	11 Aug	Fokker DVII	C821	88	Combles	1145	DES	CR/RAF 11.8
3**	11 Aug	Fokker DVII	C821	88	Combles	1145	OOC	CR/SR/?
4*	20 Sep	Fokker DVII	C922	88	S E Capinghem	0750	DES	CR/RAF 20.9
5s***	20 Sep	Fokker DVII	C922	88	S E Quesnoy	0755	DES	CR/RAF 20.9

TOTAL: 2 and 1 shared destroyed, 2 out of control = 5.
*Observer: Sgt C. Hill. **Observer: Sgt E. Antcliffe. ***Observer: Sgt C. Hill; shared with Capt E.C. Johnston/Lt W.I.N. Grant, Lt K.B. Conn/2/Lt B. Digby-Worsley E2216.

POPE Sydney Leo Gregory Lieutenant 60

Born in Dublin on 27 March 1898, 'Poppy' Pope joined the Inns of Court OTC in 1916, and in 1917 served with 60 Squadron during the summer, flying Nieuport Scouts. During June he claimed two victories with this type, but the following month converted to SE 5s, soon followed by SE 5As. His first victory with the new aircraft was gained on 16 September in SE 5 A8933, and on 8 November he claimed two two-seaters in SE 5A B533. His final victory on 11 November brought his score to six. He was wounded on 18 November and was forced to land near St Julien in B519. He remained in the RAF after the war and following service in Iraq and Egypt, he commanded 54 Squadron in 1932; he was awarded an AFC to add to his World War I MC, and in 1939 was a Wing Commander in command of RAF Debden, later becoming a Group Captain.

	1917		Nieuport					
1	8 Jun	Alb. C	B1652	60	Vitry	0745	OOC	CR/C&CB/?
2s*	20 Jun	Alb. DV	B1679	60	Equerchin	1140	OOC	CR/C&CB/?
			SE5					
3	16 Sep	Alb. DIII	A8933	60	S Houthem	1830	DES	CR/C&CB/?
			SE 5A					
4	8 Nov	C	B533	60	Gheluwe	1510	DES	CR/RFC 8.11
5	8 Nov	C	B533	60	Ypres	1530	DES	CR/RFC 8.11
6	11 Nov	Alb. DIII	B519	60	Gheluwe	1510	DES	CR/RFC 11.11

TOTAL: 4 destroyed, 1 and 1 shared out of control = 6.
*Shared with 2/Lt A.R. Penny B1569.

PRATT Harold Johnstone Lieutenant 48

An ex-member of the London Regiment, Pratt was commissioned into the Oxford and Buckinghamshire Light Infantry in October 1915. Transferring to the RFC in February 1917, he flew with 48 Squadron throughout the summer; his regular gunner was Lieutenant H. Owen. They were to claim five victories during a period of five months.

	1917		Bristol					
1s*	20 May	Alb. DIII	A7108	48	Brebieres	1230	OOC	CR/RFC 20.5
2s**	15 Jun	Alb. DIII	A7116	48	Fampoux	1945	OOC	CR/RFC 15.6

3***	16 Jun	Alb. DIII	A7116	48	Estree	1050	OOC	CR/RFC 16.6
4***	25 Aug	Alb. DV	A7217	48	Westkerke	1210	OOC	CR/RFC 25.8
5***	31 Aug	Alb. DV	A7217	48	Zarren	2105	OOC	CR/RFC 1.9

TOTAL: 4 and 1 shared out of control = 5.
*Observer: Lt H. Owen. Shared with Capt R. Raymond-Barker/Lt R.N.W. Jeff. **Observer: Lt H. Owen; shared with Lt H.M. Fraser/Lt M.A. Benjamin A7117. ***Observer: Lt H. Owen.

PRESTON J.C. Lieutenant 150

Preston served with 150 Squadron in Macedonia throughout 1918. He was involved in an intense action on 18 August during which he shared in five claims.

	1918		Camel					
1s*	23 Jul	Alb. DV	C6643	150	N E Boluntili	0730	DES	CR/BG Summ
2	23 Jul	DFW. CV	C6643	150	Husarli	1115	OOC	CR/BG Summ
3s**	18 Aug	Alb. DV	C6643	150	N Lake Doiran	0745	OOC	CR/BG Summ
4s**	18 Aug	S.S. DIII	C6643	150	Lake Doiran	0745	OOC	CR/BG Summ
5s***	18 Aug	S.S. DIII	C6643	150	Paravo	0745	OOC	CR/BG Summ
6s***	18 Aug	Alb. DV	C6643	150	N Lake Doiran	0745	OOC	CR/BG Summ
7s†	18 Aug	Alb. DV	C6643	150	N Lake Doiran	0745	OOC	CR/BG Summ

TOTAL: 2 shared destroyed, 1 and 4 shared out of control = 7.
*Shared with Lt D.A. Davies C1599. **Shared with Lt H.N. Jennings, Lt D.A. Davies C1598, Lt H.A.E. Matthews D6551. ***Shared with Lt H.N. Jennings. †Shared with Lt H.A.E. Matthews D6551.

PRICE Guy William Flight Commander 13(N), 8(N)

An Irishman, Guy Price sported a 'Captain Kettle' beard while serving in the RNAS. After service with 13(N) Squadron he joined 8(N) as acting flight commander in 1917. He was awarded the DSC and Bar, and claimed 12 victories before he was killed during a solo low ground strafing mission on 18 February 1918, when he was shot down by Leutnant Theodor Rumpel of Jasta 23.

	1917		Camel					
1	5 Dec	Alb. DV	B6311	8N	Cite St Auguste	1350	DES	CR/ORB/?
2s*	5 Dec	Alb. DV	B6311	8N	Wingles	1355	OOC	CR/RFC 5.12
3s**	6 Dec	DFW. C	----	8N	Loison S E Lens	1045	OOC	CR/RFC 6.12
4s**	27 Dec	DFW. C	----	8N	Henin-Lietard	1435	OOC	CR/RFC 27.12
5s***	28 Dec	DFW. C	B6229	8N	Vitry	1100	OOC	CR/RFC 28.12
	1918							
6†	2 Jan	Alb. DV	B6312	8N	Cite St Auguste	1113	DES(F)	CR/RFC 2.1
7	6 Jan	C	B6371	8N	Oppy-Fresnes	1255	DES	CR/RFC 6.1
8	19 Jan	Alb. DV	B6371	8N	Sailly- S Vitry	1215	OOC	CR/RFC 19.1
9	22 Jan	Alb. DV	B6379	8N	Vitry	1120	OOC	CR/RFC 22.1
10††	24 Jan	Alb. DV	B6379	8N	La Bassee	1225	DES	CR/RFC 24.1
11†††	28 Jan	C	B6379	8N	La Bassee	1105	DES(F)	CR/RFC 28.1
12s‡	16 Feb	Alb. DV	B6379	8N	Pronville	1115	DES(F)	CR/ORB/?

TOTAL: 5 and 1 shared destroyed, 2 and 4 shared out of control = 12.
*Shared with FSL W.H. Sneath B3821. **Shared with FSL H. Day. ***Shared with FSL H. Day B6379. †This was Lt Gunther Auffahrt of Jasta 29, who was killed. ††Two claims, one loss; Uffz F. Jacobs Jasta 12 was killed. †††This was a crew from Sch.St 17. ‡Shared with FSL W.H. Sneath B6356, FSL H.H. Fowler B3832.

PRICE Stephen William Major 23, 11, 33, 36

Following service with the 8th Leicestershire Regt, Price flew FE 2Bs with 23 Squadron in 1916, where he teamed up with American gunner Lieutenant Fred Libby. It is possible that this team claimed three victories before they were posted together to 11 Squadron. Here they claimed seven more victories by 9 November, and were both awarded MCs. Price then flew with 33 Squadron on home defence during 1917 as 'A' Flight commander, before becoming Commanding Officer of 36 Squadron the following year.

	1916		FE 2B					
1s*	22 Aug	Roland CII	6994	11	S Bapaume	1910	OOC	CR/RFC 22.8
2s*	22 Aug	Roland CII	6994	11	S Bapaume	1910	OOC	CR/RFC 22.8
3**	22 Aug	Roland CII	6994	11	S Bapaume	1910	OOC	CR/RFC 22.8
4**	25 Aug	Aviatik C	6994	11	Bapaume	1300	OOC	CR/RFC 25.8
5**	14 Sep	C	6994	11	S E Bapaume	0930	OOC	CR/RFC 14.9
6**	17 Oct	Alb. DI	7027	11	Mory	1115	OOC	RFC 17.10
7	20 Oct	Alb. DI	7027	11	11 Douchy-Ayette	1130	DES(F)	CR/RFC 17.10

TOTAL: 1 destroyed, 4 and 2 shared out of control = 7.
*Observer: Lt F. Libby. Shared with 2/Lt L.B.F. Morris/Lt T. Rees 6983. **Observer: Lt F. Libby.

PRICE William Thomas 2nd Lieutenant 48

Born on 15 November 1895, Price was educated at Christ College, London, and at Reading University. He served initially with the Royal Warwickshire Regiment, but transferred to the RFC, becoming one of the original pilots in 48 Squadron. By early May 1917 he had claimed seven victories and received an MC, but on 9th of that month he was shot down by Leutnant Lothar von Richthofen of Jasta 11 as his 22nd victory. Price, although wounded, managed to force-land A7110 in British lines, north-east of Fampoux, and survived. After the war he became an agricultural educationalist, finally retiring in 1962; he died in Leamington Spa, Warwickshire, on 17 January 1982.

	1917		Bristol					
1*	6 Apr	D	----	48	Douai	----	OOC	RFC 6.4
2*	9 Apr	Alb. DIII	----	48	E Arras	----	DES	RFC 9.4
3s**	23 Apr	Alb. DIII	----	48	Vitry	----	OOC	Cit/RFC 23.4
4*	25 Apr	Alb. DIII	----	48	E Arras	1900	DES	RFC 25.4
5s***	27 Apr	C	----	48	Vitry	----	DES	RFC 27.4
6s†	9 May	C	A7110	48	Vitry-Noyelles	0820	DES	CR/RFC 9.5
7††	9 May	Alb. DIII	A7110	48	E Vitry-Fampoux	1725	DES	CR/RFC 9.5

TOTAL: 3 and 2 shared destroyed, 1 and 1 shared out of control = 7.
*Observer: Lt M.A. Benjamin. **Observer: LT M.A. Benjamin; shared with Lt F.P. Holliday/Capt A.H.G. Wall, Lt R.B. Hay/Lt V.G. Nutkins. ***Observer: Lt M.A. Benjamin; shared with Lt R.B. Hay/Lt V.G. Nutkins. †Observer: Lt E.S. Moore; shared with Lt F.P. Holliday/Capt A.H.G. Wall A7108. ††Observer: Lt C.G. Claye.

PRITT Walbanke Ashby Lieutenant 66, 44

Pritt flew Pups with 66 Squadron in the summer of 1917. He was a very aggressive pilot and very youthful in appearance, looking more like a boy of 14 or 15, despite his insistence that he was 20. On 16 August he went out to strafe an enemy airfield, but after his first attack an Albatros took off to intercept him; swooping down after this, he sent it down to crash. As he turned, he saw a second fighter taking to the air, and this too he claimed to have shot down. On another patrol he ran out of ammunition before seeing a German staff car at which he dived. One of the officers in this got out and fired at him with a pistol, so Pritt dived down again and fired a Very flare at his opponent! He was awarded an MC, having claimed at least five victories. Later in 1917 he served with 44(Home Defence) Squadron.

	1917		Pup					
1	28 Jul	Alb. DIII	B1762	66	E Roulers	1835-2100	DES	ORB/RFC 28.7
2	16 Aug	Alb. DV	B1732	66	Marcke	0515	DES	CR/RFC 16.8
3	16 Aug	Alb. DV	B1732	66	Marcke	0515	DES	CR/RFC 16.8
4	21 Aug	Aviatik C	B1762	66	S W Roulers	1145	DES	CR/RFC 21.8
5	30 Sep	Alb. DV	B2162	66	----	1000-1200	DES	ORB/RFC 30.9

TOTAL: 5 destroyed = 5.

PROCTOR Anthony Wetherby Beauchamp (see BEAUCHAMP PROCTOR Anthony Wetherby)

PROTHERO Phillip Bernard Captain 24, 56

A Scotsman, born in 1894, he first saw action flying Bristol Scouts with 24 Squadron, claiming two enemy machines in 1916. Following a rest, he joined 56 Squadron in May 1917 as 'B' Flight commander, gaining a further six victories before he was killed in action on 26 July, when he was shot down by Vizefeldwebel Artur Muth of Jasta 27. A8925 was seen to spin down north-east of Houthem at 1945, with the wings shot off.

	1916		Bristol Scout					
1	30 Jun	EA	5308	24	Grandcourt	0715	DES	ORB/RFC 1.7
2	10 Jul	C	5557	24	W Grevillers Wood	0810	DES	CR/RFC 10.7
	1917		SE 5					
3s*	23 May	Alb. DIII	A8909	56	Aubigny	1900-1915	OOC	CR/RFC 23.5
4	27 May	Alb. DIII	A8909	56	E Bugnicourt	1900-2000	OOC	CR/RFC 27.5
5	28 May	Alb. DIII	A8909	56	Busigny	1145-1245	OOC	CR/RFC 28.5
6s**	15 Jun	C	A8909	56	Fort Carnot	1315	DES	CR/RFC 15.6
7	11 Jul	D	A8909	56	Houthoulst Forest	1845-1945	OOC	CR/RFC 11.7
8	21 Jul	D	A8925	56	Polygon Wood	1930-2015	OOC	CR/RFC 21.7

TOTAL: 2 and 1 shared destroyed, 4 and 1 shared out of control = 8.
*Shared with Capt E.W. Broadberry A8903. **Shared with Lt G.C. Maxwell A8921.

PUFFER Stanley Asa Lieutenant 41

From Alberta, Canada, Puffer served in 41 Squadron from 4 February to 8 July 1918. According to Canadian records he was credited with nine victories, but only seven can actually be found for him, the other two being 'driven down' claims. After the war he returned to Canada, and in the early 1920s was a pilot with the RCAF.

	1918		SE 5A					
1	25 Mar	Alb. DV	B8271	41	Sailly	1040	OOC	CR/RFC 25.3
2	15 Jun	Alb. C	D5984	41	S E Bray	1210	OOC	CR/SR/?
3	28 Jun	Fokker DVII	D6000	41	Belloy	2005	DES(F)	CR/RAF 28.6
4	28 Jun	Pfalz DIII	D6000	41	S Feuilleres	2045	OOC	CR/SR/?
5	30 Jun	DFW. C	D6000	41	S Guerbigny	0940	DES	CR/RAF 30.6
6	30 Jun	Rumpler C	D6000	41	Dompierre	0815	OOC	CR/SR/?
7	4 Jul	Balloon	D6000	41	Mericourt	0655	DES	CR/RAF WD

TOTAL: 1 balloon, 2 destroyed, 4 out of control = 7.

PURDOM Thomas Laurence Captain 15, 62

After service with the Kings's Own Scottish Borderers, Purdom flew for most of 1916 as a BE 2 pilot in 15 Squadron, participating in many combats without any decisive success. He then flew in 62 Squadron as a flight commander in spring 1918, receiving an MC. With this unit he claimed 13 victories, all but the last one being gained with Lieutenant P.V.G. Chambers in the rear cockpit of his Bristol Fighter as gunner.

	1918		Bristol					
1*	21 Mar	Alb. DV	----	62	----	----	DES	RFC 21.3
2*	21 Mar	Alb. DV	----	62	----	----	OOC	SR/BG Summ
3*	24 Mar	Alb. DV	----	62	----	----	DES(F)	RFC 24.3
4*	26 Mar	EA	----	62	----	----	DES	SR/BG Summ
5*	26 Mar	EA	----	62	----	----	OOC	SR/BG Summ
6*	28 Mar	EA	----	62	Sailly	1005	OOC	SR/BG Summ
7s**	21 Apr	Alb. DV	----	62	S E Estaires	0945	DES	SR/RAF 21.4
8*	3 May	Alb. C	B1216	62	N Merville	1100	DES	CR/RAF 3.5
9*	3 May	Alb. DV	B1216	62	S Armentieres	1100	OOC	CR/RAF 3.5
10*	15 May	C	B1216	62	Pozieres	1745	DES	CR/RAF 15.5
11*	17 May	Fokker DVII	B1216	62	Armentieres	1045	OOC	CR/RAF 17.5
12*	17 May	C	B1216	62	Armentieres	1045	OOC	CR/BG Summ
13***	19 May	Fokker DVII	----	62	N W Douai	1815	OOC	CR/RAF 19.5

TOTAL: 5 and 1 shared destroyed, 7 out of control = 13.
*Observer: 2/Lt P.V.C. Chambers. **Observer: 2/Lt P.V.C. Chambers; shared with 2/Lt W.E. Staton/Lt J.T. Gordon. ***Observer: Sgt W.N. Holmes.

QUESTED John Bowley Major 11, 40

Born on 14 December 1893, in Cheriton, Kent, he was commissioned on 11 November 1914 and flew with 11 Squadron as an observer from April 1915. Training as a pilot, he rejoined the unit in July 1916 to fly FE 2Bs, and from the late summer of that year until early 1917 he and his gunners accounted for eight enemy machines, plus another driven down damaged. On 27 December 1916 he and his observer, Lieutenant H.J.M. Dicksee, were shot down by Manfred von Richthofen and crashed one kilometre behind the Allied trenches near Ficheux — the German's 15th victory. Lieutenant Dicksee was slightly wounded on this occasion, but both were back in action in January. In July, after a period as an instructor, Quested was sent to 40 Squadron for a refresher course, where he was injured in a crash. In October 1917 he commanded No 1 Aerial Gunnery Range in France, but returned to England in February 1918 after receiving further injuries. From August 1918 to March 1919 he commanded No 2 Aeroplane Supply Depot, but was then posted to 79 Squadron in Germany. After the war he resided for some time in Australia. He received the MC and Croix de Guerre during 1917.

	1916		FE 2B					
1*	16 Aug	Roland C	6965	11	Fampoux	0835	OOC	CR/?
2*	2 Sep	Roland C	6965	11	Bapaume	1930	OOC	CR/RFC 2.9
3*	2 Sep	Roland C	6965	11	Bapaume	1930	OOC	CR/RFC 2.9
4**	15 Sep	D	6965	11	Bapaume	0915	DES	CR/RFC 15.9
5***	22 Sep	Aviatik C	----	11	Longeast Wood	----	DES	CR/RFC 22.9
6†	20 Dec	Alb. DI	7016	11	Monchy le Preux	1420	OOC	CR/RFC 20.12
7††	27 Dec	Alb. DI	7666	11	Wancourt	1115	DES	CR/RFC 27.12
	1917							
8††	25 Jan	D	A5442	11	Beaurains	1425	OOC	CR/RFC 25.1

TOTAL: 3 destroyed, 5 out of control = 8.
*Observer: 2/Lt W.J. Wyatt. **Observer: Cpl G. Monk. ***Observer: 2/Lt G.K. Welsford. †Observer: Lt F.D. Lutyens. ††Observer: 2/Lt H.J. Dicksee.

QUIGLEY Francis Grainger Captain 70

A Canadian, born on 10 July 1894, in Toronto, he joined the 5th Field Company, Canadian Army Engineers, and arrived in the United Kingdom in May 1915, going to France some weeks later. In spring 1917 he transferred to the RFC, and after training was posted to 70 Squadron in France. He was Mentioned in Despatches several times, and was awarded an MC during the autumn. In March 1918 he received a DSO and the following May a Bar to his MC. He was wounded in the ankle on 27 March, by which time his score stood at 33, and he had been promoted to Captain; after convalescing in France, he returned to Canada to become an instructor at Armour Heights. In September 1918 he requested to go back to France and sailed for England early in October. On board ship he was struck down by the influenza epidemic which was sweeping Europe, and which was to take a heavier toll than the Great War. On arrival at Liverpool on 18th he was taken to hospital where he died two days later.

	1917		Camel					
1	10 Oct	Alb. DV	B2356	70	Westroosebeke	0805	DES(F)	CR/RFC 10.10
2	10 Oct	Alb. DV	B2356	70	S Houthoulst Forest	0825	OOC	CR/RFC 10.10
3s*	20 Oct	C	B2356	70	Rumbeke a/d	1115	DES	CR/RFC 20.10
4	12 Nov	Alb. DV	B2447	70	E Houthoulst Forest	1800	OOC	CR/RFC 12.11
5	5 Dec	Alb. DV	B2447	70	E Westroosebeke	1345	DES	CR/RFC 5.12
6	12 Dec	Alb. DV	B2311	70	Westroosebeke	0930	OOC	CR/RFC 12.12
7s**	19 Dec	Alb. DV	B2447	70	20 Q 27	0945	DES(F)	CR/RFC 19.12
8	26 Dec	C	B2447	70	20 Q 23	1520	DES(F)	CR/RFC 26.12
9s***	27 Dec	C	B2447	70	Zarren	1050	DES	CR/RFC 27.12
	1918							
10	3 Jan	C	B2447	70	E Moorslede	1345	OOC	CR/RFC 3.1
11s†	6 Jan	Alb. DV	B2447	70	Stadenberg	1400	DES	CR/RFC 6.1
12s††	6 Jan	Alb. DV	B2447	70	E Passchendaele	1415	DES	CR/RFC 6.1
13s†††	22 Jan	Alb. DV	B5214	70	N E Houthoulst Wood	1414	DES(F)	CR/RFC 22.1
14s†††	22 Jan	Alb. DV	B5214	70	N E Houthoulst Wood	1420	OOC	CR/RFC 22.1
15s‡	22 Jan	Alb. DV	B5214	70	N E Houthoulst Wood	1430	DES	CR/RFC 22.1
16	24 Jan	C	B2447	70	S E Wervicq	1120	DES	CR/RFC 24.1
17	29 Jan	Alb. DV	B5251	70	N E Houthoulst Wood	1110	DES(F)	CR/RFC 29.1
18s‡‡	17 Feb	C	----	70	Houthoulst Forest	----	OOC	RFC 17.2
19	8 Mar	Alb. DV	B7475	70	Roulers	1305	OOC	CR/RFC 8.3
20	9 Mar	Alb. DV	B7475	70	Menin	0930	DES(F)	CR/RFC 9.3
21	9 Mar	Alb. DV	B7475	70	Menin	0945	DES	CR/RFC 9.3
22	9 Mar	Alb. DV	B7475	70	Quesnoy	1310	OOC	CR/RFC 9.3
23	9 Mar	Alb. DV	B7475	70	Quesnoy	1310	OOC	CR/RFC 9.3
24s‡‡‡	11 Mar	Balloon	B7475	70	Menin	1230	DES	CR/RFC 11.3
25s§	11 Mar	Pfalz DIII	B7475	70	Passchendaele	1700	DES	CR/RFC 11.3?
26	11 Mar	Pfalz DIII	B7475	70	Passchendaele	1700	OOC	CR/RFC 11.3?
27	11 Mar	Pfalz DIII	B7475	70	Passchendaele	1700	OOC	CR/RFC 11.3?
28§§	12 Mar	Alb. DV	B7475	70	Dadizeele	1245	DES	CR/RFC 12.3
29§§	12 Mar	Alb. DV	B7475	70	Dadizeele	1245	DES	CR/RFC 12.3
30§§	12 Mar	Alb. DV	B7475	70	Dadizeele	1250	OOC	CR/RFC 12.3
31	22 Mar	Alb. DV	B7475	70	Inchy-Bourlon	1535	DES	CR/RFC 22.3
32	22 Mar	Fokker DrI	B7475	70	N E Havrincourt	1430	DES	CR/RFC 22.3
33	23 Mar	Pfalz DIII	B7475	70	Morchies	1700	DES	CR/RFC 23.3

TOTAL: 1 shared balloon, 12 and 8 shared destroyed, 10 and 2 shared out of control = 33.

*Shared with 2/Lt C.W. Primeau B2349, 2/Lt E.B. Booth B6366. **Shared with Lt F.C. Gorringe B6424. ***Shared with Lt K.A. Seth-Smith B2438, 2/Lt F.H. Hobson B6251. †Shared with Capt P.G. Kemsley, and Capt W.M. Fry B3640. Lt W. von Bulow, a 28 victory ace and commander of Jasta B, was killed. ††Shared with 2/Lt F.C. Gorringe B6426. †††Shared with 2/Lt G.R. Howsam B2530. ‡Shared with Lt J. Todd B3890. ‡‡Shared with Lt F.C. Gorringe. ‡‡‡Shared with 2/Lt A. Koch, Lt K.A. Seth-Smith, Lt W.M. Carlaw. §Shared with 2/Lt A. Koch. §§One of these was Flgr Georg Boit of Jasta 51, who was killed.

QUINTIN-BRAND Christopher Joseph Major 1, 112, 151

Born near Kimberley, South Africa, on 25 May 1893, he served in the army from 1913-16, when he transferred to the RFC. He was posted to 1 Squadron, with which he gained seven victories during 1917. He then became a flight commander with 112(Home Defence) Squadron in 1918, later taking command of the first night fighter unit to go to France, 151 Squadron, and bringing his score to 12. Known as 'Flossie', he stayed in the RAF after the war, and in 1920 flew with Pierre van Ryneveld from England to the Cape of Good Hope in 109 hours, after many adventures. Both airmen were knighted by King George V. In the thirties he was seconded to the Egyptian Air Force, and by 1936 had become a Group Captain. After the outbreak of World War II he commanded 10 Group of Fighter Command with great distinction during the Battle of Britain, with the rank of

Air Vice-Marshal. He retired in 1943 as Sir Christopher Brand, KBE, DSO, MC, DFC, and died in Rhodesia on 9 March 1968.

	1917		Nieuport					
1s*	4 Mar	Roland C	A6668	1	Boesinghe-Wytschaete	1235	DES	CR/RFC 4.3
2	15 Mar	LVG. C	A6668	1	N E Zandvoorde	1545	DES(F)	CR/RFC 15.3
3	15 Mar	Alb. DV	A6668	1	St Eloi	1635	OOC	CR/RFC 15.3
4	8 Apr	Balloon	A6668	1	Moorslede	1130	DES	CR/RFC 8.4
5**	30 Apr	Alb. C	A6668	1	Houplines	0855	CAPT	CR/RFC 30.4
6	1 May	Alb. C	A6668	1	Warneton	0915	DES	CR/RFC 1.5
7s***	1 May	Alb. C	A6668	1	Ploegsteert	1000	DES	CR/RFC 1.5
	1918		Camel					
8†	19 May	Gotha GIV	D6423	112	Faversham area	2326	CAPT	C&C/OH
9††	17 Sep	Fried. G	D6423	151	Havrincourt Wood	2241	CAPT	SR/RAF 18.9
10	21 Sep	Fried. G	D6423	151	Gouzeaucourt	2126	CAPT	SR/RAF 21.9
11s†††	21 Sep	AEG. G	D6423	151	Gouzeaucourt	2135	DES	CR/RAF 21.9
12	30 Oct	Fried. G	D6423	151	Foret d'Andigny	1904	DES	SR/RAF 30.10

TOTAL: 1 balloon, 4 captured, 3 and 3 shared destroyed, 1 out of control = 12.

*Shared with Lt V.C.A. Bush A6670. **This was Vzfw M. Baatz/Lt A. Schlieper of FAA 204. ***Shared with 2/Lt L.M. Mansbridge A6670. †This was Vzfw Fritz Bloch/Oblt Rudolf Bartowski/Vzfw Heinrich Heilgers of Bogohl III, who were killed. ††This was Lt Gerlach, Lt Tillmann (POWS) and Uffz Kurth (KIA) of KSt 4. †††Shared with Lt J.H. Summers C6713.

RAE Thomas Gillies Lieutenant 48

Lieutenant Rae joined 48 Squadron in the autumn of 1918, and claimed all his victories during the closing six weeks of the war, first scoring on 4 October. One month later he claimed his sixth and final victory, all of which were Fokker DVIIs; at least four of these were credited to his front gun.

	1918		Bristol					
1*	4 Oct	Fokker DVII	E2822	48	Wambrechies	1250	DES(F)	CR/RAF 27.10
2**	9 Oct	Fokker DVII	E2281	48	N Courtrai	1045	DES	CR/RAF 9.10
3***	21 Oct	Fokker DVII	E2433	48	Poteghem	1220	OOC	CR/11 WR
4s†	26 Oct	Fokker DVII	E2413	48	Renaix	1530	DES	CR/RAF 26.10
5††	30 Oct	Fokker DVII	E2596	48	S W Audenaarde	1545	DES	CR/RAF 30.10
6†††	4 Nov	Fokker DVII	E2596	48	Lessines-Gramont	1515	DES	CR/RAF 4.11

TOTAL: 4 and 1 shared destroyed, 1 out of control = 6.

*Observer: 2/Lt C.R. Pickering. **Observer: Sgt C.F. Perkin. ***Observer: Lt H.G. Lewis. †Observer: 2/Lt F.G. Smith. Shared with Capt F.J. Phillips/2/Lt J.W. London E2608. ††Observer: Lt R. Watson. †††Observer: 2/Lt R. Evans.

RALSTON John Steele Captain 71, 84, 24

Born on 27 April 1887, in Edinburgh, Ralston received an MC while serving with the Scottish Rifles, before transferring to the RFC in March 1917 at Aboukir, Egypt. After pilot training he was posted to 71 Squadron, and then to 84 Squadron in October 1917. He claimed at least five victories before going to 24 Squadron as a flight commander. Here he shot down an Albatros on 16 February, but was wounded during the combat. Recovering, he returned to 84 Squadron as a flight commander and brought his score to at least 12, including three balloons, also being awarded the DFC. On 27 June he was shot down in flames by Unteroffizier Hausmann of Jasta 15, but managed to crash-land D333 without injury. Finally, on 25 July he dived on a German balloon but was hit and wounded, although his target went down in flames. Ralston managed to get back to the British lines before he fainted and crashed to his death.

	1917		SE 5A					
1s*	21 Oct	C	B564	84	E Roulers-Menin Rd.	1440	OOC	CR/RFC 21.10
2	31 Oct	Alb. DV	B4853	84	Menin	1450	OOC	CR/RFC 31.10
3s**	6 Dec	C	C5310	84	Cambrai	1430	OOC	CR/RFC 6.12
4	23 Dec	C	C5310	84	St Quentin	1310	OOC	CR/RFC 23.12
	1918							
5	13 Jan	C	C5310	84	Crevecoeur	1115	DES	CR/RFC 13.1
6	16 Feb	Alb. DV	B120	24	Mont d'Origny	c1230	OOC	CR/RFC 16.2
7	18 Jun	Fokker DVII	D333	84	Villers-Brettoneaux	1055	OOC	CR/?
8	27 Jun	Pfalz DIII	D333	84	N E Villers-Brettoneaux	0930	OOC	CR/RAF 27.6
9	16 Jul	Balloon	D6914	84	~~Mericourt~~	~~1350~~	~~DES~~	~~CR/RAF 16.7~~
10s***	20 Jul	Balloon	D6914	84	Warvillers	0910	DES	CR/RAF 20.7
11s†	24 Jul	Fokker DVII	D6914	84	Warfusee-Abancourt	1115	DES	CR/RAF 24.7
12	25 Jul	Balloon	D6914	84	S Warvillers	0630	DES	CR/RAF 25.7

TOTAL: 2 and 1 shared balloons, 1 and 1 shared destroyed, 5 and 2 shared out of control = 12.

*Shared with Capt K.M. StC Leask B4874. **Shared with Lt R.A. Grosvenor. ***Shared with Lt J.E. Boudwin. †Shared with Lt N.W.R. Mawle C1868.

RALSTON Orville Alfred 1st Lieutenant 85, 148US

An American from Lincoln, Nebraska, he joined the USAS and was attached to the RAF for combat experience, flying SE 5As with 85 Squadron and claiming the destruction of two Fokker DVIIs. He was then posted to the 148th Aero Squadron, USAS, now flying Camels, and accounted for three more aircraft to bring his score to five.

	1918		SE 5A					
1	24 Jul	Fokker DVII	E1398	85	N W Armentieres	1035	DES	CR/RAF 24.7
2	22 Aug	Fokker DVII	F3983	85	N W Peronne	1650	DES	CR/RAF 22.8
			Camel					
3s*	15 Sep	Halb. C	D8250	148US	Epinoy	1040	OOC	CR/USAF 133
4	26 Sep	Fokker DVII	F5943	148US	N E Bourlon Wood	1330	DES	CR/RAF 26.9
5	3 Oct	Fokker DVII	C3202	148US	Cattenielles	1120	DES	CR/RAF 3.10

TOTAL: 4 destroyed, and 1 shared out of control = 5.
*Shared with Lt Cunnius, Lt E.W. Springs, Lt H.C. Starkey.

RANDALL Arthur Clunie Captain 32, 85

'Snowy' Randall served with 32 Squadron in 1917, flying DH 2s; on this type he claimed two victories. In 1918, now a Captain, he joined 85 Squadron as a flight commander, and added a further eight to his tally, receiving the DFC.

	1917		DH 2					
1s*	23 Jan	C	----	32	Ervillers	1515	DES(F)	ORB/RFC 23.1
2	11 Mar	Alb. DII	A2548	32	Bapaume	1005	OOC	CR/RFC 11.3
	1918		SE 5A					
3s**	18 Jun	C	B7870	85	Voormezeele	0450	DES	CR/RAF 18.6
4	14 Jul	Pfalz DIII	C1928	85	N Merville	0835	DES	CR/RAF 14.7
5***	24 Jul	Fokker DVII	C1931	85	Neuve Eglise	1045	DES	CR/RAF 24.7
6	31 Jul	Alb. C	C6454	85	Vielle Chapelle	2005	DES	CR/RAF 31.7
7	9 Aug	Alb. C	C6454	85	Steenwerck	0755	DES(F)	CR/RAF 9.8
8	10 Aug	DFW. C	C6454	85	Le Touret	0640	DES	CR/RAF 10.8
9	22 Aug	Fokker DVII	C6454	85	Maricourt	1650	OOC	CR/?
10	4 Oct	DFW. C	E5487	85	N W Aubencheul aux Bois	1755	DES	CR/?

TOTAL: 6 and 2 shared destroyed, 2 out of control = 10.
*Shared with Capt L.P. Aizlewood, Lt G.J. King, Lt F. Billinge, Lt T.A. Gooch, Lt St. C.C. Tayler, 2/Lt A. Coningham. **Shared with Lt A. Cunningham-Reid D6859. ***This was Jasta 43 being shot up; at least 3 of their aircraft were forced to land.

RANDALL George Ebben Lieutenant 3, 20

Born in London on 19 January 1899, Randall was commissioned in the RFC in April 1917, joining 3 Squadron as an observer during the next month. When this unit converted to Camels, he returned to Home Establishment for pilot training. He subsequently flew with 20 Squadron throughout the summer and autumn of 1918, claiming 11 enemy scouts between 24 July and 10 November, including two on this latter date. Although flying with various gunners, his most frequent companion was Lieutenant G.V. Learmond, and six of his victories were credited to the rear gun, five claimed while Learmond was operating this. Randall was awarded a DFC, gazetted on 8 February 1919, for his victories and for leading 71 offensive patrols. During 1919 as a Flying Officer with the RAF, he served on the North-West Frontier in India, operating against dissident tribesmen in Waziristan, and for his conduct there was awarded a Bar to his DFC.

	1918		Bristol					
1*	24 Jul	Fokker DVII	D8086	20	N Wervicq	2015	DES	CR/RAF 24.7
2**	14 Aug	Pfalz DIII	D8086	20	Dadizeele	1800-1830	OOC	CR/SR/?
3*	22 Aug	Fokker DVII	E2158	20	Dadizeele	1915	DES	CR/RAF 22.8
4*	3 Sep	Fokker DVII	E2249	20	S Havrincourt Wood	1745	OOC	CR/SR/?
5*	5 Sep	Fokker DVII	E2249	20	S E Cambrai	1521	OOC	CR/SR/?
6***	24 Sep	Fokker DVII	E2470	20	S Clery	1640	DES	CR/RAF 24.9
7***	24 Sep	Fokker DVII	E2470	20	S Clery	1640	OOC	CR/SR/?
8*	3 Nov	Fokker DVII	E2429	20	1m S W Berlaimont	1330	DES	CR/RAF 3.11
9*	9 Nov	Fokker DVII	E2429	20	S E Beaumont	1130	DES	CR/SR/?
10*	10 Nov	Fokker DVII	E2429	20	W Louerval	1100	DES	CR/RAF 10.11
11*	10 Nov	Fokker DVII	E2429	20	W Louerval	1135	DES(F)	CR/RAF 10.11

TOTAL: 7 destroyed, 4 out of control = 11.
*Observer: Lt G.V. Learmond. **Observer: Sgt A Newland. ***Observer: Lt J. Hackett.

RANSLEY Frank Cecil Captain 48

Joining 48 Squadron late in 1917, Frank Ransley gained his first victory on 28 January 1918 when his gunner drove a Rumpler two-seater down out of control. The first success with the front gun followed two months later, when he claimed an LVG. By June he had become a flight commander, and was awarded a DFC during that month, gazetted on 3 August. During the latter part of June he brought his score to nine.

	1918		Bristol					
1*	28 Jan	Rumpler C	B1193	48	Beaurevoir	1240	OOC	CR/RFC 28.1
2**	27 Mar	LVG. C	C4628	48	Morlancourt	1520	DES	CR/RFC 27.3
3***	12 Apr	Pfalz DIII	C4886	48	W Moreuil Woods	1040	DES	CR/RAF 12.4
4†	1 Jun	Alb. DV	C786	48	N Lamotte	1805	DES(F)	CR/RAF 1.6
5†	1 Jun	Alb. DV	C786	48	Lamotte	1805	OOC	CR/SR/?
6s††	10 Jun	Alb. DV	----	48	Roye	1745	DES(F)	CR/RAF 10.6
7†††	14 Jun	LVG. C	C786	48	E Albert	1530	OOC	CR/SR/?
8***	25 Jun	Fokker DVII	C786	48	Foucaucourt-Rosieres	1145	OOC	CR/SR/?
9***	27 Jun	Fokker DVII	C808	48	E Lamotte	1800	DES(F)	CR/RAF 27.6

TOTAL: 4 and 1 shared destroyed, 4 out of control = 9.
*Observer: 2/Lt R.S. Herring. **Observer: 2/Lt J.M.J. Moore. ***Observer: 2/Lt L.W. Davies. †Observer: 2/Lt G. Dixon. ††Shared with Capt C.R. Steele, 2/Lt H.A. Oaks, Lt J.E. Drummond. †††Observer: Sgt W. Lauder.

RATH Henry Coyle Lieutenant 29

A Canadian from Tweed, Ontario, Rath was born on 12 November 1898, and joined the RFC in September 1917, being posted to 29 Squadron on 5 June 1918. He was awarded a DFC which was gazetted on 8 February 1919, the citation recording only his destroyed claims. Rath was fatally injured on 26 October 1918 when he collided with another SE 5A and crashed; he died next day.

	1918		SE 5A					
1s*	28 Jul	C	E5964	29	S W Merville	0815	OOC	CR/11 WS
2s*	31 Jul	C	E5964	29	N E Estaires	1347	DES	CR/RAF 31.7
3	31 Jul	C	E5964	29	N E Estaires	1350	OOC	CR/11 WS
4	1 Aug	C	E5964	29	Steenwerck	1015	OOC	CR/11 WS
5s**	8 Aug	Alb. C	----	29	E La Gorgue	1920	DES	CR/11 WS
6	9 Aug	DFW. C	E5964	29	Steenwerck	1015	OOC	CR/RAF 9.8
7	14 Aug	Hannover C	E5964	29	S E Bailleul	0817	DES	CR/RAF 14.8
8	17 Aug	Alb. DV	E5964	29	Armentieres	0755	DES	CR/RAF 17.8
9	18 Aug	DFW. C	D6940	29	N E Neuve-Eglise	1720	DES	CR/RAF 18.8
10	29 Aug	Fokker DVIII	E5964	29	Estaires-Steenwerck	0930	OOC	CR/11 WS
11	14 Oct	Fokker DVII	C1915	29	E Roulers	0835	DES	CR/RAF 14.10
12	14 Oct	Fokker DVII	C1915	29	W Inglemunster	0850	DES	CR/RAF 14.10

TOTAL: 5 and 2 shared destroyed, 4 and 1 shared out of control = 12.
*Shared with Capt R.L.C. Holme D6155. **Shared with Lt A.E. Reed, Lt R.H. Humphries, Lt D.A. O'Leary, Lt C.M. Wilson.

RAY Lewis Hector Lieutenant 19

A Canadian, Ray joined 19 Squadron on 2 April 1918, flying Sopwith Dolphins with this unit. He claimed seven victories, including four in one action on 27 September.

	1918		Dolphin					
1s*	31 May	Pfalz DIII	C4129	19	Armentieres	0750	OOC	CR/ORB/?
2	31 Jul	Pfalz DIII	C4129	19	S Douai	1950	DES	CR/RFC 31.7
3	16 Sep	Pfalz DIII	C4129	19	S Lille	0940	OOC	ORB/SR/?
4	27 Sep	Fokker DVII	E4713	19	N E Cambrai	0715	DES	ORB/RAF 27.9
5	27 Sep	Fokker DVII	E4713	19	N E Cambrai	0715	OOC	ORB/SR/?
6	27 Sep	Fokker DVII	E4713	19	N E Cambrai	0715	OOC	ORB/SR/?
7	27 Sep	Balloon	E4713	19	N E Cambrai	0720	DES	ORB/SR/?

TOTAL: 1 balloon, 2 destroyed, 3 and 1 shared out of control = 7.
*Shared with Lt J.D. Hardman C3818.

RAYMOND-BARKER Richmond Major 6, 16, 48, 11, 3

Born on 6 May 1894, he was commissioned on 30 November 1914 and transferred to the RFC on 6 August 1915. Gaining his wings in October, he was posted to France on 22 November 1915 and flew with 6 and 16 Squadrons until 29 December 1916. In 1917 he was posted on 12 May to 48 Squadron as a flight commander, flying Bristol Fighters, but he subsequently moved to the similarly equipped 11 Squadron on 2 July. With these units he and his observers claimed six victories, and he was awarded the MC. In September 1917 he was given command of 3 Squadron and promoted to Major. On 20 April 1918 he attached himself to an offensive patrol of his squadron which ran into 15 Fokker Triplanes of von Richthofen's Circus. Manfred von Richthofen personally shot down two of the squadron's Camels, one flown by Raymond-Barker, and the other by 2nd Lieutenant D.G. Lewis; they were the German's 79th and 80th victories — his last before his own demise. Lewis was taken prisoner, but Raymond-Barker went down in flames and was killed.

	1917		Bristol					
1s*	20 May	Alb. DIII	A7112	48	Brebieres	1230	OOC	CR/RFC 20.5
2**	20 May	Alb. DIII	A7112	48	Brebieres	1230	OOC	CR/RFC 20.5
3**	26 May	Alb. DIII	A7112	48	E Brebieres	1950	DES	CR/RFC 26.5
4***	5 Jun	C	A7112	48	E Bullecourt	0730	OOC	CR/RFC 5.6
5†	8 Jul	Alb. DV	A7143	11	Bohain	1900	OOC	CR/RFC 8.7
6††	17 Jul	Alb. DIII	A7168	11	Inchy	0745-0815	DES(F)	CR/RFC 17.7

TOTAL. 2 destroyed, 3 and 1 shared out of control = 6.
*Observer: Lt R.N.W. Jeff, shared with Lt H.J. Pratt/Lt H. Owen A7108. **Observer: Lt R.N.W. Jeff. ***Observer: Sgt Nicholson. †Observer: Pte J. Mason. ††Observer: 2/Lt E.J. Price.

RAYNER John William Captain 52, 89, 60

Bill Rayner was commissioned in the Northumberland Fusiliers on 14 September 1915; he transferred to the RFC, where he initially flew as an observer with 52 Squadron in 1917. He then trained as a pilot, and upon graduation became a scout instructor. He subsequently joined 89 Squadron which was working-up in England on SE 5As, but when this unit was disbanded he was posted instead to 60 Squadron, which he joined on 25 August 1918. Following the loss of Captain J.E. Doyle on 5 September, he became 'A' Flight commander. Rayner retired from the RAF after World War II as a Wing Commander, MBE, JP.

	1918		SE 5A					
1*	5 Sep	Fokker DVII	D6953	60	Avesnes-le-Sec	1820	DES(F)	CR/RAF 5.9
2	5 Sep	Fokker DVII	D6953	60	Avesnes-le-Sec	1825	OOC	CR/SR/?
3	23 Oct	Fokker DVII	D6953	60	Selesches	1430	OOC	CR/SR/?
4	25 Oct	Fokker DVII	D6953	60	Berlaimont	0950	DES(F)	CR/RAF 25.10
5	25 Oct	Fokker DVII	D6953	60	Berlaimont	0950	OOC	CR/SR/?

TOTAL: 2 destroyed, 3 out of control = 5.
*This was Lt von Winterfeldt of Jasta 4 who was killed, who was also claimed by 92 and 79 Squadrons.

REDGATE Oliver William Captain 9(N), 209

Born in Nottingham on 23 November 1898, Redgate joined the RNAS on 3 February 1917 and after training was posted to 9(N) Squadron during the summer of that year. In 1918 he was promoted to Captain in what had become 209 Squadron, RAF, and in July was awarded the DFC; he claimed at least 16 victories by the end of May.

	1917		Camel					
1s*	25 Jul	C	B3813	9N	off Westende	1730	OOC	CR/DRO/DL
2s**	5 Sep	Alb. C	----	9N	Middelkerke-Nieuport	0800	OOC	CR/DRO/DL
3s***	21 Sep	DFW. C	B3818	9N	Zarren	1700	OOC	CR/RFC 22.9
4s†	28 Sep	Alb. DIII	B3818	9N	Dixmude	1610	DES	CR/RFC 28.9
5s††	2 Oct	C	B3818	9N	Ostend-Slype	1450	DES	CR/RNAS 2.10
6s†††	15 Oct	Alb. DIII	B3818	9N	Ostend	1230	DES	CR/DRO/DL
7	17 Oct	Alb. DV	B3818	9N	S Middelkerke	1100	OOC	CR/RNAS 17.10
8	20 Nov	Alb. DV	B3818	9N	S Pervyse	1500	DES	CR/RNAS 20.11
9s‡	10 Dec	DFW. C	B3818	9N	4m E Pervyse	1515	DES(F)	CR/RNAS 10.12
	1918							
10s‡‡	3 Feb	Alb. C	D3566	9N	Staden	0845	DES	CR/RNAS 3.2
11	2 Apr	Alb. DIII	B7250	209	S Halluin	1115	OOC	CR/RAF 2.4
12	11 Apr	Alb. DIII	B7250	209	Albert	1700	OOC	CR/RAF 11.4
13	23 Apr	Pfalz DIII	B7250	209	S E Hangard	1920	DES	CR/RAF 23.4
14s‡‡‡	27 Apr	Alb. DV	B7270	209	E Villers Brettoneaux	1445	DES	CR/RAF 27.4
15	2 May	Fokker DrI	B7270	209	1m S Cerisy	1215	OOC	CR/ORB/?
16	15 May	Alb. DV	D3370	209	Belloy-Pozieres	1015	DES	CR/RAF 17.5

TOTAL: 3 and 5 shared destroyed, 4 and 4 shared out of control = 16.
*Shared with F/Lt F.E. Banbury B3820, FSL J.W. Pinder B3870, FSL Snell, FSL H.G. Mott. **Shared with F/Cdr S.T. Edwards, FSL A.R. Brown, F/Lt F.E. Banbury, FSL A.V. Wood. ***Shared with F/Cdr S.T. Edwards B6217. †Shared with F/Lt F.E. Banbury B6230, FSL M.S. Taylor B3832, FSL J.P. Hales B6217, F/Cdr S.T. Edwards B5652. ††Shared with F/Lt F.E. Banbury B6230. †††Shared with FSL F.W.J. Mellersh B3830. ‡Shared with FSL E.M. Knott B6288, FSL A.V. Wood B3884. ‡‡Shared with F/Cdr S.T. Edwards B6351. ‡‡‡Shared with Lt R.M. Foster B6276.

REDLER Herbert Bolton Lieutenant 40, 24

Redler flew with 'A' Flight of 40 Squadron in 1917, claiming at least three victories while flying Nieuport Scouts. This Scottish-South African often flew with a detachment of the squadron at an advance airfield, awaiting enemy two-seaters. In 1918 he went to 24 Squadron where he was awarded an MC and added seven more victories to bring his score to ten. On 15 March 1918, 24 Squadron had a brief fight with some Triplanes of Jasta 12 and Redler got in a burst at the leader, which spun down. Although Redler claimed only an 'out of control', he had shot down Hauptmann Adolf Ritter von Tutschek, Commander of JG II, and victor of 27 combats. Redler was killed in a flying accident on 21 June 1918, after he had left 24 Squadron; he was 21 years old.

	1917		Nieuport					
1	7 May	Balloon	B1640	40	N Henin-Lietard	0935	DES	ORB/RFC 7.5
2	7 Jun	Alb. DIII	B1558	40	N E Ypres	1100	OOC	CR/RFC 7.6
3	14 Jul	Alb. DIII	B1558	40	E Douai	0650	OOC	CR/RFC 14.7
	1918		SE 5A					
4*	15 Mar	Fokker DrI	B79	24	Premontre	1030	OOC	CR/RFC 15.3
5s**	18 Mar	C	B7824	24	Villers le Sec	1140	OOC	CR/RFC 18.3
6	23 Mar	C	B7824	24	S Berlancourt	1650	CAPT	CR/ORB/SR/?
7	24 Mar	Rumpler C	B7824	24	Pithon, near Ham	1010	DES	CR/RFC 24.3
8	26 Mar	Rumpler C	C1081	24	Estrees-Barleux	0930	DES(F)	CR/RFC 26.3
9	12 Apr	Alb. DV	D275	24	Hangard-Moreuil	1615	DES	CR/RAF 12.4
10	20 Apr	Pfalz DIII	D275	24	Bayonvillers	1015	OOC	CR/RAF 20.4

TOTAL: 1 balloon, 1 captured, 2 destroyed, 4 and 1 shared out of control = 10.
*This was Hptm Adolph von Tutschek, a 27 victory ace, and commander of Jagdgeschwader II, who was killed. **Shared with Capt B.P.G. Beanlands C1081.

REED Arthur Eden Lieutenant 29

Born on 22 August 1898, and from Pretoria, South Africa, Reed served as a Trooper in German East Africa from June 1915-August 1916. He joined the RFC in April 1917, graduating as a pilot in February 1918. He was posted to 29 Squadron in March, making his initial claims in late May. On 18 August he claimed two Halberstadt two-seaters and a balloon, and by mid-September had brought his score to 19, of which no less than 11 were two-seaters. He was awarded a DFC and Bar, the latter being gazetted on 3 December. He had been posted to Home Establishment on 22 September, but rejoined the unit in April 1919. His brother was Company Quartermaster Sergeant C.V. Reed, VC of the 4th South African Infantry Brigade.

	1918		SE 5A					
1	28 May	Pfalz DIII	D3563	29	Neuf Berquin	1115	OOC	CR/SR/?
2	6 Jun	C	D5970	29	N Estaires	1035	OOC	CR/11 WS
3s*	6 Jun	Pfalz DIII	D5970	29	N W Estaires	1800	DES	CR/RAF 6.6
4	17 Jun	Alb. C	C1116	29	E Merville	0915	DES	CR/RAF 17.6
5	22 Jul	Hannover C	C1942	29	Erquinghem	0800	DES	CR/RAF 22.7
6s**	8 Aug	Alb. C	----	29	E La Gorgue	1940	DES	CR/SR/?
7	9 Aug	Halb. C	C1942	29	S E Bailleul	0800	DES(F)	CR/RAF 9.8
8	13 Aug	Fokker DrI	C1942	29	Dixmude	1415	OOC	CR/ORB/?
9	14 Aug	DFW. C	C1942	29	N Ploegsteert Wood	0830	DES	CR/RAF 14.8
10	18 Aug	Balloon	C1942	29	N Estaires	1145	DES	CR/RAF 18.8
11	18 Aug	Halb. C	E5964	29	S Neuve Eglise	1745	DES	CR/RAF 18.8
12	18 Aug	Halb. C	E5964	29	S Neuve Eglise	1745	OOC	CR/ORB/?
13	25 Aug	Fokker DVII	E4000	29	S E Ypres	0835	DES	CR/RAF 25.8
14	31 Aug	Fokker DVII	E4000	29	E Voormezeele	1755	DES	CR/RAF 31.8
15	1 Sep	Fokker DVII	E4000	29	W Armentieres	1815	OOC	CR/ORB/?
16	5 Sep	LVG. C	E4000	29	S E Armentieres	1830	DES	CR/RAF 5.9
17	6 Sep	Fokker DVII	E4000	29	S Lille	1910	OOC	CR/ORB/?
18	7 Sep	Halb. C	E4000	29	Warneton	1205	OOC	CR/ORB/?
19	13 Sep	Halb. C	E4000	29	S E Deulemont	1750	DES	CR/RAF 13.9

TOTAL: 1 balloon, 9 and 2 shared destroyed, 7 out of control = 19.
*Shared with Lt C.G. Ross D5953. **Shared with Lt R.H. Humphries, Lt D.A. O'Leary, Lt C.M. Wilson, Lt H.C. Rath.

REED William Ernest Captain 19, 92

After joining the RFC, he went to France with 19 Squadron when it re-equipped with Spads. On 14 April 1917, while escorting bombers, he claimed the first of two victories he was to gain with this unit before being wounded by ground fire on 22 April. In 1918 he became a flight commander and went back to France with the newly-formed 92 Squadron. With this unit he claimed seven more victories, but was wounded again on 3 November. He was awarded the DFC.

	1917		Spad					
1	14 Apr	C	A6753	19	Douai	1200	OOC	CR/RFC 14.4/?
2	22 Apr	Alb. C	B1563	19	S Quiery	0715	DES(F)	CR/RFC 22.4
	1918		SE 5A					
3	25 Aug	Fokker DVII	D6959	92	S Armentieres	1115	DES	CR/RAF 25.8
4	5 Sep	Fokker DVII	D6959	92	S W Cambrai	1100	DES	CR/RAF 5.9
5s*	23 Oct	DFW. C	C1142	92	S Pont du Nord	1300	DES	CR/RAF 23.10
6	23 Oct	DFW. C	C1142	92	N E Englefontaine	1330	DES	CR/RAF 23.10
7	29 Oct	Fokker DVII	C1142	92	N E Mormal Wood	0930	OOC	CR/ORB/?
8	29 Oct	Fokker DVII	C1142	92	E Le Quesnoy	1030	DES	CR/RAF 29.10
9	29 Oct	Fokker DVII	C1142	92	E Le Quesnoy	1030	OOC	CR/ORB/?

TOTAL: 5 and 1 shared destroyed, 3 out of control = 9.
*Shared with Capt J.M. Robb, Lt T.S. Horry, Lt E.S. Robins, Lt C.H.C. Coles, Lt E. Madill, LT E. Shapard, 2/Lt J.V. Gascoyne, Lt J. Daniel.

REES Lionel Wilmot Brabazon Lieutenant-Colonel 11, 32

Lieutenant-Colonel Rees was one of the early air fighters who received both the VC and MC for aerial combat. In 1903 he was commissioned in the Royal Garrison Artillery, and in 1913-14 was attached to the West African Frontier Force until he was seconded to the RFC on 10 August 1914. Flying Vickers Fighters with 11 Squadron in the summer and autumn of 1915, he had many encounters with enemy aeroplanes and was a most aggressive pilot. In 1916 he was given command of 32 Squadron, and flying a Vickers Scout or DH 2, was in the air whenever possible during May and June, although officially he was not allowed to fly over the lines. On 1 July he went out and attacked four enemy two-seaters, which were then joined by two or three more; in the fight which followed, Rees drove off one, forced another to land, and then hit the observer of the third, forcing this down as well, although he was himself wounded. For this action he received the Victoria Cross. For the rest of the war he commanded the Air Fighting School at Ayr. He remained in the RAF after the Armistice, retiring in 1931 as a Group Captain, VC, OBE, MC, AFC, and died in the Bahamas on 28 September 1955. In 11 Squadron, where he was awarded the MC, his usual observer was Flight Sergeant Hargreaves, DCM.

	1915		Vickers Gunbus					
1*	28 Jul	Fokker E	1649	11	----	----	DD	SR/FV
2*	31 Aug	LVG. C	1649	11	Achiet le Grand	----	DES	SR/RFC 31.8
3*	21 Sep	AGO. C	----	11	Herbcourt	1100	DD	SR/RFC 21.9
4*	22 Sep	Alb. C	----	11	S E Albert	1730	DD	SR/RFC 22.9
5**	30 Sep	Alb. C	----	11	Gommecourt	----	CAPT	SR/RFC 30.9
6***	31 Oct	LVG. C	----	11	Pys-Irnes	----	DD	SR/RFC 31.10
	1916		DH 2					
7†	1 Jul	Roland C	6015	32	Festubert	0630	OOC	CR/RFC 1.7
8	1 Jul	Roland C	6015	32	La Bassee-Souchez	0635	FTL	SR/RFC 1.7

TOTAL: 1 captured, 1 destroyed, 1 forced to land, 5 driven down = 8.
*Observer F/Sgt J.M. Hargreaves. **Observer F/Sgt J.M. Hargreaves. The crew of this aircraft were killed. ***Observer: F/Sgt Raymond. †This was confirmed as out of control next day by A.A.

REEVES Harry Gosford Captain 1

Born in October 1896, Harry Reeves lived in Brackwell, Buckinghamshire, and Taunton, Somerset. Commissioned in the RFC in April 1917, he joined 1 Squadron on 10 June and flew Nieuport Scouts throughout the summer and autumn. By mid-October he had destroyed four aircraft and shared in one more such victory, while also claiming seven out of control , bringing his score to 12. He was then promoted to flight commander, but had only one more combat, when on 18 November he claimed a DFW two-seater out of control . He was killed in a flying accident on 24 January 1918.

	1917		Nieuport					
1s*	18 Jun	Alb. DIII	B1650	1	Oostaverne	1145	DES	CR/ORB/?
2	26 Jun	Alb. DIII	B1630	1	Becelaere	2100	OOC	CR/RFC 26.6
3	31 Jul	Alb. DV	B1672	1	2000y S Terhand	1425	DES	CR/RFC 31.7
4s**	13 Aug	Alb. C	B1672	1	Houthem	0920	OOC	CR/RFC 13.8

5	14 Aug	Alb. DV	B3558	1	S Moorslede	1910	DES	CR/RFC 14.8
6	21 Aug	Alb. DV	B1672	1	Houthoulst	1910	OOC	CR/RFC 22.8
7	4 Sep	DFW. C	B1672	1	S Polygon Wood	1115	OOC	CR/ORB/?
8	9 Sep	Rumpler C	B1672	1	E Polygon Wood	1035	OOC	CR/RFC 11.9
9	11 Sep	Alb. DV	B3630	1	Houthoulst Forest	1815	OOC	CR/RFC 11.9
10***	9 Oct	Alb. DV	B6774	1	S Polygon Wood	1515	DES(F)	CR/RFC 9.10
11	15 Oct	DFW. C	B6774	1	Comines	1200	DES	CR/RFC 15.10
12	17 Oct	Alb. DV	B6774	1	Gheluwe	1430	OOC	CR/RFC 17.10
13	18 Nov	DFW. C	B6774	1	Becelaere	0815	OOC	CR/RFC 18.11

TOTAL: 4 and 1 shared destroyed, 7 and 1 shared out of control = 13.
*Shared with Lt L.F. Jenkin B1681, Lt C.S.T. Lavers B3495. **Shared with Capt T.F. Hazell B3455. ***1 Sqn made 2 claims and 53 Sqn another; Lt R. Wagner of Jasta 26 was killed.

REID Ellis Vair Flight Sub Lieutenant 3W, 10(N)

Born on 31 October 1889, in Belleville, Ontario, Canada, Reid joined the RNAS and first served with 3 Wing from 1915, subsequently flying Sopwith 1½ Strutters. In April 1917 he transferred to the new 10(N) Squadron which was equipping with Sopwith Triplanes, and joined Raymond Collishaw's Flight. He first claimed on 1 June, and during the month gained nine victories. He claimed ten more in July, including three Albatros Scouts on 27th. His 19th victory occurred on 28 July, but on this day he was shot down and killed by K.Flak 21. The award of a DSC was announced on 11 August.

	1917		Triplane					
1	1 Jun	Alb. C	N5483	10N	W Wervicq	0915	DES	CR/RFC 1.6
2s*	2 Jun	C	N5483	10N	St Julien	0900	OOC	CR/ORB/AC
3	3 Jun	Alb. DIII	N5483	10N	Roubaix	1815	DES	CR/RFC 3.6
4s**	5 Jun	C	N5483	10N	Wervicq	0850	DES(F)	CR/RFC 5.6
5	6 Jun	Halb. DII	N5483	10N	N Polygon Wood	1100	DES	CR/RFC 6.6
6	7 Jun	Alb. C	N5483	10N	Clerckem	0915	DES	CR/RFC 7.6
7	15 Jun	Alb. DIII	N5483	10N	Moorslede	1745	OOC	CR/RFC 16.6
8	15 Jun	Alb. DIII	N5483	10N	Moorslede	1745	OOC	CR/RFC 16.6
9	17 Jun	Alb. DIII	N5483	10N	Roulers	1910	OOC	CR/RFC 18.6
10	6 Jul	Alb. DV	N5483	10N	Deulemont	1100	OOC	CR/RFC 6.7
11	12 Jul	Alb. DIII	N5481	10N	Menin-Polygon Wood	0845	DES	CR/RFC 12.7
12	12 Jul	Alb. DIII	N5481	10N	Veldhoek	0845	DES	CR/RFC 12.7
13	20 Jul	Alb. DV	N5483	10N	Menin-Messines	0805	OOC	CR/RFC 20.7
14	21 Jul	Fokker DV	N5483	10N	N Becelaere	2030	DES	CR/RFC 22.7
15	23 Jul	Alb. DV	N5483	10N	Houthoulst Forest	2025	OOC	CR/RFC 23.7
16	27 Jul	Alb. DV	N5483	10N	Menin	1950	DES	CR/RFC 27.7
17	27 Jul	Alb. DV	N5483	10N	Courtrai	2000	OOC	CR/RFC 27.7
18	27 Jul	Alb. DV	N5483	10N	Menin	2005	DES	CR/RFC 27.7
19	28 Jul	Alb. DV	N5483	10N	Becelaere	2000	DES	CR/ORB/DL

TOTAL: 10 and 1 shared destroyed, 7 and 1 shared out of control = 19.
*Shared with F/Lt R. Collishaw N5490, FSL W.M. Alexander N5487, FSL G.E. Nash N5492. **Shared with F/Lt R. Collishaw N5490, FSL D.F. Fitzgibbon N5466, FSL G.E. Nash N6302.

REID George Ranald Macfarlane Major 25, 20, 18, 206

Born in Scotland on 25 October 1893, he joined — and was commissioned in — the 4th Battalion, Argyll and Sutherland Highlanders, in August 1914. Going to France in January 1915 with the 2nd Battalion of the Black Watch, he served until he was wounded at the Battle of Festubert. Transferring to the RFC in August 1915, he returned to France as a pilot with the newly-formed 25 Squadron in February 1916. He flew FE 2Bs until August, he and his observer, Lieutenant J.A. Mann, late of the 5th Scottish Rifles, being involved in many combats. Both were awarded the MC for attacking eight enemy aircraft in seven days, driving down four of them and damaging another three. Of these, at least two crashed and another was forced to land. Promoted to Captain, Reid went to 20 Squadron as a flight commander in June, again flying FEs. His usual observer was now Lieutenant L.H. Scott, and with this squadron he claimed at least six more victories; Reid was awarded a Bar to his MC. Returning to England in February 1917, he commanded a Flying Training School at Norwich before taking a CFS course at Gosport. He returned to active duty in March, commanding 18 Squadron until November 1917, when he again returned home to command No 1 FTS at Stafford. In June 1918 he once more went to France, this time to command 206 Squadron at Dunkirk, equipped with DH 9As which were mainly occupied with bombing the docks at Bruges. On 1 January 1919 he was gazetted as a recipient of the DSO for his work.

In 1919 he served in Germany and then in Egypt with 206, which was then re-numbered 47 Squadron.

Returning to England, he spent several years at Halton starting the Apprentice Training School, and then in 1924 took command of 99 Squadron. From 1927-29 he was in the Sudan as a Wing Commander on the GOC Staff. This was followed in the early thirties by a spell as air attache in Washington, and then from late in the decade until 1941 he was AOC Administration. He retired in 1946 as Air Vice-Marshal Sir Ranald Reid, KCB, DSO, MC and Bar, and was living in retirement in Western Australia at the time of writing

	1916		FE 2B					
1*	16 May	Aviatik C	6330	25	Souchez	0800	FTL/DES	CR/RFC 16.5
2*	19 May	Fokker E	6330	25	Mericourt	1815	DES	CR/RFC 19.5
3*	21 May	C	6330	25	Annay-Lens	1805	DES	CR/SR/?
			FE 2D					
4**	29 Jul	Rumpler C	A22	20	Zandvoorde	1215	DES	CR/RFC 29.7
5***	31 Jul	LVG. C	A22	20	Ypres	1135	DES	CR/11 WS
6***	31 Aug	Fokker DII	A19	20	Langemarck	1025	OOC	CR/RFC 31.8
7s†	24 Sep	Fokker DII	A39	20	Rumbeke	1210	DES	CR/RFC 24.9
8***	16 Oct	LVG. C	A39	20	Wadizeele	0905	OOC	CR/RFC 16.10
9***	21 Oct	LVG. C	A39	20	Comines	1200	DES	CR/RFC 21.10

TOTAL: 6 and 1 shared destroyed, 2 out of control = 9.
*Observer: Lt I.A. Mann. **Observer: Lt L.H. Scott. This was Lt Kisker/Oblt von Hartz of FA 3. ***Observer: Lt L.H. Scott. †Observer: Lt L.H. Scott; shared with Lt A.D. Pearce/2/Lt W.F. Findlay A19.

REID Guy Patrick Spencer Lieutenant 20

Guy Reid transferred to the RFC from the Seaforth Highlanders, joining 20 Squadron in 1916. Here he flew FE 2s, generally with Captain Gerald Dixon-Spain as his observer. Their first success was gained on 7 February 1916 when they drove down a Fokker monoplane which was last seen with its engine stopped, leaving a trail of smoke. During the summer they were to claim several further victories, both being awarded MCs in September. On 11 November Reid and 1st Air Mechanic A.M. Alexander were engaged by a number of German scouts, but although Alexander was wounded twice, Reid managed to regain the safety of the British lines.

	1916		FE 2B					
1*	7 Feb	Fokker E	----	20	Roulers	0900	DD	CR/RFC 7.2
2**	1 Jul	Fokker E	A11	20	Wervicq	0530	DES	CR/RFC 1.7
3**	3 Aug	Aviatik C	A19	20	Hollebeke	0930	OOC	CR/RFC 3.8
4**	31 Aug	Fokker E	----	20	Boeschere	0855	DD	CR/RFC 31.8
5***	6 Sep	Fokker E	A19	20	Passchendaele	1245	OOC	CR/RFC 5.9

TOTAL: 1 destroyed, 2 out of control, 2 driven down = 5.
*Observer: Lt S. Billing. **Observer: Capt G. Dixon-Spain. ***Observer: 2/Lt H.M. Golding.

RHYS-DAVIDS Arthur Percival Foley Lieutenant 56

Born on 27 September 1897, this old Etonian joined the RFC in late 1916 and was posted to 56 Squadron which was in the process of forming with SE 5s; he accompanied this unit to France in April 1917. He survived his first combat, when he was attacked by Leutnant Kurt Wolff of Jasta 11 during the fight in which Albert Ball was killed. Having been Head Boy at Eton, he had obtained a scholarship to Oxford, where he intended to study Classics after the war. He always carried a volume of Blake's poetry in his pocket when flying, in case he should be shot down and taken prisoner. An intensive period of operations in late May took his score from one to six in three days, with two more following in early June. 56 Squadron was then posted to England on home defence duties. After it returned to France he became involved in his most famous combat which occurred on 23 September, when in company with McCudden, Bowman, Hoidge, Maybery and others, he fought the well-known German ace, Leutnant Werner Voss, who put up a wonderful single-handed fight in a Fokker Triplane until finally hit and killed by Rhys-Davids' fire. A lone Albatros Scout flown by Leutnant Karl Menckhoff, who had nearly shot Rhys-Davids down on 14 September, attempted to come to Voss's assistance, but this too was credited to the British pilot as shot down out of control , and indeed Menckhoff was obliged to carry out a crash-landing. By now Rhys-Davids had received both the MC and Bar, and on 2 October came the award of the DSO. Later in the month when McCudden went on leave, he took over 'B' Flight in his absence. On 27 October he led the flight into a dog-fight from which he did not return, his pilots reporting that they had last seen him making dashes at groups of enemy scouts behind the German lines; he had in fact been shot down and killed by Leutnant Karl Gallwitz of Jasta Boelcke. *Brief Glory* by Alex Revell, published by William Kimber in 1984, is a superb biography of one of the most famous aces of WW I.

	1917		SE 5					
1	23 May	Alb. DIII	A4868	56	E Lens	1900-2015	OOC	CR/RFC 23.5
2s*	24 May	Alb. DIII	A4868	56	S Douai	1900-2000	OOC	CR/RFC 24.5
3s**	24 May	C	A4868	56	Gouy sous Bellone	1900-2000	DES(F)	CR/RFC 24.5
4	24 May	C	A4868	56	Sains	1900-2000	OOC	CR/RFC 24.5

5	25 May	C	A4868	56	W Flers	0630-0730	DES	CR/RFC 25.5
6	26 May	Alb. DIII	A4868	56	Gouy sous Bellone	1900-2000	OOC	CR/RFC 26.5
7	4 Jun	Alb. DV	A8901	56	W Moorslede	0700-0845	OOC	CR/RFC 4.6
8***	7 Jun	Alb. DIII	A8901	56	Westroosebeke	0500-0645	OOC	CR/RFC 7.6
			SE 5A					
9	12 Jul	Fokker DV	A4563	63	E Roncq	1400-1500	OOC	CR/9 W WD
10†	12 Jul	DFW. C	A4563	56	N Armentieres	1400-1500	CAPT	CR/RFC 12.7
11	13 Jul	Alb. DV	A4563	56	Moorslede	1930-2100	OOC	CR/9 W WD
12s††	17 Jul	Alb. DV	A4563	56	Roulers Menin Rd.	1930-2110	OOC	CR/RFC 17.7
13	21 Jul	Alb. DIII	A4553	56	Polygon Wood	1930-2030	OOC	CR/RFC 21.7
14†††	3 Sep	Alb. DV	B511	56	Houthem	1845-1915	DES	CR/RFC 3.9
15	5 Sep	Alb. DV	A4563	56	E Menin	1815-1900	DES	CR/RFC 5.9
16‡	5 Sep	Alb. DV	A4563	56	N E Poelcapelle	1815-1900	DES	CR/RFC 5.9
17	5 Sep	Alb. DV	A4563	56	E Menin	1815-1900	OOC	CR/RFC 5.9
18	9 Sep	Alb. DV	B525	56	S E Houthoulst Forest	1740-1845	OOC	CR/RFC 9.9
19‡‡	23 Sep	Fokker DrI	B525	56	N E Ypres Salient	c1800	CAPT	CR/RFC 23.9
20‡‡‡	23 Sep	Alb. DV	B525	56	N E Ypres	c1800	OOC	CR/RFC 23.9
21§	24 Sep	C	B525	56	S Houthoulst Forest	1700-1820	DES(F)	CR/RFC 24.9
22	28 Sep	Alb. DV	B525	56	Comines	0815-0930	OOC	CR/RFC 28.9
23	1 Oct	Alb. DV	B525	56	Westroosebeke	1700-1815	OOC	CR/RFC 1.10
24s§§	1 Oct	Alb. DV	B525	56	Westroosebeke	1700-1815	OOC	CR/RFC 1.10
25	11 Oct	Alb. DV	B525	56	N E Becelaere	0730-0815	OOC	CR/RFC 11.10

TOTAL: 2 captured, 4 and 2 shared destroyed, 14 and 3 shared out of control = 25.
*Shared with Capt C.M. Crowe A8910, 2/Lt R.T.C. Hoidge A4862, 2/Lt K.K. Muspratt A4861, 2/Lt J.S. Turnbull A8913. **Shared with 2/Lt R.T.C. Hoidge A4868. ***This was probably Fl Om Fritz Kuhn of MFJ 1, who was killed. †This was Uffz Albert Hahnel/Lt Eugen Mann of FA 7, who were captured. ††Shared with Capt I.H.D. Henderson A8909, 2/Lt L.M. Barlow A8910, 2/Lt K.K. Muspratt A8913, Lt V.P. Cronyn A4856. †††Shared with Lt R.A. Mayberry B508. ‡This was Vzfw Alfred Muth of Jasta 27. ‡‡This was Lt Werner Voss, the 48 victory ace and commander of Jasta 10. ‡‡‡This was probably Lt Karl Menckhoff, an ace from Jasta 3, who crashlanded, unharmed. §56 made two claimes. One loss was Lt von Esmuth/Lt Fleischer FA 226. §§Shared with Capt J.T.B. McCudden B4853, Lt L.M. Barlow B511, Lt M.H. Coote B1, Lt D.J. Reason A8961.

RICE-OXLEY Alan Lieutenant 41, 45

Rice-Oxley transferred from the Shropshire Light Infantry to the RFC in 1916 and flew as a pilot with 15 Squadron later that same year. He was wounded in action during October, but recovered and converted to single-seaters. In 1918 he was sent to Italy to join 45 Squadron, flying Sopwith Camels. He claimed five victories in four days, and was awarded a DFC. Subsequently he made one further claim during August.

	1918		Camel					
1	12 Jul	Berg D	D8240	45	Col Fassole, Feltre	0805	DES	CR/14 W
2	12 Jul	Phonix D	D8240	45	Feltre	0805	DES	CR/14 W
3	14 Jul	Alb. DV	D9392	45	Cogolo	0800	DES	CR/14 W
4	15 Jul	Phonix D	D1975	45	Costa Alta	1010	OOC	CR/14 W
5	15 Jul	Phonix D	D1975	45	Mt Forcelluna	1010	OOC	CR/14 W
6	22 Aug	C	E1500	45	S Nazario	1310	DES	CR/14 W

TOTAL: 4 destroyed, 2 out of control = 6.

RICHARDS Cecil Roy Lieutenant 20

An Australian from Garvoc, Victoria, born on 24 July 1893, who had served in Gallipoli and France before transferring to the RFC in late 1916, Richards joined 20 Squadron in the summer of 1917, flying FE 2Ds. With Lieutenant A.E. Wear as gunner, he first claimed on 14 June. On 17 July, flying with Sergeant J. Cowell, two more claims were submitted at the end of one patrol, plus another two with Weir during the same day, and a fifth credited as driven down. Four more claims were to be made in August, and Richards was awarded an MC (gazetted on 17 September), but on 17 August he was shot down and wounded by Leutnant Ernst Hess of Jasta 28, being taken prisoner. He died on 28 March 1973 in Glenelg, South Australia.

	1917		FE 2D					
1*	14 Jun	Alb. DV	A6498	20	Becelaere	1100	OOC	CR/RFC 14.6
2**	17 Jun	Aviatik C	A6431	20	Zonnebeke	0720	DES(F)	CR/RFC 17.6
3*	6 Jul	Alb. DV	A6498	20	Wervicq	1030	OOC	CR/RFC 6.7
4*	7 Jul	Alb. DIII	A6498	20	Becelaere	1500	OOC	CR/RFC 7.7
5*	17 Jul	Alb. DV	A6468	20	Menin	1030	OOC	CR/RFC 17.7
6*	17 Jul	Alb. DV	A6468	20	Menin	1040	DES	CR/RFC 17.7
7***	17 Jul	Alb. DV	A6468	20	Polygon Wood	1945	DES(F)	CR/RFC 17.7
8***	17 Jul	Alb. DV	A6468	20	20 28Q 28	1945	DES	CR/RFC 17.7
9*	9 Aug	Alb. DV	B1890	20	N Becelaere	0950	OOC	CR/SR/11 WS

10*	10 Aug	C	B1890	20	Polygon Wood	0840	OOC	CR/SR/11 WS
11s†	10 Aug	Alb. DV	B1890	20	Wervicq	0900	OOC	CR/RFC 10.8
12	16 Aug	Alb. DV	B1890	20	E Passchendaele	0915	OOC	CR/RFC 16.8

TOTAL: 4 destroyed, 7 and 1 shared out of control = 12.
*Observer: Lt A.E. Wear. **Observer: Lt A.E. Wear. This was the crew Vzfw R. Neidhart/Uffz S. Hornung of Sch 30b. ***Observer: Sgt J.J. Cowell. †Observer: Lt A.E. Wear. Shared with Capt A.N. Solly/2/Lt J.J. Cawley A5417, Lt D.Y. Hay/2/Lt M. Todd B6456.

RICHARDSON Herbert Brian Lieutenant 24

Richardson was awarded an MC and DFC whilst serving with 24 Squadron, 14 November 1917-29 April 1918. He claimed most of his 15 victories during the March Offensive of that year, including three enemy scouts shot down in one fight on 21st of that month. He also took part in several ground attack sorties.

	1918		SE 5A					
1	18 Feb	Pfalz DIII	C1057	24	E St Quentin	1430	OOC	CR/RFC 18.2
2	26 Feb	Fokker DrI	B124	24	E Laon	0840	OOC	CR/RFC 26.2
3s*	26 Feb	Fokker DrI	B124	24	E Samoussy	0900	DES	CR/RFC 26.2
4	6 Mar	Fokker DrI	B124	24	Fontaine-Croin	1055	DES	CR/RFC 6.3
5s**	11 Mar	C	C1070	24	E Bellenglise	1315	OOC	CR/RFC 11.3
6	11 Mar	Alb. DV	C1070	24	Ribemont	1815	OOC	CR/RFC 12.3
7s***	15 Mar	Rumpler C	B8257	24	N Premonte	1020	DES	CR/RFC 15.3
8	16 Mar	Alb. DV	B176	24	Barisis	1630	DES	CR/RFC 16.3
9	17 Mar	Pfalz DIII	D279	24	S W Ramicourt	1825	OOC	CR/RFC 17.3
10	21 Mar	Pfalz DIII	D279	24	Bellicourt	1415	OOC	CR/RFC 21.3
11	21 Mar	Pfalz DIII	D279	24	Bellicourt	1415	DES	CR/RFC 21.3
12	21 Mar	Pfalz DIII	D279	24	Bellicourt	1420	DES	CR/RFC 21.3
13	22 Mar	Pfalz DIII	D279	24	Peronne	1600-1700	DES	CR/RFC 22.3
14	26 Mar	C	D279	24	Dreslincourt	1430	DES	CR/RFC 26.3
15	4 Apr	C	D279	24	Warfusee-Abancourt	1530	DES(F)	CR/RAF 4.4

TOTAL: 7 and 2 shared destroyed, 5 and 1 shared out of control = 15.
*Shared with Lt I.D.R. MacDonald C1057, 2/Lt J.J. Dawe B85, 2/Lt W.F. Poulter C9342, Lt R.T. Mark B67. **Shared with Capt A.J. Brown C9494, 2/Lt P.J. Nolan C5301, Lt R.T. Mark C6397, Lt E.W. Lindeburg B125. ***Shared with Lt A.K. Cowper C5428, Lt R.T. Mark C9494.

RICHARDSON Lancelot Lytton Captain 25

An Australian, born in 1896 at Bereen Barraba, New South Wales, Richardson joined the RFC and was posted to 25 Squadron on 3 June 1916. After several early combats, he was wounded in action on 20 July. He returned to the unit as a flight commander in early 1917, gaining two further victories. On 13 April however, he and his observer were shot down in an FE 2D by Jasta 11. The award of an MC was gazetted the following month. Richardson has in the past been incorrectly listed as an American with some ten victories.

	1916		FE 2B					
1s*	17 Jun	Fokker E	6337	25	Don	1130	OOC	CR/RFC WD
2**	26 Jun	Fokker E	4283	25	Annoeullin	0725	FTL	CR/RFC 26.6
3***	2 Jul	Alb. C	4283	25	Habourdin-Fromelles	1930	FTL	CR/RFC WD
4s†	20 Jul	Fokker E	6932	25	E Lens	1830	DES	CR/RFC WD
5s†	20 Jul	Fokker E	6932	25	E Lens	1830	OOC	CR/RFC WD
	1917							
6††	15 Feb	C	7686	25	Avion	1630	OOC	CR/RFC 15.2
7†††	17 Mar	Alb. DII	4839	25	Oppy-Beaumont	1100-1130	DES(F)	CR/RFC 17.3

TOTAL: 1 and 1 shared destroyed, 1 and 2 shared out of control, 2 forced to land = 7.
,*Observer: Lt M.V. Lewes; shared with 2/Lt J.R.B. Savage/2AM Robinson 5201, Lt H.B. Davey/2/Lt J.B. Hinchcliffe. **Observer: 2 AM L.S. Court. ***Observer: Lt M.V. Lewes. †Observer: 2 AM L.S. Court; shared with Lt H.B. Davey/Capt H.C. Morley 5238. ††Observer: Lt W.G. Meggitt. †††Observer: 2/Lt D.C. Wollen

RIDLEY Cyril Burfield Captain 1(N), 201

Joining 1(N) Squadron in summer 1917, Ridley — an Englishman, born on 15 January 1895, who had been living in Toronto, Canada — claimed four victories flying Sopwith Triplanes, and was promoted to Flight Lieutenant. The squadron converted to Camels, and on 1 April 1918 became 201 Squadron, RAF. He shared a balloon on 8 April, and added two more victories before becoming a flight commander during May. Awarded a DSC, he claimed a further two victories by early July, to raise his total to 11.

	1917		Triplane					
1s*	29 Apr	Alb. DIII	N5437	1N	Villers les Cagnicourt	1150	OOC	CR/RFC 29.4
2s**	17 Jul	Alb. DV	N6304	1N	4m E Messines	2005	OOC	CR/RFC 17.7
3	14 Aug	Alb. DV	N6296	1N	N E Ypres	0840	OOC	CR/RFC 14.8

4	10 Sep	DFW. C	N5436	1N	Zillebeke	1705	OOC	CR/RFC 10.9
			Camel					
5	6 Dec	Alb. DV	B6418	1N	N Passchendaele	1100	OOC	CR/RNAS 6.12
	1918							
6s***	12 Mar	Balloon	B6418	1N	Ypres	1315	DES	CR/DOS/?
7s†	8 Apr	Balloon	B7248	201	E Boyelles	0645	DES	CR/RFC 8.4
8	2 May	Pfalz DIII	B7248	201	E Villers Brettoneaux	1250	OOC	CR/RAF 2.5
9	6 May	Fokker DrI	B7248	201	S Albert	1920	DES	CR/RAF 16.5
10	30 Jun	Fokker DrI	B7248	201	Pozieres	0815	OOC	CR/ORB/?
11	4 Jul	Fokker DVII	B7248	201	Foucaucourt	1915	OOC	CR/ORB/?

TOTAL: 2 shared balloons, 1 destroyed, 6 and 2 shared out of control = 11.
*Shared with FSL H.V. Rowley N5425. **Shared with F/Cdr F.H.M. Maynard N5479, FSL E. Anthony N6296, FSL H.V. Rowley N5373, FSL C.G. Brock N5485, FSL G.B.G. Scott N5455, F/Lt H.L. Everett N6308, FSL A.G.A. Spence N6300. ***Shared with F/Cdr H.V. Rowley B6429. †Shared with Capt D.J. Bell C6730, 3 Sqn.

RIGBY Harry Alexander Captain 40, 1

An Australian from Melbourne, Rigby was commissioned into the RFC on 22 May 1916, and joined 40 Squadron on 1 August of that year. He remained only for a month, but was then taken ill. He joined 1 Squadron on 2 February 1918 and was shortly afterwards promoted to Captain. He was again taken ill in May, leaving the unit on 17th, but by this time he had claimed six victories and damaged a balloon.

	1918		SE 5A					
1s*	13 Mar	Pfalz DIII	C9624	1	Wieltje	1220	OOC	CR/RFC 13.3
2	26 Mar	Alb. DV	B4851	1	Bapaume	1710	DES(F)	CR/RFC 26.3
3	29 Apr	C	C1113	1	Wytschaete	0645	DES	CR/RAF 29.4
4	2 May	Pfalz DIII	C1113	1	E Bailleul	1350	DES	CR/RAF 2.5
5	3 May	Fokker DrI	C1113	1	Wytschaete	0735	OOC	CR/ORB/SR/?
6	11 May	Alb. DV	C1113	1	Bailleul	1715	OOC	CR/ORB/SR/?

TOTAL: 2 destroyed, 3 and 1 shared out of control = 6.
*Shared with Capt W.D. Patrick B641, Capt G.B. Moore B511, Capt H.J. Hamilton B32, Lt A. Hollis B520, 2/Lt L.W. Mawbey B632, 2/Lt P.J. Clayson A8908, 2/Lt A.E. Sweeting A8932, 2/Lt W.M.R. Gray A8904.

RILEY A.G. Lieutenant 48

An original member of 48 Squadron, Riley usually flew with 2nd Lieutenant L.G. Hall as the gunner in his F2A, the pair claiming four victories during their first week at the front, for which both were awarded MCs. Sometime after his fifth victory, Riley was posted to Home Establishment.

	1917		Bristol					
1s*	8 Apr	Alb. DIII	----	48	Remy	----	OOC	SR/RFC 8.4
2s**	11 Apr	Alb. DIII	----	48	Fampoux	0800	OOC	SR/RFC 11.4
3s**	11 Apr	Alb. DIII	----	48	Fampoux	0800	OOC	SR/RFC 11.4
4†	11 Apr	Alb. DIII	----	48	Fampoux	0900	DES	SR/RFC 11.4
5††	3 Jul	Alb. DV	A7153	48	Queant	0930	OOC	CR/RFC 3.7

TOTAL: 1 destroyed, 1 and 3 shared out of control = 5.
*Observer: 2/Lt L.G. Hall, shared with 2/Lt G.N. Brockhurst/2/Lt C.B. Boughton, 2/Lt R.E. Adeney/2/Lt L.G. Lovell. **Observer: 2/Lt L.G. Hall, shared with Capt D.M. Tidmarsh/2/Lt C.B. Holland A3338, 2/Lt R.E. Adeney/2/Lt L.G. Lovell A3318, 2/Lt G.N. Brockhurst/2/Lt C.B. Boughton A3327. †Observer: 2/Lt L.G. Hall. ††Observer: 2/Lt W. O'Toole.

RILEY George Raby Lieutenant 3

Born in London on 23 February 1899, Riley joined 3 Squadron on his birthday in 1918, and served throughout the spring and summer. He claimed his first victory on 22 March and his last on 28 September, being awarded an MC. His victories included four Fokker DVIIs, while on 27 September he claimed three balloons destroyed; he was also prominent in attacking targets on the ground.

	1918		Camel					
1	22 Mar	Alb. DV	C1609	3	Havrincourt Wood	1530	OOC	CR/RFC 22.3
2s*	27 Mar	LVG. C	----	3	----	0700	DES	WD/?
3	8 Apr	Balloon	D6475	3	Mory	0645	DES	CR/III BG WD
4	12 Apr	Alb. DV	D6475	3	N Pozieres	1915	DES	CR/RAF 12.4
5s**	8 Aug	Rumpler C	----	3	62 D X 30	1400	OOC	CR/WD/?
6	9 Aug	Fokker DVII	F5938	3	62 C 16	1945	OOC	CR/WD/?
7	10 Aug	Fokker DVII	F5938	3	62 C 54	1040	OOC	CR/WD/?
8***	21 Aug	Fokker DVII	F5938	3	57 C 68	1130	CAPT	CR/RAF 21.8
9s†	22 Aug	Balloon	F5938	3	Thilloy	0955	DES	CR/WD/?
10	27 Sep	Balloon	F2153	3	57 B M 14	0805	DES	CR/RAF 27.9
11	27 Sep	Balloon	F2153	3	57 B M 14	0805	DES	CR/RAF 27.9

12s††	27 Sep	Balloon	F2153	3	57 C L 29	0820	DES	CR/RAF 27.9
13	28 Sep	Fokker DVII	F2153	3	57 B M6	1620	OOC	CR/?

TOTAL: 3 and 2 shared balloons, 1 captured, 1 and 1 shared destroyed, 4 and 1 shared out of control = 13.
*Shared with Capt D.J. Bell/Lt W.C. Dennett. **Shared with Capt H.L. Wallace, 2/Lt H.S. Basfurd, Lt A.O. McManus. Lt V.B. McIntosh. ***This was Vzfw A. Bernhorster of Jasta 61 who was killed. †Shared with Capt H.L. Wallace C1698. ††Shared with 2/Lt W.H. Maxted B7905.

ROBB James Milne Captain 32, 92

'Robbo' was born in Scotland on 26 January 1895, and on the outbreak of war he joined the Northumberland Fusiliers, prior to becoming an RFC pilot in 1916. That same year he flew with 32 Squadron and claimed at least one victory before being wounded in action on 11 March. After a period on Home Establishment, he became a flight commander with 92 Squadron and on 22 July 1918 he claimed that unit's first victory. Although he was slightly wounded on 16 August, he ended the war with a total of seven victories and a DFC. He remained in the RAF after the war, commanding 30 Squadron in Kurdistan, 1923-24, but this was only the first of many commands. He became a Wing Commander in 1935 with HQ, RAF Mediterranean, and rose in rank during World War II, becoming Commander of Air Defence of Great Britain in 1944, and then of Fighter Command, as it was re-christened. He retired as Air Chief Marshal Sir James Robb, KBE, GCB, DSO, DFC in 1951, and died on 18 December 1968.

	1917		DH 2					
1s*	27 Jan	C	7937	32	Courcrelles-Achiet	0945	DES(F)	CR/RFC 27.1
	1918		SE 5A					
2	22 Jul	Alb. DV	D372	92	S Bailleul	1930	DES	CR/RAF 22.7
3	7 Aug	Fokker DVII	D372	92	Steenwerck	0815	OOC	CR/ORB/SR/?
4	14 Aug	Fokker DVII	D5973	92	S E Bray	1900	DES	CR/RAF 14.8
5s**	4 Oct	Hannover C	F5666	92	S E Bertry	0705	OOC	CR/ORB/SR/?
6	14 Oct	Fokker DVII	E3211	92	S E Le Cateau	1630	DES(F)	CR/RAF 14.10
7s***	23 Oct	DFW. C	D376	92	S Pont du Nord	1300	DES	CR/RAF 23.10

TOTAL: 3 and 1 shared destroyed, 1 and 2 shared out of control = 7.
*Shared with Lt F. Billinge 7897, Lt T.A. Gooch 7941, Lt C.G. Eccles A2535, 2/Lt H.D. Davies A2534, Lt C.E. Pickthorn A2545, Lt M.L. Taylor 7938. **Shared with Lt T.S. Horry F858, Capt W.S. Philcox D6005, Lt E. Shapard E4009. ***Shared with Lt T.S. Horry, Lt E.S. Robins, Lt C.H.E. Coles, Lt E. Madill, Capt W.E. Reed, Lt E. Shapard, Lt J.V. Gascoyne, Lt J. Daniel.

ROBERTS Norman Lieutenant 48

Lieutenant Roberts served with 48 Squadron during the spring and early summer of 1918. He was awarded a DFC, gazetted on 10 September, for three aircraft destroyed and two out of control, and for ground attack missions.

	1918		Bristol					
1*	12 Mar	Fokker DrI	C4603	48	N N E St Quentin	1200	DES	CR/RFC 12.3
2*	12 Mar	Fokker DrI	C4603	48	N N E St Quentin	1200	OOC	CR/RFC 12.3
3**	10 May	Fokker DrI	C805	48	Suzanne	1545	OOC	CR/V BG WD DFC Cit
4***	25 Jun	Fokker DVII	C983	48	E Foucaucourt	1145	DES	CR/RAF 25.6
5**	27 Jun	Fokker DVII	C943	48	1m N E Lamotte	1800	DES	CR/RAF 27.6

TOTAL: 3 destroyed, 2 out of control = 5.
*Observer: Cpl W. Lawder. **Observer: 2/Lt W.F. Hanna. ***Observer: 2/Lt C.C. Walmesley; this was probably Uffz W. Hertsch of Jasta 12 who was fatally wounded.

ROBINSON Harry Noel Cornforth Captain 46, 70

Born on 25 December 1898, Harry Robinson joined the RFC in March 1917 and was posted to 46 Squadron in July to fly Sopwith Pups. He did much good work in low ground attacks during the Battle of Cambrai, by which time the squadron had converted to Camels, and he shot down his first enemy aircraft three days after Christmas, 1917. After accounting for eight hostile machines he was promoted to Captain and awarded an MC on 28 March 1918, when he was posted to 70 Squadron as a flight commander; here he brought his score to ten. On one occasion he was forced to return from a patrol with petrol pressure dropping. Flying alone, he saw seven enemy aircraft attacking an Allied artillery observation machine and went to its aid; he drove one down, but his guns then jammed; despite this he kept up his attack and succeeded in driving the others off. From the French he received the Croix de Guerre.

	1917		Camel					
1s*	28 Dec	C	B2429	46	3m W Havrincourt	1200	CAPT	CR/RFC 28.12
	1918							
2	11 Mar	Alb. DV	B5425	46	Dury	1645	OOC	CR/III BG WD
3	21 Mar	Alb. DV	B9158	46	57 C E 20	1200	OOC	CR/RFC 21.3
4	22 Mar	Alb. C	B9158	46	Hendecourt	1730	DES	CR/RFC 23.3

5s**	22 Mar	LVG. C	B9158	46	Bullecourt	1800	OOC	CR/RFC 23.3
6	23 Mar	LVG. C	B5425	46	Vaulx	1000	DES	CR/RFC 23.3
7s***	23 Mar	LVG. C	B5425	46	Vaulx	1005	OOC	CR/RFC 23.3
8	24 Mar	Alb. C	B5425	46	Sailly-Saillisel	1630	DES	CR/RFC 24.3
9s†	6 Apr	Alb. C	C8217	70	Bray	1545	OOC	CR/RAF 6.4
10	15 May	Pfalz DIII	C8217	70	57 D R 4	0700	OOC	CR/RAF 15.5

TOTAL: 1 shared captured, 3 destroyed, 3 and 3 shared out of control = 10.

*Shared with 2/Lt G.D. Lambourn B5419; The victims were Lt K. Doring/Lt H. Dobislav, of FA 32, who were killed. **Shared with 2/Lt W.J. Shorter B9199. ***Shared with 2/Lt G. Hudson C1649. †Shared with 2/Lt S.T. Liversedge C8220.

ROCHFORD Leonard Henry Captain 3(N), 203

Born in Enfield on 10 November 1896, he tried to join the RNAS when war was declared, but was too young. He therefore learned to fly with the London Provincial Flying Club at Hendon in 1915, and then joined the RNAS in May 1916. After a period with the War Flight at Eastchurch, he was posted to 3 Naval Squadron in January 1917. He remained with this unit which later became 203 Squadron,RAF, until the end of the war, during which time he was awarded the DSC and Bar, and the DFC, claiming 29 victories. In addition, 'Titch' as he was called due to his slight stature, had over 40 indecisive combats, several of which left enemy machines in a damaged condition. Indeed he was the highest scoring pilot with 3(N)/203 Squadron. In 1918 he was Mentioned in Despatches with his CO, Ray Collishaw, when they alone bombed and strafed Dorignies aerodrome on 22 July to good effect. After the war he went into engineering, but then took up farming until World War II, when he held several training posts. 'Titch' retired first to Enfield, and later to Somerset, where he wrote an excellent autobiography, *I Chose the Sky*. He appeared on television on several occasions, and was featured in one of the British Legion Armistice Day ceremonies at the Royal Albert Hall. He remained a keen member of Cross and Cockade until his death on 17 December 1986.

	1917		Pup					
1	4 Mar	Alb. DI	N5199	3N	Manancourt	1115	OOC	CR/ORB/DL
2	20 May	Alb. DIII	N6461	3N	N E Bullecourt	0930	OOC	CR/RFC 20.5
3s*	7 Jul	Seaplane	N6162	3N	6m N Ostend	1110	DES	CR/RNAS 7.7
			Camel					
4	5 Sep	Alb. DIII	B3807	3N	Leke	1820	OOC	CR/RNAS 5.9
5	11 Sep	Alb. DV	B3798	3N	Thorout	1110	OOC	CR/RNAS 11.9
	1918							
6s**	28 Jan	DFW. CV	B6401	3N	Houthoulst Forest	1105	OOC	CR/RNAS 28.1
7s***	30 Jan	Alb. DV	B6401	3N	Gheluvelt	1045	OOC	CR/RNAS 30.1
8s***	30 Jan	Alb. DV	B6401	3N	Gheluvelt	1045	OOC	CR/RNAS 30.1
9	12 Mar	Alb. C	B7203	3N	Brebieres	1100	OOC	CR/RFC 12.3
10s†	16 Mar	Hannover C	B7203	3N	Gavrelle	1120	DES(F)	CR/RFC 16.3
11s††	21 Mar	Alb. DV	B7222	3N	Douai	1115	OOC	CR/RFC 21.3
12s†††	21 Mar	Alb. C	B7203	3N	4m E Bapaume	1645	DES(F)	CR/RFC 21.3
13	22 Mar	Alb. DV	B7203	3N	Boursies	1230	DES	CR/RFC 22.3
14	24 Mar	Alb. DV	B7203	3N	Beaumetz	1715	OOC	CR/RFC 24.3
15s‡	15 May	DFW. CV	B3353	203	N Estaires	1140	OOC	CR/RAF 15.5
16	17 May	Pfalz DIII	B7197	203	N Estaires-Beaupre	1115	DES	CR/RAF 17.5
17s‡‡	17 May	Pfalz DIII	B7197	203	N E Estaires	1130	DES(F)	CR/RAF 17.5
18	19 May	DFW. CV	D3371	203	Merville	1015	DES	CR/RAF 19.5
19s‡‡‡	21 May	DFW. CV	D3413	203	Neuf Berquin	0530	DES	CR/RAF 21.5
20	5 Jun	LVG. C	D3417	203	La Bassee	----	OOC	CR/Auto/?
21	7 Jun	Fokker DrI	D3417	203	La Bassee	1200	OOC	CR/?
22s§	20 Jul	DFW. CV	D9618	203	S E Lestrem	1800	DES	CR/AA/Auto
23	22 Jul	Fokker DVII	D9585	203	Festubert	0925	OOC	CR/RAF 22.7
24	22 Jul	Fokker DVII	D9585	203	Carvin	1035	DES	CR/RAF 22.7
25	25 Jul	Fokker DVII	D9618	203	E La Bassee	0740	DES	CR/RAF 25.7
26	11 Aug	Fokker DVII	D9618	203	E Bray	1930	OOC	CR/?
27	7 Sep	Fokker DVII	C197	203	N Bourlon Wood	0815	DES	CR/RAF 7.9
28s§§	9 Oct	Rumpler C	D4386	203	St Aubert	1630	DES(F)	CR/RAF 9.10
29	29 Oct	Fokker DVII	D4386	203	E Bruay	1515	OOC	CR/?

TOTAL: 6 and 7 shared destroyed, 11 and 5 shared out of control = 29.

*Shared with FSL J.S.T. Fall N6364, FSL J.A. Glen N6183, FSL F.C. Armstrong N6163, FSL R.F.P. Abbott. **Shared with FSL J.A. Glen B6408, FSL C.S. Devereux B3785. ***Shared with FSL J.A. Glen B6242, FSL A.B. Ellwood B6408. †Shared with FSL J.A. Glen B7185, FSL A.B. Ellwood B7229. ††Shared with FSL J.A. Glen B7185. †††Shared with FSL O.P. Adam B3798, FSL J.A. Glen B7185, FSL K.D. Macleod B7222, FSL W.H. Chisam B7223, FSL A.B. Ellwood B7229, FSL C.S. Devereux B7228, FSL L.A. Sands B7216, FSL R.C. Berlyn B7224, FSL E.T. Hayne B7231. ‡Shared with Lt C.F. Brown C61. ‡‡Shared with Lt C.F. Brown, Lt Y.E.S. Kirkpatrick, Lt E.R. Prideaux B6408. ‡‡‡Shared with Lt R.C. Berlyn. §Shared with Lt W. Sidebottom D9583. §§Shared with Lt W. Sidebottom C187.

ROGERS Bogart Lieutenant 32

An American born on 24 June 1898 in Los Angeles who joined the RFC, he was posted to 32 Squadron on 3 May 1918. He claimed five Fokkers and one Rumpler two-seater shot down by the close of hostilities. Rogers died in Burbank, California on 24 July 1966.

	1918		SE 5A					
1	22 Jul	Fokker DVII	C1856	32	Mont Notre Dame	1805	OOC	CR/ORB/?
2	6 Sep	Rumpler C	D6991	32	E Roisel	1100	OOC	CR/ORB/?
3	6 Sep	Fokker DVII	D6991	32	Holnon	1700	DES(F)	CR/ORB/?
4	16 Sep	Fokker DVII	E1399	32	Sancourton	1810	OOC	CR/ORB/?
5	27 Sep	Fokker DVII	D3443	32	Emerchicourt	0930	DES(F)	CR/RAF 27.9
6	1 Nov	Fokker DVII	D6991	32	E Valenciennes	1325	OOC	CR/ORB/?

TOTAL: 1 destroyed. 5 out of control = 6.

ROGERS William Wendell Captain 1

A Canadian from Alberton, Prince Edward Island, born in 1897, he joined the RFC in 1916 and by the following spring had been posted to 1 Squadron in France, flying Nieuport Scouts. With this unit he received the MC and claimed nine enemy aircraft. One of his most notable combats occurred on 12 December 1917 when he shot down a Gotha bomber of Bogohl 1 during a daylight raid over France. After the war he operated an automobile business in Saint John, Canada, and flew with the local Saint John Flying Club, of which he became a prominent member.

	1917		Nieup					
1s*	12 Jul	Alb. DIII	B3463	1	Menin	2055	OOC	CR/RFC 12.7
2	7 Oct	Alb. DV	B6754	1	Menin	0800	OOC	CR/RFC 7.10
3	8 Oct	Alb. DV	B6754	1	Polygon Wood	1430	OOC	CR/RFC 8.10
4	9 Oct	Alb. DV	B3629	1	N W Gheluwe	1300	OOC	CR/RFC 9.10
5	20 Oct	Alb. DV	B3629	1	Linselles	1050	OOC	CR/RFC 20.10
6	29 Oct	DFW. C	B6789	1	Quesnoy	1055	OOC	CR/RFC 29.11
7**	12 Dec	Gotha G.	B6825	1	N Frelinghien	1415	DES	CR/RFC 12.12
8s***	17 Dec	C	B6789	1	S W Moorslede	1420	OOC	CR/RFC 17.12
9	18 Dec	Alb. DV	B6789	1	Moorslede	1140	OOC	CR/RFC 18.12

TOTAL: 1 destroyed, 7 and 1 shared out of control = 9.

*Shared with 2/Lt H.S. Davies B1659. **This was Hptm R. Kleine, the commander of BG 1, and his crew Lt Bulowius, Lt von der Nahmer, Gefr Weber. ***Shared with Lt R.C. Sotham B6768, 2/Lt W.D. Patrick B6830.

ROOPER William Victor Trevor Captain 1

After service with the Denbeigh Yeomanry, Lieutenant Rooper who was born in 1897, joined 1 Squadron in early summer 1917, and first claimed on 28 July. In mid-September he was promoted to flight commander and by early November had brought his score to eight. Rooper is often reported killed in action on 9 October of that year, but he was actually shot down and crashed in the front line trenches, breaking his thigh whilst flying B6767 near Polygon Wood. He subsequently died. His victor was Leutnant Helmut Dilthey of Jasta 27.

	1917		Nieuport					
1	28 Jul	Alb. DV	B1675	1	Becelaere	1910	OOC	CR/RFC 28.7
2s*	9 Aug	C	B1675	1	Houthoulst Forest	1050	CAPT	CR/RFC 9.8
3s**	17 Aug	DFW. C	B1675	1	Tenbrielen	1015	OOC	CR/RFC 17.8
4	11 Sep	Alb. DV	B3632	1	Houthoulst	1815	OOC	CR/RFC 11.9
5	19 Sep	Alb. DV	B6767	1	E Poelcapelle	1800	DES(F)	CR/ORB/?
6	25 Sep	Alb. DV	B6767	1	E Gheluvelt	1830	DES	CR/RFC 25.9
7s***	1 Oct	DFW. C	B6767	1	Houthoulst	1110	OOC	CR/RFC 1.10
8	5 Oct	Alb. DV	B6767	1	Zandvoorde	0955	DES	CR/RFC 5.10

TOTAL: 1 shared captured, 3 destroyed, 2 and 2 shared out of control = 8.

*Shared with Capt P.F. Fullard B3459. The crew of this aircraft, Uffz W. Stulcken/Lt J. Schmidt FAA 238. **Shared with Lt C.S.T. Lavers B1692. ***Shared with Capt R.A. Birkbeck B6753, 2/Lt F.G. Baker B3630, 2/Lt L. Cumming B6790.

ROSE Oren John Captain 92

An American from Platte County, Missouri, born on 23 March 1893, Rose served in the RFC/RAF during 1918 and flew in France with 92 Squadron. He was the most successful pilot in that unit, claiming 16 victories and being awarded the DFC and Bar. He also shot down the unit's last enemy aircraft at 1045 on 4 November 1918. In 1919 he served with the RAF in Russia.

	1918		SE 5A					
1	30 Jul	Fokker DVII	D6173	92	Estaires	1850	OOC	CR/ORB/?
2	31 Jul	C	D6173	92	Sailly sur la Lys	1920	DES	CR/RAF 31.7
3	14 Aug	Fokker DVII	D6173	92	S Peronne	1130	DES(F)	CR/RAF 14.8

4	14 Aug	Fokker DVII	D6173	92	S Peronne	1130	DES	CR/RAF 14.8
5	25 Aug	Fokker DVII	B8430	92	Lille-Armentieres	1415	OOC	CR/ORB/?
6	4 Sep	Halb. C	B8430	92	E Quiery-W Douai	1110	DES	CR/RAF 4.9
7	15 Sep	Hannover C	B8430	92	W Lille	1300	DES	CR/RAF 15.9
8	29 Sep	Fokker DVII	C9064	92	E Beaurevoir	1145	DES(F)	CR/ORB/?
9	29 Sep	Halb. C	C9064	92	Bellicourt	1150	DES	CR/ORB/?
10	3 Oct	Fokker DVII	C1142	92	N Beaurevoir	0815	DES	CR/RAF 3.10
11	3 Oct	Fokker DVII	C1142	92	N Fresnoy	0845	DES	CR/RAF 3.10
12	8 Oct	Pfalz DIII	C1142	92	N Le Cateau	1430	DES	CR/RAF 8.10
13	9 Oct	Fokker DVII	B8430	92	E Proix-Montigny	1320	DES	CR/RAF 9.10
14s*	29 Oct	DFW. C	C1142	92	Favril	1605	DES	CR/RAF 29.10
15	30 Oct	DFW. C	C1142	92	W Sassegnies	0915	DES(F)	CR/RAF 30.10
16	4 Nov	Fokker DVII	C1142	92	W Landrecies	1045	DES	CR/RAF 4.11

TOTAL: 13 and 1 shared destroyed, 2 out of control = 16.
*Shared with Lt J.V. Gascoyne B8430, Capt W.S. Philcox E5771, Lt W.S. Rogers E5789.

ROSE Thomas Captain 64

'Tommy' Rose was born on 27 January 1895, and joined the RFC in 1917; he was posted to 64 Squadron later that year. This unit was flying DH 5s and was involved in the Battle of Cambrai, undertaking much ground strafing work. Subsequently the unit was re-equipped with SE 5As, following which much more success was achieved in aerial combat. Rose soon became a deputy flight commander, and when his DFC was gazetted in November 1918, he had claimed 11 victories. He remained in the RAF for a time after the war, being a flight commander with 43 Squadron during 1925-27. Leaving the service, he was Sales Manager to Phillips & Powis Aircraft Co Ltd. He also undertook a good deal of air racing in the thirties, winning the King's Cup Air Race in 1935. He took part in the race to Johannesburg the following year. Subsequently he lived in retirement in the Channel Islands, where he died on 20 June 1968.

	1918		SE 5A					
1	8 Mar	Alb. DV	----	64	Graincourt	1230	OOC	CR/RFC 8.3
2	23 Apr	C	C5393	64	Ervillers	1750	DES(F)	CR/RAF 23.4
3	29 Apr	Pfalz DIII	C5392	64	Wancourt	1735	OOC	CR/RAF 29.4
4	9 May	Rumpler C	C1860	64	Boiry	1040	DES	CR/RAF 9.5
5	9 May	Halb. C	C1860	64	Boiry	1042	OOC	CR/RAF 9.5
6	22 May	C	----	64	Bauvin-Carvin	1120	DES	CR/RAF 22.5
7	25 Jul	Fokker DVII	----	64	W Aubers	0810	OOC	CR/?
8	10 Aug	Fokker DVII	C1860	64	Roye	0840	OOC	CR/ORB/?
9s*	11 Aug	Fokker DVII	C1860	64	Roye	0815	OOC	CR/ORB/?
10	12 Aug	Fokker DVII	----	64	Chaulnes	0715	DES	CR/RAF 12.8
11**	14 Aug	Alb. C	----	64	N Roye	0910	OOC	CR/?

TOTAL: 4 destroyed, 5 and 2 shared out of control = 11.
*Shared with Capt E.R. Tempest B74, Lt G.L. Wood E1391, Capt T. St P. Bunbury E5977, Capt A.F. Buck, Capt C.W. Cudemore D6952. **Shared with Capt E.R. Tempest, Lt G.A. Wood.

ROSEVEAR Stanley Wallace Captain 1(N), 201

Rosevear was born in Walkerton, Ontario, on 9 March 1896, and lived before the war in Port Arthur in the same Canadian province. He attended the University of Toronto, and joined the RNAS in February 1917. After training he was posted to Dover on 22 June, and shortly thereafter joined 1(N) Squadron in France to fly Sopwith Triplanes. He first claimed in August, and by the end of October had eight victories to his credit. The squadron then converted to Camels, and he was awarded a DSC on 14 November. He saw very heavy action during March 1918, gaining many more victories and becoming a flight commander. On 1 April the squadron became 201, RAF, and on 17th he received a Bar to his DSC. He claimed his last two victories during this month, but on 25th crashed and was killed in B6231 when he failed to pull out of a dive on a practice target while on a test flight.

	1917		Triplane					
1	14 Aug	Alb. DV	N6299	1N	N E Ypres	0840	OOC	CR/RFC 14.8
2	16 Aug	Alb. DV	N6299	1N	Menin	0700	DES	CR/RFC 16.8
3s*	26 Aug	DFW. C	N6299	1N	E Deulemont	0750	OOC	CR/RFC 26.8
4	19 Sep	Alb. DV	N6299	1N	Becelaere	1010	DES	CR/RFC 19.9
5	17 Oct	Alb. DV	N5489	1N	S Polygon Wood	1045	DES	CR/RFC 17.10
6	21 Oct	Alb. DV	N5489	1N	S E Wervicq	0940	OOC	CR/RFC 21.10
7	24 Oct	Alb. C	N5489	1N	Comines	1200	DES(F)	CR/RFC 24.10
8	24 Oct	C	N5489	1N	Comines	1200	DES	CR/RFC 24.10
			Camel					
9	5 Dec	Alb. DV	B6428	1N	Vladsloo	1410	DES	CR/RNAS 5.12

10	6 Dec	C	B6428	1N	Ostend	0625	OOC	CR/RNAS 6.12
	1918							
11s**	19 Feb	Alb. DV	B6428	1N	S Zillebeke Lake	1150	DES(F)	CR/RNAS 19.2
12	6 Mar	Fokker DrI	B6428	1N	Bouchoir	1315	DES	CR/DOS/?
13	10 Mar	C	B6428	1N	Menin	1530	OOC	CR/RNAS 10.3
14	11 Mar	C	B6428	1N	S Armentieres	1200	OOC	CR/RNAS 11.3
15	13 Mar	Alb. DV	B6428	1N	Dixmude	0725	DES	CR/RNAS 13.3
16	15 Mar	Pfalz DIII	B6428	1N	E Dixmude	1145	DES	CR/RNAS 15.3
17	15 Mar	Pfalz DIII	B6428	1N	E Dixmude	1145	DES(F)	CR/RNAS 15.3
18	16 Mar	Alb. DV	B6428	1N	E Roulers	1155	DES	CR/RNAS 16.3
19	16 Mar	Alb. DV	B6428	1N	Roulers	1625	DES	CR/RNAS 16.3
20	21 Mar	Alb. DV	B6428	1N	Nieuport	0715	DES(F)	CR/RNAS 21.3
21	21 Mar	Alb. DV	B6428	1N	Nieuport	0720	DES	CR/RNAS 21.3
22	21 Mar	Alb. DV	B6428	1N	Nieuport	0720	OOC	CR/RNAS 21.3
23	6 Apr	Fokker DrI	B6419	201	Mericourt	1315	DES	CR/RAF 6.4
24	22 Apr	Pfalz DIII	D3363	201	Hangard	1110	DES	CR/RAF 22.4
25	22 Apr	Pfalz DIII	D3363	201	Hangard	1110	DES	CR/RAF 22.4

TOTAL: 16 and 1 shared destroyed, 7 and 1 shared out of control = 25.
*Shared with FSL H.V. Rowley N6301. **Shared with F/Cdr A.W. Carter B7202.

ROSS Charles Gordon Captain 29

Born on 12 March 1892, in Johannesburg, South Africa, he joined the RFC in August 1917, being posted to 29 Squadron on 25 March 1918. While with the unit he claimed 20 victories, on three occasions claiming two in one day. He became a flight commander during September, and was awarded a DFC and Bar. After the war he went with the squadron to Cologne in Germany, but subsequently left the RAF, joining the new SAAF in 1921. He also received the Belgian Croix de Guerre.

	1918		SE 5A					
1s*	26 May	DFW. C	----	29	S Bailleul	1835	DES	CR/RAF 26.5
2	27 May	DFW. C	D5981	29	S E Bailleul	1115	DES(F)	CR/RAF 27.5
3s**	28 May	DFW. C	D5981	29	Neuve Eglise	0905	DES(F)	CR/RAF 28.5
4	29 May	Alb. DV	D6137	29	Merville	1630	OOC	ORB/?
5s***	6 Jun	Pfalz DIII	D5953	29	N W Estaires	1800	DES	CR/RAF 6.6
6	28 Jul	DFW. C	E3917	29	Fournes	0730	DES	CR/RAF 28.7
7	8 Aug	Balloon	C9071	29	Estaires	0950	DES	CR/RAF 8.8
8	12 Aug	Fokker DVII	C9071	29	Comines	0925	DES	CR/RAF 12.8
9	16 Aug	Fokker DVII	D6939	29	Poelcapelle	1845	DES	CR/RAF 16.8
10	22 Aug	DFW. C	C9071	29	Estaires	0735	DES	CR/RAF 22.8
11	23 Aug	DFW. C	C9071	29	E Ypres	0630	DES	CR/RAF 23.8
12s†	23 Aug	Balloon	C9071	29	S E Kemmel	0630+	DES	CR/RAF 23.8
13	24 Aug	Fokker DVII	C9071	29	S Comines	1915	OOC	CR/11 WS
14	28 Sep	Fokker DVII	D6984	29	S Menin	1710	DES(F)	CR/RAF 28.9
15	28 Sep	Fokker DVII	D6984	29	Menin-Gheluvelt Rd.	1730	DES	CR/RAF 28.9
16	2 Oct	Fokker DVII	E6030	29	N E Roulers	1520	DES	CR/RAF 2.10
17	4 Oct	Fokker DVII	E6030	29	E Halluin	0935	DES	CR/RAF 4.10
18s††	9 Nov	Fokker DVII	F5543	29	Laerne	1025	DES	CR/RAF 9.11
19	9 Nov	Fokker DVII	F5543	29	Laerne	1020	DES	CR/RAF 9.11
20	10 Nov	Fokker DVII	C8904	29	N Elene	1345	DES(F)	CR/RAF 10.11

TOTAL: 1 and 1 shared balloons, 12 and 4 shared destroyed, 2 out of control = 20.
*Shared with Capt R.H. Rusby, Lt F.J. Davies. **Shared with Capt R.H. Rusby D5963, Lt H.M. Hutton D6153. ***Shared with Lt A.E. Reed D5970. †Shared with 1/Lt A.F. Diamond C8859, Capt E.C. Hoy D6939. ††Shared with lt H. Holroyde H7162.

ROWLEY Herbert Victor Captain 1(N), 201

Born on 24 October 1897, Rowley joined the RNAS in June 1916 and was posted to 1(N) Squadron in February 1917. He served throughout the year, flying Triplanes, claiming his first victory on 29 April. However, after the second of these, he was shot down and forced to land near Bethune in N5425 by an Albatros DIII. By late 1917 he had become a flight commander, and following the unit's re-equipment with Camels and its return to the front, he added three further victories plus a share in a balloon to bring his total to nine by April 1918. During World War II he served in the India-Burma theatre as an Air Commodore.

	1917		Triplane					
1s*	29 Apr	Alb. DIII	N5425	1N	Villers les Cagnicourt	1150	OOC	CR/RFC 29.4
2s**	13 Jul	C	N6308	1N	E Warneton	1025	DES	CR/RFC 13.7
3s***	17 Jul	Alb. DV	N5373	1N	4m E Messines	1805	OOC	CR/RFC 17.7
4s†	26 Aug	DFW. C	N6301	1N	E Deulemont	0750	OOC	CR/RFC 26.8
5	13 Nov	C	N5472	1N	S E Nieuport	1210	OOC	CR/RNAS 13.11
	1918		Camel					

6s††	12 Mar	Balloon	B6429	1N	Ypres	1315	DES	CR/RNAS 13.3
7	16 Mar	Alb. DV	B6429	1N	Dixmude	1145	OOC	CR/DOS/?
8	21 Mar	Alb. DV	B6429	1N	Nieuport	1550	DES	CR/RNAS 22.3
9	1 Apr	Alb. DV	B6429	201	Arras-Albert	1300	OOC	CR/ORB/?

TOTAL: 1 shared balloon, 1 and 1 shared destroyed, 3 and 3 shared out of control = 9.
*Shared with FSL C.B. Ridley N5437. **Shared with F/Cdr F.H.M. Maynard N5479, FSL A.G.A. Spence N5459. ***Shared with F/Cdr F.H.M. Maynard N5479, FSL E. Anthony N6296, FSL C.B. Ridley N6304, FSL C.G. Brock N5485, FSL G.B.G Scott N5455, F/L H.L. Everitt N6308, FSL A.G.A. Spence N6300. †Shared with FSL S.W. Rosevear N6299. ††Shared with F/Cdr C.B. Ridley B6418.

ROXBURGH-SMITH Benjamin Captain 60, 74

A former bank clerk from Bromley, Surrey, and a married man with a family, he joined the RFC, serving initially with 60 Squadron during 1917. While with the unit, he crashed his Nieuport Scout, A164, and was injured. Posted home, he served as an instructor until early 1918, when he went to France with 74 Squadron, whose pilots he had been training. Serving in Captain Mannock's 'A' Flight, he was known as 'Dad' due to his relatively advanced age of 34! He subsequently became a flight commander, claiming at least 22 victories and receiving the DFC and Bar, and the Belgian Croix de Guerre. He was shot down on 19 July, but force-landed with only slight wounds.

	1918		SE 5A					
1s*	12 Apr	Alb. DV	----	74	Bois de Phalempin	1440	DES	CR/RAF 12.4
2	29 Apr	LVG. C	----	74	Dickebusch Lake	1150	DES	CR/RAF 29.4
3s**	6 May	Fokker DrI	C1108	74	N E Ypres	1520	DES	CR/RAF 6.5
4	12 May	Pfalz DIII	C1108	74	N Wulverghem	1825	DES	CR/RAF 12.5
5	26 May	Pfalz DIII	C1108	74	Doullieu	1930	DES	CR/RAF 26.5
6	17 Jun	Fokker DVII	D6855	74	4m S E Dickebusch	0845	DES	CR/RAF 17.6
7	18 Jun	DFW. C	D6855	74	1m S Bailleul	1745	OOC	CR/11 WS
8	19 Jul	Pfalz DIII	E5949	74	N E Gheluvelt	0850	DES	CR/RAF 19.7
9	10 Aug	Fokker DVII	----	74	E Messines	1900	DES	CR/RAF 10.8
10	17 Aug	Fokker DVII	D6976	74	N Houthoulst Forest	0905	OOC	CR/11 WS
11	19 Aug	Fokker DVII	----	74	Houthem	1930	DES	CR/RAF 19.8
12	23 Aug	Fokker DVII	----	74	Passchendaele	1905	DES(F)	CR/RAF 23.8
13	23 Aug	Fokker DVII	----	74	Passchendaele	1933	DES(F)	CR/RAF 23.8
14	21 Sep	Fokker DVII	----	74	Lille	1845	OOC	CR/11 WS
15s***	24 Sep	Rumpler C	----	74	Capinghem	1045	DES	CR/RAF 24.9
16	26 Sep	Fokker DVII	D6976	74	S E Warneton	1130	DES	CR/RAF 26.9
17s†	26 Sep	DFW. C	D6976	74	3m S E Armentieres	1510	DES	CR/RAF 26.9
18	5 Oct	Fokker DVII	D6976	74	3m S W Roulers	0930	DES	CR/RAF 5.10
19	5 Oct	Fokker DVII	D6976	74	3m S W Roulers	0930	OOC	CR/RAF 5.10
20	14 Oct	Fokker DVII	----	74	Courtrai	1500	OOC	CR/11 WS
21	14 Oct	Fokker DVII	----	74	Lauwe	1520	DES	CR/RAF 14.10
22	14 Oct	Fokker DVII	----	74	Reckem	1525	DES	CR/RAF 14.10

TOTAL: 13 and 4 shared destroyed, 5 out of control = 22.
*Shared with Capt E.C. Mannock, Lt H.E. Dolan, Lt P.F.C. Howe, Lt H.G. Clements. **Shared with Major K.L. Caldwell C5396. ***Shared with Lt G.R.Hicks. †Shared with Lt G.R. Hicks D6922.

ROY Indra Lal 2nd Lieutenant 56, 40

'Laddie' was born in Calcutta, India, but was at school in England when war broke out. He joined the RFC in July 1917 and was posted to 56 Squadron on 30 October, but on 6 November he crashed SE 5A B567 and was sent back to England for further training. After some additional flying he was pronounced unfit by the medical staff, a decision which he was able to get reversed, and he returned to France on 19 June 1918, joining George McElroy's flight in 40 Squadron. Between 6th and 19 July he claimed ten victories, but he was killed in a fight with Fokker DVIIs of Jasta 29 on 22nd, his SE 5A (B180) going down in flames over Carvin at 0850. His total flying time was just 170 hours 15 minutes, and in September a DFC was gazetted for this 19 year-old, the first — and to date the only — Indian fighter ace.

	1918		SE 5A					
1	6 Jul	Hannover C	B180	40	Drocourt	0545	OOC	CR/Air 1/1414
2	8 Jul	Hannover C	B180	40	Drocourt	0645	OOC	CR/Air 1/1414
3s*	8 Jul	Hannover C	B180	40	E Monchy	0925	OOC	CR/Air 1/1414
4	8 Jul	Fokker DVII	B180	40	S E Douai	1025	OOC	CR/Air 1/1414
5s**	13 Jul	Hannover C	B180	40	W Estaires	0645	DES	CR/RAF 13.7
6	13 Jul	Pfalz DIII	B180	40	Vitry-Brebieres	2005	DES	CR/RAF 13.7
7	15 Jul	Fokker DVII	B180	40	Hulloch	2005	DES	CR/RAF 15.7
8	15 Jul	Fokker DVII	B180	40	Hulloch	2005	OOC	CR/?

9	18 Jul	DFW. C	B180	40	S E Arras	2040	DES	CR/RAF 18.7
10	19 Jul	Hannover C	B180	40	Cagnicourt	1025	DES	CR/AIR 1/1414

TOTAL: 4 and 1 shared destroyed, 4 and 1 shared out of control = 10.
*Shared with Capt G.E.H. McElroy C8869, Lt G.J. Strange B191. **Shared with Capt G.E.H. McElroy C8869, Lt F.H. Knobel D3528, Lt G.J. Strange B191.

RUSBY Reginald Howard Captain 22, 29

Born on 4 September 1893, Rusby was a Londoner who served with the Gloucestershire Regiment in 1916, before transferring to the RFC. He flew briefly as an observer with 22 Squadron, but was wounded on 24 January 1917. Later that year he trained as a pilot and then joined 29 Squadron as a flight commander in October 1917, flying Nieuports, and later in 1918, SE 5As. During the opening months of 1918 he brought his score to three before converting to the SE, after being slightly wounded on 7 January. In the heavy fighting in May he made a further seven claims. He received the DFC, gazetted on 2 July, for six destroyed plus a balloon damaged, but his final score of 10 included four out of control claims. He returned to Home Establishment on 9 June.

	1917		Nieuport					
1	16 Dec	Alb. DV	----	29	Roulers area	1025	OOC	CR/RFC 16.12
	1918							
2	18 Feb	Alb. DV	B3622	29	W Houthoulst	1210	OOC	CR/RFC 18.2
3	23 Mar	C	B3622	29	E Passchendaele	1050	DES(F)	CR/RFC 23.3
			SE 5A					
4	15 May	C	D5963	29	S E Merris	1505	DES(F)	CR/RAF 15.5
5	18 May	Pfalz DIII	D3915	29	E Merville	1150	DES	CR/RAF 18.8
6	20 May	DFW. C	D5963	29	Kemmel Hill	0950	OOC	CR/11 WS
7	23 May	C	D3915	29	S E Bailleul	0945	OOC	CR/11 WS
8s*	26 May	DFW. C	D5963	29	S Bailleul	1835	DES	CR/RAF 26.5
9s**	28 May	DFW. C	D5963	29	Neuve Eglise	0905	DES(F)	CR/RAF 28.5
10	31 May	Fokker DrI	D5970	29	W Bailleul	1655	CAPT	CR/RAF 31.5

TOTAL: 1 captured, 3 and 2 shared destroyed, 4 out of control = 10.
*Shared with Lt F.J. Davies, Lt C.G. Ross. **Shared with Lt C.G. Ross D5981, Lt H.M. Hutton D6153.

RUTHERFORD William James Captain 60

A Canadian from Montreal who joined the RFC from the 23rd Canadian Battalion, Rutherford was posted to 60 Squadron in 1917, flying Nieuport Scouts. Later that year he was promoted to Captain, taking command of 'C' Flight. Known to his friends as 'Jack', he had claimed eight victories before he returned to Home Establishment on 5 December 1917. In 1918 he commanded Beamsville Camp, Ontario.

	1917		Nieuport					
1s*	25 Jun	Alb. DIII	B1602	60	Dury	1025	OOC	CR/RFC 25.6
			SE 5A					
2	22 Sep	C	B6	60	Ypres-Roulers	1845	DES	CR/RFC 22.9
3s**	21 Oct	C	B533	60	Houthoulst	1615	DES	CR/RFC 21.10
4	28 Oct	Alb. DV	A8901	60	Westroosebeke	0930	OOC	CR/RFC 28.10
5s***	1 Nov	C	A8934	60	Moorslede	1345	OOC	CR/RFC 1.11
6s***	1 Nov	C	A8934	60	Moorslede	1410	OOC	CR/RFC 1.11
7s†	6 Nov	C	A8934	60	Zonnebeke	0730	DES	CR/RFC 6.11
8	8 Nov	Alb. DV	B608	60	Westroosebeke	1545	OOC	CR/RFC 8.11

TOTAL: 1 and 2 shared destroyed, 2 and 3 shared out of control = 8.
*Shared with Lt F.O. Soden B1598, 2/Lt G.C. Young B1619. ** Shared with Lt F.O. Soden B543, Lt G.L. Young B580. ***Shared with Lt F.O. Soden A8898. †Shared with Lt F.O. Soden B543.

SAINT Howard John Thomas Captain 10(N)

Howard Saint was from Ruabon, North Wales, where he was born on 21 January 1893. He served as a Chief Petty Officer with the Royal Naval Armoured Cars in France during 1915-16, being commissioned as a Sub Lieutenant in August 1915. Early in 1916 he undertook pilot training, and on graduation was posted to 5 Wing as a bomber pilot on 2 September of that year. On 26 July 1917 he joined 10(N) Squadron, where he became a flight commander and was awarded the DSC, which was gazetted in November. He was wounded in the leg on 16 August, though not seriously. Flying Sopwith Triplanes and Camels, he claimed seven victories before leaving the unit on 14 November. After the war he became Chief Test Pilot for the Gloster Aircraft Company, being responsible for the development of the Gamecock fighter.

	1917		Triplane					
1	9 Aug	Alb. DIII	N5380	10N	Polygon Wood	1550	OOC	CR/DOS/DL/?
2	14 Aug	Alb. DIII	N5380	10N	Houthoulst Forest	1615	DES(F)	CR/DOS/DL/?
3	21 Aug	C	N6295	10N	1m S Roulers	0740	OOC	CR/RFC 21.8

4	25 Aug	Alb. DV	N6295	10N	S Roulers	0700	OOC	CR/RFC 25.8
			Camel					
5	21 Sep	Alb. DV	B6201	10N	Wervicq	1100	OOC	CR/RFC 21.9
6	23 Sep	Alb. DV	N6341	10N	Westroosebeke	1130	OOC	CR/RFC 23.9
7	20 Oct	Alb. DV	N6341	10N	N E Dixmude	1340	DES	CR/RFC 20.10

TOTAL: 2 destroyed, 5 out of control = 7.

SALTER Ernest James Captain 54

A Canadian, Salter joined 54 Squadron in early summer 1918, gaining his first victory on 9 June. On 21 July he claimed two two-seaters in one sortie and a Fokker DVII in flames in another. He was promoted to flight commander the following month, and brought his score to nine, the highest for a 54 Squadron pilot. He was awarded the Croix de Guerre avec Palme and created a Chevalier of the Legion d'Honneur by the French. He died in 1970.

	1918		Camel					
1	9 Jun	C	B7171	54	E Zandvoorde	0715	OOC	CR/?
2	4 Jul	Hannover C	D1948	54	Herleville	1430	OOC	CR/?
3	5 Jul	Alb. DV	D1948	54	N E Lamotte	1050	OOC	CR/?
4	21 Jul	Halb. C	D1946	54	E Dravegny	1555	DES	CR/RAF 21.7
5	21 Jul	Halb. C	D1946	54	.5m E Chery	1600	DES	CR/RAF 21.7
6	21 Jul	Fokker DVII	D9497	54	Fere en Tardenois	1915	DES(F)	CR/RAF 21.7
7s*	22 Aug	Alb. C	D1946	54	200y W Greyvillers	1745	DES	CR/RAF 22.8
8	25 Aug	Fokker DVII	D1946	54	Combles	1045	OOC	CR/?
9	30 Aug	Fokker DVII	E5168	54	S E Riencourt	0645	OOC	CR/?

TOTAL: 3 and 1 shared destroyed, 5 out of control = 9.
*Shared with Lt Crosse E5174, Lt Bellivaux E5149, Lt A.S. Crompton D9567.

SANDAY William Douglas Stock Major 2, 70, 19

Sanday went to France with 2 Squadron in 1915, and on 11 October with two other aircraft, forced down a two-seater of FlgAbt 202, capturing the crew. In 1916 he went to 70 Squadron, which was flying Sopwith 1½ Strutters. Here he flew many reconnaissance and escort missions during the summer, receiving the MC, followed in October by the award of the DSO; by this time he had flown over 35 patrols and accounted for at least four enemy machines, one in flames. On 6 August he led his patrol after ten German bombers which were observed flying towards the Allied lines, forcing them back and causing them to land without being able to drop a single bomb. In 1917 he took command of 19 Squadron after the death in action of Major G.H. Harvey-Kelly, and led this unit until the new year. He often went out on patrols with his pilots, and also frequently flew on his own along the front line. He had several encounters, claiming a victory and damaging several other enemy machines, bringing his score to five.

	1915		BE 2C					
1s*	11 Oct	Alb. C	----	2	Noyelles-les-Vermelles	0900	CAPT	RFC 11.10
	1916		Strutter					
2s**	6 Aug	Alb. C	----	70	Gouzeacourt	1845	FTL	C&CA 20.4 RFC 6.8
3s**	6 Aug	Alb. C	----	70	Gouzeacourt	1845	FTL	C&CA 20.4 RFC 6.8
4s***	6 Sep	Roland CII	A3431	70	Elincourt	1845	DES(F)	CR/RFC 6.9
	1917		Spad					
5	13 Jul	C	B1563	19	Lille	1338-1515	DES	ORB/RFC 13.7

TOTAL: 1 shared captured, 1 and 1 shared destroyed, 2 shared forced to land = 5.
*Observer: 2/Lt Ellison: shared with Capt Barrat/Lt Cleaver 3 Sqn, and Lt Clark/Lt Stammers. The crew OffzSt George Reimann/Lt Arthur Reinhardt of FA 202, were captured. **Observer: Lt Busk. Shared with Lt Mase/?, 2/Lt E.W. Blain/2/Lt Griffiths. ***Observer: Lt Busk: shared with Lt B.P.G. Beanlands/Lt Goode A1902, Lt Selby/Lt Thomas A394. This was Vzfw F. Fahlbusch/Lt H. Rosenkrantz of Kampfstaffel 1, a 5 victory ace crew, who were killed.
NB: Although Sanday's DSO citation in 1916 specifically states 4 destroyed, it is believed that his score was derived as above.

SANDERSON Ivan Couper Lieutenant 210

Sanderson was born on 21 December 1899, and came from Gerrards Cross, Buckinghamshire. He joined 210 Squadron on 9 May 1918 after only 40 hours flying time and took part in many joint successes. Between 23 June and 5 September he was involved in victories over 11 enemy scouts, but only four of these were claimed shot down by his guns alone, seven being shared with one or two other pilots. He was wounded in action on 17 September 1918.

	1918		Camel					
1	23 Jun	Pfalz DIII	B7153	210	E Zillebeke Lake	1215	DES	CR/ORB/?
2s*	26 Jun	Fokker DVII	B7153	210	1m W Armentieres	1920	DES	CR/RAF 26.6
3s**	26 Jun	Fokker DVII	B7153	210	1m W Armentieres	1920	OOC	CR/RAF 26.6

4s**	26 Jun	Fokker DVII	B7153	210	1m W Armentieres	1920	OOC	CR/RAF 26.6
5s**	26 Jun	Fokker DVII	B7153	210	1m W Armentieres	1920	OOC	CR/RAF 26.6
6s***	31 Jul	Fokker DVII	E1405	210	Nieuport-Dixmude	1115	OOC	CR/5 GP Comm
7s***	31 Jul	Fokker DVII	E1405	210	Wervicq	1825	OOC	CR/5 GP Comm
8	11 Aug	Fokker DVII	E1405	210	S E Dixmude	1845	DES	CR/5 GP Comm
9	12 Aug	Fokker DVII	E1405	210	Nieuport-Westende	0900	DES	CR/5 GP Comm
10s†	3 Sep	Fokker DVII	E1405	210	Menin-Courtrai	1830	DES	CR/5 GP Comm
11	5 Sep	Fokker DVII	E1405	210	S E Roulers	1730	DES	CR/5 GP Comm

TOTAL: 4 and 2 shared destroyed, 5 shared out of control = 11.
*Shared with Lt L.P. Coombes D3387, Lt K.R. Unger D9608. This was Obflgm Schonfelder of Jasta 7, who was killed. **Shared with Lt L.P. Coombes D3387, Lt K.R. Unger D9608. ***Shared with Capt L.P. Coombes D9673. '†Shared with Capt S.C. Joseph D3374, Lt C.W. Payton D9655, Lt J.A. Lewis D3351, Lt H.R. Hughes B7222.

SATCHELL Harold Leslie Captain 20

Seconded to the RFC from the Royal Warwickshire Regiment in June 1916, Satchell trained at Thetford before joining 20 Squadron in February 1917 with a total of 26 hours 50 minutes flying time in his logbook. He claimed his first victory on 26 April, flying an FE 2. His fourth victory, on 5 June, while flying with Lieutenant T.A.M.S. Lewis in place of his usual gunner, Lieutenant A.N. Jenks, was over an Albatros Scout flown by the German ace Leutnant Karl Schaefer of Jasta 28, victor of 30 combats. Promoted to flight commander during June, he added several more victories to his score by the end of July for a total of eight. He was posted to Home Establishment on 11 September 1917, where he formed 103 Squadron in 33 Wing, Southern Training Brigade; he later became Inspector of Instructors within this Brigade. He was demobilized in 1919 and lived in England until his death on 8 June 1983.

	1917		FE 2D					
1*	26 Apr	Alb. DIII	A5149	20	S W Roulers	1915	OOC	CR/RFC 26.4
2**	26 May	Alb. DIII	A6469	20	Comines	1030	DES	CR/RFC 26.5
3**	26 May	Alb. DIII	A6469	20	Comines	1040	OOC	CR/RFC 26.5
4***	5 Jun	Alb. DIII	A6469	20	Becelaere-Zandvoorde	1435	DES	CR/RFC 5.6
5**	29 Jun	Alb. DIII	A6431	20	Becelaere	1610	DES	CR/RFC 29.6
6**	2 Jul	Alb. DV	A6431	20	Comines-Houthem	1245	DES(F)	CR/RFC 2.7
7**	22 Jul	Alb. DV	A6512	20	Menin-Wervicq	1900	OOC	CR/RFC 22.7
8**	28 Jul	Alb. DV	A3	20	N E Tourcoing	1830	OOC	CR/RFC 28.7

TOTAL: 4 destroyed and 4 out of control = 8.
*Observer: 2/AM M. Todd. **Observer: Lt A.N. Jenks. ***Observer: Lt T.A.M.S. Lewis; this was Lt Karl Emil Schaefer, a 30 victory ace, and commander of Jasta 28.

SAUNDBY Robert Henry Magnus Spencer Captain 24, 41

Born on 26 April 1896, Robert Saundby was commissioned in the Royal Warwickshire Regiment in 1914, but was seconded to the RFC in January 1916. He went to France as one of the original pilots with 24 Squadron flying DH 2s in 1916, when he shot down one enemy aircraft on the last day of July, although he was slightly wounded. During the autumn he gained two further victories and was then posted to 41 Squadron on 26 January 1917, flying FE 8s. He shared in one victory, but was then rested, being attached to a Home Defence unit in England on 31 March 1917. On the night of 16/17 June 1917 he and Lieutenant L.P. Watkins shot down the Zeppelin L 48 near Theberton in Suffolk. This brought his score to five and he received the MC. Remaining in the RAF after the war, he served in Iraq and Aden, and was awarded the DFC in Egypt. By the early thirties he was a Wing Commander, while during World War II he served as Deputy Commander-in-Chief, Bomber Command. He retired in 1946 as Air Vice-Marshal Sir Robert Saundby, KCB, KBE, MC, DFC, AFC, and died on 25 September 1971.

	1916		DH 2					
1	31 Jul	Fokker E	5967	24	E Roisel	1015	OOC	CR/RFC 31.7
2s*	6 Sep	C	5928	24	E Flers	1830	DES(F)	CR/RFC 6.9
3	23 Nov	Alb. DII	5925	24	Bapaume	1350	OOC	CR/RFC 23.11
	1917		FE 8					
4s**	4 Mar	SS DI	6431	41	E Polygon Wood	1218	DES	CR/RFC 4.3
			DH 2					
5s***	17 Jun	Zeppelin	A5058	HD	Orfordness Theberton	0330	DES	CR/OH

TOTAL: 1 shared Zeppelin, 2 shared destroyed, 2 out of control = 5.
*Shared with Capt J.O. Andrews 5998. **Shared with 2/Lt A.Fraser 7622. ***Shared with 2/Lt F.D. Holder/Sgt S. Ashby FE 2B B401, 2/Lt L.P. Watkins BE 12 of 37 Sqn. The Zeppelin was L48.

SAUNDERS Alfred William Captain 60

Saunders served with the Royal Field Artillery in the Dardanelles campaign before joining the RFC in September 1917. He was posted to 60 Squadron in October, and in July 1918 took command of 'A' Flight. By the time he left the squadron in August, he had claimed twelve victories and received the DFC for his actions on 2 July.

	1918		SE 5A					
1	10 May	Pfalz DIII	C5450	60	Bapaume-Peronne	1735	DES	CR/RAF 10.5
2	16 May	Alb. DV	C5450	60	Beaulencourt	1615	DES	CR/RAF 16.5
3s*	23 May	Alb. DV	B137	60	Fricourt	0550	DES	CR/RAF 23.5
4s*	9 Jun	Hannover C	B137	60	Arras	1045	DES(F)	CR/RAF 9.6
5s*	9 Jun	Hannover C	B137	60	Arras	1050	OOC	CR/SR/?
6	2 Jul	Pfalz DIII	E1279	60	Villers-Brettoneaux	1045	DES	CR/RAF 2.7
7**	2 Jul	Pfalz DIII	E1279	60	Bois de Pierret	1050	DES	CR/RAF 2.7
8**	2 Jul	Pfalz DIII	E1279	60	Bois de Pierret	1050	DES	CR/RAF 2.7
9	1 Aug	Fokker DVII	E3916	60	Bapaume	2020	OOC	CR/SR/?
10	8 Aug	C	E3916	60	Chaulnes	1315	OOC	CR/SR/?
11	9 Aug	Fokker DVII	E3916	60	Chaulnes	1545	DES	CR/RAF 9.8
12	9 Aug	Fokker DVII	E3916	60	Nesle	1547	DES	CR/SR/?

TOTAL: 7 and 2 shared destroyed, 2 and 1 shared out of control = 12.
*Shared with Capt J.D. Belgrave D5988. **The above two Pfalz collided.

SAUNDERS Franklin Geoffrey Captain 47, 150

After initial service with the 7th Dragoon Guards, he transferred to the RFC in May 1916, serving in Salonica during 1917. With Captain Murlis-Green he was one of the two most successful British pilots in the area during that year. Flying the generally unsuccessful BE 12, he claimed three victories during the spring, was promoted to flight commander, and claimed a fourth success in the summer. After his second victory on 18 March 1917, he was shot-up and forced to land, but was unhurt. His aircraft was sufficiently repaired for him to gain his third victory in it two days later. Early in 1918 SE 5As became available, and flying these he added four more victories during January and February, to bring his score to eight. He was awarded an MC and Bar. In 1939 he rejoined the RAF as a Flight Lieutenant.

	1917		BE 12					
1s*	14 Jan	Alb. C	6603	47	Lahana	1115	CAPT	CR/Bg SUM
2	18 Mar	Fried G	6675	47	Karasouli	1750	OOC	CR/Bg SUM
3	20 Mar	Alb. C	6675	47	W Davista	1230	DES	CR/Bg SUM
4	25 Jun	Alb. DIII	6600	47	----	----	DES	SR/?
			SE 5A					
5	22 Jan	DFW. C	B28	150	Porna	1350	CAPT	CR/Bg SUM
6s**	31 Jan	Rumpler C	B28	150	2m N N E Kajendra	1220	DES	CR/Bg SUM
7s**	5 Feb	Alb. DIII	B28	150	Vernak Farm	1510	OOC	CR/Bg SUM
8	5 Feb	DFW. C	B28	150	N W Topoljani	1715	DES(F)	CR/Bg SUM

TOTAL: 1 and 1 shared captured, 3 and 1 shared destroyed, 1 and 1 shared out of control = 8.
*Shared with Capt G.W. Murlis-Green 6601. Two crew were captured. **Shared with Lt G.E. Gibbs B613.

SAUNDERS Hugh William Lumsden Captain 84

Born in South Africa on 24 August 1894, Hugh Saunders served in the Witwatersrand Rifles and the South African Horse, receiving the MM and becoming known to his friends as 'Dingbat'. Joining the RFC, he received his 'wings' and was posted to 84 Squadron in November 1917. In April the following year he was promoted to command 'C' Flight, which he led until August. By this time he had been awarded the MC and DFC, having claimed 15 victories, including two kite balloons. Remaining in the RAF, he again served in 84 Squadron in Iraq from 1920 to 1923, and was awarded a Bar to his DFC. He then held various staff positions until he took command of 45 Squadron in Egypt from 1931-34. During World War II he held high positions at home and abroad, and in 1947 was Commander-in-Chief, Bomber Command. He retired in 1953 as Marshal of the RAF Sir Hugh Saunders, GCB, KBE, MC, DFC, MM; and died on 8 May 1987.

	1918		SE 5A					
1	25 Jan	C	C9500	84	Malincourt	1440	OOC	CR/SR/?
2	18 Feb	LVG. C	C9500	84	Beaurevoir	1100	OOC	CR/RFC 18.2
3	3 Apr	Pfalz DIII	C1794	84	Rosieres	1950	DES	CR/RAF 3.4
4s*	6 Apr	LVG. C	C1794	84	N Hangard	1120	CAPT	CR/RAF 6.4
5	25 Apr	Pfalz DIII	B8403	84	Wiencourt	1700	OOC	CR/RAF 25.4
6s**	29 Apr	DFW. C	B8403	84	S E St Gratien	1900	CAPT	CR/RAF 29.4
7	16 May	Alb. DV	B8403	84	Chipilly	0745	OOC	CR/RAF 16.5
8***	16 May	Fokker DrI	B8403	84	S Herleville	1805	OOC	CR/RAF 16.5

9	17 May	Alb. DV	B8403	84	S E Hangest	1330	DES	CR/RAF 17.5
10	28 May	Alb. DV	B8403	84	S Wiencourt	0920	OOC	CR/SR/?
11	28 Jun	LVG. C	B6496	84	Fricourt	0650	DES	CR/RAF 28.6
12	16 Jul	Balloon	B6496	84	S W Proyart	1345	DES	CR/RAF 16.7
13†	20 Jul	Fokker DVII	B6496	84	Morcourt	1015	DES	CR/RAF 20.7
14	22 Jul	Balloon	B6496	84	N Fricourt	1345	DES	CR/RAF 22.7
15	29 Jul	LVG. C	B6496	84	N Bois de Tailles	0800	DES	CR/RAF 29.7

TOTAL: 2 balloons, 2 shared captured, 5 destroyed, 6 out of control = 15.
*Shared with Lt J.F. Larson C1772, Lt C.L. Stubbs C9519, Lt H.O. MacDonald C1694. The crew of Uffz Drexler/Lt Kalfeken of FAA 205 were captured. **Shared with Lt C.F. Falkenberg and Lt J. Todd C1670/Lt V.C. Chapman B7471 of 70 Sqn. The crew, Uffz Krug/Lt Adler of FAA 218 were captured. ***84 made two claims; Vzfw Schmutzler of Jasta 4 was killed †This was Werner Meyer of Jasta 34, who was killed.

SAVAGE Douglas Alfred Lieutenant 62

After service with the trench mortars, Savage transferred to the RFC and joined 62 Squadron in 1918, making his first claim on 26 March. He claimed two on 12 April and two more on 21st. After his sixth victory on 19 May, he was shot-up and force landed in B1336. In June he was posted to Home Establishment, having been awarded an MC.

	1918		Bristol					
1*	26 Mar	EA	----	62	----	----	OOC	CR/BG WD
2*	12 Apr	Pfalz DIII	B1234	62	E Estaires	1420	OOC	CR/RAF 12.4
3*	12 Apr	Alb. DV	B1234	62	Aubers	1515	OOC	CR/SR/?
4*	21 Apr	Alb. DV	B1234	62	3m W Lille	0945	DES	CR/RAF 21.4
5*	21 Apr	Pfalz DIII	B1234	62	W Lille	0950	DES	CR/RAF 21.4
6**	19 May	Alb. DV	B1336	62	Bray	1030	OOC	CR/RAF 19.5
7***	2 Jun	Fokker DrI	C953	62	S Pozieres	1945	OOC	CR/SR/?

TOTAL: 2 destroyed, 5 out of control = 7.
*Observer: 2/Lt L.M. Thompson. **Observer: Lt E.W. Collis. Probably Lt Karl Bauernfeind of Jasta 34, who was wounded. ***Observer: Sgt W.N. Holmes

SAWYER Cyril Hayes Lieutenant 46

Born on 5 April 1899, in Surbiton, Surrey, he joined the RFC on 29 August 1917 and was posted to 46 Squadron on 11 May 1918. He claimed six victories during August and September, five of which were shared.

	1918		Camel					
1	3 Aug	Fokker DVII	B9253	46	E Lens	1835	DES	CR/RAF 3.8
2s*	16 Sep	Fokker DVII	D6693	46	Cambrai	1815	DES(F)	CR/RAF 16.9
3s**	17 Sep	Fokker DVII	D6693	46	Cambrai	1200	OOC	CR/V BG WD
4s**	17 Sep	Fokker DVII	D6693	46	Cambrai	1200	OOC	CR/V BG WD
5s***	29 Sep	Fokker DVII	D9457	46	S Beaurevoir Rd	1640	OOC	CR/V BG WD
6s†	2 Oct	Fokker DVII	F1974	46	Morcourt	1030	OOC	CR/V BG WD

TOTAL: 1 and 1 shared destroyed, 4 shared out of control = 6.
*Shared with Capt D.R. MacLaren F2137, Lt R. Viall F1971. **Shared with Capt D.R. MacLaren F2137, 2/Lt R.D. Gilpin-Brown F5950, Lt P.M. Tudhope F1966, Capt C.W. Odell D1942, 2/Lt L.S. Skerrington. ***Shared with Capt D.R. MacLaren F2137. †Shared with Capt D.R. MacLaren F2137, Capt J.L. Leith H7279.

SCANDRETT Harry Lieutenant 25, 11

Harry Scandrett was born in 1892, and at the outbreak of war was living in Strawberry Hill, South London, with his wife. He served initially with 25 Squadron as an observer on FE 2Bs, claiming one shared victory. Re-training as a pilot, he was posted to 11 Squadron in early summer 1917, where he was to add six further victories whilst flying F2Bs.

	1916		FE 2B					
1s*	17 Nov	EA	7024	25	Vitry	1930	DES	CR/RFC 17.11
	1917		Bristol					
2**	7 Jul	Alb. DV	A7147	11	N W Cambrai	1440	OOC	CR/RFC 7.7
3***	17 Jul	Alb. DV	A7156	11	5m E Bullecourt	1915	OOC	CR/RFC 17.7
4†	5 Aug	Alb. DV	A7156	11	Queant-Pronville	1915	OOC	CR/RFC 5.8
5s††	12 Sep	Alb. DV	----	11	Havrincourt	1905	OOC	CR/RFC 12.9
6†††	30 Sep	Alb. DV	A7231	11	Etaing	1550	OOC	CR/RFC 30.9
7†††	30 Sep	Alb. DV	A7231	11	Etaing	1600	OOC	CR/RFC 30.9

TOTAL: 1 destroyed, 4 and 2 shared out of control = 7.
*Pilot: Lt C. Dunlop; shared with Capt R. Chadwick/Lt W.G. Meggitt 7022, 2/Lt H.L. Chadwick/2/Lt C.J. Butler 7025, 2/Lt D.S. Johnson/Lt I. Heald 6990, Sgt J.H.R. Green/Cpl A.G. Bower 4877. **Observer: Cpl S.A. Mee. ***Observer: Cpl J.W. Ross. †Observer: Lt F.A. Herron. ††Observer: Lt G. Watson; shared with Capt E.H.G. Sharples/2/Lt S. Sutcliffe. †††Observer: Lt G. Watson.

SCHOLTE Owen John Fredrick Captain 18, 51, 48, 60

Born in Hampstead, London, in 1894, he became a dispatch rider with the Royal Engineers on the outbreak of war, before being commissioned in the Bedfordshire Regiment; he then transferred to the RFC in 1915. He flew as an observer with 18 Squadron on Vickers Fighters, and during one fight on 21 February 1916 his machine was shot down in flames. His pilot, Lieutenant M. Henderson, had his leg almost severed by a shell, but was then trapped in the wreckage by his injured limb. Scholte was forced to complete the amputation of the damaged leg in order to free Henderson and get him clear of the flames. Following pilot training, Scholte flew in 51(Home Defence) Squadron, before being posted as one of the original members of 48 Squadron in 1917. While flying Bristol Fighters on reconnaissance and escort missions with this unit, he claimed six victories and was awarded an MC. On 13 September he went up at night after a Gotha which he hit and damaged, seeing it go down with one engine stopped. In 1918, after a period in England, he went on 60 Squadron as a flight commander, flying SE 5As. On these he claimed two more enemy aircraft shot down before he was killed in a motor accident on 30 July while returning from a party at a neighbouring squadron. His brother, Llewelyn, was an engineer officer with the RFC and RAF, who became a Lieutenant Colonel, OBE.

	1917		Bristol					
1*	2 May	Alb. DIII	A3347	48	Biache-Vitry	1945	DES(F)	CR/RFC 2.5
2*	2 May	Alb. DIII	A3347	48	Biache-Vitry	1945	OOC	CR/III BG WD
3**	29 Jun	Alb. DIII	A7118	48	Brebieres	2000	OOC	CR/RFC 30.6
4**	6 Jul	Alb. DV	A7118	48	E Cambrai	0930	DES	CR/RFC 6.7
5***	13 Jul	Alb. DV	A7155	48	Slype	0940	OOC	CR/RFC WD
6†	5 Sep	Alb. DV	A7221	48	Mariakerke	1200	OOC	CR/SR/?
	1918		SE 5A					
7	15 May	Rumpler C	C5385	60	Lamotte	1220	DES(F)	CR/RAF 15.5
8	19 May	Hanover C	C5385	60	Arras	1010	DES(F)	CR/RAF 19.5

TOTAL: 4 destroyed, 4 out of control = 8.
*Observer: 2 AM F.W. Dame. **Observer: 2/Lt A.W. Merchant. ***Observer: Lt A.D. Light. †Observer: 2/Lt G.R. Horsfall.

SCOTT Alan John Lance Lieutenant Colonel 43, 60

Born on 29 August 1884, 'Jack' Scott was a New Zealander and a former barrister who initially joined the Sussex Yeomanry, and subsequently transferred to the RFC. During his training he had a serious crash which resulted in two broken legs, but he recovered, although he had to walk with sticks and often had to be helped into the cockpit. In 1917 he flew 1½ Strutters with 43 Squadron and later that year was given command of 60 Squadron. He was never a good pilot, but was a most determined air fighter; he had the habit of flying off alone over the lines, and often got into trouble. Indeed on 28 May 1917 in Nieuport B1575, he was forced to land near Monchy-le-Preux by Leutnant Karl Allmenröder of Jasta 11 as the latter's 21st victory. Scott decorated his office with pieces of his own machines which had been shot-up, but nonetheless received credit for five victories and received the MC before being wounded in the left arm on 10 July. Sent to 11 Wing Headquarters, he later took command of the Central Flying School, a post which he held until the end of the war, receiving an AFC and being promoted to Lieutenant Colonel. He wrote a history of 60 Squadron, but in 1919 he died, a victim of the influenza epidemic.

	1917		Nieuport					
1s*	31 Mar	Alb. DIII	A6477	60	Heninel	0730	DES	CR/RFC 31.3
2	8 Apr	Alb. CV	A6647	60	Douai-Fouquieres	0930	DES	CR/RFC 8.4
3	2 May	Alb. DIII	B1575	60	Eterpigny	1630	DES	CR/RFC 2.5
4**	5 Jun	Alb. DIII	B1575	60	Monchy	2035	CAPT	CR/RFC 5.6
5	10 Jul	Alb. DIII	B1575	60	Quiery la Motte	2010	DES(F)	CR/SR/?

TOTAL: 1 captured, 4 destroyed = 5.
*Shared with Capt C.T. Black A6770. **This was Lt Oscar von Neudorff, of Jasta 3, who was killed.

SCOTT Maurice Douglas Guest Captain 18, 54, 46

Born on 13 November 1895, Maurice Scott served with the 3rd Loyal North Lancashires before transferring to the RFC in February 1916. He became an observer with 18 Squadron, where with his pilot, Lieutenant Findley, he shot down and captured a two-seater as one of the unit's first claims. Subsequently trained as a pilot, he flew Sopwith Pups in 54 Squadron during spring 1917, claiming four victories with this unit. He was then posted to 46 Squadron as a flight commander in August, this unit also flying Pups; during September he claimed seven more victories. He was awarded an MC, gazetted on 27 October 1917, and on 8th of that month had been posted to Home Establishment. On 17 March 1918 he was killed in a flying accident at Shoreham.

	1916		Vickers FB5					
1s*	3 Apr	C	2882	18	Souchez	1015	CAPT	CR/RFC 3.4

	1917		Pup					
2s**	5 Apr	Balloon	----	54	Gouy	----	DES	RFC 5.4
3	9 May	C	A7330	54	Seranvillers	1530	DES	CR/RFC 9.5
4s***	11 May	C	A6165	54	Walincourt	1840	DES	CR/RFC 11.5
5s†	1 Jun	Alb. DIII	A7330	54	Honnecourt	1135	OOC	CR/RFC 1.6
6s††	4 Sep	Alb. C	B1843	46	S Scarpe	0930	OOC	CR/11 WS
7s†††	11 Sep	C	B2191	46	S Scarpe	1055	OOC	CR/RFC 11.9
8s‡	21 Sep	C	B2191	46	S Scarpe	0820	OOC	CR/RFC 21.9
9	22 Sep	Alb. DV	B2191	46	Sailly en Ostrevent	1030	OOC	CR/III BG WD
10s‡‡	24 Sep	DFW. C	B2191	46	S E Honnecourt	1030	DES	CR/RFC 24.9
11	30 Sep	Alb. DV	B2191	46	Vitry	1630	OOC	CR/RFC 1.10
12	30 Sep	Alb. DV	B2191	46	Vitry	1636	OOC	CR/RFC 1.10

TOTAL: 1 shared balloon, 1 shared captured, 1 and 2 shared destroyed, 3 and 4 shared out of control = 12.
*Pilot: Lt Findlay; shared with Capt Rawcliffe/Sgt Woodfield. The two crew were killed. **Shared with Capt R.G.H. Pixley, Capt F.N. Hudson, 2/Lt R.M. Charley. ***Shared with Capt W.V. Strugnell A6168, Lt O.M. Sutton A6183, Major C.E. Sutcliffe A7306, Lt E.J.Y. Grevelinck A7330, Lt M.B. Cole A640. †Shared with Lt O.M. Sutton A6183. ††Shared with Lt C.W. Odell B1842, Lt E. Armitage B1837, 2/Lt C. Courtneidge B1802, Lt E.Y. Hughes B6188. †††Shared with Lt A.G. Lee B1777, Lt E.Y Hughes, Lt E Armitage. ‡Shared with Lt A.G. Lee B1777, Lt E.Y. Hughes A6188. ‡‡Shared with Lt E. Armitage B1829, Lt C.W. Odell B1802, 2/Lt C. Courtneidge B1837.

SEABROOK Joseph Powell Captain 60, 8, 11

After training, he was posted to 60 Squadron on 27 November 1916. After one week, he was sent to 8 Squadron to fly BE 2s, but on 20 January 1918 he began a second tour with 11 Squadron on Bristol Fighters, where he was later promoted to the rank of Captain. He returned to Home Establishment on 12 September 1918.

	1918		Bristol					
1*	12 Mar	Alb. DV	A7153	11	S E Cambrai	1155	DES	CR/RFC 12.3
2**	22 Mar	Alb. DV	B1194	11	Queant	1835	DES(F)	CR/RFC 22.3
3*	15 May	Pfalz DIII	C867	11	S E Albert	1722	OOC	CR/RAF 15.5
4*	16 May	C	C867	11	E Cambrai	0635	DES	CR/RAF 16.5
5s***	9 Aug	Fokker DVII	----	11	Bray-Peronne	0745	OOC	CR/?

TOTAL: 3 destroyed, 1 and 1 shared out of control = 5.
*Observer: 2/Lt C. Wrigglesworth. **Observer: Lt A. Reeve. ***Observer: 2/Lt C. Wrigglesworth; shared with Lt R.K. Harrison/2/Lt L.W. King C 878.

SELLARS Herbert Whiteley Lieutenant 25, 11

Born in 1896 in Westwork, Hoylake, Cheshire, Sellars was commissioned in the RFC in June 1916, joining 25 Squadron on 2 August but was severely injured in a crash on 16 September. On recovery, he re-joined 25 Squadron in July 1917, serving for three months, but was then posted to 11 Squadron on 19 October. He claimed six victories in March 1918 and a seventh in April, and was awarded the MC. His usual observer was Lieutenant C.C. Robson, and it was this officer who, while flying with Sellars on 21 March, shot down an Albatros Scout flown by Leutnant Ludwig Hanstein, leader of Jasta 35, and victor of 16 combats. On 15 May however, this team was shot down over Bouchou in C845 by either OffizierStv Josef Mai of Jasta 5 or Leutnant Hans Kirschtein of Jasta 6, Sellars being killed and Robson taken prisoner.

	1918		Bristol					
1*	12 Mar	LVG. CVI	C4673	11	Doignies	1440	CAPT	CR/RFC 12.3
2**	13 Mar	Alb. DV	C4673	11	Oisy	1400	OOC	CR/RFC 13.3
3**	15 Mar	Alb. DV	C4673	11	Rumilly	1115	OOC	CR/RFC 15.3
4**	18 Mar	Alb. DV	C4673	11	N St Quentin	1100	OOC	CR/RFC 18.3
5***	21 Mar	Alb. C	C4673	11	Morchies	1615	DES	CR/RFC 21.3
6†	21 Mar	Alb. DV	C4673	11	Morchies	1615	DES(F)	CR/RFC 21.3
7**	2 Apr	Fokker DrI	C4673	11	S E Albert	1820	OOC	CR/RFC 2.4
8s††	15 May	Fokker DrI	C4673	11	Mametz	1720	OOC	CR/RFC 15.5

TOTAL: 1 captured, 2 destroyed, 4 and 1 shared out of control = 8.
*Observer: Lt C.C. Robson; the crew were Vzfw R. Mischke/Lt H. Reissig of FA 263. **Observer: Lt C.C. Robson. ***Observer: Lt C.C. Robson. Possibly Gefr J. Voight/Lt J. Szejkowski of FAA 228. †Observer: Lt C.C. Robson. This was Lt Ludwig Hanstein, an ace and commander of Jasta 35b. ††Observer: Lt C.C. Robson; shared with Capt J.V. Aspinall/Lt de la Cour.

SETH-SMITH Kenneth Gordon Lieutenant 70

Joining 70 Squadron in France to fly as an observer in Sopwith 1½ Strutters, Lieutenant Seth-Smith gained his first victory on 4 May 1917. Remustering as a pilot, he subsequently rejoined the unit later in the year, by which time it had been re-equipped with Camels. With these fighters, he claimed two victories in December, two in January 1918, and two the following March, including a share in the destruction of a balloon. He was wounded in action on 23 March. During World War II he was a test pilot with Hawker Aviation, and was killed on 11 August 1942 when he crashed in one of the prototype Typhoon fighters.

	1917		Strutter					
1*	4 May	Alb. DIII	A8211	70	E Tournai	1025	OOC	CR/RFC 4.5
			Camel					
2	12 Dec	Alb. DV	B2499	70	Westroosebeke	0930	OOC	CR/RFC 12.12
3s**	27 Dec	Alb. C	B2438	70	Zarren	1050	DES	CR/RFC 27.12
	1918							
4	22 Jan	Alb. DV	B2438	70	Oostnieuwkerke	1035	OOC	CR/RFC 22.1
5	29 Jan	Alb. DV	B2438	70	Moorslede	1255	OOC	CR/RFC 29.1
6s***	11 Mar	Balloon	----	70	Menin	1230	DES	CR/RFC 11.3
7	12 Mar	Alb. DV	B7474	70	N Wervicq	1250	OOC	CR/RFC 12.3

TOTAL: 1 shared balloon, 1 shared destroyed, 5 out of control = 7.
*Pilot: Sgt Skinner. **Shared with 2/Lt F.G. Quigley, 2/Lt F.H. Hobson B6251. ***Shared with Capt F.G. Quigley, Lt A. Koch, Lt W.M. Carlaw.

SHARMAN John Edward Flight Commander 3W, 10(N)

Born on 11 September 1892, in Oak Lake, Manitoba, Canada, John Sharman joined the RNAS on 3 February 1916 and served from the middle of that year in 3 Wing, flying Sopwith 1½ Strutters on at least 29 raids during which he claimed one victory. The Wing was disbanded in April and from 1 May he was one of the pilots forming the nucleus of 10(N) Squadron with Sopwith Triplanes; he was assigned to Raymond Collishaw's flight. During June and July he claimed seven victories, becoming a flight commander on 9 July, but on 22nd of that month he was shot down and killed, probably by Flak Batterie 503. In the past he has been recorded as a victim of Oberleutnant Willi Reinhardt of Jasta 11, but this was not in fact the case. He was awarded both a DSC on 12 May and a Bar, announced posthumously on 11 August, as well as a Croix de Guerre from the French.

	1917		Strutter					
1	25 Feb	Fokker E	----	3W	Burbach	----	OOC	AIR 1/149
			Triplane					
2	6 Jun	Alb. DIII	N6307	10N	Polygon Wood	1110	OOC	CR/RFC 6.6
3	7 Jun	Alb. DIII	N6307	10N	Moorslede	0915	DES	CR/RFC 7.6
4	7 Jun	Alb. DIII	N6307	10N	Moorslede	0917	OOC	CR/RFC 7.6
5	14 Jun	Alb. DIII	N6307	10N	Zonnebeke	1925	OOC	CR/RFC 14.6
6s*	15 Jun	C	N6307	10N	St Julien-Houthem	1050	OOC	CR/RFC 15.6
7	24 Jun	Alb. DV	N6307	10N	Zonnebeke	0810	DES	CR/RFC 24.6
8	12 Jul	Alb. DV	N6307	10N	Polygon Wood	1215	DES	CR/RFC 12.7

TOTAL: 3 destroyed, 4 and 1 shared out of contol = 8
*Shared with F/Lt R. Collishaw N5492.

SHARPE Frank Lieutenant 1

Born in 1896, Frank Sharpe was a Londoner from Eversham. After service with the Notts and Derby Regiment, he transferred to the RFC and was posted to 1 Squadron as an observer in June 1916. On 26 November he was sent back to England for pilot training, rejoining the unit on 10 April 1917. He accounted for four aircraft and a balloon, and drove down a second balloon in a deflated condition. Out after balloons again on 9 June, he was shot down in Nieuport Scout B3481 by Oberleutnant Kurt von Döring of Jasta 4, and became a prisoner.

	1917		Nieuport					
1s*	1 May	Alb. DIII	B1550	1	Ypres-Roulers	1200	DES(F)	CR/RFC 1.5
2	26 May	Alb. DV	B1550	1	Lompret	1040	OOC	CR/RFC 26.5
3	4 Jun	Rumpler C	B1550	1	Perenchies	2040	DES	CR/RFC 4.6
4s**	7 Jun	Alb. DV	B3481	1	Zandvoorde	0940	DES	CR/RFC 7.6
5	7 Jun	Balloon	B3481	1	Quesnoy	1325	DES	CR/ORB/11 WS

TOTAL: 1 balloon, 1 and 2 shared destroyed, 1 out of control = 5.
*Shared with 2/Lt E.S.T. Cole B1508. **Shared with Lt L.F. Jenkin B1547.

SHARPE, Thomas Sydney Captain 24, 73

Following service with the Gloucestershire Regiment, Tommy Sharpe joined the RFC and flew with 24 Squadron from May to July 1916. In 1918 he became a flight commander in 73 Squadron; flying Camels with this unit he claimed six victories during March, and was later awarded the DFC. By that time however, he was a prisoner of war, having been shot down and wounded on 27 March, probably by Leutnant Hans Kirschtein of Jasta 6 whilst in C6733 near Albert.

	1918		Camel					
1	11 Mar	Fokker DrI	B5627	73	3m S W Caudry	1355	DES	CR/RFC 11.3
2	22 Mar	Alb. DV	C1619	73	Douchy	1430	DES	CR/RFC 23.3
3	22 Mar	LVG. C	C1619	73	Roisel	1510	DES	CR/RFC 23.3
4	22 Mar	LVG. C	C1619	73	N Roisel	1510	DES	CR/RFC 23.3
5	24 Mar	Alb. DV	C1619	73	1m N W St Simon	0945	DES	CR/RFC 24.3
6	24 Mar	Alb. DV	C1619	73	Vermand	1030	DES	CR/RFC 24.3

TOTAL: 6 destroyed = 6.

SHEPHERD Alfred Seymour Captain 29

Born in New South Wales, Australia, on 13 April 1893, he enlisted on 8 September 1915, serving as an officer with the 30th and 46th Battalions of the Australian Infantry before transferring to the RFC on 23 October 1916. On 25 April 1917 he joined 29 Squadron, flying Nieuport Scouts, and in just over two months claimed 10 victories, receiving an MC. On one occasion he was attacking a balloon when he came under fire from a German rocket battery; he at once dived down and shot up the site, scattering the enemy gunners. He was made a flight commander on 13 July, and was awarded the DSO on 15th. Five days later however, he was shot down and killed in B1504 during the late evening, probably falling victim to Leutnant Kurt von Döring of Jasta 4 at Zandvoort.

	1917		Nieuport					
1	11 May	Alb. DIII	A6787	29	Sailly	1015	DES	CR/RFC 11.5
2	20 May	Alb. DIII	B1504	29	E Douai	1245	DES(F)	CR/RFC 20.5
3	24 May	Alb. DIII	B1504	29	Vitry	0800	DES(F)	CR/RFC 24.5
4	1 Jun	Alb. DIII	B1504	29	Brebieres	0515	OOC	CR/RFC 1.6
5	21 Jun	Alb. DIII	B1504	29	Ecourt St Quentin	0800	OOC	CR/RFC 21.6
6	24 Jun	Alb. DIII	B1504	29	Douai	1900	OOC	CR/RFC 25.6
7	27 Jun	Alb. DIII	B1504	29	Bullecourt	1920	DES	CR/RFC 27.6
8	27 Jun	Alb. DIII	B1504	29	Brebieres	1925	OOC	CR/RFC 27.6
9	29 Jun	Alb. DIII	B1504	29	Bullecourt	0720	OOC	CR/RFC 29.6
10	29 Jun	Alb. DIII	B1504	29	Henin-Lietard	0830	OOC	CR/RFC 29.6

TOTAL: 4 destroyed, 6 out of control = 10.

SHIELDS William Ernest Captain 41

Shields was born in Lipton, Saskatchewan, Canada, on 15 October 1892. After joining the RFC he was posted to France on 20 March 1918, to fly with 41 Squadron. Although rather overshadowed by two illustrious countrymen of his in the squadron at this time (Claxton and McCall), Bill Shields quietly built up a steady score, being awarded a DFC and Bar and becoming a flight commander in September. His best day was 3 July 1918, when he claimed three Pfalz DIIIs; his score of 24 included five balloons. Shields was killed in a flying accident in 1920 when serving with the Canadian Air Force.

	1918		SE 5A					
1	12 Jun	Alb. DV	D6023	41	Guerbigny	1300	OOC	CR/SR/?
2	28 Jun	C	D5984	41	N Lignieres	1230	DES	CR/RAF 28.6
3	29 Jun	Pfalz DIII	D5984	41	N W Fouquescourt	1930	DES	CR/RAF 29.6
4	29 Jun	Pfalz DIII	D5984	41	E Fouquescourt	1932	OOC	CR/SR/RAF WD
5	3 Jul	Pfalz DIII	D3567	41	E Villers Brettoneaux	1910	OOC	CR/SR/?
6	3 Jul	Pfalz DIII	D3567	41	E Villers Brettoneaux	1912	DES	CR/RAF 3.7
7	3 Jul	Pfalz DIII	D3567	41	Villers Brettoneaux	1915	DES	CR/RAF 3.7
8	5 Jul	Pfalz DIII	D3567	41	E Hangest	0710	DES	CR/RAF 5.7
9	31 Jul	Pfalz DIII	D3984	41	Guerbigny	1845	OOC	CR/SR/?
10	3 Aug	Halb. C	D5984	41	E Proyart	1935	OOC	CR/SR/?
11	11 Aug	DFW. C	D5984	41	N E Proyart	1455	DES(F)	CR/RAF 11.8
12	17 Aug	Pfalz DIII	----	41	E Deulemont	0915	DES	CR/RAF 17.8
13	31 Aug	Fokker DVII	E1300	41	N E Armentieres	1545	OOC	CR/SR/?
14	15 Sep	Fokker DVII	C1912	41	Houthem	1645	OOC	CR/SR/?
15*	21 Sep	Fokker DVII	C1912	41	Don	1810	DES	CR/RAF 21.9
16*	21 Sep	Fokker DVII	C1912	41	Don	1810	OOC	CR/SR/?
17	24 Sep	Fokker DVII	C1912	41	W Comines	1715	DES(F)	CR/RAF 24.9
18	29 Sep	Balloon	C1912	41	S E Comines	1240	DES	CR/RAF 29.9

19	27 Oct	Balloon	C1912	41	Mellen	0940	DES	CR/RAF 27.10
20	28 Oct	Balloon	C1912	41	Audenarde	0810	DES	CR/RAF 28.10
21	30 Oct	Fokker DVII	C1912	41	E Tournai	1045	DES	CR/RAF 30.10
22	30 Oct	DFW. C	C1912	41	Mansart Station	1135	DES	CR/RAF 30.10
23	4 Nov	Balloon	C1912	41	S Gaillaix	1120	DES	CR/RAF 4.11
24s**	4 Nov	Balloon	C1912	41	Pipaix	1125	DES	CR/RAF 4.11

TOTAL: 4 and 1 shared balloons, 11 destroyed, 8 out of control = 24.
*The above two aircraft collided. **Shared with Lt M.P. MacLeod H683.

SHOEMAKER Harold Goodman 1st Lieutenant 74, 17US

A member of the USAS attached to the RAF for training and experience, he was posted to 74 Squadron on 3 July 1918, making his first claim on 30th of that month. His total had risen to five by the end of August, but he was then posted to the 17th Aero Squadron, USAS, flying Camels with the British 65th Wing. Here he was involved in a mid-air collision over the German lines on 6 October, and was killed in F6194. He was buried at Bony with 1st Lieutenant Glenn D. Wicks with whom he had collided.

	1918		SE 5A					
1s*	30 Jul	Rumpler C	E1389	74	Cassell-Ypres	1210	DES(F)	CR/RAF 30.7
2s**	16 Aug	Rumpler C	E4685	74	E Kemmel Hill	1250	DES(F)	CR/RAF 16.8
3s***	19 Aug	DFW. C	----	74	Ploegsteert Wood	2010	DES	CR/RAF 19.8
4	23 Aug	Fokker DVII	----	74	Passchendaele	1925	OOC	CR/11 WS
5	25 Aug	Fokker DVII	----	74	Warneton	1845	DES	CR/RAF 25.8

TOTAL: 1 and 3 shared destroyed, 1 out of control = 5.
*Shared with Capt J.I.T. Jones D6895, Lt G.W.G. Gauld. **Shared with Lt F.S. Gordon D3438. ***Shared with Lt G.R. Hicks.

SHOOK Alexander MacDonald Major 4(N), 204

Born on 2 December 1888, in Tioga, Ontario, Canada, Shook joined the RNAS, serving throughout 1916 with 5 Wing on Sopwith 1½ Strutters. He joined 4(N) Squadron on its formation in April 1917 on Pups, becoming a flight commander during the following month, when this unit received the first Camels. To him went the honour of claiming this aircraft's first victories of the war on 5 June 1917. He was awarded a DSC on 1 August. He was wounded in action on 21 October, but returned to the squadron on 4 January 1918, remaining until 15 April. He was awarded a DSO and a Croix de Guerre during 1918, and after leaving the squadron he rose to the rank of Major in the new RAF, where he was awarded an AFC. On 2 October 1918 his younger brother was lost in action whilst flying Camels with 46 Squadron, and was taken prisoner.

	1917		Pup					
1	24 Apr	Fokker DII	N6200	4N	Ghistelles	1010	OOC	CR/RNAS24.4
2s*	9 May	C	N6200	4N	.5m S E Ghistelles	1715	DES	CR/DOS/DL/?
3	12 May	Seaplane	N6200	4N	off Zeebrugge	0730	DES	CR/DOS/DL/?
			Camel					
4	5 Jun	Alb. DIII	N6347	4N	Ostend	1900	DES	CR/DOS/DL/?
5	5 Jun	C	N6357	4N	Ostend	1910	OOC	CR/DOS/DL/?
6	4 Jul	Gotha G	N6363	4N	30m N W Ostend	0830	DES(F)	CR/RNAS 4.7
7	18 Aug	Alb. DV	N6363	4N	Ghistelles	0910	DES	CR/RNAS 18.8
8	21 Oct	Alb. DIII	N6363	4N	S Ghistelles	1025	OOC	CR/RNAS 21.10
	1918							
9	11 Mar	Alb. DV	B6300	4N	Keyem	1640	OOC	CR/RNAS11.3
10**	22 Mar	Alb. DV	B6300	4N	Slype	1400	DES(F)	CR/RNAS 22.3
11	22 Mar	Alb. DV	B6300	4N	Slype	1400	DES(F)	CR/RNAS 22.3
12	22 Mar	Alb. DV	B6300	4N	Slype	1430	OOC	CR/RNAS 22.3

TOTAL: 6 and 1 shared destroyed, 5 out of control = 12.
*Shared with FSL L.W.F. Smith N6168. **Possible Lt Bertram Heinrich, an ace of MFJ 1, who was wounded.

SIDDALL Joseph Henry Lieutenant 209

Siddall was born in St Helens, Lancashire, on 28 March 1896. After service with the RNAS at Dunkirk, he flew with 209 Squadron during 1918, claiming nine victories. He was reported missing on 25 July after a fight with several enemy machines west of Houthem at 0840, when he was flying Camel D9636. He was shot down by Leutnant Karl Degelow, commander of Jasta 40, over Wytschaete.

	1918		Camel					
1s*	2 Apr	Alb. DIII	----	209	S Halluin	1115	OOC	CR/SR/?
2	11 Apr	Alb. DV	D3327	209	Albert	1700	OOC	CR/RAF 11.4
3	2 May	Alb. DV	D3327	209	Cayeaux	1830	OOC	CR/SR/?
4	19 May	Alb. DV	D3327	209	Marcelcave	2035	OOC	CR/RAF 19.5
5	31 May	LVG. C	B6369	209	Ovillers	0820	DES	CR/SR/?

6	3 Jun	Pfalz DIII	B6369	209	Fignieres	2000	DES	CR/RAF 3.6
7	6 Jun	LVG. C	B6369	209	Cappy	0830	OOC	CR/SR/?
8s**	9 Jun	LVG. C	B6369	209	Proyart	1130	OOC	CR/SR/?
9	9 Jun	LVG. C	B6369	209	S Morcourt	1135	DES(F)	CR/RAF 9.6

TOTAL: 3 destroyed, 4 and 2 shared out of control = 9
*Shared with Capt S.T. Edwards B7199. Probably Uffz Meyer of Jasta 57, who was wounded. **Shared with Lt C.G. Edwards B6371.

SIDEBOTTOM William Lieutenant 203

He joined the RFC on 11 October 1917 and was posted to 203 Squadron in 1918. In less than four months he claimed 14 victories and received the DFC. In 1919 he served with the RAF in South Russia.

	1918		Camel					
1s*	16 Jun	DFW. C	B7185	203	Estaires	0610	DES	CR/SR/?
2s**	20 Jul	DFW. C	D9583	203	S E Lestrem	1800	DES	CR/RAF 20.7
3	22 Jul	Fokker DVII	D9583	203	Carvin	1035	DES	CR/RAF 22.7
4	25 Jul	Fokker DVII	D9583	203	2m S E La Bassee	0745	OOC	CR/SR/?
5	11 Aug	Fokker DVII	D9595	203	Bray	1930	OOC	CR/SR/?
6s***	22 Aug	DFW. C	D9595	203	S Mericourt	0630	DES	CR/SR/?
7s†	24 Sep	Fokker DVII	C197	203	S E Lens	0900	DES	CR/RAF 24.9
8	28 Sep	Fokker DVII	C197	203	Hem-Langlet	0830	OOC	CR/SR/?
9	1 Oct	Fokker DVII	C197	203	Naves, E Cambrai	1330	DES	CR/RAF 1.10
10	2 Oct	Fokker DVII	C197	203	Caurior	0845	OOC	CR/RAF 2.10
11s††	9 Oct	Rumpler C	C197	203	St Aubert	1630	DES(F)	CR/RAF 9.10
12	23 Oct	Fokker DVII	C197	203	Vertain	1635	OOC	CR/SR/?
13s†††	23 Oct	Fokker DVII	C197	203	Vertain	1635	OOC	CR/SR/?
14s‡	29 Oct	Fokker DVII	C197	203	Bruay	1515	OOC	CR/SR/?

TOTAL: 2 and 5 shared destroyed, 5 and 2 shared out of control = 14.
*Shared with Lt E.T. Hayne D3417, Lt C.F. Brown D9535, Lt R. Stone D3571, Lt Y. Kirkpatrick D3414. **Shared with Capt L.H. Rochford D9618. ***Shared with Capt A.T. Whealy D9641. †Shared with 2/Lt W.H. Coghill D9597. ††Shared with Capt L.H. Rochford D3938. †††Shared with Lt D.B. Barbour D9597. ‡Shared with Sgt W.G. Jones F3098.

SIMON Walter Carl Lieutenant 139

An American who joined the RFC in March 1918, Simon flew Bristol Fighters with 139 Squadron in Italy from mid summer of that year, his usual observer being Lieutenant W.W. Smith. He claimed eight victories, including five in a single combat on 30 July. It must be stated that Austro-Hungarian records indicate no losses at all on this date. Simon was awarded a DFC for this combat.

	1918		Bristol					
1*	4 Jul	Alb. DIII	C999	139	Levico	1030	OOC	SR/14 W
2*	15 Jul	Alb. DIII	C999	139	Migazone	c0800	DES	SR/14 W
3*	30 Jul	LVG. C	C999	139	Torre di Mosto	0630	DES	SR/14 W
4*	30 Jul	C	C999	139	Caorle	0630	OOC	SR/14 W
5*	30 Jul	Alb. DIII	C999	139	Motta	0630	DES(F)	SR/14 W
6*	30 Jul	Alb. DIII	C999	139	Motta	0630	DES(F)	SR/14 W
7*	30 Jul	Alb. DIII	C999	139	Caorle	0630	OOC	SR/14 W
8**	10 Aug	Alb. DV	D8075	139	Caldonazzo	----	DES	SR/14 W

TOTAL: 5 destroyed, 3 out of control = 8.
*Observer: Lt W.W. Smith. **Observer: Sgt M. Akam.

SIMONSON Eric Landon Captain 2AFC

Simonson was born on 23 January 1894 in Melbourne, Australia, and was studying engineering when war broke out; he then joined the infantry, serving initially with the 8th Battalion from 9 September 1915. In January 1916 he was posted to the 14th Battalion, serving in France until September 1917, during which year he was promoted to Captain. He transferred to the AFC late in 1917 and was posted to 2AFC Squadron in France on 15 May 1918 where he claimed five victories during the last two months of the war, putting in over 200 hours flying. He was demobilized on 26 December 1919 and joined his family's business.

	1918		SE 5A					
1	24 Sep	Fokker DVII	D406	2AFC	Habourdin	1820	DES(F)	CR/RAF 24.9
2	24 Sep	Pfalz DXII	D406	2AFC	S Habourdin	1820	OOC	CR/ORB/OH
3	28 Oct	Fokker DVII	C1125	2AFC	3m W Lessines	1525	DES	CR/RAF 28.10
4	30 Oct	Fokker DVII	C1125	2AFC	2m N Tournai	0845	OOC	CR/ORB/OH
5	4 Nov	Fokker DVII	C1129	2AFC	Tombelle	0810	DES	CR/RAF 4.11

3 destroyed, 2 out of control = 5.

SIMPSON George Goodman Captain 1(W), 8(N), 9(N)

A Londoner, born on 14 September 1896, George Simpson joined the RNAS on 8 August 1915. On completion of training, he flew Nieuports, Pups and Triplanes with 1 Wing, RNAS, and then with 8(N) Squadron during 1916-17, becoming 'A' Flight commander. He claimed six victories and was awarded the DSC. In June he was posted to 9(N) Squadron, where he claimed two more victories. In 1918 he was a test pilot at Martlesham Heath.

	1916		Nieuport					
1s*	4 Dec	Alb. DI	3958	8N	N E Bapaume	1100	OOC	CR/SR/DL/?
	1917		Triplane					
2	24 Apr	Alb. DIII	N5460	8N	Sailly	0840	OOC	CR/RFC 24.4
3	2 May	C	N5460	8N	Douai	0945	OOC	CR/RFC 2.5
4	11 May	Alb. DIII	N5460	8N	Douai	1950	OOC	CR/RFC 11.5
5	11 May	Alb. DIII	N5460	8N	Douai	1950	DES(F)	CR/RFC 11.5
6	23 May	Alb. DIII	N5460	8N	Douai	1800	OOC	CR/ORB/SR/?
7	24 Jul	C	N5462	9N	Leffinghe	0635	OOC	CR/ORB/SR/?
8s**	28 Jul	C	N5462	9N	Middelkerke	1735	OOC	CR/RFC 28.7

TOTAL: 1 destroyed, 5 and 2 shared out of control = 8.
*Shared with F/Lt C.R. Mackenzie. **Shared with FSL F.J.W. Mellersh N5377.

SIMS Charles John Lieutenant 213

Born in Bournemouth on 20 December 1899, he was commissioned in the RNAS on 23 October 1917. In 1918 he was posted to 13(N) Squadron, which then became 213 Squadron, RAF. He took part in many ground attacks and was awarded the DFC in September; in air combat he claimed nine victories; on 25 September he reported shooting down one Fokker which spun down and collided with another, both subsequently crashing.

	1918		Camel					
1s	7 Jul	Alb. DV	D9672	213	Middelkerke	1140	OOC	CR/5 GP Comm
2	31 Jul	Seaplane	D9490	213	15m N W Ostend	1935	DES	CR/5 GP Comm
3	11 Aug	Fokker DVII	D9490	213	5 m S E Ostend	1550	DES	CR/5 GP Comm
4s	25 Sep	Fokker DVII	D7272	213	S W Ostend	1835	DES	CR/5 GP Comm
5s	25 Sep	Fokker DVII	D7272	213	S W Ostend	1835	DES	CR/5 GP Comm
6	14 Oct	Fokker DVII	D7272	213	Leke	1430	DES	CR/5 GP Comm
7	14 Oct	Fokker DVII	D7272	213	Leke	1430	OOC	CR/5 GP Comm
8	14 Oct	Fokker DVII	D7272	213	Leke	1430	DES	CR/5 GP Comm
9	9 Nov	Balloon	D7272	213	5m N W Ghent	1025	DES	CR/5 GP Comm

TOTAL: 1 balloon, 4 and 2 shared destroyed, 2 out of control = 9.

SLATER James Anderson Captain 18, 1, 64

Born on 27 November 1896, Slater joined the Royal Sussex Regiment in 1914 as a private, and was later commissioned in the Irish Rifles. In 1915 he transferred to the RFC as an observer and flew in France with 18 Squadron from November until March 1916. Accepted for pilot training, he returned to France to join 1 Squadron in August, flying with this unit until May 1917, during which time he claimed one victory and shared one more. After a period as an instructor, he was promoted to Captain and became a flight commander with the newly-formed 64 Squadron which was equipped with DH 5s. Going to France in October 1917, he shot down the squadron's first enemy aircraft; when the unit was re-equipped with SE 5As Jimmy Slater really began to show his fighting skill, and soon brought his score to 24, receiving an MC and Bar, and a DFC. In 18 days in May he engaged in 25 combats and claimed eight enemy aircraft shot down. He returned to Home Establishment in July and finished the war as an instructor again. After the war he continued to instruct both at home and in the Middle East. He also flew with 20,216 and 1 Squadrons and in 1925 with 3 Squadron. While an instructor at CFS, this gallant and popular pilot was killed in a flying accident the day before his 29th birthday.

	1917		Nieuport					
1	15 Feb	Alb. DII	A6613	1	Warneton	1230	OOC	CR/ORB/?
2s*	17 Mar	Alb. DIII	A6624	1	Courtrai-Menin	1045	OOC	CR/RFC 17.3
			DH 5					
3	30 Nov	DFW. C	A9458	64	Bourlon Wood	1045	OOC	CR/RFC 30.11
	1918		SE 5A					
4	8 Mar	Pfalz DIII	----	64	Cambrai	1040	OOC	CR/RFC 8.3
5	11 Mar	Pfalz DIII	B147	64	Cambrai	1130	OOC	CR/RFC 11.3
6	11 Mar	Alb. DV	B147	64	Douai	1157	DES(F)	CR/RFC 11.3
7	15 Mar	Alb. DV	B147	64	Masnieres	1120	OOC	CR/RFC 15.3
8	21 Mar	Alb. DV	B147	64	Inchy en Artois	1205	DES	CR/RFC 21.3
9s**	21 Mar	Fokker DrI	B147	64	Bourlon Wood	1335	OOC	CR/RFC 21.3

10s**	21 Mar	Alb. DV	B147	64	Bourlon Wood	1335	OOC	CR/RFC 21.3
11	23 Mar	Pfalz DIII	----	64	Pronville	1040	DES	CR/RFC 23.3
12	23 Mar	Fokker DrI	B147	64	Graincourt	1555	OOC	CR/RFC 23.3
13s***	30 Mar	C	D289	64	Croiselles	1150	DES	CR/RFC 30.3
14	1 Apr	Pfalz DIII	D289	64	Maricourt	0715	DES(F)	CR/RAF 1.4
15	20 Apr	Alb. DV	D289	64	Neuf Berquin	0945	OOC	CR/RAF 20.4
16	20 Apr	Pfalz DIII	D289	64	Neuf Berquin	0945	OOC	CR/RAF 20.4
17	16 May	Alb. DV	B7786	64	S W Brebieres	0940	DES(F)	CR/RAF 16.5
18	19 May	Alb. DV	B7786	64	E Oppy	1955	DES	CR/RAF 19.5
19	19 May	Pfalz DIII	B7786	64	Brebieres	2000	DES	CR/RAF 19.5
20	26 May	Alb. DV	B7786	64	Erquinghem-Lys	1930	DES(F)	CR/RAF 20.5
21	27 May	Alb. DV	B7786	64	Cagnicourt	1055	DES	CR/RAF 27.5
22	29 May	Pfalz DIII	C1880	64	La Bassee-Boyelles	1940	DES	CR/RAF 29.5
23	31 May	Pfalz DIII	----	64	La Bassee	1940	DES	CR/RAF 31.5
24	31 May	Pfalz DIII	----	64	La Bassee	1942	OOC	CR/I BG WD

TOTAL: 11 and 1 shared destroyed, 9 and 3 shared out of control = 24.
*Shared with 2/Lt C.C. Clark A6672. **Shared with Lt V.W. Thompson B124. ***Shared with Lt P.S. Burge B76.

SLATTER Leonard Horatio Captain SDF, 13(N), 213, 4ASD

Born on 8 December 1894, and educated in South Africa, Leonard Slatter became a civil engineer. On the outbreak of war he served as a dispatch rider with an armoured car unit, and then in 1916 he joined the RNAS as an observer. He flew over 100 hours on Short seaplanes with the Seaplane Squadron at Dunkirk, attacking submarines and land targets. On 30 March he and his pilot, Lieutenant Tooke, bombed one of four submarines single-handed. Selected for pilot training in July, he eventually returned to his old unit in February 1917, but this was now flying Sopwith 1½ Strutters and Shorts on a variety of operations along the coast and over the British Fleet. In July 1917 it re-equipped with Pups and became the Seaplane Defence Flight at St Pol, later converting to Camels. Flying escorts, bombing raids and patrols over the Fleet, Slatter now claimed six victories, plus a Gotha forced to land during a night patrol on 29 September. He was awarded a DSC and Bar. On 4 September he and his flight strafed a German destroyer with machine gun fire. He left the unit at the beginning of July 1918, by which time it had become 13(N) Squadron, and then 213 Squadron, RAF, and went to No 4 ASD — Pilot Pool — in France with the object of training pilots before posting to an operational squadron. On 30 August he flew over the lines and shot down a Halberstadt two-seater for his seventh victory, for which he received the DFC. In 1919 he served in South Russia with 47 Squadron, and during the following years commanded 19,111 and 43 Squadrons before taking command of RAF Tangmere in 1935 as a Wing Commander. He was often attached to the Naval Flying side of the RAF, and during World War II commanded 15 Group, Coastal Command, before becoming Commander-in-Chief, Coastal Command in 1945, with the rank of Air Marshal. He had been awarded the OBE in 1919, and died in 1961.

	1917		Pup					
1s*	12 Aug	Seaplane	N6459	SDF	off Ostend	2000	DES	CR/RNAS 13.8
2s**	15 Sep	Seaplane	B3793	SDF	12m N E Nieuport	1910	DES(F)	DL/RNAS 16.9
			Camel					
3***	25 Sep	Seaplane	N6348	SDF	near Ostend	1700	DES	CR/RNAS 25.9
4	27 Oct	Alb. DIII	B3936	SDF	N W Ostend	1500	DES	CR/RNAS27.10
	1918							
5s†	29 Jan	Seaplane	B7186	13N	100y off Blankenberghe Pier	1400	DES	CR/RNAS29.1
6	11 Mar	Alb. DV	B6400	213	2m M Mariakerke	1445	DES	CR/5 GP Comm
7	30 Aug	Halb. C	D3346	4ASD	S Stalhille	c1400	DES	CR/5 GP Comm

TOTAL: 4 and 3 shared destroyed = 7.
*Shared with F/Cdr R. Graham N6478, F/L P. Fisher N6437; This was Flgm Paatz/Vzflgm Putz of Seeflug 1, killed in FF 33L No.1246. **Shared with F/Cdr R. Graham B3794. ***This was Vzflgm Plattenberg of Seeflug 1, who was wounded. †Shared with FSL J. deC Paynter B3782, FSL J.E. Greene B3919, FSL G.C. Mackay B6407, FSL M.L. Cooper B6410.

SLOLEY Robert Hugh Lieutenant 56

After serving in the Royal Artillery, he joined the RFC and was posted to fly with 56 Squadron in 1917, serving with 'A' Flight. He was credited with nine victories before he was killed on 1 October 1917 in a fight with several Albatros Scouts, his SE 5 being shot to pieces in the air by Leutnant Xaver Dannhuber of Jasta 26.

	1917		SE 5A					
1s*	14 Aug	C	A4868	56	E Westroosebeke	1730-1830	OOC	CR/RFC 14.8
2s**	18 Aug	Alb. DV	A4868	56	Menin	0630-0710	OOC	CR/RFC 18.8
3	20 Aug	Alb. DV	A4868	56	Moorslede	1910-1930	OOC	CR/RFC 20.8
4	22 Aug	Alb. DV	A4868	56	Houthoulst Forest	0615-0715	OOC	CR/RFC 22.8

5	5 Sep	C	A4868	56	E Houthoulst Forest	1815	OOC	CR/RFC 5.9
6	14 Sep	Alb. DV	A4868	56	S Houthoulst Forest	0845-0915	OOC	CR/RFC 14.9
7	16 Sep	Alb. DV	A8944	56	Roulers	1630	OOC	CR/RFC 16.9
8	20 Sep	Alb. DV	A4868	56	Moorslede	1200	OOC	CR/RFC 20.9
9s***	29 Sep	Alb. DV	A8928	56	Staden	1750-1810	OOC	CR/RFC 29.9

TOTAL: 6 and 3 shared out of control = 9.

*Shared with Capt G.C. Maxwell B502. **Shared with Capt G.C. Maxwell B502, Lt J.S. Turnbull A8946, Lt D.S. Wilkinson B521, 2/Lt W.J. Potts B4857, Capt H.M. Rushworth B517. ***Shared with Capt G.C. Maxwell B502, Lt H.A. Johnston B12, Lt C.H. Jeffs B524, Lt R.W. Young A8946, Lt R.J. Preston-Cobb B527.

SMART Wallace Alexander Lieutenant 1

Born on 7 January 1898 in Cardiff, Smart was commissioned in the RFC on 29 September 1917 and was posted to 1 Squadron in France on 10 April 1918. He remained with the unit until the end of the war, being involved in the squadron's last successful engagement of the conflict.

	1918		SE 5A					
1	31 May	Alb. DV	C1092	1	Dranoutre	0850	OOC	CR/ORB/?
2s*	1 Jun	Pfalz DIII	C1092	1	Armentieres	1940	OOC	CR/ORB/?
3s**	1 Jul	Halb. C	C1092	1	Messines	0805	DES(F)	CR/RAF 1.7
4s***	1 Oct	Fokker DVII	D6973	1	N E St Quentin	1710	OOC	CR/ORB/?
5	29 Oct	Fokker DVII	D6973	1	Landrecies	1420	DES(F)	CR/RAF 29.10

TOTAL: 1 and 1 shared destroyed, 1 and 2 shared out of control = 5.

*Shared with Capt C.S.T. Lavers C1110, Lt D. Knight C1106, Lt L.W. Mawbey B130, Lt E.M. Newman C1101, Capt P.J. Clayson C1114, Lt H.A. Kullberg B8512, Lt C.B. Henderson C1849, 2/Lt H.S. Hennessy D337, Lt E.T.S. Kelly B733. **Shared with Lt H.A. Kullberg C1835, Lt J.C. Bateman B8254. ***Shared with Capt C.S.T. Lavers C9292, Lt B.H. Moody B8501, Lt F.M. Squires E6009, 2/Lt F.A.S. Nesbitt B7881, 2/Lt C.R. Boyd C9065, Lt D.E. Cameron H7257, 2/Lt L.H. Phinney D6951, Capt W. Pallister F5473, Lt W. Newby E1353, Lt C.W. Arning E4023, 2/Lt W. Joffe B8427, 2/Lt Dickenson C1812.

SMITH David Esplin Lieutenant 20

Lieutenant Smith was commissioned in July 1917 and flew Bristol Fighters with 20 Squadron in 1918, claiming six victories before he was reported missing on 14 August. The aircraft C987 had been shot down by Leutnant Schramm of Jasta 56, Smith being killed while his regular observer, Lieutenant J. Hills, was taken prisoner.

	1918		Bristol					
1*	9 May	Fokker DrI	----	20	S W Merris	1650	DES	CR/RAF 9.5
2*	16 Jun	Pfalz DIII	C859	20	S Comines	1915	DES	CR/RAF 16.6
3**	2 Jul	Pfalz DIII	C859	20	S W Ypres	0845	OOC	CR/SR/11 WS
4**	25 Jul	Fokker DVII	C4672	20	Comines Canal	0850	DES	CR/RAF 25.7
5**	25 Jul	Fokker DVII	C4672	20	Comines Canal	0855	DES(F)	CR/RAF 25.7
6s***	25 Jul	Fokker DVII	C4672	20	Comines Canal	0850	DES(F)	CR/RAF 25.7

TOTAL: 4 and 1 destroyed, 1 out of control = 6.

*Observer: Pbr F.J. Ralph. **Observer: Pbr J. Hills. ***Observer: Pbr J. Hills. Shared with Capt H.P. Lale/2/Lt F.J. Ralph C4718, Lt W.M. Thompson/ Sgt J.D.C. Summers C843.

SMITH Emerson Arthur Lincoln Fisher Lieutenant 45

Emerson Smith was a Canadian who initially flew 1½ Strutters, and later Camels, with 'A' Flight of 45 Squadron in the summer and autumn of 1917, claiming seven victories. On 9 September while out alone, he encountered 15 Albatros two-seaters which he attacked single-handed, claiming one destroyed and one out of control. He flew a ground strafing mission on 28 October during which he was attacked by Leutnant von Busse of Jasta 3; wounded in one lung and the left arm, he crashed and was taken prisoner.

	1917		Strutter					
1*	21 Aug	Alb. DIII	----	45	S E Ypres	1000	DES	CR/RFC 21.8
			Camel					
2	9 Sep	Alb. C	B3791	45	Comines	1630	DES(F)	CR/RFC 9.9
3	9 Sep	Alb. C	B3791	45	3m E Ypres	1635	OOC	CR/RFC 9.9
4	10 Sep	Alb. DIII	----	45	Houthoulst Forest	1730	OOC	CR/RFC 10.9
5s**	20 Sep	C	----	45	Passchendaele	1825	DES(F)	CR/RFC 20.9
6	21 Sep	Alb. DV	----	45	Passchendaele	1840	OOC	CR/RFC 22.9
7	1 Oct	Alb. DV	----	45	Quesnoy	1220	OOC	CR/RFC 1.10

TOTAL: 3 destroyed, 4 out of control = 7.

*Observer: Gnr H. Grenner. **Shared with Lt H.M. Moody, Lt R.J. Brownell.

SMITH Francis Ryan Captain 2AFC

Frank Smith was born in 1896 in Brisbane, Queensland, and worked as a clerk before joining the Australian infantry after the start of the war, receiving an MC in 1916. Transferred to the AFC, he was posted to 2AFC Squadron in France on 28 February 1918, first claiming in May. Further victories followed in July and August, while in September he claimed two destroyed and four out of control. He was awarded a DFC, gazetted on 24 October, and was promoted to flight commander. On 14 October he claimed three Fokker DVIIs destroyed and a fourth out of control to bring his score to 16. On 10 November he was shot down by ground fire while strafing, but evaded capture and came back through the lines on foot three days after the Armistice, by which time he had flown 238 hours.

	1918		SE 5A					
1s*	9 May	Pfalz DIII	C9496	2AFC	Marcoing	1750	DES	CR/RAF 9.5
2s**	2 Jun	Pfalz DIII	----	2AFC	Clery	1905	OOC	CR/ORB/OH/?
3	4 Jul	Fokker DVII	D6190	2AFC	Capinghem	1920	DES	CR/RAF 4.7
4	7 Aug	Fokker DVII	C6403	2AFC	Wavrin	0630	OOC	CR/ORB/OH
5	3 Sep	Fokker DVII	C6403	2AFC	3m N W Cambrai	1720	OOC	CR/ORB/OH
6	6 Sep	Fokker DVII	C6403	2AFC	2m N N E Douai	1900	DES	CR/RAF 6.9
7	16 Sep	Fokker DVII	C6403	2AFC	Lille	0730	OOC	CR/ORB/OH
8	16 Sep	Fokker DVII	C6403	2AFC	Lille	0730	OOC	CR/ORB/OH
9s***	24 Sep	Alb. C	C6403	2AFC	La Bassee-Bethune	1030	OOC	CR/ORB/AA
10	24 Sep	Fokker DVII	C6403	2AFC	S Capinghem	1820	DES	CR/RAF 24.9
11	9 Oct	Fokker DVII	C6403	2AFC	Lille-Armentieres	1015	OOC	CR/ORB/OH
12	9 Oct	Fokker DVII	C6403	2AFC	Lille-Armentieres	1015	OOC	CR/ORB/OH
13	14 Oct	Fokker DVII	C6403	2AFC	W Roubiax	1100	DES	CR/RAF 14.10
14	14 Oct	Fokker DVII	C6403	2AFC	.5m N Mouvaux	1100	DES	CR/RAF 14.10
15	14 Oct	Fokker DVII	C6403	2AFC	Havron	1600	DES	CR/RAF 14.10
16	14 Oct	Fokker DVII	C6403	2AFC	Havron	1600	OOC	CR/RAF 14.10

TOTAL: 6 and 1 shared destroyed, 7 and 2 shared out of control = 16.
*Shared with Lt J.A. Adam D4895. **Shared with Lt W.Q. Adams D3429, Capt A.T. Cole D3962, Lt H.E. Hamilton. ***Shared with Capt R.L. Manuel C1948.

SMITH Harry Coleman Lieutenant 213

Harry Smith joined the RNAS in June 1917, going to France to join 213 Squadron on 28 May 1918. He claimed five victories and took part in 12 low-level bombing raids.

	1918		Camel					
1s*	21 Aug	LVG. C	D3341	213	S Zevecote	1650	DES	CR/5 BG Comm
2s**	15 Sep	Rumpler C	D3378	213	Ostend	1400	DES	CR/5 GP Comm
3s***	18 Sep	Balloon	D3378	213	La Barriere	1050	DES	CR/5 GP Comm
4	14 Oct	LVG. C	D3400	213	E Gits	0630	DES	CR/5 GP Comm
5	9 Nov	Fokker DVII	D3400	213	10m N E Ghent	1030	DES	CR/5 GP Comm

TOTAL: 1 shared balloon, 2 and 2 shared destroyed = 5.
*Shared with Capt C.P. Brown D9649, Lt D.S. Ingalls N6376. **Shared with Lt D.S. Ingalls D9649. ***Shared with Lt D.S. Ingalls D9649, Lt G.S. Hodson D3741.

SMITH John Henry Lieutenant 46

John Smith was born on 9 March 1894, in Cambellford, Ontario, Canada, and joined the RFC on 29 June 1917. He was commissioned the following November and on 3 March 1918 was posted to 46 Squadron. He began claiming straight away, the culmination coming on 22 May when he claimed two scouts. On 2 July he was hospitalized and had to cease operational flying.

	1918		Camel					
1s*	23 Mar	Alb. C	C1685	46	N Croisilles	0930	OOC	CR/RFC 23.3
2	23 Mar	Alb. DV	C1685	46	Vaulx	1800	DES	CR/RFC 23.3
3s**	2 Apr	Balloon	C1617	46	----	1315	DES	CR/RAF 3.4
4s***	2 May	Pfalz DIII	C1575	46	Estaires	1700	OOC	CR/RAF 2.5
5s†	6 May	DFW. C	----	46	St Venant	1800	CAPT	CR/RAF 6.5
6s††	9 May	Fokker DrI	C1575	46	S Lestrem	1200	DES	CR/RAF 9.5
7	22 May	Alb. DV	D6509	46	Richebourg St Vaast	1815	OOC	CR/SR/?
8	22 May	Alb. DV	D6509	46	Richebourg St Vaast	1815	OOC	CR/SR/?

TOTAL: 1 shared balloon, 1 shared captured, 1 and 1 destroyed, 2 and 2 shared out of control = 8.
*Shared with 2/Lt D.R. MacLaren B9153, 2/Lt H.P. Blakely B5435. **Shared with 2/Lt D.R. MacLaren B9153. ***Shared with Capt C.J. Marchant B9211. †Shared with Capt D.R. MacLaren, Capt C.J. Marchant, Lt V.M. Yeates, 2/Lt H.T.W. Manwaring. This was Lt Junemann/Lt Barth of FA 14. ††Shared with Lt H.L.M. Dodson C1643.

SMITH Langley Frank Willard Flight Sub Lieutenant 4(N)

Born on 15 August 1897, Flight Sub Lieutenant Smith is believed to have been an American from Chicago, who joined the RNAS in September 1916. He was posted to 4(N) Squadron on 25 April 1917, claiming eight victories plus at least three forced to land. He was awarded a DSC just before he was reported missing in action on 13 June 1917 in N6362. It is believed that this Camel broke up while stunting over the German fighter airfield at Neumünster. He was a recipient of the Belgian Croix de Guerre, and was made a Chevalier de la Couronne.

	1917		Pup					
1	30 Apr	Alb. DII	N6168	4N	E Nieuport	1245	OOC	CR/RNAS 30.4
2	9 May	Balloon	N6168	4N	Ghistelles	0800	DES	CR/DOS/SR/
3s*	9 May	C	N6168	4N	.5m S E Ghistelles	1715	DES	CR/DOS/DL/?
4	12 May	Alb. DIII	N6168	4N	off Zeebrugge	0730	DES	CR/DOS/?
5s**	25 May	Gotha G.	N6168	4N	15m N Westende	1830	DES	CR/DOS/DL/?
6	5 Jun	Balloon	N6168	4N	Ostend	0440	DES	CR/DOS/?
7	6 Jun	Alb. DV	N6168	4N	N Handzaeme	1520	DES	CR/DOS/DL/?
8	6 Jun	Alb. DV	N6168	4N	N Handzaeme	1520	OOC	CR/DOS/DL/?

TOTAL: 2 balloons, 2 and 2 shared destroyed, 2 out of control = 8.
*Shared with F/Lt A.M. Shook N6200. **Shared with FSL A.J. Chadwick N6176, F/Lt G.H.T. Rouse N6168, FSL E.W. Busby N5796.

SMITH Ross Macpherson Captain 67, 1AFC

Born in Adelaide, South Australia, on 4 December 1892, Ross Smith served with the Australian Light Horse before joining the AFC. He was posted to the Middle East and flew with 67 Squadron, which later became 1AFC Squadron, and was equipped with Bristol Fighters in early 1918. A very aggressive pilot, he was to receive an MC and Bar, followed by a DFC and two Bars. On 19 October he forced an enemy two-seater to land behind its own lines, then landed next to it; while his observer, Lieutenant A.V. McCann, covered the crew with the rear guns, Ross jumped down and set fire to the enemy machine, then flew back home! Known as 'Hadji' to his friends, he was wounded in action on two occasions, in neither case seriously. In 1919 he and his brother Keith made the first flight from England to Australia in a Vickers Vimy, leaving Hounslow on 12 November and arriving at Darwin on 10 December. Both brothers were knighted for this epic flight, but 'Hadji' lost his life in a flying accident on 14 April 1922.

	1917		BE 2E					
1s*	1 Sep	Alb. DIII	6311	1AFC	Beersheba	0920	FTL/DES	CR/5 W WD
	1918		Bristol					
2s**	7 May	C	B1229	1AFC	1m S E Jenin a/d	1515	DES(F)	CR/40 W WD
3***	22 May	Alb. DIII	B1229	1AFC	3m N Nablus	0645	OOC	CR/40 W WD
4s†	11 Jun	C	B1229	1AFC	8m N Tulkeram	0615	FTL/DES	CR/40 W WD
5***	19 Jun	C	B1229	1AFC	Jericho-Domie	0605	FTL/DES	CR/40 W WD
6††	17 Jul	Alb. DIII	B1229	1AFC	3m W Huwarra	0640	FTL/DES	CR/40 W WD
7††	17 Jul	Alb. DIII	B1229	1AFC	Wadi Auja	0645	FTL/DES	CR/40 W WD
8†††	22 Sep	C	B1229	1AFC	Mafrak, E Deraa	1000	DES	ORB/WS/oH
9‡	22 Sep	Pfalz DIII	B1229	1AFC	Mafrak	1045	FTL/DES	ORB/WS/OH
10‡	22 Sep	Pfalz DIII	B1229	1AFC	Mafrak	1045	FTL/DES	ORB/WS/OH
11	19 Oct	DFW. C	B1229	1AFC	25m S W Aleppo	1030	DES	ORB/WS/OH

TOTAL: 6 and 4 shared destroyed 1 out of control = 11.
*Shared with Major A.W.L. Ellis: This aircraft was confirmed when a wireless message was intercepted, stating that 'Lt Schmarje had crashed'. Schmarje, from FA 300, had scored at least twice. **Observer: Lt E.A. Mustard; shared with Lt A.V. Tonkin/Lt R.A. Camm B1276. ***Observer: Lt W.A. Kirk. †Observer: Lt W.A. Kirk; shared with Lt E.G.C. Stooke/Lt L.P. Kreig B1276. ††Observer: Lt W.A. Kirk. The ORB has photographs taken at the time of these combats of both wrecks. †††Observer: Lt E.A. Mustard. Shared with Lt E.S. Headlam/Lt W.H. Lilly B1286. ‡Observer: Lt E.A. Mustard.

SMITH Sydney Philip Captain 6, 46

Born on 10 May 1895, in Aldershot, Smith served with the Wessex Division Training ASC(TF) until he transferred to the RFC in 1916. He qualified as a pilot in June, and by December was a Captain flying BE 2s with 6 Squadron. On 17 March 1917 he and his observer claimed an Albatros Scout shot down. Following a period off operations, he joined 46 Squadron as a flight commander on 6 March 1918. Here he claimed four victories, but on 6 April he was shot down and killed by Manfred von Richthofen. He was awarded the DSO and Croix de Guerre.

	1917		BE 2D					
1*	17 Mar	Alb. DII	6278	6	Becelaere	1205	DES	CR/RFC 17.3
	1918		Camel					

2s**	16 Mar	C	C1617	46	S Brebieres	1130	OOC	CR/RFC 16.3
3s**	16 Mar	C	C1617	46	S Brebieres	1200	OOC	CR/RFC 16.3
4	24 Mar	C	D6407	46	57 C I 17c	1600	DES	CR/RFC 24.3
5s***	2 Apr	C	----	46	Courcelles	1245	DES	CR/RAF 2.4

TOTAL: 2 and 1 shared destroyed, 2 shared out of control = 5.
*Observer: 2 AM Backhouse. **Shared with Capt G.E. Thomson C1627. ***Shared with Lt A.G. Vlasto, Lt H.G.W. Debenham, 2/Lt D.R. MacLaren, 2/Lt R.K. McConnell.

SMUTS Neil Ritz Captain 3

Born in Johannesburg, South Africa, on 23 December 1898, Smuts was commissioned in the RFC in August 1917 and joined 3 Squadron on 1 January 1918, becoming a flight commander during the late summer.

	1918		Camel					
1	6 Apr	Alb. DV	D6455	3	Morlancourt	1200	OOC	CR/RAF 6.4
2s*	9 Aug	Fokker DVII	----	3	----	1945	OOC	SR/ORB/?
3	1 Oct	Fokker DVII	C8343	3	57 B Z 6	1310	OOC	CR/SR/?
4	4 Oct	Fokker DVII	F6180	3	62 B J 31	1030	OOC	CR/SR/?
5	4 Oct	Fokker DVII	F6180	3	62 B J 31	1030	OOC	CR/SR/?

TOTAL: 4 and 1 shared out of control = 5.
*Shared with Lt L.H. McIntyre.

SMYTHE Cyril Richard Lieutenant 11

Born on 2 July 1899 in Hampton Hill, Middlesex, Smythe was commissioned in the RFC on 30 May 1917 and served with 11 Squadron during the summer and autumn of 1918, claiming six Fokker DVIIs; four of these were credited to the rear gun, manned by Lieutenant W.T. Barnes.

	1918		Bristol					
1*	22 Aug	Fokker DVII	D7981	11	Bapaume	0740	DES(F)	CR/RAF 22.8
2*	29 Aug	Fokker DVII	D7981	11	Bourlon Wood	1830	OOC	CR/?
3*	4 Sep	Fokker DVII	B8941	11	S St Hilaire	1045	DES(F)	CR/RAF 4.9
4*	1 Oct	Fokker DVII	E2573	11	S Le Cateau	0820	DES	CR/RAF 1.10
5*	1 Oct	Fokker DVII	E2573	11	S Le Cateau	0825	OOC	CR/RAF 1.10
6*	3 Oct	Fokker DVII	B8941	11	N E Cambrai	1800	OOC	CR/?

TOTAL: 3 destroyed and 3 out of control = 6.
*Observer: Lt W.T. Barnes.

SNEATH Wilfred Henry Lieutenant 8(N), 208

Harry Sneath was born in Hendon, North London, on 19 March 1899. Joining the RNAS, he was posted to 'C' Flight of 8(N) Squadron as a Flight Sub Lieutenant in late 1917, claiming four shared and one individual victory by April 1918. After sharing his fifth and last victory on 6th of that month, he was reported missing in action, shot down in flames in B7187 by Leutnant Hertz of Jasta 59 near Lens.

	1917		Camel					
1s*	5 Dec	Alb. DV	B3821	8N	Wingles	1355	OOC	CR/RFC 5.12
	1918							
2	24 Jan	Alb. DV	B3821	8N	E Lens	1500	DES	CR/RFC 24.1
3s**	5 Feb	Alb. DV	N6356	8N	S Pont a Vendin	1245	DES	CR/RFC 5.2
4s***	16 Feb	Alb. DV	N6356	8N	Pronville	1115	DES(F)	CR/I BG WD
5s†	6 Apr	Fokker DrI	B7187	208	Lens	1130	OOC	CR/RAF 6.4

TOTAL: 1 and 2 shared destroyed, 2 shared out of control = 5.
*Shared with F/Cdr G.W. Price B6311. **Shared with F/Cdr R. Macdonald N6387, FSL H. Day N6379, FSL H.H.S. Fowler B3832. ***Shared with F/Cdr G.W. Price N6379, FSL H.H.S. Fowler B3832. †Shared with Capt T.F.N. Gerrard B7196, Lt G.K. Cooper B7189.

SOAR Reginald Rhys Captain 5W, 8(N),

Born on 24 August 1893, Reggie Soar joined the RNAS on 10 August 1915 and served with 5 Naval Wing, flying 1½ Strutters early in 1916; this was the first unit to operate these aircraft. He then flew with 8(N) Squadron during 1916-17; in company with his flight commander, R.A. Little, he was involved in several engagements and claimed 12 victories at least. In one action on 3 July 1917 he took on seven enemy fighters single-handed and claimed one of these shot down. The award of the DSC was gazetted in August 1917. He died in 1971.

	1916		Pup					
1	20 Dec	Halb. D	N5181	8N	Remy	1050	OOC	CR/ORB/DL
2	20 Dec	Halb. D	N5181	8N	Fontaine	1130	OOC	CR/ORB/DL
	1917		Triplane					
3s*	23 May	C	N6292	8N	La Bassee	1000	OOC	CR/RFC 23.5
4	12 Jun	Aviatik C	----	8N	Arras	0835	OOC	CR/RFC 12.6

5s**	12 Jun	Aviatik C	----	8N	N Arras	0855	CAPT	CR/RFC 12.6
6s***	29 Jun	Alb. DIII	N6292	8N	E Lens	0655	OOC	CR/RFC 29.6
7	3 Jul	Alb. DIII	N6292	8N	Pont a Vendin	2100	OOC	CR/RFC 4.7
8	5 Jul	Aviatik C	N6292	8N	E Wingles	1830	OOC	CR/RFC 5.7
			Camel					
9s†	11 Jul	C	N3758	8N	E Izel	1815	CAPT	CR/ORB/?
10s††	13 Jul	C	N6376	8N	Lens	1015	DES	CR/RFC 13.7
			Triplane					
11s†††	17 Jul	Alb. DIII	N6292	8N	Quiery la Motte	0930	OOC	CR/RFC 17.7
12s†††	22 Jul	Alb. DIII	N6292	8N	Quiery la Motte	0735	OOC	CR/RFC 22.7

TOTAL: 2 shared captured, 1 shared destroyed, 5 and 4 shared out of control = 12.
*Shared with FSL C. Jenner-Parsons. **Shared with F/Cdr C.D. Booker, FSL C. Jenner Parsons. This was the crew of Lt von Pieveling/Lt Nieberie FAA 288. ***Shared with F/Lt R.A. Little N5493. †Shared with FSL J.H. Thompson N5460. ††Shared with F/Lt R.A. Little N6378. †††Shared with F/Cdr C.D. Booker N5482.

SODEN Frank Ormond Captain 60, 41

Although born in Canada at Petit Codiac, New Brunswick, on 3 November 1895, Soden returned with his family to the United Kingdom in 1904. He was a member of the Inns of Court OTC before joining the army, and was commissioned in the 8th South Staffordshire Regiment in November 1914. He took private flying lessons, qualifying as a pilot on 9 September 1916, and then transferred to the RFC. He was posted to 60 Squadron in France in June 1917, initially flying Nieuport 17s. He made two claims while flying these aircraft, but then converted to SE 5s, followed by 5As. By February 1918 he had flown 159 patrols and claimed five aircraft destroyed, and sent down 11 more out of control. During the month he was posted to Home Establishment as an instructor, and returned to the front on 13 July 1918 as a flight commander in 41 Squadron. During the next three and a half months he claimed 11 more victories to bring his score to 27; he received a DFC on 27 October. He remained in the RAF after the war, serving in South Russia in 1919. In 1922 as a flight commander in 1 Squadron in Iraq, he led his flight of Snipes against Turkish Army units that attempted to invade that country, being awarded a Bar to his DFC. In 1934 he was promoted Squadron Leader and commanded 65 Squadron. He became a Wing Commander in 1939, and during the 1940-45 period held several posts including that of station commander at Biggin Hill in 1941. He died in London on 12 February 1961.

	1917		Nieuport					
1s*	25 Jun	Alb. DIII	B1598	60	Dury	1025	OOC	CR/RFC 25.6
2	3 Jul	Alb. DV	B1602	60	Graincourt	1830	OOC	CR/SR/?
			SE 5A					
3	17 Sep	Alb. DV	B543	60	Polygon Wood	1830	OOC	CR/SR/?
4	20 Sep	Alb. DV	B510	60	N E Zonnebeke	1110	DES	CR/RFC 20.9
5	21 Sep	Alb. DV	B523	60	Langemarck	0700	OOC	CR/RFC 21.9/?
6s**	21 Oct	C	B543	60	Houthoulst	1615	DES	CR/RFC 21.10
7s***	1 Nov	C	A8898	60	Moorslede	1345	OOC	CR/RFC 1.11
8s***	1 Nov	C	A8898	60	Moorslede	1410	OOC	CR/SR/?
9	5 Nov	Alb. DV	B543	60	Houthoulst	1215	DES	CR/RFC 5.11
10s***	6 Nov	C	B543	60	Zonnebeke	0730	DES	CR/RFC 6.11
11s†	18 Dec	Alb. C	A8934	60	Gheluvelt	0815	OOC	CR/SR/?
	1918							
12s††	1 Jan	DFW. C	C5332	60	W Roulers	1050	OOC	CR/RFC 1.1
13s†††	9 Jan	Alb. DV	C5332	60	Moorslede	1645	DES(F)	CR/RFC 9.1
14	28 Jan	Alb. DV	C5332	60	Handzaeme	1330	OOC	CR/SR/?
15	5 Feb	Alb. DV	C5332	60	N Becelaere	1130	OOC	CR/RFC 5.2
16	5 Feb	Alb. DV	C5332	60	N Becelaere	1130	OOC	CR/RFC 5.2
17	8 Aug	Fokker DVII	E1300	41	W Proyart	1145	DES(F)	CR/RAF 8.8
18	25 Aug	Fokker DVII	E1300	41	S Comines	1900	DES(F)	CR/RAF 25.8
19	29 Aug	Fokker DVII	E4048	41	Steenwerck	0920	OOC	CR/SR/?
20	15 Sep	Balloon	C1913	41	Beaucamps	1700	DES	CR/RAF 15.9
21s‡	8 Oct	DFW. C	F5545	41	Ledeghem	1233	DES	CR/11 WS
22s‡‡	10 Oct	Fokker DVII	F5545	41	N Moorslede	1645	DES(F)	CR/RAF 10.10
23	14 Oct	Fokker DVII	F5545	41	W Roulers	0920	DES	CR/11 WS
24	14 Oct	Fokker DVII	F5545	41	Inglemunster	1620	DES	CR/RAF 14.10
25	26 Oct	Balloon	F5545	41	Mellen	1440	DES	CR/RAF 26.10
26‡‡‡	28 Oct	Fokker DVII	F5545	41	Ooteghem	1530	CAPT	CR/RAF 28.10
27	31 Oct	Fokker DVII	E4082	41	S Audenarde	1010	OOC	CR/11 WS

TOTAL: 1 captured, 2 balloons, 4 and 5 shared destroyed, 8 and 5 shared out of control = 27.
*Shared with Lt W.J. Rutherford B1602, 2/Lt G.C. Young B1619. **Shared with Lt W.J. Rutherford B533, Lt G.C. Young B580 ***Shared with Capt W.J. Rutherford A8934 †Shared with Lt A.W. Morey B510 ††Shared with 2/Lt J.B. Crompton A8901. †††Shared with Capt R.L. Chidlaw-Roberts B626. Shared with 21 Squadron, this was Lt Max Muller, the commander of Jasta B. ‡Shared with Lt E.J. Stephens F5469. ‡‡Shared with Major G.H. Bowman E4092. This was Lt Schafer of Jasta 16, who was killed. ‡‡‡This was Lt Adolph Auer of Jasta 40, who was captured.

SOLLY Arthur N. Captain 23, 20

Solly flew as an observer in 23 Squadron in 1916, sharing with his pilots in two victories. After training as a pilot, he joined 20 Squadron on FE 2Ds during spring 1917; here he claimed seven further victories before being wounded in action on 1 July 1916. Solly, with Lieutenant D.Y. Hay, was killed in a flying accident when he crashed A7108, one of the unit's first Bristol Fighters, on 11 August 1917.

	1916		FE 2B					
1s*	31 May	EA	5215	23	Marquion	0920	OOC	CR/RFC 31.5
2**	2 Aug	D	5213	23	Douai	2000	OOC	CR/III BG WD
	1917		FE 2D					
3***	13 May	C	A6354	20	Menin	1100	DES	CR/11 WS
4***	15 May	Alb. DIII	A6354	20	Quesnoy	0700	OOC	CR/RFC 15.5
5†	12 Jun	Alb. DIII	A6354	20	Zandvoorde	1215	OOC	CR/RFC 12.6
6††	18 Jun	Alb. DIII	A6516	20	E Quesnoy	1315	OOC	CR/RFC 18.6
7†††	9 Aug	Alb. DIII	A5147	20	Polygon Wood	1815	OOC	CR/RFC 10.8
8‡	10 Aug	C	A5147	20	Becelaere	0845	OOC	CR/RFC 10.8
9s‡‡	10 Aug	Alb. DV	A5147	20	Wervicq	0900	OOC	CR/RFC 10.8

TOTAL: 1 destroyed, 6 and 2 shared out of control = 9.

*Pilot: Capt H. Wyllie; shared with 2/Lt D. Cloete/ 2/Lt C.E. Pither 6354, 2/Lt A.T. Watson/2/Lt C.L. Blake 5249, 2/Lt E.F. Allen/Lt L.C. Powell 5235, and a Martinsyde, 1 AM D.R. Chapman 7280. **Pilot: Lt J.C. Griffiths. ***Observer: 2 AM C. Beminster. †Observer: 2/Lt F.J. Kydd. ††Observer: Lt W.C. Cambray. †††Observer: Lt C.A. Hoy. ‡Observer: 2/Lt J. Cawley. ‡‡Observer: 2/Lt J. Cawley; shared with Lt C.R. Richards/Lt A.E. Wear B1890, Lt D.Y. Hay/2/Lt M. Tod A6456.

SORSOLEIL Jack Victor Captain 84

Born in Toronto on 2 June 1898, this Canadian served with 84 Squadron from November 1917 to July 1918, becoming a flight commander and receiving an MC. After claiming 14 victories he was posted to England, where he ended the war as an instructor. He then returned to Canada where he became a successful businessman. During World War II he served as a Squadron Leader with the RCAF, but he died in 1946.

	1918		SE 5A					
1	13 Jan	C	B5463	84	N W Graincourt	1130	DES	CR/RFC 13.1
2	16 Feb	Alb. DV	B5463	84	St Quentin	0945	DES(F)	CR/RFC 16.2
3	19 Feb	Alb. DV	B5463	84	St Gobain Wood	1015	DES	CR/RFC 19.2
4	19 Feb	Alb. DV	B5463	84	N St Gobain Wood	1015	DES	CR/RFC 19.2
5	17 Mar	Pfalz DIII	B8233	84	1m E Mametz	1145	DES	CR/RFC 17.3
6	11 Apr	Fokker DrI	B8233	84	E Albert	1705	OOC	CR/RAF 11.4
7	25 Apr	Alb. DV	B8233	84	E Wiencourt	1700	OOC	CR/RAF 25.4
8*	25 Apr	Pfalz DIII	B8233	84	Wiencourt	1705	DES(F)	CR/RAF 25.4
9	7 May	Fokker DrI	B8233	84	Bray sur Somme	1915	DES(F)	CR/RAF 7.5
10	3 Jun	Fokker DrI	B8233	84	E Montdidier	2010	DES	CR/RAF 3.6
11	3 Jun	Fokker DrI	B8233	84	E Montdidier	2010	OOC	CR/?
12s**	17 Jun	Fokker DrI	C1834	84	Chaulnes	0940	OOC	CR/?
13	25 Jun	Pfalz DIII	C1874	84	Chipilly	1330	OOC	CR/?
14	27 Jun	Pfalz DIII	C1834	84	2.5m E Villers Brettoneaux	0945	DES	CR/RAF 27.6

TOTAL: 9 destroyed, 4 and 1 shared out of control = 14

*This was probably Lt Werner Meyer of Jasta 34 who was killed. 84 made 8 claims for 2 lost by Jasta 34. **Shared with Lt C.F. Falkenberg D6890, Lt A.F. Matthews B682.

SOUTHEY Walter Alfred Captain 48, 84

Born on 29 April 1897, in South Africa he served with the army for seven months before joining the RFC in August 1916. During spring 1917 he served in 48 Squadron, flying Bristol Fighters, but apparently made no claims. In April 1918 he joined 84 Squadron on SE 5As, where he was awarded the DFC and Bar and claimed 20 victories. During a late patrol on 25 July, the evening became very cloudy and he lost his bearings; he actually touched down behind the German lines before realising that he was in enemy territory. He very rapidly took off again and reached his own airfield. He became a flight commander during the summer.

	1918		SE 5A					
1	2 May	Alb. DV	D5399	84	E Abancourt	1450	OOC	CR/RAF 2.5
2	16 May	Fokker DrI	D5399	84	N N W Abancourt	1620	DES	CR/RAF 16.5
3s*	5 Jun	Rumpler C	D5399	84	200y W Moreuil	1235	DES	CR/RAF 5.6
4	18 Jun	Fokker DVII	B8399	84	Abancourt	1055	OOC	CR/?
5	1 Aug	Fokker DVII	C1834	84	Suzanne a/d	1005	DES	CR/RAF 1.8
6	7 Aug	Rumpler C	C1834	84	E Arvillers	0955	DES	CR/RAF 7.8
7	10 Aug	Fokker DVII	C1834	84	Peronne-Brie	1800	OOC	CR/?
8	17 Aug	Fokker DVII	C1834	84	Estrees	0900	OOC	CR/?

9s**	25 Aug	LVG. C	C1834	84	N Foucaucourt	0945	OOC	CR/?
10	29 Aug	Fokker DVII	C1834	84	W Athies	1445	OOC	CR/?
11s***	3 Sep	C	C1834	84	S Manancourt-Nurlu Rd	0615	DES(F)	CR/RAF 3.9
12	3 Sep	Balloon	C1834	84	Fins	0645	DES	CR/RAF 3.9
13	3 Sep	Balloon	C1834	84	N Fins	1530	DES	CR/RAF 3.9
14	14 Sep	Balloon	E6008	84	Gonnlieu	1030	DES	CR/RAF 14.9
15	14 Oct	Balloon	E4071	84	E Mont d'Origny	0700-0900	DES	CR/?
16	22 Oct	Balloon	F5625	84	Prisches	0915	DES	CR/RAF 22.10
17	23 Oct	Fokker DVII	F5625	84	S Fontaine	1115	DES	CR/RAF 23.10
18	27 Oct	Fokker DVII	E4071	84	Esqueheries	0910	OOC	CR/?
19	28 Oct	LVG. C	E5963	84	La Queue de Boue	0750	DES	CR/RAF 28.10
20	30 Oct	Fokker DVII	H685	84	Foret de Nouvion	0930	DES	CR/?

TOTAL: 5 balloons, 6 and 2 shared destroyed, 6 and 1 shared out of control = 20.
*Shared with Capt A.W. Beauchamp Proctor D333. **Shared with 2/Lt C.F.C. Wilson B6430. ***Shared with Lt A.E. Hill, 2/Lt C.F.C. Wilson,Lt E.R.W. Miller, 2/Lt F.R. Christiani.

SOWREY Frederick Major 39, 37, 19, 143

Born on 25 August 1893, he was one of three brothers to fly during the war, but was first commissioned in the Royal Fusiliers, in 1914. He served in France until he transferred to the RFC in December 1915. After training at Thetford he joined 39 (Home Defence) Squadron, and on the night of 23/24 September 1916, he engaged and shot down the Zeppelin L 32, which crashed at Billericay in Essex. For this action he was awarded the DSO, and shortly afterwards joined 37 (Home Defence) Squadron. The following year he went to France on liaison work, but on 14 June was posted to 19 Squadron as a flight commander, where he claimed at least 12 victories and received the MC. Returning to England, he took command of 143 (Home Defence) Squadron, a post he held until the war's end. He remained in the RAF after the war, commanding 100 Squadron in Ireland, 8 Squadron in Baghdad and then 41 Squadron at Northolt. He became a Group Captain in 1934 and retired from the service in 1940, to live in Eastbourne, Sussex, where he died in 1969. His son, Air Vice-Marshal F.B. Sowrey, CB, CBE, AFC, is President of Cross & Cockade International at the date of writing.

	1916		BE 2C					
1*	24 Sep	Zeppelin	4112	39	Billericay	c0110	DES	C&C RLR
	1917		Spad					
2	17 Jun	Alb. DIII	B1660	19	S E Houthoulst Forest	1845	DES	ORB/RFC 27.6
3	13 Jul	C	B3479	19	----	1338-1515	OOC	ORB/RFC 13.7
4s**	20 Jul	C	B3616	19	Houthoulst Forest	0625	DES	ORB/?
5	21 Jul	Alb. DIII	B3479	19	N E Ypres	1930	OOC	ORB/RFC 21.7
6	17 Aug	Alb. DIII	B3620	19	W Roulers	0630	DES	CR/RFC 17.8
7s***	20 Aug	Alb. C	B3616	19	S E Houthoulst Forest	0625	OOC	ORB/RFC 20.8
8s†	11 Sep	Rumpler C	B3616	19	E Quesnoy	1320	DES	CR/RFC 11.9
9	20 Sep	Alb. DV	B3520	19	N Menin	1820	OOC	CR/RFC 20.9
10s††	30 Sep	Alb. C	A6777	19	Gheluwe	0900	OOC	CR/RFC 30.9
11	7 Oct	Fokker DV	A6777	19	2m E Gheluvelt	1005	DES	CR/RFC 7.10
12s†††	9 Oct	Alb. C	A6667	19	Moorslede-Passchendaele	1040	OOC	CR/RFC 9.10
13	15 Oct	Alb. C	A6709	19	N E Moorslede	1645	DES(F)	CR/RFC 15.10

TOTAL: 1 Zeppelin, 4 and 2 shared destroyed, 3 and 3 shared out of control = 13.
*This was L32, commanded by Oblt z S. Werner Peterson. **Shared with 2/Lt A.A.N.D. Pentland. ***Shared with Lt A.A.N.D. Pentland B3620, Lt H.C. Ainger B3564. †Shared with Lt H.C. Ainger B3535. ††Shared with Lt Delamere B3489, Lt R.M. Strang B1697, Lt R.A. Hewat A6662, Lt J.G.S. Candy B3615 and an SE 5A. †††Shared with Lt R.A. Hewat A6662, Lt J.G.S. Candy B3615.

SPENCE Anthony George Allen Lieutenant 1(N), 201

A native of Toronto, Canada, Spence was born on 27 May 1897, attending Toronto University where he became a BA. He joined the RNAS in November 1916, completing his training in March the following year. He was posted to 1(N) Squadron in France to fly Sopwith Triplanes. By the end of October he had claimed six victories, but was wounded on 8 November. On recovery he returned to the squadron which had in the meantime converted to Camels, and claimed one further victory before the unit became 201 Squadron, RAF on 1 April 1918. He gained another victory and shared a second with five other pilots, but then on 10 May he was posted to Home Establishment, spending the rest of the war at the School of Special Flying, Gosport. He was demobilized in February 1919.

	1917		Triplane					
1	7 Jul	Alb. DV	N6300	1N	N Gheluvelt	1000	OOC	CR/DOS/DL
2s*	13 Jul	C	N5459	1N	E Warneton	1025	DES	CR/DOS/DL
3s**	17 Jul	Alb. DV	N6300	1N	4m E Messines	1805	OOC	CR/DOS/?
4	9 Aug	Alb. DV	N6300	1N	Moorslede	0740	OOC	CR/RFC 9.8

5	21 Oct	C	N5449	1N	S Comines	1100	OOC	CR/RFC 21.10
6	26 Oct	C	N5449	1N	Moorslede-Passchendaele	1010	OOC	CR/RFC 27.10
	1918		Camel					
7	6 Mar	Fokker DrI	B7267	1N	Bouchoir	1320	DES	CR/RNAS 16.3
8	6 Apr	Fokker DrI	B7267	201	Mericourt	1315	DES	CR/RAF 6.4
9s***	2 May	C	B7278	201	N Albert	1010	OOC	CR/RAF 2.5

TOTAL: 2 and 1 shared destroyed, 4 and 2 shared out of control = 9.

*Shared with F/Cdr F.H.M. Maynard N5479, FSL H.V. Rowley N6308. **Shared with FSL E. Anthony N6296, F/Lt C.B. Ridley N6304, FSL G.B. Scott N5455, FSL H.L. Everitt N6308, FSL H.V. Rowley N5373, F/Cdr F.H.M. Maynard N5479, FSL C.G. Brock N5485. ***Shared with Capt S.M. Kinkead B6429, Lt H.L. Wallace B6359, Lt R.E. Bright B7267, 2/Lt H. Riddell B7225, Lt R.C.B. Brading B6421.

SPRINGS Elliot White Captain 85, 148US

An American, born on 31 July 1896 at Fort Hill, South Carolina, he was educated at Culver Military Academy and Princeton University. He trained as an aviation cadet and in autumn 1917 was posted to England with 209 others to gain operational training and experience with British units. In the summer of 1918 he joined 85 Squadron and was credited with four victories before his SE 5A was shot down and he was wounded on 27 June, probably by Leutnant Josef Raesch of Jasta 43. On recovery he was posted to the 148th Aero Squadron, USAS, flying Camels attached to the British 65th Wing. As a flight commander he claimed 13 more victories, one of which was disallowed (a semi-official American list gives him 11 victories with the 148th Squadron, but this ignores his claims with 85 Squadron). In October the 148th and 17th Aero Squadrons joined the US 4th Pursuit Group and he became squadron commander; by this time he had received a DFC and DSC(US). Released in 1919, he became a barn-storming pilot in the US, and while travelling, wrote *War Birds*, a book based on the diaries of his dead squadron companion, John Grider. This book earned him half a million dollars when it captured the imagination of the English-speaking world. Following this success, he wrote numerous novels based loosely on his war experiences. He became Vice-President of his father's cotton mills until 1941, when he was recalled to active service with the USAAF. He retired after the war and died on 15 October 1959, worth $200 million.

	1918		SE 5A					
1	1 Jun	Pfalz DIII	C1885	85	La Gorgue	2015	OOC	CR/11 WS
2s*	17 Jun	C	D6851	85	S Merris	0645	DES	CR/RAF 17.6
3	18 Jun	C	D6851	85	Menin	1005	DES	CR/RAF 18.6
4	25 Jun	C	D6851	85	3m E Kemmel	1610	DES	CR/RAF 25.6
			Camel					
5	3 Aug	Fokker DVII	D8250	148US	S E Ostend	0940	DES(F)	CR/US 133
6	13 Aug	Fokker DVII	D8250	148US	7m S E Roye	1950	DES	CR/US 133
7	22 Aug	Fokker DVII	D8250	148US	S Velu	1010	DES	CR/RAF 22.8
8	22 Aug	Fokker DVII	D8250	148US	S Velu	1010	OOC	CR/US 133
9	22 Aug	Fokker DVII	D8250	148US	S Velu	1010	DES	CR/US 133
10	27 Aug	Fokker DVII	----	148US	Souchez-Pronville	1330	DES	CR/RAF 27.8
11	5 Sep	Fokker DVII	D8203	148US	Canal du Nord	1715	DES	CR/10 BG WD
12	5 Sep	Fokker DVII	D8203	148US	Canal du Nord	1720	OOC	CR/US 133
13s**	15 Sep	Halb. C	D8250	148US	Epinoy	1040	OOC	CR/US 133
14	20 Sep	Fokker DVII	D8250	148US	Aubigny	1455	DES	CR/RAF 20.9
15	24 Sep	Fokker DVII	D8250	148US	N E Bourlon	0740	DES	CR/RAF 24.9
16s***	27 Sep	Halb. C	E1550	148US	Fontaine-Notre-Dame	0955	DES	CR/RAF 27.9

TOTAL: 10 and 2 shared destroyed, 3 and 1 shared out of control = 16.

*Shared with Lt J. MacG. Grider C1883, Lt J.D. Canning C1922. **Shared with 1/Lt Cunnius, 1/Lt O.A. Ralston, 1/Lt H.C. Starkey. ***Shared with 1/Lt H.R. Clay E1580.

STACKARD Harold Francis Flight Sub Lieutenant 9(N)

A North Londoner from Muswell Hill, Stackard was born on 2 March 1895. He saw much action with the Royal Navy Division early in the war, serving at Antwerp in 1914, Gallipoli in 1915 and in France in 1916. Transferring to the RNAS, he joined 9(N) Squadron during March 1917 where he made two claims in May and one in June. He was shot down and force-landed on 8 June, following which he was rested. Returning to action in September, he claimed eleven further victories during that month and one more in October to bring his total to 15, all but one of which were shared.

	1917		Pup					
1s*	2 May	C	9916	9N	Middelkerke	2030	DES	CR/RNAS 3.5
2s**	31 May	C	----	9N	Ostend	1415	OOC	CR/DOS/DL
			Triplane					
3	8 Jun	Alb. DIII	N5451	9N	Dixmude	1145	OOC	CR/DOS/DL
			Camel					

4s***	3 Sep	Alb. DIII	B6204	9N	S E Pervyse	1830	DES	CR/RFC 3.9
5s†	4 Sep	DFW. C	B6204	9N	Nieuport-Middelkerke	2140	DES	CR/RFC 4.9
6s††	6 Sep	Alb. C	----	9N	Middelkerke	1335	OOC	CR/ORB/DL
7s†††	9 Sep	Alb. DV	B6204	9N	E Middelkerke	1905	OOC	CR/RFC 9.9
8s‡	11 Sep	Alb. DV	B3863	9N	Leke	1730	DES(F)	CR/RFC 12.9
9s‡	11 Sep	Alb. DV	B3863	9N	Leke	1730	DES	CR/RFC 12.9
10s‡‡	13 Sep	Alb. DV	----	9N	E Leke	----	OOC	ORB/DL/?
11s‡‡‡	24 Sep	Alb. DIII	B3883	9N	Leke	1545	OOC	CR/RFC 24.9
12	24 Sep	Alb. DV	B3883	9N	Middelkerke	1630	OOC	CR/ORB/DL
13s‡	30 Sep	Alb. C	B3883	9N	S Middelkerke	1055	DES	CR/RFC 30.9
14	30 Sep	Alb. C	B3883	9N	S Middelkerke	1155	OOC	CR/RFC 30.9
15s§	27 Oct	Alb. DV	B6327	9N	Slype	1040	OOC	CR/RFC 27.10

TOTAL: 6 shared destroyed, 3 and 6 shared out of control = 15.
*Shared with FSL H.G. Mott N5188. **Shared with F/Cdr F.E. Banbury, FSL Shearer. ***Shared with F/Cdr J.S.T. Fall B3898, FSL J.E. Scott B3884, FSL A.V. Wood B3907. †Shared with F/Cdr J.S.T. Fall B3898, FSL J.E Scott B3905. ††Shared with F/Cdr J.S.T. Fall, FSL H.L. Wallace, FSL J.E. Scott, FSL A.V. Wood. †††Shared with F/Cdr J.S.T. Fall B3898. ‡Shared with F/Cdr J.S.T Fall B3898, FSL A.V. Wood B3884. ‡‡Shared with FSL S.T. Edwards. ‡‡‡Shared with F/Cdr J.S.T. Fall B3892, FSL A.V. Wood B3885. §Shared with F/Cdr S.T. Edwards and others.

STANGER Stanley Captain 66, 28

Born in Montreal, Canada, on 10 July 1894, 'Stan' Stanger joined the RFC after two and a half years in the Canadian Army. He was commissioned on 10 May 1917 and joined 66 Squadron on 18 October 1917, serving in France and Italy, during which time he claimed three victories. He was then posted to 28 Squadron on 27 April 1918 where he claimed a further ten victories and was awarded the MC and DFC. He was wounded by anti-aircraft fire on 23 August and was out of action until 20 September. One day in October he felt ill while in the air and landed on an aerodrome only to find that it was in Austrian hands. He had switched his engine off, but by using his boots as chocks, he swung the propeller and took off before the enemy could prevent him. After the war he returned to Canada and joined his family's business, The Guardian Trust Co of Montreal. He became President of the company in 1939 and remained so until a few months before his death on 10 September 1967.

	1917		Camel					
1	14 Dec	Alb. DV	B6326	66	Ormelle	1015	OOC	ORB/SR/7 BG
	1918							
2	18 Mar	Berg DI	B2497	66	Cimadolmo	1550	DES	ORB/SR/7 BG
3	17 Apr	Alb. DV	B7358	66	Vittorio	1100	DES(F)	ORB/SR/7 BG
4	2 May	C	B6413	28	Valdobbiadene	1035	DES	CR/7 BG
5	3 May	C	B6413	28	Conegliano	1040	DES(F)	CR/7 BG
6	13 May	C	B6413	28	E Quero, into Piave	0845	DES	CR/14 W
7	23 May	Alb. DV	B6413	28	2km W Grigno	0725	DES	CR/14 W
8	3 Jun	Berg DI	D8103	28	S W Motta a/d	1500	DES	CR/14 W
9	27 Jul	Alb. DV	D8103	28	Grigno	0925	DES	CR/14 W
10	28 Jul	C	B8103	28	E Segasino	0825	DES(F)	CR/14 W
11s*	26 Sep	Alb. DV	D1581	28	10km S W Belluna	1100	DES	CR/14 W
12	4 Oct	Alb. DV	D8241	28	Tagliamento River	1345	DES	CR/14 W
13	4 Oct	Alb. DV	D8241	28	Tagliamento River	1345	DES	CR/14 W

TOTAL: 11 and 1 shared destroyed, 1 out of control = 13.
*Shared with Capt C.M. McEwan D8239.

STANTON Frederick Cecil Lieutenant 22

Commissioned on 26 September 1917, Lieutenant Stanton joined 22 Squadron in summer 1918; flying with observer Lieutenant C.J. Tolman, they were first in action on 10 July, when they claimed two scouts and a DFW two-seater.

	1918		Bristol					
1*	10 Jul	Pfalz DIII	D8089	22	S Lille	1015	DES	CR/RAF 10.7
2*	10 Jul	Pfalz DIII	D8089	22	S Lille	1015	DES	CR/RAF 10.7
3*	10 Jul	DFW. C	D8089	22	S Lille	1030	OOC	CR/SR/?
4*	13 Aug	Fokker DVII	----	22	Auberchicourt	1120	DES	CR/RAF 13.8
5*	13 Aug	Fokker DVII	----	22	Auberchicourt	1120	DES(F)	CR/RAF 13.8
6*	21 Aug	C	E2500	22	Albert	1945	OOC	CR/SR/?
7*	27 Aug	Fokker DVII	E2500	22	S E Senlemont	1400	OOC	CR/SR/?

TOTAL: 4 destroyed and 3 out of control = 7.
*Observer: Lt C.J. Tolman.

STATON William Ernest Captain 62

'Bull' Staton was born on 27 August 1898, and joined 62 Squadron, where he teamed up with Lieutenant J.R. Gordon as his gunner. He ultimately became the squadron's out standing exponent of the Bristol Fighter, and was awarded an MC, gazetted on 22 June 1918, Gordon also receiving a similar decoration. Staton was promoted to flight commander early in June, and having added 11 more victories to his total, was awarded a DFC, gazetted on 21 September. During August and September he flew with several gunners before operating regularly with 2nd Lieutenant L.E. Mitchell; by the end of September he had added a further six victories to bring his score to 26. He was then wounded, but was awarded a Bar to his DFC, gazetted on 3 December. He remained in the RAF, and being an excellent shot with rifle and pistol, represented the service at Bisley. In July 1934 he was a Flight Lieutenant in 501 Squadron, and the following year was promoted to Squadron Leader. June 1938 found him a Wing Commander leading 10 Squadron on Whitley bombers, and in 1940 he was awarded a DSO. Serving in the Far East in 1942, he was captured on Singapore and suffered considerably during the three years he spent in Japanese hands. In 1952, having reached the rank of Air Vice-Marshal two years earlier, he retired; he was made a CB. He enjoyed sailing in his later years, but he died on 22 July 1983 in Emsworth, Hampshire.

	1918		Bristol					
1*	13 Mar	Fokker DrI	C4619	62	Cambrai	1030	OOC	CR/RFC 13.3
2*	13 Mar	Alb. DV	C4619	62	Cambrai	1030	OOC	CR/RFC 13.3
3**	21 Mar	Fokker DrI	----	62	----	----	DES(F)	9 WS/RFC 21.3
4**	26 Mar	EA	----	62	----	----	DES	9 WS/?
5**	26 Mar	EA	----	62	----	----	DES	9 WS/?
6**	26 Mar	EA	----	62	----	----	OOC	9 WS/?
7**	1 Apr	Alb. DV	C4619	62	Bouchoir	1700	OOC	CR/RAF 1.4
8s***	21 Apr	Fokker DrI	----	62	S E Estaires	0945	DES	SR/RAF 21.4
9**	3 May	Alb. DV	C4619	62	2m S Armentieres	1130	DES	CR/RAF 3.5
10**	3 May	C	C4619	62	1m S E Ploegsteert	1140	DES	CR/RAF 3.5
11**	22 May	LVG. C	C874	62	N Laventie	0800	DES	CR/RAF 22.5
12**	29 May	LVG. C	C874	62	Aubigny	1915	DES	CR/RAF 29.5
13**	30 May	C	C874	62	Arras-Cambrai	1340	OOC	CR/9 WS
14**	2 Jun	Fokker DrI	C874	62	S Pozieres	1945	DES	CR/9 WS
15**	5 Jun	Pfalz DIII	C874	62	Douai	1645	DES	CR/RAF 5.6
16**	5 Jun	Pfalz DIII	C874	62	N W Douai	1650	DES	CR/RAF 5.6
17**	8 Jun	Pfalz DIII	C874	62	S E Bray	1745	OOC	CR/9 WS
18†	8 Jul	Fokker DrI	D7899	62	N W Carvin	0710	DES	CR/RAF 8.7
19††	12 Aug	EA	----	62	----	----	DES	SR/RAF 12.8
20††	12 Aug	EA	----	62	----	----	DES	SR/RAF 12.8
21††	13 Aug	Fokker DVII	----	62	Bullecourt	1030	OOC	SR/9 WS
22††	22 Aug	Fokker DVII	D7899	62	Pronville	0945	DES(F)	CR/RAF 22.8
23††	3 Sep	Fokker DVII	D7899	62	S E Marquion	1830	DES	CR/RAF 3.9
24††	4 Sep	Fokker DVII	D7899	62	Marquette, N Cambrai	0930	OOC	CR/9 WS
25s†††	15 Sep	Pfalz DXII	----	62	Marquion	1705	CAPT	SR/RAF 15.9
26††	24 Sep	Fokker DVII	----	62	E Cambrai	----	OOC	SR/9 WS

TOTAL: 1 shared captured, 15 and 1 shared destroyed, 9 out of control = 26.
*Observer: Lt H.E. Merritt. **Observer: Lt J.R. Gordon. ***Observer: Lt J.R. Gordon. Shared with Capt T.L. Purdom/ 2/Lt P.V.G. Chambers. †Observer: Sgt W.N. Holmes. ††Observer: Lt L.E. Mitchell. †††Observer: Lt L.E. Mitchell. Shared with 1 Sqn. Lt P. Vogel of Jasta 23 was killed.

STEAD Ian Oliver Lieutenant 22

A South African who joined the RFC in July 1917, Lieutenant Stead served with 22 Squadron, flying Bristol Fighters during the spring and summer of 1918, during which period he was credited with five victories, three with the front gun and two with the rear. He was reported missing in action with Lieutenant W.A. Cowie in E2516, shot down by Fokker DVIIs in the Cambrai area on 2 September.

	1918		Bristol					
1*	22 May	Pfalz DIII	C4706	22	Merville-Bailleul	1920	OOC	CR/ORB/SR/?
2**	16 Aug	Pfalz DIII	E1330	22	S S E Lille	1045	OOC	CR/ORB/SR/?
3s***	22 Aug	Halb. C	----	22	N E Bailleul	1910	DES	CR/RAF 22.8
4†	31 Aug	Fokker DVII	F4820	22	Douai	1710	DES	CR/RAF 31.8
5**	2 Sep	Fokker DVII	E2516	22	Arras-Cambrai Rd.	0915	OOC	CR/ORB/SR/?

TOTAL: 1 and 1 shared destroyed, 3 out of control = 5.
*Observer: Sgt C. Williams. **Observer: 2/Lt W.A. Cowie. ***Observer: 2/Lt W.A. Cowie. Shared with Capt W.F.J. Harvey/Capt D.E. Waight, Lt H.H. Beddow/Lt T.J. Birmingham. †Observer: Capt D.E. Waight.

STEELE Charles Ronald Captain 15, 20, 48

Born on 26 January 1896, Steele was seconded to the RFC from Sandhurst after receiving a commission in the Yorkshire Regiment. Following training at Farnborough and Montrose, he joined 15 Squadron in April 1916 as a BE 2C pilot. He flew many reconnaissance sorties and was with the squadron until April 1917, when he returned home for a rest, becoming an instructor at Stirling and Turnberry. He went through the SSF course at Gosport, and in November went to the School of Aerial Fighting at Ayr. He was attached to 20 Squadron for four weeks, and then went to 48 Squadron in February 1918, where he claimed seven victories and was awarded the DFC. He was wounded during an enemy air raid on his aerodrome on 24 August, which ended his flying during the war. In 1919 he went to Cranwell, then to Netheravon, before going out to India with 28 Squadron in August. He remained in the RAF, passing the Staff College Course in December 1935, following which he took command of 18 Squadron. He retired from the service as Air Marshal Sir Charles Steele, KCB, DFC.

	1918		Bristol					
1*	18 Mar	Fokker DrI	----	48	----	----	OOC	Citation
2s**	10 Jun	Alb. DV	----	48	Roye	1745	DES(F)	CR/RAF 10.6
3***	7 Jul	Pfalz DIII	D7909	48	S W Proyart	1130	DES(F)	CR/RAF 7.7
4†	8 Aug	DFW. C	F5811	48	Rosieres-Chaulnes	0950	OOC	CR/V BG WD
5††	13 Aug	Fokker DVII	C940	48	E Roye	1700	DES	CR/RAF 13.8
6††	13 Aug	Fokker DVII	C940	48	E Roye	1700	OOC	CR/V BG WD
7††	13 Aug	Fokker DVII	C940	48	E Roye	1700	OOC	CR/V BG WD

TOTAL: 2 and 1 shared destroyed, 4 out of control = 7.

*Observer: unknown. **Observer: unknown. Shared with Capt F.C. Ransley, Lt H.A. Oaks, Lt J.E. Drummond. ***Observer: Lt A.E. Ansell. †Observer: 2/Lt E. Vickers. ††Observer: Lt J.B. Jameson.

STEPHENS Eric John Captain 41

Born in Western Australia on 13 September 1895, he was commissioned in the RFC on 13 April 1917, becoming a pilot on 30 June. After a period as an instructor, he joined 41 Squadron on 16 March 1918, just before the German spring offensive. He claimed his first victory on 28 June, when he and Freddie McCall brought down a Rumpler two-seater. After this he began to claim quite regularly against German fighters, and by the war's end he had been made a flight commander. He was recommended for the DFC, which was gazetted in June 1919, having been credited with 13 victories. He flew for Qantas, the Australian airline, during the 1930s.

	1918		SE 5A					
1s*	28 Jun	Rumpler C	D5961	41	Belloy en Santerre	1150	DES	CR/RAF 28.6
2	30 Jun	Pfalz DIII	D5961	41	Bray-Peronne	0815	OOC	CR/SR/?
3	3 Jul	Pfalz DIII	C5359	41	E Lamotte	1915	OOC	CR/SR/?
4	29 Aug	Fokker DVII	C8868	41	S Armentieres	0850	OOC	CR/SR/11 WS
5	29 Aug	Fokker DVII	C8868	41	E Comines	0930	DES	CR/RAF 29.8
6	3 Sep	Fokker DVII	E1344	41	S Vitry	1845	OOC	CR/SR/11 WS
7	29 Sep	Fokker DVII	F5519	41	N E Roulers	1145	DES	CR/RAF 29.9
8	1 Oct	Fokker DVII	F5519	41	S W Roulers	1110	OOC	CR/SR/11 WS
9	1 Oct	Fokker DVII	F5519	41	S E Armentieres	1510	OOC	CR/SR/11 WS
10	8 Oct	DFW. C	F5469	41	Ledeghem	1233	DES	CR/11 WS
11	14 Oct	Fokker DVII	F5469	41	W Roulers	0855	OOC	CR/11 WS
12	28 Oct	Fokker DVII	F912	41	W Audenaarde	1530	DES	CR/RAF 28.10
13	1 Nov	Fokker DVII	F912	41	E Tournai	1520	OOC	CR/SR/11 WS

TOTAL: 4 and 1 shared destroyed, 8 out of control = 13.

*Shared with Capt F.R. McCall D3927.

STEPHENSON Thomas Frederick Sergeant 11

Stephenson flew Bristol Fighters in 11 Squadron in 1917, being awarded a DCM. On 31 October he and his observer, 1st Air Mechanic S.H. Platel, claimed two Albatros Scouts shot down, but were then hit and crash-landed, claimed by Oberleutnant Hans Bethge of Jasta 30 as his 18th victory. Sergeant Stephenson and Lieutenant T.W. Morse were subsequently reported missing in action in A7292 on the morning of 20 November 1917, shot down by Flakbatterie 710, 572, or Flak 4 and 9 Kompanie of Infanterie Regiment 184 west of Beaurevoir.

	1917		Bristol					
1*	23 Sep	Alb. DV	A7209	11	Vitry	1625	OOC	CR/RFC 23.9
2*	20 Oct	Alb. DV	----	11	N W Cambrai	1640	OOC	CR/RFC 20.10
3*	20 Oct	Alb. DV	----	11	N W Cambrai	1640	OOC	CR/RFC 20.10
4*	31 Oct	Alb. DV	A7235	11	Fresse	1530	DES(F)	CR/SR/?
5**	31 Oct	Alb. DV	A7235	11	Fresse	1530	DES	CR/SR/?

TOTAL: 2 destroyed, 3 out of control = 5.

*Observer: 1 AM S. Platel. **Observer: 1 AM S. Platel. Stephenson and Platel were shot down and crash-landed after this combat. Consequently the fight is not in the communiques.

STEPHENSON William Samuel Captain 73

Born in Winnipeg, Canada on 11 January 1896, he joined the Canadian Engineers and was badly gassed in France as a Sergeant, but continued to serve throughout 1916. He then transferred to the RFC, joining 73 Camel Squadron in 1918. He claimed 12 victories with this unit, and was awarded an MC and DFC. He also engaged in many ground strafing attacks. On 28 July he failed to return and was reported missing after a fight with several Fokkers, one of which he had brought down. He was only wounded however, becoming a prisoner of war; he later escaped from prison camp and returned to his squadron. After the war he became a successful businessman, but before and during World War II played a prominent role in counter-intelligence work in North America (fully recorded in his biography *A Man Called Intrepid*). For this service he was knighted by King George VI and decorated with the US Presidential Medal for Merit. He died in late January 1989 in Bermuda.

	1918		Camel					
1	22 Mar	Alb. DV	B7302	73	Marteville	1505	DES	CR/RFC 22.3
2	24 Mar	LVG. C	B6421	73	Poeuilly	1040	DES(F)	CR/RFC 24.3
3	3 May	Fokker DrI	----	73	Ploegsteert	1230	DES	SR/RAF 3.5
4	9 Jul	Fokker DrI	C8296	73	W Moncheaux	1205	DES	CR/RAF 9.7
5	16 Jul	Fokker DVII	C8296	73	Roncheres	2000	DES	CR/RAF 16.7
6	16 Jul	C	C8296	73	Roncheres	2000	OOC	CR/SR/?
7s*	21 Jul	Fokker DrI	C8296	73	N E Oulchy le Chateau	2000	DES	CR/RAF 21.7
8	22 Jul	Fokker DrI	C8296	73	Bazoches	1810	DES	CR/RAF 22.7
9	22 Jul	Fokker DVII	C8296	73	Bazoches	1815	DES(F)	CR/RAF 22.7
10	25 Jul	Fokker DVII	C8296	73	E Courmont	1900	DES	CR/RAF 25.7
11s**	25 Jul	LVG. C	C8296	73	Cohan	1945	DES	CR/RAF 25.7
12	28 Jul	Fokker DVII	C8296	73	N W Fere en Tardenois	1400	DES(F)	CR/RAF 28.7

TOTAL: 9 and 2 shared destroyed, 1 out of control = 12.

*Shared with Major R.H. Freeman D1918, Capt M.LeB. Smith D8164, Lt G.L. Graham D1958, 2/Lt K.S. Laurie B7874, Lt W. Sidebottom B8199, 2/Lt R.W. Chandler D1922, Lt J. Balfour D8114, Lt W.G. Peters B5449. **Shared with 2/Lt N. Cooper D6984.

STEVENS Frank Douglas Captain 20

An FE 2 pilot with 20 Squadron in 1917, 'Inky' Stevens with his various observers, claimed five victories and was promoted to Captain.

	1917		FE 2D					
1*	3 May	Alb. DIII	A6444	20	Westroosebeke	1715	OOC	CR/RFC 3.5
2**	3 Jul	Alb. DIII	A6516	20	Becelaere	1600	OOC	CR/RFC 4.7
3***	6 Jul	Alb. DIII	A6516	20	Comines	1830	OOC	CR/RFC 6.7
4†	17 Jul	Alb. DIII	A6516	20	Polygon Wood	1955	OOC	CR/RFC 17.7
5†	16 Aug	Alb. DIII	A6516	20	S E Polygon Wood	1100	OOC	CR/RFC 16.8

TOTAL: 5 out of control = 5.

*Observer: Lt H.R. Wilkenson. **Observer: Lt F.J. Kydd. ***Observer: Lt A.N. Jenks. †Observer: W.C. Cambray.

STEWART David Arthur Captain 20, 18

Second Air Mechanic D.A. Stewart shared in two victories with his pilots and participated in many other combats whilst flying as an observer/gunner in 20 Squadron FE 2Ds during the summer of 1916. It is believed that he was posted back to England for pilot training and subsequently joined 18 Squadron in the autumn of 1917 as a 2nd Lieutenant to fly DH 4s. Here he added 14 further victories, becoming one of the top-scoring bomber pilots of the war. Promoted to Captain in May 1918, he was awarded an MC and Bar, gazetted respectively on 22 April and 22 June, followed by a DFC in August.

	1916		FE 2D					
1*	1 Aug	Fokker EIII	A13	20	Moorslede	1600	DES	CR/RFC 1.8
2**	3 Aug	D	A23	20	Ypres	1010	DES	CR/RFC 3.8
	1918		DH 4					
3***	6 Jan	Alb. DV	A7653	18	Valenciennes	1205	OOC	CR/RFC 6.1
4***	6 Mar	Pfalz DIII	A7797	18	Lens-Pont a Vendin	1115	DES	CR/RFC 6.3
5***	6 Mar	Pfalz DIII	A7797	18	Lens-Pont a Vendin	1115	OOC	CR/RFC 6.3
6***	6 Mar	Alb. DV	A7797	18	Lens-Pont a Vendin	1120	OOC	CR/RFC 6.3
7***	6 Mar	Alb. DV	A7797	18	Lens-Pont a Vendin	1120	OOC	CR/RFC 6.3
8†	10 Mar	Pfalz DIII	A7799	18	Carvin-Fromelles	1245	OOC	CR/RFC 10.3
9††	15 Mar	Pfalz DIII	A8038	18	Avelin	1255	DES	CR/RFC 15.3
10†††	25 Mar	C	A8038	18	Loupart Wood	1715	DES	CR/RFC 25.3
11†††	27 Mar	Fokker DrI	A7800	18	S W Albert	1130	DES	CR/RFC 27.3
12†††	28 May	Alb. DV	A8038	18	W Douai	1140	DES	CR/RAF 28.5

13‡	30 May	Pfalz DIII	A8038	18	Neuve Chapelle	1300	DES	CR/RAF 30.5
14‡	30 May	Pfalz DIII	A8038	18	Richebourg St Vaast	1305	OOC	CR/?
15†††	17 Jun	Pfalz DIII	----	18	Hulloch	0845	DES	CR/RAF 17.6
16†††	17 Jun	Pfalz DIII	----	18	Loos	0850	OOC	CR/RAF 17.6

TOTAL: 9 destroyed, 7 out of control = 16.
*Pilot: Lt D.H. Dabbs. **Pilot: Capt R.S. Maxwell. ***Observer: 2/Lt H.W. Mackay. †Observer: Sgt C. Beardmore. ††Observer: Sgt A. Pollard. †††Observer: Capt L.I. Collins. ‡Observer: Lt W. Miller.

STEWART Oliver Major 22, 54

Oliver Stewart joined the 9th Middlesex Regiment as a 2nd Lieutenant in October 1914. He transferred to the RFC in 1915, served briefly with 22 Squadron, and then went to 54 Squadron in 1917, flying Sopwith Pups. He claimed five victories and received the MC, becoming a flight commander; his nickname in the squadron was 'Stewpot'. Returning to Home Establishment, he was promoted to Major in June 1918 and took command of the Aeroplane and Armament Experimental Establishment at Orfordness and Martlesham Heath; for his services he received the AFC. He retired from the RAF in 1921, becoming a well-known aviation writer; from 1939-62 he was Editor of *Aeronautics* magazine. He died in 1976, *Words and Music of a Mechanical Man*, his autobiography, having just been published.

	1917		Pup					
1	6 Apr	Alb. DIII	A6156	54	St Quentin	0800	DES	CR/RFC 6.4
2	24 May	Alb. DIII	A6156	54	Premont	0800	OOC	CR/RFC 24.5
3	6 Jun	Alb. DIII	A6156	54	S W Cambrai	1200	DES	CR/RFC 6.6
4s*	15 Aug	C	----	54	----	----	DES	RFC 15.8
5	25 Sep	Alb. DV	A6211	54	N Middelkerke	1130	DES	CR/RFC 25.9

TOTAL: 3 and 1 shared destroyed, 1 out of control = 5.
*Shared with 2/Lt C.G. Wood, 2/Lt G. Clapham.

STONE C.O. Lieutenant 2AFC

Born at Chingford, Essex, in September 1893, Stone emigrated with his family to Australia, and was employed in that country as a chauffeur when the war broke out. He joined the AFC and was posted to France, serving in 2AFC Squadron. He made one claim in July 1918, but his other six victories were all claimed during the last two months of the war, including two Fokker DVIIs in a day on two occasions.

	1918		SE 5A					
1s*	17 Jul	Fokker DrI	D6919	2AFC	Armentieres	1730	DES(F)	CR/RAF 18.7
2	3 Sep	Fokker DVII	D6919	2AFC	3m N W Cambrai	1720	OOC	CR/ORB/OH/?
3	14 Oct	Fokker DVII	D6919	2AFC	Tournai	1610	OOC	CR/RAF 14.10
4	14 Oct	Fokker DVII	D6919	2AFC	Havron	1610	DES	CR/RAF 14.10
5	28 Oct	Fokker DVII	A6919	2AFC	Mons	1120	OOC	CR/ORB/OH/?
6	4 Nov	Fokker DVII	D6919	2AFC	Renaix	0810	DES	CR/RAF 4.11
7	4 Nov	Fokker DVII	D6919	2AFC	Houtaing	1310	OOC	CR/ORB/OH/?

TOTAL: 2 and 1 shared destroyed, 4 out of control = 7.
*Shared with Capt A.T. Cole C1934. This was Lt O. Francke of Jasta 30, who was killed.

STRANGE Gilbert John Captain 40

Known as 'Ben', he was the younger brother of Lieutenant Colonel L.A. Strange, DSO, MC, DFC. After leaving school, he went to Sandhurst, and then to the CFS for pilot training. For a while he remained at the school as an instructor, but was then posted to 40 Squadron. In a fight with several Fokker DVIIs on 24 September 1918, he was seen to shoot one down, but was then shot down himself and killed. He had only been promoted to Captain a few days earlier.

	1918		SE 5A					
1s*	30 Jun	Balloon	D8197	40	Annay	1045	DES	CR/RAF 30.6
2s**	8 Jul	Hannover C	B191	40	E Monchy	0925	OOC	CR/SR/?
3s***	13 Jul	Hannover C	B191	40	W Estaires	0645	DES	CR/RAF 13.7
4	13 Jul	Pfalz DIII	B191	40	E Brebieres	2005	DES	CR/RAF 13.7
5	22 Jul	Fokker DVII	D3527	40	Carvin-Pont a Vendin	0850	DES	CR/RAF 22.7
6	8 Aug	Fokker DrI	B191	40	Don	1030	OOC	CR/SR/?
7	24 Sep	Fokker DVII	E4054	40	Cambrai	0700	DES	CR/RAF 24.9

TOTAL: 1 shared balloon, 3 and 1 shared destroyed, 1 and 1 shared out of control = 7.
*Shared with Capt G.E.H. McElroy C8869, Lt A.R. Whitton B191. **Shared with Capt G.E.H. McElroy C8869, Lt I.L. Roy B189. ***Shared with Capt G.E.H. McElroy C8869, Lt F.H. Knobel D3528, Lt I.L. Roy B189.

STRUGNELL William Victor Major 1, 54

Born on 23 July 1892, the son of a Regular Army family, 'Struggy' was one of the first aviators possessing a private pilot's licence as early as 1912; he was the third NCO pilot to receive a flying certificate. He joined the RFC and served with 3 and 5 Squadrons before the war; soon after hostilities began he went to France with 1 Squadron, with which he flew from mid 1915 to 1916. He saw a good deal of action, claimed at least one victory, and was awarded the MC, having been commissioned at an earlier date. After a period of instructing, he returned to France and commanded 'A' Flight of 54 Squadron in 1917. A Bar to his MC was gazetted in July. Ending the war with the rank of Major, he remained in the RAF, later serving in Iraq and Egypt. He became a Group Captain in July 1934, and retired in 1945. Long associated with the Air Training Corps in Cornwall, he died in 1977.

	1916		Morane					
1	5 Feb	Aviatik C	5068	1	S E Armentieres	----	OOC	CR/RFC 5.2
	1917		Pup					
2s*	19 Mar	C	----	54	Roisel	0745	DES(F)	CR/RFC 19.3
3	14 Apr	C	A7306	54	Buissy-Inchy	0815	OOC	CR/RFC 14.4
4	1 May	Alb. DIII	A7306	54	E St Quentin	0710	OOC	CR/RFC 1.5
5s**	11 May	C	A6168	54	Walincourt	1840	DES	CR/RFC 11.5
6	11 May	Alb. DIII	A6168	54	Beaurevoir	1910	DES	CR/RFC 11.5

TOTAL: 1 and 2 shared destroyed, 3 out of control = 6.

*Shared with Lt E.J.Y. Grevelink A7308. **Shared with Lt M.D.G. Scott, Lt O.M. Sutton, Major C.E. Sutcliffe, Lt E.J.Y. Grevelink, Lt M.B. Cole.

STUART-WORTLEY Rothesay Nicholas Montague Major 22, 44, 88

Born on 9 January 1892, at Highcliffe Castle, Hampshire, he was educated at Eton and Oxford, where he gained Honours in History. In mid 1914 he joined the Hampshire Yeomanry, and when war was declared he went onto the staff of his father — a Brigadier General — in an infantry brigade. He joined the RFC early in 1917 and in August went to 22 Squadron where he became a flight commander and was awarded an MC. With his observers, he claimed at least six victories. Returning to England, he took command of 44 (Home Defence) Squadron and then in September 1918 went back to France to take command of 88 Squadron in the 80th Wing. After the war he was taken ill and died in the South of France in 1920.

	1917		Bristol					
1*	6 Sep	C	----	22	S E Zonnebeke	c0745	OOC	CR/RFC 6.9
2	6 Sep	Alb. DV	----	22	S E Zonnebeke	c0745	OOC	CR/RFC 6.9
3	22 Sep	Alb. DV	A7118	22	Houthoulst Forest	0900	DES	CR/RFC 22.9
4	22 Sep	Alb. DV	A7118	22	Houthoulst Forest	0900	DES	CR/RFC 22.9
5**	17 Oct	Alb. DIII	A7268	22	Ypres	1110	CAPT	CR/RFC 17.10
	1918							
6***	28 Jan	Alb. DV	C4835	22	Douvrin	1110	DES(F)	CR/?

TOTAL: 1 captured, 3 destroyed, 2 out of control = 6.

*Observer: 2/Lt P.V. Burton. **Observer: Lt H.D. McGrath. This was G.81 on the captured aircraft list. ***Observer: Lt D.W. Kent-Jones.

STUBBS Charles Lionel Lieutenant 84

Born in 1898 in Liverpool, Charles Stubbs joined the RFC on 15 February 1917, qualifying as a pilot in July with 84 Squadron as it was forming. One of the original members of this unit, he claimed six victories but was wounded on 8 May 1918. He returned to the squadron late in the war, making one final claim at the end of October.

	1918		SE 5A					
1	18 Feb	C	C5303	84	Beaurevoir	1100	OOC	CR/SR/?
2*	13 Mar	Alb. DV	C5303	84	N E St Quentin	1010	OOC	CR/RFC 13.3
3**	17 Mar	Alb. DV	C5303	84	Busigny	1145	DES	CR/RFC 17.3
4s***	12 Apr	C	C9519	84	N Hangard	1120	CAPT	CR/RAF 12.4
5s†	12 Apr	DFW. C	C9519	84	Bapaume	1150	OOC	CR/RAF 12.4
6	23 Apr	Fokker DrI	C9519	84	Framerville	1640	DES	CR/RAF 23.4
7	30 Oct	Halb. C	B8010	84	N Mormal Wood	1030	OOC	CR/SR/?

TOTAL: 1 shared captured, 2 destroyed, 3 and 1 shared out of control = 7.

*Probably Vzfw A. Bleymuller of Jasta 8, who was killed. **84 made 3 claims in this area at this time. One victim was probably Vzfw Adolf Schreder of Jasta 17. ***Shared with Lt J.F. Larson C1772, Lt H.W.L. Saunders C1794, Lt H.O. MacDonald C6410. The crew were Uffz Drexler/Lt Kalfeken of FAA 205. †Shared with LT W.E. Lunnon D276.

SUMMERS John Kenneth Captain 3, 209

Born on 22 December 1894, he was commissioned in the Royal Warwickshire Regiment on 25 January 1915, then joining the RFC as an observer. In May he went to 3 Squadron, flying in Morane Parasols; after five months of operations he returned to Castle Bromwich for pilot training. He rejoined 3 Squadron in June 1917, serving until October, and being awarded an MC. 'Boom' Trenchard then insisted that he should be rested, but Summers managed to get a job as liaison officer with the 1st Brigade Headquarters, and then got himself posted back to his squadron. He eventually returned to Home Establishment, but came back to France in June 1918, where he was given a flight in 209 Squadron, flying Camels. He flew many ground attack missions and in air fighting claimed eight victories. On 12 August his flight was engaged by JG I and he and two of his pilots were shot down. Summers was taken prisoner and was 'entertained' by his captors of the famed Richthofen Circus, meeting the man who had shot him down — Leutnant Lothar von Richthofen of Jasta 11; he had been the German's 40th and last victory. After the war Summers undertook two navigation courses, and in 1923 joined 45 Squadron in Iraq, taking command in 1926. At the end of 1928 he went to Headquarters, Air Defence of Great Britain at Uxbridge; several postings in Bomber Command followed, and in 1940 he became Commanding Officer of the Blenheim Operational Training Unit. In 1941 he went to Rhodesia to form the Combined Air Observers' School, but he retired in 1943, settling in Rhodesia where he became a farmer.

	1918		Camel					
1s*	23 Jun	LVG. C	D3338	209	Martinpuich	0710	OOC	CR/ORB/?
2	1 Jul	Alb. DV	D9607	209	Bray	1940	OOC	CR/ORB/?
3s**	18 Jul	Alb. C	C198	209	Grivesnes-Plessier	1100	DES	CR/RAF 18.7
4s***	26 Jul	Fokker DVII	----	209	N Comines	0720	OOC	CR/ORB/?
5	8 Aug	Fokker DVII	B7471	209	Caix	1915	DES(F)	CR/RAF 8.8
6	8 Aug	Fokker DVII	B7471	209	Caix	1915	DES	CR/RAF 8.8
7s†	10 Aug	Fokker DVII	D9637	209	E Bouchoir	1155	CAPT	CR/RAF 10.8
8	11 Aug	Fokker DVII	D9637	209	Peronne	0755	DES	CR/RAF 11.8

TOTAL: 1 shared captured, 3 and 1 destroyed, 1 and 2 shared out of control = 8.
*Shared with Lt W.J. Armstrong D3398. **Shared with Lt K.M. Walker D1891. ***Shared with Lt A.L. Porter, Lt K.M. Walker. †Shared with Lt K.M. Walker D9657. Probably Lt Muhs of Jasta 12.

SUTTON Oliver Manners Captain 21, 54, 28

Oliver Sutton transferred to the RFC from the South Lancashire Regiment (SR), flying BE 12s in 21 Squadron in late 1916, before he flew Pups with 54 Squadron in 1917. On 24 May during a patrol led by his flight commander, Oliver Stewart, they got into a fight during which Sutton collided with an Albatros and lost about a foot off his starboard top wing. He managed to get his damaged aircraft back to base, but the incident was reported and gave rise to a story that RFC pilots were using ramming tactics. After a period with 91 and 93 Squadrons at Martlesham Heath, he was posted to Italy as a flight commander with 28 Squadron. He claimed seven victories and was subsequently awarded an MC. He was killed in a flying accident testing a four-engine triplane, on 16 August 1921.

	1917		Pup					
1	2 Apr	C	A637	54	E Peronne	0800	OOC	CR/RFC 2.4
2s*	11 May	C	A6183	54	Walincourt	1840	DES	CR/RFC 11.5
3**	24 May	Alb. DIII	A6183	54	Premont	0810	DES	CR/RFC 24.5
4s***	1 Jun	Alb. DIII	A6183	54	Honnecourt	1125	DES	CR/RFC 1.6
5	5 Jun	Alb. DIII	A6183	54	Brebieres	0700	OOC	CR/RFC 5.6
6	6 Jun	Alb. DIII	A6183	54	S W Cambrai	1200	DES	CR/RFC 6.6
	1918		Camel					
7	15 Aug	D	B6344	28	4km S E Feltre	1200	OOC	CR/ORB/?

TOTAL: 2 and 2 shared destroyed, 3 out of control = 7.
*Shared with Capt V.W. Strugnell A6168, Lt M.D.G. Scott, Major C.E. Sutcliffe, Lt E.J.Y Grevelink, Lt M.B. Cole. **Sutton collided with this aircraft. ***Shared with Lt M.D.G. Scott A7336.

SWALE Edwin Captain 10(N), 210

Born on 28 June 1899 in Chesterfield, he joined the RNAS on 19 August 1917. After training he was posted to 10(N) on 21 March 1918, becoming 'A' Flight commander on 5 September. He was awarded a DFC in September and a Bar in late October, claiming a total of 17 victories during 440 hours operational flying. Posted to Home Establishment on 21 October, he left the RAF after the war and entered the family business. He was later prominent in local politics in Chesterfield, serving on the Town Council between 1927-33, and 1946-71; he was Mayor in 1953. During World War II he served in the RAF as a Wing Commander, connected with 'Ultra' code-breaking intelligence. He received an OBE in 1958 and a CBE in 1964; he died in 1978.

	1918		Camel					
1	30 May	Pfalz DIII	D3392	210	W Armentieres	1130	DES	CR/RAF 30.5
2	5 Jun	Balloon	D3392	210	Estaires	1000	DES	CR/RAF 5.6

3	17 Jun	Alb. DV	D9613	210	S E Zillebeke Lake	0800	DES	CR/RAF 17.6
4	20 Jul	Fokker DVII	D9613	210	S E Ostend	0945	OOC	CR/5 GP Comm
5	20 Jul	Fokker DVII	D9613	210	S E Ostend	0945	OOC	CR/5 GP Comm
6	22 Jul	Fokker DVII	D9613	210	S Ostend	1755	DES	CR/5 GP Comm
7	1 Aug	Fokker DVII	D9675	210	N Lille	1925	OOC	CR/5 GP Comm
8	11 Aug	Fokker DVII	D9675	210	W Roulers	0930	DES	CR/5 GP Comm
9	15 Aug	Fokker DVII	D9675	210	S E Brugge	1620	DES	CR/5 GP Comm
10	1 Sep	Fokker DVII	E4406	210	E Ypres	1830	OOC	CR/5 GP Comm
11	3 Sep	Fokker DVII	E4406	210	Courtrai	1830	DES	CR/5 GP Comm
12	6 Sep	Fokker DVII	E4406	210	W Ostend	1835	DES	CR/5 GP Comm
13	24 Sep	Fokker DVII	D3332	210	S St Pierre Capelle	1440	DES	CR/5 GP Comm
14	29 Sep	Fokker DVII	F3116	210	Courtemarck	0800	DES	CR/5 GP Comm
15	1 Oct	Fokker DVII	D3332	210	S E Roulers	1710	DES	CR/5 GP Comm
16	1 Oct	Fokker DVII	D3332	210	Roulers	1715	OOC	CR/5 GP Comm
17	8 Oct	Fokker DVII	D3332	210	4m N E Roulers	0920	DES(F)	CR/5 GP Comm

TOTAL: 12 destroyed, 5 out of control = 17.

SWAYZE William Keith Lieutenant 62

'Pete' Swayze joined 62 Squadron on 4 January 1918, claiming his first victory on 22 May. By mid August his total had reached six. However on 4 September, while flying Bristol Fighter D7945 with 2nd Lieutenant W.E. Hall as observer, Swayze experienced an engine failure over the German lines. He was then attacked and forced to land by Leutnant Martin Demisch of Jasta 58, coming down on that unit's airfield. Swayze returned to Toronto on 11 February 1919, but was seriously ill and died in 1920.

	1918		Bristol					
1*	22 May	LVG. C	C4633	62	2m N W Merville	0800	DES	CR/RAF 22.5
2**	9 Jun	Pfalz DIII	B1238	62	N W Cambrai	1040	DES(F)	CR/RAF 9.6
3**	9 Jun	Pfalz DIII	B1238	62	N W Cambrai	1040	DES(F)	CR/RAF 9.6
4***	3 Aug	EA	----	62	----	----	OOC	SR/C&C V17 N4
5***	12 Aug	EA	----	62	----	----	OOC	SR/C&C V17 N4
6	12 Aug	EA	----	62	----	----	OOC	SR/C&C V17 N4

TOTAL: 3 destroyed, 3 out of control = 6.
*Observer: 2/Lt T. Elliott. **Observer: 2/Lt E.M. Nicholas. ***Observer: 2/Lt W.E. Hall.

SYKES Ronald Captain 9(N), 3(N), 201

Born in Stockton-on-Tees on 3 March 1899, Sykes joined the RNAS in April 1917. Posted to 9(N) Squadron in September, he became a member of Roy Brown's flight. Within days of joining the unit he was shot down behind enemy lines on 20 September by Unteroffizier Paul Baumer of Jasta Boelcke as the fifth of his 43 victories, coming down near St Pierre Capelle in Camel B3906. Sykes successfully avoided capture, swimming across the Yser River and regaining Allied lines. In March 1918 he joined 3(N) Squadron under Ray Collishaw and flew during the battles of Bapaume and Merville, during which time he brought down his second enemy machine. In August he went to 201 Squadron where he became a flight commander, bringing his score to six and receiving a DFC. In 1919 Sykes served with the RAF in North Russia where he again flew Camels, until he was forced down behind Red lines when his tension wires snapped. He was taken as a prisoner to Moscow, and later exchanged in 1920. Leaving the RAF, he became a chartered engineer with ICI. He contributed two articles to *Cross & Cockade* during the 1970s, shortly before his death.

	1917		Camel					
1	20 Sep	Alb. DIII	B3906	9N	St Pierre Capelle	1510	OOC	CR/RFC 22.9
	1918							
2	30 May	Fokker DrI	B6378	203	Fournes en Weppes	1810	OOC	CR/I BG WD
3s*	12 Aug	Fokker DVII	B7190	201	St Christ	1100	DES	CR/RFC 12.8
4s*	12 Aug	Fokker DVII	B7190	201	St Christ	1100	DES	CR/RAF 12.8
5	2 Sep	Fokker DVII	D9669	201	Lagnicourt	0715	DES	CR/RAF 2.9
6	9 Nov	Fokker DVII	F5941	201	Bois de Princemaille	1445	OOC	CR/SR/?

TOTAL: 1 and 2 shared destroyed, 3 out of control = 6.
*Shared with Capt H.R. de Wilde C143, Lt R. McLoughlin B6398.

SYMONDSON Francis Stanley Captain 29, 66

From Bromley, Kent, Symondson transferred to the RFC after serving for three and a half years overseas in the Glamorgan Yeomanry. Posted to 29 Squadron on 4 September 1917 aged 20, he was with the unit for 16 days during which time he crashed three Nieuports; he was then despatched home for further training. He subsequently joined 66 Squadron in Italy where he was to claim 11 aircraft and two balloons shot down. He received awards of the MC and the Italian Medal for Military Valour, ending the war as a Captain. His interest in flying remained, and he flew light aircraft for pleasure during the 1930s. In May 1935 he flew a Gipsy Moth in an air display during Jubilee Week. He died on 1 May 1975.

	1918		Camel					
1	7 Mar	Balloon	B2445	66	Chiarano	1015	DES(F)	ORB/SR/7 BG
2	16 Mar	Berg DI	B2445	66	Col la Parada	1200	DES	ORB/SR/7 BG
3	30 Mar	Alb. DIII	B7353	66	Mt Maletto	1315	DES	ORB/SR/7 BG
4*	4 Apr	Alb. DV	B7353	66	R Brenta at Cismon	0915	DES	ORB/SR/7 BG
5	17 Apr	Alb. DIII	B7353	66	S Giacomo	1415	DES(F)	ORB/SR/14 W
6	17 Apr	Alb. DIII	B7353	66	S Giacomo	1425	DES(F)	ORB/SR/14 W
7	6 May	Alb. DIII	B7353	66	Motta	1040	DES	ORB/SR/14 W
8	6 May	Alb. DIII	B7353	66	Motta	1042	DES	ORB/SR/14 W
9	6 Jun	Alb. DV	D1912	66	Zangetti	1225	DES	ORB/SR/14 W
10	15 Jun	Alb. DV	D9406	66	Val d'Assa	0810	DES	ORB/SR/14 W
11	13 Aug	Balloon	D9390	66	W Conegliano	0935	DES	ORB/SR/14 W
12	28 Aug	Aviatik C	D9390	66	S Feltre	1705	DES	ORB/SR/14 W
13	15 Sep	Berg DI	E1577	66	N E Feltre	0830	OOC	ORB/SR/14 W

TOTAL: 2 balloons, 10 destroyed, 1 out of control = 13.
*66 made 3 claims. Offstvtrt Kurt Gruber of Flik 60j was killed in Phonix DI 228:24.

SYMONS Harry Lutz Captain 65

Symons first served with the Canadian Engineers before joining the RFC in August 1917; he was posted to 65 Squadron late in the year, claiming his first victory during November. He claimed three more during the following January and another two next month to bring his score to six, two destroyed and four out of control. He was promoted to flight commander while with the squadron.

	1917		Camel					
1	15 Nov	Alb. DIII	B2418	65	Dadizeele	0740	OOC	CR/RFC 15.11
	1918							
2	10 Jan	Alb. DV	B5600	65	Frelinghien	1530	OOC	CR/RFC 10.1
3	29 Jan	Alb. DV	B5600	65	S W Roulers	1255	OOC	CR/RFC 29.1
4	29 Jan	C	B5600	65	S W Roulers	1300	OOC	CR/RFC 29.1
5	18 Feb	C	B5599	65	Kestelhoek	1010	DES	CR/??
6s*	21 Feb	Alb. DV	B5600	65	3m E Dixmude	1450	DES(F)	CR/RFC 21.2

TOTAL: 2 destroyed, 4 out of control = 6.
*Shared with Lt Andre de Meeulemeester, of the Belgian Flying Corps.

TAPLIN Leonard Thomas Eaton Lieutenant 67, 1AFC, 4 AFC

Born on 16 December 1895, in Adelaide, South Australia, Taplin worked in Sydney as an electrical engineer until the outbreak of war, when he joined the Australian Army Engineers. He later transferred to the AFC, and in 1917 joined 67 Squadron (soon to become 1AFC Squadron) in Palestine. On 17 January 1918, flying the unit's only BE 12A, he was trying to take air to ground photographs when his camera jammed. While repairing it, he was attacked by an Albatros Scout. He fired at this, but after one shot his gun also jammed. Disengaging, he cleared the stoppage, attacked and drove down the Albatros then continued his sortie. In July he was posted to France, joining 4 AFC Squadron, where he flew Camels. He shot down a two-seater on 17 July, but on 26th while taking off laden with bombs, the axle of his undercarriage snapped. Hastily, he switched off the engine and unfastened his safety belt; as his aircraft touched the ground and the bombs exploded, he was thrown clear, unhurt! During the next six weeks he claimed ten victories, four of them over balloons, and on 5 September flew in a patrol of five aircraft which met a larger formation of JG III Fokker DVIIs from Jasta 26 and 27. The leader of the Camels gave the signal to disengage and broke away, but the others did not see this, and became involved in a dogfight. Taplin claimed one out of control (which he claimed on his return after the war) and damaged a second, but all four Camels were shot down, only Taplin surviving. Wounded, he became a prisoner for the rest of the war. He was awarded a DFC.

	1918		Camel					
1	17 Jul	Alb. C	C8226	4AFC	S W Estaires	0620	DES	CR/RAF 17.7
2	30 Jul	Fokker DVII	E1407	4AFC	N Armentieres	2005	OOC	CR/ORB/OH
3	31 Jul	Fokker DVII	E1407	4AFC	S Lestrem	1135	DES	CR/RAF 31.7
4	31 Jul	Fokker DVII	E1407	4AFC	S W Estaires	1135	OOC	CR/ORB/OH
5	7 Aug	Alb. DV	E1407	4AFC	S Laventie	1405	DES(F)	CR/RAF 7.8
6	9 Aug	Hannover C	D9432	4AFC	N Marquillies	1050	DES	CR/RAF 9.8
7	1 Sep	Balloon	E1407	4AFC	Fromelles	0740	DES	CR/RAF 1.9
8	2 Sep	Halb. C	E1407	4AFC	E Aubers	1900	DES	CR/RAF 2.9
9	3 Sep	Balloon	E1407	4AFC	Le Plouich	0705	DES	CR/RAF 3.9
10	3 Sep	Balloon	E1407	4AFC	Herlies	1900	DES	CR/80 W/OH
11	5 Sep	Balloon	E1407	4AFC	Perenchies	0630	DES	CR/RAF 5.9
12	5 Sep	Fokker DVII	E1407	4AFC	Brebieres	c1800	OOC	SR/OH

TOTAL: 4 balloons, 5 destroyed, 3 out of control = 12.

TAYLER St Cyprian Churchill Captain 32, 80

He joined the RFC in 1916 from the Royal Sussex Regiment, and was posted to 32 Squadron. During the first half of 1917 he flew in Captain Coningham's DH 5 flight with which he claimed six victories before he was wounded on 31 July. Recovering, he was promoted to Captain and in late 1917 joined 80 Squadron as a flight commander as the unit was forming, moving to France with it in January 1918. Here he added three more victories to his total before he was killed in action in Camel B9209 on 17 March, probably shot down by Leutnant Heinrich Kroll of Jasta 24 south of Cambrai. Tayler had been awarded an MC on 26 September 1917.

	1917		DH 2					
1*	23 Jan	C	----	32	Ervillers	1515	DES(F)	ORB/SD/?
			DH 5					
2	14 May	Alb. DIII	A4800	32	S E Baralle	1030	DES	CR/RFC 14.5
3	11 Jul	Alb. DIII	A9385	32	Hooge	0915	OOC	ORB/RFC 11.7
4	12 Jul	Alb. DIII	A9185	32	Polygon Wood	0955	OOC	CR/RFC 12.7
5s**	27 Jul	C	A9213	32	Gheluvelt	1445	DES	ORB/RFC 27.7
6s***	28 Jul	Alb. C	A9213	32	Pilkem	0530	DES	ORB/RFC 28.7
7s†	29 Jul	A.G.O. C	A9213	32	Langemarck	0800	CAPT	CR/RFC 29.7
	1918		Camel					
8	10 Mar	Alb. DV	----	80	Bohain-Ribemont	----	DES	SR/RFC 10.3
9	10 Mar	Alb. DV	----	80	Bohain-Ribemont	----	OOC	SR/RFC 10.3
10	13 Mar	Alb. DV	----	80	----	----	DES	SR/RFC 13.3

TOTAL: 1 shared captured, 2 and 3 shared destroyed, 4 out of control = 10.
*Shared with Capt L.P. Aizlewood, Lt G.J. King, Lt F.Billinge, Lt T.A. Gooch, Lt A.C. Randall, 2/Lt A. Coningham. **Shared with Lt W.R.G. Pearson A9399, 2/Lt E. Pownall A9396, 2/Lt R.G. Ottey B353. ***Shared with Capt R.M. Williams B353, Lt W.R.G. Pearson A9207, 2/Lt T.E. Salt A9421. †Shared with Capt R.M. Williams A9398, Lt W.R.G. Pearson A9424, 2/Lt C. Turner A9207. This was a crew from FAA 202.

TAYLOR A.G.V. Captain 20

After service with the Indian Infantry, Taylor transferred to the RFC in 1917 and flew with 20 Squadron during the summer and autumn of that year. He flew FE 2Ds and later, Bristol Fighters, gaining three of his victories on the former type. On 19 September he and his observer were involved in a fight with several Albatros Scouts, claiming three of their assailants shot down, although the observer was wounded. Taylor was shot down and killed in A7271 on 17 October 1917 over Poelcapelle at 0930, victim of either Leutnant T. Quandt or H. Bongartz of Jasta 36; his observer, Sergeant W.J. Berger, also died of his wounds.

	1917		FE 2D					
1*	16 Aug	Alb. DIII	A6456	20	Zonnebeke	0930	OOC	CR/RFC 16.8
2*	17 Aug	Alb. DIII	B1890	20	E Polygon Wood	2000	DES	CR/RFC 17.8
3**	11 Sep	Alb. DV	A6458	20	N Wervicq	1430	OOC	CR/RFC 11.9
			Bristol					
4***	19 Sep	Alb. DV	A7246	20	Becelaere-Polygon Wood	1000	DES(F)	CR/RFC 19.9
5***	19 Sep	Alb. DV	A7246	20	Becelaere-Polygon Wood	1000	OOC	CR/RFC 19.9
6***	19 Sep	Alb. DV	A7246	20	Becelaere-Polygon Wood	1000	OOC	CR/RFC 19.9
7†	3 Oct	Alb. DV	A7271	20	Wervicq	1500	OOC	CR/RFC 3.10

TOTAL: 2 destroyed, 5 out of control = 7.
*Observer: 2/Lt M. Todd. **Observer: Lt G.A. Brooke. ***Observer: 2/Lt H. Dandy. †Observer: Sgt W.J. Benger.

TAYLOR Edgar Lieutenant 79

An American from Central Falls, Long Island, Taylor flew Sopwith Dolphins with 79 Squadron, joining the unit on 24 April 1918. During August he claimed four balloons in rapid succession, but failed to return after shooting down the last of these on 24th of that month. He was shot down by anti-aircraft fire in C3727 and killed.

	1918		Dolphin					
1	4 Aug	Fokker DVII	C3727	79	Neuve-Eglise	0840	OOC	CR/11 WS
2	15 Aug	Balloon	C3727	79	N Estaires	0720	DES	CR/RAF 15.8
3	23 Aug	Balloon	C3727	79	3m E Ypres	0830	DES	CR/RAF 23.8
4	23 Aug	Balloon	C3727	79	3m E Ypres	0830	DES	CR/RAF 23.8
5	24 Aug	Balloon	C3727	79	Sailly sur la Lys	1730	DES	CR/RAF 24.8

TOTAL: 4 balloons, 1 out of control = 5.

TAYLOR Frank Harold Lieutenant 41, 84

A Canadian from Toronto, Taylor was born on 11 August 1896, and joined the RFC in 1917. He first served with 41 Squadron from 7 December of that year until 13 May 1918, claiming eight victories and receiving an MC. He was then off operations for some months, joining 84 Squadron on 26 September and adding two further victories to his score, one of these on the day before the Armistice.

	1917		DH 5					
1s*	30 Nov	C	B667	41	Rumilly	1400	DES	CR/RFC 30.11
	1918		SE 5A					
2s**	25 Jan	Alb. DV	C1752	41	Vitry	1430	DES	CR/RFC 25.1
3	16 Mar	LVG. C	C1752	41	Bourlon Wood	1600	DES	CR/RFC 16.3
4	18 Mar	C	C1752	41	Lecluse	1415	DES	CR/RFC 18.3
5	23 Mar	Alb. DV	C1752	41	Bourlon Wood	1130	DES(F)	CR/RFC 23.3
6	23 Mar	Alb. DV	C1752	41	Bourlon Wood	1130	OOC	CR/RFC 23.3
7	24 Mar	Alb. DV	C1752	41	Vaulx	0900	DES	CR/RFC 24.3
8	24 Mar	Balloon	C1752	41	Fontaine les Croiselles	0950	DES	CR/RFC 24.3
9	3 Nov	Fokker DVII	F855	84	Mormal Wood	1530	OOC	CR/?
10	10 Nov	Fokker DVII	F855	84	S E Faynolle	1000	DES	CR/RAF 10.11

TOTAL: 1 balloon, 5 and 2 shared destroyed, 2 out of control = 10.
*Shared with Capt M. Thomas B38, Capt L. MacLean B633, Lt R. Winnicott B596. **Shared with 2/Lt H.E. Watson B8235.

TAYLOR Merril Samuel Lieutenant 9(N), 209

Born in Regina, Saskatchewan, Canada on 15 April 1893, and educated at Toronto University, where he became a keen rugby player, Taylor joined the RNAS in February 1917, and was commissioned as a Flight Sub Lieutenant on 23 July. Posted to 9(N) Squadron at the end of 1917, he flew with the unit until July 1918. On 2 May 1918 he shot down an all-white Fokker Triplane flown by Leutnant Hans Weiss of Jasta 11, victor over 16 Allied machines. Taylor was credited with a total of seven German aircraft shot down before he was killed over Hamel on 7 July in D3329, shot down by Leutnant Franz Büchner as the eighth of his 40 victories. Taylor's only award was the French Croix de Guerre.

	1917		Camel					
1s*	28 Sep	Alb. DIII	B5652	9N	Dixmude	1620	DES	CR/RFC 28.9
	1918							
2	21 Apr	C	B7200	209	Beaucourt	1025	DES(F)	CR/RAF 21.4
3s**	22 Apr	C	----	209	Albert	0610	CAPT	CR/RAF 22.4
4	27 Apr	Alb. DV	B3858	209	E Villers-Brettoneaux	1445	OOC	CR/RAF 27.4
5***	2 May	Fokker DrI	D3326	209	1m S Cerisy	1200	DES	CR/RAF 2.5
6	15 May	Alb. DV	D3329	209	Belloy-Pozieres	1015	OOC	CR/ORB/?
7s†	16 May	Fokker DrI	D3329	209	Corbie	1615	CAPT	CR/RAF 16.5

*Shared with FSL F.E. Banbury B6330, FSL O.M. Redgate B3818, FSL J.P. Hales B3832, F/Cdr S.T. Edwards B6217. **Shared with Capt O.C. Le Boutillier, Lt M.A. Harker, Lt R.M. Foster, Lt C.G. Brock; Flgr Raschke/Lt K. Schneider KIA, of FAA 219. ***This was Lt Hans Weiss, a 16 victory ace, of Jasta 11, who was killed. †Shared with Capt S.T. Edwards B7199, Lt W.R. May D6398. Lt Hubner of Jasta 4, was captured.

TEMPEST Edmund Roger Captain 6, 29, 15, 64

Although he was born in England, he and his brother Wulstan both went farming in Saskatchewan, Canada. On the outbreak of war both returned to join the King's Own Yorkshire Light Infantry, and then the RFC. Wulstan later won fame when he shot down Zeppelin L 31. Edmund joined 6 Squadron in May 1916, and in August was briefly posted to 29 Squadron, then serving with 15 Squadron. In July 1917 he was posted to 64 Squadron flying DH 5s, and later in 1918, SE 5As. Becoming a flight commander, he claimed 17 victories, 15 of them scouts. He returned to England at the end of August 1918 with the MC and DFC.

	1917		DH 5					
1	30 Nov	Alb. DV	A9507	64	N W Bourlon Wood	1520	OOC	CR/RFC 30.11
	1918		SE 5A					
2	8 Mar	Alb. DV	----	64	Graincourt	1230	DES	CR/RFC 8.3
3	17 Mar	Pfalz DIII	----	64	Douai	1130	DES	CR/RFC 17.3
4s*	17 Mar	Pfalz DIII	----	64	Biache	1135	OOC	CR/RFC 17.3
5	18 Mar	Alb. DV	----	64	Cambrai	1235	OOC	CR/RFC 18.3
6	22 Mar	Pfalz DIII	C5392	64	Pronville	1745	DES	CR/RFC 22.3
7	2 Apr	Alb. DV	B74	64	Ervillers	1835	DES(F)	CR/RAF 2.4
8	23 Apr	Alb. DV	B74	64	Boiry Notre Dame	1835	DES	CR/RAF 23.4
9	3 May	Pfalz DIII	B74	64	Vitry en Artois	1645	DES	CR/RAF 3.5

10	31 May	Alb. DV	C1860	64	N W Steenwerck	0625	DES	CR/RAF 31.5
11	12 Jun	Alb. C	B74	64	Festubert	1230	DES(F)	CR/RAF 12.6
12s**	20 Jul	Rumpler C	----	64	Drocourt	0925	DES	CR/RAF 20.7
13	10 Aug	Fokker DVII	B74	64	Roye	0840	DES	CR/RAF 10.8
14s***	11 Aug	Fokker DVII	B74	64	Roye	0815	OOC	CR/ORB/SR/?
15	11 Aug	Fokker DVII	B74	64	Roye	1515	DES	CR/RAF 11.8
16	12 Aug	Fokker DVII	----	64	Chaulnes	0715	DES	CR/RAF 12.8
17s†	14 Aug	C	----	64	N Roye	0910	OOC	CR/SR/?

TOTAL: 11 and 1 shared destroyed, 3 and 2 shared out of control = 17.
*Shared with Lt J.F.T. Barrett, 2/Lt C.B. Stringer, Lt C.A. Bissonette, 2/Lt K.G.P. Hendrie. **Shared with Capt P.S. Burge, Lt W.R. Henderson. ***Shared with Lt T. Rose C1860, Lt G.L. Wood E1391, Capt T. St P. Bunbury E5977, Capt A.F. Buck, Capt C.W. Cudemore D6952. †Shared with Lt T. Rose, Lt G.L. Wood.

THAYRE Frederick James Harry Captain 16, 20

Thayre first served in 16 Squadron in 1916, flying BEs. His first victory was claimed on 18 March when his observer shot down a German scout while it was attacking their aircraft. Thayre was later posted to 20 Squadron to fly FE 2Ds, and here he teamed up with Lieutenant (later Captain) Francis Cubbon, this proving to be a most successful partnership. Their first two victories were claimed on 29 April, while during May they accounted for no less than 15 of the enemy, both men receiving the MC and Bar. On 3 May, after forcing a two-seater to land, they fought an epic battle with 26 Albatros Scouts, claiming two of their attackers shot down and driving off the others; by this time they had exhausted their machine gun ammunition, and were firing their automatic pistols! Their last two victories were gained in June, making Thayre's personal score 20, 19 of them on FEs. Cubbon, with a score of 21, became the RFC's most successful observer/gunner, a position he retained well into 1918. After this great run of successes, both officers were killed when their FE 2D, A6430, received a direct hit from anti-aircraft battery K Flak 60 near Warneton on 9 June 1917.

	1916		BE 2					
1*	18 Mar	E	----	16	----	1630	DES	RFC 18.3
	1917		FE 2D					
2**	29 Apr	Alb. DIII	A6430	20	E Menin	1705	DES(F)	CR/RFC 29.4
3**	29 Apr	Alb. DIII	A6430	20	1m E Zillebeke	1710	DES(F)	CR/RFC 29.4
4***	1 May	Alb. C	A6390	20	Ploegsteert Wood	1120	DES(F)	CR/RFC 1.5
5**	3 May	Alb. DIII	A6430	20	Moorslede	1720	DES	CR/RFC 3.5
6**	3 May	Alb. DIII	A6430	20	Westroosebeke	1725	DES	CR/RFC 3.5
7**	5 May	Alb. DIII	A6430	20	Poelcapelle	1700	DES	CR/RFC 6.5
8†	5 May	Alb. DIII	A6430	20	Houthem	1720	DES(F)	CR/RFC 6.5
9††	5 May	Alb. DIII	A6430	20	Houthem	1730	DES	CR/RFC 6.5
10**	12 May	Alb. DIII	A6430	20	Tournai	0810	OOC	CR/11 WS
11**	13 May	Alb. DIII	A6430	20	Gheluvelt	1045	DES(F)	CR/RFC 13.5
12**	13 May	Alb. DIII	A6430	20	Gheluvelt	1045	DES	CR/RFC 13.5
13**	23 May	Alb. DIII	A6430	20	Zandvoorde	1510	DES	CR/RFC 23.5
14**	23 May	Alb. DIII	A6430	20	N E Ploegsteert	1515	OOC	CR/RFC 23.5
15**	25 May	Alb. DIII	A6430	20	Reckem	0730	DES	CR/RFC 25.5
16**	25 May	Alb. DIII	A6430	20	Wervicq	0900	DES(F)	CR/RFC 25.5
17**	27 May	Alb. C	A6430	20	Ypres	0730	DES	CR/RFC 27.5
18**	27 May	Alb. DIII	A6430	20	Ypres	0735	DES	CR/RFC 27.5
19**	5 Jun	Alb. DIII	A6430	20	Coucou	0810	DES	CR/RFC 5.6
20**	7 Jun	Alb. DIII	A6430	20	Houthem	1700	DES	CR/RFC 7.6

TOTAL: 17 and 1 shared destroyed, 2 out of control = 20.
*Observer: Lt C.R. Davidson. **Observer: Capt F.R. Cubbon. ***Observer:Capt F.R. Cubbon. Probably Uffz Gottwald/Lt Heinemann of FA 6. †Observer: Capt F.R. Cubbon. This was Vzfw F. Glasmacher of Jasta 8, who was killed. ††Observer: Capt F.R. Cubbon; shared with 2/Lt G.C. Heseltine/2/Lt F.G. Kydd.

THOMAS Meredith Captain 41

Born on 6 July 1892, he joined the Queen's Westminster Rifles in August 1914, going to France in January 1915. He served in the trenches for nearly two years, being commissioned in December 1915. Transferring to the RFC in October 1916, he was trained as a pilot and sent to 41 Squadron the following year. With this unit he flew FE 8s, DH 5s, and later, SE 5As, claiming five enemy machines before returning to England as an instructor. After serving in Germany in 1919, he went to Iraq from 1920 to 1923 and was awarded the DFC in 1922 when a Flight Lieutenant. He rose to the rank of Air Vice-Marshal, CSI, CBE, DFC, AFC. During World War II he was AOC, RAF in India. He died on 20 May 1984.

	1917		DH 5					
1	25 Sep	Alb. DIII	B340	41	S W Cambrai	1810	DES	CR/RFC 25.9
2	28 Sep	Alb. DIII	B340	41	Bugnicourt	1810	DES	CR/RFC 28.9

			SE 5A					
3	30 Nov	Alb. DV	B38	41	Rumilly	1345	DES	CR/RFC 30.11
4s*	30 Nov	Alb. DV	B38	41	Rumilly	1400	OOC	CR/30.11
5	6 Dec	Alb. DV	B633	41	Sailly	1450	OOC	CR/RFC 6.12

TOTAL: 3 destroyed, 1 and 1 shared out of control = 5.
*Shared with Capt L.J. MacLean B633, Lt R. Winnicott B596, Lt F.H. Taylor B667.

THOMPSON Cecil Robert Lieutenant 84

Born in South Africa on 4 December 1894, 'Ruggles' Thompson served in the army for two and a half years during the German East and West African Campaigns. He then joined the RFC in August 1917, and flew with 84 Squadron, which he joined in April 1918. He made no early claims, going into hospital during June and July, but on his return to the front he very rapidly claimed three enemy machines, then turning his attention to balloons. He shot down two of these early in September, but on 15th, having just shot down another, he was set upon by several Fokker DVIIs. He fought his way back, but was hit in the face and shoulder. For this action, and for his seven victories, he received the DFC. Thompson died in the mid 1970s.

	1918		SE 5A					
1	4 Aug	Alb. DV	D6906	84	E Warfusee-Abancourt	0830	DES	CR/RAF 4.8
2	7 Aug	Pfalz DIII	D6906	84	Le Quesnel	0910	OOC	CR/?
3	11 Aug	Fokker DVII	D6906	84	Villers-Carbonnel	1800	DES	CR/RAF 11.8
4s*	4 Sep	Balloon	F6420	84	Douvieux	1330	DES	CR/RAF 4.9
5	5 Sep	Balloon	F6420	84	S Poeuilly	0950	DES	CR/RAF 5.9
6	15 Sep	Balloon	F6420	84	E St Quentin	0955	DES	CR/RAF 15.9

TOTAL: 2 and 1 shared balloons, 2 destroyed, 1 out of control = 6.
*Shared with Lt S.W. Highwood B6920.

THOMPSON Claud Robert James Lieutenant 19

An Australian from Melbourne who was born on 15 June 1892, Claud Thompson served with 19 Squadron, flying Spads from 4 June to 14 November 1917. He undertook many offensive patrols and ground attack missions, during which he claimed at least six enemy machines. He was killed in a flying accident on 17 July 1918 while with 63 Training Squadron.

	1917		Spad					
1	19 Jul	Alb. DIII	B3498	19	Kruiesik	2000	OOC	ORB/RFC 21.7
2	14 Oct	Alb. DV	B6776	19	Coucou	1030	DES	CR/RFC 14.10
3	27 Oct	Rumpler C	B6817	19	S E'Passchendaele	0620	OOC	CR/RFC WD
4s*	30 Oct	DFW. C	B6817	19	W Dadizeele	0620	OOC	CR/RFC WD
5	9 Nov	Alb. DV	A6784	19	Zuidhoek	1000	DES	CR/RFC 9.11
6	9 Nov	Alb. DV	A6784	19	Zandvoorde	1030	OOC	CR/RFC 9.11

TOTAL: 2 destroyed, 3 and 1 shared out of control = 6.
*Shared with Lt J. de Pencier A6971.

THOMPSON Chester William McKinley Lieutenant 22

Lieutenant Thompson, commissioned on 27 September 1917, served with 22 Squadron throughout the spring and summer of 1918, claiming twelve victories. On at least two occasions he and his gunners claimed two Fokker DVIIs in one day. Shot down in E2517 east of Cambrai on 29 September, by aircraft of Jasta B, he and his observer, Lieutenant James, were taken prisoner.

	1918		Bristol					
1*	28 May	C	C4894	22	Merville-La Bassee	1100	OOC	CR/ORB/SR
2**	11 Aug	Fokker DVII	C1035	22	S E Arras	1940	OOC	CR/ORB/SR
3**	13 Aug	Pfalz DIII	C1035	22	S E Douai	1100	OOC	CR/ORB/SR
4***	3 Sep	Pfalz DIII	F5820	22	Sailly-Saillisel	0700	DES	CR/RAF 3.9
5***	5 Sep	Fokker DVII	F5820	22	Douai	1700	OOC	CR/ORB/SR
6***	17 Sep	Fokker DVII	C1045	22	S W Douai	1830	DES(F)	CR/RAF 17.9
7***	17 Sep	Fokker DVII	C1045	22	Brebieres	1835	DES	CR/RAF 17.9
8***	24 Sep	Fokker DVII	C1035	22	Cambrai	1700	OOC	CR/ORB/SR
9†	25 Sep	Fokker DVII	C1035	22	Bourlon Wood	1810	OOC	CR/ORB/SR
10††	26 Sep	Fokker DVII	C1035	22	Arras-Cambrai Rd	1300	DES	CR/RAF 26.9
11††	26 Sep	Fokker DVII	C1035	22	Arras-Cambrai Rd	1300	DES	CR/RAF 26.9
12s†††	27 Sep	Fokker DVII	F5820	22	Oisy le Verger	0730	DES	CR/RAF 27.9

TOTAL: 5 and 1 shared destroyed, 6 out of control = 12.
*Observer: Sgt H.C. Hunt. **Observer: 2/Lt J. Amos. ***Observer: 2/Lt G. McCormack. †Observer: Lt L.R. James. ††Observer: Lt W.U. Tyrrell. †††Observer: Lt L.R. James; shared with Lt L.C. Rowney/Lt W.U. Tyrrell E2517.

THOMPSON Samuel Frederick Henry Captain 20, 22

'Siffy' Thompson served initially with the Royal Army Service Corps before transferring to the RFC. In late 1917 he joined 20 Squadron, but crashed B1102 on 27 October. At a later date he was posted to 22 Squadron which was also flying Bristol Fighters, and claimed his first victory on 22 April 1918. A most aggressive pilot, he claimed five aircraft, while his observer got a sixth prior to 21 May; he then teamed up with Sergeant R.M. Fletcher, with whom he was to do most of the remainder of his fighting. Engaged mainly against enemy scouts, this pair claimed, generally two at a time, throughout the summer. Thompson received an MC, gazetted on 16 September, and a DFC, gazetted on 2 November, while Fletcher was awarded a DFM for their actions. When he claimed a Halberstadt two-seater on 27 September, Thompson brought his score to 30; at least 18 of these had been claimed with the front gun, while of eight known to have been claimed by the gunner, six were credited to Fletcher, whose personal score, including victories gained with other pilots, was a minimum of 11. Soon after their final victory, Thompson was reported missing in action near Cambrai during an afternoon sortie on 27 September, with Lieutenant C.J. Tolman in the rear seat; both men were killed. Thompson was the second most successful Bristol Fighter pilot after Andrew McKeever.

	1918		Bristol					
1*	22 Apr	Alb. DV	B1136	22	E Merville	0840	OOC	CR/RAF 22.4
2**	8 May	C	B1162	22	Arras	1015	DES(F)	CR/RAF 8.5
3**	9 May	Pfalz DIII	B1164	22	N Douai	1845	OOC	CR/RAF 9.5
4***	16 May	Pfalz DIII	B1213	22	Douai	1005	DES	CR/RAF 16.5
5***	16 May	Pfalz DIII	B1213	22	S Douai	1005	DES	CR/RAF 16.5
6***	16 May	Pfalz DIII	B1213	22	Douai	1015	DES	CR/RAF 16.5
7***	21 May	Pfalz DIII	B1213	22	S W Vitry	1015	DES	CR/RAF 21.5
8***	21 May	Pfalz DIII	B1213	22	S W Vitry	1015	OOC	CR/ORB/SR
9***	22 May	Alb. DV	B1213	22	Hancourt	1030	DES	CR/RAF 22.5
10***	25 May	Alb. DV	B1213	22	W Carvin	1130	DES(F)	CR/RAF 25.5
11***	1 Jun	Alb. C	C929	22	Erquinghem	1915	DES	CR/RAF 1.6
12***	1 Jun	Alb. DV	C929	22	Erquinghem	1915	DES	CR/RAF 1.6
13***	2 Jun	Pfalz DIII	C929	22	N E Lens	1030	DES(F)	CR/RAF 2.6
14***	2 Jun	Pfalz DIII	C929	22	N E Lens	1030	OOC	CR/ORB/SR
15***	5 Jun	Alb. DV	C929	22	S Laventie	1030	DES	CR/RAF 5.6
16***	5 Jun	Alb. DV	C929	22	S Laventie	1030	DES	CR/RAF 5.6
17***	23 Jun	Pfalz DIII	C929	22	La Bassee	2045	OOC	CR/ORB/SR
18***	23 Jun	Pfalz DIII	C929	22	La Bassee	2045	OOC	CR/ORB/SR
19*	26 Jul	Fokker DrI	D7896	22	Laventie	0900	OOC	CR/ORB/SR
20***	8 Aug	Fokker DrI	E2477	22	Dechy	1040	DES	CR/RAF 8.8
21***	13 Aug	Alb. DV	----	22	Arras-Cambrai Rd	1130	DES	CR/RAF 13.8
22***	13 Aug	Alb. DV	----	22	S E Douai	1135	OOC	CR/ORB/SR
23***	13 Aug	Fokker DVII	----	22	S E Douai	1135	DES	CR/RAF 13.8
24***	27 Aug	Fokker DVII	E2477	22	Senlemont	1400	OOC	CR/ORB/SR
25***	27 Aug	Fokker DVII	E2477	22	Senlemont	1400	OOC	CR/ORB/SR
26***	2 Sep	Fokker DVII	E2477	22	Haynecourt	1115	DES	CR/RAF 2.9
27***	5 Sep	Fokker DVII	E2477	22	Douai	1700	DES(F)	CR/RAF 5.9
28***	5 Sep	Fokker DVII	E2477	22	Douai	1700	OOC	CR/ORB/SR
29***	24 Sep	Fokker DVII	E2477	22	Cambrai	1700	OOC	CR/ORB/SR
30†	27 Sep	Halb. C	E2477	22	N Noyelles	0720	DES	CR/RAF 27.9

TOTAL: 18 destroyed, 12 out of control = 30.
*Observer: Lt C.G. Gass. **Observer: Sgt L. Kendrick. ***Observer: Sgt R.M. Fletcher. †Observer: 2/Lt C.J. Tolman.

THOMSON George Edwin Captain 46

George Thomson was born on 19 September 1897, serving early in the war with the King's Own Scottish Borderers. He was seconded to the RFC in September 1916 and ten months later joined 46 Squadron in France, flying Sopwith Pups. He had been delayed by a crash during training which had scarred his face. On 25 September, one year after joining the RFC, he shared in his first victory. Shortly after this, the squadron began converting to Sopwith Camels, and on 23 November, having displayed both piloting skill and leadership early in his flying career, he was promoted to flight commander. He claimed his first two victories on Camels on 30 November, and gained one more before the end of the year. Another two followed during January and February 1918, but it was in March that he really shone, and by 25th of that month his score had risen to 21. On that date, having received an MC during the month, he was posted to Home Establishment, joining 7 TDS at Feltwell. The award of a DSO was announced in April. His career came to an abrupt end when taking off from Port Meadow, Oxford, on 23 May 1918, his machine suddenly burst into flames and crashed, and he was killed.

	1917		Pup					
1s	25 Sep	C	B2196	46	Pelves	1150	DES	CR/RFC 25.9

			Camel					
2	30 Nov	Alb. DV	B3514	46	Bourlon Wood	1125	DES	CR/RFC 30.11
3*	30 Nov	Pfalz DIII	B3514	46	N E Flesquieres	1510	CAPT	CR/RFC 30.11
4	10 Dec	Alb. DV	B2451	46	6m N E St Quentin	1100	OOC	CR/RFC 10.12
	1918							
5	18 Jan	C	B2451	46	51 B V 22	1145	OOC	CR/III BG WD
6s**	16 Feb	Alb. C	B9131	46	51 B V 2	0830	OOC	CR/RFC 16.2
7	6 Mar	Hannover C	B9197	46	E Douai	1345	OOC	CR/RFC 6.3
8	8 Mar	C	C1627	46	Ecourt St Quentin	1215	OOC	CR/RFC 8.3
9	11 Mar	Alb. DV	C1627	46	Cherisy	1215	OOC	CR/III BG WD
10	12 Mar	Pfalz DIII	C1627	46	Ecourt St Quentin	1300	OOC	CR/RFC 12.3
11	16 Mar	C	C1627	46	S Brebieres	1130	OOC	CR/RFC 16.3
12s***	16 Mar	C	C1627	46	Brebieres	1200	DES(F)	CR/RFC 16.3
13	16 Mar	C	C1627	46	Brebieres	1200	OOC	CR/RFC 16.3
14s***	16 Mar	C	C1627	46	S Brebieres	1200	OOC	CR/RFC 16.3
15	17 Mar	Alb. DV	C1627	46	Cambrai	0845	OOC	CR/RFC 17.3
16	17 Mar	C	C1627	46	Cambrai	0930	OOC	CR/III BG WD
17	22 Mar	Alb. DV	C1837	46	Bullecourt	1800	DES	CR/RFC 22.3
18	22 Mar	Alb. DV	C1837	46	W Boursies	1830	OOC	CR/RFC 22.3
19	23 Mar	Alb. DV	D6407	46	Morchies	1400	DES	CR/RFC 23.3
20	23 Mar	Alb. DV	D6407	46	Morchies	1400	OOC	CR/RFC 23.3
21	23 Mar	Alb. DV	D6407	46	Morchies	1400	OOC	CR/RFC 23.3

TOTAL: 1 captured, 3 and 2 shared destroyed, 13 and 2 shared out of control = 21.
*This was Lt Hans Hofacker of Jasta 33, who was captured. **Shared with Lt H.G.W. Debenham B9195. ***Shared with Capt S.P. Smith C1617.

THOMSON William McKenzie Captain 20

William Thomson, a Canadian, joined 20 Squadron early in 1918 and was in action during the spring, flying mainly with Lieutenant G.H. Kemp as his observer. His score quickly mounted and he was awarded the MC on 5 June, followed by a DFC on 25 August. During June he began to fly with a number of different observers, but by September he had teamed up with a very successful gunner, Lieutenant H.L. Edwards. By the end of that month Thomson had brought his score to 26 and been promoted to Captain. He was still alive at the time of writing.

	1918		Bristol					
1*	9 May	Alb. DV	C4851	20	W Comines	1330	DES	CR/RAF 9.5
2**	14 May	Alb. DV	C859	20	Wervicq-Zillebeke	1845	CAPT	CR/RAF 14.5
3*	17 May	Alb. DV	C859	20	E Armentieres	0815	DES	CR/RFC 17.5
4*	17 May	Alb. DV	C859	20	Armentieres	0815	OOC	CR/11 WS
5*	18 May	Pfalz DIII	C859	20	S Merville	c1140	OOC	CR/11 WS
6*	19 May	Pfalz DIII	C843	20	Estaires	1045	DES	CR/RAF 19.5
7*	21 May	Alb. DV	C843	20	Warneton	0835	DES(F)	CR/RAF 21.5
8***	22 May	Alb. DV	C843	20	Warneton	1840	OOC	CR/11 WS
9***	29 May	Alb. DV	C843	20	Bac St Maur	1830	OOC	CR/11 WS
10*	31 May	Pfalz DIII	C843	20	Bois Grenier	1850	DES	CR/RAF 31.5
11*	31 May	Alb. DV	C843	20	Armentieres	1855	OOC	CR/11 WS
12*	1 Jun	Pfalz DIII	C843	20	Comines	0630	DES	CR/RAF 1.6
13*	1 Jun	Pfalz DIII	C843	20	Comines	0630	DES	CR/RAF 1.6
14†	9 Jun	Pfalz DIII	C843	20	Comines-Houthem	0945	DES	CR/RAF 9.6
15s††	17 Jun	Fokker DVII	C843	20	Boesinghe	0745	OOC	CR/11 WS
16†††	19 Jul	Fokker DrI	C843	20	S Gheluvelt	0845	DES	CR/RAF 19.7
17†††	25 Jul	Fokker DVII	C843	20	Gheluvelt	0855	DES	CR/RAF 25.7
18s‡	25 Jul	Fokker DVII	C843	20	Comines	0855	DES(F)	CR/RAF 25.7
19‡‡	14 Aug	Fokker DVII	E2154	20	Dadizeele	1800-1830	DES(F)	CR/RAF 14.8
20‡‡	14 Aug	Fokker DVII	E2154	20	E Dadizeele	1830	OOC	CR/SR/?
21‡‡	15 Aug	Fokker DVII	E2154	20	Becelaere	0710	DES	CR/RAF 15.8
22‡‡‡	15 Sep	Fokker DVII	E2514	20	Omissy-St Quentin	1120	DES	CR/RAF 15.9
23‡‡‡	15 Sep	Fokker DVII	E2514	20	S E St Quentin	1120	DES	CR/RAF 15.9
24‡‡‡	16 Sep	Fokker DVII	E2514	20	N E St Quentin	0815	DES(F)	CR/RAF 16.9
25‡‡‡	16 Sep	Fokker DVII	E2514	20	St Quentin	0820	DES	CR/RAF 16.9
26s§	16 Sep	Fokker DVII	E2514	20	N W St Quentin	0820	DES	CR/RAF 16.9

TOTAL: 1 captured, 16 and 2 shared destroyed, 6 and 1 shared out of control = 26.
*Observer: 2/Lt G.H. Kemp. **Observer: 2/Lt G.H. Kemp. Lt E.Weiss of Jasta 33 was killed. ***Observer: Lt C.G. Gass. †Observer: Pbr F.J. Ralphs. ††Observer: Pbr F.J. Ralphs. Shared with Capt D. Latimer/Lt T.C. Noel C987. †††Observer: Sgt J.D.C. Summers. ‡Observer: Sgt J.D.C. Summers. Shared with Capt H.P. Lale/2/Lt F.J. Ralph C4718, Lt D.E. Smith/Prb J. Hills C4672. ‡‡Observer: Lt M.A. McKenzie. ‡‡‡Observer: Lt H.L. Edwards. §Observer: Lt H.L. Edwards. Shared with Lt A.R. Strachan/2/Lt D.M. Calderwood C951.

THORNELY Ronald Roscoe Captain 8(N)

Ronald Thornely served in Gallipoli with the Royal Naval Armoured Car Squadron before joining the RNAS in May 1916. He was commissioned in October and posted to 8(N) Squadron in March 1917. With this unit he claimed nine victories, the award of a DSC being gazetted in November. In January 1919 he was Mentioned in Despatches.

	1917		Triplane					
1s*	4 Jun	C	N5465	8N	E Lens	0945	DES(F)	CR/RFC 4.6
2	7 Jun	Alb. DV	N5465	8N	Henin-Lietard	1015	OOC	CR/RFC 7.6
			Camel					
3s**	16 Jun	C	N5465	8N	Loos-E Lens	0830	CAPT	CR/RFC 16.6
4	22 Jul	Alb. DIII	B3845	8N	S E Gavrelle	0630	OOC	CR/RFC 22.7
5	28 Jul	Alb. DIII	B3845	8N	Lens-La Bassee	0915	OOC	CR/ORB/DL
6s***	9 Aug	Alb. DV	B3845	8N	E Henin-Lietard	0915	OOC	CR/ORB/DL
7	15 Aug	Alb. DIII	B3845	8N	Lens	2015	OOC	CR/RFC 15.8
8s†	19 Aug	C	----	8N	E Lens	0850	OOC	CR/RFC 19.8
9	11 Sep	C	B3845	8N	Pont a Vendin	1150	OOC	CR/RFC 11.9

TOTAL: 1 shared captured, 1 shared destroyed, 5 and 2 shared out of control = 9.

*Shared with FSL R.J.O. Compston N5471, FSL E.A. Bennetts N5492. **Shared with F/Lt R.J.O. Compston N6299; the crew were Vxfw H. Totsch/Lt K. Riegel of FAA 211. ***Shared with FSL W.L. Jordan. †Shared with FSL W.L. Jordan, FSL R. Macdonald, FSL J.H. Thompson.

TIDMARSH David Mary Captain 24, 48

Tidmarsh, an Irishman, went to France with 24 Squadron in 1916, having transferred from the 4th Regiment, Irish Rifles Special Reserve. On 2 April he and Lieutenant S.J. Sibley made the first confirmed claim for the new squadron. Altogether he was given credit for three victories and was awarded an MC before being rested. On a patrol on 21 April 1916 an enemy AA shell passed through his cockpit nascelle without exploding or hitting the pilot. Early in 1917 he was given a flight in 48 Squadron which had just been formed, as the first unit to go into action with Bristol Fighters. On 11 April 1917 Tidmarsh and two companions engaged a formation of Albatros Scouts; Tidmarsh and one other crew were credited with two shot down on the evidence of AA crews, but shortly thereafter they were engaged in a fight with Jasta 11, and both crews failed to return. Tidmarsh was shot down by Leutnant Kurt Wolff as the ninth of his 33 claims, and became a prisoner.

	1916		DH 2					
1s*	2 Apr	Alb. C	5924	24	Grandcourt-Albert	0655	DES	CR/SR/?
2**	30 Apr	Fokker E	5965	24	Bapaume	1045	DES	CR/RFC 30.4
3s***	20 May	C	5965	24	S Pozieres	0415	DES(F)	CR/RFC 20.5
	1917		Bristol					
4s†	8 Apr	Alb. DIII	----	48	Remy	----	OOC	SR/RFC 8.4
5s††	10 Apr	EA	A3338	48	Remy	----	OOC	SR/RFC 10.4
6s†††	11 Apr	Alb. DIII	A3338	48	Fampoux	0830-0900	DES	CR/RFC 11.4
7s‡	11 Apr	Alb. DIII	A3338	48	Fampoux	0830-0900	DES	CR/RFC 11.4

TOTAL: 1 and 4 shared destroyed, 2 shared out of control = 7.

*Shared with 2/Lt S.J. Sibley 5498. **This was Lt Schmeckes of KEK B, who was killed. ***Shared with Capt W.A. Summers 7284, of 22 Sqn. †Observer: 2/Lt C.B. Holland, shared with 2/Lt O.W. Berry/2/Lt F.B. Goodison. ††Observer: 2/Lt C.B. Holland, shared with 2/Lt G.N. Brockhurst/2/Lt C.B. Boughton A3323. †††Observer: 2/Lt C.B. Holland, shared with 2/Lt G.N. Brockhurst/2/Lt C.B. Boughton A3323, 2/Lt R.F. Adeney/2/Lt L.G. Lovell A3318, 2/Lt A.G. Riley/2/Lt L.G. Hall. ‡Observer: 2/Lt C.B. Holland, shared with 2/Lt G.N. Brockhurst/2/Lt C.B. Boughton A3323, 2/Lt R.F. Adeney/2/Lt L.G. Lovell A3318, 2/Lt A.G. Riley/2/Lt L.G. Hall.

TIPTON William Duncan 1st Lieutenant 3, 17US

An American from Jarretsville, Maryland, where he was born on 11 December 1892, Bill Tipton joined the USAS and was sent for advanced training and early combat experience with the RFC. By the time he joined 3 Squadron, the RAF had been formed, and during the heavy fighting in late spring 1918 he shared in two victories with this British unit. He was then transferred to the 17th Aero Squadron, USAS, which was operating under RAF control. He gained a further three victories, the last two on 26 August in a combat with several Fokkers of JG III. In the fight seven American Camels were brought down, Tipton's being one of them; he was probably the victim of Leutnant Hermann Frommherz, the commander of Jasta 27, who claimed three of the seven. Tipton spent the rest of the war as a prisoner. He served in the USAAF during World War II, but was killed in a flying accident in a P-47 at Odema, Ohio, as a Colonel on 12 December 1945.

	1918		Camel					
1s*	2 May	DFW. C	D6519	3	Arras	1615	OOC	CR/RAF 2.5
2s**	18 May	Alb. C	----	3	57 C S 17	0800	OOC	CR/RAF 18.5
3s***	22 Aug	Balloon	F2157	17US	57 C H 22	0955	DES	CR/RAF 22.8

4	26 Aug	Fokker DVII	F5951	17US	Bapaume-Queant	1700	DES	CR/US 133
5	26 Aug	Fokker DVII	F5951	17US	Bapaume-Queant	1700	DES	CR/US 133

TOTAL: 1 shared balloon, 2 destroyed, 2 shared out of control = 5.
*Shared with Lt W. Hubbard D9297. **Shared with Lt L.A. Hamilton, Lt Macklin. ***Shared with 1/Lt R.D. Williams D6595.

TOD G.O.D. Lieutenant 65

An American, Tod served with 65 Squadron from April 1918, flying Camels. He claimed three victories during the early summer, and then on 8 August, the first day of the Amiens offensive, participated in forcing down two Fokker DVIIs, both of which crashed in Allied lines. Next day he was shot down in D1810 near Vauxvillers and while reported missing, was later found to have crashed in British lines after being wounded.

	1918		Camel					
1	9 May	Alb. DV	D1921	65	E Villers-Brettoneaux	1940	OOC	CR/SR/ORB/?
2	15 May	Alb. DV	D1921	65	S E Villers-Brettoneaux	0840	DES	CR/RAF 15.5
3	3 Jun	Pfalz DIII	D1921	65	Villers-Brettoneaux	1305	OOC	CR/SR/ORB/?
4s*	8 Aug	Fokker DVII	D1810	65	Proyart	1225	CAPT	CR/RAF 8.8
5s*	8 Aug	Fokker DVII	D1810	65	Proyart	1225	CAPT	CR/RAF 8.8

TOTAL: 2 shared captured, 1 destroyed, 2 out of control = 5.
*Shared with Lt J.L.M. White, Lt F. Edsted, Lt C. Tolley, Lt D. Oxley, Capt E.G. Brookes.

TODD John Captain 70

Joining 70 Squadron in the winter of 1917-18, Lieutenant Todd, previously a student at Edinburgh University, claimed his first victory on 22 January. By the end of March his score had risen to five, and he was promoted to flight commander, having received the award of an MC. He continued scoring throughout the spring and early summer, receiving a DFC after his ninth victory, gazetted on 3 August, and by the end of July his total had risen to 18. He then served with 204 Training Squadron as a fighting instructor.

	1918		Camel					
1s*	22 Jan	Alb. DV	B3890	70	N E Houthoulst Forest	1430	DES	CR/RFC 22.1
2	28 Jan	Fokker DrI	B3890	70	N W Menin	1550	OOC	CR/RFC 28.1
3	18 Feb	Alb. DV	B7320	70	Staden	1215	OOC	CR/RFC 18.2
4	12 Mar	Alb. DV	C8213	70	N Menin	1245	OOC	CR/RFC 12.3
5	22 Mar	Fokker DrI	C8213	70	S W Cambrai	1550	OOC	CR/SR/?
6	22 Apr	C	C1670	70	S E Wancourt	1630	DES	CR/SR/?
8s**	29 Apr	C	C1670	70	N E Querrieu	1910	CAPT	CR/RAF 29.4
9	27 May	Alb. DV	C1670	70	Ribemont	1000	OOC	CR/III BG WD
10s***	27 May	LVG. C	C1670	70	Ribemont	1155	DES(F)	CR/RAF 27.5
11	30 May	Alb. DV	C1670	70	Albert-Bruay	1110	DES(F)	CR/RAF 30.5
12	30 May	Alb. DV	C1670	70	Albert-Bruay	1110	DES	CR/RAF 30.5
13	31 May	Alb. DV	C1670	70	S E Albert	1000	DES	CR/RAF 31.5
14	31 May	Alb. DV	C1670	70	S E Albert	1800	DES(F)	CR/RAF 31.5
15	27 Jun	Alb. DV	C1670	70	.5m E Lakes at Albert	2045	DES	CR/RAF 27.6
16	30 Jun	Alb. DV	C1670	70	Bray	1835	OOC	CR/III BG WD
17	30 Jun	Fokker DrI	C1670	70	S Bray	1840	DES	CR/RAF 30.6
18	1 Jul	Alb. DV	C1670	70	Bray	0920	OOC	CR/III BG WD

TOTAL: 1 shared captured, 8 and 2 shared destroyed, 7 out of control = 18.
*Shared with Capt F.G. Quigley B5214. **Shared with Lt V.C. Chapman C7471, and Lt C.F. Falkenberg and Lt H.W.L. Saunders B8403 of 84 Sqn. Uffz Krug/Lt Adler of FAA 218 were captured.***Shared with Lt S.T. Liversedge C8220.

TODD Robert Miles 2nd Lieutenant 17US

Robert Todd, an American citizen from Cincinatti, Ohio born on 24 June 1897, joined the USAS and served in France with the 17th Aero Squadron, which was operating under RAF control. He claimed four victories, three destroyed and one out of control, during August 1918, and then on 26th of that month was one of seven Camel pilots shot down in a fight with JG III Fokker DVIIs. Before crashing and becoming a prisoner, he brought down one of his attackers to bring his score to five. It is believed that he was shot down by Leutnant Rudolf Klimke of Jasta 27. He died on 20 January 1988 in La Jolla, California.

	1918		Camel					
1	1 Aug	Fokker DrI	D9513	17US	Provin	0900	DES	CR/RAF 1.8
2s*	14 Aug	Fokker DVII	D9513	17US	S W Bruges	1130	DES	CR/RAF 14.8
3s**	21 Aug	Balloon	D9513	17US	57 C H 17	1845	DES	CR/RAF 21.8
4	22 Aug	Fokker DVII	D9513	17US	57 C H 32	1000	DES	CR/US 133
5	26 Aug	Fokker DVII	D6545	17US	Bapaume-Queant	1700	DES	CR/US 133

TOTAL: 1 shared balloon, 3 and 1 shared destroyed = 5.
*Shared with 1/Lt L.A. Hamilton D1940, 1/Lt J.F. Campbell D9399. **Shared with 1/Lt L.A. Hamilton D1940.

TONKS Adrian James Boswell Captain 4(N), 204

Born on 10 May 1898, in Kensington, London, Tonks joined 4(N) Squadron on 17 August 1917, claiming four victories during the rest of the year. After a seven month gap, he started claiming again in June 1918, and was promoted to flight commander on 10 July. During August he claimed several victories, including two on 15th, and on 10 September was awarded a DFC, a Bar to this following on 30 October. Meanwhile, he had been posted to the Air Ministry for a rest from operations on 13 October. He died from injuries suffered in a crash on 14 July 1919.

	1917		Camel					
1	22 Aug	Alb. DV	B3856	4N	S E Ostend	0945	OOC	CR/RNAS 22.8
2	22 Aug	Alb. DV	B3856	4N	S E Ostend	0945	OOC	CR/RNAS 22.8
3	9 Nov	DFW. C	B6256	4N	N Pervyse	1330	OOC	CR/RNAS 9.11
4	23 Nov	Alb. DV	B6243	4N	E Keyem	1400	OOC	CR/RNAS 23.11
	1918							
5	30 Jun	Fokker DVII	D1824	204	Zeebrugge	1430	OOC	CR/5 GP Comm
6	10 Aug	Fokker DVII	C66	204	Ghistelles	1840	OOC	CR/5 GP Comm
7s*	13 Aug	Fokker DVII	C66	204	S E Bailleul	1915	OOC	CR/5 GP Comm
8	15 Aug	Fokker DVII	C66	204	E Ypres	0830	OOC	CR/5 GP Comm
9	15 Aug	Fokker DVII	C66	204	E Ypres	0830	OOC	CR/SR/?
10	15 Aug	Fokker DVII	C66	204	E Ypres	0830	OOC	CR/SR/?
11	28 Sep	Fokker DVII	D9600	204	Wercken	1230	DES	CR/5 GP Comm
12	28 Sep	Fokker DVII	D9600	204	Wercken	1230	OOC	CR/5 GP Comm

TOTAL: 1 destroyed, 11 out of control = 12.
*Shared with Lt H.W.M. Cumming D9628.

TRAILL Thomas Caithcart Captain 20

Born on 6 August 1899, Tommy Traill joined the Royal Navy as a young man, serving as a midshipman during the Dardanelles Campaign. In 1917 he joined the RFC, and the following year was posted to 20 Squadron, flying Bristol Fighters. He served with this unit until the end of the war, becoming a flight commander, receiving the DFC, and with his observers gained at least eight victories. He had several narrow escapes; on one occasion his observer, Lieutenant P.G. Jones, was killed a second after giving warning of an attack. In that same instant, Traill ducked down as he went into a sharp turn, and a bullet from a German fighter behind, went through his windshield. During another fight his observer, Lieutenant Gordon-Bennett, was hit in the leg by an incendiary bullet. On 23 October 1918, while returning from a patrol, he collided with another Bristol, losing part of the right-hand plane, which sent the machine into a spin. His observer on this occasion, Captain Burbidge, gallantly climbed out onto the lower plane to counter the spin. The Bristol partially recovered before it hit the ground, but Burbidge was hurled into the air and landed on his face, breaking his nose and biting through his tongue, although Traill was again unhurt. He remained in the RAF after the war, later commanding 14 Squadron in Amman; he eventually rose to the rank of Air Vice-Marshal, commanding 19 Group, Coastal Command until his retirement in 1954. He received the OBE in 1940 and the CBE in 1948. He died soon after, in the 1970s.

	1918		Bristol					
1*	29 May	Fokker DrI	C856	20	W Armentieres	1840	OOC	CR/11 WS
2*	30 Jun	Alb. DV	C938	20	N Comines	0730	OOC	CR/11 WS
3*	2 Jul	Fokker DVII	B1344	20	S E Gheluvelt	0840	DES(F)	CR/11 WS
4**	29 Jul	Fokker DVII	E2452	20	Gheluwe	1955	OOC	CR/11 WS
5**	24 Sep	Fokker DVII	E2252	20	W Busigny	1600	OOC	CR/?
6**	25 Sep	Fokker DVII	E2252	20	N E St Quentin	1820	DES(F)	CR/RAF 25.9
7***	29 Sep	Fokker DVII	E2370	20	N St Quentin	1025	DES	CR/?
8***	23 Oct	Fokker DVII	E2403	20	W Aulnoye	1520	DES	CR/RAF 23.10

TOTAL: 4 destroyed, 4 out of control = 8.
*Observer: 2/Lt P.G. Jones. **Observer: Lt R. Gordon-Bennett. ***Observer: Capt L.W. Burbidge.

TRAPP George Leonard Flight Lieutenant 10(N)

Born on 1 July 1894, in New Westminster, British Columbia, Canada, he joined the RNAS in 1917, going to 10(N) Squadron after training. He was one of three brothers in the air service, all three giving their lives during the war. George Trapp was shot down and killed in action on 13 November 1917, by Oberleutnant Bruno Justinius of Jasta 35. He had claimed six victories and attacked many ground targets prior to his death; his sister was married to the great RNAS ace, Raymond Collishaw.

	1917		Triplane					
1	12 Aug	Alb. DIII	N5354	10N	Roulers	0745	OOC	CR/RFC 12.8
2	17 Aug	Alb. DIII	N5354	10N	Ledeghem	0830	OOC	CR/RFC 17.8

3	21 Aug	Alb. DIII	N5366	10N	E Menin	1835	OOC	CR/RFC 21.8
			Camel					
4	9 Sep	Alb. DV	B3822	10N	E Zonnebeke	1630	OOC	CR/ORB/DL
5	28 Sep	Alb. DV	B3822	10N	Moorslede	1045	DES	CR/RFC 28.9
6s*	12 Nov	C	B6341	10N	Couckelaere	0800	DES	CR/RFC 12.11

TOTAL: 1 and 1 shared destroyed, 4 out of control = 6.
*Shared with FSL A.G. Beattie B5659.

TRAVERS Frederick Dudley Captain 47, 17, 150

Born on 15 February 1897, he first became interested in flying during his school days, looking through the airfield fence at Hendon. He joined the Inns of Court OTC, and was commissioned in the Hertfordshire Yeomanry in 1916, serving during the attempted relief of Kut-el-Amara in the Middle East. Seconded to the RFC in April 1917, he trained in Egypt, going solo in only two and a half hours. He then flew operationally with 47, 17 and 150 Squadrons in Macedonia, 1917-18, where he was awarded the DFC for leading three British machines against 12 German aircraft, four of the latter being claimed shot down. After the war he flew in Rumania and South Russia, and later with 25 Squadron under Sholto Douglas. He joined Imperial Airways in 1926 and did much to pioneer the early routes for civil airlines over Africa, Europe and the Far East. Later he joined BOAC, holding Master Pilot's Certificate No 2 for landplanes and No 37 for seaplanes, amassing over 19,500 hours flying in command. In 1943 he received the King's Commendation for Valuable Service in the Air. He subsequently retired to Kenya.

	1917		BE 12					
1	19 Dec	Alb. DIII	4046	17	W Lake Doiran	1230	OOC	CR/BG Summ
	1918		SE 5A					
2s*	15 May	Alb. DV	B688	150	Hudova a/d	0630	OOC	CR/BG Summ
3s**	28 May	DFW. C	B688	150	E Vardarhohe	1500	DES(F)	CR/BG Summ
4	1 Jun	Alb. DV	B690	150	Bogdanci	1510	DES	CR/BG Summ
			Bristol M1C					
5s***	2 Sep	LVG. C	C4976	150	Nihor	0815	DES(F)	CR/BG Summ
6	3 Sep	Alb. DV	----	150	N W Lake Doiran	0815	DES	CR/BG Summ
7	3 Sep	Alb. DV	----	150	E Cerniste	0820	DES	CR/BG Summ
8s†	4 Sep	C	C4976	150	N Karusu Bridge	1055	DES	CR/BG Summ
9	16 Sep	Fokker DVII	C4976	150	Lake Doiran	1205	OOC	CR/BG Summ

TOTAL: 3 and 3 shared destroyed, 2 and 1 shared out of control = 9.
*Shared with Capt G.G. Bell B28. **Shared with Capt A.G. Goulding B690. ***Shared with Lt J.P. Cavers C4907. †Shared with Lt L. Hamilton.

TRAVERS Herbert Gardner Flight Commander 1W, 3(N)

'Tiny' Travers was born on 1 April 1891, and transferred to the RNAS on 14 December 1915 after serving as a machine gunner with the Honourable Artillery Company. He joined 1(N) Wing on 27 May 1916 and served for the rest of the year with that unit, flying scouts. He was sent home at the end of 1916 for a rest, returning in 1917 to join 3(N) Squadron in France. He claimed five victories, following which he was awarded a DSC, gazetted in June, by which time he had left the unit to take up a post at Dunkirk. Leaving the service after the war, he re-enlisted in the RAF in January 1939 with the rank of Flight Lieutenant.

	1917		Pup					
1	11 Mar	Alb. C	N6175	3N	Bapaume	1150	OOC	CR/RFC 11.3
2	17 Mar	Alb. DIII	N6175	3N	Pronville	1050	OOC	CR/RFC 17.3
3	8 Apr	Alb. DIII	N6169	3N	N E Pronville	1510	OOC	CR/RFC 8.4
4	21 Apr	Alb. DIII	N6169	3N	Cagnicourt	1730	OOC	CR/RFC 21.4
5s*	21 Apr	DFW. CV	N6169	3N	Morchies-Louverval	1650	CAPT	CR/RFC 24.4

TOTAL: 1 shared captured, 4 out of control = 5.
*Shared with FSL F.D. Casey N6182, FSL J.J. Malone N6208. This was Uffz M. Haase/Lt R. Kelm of FA 26.

TRESCOWTHICK Norman Charles Lieutenant 4 AFC

An Australian boot manufacturer from Melbourne, Victoria, Norman Trescowthick was born on 18 July 1895. He joined the AFC, and in mid 1918 was posted to 4 AFC Squadron in France. Promotion to flight commander followed in September, together with the award of a DFC, and in mid-October the squadron converted to Snipes. Flying one of these he claimed his last victory on 30 October to bring his total to seven.

	1918		Camel					
1	14 Jul	AGO. C	D1927	4AFC	Laventie	0715	DES	CR/RAF 14.7
2	30 Jul	Fokker DVII	D1927	4AFC	N Armentieres	2005	OOC	CR/ORB/OH
3	7 Aug	Pfalz DIII	D1927	4AFC	S Armentieres	1245	DES	CR/RAF 7.8
4	7 Aug	Pfalz DIII	D1927	4AFC	S Armentieres	1245	DES(F)	CR/RAF 7.8

5s*	13 Aug	C	----	4AFC	Cartigny	1700	DES	CR/ORB/OH
6s**	16 Aug	Fokker DVII	----	4AFC	Wavrin	1315	DES	CR/ORB/OH
			Snipe					
7	30 Oct	Fokker DVII	E8064	4AFC	Leuze	1455	DES	CR/RAF 30.10

TOTAL: 4 and 2 shared destroyed, 1 out of control = 7.
*Shared with Lt R. King, Lt D.C. Carter, Lt R.G. Smallwood. **Shared with Capt A.H. Cobby, Lt D.C. Carter, Lt R. King, Lt T.R. Edols, Lt M.H. Eddie.

TREVETHAN Richard Michael Captain 20

Another of 20 Squadron's successful FE 2D pilots of 1917, Trevethan claimed at least 12 enemy scouts between 2 June and 9 August, and was awarded the MC, which was gazetted on 17 September. He became a flight commander, but was wounded in action on 18 September, and returned to England. In 1919 he served in North Russia, and by 1934 was a Squadron Leader at RAF Henlow.

	1917		FE 2D					
1*	2 Jun	Alb. DIII	A6480	20	Gheluvelt	0945	DES	CR/RFC 2.6
2**	9 Jun	Alb. DIII	A6341	20	E Ploegsteert	0600	DES(F)	CR/RFC 9.6
3***	2 Jul	Alb. DIII	A6523	20	Comines-Houthem	1245	OOC	CR/RFC 2.7
4***	7 Jul	Alb. DIII	A6498	20	Wervicq	1900	DES(F)	CR/RFC 7.7
5†	12 Jul	Alb. DV	A6528	20	E Ploegsteert Wood	1725	DES(F)	CR/RFC 12.7
6***	17 Jul	Alb. DV	A6512	20	Ploegsteert Wood	1955	DES	CR/RFC 17.7
7***	22 Jul	Alb. DV	A6528	20	Menin-N Wervicq	1650	DES(F)	CR/RFC 22.7
8***	27 Jul	Alb. DV	A6528	20	Lille-Menin	1945-2045	OOC	CR/RFC 27.7
9***	28 Jul	Alb. DV	A6528	20	Kezelbars	0915	OOC	CR/RFC 28.7
10***	8 Aug	Alb. DV	A6527	20	E Messines	1030	OOC	CR/RFC 8.8
11***	8 Aug	Alb. DV	A6527	20	E Messines	1040	OOC	CR/RFC 8.8
12***	9 Aug	Alb. DV	A6527	20	Becelaere-Roulers	0950	OOC	CR/RFC 8.8

TOTAL: 6 destroyed, 7 out of control = 12.
*Observer: 2 AM J.J. Cowell. **Observer: 2/Lt M. Dudbridge. ***Observer: Lt C.A. Hoy. †Observer: Pte Arkley.

TROLLOPE John Lightfoot Captain 70, 43

Born in 1898, he initially served as a dispatch rider in 1915 before training as a pilot. He flew 1½ Strutters with 70 Squadron on reconnaissance and fighter escort missions. Converting to single-seaters, he was posted to 43 Squadron in 1917 with the rank of Captain, and was awarded an MC in March 1918 for his initial five victories. On 24 March he flew two patrols, one in the morning during which he claimed three German machines. Leading a second patrol that afternoon he attacked nine two-seaters and again claimed three, making a total of six in one day — the second pilot to achieve this. On 12 April another pilot in the same squadron, H.W. Woollett, equalled this record, but by that time John Trollope was a prisoner of war. He was shot down on 28 March in Camel C8270 by Leutnant Paul Billik of Jasta 52, and was badly wounded in the left hand. In a German hospital the hand was amputated, and in June he was repatriated, returning to find that he had been awarded a Bar to his MC. On arrival he claimed that his Flight had achieved six victories during his last fight, three of them by himself. These claims were announced in an RAF Communique in October 1918, thereby raising his total to 18. His arm continued to give him a great deal of trouble, and eventually it had to be amputated at the shoulder. His injuries troubled him for most of his life, but he never showed his pain. During World War II he was stationed at St Athan as a Wing Commander between 1940-43, working with Maintenance Command.

	1918		Camel					
1	19 Jan	DFW. C	B6210	43	Vitry	1025	DES	CR/RFC 19.1
2	16 Feb	DFW. C	B6210	43	Vitry	1145	DES	CR/RFC 16.2
3	17 Feb	DFW. C	B6210	43	Brebieres	0930	OOC	CR/RFC 17.2
4	5 Mar	DFW. C	B6210	43	E La Bassee	1520	OOC	CR/RFC 5.3
5	11 Mar	Alb. DV	B6210	43	Sainghin	1350	OOC	CR/RFC 11.3
6	17 Mar	Alb. DV	C8270	43	Maugne	1145	OOC	CR/RFC 17.3
7	17 Mar	Alb. DV	C8270	43	4m E Armentieres	1200	DES(F)	CR/RFC 17.3
8	23 Mar	DFW. C	C8270	43	Mercatel	1300	CAPT	CR/RFC 23.3
9	24 Mar	DFW. C	C8270	43	E Mercatel	1100	DES	CR/RFC 24.3
10s*	24 Mar	DFW. C	C8270	43	S E Mercatel	1100	DES(F)	CR/RFC 24.3
11	24 Mar	Alb. DV	C8270	43	E Mercatel	1105	DES	CR/RFC 24.3
12	24 Mar	Alb. C	C8270	43	Sailly-Saillisel	1520	DES	CR/RFC 24.3
13	24 Mar	Alb. C	C8270	43	Sailly-Saillisel	1520	DES	CR/RFC 24.3
14	24 Mar	Alb. C	C8270	43	Sailly-Saillisel	1520	DES	CR/RFC 24.3
15	24 Mar	C	C8270	43	Sailly-Saillisel	1530	DES	CR/RFC 24.3

16	28 Mar	Balloon	C8270	43	E Albert	0930	DES	CR/RAF 10.18
17	28 Mar	Alb. DV	C8270	43	E Albert	0930	DES	CR/RAF 10.18
18	28 Mar	Alb. DV	C8270	43	E Albert	0930	DES	CR/RAF 10.18

TOTAL: 1 balloon, 1 captured, 11 and 1 shared destroyed, 4 out f control = 18.
*Shared with 2/Lt R.J. Owen C8259.

TUDHOPE John Henry Captain 40

Born in Johannesburg, South Africa, on 17 April 1891, he first saw service in German South-West Africa from 1914-15, before joining the RFC. In 1917 'Tud' was posted to 40 Squadron and flew both Nieuports and SE 5s. He received the MC and Bar, claiming ten victories before returning to Home Establishment in 1918. In 1935 he was a Squadron Leader in the RCAF.

	1917		Nieuport					
1	22 Sep	Alb. DV	B3617	40	E Pont a Vendin	0830	DES	CR/RFC 22.9
2s*	27 Sep	Alb. DV	B3617	40	Souchez	1835	CAPT	CR/RFC 27.9
			SE 5A					
3	15 Dec	Alb. DV	B589	40	Douai	1510	OOC	CR/RFC 15.12
4	19 Dec	Alb. DV	B589	40	Lens-Pont a Vendin	1055	OOC	CR/RFC 19.12
	1918							
5	13 Jan	DFW. C	B589	40	Pont- a Vendin	1055	OOC	CR/RFC 13.1
6	6 Mar	Alb. DV	B589	40	E Lorgies	1200	OOC	CR/RFC 6.3
7	9 Mar	Alb. DV	B589	40	Pont a Vendin	1215	DES(F)	CR/RFC 9.3
8	23 Mar	DFW. C	B589	40	Cherisy	1025	DES	CR/RFC 23.3
9	10 Apr	Alb. DV	B189	40	Neuve Chapelle	1005	OOC	CR/RAF 10.4
10	11 Apr	Fokker DrI	B189	40	N E Lens	1640	DES	CR/RAF 11.4

TOTAL: 1 shared captured, 4 destroyed, 5 out of control = 10.
*Shared with F/Cdr C.D. Booker C227, FSL J.H. Thompson. This was Oblt Hans Waldhausen, an ace from Jasta 37, who was captured.

TUDHOPE Philip Murray Lieutenant 46

Born on 27 September 1898, in the Orange Free State, this South African joined the RFC in May 1917 and was posted to 46 Squadron on 3 March 1918. He was involved in several combats and claimed six victories. Two of the latter were Fokker DVIIs, both of which were seen to go down colliding with each other during a fight on 17 September. He was awarded a DFC.

	1918		Camel					
1s*	25 Apr	LVG. C	----	46	W Lens	----	DES	SR/I BG WD
2	30 May	Pfalz DIII	C1671	46	Estaires	1930	DES(F)	CR/RAF 30.5
3	17 Jun	Fokker DVII	C1671	46	Estaires	1730	OOC	CR/?
4	4 Sep	Fokker DVII	F1971	46	Pronville	1015	OOC	CR/V BG WD
5s**	17 Sep	Fokker DVII	F1966	46	Cambrai	1200	OOC	CR/V BG WD
6s**	17 Sep	Fokker DVII	F1966	46	Cambrai	1200	OOC	CR/V BG WD

TOTAL: 1 and 1 shared destroyed, 2 and 2 shared out of control = 6.
*Shared with Capt C.J. Marchant, 2/Lt E.Smith. **Shared with Capt D.R. MacLaren F2137, 2/Lt R.D. Gilpin-Brown F5950, 2/Lt C.H. Sawyer D6693, Capt C.W. Odell D1942, 2/Lt L.S. Skerrington F6230. The above two aircraft collided.

TURNBULL John Seymour Lieutenant 56, 41

After service with the Worcestershire Regiment, Turnbull joined 56 Squadron in May 1917, aged 21, flying SE 5s. With this unit he claimed two victories before being shot down and wounded on 12 July in A4861, either by Jasta 4 or Marinefeldjasta 1. On recovery he claimed one further victory, but was then rested. In April 1918 he joined 41 Squadron, where he added two more victories by 12 June. On 17th of that month he was shot down and killed in D3955 near Chuignes by Leutnant August Delling of Jasta 34.

	1917		SE 5					
1s*	24 May	Alb. DIII	A8913	56	S Douai	1900-2000	OOC	CR/RFC 24.5
2	11 Jul	Alb. DIII	A8911	56	Houthoulst Forest	1845-1945	OOC	CR/RFC 11.7
			SE 5A					
3s**	18 Aug	Alb. DV	A8946	56	Menin	0630-0710	OOC	CR/RFC 18.8
	1918							
4	28 May	Pfalz DIII	D3955	41	Douai	1115	OOC	CR/SR/?
5	12 Jun	Alb. DV	D3955	41	Guerbigny	1300	OOC	CR/SR/?

TOTAL: 3 and 2 shared out of control = 5.
*Shared with Capt C.M. Crowe A8910, 2/Lt R.T.C. Hoidge A4862, 2/Lt A.P. F. Rhys Davids A4868, 2/Lt K.K. Muspratt A4861. **Shared with Capt G.C. Maxwell B502, Lt D.S. Wilkinson B521, 2/Lt R.H. Sloley A4868, 2/Lt W.J. Potts B4857, Capt H.M. Rushworth B517.

TURNER Arthur Henry Lieutenant 204, 213

Born in Birmingham on 16 April 1899, Turner joined the RNAS in September 1917. After qualifying as a pilot, he arrived at Dunkirk on 3 March 1918 and on 2 April was posted to 204 Squadron. On 25 May he went to 4 ASD to await re-posting, joining 213 Squadron in the summer. He claimed five victories with this unit and took part in 11 low-level bombing raids.

	1918		Camel					
1s*	11 Aug	Alb. C	D9964	213	4m S E Dixmude	1940	DES	CR/5 GP Comm
2	25 Aug	Fokker DVII	D3349	213	10m S Ostend	0730	OOC	CR/ORB/SR/?
3s**	6 Sep	Rumpler C	D3349	213	1m N Zevecote	1500	DES	CR/5 GP Comm
4	4 Oct	Fokker DVII	F3944	213	E Thorout	0930	DES(F)	CR/5 GP Comm
5s***	1 Nov	C	F3944	213	S Ghent	1430	DES	CR/5 GP Comm

TOTAL: 2 and 2 shared destroyed, 1 out of control = 5.

*Shared with Lt W.E. Gray D8189, Lt C.P. Sparkes B7252, 2/Lt E. Toy D3409. **Shared with Lt G.C. Mackay F5913. ***Shared with Capt G.C. Mackay F3944, Lt M.N. Hancock F5913.

TYRRELL Walter Alexander Captain 32

One of three soldier sons of Alderman Tyrrell of Belfast, he joined the RFC and flew DH 5s with 32 Squadron in 1917, and SE 5As in 1918. On three occasions he claimed three enemy aircraft shot down in one day; for this he was awarded an MC. Returning over the lines from a patrol on 9 June, his SE 5A B8391, was seen suddenly to roll over and dive into the ground, and he was killed, aged 19. It was thought that he had been hit by machine gun fire from the trenches.

	1917		DH 5					
1s*	30 Oct	Alb. DV	B4916	32	Passchendaele	0845-0925	DES	ORB/SR/?
2	11 Nov	Alb. DV	B4916	32	Poelcapelle	1550	OOC	ORB/SR/?
3s**	13 Nov	C	B4916	32	S E Houthoulst Forest	1530	OOC	CR/RFC 13.11
4s***	20 Nov	Alb. C	B4916	32	Passchendaele	0800	DES(F)	CR/RFC 20.11
5s†	5 Dec	C	B4916	32	Becelaere	0855	OOC	CR/RFC 5.12
	1918		SE 5A					
6	7 Apr	Fokker DrI	B8374	32	N E Lamotte	1115	DES	CR/RAF 7.4
7	7 Apr	Alb. DV	B8374	32	N E Lamotte	1120	DES	CR/RAF 7.4
8	7 Apr	Alb. DV	B8374	32	N E Lamotte	1130	OOC	CR/RAF 7.4
9	11 Apr	AGO. C	B8374	32	N E Bray	1930	DES(F)	CR/RAF 11.4
10	12 Apr	Pfalz DIII	B8374	32	W Steenwercke	1210	OOC	CR/RAF 12.4
11	3 May	Fokker DrI	B8374	32	Frelinghem	1220	OOC	CR/RAF 3.5
12	3 May	Fokker DrI	B8374	32	Frelinghem	1230	OOC	CR/RAF 3.5
13††	3 May	LVG. C	B8374	32	1m W S W Poperinghe	1235	CAPT	CR/RAF 3.5
14	8 May	Pfalz DIII	B8374	32	Sailly-en-Ostrevent	0940	DES	CR/RAF 8.5
15s†††	6 Jun	Pfalz DIII	B8374	32	Romagnies	0550	DES(F)	CR/RAF 6.6
16	6 Jun	Fokker DVII	B8374	32	Montdidier	1845	DES(F)	CR/RAF 6.6
17	6 Jun	Fokker DVII	B8374	32	Montdidier	1850	OOC	CR/ORB/SR/?

TOTAL: 1 captured, 5 and 3 shared destroyed, 6 and 2 shared out of control = 17.

*Shared with Capt W.R. Fish A9300. **Shared with 2/Lt H.C. Leese B4914, 2/Lt A.L. Cuffe B4924, Capt W.R. Fish A9300. ***Shared with 2/Lt A.L. Cuffe B4924, Lt A. Claydon A9300. †Shared with Capt W.R.G. Pearson A9300. ††This crew were Uffz Nievitecki/Uffz Priehs of FAA 266, who were captured. †††Shared with Lt J.W. Trusler C9612.

UNGER Kenneth Russell Lieutenant 210

An American, born in Newark, New Jersey, on 19 April 1898, he was turned down by the USAS, even though he had received flying instruction and held US Aero Club Certificate No 1356. He therefore went to Canada and joined the RFC in June 1917. After completing training in Canada and Texas, he went to England and then to France, where he joined 210 Squadron, flying Camels. During the closing months of the war, Unger claimed 14 victories and was awarded the DFC. Subsequently, Unger became a pilot for the US Air Mail, operating between Salt Lake City and Oakland. During World War II he flew cargo planes for the US Navy with the rank of Lieutenant Commander. He died in Florida on 6 January 1979.

	1918		Camel					
1s*	26 Jun	Fokker DVII	D9608	210	1m W Armentieres	1920	DES	CR/RAF 26.6
2s**	26 Jun	Fokker DVII	D9608	210	Ypres-Dickebusch	1945	OOC	CR/ORB/?
3s**	26 Jun	Pfalz DIII	D9608	210	Ypres-Dickebusch	1945	OOC	CR/ORB/?
4s**	26 Jun	Pfalz DIII	D9608	210	Ypres-Dickebusch	1945	OOC	CR/ORB/?
5	20 Jul	Fokker DVII	D9608	210	S E Ostend	0950	OOC	CR/5 GP Comm
6	31 Jul	Fokker DVII	D9608	210	Nieuport-Dixmude	1115	OOC	CR/5 GP Comm
7	24 Sep	Fokker DVII	F3930	210	S St Pierre Capelle	1440	OOC	CR/5 GP Comm
8	27 Sep	Halb. C	F3930	210	S E Nieuport	1745	DES	CR/5 GP Comm
9	28 Sep	Fokker DVII	D3336	210	4m N E Dixmude	1745	DES	CR/5 GP Comm

10	1 Oct	Pfalz DXII	F3930	210	8m N E Ypres	0945	DES(F)	CR/5 GP Comm
11	14 Oct	Fokker DrI	F3930	210	2m S Lichtervelde	1040	OOC	CR/5 GP Comm
12	27 Oct	Fokker DVII	F3930	210	2m W Locquignol	1030	DES	CR/5 GP Comm
13	30 Oct	Fokker DVII	F3930	210	200y E Rombies	1115	DES(F)	CR/RAF 30.10
14	1 Nov	Balloon	F3930	210	Estreaux	1210	DES	CR/RAF 1.11

TOTAL: 1 balloon, 5 and 1 shared destroyed, 4 and 3 shared out of control = 14.
*Shared with Capt L.P. Coombes D3387, Lt I.C. Sanderson B7155. This was Obflgm Schonfelder, an ace from Jasta 7. **Shared with Capt L.P. Coombes D3387, Lt I.C. Sanderson B7155.

VAUCOUR Awdry Morris Major 10, 70, 45

'Bunny' Vaucour was born in Upper Norwood, South London, in 1890, the only son of the Reverend H.M. Vaucour. After serving in the Royal Artillery, he joined the RFC, going to 10 Squadron as an observer in late 1915, and then to 70 Squadron as a pilot flying 1½ Strutters in 1916, where he was awarded an MC. In January 1917 he commanded 'B' Flight of the CFS, following which he took command of 45 Squadron in August, leading that unit to Italy in November. In Italy he received a Bar to his MC and the Italian Silver Medal for Military Valour. Flying alone on 16 July 1918, he was attacked by an Italian pilot who shot him down before realising that he was attacking a British Camel; Vaucour was hit in the head and killed. His advice to his young pilots when joining his squadron was "never break formation, should you ever find yourself alone in a fight, turn straight at the nearest enemy machine and fly for a collision...and never give way!" He had also received the DFC shortly before his death.

	1916		Strutter					
1*	2 Sep	Fokker E	A892	70	Bourlon Wood	1905	DES	CR/RFC 2.9
2*	2 Sep	Fokker E	A892	70	Ytres-Sailly	1925	OOC	CR/RFC 2.9
3*	15 Sep	Fokker E	A892	70	Hendicourt	1840	DES	CR/RFC 15.9
	1918		Camel					
4	27 Feb	Alb. DIII	B6354	45	Oderzo-Ponte di Piave	1250	DES	CR/7 BG
5	27 Feb	Alb. DIII	B6354	45	Orderzo-Ponte di Piave	1250	OOC	CR/7 BG
6	19 Jun	C	D1975	45	Postiama	1015	DES	ORB/14 W
7	25 Jun	C	D1910	45	3m E Treviso	1135	DES	ORB/14 W

TOTAL: 5 destroyed, 2 out of control = 7.
*Observer: Lt A.J. Bott.

VAUGHN Jnr George Augustus 1st Lieutenant 84, 17US

Born on 20 May 1897, this native of Brooklyn, New York, joined the USAS and in September 1917 was posted to the United Kingdom for operational training and combat experience in British units. He was sent to 84 Squadron, RAF on 28 May 1918, where during the summer he was credited with seven victories, being awarded the DFC. At the end of August he was re-assigned to the 17th US Aero Squadron as a flight commander, and flying Camels claimed six more enemy machines to bring his total to 13. He was then awarded the American DSC. After the war he remained very interested in aviation, becoming an aeronautical engineer, and a partner in the Casey Jones Academy of Aeronautics at La Guardia Field, New York. His biography was published during the 1980s. He was for many years an active member of the American Fighter Aces Association, and in early 1989 attended the unveiling of a rebuilt SE 5A in the US. He died suddenly on 31 July 1989.

	1918		SE 5A					
1	16 Jun	Pfalz DIII	D6149	84	Beaucourt	2000	DES(F)	CR/RAF 16.6
2	24 Jul	Fokker DVII	C6457	84	E Bray	2035	OOC	CR/AIR I/1794
3s*	28 Jul	Rumpler C	C6457	84	Harbonnieres	0940	DES	CR/RAF 28.7
4s*	29 Jul	Rumpler C	C6457	84	N Bois de Tailles	0800	DES	CR/RAF 29.7
5s**	22 Aug	Rumpler C	E4012	84	S E Villers Carbonnel	1100	DES	CR/RAF 22.8
6	23 Aug	Balloon	E4012	84	Hem	1015	DES	CR/AIR I/1794
7s***	23 Aug	Rumpler C	E4012	84	Maricourt	1120	DES	CR/RAF 23.8
			Camel					
8†	22 Sep	Fokker DVII	F6034	17US	S E Fontaine Notre Dame	0845	DES	CR/RAF 22.9
9††	22 Sep	Fokker DVII	F6034	17US	S W Cambrai	1205	DES(F)	CR/RAF 22.9
10	28 Sep	LVG. C	H828	17US	51 A M 34	1745	DES	CR/US 133
11s†††	2 Oct	DFW. C	H828	17US	E Awoignt	0910	DES	CR/RAF 2.10
12s‡	14 Oct	Halb. C	H828	17US	E Bazael	0710	DES	CR/RAF 14.10
13s‡‡	14 Oct	Fokker DVII	H828	17US	N E Hausey	1400	DES	CR/US 133

TOTAL: 1 balloon, 4 and 7 shared destroyed, 1 out of control = 13.
*Shared with Lt R. Manzer C8732. **Shared with 2/Lt S.W. Highwood C9869. ***Shared with Lt C.F. Falkenberg D6920. †This was Lt F. Noltenius of Jasta 27, who was damaged. ††This was Karl Bauerbfeind of Jasta 34, who was killed. †††Shared with 2/Lt H. Burdick F2141. ‡Shared with 2/Lt H. Burdick H830, 2/Lt L. Myers F2007. ‡‡Shared with 2/Lt H. Burdick H830.

VENTER Cristoffel Johannes Captain 29

'Boetie' Venter was born in South Africa on 1 November 1893. He travelled to England in March 1917 to join the RFC, and was posted to 29 Squadron in France on 19 April 1918 as the unit was re-equipping with SE 5As. In August he was awarded a DFC for five victories, but on 18th of that month, his score having reached 16, he was shot down in D6965 near Kemmel, probably by the rear gunner of a two-seater, and was taken prisoner. In November a Bar to his DFC was gazetted. After the war he joined the SAAF, rising to high rank. At the beginning of World War II he was OC, Cape Command, and later Director-General of Air Services. He subsequently managed South African Airways, and then became a Director of the English Electric Company of South Africa. He died on 20 February 1977.

	1918		SE 5A					
1	16 May	C	D3359	29	Merville	0930	DES	CR/RAF 16.5
2	18 May	Pfalz DIII	D3937	29	W Estaires	1150	DES(F)	CR/RAF 18.5
3	19 May	C	D5969	29	N W Estaires	1150	DES	CR/RAF 19.5
4s*	2 Jun	C	B8240	29	Bailleul-Armentieres	0815	OOC	ORB/?
5	6 Jun	Pfalz DIII	D3359	29	Estaires-Bailleul	1755	OOC	CR/ORB/11 WS
6	8 Jun	C	D3359	29	E Merville	1930	DES(F)	CR/RAF 8.6
7	17 Jun	Alb. C	C1116	29	E Merville	0915	DES	CR/RAF 17.6
8	18 Jun	Fokker DVII	B8504	29	N E Estaires	0825	OOC	CR/ORB/11 WS
9	26 Jun	Hannover C	C1116	29	S E Mt Kemmel	1745	DES	CR/RAF 26.6
10	2 Jul	Halb. C	C1116	29	W Houthem	1030	DES	CR/RAF 2.7
11	8 Jul	Hannover C	C1116	29	Messines	0930	DES(F)	CR/RAF 8.7
12	19 Jul	Halb. C	C1116	29	Outtersteene	1230	DES	CR/RAF 19.7
13	12 Aug	Fokker DVII	D6965	29	Comines	0925	OOC	CR/ORB/11 WS
14	12 Aug	Fokker DVII	D6965	29	N E Armentieres	0930	DES	CR/RAF 12.8
15**	12 Aug	Fokker DVII	D6965	29	S E Bailleul	1940	DES(F)	CR/RAF 12.8
16s***	14 Aug	Halb. C	D6965	29	Armentieres	1010	DES(F)	CR/RAF 14.8

TOTAL: 11 and 1 shared destroyed, 3 and 1 shared out of control = 16.
*Shared with Lt C.H.R. Lagesse D5969. **The pilot of this aircraft baled out successfully. ***Shared with Lt E.C. Hoy C9071.

VICKERS Oliver Henry Douglas Captain 20

A Londoner, born on 12 September 1898, he flew FE 2Ds in 20 Squadron in summer 1917. Vickers first claimed on 29 June, and in July added six further victories, flying mainly with the highly successful gunner, Sergeant J. Cowell. On 16 August, flying with Lieutenant J.A. Hone, two Albatros Scouts were claimed, while next day this pair added four more to bring Vickers' score to 13. He was promoted to flight commander whilst with the squadron.

	1917		FE 2D					
1*	29 Jun	Alb. DV	A6376	20	Becelaere	1610	OOC	CR/RFC 29.6
2**	3 Jul	Alb. DV	A6376	20	Becelaere	1700	OOC	CR/RFC 4.7
3*	12 Jul	Alb. DIII	A6376	20	E Ploegsteert Wood	1700	DES	CR/RFC 12.7
4*	12 Jul	Alb. DIII	A6376	20	E Ploegsteert Wood	1715	OOC	CR/RFC 12.7
5*	20 Jul	Alb. DV	A6376	20	Wervicq	0955	OOC	CR/ORB/11 WS
6*	22 Jul	Alb. DV	A6376	20	Menin-Wervicq	1650	OOC	CR/RFC 22.7
7*	28 Jul	Alb. DV	A6376	20	E Messines	1845	OOC	CR/RFC 28.7
8***	16 Aug	Alb. DV	A6376	20	E Passchendaele	0855	OOC	CR/RFC 16.8
9***	16 Aug	Alb. DV	A6376	20	N E Zonnebeke	0917	DES	CR/RFC 16.8
10***	17 Aug	Alb. DV	A6376	20	Halluin	1010	OOC	CR/RFC 17.8
11***	17 Aug	Alb. DV	A6376	20	Halluin	1012	OOC	CR/RFC 17.8
12***	17 Aug	Alb. DV	A6376	20	Halluin	1015	OOC	CR/RFC 17.8
13***	17 Aug	Alb. DV	A6376	20	Halluin	1015	OOC	CR/RFC 17.8

TOTAL: 2 destroyed, 11 out of control = 13.
*Observer: Sgt J.J. Cowell. **Observer: 2/Lt S.F. Thompson. ***Observer: Lt J.A. Hone.

VIGERS Arthur Whitehair Captain 15, 87

Born on 20 January 1890, and known as 'Wiggy' due to his unusual second name, he first saw service with the Signal Service (TF) of the Royal Engineers, receiving the MC in late 1915 and being Mentioned in Despatches. Seconded to the RFC, he flew as an observer in 15 Squadron before being selected for pilot training in 1917. In April 1918 he flew in France with 87 Squadron on Dolphins, and remained with that unit until 1919. He was awarded the DFC, and in August 1918 took command of 'C' Flight. On one occasion he and Lieutenant C.K.

Oliver (four victories) pursued a German two-seater over Amiens. When the two Dolphins closed in, the pilots found that their guns had become frozen with the cold, and the guns of their adversary were obviously similarly affected. All the four airman could do was to wave at each other! However on other occasions he was more successful, claiming a total of 14 victories. He was Mentioned in Despatches again in 1919. He emigrated to Australia after the war, serving with the RAAF: he died in September 1968.

	1918		Dolphin					
1	3 Jun	Fokker DrI	C4159	87	Bray	1835	DES	CR/RAF 3.6
2	3 Jun	Alb. DV	C4159	87	Bray-Herbecourt	1835	OOC	CR/?
3	10 Aug	Fokker DVII	C4159	87	Misery	0920	DES	CR/RAF 10.8
4	10 Aug	Fokker DVII	C4159	87	Misery	0920	DES	CR/RAF 10.8
5	10 Aug	Fokker DVII	C4159	87	Misery	0920	OOC	CR/?
6	21 Aug	Fokker DVII	C4159	87	Biefvillers	1745	DES	CR/RAF 21.8
7	21 Aug	Fokker DVII	C4159	87	Biefvillers	1745	OOC	CR/?
8	25 Aug	Fokker DVII	C4159	87	Velu Wood	1800	OOC	CR/?
9	3 Sep	Fokker DVII	C4159	87	Epinoy	1830	DES	CR/RAF 3.9
10	3 Sep	Fokker DVII	C4159	87	Epinoy	1830	OOC	CR/?
11	16 Sep	Rumpler C	C4159	87	N Cambrai	1030	DES	CR/RAF 16.9
12s*	22 Sep	Rumpler C	C4159	87	N E Bapaume	0910	OOC	CR/?
13	23 Sep	Fokker DVII	C4159	87	N E Cambrai	1745	OOC	CR/?
14	23 Sep	Fokker DVII	C4159	87	Bourlon Wood	1816	OOC	CR/?

TOTAL: 6 destroyed, 7 and 1 shared out of control = 14.
*Shared with Lt R.M. Macdonald C4156.

VLASTO Alexander George Lieutenant 46

Born on 12 September 1897, Alexander Vlasto was from Bracknell, Berkshire, and joined the Royal Field Artillery in July 1915; he transferred to the RFC two years later. After training, he joined 46 Squadron in November 1917, and first claimed on 21 March 1918. He was posted to Home Establishment on 15 July, and died during the 1930s of TB.

	1918		Camel					
1	21 Mar	Alb. DV	B9195	46	Lagnicourt	1145	DES	CR/RFC 21.3
2	23 Mar	LVG. C	B5428	46	S Vaulx	1000	OOC	CR/RFC 23.3
3s*	2 Apr	Alb. C	----	46	Courcelles	1245	DES	CR/RAF 2.4
4	3 May	Pfalz DIII	B2522	46	Fleurbaix	1330	OOC	CR/RAF 3.5
5	9 May	Pfalz DIII	B2522	46	Neuf Berquin	1915	OOC	CR/RAF 9.5
6	15 May	Pfalz DIII	B2522	46	Armentieres	1245	OOC	CR/RAF 15.5
7	15 May	Pfalz DIII	B2522	46	Armentieres	1245	OOC	CR/RAF 15.5
8s**	22 May	LVG. C	----	46	W Estaires	0920	DES	CR/RAF 22.5

TOTAL: 1 and 2 shared destroyed, 5 out of control = 8.
*Shared with Capt S.P. Smith, Lt H.G.W. Debenham, 2/Lt D.R. MacLaren, 2/Lt R.K. McConnell. **Shared with Lt V.M. Yeates, Lt J.R. Cote, Lt N. Bruce.

WALKER K.M. Lieutenant 209

He flew Sopwith Camels with 209 Squadron during the summer of 1918, serving in Captain J.K. Summers' flight. He claimed five victories, all shared but on 12 August Walker, Captain Summers and one other pilot were all shot down in a fight with Jastas 5 and 11, Walker in D9057 falling east of Peronne, possibly the victim of Leutnant Josef Mai of Jasta 5.

	1918		Camel					
1s*	18 Jul	Alb. C	D1891	209	Grivesnes-Plessier	1100	DES	CR/RAF 18.7
2s**	26 Jul	Fokker DVII	----	209	N Comines	0720	OOC	CR/?
3s***	8 Aug	Halb. C	----	209	Harbonnieres	1905	DES(F)	CR/RAF 8.8
4s†	10 Aug	Fokker DVII	D9657	209	E Bouchoir	1155	CAPT	CR/RAF 10.8
5††	11 Aug	Fokker DVII	D9657	209	Peronne	0810	DES(F)	CR/RAF 11.8

TOTAL: 1 shared captured, 1 and 2 shared destroyed, 1 shared out of control = 5.
*Shared with Capt J.K. Summers C198. **Shared with Capt J.K. Summers, Lt A.L. Porter. ***Shared with Capt R.M. Foster, Lt C.G. Edwards, Capt T.C. Luke, Lt M.A. Harker. †Shared with Capt J.K. Summers D9637. This was probably Lt Muhs of Jasta 12. ††Probably Lt Festler of Jasta 11, who was killed.

WALKERDINE Bernard Albert Lieutenant 64

Walkerdine joined the RFC on 26 July 1917 and claimed six victories while flying with 64 Squadron, which he joined on 5 December 1917. All his claims were made in May 1918, although he was with the unit for nearly eight months. His combat career ended when he was injured in a crash on 15 July.

	1918		SE 5A					
1s*	3 May	Rumpler C	C6447	64	Mercatel	1055	DES(F)	CR/RAF 3.5
2	16 May	Alb. DV	C6470	64	Brebieres	0930	DES	CR/RAF 16.5
3	16 May	Alb. DV	C6470	64	Brebieres	0940	OOC	CR/RAF 16.5
4	21 May	Halb. C	C1857	64	Ligny le Petit	1055	OOC	CR/?
5	28 May	Alb. DV	C1857	64	Pont Ricqueul	0755	DES	CR/RAF 28.5
6	31 May	Alb. DV	C1857	64	Monchy le Preux	1050	OOC	CR/?

TOTAL: 2 and 1 shared destroyed, 3 out of control = 6.
*Shared with Capt P.S. Burge B58, Lt W.C. Daniel B2.

WALKERDINE Harold John Lieutenant 56

Born on 13 January 1899, Walkerdine was commissioned in the RFC during September 1917 and was then posted to France, where he joined 56 Squadron on 2 November, to fly SE 5s. He claimed seven victories and received an MC for an action he fought on 18 March 1918, when he claimed two Pfalz Scouts shot down in one fight.

	1917		SE 5A					
1	29 Nov	DFW. C	B610	56	Neuvireuil	1320	DES	CR/RFC 29.11
	1918							
2	15 Mar	Alb. DV	B8266	56	N Bourlon Wood	1050	OOC	CR/RFC 15.3
3	16 Mar	Alb. DV	C5303	56	E Sancourt	1200	OOC	CR/RFC 16.3
4	18 Mar	Pfalz DIII	C5389	56	N E Marquion	0650-0715	DES	CR/RFC 18.3
5	18 Mar	Pfalz DIII	C5389	56	N Baralle	0650-0715	DES	CR/RFC 18.3
6s*	23 Mar	C	B8266	56	Moreuil	0740	DES	CR/RFC 23.3
7s**	27 Mar	Alb. DV	B8266	56	S E Bray	1315	DES	CR/RFC 27.3

TOTAL: 3 and 2 shared destroyed, 2 out of control = 7.
*Shared with Lt M.E. Mealing C5389, Capt L.W. Jarvis C5430, Lt E.D.G. Galley B59, Lt H.J. Burden D283, 2/Lt W.S. Maxwell B119. **Shared with Capt L.W. Jarvis C5430.

WALLACE Hazel LeRoy Captain 9(N), 201, 3

Born on 13 November 1897 in Earls Court, London, Wallace served in 9(N) Squadron for a short time before being posted to 201 Squadron in spring 1918. With this unit he claimed three victories in a week during May — one destroyed and two out of control. In the summer he was posted to 3 Squadron as 'C' Flight commander, and here he claimed several more victories. He was awarded a DFC, gazetted on 2 November; on 22 August he added a share in a balloon to bring his total to 11.

	1917		Camel					
1s*	6 Sep	Alb. C	B3892	9N	Middelkerke	1335	OOC	CR/ORB/?
2s**	16 Sep	DFW. C	B3883	9N	E Mariakerke	1645	DES(F)	CR/RFC 16.9
	1918							
3	11 Mar	Alb. DV	B6359	1N	E Armentieres	1000	OOC	CR/RNAS 11.3
4s***	16 Mar	Alb. DV	B6359	1N	E Roulers	1625	OOC	CR/RNAS 16.3
5s†	2 May	C	B6359	201	N Albert	1010	OOC	CR/RAF 2.5
6s††	15 May	Alb. DV	----	201	Bapaume	0645	DES	CR/RAF 15.5
7	15 May	Alb. DV	B6421	201	E Albert	1745	OOC	CR/RAF 15.5
8	17 May	Alb. DV	B7191	201	Albert	1930	OOC	CR/RAF 17.5
9s†††	20 Jul	Hannover C	C1698	3	Ayette	1020	OOC	CR/?
10	3 Aug	DFW. C	C1698	3	S Arras	1620	DES	CR/RAF 3.8
11s‡	8 Aug	Rumpler C	----	3	62 D X 30	1400	OOC	CR/?
12	10 Aug	Fokker DVII	----	3	62 C C54	1040	DES	CR/RAF 10.8
13	21 Aug	Fokker DVII	C1698	3	57 C G 8	1120	OOC	CR/?
14s‡‡	22 Aug	Balloon	C1698	3	Tilloy	0955	DES	CR/?

TOTAL: 1 shared balloon, 2 and 2 shared destroyed, 4 and 5 shared out of control = 14.
*Shared with F/Cdr J.S.T Fall B3898 FSL A.W. Wood B3884, FSL H.F. Stackard B6204, FSL J.E. Scott B3907. **Shared with Capt J.S.T. Fall B3883, FSL A.W. Wood B3905. ***Shared with FSL M.H. Findlay B6419. †Shared with Capt S.M. Kinkead B6429, Capt R.C.B. Brading B6421, Lt R.E. Bright B7267, 2/Lt H. Riddell B7225, Lt A.G.A. Spence B7278. ††Shared with Maj C.D. Booker, Capt S.M. Kinkead, Lt M.H. Findlay, Lt R. Hemmens, Lt J.H. Forman, Lt R. McLaughlin, Lt R.C.B. Brading, Lt R.S.S. Orr. †††Shared with Lt A.W. Franklyn D6628. ‡Shared with 2/Lt H.S. Basford, Lt A.D. McManus, Lt G.R. Riley, Lt V.B. McIntosh. ‡‡Shared with Lt G.R. Riley F5930.

WALLAGE Stanley Harry Captain 22

Stanley Wallage served with 22 Squadron early in 1917, flying Bristol Fighters with various gunners. Having gained one victory in February and two in March, he claimed six more in May. Of this total of nine, five were credited to the front gun and four to the rear. He was awarded an MC, and was promoted to flight commander while with the unit. After a period off operations, he returned to the unit in October, making one of the last two claims by the squadron on 4 November.

	1918		Bristol					
1*	18 Feb	C	C4808	22	Seclin	1400	OOC	CR/RFC 18.2
2*	11 Mar	Alb. DV	A7286	22	Lomme	1420	OOC	CR/RFC 11.3
3*	11 Mar	Alb. DV	A7286	22	Ligny	1420	OOC	CR/RFC 11.3
4**	8 May	Pfalz DIII	C795	22	N La Bassee	1900	DES	CR/RAF 8.5
5**	15 May	DFW C	C795	22	La Bassee	1040	OOC	CR/RAF 15.5
6**	15 May	DFW. C	C795	22	La Bassee	1045	OOC	CR/ORB/SR
7***	22 May	Alb. DV	C795	22	Hancourt	1030	DES	CR/RAF 22.5
8***	22 May	Alb. DV	C795	22	Hancourt	1030	OOC	CR/RAF 22.5
9***	26 May	Alb. DV	----	22	S E Armentieres	1945	DES	CR/RAF 26.5
10†	4 Nov	Pfalz DXII	E2454	22	N W Bavay	1415	OOC	CR/ORB/SR

TOTAL: 3 destroyed, 7 out of control = 10.
*Observer: Sgt J.H. Jones. **Observer: Lt G. Thompson. ***Observer: Lt A.P. Stoyle. †Observer: Capt D.E. Waight.

WALLWORK John Wilson Lieutenant 40

He claimed five victories flying SE 5As in 40 Squadron in 1918. The award of an MC was gazetted in July.

	1918		SE 5A					
1	6 Mar	Alb. DV	C1068	40	N W Lens	1620	DES	CR/RFC 6.3
2	9 Mar	Alb. DV	C1068	40	S Pont a Vendin	1155	OOC	CR/RFC 9.3
3	9 Mar	Alb. DV	C1068	40	Henin-Lietard	1615	OOC	CR/RFC 9.3
4	24 Mar	Fokker DrI	C1068	40	Croiselles	1030	OOC	CR/AIR 1/1222
5	12 Apr	Pfalz DIII	D3510	40	Bethune	1730	OOC	CR/RAF 12.4

TOTAL: 1 destroyed, 4 out of control = 5.

WALTER Stephen Reginald Parke 2nd Lieutenant 32

Walter transferred from the Queen's Royal West Surrey Regiment to the RFC late in 1916. Like his flight commander, Captain A. Coningham, he was one of the little-known DH 5 pilots who did a great deal of air fighting with 32 Squadron in July 1917. During that month he claimed six victories, but was killed on 31st when while returning from patrol he flew into the cable of a kite balloon and crashed.

	1917		DH 5					
1	11 Jul	Alb. DIII	B349	32	W Gheluvelt	1730	OOC	CR/RFC 11.7
2	12 Jul	Alb. DIII	B349	32	Polygon Wood	0955	DES	CR/RFC 12.7
3	17 Jul	Alb. DIII	A9199	32	Polygon Wood	2040	OOC	CR/RFC 18.7
4	22 Jul	Alb. DIII	A9199	32	Comines	0835	OOC	CR/RFC 22.7
5*	25 Jul	Alb. DIII	A9407	32	N Polygon Wood	c0830	OOC	ORB/SD/?
6	28 Jul	Alb. DIII	A9199	32	N E Bixschoote	1955	OOC	CR/RFC 28.7

TOTAL: 1 destroyed, 4 and 1 shared out of control = 6.
*Shared with 2/Lt J. Simpson A9404, 2/Lt H.J. Edwards A9374, 2/Lt W.R. Fish A9396.

WAREING Guy Wilbraham Captain 29

Born on 23 July 1899, in Warrington, Lancashire, Wareing joined the RFC in August 1917 and was posted to 29 Squadron on 9 June 1918. He claimed five aircraft and a balloon shot down by mid-September, being awarded a DFC which was gazetted on 3 December. He was promoted to flight commander, and by the end of September had accounted for three more balloons to bring his score to nine. He was then killed in action on 27 October in H676 east of Tournai, shot down by a Fokker DVII.

	1918		SE 5A					
1	12 Aug	Pfalz DIII	C1133	29	Ploegsteert	0920	DES	CR/RAF 12.8
2	19 Aug	DFW. C	C1133	29	E Bailleul	1115	DES	CR/RAF 19.8
3	31 Aug	LVG. C	C1133	29	E Estaires	1450	OOC	CR/ORB/11 WS
4	6 Sep	DFW. C	C1133	29	S E Perenchies	1800	DES	CR/RAF 6.9
5	7 Sep	Balloon	C1133	29	Gheluvelt	0655	DES	CR/RAF 7.9
6	15 Sep	Fokker DVII	C1133	29	Roulers-Rumbeke	1845	DES(F)	CR/RAF 15.9
7	27 Sep	Balloon	C1133	29	Moorslede	0845	DES	CR/RAF 27.9
8	29 Sep	Balloon	D6940	29	S E Armentieres	1000	DES	CR/RAF 29.9
9	29 Sep	Balloon	C1133	29	E Comines	1410	DES	CR/RAF 29.9

TOTAL: 4 balloons, 4 destroyed, 1 out of control = 9.

WARMAN Clive Wilson Captain 23

An American born in Norfolk, Virginia on 30 June 1892, Clive Warman joined the RFC after service with the Canadian infantry, and in 1917 was posted to 23 Squadron in France to fly Spad S VIIs. He showed immediate promise, claiming his first victory on 6 July, and by the end of the month had added three more to this score. In August he claimed two Albatros Scouts on 12th and again late on 15th. Early on 16th he claimed a balloon and a DFW two-seater. While fighting three scouts his gun finally jammed and he fired all his Very lights at them, finally hurling his hammer, kept for clearing jams in his machine gun, at the nearest before returning to base in disgust. He added another victory on 18th, bringing his score to 12. Awarded a DSO and MC, he was promoted to flight commander, but was then wounded in action before the end of the month, and did not return to combat. Warman's score is often given as 15, but this is because three of his victories were claimed in the late evening (15th and 18 August) and were reported in the next day's communiques, thereby being double-counted. He was killed in a flying accident with 1 Canadian Squadron on 12 June 1919.

	1917		Spad					
1	6 Jul	Alb. DIII	B1698	23	Thorout Houthoulst Forest	1520	DES	CR/RFC 6.7
2	13 Jul	C	----	23	----	----	DES	RFC 14.7
3*	27 Jul	Alb. DIII	B1581	23	Menin	2015-2030	OOC	CR/RFC 27.7
4	31 Jul	Alb. DIII	B1581	23	.5m S W Westroosebeke	1215	DES	CR/RFC 31.7
5	9 Aug	Balloon	----	23	----	----	DES	????
6s**	12 Aug	Alb. DV	B1581	23	Gheluvelt	0620	DES	CR/RFC 12.8
7	12 Aug	Alb. DV	B1698	23	E Polygon Wood	1245	DES(F)	CR/RFC 12.8
8	15 Aug	Alb. DV	----	23	Houthoulst Forest	1825	DES	CR/RFC 15.8
9	15 Aug	Alb. DV	----	23	Zonnebeke	2000	OOC	CR/RFC 15.8
10	16 Aug	DFW. C	----	23	Beveren a/d	0450	DES	CR/RFC 16.8
11	16 Aug	Balloon	----	23	Passchendaele	0500	DES	CR/RFC 16.8
12	18 Aug	Alb. DV	B1581	23	Passchendaele	1940	DES	CR/RFC 18.8

TOTAL: 2 balloons, 7 and 1 shared destroyed, 2 out of control = 12.
*Probably Lt H. Kroll, of Jasta 24, who crash-landed. **Shared with Lt S.C. O'Grady B3556.

WARNER John Weston Lieutenant 85

From Yorkshire, he joined the RFC in September 1917, and the following year went to France with 85 Squadron. He claimed eight victories and was awarded a DFC. He was shot down and killed on 4 October at the age of 19 by a Fokker DVII.

	1918		SE 5A					
1	29 Jun	Pfalz DIII	C1678	85	Kemmel	2017	OOC	CR/?
2	7 Jul	Fokker DVII	C1922	85	Doulieu	2015	OOC	CR/?
3	22 Aug	Fokker DVII	E3922	85	Clery sur Somme	1650	DES	CR/RAF 22.8
4	23 Aug	Fokker DVII	E3922	85	Suzanne/Peronne	0905	OOC	CR/?
5	15 Sep	Fokker DVII	E3922	85	Bourlon Wood	1805	DES	CR/RAF 15.9
6	20 Sep	Fokker DVII	E3922	85	E Bourlon Wood	1550	DES	CR/RAF 20.9
7	25 Sep	Fokker DVII	E3922	85	Urvillers	1755	DES	CR/RAF 25.9
8	2 Oct	Fokker DVII	E3922	85	S E Bohain	0855	DES	CR/?

TOTAL: 5 destroyed, 3 out of control = 8.

WATSON Henry Ellis Lieutenant 41

'Harry' Watson was commissioned in the RFC on 29 August 1917, and flew SE 5As with 41 Squadron from 23 November until 21 July 1918.

	1918		SE 5A					
1s*	25 Jan	Alb. DV	B8235	41	Vitry	1430	DES	CR/RFC 25.1
2	21 Mar	Fokker DrI	B8235	41	Bullecourt-Bourlon Wood	1350	OOC	CR/SR/?
3	30 Jun	Pfalz DIII	D6186	41	E Bray	0815	DES	CR/RAF 30.6
4	30 Jun	Pfalz DIII	D6186	41	Bray	0845	OOC	CR/RAF WD
5	1 Jul	C	D6125	41	E Adinfer Wood	1935	OOC	CR/SR/?
6	4 Jul	LVG. C	C8879	41	Bayonvillers	0710	OOC	CR/SR/?

TOTAL: 1 and 1 shared destroyed, 4 out of control = 6.
*Shared with Lt F.H. Taylor C1752.

WATSON Herbert Gillis Captain 4 AFC

Born on 30 March 1890, in Dunedin, New Zealand, Watson was working in Australia as a depot manager in Sydney at the outbreak of war, and enlisted in the Australian Army Service Corps. He transferred to the AFC in 1917 and was trained in England, being posted to 4 AFC Squadron on 5 February 1918. He first claimed in April 1918, and had eight victories by the end of June. He was awarded a DFC in mid-July, and by early

October when he became a flight commander, had brought his score to 14, three of these being balloons. Postwar he bred racehorses in Victoria until his death in the early 1940s.

	1918		Camel					
1	19 Apr	Alb. DV	B7406	4AFC	E Loos	1215	OOC	CR/RAF 19.4
2	11 May	Pfalz DIII	B7406	4AFC	N E Armentieres	1805	DES	CR/RAF 11.5
3	30 May	Alb. DV	D8116	4AFC	Estaires	1650	OOC	CR/ORB/OH
4	6 May	Balloon	D8116	4AFC	N Sailly	1630	DES	CR/RAF 6.6
5	17 Jun	Pfalz DIII	D9422	4AFC	E Laventie	1950	DES	CR/RAF 17.6
6	17 Jun	Pfalz DIII	D9422	4AFC	E Laventie	1950	DES	CR/RAF 17.6
7	25 Jun	AGO. C	C8300	4AFC	Bac St Maur	1940	DES	CR/RAF 25.6
8	26 Jun	Pfalz DIII	C8300	4AFC	S E Armentieres	1810	DES(F)	CR/RAF 26.6
9	15 Jul	Pfalz DIII	D8159	4AFC	Armentieres	1725	OOC	CR/ORB/OH
10	25 Jul	Balloon	D8159	4AFC	S Comines	0410	DES	CR/RAF 25.7
11s*	4 Aug	AGO. C	D8159	4AFC	S Laventie	2015	DES	CR/RAF 4.8
12	8 Aug	DFW. C	D8159	4AFC	Comines	2015	OOC	CR/ORB/?
13	16 Sep	Fokker DVII	D8159	4AFC	Le Quesnoy	0625	OOC	CR/ORB/OH
14	2 Oct	Balloon	D8159	4AFC	Capinghem-Wez Macquart	0615	DES	CR/RAF 2.10

TOTAL: 3 balloons, 5 and 1 shared destroyed, 5 out of control = 14.
*Shared with Lt R. King E1416.

WATSON Kenneth Bowman Lieutenant 10, 70

A Canadian from Ontario, he trained in Canada and was then posted overseas, flying with 10 Squadron in France in 1917. He later went to 70 Squadron, claiming nine victories and receiving the DFC. His last victory, on 4 November, was also the last claimed by his squadron before the Armistice.

	1918		Camel					
1	31 May	Alb. DV	C8218	70	S E Bapaume	1750	DES	CR/RAF 31.5
2	29 Jun	Alb. DV	C8218	70	Irles	0920	OOC	CR/III BG WD
3	4 Sep	Fokker DVII	E7173	70	Escaillon	0815	DES(F)	CR/RAF 4.9
4	29 Sep	Fokker DVII	E7173	70	Oostnieuwkerke	1140	DES	CR/RAF 29.9
5	8 Oct	C	E7173	70	E Menin	1750	DES	CR/RAF 8.10
6	9 Oct	Fokker DVII	E7173	70	S Roulers	0945	CAPT	CR/RAF 9.10
7s*	9 Oct	Fokker DVII	E7173	70	W Mayerneine	0945	CAPT	CR/RAF 9.10
8	28 Oct	Fokker DVII	E7183	70	Bois du Biez	1145	DES	CR/RAF 28.10
9	4 Nov	Fokker DVII	E7183	70	S W Renaix	1145	DES	CR/RAF 4.11

TOTAL: 1 and 1 shared captured, 6 destroyed, 1 out of control = 9.
*Shared with Capt S.T. Liversedge E7161, Lt O.A. Heron E7277, Lt E.A. Copp E7161, Lt A. Webster D6676.

WEARE Frank Gerald Craven Captain 22

'Weary' Weare transferred from the East Kent Regiment ('The Buffs') to the RFC in July 1917, and after training joined 22 Squadron to fly Bristol Fighters, teaming up with Lieutenant G.S.L. Hayward as his observer. He first claimed on 13 March 1918, and before the big German 'push' began, already had three to his credit. From then onwards his unit was continually in action, and he had claimed five more victories before the end of the month. Another seven were added during April, the last two falling on 22nd, by which time 11 of his 15 victories had been gained with the front gun, and four by Hayward's rear gun. Both crew members were awarded MCs, gazetted on 22 June; Hayward, flying also with other pilots, had a final personal score of 25. Weare later became a Lieutenant Colonel, a Justice of the Peace, and a prominent member of Tunbridge Wells Council. He died on 6 July 1971.

	1918		Bristol					
1*	13 Mar	Alb. DV	A7254	22	Seclin-Houplines	1615	DES	CR/RFC 13.3
2*	16 Mar	Pfalz DIII	B1152	22	S W Esquerchin	1155	DES	CR/RFC 16.3
3**	18 Mar	Alb. DV	B1152	22	Carvin	1015	DES	CR/RFC 18.3
4**	24 Mar	Alb. DV	C4828	22	Cherisy	1115	DES	CR/RFC 24.3
5**	24 Mar	Alb. DV	C4828	22	Vis-en-Artois	1120	DES	CR/RFC 24.3
6**	26 Mar	Pfalz DIII	B1217	22	E Albert	1245	DES	CR/RFC 26.3
7**	26 Mar	Pfalz DIII	B1217	22	E Albert	1245	OOC	CR/RFC 26.3
8**	29 Mar	Alb. DV	B1164	22	Guillancourt	1545	OOC	CR/RFC 29.3
9**	2 Apr	Alb. DV	B1164	22	Vauvillers	1645	DES	CR/RAF 2.4
10**	2 Apr	Alb. DV	B1164	22	Vauvillers	1645	DES(F)	CR/RAF 2.4
11**	12 Apr	Pfalz DIII	B1253	22	S W Sailly	1455	DES	CR/RAF 12.4
12**	12 Apr	Pfalz DIII	B1253	22	S W Sailly	1455	DES	CR/RAF 12.4
13**	12 Apr	Pfalz DIII	B1253	22	Sailly	1500	DES	CR/RAF 12.4
14**	22 Apr	Alb. DV	B1253	22	E Merville	0940	OOC	CR/RAF 22.4
15	22 Apr	Alb. DV	B1253	22	E Merville	0940	OOC	CR/RAF 22.4

TOTAL: 11 destroyed, 4 out of control = 15.
*Observer: 2/Lt S.J. Hunter. **Observer: Lt G.S.L. Hayward.

WEBB Noel William Ward Captain 25, 70

Webb, from Kensington, London, born in 1897, received a commission in the RFC in March 1916 and won his wings in June; he then went to France on 4 July to join 25 Squadron, flying two-seaters. During his first tour at the front he and his observer claimed five victories, and he received an MC. On 2 September he volunteered to attack the enemy balloon line, forcing down two although his FE 2 was hit several times and the fuel tank holed. Promoted to Captain, he returned to Home Establishment as an instructor. He returned to France on 21 June 1917 and joined 70 Squadron, flying Camels. With this unit he made the first RFC claim by a Camel on 12 July while flying on an air test, when he encountered a German two-seater, and forced it down, wounding the pilot and observer. The German was obliged to land on a British airfield to be captured. Webb subsequently added eight more victories and received a Bar to his MC during a very short period. On 16 August while leading a patrol, he was seen to dive after two German aircraft, but failed to return; he had been shot down by the great German ace, Leutnant Werner Voss of Jasta 10, and killed near Polygon Wood in B3756.

	1916		FE 2B					
1*	19 Jul	Fokker E	5245	25	E Provin	0645	DES	CR/RFC 19.7
2**	9 Aug	Alb. C	4839	25	Beaumont	1215	FTL	CR/?
3s***	7 Sep	Fokker E	7003	25	Pont a Vendin	1750	OOC	CR/RAF 8.9
4†	9 Sep	C	6993	25	Pont a Vendin	1600	DES	CR/RFC 9.9
5**	15 Sep	Fokker E	4841	25	Fresnoy	1720	DES	CR/?
	1917		Camel					
6††	12 Jul	C	B3756	70	Bellevue	1215	CAPT	CR/RFC 12.7
7†††	17 Jul	Alb. DV	B3756	70	S Gheluvelt	2000	OOC	CR/RFC 17.7
8	17 Jul	Alb. DV	B3756	70	S Gheluvelt	2055	OOC	CR/RFC 17.7
9‡	26 Jul	Alb. DV	B3756	70	E Zonnebeke	1930	DES	CR/RFC 26.7
10	28 Jul	Alb. DIII	B3756	70	Roulers	1940	DES	CR/RFC 28.7
11	28 Jul	Alb. DIII	B3756	70	E Polygon Wood	1950	OOC	CR/RFC 28.7
12	13 Aug	DFW. C	B3756	70	N E Dixmude	1930	OOC	CR/RFC 13.8
13	13 Aug	DFW. C	B3756	70	E Dixmude	1930	DES	CR/RFC 13.8
14s‡‡	13 Aug	DFW. C	B3756	70	N E Dixmude	1945	OOC	CR/RFC 13.8

TOTAL: 1 captured, 1 forced to land, 6 destroyed, 5 and 1 shared out of control = 14.

*Observer: 2/Lt I.A. Mann. **Observer: Lt C.S. Workman. ***Observer: Corp H. Brown, shared with Capt A.T. Loyd/2/Lt C.S. Workman 6993, Capt C.H. Dixon/AM J.H. Booth 6997. †Observer: Sgt L.S. Court. ††This crew were Lt J. Wollenhaupt/Lt H. Bohm of FA 18, who were captured. †††This was Lt Karl Meyer of Jasta 11, who was wounded. ‡This was Lt Otto Brauneck an ace of Jasta 11, who was killed. ‡‡Shared with Capt A.R. Hudson.

WELLS William Lewis Captain 22, 48

After serving with the Middlesex Regiment, Lewis Wells transferred to the RFC and flew as a Lieutenant in 22 Squadron from early October 1917, claiming six victories with the unit during the first months of the new year, five of these being credited to the front gun and one to the rear. He was awarded an MC, gazetted on 13 May. After claiming three scouts on 16 March, he was posted to 48 Squadron as a flight commander. He gained his first victory with his new unit on 21 March, and two days later shared an LVG two-seater with an SE 5A of 24 Squadron, then shot down a second and also claimed a Pfalz DIII. On 28 March he was mortally wounded in action and died on 6 May; a Bar to his MC was announced later.

	1918		Bristol					
1*	25 Jan	Alb. DIII	A7236	22	Emmerin, S W Lille	1340	OOC	CR/RFC 25.1
2*	18 Feb	C	A7251	22	Seclin	1400	OOC	CR/RFC 18.2
3**	13 Mar	Alb. DV	A7286	22	W Emmerin	1630	DES	CR/RFC 13.3
4***	16 Mar	Pfalz DIII	C4808	22	Oignies	1045	OOC	CR/RFC 16.3
5***	16 Mar	Pfalz DIII	C4808	22	Oignies	1100	OOC	CR/RFC 16.3
6***	16 Mar	Pfalz DIII	C4808	22	Beaumont	1115	DES	CR/RFC 16.3
7†	21 Mar	Pfalz DIII	C4707	48	S W Honnecourt	1420	DES	CR/RFC 21.3
8s††	23 Mar	LVG. C	C4707	48	N W Hem	1124	DES	CR/RFC 23.3
9†	23 Mar	LVG. C	C4707	48	Matigny	1625	DES	CR/RFC 23.3
10†	23 Mar	Pfalz DIII	C4707	48	Matigny	1625	DES	CR/RFC 23.3

TOTAL: 5 and 1 shared destroyed, 4 out of control = 10.

*Observer: Lt H.E. Moore. **Observer: 2/Lt P.S. Williams ***Observer: Lt G.S.L. Hayward. †Observer: Cpl W. Beales. ††Observer: Cpl W. Beales; shared with Lt A.K. Cowper B8407.

WELLWOOD James Joseph Lieutenant 2AFC

An Australian, Wellwood was born in Drouin, Victoria, on 15 October 1892, and worked as a motor engineer until he joined the Australian artillery after the outbreak of war. He later transferred to the AFC, and was posted to 2 AFC Squadron in France in the summer of 1918. In the next three months before the end of the war, he claimed six victories, the last on 4 November. He was awarded a DFC.

	1918		SE 5A					
1	1 Aug	Rumpler C	D6913	2AFC	3m S E Lille	1150	DES	CR/RAF 1.8
2	12 Aug	Fokker DVII	D6913	2AFC	Licourt	1110	DES	CR/RAF 12.8
3s*	25 Aug	DFW. C	D6968	2AFC	Epinoy	1130	DES	CR/RAF 25.8
4	6 Sep	Fokker DVII	D6968	2AFC	2m N W Douai	1900	OOC	CR/ORB/OH
5	24 Sep	Pfalz DIII	D6968	2AFC	N W Habourdin	1810	DES(F)	CR/RAF 24.9
6	4 Nov	Fokker DVII	F5511	2AFC	Tombelle	1110	DES	CR/RAF 4.11

TOTAL: 5 destroyed, 1 out of control = 6.
Shared with Capt A.T. Cole D6948.

WELSH George Arthur Lieutenant 210

Born on 28 July 1896 in Sunderland, Ontario, this Canadian flew with 210 Squadron in France from 22 June 1918. Flying Camels B7277 and F3106 he claimed five Fokker DVIIs shot down.

	1918		Camel					
1	11 Aug	Fokker DVII	B7277	210	W Roulers	0910	OOC	CR/5 GP Comm
2	24 Sep	Fokker DVII	F3106	210	5m N E Nieuport	1440	OOC	CR/5 GP Comm
3	28 Sep	Fokker DVII	F3106	210	7m S E Nieuport	1745	OOC	CR/ORB/SR/?
4	28 Sep	Fokker DVII	F3106	210	7m S E Nieuport	1750	DES	CR/5 GP Comm
5*	29 Sep	Fokker DVII	F3106	210	W Wijnendaele Wood	0800	DES	CR/5 GP Comm

TOTAL: 2 destroyed, 3 out of control = 5.
*The Pilot jumped out, without any parachute being seen.

WEST Mortimer Sackville 2nd Lieutenant 11

West served with 11 Squadron during 1917, flying Bristol Fighters. He made his first two claims on 17 July, and his fifth on 11 September.

	1917		Bristol					
1*	17 Jul	C	A7138	11	Sandemont	0835	OOC	CR/RFC 17.7
2*	17 Jul	Alb. DV	A7138	11	Bourlon Wood	1915	DES	CR/RFC 17.7
3*	20 Jul	Alb. DV	A7138	11	N W Blecourt	1915	DES(F)	CR/RFC 20.7
4**	17 Aug	Alb. DV	A7138	11	S W Douai	1510	DES(F)	CR/RFC 17.8
5**	11 Sep	Alb. DV	----	11	Cagnicourt	1845	OOC	CR/RFC 12.9

TOTAL: 3 destroyed, 2 out of control = 5.
*Observer: 2/Lt F.A. Adams. **Observer: 2/Lt F.A. Herron.

WESTON David John Lieutenant 20

David Weston joined 20 Squadron late in 1917; during May 1918 his observer was Corporal E.A. Deighton, an ace gunner who gained three of his victories whilst flying with Weston. The latter then teamed up with Lieutenant W. Noble with whom he had flown briefly earlier in the year, and who was himself to gain at least five victories. During the next few weeks they claimed six victories, including three Pfalz Scouts on 30 June. Weston was awarded the DFC, gazetted on 3 August, his final total being 13.

	1918		Bristol					
1*	25 Jan	Alb. DV	B1177	20	S E Staden	1225	OOC	CR/RFC 25.1
2*	25 Jan	Alb. DV	B1177	20	S E Staden	1225	DES	CR/RFC 25.1
3*	4 Feb	Alb. DV	----	20	Menin-Roulers Rd	1415	OOC	SR/RFC 4.2
4**	16 May	Alb. DV	C4763	20	Wervicq	1830	DES	CR/RAF 16.5
5**	19 May	Pfalz DIII	C4763	20	Armentieres	1035	OOC	CR/11 WS
6**	19 May	Pfalz DIII	C4763	20	Merville	1035	DES(F)	CR/RAF 19.5
7**	19 May	Pfalz DIII	C4763	20	N Frelinghien	1040	DES	CR/RAF 19.5
8***	30 May	Pfalz DIII	C979	20	Lille Citadel	1725	DES	CR/RAF 30.5
9***	31 May	Alb. DV	C4699	20	Estaires	0740	OOC	CR/11 WS
10***	30 Jun	Pfalz DIII	B1307	20	Wervicq	0730	DES	CR/RAF 30.6
11***	30 Jun	Pfalz DIII	B1307	20	Wervicq	0730	OOC	CR/11 WS
12***	30 Jun	Pfalz DIII	B1307	20	Wervicq	0730	OOC	CR/11 WS
13***	2 Jul	Fokker DVII	B1168	20	Gheluvelt-Menin	0845	DES	CR/RAF 2.7

TOTAL: 7 destroyed, 6 out of control = 13.
*Observer: 2/Lt W. Noble. **Observer: Cpl E.A. Deighton. ***Observer: Lt W. Noble.

WESTWOOD William Graham Captain 88

Born on 3 May 1891, in Pietermaritzberg, South Africa, he enlisted in August 1917, joining 88 Squadron on graduating as a pilot. He accompanied the unit to France in April 1918, where he operated with Lieutenant W. Tinsley as his usual observer throughout the summer, claiming six victories. He was promoted to Captain on 10 September.

	1918		Bristol					
1*	2 Jun	Alb. DV	----	88	Ostend	1945	OOC	CR/SR/?
2*	29 Jul	Fokker DVII	D7942	88	Bois Grenier	1830	OOC	CR/SR/?
3*	31 Jul	Pfalz DIII	D7942	88	S Merville	1000	DES(F)	CR/RAF 31.7
4*	11 Aug	Fokker DVII	D7942	88	Barleux	1610	OOC	CR/SR/?
5*	12 Aug	Fokker DVII	D7942	88	La Chapellette	1000	OOC	CR/SR/?
6**	14 Oct	Fokker DVII	----	88	E Lille	----	OOC	SR/?

TOTAL: 1 destroyed, 5 out of control = 6.
*Observer: 2/Lt W. Tinsley. **Observer: Lt A. Trantor.

WHEALY Arthur Treloar Captain 3W, 3(N), 9(N), 203

Born in Canada on 2 November 1893, Art Whealy joined the RNAS in Canada in 1915. Coming to England, he was commissioned Flight Sub Lieutenant in February 1916 and in June was posted to 3 Wing. In April 1917 he joined 'C' Flight of 3(N) Squadron, claiming three victories with this unit before being posted to 9(N) Squadron in May. He rejoined 3(N) in November, having increased his score to seven. He then claimed a further 20 victories between 17 February and 4 September 1918. Captain Whealy was rewarded with the DSC and Bar and the DFC for 27 victories and numerous ground strafing attacks. He left for Home Establishment on 24 September 1918.

	1917		Pup					
1	12 Apr	Alb. DIII	N6194	3N	Pronville	1030	OOC	CR/RFC 12.4
2	23 Apr	Alb. DIII	N6194	3N	N Arras-Cambrai Rd	1800	OOC	CR/RFC 24.4
3s*	2 May	Alb. C	N6194	3N	Bourlon Wood	0700	DES(F)	CR/ORB/DL
4	9 May	Halb. DII	N6167	9N	----	1230	OOC	ORB/SR/DL/?
5s**	7 Jul	Alb. DV	N6174	9N	S W Haynecourt	1730	OOC	CR/RFC 8.7
			Triplane					
6	29 Jul	Alb. DV	N5490	9N	Ostend	0520	OOC	CR/ORB/DL
7	29 Jul	Alb. DV	N5490	9N	Lombartzyde	0610	DES(F)	CR/RFC 29.7
			Camel					
8	5 Sep	Alb. DV	B3893	3N	N E Dixmude	1700	OOC	CR/DOS/DL
	1918							
9	17 Feb	Alb. DV	B7196	3N	Quesnoy	1055	OOC	CR/RNAS 17.2
10***	10 Mar	Alb. DV	B7220	3N	2m E Lens	1315	DES	CR/RFC 10.3
11	17 Mar	C	B7220	3N	Armentieres	1050	OOC	CR/RFC 17.3
12	22 Mar	Alb. DV	B7220	3N	Marquion	1230	CAPT	CR/RFC 22.3
13	23 Mar	Pfalz DIII	B7220	3N	Vaulx	1655	OOC	CR/RFC 23.3
14s†	24 Mar	Alb. DV	B7220	3N	Vaulx	1530	OOC	CR/RFC 24.3
15	11 Apr	LVG. C	B7220	203	1m E Estaires	1420	DES	CR/RAF 11.4
16	22 Apr	Alb. DV	B7220	203	Merville	0930	DES	CR/RAF 22.4
17	22 Apr	Alb. DV	B7220	203	Merville-Estaires	0932	DES	CR/RAF 22.4
18	3 May	C	B7220	203	1m N E Lens	1110	DES	CR/RAF 3.5
19	9 May	Pfalz DIII	B7220	203	1m N La Bassee	1130	DES	CR/RAF 9.5
20	14 May	LVG. C	B7220	203	N La Bassee	1950	DES	CR/RAF 14.5
21s††	15 May	DFW. C	B7220	203	1m E Pont du Hem	1050	DES	CR/RAF 15.5
22	16 May	Pfalz DIII	B7220	203	N La Bassee	1120	OOC	CR/ORB/?
23	16 May	C	B7220	203	Estaires	1135	DES	CR/ORB/?
24	7 Jun	Fokker DrI	D9594	203	1m S E Lestrem	1145	OOC	CR/ORB/?
25s†††	22 Aug	DFW. C	D9641	203	S Mericourt	0630	DES	CR/?
26s‡	27 Aug	DFW. C	D9641	203	S Combles	1210	DES	CR/RAF 27.8
27	4 Sep	Fokker DVII	D9641	203	Trescault	1615	DES	CR/RAF 4.9

TOTAL: 1 captured, 12 and 4 shared destroyed, 8 and 2 shared out of control = 27.
*Shared with FSL F.C. Armstrong N6178, FSL E. Pierce N6171. **Shared with F/Cdr H.E. Hervey N6162, FSL J.W. Pinder B6475, FSL H.G. Mott N6469, FSL J.C. Tanner N6166. ***3N claimed 1 destroyed, 3 out of control in this fight. Oblt H.J. Buddecke was killed and Oblt R. Berthold was wounded. †Shared with F/Cdr F.C. Armstrong B7218, FSL S. Smith B7274, FSL R.C. Berlyn B7274, FSL L.D. Bawlf B7192, F/Lt E. Pierce B7227, FSL F.J.S. Britnell B7229. ††Shared with Lt F.J.S. Britnell B7251. †††Shared with Lt W. Sidebottom D9645. ‡Shared with Lt F.J.S. Britnell D9611.

WHEELER William Allan Lieutenant 88

Born on 5 April 1888 in Coventry, Wheeler joined the RFC in August 1917 and flew Bristol Fighters from 22 May 1918 with 88 Squadron in France. With three observers, he claimed a total of six victories, and took part in several bombing raids on German aerodromes and dumps.

	1918		Bristol					
1*	29 Jun	Fokker DVII	C774	88	N N W Dixmude	2010	DES(F)	CR/RAF 29.6
2**	11 Aug	Fokker DVII	----	88	Combles	1135	OOC	CR/SR/?
3**	11 Aug	Fokker DVII	----	88	N W Peronne	1145	OOC	CR/SR/?
4***	29 Aug	Fokker DVII	D8064	88	E Lille	0815	DES	CR/SR/X BG S
5†	23 Oct	Fokker DVII	E2458	88	Leuze	1710	DES(F)	CR/RAF 23.10
6†	30 Oct	Fokker DVII	E2458	88	Peruwelz	0930	OOC	CR/SR/?

TOTAL: 3 destroyed, 3 out of control = 6.
*Observer: Lt T.S. Chiltern. **Observer: Lt G.N. Howard. ***Observer: 2/Lt W. Tinsley. †Observer: 2/Lt W.B. Clarke

WHISTLER Harold Alfred Captain 3, 80

'Willy' Whistler was born on 30 December 1896, and attended the Royal Military College at Sandhurst, being commissioned in the Dorsetshire Regiment. Transferred to the RFC in 1916, he flew Morane Parasols with 3 Squadron that same year until he was wounded on 29 January 1917. Later in 1917 he joined 80 Squadron as a flight commander, going to France with the unit in the new year, and becoming its most outstanding pilot. In short order he received the DSO, DFC and Bar, claiming 23 victories as well as flying many army support and ground attack sorties. During one combat on 1 June, the plywood behind his seat was set on fire by a tracer bullet, but he put out the flames and got his Camel safely home. He remained in the RAF, being stationed at the new College at Cranwell as an instructor. He subsequently also instructed at CFS from 1930-32, later becoming a Wing Commander. In 1929 a second Bar to his DFC was announced for operations against Najd Bedouin tribesmen whilst commanding 55 Squadron.

	1918		Camel					
1	17 Mar	Alb. DV	----	80	S Cambrai	1020	DES	SR/RFC 17.3
2	17 Mar	Alb. DV	----	80	S Cambrai	1020	OOC	SR/RFC 17.3
3	24 Mar	Alb. DV	----	80	----	----	DES	RFC 24.3
4	24 Mar	Alb. DV	----	80	----	----	DES	RFC 24.3
5	17 May	Alb. C	B7346	80	----	1800	OOC	SR/RAF 17.5
6	1 Jun	Pfalz DIII	B7346	80	Dompierre	0725	DES	CR/RAF 1.6
7	1 Jun	Pfalz DIII	B7346	80	Curlu-Eclusier-Vaux	0815	DES	CR/RAF 1.6
8	12 Jun	Fokker DrI	B7346	80	W Noyon	----	DES(F)	SR/RAF 12.6
9	12 Jun	Pfalz DIII	B7346	80	W Noyon	----	DES	SR/RAF 12.6
10	2 Jul	Fokker DrI	----	80	----	----	DES	RAF WD
11	9 Jul	Fokker DVII	C8205	80	La Bassee	0930	OOC	CR/SR/?
12	30 Jul	Fokker DVII	D9485	80	Fismes	----	DES(F)	SR/RAF 30.7
13	30 Jul	Fokker DVII	D9485	80	Fismes	----	OOC	SR/?
14	4 Aug	D	----	80	----	----	DES	SR/?
15	9 Aug	Fokker DVII	D9485	80	Framerville	1050	OOC	CR/V BG WD
16	14 Aug	Fokker DVII	----	80	Roye	2000	OOC	CR/V BG WD
17	14 Aug	Fokker DVII	----	80	Roye	2000	OOC	CR/V BG WD
18	15 Sep	Balloon	D9485	80	Etricourt	1320	DES	CR/RAF 15.9
19	18 Sep	Fokker DVII	D9485	80	E Pontruet	1445	DES	CR/V BG WD
20	29 Sep	Fokker DVII	D9485	80	N Fontaine	1015	DES	CR/RAF 29.9
21	29 Sep	Fokker DVII	D9485	80	Joncourt	1035	DES	CR/RAF 29.9
22	2 Oct	Halb. C	D9485	80	E Bohain	1230	OOC	CR/V BG WD
23	2 Oct	Fokker DVII	D9485	80	E Bohain	1235	OOC	CR/V BG WD

TOTAL: 1 balloon, 13 destroyed, 9 out of control = 23.

WHITE Harold Albert Lieutenant 23

Lieutenant White, an American, flew Sopwith Dolphins with 23 Squadron from September 1918, claiming seven victories.

	1918		Dolphin					
1	28 Jun	Pfalz DIII	D3715	23	E Bray	1000	OOC	CR/V BG WD
2s*	29 Jun	Fokker DVII	C3786	23	Hangard	1030	DES(F)	CR/RAF 29.6
3	24 Aug	Fokker DVII	D3706	23	Peronne	1825	OOC	CR/V BG WD
4s**	7 Sep	Fokker DVII	D3706	23	Ronnssoy	1845	OOC	CR/V BG WD
5s***	16 Sep	Fokker DVII	C8187	23	St Quentin	0830	OOC	CR/V BG WD
6	16 Sep	Fokker DVII	C8187	23	St Quentin	0830	DES(F)	CR/V BG WD
7	20 Sep	Fokker DVII	E4513	23	N St Quentin	1215	DES(F)	CR/V BG WD

TOTAL: 2 and 1 shared destroyed, 2 and 2 shared out of control = 7.
*Shared with Capt A.B. Fairclough D3669, Lt A.P. Pehrson C4181, Lt C.C.A. Sherwood C3903, Lt A.D. Bentley D3715, Lt J. Adam C8063, Lt K.D. Macpherson C8070. **Shared with 2/Lt E.J. Taylor D3751. ***Shared with Lt A.P. Pehrson F5965.

WHITE Hugh Granville Captain 20, 29

Born in Maidstone, Kent, on 1 March 1898, he had originally decided upon a naval career, but he entered the Royal Military College, Sandhurst, when he was 17. Commissioned in the East Kent Regiment, he was attached to the RFC in 1916. Posted in July to 20 Squadron as a pilot flying FE 2Bs and 2Ds, he was called the 'Child Pilot' because of his age. He survived however, to become a flight commander and claimed three victories, including a scout forced down inside the Allied lines, where its pilot, Leutnant Josef Flintz of Jasta 18, was captured. After 11 months with 20 he returned to the United Kingdom as an instructor. In February 1918 he returned to France to command a flight of 29 Squadron on Nieuports and then SE 5As. Due to the conversion to SEs, he did not claim any further victories until mid-May. However on 19 May he became involved in an engagement so dramatic that it is worthy of recording in some detail.

Leading a patrol, he and his pilots were shooting-up a line of observation balloons when nine Pfalz DIIIs of Jasta 29 attacked. Three of the patrol were driven away westwards immediately, and Captain White was left alone. He dived on one of the Pfalz and fired about 100 rounds from very close range. The German scout zoomed to the left and its top plane caught the leading edge of the right-hand top plane of the SE, causing the Pfalz to turn a cartwheel over the British aircraft. The shock of the collision flung White forward onto the gun mounting and stopped the engine. The Pfalz went into a dive and White — expecting his machine to break up at any moment — dived after it, firing a further 100 rounds. The right-hand wings of the Pfalz then fell off, and it went down completely out of control. The pilot of this aircraft is now known to have been Vizefeldwebel Karl Pech, a nine victory ace who had shot down two Camels of 210 Squadron exactly 24 hours earlier in the same area, and who was killed. White turned west to endeavour to recross the lines and was followed back by five Pfalz for some distance, until these were driven off by friendly aircraft. He managed to keep his aircraft fairly straight by putting on hard left bank, left rudder, and leaning over the side of the cockpit. Near the ground, the SE became uncontrollable and it crashed on landing — the centre section wires of the machine had broken, and the right-hand top plane had anhedral, rather than dihedral! Despite the damage to this wing, the main spars had held, although the fabric covering was completely torn away. Following this epic fight, White was posted home for a rest on 22 May, and was recommended for a decoration which he never received. At the beginning of 1919 he took command of 64 Squadron, and then of his old 29 Squadron in Germany. He later spent five years in India with 28 Squadron. In 1942 with the rank of Air Commodore, he became AOC Halton, and later reached the rank of Air Vice-Marshal in July 1949, retiring as a CB, CBE, in 1955. During his career he had also played rugby for the RAF. He died on 23 September 1983.

	1917		FE 2D					
1*	5 Apr	Alb. DIII	A6385	20	Neuve Eglise	1145	CAPT	CR/RFC 5.4
2**	23 May	Alb. DIII	A6412	20	Zandvoorde	1045	OOC	CR/RFC 23.5
3**	26 May	Alb. DIII	A6412	20	Comines-Quesnoy	1045	OOC	CR/RFC 26.5
	1918		SE 5A					
4	15 May	Alb. DV	D3937	29	Bailleul	1955	OOC	ORB/?
5	17 May	Pfalz DIII	D5970	29	Merville	0745	DES(F)	CR/RAF 17.5
6	18 May	Pfalz DIII	D3942	29	1.5m W Estaires	1140	DES	CR/RAF 18.5
7***	19 May	Pfalz DIII	D3942	29	Bailleul	1140	DES	CR/RAF 19.5

TOTAL: 1 captured, 3 destroyed, 3 out of control = 7.
*Observer: Pt T. Allum; This was Lt J. Flintz of Jasta 18, who was captured. **Observer: 2/Lt T.A.M.S. Lewis. ***White collided with this aircraft, piloted by Vzfw Karl Pech, an ace from Jasta 29, who was killed.

WHITE James Butler Captain 8(N), 208

A Canadian from Manitoulin Island, Ontario, born on 7 July 1893, White joined the RNAS and was posted to 8(N) Squadron as a Flight Sub Lieutenant in the winter of 1917-18. He claimed one victory on 24 January, and in the following September was promoted to flight commander and awarded a DFC, which was gazetted on 3 December. He took part in many ground attack sorties, remaining with the squadron until the autumn, claiming two final victories on 3 October to bring his score to 12. He became a stockbroker after the war.

	1918		Camel					
1	24 Jan	Alb. DV	B6321	8N	Fresnes-Vitry	1140	DES	CR/RFC 24.1
2	3 Feb	Alb. DV	B6321	8N	Vitry	1230	OOC	CR/RFC 3.2
3	8 May	Alb. DV	D1867	208	Provin	1115	OOC	CR/RAF 8.5
4s*	28 Jul	Rumpler C	----	208	S Estaires	0950	OOC	CR/RAF 28.7
5	29 Jul	C	----	208	S Estaires	2040	OOC	CR/?
6	31 Jul	Pfalz DIII	D1417	208	S Pont a Vendin	1140	DES	CR/RAF 31.7
7s**	14 Aug	DFW. C	----	208	E Oppy	0600	OOC	CR/?
8	6 Sep	Fokker DVII	----	208	Arras-Cambrai Rd	1830	DES(F)	CR/RAF 6.9
9	26 Sep	Pfalz DXII	----	208	S Gouy	1220	DES	CR/RAF 26.9

10	29 Sep	Fokker DVII	----	208	N Lesdains	1230	DES	CR/RAF 29.9
11	3 Oct	Fokker DVII	E7165	208	Brancourt	1810	DES	CR/RAF 3.10
12	3 Oct	Fokker DVII	E7165	208	Premont	1815	DES(F)	CR/RAF 3.10

TOTAL: 7 destroyed, 3 and 2 shared out of control = 12.
*Shared with Lt M.C. Howell, Lt G.A. Wightman. **Shared with Lt Allison, Lt E.G. Johnstone, Lt R.G. Gifford.

WHITE Joseph Leonard Maries Captain 65

'John' White, a Canadian, first served with the Canadian Machine Gun Corps. Becoming a pilot in the RFC in September 1917, he flew with 65 Squadron from April 1918. He remained with the unit until the Armistice, and was able to claim 22 victories and engage in much ground attack work, becoming a flight commander in August, and receiving both DFC and Bar, and the Croix de Guerre. His final combat on 4 November was his most successful when he claimed four of 17 victories reported by the squadron. In 1924 White joined the newly-formed Royal Canadian Air Force, but on 24 February 1925 was killed in a flying accident.

	1918		Camel					
1	9 May	Alb. DV	D6562	65	Lamotte	1930	OOC	CR/ORB/?
2	18 May	Alb. DV	C8264	65	Bray-Albert	1020	DES	CR/RAF 18.5
3	19 May	C	D6562	65	2m S E Villers Brettoneaux	0700	DES	CR/RAF 19.5
4	25 May	Alb. DV	C8275	65	1m S E Albert	1940	DES	CR/ORB/?
5	28 May	Alb. DV	C8272	65	N Lamotte	0930	OOC	CR/?
6	2 Jun	Alb. DV	C8272	65	Mezieres	1900	OOC	CR/ORB/?
7	9 Jun	C	D8119	65	E Morlancourt	0800	DES	CR/ORB/?
8	2 Jul	Pfalz DIII	C8204	65	Proyart	2025	OOC	CR/ORB/?
9	3 Jul	Pfalz DIII	C8204	65	Beaucourt	2025	OOC	CR/ORB/?
10s*	8 Aug	Fokker DVII	----	65	Proyart	1225	CAPT	CR/RAF 8.8
11s*	8 Aug	Fokker DVII	----	65	Proyart	1225	CAPT	CR/RAF 8.8
12	9 Aug	Fokker DVII	D8193	65	S Foucaucourt	1735	DES(F)	CR/RAF 9.8
13	9 Aug	Fokker DVII	D8193	65	S Foucaucourt	1735	OOC	CR/?
14	3 Sep	Fokker DVII	D8193	65	Engel	1055	OOC	CR/ORB/?
15	3 Sep	Fokker DVII	D8193	65	Engel	1100	OOC	CR/ORB/?
16	14 Oct	Fokker DVII	D8193	65	Courtrai	0755	DES(F)	CR/RAF 14.10
17	14 Oct	Fokker DVII	D8193	65	Courtrai	0755	DES	CR/RAF 14.10
18	26 Oct	Fokker DVII	H7007	65	Helderghem	1335	DES	CR/RAF 26.10
19	4 Nov	Fokker DVII	H7007	65	S E Ghent	0850	DES	CR/RAF 4.11
20	4 Nov	Fokker DVII	H7007	65	S E Ghent	0850	DES(F)	CR/RAF 4.11
21	4 Nov	Fokker DVII	H7007	65	S E Ghent	0850	DES(F)	CR/RAF 4.11
22	4 Nov	Fokker DVII	H7007	65	S E Ghent	0850	OOC	CR/RAF 4.11

TOTAL: 2 shared captured, 10 destroyed, 10 out of control = 22.
*Shared with Capt E.G. Brookes, Lt G.D. Tod, Lt F. Edsted, Lt C. Tolley, Lt D. Oxley.

WHITEHEAD Lewis Ewart Captain 60, 65

Whitehead flew Nieuport Scouts with 60 Squadron in the summer of 1916 and was wounded in combat on 26 July. Back in action later in the year, he assisted in bringing down an Albatros two-seater on 11 December, which was forced to land in Allied lines. In 1917 he served with 65 Squadron as it was forming, on occasions undertaking home defence sorties in its Camels. But he did not accompany the unit to France in November 1917. In April 1918, however, he rejoined the squadron as a flight commander, and during May claimed four victims, two of which were again brought down and captured within Allied lines. Whitehead was reported missing in Camel D1876 on 20 May, seen by his comrades to be shot down by a Fokker Triplane south-east of Albert at 1820 hours. He was the victim of OffStellv Fritz Rumey of Jasta 5 (45 victories).

	1916		Nieup					
1s*	11 Dec	Alb. CIII	----	60	Dainville	1030	CAPT	CR/RFC 11.12
	1918		Camel					
2	2 May	C	D1876	65	Cerisy-Lamotte	1325	DES	CR/?
3s**	3 May	Hannover C	D1876	65	Heilly	0645	CAPT	CR/RFC 3.5
4***	15 May	Alb. DV	D1876	65	S E Villers-Brettoneaux	0845	DES	CR/RAF 15.5
5†	17 May	Alb. DV	D1876	65	N E Villers-Brettoneaux	1100	CAPT	CR/RAF 17.5

TOTAL: 1 and 2 shared captured, 2 destroyed = 5.
*Shared with Capt E.O. Grenfell, Lt H. Meintjes, Lt Daly, Lt L.S. Weedon, Lt K.L. Caldwell. Lt Baldamus, observer, was captured. **Shared with 2/Lt S.W. Crane B1791; this was the crew of ?/Gefr M. Lang of Schl 31. ***65 made 3 claims. Oblt W. Ewers, commander of Jasta 77 was killed. †This was Gefr A. Wendt of Jasta 63, who was killed.

WHITNEY Robert Kenneth Lieutenant 60

Whitney, a Canadian, joined 60 Squadron on 21 February 1918, flying SE 5As. Before being wounded in the hand on 11 August, he claimed five victories, all whilst flying C8886, and received the DFC. He also attacked and forced down several kite balloons. It is noteworthy that both crew members of a two-seater shot down by him at 1640 hours on 8 August, baled out successfully.

	1918		SE 5A					
1	7 Jul	DFW. C	B186	60	Achiet le Grand	1145	DES(F)	CR/SR/?
2	18 Jul	DFW. C	B186	60	Boiry Notre Dame	0500	DES	CR/RAF 18.7
3s*	8 Aug	Hannover C	C8886	60	Foucaucourt	1640	DES	CR/RAF 8.8
4s**	8 Aug	DFW. C	C8886	60	Estrees	1650	DES(F)	CR/SR/?
5s***	9 Aug	Hannover C	C8886	60	Croisilles	0835	DES	CR/RAF 9.8

TOTAL: 2 and 3 shared destroyed = 5.

*Shared with Capt J.E. Doyle E1397; both crew baled out safely. **Shared with Lt F.W. Clark E3919. ***Shared with Capt J.E. Doyle E1288.

WILKINSON Alan Machin Lieutenant Colonel 24, 48, 23

Born in Eastbourne, Sussex, on 21 November 1891, and educated at Oxford, he first served with the Hampshire Regiment of the Territorial Force. Transferring to the RFC, he became one of the first pilots to fly fighting scouts in action, joining 24 Squadron on 16 January 1916. Going to France during the spring, he soon adapted his DH 2 to carry two Lewis guns, though higher authority later ordered that only one should be carried. He first claimed on 16 May when he shot down two aircraft out of control. By 19 July he had become one of the RFC's first aces, by which time he had also been promoted to flight commander; he was slightly wounded in action next day. By 31 August he had claimed one captured, four destroyed, four out of control, two forced to land and one driven down. At this stage he was probably one of the two most successful scout pilots in the RFC. He was awarded a DSO, gazetted on 20 October, but on 13 October he returned to Home Establishment. Posted as a flight commander to 48 Squadron which was forming with the first Bristol F2A Fighters, he accompanied this unit to France in spring 1917. It has often been stated that not until Andrew McKeever began his run of successes later in the year was the Bristol properly flown in action. However Wilkinson and one of the other flight commanders, D.M. Tidmarsh, employed correct tactics from the beginning. Within a month Wilkinson and four other crews had achieved considerable success; indeed in a short space of time Wilkinson claimed nine victories, seven in the course of four days — four of them in one day! Wilkinson received an immediate Bar to his DSO, gazetted on 26 May. However during the month he had already been posted again, this time to command 23 Squadron, equipped with Spad S VIIs. Tied down with administrative work demanded of commanding officers at that time, Major Wilkinson had little opportunity to fly, and the combat career of one of the truly outstanding fighters of the RFC came to an end. Later he commanded No 8 Aerial Fighting School until 1919, achieving the rank of Lieutenant Colonel.

	1916		DH 2					
1	16 May	AGO GII	5966	24	Peronne	0700	OOC	CR/ORB/?
2	16 May	Fokker E	5966	24	Peronne	0730	OOC	CR/ORB/?
3	17 Jun	Fokker E	5966	24	Miraumont	1825	DES	CR/RFC 17.6
4	17 Jun	Alb. C	5966	24	Grevillers	1900	FTL	CR/RFC 17.6
5	18 Jun	C	5966	24	S E Achiet le Grand	1950	DES	CR/RFC 18.6
6	19 Jul	Fokker E	5966	24	Bapaume-Peronne Rd	1015	OOC	CR/ORB/?
7s*	21 Aug	C	----	24	Le Sars	----	DES	RFC 21.8
8	28 Aug	EA	7880	24	Le Sars-Flers	1840	DES	CR/RFC 28.8
9	31 Aug	Roland C	7880	24	Villers	1100	DES	CR/RFC 31.8
10	31 Aug	LVG. C	7880	24	High Wood	1130	OOC	CR/RFC 31.8
	1917		Bristol					
11**	5 Apr	Alb. DIII	----	48	Douai	c1200	OOC	RFC 5.4
12***	9 Apr	C	----	48	Lens	----	DES	RFC 9.4
13***	9 Apr	Alb. DIII	----	48	Lens	----	OOC	RFC 9.4
14s†	9 Apr	Alb. DIII	----	48	Arras	----	DES	RFC 9.4
15s†	9 Apr	Alb. DIII	----	48	Arras	----	OOC	RFC 9.4
16s††	12 Apr	Alb. DIII	----	48	----	----	OOC	RFC 12.4
17s†††	13 Apr	Alb. DIII	----	48	Vitry en Artois	----	DES	RFC 13.4
18s†††	13 Apr	Alb. DIII	----	48	Vitry en Artois	----	OOC	RFC 13.4
19‡	22 Apr	Alb. DIII	----	48	----	----	OOC	RFC 22.4

TOTAL: 6 and 2 shared destroyed, 6 and 4 shared out of control, 1 forced to land = 19.

*Shared with 2/Lt H.A. Wood, 2/Lt S.J. Sibley. **Observer: Lt L.W. Allen. ***Observer: Lt H.B. Griffiths. †Observer: Lt L.W. Allen. Shared with Capt J.H.T. Letts/Lt H.G. Collins. ††Observer: Lt L.W. Allen. Shared with Lt W.O.B. Winkler/2/Lt E.S. Moore. †††Observer: Lt L.W. Allen. Shared with Lt J.W. Warren/2/Lt H.B. Griffiths. ‡Observer: Lt L.W. Allen.

WILLIAMS Edward George Herbert Caradoc Lieutenant 48

Williams flew F2B Fighters with 48 Squadron during the latter half of 1917, claiming five victories.

	1917		Bristol					
1*	9 Sep	Alb. DIII	A7213	48	Middelkerke	1615	OOC	CR/?
2**	11 Sep	Alb. DIII	A7216	48	Ostend	1900	OOC	CR/?
3***	15 Sep	Alb. DV	A7216	48	N E Dixmude	1830	OOC	CR/RFC 15.9
4†	29 Oct	Pfalz DIII	A7216	48	N E Dixmude	1625	DES	CR/RFC 29.10
5††	13 Nov	Alb. DIII	A7216	48	N E Ostend	1315	DES	CR/RFC 13.11

TOTAL: 2 destroyed, 3 out of control = 5.
*Observer: 2 AM B. Jackman. **Observer: 2 AM H. Lindfield. ***Observer: 2/Lt J.C. Boughton. †Observer: 2/Lt G.W. Croft. ††Observer: 2 AM T.W. Jones.

WILLIAMS Francis Jefferies Lieutenant 29

Born on 1 February 1898, Williams was commissioned on 15 April 1917 in the RFC, and was posted to 29 Squadron on Nieuports on 4 September. He claimed five victories by the end of March 1918.

	1917		Nieuport					
1	26 Oct	C	B6826	29	E Houthoulst Forest	1705	OOC	CR/RFC 26.10
2s*	5 Dec	Alb. DV	B6826	29	E Staden	1545	OOC	CR/RFC 5.12
	1918							
3	3 Jan	Alb. DV	B6826	29	S Moorslede	1535	OOC	CR/RFC 3.1
4	5 Feb	C	B6826	29	Moorslede	1030	OOC	CR/RFC 5.2
5	18 Mar	Pfalz DIII	B3605	29	S E Rumbeke	1145	DES	CR/RFC 18.3

TOTAL: 1 destroyed, 3 and 1 shared out of control = 5.
*Shared with Capt H.J. Hamilton B3631.

WILLIAMS Thomas Frederick Captain 45, 28

Born in Ontario, Canada, on 12 October 1885, he joined the 1st Canadian Division in August 1914, and sailed to England. He transferred to the RFC in 1916, and after pilot training was posted to 45 Squadron in France. Before the unit moved to Italy, he was shot down twice, firstly on 22 September during a fight with the Richthofen Circus (JG I), and then on 6 November by a Canadian machine gunner who thought he and Captain Firth were Germans as they flew back through a barrage over Passchendaele. He did, however, claim four victories during this period, the first during a spectacular lone fight with seven Albatros Scouts, the leader of which was reported to have crashed. It was because of this battle at odds that he was nicknamed 'Voss' by his comrades. In Italy he claimed four more victories before being posted to 28 Squadron as a flight commander. With this new unit he claimed a further six, bringing his total to 14. He flew 199 patrols, receiving the MC and Italian Valore Militaire. He was recommended for a DFC, but never received it. Returning to Canada, he became a barnstormer in the twenties, holding Flying Certificate No 91. From 1939-48 he was chief test pilot for Fleet Aircraft Company of Ontario, continuing thereafter to fly up to the age of 87; he was also an active organiser and participator in Canadian World War I veteran reunions. He attended the Aces' Reunion in Paris in 1981, and published a book of poetry at the age of 97, but died in July 1985, two months short of his 100th birthday.

	1917		Camel					
1	24 Oct	Alb. DV	----	45	Menin-Coucou	1410	DES	CR/RFC 24.10
2	8 Nov	Alb. DV	----	45	Westroosebeke	1605	DES(F)	CR/RFC 8.11
3	8 Nov	Alb. DV	----	45	Houthoulst Forest	1610	OOC	CR/RFC 8.11
4	13 Nov	Junkers JI	B6282	45	N W Westroosebeke	1155	DES	CR/RFC 13.11
	1918							
5	10 Jan	Alb. DIII	B6282	45	Porto Buffole	1615	OOC	CR/ORB/14 W
6	11 Jan	Alb. DIII	B6282	45	Vittorio	1145	OOC	CR/7 BG S
7*	26 Jan	Alb. DIII	B6282	45	Roncade-Treviso	1335	CAPT	CR/7 BG S
8	27 Mar	Alb. DIII	B3887	45	Ceggia	1205	DES(F)	CR/7 BG S
9	19 Jun	Alb. DV	D8208	28	Borgo	0940	DES	CR/14 W
10s**	25 Jun	Berg DI	D8208	28	Udine	1010	OOC	CR/14 W
11***	15 Jul	Alb. DV	D8208	28	N Roana	1005	DES	CR/14 W
12†	15 Jul	Alb. DV	D8208	28	N Roana	1015	DES(F)	CR/14 W
13s††	23 Jul	Alb. DV	D6342	28	2km N E S Paolo di Piave	0830	DES	CR/14 W
14†††	27 Jul	C	D8208	28	.5km N E Gallio	0855	DES(F)	CR/14 W

TOTAL: 1 captured, 8 and 1 shared destroyed, 3 and 1 shared out of control = 14.
*This was KorpP Ignatz Stiegl of Flik 12D who was killed in 153:84. **Shared with Lt A.G. Jarvis D8170, Lt C. Costanduros D8206. ***This was Fl O. Spenn of Flik 55J, killed in 122:90. †This was Oblt E. von Hebra, also of Flik 55j, who managed to crash-land his burning Phonix DII. ††Shared with Lt A.G. Jarvis D8170. This was Fp Salm of Flik 74j, killed in 38:61. †††This was the crew Schuff/Nather killed in 369:59 of Flik 45D.

WILLIAMS Thomas Mellings Captain 65

Born in South Africa, Tommy Williams came to England and joined the RFC in 1917. He was posted to 65 Squadron and with this unit claimed nine victories, also taking part in numerous ground attack operations. The awards of the MC and DFC were gazetted in September and November 1918. He remained in the RAF, and as a Flight Lieutenant was adjutant to the Cambridge University Air Squadron in the early thirties. In 1935, with the rank of Squadron Leader, he attended the RAF Staff College. During the early years of World War II he served with Bomber Command, while he later held commands in India and the Far East. After the war he became Inspector General of the RAF, 1948-51, and retired in 1952 as Air Marshal Sir Thomas Williams, KCB, OBE, MC, DFC, MA. He died in 1956.

	1918		Camel					
1	29 Jan	Alb. DV	B9166	65	S W Roulers	1257	OOC	CR/RFC 29.1
2	1 Apr	Alb. DV	D1817	65	Froissy	1625	OOC	CR/RAF 1.4
3	23 Apr	Alb. DV	D1817	65	Morlancourt	1835	DES	CR/RAF 23.4
4	2 May	C	D1817	65	Villers-Brettoneaux	1155	DES(F)	CR/RAF 2.5
5s*	10 May	Alb. DV	----	65	N Villers-Brettoneaux	1930	DES	CR/RAF 10.5
6	18 May	C	D1817	65	W Wiencourt	1030	DES	CR/RAF 18.5
7	28 May	Pfalz DIII	B7347	65	Bois de Tailleux	0955	OOC	CR/ORB/?
8s**	3 Jul	Pfalz DIII	D1817	65	Aubercourt	1918	DES(F)	CR/RAF 3.7
9s***	1 Aug	C	D1817	65	N Entineham	0830	OOC	CR/?

TOTAL: 3 and 2 shared destroyed, 3 and 1 shared out of control = 9.
*Shared with Capt J.I. Gilmour, 2/Lt H. Brown, 2/Lt W.F. Scott-Kerr, 2/Lt H. Spreadbury, 2/Lt M.A. Newnham. **Shared by Lt D.M. John D1878. ***Shared with 2/Lt F. Niseroi E1415.

WILLIAMSON Alec Lieutenant 88

Born on 8 November 1898, in Leek, Staffordshire, he claimed five victories and his observers another four while flying Bristol Fighters with 88 Squadron in 1918. His two successful observers were Lieutenant W.I.N. Grant and Air Gunner E. Hoare.

	1918		Bristol					
1*	28 Jun	Halb. C	C4720	88	Houthoulst Forest	2000	DES(F)	CR/RAF 28.6
2*	28 Jun	Halb. C	C4720	88	Houthoulst Forest	2000	DES(F)	CR/RAF 28.6
3*	6 Aug	Fokker DVII	C4720	88	Ploegsteert	1045	OOC	CR/SR/?
4*	11 Aug	Fokker DVII	C787	88	Combles	1130	DES(F)	CR/RAF 11.8
5*	11 Aug	Fokker DVII	E2183	88	Herbecourt	1615	OOC	CR/SR/?
6*	14 Aug	Fokker DVII	E2183	88	Dompierre	1745	OOC	CR/SR/?
7**	19 Aug	Fokker DVII	E2153	88	Bauvin-Douai	1025	OOC	CR/SR/?
8***	23 Oct	Fokker DVII	E2481	88	Beclers	1710	DES	CR/RAF 23.10
9***	23 Oct	Fokker DVII	E2481	88	Beclers	1710	DES(F)	CR/RAF 23.10

TOTAL: 5 destroyed, 4 out of control = 9.
*Observer: Gnr E. Hoare. **Observer: Pte T. Proctor. ***Observer: Lt W.I.N. Grant.

WILSON Cecil Frederick Charles Lieutenant 84

Born on 18 July 1897 in Newport, Monmouthshire, Wilson was commissioned on 9 September 1917. He joined 84 Squadron on 12 April 1918, but after claiming one victory during May, was hospitalized in June. On return to the unit he added four more to his total. The last of these was a Fokker DVII, shot down on 3 November, the pilot of this aircraft baling out.

	1918		SE 5A					
1	28 May	Alb. DV	D8223	84	S Wiencourt	0920	OOC	CR/?
2s*	25 Aug	LVG. C	C6430	84	N Foucaucourt	0945	OOC	CR/?
3s**	3 Sep	Rumpler C	----	84	S Manacourt-Nurlu	0625	DES	CR/RAF 3.9
4s***	16 Sep	Rumpler C	B8420	84	Selenoy	0630	DES	CR/RAF 16.9
5†	3 Nov	Fokker DVII	E6008	84	Mormal Wood	1530	DES	CR/RAF 3.11

TOTAL: 1 and 2 shared destroyed, 2 out of control = 5.
*Shared with Capt W.A. Southey C1834. **Shared with Capt W.A. Southey, Lt A.E. Hill, Lt E.R.W. Miller, 2/Lt F.R. Christiani. ***Shared with 2/Lt S.W. Highwood C6490. †The pilot baled out successfully.

WILSON Claude Melnot Lieutenant 29

Born on 6 July 1898, in Vancouver, British Columbia, Wilson joined the RFC in July 1917, being posted to 29 Squadron on 4 May 1918. However he was taken into hospital on 15 May and did not return until 23 June. He claimed his first victory over a Hannover two-seater on 22 July. He had added victories over five more aircraft and a balloon by September, when he was awarded a DFC. However Wilson was killed on 14 October when shot down east of Roulers in F5516 by a Fokker DVII.

	1918		SE 5A					
1	22 Jul	Hannover C	C9582	29	Armentieres	0825	OOC	CR/ORB/?
2s*	8 Aug	Alb. C	----	29	E La Gorgue	1940	DES	CR/ORB/?
3	9 Aug	Hannover C	D6949	29	S Lestrem	2025	DES	CR/RAF 9.8
4	18 Aug	DFW. C	C8859	29	N Neuve Eglise	1720	DES	CR/RAF 18.8
5	24 Aug	Balloon	D6940	29	E Steenwerck	0945	DES	CR/RAF 24.8
6	25 Aug	Fokker DVII	D6940	29	Hollebeke	0835	DES	CR/RAF 25.8
7	25 Aug	Fokker DVII	D6940	29	Hollebeke	0840	OOC	CR/11 WS
8	16 Sep	Fokker DVII	D6940	29	N Loos a/d	0917	DES	CR/RAF 16.9

TOTAL: 1 balloon, 4 and 1 shared destroyed, 2 out of control = 8.
*Shared with Lt A.E. Reed, Lt H.R. Humphries, Lt D.A. O'Leary, Lt H.C. Rath.

WILSON Percy Captain 28

Born in Cheshire on 11 April 1895, Wilson initially joined 28 Squadron in November 1917, accompanying this unit to Italy, where he was promoted to flight commander in April 1918. He was also awarded the MC and Italian Bronze Medal for Military Valour, claiming seven victories, including a balloon. On 3 May he shot down one of five enemy scouts that were escorting an Aviatik two-seater, while on 11th, when escorting an RE 8 of 34 Squadron, he and Lieutenant O.W. Frayne (four victories) each claimed an Albatros shot down when these attempted to attack their charge. In April 1919 he served with 79 Squadron in Germany.

	1918		Camel					
1	25 Jan	C	B6363	28	St Fior di Sopra	1145	DES	CR/7 BG S
2*	4 Feb	Alb. DV	B6363	28	1km S Motta	1005	DES	CR/7 BG S
3**	27 Feb	C	B5183	28	Nerversa	1030	DES	CR/7 BG S
4	3 May	Alb. DV	B5187	28	Mt Santo	0915	DES	CR/7 BG S
5	10 May	Balloon	B6363	28	Mareno	1425	DES	CR/14 W
6	11 May	Alb. DV	B6363	28	Follina	1000	DES(F)	CR/14 W
7	19 May	Alb. DV	B6363	28	Arsie	0715	DES(F)	CR/14 W

TOTAL: 1 balloon, 6 destroyed = 7
*This was Uffz Deerenfeld of Jasta 39, who was wounded. **This was the crew KorpP Rettmann/Lt Capponi Flik 47B killed in 165:64.

WINKLER William Otto Braasch Lieutenant 48

An Englishman despite his Germanic name, Winkler was one of the original members of 48 Squadron, and was posted to France with this unit on 8 March 1917. Although the unit suffered heavily at the hands of Jasta 11 during April and May, Winkler had made six claims by 2 May. During the evening of 11 May he and his observer, 2nd Lieutenant E.S. Moore, were shot down near Gavrelle in A7111, another Bristol also being lost in this engagement; the two British aircraft fell to Leutnant Wilhelm Allmenröder and Leutnant Lother von Richthofen of Jasta 11. Winkler was killed but Moore survived as a prisoner, returning after the war.

	1917		Bristol					
1s*	12 Apr	Alb. DIII	----	48	----	----	OOC	SR/RFC 12.4
2s**	23 Apr	Alb. DIII	----	48	Vimy	----	OOC	SR/RFC 23.4
3s***	24 Apr	Alb. DIII	----	48	Cagnicourt	----	OOC	SR/RFC 23.4
4†	2 May	Alb. DIII	A3348	48	Brebieres-Biache	1930	OOC	CR/RFC 2.5
5†	2 May	Alb. DIII	A3348	48	Brebieres-Biache	1935	OOC	CR/III BG WD
6†	2 May	Alb. DIII	A3348	48	Brebieres-Biache	1940	DES	CR/RFC 2.5

TOTAL: 1 destroyed, 2 and 3 shared out of control = 6.
*Observer: 2/Lt E.S. Moore, shared with Capt A.M. Wilkenson/Lt L.W. Allen. **Observer: 2/Lt E.S. Moore, shared with Lt F.P. Holliday/Capt A.H.W. Wall, Lt R.B. Hay/?, Lt W.T. Price/Lt M.A. Benjamin. ***Observer: 2/Lt E.S. Moore, shared with Lt F.P. Holliday/Capt A.H.W. Wall, Lt R.B. Hay/? †Observer: 2/Lt E.S. Moore.

WINNICOTT Russell Lieutenant 41

Born in Plymouth, the youngest son of Alderman R.W. Winnicott, he joined the RFC and was posted to 41 Squadron in 1917, where he flew both DH 5s and SE 5As, receiving an MC. He was killed in a mid-air collision on 6 December at the age of 19.

	1917		DH 5					
1	6 Sep	Alb. C	A9218	41	Masnieres-Lesdain	1335	OOC	CR/RFC 6.9
2	18 Sep	Alb. DV	A9218	41	Cambrai	1115	OOC	CR/RFC 18.9
3	25 Sep	Alb. DV	A9218	41	S W Cambrai	1810	DES	CR/RFC 25.9
4	28 Sep	Alb. DV	A9218	41	Bugnicourt	1810	OOC	CR/RFC 28.9
5	30 Sep	Alb. DV	A9218	41	Eterpigny	1600	OOC	CR/RFC 30.9
6	30 Sep	Alb. DV	A9218	41	E Marquion	1630	OOC	CR/RFC 30.9
7	18 Oct	Alb. DV	A9218	41	Arleux	1530	OOC	CR/RFC 18.10
			SE 5A					

8s*	29 Nov	Alb. DV	B667	41	Douai	1050	OOC	CR/RFC 29.11
9	30 Nov	Alb. DV	B667	41	N Bourlon	1340	DES	CR/RFC 30.11
10s**	30 Nov	C	B667	41	Rumilly	1400	OOC	CR/RFC 30.11

TOTAL: 2 destroyed, 6 and 2 shared out of control = 10.

*Shared with Capt L.J. MacLean B642, Lt D.A. MacGregor B644, Lt E.M. Essell B65. **Shared with Capt M. Thomas B38, Capt L.J. MacLean B633, Lt F.H. Taylor B596.

WINTER Rupert Randolph Flight Commander 6(N), 9(N)

Born on 24 April 1896 in Woodside Park, North London, Winter joined the RNAS on 25 April 1916. He was posted to 4(N) Wing on 17 January 1917, but soon afterwards moved to 6(N) Squadron, remaining with this unit until it was disbanded in August. Thereafter he was posted to 9(N) Squadron, but was killed on 3 February 1918 immediately after achieving his fifth victory, when his Camel, B6430, was shot down south-west of Roulers by pilots of Jasta 26. It is interesting to note that on this occasion the German pilots made claims for five victories, although his was the only British aircraft to fall!

	1917		Nieuport					
1	29 Apr	Alb. DIII	N3199	6N	Guise	1850	OOC	CR/RFC 29.4
			Camel					
2	21 Jul	Alb. DV	N6379	6N	Westende	2005	DES	CR/DRO/Cit
3s*	28 Jul	DFW. C	B3821	6N	N 5 Central	1600	DES	CR/RFC 28.7
4s**	6 Dec	Alb. C	B6317	9N	2m N W Courtrai	1345	DES	CR/RNAS 6.12
	1918							
5s***	3 Feb	Fokker DrI	B6430	9N	2m S W Roulers	1400	DES	CR/RNAS 3.2

TOTAL: 1 and 3 shared destroyed, 1 out of control = 5.

*Shared with FSL N.M. MacGregor B3833. **Shared with FSL E.M. Knott B6288. ***Shared with FSL M.A. Harker N7381.

WOMERSLEY John Herbert Greenwood Captain 43

John Womersley was commissioned into the East Riding Regiment from the Leeds University OTC on 27 October 1915. He transferred to the RFC later in the war, and flew Sopwith 1½ Strutters with 43 Squadron during the summer of 1917. He claimed two victories before the unit converted to Camels, then making three more claims. The last of these was on 12 November 1917, but before he could make out any reports, he took off for a practice flight and crashed, severely injuring himself. The victory was subsequently confirmed by his MC citation.

	1917		Strutter					
1s*	16 Jun	Alb. DIII	A8244	43	N Lens	0830	DES(F)	CR/RFC 16.6
2**	23 Jul	Alb. DV	A8247	43	N E Lens	1745	OOC	CR/43 WD/AA
			Camel					
3	24 Oct	DFW. C	B6365	43	N Loison-Lens	0800	DES	CR/RFC 24.10
4	31 Oct	DFW. C	B6365	43	Habourdin	1100	OOC	CR/RFC 31.10
5	12 Nov	Alb. DV	B2437	43	E Annay	1215	OOC	SR/Cit

TOTAL: 1 and 1 shared destroyed, 3 out of control = 5.

*Observer: 2 AM J.M. O'Shea; shared with Capt K.L. Gopsill/2/Lt J. Bonner-Smith A8335, 2/Lt C.H. Harriman/2/Lt G.J. Dickson A8785, Sgt A.V. Webb/Lt C.E. Day A7798, 2/Lt L.S.V. Gedge/Pte C.B. Blatherwick A8829, 2/Lt C.G. Moore/Lt W.B. Giles A1903. **Observer: 2/Lt C.J. Agelasto.

WOOD Arthur William Flight Sub Lieutenant 9(N)

Born on 9 April 1898 in Heaton, Bradford, in West Yorkshire, Wood joined the RNAS on 15 October 1916. After training with 12(N) Squadron during August 1917, he was posted to 9(N) Squadron where he participated in 11 shared victories before the end of the year, eight of them during September.

	1917		Camel					
1s*	3 Sep	Alb. DV	B3884	9N	S E Pervyse	1830	DES	CR/RFC 3.9
2s**	5 Sep	Alb. C	B3897	9N	Middelkerke	0800	OOC	CR/ORB/?
3s***	6 Sep	Alb. C	B3884	9N	Middelkerke	1335	OOC	CR/ORB/?
4s†	11 Sep	Alb. DV	B3884	9N	Leke	1730	DES(F)	CR/RFC 11.9
5s††	11 Sep	Alb. DV	B3884	9N	Leke	1730	DES	CR/RFC 11.9
6s†††	16 Sep	DFW. C	B3905	9N	E Mariakerke	1645	DES(F)	CR/RFC 16.9
7s‡	24 Sep	Alb. DIII	----	9N	Leke	1545	OOC	CR/ORB/?
8s‡	30 Sep	Alb. C	B3884	9N	S Middelkerke	1055	DES	CR/RNAS 30.9
9s‡‡	21 Oct	C	N6348	9N	N Slype	1300	DES(F)	CR/DOS/?
10s‡‡‡	13 Nov	Alb. DV	B3884	9N	Pervyse	1435	DES	CR/RNAS 13.11
11s§	10 Dec	DFW. C	B3884	9N	4m E Pervyse	1515	DES(F)	CR/RNAS 10.12

TOTAL: 8 shared destroyed, 3 shared out of control = 11.

*Shared with F/Cdr J.S.T. Fall B3898, FSL J.E. Scott B3907, FSL H.F. Stackard B6204. **Shared with F/Cdr S.T.

Edwards B6217, FSL F.E. Banbury B6330, FSL O.M. Redgate B3818, FSL J.P. Hales B3832, FSL M.S. Taylor B5652. ***Shared with F/Cdr J.S.T. Fall B3898, FSL H.F. Stackard B6204, FSL J.E. Scott B3907, FSL H.L. Wallace B3892. †Shared with F/Cdr J.S.T. Fall B3898, FSL H.F. Stackard B3863, This was probably Lt Z.S. Gotz of MFJ 1. ††Shared with F/Cdr J.S.T Fall B3898, FSL H.F. Stackard B3863. †††Shared with F/Cdr J.S.T. Fall B3883, FSL H.L. Wallace B3892. ‡Shared with F/Cdr J.S.T. Fall B3892, FSL H.F. Stackard B3885. ‡‡Shared with F/Cdr J.S.T. Fall B3898. ‡‡‡Shared with F/Cdr J.S.T. Fall B3883. §Shared with FSL O.M. Redgate B3818, FSL E.M. Knott B6288.

WOOD Walter Bertram Lieutenant 29, 44

Bert Wood was born in Grimsby, Lincolnshire, on 25 October 1898, the younger son of a local magistrate. After initial coast-watching duties as a Boy Scout, he joined the army in 1915 and was commissioned in the 2/8th Hampshire Regiment; on 2 June 1916 he transferred to the RFC. After training he went to France on 30 March 1917, and joined 29 Squadron on 23 April. He made his first claim on 11 May, and by the summer had claimed 13 victories and five driven down. He was awarded an MC on 15 July and a Bar on 10 August. His last victory on 9 August was gained after he was given permission to fly a 'joy-ride' before leaving for England. He went over the lines, attacked three two-seaters and shot down one which was last seen going down over Menin Town Hall. He left for home on 11th, and joined 44(Home Defence) Squadron at Hainault Farm. During his last days in France he had gone down with influenza and in all probability had not fully recovered from this when he took off in a Camel in company with another machine to practice air-fighting tactics — the date was 11 November 1917, ten days after his 19th birthday. For no apparent reason, his Camel dived into the ground and he was killed; it was thought that he had probably fainted.

	1917		Nieuport					
1	11 May	Alb. DIII	A6721	29	Biache	1040	OOC	CR/RFC 11.5
2	5 Jun	Alb. DIII	B1609	29	E Biache	2030	OOC	CR/11 WS
3	18 Jun	Alb. C	B1609	29	E Haucourt	0830	DES(F)	CR/RFC 18.6
4	23 Jun	Alb. DIII	B1609	29	Estrees	1600	DES	CR/RFC 23.6
5	24 Jun	Alb. DIII	B1609	29	Douai	1900	OOC	CR/RFC 25.6
6	25 Jun	Alb. C	B1609	29	Douai	1915	DES	CR/RFC 25.6
7	25 Jun	Alb. C	B1609	29	Douai	1915	OOC	CR/RFC 25.6
8	16 Jul	Alb. DV	B1665	29	4m E Ypres	0850	OOC	CR/RFC 16.7
9	23 Jul	Alb. DV	B1646	29	E Ypres	1955	DES	CR/RFC 23.7
10	23 Jul	Alb. DV	B1646	29	E Ypres	1955	OOC	CR/RFC 23.7
11	31 Jul	Alb. DV	B1553	29	3m N Polygon Wood	1300	DES	CR/RFC 31.7
12	31 Jul	Alb. DV	B1553	29	N Polygon Wood	1305	DES	CR/RFC 31.7
13	9 Aug	C	B1553	29	Menin	1830	OOC	CR/RFC 9.8

TOTAL: 6 destroyed, 7 out of control = 13.

WOOLLETT Henry Winslow Captain 24, 43

From Southwold, Suffolk, the son of a doctor, Henry Woollett was a medical student at the outbreak of war, and was commissioned in the Lincolnshire Regiment in August 1914. A year later he took part in the Suvla Bay landings in the Dardanelles. In 1916 he transferred to the RFC and gained his wings after only three and a half hours of dual instruction; however he crashed an Avro 504 later, and as a result was posted to a single-seater scout unit, joining 24 Squadron in France in November. This unit was flying DH 2s, which were becoming obsolescent, but Woollett managed to gain a victory on this type before converting to DH 5s, in which he claimed a further four. In August 1917 he returned to England, having become a flight commander and received an MC; here he became an instructor. He was posted back to France in March 1918, to 43 Squadron to fly Camels, and here he decorated his aircraft with a special spinner painted to represent the face of a Red Indian, while personally sporting a leopardskin flying helmet and gauntlets, which created quite a stir. Leading 'C' Flight, he brought his score to 35 by early August, many of these being balloons. On 12 April he became the RFC pilot to claim six aircraft in a day, the first also having been a member of 43 Squadron. Having received a DSO and a Bar to his MC, together with the French Legion d'Honneur and Croix de Guerre, he returned to England in August to command three training squadrons at Eastbourne. He served in Iraq in 1924, and commanded 23 Squadron in 1930-31. He died on 31 October 1969.

	1917		DH 2					
1	5 Apr	Alb. DIII	6008	24	1.5m E Honnecourt	1100	DES	CR/RFC 5.4
			DH 5					
2	23 Jul	C	A9165	24	N E Havrincourt	1845	DES	CR/RFC 23.7
3	23 Jul	Alb. DV	A9165	24	Marcoing	1850	DES	CR/RFC 23.7
4	28 Jul	Rumpler C	A9165	24	Scarpe Valley	2025	DES	CR/RFC 28.7
5	17 Aug	Alb. DV	A9165	24	Ribecourt	0810	OOC	CR/RFC 17.8
	1918		Camel					
6	8 Mar	Alb. DV	B7356	43	N E La Bassee	1215	DES(F)	CR/RFC 8.3
7	11 Mar	Alb. DV	B7356	43	La Bassee	1425	OOC	CR/RFC 11.3

8	13 Mar	Alb. DV	B7356	43	La Bassee	1300	DES	CR/RFC 13.3
9*	13 Mar	Alb. DV	B7356	43	La Bassee	1300	DES	CR/RFC 13.3
10	18 Mar	C	C8247	43	E La Bassee	1030	DES	CR/RFC 18.3
11	24 Mar	DFW. C	D6402	43	S E Arras	1100	DES(F)	CR/RFC 24.3
12	24 Mar	DFW. C	D6402	43	S E Arras	1100	DES	CR/RFC 24.3
13	25 Mar	Alb. DV	D6402	43	S Arras	1250	DES	CR/RFC 25.3
14	27 Mar	Balloon	D6402	43	S Arras	1625	DES	ORB/RFC WD
15	27 Mar	Balloon	D6402	43	S Arras	1625	DES	ORB/RFC WD
16	2 Apr	Balloon	D6402	43	Thiepval	1240	DES	CR/RAF 2.4
17	2 Apr	Balloon	D6402	43	N Bray, S W Somme R.	1255	DES	CR/RAF 2.4
18	2 Apr	Balloon	D6402	43	Mericourt	1355	DES	CR/RAF 2.4
19	12 Apr	Alb. DV	D6402	43	W La Gorgue	1030	DES(F)	CR/RAF 12.4
20	12 Apr	C	D6402	43	N E La Gorgue	1030	DES	CR/RAF 12.4
21	12 Apr	Alb. DV	D6402	43	N E La Gorgue	1040	DES(F)	CR/RAF 12.4
22	12 Apr	Alb. DV	D6402	43	N La Gorgue	1700	DES	CR/RAF 12.4
23	12 Apr	Alb. DV	D6402	43	N E La Gorgue	1700	DES	CR/RAF 12.4
24	12 Apr	Alb. DV	D6402	43	N E La Gorgue	1700	DES	CR/RAF 12.4
25	22 Apr	Balloon	D6402	43	N Scarpe River	1535	DES	CR/RAF 22.4
26	22 Apr	Balloon	D6402	43	N Scarpe River	1540	DES	CR/RAF 22.4
27	9 May	Alb. DV	D6402	43	S La Gorgue	1510	DES	CR/RAF 9.5
28	9 May	Balloon	D6402	43	N E La Gorgue	1520	DES	CR/RAF 9.5
29	16 May	LVG. C	D6402	43	Croisilles	1745	OOC	CR/RAF 16.5
30	9 Jul	Pfalz DIII	D6402	43	N W La Bassee	1050	DES	CR/RAF 9.7
31	15 Jul	Balloon	D6402	43	Dormans	1250	DES	CR/RAF 15.7
32	19 Jul	Balloon	D6402	43	E Bezu	1025	DES	CR/RAF 18.7
33	19 Jul	Balloon	D6402	43	S E Bonnes	1040	DES	CR/RAF 18.7
34	24 Jul	Fokker DVII	E1467	43	Fere en Tardenois	1930	OOC	CR/ORB/?
35	9 Aug	Fokker DVII	E1467	43	Pertain	0630	DES	CR/RAF 9.8

TOTAL: 11 balloons, 20 destroyed, 4 out of control = 35.
*43 claimed 5 destroyed and 3 out of control; Lt Hafner of Jasta 57 was killed.

WOOLLVEN Charles Henry Chapman Captain 25

A native of Plymouth, Woollven saw service in the Devon Regiment before transferring to the RFC. He joined 25 Squadron on 19 June 1916 at the age 19, to fly FE 2s, and became a flight commander in early 1917. His fifth and last claim was made on 1 May of that year.

	1916		FE 2B					
1*	8 Aug	Roland CII	6991	25	Don	0640	OOC	CR/RFC 8.8
2**	16 Nov	Alb. DI	7024	25	Somain	1300	DES(F)	CR/RFC 16.11
3***	23 Nov	Alb. DI	7024	25	E Oppy	1545	DES	CR/RFC 23.11
	1917							
4†	17 Mar	Alb. DII	A5484	25	Oppy-Beaumont	1100-1130	OOC	CR/RFC 17.3
5††	1 May	Alb. DIII	7003	25	S E Fresnoy	1800	DES	CR/RFC 1.5

TOTAL: 3 destroyed, 2 out of control = 5.
*Observer: Lt C. Nelson. **Observer: 2/Lt C.H. Marchant. ***Observer: Sgt G.R. Horrocks. †Observer: Sgt J.H. Booth. ††Observer: Sgt J.H. Brown.

WORTHINGTON Charles Edward Lieutenant 87

He went to France as a pilot with 87 Squadron, flying Sopwith Dolphins, in April 1918. Here he became a deputy flight leader and claimed five victories.

	1918		Dolphin					
1	16 May	Alb. DV	C4056	87	3m off Ostend	1730	DES	CR/RAF 16.5
2	14 Aug	Alb. DV	C4157	87	Nesle	0905	OOC	CR/?
3s*	25 Aug	Fokker DVII	C4156	87	Velu Wood	1800	DES	CR/RAF 25.8
4	30 Aug	Fokker DVII	C4157	87	Velu Wood	1810	DES(F)	CR/?
5s**	4 Oct	Fokker DVII	D3590	87	Deseries	1800	DES	CR/RAF 4.10

TOTAL: 2 and 2 shared destroyed, 1 out of control = 5.
*Shared with Lt L. Murray-Stewart C4156. **Shared with Capt L.N. Hollinghurst.

WRIGHT William Allan Captain 45

Wright was credited with eight victories while serving with 45 Squadron in 1917. His first four claims were made while flying Sopwith 1½ Strutters, and he added four more on Camels, the last of them an Albatros DV of Jasta 33 flown by Leutnant Fritz Cleiss, as it was attacking a 53 Squadron RE 8. He was promoted to Captain in September, and after the war became a very senior civil servant.

	1917		Strutter					
1s*	9 May	Alb. DIII	A8225	45	N W Seclin	1700	DES	CR/RFC 9.5
2**	24 May	Alb. DIII	A8269	45	Zonnebeke	1945	DES(F)	CR/RFC 25.5
3**	24 May	Alb. DIII	A8269	45	Zonnebeke	1945	DES	CR/RFC 25.5
4**	28 May	Alb. DIII	A8269	45	Comines	1345	DES(F)	CR/RFC 28.5
			Camel					
5	5 Sep	DFW. C	----	45	Comines	0800	OOC	CR/RFC 5.9
6	11 Sep	C	----	45	1m S E Moorslede	1830	OOC	CR/RFC 12.9
7	20 Sep	C	B3903	45	Westroosebeke	1145	DES	CR/RFC 20.9
8s**	1 Oct	Alb. DV	----	45	E Polygon Wood	1600	CAPT	CR/RFC 1.10

TOTAL: 1 shared captured, 4 and 1 shared destroyed, 2 out of control = 8.
*Observer: 2/Lt E.T. Caulfield-Kelly; shared with 2/Lt G.H. Cock/2/Lt J.T.G. Murison. **Observer: 2/Lt E.T. Caulfield-Kelly. ***Shared with Lt R. Reeder/Cpl G. Holmes A3402, of 53 Sqn. Lt F. Cleiss of Jasta 33 was killed.

YEATES Victor Maslin Lieutenant 46

Born on 30 September 1897, he joined the RFC in May 1917 and was posted to 46 Squadron in February 1918; he was the author of the famous novel *Winged Victory*, which was closely based on his experiences whilst serving with this unit. Yeates was one of the RAF's relatively rare married pilots. He later became a deputy flight leader, claiming a total of five victories, four of them shared, by 9 August. By this time he had flown 248 hours on Camels and been shot down twice. His health suffered through his war service, and after writing his book, he died of tuberculosis on 15 December 1934, aged 37.

	1918		Camel					
1s*	3 May	C	C1637	46	N W Don	1300	DES	CR/RAF 3.5
2s**	6 May	DFW. C	----	46	St Venant	1800	CAPT	CR/RAF 6.5
3	15 May	Pfalz DIII	D6565	46	Armentieres	1250	OOC	CR/RAF 15.5
4s***	22 May	C	----	46	W Estaires	0920	DES	CR/RAF 22.5
5	3 Aug	Fokker DVII	D9405	46	E Lens	1835	DES	CR/RAF 3.8

TOTAL: 1 shared captured, 1 and 2 shared destroyed, 1 out of control = 5.
*Shared with Capt D.R. MacLaren B9153. **Shared with Capt D.R. MacLaren, Capt C.H. Marchant, 2/Lt J.H. Smith, 2/Lt H.T.W. Manwaring. This was Lt Junemann/Lt Barth of FA 14. ***Shared with Lt A.G. Vlasto, Lt J.A. Cote, Lt N. Bruce.

YOUNG Graham C. 2nd Lieutenant 60

From Perth, Graham Young joined 60 Squadron in March 1917 and was one of that unit's very few pilots to survive 'Bloody April'. He served until December 1917 when he was posted to Home Establishment.

	1917		Nieuport					
1s*	25 Jun	Alb. DIII	B1619	60	Dury	1025	OOC	CR/RFC 25.6
			SE 5A					
2	21 Sep	Alb. DV	B533	60	Langemarck	1400	DES	CR/RFC 21.9
3s**	25 Sep	Alb. DV	B533	60	Goenberg	1200	DES	CR/RFC 25.9
4s***	21 Oct	C	B580	60	Houthoulst	1615	DES	CR/RFC 21.10
5	1 Nov	Alb. DV	A8901	60	Houthoulst	1430	OOC	CR/RFC 1.11

TOTAL: 1 and 2 shared destroyed, 1 and 1 shared out of control = 5.
*Shared with Lt W.J. Rutherford B1602, Lt F.O. Soden B1598. **Shared with 2/Lt J.B. Crompton B512. ***Shared with Lt W.J. Rutherford B533, Lt F.O. Soden B543.

YOUNG Wilfred Ernest Major 6, 19, 74, 1

Born on 28 December 1891 and from Bournemouth, Young was commissioned into the Dorset Regiment on 23 January 1915, but on 15 December of that year, having transferred to the RFC, he was posted to 6 Squadron. On 12 August 1916 he returned to Home Establishment, next returning to France on 5 June 1917 as a flight commander on Spads in 19 Squadron, where he claimed three victories. He was wounded in action on 22 July, on recovery from which he took command of a flight in the new 74 Squadron in March 1918, returning to France with the unit during April. On 8 May, while leading six SEs over Ypres, his flight was surprised by ten Fokker Triplanes of Jasta 26, four SEs being shot down and Young's machine badly damaged, causing him to force-land at Marie Capelle. By early June he had claimed eight more victories with the squadron, but on 3 August he was promoted to Major and posted to command 1 Squadron. He received the DFC.

	1917		Spad					
1	17 Jun	Alb. DIII	B1628	19	Gheluwe-Wervicq	1930	DES	CR/RFC 17.6
2s*	3 Jul	C	----	19	----	0855-1040	OOC	ORB/23 Sqn
3	22 Jul	Alb. DIII	B1628	19	E Boesinghe	2050	OOC	TMBP/9 WS/?
	1918		SE 5A					
4	12 Apr	Alb. DV	D271	74	W Armentieres	1940	DES	CR/11 BG WD

5	12 May	Pfalz DIII	C6474	74	N Wulverghem	1825	DES	CR/RAF 12.5
6	21 May	Pfalz DIII	C6474	74	Hollebeke	1905	DES(F)	CR/RAF 21.5
7	1 Jun	Hannover C	C1116	74	Estaires	0430	DES(F)	CR/11 WS
8	1 Jun	Hannover C	C1116	74	Robecq	0500	DES	CR/11 WS
9s**	6 Jun	Pfalz DIII	----	74	2m W Roulers	1935	DES	CR/RAF 6.6
10s***	9 Jun	Alb. C	----	74	S Mt Kemmel	0810	DES	CR/11 WS
11s†	9 Jul	DFW. C	----	74	Merris	1425	OOC	CR/11 WS

TOTAL: 6 and 2 shared destroyed, 1 and 2 shared out of control = 11.
*Shared with Lt C.D. Thompson B1628. **Shared with Capt E.C. Mannock, Lt H.G. Clements, Lt A.C. Kiddie, and 5 others. ***Shared with Capt E.C. Mannock. †Shared with flight.

ZINK Edmund Leonard Captain 18, 32

Commissioned in the Suffolk Regiment on 7 October 1915, Zink transferred to the RFC in 1916, flying FE 2s in 18 Squadron from that summer, claiming four victories by the end of April 1917. Rested, he served as an instructor at Turnberry before joining 32 Squadron in September 1918 as a flight commander. With this unit he claimed one further victory.

	1916		FE 2B					
1*	26 Dec	Alb. DII	----	18	Velu	0950	OOC	CR/RFC 26.12
	1917							
2**	24 Mar	Alb. DII	4898	18	Reincourt	1500	OOC	CR/RFC 24.3
3***	12 Apr	Alb. DIII	A823	18	Cagnicourt	1230	OOC	CR/V BG WD
4†	23 Apr	Alb. DIII	A823	18	Baralle	1730	OOC	CR/RFC 24.4
	1918		SE 5A					
5	5 Sep	C	C1836	32	N Equancourt	1215	DES	CR/RAF 5.9

TOTAL: 1 destroyed, 4 out of control = 5.
*Observer: 2/Lt Mayhew. **Observer: 2 AM J. Walker. ***Observer: Pte N.G. Jones. †Observer: 2/Lt G.B. Bate.

Statistics and Map

The "Balloon Strafers"

Name	Unit	Balloons Destroyed
Beauchamp Proctor, Captain A.W.	84 Squadron	16
Woollett, Captain H.W.	43 Squadron	11
Hazell, Major T.F.	24 Squadron	10
Barker, Major W.G.	28 Squadron	9
Bennett, Lieutenant L. Jr	40 Squadron	9
Highwood, Captain S.W.	84 Squadron	9
Goode, Lieutenant H.K.	66 Squadron	7
Hudson, Lieutenant H.B.	28 Squadron	7
MacLaren, Captain D.R.	46 Squadron	6
Campbell, Captain W.C.	1 Squadron	5
Carlin, Captain S.	74 Squadron	5
Cobby, Captain A.H.	4 AFC Squadron	5
Munday, Flight Commander R.B.	8(Naval) Squadron	5
Shields, Captain W.E.	41 Squadron	5
Southey, Captain W.A.	84 Squadron	5

Top-Scoring Pilots on a Monthly Basis from August 1916 – October 1918

(NB August 1916 was the first month in which any pilot claimed more than five victories in one month.)

1916	Name	Unit	Aircraft	Victories
August	Lt A. Ball	11,60	Nieuport	10
September	Lt A. Ball	60	Nieuport	14
October	Lt H.H. Turk	11	FE 2	3
November	Lt E.C. Pashley	24	DH 2	4
December	Capt S.H. Long	24	DH 2	4
1917				
January	Ten pilots each claimed 2			
February	Three pilots each claimed 3			
March	Flt Cdr B.C. Bell	3(N)	Sopwith Pup	4
	Flt Sub Lt J.J. Malone	3(N)	Sopwith Pup	4
April	Flt Lt W.A. Bishop	60	Nieuport	12
May	Capt F.J.H. Thayre	20	FE 2D	15
June	Flt Lt R. Collishaw	10(N)	Sopwith Triplane	16
July	Flt Cdr R. Collishaw	10(N)	Sopwith Triplane	14
August	Capt P.F. Fullard	1	Nieuport	12
September	Flt Cdr J.S.T. Fall	9(N)	Sopwith Camel	11
October	Capt P.F. Fullard	1	Nieuport	11
November	Maj A.D. Carter	19	Spad	6
December	Capt J.T.B. McCudden	56	SE 5A	14
1918				
January	Flt Sub Lt W.L. Jordan	8(N)	Sopwith Camel	9
	Capt J.T.B. McCudden	56	SE 5A	9
February	Capt J.T.B. McCudden	56	SE 5A	11
March	Capt G.E. Thomson	46	Sopwith Camel	15
April	Capt H.W. Woollett	43	Sopwith Camel	11
May	Capt A.C. Atkey	22	Bristol F2B	27
June	Lt W.G. Claxton	41	SE 5A	17
July	Capt G.E.H. McElroy	40	SE 5A	16+
August	Capt A.W. Beauchamp-Proctor	84	SE 5A	15
September	Capt S.W. Highwood	84	SE 5A	10
October	Capt O.A.P. Heron	70	Sopwith Camel	9
	Capt C.H.R. Lagesse	29	SE 5A	9

Top-Scoring Pilots by Types of Aircraft

Aircraft Type	Pilot Name	Score on Type	Squadron
Bristol Scout	Maj C.G. Bell	5+	10
Vickers FB 5 Gun Bus	Capt L.W.B. Rees	6	11
DH 2	Capt A.M. Wilkinson	10	24
FE 2B	Capt S.W. Price	8+	23,11
	Capt C.M. Clement	8	22
FE 2D	Capt F.J.H. Thayre	19	20
Fe 8	Capt E.L. Benbow	8	40
Martinsyde G 100 Elephant	Capt D.J. Bell	3	27
	Lt J.I. Gilmour	3	27
BE 12	Capt G.W. Murlis-Green	6	47
Sopwith 1½ Strutter	Capt G.H. Cock	13	45
Sopwith Pup	Capt M.D.G. Scott	11	54,46
Nieuport 17, 23 & 27 Scouts	Capt P.F. Fullard	40	1
Sopwith Triplane	Flt Cdr R. Collishaw	33	10(N)
Spad S VII & XIII	Maj W.J.C.K. Cochran-Patrick	18	23
Bristol F2B Fighter	Capt A.E. McKeever	31	11
SE 5 & 5A	Capt A.W. Beauchamp-Proctor	54	84
Sopwith Camel	Capt D.R. MacLaren	54	46
DH 5	Capt A. Coningham	9	32
Sopwith Dolphin	Capt F.W. Gillett	20	79
Bristol MIC	Capt F.D. Travers	5	150
Sopwith Snipe	Capt E.R. King	7	4 AFC
RE 8	Lt C.R. Pithey	10	12
DH 4 & DH 9	Capt E. Dickson	14	5(N), 205
	Capt D.A. Stewart	14	18

Gunner Aces of the Bomber and Corps Squadrons

The following personnel were observer/gunners in a variety of aircraft types who were involved in five or more victories in conjunction with their pilots.

Name	Squadron	Score	Name	Squadron	Score
Naylor	5(N)/205	13	2nd Lt E.A. Simpson	49	6
Lt H. Rhodes	12	11	Lt E. Walker	18	6
Lt L.A. Christian	206	9	Capt L.I. Collins	18	5
2nd Lt G.N. Blennerhasset	18	8	Sgt L.S. Court	25	5
Cpl L. Emsden	25	8	2nd Lt F.C. Craig	57	5
Sgt J. Grant	57	8	2nd Lt C.C. Dance	103	5
Lt F. Leathley	57	8	Sgt W. Dyke	18	5
Lt D.L. Burgess	25	7	Lt C.E. Eddy	103	5
Gnr C.V. Robinson	5(N)/205	7	Lt H.C.T. Gompertz	55	5
Sgt F.W. Bell	49	6	Lt C.P. Harrison	98	5
Lt A.F. Britton	57	6	2nd Lt E.P. Hartigan	57	5
2nd Lt S.H. Hamblin	205	6	Sgt M.B. Kilroy	18	5
Lt P.J. Holligan	49	6	Sgt S.F. Langstone	205	5
AGL Jackson	5(N)	6	2nd Lt H.W.N. Mackay	18	5
Lt F.T.S. Menendez	57	6	2nd Lt L.L.T. Sloot	57	5
Sgt W.J. Middleton	205	6	2nd Lt J.R. Smith	18	5
Lt W. Miller	18	6	2nd Lt C.N. Whitham	205	5
Lt Scott	5(N)/205	6			

Gunner Aces of the Scout Squadrons

The following personnel were observer/gunners in FE 2, Sopwith 1½ Strutter or Bristol Fighter units, and were involved in five or more victories while flying with various pilots in their units. These names have appeared in the main text alongside those of the successful pilots.

Name	Squadron	Score	Name	Squadron	Score
Lt C.G. Gass	22	39	Lt A.W. Merchant	48	9
Sgt R.M. Fletcher	22	26	Lt H.E. Merritt	62	9
2nd Lt G.S.L. Hayward	22	25	2nd Lt A.R. Ness	48	9
Lt T.C. Noel	20	24	Lt S. Parry	62	9
Capt F.R. Cubbon	20	21	Cpl V. Reed	48	9
2nd Lt H.L. Edwards	20	21	Lt L.M. Thompson	62	9
Sgt A. Newland	20	21	2nd Lt R.W. Turner	20	9
Lt L.A. Powell	11	20	2nd Lt A.E. Wear	20	9
Capt A.H.W. Wall	48	16	2nd Lt S.W. Bunting	22	8
Sgt J.J. Cowell	20	15(16)	Lt H.G. Crowe	20	8
Sgt E.A. Deighton	20	15	2nd Lt P. Douglas	11	8
2nd Lt B. Digby-Worsley	88	15	Lt C.W. Gladman	11	8
Lt J.R. Gordon	62	15	Sgt W.N. Holmes	62	8
Sgt J.H. Jones	22	15	Sgt H.C. Hunt	22	8
Lt A. Mills	20	15	Lt A.N. Jenks	20	8
Lt G. Thomson	22	14	Lt S.A.W. Knights	62	8
2nd Lt F.J. Ralphs	20	13	Lt A.D. Light	48	8
2nd Lt J.H. Umney	22	13	Cpl M. Mather	20	8
2nd Lt D.P.F. Uniacke	48	13	2nd Lt L.E. Mitchell	62	8
2nd Lt C.G. Boothroyd	20	12	2nd Lt W. O'Toole	48	8
2nd Lt P.V.G. Chambers	62	12	Lt C.C. Robson	11	8
Capt F. Godfrey	20	12	Lt W.W. Smith	139	8
2nd Lt E. Hardcastle	20	12	Lt L.W. Sutherland	1AFC	8
2nd Lt G.H. Kemp	20	12	Lt C.J. Tolman	22	8
2nd Lt J.L. Morgan	22	12	Lt I.W.F. Agabeg	88	7
Lt W. Noble	20	12	Lt L.W. Allen	48	7
Lt J.J. Scaramanga	20,22	12	Sgt D. Antcliffe	88	7
Lt M.W. Waddington	20	12	Lt T.J. Birmingham	22	7
Capt D.E. Waight	22	12	Lt G.A. Brooke	45,20	7
Capt H. Claye	62	11	Capt L.W. Burbidge	20	7
2nd Lt T.E. Elliott	62	11	Lt A.C. Cooper	48	7
Capt J.H. Hedley	20	11	2nd Lt R. Critchley	22	7
Lt V. St B. Collins	45,22	10	Lt A.S. Draisey	20	7
Lt C.A. Hoy	20	10	2nd Lt H.E. Easton	20	7
Lt F. Libby	23,11	10(14)	Lt G. Finlay	1AFC	7
2nd Lt J. Rudkin	88	10	Lt E.C. Gilroy	11	7
2nd Lt C.J. Agelasto	43,20	9	Lt W.J.N. Grant	88	7
2nd Lt W.T. Barnes	11	9	2nd Lt R.F. Hill	20	7
Sgt W. Beales	48	9	Pbr J. Hills	20	7
2nd Lt G.V. Learmond	20	9	1 AM E. Hoare	88	7
Lt J. McDonald	22	9	Lt A.W. Kirk	1AFC	7

Cpl F.J. Knowles	111	7
2nd Lt H. Owen	48	7
Pvt F.A. Potter	20	7
Lt L.H. Scott	20	7
Lt B.H. Smyth	88	7
Lt J. Tennant	20	7
2nd Lt W. Tinsley	88	7
2nd Lt A. Trantor	88	7
2nd Lt P.S. Williams	22	7
Lt M.A. Benjamin	48	6
Lt W.C. Cambray	20	6
2nd Lt T.S. Chiltern	88	6
Sgt C. Hill	88	6
2 AM B Jackson	48	6
Cpl F.J. Knowles	111	6
Lt T.A.M.S. Lewis	20	6
2 AM H. Lingfield	48	6
2nd Lt L.H. McRobert	11	6
2nd Lt E.S. Moore	48	6
2nd Lt M.K. Parlee	22	6
Sgt E.H. Sayers	20	6
Lt T.C.S. Tuffield	48	6
Lt W.U. Tyrrell	22	6
Lt V.R.S. White	45,20	6
Lt A.E. Ansell	48	5
Sgt W.J. Benger	20	5
Lt R. Gordon-Bennett	20	5
Lt G.W. Blaicklock	45	5
Lt J. Bruce-Norton	62	5
2nd Lt C.W. Davies	48	5
Lt H.R. Eldon	88	5
Lt H. Fysh	1AFC	5
Lt W.T. Gilson	20	5
Sgt J.H. Hall	22	5
Lt R.S. Herring	48	5
Sgt G.F. Hines	62	5
2nd Lt W. Hodgkinson	62	5
2nd Lt P.G. Jones	20	5
2nd Lt E.T. Caulfield-Kelly	45	5
Lt F.J. Kydd	20	5
Capt J.L. Lloyd-Williams	111	5
2nd Lt R. Lowe	62	5
2nd Lt S.H.P. Masding	20	5
Cpl J. Mason	11	5
Lt G. McCormack	22	5
Lt M.A. McKenzie	20	5
Lt H.E. Moore	22	5
Lt J.G. Murison	45	5
Lt E.A. Mustard	1AFC	5
1 AM S.H. Platel	11	5
Pvt T. Proctor	88	5
Lt J.H. Robertson	48	5
Sgt G. Shannon	22	5
2nd Lt A.J.H. Thornton	22	5
Lt J.A. Vessey	45	5
2nd Lt E.H. Ward	88	5
Lt W.J.A. Weir	1AFC	5

NB A figure in brackets after the score indicates further victories subsequently achieved as a pilot.

Bomber and Corps Pilot Aces

The following personnel claimed five or more victories whilst flying Bomber or Corps aircraft. This does not include pilots who subsequently served with Scout units.

Name	Squadron	Score
Capt E. Dickson	5(N)/205	14
Capt D.A. Stewart	20,18	14(16)
Capt A.G. Waller	18	11
Lt C.R. Pithey	12	10
Lt G. Darvill	18	9
Flt Cdr C.P.O. Bartlett	5(N)	8
Capt L.R. Warren	206	8
Capt W.E. Green	57	8
Maj E.G. Joy	55,205	8
Capt J.S. Stubbs	103	8
Capt J. Gamon	5(N)/205	7
Flt Cdr T.F. Le Mesurier	5(N)	7
Capt A. Roulstone	25,57	7
Capt G. Fox-Rule	49	7
Capt F. McD. C. Turner	55,57	7
Lt L.A. Ashfield	202	6
Lt R.L.M. Barbour	205	6
Capt G. Bowman	49	6
2nd Lt R. Chalmers	205	6
Sgt D.E. Edgley	57	6
Capt H.R. Gould	18	6
Capt D.S. Hall	57	6
Lt C.J.H. Heywood	205	6
Lt J.A. Keating	49	6
2nd Lt P. O'Leiff	1,55	6
Capt A. MacGregor	57	6
Capt L. Minot	57	6
Lt A.R. Spurling	49	6
2nd Lt F.C. Wilton	98	6
Lt P.E. Appleby	104	5
Capt E.D. Asbury	49	5
Capt R.N.G. Atkinson	98,206	5
Capt D.H.M. Carberry	52,59	5
Lt W.H. Clarke	205	5
Lt W.B. Elliott	205	5
Lt W. Grossart	205	5
Capt O.C.W. Johnsen	98	5
Lt C.I. Lally	25	5
Capt C.R. Lupton	5(N)/205	5
Capt W.J. Pace	55	5
Lt L.H. Pearson	202	5
Capt J.E. Pugh	25	5
Capt C.H. Stokes	57	5

NB: Capt Stewart also claimed two victories as a gunner to bring his total score to 16. Lt O'Leiff also claimed two victories as an Air Mechanic observer in 1 Squadron in 1916; these are included in his total of 6.

Aircraft Types:

1 Squadron	Morane
12 Squadron	RE 8
18 Squadron	DH 4, DH 9
20 Squadron	FE 2D
25 Squadron	FE 2, DH 4
49 Squadron	DH 9
52 Squadron	BE 2
55 Squadron	DH 4
57 Squadron	FE 2, DH 4, D 9
59 Squadron	RE 8
98 Squadron	DH 9
103 Squadron	DH 9
104 Squadron	DH 9
202 Squadron	DH 4
5(N)/205 Squadron	DH 4, DH 9A
206 Squadron	DH 4, DH 9, DH 9A

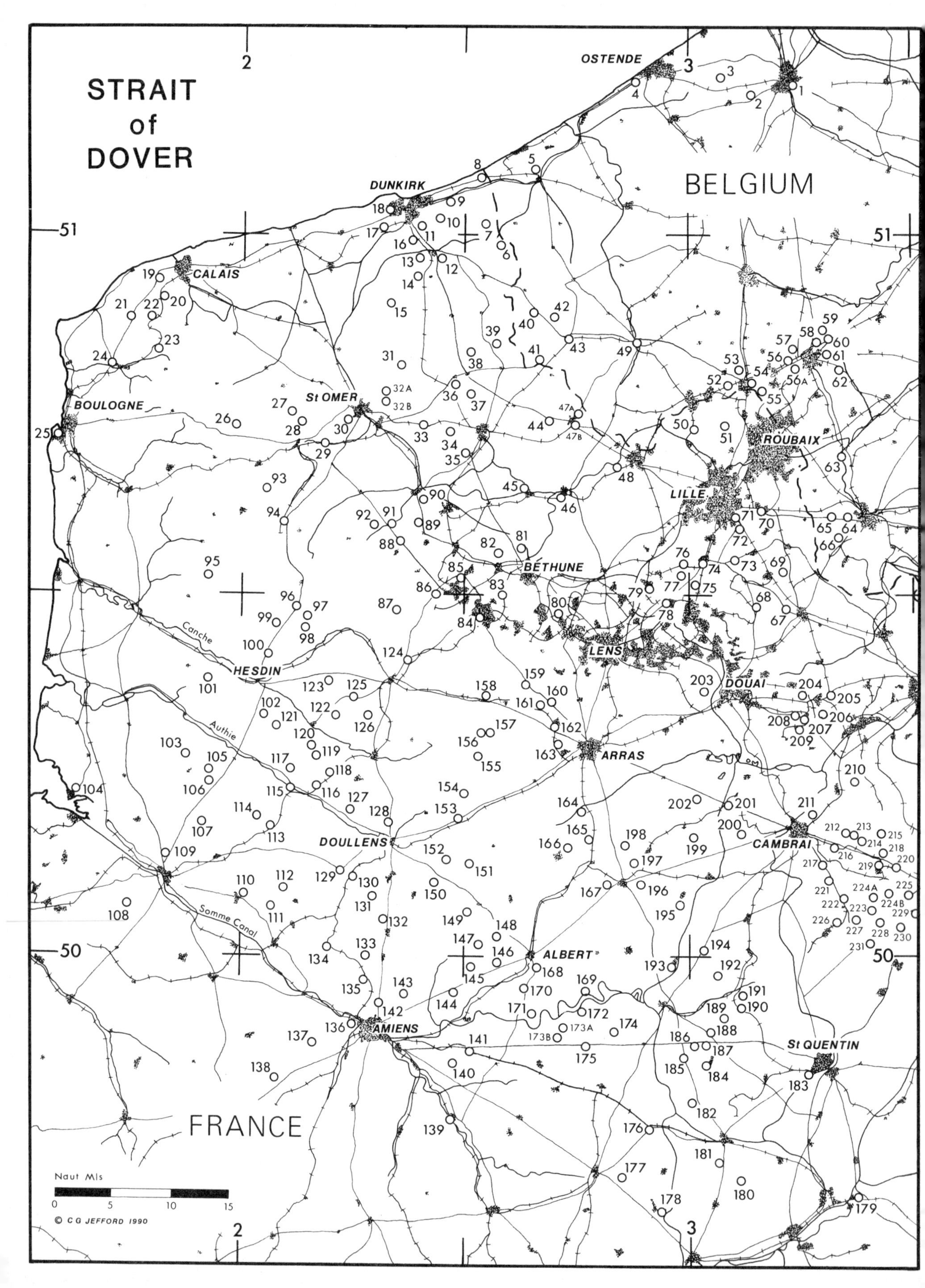
STRAIT
of
DOVER
BELGIUM
FRANCE
OSTENDE
DUNKIRK
CALAIS
BOULOGNE
St OMER
ROUBAIX
LILLE
BÉTHUNE
LENS
DOUAI
ARRAS
HESDIN
DOULLENS
CAMBRAI
ALBERT
AMIENS
St QUENTIN
Canche
Authie
Somme Canal
Naut Mls
0 5 10 15
© C G JEFFORD 1990

The Western Front – France and Belgium, 1914-19

1 Bruges
2 Varssenaere
3 Stalhille
4 Ostende
5 Furnes
6 Hondschoote
7 Les Moëres
8 Bray Dunes (Frontier Aerodrome)
9 Leffrinckhoucke
10 Teteghem
11 Coudekerque
12 Bergues
13 Bierne
14 Crochte
15 Eringhem
16 Cappelle
17 Petite Synthe
18 St-Pol
19 Calais
20 Fréthun/Nielles-lès-Calais
21 St-Inglevert
22 Beauregard
23 Caffiers
24 Marquise
25 Boulogne
26 Alquines
27 Boisdinghem
28 Quelmes
29 Esquerdes
30 St-Omer
31 Hoog Huis/Huys
32A Clairmarais North
32B Clairmarais South
33 Ebblinghem
34 Wallon-Cappel
35 Morbecque
36 Oxelaere
37 Ste-Marie-Cappel
38 Oudezeele
39 Droglandt
40 Proven
41 Abeele
42 La Lovie
43 Poperinghe
44 Meteren
45 Merville
46 La Gorgue
47A Bailleul (Asylum Ground)
47B Bailleul (Town Ground)
48 Erquinghem
49 Ypres
50 Ste-Marguerite
51 Linselles
52 Coucou
53 Menin
54 Halluin
55 Reckem
56 Bisseghem
56A Marcke
57 Heule
58 Cuerne
59 Bavichove
60 Harlebeke
61 Staceghem
62 Sweveghem
63 Pecq
64 Orcq
65 Marquain
66 Froidmont
67 Auchy
68 Bersée
69 Genech
70 Asq/Ascq
71 Lille/Ronchin
72 Merchin
73 Ennetières
74 Lille/Seclin
75 Phalempin
76 Gondecourt
77 Chemy
78 Carvin
79 Provin
80 Mazingarbe
81 Hinges
82 Chocques/Gonneham
83 Hesdigneul
84 Bruay
85 Auchel/Lozinghem
86 Floringhem
87 Sains-lès-Pernes
88 Rely
89 Norrent-Fontes
90 Aire/Treizennes
91 Estrée-Blanche/Liettres
92 Serny
93 Drionville
94 Fauquembergues
95 Quilen
96 Ruisseauville
97 Tramecourt
98 Maisoncelle
99 Planques
100 Wamin
101 St-André-aux Bois
102 Le Quesnoy
103 Ligescourt/Crécy-en-Ponthieu
104 Le Crotoy
105 Estrées-lès-Crécy
106 Fontaine-sur-Maye
107 Agenvillers
108 Moyenneville
109 Abbeville
110 Famechon
111 Surcamps
112 Franqueville
113 Conteville
114 Bois-de-Roche
115 Auxi-le-Château
116 Nouex-les-Auxi
117 Le Planty
118 Boffles
119 Rougefay
120 Belleville Farm
121 Les Eauvis
122 Blangermont
123 Beauvois/Humières
124 Bryas
125 Croisette
126 Ecoivres
127 Remaisnil
128 Haute Visée
129 Fienvillers
130 Candas
131 Valheureux
132 Vert Galand
133 Flesselles/Villers-Bocage
134 Vignacourt
135 Bertangles
136 Amiens
137 Bovelles
138 Quevauvillers
139 Moreuil
140 Cachy
141 Villers-Bretonneux
142 Poulainville
143 Allonville
144 Lahoussoye
145 Baizieux
146 Laviéville
147 Warloy-Baillon
148 Senlis-le-Sec
149 Léalvillers/Clairfaye Farm
150 Marieux
151 St-Léger-les-Authie
152 Hurtebise Farm
153 La Bellevue
154 Soncamp
155 Avesnes-le-Comte
156 Le Hameau/Izel le Hameau
157 Filescamp Farm
158 Savy
159 Camblain-l'Abbé
160 St-Eloi
161 Acq
162 Etrun
163 Wagnonlieu
164 Boiry-St-Martin
165 Courcelles-le-Comte
166 Ablainzevelle
167 Bapaume
168 Méaulte/Citadel
169 Suzanne
170 Morlancourt
171 Chipilly
172 Cappy
173A Proyart East
173B Proyart South
174 Assevillers
175 Foucaucourt
176 Nesle
177 Champien
178 Catigny
179 La Fère
180 Villeselve
181 Golancourt (Bonneuil)
182 Matigny
183 St-Quentin
184 Flez
185 Athies
186 Mons-en-Chaussée
187 Estrées-en-Chaussée
188 Bouvincourt
189 Hancourt
190 Montigny Farm
191 Hervilly
192 Longavesnes
193 Moislains
194 Nurlu
195 Léchelle
196 Bancourt
197 Beugnâtre
198 Mory
199 Pronville
200 Bourlon
201 Marquion
202 Villers-lès-Cagnicourt
203 La Brayelle
204 Bruille
205 Erre
206 Abscon
207 Aniche
208 Auberchicourt
209 Emerchicourt
210 Avesnes-le-Sec
211 Escaudoeuvres
212 Carnières
213 Boussières
214 Bévillers
215 Quiévy
216 Estourmel
217 La Targette
218 Béthencourt
219 Caudry
220 Inchy
221 Esnes
222 Selvigny/Ferme Guillemin
223 Iris Farm (Clary)
224A Bertry West
224B Bertry East
225 Reumont
226 Malincourt
227 Elincourt
228 Maretz
229 Escaufourt
230 Busigny
231 Prémont Farm